用心字里行间　雕刻名著经典

經濟學

GOVERNMENT DEBT SINCE THE AMERICAN REVOLUTION

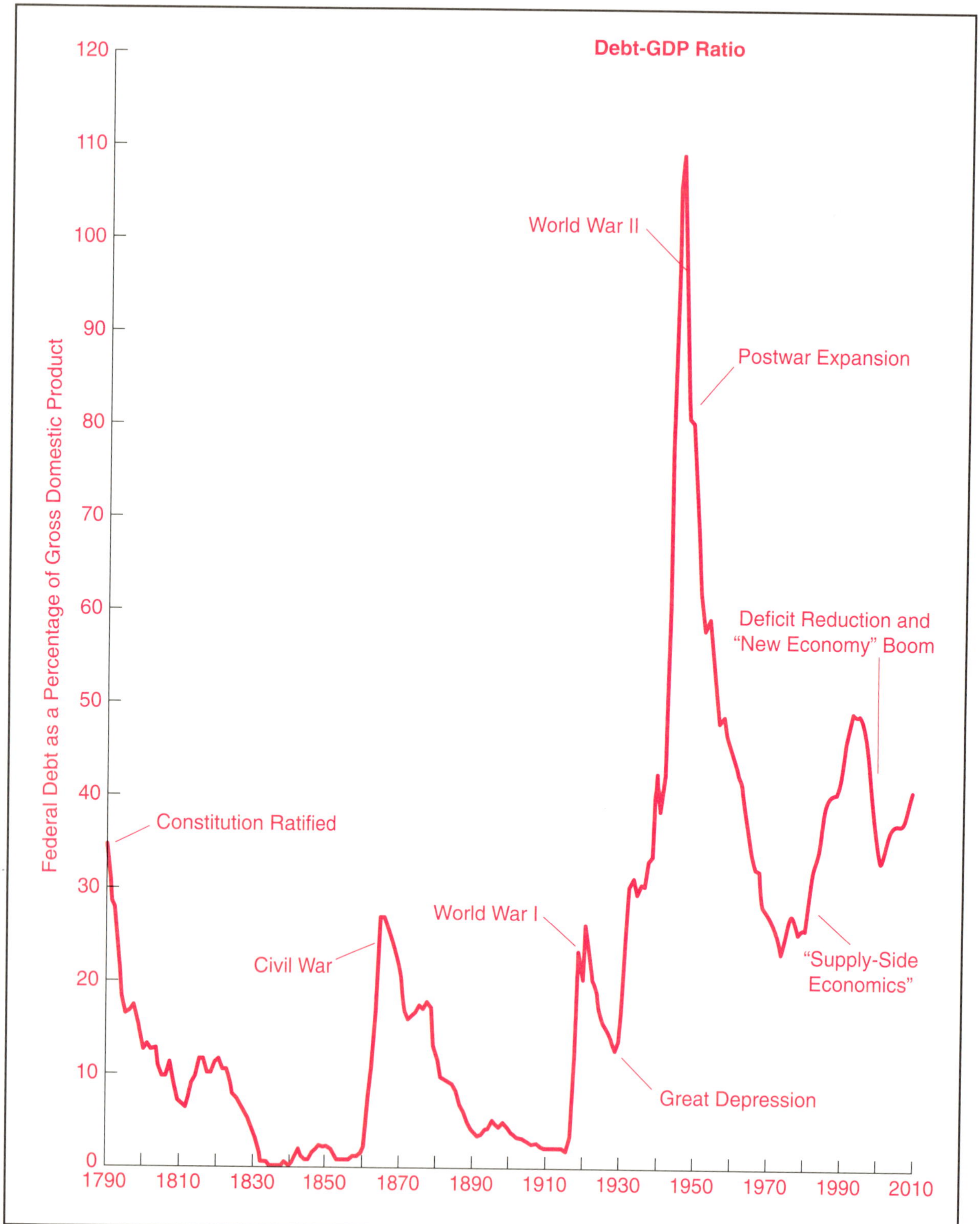

GOVERNMENT DEBT SINCE THE AMERICAN REVOLUTION

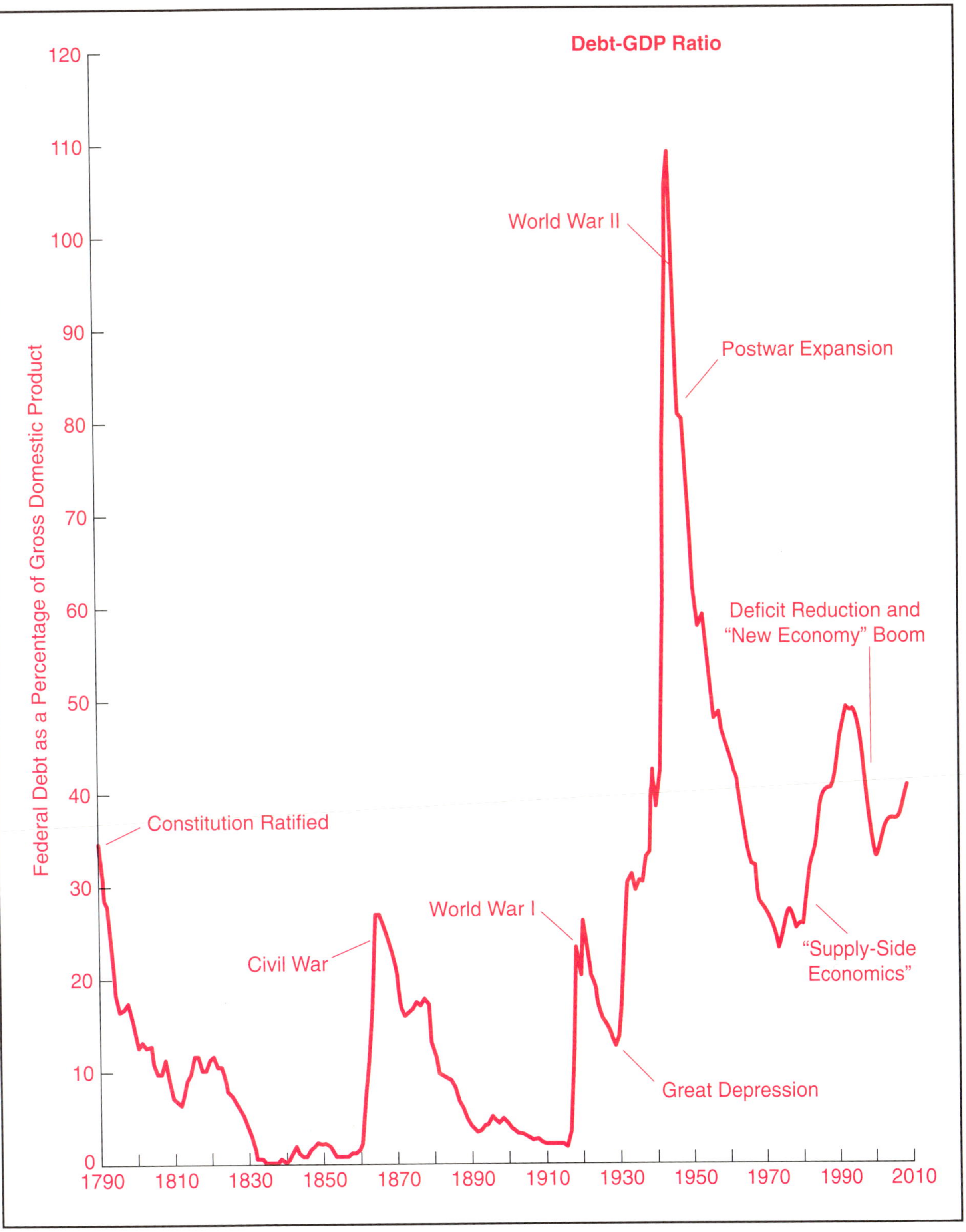

ECONOMICS

Nineteenth Edition

Commentated Version

PAUL A. SAMUELSON

Institute Professor Emeritus

Massachusetts Institute of Technology

WILLIAM D. NORDHAUS

Sterling Professor of Economics

Yale University

YU JIAN

Professor

China University of Political Science and Law

经济学

第 19 版

双语注疏版

〔美〕保罗·萨缪尔森　威廉·诺德豪斯　著

译·注·疏
于　健

人民邮电出版社
北　　京

图书在版编目（CIP）数据

经济学（第 19 版）：双语注疏版 /（美）萨缪尔森（Samuelson，P. A.），（美）诺德豪斯（Nordhaus，W. D.）著；于健 译注疏 .

- 北京：人民邮电出版社，2013.11（2018.12重印）

高等学校教材

ISBN 978-7-115-32871-7

Ⅰ. ①经… Ⅱ. ①萨… ②诺… ③于… Ⅲ. ①经济学—高等学校—教材 Ⅳ. ① F0

中国版本图书馆 CIP 数据核字（2013）第 192116 号

Paul A. Samuelson, William D. Nordhaus

Economics, 19th Edition

ISBN 0-07-351129-3

经济学（第 19 版）：双语注疏版

◆ 著 ［美］保罗 · 萨缪尔森 威廉 · 诺德豪斯
译 · 注 · 疏 于 健
策 划 刘 力 陆 瑜
责任编辑 徐向娟
装帧设计 陶建胜

◆ 人民邮电出版社出版发行 北京市东城区夕照寺街 14 号 A 座
邮编 100061 电子邮件 315@ptpress.com.cn
网址 http://www.ptpress.com.cn
电话 （编辑部）010-84937150 （市场部）010-84937152
申请课件：ncceco@163.com
三河市少明印务有限公司印刷
新华书店经销

◆ 开本：850 × 1092 1/16
印张：48.75 插页 12
字数：1463 千字 2013 年 11 月第 1 版 2018 年 12月第 5次印刷
著作权合同登记号 图字：01-2011-7067

ISBN 978-7-115-32871-7/F

定价：158.00 元

本书如有印装质量问题，请与本社联系 电话：(010) 84937153

内容提要

本书是萨缪尔森先生的绝笔《经济学》19版的双语注疏版。本书自1948年问世以来就广受赞誉，先后被翻译成40多种文字，是有史以来发行量最大、至今在全球范围内仍然被广泛采用的经济学教科书。本书在经历了前18个版本的积累和沉淀后，融入了时代变革的元素和新的案例及数据。以此为基础，为了让广大读者对萨翁经典有更好的了解，我们添加了词句解释和注疏——既有译者对标题和难懂的词句的中文注释，也有译者对英文原文中的语言、原作者的写作背景以及经济学家和企业等的注疏。

本书共31章，包括经济学核心概念、现代混合经济、供给与需求、竞争市场、商业周期与总需求、货币与金融体系、货币政策与经济、经济增长、经济发展的挑战以及汇率与国际金融体系、失业、通货膨胀等。每章都有译者的详尽注释和精彩注疏。

本书适合于经济学专业、财经类专业的本科生及教师，MPA、MBA、EMBA、IMBA学员及教师，理论研究者，政府工作人员及企事业管理者学习和研究之用。

To our families, students, and colleagues

ABOUT THE AUTHORS

PAUL A. SAMUELSON, founder of the renowned MIT graduate department of economics, was trained at the University of Chicago and Harvard. His many scientific writings brought him world fame at a young age, and in 1970 he was the first American to receive a Nobel Prize in economics. One of those rare scientists who can communicate with the lay public, Professor Samuelson wrote an economics column for *Newsweek* for many years and was economic adviser to President John F. Kennedy. He testifies often before Congress and serves as academic consultant to the Federal Reserve, the U.S. Treasury, and various private, nonprofit organizations. Professor Samuelson, between researches at MIT and tennis games, is a visiting professor at New York University. His six children (including triplet boys) have contributed 15 grandchildren.

[1] **保罗·萨缪尔森**（Paul A. Samuelson），1915 年 5 月 15 日出生在美国印第安纳州盖瑞市一位波兰裔的犹太移民家庭。2009 年 12 月 14 日，在麻省贝尔蒙市的家中逝世，离开了 70 年来为之倾注毕生心血的现代经济学科。萨缪尔森 20 岁（1935）毕业于芝加哥大学。同年以全美 8 位最杰出的本科生的身份被选送哈佛大学攻读文学硕士和哲学博士学位。1941 年，其博士论文《经济理论的运行意义》（*The Operational Significance of Economic Theory*）获著名的哈佛大学威尔斯博士论文奖（David A. Wells Prize），并受聘留校任讲师，但麻省理工学院以助理教授的职位将其挖走直至逝世。正如麻省理工学院校长苏珊·霍克菲尔德对萨氏一生所作的评价："保罗·萨缪尔森在其一生所从事的每一个学术领域都做出了革命性的贡献——经济学的理论基础、全球经济学科的教学方法、麻省理工学院经济系学派思想体系的建立和思潮的发展、学校的战略发展和资金募集、学术团队与学生人生和学术道路的塑造等。总而言之，无论是人品还是学品，萨缪尔森都是麻省理工学院经济系团队精神的杰出代表，他所做的一切都是 MIT 精神的集中体现。" 1947 年，32 岁的保罗被美国经济学会授予 40 岁以下最有成就的克拉克奖（John Bates Clark Medal）。1970 年获诺贝尔经济学奖，是美国获此殊荣的第一人。

WILLIAM D. NORDHAUS is one of America's eminent economists. Born in Albuquerque, New Mexico, he received his B.A. from Yale and his Ph.D. in economics at MIT. He is Sterling Professor of Economics at Yale University and on the staff of the Cowles Foundation for Research in Economics and the National Bureau of Economic Research. His research has spanned much of economics—including the environment, energy, technological change, economic growth, and trends in profits and productivity. In addition, Professor Nordhaus takes a keen interest in economic policy. He served as a member of President Carter's Council of Economic Advisers from 1977 to 1979, serves on many government advisory boards and committees, and writes occasionally for *The New York Review of Books* and other periodicals. He regularly teaches the Principles of Economics course at Yale. Professor Nordhaus lives in New Haven, Connecticut, with his wife, Barbara. When not writing or teaching, he devotes his time to music, travel, skiing, and family.

[2] **威廉·诺德豪斯**（William A. Nordhaus），1941 年 5 月 31 日出生于新墨西哥州的阿布科克市，耶鲁大学经济学讲座教授，美国国家科学院院士和瑞典皇家工程科学院外籍院士，1986~1988 年任耶鲁大学教务长，1992~1993 年任耶鲁大学副校长。从 1985 年的第 12 版起，诺德豪斯即成为萨缪尔森《经济学》教材所有版本的合作编写者，现与妻子居住在康州的纽黑文市（New Haven）。

注疏者简介

于 健，中国政法大学教授，国内重点高校教学中率先同步使用萨缪尔森各版次经典的经济学教材，18 年如一日，用中西哲学的不同思维研究萨缪尔森经济学、采用中英双语教育的学者。于健教授先后求学和任教于北京大学、中国政法大学、首都师范大学、辽宁师范大学、沈阳师范大学、北京工商大学、山西晋中学院等，曾应邀出任了欧盟 *EuroSinoEducationalNetwork* 项目的中方首席主持人、国家级火炬计划《中小学数字化图书馆》和《全国中小学通用校园网》等项目主持人。代表性著作有萨缪尔森《微观经济学》（第 19 版注疏本）、《宏观经济学》（第 19 版注疏本）、《中国教育的出路问题》和《中国英语教育改革探思录》等。

永远的萨缪尔森，定格的19版

——写在《经济学》第19版注疏本出版之际

公元2009年12月14日，周一，课满。习惯于早早出门，地铁，班车……。突然，手机铃声划破天际，从遥远的南国而至，萨翁去世了。噩耗传来，思绪难抑，三站地铁之隙，即咏而就：

萨翁噩耗惊天地，
巨著十九泣鬼神；
四八首版逾甲子，
天翻地覆功一人。

萨翁《经济学》第19版的出版在全球经济学界是谈论久已和期待的事情了，尤其是自己。从2000年的第17版开始，我就始终是全球范围内能在第一时间享受到样书的人。19版对我而言更有其特殊意义。从这一版开始，应约为200多年来的西方经济学经典做一套注疏本。这是一项国内学术界开创性的工程，既兴奋，又倍感责任重大。萨翁《微观经济学》19版的注疏本是这套丛书的第一本，萨翁《宏观经济学》第19版的注疏本为第二本。第三本即本书，萨缪尔森的绝笔——《经济学》第19版注疏本。

2009年9月6日，周日，正逢北京国际书展，与麦格劳–希尔教育出版公司参加书展的小张将19版的样书在亮马桥地铁站交割。那是一个兴奋而又难以忘却的时刻，这本书我已经等待太久。第二天周一是新学期的第一节课，弟子们又可以再一次在全球范围内率先享受到萨翁的最新版，先睹为快和第一使用者的幸福感难以言表。

按照麦格劳–希尔的出版计划，19版的出版时间刚好赶上金融危机爆发。这就是萨氏的经济学，始终与战后60多年人类历史的脚步同行。这一次也不例外，萨翁的“收官之作”只有加入了金融危机的内容，才可能真正定格。麦格劳–希尔也为此而不得不数次“毁约”。

本书的第一版从1948年推出至今已经走过了65年的历史。所有的19个版本版版经典，版版畅销。2008年，恰逢第一版60周年，动议中的该版中文版也正式进入出版程序，我很快地进入角色，翻译工作按部就班地进行。但是，酝酿数年之久的个人文集突然在2009年的3月由现代教育出版社正式批复书号，手头正在翻译中的萨翁《经济学》第一版被迫暂停，致使本已在安排之中的有萨缪尔森亲撰序的60周年中文纪念版成了永远的遗憾。第一版的中文版也纯粹因为我个人的原因而被迫延后，愧以告慰天国的萨翁。谨以此文及这三本书的问世，聊以慰之。

26年前的一天，在校园门口二手书摊上摆售的萨翁经济学第12版在纷纷杂杂的原版书中，其夺目的装帧设计一跃进入了我的视线，前言里萨氏语言逻辑的独特吸力，将我和萨翁从此连在了一起。在那之前的近40年时间里，这样的书对于中国学者来讲，绝对是另外一个世界。

第二次世界大战刚刚结束后的麻省理工学院学生有一学年的经济学必修课，教材沉闷、教授低迷、学生厌学。“务必请您编写一本既能引起学生兴趣，学术态度还必须严谨的经济学教科书，将一个学期或一个学年枯燥的经济学课程变得轻松起来。”系主任的一席话让刚刚因为博士论文的发表而在美国声名鹊起的萨缪尔森遇到了难得的机会。

1938年，23岁的萨缪尔森与小其一岁的同窗师妹玛丽昂·克劳福德（1916~1978）结婚，由于战争及玛丽昂攻读博士学位的缘故，直到战后两人才开始组织自己的小家。玛丽昂不仅是年轻的萨缪尔森事业上的得力推手，更是其温暖舒适的避风港湾。在其第四次怀孕时，一胎送给了丈夫三个儿子。1978年，62岁的爱妻死于癌症。三年后，丽莎·伊卡思走进了他的生活，为萨缪尔森承担起抚养前妻6个孩子的责任，让萨翁的晚年在夫人、6个子女、15个孙辈的天伦之乐中含着微笑走到了人生的尽头。

萨缪尔森是幸福的，他走得自然，走得安详，他在家人的陪伴下走入他早已为自己建构好的永恒世界。

“在中世纪末期，英国有一位伟大的诗人乔叟。一天，他看见三个人正在忙碌，遂上前问道：‘诸位在忙些什么？’第一个人随口答道：‘我在挣钱，这活挣得多。’第二个人慢条斯理地说：‘我在把这些宝石和玻璃镜片雕拼成神圣的图案。’第三个人振振有词：‘我在建一座伟大的教堂。’”这段话是1998年萨缪尔森在麦格劳－希尔出版公司为其重印第1版50周年纪念版时专门撰序的开头所讲的一段故事。在完成第1版写作任务的艰难的三个月时间里，萨缪尔森讲自己“始终同时扮演着这三个不同的角色”。

这就是只属于萨缪尔森的永恒世界，三者兼而有之。

1948年第一版的畅销，几乎使萨缪尔森一夜之间成为拜伦式的英雄。这一奇迹，保持了30年之久。过去的四五十年中，出现了几本经济学教科书，对萨翁的经济学教科书形成了挑战，有的甚至一度超过了该书的销量。但迄今仍然没有一本经济学的教科书能够历经61年，18次再版，版版精品，版版畅销。从某种程度上我们可以说，既是麦格劳－希尔出版公司造就了萨缪尔森，也是萨缪尔森造就了麦格劳－希尔。对于幼年艰难经历的保罗而言，19个版次的出版发行，历时60余年源源不断的版税收入对于其儿孙满堂的晚年生活更有其作为一个普通人的实质意义。这一点萨缪尔森更像东方人，一个地地道道的犹太人。

1915年的5月15日，萨缪尔森出生在印第安纳州的盖瑞市。父亲是一位来自波兰的犹太移民，依托当地新兴的钢铁工业，一家人的日子靠父亲经营的药店过得红红火火。然而，好景不长，第一次世界大战的持续使全家几乎濒临破落，只好举家迁往芝加哥。此时的芝加哥，百业凋零，即便是中产阶级的家庭，也只能是“我们在饥饿中挣扎，谁又能施舍我们一颗土豆？”这就是留在萨缪尔森心中挥之不去的关于芝加哥的童年记忆。这样的早期生活经历促使正在海德高中读高一的保罗开始研究股票市场。在 20 年代的牛市期，一次偶然的机会，萨缪尔森帮助自己的代数老师买进的几支股票，着实让老师猛赚了一把。直到 70 多年后的一次专访中，萨翁还能如数家珍、津津有味地形容它是针对于人之本能思维惰性的“系统误导性检验”（proof of the fallibility of systems）理论。从此，萨缪尔森走上了一条天才经济学家的道路，让我们这个前 50 年危机（两次世界大战和一次大萧条）后 50 年和平（萨缪尔森在 17 版的前言中对 20 世纪的精辟断代）的世界拥有了一位真正的经济学大师。

这是萨缪尔森的第一个永恒世界。

早在芝加哥和哈佛大学读书期间，萨缪尔森就是一位“既不考虑资历也不考虑地位、率直批评教授们的弟子”，这是耶鲁大学的诺奖得主詹姆斯·托宾对萨翁的回忆和评价。萨缪尔森这种在学术上桀骜不驯的精神也使其与具有同样个性的哈佛大学经济系主任哈罗德·伯班克的关系既牢固又飘忽不定的微妙，学术观点上针锋相对，个人关系上融洽温暖。在萨缪尔森被美国经济学会授予 40 岁以下最有成就的克拉克奖（John Bates Clark Medal）时，就受到了来自哈罗德的强烈抵制。这个奖项也最终导致萨缪尔森成为第一位获得诺贝尔经济学奖的美国人。被伯班克教授强烈批评的萨缪尔森的博士论文，也在其后被全世界的经济学家们热捧 20 多年之久。保罗常把这件事笑谈为“甜蜜的报复”。

直到弗里德曼去世之前，萨缪尔森与米尔顿·弗里德曼（1976 年诺贝尔经济学奖得主）之间的学术纷争在经济学界始终是家喻户晓的事情。两人都是芝加哥大学的同门弟子，弗里德曼是师兄，萨缪尔森是学弟。从那时开始，在半个多世纪的学术生涯中，两人几乎在任何问题上都是针锋相对的对手。然而，很少有人知道萨弗二人在学术之外却是非常要好的朋友，相互嘘寒问暖的兄弟。

萨缪尔森一生高徒满堂，最有影响的学生当属肯尼迪总统。肯尼迪在竞选成功后的第一时间所做的第一件事情就是邀请萨缪尔森为他授课。两人课前坐在马萨诸塞州避暑胜地海恩尼斯海边的岩石上有一次深入的心与心的交流。按照肯尼迪家族的惯例，课前必须在其私人游艇上举行一次盛宴款待老师，萨缪尔森对此颇感失望。然而，他却另有一番调侃：“我们举行了一次大脑与内心深度交流的思想大餐。”总统与学者之间这样心与心的交流使肯尼迪政府领导下的美国成功地避免了一次潜在的经济危机。作为肯尼迪总统的高级智囊，萨缪尔森谢绝了肯尼迪的入阁邀请。在他看来，担任了总统经济顾问委员会主席后，将无法按照自己的判断去讲话，去写文章。

上任伊始，肯尼迪如沐春风，搭建了一个强有力的财政团队，预算也已平衡，只欠大刀阔斧地施政而已。然而，萨缪尔森给他的谏言却是美国经济正在走向衰退的警告，必须通过减税来规避这场危机。肯尼迪对此极为恼怒。但总统最终还是接受了保罗的劝告，按照萨的设计，推出了著名的“肯尼迪减税方案”。即使发生了举世瞩目的遇刺身亡事件，其继任的约翰逊总统还是成功地实施了这项方案，使美国的经济很快地得以恢复。

这就是萨缪尔森的第二个永恒世界。把那些漂亮的各自相左的宝石和玻璃镜片兼收并蓄，雕拼成神圣的图案。这是他的信仰，他的追求，义无反顾，勇往直前。

晚年的萨缪尔森思维更加敏锐而冷静。"适度的中间路线"是其晚年对崛起中的中国发自肺腑的箴言。他在寻找一条人类社会健康发展的既不左也不右的中庸之道。如果上苍能够再给萨缪尔森几年的时间，我确信，他一定会深入到孔子和老子的研究中去。

萨缪尔森的这一思想集中体现在最新的第 19 版中。94 岁的老人不但亲自大动干戈地将第 18 版的内容删去了 10%，并与时俱进地更新了 30% 以上的数据和内容，而且亲自执笔写就了那篇置于本书序言之前的空前绝后的"一个中道老者的宣言"。这篇自序对战后经济科学的发展进行了深入的反思，对功过得失进行了彻底的梳理，是 19 版得以在历史上定格的基石。7 个月后的 2009 年 9 月 2 日，获奖不到一年的诺奖得主保罗·克鲁格曼在《纽约时报》发表了一篇极其重要的专栏文章《经济学家们为什么会如此错误百出》（*How Did Economists Get It So Wrong?*）。这篇文章应该是克鲁格曼对萨翁这篇自序的回应，一个后生对前辈的继承。

这就是萨缪尔森的第三个永恒世界。他倾其一生在努力"建一座伟大的教堂"——一座东西兼容、南北并包、天下和谐大同而又个性张扬，全球化的世界经济按照其提出的乘数加速模型发展的大教堂，这也是崛起的中国所矢志追求的和谐世界，中华民族迎接两个百年所要圆就的中国梦。

萨缪尔森一生所追求的这三个永恒世界，同时也是萨缪尔森集 19 个版本的经济学教材为我们今天这个全球化的世界所建构的三层结构的金字塔。概括起来即：力图多挣钱，养家糊口的底座结构，这是人类解决生存问题的必需；用宝石和玻璃镜片雕拼神圣图案的中阶结构，这是两百多年来经济学巨匠们的同心协力之作，凯恩斯即是这些巨匠中间杰出的代表；能进入到建构伟大教堂行列的则只有萨缪尔森的《经济学》，以及亚当·斯密以《道德情操论》为哲学基础所构建的思想，这也是萨缪尔森《经济学》被誉为学界"圣经"和"天书"的本质原因所在。

莎士比亚的 37 部戏剧中有四大悲剧，500 多年来历久而弥新，铺就了人类现代文明的重要基石。无独有偶，萨缪尔森的 19 个版本中，第 1 版、第 12 版、第 17 版及第 19 版四个版本，则是经典中的经典，天书中的天书。而绝笔之作的第 19 版，则是塔尖上最耀眼的一部。著名的米兰大教堂始建于 1386 年，正好与乔叟同期，到 1960 年最后一扇铜门安装到位，历时 574 年。这 574 年，是西方社会从黑暗的中世纪将全世界推入美国式全球化的半个千年。萨缪尔森的经济学教科书，站在亚当·斯密的肩上，融两百多年来经济学各流派之大同，集古希腊古罗马以来西方文明之大成，迎接和拥抱了中华民族开始崛起的中国式全球化的曙光。

一向保守自恃的印度学者在印度"塔塔"版的萨缪尔森 *Economics* 第 19 版中，夹进了几百字的前言，开头有这样一段话：

> 萨缪尔森的经济学教材从 1948 年的第 1 版一问世，即在经济学界树立了一个既学术严谨又通俗易懂的教材样板。……其所倡导的新古典主义综合模式，成为后来经济学的主流思想。萨缪尔森的经济学教材始终坚持了这一原则，不为激进思想或者昙花一现的时尚潮流所左右。但与此同时，又毫无学派成见地对经济学领域固守的普世价值的新思想，不吝笔墨地在第一时间予以推介。
>
> 现在，经济学教材的版本繁多，对经济学的基本原理都有很好的论述。但萨缪尔森的这部堪称凤凰涅槃之作的 19 版，依然是其中论述最为准确和清晰、最通俗易懂者之一。

“最为准确和清晰、最通俗易懂”之说即底座结构的“养家糊口”层面，目前在业界享有口碑的原版经济学教材都属于这个层面，给学生和老师以基本的生存技能。而由经济学巨匠所编撰的经典教材，则非萨缪尔森莫属。

国人所作注疏体应始于先秦时期对典籍的注释。汉武帝的“罢黜百家，独尊儒术”催生了经注，两汉之后出现了义疏，范围逐渐扩大到了经、史、子、集各类。义疏又称讲疏，原本为佛门讲经和清谈玄学的一种方式，以疏通文字、讲解义理为主，方式自由，内容详尽。宋、元、明时期“求变求新”，摒弃门户之见，出现了一批理学注疏大家。清代的典籍注疏更是盛极一时，倡导了以训诂考据为主流的务实学风，考据学兴盛，注疏也迅速发展，出现了补注、集注、评注、校注等一系列的注疏方法。

如果说佛经的翻译在唐代达到顶峰，以及与之相伴随的讲经是国人对外来经典的最早的注疏的话，国人对西方经典的注疏则是一项两千多年以来几近空白的领域。从这个意义上讲来，作为对“圣经”和“天书”注疏的萨缪尔森《微观经济学》19 版注疏本和萨缪尔森《宏观经济学》19 版注疏本，以及本书的出现，即是国内学术界一项开创性的探索。

在美国的知识产权保护领域有一个很著名的案例。作者 X 就其经济学教材涉嫌被 Y 剽窃的侵权行为向法院提起诉讼，愤怒的法官不屑一顾地拒绝受理这一诉讼:“无论从哪个角度看，你们双方的版本都是从萨缪尔森那里克隆来的。”（见即将出版的萨氏经济学 1948 年首版中文版）。所以，微缩到经济学教材领域，萨翁为期 61 年的 19 个经济学教材版本已成为其各个历史时期的母本，定格在了人类战后的伟大和平时期（萨翁第 17 版的伟大断代说）。在世界经济从 20 世纪的美国式全球化到 21 世纪走向中国式全球化的进程中，萨缪尔森的经济学教材及其模式必将与时俱进。

第 12 版是全部 19 版中具有转折意义的一个版本。它不但为萨氏经济学教材作为模板做了铺垫——引领所有的经济学教材采纳;更重要的,它是冷战结束的丧钟。丧钟为谁而鸣（*For Whom the Bell Tolls*）？我们真希望今天的奥巴马能像当年的肯尼迪一样，有萨缪尔森这样的学者为其撞钟，再不要出现迪思莉·罗杰斯那样的美女幕僚为蹭一顿国宴而小脑动尽，被顶尖权威的媒体将其与伍兹的绯闻放在一起让社会所诟病［《纽约时报》2009 年 12 月 5 日的专栏文章《美女与猛虎》(*The Beauty and the Tiger*)］。

与学术界和社会大众对萨翁定位的不同，萨缪尔森认为自己首先是一位哲学家。从第 12 版开始，萨翁极其深厚的人文修养在新的版式设计中表现得淋漓尽致，这一点令克隆其模式的所有经济学教材只能是班门弄斧。曼昆本人对此有坦诚的表述，他认为现在流行的经济学教材比起萨翁的所有版本来讲只是小巫见大巫。

国外的权威媒体在关注并赞赏中国崛起的同时，谈到中国的教育时，往往使用一个极其令人警惕的词“collapse”，应该说这是一种善意的警告。60 多年来我们的教育培养出大批国家建设亟需的工程师，基本扫除了文盲，成就巨大。但比起中国今天的发展和迅速提高中的国际地位来讲，在国家政治、经济、社会和文化的高端，我们还缺少与之相适应的人才储备。这一点正是“collapse”之所在，我们必须对此倍加重视。回到西方经济学这门纯粹的舶来学科就更为明显。作为改革开放重要指标之一的西方经济学课程的建设和教材的翻译，从萨翁第 10 版开始，在每个版本中集中体现萨缪尔森思想精髓的 30% 部分，与萨氏原著相悖的距离始终很大，很大。这也正是笔者矢志编写注疏本的初衷和目的——帮助读者免受所有译本中随处可见的“关公战秦琼”式的“善意误导”和人文史哲以及语言逻辑方面的误解陷阱。

萨翁的经济学教材从根本上讲是一本哲学教科书，一本特殊的哲学论著，萨缪尔森本人也在这一最新版本的前言部分第一次作了明确的表达。这也是萨翁经济学教材 60 多年长盛不衰的关键所在。即便是美国大学的经济学教授也普遍认为读懂萨翁的经济学教材着实不是一件容易做到的事情。这当然指的是本书内容约 30% 以上的部分，这些内容是萨缪尔森将人类几千年文明（当然是欧洲文明），特别是文艺复兴 600 多年以来的现代文明精髓矢志以求的集大成之作。它们是每个新的版本重点修订的内容之一，散布于全书的各个章节。

这些内容就是笔者对本书的重点注疏部分。* 它集中了笔者几十年来的探索与思考，其所涉范围绝不仅仅局限于萨翁第 19 版的经济学教材，同时覆盖了从第 1 版到第 19 版的每一个版本的精华。更为重要的是，这些内容是对与萨翁的 19 个版本同步走来的战后世界伟大和平的半个多世纪的反思，是对 1949 年之后新中国崛起过程的深层次思考，是对未来构建大中华（the Grand China）文化的冷静思索（cool heads at the service of warm hearts，萨翁语）。由于能力所限，这些注疏部分一定会有一些有待商榷之处，衷心希望读者不吝赐教。同时，也借此机会希望此书的读者能够回归到拜读原著的原生状态。像萨翁经济学这样的经典原著，必须依赖于经典而权威的英文原版词典阅读，所谓的电子词典乃少儿不宜之物，严重一点讲犹如毒品，应尽可能地远离为好。这里，顺便向读者推荐欧美学术界公认的三本各具特色的案头词典：

* 注：本书的注疏文字以 [1][2][3]……标记，翻译文字以①②③……标记。

1. *Webster's New World Dictionary of American English*
2. *Merriam–Webster's Collegiate Dictionary*
3. *The American Heritage Dictionary of the English Language*

这在一定程度上是代表读书人“身份”的权威工具书，有条件的读者最好同时拥有。此乃读书人之一大幸事，个中定有黄金屋，其乐无穷。某种程度讲来，无论英语是否为母语，会不会使用权威经典的工具书乃衡量读者是否已经进入英文自由王国的终极指标。阅读中遇到生词，希望读者养成一个以词典为师的好习惯。在空白处用中文解释没有歧义的生词，弊多利少，本书基本未予提供，此乃笔者的良苦用心，还望读者理解。如果您能静下心来，借助于上述词典和笔者的注疏，认认真真地读几遍本书，一定会有胜读 20 年书的感觉。

西方但凡受过良好教育的人都有很好的文学和哲学修养，作为一代宗师的萨缪尔森更为突出。萨翁是一位极富唯美思想的唯美主义哲学家，对莎士比亚的作品更是情有独钟。2009 年 12 月 14 日萨翁逝世的噩耗传来的当晚，笔者彻夜难眠，遂步莎士比亚 14 行诗为韵，填英文古典诗一首，以悼萨翁。值此开创性的萨翁 19 版注疏本付梓之际，笔者特将此诗附于此。我想，这首 14 行诗一定能飞到天外的保罗身边，让萨翁的思想随着诗行的吟诵，永远寄托着一位中国学者对他的追念。同时，也愿已经进入自己永恒世界的萨翁，为其绝笔之作在中国有了他的注疏本而感到欣慰。

SONNET

In Memory of Paul Samuelson

Shall I compare you to a super star?
You're at all much brighter and much bigger;
Cold winds blow the leaves away from trees far,
Your thoughts along with the flying leaves linger;
Sometime warmer the eye of heaven shines,
And it rains or boils with cloudless often,
And every truth from truth sometime declines,
By changing nature, new science opens;
But your eternal theory shall not fade,
Nor lose possession of that truth you have;
Nor's Death taken you away in his shade,
When in eternal lines to time you save:
    Nobody else could smooth what we grieve,

Nothing else would make up what you leave.

December 14, 2009

为便于广大读者阅读，特将拙作的中文版本附后。中英文诗歌，特别是古体诗歌是不可能互译的。因此，中文版本虽是笔者根据本诗意境创作的，但还是建议有英文基础的读者最好不要比照吟之。

悼萨翁仙逝

我欲比公似巨星，
巨星岂敢见萨翁；
寒风淩叶扬天外，
片片洌叶捲君腾；
天眼偶尔送温暖，
阴雨连绵烈日蒸；
与时俱进新知现，
人间真理难永恒；
巨著十九部部精，
珠玑字字阅真诚；
死神阴影谋罩君，
等身巨著伴君生；
先生仙逝难弥补，
天地动容人间芃。

己丑十一月二十九

于 健

2010 年 1 月 3 日于京都万科星园“守中和”，以致《微观经济学》。

时窗外漫天飞雪，万物已尺厚银装，京城半个世纪之最大雪，近半个世纪以来最低温。然斗室如春，心潮温动，虽序至此，难以抑止，只有萨翁一句名言落此，聊以表达完成本书近一年来的状态而已：

Cool heads at the service of warm hearts。

2012 年 8 月 21 第二稿，以序《宏观经济学》。

2013 年 7 月 1 日第三稿，序《经济学》第 19 版双语注疏本，以祭于文襄公敏中天祖总裁《四库全书》241 周年。

Contents in Brief

简要目录

Contents

目　录

A Centrist Proclamation [1]

一位中道老者的宣言

Sciences advance. But they can also recede. That is true of economics as well. By the end of World War II, the leading introductory textbooks in economics had lost their vitality and relevance. Nature abhors a vacuum. The first edition of this textbook [2] appeared as the 1948 edition of Samuelson's *ECONOMICS*. It introduced macroeconomics into our colleges and served as the gold standard for teaching economics in an increasingly globalized world.

Both the economy and economics have changed greatly over the years. Successive editions of this textbook, which became Samuelson-Nordhaus *ECONOMICS*, have documented the evolutionary changes in the world economy [3] and have provided the latest rigorous economic thinking at the frontier of the discipline.

To our surprise, this nineteenth edition may be one of the most significant of all revisions. We call this the *centrist edition*. It proclaims the value of the mixed economy—an economy that combines the tough discipline of the market with fair-minded governmental oversight.

Centrism is of vital importance today because the global economy is in a terrible meltdown—perhaps worse than any cyclical slump since the Great Depression [4] of the 1930s. Alas, many textbooks have strayed too far toward over-complacent libertarianism. They joined the celebration of free-market finance and supported dismantling regulations and abolishing oversight. The bitter harvest of this celebration was seen in the irrationally exuberant housing and stock markets that collapsed and led to the current financial crisis.

The centrism we describe is not a prescription that is intended to persuade readers away from their beliefs. We are analysts and not cult prescribers. It is not ideology that breeds centrism as our theme. We sift facts and theories to determine the consequences of Hayek-Friedman libertarianism. All readers are free to make [5] up their own minds about best ethics and value judgments.

Having surveyed the terrain, this is our reading: Economic history confirms that neither unregulated capitalism nor overregulated central planning can organize a modern society effectively.

The follies of the left and right both mandate centrism. Tightly controlled central planning, which was widely advocated in the middle decades of the last century, was abandoned after it produced stagnation and unhappy consumers in communist countries.

What exactly was the road to serfdom that Hayek and Friedman warned us against? They were arguing against social security, a minimum wage, national parks, progressive taxation, and government rules to clean up the environment or slow global warming. People who live in high-income societies support these programs with great majorities. Such mixed economies involve both the rule of law and the limited liberty to compete.

[1] Centrism，中间路线；centrist，中道之人；萨翁笃信中间路线，笃行中庸之道，晚年尤甚；此乃萨翁自封。

[2] Nature abhors a vacuum. 英文谚语，出自公元一世纪古希腊哲学家普卢塔克（Plutarch）的论文及讲演集（*Plutarch of Delphi*）中的风俗与道德问题（*Moralia*）篇，莎士比亚的历史剧和后来许多欧洲人文大家常引用。意为：新陈代谢，推陈出新，自然界的发展规律永远不可能出现停滞不前的空洞状态。

[3] Macroeconomics, 宏观经济学，它和微观经济学（microeconomics）两个词首次于 1941 年出现在肯尼思・艾瓦特・博尔丁（1910~1993，一位笃信基督教的美国经济学家，出生于英国利物浦，美国十大教授之一，曾任美国经济学会会长，美国文理研究院院长）的《经济分析》（*Economic Analysis*），是本书第 1 版（1948）出版之前最畅销的经济学教科书。此时 macroeconomics 一词尚未收录到英文词典，萨翁《经济学》第一版所附索引也未列出。

Samuelson-Nordhaus *ECONOMICS*，从第 12 版开始，萨缪尔森的《经济学》成了与威廉・诺德豪斯的合著，这一版本记录了世界经济的深刻变化和经济科学思想蓬勃发展的最新前沿，同时，也预示着冷战的结束。所以，第 12 版在所有 19 个版本中具有转折性的历史意义。

[4] Cyclical，此处与 *Nature abhors a vacuum* 呼应。本段所表达的思想萨翁在 2005 年 12 月接受《人民日报》记者专访时即已做出预警，实质上预测到了两年后从房贷危机开始的金融危机（详见 2005 年 12 月 26 日人民日报第 7 版）。

[5] 哈耶克（Friedrich August von Hayek，1899~1992），奥地利经济学派的杰出代表人物之一，1938 年入英国国籍，著名的经济学家和哲学家，终身维护古典自由主义的资本主义自由市场经济理论，强烈反对社会主义。米尔顿・弗里德曼（Milton Friedman，1912~2006），美国芝加哥自由主义经济学派的杰出代表人物之一，萨缪尔森的师兄，两人终身观点相左，但平时生活中又是极其要好的朋友，在学术界颇为称道。

We survey the centrist approach to economics in the pages that follow. Millions of students in China, India, Latin America, and emerging societies have sought economic wisdom from these pages. Our task is to make sure that the latest and best thinking of economists is contained here, describing the logic of the modern mixed economy, but always presenting in a fair manner the views of those who criticize it from the left and the right.

limited centrism 可控型中间路线。

But we go a step further in our proclamation. We hold that there must be a *limited centrism.* Our knowledge is imperfect, and society's resources are limited. We are also mindful of our current predicament. We see that unfettered capitalism has generated painful inequalities of income and wealth, and that supply-side fiscal doctrines have produced large government deficits. We observe that the major innovations of modern finance, when operating in an unregulated system, have produced trillions of dollars of losses and led to the ruin of many venerable financial institutions.

limited center 可控型中间道路。

Only by steering our societies back to the limited center can we ensure that the global economy returns to full employment where the fruits of progress are more equally shared.

Paul A. Samuelson
February 2009

Preface

前 言

As we complete this nineteenth edition of *Economics*, the U.S. economy has fallen into a deep recession as well as the most serious financial crisis since the Great Depression of the 1930s. The federal government [1] has invested hundreds of billions of dollars to protect the fragile network of the U.S. and indeed the world financial system. The new Obama administration has worked with Congress to pass the largest stimulus package in American history. The economic turmoil, and the manner in which countries respond to it, will shape the American economy, its labor market, and the world financial system for years to come.

We should remember, however, that the financial crisis of 2007–2009 came after more than a half-century of spectacular increases in the living standards of most of the world, particularly those living in the affluent countries of North America, [2] Western Europe, and East Asia. People are asking, "Will the twenty-first century repeat the successes of the last century? Will the affluence of the few spread to poor countries? Alternatively, will the four horsemen of the economic apocalypse [3] — famine, war, environmental degradation, and depression — spread to the North? [4] Do we have the wisdom to reshape our financial systems so that they can continue to provide the investments that have fueled economic growth up to now? And what should we think about environmental threats such as global warming?"

These are ultimately the questions we address in this new edition of *Economics*.

市场日益重要

The Growing Role of Markets

You might think that prosperity would lead to a declining interest in economic affairs, but paradoxically an understanding of the enduring truths of economics has become even more vital in the affairs of people and nations. Those who remember history recognize that the crises that threatened financial markets in the twenty-first century were the modern counterpart of banking panics of an earlier era.

In the larger scene, the world has become increasingly interconnected as computers and communications create an ever more competitive global marketplace. Developing countries like China and India—two giants that relied heavily on central planning until recently—need a firm understanding of the institutions of a market economy if they are to attain the living standards of the affluent. At the same time, there is growing concern about international environmental problems and the need to forge agreements to preserve our precious natural heritage. All these fascinating changes are part of the modern drama that we call ⑤ economics.

新版经济学

ECONOMICS Reborn [6]

For more than half a century, this book has served as the standard-bearer for the teaching of introductory economics in classrooms in America and throughout the world. Each new edition distills the best thinking of economists about how markets function and about what countries can do to improve people's living standards. But economics has changed profoundly since the first edition of this text appeared in 1948. Moreover, because economics is above all a living and evolving organism, *Economics* is born anew each edition as the authors have the exciting opportunity to present the latest thinking of modern economists and to show how the subject can contribute to a more prosperous world.

Our task then is this: We strive to present a clear, accurate, and interesting introduction to the principles of modern economics and to the institutions of the American and world economies. Our primary goal is to emphasize the core economic principles that will endure beyond today's headlines.

---

[1] 世纪元年出版的第 17 版在萨缪尔森长达 61 年的 19 个版本中占有比较重要的地位。其中重要的原因之一是在前言中，萨翁看似不经意间将刚刚结束的 20 世纪做了一个全新的断代界定，即前 50 年的 *The Great Depression* 和后 50 年的 *The Great Peace*。这一断代学说正好与长波论（*Long Wave Cycles*）创始人、前苏联经济学家尼古拉·康德拉季耶夫（Nikolai D. Kondratieff，1892~1938）的著名周期理论相契合。

[2] affluent：巨富之意，源自古法语，此词的使用某种程度上反映作者的人文功底。affluence 为其名词形式。

[3] four horsemen of the apocalypse 源自 1921 年发行并获巨大成功的同名好莱坞反战影片，1961 年重拍，故事情节由第一次大战转移到了第二次大战。apocalypse 源自圣经，即启示录，有吉凶启征之意。

[4] the North：富国集团，因最富的国家基本在北半球而得名，与 the South 相对。

⑤ the modern drama that we call economics: 经济学的现代大戏。

[6] *ECONOMICS* reborn：*ECONOMICS* 特指本教材的所有版本（详见注疏者序），reborn，涅槃之意。

第 19 版
THE NINETEENTH EDITION

[1] philosophy 是奠定萨氏经济学 19 个版本版版经典的关键基石，也是其过人之处。从 1998 年的第 16 版开始基本成型，在本版的 THE NIETEENTH EDITION 这一节第一次明确地提出了哲学思想的概念，共 6 点（16 版 10 点，17 版 9 点，18 版 7 点）。自此，标志着萨缪尔森的经济学教材开创性地成为**经济哲学**教科书。

As economics and the world around it evolve, so does this book. Our philosophy continues to emphasize [1] six basic principles that underlie earlier editions and this revision:

1. The Core Truths of Economics. Often, economics ② appears to be an endless procession of new puzzles, problems, and dilemmas. But as experienced teachers have learned, there are a few basic concepts that underpin all of economics. Once these concepts have been mastered, learning is much quicker and more enjoyable. *We have therefore chosen to focus on the central core of economics—on those enduring truths that will be just as important in the twenty-first century as they were in the twentieth.* Microeconomic concepts such as scarcity, efficiency, the gains from specialization, and the principle of comparative advantage will be crucial concepts as long as scarcity itself exists. In macroeconomics, we emphasize the two central approaches: Keynesian economics to understand business cycles, and the neoclassical growth model to understand longer-term growth trends. Within these frameworks, established approaches such as the consumption function take place alongside new developments in financial macroeconomics.

2. Innovation in Economics. Economics has made many advances in understanding the role of inno- [3] vation. We are accustomed to the dizzying speed of invention in software, where new products appear monthly. The Internet is revolutionizing communications and study habits and is making inroads into commerce.

In addition, we emphasize innovations in economics itself. Economists are innovators and inventors in their own way. History shows that economic ideas can produce tidal waves when they are applied to real-world problems. Among the important innovations we survey is the application of economics to our environmental problems through emissions-trading plans. We explain how behavioral economics has changed views of consumer theory and finance. One of the most important innovations for our common future is dealing with global public goods like climate change, and we analyze new ways to deal with international environmental problems, including approaches such as the Kyoto Protocol. We must also track innovations in policy, such as the changing approach to monetary policy in the Federal Reserve.

3. Small Is Beautiful. Economics has increased its [4] scope greatly over the past half-century. The flag of economics flies over its traditional territory of the marketplace, but it also covers the environment, legal studies, statistical and historical methods, gender and racial discrimination, and even family life. But at its core, economics is the science of choice. That means that we, as authors, must choose the most important and enduring issues for this text. In a survey, as in a meal, small is beautiful because it is digestible.

Choosing the subjects for this text required many hard choices. To select these topics, we continually survey teachers and leading scholars to determine the issues most crucial for an informed citizenry and a new generation of economists. We drew up a list of key ideas and bid farewell to material we judged inessential or dated. *At every stage, we asked whether the material was, as best we could judge, necessary for a student's understanding of the economics of the twenty-first century.* Only when a subject passed this test was it included. The result of this campaign is a book that has lost more than one-quarter of its weight in the last few editions and has trimmed three chapters for this edition. Farm economics, the history of labor unions, Marxian economics, advanced treatment of general equilibrium, regulatory developments, and the lump-of-labor fallacy have been trimmed to make room for modern financial theory, real business cycles, and global public goods.

4. Policy Issues for Today. For many students, the ⑤ lure of economics is its relevance to public policy. The nineteenth edition emphasizes policy in both microeconomics and macroeconomics. As human societies grow, they begin to overwhelm the environment and ecosystems of the natural world. Environmental economics helps students understand the externalities associated with economic activity and then analyzes different approaches to making human economies compatible with natural systems. New examples bring the core principles of microeconomics to life.

A second area of central importance is financial and monetary economics. We have completely revised our treatment here. Previous treatment emphasized the quantity of money as the prime channel through which the central bank influences the economy. This

---

② the Core Truths：本质。

[3] Innovation：动态（在 17 版的同节开头萨翁特别强调了经济学的动态特性）创新。

[4] Small Is Beautiful：著名英国德裔经济学家舒马赫（Ernst Friedrich Schumacher，1911~1977）代表作的书名，1973 年首版，1999 年再版，是一本从信仰和道德的高度，思考和批判经济学及其主导下的现代西方社会经济形态顽症的经典之作，是规范经济学的哲学原理。它不宜用"小的是美的"简而盖之。

⑤ Policy Issues for Today：当前的政策问题。

approach no longer reflects the realities of a modern financial system. Today, the Fed exercises its policies by targeting the short-run interest rate and providing liquidity to financial markets. With the nineteenth edition, we fully incorporate these changes in three central chapters.

5. Debates about Globalization. The last decade has [1] witnessed pitched battles over the role of international trade in our economies. Some argue that "outsourcing" is leading to the loss of thousands of jobs to India and China. Immigration has been a hot-burner issue, particularly in communities with high unemployment rates. Whatever the causes, the United States was definitely faced with the puzzle of rapid output growth and a very slow growth in employment in the first decade of the twenty-first century.

One of the major debates of recent years has been over "globalization," which concerns the increasing economic integration of different countries. Americans have learned that no country is an economic island. Immigration and international trade have profound effects on the goods that are available, the prices we pay, and the wages we earn. Terrorism can wreak havoc on the economy at home, while war causes famines, migration, and reduced living standards in Africa. No one can fully understand the impact of growing trade and capital flows without a careful study of the theory of comparative advantage. We will see how the flow of financial capital has an enormous influence on trading patterns as well as understand why poor countries like China save while rich countries like the United States are borrowers. The nineteenth edition continues to increase the material devoted to international economics and the interaction between international trade and domestic economic events.

6. Clarity. Although there are many new features in [2] the nineteenth edition, the pole star for our pilgrimage for this edition has been to present economics clearly and simply. Students enter the classroom with a wide range of backgrounds and with many preconceptions about how the world works. Our task is not to change students' values. Rather, we strive to help students understand enduring economic principles so that they may better be able to apply them—to make the world a better place for themselves, their families, and their communities. Nothing aids understanding better than clear, simple exposition. We have labored over every page to improve this survey of introductory economics. We have received thousands of comments and suggestions from teachers and students and have incorporated their counsel in the nineteenth edition.

内容选择
Optional Matter

Economics courses range from one-quarter surveys to year-long intensive honors courses. This textbook has been carefully designed to meet all situations. If yours is a fast-paced course, you will appreciate the careful layering of the more advanced material. Hard-pressed courses can skip the advanced sections and chapters, covering the core of economic analysis without losing the thread of the economic reasoning. This book will challenge the most advanced young scholar. Indeed, many of today's leading economists have written to say they have relied upon *Economics* all along their pilgrimage to the Ph.D.

版　式
Format

The nineteenth edition employs in-text logos and material to help illustrate the central topics. You will find a distinctive logo indicating warnings for the fledgling economist, examples of economics in action, and biographical material on the great economists of the past and present. But these central topics are not drifting off by themselves in unattached boxes. Rather, they are integrated right into the chapter so that students can read them and see how they illustrate the core material. Keep these sections in mind as you read through the text. Each one is either:

- A warning that students should pause to ensure that they understand a difficult or subtle point.
- An interesting example or application of the analysis, often representing one of the major innovations of modern economics.
- A biography of an important economic figure.

New features in this edition include fresh end-of-chapter questions, with a special accent on short problems that reinforce the major concepts surveyed in the chapter.

Terms printed in **bold type** in the text mark the first occurrence and definition of the most important words that constitute the language of economics.

But these many changes have not altered one bit the central stylistic beacon that has guided *Economics* since the first edition: to use simple sentences, clear explanations, and concise tables and graphs.

---

[1] Debates about Globalization：本版较之 18 版删去了 *The Contending Schools of Macroeconomics* 小节，而在本小节中强调了中美之间文化传统形态对各自经济的深远影响，映射了从美式全球化向中国式全球化的过渡过程中不可避免的文化和经济形态的冲突。

[2] Clarity：明确清晰，一目了然；这一思想是本教材所有版本贯穿始终的不变目标，正如萨翁所言，这一目标就是朝圣者心中永恒的北斗七星。

致喜欢先教宏观部分的教师

For Those Who Prefer Macro First

Although, like the previous edition, this new edition has been designed to cover microeconomics first, many teachers continue to prefer beginning with macroeconomics. Many believe that the beginning student finds macro more approachable and will more quickly develop a keen interest in economics when the issues of macroeconomics are encountered first. We have taught economics in both sequences and find both sequences work well.

Whatever your philosophy, this text has been carefully designed for it. Instructors who deal with microeconomics first can move straight through the chapters. Those who wish to tackle macroeconomics first should skip from Part One directly to Part Five, knowing that the exposition and cross-references have been tailored with their needs in mind.

In addition, for those courses that do not cover the entire subject, the nineteenth edition is available in two paperback volumes, *Microeconomics* (Chapters 1 to 18 of the full text) and *Macroeconomics* (Chapters 1 to 3, 15, and 19 to 31 of the full text).

教学参考书和其他教辅材料

Auxiliary Teaching and Study Aids

Students of this edition will benefit greatly from the *Study Guide*. This carefully designed supplement was updated by Walter Park of the American University. When used alongside classroom discussions and when employed independently for self-study, the *Study Guide* has proved to be an impressive success. There is a full-text *Study Guide*, as well as micro and macro versions. The *Study Guides* are available electronically for online purchase or packaged with the text via code-card access.

In addition, instructors will find both the *Instructor's Resource Manual*, updated for this edition by Carlos Liard-Muriente of Central Connecticut State University, and the *Test Bank*, fully revised by Craig Jumper of Rich Mountain Community College. These supplements are incredibly useful for instructors planning their courses and preparing multiple sets of test questions in both print and computerized formats. The graphs and figures in this edition can also be viewed electronically as PowerPoint slides. The slides can be downloaded from our website (*www.mhhe.com/samuelson19e*). The website also contains chapter summaries, self-grading practice quizzes, and links to the websites suggested for further research at the end of each chapter.

电子书

CourseSmart eTextbook

For roughly half the cost of a print book, you can reduce your impact on the environment by purchasing the electronic edition of the nineteenth edition of Samuelson and Nordhaus, *Economics*. CourseSmart eTextbooks, available in a standard online reader, retain the exact content and layout of the print text, plus offer the advantage of digital navigation to which students are accustomed. Students can search the text, highlight, take notes, and use e-mail tools to share notes with their classmates. CourseSmart also includes tech support in case help is ever needed. To buy *Economics*, 19e as an eTextbook, or to learn more about this digital solution, visit ***www.CourseSmart.com*** and search by title, author, or ISBN.

计算机时代的经济学

Economics in the Computer Age

The electronic age has revolutionized the way that scholars and students can access information. In economics, the information revolution allows us quick access to economic statistics and research. An important feature of the nineteenth edition is the section "Economics and the Internet," which appears just before Chapter 1. This little section provides a road map for the state of economics on the Information Superhighway.

In addition, each chapter has an updated section at the end with suggestions for further reading and addresses of websites that can be used to deepen student understanding or find data and case studies.

致　谢

Acknowledgments

This book has two authors but a multitude of collaborators. We are profoundly grateful to colleagues, reviewers, students, and McGraw-Hill's staff for contributing to the timely completion of the nineteenth edition of *Economics*. Colleagues at MIT, Yale, and elsewhere who have graciously contributed their comments and suggestions over the years include William C. Brainard, E. Cary Brown, John Geanakoplos, Robert J. Gordon, Lyle Gramley, Gerald Jaynes, Paul Joskow, Alfred Kahn, Richard Levin, Robert Litan, Barry Nalebuff, Merton J. Peck, Gustav Ranis, Herbert Scarf, Robert M. Solow, James Tobin, Janet Yellen, and Gary Yohe.

In addition, we have benefited from the tireless devotion of those whose experience in teaching elementary economics is embodied in this edition. We are particularly grateful to the reviewers of the nineteenth edition. They include:

Esmael Adibi, *Chapman University*
Abu Dowlah, *Saint Francis College*
Adam Forest, *University of Washington, Tacoma*
Harold Horowitz, *Touro College*
Jui-Chi Huang, *Harrisburg Area Community College*
Carl Jensen, *Iona College, New Rochelle*
Craig Jumper, *Rich Mountain Community College*
Carlos Liard-Muriente, *Central Connecticut State University*
Phillip Letting, *Harrisburg Area Community College*
Ibrahim Oweiss, *Georgetown University*
Walter Park, *American University*
Gordana Pesakovic, *Argosy University, Sarasota*
Harold Peterson, *Boston College*
David Ruccio, *University of Notre Dame*
Derek Trunkey, *George Washington University*
Mark Witte, *Northwestern University*
Jiawen Yang, *George Washington University*

Students at MIT, Yale, and other colleges and universities have served as an "invisible college." They [1] constantly challenge and test us, helping to make this edition less imperfect than its predecessor. Although they are too numerous to enumerate, their influence is woven through every chapter. Nancy King helped in logistics at the New Haven end of the operation. We are particularly grateful for the contribution of Caroleen Verly, who read the manuscript and made many suggestions for improvement. We are grateful to Dr. Xi Chen, who prepared the economic globes and reviewed the manuscript.

This project would have been impossible without the skilled team from McGraw-Hill who nurtured the book at every stage. We particularly would like to thank, in chronological order to their appearance on the scene: Douglas Reiner, Karen Fisher, Noelle Fox, Susanne Reidell, Lori Hazzard, Matt Baldwin, and Jen Lambert. This group of skilled professionals turned many megabytes and a mountain of paper into a finely polished work of art.

致我行我素的学生
A WORD TO THE SOVEREIGN STUDENT

思想的市场
The Intellectual Marketplace

Just what is the market that students in repressed societies are agitating for? In the pages that follow, you will learn about the promise and perils of globalization, about the fragility of financial markets, about unskilled labor and highly trained neurosurgeons. You have probably read in the newspaper about the gross domestic product, the consumer price index, the Federal Reserve, and the unemployment rate. After you have completed a thorough study of this textbook, you will know precisely what these words mean. Even more important, you will also understand the economic forces that influence and determine them.

There is also a marketplace of ideas, where contending schools of economists fashion their theories and try to persuade their scientific peers. You will find in the chapters that follow a fair and impartial review of the thinking of the intellectual giants of our profession—from the early economists like Adam Smith, David Ricardo, and Karl Marx to modern-day titans like John Maynard Keynes, Milton Friedman, and James Tobin.

祝 愿
Skoal!

As you begin your journey into the land of the mixed economy, it would be understandable if you are anxious. But take heart. The fact is that we envy you, the beginning student, as you set out to explore the exciting world of economics for the first time. This is a thrill that, alas, you can experience only once in a lifetime. So, as you embark, we wish you bon voyage!

Paul A. Samuelson
William D. Nordhaus

[1] invisible college：从第 16 版开始版版出现，是萨翁对在麻省理工和耶鲁大学这样顶尖的高校就读的学生赋予的最深情的称谓。同时也从另一个侧面折射了萨翁与哈佛大学之间一段 60 多年来的不解之怨，萨翁甚至在 1947 年获得克拉克奖之后用“甜蜜的报复”这样的笑谈来形容其与上世纪 40 年代末期哈佛经济系主任哈罗德·伯班克之间的恩恩怨怨。

For the Student: Economics and the Internet

经济学与互联网（供学生参用）

The Information Age is revolutionizing our lives. Its impact on scholars and students has been particularly profound because it allows inexpensive and rapid access to vast quantities of information. The Internet, which is a huge and growing public network of linked computers and information, is changing the way we study, shop, share our culture, and communicate with our friends and family.

In economics, the Internet allows us quick access to economics statistics and research. With just a few clicks of a mouse, we can find out about the most recent unemployment rate, track down information on poverty and incomes, or investigate the intricacies of our banking system. A few years ago, it might have taken weeks to dig out the data necessary to analyze an economic problem. Today, with a computer and a little practice, that same task can be done in a few minutes.

This book is not a manual for driving on the Information Superhighway. That skill can be learned in classes on the subject or from informal tutorials. Rather, we want to provide a road map that shows the locations of major sources of economic data and research. With this map and some rudimentary navigational skills, you can explore the various sites and find a rich array of data, information, studies, and chat rooms. Additionally, at the end of each chapter there is a list of useful websites that can be used to follow up the major themes of that chapter.

Note that some of these sites may be free, some may require a registration or be available through your college or university, and others may require paying a fee. Pricing practices change rapidly, so while we have attempted to include primarily free sites, we have not excluded high-quality sites that may charge a fee.

数据和机构
Data and Institutions

The Internet is an indispensable source of useful data and other information. Since most economic data are provided by governments, the first place to look is the web pages of government agencies and international organizations. The starting point for U.S. government statistics, *www.fedstats.gov,* provides one-stop shopping for federal statistics with links to over 70 government agencies that produce statistical information. Sources are organized by subject or by agency, and the contents are fully searchable. Another good launching site into the federal statistical system is the Economic Statistics Briefing Room at *www.whitehouse.gov/fsbr/esbr.html.* Additionally, the Commerce Department operates a huge database at *www.stat-usa.gov,* but use of parts of this database requires a subscription (which may be available at your college or university).

The best single statistical source for data on the United States is the *Statistical Abstract of the United States,* published annually. It is available online at *www.census.gov/compendia/statab.* If you want an overview of the U.S. economy, you can read the *Economic Report of the President* at *www.gpoaccess.gov/eop/index.html.*

Most of the major economic data are produced by specialized agencies. One place to find general data is the Department of Commerce, which encompasses the Bureau of Economic Analysis (BEA) (*www.bea.gov*) and the Census Bureau (*www.census.gov*). The BEA site includes all data and articles published in the *Survey of Current Business,* including the national income and product accounts, international trade and investment flows, output by industry, economic growth, personal income and labor series, and regional data.

The Census Bureau site goes well beyond a nose count of the population. It also includes the economic census as well as information on housing, income and poverty, government finance, agriculture, foreign trade, construction, manufacturing, transportation, and retail and wholesale trade. In addition to making Census Bureau publications available, the site allows users to create custom extracts of popular microdata sources including the Survey of Income and Program Participation,

Consumer Expenditure Survey, Current Population Survey, American Housing Survey, and, of course, the most recent census.

The Bureau of Labor Statistics (at *www.bls.gov*) provides easy access to commonly requested labor data, including employment and unemployment, prices and living conditions, compensation, productivity, and technology. Also available are labor-force data from the Current Population Survey and payroll statistics from the Current Employment Statistics Survey.

A useful source for financial data is the website of the Federal Reserve Board at *www.federalreserve.gov*. This site provides historical U.S. economic and financial data, including daily interest rates, monetary and business indicators, exchange rates, balance-of-payments data, and price indexes. In addition, the Office of Management and Budget at *www.gpo.gov/usbudget/index.html* makes available the federal budget and related documents.

International statistics are often harder to find. The World Bank, at *www.worldbank.org*, has information on its programs and publications at its site, as does the International Monetary Fund, or IMF, at *www.imf.org*. The United Nations website (*www.unsystem.org*) is slow and confusing but has links to most international institutions and their databases. A good source of information about high-income countries is the Organisation for Economic Cooperation and Development, or OECD, at *www.oecd.org*. The OECD's website contains an array of data on economics, education, health, science and technology, agriculture, energy, public management, and other topics.

经济研究和文献查询
Economic Research and Journalism

The Internet is rapidly becoming the world's library. Newspapers, magazines, and scholarly publications are increasingly posting their writing in electronic form. Most of these present what is already available in the paper publications. Some interesting sources can be found at the *Economist* at *www.economist.com* and the *Financial Times* (*www.ft.com*). The *Wall Street Journal* at *www.wsj.com* is currently expensive and not a cost-effective resource. Current policy issues are discussed at *www.policy.com*. The online magazine *Slate* at *www.slate.com* occasionally contains excellent essays on economics.

For scholarly writings, many journals are making their contents available online. WebEc at *www.helsinki.fi/WebEc/* contains a listing of websites for many economic journals. The archives of many journals are available at *www.jstor.org*.

There are now a few websites that bring many resources together at one location. One place to start is *Resources for Economists on the Internet*, sponsored by the American Economic Association and edited by Bill Goffe, at *www.rfe.org*. Also see *WWW Resources in Economics*, which has links to many different branches of economics at *netec.wustl.edu/WebEc/WebEc.html*. For working papers, the National Bureau of Economic Research (NBER) website at *www.nber.org* contains current economic research. The NBER site also contains general resources, including links to data sources and the official U.S. business-cycle dates.

An excellent site that archives and serves as a depository for working papers is located at *econwpa.wustl.edu/wpawelcome.html*. This site is particularly useful for finding background material for research papers.

Did someone tell you that economics is the dismal science? You can chuckle over economist jokes (mostly at the expense of economists) at *netec.mcc.ac.uk/JokEc.html*.

提醒一句
A Word of Warning

It is an unfortunate fact that, because of rapid technological change, this list will soon be out of date. New sites with valuable information and data are appearing every day . . . and others are disappearing almost as rapidly.

Before you set off into the wonderful world of the Web, we would pass on to you some wisdom from experts. Remember the old adage: You only get what you pay for.

Warning: Be careful to determine that your sources and data are reliable. The Internet and other electronic media are easy to use and equally easy to abuse.

The Web is the closest thing in economics to a free lunch. But you must select your items carefully to ensure that they are palatable and digestible.

PART ONE

Basic Concepts
基本概念

CHAPTER

1

The Central Concepts of Economics

经济学的主要概念

[1] 埃德蒙·伯克（Edmund Burke, 1729~1797），爱尔兰出生的英国政论家，北美殖民政策的捍卫者，以出色的演说才能称雄于当时的英国政坛。本段话出自其 1790 年出版的代表性著作《法国革命感思录》（*Reflections on the Revolution in France*）的第 76 页——批判法国国王路易十六世奢侈跋扈的王后 Marie Antoinette（1755~1793）的一段话，原文为：I thought ten thousand swords must have leaped from their scabbards to avenge even a look that threatened her with insult. But the age of chivalry is gone. That of sophisters, economists, and calculators, has succeeded; and the glory of Europe is extinguished for ever.

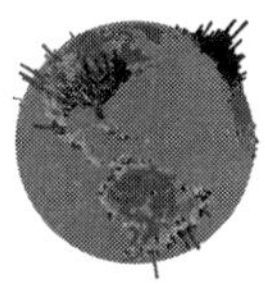

这段话语法规则严密，文化历史背景和语言结构本身以及几个关键词都有很深的含义。除个别版次作者将其位置调整外（如第 16 版置于第二编的第 4 章），从内容和章次结构彻底改观的第 12 版开始，本段话几乎均安排在第一编的第 1 章，是为数不多的几段始终保留下来的名言之一。本书中大多数章首的名言基本上均经萨缪尔森之手演绎，为其所妙用。根据原文及相关历史背景，这句话拟应翻译如下：

The Age of Chivalry is gone; that of sophisters, economists, and calculators has succeeded.

Edmund Burke [1]

骑士时代已经一去不复返了，取而代之的是学者、经济学家和政客的时代。——埃德蒙·伯克

为什么学经济学

A. WHY STUDY ECONOMICS?

As you open this textbook, you may be wondering, Why should I study economics? Let us count the ways.

Many study economics to help them get a good job.

Some people feel they should understand more deeply what lies behind reports on inflation and unemployment.

Or people want to understand what kinds of policies might slow global warming or what it means to say an iPod is "made in China."

战地钟声

For Whom the Bell Tolls [2]

All these reasons, and many more, make good sense. Still, as we have come to realize, there is one overriding reason to learn the basic lessons of economics: All your life—from cradle to grave and beyond—you will run up against the brutal truths of economics.

As a voter, you will make decisions on issues that cannot be understood until you have mastered the rudiments of this subject. Without studying economics, you cannot be fully informed about international trade, tax policy, or the causes of recessions and high unemployment.

Choosing your life's occupation is the most important economic decision you will make. Your future depends not only on your own abilities but also on how national and regional economic forces affect your wages. Also, your knowledge of economics can help you make wise decisions about how to buy a home, pay for your children's education, and set aside a nest egg for retirement. Of course, studying economics will not make you a genius. But without economics the dice of life are loaded against you.

[3] 出自希腊谚语 When God throws the dice are loaded。美国著名作家马克·吐温（Mark Twain，1835~1910）的短篇小说《竞选州长》（*Running for Governor*）中的跳蛙情节也源自于此。拟译为：注定要吃亏的。

There is no need to belabor the point. We hope you will find that, in addition to being useful, economics is even a fascinating field. Generations of students, often to their surprise, have discovered how stimulating it is to look beneath the surface and understand the fundamental laws of economics.

稀缺与效率——经济学的双重主题

SCARCITY AND EFFICIENCY: THE TWIN THEMES OF ECONOMICS

Definitions of Economics 经济学的定义

Let us begin with a definition of economics. Over the last half-century, the study of economics has expanded to include a vast range of topics. Here are [4]

[2] 出自 16 世纪英国玄学派诗人的主要代表人物约翰·邓恩（John Donne，1572~1631）1624 年出版的《适时祈祷》（*Devotions Upon Emergent Occasions*）。1954 年诺贝尔文学奖获得者、著名美国作家欧内斯特·海明威（Ernest Hemingway，1899~1961），以自己参加西班牙内战的亲身经历为背景写的一部著名的长篇小说以此冠名（中译本《丧钟为谁而鸣》），改编的同名电影《战地钟声》曾获 1943 年的奥斯卡单项奖。

根据上下文，此处拟借译为“战地钟声”。意指经济学的研习犹如战地的钟声，看似与己毫无关联，却与每一个人和整个世界的命运息息相关。

[4] over the last half-century 译为上世纪战后 50 年

作者在其第 17 版（*Economics*, 17th, Samuelson & Nordhaus, 2001）中将这半个世纪定义为伟大和平的 50 年（*the Great Peace*, page xvii），系相对于其对上世纪前 50 年定义的“危机四伏的 50 年”（*the Great Depression*, page xvii）而言。这是萨缪尔森根据前苏联经济学家尼古拉·康德拉季耶夫著名的周期学说长波论，对 20 世纪的断代研究做出的特殊贡献。

some of the major subjects that are covered in this book:[1]

- Economics explores the behavior of the financial markets, including interest rates, exchange rates, and stock prices.
- The subject examines the reasons why some people or countries have high incomes while others are poor; it goes on to analyze ways that poverty can be reduced without harming the economy.
- It studies business cycles—the fluctuations in credit, unemployment, and inflation—along with policies to moderate them.
- Economics studies international trade and finance and the impacts of globalization, and it particularly examines the thorny issues involved in opening up borders to free trade.
- It asks how government policies can be used to pursue important goals such as rapid economic growth, efficient use of resources, full employment, price stability, and a fair distribution of income.

business cycles 商业周期

This is a long list, but we could extend it many times. However, if we boil down all these definitions, we find one common theme:

boil down 浓缩，概括

major-league baseball 美国职业棒球大联盟

Economics is the study of how societies use scarce ① resources to produce valuable goods and services and distribute them among different individuals.

稀缺与效率
Scarcity and Efficiency

If we think about the definitions, we find two key ideas that run through all of economics: that goods are scarce and that society must use its resources efficiently. *Indeed, the concerns of economics will not go away because of the fact of scarcity and the desire for efficiency.*

Consider a world without scarcity. If infinite quan- ② tities of every good could be produced or if human desires were fully satisfied, what would be the consequences? People would not worry about stretching out their limited incomes because they could have everything they wanted; businesses would not need to fret over the cost of labor or health care; governments would not need to struggle over taxes or spending or pollution because nobody would care. Moreover, since all of us could have as much as we pleased, no one would be concerned about the distribution of incomes among different people or classes.

In such an Eden of affluence, all goods would be ③ free, like sand in the desert or seawater at the beach. All prices would be zero, and markets would be unnecessary. Indeed, economics would no longer be a useful subject.

But no society has reached a utopia of limitless possibilities. Ours is a world of **scarcity,** full of **economic goods.** A situation of scarcity is one in which goods are limited relative to desires. An objective observer would have to agree that, even after two centuries of rapid economic growth, production in the United States is simply not high enough to meet everyone's desires. If you add up all the wants, you quickly find that there are simply not enough goods and services to satisfy even a small fraction of everyone's consumption desires. Our national output would have to be many times larger before the average American could live at the level of the average doctor or major-league baseball player. Moreover, outside the United States, particularly in Africa, hundreds of millions of people suffer from hunger and material deprivation.

Given unlimited wants, it is important that an economy make the best use of its limited resources. That brings us to the critical notion of efficiency. **Efficiency** denotes the most effective use of a society's resources in satisfying people's wants and needs. By contrast, consider an economy with unchecked monopolies or unhealthy pollution or government corruption. Such an economy may produce less than would be possible without these factors, or it may produce a distorted bundle of goods that leaves consumers worse off than they otherwise could be—either situation is an inefficient allocation of resources.

Economic efficiency requires that an economy ④ produce the highest combination of quantity and quality of goods and services given its technology and scarce resources. An economy is producing efficiently when no individual's economic welfare can be improved unless someone else is made worse off.

The essence of economics is to acknowledge the reality of scarcity and then figure out how to organize

[1] This list contains several specialized terms that you will need to understand. If you are not familiar with a particular word or phrase, you should consult the Glossary at the back of this book. The Glossary contains most of the major technical economic terms used in this book. All terms printed in boldface are defined in the Glossary.

---

① **经济学**研究人类社会如何使用稀缺的资源来生产有价值的商品和服务，并将其在不同的个体中进行分配。

② 让我们设想一个不存在稀缺的世界。

③ 在这样一个物质极大丰富的伊甸园里。此处 affluence 与前言中 affluent countries 呼应。

④ **经济效率**强调的是，一个经济体在依赖于自身的科学技术和有限资源的基础上，所能生产出的有形和无形商品在数量和质量上双双实现最佳。当任何个体在不使其他个体的经济福利变差的情况下，其经济福利仍然无法得到改善时，则其所在经济体的经济活动就是有效率的。

society in a way which produces the most efficient use of resources. That is where economics makes its unique contribution.

微观经济学与宏观经济学 *Microeconomics and Macroeconomics*

Economics is today divided into two major subfields, microeconomics and macroeconomics. Adam Smith is usually considered the founder of **microeconomics,** the branch of economics which today is concerned with the behavior of individual entities such as markets, firms, and households. In *The Wealth of Nations* [1] (1776), Smith considered how individual prices are set, studied the determination of prices of land, labor, and capital, and inquired into the strengths and weaknesses of the market mechanism. Most important, he identified the remarkable efficiency properties of markets and explained how the self-interest of individuals working through the competitive market can produce a societal economic benefit. Microeconomics today has moved beyond the early concerns to include the study of monopoly, the role of international trade, finance, and many other vital subjects.

The other major branch of our subject is **macroeconomics,** which is concerned with the overall performance of the economy. Macroeconomics did not even exist in its modern form until 1936, when John [2] Maynard Keynes published his revolutionary *General Theory of Employment, Interest and Money.* At the time, England and the United States were still stuck in the Great Depression of the 1930s, with over one-quarter [3] of the American labor force unemployed. In his new theory Keynes developed an analysis of what causes business cycles, with alternating spells of high unemployment and high inflation. Today, macroeconomics examines a wide variety of areas, such as how total investment and consumption are determined, how central banks manage money and interest rates, what causes international financial crises, and why some nations grow rapidly while others stagnate. Although macroeconomics has progressed far since his first insights, the issues addressed by Keynes still define the study of macroeconomics today.

经济学的逻辑 THE LOGIC OF ECONOMICS

Economic life is an enormously complicated hive of activity, with people buying, selling, bargaining, investing, and persuading. The ultimate purpose of economic science and of this text is to understand this complex undertaking. How do economists go about their task?

Economists use the *scientific approach* to understand economic life. This involves observing economic affairs and drawing upon statistics and the historical record. For complex phenomena like the impacts of budget deficits or the causes of inflation, historical research has provided a rich mine of insights.

Often, economics relies upon analyses and theories. Theoretical approaches allow economists to make broad generalizations, such as those concerning the advantages of international trade and specialization or the disadvantages of tariffs and quotas.

In addition, economists have developed a specialized technique known as *econometrics,* which applies the tools of statistics to economic problems. Using econometrics, economists can sift through mountains of data to extract simple relationships.

Budding economists must also be alert to common fallacies in economic reasoning. Because economic relationships are often complex, involving many different variables, it is easy to become confused about the exact reason behind events or the impact of policies on the economy. The following are some of the common fallacies encountered in economic reasoning:

- *The **post hoc fallacy.*** The first fallacy involves the [4] inference of causality. *The post hoc fallacy occurs when we assume that, because one event occurred before another event, the first event caused the second event.*[2] An example of this syndrome occurred in the Great Depression of the 1930s in the United States. Some people had observed that periods of business expansion were preceded or accompanied by rising prices. From this, they concluded that the appropriate remedy for depression was to raise wages and prices. This idea led to a host of legislation and regulations to prop up wages and prices in an inefficient manner. Did these measures promote economic recovery? Almost surely not. Indeed, they probably slowed recovery, which did not occur until total spending began to rise as the government increased military spending in preparation for World War II.

---

2 "Post hoc" is shorthand for *post hoc, ergo propter hoc.* Translated from the Latin, the full expression means "after this, therefore necessarily because of this."

[3] Great Depression：指上世纪30年代的大萧条时期，萨翁在17版的前言中将上世纪的前半个50年用它来定义（笔者译为“危机四伏时期”），后半个50年则相应地定义为“伟大的和平时期”（the Great Peace）。这是迄今为止国际学术界对上世纪100年符合“长波论”断代思想的唯一论述，但在此后的18版即予删除（见本书前言部分笔者对此的注疏内容）。因此，本书的17版在学术上由于这个断代说和对美国网络经济泡沫破灭的反思，更有其独特的价值所在。有关论述详见笔者《中国英语教育改革探思录》（现代教育出版社，2009.5）和《中国教育的出路问题》（中国书籍出版社，2012.9）。

[4] The post hoc fallacy：逻辑学名词，因果误导。观察到事件A在事件B之前发生的事实，并不能证明事件A是事件B发生的原因。由此而认为“事件后”的说法便意味着“该事件即原因说”就是前因后果的误导。

---

[1]《国富论》（*The Wealth of Nations*，1776），亚当·斯密还有一部与之称为姊妹篇的经典：《道德情操论》（*The Theory of Moral Sentiments*，1759）。两者建构了斯密完整的经济学思想，先有利他，才有利己。而多年来学术界几乎忘却了利他主义的《道德情操论》，严重曲解了斯密的经济学理论。

亚当·斯密（Adam Smith，1723~1790），古典经济学之父，苏格兰道德哲学家，老亚当·斯密的遗腹子，一生与母亲相依为命，终身未娶。上述两部书是斯密留给全人类的跨世经典。

[2] 凯恩斯（John Maynard Keynes，1883~1946），英国经济学家，开创了经济学的“凯恩斯革命”，是现代西方经济学最具影响的经济学家之一，被誉为上世纪30年代经济大萧条的终结者，他创立的宏观经济学被称为20世纪人类知识界的三大革命之一。《就业、利息与货币通论》（*General Theory of Employment, Interest and Money*，简称《通论》），是其革命性的代表作。

- *Failure to hold other things constant.* A second pitfall is failure to hold other things constant when thinking about an issue. ① For example, we might want to know whether raising tax rates will raise or lower tax revenues. Some people have put forth the seductive argument that we can eat our fiscal cake and have it too. They argue that cutting tax rates will at the same time raise government revenues and lower the budget deficit. They point to the Kennedy-Johnson tax cuts of 1964, which lowered tax rates sharply and were followed by an increase in government revenues in 1965. Hence, they argue, lower tax rates produce higher revenues.

  Why is this reasoning fallacious? The argument assumes that other things were constant—in particular, it overlooked the growth in the overall economy from 1964 to 1965. Because people's incomes grew during that period, total tax revenues grew even though tax rates were lower. Careful econometric studies indicate that total tax revenues would have been *even higher* in 1965 if tax rates had been held at the same level as in 1964. Hence, this analysis fails to hold other things constant in making the calculations.

  Remember to hold other things constant when you are analyzing the impact of a variable on the economic system.

- *The **fallacy of composition.*** Sometimes we assume ② that what holds true for part of a system also holds true for the whole. In economics, however, we often find that the whole is different from the sum of the parts. *When you assume that what is true for the part is also true for the whole, you are committing the fallacy of composition.*

  Here are some true statements that might surprise you if you ignored the fallacy of composition: (1) If one farmer has a bumper crop, she has a higher income; if all farmers produce a record crop, farm incomes will fall. (2) If one person receives a great deal more money, that person will be better off; if everyone receives a great deal more money, the society is likely to be worse off. (3) If a high tariff is put on a product such as shoes or steel, the producers in that industry are likely to profit; if high tariffs are put on all products, the economic welfare of the nation is likely to be worse off.

  These examples contain no tricks or magic. Rather, they are the results of systems of interacting individuals. Often the behavior of the aggregate looks very different from the behavior of individual people.

We mention these fallacies only briefly in this introduction. Later, as we introduce the tools of economics, we will provide examples of how inattention to the logic of economics can lead to false and sometimes costly errors. When you reach the end of this book, you can look back to see why each of these paradoxical examples is true.

Positive Economics versus Normative Economics

When considering economic issues, we must carefully distinguish questions of fact from questions of fairness. Positive economics describes the facts of an economy, while normative economics involves value judgments.

Positive economics deals with questions such as: ③
Why do doctors earn more than janitors? Did the North ④
American Free Trade Agreement (NAFTA) raise or lower the incomes of most Americans? Do higher interest rates slow the economy and lower inflation? Although these may be difficult questions to answer, they can all be resolved by reference to analysis and empirical evidence. That puts them in the realm of positive economics.

Normative economics involves ethical precepts ⑤
and norms of fairness. Should unemployment be raised to ensure that price inflation does not become too rapid? Should the United States negotiate further agreements to lower tariffs on imports? Has the distribution of income in the United States become too unequal? There are no right or wrong answers to these questions because they involve ethics and values rather than facts. While economic analysis can *inform* these debates by examining the likely consequences of alternative policies, the answers can be resolved only by discussions and debates over society's fundamental values.

热切的心情，冷静的头脑
COOL HEADS AT THE SERVICE OF WARM HEARTS

Economics has, over the last century, grown from a tiny acorn into a mighty oak. Under its spreading branches we find explanations of the gains from international trade, advice on how to reduce

---

① 无法保证其他条件保持不变
② 以点代面的谬误（也译作“合成谬误”）
③ 实证经济学
④ 北美自由贸易协定
⑤ 规范经济学

unemployment and inflation, formulas for investing your retirement funds, and proposals to auction limited carbon dioxide emissions permits ① to help slow global warming ②. Throughout the world, economists are laboring to collect data and improve our understanding of economic trends.

You might well ask, What is the purpose of this army of economists measuring, analyzing, and calculating? *The ultimate goal of economic science is to improve the living conditions of people in their everyday lives.* ③ Increasing the gross domestic product is not just a numbers game. Higher incomes mean good food, warm houses, and hot water. They mean safe drinking water and inoculations against the perennial plagues of humanity.

Higher incomes produce more than food and shelter. Rich countries have the resources to build schools so that young people can learn to read and develop the skills necessary to use modern machinery and computers. As incomes rise further, nations can afford scientific research to determine agricultural techniques appropriate for a country's climate and soils or to develop vaccines against local diseases. With the resources freed up by economic growth, people have free time for artistic pursuits, such as poetry and music, and the population has the leisure time to read, to listen, and to perform. Although there is no single pattern of economic development, and cultures differ around the world, freedom from hunger, disease, and the elements is a universal human goal.

But centuries of human history also show that warm hearts alone will not feed the hungry or heal the sick. A free and efficient market will not necessarily produce a distribution of income that is socially acceptable. Determining the best route to economic progress or an equitable distribution of society's output requires cool heads that objectively weigh the costs and benefits of different approaches, trying as hard as humanly possible to keep the analysis free from the taint of wishful thinking. Sometimes, economic progress will require shutting down an outmoded factory. Sometimes, as when centrally planned countries adopted market principles, things get worse before they get better. Choices are particularly difficult in the field of health care, where limited resources literally involve life and death.

You may have heard the saying, "From each according to his ability, to each according to his need." ④ Governments have learned that no society can long operate solely on this utopian principle. To maintain a healthy economy, governments must preserve incentives for people to work and to save.

Societies can support the unemployed for a while, but when unemployment insurance pays too much for too long, people may come to depend upon the government and stop looking for work. If they begin to believe that the government owes them a living, this may dull the cutting edge of enterprise. Just because government programs pursue lofty goals cannot exempt them from careful scrutiny and efficient management.

Society must strive to combine the discipline of the marketplace with the compassion of social programs. ⑤ By using cool heads to inform warm hearts, economic science can do its part in finding the appropriate balance for an efficient, prosperous, and just society.

经济组织的三个问题

B. THE THREE PROBLEMS OF ECONOMIC ORGANIZATION

Every human society—whether it is an advanced industrial nation, a centrally planned economy, or an isolated tribal nation—must confront and resolve three fundamental economic problems. Every society must have a way of determining *what* commodities are produced, *how* these goods are made, and *for whom* they are produced.

Indeed, these three fundamental questions of economic organization—***what, how,* and *for whom***—are as crucial today as they were at the dawn of human civilization ⑥. Let's look more closely at them:

- *What* commodities are produced and in what quantities? A society must determine how much of each of the many possible goods and services it will make and when they will be produced. Will we produce pizzas or shirts today? A few high-quality shirts or many cheap shirts? Will we use scarce resources to produce many consumption goods (like pizzas)? Or will we produce fewer consumption goods and more investment goods (like pizza-making machines), which will boost production and consumption tomorrow?
- *How* are goods produced? A society must determine who will do the production, with what resources, and what production techniques they will use. Who farms and who teaches? Is electricity

---

① 限制二氧化碳排放的交易，即碳交易。
② 有助于减缓全球变暖的速度。
③ 经济学研究的终极目标是改善人们日常生活的条件。
④ 各尽所能，按需分配。
⑤ 社会必须竭尽全力地将市场的运行规则与社会福利整合为一体。经济学的研究在提供热情服务的同时，还应保持冷静的头脑去发挥自身的优势。这样，才可以为构建一个有效率、繁荣和公平的社会找到合适的平衡关系。
⑥ 人类文明的曙光。

generated from oil, from coal, or from the sun? Will factories be run by people or robots?

- *For whom* are goods produced? Who gets to eat the fruit of economic activity? Is the distribution of income and wealth fair and equitable? How is the national product divided among different households? Are many people poor and a few rich? Do high incomes go to teachers or athletes or autoworkers or venture capitalists? Will society provide minimal consumption to the poor, or must people work if they are to eat?

市场经济、指令经济与混合经济
MARKET, COMMAND, AND MIXED ECONOMIES

mixed economy 混合经济，即市场和计划兼而有之的经济

What are the different ways that a society can answer the questions of *what, how,* and *for whom?* Different societies are organized through *alternative economic systems,* and economics studies the various mechanisms that a society can use to allocate its scarce resources. ①

We generally distinguish two fundamentally different ways of organizing an economy. At one extreme, government makes most economic decisions, with those on top of the hierarchy giving economic commands to those further down the ladder. At the other extreme, decisions are made in markets, where individuals or enterprises voluntarily agree to exchange goods and services, usually through payments of money. Let's briefly examine each of these two forms of economic organization.

market economy 市场经济

a stock of limited resources 有限的资源存量

laissez-faire economy 放任主义的市场经济

command economy 指令经济

In the United States, and increasingly around the world, most economic questions are settled by the market mechanism. Hence their economic systems are called market economies. A **market economy** is one in which individuals and private firms make the major decisions about production and consumption. A system of prices, of markets, of profits and losses, of incentives and rewards determines *what, how,* and *for whom.* Firms produce the commodities that yield the highest profits (the *what*) by the techniques of production that are least costly (the *how*). Consumption is determined by individuals' decisions about how to spend the wages and property incomes generated by their labor and property ownership (the *for whom*). The extreme case of a market economy, in which the government keeps its hands off economic decisions, is called a **laissez-faire** economy.

By contrast, a **command economy** is one in which the government makes all important decisions about production and distribution. In a command economy, such as the one which operated in the Soviet Union during most of the twentieth century, the government owns most of the means of production (land and capital); it also owns and directs the operations of enterprises in most industries; it is the employer of most workers and tells them how to do their jobs; and it decides how the output of the society is to be divided among different goods and services. In short, in a command economy, the government answers the major economic questions through its ownership of resources and its power to enforce decisions.

No contemporary society falls completely into either of these polar categories. Rather, all societies are **mixed economies,** with elements of market and command.

Economic life is organized either through hierarchical command or decentralized voluntary markets. Today most decisions in the United States and other high-income economies are made in the marketplace. But the government plays an important role in overseeing the functioning of the market; governments pass laws that regulate economic life, produce educational and police services, and control pollution. Most societies today operate mixed economies. ②

社会的技术可能性
C. SOCIETY'S TECHNOLOGICAL POSSIBILITIES

Every gun that is made, every warship launched, every rocket fired signifies, in the final sense, a theft from those who hunger and are not fed. ③

President Dwight D. Eisenhower

Each economy has a stock of limited resources—labor, technical knowledge, factories and tools, land, energy. In deciding *what* and *how* things should be produced, the economy is in reality deciding how to allocate its resources among the thousands of different possible commodities and services. How much land will go into growing wheat? Or into housing the population? How many factories will produce computers? How many will make pizzas? How many children will grow up to play professional sports or to be professional economists or to program computers?

Faced with the undeniable fact that goods are scarce relative to wants, an economy must decide

---

① 经济学就是这样一门研究用于配置稀缺资源的各种相应机制的科学。

② 经济生活是通过各级政府或者分权制的自发性市场行为来组织的。在今天的美国以及其他高收入型的社会中，大多数政策都由市场来决定。但是，政府对市场的运行起着极其重要的监管作用。政府通过立法来规范经济生活，提供教育和治安服务产品，以及控制污染等。今天，大多数经济体都实施了混合型的经济。

③ 所造的每一支枪，下水的每一艘战舰，发射的每一枚火箭，归根结底，都是一种从那些忍饥挨饿的人们口中窃取救命食物的行为。

——美国第 34 任总统艾森豪威尔

how to cope with limited resources. It must choose among different potential bundles of goods (the *what*), select from different techniques of production (the *how*), and decide in the end who will consume the goods (the *for whom*).

投入和产出
INPUTS AND OUTPUTS

To answer these three questions, every society must make choices about the economy's inputs and outputs. **Inputs** are commodities or services that are used to produce goods and services. An economy uses its existing technology to combine inputs to produce outputs. **Outputs** are the various useful goods or services that result from the production process and are either consumed or employed in further production. Consider the "production" of pizza. We say that the eggs, flour, heat, pizza oven, and chef's skilled labor are the inputs. The tasty pizza is the output. In education, the inputs are the time of the faculty and students, the laboratories and classrooms, the textbooks, and so on, while the outputs are informed, productive, and well-paid citizens.

Another term for inputs is **factors of production.** ① These can be classified into three broad categories: land, labor, and capital.

- *Land*—or, more generally, natural resources—represents the gift of nature to our societies. It consists of the land used for farming or for underpinning houses, factories, and roads; the energy resources that fuel our cars and heat our homes; and the nonenergy resources like copper and iron ore and sand. In today's congested world, we must broaden the scope of natural resources to include our environmental resources, such as clean air and drinkable water.
- *Labor* consists of the human time spent in production—working in automobile factories, writing software, teaching school, or baking pizzas. Thousands of occupations and tasks, at all skill levels, are performed by labor. It is at once the most familiar and the most crucial input for an advanced industrial economy.
- *Capital* resources form the durable goods of an economy, produced in order to produce yet other goods. Capital goods include machines, roads, computers, software, trucks, steel mills, automobiles, washing machines, and buildings. As we will see later, the accumulation of specialized capital goods is essential to the task of economic development.

Restating the three economic problems in these terms, society must decide (1) *what* outputs to produce, and in what quantity; (2) *how,* or with what inputs and techniques, to produce the desired outputs; and (3) *for whom* the outputs should be produced and distributed.

生产的可能性边界
THE PRODUCTION-POSSIBILITY FRONTIER

We learn early in life that we can't have everything. "You can have chocolate or vanilla ice cream. No, not both," we might hear. Similarly, the consumption opportunities of countries are limited by the resources and the technologies available to them. [2]

The need to choose among limited opportunities is dramatized during wartime. In debating whether the United States should invade Iraq in 2003, people wanted to know how much the war would cost. The administration said it would cost only $50 billion, while some economists said it might cost as much as $2000 billion. These are not just mountains of dollar bills. These numbers represent resources diverted from other purchases. As the numbers began to climb, people naturally asked, Why are we policing Baghdad rather than New York, or repairing the electrical system in the Middle East rather than in the U.S. Midwest? People understand, as did former general and president Eisenhower, that when output is devoted to military tasks, there is less available for civilian consumption and investment.

dramatize 戏剧性地描述一下

Let us dramatize this choice by considering an economy which produces only two economic goods, guns and butter. The guns, of course, represent military spending, and the butter stands for civilian spending. Suppose that our economy decides to throw all its energy into producing the civilian good, butter. There is a maximum amount of butter that can be produced per year. The maximal amount of butter depends on the quantity and quality of the economy's resources and the productive efficiency with which they are used. Suppose 5 million pounds of butter is the maximum amount that can be produced with the existing technology and resources.

At the other extreme, imagine that all resources are instead devoted to the production of guns. Again, because of resource limitations, the economy can produce only a limited quantity of guns. For this example, assume that the economy can produce 15,000 guns of a certain kind if no butter is produced.

at the other extreme 另一个极端的例子

---

① 投入的另外一个专用术语为**生产要素**，广义来讲，可以归为三类：土地、劳动和资本。

[2] 最好的巧克力产自欧洲，而最好的 vanilla（香草）产自南美。这一段为作者为本版新加，用意颇深。

Alternative Production Possibilities

Possibilities	Butter (millions of pounds)	Guns (thousands)
A	0	15
B	1	14
C	2	12
D	3	9
E	4	5
F	5	0

TABLE 1-1. Limitation of Scarce Resources Implies the Guns-Butter Tradeoff ①

Scarce inputs and technology imply that the production of guns and butter is limited. As we go from A to B . . . to F, we are transferring labor, machines, and land from the gun industry to butter and can thereby increase butter production.

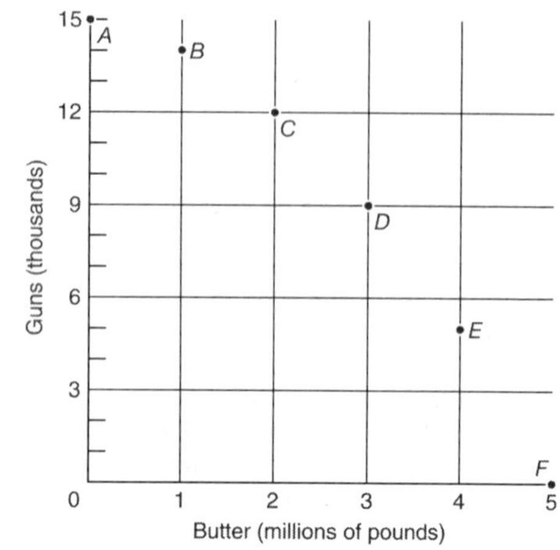

FIGURE 1-1. The Production Possibilities in a Graph ⑤

This figure displays the alternative combinations of production pairs from Table 1-1.

These are two extreme possibilities. In between are many others. If we are willing to give up some butter, we can have some guns. If we are willing to give up still more butter, we can have still more guns.

A schedule of possibilities is given in Table 1-1. Combination F shows the extreme, where all butter and no guns are produced, while A depicts the opposite extreme, where all resources go into guns. In between—at E, D, C, and B—increasing amounts of butter are given up in return for more guns.

How, you might well ask, can a nation turn butter ② into guns? Butter is transformed into guns not physically but by the alchemy of diverting the economy's [3] resources from one use to the other.

We can represent our economy's production possibilities more vividly in the diagram shown in Figure 1-1. This diagram measures butter along the horizontal axis and guns along the vertical one. (If you are unsure about the different kinds of graphs or about how to turn a table into a graph, consult the appendix to this chapter.) We plot point *F* in Figure 1-1 from the data in Table 1-1 by counting over 5 butter units to the right on the horizontal axis and going up 0 gun units on the vertical axis; similarly, *E* is obtained by going 4 butter units to the right and going up 5 gun units; and finally, we get *A* by going over 0 butter units and up 15 gun units.

If we fill in all intermediate positions with new [4] green-colored points representing all the different combinations of guns and butter, we have the continuous green curve shown as the *production-possibility frontier,* or *PPF,* in Figure 1-2.

The **production-possibility frontier** (or ***PPF***) shows ⑥ the maximum quantity of goods that can be efficiently produced by an economy, given its technological knowledge and the quantity of available inputs.

生产可能性边界的应用
Applying the PPF to Society's Choices

The *PPF* is the menu of choices that an economy has to choose from. Figure 1-2 shows a choice between guns and butter, but this concept can be applied to a broad range of economic choices. Thus the more resources the government uses to spend on public highways, the less will be left to produce private goods like houses; the more we choose to consume of food, the less we can consume of clothing; the more an economy consumes today, the less can be its production of capital goods to turn out more consumption goods in the future.

The graphs in Figures 1-3 to 1-5 present some important applications of *PPF*s. Figure 1-3 shows the effect of economic growth on a country's production possibilities. An increase in inputs, or improved technological knowledge, enables a country to produce more of all goods and services, thus shifting

---

① 表 1-1. 稀缺资源的制约意味着在大炮与黄油之间的抉择

② 这时，你可能会提出一个很好的问题：一个国家怎么可能将黄油转变为大炮？这里所讲的并不是物理意义上的转换，而是像炼丹术一样，将这个国家生产某种产品的资源转而生产完全不同的另一种产品。

[3] the economy，这个国家，与 a nation 呼应。

[4] 原版全书用绿色的不同明度印刷

⑤ 图 1-1. 生产可能性图

⑥ **生产可能性边界**（PPF）表示在技术知识和可获得的生产要素数量既定的条件下，一个经济体有能力高效率地生产有形产品的最大量值。

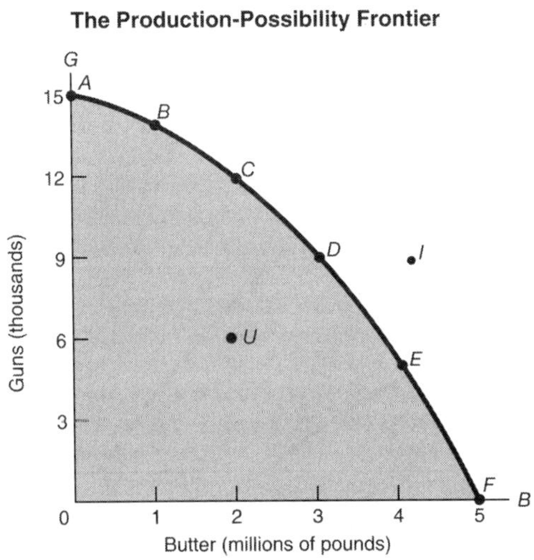

FIGURE 1-2. A Smooth Curve Connects the Plotted Points of the Numerical Production Possibilities ①

This frontier shows the schedule along which society can choose to substitute guns for butter. It assumes a given state of technology and a given quantity of inputs. Points outside the frontier (such as point *I*) are infeasible or unattainable. Any point inside the curve, such as *U*, indicates that the economy has not attained productive efficiency, as is the case, for instance, when unemployment is high during severe business cycles.

infeasible or unattainable 不可行的或者是很难达到的

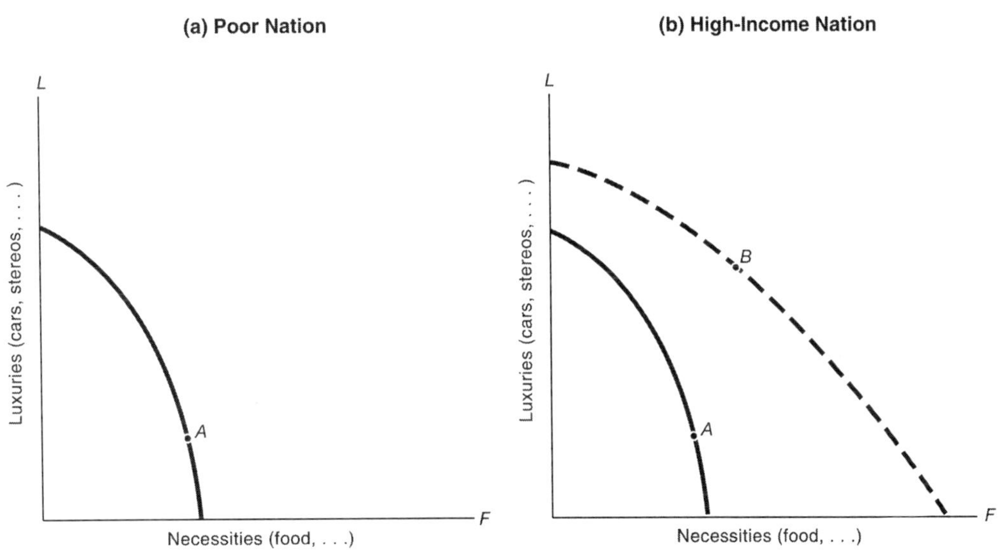

FIGURE 1-3. Economic Growth Shifts the *PPF* Outward ②

(**a**) Before development, the nation is poor. It must devote almost all its resources to food and enjoys few comforts. (**b**) Growth of inputs and technological change shift out the *PPF*. With economic growth, a nation moves from *A* to *B*, expanding its food consumption little compared with its increased consumption of luxuries. It can increase its consumption of both goods if it desires.

necessities 生活必需品

luxuries 奢侈消费品

① 图 1-2. 连接生产可能性数值各点的平滑曲线 ② 图 1-3. 经济增长使生产可能性边界外移

Frontier society
发展中国家
Urban society
发达国家

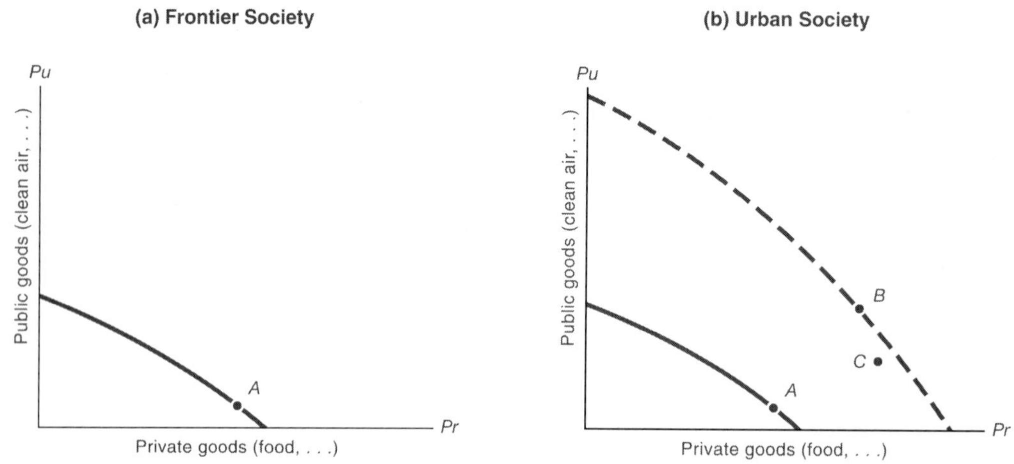

FIGURE 1-4. Economies Must Choose between Public Goods and Private Goods ①

(a) A poor frontier society lives from hand to mouth, with little left over for public goods like clean air or public health. **(b)** A modern urbanized economy is more prosperous and chooses to spend more of its higher income on public goods and government services (roads, environmental protection, and education).

Today's choices
当前选择
Future consequences
未来的结果

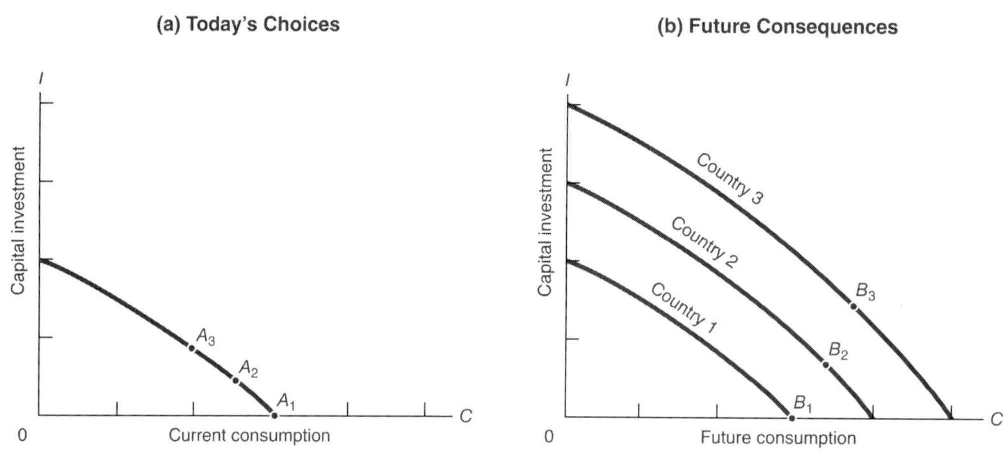

FIGURE 1-5. Investment for Future Consumption Requires Sacrificing Current Consumption ②

A nation can produce either current-consumption goods (pizzas and concerts) or investment goods (pizza ovens and concert halls). **(a)** Three countries start out even. They have the same *PPF,* shown in the panel on the left, but they have different investment rates. Country 1 does not invest for the future and remains at A_1 (merely replacing machines). Country 2 abstains modestly from consumption and invests at A_2. Country 3 sacrifices a great deal of current consumption and invests heavily. **(b)** In the following years, countries that invest more heavily forge ahead. Thus thrifty Country 3 has shifted its *PPF* far out, while Country 1's *PPF* has not moved at all. Countries that invest heavily can have *both* higher investment and consumption in the future.

① 图 1-4. 相应国家必须在公共物品和私人物品之间作出选择

② 图 1-5. 投资于未来消费就要牺牲当前消费

out the *PPF*. The figure also illustrates that poor countries must devote most of their resources to food production while rich countries can afford more luxuries as productive potential increases.

Figure 1-4 depicts the choice between private goods (bought at a price) and public goods (paid for by taxes). Poor countries can afford little of public goods like public health and primary education. But with economic growth, public goods as well as environmental quality take a larger share of output.

Figure 1-5 portrays an economy's choice between (*a*) current-consumption goods and (*b*) investment in capital goods (machines, factories, etc.). By sacrificing current consumption and producing more capital goods, a nation's economy can grow more rapidly, making possible more of *both* goods (consumption and investment) in the future.

Be Not Time's Fool [1]

The great American poet Carl Sandburg [2] wrote, "Time is the coin of your life. It is the only coin you have, and only you can determine how it will be spent. Be careful lest you let other people spend it for you." This emphasizes that one of the most important decisions that people confront is how to use their time.

We can illustrate this choice using the production-possibility frontier. For example, as a student, you might have 10 hours to study for upcoming tests in both economics and history. If you study only history, you will get a high grade there and do poorly in economics, and vice versa. Treating the grades on the two tests as the "output" of your studying, sketch out the *PPF* for grades, given your limited time resources. Alternatively, if the two student commodities are "grades" and "fun," how would you draw this *PPF*? Where are you on this frontier? Where are your lazy friends?

Recently, the United States collected data on how Americans use their time. Keep a diary of your time use for two or three days. Then go to *www.bls.gov/tus/home.htm* and compare how you spend your time with the results for other people.

机会成本
Opportunity Costs

When Robert Frost wrote of the road not taken, he [3] pointed to one of the deepest concepts of economics, *opportunity cost*. Because our resources are limited, we must decide how to allocate our incomes or time. When you decide whether to study economics, buy a car, or go to college, you will give something up—there will be a forgone opportunity. The next-best good that is forgone represents the opportunity cost of a decision.

The concept of opportunity cost can be illustrated using the *PPF*. Examine the frontier in Figure 1-2, which shows the tradeoff between guns and butter. Suppose the country decides to increase its gun purchases from 9000 guns at *D* to 12,000 units at *C*. What is the opportunity cost of this decision? You might calculate the cost in dollar terms. But in economics we always need to "pierce the veil" of money to examine the *real* impacts of alternative decisions. On the most fundamental level, the opportunity cost of moving from *D* to *C* is the butter that must be given up to produce the extra guns. In this example, the opportunity cost of the 3000 extra guns is 1 million pounds of butter forgone.

Or consider the real-world example of the cost of opening a gold mine near Yellowstone National Park. The developer argues that the mine will have but a small cost because Yellowstone's revenues will hardly be affected. But an economist would answer that the dollar receipts are too narrow a measure of cost. We should ask whether the unique and precious qualities of Yellowstone might be degraded if a gold mine were to operate, with the accompanying noise, water and air pollution, and decline in amenity values for visitors. While the dollar cost might be small, the opportunity cost in lost wilderness values might be large indeed.

[3] Robert Frost：罗伯特·弗罗斯特（1874~1963），一位兼跨古典和现代的美国诗人，曾四次获得普利策诗歌奖；其诗歌从乡村生活中汲取营养，作品既崇尚生活的现实，又富有神秘的色彩。"*the road not taken*"出自其发表于1916年的著名诗篇 *The Road Not Taken*。本诗寓意颇深，系世界文学史上的经典名篇。该诗结构严谨，格式规范，全诗四节，每节五行，均为五步抑扬格的abaab结构（Iambic Pentameter）。

In a world of scarcity, choosing one thing means giving up something else. The **opportunity cost** of a decision is the value of the good or service forgone. ④

④ 在我们这样一个资源稀缺的世界，对一种物品的选择就意味着对另一种物品的舍弃。决定这种选择的**机会成本**就是所放弃的物品或服务的价值。

效　率
Efficiency

Economists devote much of their study to exploring the efficiency of different kinds of market structures, incentives, and taxes. Remember that efficiency means that the economy's resources are being used as effectively as possible to satisfy people's desires. One important aspect of overall economic efficiency is productive efficiency, which is easily pictured in terms of the *PPF*. Efficiency means that the economy is *on* the frontier rather than *inside* the production-possibility frontier.

Productive efficiency occurs when an economy cannot produce more of one good without producing less of another good; this implies that the economy is on its production-possibility frontier. ⑤

---

[1] 做时间的主人。从第17版起，每章均开辟若干专栏，重点阐述与本章内容相关的经济生活中的重要概念或术语。本专栏前两版的题目均为 *The Tradeoff of Time*。这一修改同样呼应了作者对经济学赋予新的定义的哲学思考。

[2] 卡尔·桑德伯格（Carl Sandburg，1878~1967），著名的美国现代诗人和传记作家，先后三次获普利策奖。被誉为"巴尔迪莫圣人"的美国著名批评家门肯（H. L. Mencken, 1880~1956）称赞桑德伯格生命中的"每一次心脏搏动都是为美国人民的"。

⑤ **生产效率**是指当一个经济体在不减少另外一种产品数量的前提下，就无法增加某一种产品的产量，即该经济体的经济运行状况处于生产可能性边界状态，也可称作有效率的生产。

Let's see why productive efficiency requires being on the *PPF.* Start in the situation shown by point *D* in Figure 1-2. Say the market calls for another million pounds of butter. If we ignored the constraint shown by the *PPF,* we might think it possible to produce more butter without reducing gun production, say, by moving to point *I,* to the right of point *D.* But point *I* is outside the frontier, in the "infeasible" region. Starting from *D,* we cannot get more butter without giving up some guns. Hence point *D* displays productive efficiency, while point *I* is infeasible.

One further point about productive efficiency can be illustrated using the *PPF:* Being on the *PPF* means that producing more of one good inevitably requires sacrificing other goods. When we produce more guns, we are substituting guns for butter. *Substitution* is the law of life in a full-employment economy, and the production-possibility frontier depicts the menu of society's choices.

Waste from Business Cycles and Environmental Degradation. Economies suffer from inefficient use of resources for many reasons. When there are unemployed resources, the economy is not on its production-possibility frontier at all but, rather, somewhere *inside* it. In Figure 1-2, point *U* represents a point inside the *PPF;* at *U,* society is producing only 2 units of butter and 6 units of guns. Some resources are unemployed, and by putting them to work, we can increase our output of all goods; the economy can move from *U* to *D,* producing more butter and more guns, thus improving the economy's efficiency. We can have our guns and eat more butter too.

Historically, one source of inefficiency occurs during business cycles. From 1929 to 1933, in the Great Depression, the total output produced in the American economy declined by 25 percent. The economy did not suffer from an inward shift of the *PPF* because of technological forgetting. Rather, panics, bank failures, bankruptcies, and reduced spending moved the economy *inside* its *PPF.* A decade later, the military expenditures for World War II expanded demand, and output grew rapidly as the economy pushed back to the *PPF.*

Similar situations occur periodically during business-cycle recessions. The latest growth slowdown occurred in 2007–2008 when problems in housing and credit markets spread through the entire economy. The economy's underlying productivity had not suddenly declined during those years. Rather, reduced overall spending pushed the economy temporarily inside its *PPF* for that period.

A different kind of inefficiency occurs when markets are failing to reflect true scarcities, as with environmental degradation. Suppose that an unregulated business decides to dump chemicals in a river, killing fish and ruining recreational opportunities. The firm is not necessarily doing this because it has evil intent. Rather, the prices in the marketplace do not reflect true social priorities—the price on polluting in an unregulated environment is zero rather than the true opportunity cost in terms of lost fish and recreation.

Environmental degradation can also push the economy inside its *PPF.* The situation is illustrated in Figure 1-4(*b*). Because businesses do not face correct prices, the economy moves from point *B* to point *C.* Private goods are increased, but public goods (like clean air and water) are decreased. Efficient regulation of the environment could move northeast back to the dashed efficient frontier.

As we close this introductory chapter, let us return briefly to our opening theme, Why study economics? Perhaps the best answer to the question is a famous one given by Keynes in the final lines of *The General Theory of Employment, Interest and Money:*

> The ideas of economists and political philosophers, both when they are right and when they are wrong, are more powerful than is commonly understood. Indeed the world is ruled by little else. Practical men, who believe themselves to be quite exempt from any intellectual influences, are usually the slaves of some defunct economist. Madmen in authority, who hear voices in the air, are distilling their frenzy from some academic scribbler of a few years back. I am sure that the power of vested interests is vastly exaggerated compared with the gradual encroachment of ideas. Not, indeed, immediately, but after a certain interval; for in the field of economic and political philosophy there are not many who are influenced by new theories after they are twenty-five or thirty years of age, so that the ideas which civil servants and politicians and even agitators apply to current events are not likely to be the newest. But, soon or late, it is ideas, not vested interests, which are dangerous for good or evil. ①

To understand how the powerful ideas of economics apply to the central issues of human societies—ultimately, this is why we study economics.

---

① 无论经济学家和政论家们的观点正确与否，都比普通人的理解更具影响力。这个世界的确由极少数人统治着。阅历丰富的人自认为自己不会受到任何学究的影响，却往往是某位已故经济学家的奴隶。那些高高在上的有权有势的狂人，一直在从若干年前过世的某位拙劣文人那里攫取其狂妄荒诞之举。我确信，与那些渐被侵蚀的观念相比，这种既得利益的威力被夸大其辞了。确实，这种现象既是一时的权宜之计，同时也是经过了一段时间形成的。因为，在经济学和政治哲学领域，在 25~30 岁这个年龄段以后还受新思潮影响的人是不多的。因此，公务员和政客，甚至那些煽风点火的人所左右局势的理论都不太可能是最新的。但是，无论早晚，终究不是既得利益，而是对善与恶这一人类永恒主题相悖的思想。

SUMMARY

A. Why Study Economics?

1. What is economics? Economics is the study of how societies choose to use scarce productive resources that have alternative uses, to produce commodities of various kinds, and to distribute them among different groups. We study economics to understand not only the world we live in but also the many potential worlds that reformers are constantly proposing to us.
2. Goods are scarce because people desire much more than the economy can produce. Economic goods are scarce, not free, and society must choose among the limited goods that can be produced with its available resources.
3. Microeconomics is concerned with the behavior of individual entities such as markets, firms, and households. Macroeconomics views the performance of the economy as a whole. Through all economics, beware of the fallacy of composition and the post hoc fallacy, and remember to keep other things constant.

B. The Three Problems of Economic Organization

4. Every society must answer three fundamental questions: *what, how,* and *for whom? What* kinds and quantities are produced among the wide range of all possible goods and services? *How* are resources used in producing these goods? And *for whom* are the goods produced (that is, what is the distribution of income and consumption among different individuals and classes)?
5. Societies answer these questions in different ways. The most important forms of economic organization today are *command* and *market.* The command economy is directed by centralized government control; a market economy is guided by an informal system of prices and profits in which most decisions are made by private individuals and firms. All societies have different combinations of command and market; all societies are mixed economies.

C. Society's Technological Possibilities

6. With given resources and technology, the production choices between two goods such as butter and guns can be summarized in the *production-possibility frontier* (*PPF*). The *PPF* shows how the production of one good (such as guns) is traded off against the production of another good (such as butter). In a world of scarcity, choosing one thing means giving up something else. The value of the good or service forgone is its opportunity cost.
7. Productive efficiency occurs when production of one good cannot be increased without curtailing production of another good. This is illustrated by the *PPF.* When an economy is on its *PPF,* it can produce more of one good only by producing less of another good.
8. Production-possibility frontiers illustrate many basic economic processes: how economic growth pushes out the frontier, how a nation chooses relatively less food and other necessities as it develops, how a country chooses between private goods and public goods, and how societies choose between consumption goods and capital goods that enhance future consumption.
9. Societies are sometimes inside their production-possibility frontier because of macroeconomic business cycles or microeconomic market failures. When credit conditions are tight or spending suddenly declines, a society moves inside its *PPF* in recessions; this occurs because of macroeconomic rigidities, not because of technological forgetting. A society can also be inside its *PPF* if markets fail because prices do not reflect social priorities, such as with environmental degradation from air and water pollution.

CONCEPTS FOR REVIEW

Fundamental Concepts

scarcity and efficiency
free goods vs. economic goods
macroeconomics and microeconomics
normative vs. positive economics
fallacy of composition, post hoc fallacy
"keep other things constant"

Key Problems of Economic Organization

what, how, and *for whom*
alternative economic systems:
command vs. market
laissez-faire
mixed economies

Choice among Production Possibilities

inputs and outputs
production-possibility frontier (*PPF*)
productive efficiency and inefficiency
opportunity cost

FURTHER READING AND INTERNET WEBSITES

Further Reading

Robert Heilbroner, *The Worldly Philosophers,* 7th ed. (Touchstone Books, 1999), provides a lively biography of the great economists along with their ideas and impact. The authoritative work on the history of economic analysis is Joseph Schumpeter, *History of Economic Analysis* (McGraw-Hill, New York, 1954).

Websites

One of the greatest books of all economics is Adam Smith, *The Wealth of Nations* (many publishers, 1776). Every economics student should read a few pages to get the flavor of his writing. *The Wealth of Nations* can be found at *www.bibliomania.com/NonFiction/Smith/Wealth/index.html.*

Log on to one of the Internet reference sites for economics such as *Resources for Economists on the Internet* (*www.rfe.org*). Browse through some of the sections to familiarize yourself with the site. You might want to look up your college or university, look at recent news in a newspaper or magazine, or check some economic data.

Two sites for excellent analyses of public policy issues in economics are those of the Brookings Institution (*www.brook.edu*) and of the American Enterprise Institute (*www.aei.org*). Each of these publishes books and has policy briefs online.

QUESTIONS FOR DISCUSSION

1. The great English economist Alfred Marshall (1842–1924) invented many of the tools of modern economics, but he was most concerned with the application of these tools to the problems of society. In his inaugural lecture, Marshall wrote:

   > It will be my most cherished ambition to increase the numbers who Cambridge University sends out into the world with cool heads but warm hearts, willing to give some of their best powers to grappling with the social suffering around them; resolved not to rest content till they have opened up to all the material means of a refined and noble life. [*Memorials of Alfred Marshall,* A. C. Pigou, ed. (Macmillan and Co., London, 1925), p. 174, with minor edits.]

   Explain how the cool head might provide the essential positive economic analysis to implement the normative value judgments of the warm heart. Do you agree with Marshall's view of the role of the teacher? Do you accept his challenge?
2. The late George Stigler, an eminent conservative Chicago economist, wrote as follows:

   > No thoroughly egalitarian society has ever been able to construct or maintain an efficient and progressive economic system. It has been universal experience that some system of differential rewards is necessary to stimulate workers. [*The Theory of Price,* 3d ed. (Macmillan, New York, 1966), p. 19.]

   Are these statements positive or normative economics? Discuss Stigler's view in light of Alfred Marshall's quote in question 1. Is there a conflict?
3. Define each of the following terms carefully and give examples: *PPF,* scarcity, productive efficiency, inputs, outputs.
4. Read the special section on time use (p. 13). Then do the exercise in the last paragraph. Construct a table that compares your time use with that of the average American. (For a graphical analysis, see question 5 of the appendix to this chapter.)
5. Assume that Econoland produces haircuts and shirts with inputs of labor. Econoland has 1000 hours of labor available. A haircut requires ½ hour of labor, while a shirt requires 5 hours of labor. Construct Econoland's production-possibility frontier.
6. Assume that scientific inventions have doubled the productivity of society's resources in butter production without altering the productivity of gun manufacture. Redraw society's production-possibility frontier in Figure 1-2 to illustrate the new tradeoff.
7. Some scientists believe that we are rapidly depleting our natural resources. Assume that there are only two inputs (labor and natural resources) producing two goods (concerts and gasoline) with no improvement in society's technology over time. Show what would happen to the *PPF* over time as natural resources are exhausted. How would invention and technological improvement modify your answer? On the basis of this example, explain why it is said that "economic growth is a race between depletion and invention."
8. Say that Diligent has 10 hours to study for upcoming tests in economics and history. Draw a *PPF* for grades, given Diligent's limited time resources. If Diligent

studies inefficiently by listening to loud music and chatting with friends, where will Diligent's grade "output" be relative to the *PPF*? What will happen to the grade *PPF* if Diligent increases study inputs from 10 hours to 15 hours?

9. Consider the *PPF* for clean air and automobile travel.
   a. Explain why unregulated air pollution in automobiles would push a country inside its *PPF*. Illustrate your discussion with a carefully drawn *PPF* for these two goods.
   b. Next explain how putting a price on harmful automobile emissions would increase both goods and move the country to its *PPF*. Illustrate by showing how correcting the "market failure" would change the final outcome.

Appendix I

HOW TO READ GRAPHS

第 1 章附录　如何看图

A picture is worth a thousand words. [1]

Chinese Proverb

Before you can master economics, you must have a working knowledge of graphs. They are as indispensable to the economist as a hammer is to a carpenter. So if you are not familiar with the use of diagrams, invest some time in learning how to read them—it will be time well spent.

What is a *graph?* It is a diagram showing how two or more sets of data or variables are related to one another. Graphs are essential in economics because, among other reasons, they allow us to analyze economic concepts and examine historical trends.

You will encounter many different kinds of graphs in this book. Some graphs show how variables change over time (see, for example, the inside of the front cover); other graphs show the relationship between different variables (such as the example we will turn to in a moment). Each graph in the book will help you understand an important economic relationship or trend.

生产可能性边界

THE PRODUCTION-POSSIBILITY FRONTIER

The first graph that you encountered in this text was the production-possibility frontier. As we showed in the body of this chapter, the production-possibility frontier, or *PPF*, represents the maximum amounts of a pair of goods or services that can both be produced with an economy's given resources, assuming that all resources are fully employed.

Let's follow up an important application, that of choosing between food and machines. The essential data for the *PPF* are shown in Table 1A-1, which is very much like the example in Table 1-1. Recall that each of the possibilities gives one level of food production and one level of machine production. As the quantity of food produced increases, the production of machines falls. Thus, if the economy produced 10 units of food, it could produce a maximum of 140 machines, but when the output of food is 20 units, only 120 machines can be manufactured.

生产可能性图表

Production-Possibility Graph

The data shown in Table 1A-1 can also be presented as a graph. To construct the graph, we represent each of the table's pairs of data by a single point on a two-dimensional plane. Figure 1A-1 displays in a graph

Alternative Production Possibilities

Possibilities	Food	Machines
A	0	150
B	10	140
C	20	120
D	30	90
E	40	50
F	50	0

TABLE 1A-1. The Pairs of Possible Outputs of Food and Machines ②

The table shows six potential pairs of outputs that can be produced with the given resources of a country. The country can choose one of the six possible combinations.

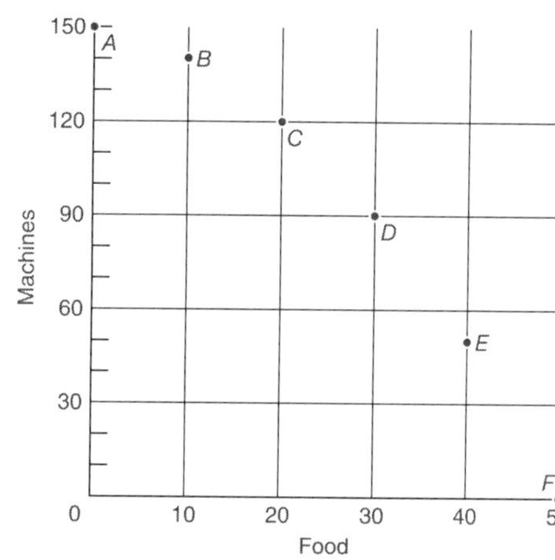

FIGURE 1A-1. Six Possible Pairs of Food-Machine Production Levels ③

This figure shows the data of Table 1A-1 in graphical form. The data are exactly the same, but the visual display presents the data more vividly.

---

[1] 中国谚语:"百闻不如一见"。距今两千多年前的公元前1世纪,西汉宣帝刘询时期,羌人入侵,所到之处烧杀掳抢,攻夺城池,掠夺土地,形势十万火急。宣帝遂召集文武百官询问谁愿统兵前去拒敌。这时,早已过耄耋之年的老将赵充国自告奋勇,集自己几十年镇守边关和羌人打交道的经验,自愿担当这一重任。当宣帝问他需要多少兵马时,他讲了这样一段话:"百闻不如一见。兵难渝度,臣愿驰至金城,图上方略。"

这就是我们中国人家喻户晓的成语"百闻不如一见"的典故及其来历。

赵充国以76岁的高龄亲自率小队人马过黄河、擒俘虏、察地形、摸敌情,确定攻守计划,画好作战地图,向宣帝奏上。随后朝廷按图屯兵,整治边境,分化瓦解羌人并平定了羌人的侵扰,安定了西北边疆。这里,"图"的作用可见一斑。因此我们说,"百闻不如一见"这句成语中的"见"意为"图","百闻不如一见"应理解为"百闻不如一图"。西方学术界熟悉的中国谚语大多是当年的传教士翻译的,这条翻译亦不例外。从这里我们也不难看出当年的传教士们对中国文化的了解之深。

图解和识图能力对于经济学家来讲,其作用犹如木匠之板斧,为其器之首。

② 表1A-1. 食品与机器产量的可能性组合

③ 图1A-1. 食品与机器产量的六种可能组合

the relationship between the food and machine outputs shown in Table 1A-1. Each pair of numbers is represented by a single point in the graph. Thus the row labeled "A" in Table 1A-1 is graphed as point *A* in Figure 1A-1, and similarly for points *B*, *C*, and so on.

In Figure 1A-1, the vertical line at left and the horizontal line at the bottom correspond to the two variables—food and machines. A **variable** is an item of interest that can be defined and measured and that takes on different values at different times or places. Important variables studied in economics are prices, quantities, hours of work, acres of land, dollars of income, and so forth.

The horizontal line on a graph is referred to as the *horizontal axis*, or sometimes the *X axis*. In Figure 1A-1, food output is measured on the black horizontal axis. The vertical line is known as the *vertical axis*, or *Y axis*. In Figure 1A-1, it measures the number of machines produced. Point *A* on the vertical axis stands for 150 machines. The lower left-hand corner, where the two axes meet, is called the *origin*. It signifies 0 food and 0 machines in Figure 1A-1.

一条平滑的曲线

A Smooth Curve

In most economic relationships, variables can change by small amounts as well as by the large increments shown in Figure 1A-1. We therefore generally draw economic relationships as continuous curves. Figure 1A-2 shows the *PPF* as a smooth curve in which the points from *A* to *F* have been connected.

By comparing Table 1A-1 and Figure 1A-2, we can see why graphs are so often used in economics. The smooth *PPF* reflects the menu of choice for the economy. It is a visual device for showing what types of goods are available in what quantities. Your eye can see at a glance the relationship between machine and food production.

斜率和线段

Slopes and Lines

Figure 1A-2 depicts the relationship between maximum food and machine production. One important way to describe the relationship between two variables is by the slope of the graph line.

The **slope** of a line represents the change in one variable that occurs when another variable changes. More precisely, it is the change in the variable *Y* on the vertical axis per unit change in the variable *X* on the horizontal axis. For example, in Figure 1A-2, say that food production rose from 25 to 26 units. The

The Production-Possibility Frontier

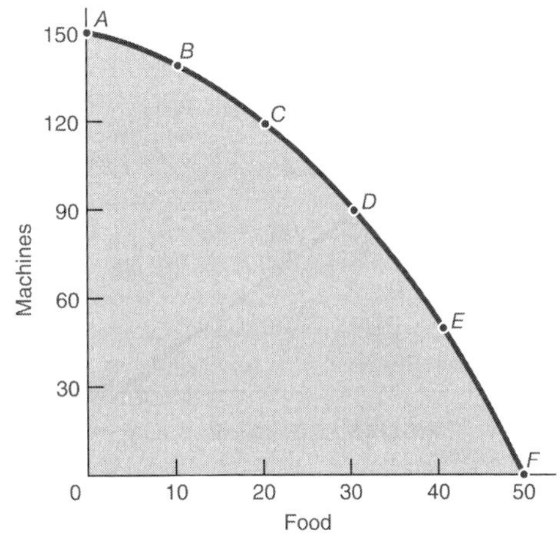

FIGURE 1A-2. A Production-Possibility Frontier ①

A smooth curve fills in between the plotted points, creating the production-possibility frontier.

slope of the curve in Figure 1A-2 tells us the precise change in machinery production that would take place. *Slope is an exact numerical measure of the relationship between the change in* Y *and the change in* X.

We can use Figure 1A-3 to show how to measure the slope of a straight line, say, the slope of the line between points *B* and *D*. Think of the movement from *B* to *D* as occurring in two stages. First comes a horizontal movement from *B* to *C* indicating a 1-unit increase in the *X* value (with no change in *Y*). Second comes a compensating vertical movement up or down, shown as *s* in Figure 1A-3. (The movement of 1 horizontal unit is purely for convenience. The formula holds for movements of any size.) The two-step movement brings us from one point to another on the straight line.

Because the *BC* movement is a 1-unit increase in *X*, the length of *CD* (shown as *s* in Figure 1A-3) indicates the change in *Y* per unit change in *X*. On a graph, this change is called the *slope* of the line *ABDE*.

Often slope is defined as "the rise over the run." The *rise* is the vertical distance; in Figure 1A-3, the rise is the distance from *C* to *D*. The run is the horizontal distance; it is *BC* in Figure 1A-3. The rise over the run in this instance would be *CD* over *BC*. Thus

① 图 1A-2. 生产可能性边界

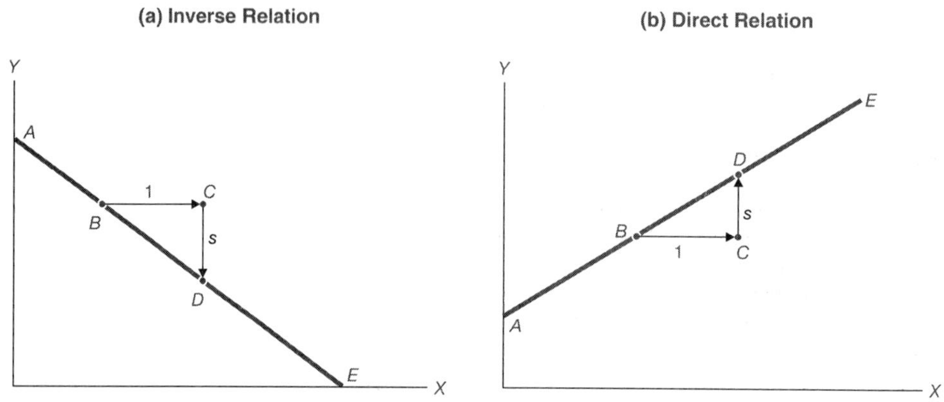

FIGURE 1A-3. Calculation of Slope for Straight Lines ①

It is easy to calculate slopes for straight lines as "rise over run." Thus in both **(a)** and **(b)**, the numerical value of the slope is rise/run = $CD/BC = s/1 = s$. Note that in **(a)**, *CD* is negative, indicating a negative slope, or an inverse relationship between *X* and *Y*.

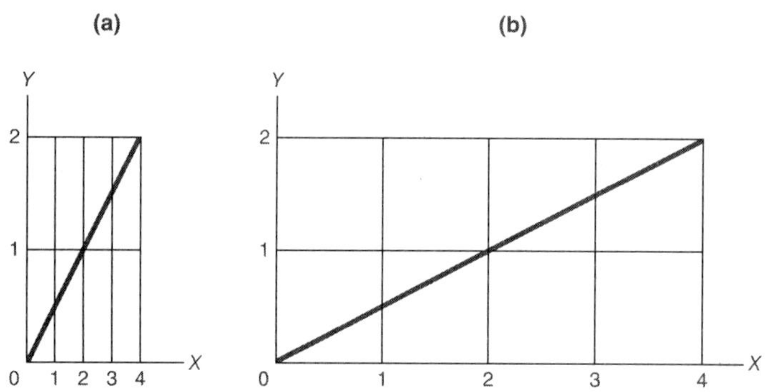

FIGURE 1A-4. Steepness Is Not the Same as Slope ②

Note that even though **(a)** looks steeper than **(b)**, they display the same relationship. Both have a slope of ½, but the *X* axis has been stretched out in **(b)**.

the slope of *BD* is *CD/BC*. (For those who have studied calculus, question 7 at the end of this appendix relates slopes to derivatives.)

The key points to understand about slopes are the following:

1. The slope can be expressed as a number. It measures the change in *Y* per unit change in *X*, or "the rise over the run."
2. If the line is straight, its slope is constant everywhere.
3. The slope of the line indicates whether the relationship between *X* and *Y* is direct or inverse.

Direct relationships occur when variables move in the same direction (that is, they increase or decrease together); *inverse relationships* occur when the variables move in opposite directions (that is, one increases as the other decreases).

Thus a negative slope indicates the *X-Y* relation is inverse, as it is in Figure 1A-3(*a*). Why? Because an increase in *X* calls for a decrease in *Y*.

People sometimes confuse slope with the appearance of steepness. This conclusion is often but not always valid. The steepness depends on the scale of the graph. Panels (*a*) and (*b*) in Figure 1A-4 both

① 图 1A-3. 直线斜率的计算
② 图 1A-4. 斜率不同于坡度

portray exactly the same relationship. But in (*b*), the horizontal scale has been stretched out compared with (*a*). If you calculate carefully, you will see that the slopes are exactly the same (and are equal to ½).

曲线的斜率

Slope of a Curved Line

A curved or nonlinear line is one whose slope changes. Sometimes we want to know the slope at *a given point,* such as point *B* in Figure 1A-5. We see that the slope at point *B* is positive, but it is not obvious exactly how to calculate the slope.

To find the slope of a smooth curved line at a point, we calculate the slope of the straight line that just touches, but does not cross, the curved line at the point in question. Such a straight line is called a *tangent* to the curved line. Put differently, the slope of a curved line at a point is given by the slope of the straight line that is tangent to the curve at the given point. Once we draw the tangent line, we find the slope of the tangent line with the usual right-angle measuring technique discussed earlier.

To find the slope at point *B* in Figure 1A-5, we simply construct straight line *FBJ* as a tangent to the curved line at point *B*. We then calculate the slope of the tangent as *NJ/MN*. Similarly, the tangent line *GH* gives the slope of the curved line at point *D*.

Another example of the slope of a nonlinear line is shown in Figure 1A-6. This shows a typical microeconomics curve, which is dome-shaped and has a maximum at point *C*. We can use our method of slopes as tangents to see that the slope of the curve is always positive in the region where the curve is rising and negative in the falling region. At the peak or maximum of the curve, the slope is exactly zero. A zero slope signifies that a tiny movement in the *X* variable around the maximum has no effect on the value of the *Y* variable.[1]

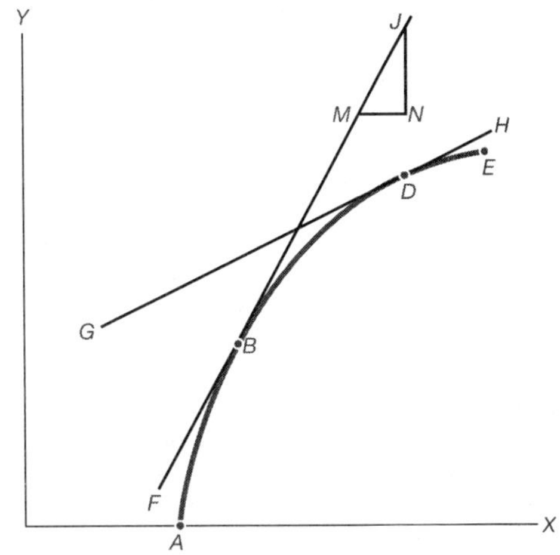

FIGURE 1A-5. Tangent as Slope of Curved Line ①

By constructing a tangent line, we can calculate the slope of a curved line at a given point. Thus the line *FBMJ* is tangent to smooth curve *ABDE* at point *B*. The slope at *B* is calculated as the slope of the tangent line, that is, as *NJ/MN*.

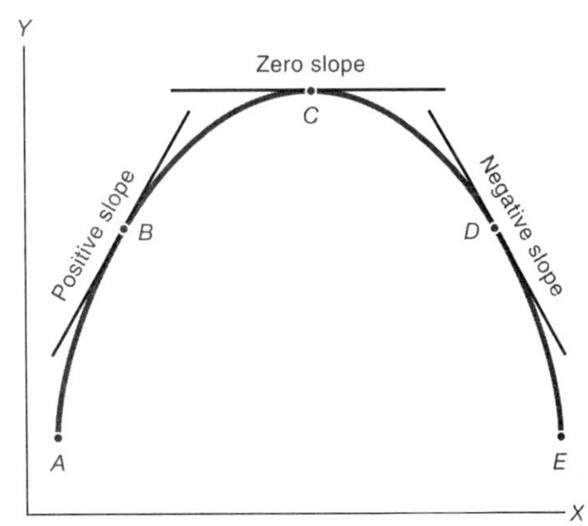

FIGURE 1A-6. Different Slopes of Nonlinear Curves ②

Many curves in economics first rise, then reach a maximum, then fall. In the rising region from *A* to *C* the slope is positive (see point *B*). In the falling region from *C* to *E* the slope is negative (see point *D*). At the curve's maximum, point *C*, the slope is zero. (What about a U-shaped curve? What is the slope at its minimum?)

[1] For those who enjoy algebra, the slope of a line can be remembered as follows: A straight line (or linear relationship) is written as $Y = a + bX$. For this line, the slope of the curve is b, which measures the change in Y per unit change in X.

A curved line or nonlinear relationship is one involving terms other than constants and the X term. An example of a nonlinear relationship is the quadratic equation $Y = (X - 2)^2$. You can verify that the slope of this equation is negative for $X < 2$ and positive for $X > 2$. What is its slope for $X = 2$?

For those who know calculus: A zero slope comes where the derivative of a smooth curve is equal to zero. For example, plot and use calculus to find the zero-slope point of a curve defined by the function $Y = (X - 2)^2$.

① 图 1A-5. 曲线斜率的切线

② 图 1A-6. 非线性曲线的不同斜率

作为边际值的斜率

Slope as the Marginal Value [1]

One of the most important concepts in economics is *marginal*, which always means "additional" or "extra." For example, we talk about "marginal cost," which means the extra cost that is incurred when a firm produces an extra unit of output. Similarly, in fiscal economics, we discuss the "marginal tax rate," which denotes the additional taxes that are paid when an individual earns an additional dollar of income.

We can calculate the marginal value in a relationship from the slope. Figure 1A-3 shows the marginal values for two straight lines. Look first at Figure 1A-3(*b*). Perhaps the *Y* variable is taxes and the *X* variable is income. Then the slope *s* represents the marginal tax rate. For every unit of *X*, taxes go up by *s* units. For many taxpayers, the marginal tax rate would be between 0.20 and 0.40.

Next examine Figure 1A-3(*a*). Here, the marginal value is negative. This might represent what happens when a particular area is overfished, where the *X* variable is number of boats and the *Y* variable is total fish catch. Because of overfishing, the marginal catch per boat is actually negative because the stock of fish is being depleted.

We can also apply this concept to curved lines. What is the marginal value at point *B* in Figure 1A-5? You can calculate that each *MN* units of *X* produce *NJ* units of *Y*. The marginal value at *B* is also the slope, which is *NJ*/*MN*. Note that the marginal value is declining as *X* increases because the curve is concave or dome-shaped.

Query: What is the marginal value of the relationship in Figure 1A-6 at point *C*? Make sure you can explain why the marginal value is zero.

曲线的移动和沿着曲线移动

Shifts of and Movement along Curves [2]

An important distinction in economics is that between shifts of curves and movement along curves. We can examine this distinction in Figure 1A-7. The inner production-possibility frontier reproduces the *PPF* in Figure 1A-2. At point *D* society chooses to produce 30 units of food and 90 units of machines. If society decides to consume more food with a given *PPF*, then it can *move along* the *PPF* to point *E*. This movement along the curve represents choosing more food and fewer machines.

Suppose that the inner *PPF* represents society's production possibilities for 1990. If we return to the same country in 2000, we see that the *PPF* has *shifted* from the inner 1990 curve to the outer 2000 curve. (This shift would occur because of technological change or because of an increase in labor or capital available.) In the later year, society might choose to be at point *G*, with more food and machines than at either *D* or *E*.

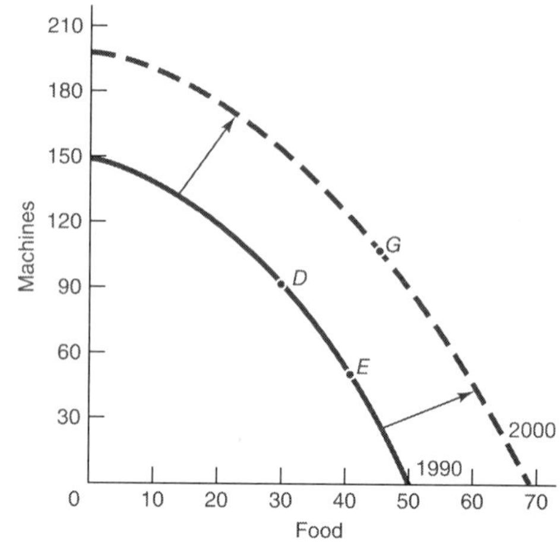

FIGURE 1A-7. Shift of Curves versus Movement along Curves ③

In using graphs, it is essential to distinguish *movement along* a curve (such as from high-investment *D* to low- investment *E*) from a *shift* of a curve (as from *D* in an early year to *G* in a later year).

The point of this example is that in the first case (moving from *D* to *E*) we see movement along the curve, while in the second case (from *D* to *G*) we see a shift of the curve.

某些特殊的图

Some Special Graphs

The *PPF* is one of the most important graphs of economics, one depicting the relationship between two economic variables (such as food and machines or guns and butter). You will encounter other types of graphs in the pages that follow.

Time Series Some graphs show how a particular variable has changed over time. Look, for example, at the graphs on the inside front cover of this text.

[1] 边际值的斜率。这一部分是本版新加的内容，强调读者应该着重理解图 1A-6 中 C 点的边际值含义，读懂图中其值为零的原因。

[2] 沿曲线移动及曲线的移动，此处英文为 Shifts of Curves and Movement along Curves 的缩略表述。

③ 图 1A-7. 曲线位移与沿曲线移动

The left-hand graph shows a time series, since the American Revolution, of a significant macroeconomic variable, the ratio of the federal government debt to total gross domestic product—this ratio is the *debt-GDP ratio.* Time-series graphs have time on the horizontal axis and variables of interest (in this case, the debt-GDP ratio) on the vertical axis. This graph shows that the debt-GDP ratio has risen sharply during every major war.

Scatter Diagrams Sometimes individual data points will be plotted, as in Figure 1A-1. Often, combinations of variables for different years will be plotted. An important example of a scatter diagram from macroeconomics is the *consumption function,* shown in Figure 1A-8. This scatter diagram shows the nation's total disposable income on the horizontal axis and total consumption (spending by households on goods like food, clothing, and housing) on the vertical axis. Note that consumption is very closely linked to income, a vital clue for understanding changes in national income and output.

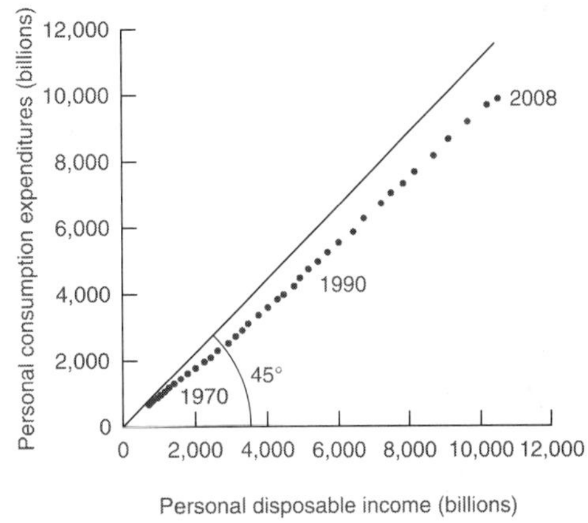

FIGURE 1A-8. Scatter Diagram of Consumption Function Shows Important Macroeconomic Law ①

The dots show a scatter diagram of income and consumption. Note how close the relationship is between the two. This forms the basis for the *consumption function* of macroeconomics.

Diagrams with More than One Curve Often it is useful to put two curves in the same graph, thus obtaining a "multicurve diagram." The most important example is the *supply-and-demand diagram,* shown in Chapter 3 (see page 55). Such graphs can show two different relationships simultaneously, such as how consumer purchases respond to price (demand) and how business production responds to price (supply). By graphing the two relationships together, we can determine the price and quantity that will hold in a market.

This concludes our brief excursion into graphs. Once you have mastered these basic principles, the graphs in this book, and in other areas, can be both fun and instructive.

SUMMARY TO APPENDIX

1. Graphs are an essential tool of modern economics. They provide a convenient presentation of data or of the relationships among variables.
2. The important points to understand about a graph are: What is on each of the two axes (horizontal and vertical)? What are the units on each axis? What kind of relationship is depicted in the curve or curves shown in the graph?
3. The relationship between the two variables in a curve is given by its slope. The slope is defined as "the rise over the run," or the increase in Y per unit increase in X. If it is upward- (or positively) sloping, the two variables are directly related; they move upward or downward together. If the curve has a downward (or negative) slope, the two variables are inversely related.
4. In addition, we sometimes see special types of graphs: time series, which show how a particular variable moves over time; scatter diagrams, which show observations on a pair of variables; and multicurve diagrams, which show two or more relationships in a single graph.

① 图 1A-8. 通过消费函数散点图的重要宏观经济规律

CONCEPTS FOR REVIEW

Elements of Graphs

horizontal, or *X*, axis
vertical, or *Y*, axis
slope as "rise over run"
slope (negative, positive, zero)
tangent as slope of curved line

Examples of Graphs

time-series graphs
scatter diagrams
multicurve graphs

QUESTIONS FOR DISCUSSION

1. Consider the following problem: After your 8 hours a day of sleep, you have 16 hours a day to divide between leisure and study. Let leisure hours be the *X* variable and study hours be the *Y* variable. Plot the straight-line relationship between all combinations of *X* and *Y* on a blank piece of graph paper. Be careful to label the axes and mark the origin.
2. In question 1, what is the slope of the line showing the relationship between study and leisure hours? Is it a straight line?
3. Let us say that you absolutely need 6 hours of leisure per day, no more, no less. On the graph, mark the point that corresponds to 6 hours of leisure. Now consider a *movement along the curve:* Assume that you decide that you need only 4 hours of leisure a day. Plot the new point.
4. Next show a *shift of the curve:* You find that you need less sleep, so you have 18 hours a day to devote to leisure and study. Draw the new (shifted) curve.
5. As suggested in the special section on time use, keep a diary of your time use by half-hour increments for 3 days; record studying, sleeping, working, leisure, and other uses. Then draw a time production-possibility curve, like Figure 1A-2, between leisure and all other activities. Locate each of your 3 days on the time *PPF.* Then put the average for all Americans on the same graph. How do you compare with the average person?
6. Go to the website of the Bureau of Economic Analysis at *www.bea.gov.* Then click on "Gross Domestic Product." On the next page, click on "Interactive NIPA data." Then click on "Frequently Requested NIPA Tables." Click on "Table 1.2 (Real Gross Domestic Product)," which is the total output of the economy. This will probably come up with the quarterly data.
   a. Construct a graph that shows the time series for real GDP for the last six quarters. Is the general trend upward or downward? (In macroeconomics, we will learn that the slope is downward in recessions.)
   b. Construct a scatter plot showing "Imports" on the vertical axis and "Gross domestic product" on the horizontal axis. Describe the relationship between the numbers. (In macroeconomics, this will be the marginal propensity to import.)
7. *For those who have studied calculus:* The slope of a smooth line or curve is its derivative. The following are the equations for two inverse demand curves (where price is a function of output). For each curve, assume that the function holds only when $P \geqslant 0$ and $X \geqslant 0$.
   a. $P = 100 - 5X$
   b. $P = 100 - 20X + 1X^2$
   For each demand curve, determine its slope when $X = 0$ and when $X = 1$. For linear demand curves such as **a**, what is the condition under which the law of downward-sloping demand holds? Is curve **b** concave (like a dome) or convex (like a cup)?
8. The marginal value of a curve is its slope, which is the same as the first derivative of a function. Calculate algebraically the marginal effect of output on price for the inverse demand curves **a** and **b** in question 7. Provide the numerical marginal values at $X = 10$ for both demand curves.

The Modern Mixed Economy
现代混合经济

CHAPTER

2

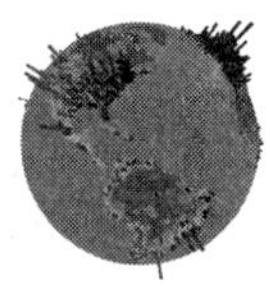

Every individual endeavors to employ his capital so that its produce may be of greatest value. He generally neither intends to promote the public interest, nor knows how much he is promoting it. He intends only his own security, only his own gain. And he is in this led by an invisible hand to promote an end which was no part of his intention. By pursuing his own interest he frequently promotes that of society more effectually than when he really intends to promote it.

Adam Smith

The Wealth of Nations (1776) [1]

[1] 美国的《独立宣言》同年发表，是学术界公认的1776年最为重要的两部文献。1902年，严复先生使用文言文开中文节选意译本先河，取名《原富》，使一个世纪之前处于彷徨之中的中国人开始认识亚当·斯密和他的《国富论》。1928年，郭大力和王亚南两先生为了更好地翻译《资本论》，先期合作重新翻译全书，1931年由上海神州国光社出版，译名根据英文书名的缩写定为《国富论》。从此，《国富论》成为亚当·斯密这本经典著作普遍认可的中文译名和迄今为止在国内传播最广、影响最大和引用次数最多的译本。进入21世纪后，国内先后又出现了唐日松（华夏出版社，2005年）和杨敬年（陕西人民出版社，2006年）的两个译本。

这一章是作者修订量最大的章之一，是作者冷静而深刻地思考本次金融危机成因的重要表现，也是本版《经济学》学术价值和历史地位的重要体现。这一段文字凝练自《国富论》第四篇的第二章（Book IV, Chapter II）中第九自然段（目前常用版本为1904年伦敦 Methuen & Co., Ltd. 出版的第5版）中间的一段，原文如下：

As every individual, therefore, endeavors as much as he can both to employ his capital in the support of domestic industry, and so to direct that industry that its produce may be of the greatest value; every individual necessarily labors to render the annual revenue of the society as great as he can. He generally, indeed, neither intends to promote the public interest, nor knows how much he is promoting it. By preferring the support of domestic to that of foreign industry, he intends only his own security; and by directing that industry in such a manner as its produce may be of the greatest value, he intends only his own gain, and he is in this, as in many other cases, led by an invisible hand to promote an end which was no part of his intention. Nor is it always the worse for the society that it was no part of it. By pursuing his own interest he frequently promotes that of the society more effectually than when he really intends to promote it.

结合原文，拟译为：

每个个人都在竭尽全力地使用好自己的资本，以使其有可能产生最大的价值。总的来讲，他既不试图促进公共利益，也不知晓究竟对此能促进到什么程度。通常情况下，他只是在核计自己的证券，盘算自己的利润。因此，他总受着一只看不见的手的引导，促进实现一种丝毫与自己的意图无关的目标。通过追求自己的利益所产生的社会利益，往往使他能比真正出于本意去刻意追求的社会利益更为有效。

——亚当·斯密

《国富论》（1776）

Think for a moment about some of the goods and services that you consumed over the last few days. Perhaps you took an airline flight to school or bought some gasoline for the family car. You surely had some home-cooked food bought in a grocery store or a meal purchased at a restaurant. You might have bought a book (such as this textbook) or some pharmaceutical drugs.

Now consider some of the many steps that preceded your purchases. The airplane flight will illustrate the point very well. You may have purchased an airline ticket on the Internet. This simple-sounding purchase involves much tangible capital such as your computer, intellectual property (in software and designs), and sophisticated fiber-optic transmission lines, as well as complicated airline reservation systems and pricing models. The airlines do all this to make profits (although profits have been very modest in that sector).

At the same time, government plays an important role in air travel. It regulates airline safety, owns many airports, manages the traffic-control system, produces the public good of weather data and forecasting, and provides information on flight delays. And this list could go on into the public and private support of aircraft manufacturing, international agreements on airline competition, energy policy on fuels, and other areas.

The same point would apply—in different degrees depending upon the sector—to your purchases of clothing or gasoline or pharmaceuticals or just about any item. The economy of every country in the world [2] is a **mixed economy**—a combination of private enterprise working through the marketplace and government regulation, taxation, and programs. What exactly is a market economy, and what makes it such a powerful engine of growth? What is the "capital" in "capitalism"? What government controls are needed

[2] 当今世界上任何一个国家的经济形态都是**混合型**的。

这是作者在本章前面所加的四段文字中极其重要的一句话，它用经济学的观点和方法为当今世界的政治格局以及金融危机之后新的国与国关系奠定了一个很好的经济哲学基础，意义重大。所以，作者也将在第17和18版中一直沿用的题目 *Markets and Government in a Modern Economy* 改成了 *The Modern Mixed Economy*（现代混合经济）。

to make markets function effectively? The time has come to understand the principles that lie behind the market economy and to review government's role in economic life.

市场机制

A. THE MARKET MECHANISM

Most economic activity in most high-income countries takes place in private markets—through the market mechanism—so we begin our systematic study there. Who is responsible for making the decisions in a market economy? You may be surprised to learn that *no single individual or organization or govern-* ①
ment is responsible for solving the economic problems in a market economy. Instead, millions of businesses and consumers engage in voluntary trade, intending to improve their own economic situations, and their actions are invisibly coordinated by a system of prices and markets.

To see how remarkable this is, consider the city of New York. Without a constant flow of goods into and out of the city, New Yorkers would be on the verge of starvation within a week. But New Yorkers actually do very well economically. The reason is that goods travel for days and weeks from the surrounding counties, from 50 states, and from the far corners of the world, with New York as their destination.

How is it that 10 million people can sleep easily at night, without living in mortal terror of a breakdown in the elaborate economic processes upon which they rely? The surprising answer is that, without coercion or centralized direction by anyone, these economic activities are coordinated through the market.

Everyone in the United States notices how much the government does to control economic activity: it regulates drugs, fights fires, levies taxes, sends armies around the world, and so forth. But we seldom think about how much of our ordinary economic life proceeds without government intervention. Thousands of commodities are produced by millions of people every day, willingly, without central direction or master plan.

不是混乱，而是经济秩序
Not Chaos, but Economic Order

The market looks like a jumble of sellers and buyers. It seems almost a miracle that food is produced in suitable amounts, gets transported to the right place, and arrives in a palatable form at the dinner table. But a close look at New York or other economies is convincing proof that a market system is neither chaos nor miracle. It is a system with its own internal logic. And it works.

A market economy is an elaborate mechanism for coordinating people, activities, and businesses through a system of prices and markets. It is a communication device for pooling the knowledge and actions of billions of diverse individuals. Without central intelligence or computation, it solves problems of production and distribution involving billions of unknown variables and relations, problems that are far beyond the reach of even today's fastest supercomputer. Nobody designed the market, yet it functions remarkably well. In a market economy, no single individual or organization is responsible for production, consumption, distribution, or pricing.

How do markets determine prices, wages, and outputs? Originally, a market was an actual place where buyers and sellers could engage in face-to-face bargaining. The *marketplace*—filled with slabs of butter, pyramids of cheese, layers of wet fish, and heaps of vegetables—used to be a familiar sight in many villages and towns, where farmers brought their goods to sell. In the United States today there are still important markets where many traders gather together to do business. For example, wheat and corn are traded at the Chicago Board of Trade, oil and platinum are traded at the New York Mercantile Exchange, and gems are traded at the Diamond District in New York City.

Markets are places where buyers and sellers interact, exchange goods and services or assets, and determine prices. There are markets for almost everything. You can buy artwork by old masters at auction houses in New York or pollution permits at the Chicago Board of Trade. A market may be centralized, like the stock market. It may be decentralized, as is the case for most workers. Or it may exist only electronically, as is increasingly the case with "e-commerce" on the Internet. Some of the most important markets are for financial assets, such as stocks, bonds, foreign exchange, and mortgages.

A **market** is a mechanism through which buyers ②
and sellers interact to determine prices and exchange goods, services, and assets.

---

① 没有任何一个个人、组织或者政府负责解决市场经济中所产生的大大小小的经济问题。

② 所谓**市场**就是一种机制，买家和卖家通过这一机制相互作用来决定价格，以及交换商品、服务和资产。

The central role of markets is to determine the **price** of goods. A price is the value of the good in terms of money (the role of money will be discussed later in this chapter). At a deeper level, prices represent the terms on which different items can be exchanged. The market price of a bicycle might be $500, while that of a pair of shoes is $50. In essence, the market is saying that shoes and bicycles trade on a 10-to-1 basis.

In addition, prices serve as *signals* to producers and consumers. If consumers want more of any good, the price will rise, sending a signal to producers that more supply is needed. When a terrible disease reduces beef production, the supply of beef decreases and raises the price of hamburgers. The higher price encourages farmers to increase their production of beef and, at the same time, encourages consumers to substitute other foods for hamburgers and beef products.

What is true of the markets for consumer goods is also true of markets for factors of production, such as land or labor. If more computer programmers are needed to run Internet businesses, the price of computer programmers (their hourly wage) will tend to rise. The rise in relative wages will attract workers into the growing occupation.

Prices coordinate the decisions of producers and ① consumers in a market. Higher prices tend to reduce consumer purchases and encourage production. Lower prices encourage consumption and discourage production. Prices are the balance wheel of the market mechanism.

Market Equilibrium. At every moment, some people are buying while others are selling; firms are inventing new products while governments are passing laws to regulate old ones; foreign companies are opening plants in America while American firms are selling their products abroad. Yet in the midst of all this turmoil, markets are constantly solving the *what, how,* and *for whom*. As they balance all the forces operat- ② ing on the economy, markets are finding a **market equilibrium of supply and demand.**

A market equilibrium represents a balance among all ③ *the different buyers and sellers.* Depending upon the price, households and firms all want to buy or sell different quantities. The market finds the equilibrium price that simultaneously meets the desires of buyers and sellers. Too high a price would mean a glut of goods with too much output; too low a price would produce long lines in stores and a deficiency of goods. Those prices for which buyers desire to buy exactly the quantity that sellers desire to sell yield an equilibrium of supply and demand.

市场如何解决三个经济问题
How Markets Solve the Three Economic Problems

We have just described how prices help balance consumption and production (or demand and supply) in an individual market. What happens when we put all the different markets together—beef, cars, land, labor, capital, and everything else? These markets work simultaneously to determine a general equilibrium of prices and production.

By matching sellers and buyers (supply and demand) in each market, a market economy simultaneously solves the three problems of *what, how,* and *for whom*. Here is an outline of a market equilibrium:

1. *What* goods and services will be produced is determined by the dollar votes of consumers in their daily purchase decisions. A century ago, many dollar votes for transportation went for horses and horseshoes; today, much is spent on automobiles and tires.

   Firms, in turn, are motivated by the desire to maximize profits. **Profits** are net revenues, or ④ the difference between total sales and total costs. Firms abandon areas where they are losing profits; by the same token, firms are lured by high profits into production of goods in high demand. Some of the most profitable activities today are producing and marketing drugs—drugs for depression, anxiety, and all other manner of human frailty. Lured by the high profits, companies are investing billions of dollars each year in research to come up with yet more new and improved medicines.
2. *How* things are produced is determined by the competition among different producers. The best way for producers to meet price competition and maximize profits is to keep costs at a minimum by adopting the most efficient methods of production. Sometimes change is incremental and consists of little more than tinkering with the machinery or adjusting the input mix to gain a cost advantage. At other times there are drastic

market equilibrium
市场均衡

---

① 价格是市场活动中生产商与消费者各自决策的协调者。较高的物价在抑制消费者购买力的同时也刺激了生产。较低的价格在鼓励消费的同时也抑制了生产。因此，价格是在市场机制中起平衡作用的摆轮。

② 市场在平衡经济体中所有影响其运行的力量的过程，就是市场本身在发现**供给与需求的市场均衡**的过程。

③ 市场均衡代表了在所有不同的卖家和买家之间达到的一种平衡。

④ **利润**即净收益，等于销售总额与总成本之差。

shifts in technology, as with steam engines displacing horses because steam was cheaper per unit of useful work, or airplanes replacing railroads as the most efficient mode for long-distance travel. Right now we are in the midst of just such a transition to a radically different technology, with computers revolutionizing many tasks in the workplace, from the checkout counter to the lecture room.

3. *For whom* things are produced—who is consuming and how much—depends, in large part, on the supply and demand in the markets for factors of production. Factor markets (i.e., markets for factors of production) determine wage rates, land rents, interest rates, and profits. Such prices are called *factor prices*. The same person may receive wages from a job, dividends from stocks, interest on a bond, and rent from a piece of property. By adding up all the revenues from all the factors, we can calculate the person's market income. The distribution of income among the population is thus determined by the quantity of factor services (person-hours, acres, etc.) and the prices of the factors (wage rates, land rents, etc.).

factor markets 生产要素市场

两大主宰

The Dual Monarchy

Who are the rulers in a market economy? Do giant companies like Microsoft and Toyota call the tune? Or perhaps Congress and the president? Or advertising moguls from Madison Avenue? All these people [1] and institutions affect us, but in the end the major ② forces affecting the shape of the economy are the dual monarchs of *tastes* and *technology*.

[1] Madison Avenue，纽约的麦迪逊大道，美国广告业的代名词。

② 所有这些人和机构都影响着我们，但最终对经济形态发挥主要作用的还是消费倾向和技术这两大主宰。

One fundamental determinant is the tastes of the population. These innate and acquired tastes—as expressed in the dollar votes of consumer demands—direct the uses of society's resources. They pick the point on the production-possibility frontier (*PPF*).

The other major factor is the resources and technology available to a society. The economy cannot go outside its *PPF*. You can fly to Hong Kong, but there are no flights yet to Mars. Therefore, the economy's resources limit the candidates for the dollar votes of consumers. Consumer demand has to dovetail with business supply of goods and services to determine what is ultimately produced.

You will find it helpful to recall the dual monarchy when you wonder why some technologies fail in the marketplace. From the Stanley Steamer—a car that [3] ran on steam—to the Premiere smokeless cigarette, [4] which was smokeless but also tasteless, history is full of products that found no markets. How do useless products die off? Is there a government agency that pronounces upon the value of new products? No such agency is necessary. Rather, they become extinct because there is no consumer demand for the products at the going market price. These products make losses rather than profits. This reminds us that profits serve as the rewards and penalties for businesses and guide the market mechanism.

Like a farmer using a carrot and a stick to coax a ⑤ donkey forward, the market system deals out profits and losses to induce firms to produce desired goods efficiently.

价格和市场关系图

A Picture of Prices and Markets

We can picture the circular flow of economic life in Figure 2-1. The diagram provides an overview of how consumers and producers interact to determine prices and quantities for both inputs and outputs. Note the two different kinds of markets in the circular flow. At the top are the product markets, or the flow of outputs like pizza and shoes; at the bottom are the markets for inputs or factors of production like land and labor. Further, see how decisions are made by two different entities, consumers and businesses.

Consumers buy goods and sell factors of production; businesses sell goods and buy factors of production. Consumers use their income from the sale of labor and other inputs to buy goods from businesses; businesses base their prices of goods on the costs of labor and property. Prices in goods markets are set to balance consumer demand with business supply; prices in factor markets are set to balance household supply with business demand.

All this sounds complicated. But it is simply the total picture of the intricate web of supplies and demands connected through a market mechanism to solve the economic problems of *what, how,* and *for whom*.

看不见的手

The Invisible Hand

It was Adam Smith who first recognized how a market economy organizes the complicated forces of supply and demand. In one of the most famous passages of all economics, quoted from *The Wealth of Nations* at the opening of this chapter, Smith saw the harmony between private profit and public interest. Go back and reread these paradoxical words. Particularly note

---

[3] 著名的斯坦利机车，美国的孪生兄弟发明家 Francis Edgar Stanley（1849~1918）和 Freelan O. Stanley（1849~1940）于 1897 年发明。

[4] 美国雷诺兹烟草公司（R. J. Reynolds Tobacco Company）于 1988 年推出的一款 *Premier* 牌“无烟、无灰、无尼古丁”的健康香烟作为传统香烟的替代品上市，该产品还有环保和避免被动吸烟的显著优点。但终因不符合目标市场的消费倾向而未获成功。

⑤ 正如农民用胡萝卜加棒子来驱使牲畜干农活的办法一样，市场机制就是同时使用收益和亏损来引导企业高效率地生产消费者期望的产品。

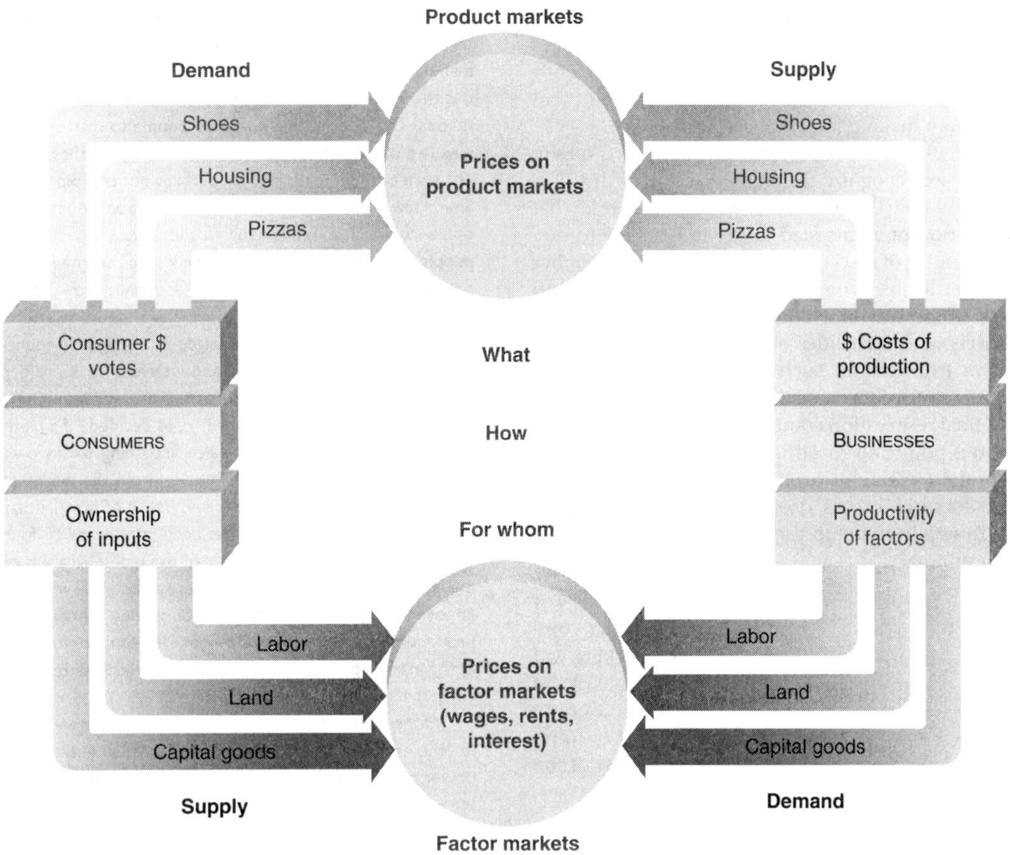

FIGURE 2-1. The Market System Relies on Supply and Demand to Solve the Trio ① of Economic Problems

We see here the circular flow of a market economy. Dollar votes of consumers (households, governments, and foreigners) interact with business supply in the product markets at top, helping to determine *what* is produced. Business demand for inputs meets the supply of labor and other inputs in the factor markets below, determining wage, rent, and interest payments; incomes thus influence *for whom* goods are delivered. Business competition to buy factor inputs and sell goods most cheaply determines *how* goods are produced.

the subtle point about the **invisible hand**—that private interest can lead to public gain *when it takes place* ② *in a well-functioning market mechanism.*

Smith's words were written in 1776. That same year was also marked by the American Declaration of Independence. It is no coincidence that both ideas appeared at the same time. Just as Americans were ③ proclaiming freedom from tyranny, Adam Smith was preaching a revolutionary doctrine emancipating trade and industry from the shackles of a feudal aristocracy. Smith held that government interference with market competition is almost certain to be injurious.

Smith's insight about the functioning of the market mechanism has inspired modern economists—both the admirers and the critics of capitalism.

① 图 2-1. 市场机制依赖于供求关系来解决经济学的三大问题

② 当这只看不见的手在市场体系中有效地发挥作用时。

③ 当美国人民在为摆脱英国的殖民暴政浴血奋斗之时，亚当·斯密也一直在宣传自己的革命学说，呼吁把贸易和工业生产从封建贵族统治的桎梏中解放出来。斯密坚持认为，政府对市场竞争的干预行为几乎可以肯定是有害无益的（注：作者在这里删去了本句中从 16 版开始，连续三版均有的介词短语：in this best of all possible worlds，意为“在所有可能的手段中最行之有效的”）。

Economic theorists have proved that under limited conditions a perfectly competitive economy is efficient (remember that an economy is producing efficiently when it cannot increase the economic welfare of anyone without making someone else worse off).

After two centuries of experience and thought, however, we recognize the limited scope of this doctrine. We know that there are "market failures," that markets do not always lead to the most efficient outcome. One set of market failures concerns monopolies and other forms of imperfect competition. A second failure of the "invisible hand" comes when there are spillovers or externalities outside the marketplace—positive externalities such as scientific discoveries and negative spillovers such as pollution.

A final reservation comes when the income distribution is politically or ethically unacceptable. When any of these elements occur, Adam Smith's invisible-hand doctrine breaks down and government may want to step in to mend the flawed invisible hand.

In summary:

Adam Smith discovered a remarkable property of ① a competitive market economy. Under perfect competition and with no market failures, markets will squeeze as many useful goods and services out of the available resources as is possible. But where monopolies or pollution or similar market failures become pervasive, the remarkable efficiency properties of the invisible hand may be destroyed.

① 亚当·斯密发现了市场经济的竞争性本身所具有的极其重要的价值。在完全竞争和不存在市场失灵的情况下，市场会用可供支配的资源尽可能多地生产出有用的物品和劳务。但在垄断、污染或者类似市场失灵的情况下，这只看不见的手的神奇效率特征就可能遭到破坏。

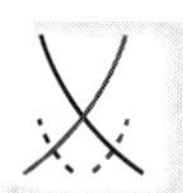

Adam Smith: Founding Father of Economics

"For what purpose is all the toil and bustle of this world? What is the end of avarice and ambition, of the pursuit of wealth, of power, and pre-eminence?" ② [3] Thus wrote Adam Smith (1723–1790), of Scotland, who glimpsed for the social world of economics what Isaac Newton recognized for the physical world of the heavens. Smith answered his questions in *The Wealth of Nations* (1776), where he explained the self-regulating natural order by which the oil of self-interest lubricates the economic machinery in an almost miraculous fashion. Smith believed that the toil and bustle had the effect of improving the lot of the common man and woman. "Consumption is the sole end and purpose of all production."

Smith was the first apostle of economic growth. At the dawn of the Industrial Revolution, he pointed to the great strides in productivity brought about by specialization and the division of labor. In a famous example, he described the manufacturing of a pin factory in which "one man draws out the wire, another straightens it, a third cuts it," and so it goes. This operation allowed 10 people to make 48,000 pins in a day, whereas if "all wrought separately, they could not each of them make twenty, perhaps not one pin a day." Smith saw the result of this division of labor as "universal opulence which extends itself to the lowest ranks of the people." Imagine what he would think if he returned today to see what two more centuries of economic growth have produced!

Smith wrote hundreds of pages railing against countless cases of government folly and interference. Consider the seventeenth-century guild master who was attempting to improve his weaving. The town guild decided, "If a cloth weaver intends to process a piece according to his own invention, he should obtain permission from the judges of the town to employ the number and length of threads that he desires after the question has been considered by four of the oldest merchants and four of the oldest weavers of the guild." Smith argued that such restrictions—whether imposed by government or by monopolies, whether on production or on foreign trade—limit the proper workings of the market system and ultimately hurt both workers and consumers.

None of this should suggest that Smith was an apologist for the establishment. He had a distrust of all entrenched power, private monopolies as much as public monarchies. He was for the common people. But, like many of the great economists, he had learned from his research that the road to waste is paved with good intentions.

Above all, it is Adam Smith's vision of the self-regulating ④ "invisible hand" that is his enduring contribution to modern economics.

贸易、货币和资本

B. TRADE, MONEY, AND CAPITAL

What are some of the distinguishing features of a modern economy? Three important ones are considered in this section:

1. An advanced economy is characterized by an elaborate network of trade that depends on specialization and an intricate division of labor.

---

② 这个世界上的一切艰辛和劳碌究竟都是为了什么？是追求财富、权势，还是出人头地？什么时候才是这些贪婪和野心的尽头？

[3] 这段话的原文出自斯密在出版《国富论》之前出版的经典名著《道德情操论》的第一卷第三篇的第二章，该书是亚当·斯密《国富论》经济学理论的灵魂，是利他主义的伦理学著作。

④ 总而言之，亚当·斯密关于市场这只“看不见的手”具有自我调节功能的理论正是其对现代经济学做出的不朽贡献。

2. Modern economies today make extensive use of money, which provides the yardstick for measuring economic values and is the means of payment.
3. Modern industrial technologies rest on the use of vast stocks of capital. Capital leverages human labor into a much more efficient factor of production and allows productivity many times greater than that possible in an earlier age.

贸易、专业化和劳动分工
TRADE, SPECIALIZATION, AND DIVISION OF LABOR

As compared to the economies of the 1700s, today's economies depend heavily on the specialization of individuals and firms, connected by an extensive network of trade. Modern economies have enjoyed rapid economic growth as increasing specialization has allowed workers to become highly productive in particular occupations and to trade their output for the commodities they need.

Specialization occurs when people and countries concentrate their efforts on a particular set of tasks—it permits each person and country to use to best advantage the specific skills and resources that are available. One of the facts of economic life is that, rather than have everyone do everything in a mediocre way, it is better to establish a *division of labor*—dividing production into a number of small specialized steps or tasks. A division of labor permits tall people to play basketball, numerate people to teach, and persuasive people to sell cars. It sometimes takes many years to receive the training for particular careers—it usually takes 14 postgraduate years to become a certified neurosurgeon.

Capital and land are also highly specialized. In the case of land, some lands form the precious sandy strips of beach between populous cities and warm oceans; others are valuable vineyard lands of France or California; still other lands border on deepwater ports and serve as centers of trade for the world.

Capital also is highly specialized. The computer software that went along with the labor to write this textbook took over a decade to be developed, but it is useless at managing an oil refinery or solving large numerical problems. One of the most impressive examples of specialization is the computer chip that manages automobiles, increases their efficiency, and can even serve as a "black box" to record accident data.

The enormous efficiency of specialization allows the intricate network of trade among people and nations that we see today. Very few of us produce a single finished good; we make but the tiniest fraction of what we consume. We might teach a small part of one college's curriculum, or empty coins from parking meters, or separate the genetic material of fruit flies. In exchange for this specialized labor, we will receive an income adequate to buy goods from all over the world.

The idea of *gains from trade* forms one of the central insights of economics. Different people or countries tend to specialize in certain areas; they then engage in the voluntary exchange of what they produce for what they need. Japan has grown enormously productive by specializing in manufacturing goods such as automobiles and consumer electronics; it exports much of its manufacturing output to pay for imports of raw materials. By contrast, countries which have tried the strategy of becoming self-sufficient—attempting to produce most of what they consume—have discovered that this is the road to stagnation. Trade can enrich all nations and increase *everyone's* living standards. ①

gains from trade 贸易增益

To summarize:

> Specialization and trade are the key to high living standards. By specializing, people can become highly productive in a very narrow field of expertise. People can then trade their specialized goods for others' products, vastly increasing the range and quality of consumption and having the potential to raise everyone's living standards. ② [3]

Globalization

You can hardly open a newspaper today without reading about the most recent trends in "globalization." What exactly does this term mean? How can economics contribute to understanding the issues?

Globalization is a term that is used to *denote an increase in economic integration among nations*. Increasing integration is seen today in the dramatic growth in the flows of goods, services, and finance across national borders.

One major component of globalization is the steady increase in the share of national output devoted to imports and exports. With a continuous drop in transportation and communication costs, along with declining tariffs and other

① 贸易可以惠及所有的国家，并有可能改善每一位公民的生活水平。

② 专业化与贸易是高生活水平的关键所在。通过专业化，人们可以在很窄的专业领域变得高效。然后，将他们专业化的产品与他人生产的商品进行交换，大大增加了消费的范围和质量，同时也潜在提高了每个人的生活水平。

[3] 本段文字的前半部分相较于前几个版本做了彻底的修订，之前强调的是发达经济体。本版的这段文字客观地论述了当前世界经济的全球化格局。

barriers to trade, the share of trade in U.S. national output has more than doubled over the last half-century. Domestic producers now compete with producers from around the world in their prices and design decisions.

At a deeper level, however, globalization reflects an extension of specialization and division of labor to the entire world. Two centuries ago, most people lived on farms and produced virtually everything they consumed: food, shelter, clothing, fuel, and so on. Gradually, people specialized and bought much of their consumption from others in their community or nation. Today, many goods are produced in several countries and shipped around the world.

An interesting example of the globalized economy is the production of the iPod. Who makes the iPod? You might think that it is made by Apple, while if you look at the back of the iPod, it says "Made in China." What is the truth here? The iPod is actually a small portable computer for delivering music. It has at least 451 parts, which are made all around the world. Apple designed the software and manages the production process, earning about $80 for each $299 of sales. China's part consists primarily of assembly, with about $5 of labor costs. So, while the trade statistics record that an iPod sold in the United States incurs $150 of trade deficit with China, only a tiny fraction of the $150 was actually earned by China.

Hal Varian, chief economist for Google, summarized the results of this study very nicely:

> Ultimately, there is no simple answer to who makes the iPod or where it is made. The iPod, like many other products, is made in several countries by dozens of companies, with each stage of production contributing a different amount to the final value. The real value of the iPod doesn't lie in its parts or even in putting those parts together. The bulk of the iPod's value is in the conception and design of the iPod. That is why Apple gets $80 for each of these video iPods it sells, which is by far the largest piece of value added in the entire supply chain. Those clever folks at Apple figured out how to combine 451 mostly generic parts into a valuable product. They may not make the iPod, but they created it. In the end, that's what really matters.[1]

Evidence indicates that this process of "slicing up the value added" is typical of manufacturing activities in the United States and other high-income countries.

Globalization occurs in financial markets as well as in goods markets. Financial integration is seen in the accelerated pace of lending and borrowing among nations as well as in the convergence of interest rates among different countries. The major causes of financial-market integration have been the dismantling of restrictions on capital flows among nations, cost reductions, and innovations in financial markets, particularly the use of new kinds of financial instruments.

Financial integration among nations has undoubtedly led to gains from trade, as nations with productive uses for capital can borrow from countries with excess savings. In the last two decades, Japan and China have served as the world's major lending countries. Surprisingly, the United
[1] States has been the world's largest borrower—partly because of its low national saving rate and partly because of the dynamism of its industries, such as information and biomedical technologies.

Global integration of goods and financial markets has produced impressive gains from trade in the form of lower prices, increased innovation, and more rapid economic growth. But these gains have been accompanied by painful side effects.

One consequence of economic integration is the unemployment and lost profits that occur when low-cost foreign producers displace domestic production. For example, from 1980 to 2007, U.S. employment in textiles
[2] and apparel fell from 2 million to 0.6 million workers. The unemployed textile workers found little solace in the fact that consumers were enjoying declining prices for Chinese clothing. Those who lose from increased international trade are the tireless advocates of "protectionism" in the form of tariffs and quotas on international trade.

A second consequence comes when financial integration triggers international financial crises. The latest crisis began in mid-2007 when a decline in U.S. housing prices spilled over into stock and bond markets around the world. One might ask why the Indian stock market should decline 20 or 30 percent because of problems in the U.S. housing market. The contagion arising from such disturbances is the result of closely linked markets. The irrational exuberance in financial markets in the 2000s led to extremely small risk premiums, raising asset prices around the world. When investors turned pessimistic in 2007 and 2008, risk premiums rose everywhere, including on Indian assets.

Globalization raises many new issues for policymakers. Are the gains from trade worth the domestic costs in terms of social disruption and dislocation? Should countries attempt to insulate themselves from global financial crises by walling off their financial markets? Does integration lead to greater income inequality? How should central

[1] See the website listings in the Further Reading section at the end of this chapter.

---

[1] 苹果产品的定位是约占美国人口 5% 的时尚和专业群体。作者在此引用美国人引以为豪的 iPod 产品的国际化分工生产的典型案例，对全球化做了很好的诠释。这也是本教材经久不衰的重要原因之一，案例新，数据新，与时俱进。这一段专门论述全球化的文字全部用新的典型案例和新的数据更新，篇幅也稍有扩大。

[2] 哈尔·瓦里安（Hal Varian），1947 年生于俄亥俄州的伍斯特，美国加州大学柏克莱信息学院教授，现正学术休假，期间应邀出任谷歌公司的首席经济学家。其编写的《中级微观经济学》（*Interme-diate Microeconomics*）和《微观经济学分析》（*Microeconomics Analysis*）都是发行量很大的教科书。

banks respond to financial instabilities that spread around the world? These questions are on the minds of policymakers who are attempting to deal with globalization.

货币：交换的润滑剂 MONEY: THE LUBRICANT OF EXCHANGE

If specialization permits people to concentrate on particular tasks, money then allows people to trade their specialized outputs for the vast array of goods and services produced by others.

Money is the means of payment in the form of currency and checks used to buy things. Money is a lubricant that facilitates exchange. When everyone trusts and accepts money as payment for goods and debts, trade is facilitated. Just imagine how complicated economic life would be if you had to barter goods for goods every time you wanted to buy a pizza or go to a concert. What services could you offer Sal's Pizza? What could you barter with your college [1] to cover your tuition? Money acts as a matchmaker between buyers and sellers, effortlessly effecting little marriages of mutual self-interest billions of times every day.

Governments control the money supply through their central banks. But like other lubricants, money can get overheated and damage the economic engine. It can grow out of control and cause a hyperinflation, in which prices increase very rapidly. When that happens, people concentrate on spending their money quickly, before it loses its value, rather than investing it for the future. That's what happened to several Latin American countries in the 1980s, and many former socialist economies in the 1990s, when they had inflation rates exceeding 1000 percent or even 10,000 percent per year. Imagine getting your paycheck and having it lose 20 percent of its value by the end of the week!

Money is the medium of exchange. Proper man- ② agement of the financial system is one of the major [3] issues for government macroeconomic policy in all countries.

资 本 CAPITAL

The two great input partners in the productive process are labor and capital. We know what labor is, because we are all workers who rent our time for wages. The other partner is **capital**—a produced and durable input which is itself an output of the economy. Capital consists of a vast and specialized array of machines, buildings, computers, software, and so on.

Most of us do not realize how much our daily activities depend upon capital, including the houses where we live, the highways on which we drive, and the wires that bring electricity and cable TV to our homes. The total net capital stock in the U.S. economy in 2008, including government-owned, business, and residential capital, amounted to more than $150,000 per person.

Unlike land and labor, capital has to be produced before you can use it. For example, some companies build textile machines, which are then used to make shirts; some companies build farm tractors, which are then used to help produce corn.

Use of capital involves time-consuming, roundabout methods of production. People learned long ago that indirect and roundabout production techniques often are more efficient than direct methods of production. For example, the most direct method of catching fish is to wade into a stream and grab fish with your hands, but this yields more frustration than fish. By using a fishing rod (which is capital equipment), fishing time becomes more productive in terms of fish caught per day. By using even more capital, in the form of nets and fishing boats, fishing becomes productive enough to feed many people and provide a good living to those who operate the specialized nets and equipment.

Growth from the Sacrifice of Current Consumption. If people are willing to save—to abstain from present consumption and wait for future consumption—society can devote resources to new capital goods. A larger stock of capital helps the economy grow faster by pushing out the *PPF*. Look back at Figure 1-5 to see how forgoing current consumption in favor of investment adds to future production possibilities. High rates of saving and investment help explain how China and other Asian countries have grown so fast over the last three decades. By contrast, many poor countries are caught in a vicious circle called the "poverty trap." They have low incomes and few productive outlets for their savings, they save and invest little, they grow slowly, and as a consequence they fall further behind in the economic standings of nations.

[1] Sal's Pizza，美国一家著名的特许经营的比萨快餐外卖餐厅，老板 Sal Lupoli 曾在波士顿著名的意大利餐厅 North End 帮厨学艺，这段经历对他发明自己独特的比萨配方起了重要的作用。

② 货币是交易的媒介。对于所有国家来说，对金融体系的有效管理是政府宏观经济政策的主要问题之一。

[3] 作者在本版将前几个版本一直沿用的货币供应 *money supply* 改为金融体系 *financial system*，突显了作者对此次金融危机成因的反思。

We summarize as follows:

Economic activity involves forgoing current ① consumption to increase our capital. Every time we invest—building a new factory or road, increasing the years or quality of education, or increasing the stock of useful technical knowledge—we are enhancing the future productivity of our economy and increasing future consumption.

资本和私有财产

Capital and Private Property

In a market economy, capital typically is privately owned, and the income from capital goes to individuals. Every patch of land has a deed, or title of ownership; almost every machine and building belongs to an individual or corporation. *Property rights* bestow on their owners the ability to use, exchange, paint, dig, drill, or exploit their capital goods. These capital goods also have market values, and people can buy and sell the capital goods for whatever price the goods will fetch. *The ability of individuals to own and profit from capital is what gives capitalism its name.*

However, while our society is one built on private property, property rights are limited. Society determines how much of "your" property you may bequeath to your heirs and how much must go in inheritance taxes to the government. Society determines how much your factory can pollute and where you can park your car. Even your home is not your castle: you must obey zoning laws and, if necessary, make way for a road.

Interestingly enough, the most valuable economic resource, labor, cannot be turned into a commodity that is bought and sold as private property. Since the abolition of slavery, it has been illegal to treat human earning power like other capital assets. You are not free to sell yourself; you must rent yourself at a wage.

Property Rights for Capital and Pollution ②

Economists often emphasize the importance of property rights in an efficient market economy. Property rights define how individuals or firms can own, buy, sell, and use capital goods and other property. These rights are enforced through the legal framework, which constitutes the set of laws within which a society operates. An efficient and acceptable legal framework for a market economy includes the definition of clear property rights, the laws of contract, and a system for adjudicating disputes.

Poor countries have discovered that it is difficult to have an efficient market economy when there are no laws enforcing contracts or guaranteeing that a company can keep its own profits. And when the legal framework breaks down, as in war-torn Iraq after 2003, people begin to fear for their lives. They have little time or inclination to make long-term investments for the future. Production falls and the quality of life deteriorates. Indeed, many of the most horrifying African famines were caused by civil war and the breakdown in the legal order, not by bad weather.

The environment is another example where poorly designed property rights harm the economy. Water and air are generally open-access resources, meaning that no one owns or controls them. As the saying goes, "Everyone's ③ business is nobody's business." In this area, people do not weigh all the costs of their actions. Someone might throw trash into the water or emit smoke into the air because the costs of dirty water or foul air are borne by other people. By contrast, people are less likely to throw trash on their own lawn or burn coal in their own living room because they themselves will bear the costs.

In recent years, economists have proposed extending property rights to environmental commodities by selling or auctioning permits to pollute and allowing them to be traded on markets. Preliminary evidence suggests that this extension of property rights has given much more powerful incentives to reduce pollution efficiently.

We have highlighted some key features of a modern economy: Specialization and the division of labor among people and countries create great efficiencies; increased production makes trade possible; money allows trade to take place efficiently; and a sophisticated financial system allows people's savings to flow smoothly into other people's capital.

政府的看得见的手

C. THE VISIBLE HAND OF GOVERNMENT

In an idealized market economy, all goods and services are voluntarily exchanged for money at competitive market prices that reflect consumer valuations and social costs. Such a system squeezes the maximum in consumer satisfaction out of a society's available resources. In reality, however, no economy actually conforms totally to the idealized world of the smoothly

① 经济活动涉及放弃当前的消费以增加资本。新建一座工厂或者新修一条公路，延长受教育的时间，提高教育质量，或者逐渐增加有用的技术知识，每一次这样的投资都是在提高经济的未来生产效率，进而扩大未来消费。

② 资本以及污染的产权问题

③ 人人都有责任等于没有人负责任

functioning invisible hand. Rather, economic imperfections lead to such ills as pollution, unemployment, financial panics, and extremes of wealth and poverty.

No government anywhere in the world, at any time, no matter how conservative it claims to be, keeps its hands off the economy. Governments take on many tasks in response to the flaws in the market mechanism. The military, the police, and the national weather service are typical areas of government activity. Socially useful ventures such as space exploration and scientific research benefit from government funding. Governments may regulate some businesses (such as finance and drugs) while subsidizing others (such as education and biomedical research). Governments tax their citizens and redistribute some of the proceeds to the elderly and needy.

How do governments perform their functions? Governments operate by requiring people to pay taxes, obey regulations, and consume certain collective goods and services. Because of its coercive powers, the government can perform functions that would not be possible under voluntary exchange. Government coercion increases the freedoms and consumption of those who benefit while reducing the incomes and opportunities of those who are taxed or regulated.

Governments have three main economic func- ①
tions in a market economy:

1. Governments increase *efficiency* by promoting competition, curbing externalities like pollution, and providing public goods.
2. Governments promote *equity* by using tax and expenditure programs to redistribute income toward particular groups.
3. Governments foster *macroeconomic stability and growth*—reducing unemployment and inflation while encouraging economic growth—through fiscal and monetary policy.

We will examine briefly each function.

效　率
EFFICIENCY

Adam Smith recognized that the virtues of the market mechanism are fully realized only when the checks and balances of perfect competition are present. What is meant by **perfect competition?** This techni- ②
cal term refers to a market in which no firm or consumer is large enough to affect the market price. For example, the wheat market is perfectly competitive because the largest wheat farm, producing only a minuscule fraction of the world's wheat, can have no appreciable effect upon the price of wheat.

The invisible-hand doctrine applies to economies in which all markets are perfectly competitive. Perfectly competitive markets will produce an efficient allocation of resources, so the economy is on its production-possibility frontier. When all industries are subject to the checks and balances of perfect competition, as we will see later in this book, markets will produce the bundle of outputs most desired by consumers using the most efficient techniques and the minimum amount of inputs.

Alas, there are many ways that markets can fall short of efficient perfect competition. The three most important ones involve imperfect competition, such as monopolies; externalities, such as pollution; and public goods, such as national defense and lighthouses. In each case, market failure leads to inefficient production or consumption, and government can play a useful role in curing the disease.

不完全竞争
Imperfect Competition

One serious deviation from an efficient market comes from *imperfect competition* or *monopoly* elements. Whereas under perfect competition no firm or consumer can affect prices, **imperfect competition** occurs when a ③
buyer or seller can affect a good's price. For example, if the TV company or a labor union is large enough to influence the price of TV service or labor, respectively, some degree of imperfect competition has set in. When imperfect competition arises, society may move inside its *PPF*. This would occur, for example, if a single seller (a monopolist) raised the price to earn extra profits. The output of that good would be reduced below the most efficient level, and the efficiency of the economy would thereby suffer. In such a situation, the invisible-hand property of markets may be violated.

What is the effect of imperfect competition? Imperfect competition leads to prices that rise above cost and to consumer purchases that are reduced below efficient levels. The pattern of too high price and too low output is the hallmark of the inefficiencies associated with imperfect competition.

In reality, almost all industries possess some measure of imperfect competition. Airlines, for example, may have no competition on some of their routes but face several rivals on others. The extreme case of imperfect competition is the *monopolist*—a single

---

① 在市场经济中，政府有三个主要的经济职能：
1. 政府通过鼓励竞争，控制诸如污染的外部性问题，以及提供公共产品等行为来提高经济效率。
2. 政府利用税收和财政支出手段来实现针对特殊群体的收入再分配，以促进社会公平。
3. 政府通过财政政策和货币政策来促进宏观经济的稳定和增长，在鼓励经济增长的同时降低失业率，减少通货膨胀的发生。

② **完全竞争**这一专业术语指的是没有任何企业或者消费者有足够的能力来影响市场价格。

③ 当买家或者卖家有能力影响产品价格时，就会出现**不完全竞争**。

supplier who alone determines the price of a particular good or service. For example, Microsoft has been a monopolist in the production of Windows operating systems.

Over the last century, most governments have taken steps to curb the most extreme forms of imperfect competition. Governments sometimes regulate the price and profits of monopolies such as local water, telephone, and electric utilities. In addition, government antitrust laws prohibit actions such as price fixing and agreements to divide up markets. The most important check to imperfect competition, however, is the opening of markets to competitors, whether they be domestic or foreign. Few monopolies can long withstand the attack of competitors unless governments protect them through tariffs or regulations.

外部性

Externalities

A second type of inefficiency arises when there are spillovers or externalities, which involve involuntary imposition of costs or benefits. Market transactions involve voluntary exchange in which people exchange goods or services for money. When a firm buys a chicken to make frozen drumsticks, it buys the chicken from its owner in the chicken market, and the seller receives the full value of the hen. When you buy a haircut, the barber receives the full value for time, skills, and rent.

But many interactions take place outside markets. While airports produce a lot of noise, they generally do not compensate the people living around the airport for disturbing their peace. On the other hand, some companies which spend heavily on research and development have positive spillover effects for the rest of society. For example, researchers at AT&T [1] invented the transistor and launched the electronic revolution, but AT&T's profits increased by only a small fraction of the global social gains. In each case, an activity has helped or hurt people outside the marketplace; that is, there was an economic transaction without an economic payment.

Externalities (or spillover effects) occur when ② firms or people impose costs or benefits on others outside the marketplace.

Negative externalities get most of the attention in today's world. As our society has become more densely populated and as the production of energy, chemicals, and other materials increases, negative externalities or spillover effects have grown from little nuisances into major threats. This is where governments come in. Government *regulations* are designed to control externalities like air and water pollution, damage from strip mining, hazardous wastes, unsafe drugs and foods, and radioactive materials.

In many ways, governments are like parents, always saying no: Thou shalt not expose thy workers to dangerous conditions. Thou shalt not pour out poisonous smoke from thy factory chimney. Thou shalt not sell mind-altering drugs. Thou shalt not drive without wearing thy seat belt. And so forth. Finding the correct balance between free markets and government regulation is a difficult task that requires careful analysis of the costs and benefits of each approach. But few people today would argue for returning to the unregulated economic jungle where firms would be allowed to dump pollutants like plutonium wherever they wanted.

公共物品

Public Goods

While negative externalities like pollution or global warming get most of the headlines, positive externalities are in fact of great economic significance. Consider the gradual elimination of smallpox, a disease which claimed millions of lives and disfigured even more. No private firm would undertake the research and vaccinations and fieldwork in far corners of the world that were needed to combat the disease. Incentives for private production were inadequate because the benefits were so widely dispersed around the world that firms could not capture the returns. The benefits of eliminating communicable diseases cannot be bought and sold in markets. Similar cases of positive externalities are construction of a highway network, operation of a national weather service, and support of basic science.

The polar case of a positive externality is a public good. **Public goods** are commodities which can ③ be enjoyed by everyone and from which no one can be excluded. The classic example of a public good is national defense. Suppose a country decides to increase spending to defend its borders or to send peacekeepers to troubled lands. All must pay the piper and all will suffer the consequences, whether they want to or not.

---

[1] AT&T：美国电话电报公司（American Telephone & Telegraph Company），始于 1877 年创建的著名的贝尔（Bell）电话公司，曾长期垄断美国长途和本地电话市场。近 20 年来曾多次分拆和重组，故已不用全名。公司总部在 2008 年从位于德州南部的圣安东尼奥搬到了北部的达拉斯。

② 当企业或个人将市场活动之外的成本或者收益强加于其他企业或个人时，即出现了**外部性**（或称溢出效应）。

③ 外部性的最典型案例就是公共物品。**公共物品**就是每个人都可以享用并且无法排除他人享用的物品。

However, once the government decides to buy the public good, the market mechanism is still at work. In providing public goods like national defense or lighthouses, the government is behaving exactly like any other large spender. By casting its dollar votes on these items, it causes resources to flow there. Once the dollar votes are cast, the market mechanism then takes over and channels resources to firms so that the lighthouses or tanks get produced.

Lighthouses as Public Goods ①

Lighthouses are an example of the concept of public goods. They save lives and cargoes. But lighthouse keepers cannot reach out to collect fees from ships; nor, if they could, would it serve an efficient social purpose for them to exact an economic penalty on ships that use their services. The light can be provided most efficiently free of charge, for it costs no more to warn 100 ships than to warn a single ship of the nearby rocks.

But wait a moment. A recent history determined that lighthouses in England and Wales were in fact *privately* and *profitably* operated in the early days. They were financed by government-authorized "light duties" levied on ships which used nearby ports. Perhaps, we might conclude, lighthouses are not really public goods.

To understand the issues here, we need to return to fundamentals. The two key attributes of a public good are (1) that the cost of extending the service to an additional person is zero ("nonrivalry") and (2) that it is impossible to exclude individuals from enjoying it ("nonexcludability"). Both these characteristics are applicable to lighthouses.

But a "public" good is not necessarily publicly provided. Often, it is provided by no one. Moreover, just because it is privately provided does not indicate that it is efficiently provided or that a market mechanism can pay for the lighthouse. The English example shows the interesting case where, *if* provision of the public good can be tied to another good or service (in this case, vessel tonnage), and *if* the government gives private persons the right to collect what are essentially taxes, then an alternative mechanism for *financing* the public good can be found. Such an approach would work poorly where the fees could not be easily tied to tonnage (such as in international waterways). And it would not work at all if the government refused to privatize the right to collect light duties on shipping.

America shows quite a different experience. From its earliest days, the United States believed that navigational aids should be government-provided. Indeed, one of the first acts of the first Congress, and America's first public-works law, provided that "the necessary support, maintenance, and repairs of all lighthouses, beacons, [and] buoys . . . shall be defrayed out of the Treasury of the United States."

But, like many public goods, lighthouses were provided meager funding, and it is interesting to note what happened in the absence of navigational aids. A fascinating case lies off the east coast of Florida, which is a treacherous waterway with a 200-mile reef lying submerged a few feet below the surface in the most active hurricane track of the Atlantic Ocean. This heavily used channel was prime territory for storm, shipwreck, and piracy.

There were no lighthouses in Florida until 1825, and no private-sector lighthouses were ever built in this area. The market responded vigorously to the perils, however. What arose from the private sector was a thriving "wrecking" industry. Wreckers were ships that lurked near the dangerous reefs waiting for an unfortunate boat to become disabled. The wreckers would then appear, offer their help in saving lives and cargo, tow the boat into the appropriate port, and then claim a substantial part of the value of the cargo. Wrecking was the major industry of south Florida in the mid-nineteenth century and made Key West the rich- [2]
est town in America at that time.

While wreckers probably had positive value added, they provided none of the public-good attributes of lighthouses. Indeed, because many cargoes were insured, there was significant "moral hazard" involved in navigation. Connivance between wreckers and captains often enriched both at the expense of owners and insurance companies. It was only when the U.S. Lighthouse Service, financed by government revenues, began to build lighthouses through the Florida channel that the number of shipwrecks began to decrease—and the wreckers were gradually driven out of business.

Lighthouses are no longer a central issue of public policy today and are mainly of interest to tourists. They have been largely replaced by the satellite-based Global Positioning System (GPS), which is also a public good provided free by the government. But the history of lighthouses reminds us of the problems that can arise when public goods are inefficiently provided.

---

① 灯塔作为公共物品的历史

[2] Key West：基韦斯特，墨西哥湾内佛罗里达群岛最西端的同名岛上的一个小城，人口 24 000 多人，渔业和旅游业发达。

Taxes. The government must find the revenues to pay for its public goods and for its income-redistribution programs. Such revenues come from taxes levied on personal and corporate incomes, on wages, on sales of consumer goods, and on other items. All levels of government—city, state, and federal—collect taxes to pay for their spending.

Taxes sound like another "price"—in this case the price we pay for public goods. But taxes differ from prices in one crucial respect: taxes are not voluntary. Everyone is subject to the tax laws; we are all obligated to pay for our share of the cost of public goods. Of course, through our democratic process, we as citizens choose both the public goods and the taxes to pay for them. However, the close connection between spending and consumption that we see for private goods does not hold for taxes and public goods. I pay for a hamburger only if I want one, but I must pay my share of the taxes used to finance defense and public schools even if I don't care a bit for these activities.

公 平
EQUITY

Our discussion of market failures like monopoly or externalities focused on defects in the allocative role of markets—imperfections that can be corrected by careful intervention. But assume for the moment that the economy functioned with complete efficiency—always on the production-possibility frontier and never inside it, always choosing the right amount of public versus private goods, and so forth. Even if the market system worked perfectly, it might still lead to a flawed outcome.

Markets do not necessarily produce a fair distribution of income. A market economy may produce inequalities in income and consumption that are not acceptable to the electorate. ①

Why might the market mechanism produce an unacceptable solution to the question *for whom?* The reason is that incomes are determined by a wide variety of factors, including effort, education, inheritance, factor prices, and luck. The resulting income distribution may not correspond to a fair outcome. Moreover, recall that goods follow dollar votes and not the greatest need. A rich man's cat may drink the milk that a poor boy needs to remain healthy. Does this happen because the market is failing? Not at all, for the market mechanism is doing its job—putting goods in the hands of those who have the dollar votes. Even the most efficient market system may generate great inequality.

Often the income distribution in a market system is the result of accidents of birth. Every year *Forbes* magazine lists the 400 richest Americans, and it's impressive how many of them either received their wealth by inheritance or used inherited wealth as a springboard to even greater wealth. Would everyone regard that as necessarily right or ideal? Should someone be allowed to become a billionaire simply by inheriting 5000 square miles of rangeland or the family's holding of oil wells? That's the way the cookie crumbles under laissez-faire capitalism.

For most of American history, economic growth was a rising tide that lifted all boats, raising the incomes of the poor as well as those of the rich. But over the last three decades, changes in family structure and declining wages of the less skilled and less educated have reversed the trend. With a return to greater emphasis on the market has come greater homelessness, more children living in poverty, and deterioration of many of America's central cities.

Income inequalities may be politically or ethically unacceptable. A nation does not need to accept the outcome of competitive markets as predetermined and immutable; people may examine the distribution of income and decide it is unfair. If a democratic society does not like the distribution of dollar votes under a laissez-faire market system, it can take steps to change the distribution of income.

Let's say that voters decide to reduce income inequality. What tools could the government use to implement that decision? First, it can engage in *progressive taxation,* taxing large incomes at a higher rate than small incomes. It might impose heavy taxes on wealth or on large inheritances to break the chain of privilege. The federal income and inheritance taxes are examples of such redistributive progressive taxation.

Second, because low tax rates cannot help those who have no income at all, governments can make *transfer payments,* which are money payments to people. Such transfers today include aid for the elderly, blind, and disabled and for those with dependent children, as well as unemployment insurance for the jobless. This system of transfer payments provides a "safety net" to protect the unfortunate from

transfer payments 转移支付

safety net 安全网

---

① 市场不一定就带来公平的收入分配。市场经济很可能出现令选民无法接受的收入和消费水平之间的不公平现象。

privation. And, finally, governments sometimes subsidize consumption of low-income groups by providing food stamps, subsidized medical care, and low-cost housing—though in the United States, such spending comprises a relatively small share of total spending.

Low-income groups 低收入群体

Tax and transfer programs have always been controversial. Few people think about the public goods that their tax dollars are buying when they fill out their tax returns or look at the big deductions in their paychecks. Yet people also feel that societies must provide the basic necessities to everyone—for food, schooling, and health care.

What can economics contribute to debates about equality? Economics as a science cannot answer such normative questions as how much of our incomes should be taxed, how much income should be transferred to poor families, or what is the proper size of the public sector. These are political questions that are answered at the ballot box in our democratic societies.

Economics can, however, analyze the costs and benefits of different redistributive systems. Economists have devoted much time to analyzing the impact of different tax systems (such as those based on income or consumption). They have also studied whether giving poor people cash rather than goods and services is likely to be a more efficient way of reducing poverty.

And economics can remind us that the market ① giveth and the market taketh away. In a world of [2] rapid structural change, we should always remember, "There, but for the grace of supply and demand, go I."

宏观经济增长与稳定 MACROECONOMIC GROWTH AND STABILITY

Since its origins, capitalism has been plagued by periodic bouts of inflation (rising prices) and recession (high unemployment). Since World War II, for ③ example, there have been 10 recessions in the United States, some putting millions of people out of work. These fluctuations are known as the *business cycle.*

Today, thanks to the intellectual contribution of John Maynard Keynes and his followers, we know how to control the worst excesses of the business cycle. By careful use of fiscal and monetary policies, governments can affect output, employment, and inflation. The *fiscal policies* of government involve the power to tax and the power to spend. *Monetary policy* involves determining the supply of money and interest rates; these affect investment in capital goods and other interest-rate-sensitive spending. Using these two fundamental tools of macroeconomic policy, governments can influence the level of total spending, the rate of growth and level of output, the levels of employment and unemployment, and the price level and rate of inflation in an economy.

Governments in advanced industrial countries have successfully applied the lessons of the Keynesian revolution over the last half-century. Spurred on by active monetary and fiscal policies, the market economies witnessed a period of unprecedented economic growth in the three decades after World War II.

In the 1980s, governments became more concerned with designing macroeconomic policies to promote long-term objectives, such as economic growth and productivity. (*Economic growth* denotes the growth in a nation's total output, while *productivity* represents the output per unit input or the efficiency with which resources are used.) For example, tax rates were lowered in most industrial countries in order to improve incentives for saving and production. Many economists emphasize the importance of public saving through smaller budget deficits as a way to increase national saving and investment.

Macroeconomic policies for stabilization and ④ economic growth include fiscal policies (of taxing and spending) along with monetary policies (which affect interest rates and credit conditions). Since the development of macroeconomics in the 1930s, governments have succeeded in curbing the worst excesses of inflation and unemployment.

Table 2-1 summarizes the economic role played by government today. It shows the important governmental functions of promoting efficiency, achieving a fairer distribution of income, and pursuing the macroeconomic objectives of economic growth and stability. In all advanced industrial societies we find some variant of a **mixed economy,** in which the market determines output and prices in most individual sectors while government steers the overall economy with programs of taxation, spending, and monetary regulation.

[2] 此段文字为本版新加内容。The market giveth and the market taketh away 系作者改编自《旧约圣经》(*The Books of the Old Testament*)中的《约伯记》(*Book of Job*)篇第一章第21节。英文经典文献中常见的所谓原文 *The Lord giveth and the Lord taketh away* 系中古英文版本，giveth 和 taketh 均为中古英文(Middle English，从1066年诺曼底公爵征服英格兰建立诺曼底王朝始，至文艺复兴兴盛期，即约1400年止)的用法。权威的《钦定圣经》(*The Holy Bible of King James Version*)中这句话的原文为：……the LORD gave, and the LORD hath taken away;……《钦定圣经》的英文与莎士比亚剧本中的英文一样，属于早期现代英文(Early Modern English)。

"There, but for the grace of supply and demand, go I." 系作者改编自谚语 *There, but for the grace of God, go I.* 出自16世纪英国新教殉教者，著名的宗教改革派人物约翰·布雷德福德(John Bradford，1510~1555)的一段因崇奉异端遭火刑处死的悲剧传奇。

---

① 因此，经济学能够提醒我们的是，市场给予我们的一切终归要还给市场。在这样一个形态飞速变化的世界中，我们应该始终牢记一句话："如果不求助于供给与需求，吃亏的肯定是我们自己。"（接旁注）

③ 比如，自第二次世界大战以来，美国已经经历了10次衰退，其中有几次曾导致数百万人失业。这些波动就是著名的商业周期。

④ 保障社会稳定和经济增长的宏观经济政策包括（税收和支出）财政政策及与之相匹配的货币政策（货币政策影响利率和信贷条件）。随着20世纪30年代宏观经济学的出现和发展，政府已经成功地抑制了通货膨胀和失业出现失控的最坏局面。

Failure of market economy	Government intervention	Current examples of government policy
Inefficiency:		
Monopoly	Encourage competition	Antitrust laws, deregulation
Externalities	Intervene in markets	Antipollution laws, antismoking ordinances
Public goods	Encourage beneficial activities	Provide public education, build roads
Inequality:		
Unacceptable inequalities of income and wealth	Redistribute income	Progressive taxation of income and wealth
		Income-support or transfer programs (e.g., subsidize health care)
Macroeconomic problems:		
Business cycles (high inflation and unemployment)	Stabilize through macroeconomic policies	Monetary policies (e.g., changes in money supply and interest rates)
		Fiscal policies (e.g., taxes and spending programs)
Slow economic growth	Stimulate growth	Improve efficiency of tax system
		Raise national savings rate by reducing budget deficit or increasing budget surplus

TABLE 2-1. Government Can Remedy the Shortcomings of the Market ①

福利国家的产生
THE RISE OF THE WELFARE STATE

Our textbook focuses on the mixed market economy of modern industrialized nations. It will be useful to trace its history briefly. Before the rise of the market economy, going back to medieval times, aristocracies and town guilds directed much of the economic activity in Europe and Asia. However, about two centuries ago, governments began to exercise less and less power over prices and production methods. Feudalism gradually gave way to markets, or what we call the "market mechanism."

In most of Europe and North America, the nineteenth century became the age of **laissez-faire.** This doctrine, which translates as "leave us alone," holds that government should interfere as little as possible in economic affairs and leave economic decisions to the private decision making of buyers and sellers. Many governments adopted this economic philosophy starting in the middle of the nineteenth century.

Nevertheless, a century ago, the many excesses of capitalism—including monopolies and trusts, corruption, dangerous products, and poverty—led most industrialized countries to retreat from unbridled laissez-faire. Government's role expanded steadily as it regulated businesses, levied income taxes, and provided a social safety net for the elderly, unemployed, and impoverished.

This new system, called the **welfare state,** is one in which markets direct the detailed activities of day-to-day economic life while government regulates social conditions and provides pensions, health care, and other necessities for poor families. ②

保守派的反击
Conservative Backlash

Many critics of the welfare state worried that government interventions were tilting the scales in favor of *socialism,* in which the state owns, operates, and regulates much of the economy. In 1942, the great Harvard economist Joseph Schumpeter argued that [3] the United States was "capitalism living in an oxygen tent" on its march to socialism. Capitalism's success would breed alienation and self-doubt, sapping its efficiency and innovation.

Libertarian critics like Friedrich Hayek and [4] Milton Friedman argued for a return to free mar- [5] kets and minimal government. This group argued the state is overly intrusive; governments create monopoly; government failures are just as pervasive as market failures; high taxes distort the allocation of resources; social security threatens to drain the public purse; environmental regulations dull the spirit of

[3] 约瑟夫·熊彼特（Joseph Schumpeter, 1883~1950），著名的奥地利经济学家和政治学家，借用“创造性毁灭”（creative destruction）提出了其关于资本主义制度由自身力量实现涅槃重生的著名理论。该段引述出自《熊彼特论文集》（*Essays by Joseph Schumpeter*）中所收入的《资本主义的衰亡》（*Decay of Capitalism*）一文。

① 表 2-1. 政府有能力修补市场本身的缺陷

② 这种新的体制叫做**福利国家**。在这种体制下，市场主导着日复一日的经济生活中每一个细微的环节，而政府的角色是管控社会、提供退休养老金和医疗保健，以及贫穷家庭所必需的其他帮助。

[4] 弗里德里希·哈耶克（Friedrich Hayek，1899~1992），1974 年经济学诺奖得主之一，奥地利经济学派、古典自由主义和自由市场资本主义的主要代表人物之一。

[5] 米尔顿·弗里德曼（Milton Friedman，1912~2006），芝加哥经济学派的代表人物，1976 年经济学诺奖得主，萨缪尔森的师兄，两人终身学术观点相左，但生活上却是相互嘘寒问暖的好朋友。

enterprise; and government attempts to stabilize the economy only reduce growth and increase inflation. In short, for some, government is the problem rather than the solution.

Beginning around 1980, the tide turned as conservative governments in many countries began to reduce taxes and deregulate government's control over the economy. Many government-owned industries were privatized, income-tax rates were lowered, and the generosity of many welfare programs was reduced.

The most dramatic turn toward the market came in Russia and the socialist countries of Eastern Europe. After decades of extolling the advantages of a government-run command economy, beginning around 1990, these countries scrapped central planning and made the difficult transition to a decentralized market economy. China, while still run by the Communist party, has enjoyed an economic boom in the last three decades by allowing private enterprises and foreign firms to operate within its borders. Many formerly socialist regimes in India, Africa, and Latin America have embraced capitalism and reduced the role of government in their economies.

当今的混合经济
The Mixed Economy Today

In weighing the relative merits of state and market, public debate often oversimplifies the complex choices that societies face. Markets have worked miracles in some countries. But markets need well-crafted legal and political structures, along with the social overhead capital that promotes trade and ensures a stable financial system. Without these governmental structures, markets often produce corrupt capitalism, great inequality, pervasive poverty, and declining living standards.

In economic affairs, success has many parents, ① while failure is an orphan. The success of market economies may lead people to overlook the important contribution of collective actions. Government programs have helped reduce poverty and malnutrition and have reduced the scourge of terrible diseases like tuberculosis and polio. Even as the world's largest economies head into a deep recession in 2008–2009, macroeconomic policies help to stem financial-market panics and reduce the length and severity of business cycles. State-supported science has split the atom, discovered the DNA molecule, and explored space.

The debate about government's successes and failures ② demonstrates that drawing the boundary between market and government is an enduring problem. The tools of economics are indispensable to help societies find the golden mean between an efficient market mechanism and publicly decided regulation and redistribution. The good mixed economy is, perforce, the limited mixed economy. But those who would reduce government to the constable plus a few lighthouses are living in a dream world. An efficient and humane society requires both halves of the mixed system—market and government. Operating a modern economy without both is like trying to clap with one hand.

SUMMARY

A. The Market Mechanism

1. In an economy like the United States, most economic decisions are made in markets, which are mechanisms through which buyers and sellers meet to trade and to determine prices and quantities for goods and services. Adam Smith proclaimed that the *invisible hand* of markets would lead to the optimal economic outcome as individuals pursue their own self-interest. And while markets are far from perfect, they have proved remarkably effective at solving the problems of *how, what,* and *for whom.*
2. The market mechanism works as follows to determine the *what* and the *how:* The dollar votes of people affect prices of goods; these prices serve as guides for the amounts of the different goods to be produced. When people demand more of a good, its price will increase and businesses can profit by expanding production of that good. Under perfect competition, a business must find the cheapest method of production, efficiently using labor, land, and other factors; otherwise, it will incur losses and be eliminated from the market.
3. At the same time that the *what* and *how* problems are being resolved by prices, so is the problem of *for whom.* The distribution of income is determined by the ownership of factors of production (land, labor, and capital) and by factor prices. People possessing fertile land or the ability to hit home runs will earn many dollar

① 经济活动的成功是方方面面的原因作用的结果，而失败却总是被某件已经遗忘的小事所致。

② 关于强势政府与弱势政府问题的争论告诉我们，合理地划分市场和政府之间的界限是一个旷日持久的问题。要在高效的市场机制与政府规制和再分配的公共决策之间找到黄金分割，经济学的工具是不可或缺的。一个好的混合经济体必然是一个受到限制的混合经济体。但那些主张把政府的功能局限于警察加几座灯塔的人，始终生活在梦幻中的世界。一个高效和人本的社会同时需要市场和政府这个混合经济体的两部分。离开其中任一部分，要想管理好一个现代国家只能是孤掌难鸣之事。

votes to buy consumer goods. Those without property or with skills, color, or sex that the market undervalues will receive low incomes.

B. Trade, Money, and Capital

4. As economies develop, they become more specialized. Division of labor allows a task to be broken into a number of smaller chores that can each be mastered and performed more quickly by a single worker. Specialization arises from the increasing tendency to use roundabout methods of production that require many specialized skills. As individuals and countries become increasingly specialized, they tend to concentrate on particular commodities and trade their surplus output for goods produced by others. Voluntary trade, based on specialization, benefits all.
5. Trade in specialized goods and services today relies on money to lubricate its wheels. Money is the universally acceptable medium of exchange—including primarily currency and checking deposits. It is used to pay for everything from apple tarts to zebra skins. By accepting money, people and nations can specialize in producing a few goods and can then trade them for others; without money, we would waste much time negotiating and bartering.
6. Capital goods—produced inputs such as machinery, structures, and inventories of goods in process—permit roundabout methods of production that add much to a nation's output. These roundabout methods take time and resources to get started and therefore require a temporary sacrifice of present consumption in order to increase future consumption. The rules that define how capital and other assets can be bought, sold, and used are the system of property rights. In no economic system are private-property rights unlimited.

C. The Visible Hand of Government

7. Although the market mechanism is an admirable way of producing and allocating goods, sometimes market failures lead to deficiencies in the economic outcomes. The government may step in to correct these failures. Its role in a modern economy is to ensure efficiency, to correct an unfair distribution of income, and to promote economic growth and stability.
8. Markets fail to provide an efficient allocation of resources in the presence of imperfect competition or externalities. Imperfect competition, such as monopoly, produces high prices and low levels of output. To combat these conditions, governments regulate businesses or put legal antitrust constraints on business behavior. Externalities arise when activities impose costs or bestow benefits that are not paid for in the marketplace. The government may decide to step in and regulate these spillovers (as it does with air pollution) or provide for public goods (as in the case of public health).
9. Markets do not necessarily produce a fair distribution of income; they may spin off unacceptably high inequality of income and consumption. In response, governments can alter the pattern of incomes (the *for whom*) generated by market wages, rents, interest, and dividends. Modern governments use taxation to raise revenues for transfers or income-support programs that place a financial safety net under the needy.
10. Since the development of macroeconomics in the 1930s, the government has undertaken a third role: using fiscal powers (of taxing and spending) and monetary policy (affecting credit and interest rates) to promote long-run economic growth and productivity and to tame the business cycle's excesses of inflation and unemployment.
11. Drawing the right boundary between market and government is an enduring problem for societies. Economics is indispensable in finding the golden mean between an efficient market and publicly decided regulation and redistribution. An efficient and humane society requires both halves of the mixed system—market and government.

CONCEPTS FOR REVIEW

The Market Mechanism

market, market mechanism
markets for goods and for factors of production
prices as signals
market equilibrium
perfect and imperfect competition
Adam Smith's invisible-hand doctrine

Features of a Modern Economy

specialization and division of labor
money
factors of production (land, labor, capital)
capital, private property, and property rights

Government's Economic Role

efficiency, equity, stability
inefficiencies: monopoly and externalities
inequity of incomes under markets
macroeconomic policies:
  fiscal and monetary policies
  stabilization and growth

FURTHER READING AND INTERNET WEBSITES

Further Reading

A useful discussion of globalization is contained in "Symposium on Globalization in Perspective," *Journal of Economic Perspectives,* Fall 1998.

For examples of the writings of libertarian economists, see Milton Friedman, *Capitalism and Freedom* (University of Chicago Press, 1963), and Friedrich Hayek, *The Road to Serfdom* (University of Chicago Press, 1994).

A strong defense of government interventions is found in a history of the 1990s by Nobel Prize winner Joseph E. Stiglitz, *The Roaring Nineties: A New History of the World's Most Prosperous Decade* (Norton, New York, 2003). Paul Krugman's columns in *The New York Times* are a guide to current economic issues from the perspective of one of America's most distinguished economists; his most recent book, *The Great Unraveling: Losing Our Way in the New Century* (Norton, New York, 2003), collects his columns from the early 2000s.

A fascinating example of how a small economy is organized without money is found in R. A. Radford, "The Economic Organization of a P.O.W. Camp," *Economica,* vol. 12, November 1945, pp. 189–201.

Websites

You can explore recent analyses of the economy along with a discussion of major economic policy issues in the *Economic Report of the President* at *www.access.gpo.gov/eop/*. See *www.whitehouse.gov* for federal budget information and as an entry point into the useful Economic Statistics Briefing Room.

The study of the iPod is Jason Dedrick, Kenneth L. Kraemer, and Greg Linden, "Who Profits from Innovation in Global Value Chains? A Study of the iPod and Notebook PCs," available at *http://pcic.merage.uci.edu/papers/2008/WhoProfits.pdf*. Hal Varian's review is Hal R. Varian, "An iPod Has Global Value: Ask the (Many) Countries That Make It," *The New York Times,* June 28, 2007, available by Internet search.

QUESTIONS FOR DISCUSSION

1. What determines the composition of national output? In some cases, we say that there is "consumer sovereignty," meaning that consumers decide how to spend their incomes on the basis of their tastes and market prices. In other cases, decisions are made by political choices of legislatures. Consider the following examples: transportation, education, police, energy efficiency of appliances, health-care coverage, television advertising. For each, describe whether the allocation is by consumer sovereignty or by political decision. Would you change the method of allocation for any of these goods?
2. When a good is limited, some means must be found to ration the scarce commodity. Some examples of rationing devices are auctions, ration coupons, and first-come, first-served systems. What are the strengths and weaknesses of each? Explain carefully in what sense a market mechanism "rations" scarce goods and services.
3. This chapter discusses many "market failures," areas in which the invisible hand guides the economy poorly, and describes the role of government. Is it possible that there are, as well, "government failures," government attempts to curb market failures that are worse than the original market failures? Think of some examples of government failures. Give some examples in which government failures are so bad that it is better to live with the market failures than to try to correct them.
4. Consider the following cases of government intervention: regulations to limit air pollution, income support for the poor, and price regulation of a telephone monopoly. For each case, (*a*) explain the market failure, (*b*) describe a government intervention to treat the problem, and (*c*) explain how "government failure" (see the definition in question 3) might arise because of the intervention.
5. The circular flow of goods and inputs illustrated in Figure 2-1 has a corresponding flow of dollar incomes and spending. Draw a circular-flow diagram for the dollar flows in the economy, and compare it with the circular flow of goods and inputs. What is the role of money in the dollar circular flow?
6. Consider three periods of American history: (*a*) the early 1800s, when Jones lived on an isolated farm cut off from the rest of the world; (*b*) the late 1940s, when Smith lived in a country where domestic trade

and exchange was extensive but international trade was cut off because of damage from World War II; and (*c*) 2009, when Hall lives in a globalized world that promotes trade with all countries.

Suppose you were living in each of these situations. Describe the opportunities for specialization and division of labor of Jones, Smith, and Hall. Explain how the globalized world in (*c*) both allows greater productivity of Hall and allows a much greater variety of consumption goods. Give specific examples in each case.

7. "Lincoln freed the slaves. With one pen stroke he destroyed much of the capital the South had accumulated over the years." Comment.
8. The table to the right shows some of the major expenditures of the federal government. Explain how each one relates to the economic role of government.
9. Why does the saying "No taxation without representation" make sense for public goods but not private goods? Explain the mechanisms by which individuals can "protest" against (*a*) taxes that are thought excessive to pay for defense spending, (*b*) tolls that are thought excessive to pay for a bridge, and (*c*) prices that are thought excessive for an airline flight from New York to Miami.

Major Expenditure Categories for Federal Government

Budget category	Federal spending, 2009 ($, billion)
Health care	713
National defense	675
Social security	649
Income security	401
Natural resources and environment	36
International affairs	38

Source: Office of Management and Budget, *Budget of the United States Government*, Fiscal Year 2009.

CHAPTER

3

Basic Elements of Supply and Demand

供给与需求的基本原理

[1] 奥斯卡·王尔德（Oscar Wilde，1854~1900），著名的爱尔兰唯美主义印象派作家、诗人和剧作家。代表作有《道林·格雷的画像》（*The Picture of Dorian Gray*，1891），《温德密尔夫人的扇子》（*Lady Windermere's Fan*，1892；本段文字出自该剧第三幕中的一段对话，在《道林·格雷的画像》一书中有更为明确的表达，见译文）等。1895~1897 年，王尔德因同性恋被判入狱两年。近年来，在一些发达国家由于同性恋问题不再被视为异端，王尔德也成了同性恋社群的一个文化偶像。1998 年，当年判其有罪的英国，还在伦敦特拉法尔加广场附近的阿德莱德街为王尔德塑立了雕像，并刻录了他的名言"我们都在阴沟里，但仍有人始终在抬头仰望着星空"（We are all in the gutter, but some of us are looking at the stars）。

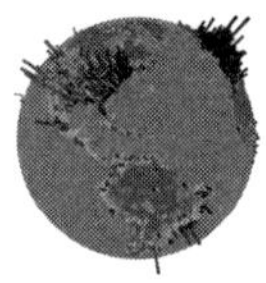

What is a cynic? A man who knows the price of everything and the value of nothing.

Oscar Wilde [1]

谁是愤世疾俗者？现实中的人只知道所有事物的价格，而对其相应的价值却毫无所知。——奥斯卡·王尔德

The first two chapters introduced the basic problems that every economy must solve: *What* shall be produced? *How* shall goods be produced? And *for whom* should goods be produced?

We also saw that the modern mixed economy relies primarily on a system of markets and prices to solve the three central problems. Recall that the fundamental building blocks of an economy are the dual monarchy of tastes and technology. "Consumer sovereignty" operating through dollar votes determines what gets produced and where the goods go, but technologies influence costs, prices, and what goods are available. Our task in this chapter is to describe in detail how this process works in a market economy.

Markets are like the weather—sometimes stormy, ② sometimes calm, but always changing. Yet a careful study of markets will reveal certain forces underlying the apparently random movements. To forecast prices and outputs in individual markets, you must first master the analysis of supply and demand.

Take the example of gasoline prices, illustrated in Figure 3-1. (This graph shows the "real gasoline ③ price," or the price corrected for movements in the general price level.) Demand for gasoline and other oil products rose sharply after World War II as real gasoline prices fell and people moved increasingly to the suburbs. Then, in the 1970s, supply restrictions, wars among producers, and political revolutions reduced production, with the consequent price spikes seen after 1973 and 1979. In the years that followed, a combination of energy conservation, smaller cars, the growth of the information economy, and expanded production around the world led to falling oil prices. War in Iraq and growing world demand for petroleum after 2002 produced yet further turmoil in oil markets. As Figure 3-1 shows, the real price of gasoline (in 2008 prices) fell from around $3.50 per gallon in 1980 to around $1.50 per gallon in the 1990s and then rose to $4 per gallon by the summer of 2008.

Consumer sovereignty
消费者上帝

What lay behind these dramatic shifts? Economics ④ has a very powerful tool for explaining such changes in the economic environment. It is called the *theory of supply and demand.* This theory shows how consumer preferences determine consumer demand for commodities, while business costs are the foundation of the supply of commodities. The increases in the price of gasoline occurred either because the demand for gasoline had increased or because the supply of oil had decreased. The same is true for every market, from Internet stocks to diamonds to land: changes in supply and demand drive changes in output and prices. If you understand how supply and demand work, you have gone a long way toward understanding a market economy.

---

② 市场犹如天气一样，时而暴风骤雨，时而风和日丽，变幻莫测。

③ 该图标示的是"汽油的实际价格"，或根据总体价格水平的波动情况进行校正以后的价格。

④ 是什么力量在背后左右了这些戏剧性的变化？经济学有一个非常有力的工具来解释经济环境中的这些变化，这就是供给与需求理论。

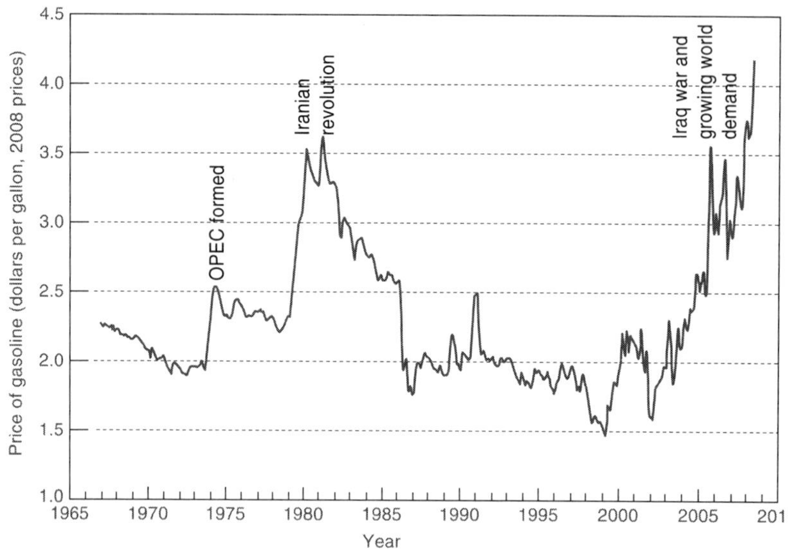

FIGURE 3-1. Gasoline Prices Move with Demand and Supply Changes ①

Gasoline prices have fluctuated sharply over the last half-century. Supply reductions in the 1970s produced two dramatic "oil shocks," which provoked social unrest and calls for increased regulation. Reductions in demand from new energy-saving technologies led to the long decline in price after 1980. Rapid growth in world demand for oil relative to supply produced steeply growing price trends in the 2000s. The tools of supply and demand are crucial for understanding these trends. ②

Source: U.S. Departments of Energy and Labor. The price of gasoline has been converted into 2008 prices using the consumer price index.

individual commodities
单一商品

This chapter introduces the notions of supply and demand and shows how they operate in competitive markets for *individual commodities*. We begin with demand curves and then discuss supply curves. Using these basic tools, we will see how the market price is determined where these two curves intersect—where the forces of demand and supply are just in balance. It is the movement of prices—the price mechanism—which brings supply and demand into balance or equilibrium. This chapter closes with some examples of how supply-and-demand analysis can be applied.

需求表

A. THE DEMAND SCHEDULE

Both common sense and careful scientific observation show that the amount of a commodity people buy depends on its price. The higher the price of an article, other things held constant,[1] the fewer units consumers are willing to buy. The lower its market price, the more units of it are bought.

There exists a definite relationship between the market price of a good and the quantity demanded of that good, other things held constant. This relationship between price and quantity bought is called the **demand schedule,** or the **demand curve.** ③

Let's look at a simple example. Table 3-1 presents a hypothetical demand schedule for cornflakes. At each price, we can determine the quantity of cornflakes that consumers purchase. For example,

[1] Later in this chapter we discuss the other factors that influence demand, including income and tastes. The term "other things held constant" simply means we are varying the price without changing any of these other determinants of demand. ④

① 图 3-1. 随供给与需求变化而波动的汽油价格
② 在上世纪的后 50 年中，汽油价格始终在剧烈的波动之中。20 世纪 70 年代供给量的减少导致了两次戏剧性的石油危机，诱发了社会动荡，引发了规范社会管理的高涨呼声。
③ 在其他条件保持不变的情况下，某种商品的市场价格与其市场需求量之间存在着一定的关系。这种价格与购买量之间的关系可以用**需求表**或者**需求曲线**来表示。
④ 本章后面的部分我们将讨论影响需求的其他因素，包括收入以及消费倾向。"其他条件保持不变"可以简单地理解为：在决定需求的其他因素保持不变的情况下，我们拟对价格进行的调整。

Demand Schedule for Cornflakes

	(1) Price ($ per box) *P*	(2) Quantity demanded (millions of boxes per year) *Q*
A	5	9
B	4	10
C	3	12
D	2	15
E	1	20

TABLE 3-1. The Demand Schedule Relates Quantity Demanded to Price ①

At each market price, consumers will want to buy a certain quantity of cornflakes. As the price of cornflakes falls, the quantity of cornflakes demanded will rise.

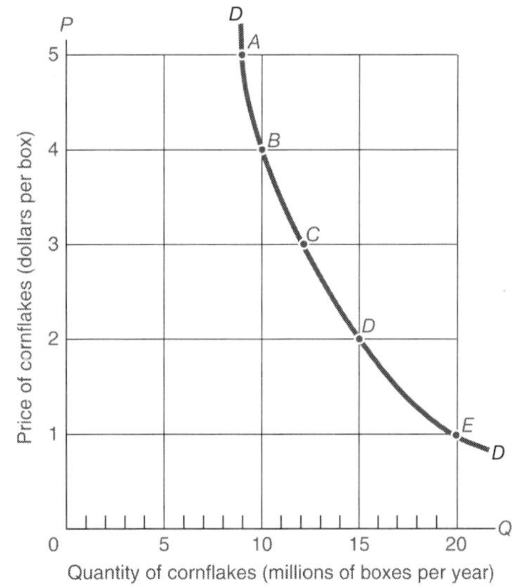

FIGURE 3-2. A Downward-Sloping Demand Curve Relates Quantity Demanded to Price ④

In the demand curve for cornflakes, price (P) is measured on the vertical axis while quantity demanded (Q) is measured on the horizontal axis. Each pair of (P, Q) numbers from Table 3-1 is plotted as a point, and then a smooth curve is passed through the points to give us a demand curve, *DD*. The negative slope of the demand curve illustrates the law of downward-sloping demand.

at $5 per box, consumers will buy 9 million boxes per year.

At a lower price, more cornflakes are bought. Thus, at a price of $4, the quantity bought is 10 million boxes. At yet a lower price (P) equal to $3, the quantity demanded (Q) is still greater, at 12 million. And so forth. We can determine the quantity demanded at each listed price in Table 3-1.

需求曲线
THE DEMAND CURVE

The graphical representation of the demand schedule is the *demand curve*. We show the demand curve in ② Figure 3-2, which graphs the quantity of cornflakes demanded on the horizontal axis and the price of cornflakes on the vertical axis. Note that quantity and price are inversely related; that is, Q goes up when P goes down. The curve slopes downward, going from northwest to southeast. This important property is called the *law of downward-sloping demand*. It is based on common sense as well as economic theory and has been empirically tested and verified for practically all commodities—cornflakes, gasoline, college education, and illegal drugs being a few examples.

Law of downward-sloping demand: When the ③ price of a commodity is raised (and other things are held constant), buyers tend to buy less of the commodity. Similarly, when the price is lowered, other things being constant, quantity demanded increases.

Quantity demanded tends to fall as price rises for two reasons:

1. First is the **substitution effect,** which occurs because a good becomes relatively more expensive when its price rises. When the price of good A rises, I will generally substitute goods B, C, D, . . . for it. For example, as the price of beef rises, I eat more chicken.
2. A higher price generally also reduces quantity demanded through the **income effect.** This comes into play because when a price goes up, I find myself somewhat poorer than I was before. If gasoline prices double, I have in effect less real income, so I will naturally curb my consumption of gasoline and other goods.

substitution effect 替代效应

law of downward-sloping demand 需求曲线向下倾斜规律

income effect 收入效应

---

① 表 3-1. 需求量与价格关系之需求表

② 图 3-2 描绘了需求的变化曲线，横轴表示玉米片的需求量变化，其价格波动则由纵轴表示。

③ **需求曲线向下倾斜规律：**当一种商品的价格上升（同时决定需求的其他因素保持不变）时，买家便会出现减少购买该种商品数量的倾向。同理，当该价格下降时，如果决定需求的其他因素仍然保持不变，需求量就会增加。

④ 图 3-2. 需求量与价格关系的需求曲线向下倾斜

市场需求

Market Demand

Our discussion of demand has so far referred to "the" demand curve. But whose demand is it? Mine? Yours? Everybody's? The fundamental building block for demand is individual preferences. However, in this chapter we will always focus on the *market demand*, which represents the sum total of all individual demands. The market demand is what is observable in the real world.

average income 平均收入

The market demand curve is found by adding together the quantities demanded by all individuals at each price. ①

Does the market demand curve obey the law of downward-sloping demand? It certainly does. If prices drop, for example, the lower prices attract new customers through the substitution effect. In addition, a price reduction will induce extra purchases of goods by existing consumers through both the income and the substitution effects. Conversely, a rise in the price of a good will cause some of us to buy less.

the size of the market 市场规模

related goods 相关商品

The Explosive Growth in Computer Use

We can illustrate the law of downward-sloping demand for the case of personal computers (PCs). The prices of the first PCs were high, and their computing power was relatively modest. They were found in few businesses and even fewer homes. It is hard to believe that just 20 years ago students wrote most of their papers in longhand and did most calculations by hand or with simple calculators!

tastes or preferences 爱好或偏好

But the prices of computing power fell sharply over the last four decades. As the prices fell, new buyers were enticed to buy their first computers. PCs came to be widely used for work, for school, and for fun. In the 2000s, as the value of computers increased with the development of the Internet, including video and personal Web pages, yet more people jumped on the computer bandwagon. ② Worldwide, PC sales totaled around 250 million in 2007.

special influences 特殊影响因素

Figure 3-3 shows the prices and quantities of computers and peripheral equipment in the United States as calculated by government statisticians. The prices reflect the cost of purchasing computers with constant quality—that is, they take into account the rapid quality change of the average computer purchased. You can see how falling prices along with improved software, increased utility of the Internet and e-mail, and other factors have led to an explosive growth in computer output.

需求曲线背后的因素

Forces behind the Demand Curve

What determines the market demand curve for cornflakes or gasoline or computers? A whole array of factors influences how much will be demanded at a given price: average levels of income, the size of the population, the prices and availability of related goods, individual and social tastes, and special influences.

- The *average income* of consumers is a key determinant of demand. As people's incomes rise, individuals tend to buy more of almost everything, even if prices don't change. Automobile purchases tend to rise sharply with higher levels of income.
- The *size of the market*—measured, say, by the population—clearly affects the market demand curve. California's 40 million people tend to buy 40 times more apples and cars than do Rhode Island's 1 million people.
- The prices and availability of *related goods* influence the demand for a commodity. A particularly important connection exists among substitute goods—ones that tend to perform the same function, such as cornflakes and oatmeal, pens and pencils, small cars and large cars, or oil and natural gas. Demand for good A tends to be low if the price of substitute product B is low. (For example, as computer prices fell, what do you think happened to the demand for typewriters?)
- In addition to these objective elements, there is a set of subjective elements called *tastes* or *preferences.* Tastes represent a variety of cultural and historical influences. They may reflect genuine psychological or physiological needs (for liquids, love, or excitement). And they may include artificially contrived cravings (for cigarettes, drugs, or fancy sports cars). They may also contain a large element of tradition or religion (eating beef is popular in America but taboo in India, while curried jellyfish is a delicacy in Japan but would make many Americans gag).
- Finally, *special influences* will affect the demand for particular goods. The demand for umbrellas is high in rainy Seattle but low in sunny Phoenix; the demand for air conditioners will rise in hot weather; the demand for automobiles will be low in New York, where public transportation is plentiful and parking is a nightmare.

The determinants of demand are summarized in Table 3-2, which uses automobiles as an example.

① 市场需求曲线是每一价格水平下所有个人的需求量的总和。

② 于是更多的人成为计算机大潮的弄潮儿。

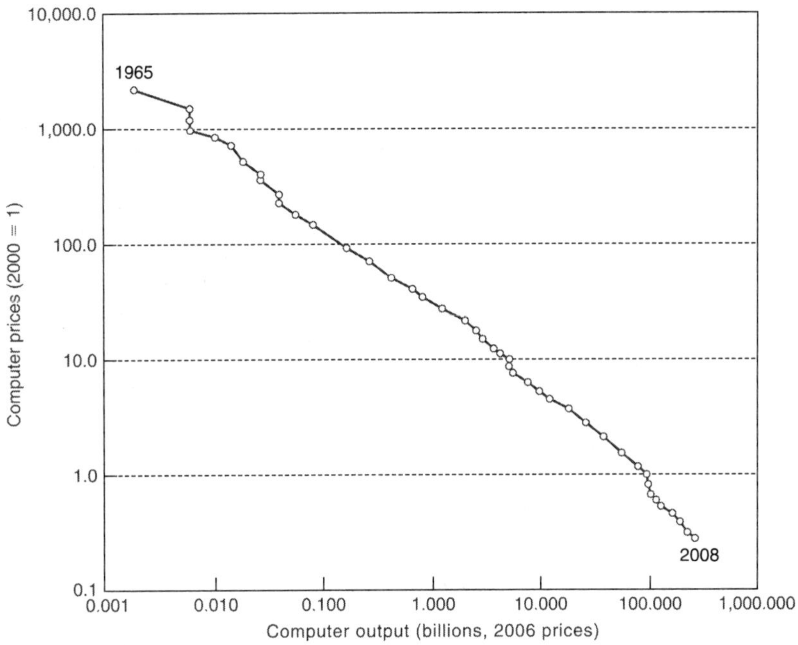

FIGURE 3-3. Declining Computer Prices Have Fueled an Explosive Growth in Computer Power ①

The prices of computers and peripheral devices are measured in terms of the cost of purchasing a given bundle of characteristics (such as memory or speed of calculations). The real price of computer power has fallen by a factor of 8000 since 1965. Falling prices along with higher incomes and a growing variety of uses have led to a 140,000-fold growth in the quantity of computers (or, really, computational power) produced.

Source: Department of Commerce estimates of real output and prices. Note that the data are plotted on ratio scales.

The real price of computer power
计算机计算能力的实际价格
a factor of 8000
8000 倍
140,000-fold
140 000 倍

Factors affecting the demand curve	Example for automobiles
1. **Average income**	As incomes rise, people increase car purchases.
2. **Population**	A growth in population increases car purchases.
3. **Prices of related goods**	Lower gasoline prices raise the demand for cars.
4. **Tastes**	Having a new car becomes a status symbol.
5. **Special influences**	Special influences include availability of alternative forms of transportation, safety of automobiles, expectations of future price increases, etc.

TABLE 3-2. Many Factors Affect the Demand Curve ②

① 图 3-3. 计算机价格的下降刺激了计算机计算能力的迅猛增长

② 表 3-2. 影响需求曲线的诸多因素

需求的变动

Shifts in Demand

As economic life evolves, demand changes incessantly. Demand curves sit still only in textbooks.

Why does the demand curve shift? Because influences other than the good's price change. Let's work through an example of how a change in a nonprice variable shifts the demand curve. We know that the ① average income of Americans rose sharply during the long economic boom of the 1990s. Because there is a powerful income effect on the demand for automobiles, this means that the quantity of automobiles demanded at each price will rise. For example, if average incomes rose by 10 percent, the quantity demanded at a price of $10,000 might rise from 10 million to 12 million units. This would be a shift in the demand curve because the increase in quantity demanded reflects factors other than the good's own price.

The net effect of the changes in underlying influences is what we call an *increase in demand.* An increase in the demand for automobiles is illustrated in Figure 3-4 as a rightward shift in the demand curve. Note that the shift means that more cars will be bought at every price.

You can test yourself by answering the following questions: Will a warm winter shift the demand curve for heating oil leftward or rightward? Why? What will happen to the demand for baseball tickets if young people lose interest in baseball and watch basketball instead? What will a sharp fall in the price of personal computers do to the demand for typewriters? What happens to the demand for a college education if wages are falling for blue-collar jobs while salaries for college-educated workers are rising rapidly?

When there are changes in factors other than a ③ good's own price which affect the quantity purchased, we call these changes shifts in demand. Demand increases (or decreases) when the quantity demanded at each price increases (or decreases).

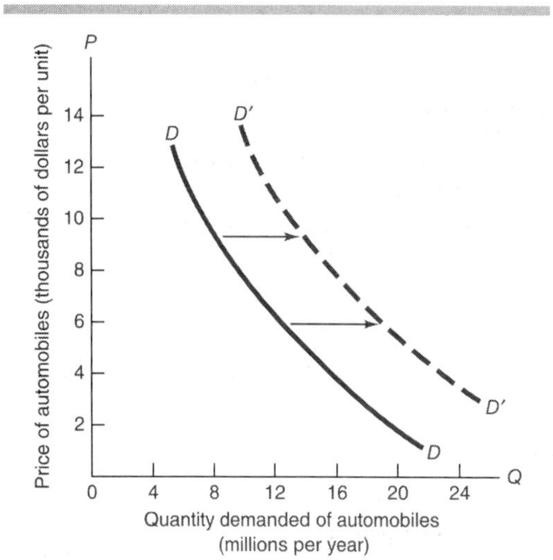

FIGURE 3-4. Increase in Demand for Automobiles ②

As elements underlying demand change, the demand for automobiles is affected. Here we see the effect of rising average income, increased population, and lower gasoline prices on the demand for automobiles. We call this shift of the demand curve an increase in demand.

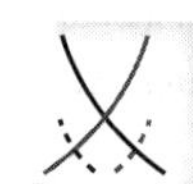

Movements along Curves versus Shifts of Curves ④

One of the most important points that you must understand in economics is the difference between movements along a curve and shifts of a curve. In the present case, do not confuse a *change in demand* (which denotes a *shift* of the demand curve) with a *change in the quantity demanded* (which means *moving along*, or moving to a different point, on the same demand curve after a price change).

A change in demand occurs when one of the elements underlying the demand curve shifts. Take the case of pizzas. Suppose incomes increase and people want to spend part of their extra income on pizzas for a given pizza price. In other words, higher incomes will increase demand and shift the demand curve for pizzas out and to the right. This is a shift in the demand for pizzas.

By contrast, suppose that a new technology reduces pizza costs and prices. This leads to a change in quantity demanded that occurs because consumers tend to buy more pizzas as pizza prices fall, all other things remaining constant. Here, the increased purchases result not from an increase in demand but from the pizza-price decrease. This change represents a *movement along* the demand curve, not a *shift of* the demand curve.

---

① 我们知道，在 20 世纪 90 年代美国经济的持续繁荣时期，美国人的平均收入迅猛增长。

② 图 3-4. 汽车需求的增加

③ 商品价格之外的因素引起购买数量发生变化时，我们称这些变化为需求的变动。需求的变动随着每一价格水平的上升或下降而增加或者减少。

④ 沿曲线运动与曲线位移

供给表

B. THE SUPPLY SCHEDULE

Let us now turn from demand to supply. The supply side of a market typically involves the terms on which businesses produce and sell their products. The supply of tomatoes tells us the quantity of tomatoes that will be sold at each tomato price. More precisely, the supply schedule relates the quantity supplied of a good to its market price, other things constant. In considering supply, the other things that are held constant include input prices, prices of related goods, and government policies.

The **supply schedule** (or **supply curve**) for a commodity shows the relationship between its market price and the amount of that commodity that producers are willing to produce and sell, other things held constant. ①

供给曲线
THE SUPPLY CURVE

Table 3-3 shows a hypothetical supply schedule for cornflakes, and Figure 3-5 plots the data from the table in the form of a supply curve. These data show that at a cornflakes price of $1 per box, no cornflakes at all will be produced. At such a low price, breakfast cereal manufacturers might want to devote their factories to producing other types of cereal, like bran flakes, that earn them more profit than cornflakes. As the price of cornflakes increases, ever more cornflakes will be produced. At ever-higher cornflakes prices, cereal makers will find it profitable to add more workers and to buy more automated cornflakes-stuffing machines and even more cornflakes factories. All these will increase the output of cornflakes at the higher market prices.

Figure 3-5 shows the typical case of an upward-sloping supply curve for an individual commodity. One important reason for the upward slope is "the law of diminishing returns" (a concept we will learn more about later). Wine will illustrate this important law. If society wants more wine, then additional labor will have to be added to the limited land sites suitable for producing wine grapes. Each new worker will be adding less and less extra product. The price needed to coax out additional wine output is therefore higher. By raising the price of wine, society can persuade wine producers to produce and sell more wine; the supply curve for wine is therefore upward-sloping. Similar reasoning applies to many other goods as well.

Supply Schedule for Cornflakes

	(1) Price ($ per box) *P*	(2) Quantity supplied (millions of boxes per year) *Q*
A	5	18
B	4	16
C	3	12
D	2	7
E	1	0

TABLE 3-3. Supply Schedule Relates Quantity Supplied to Price ②

The table shows, for each price, the quantity of cornflakes that cereal makers want to produce and sell. Note the positive relation between price and quantity supplied.

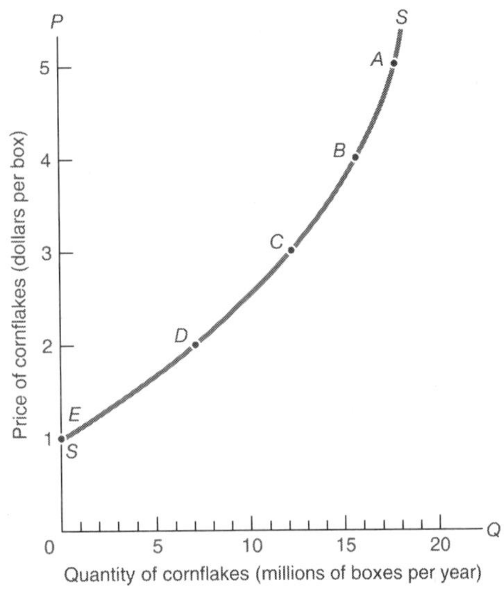

FIGURE 3-5. Supply Curve Relates Quantity Supplied to Price ③

The supply curve plots the price and quantity pairs from Table 3-3. A smooth curve is passed through these points to give the upward-sloping supply curve, *SS*.

upward-sloping supply curve *SS*
向上倾斜的供给曲线 *SS*

① 在其他因素保持不变的情况下，一种商品的**供给表**（或者**供给曲线**）表示其市场价格与生产商愿意生产和销售的数量之间的关系。

② 表 3-3. 供给量与价格关系的供给表

③ 图 3-5. 供给量与价格关系的供给曲线

供给曲线背后的因素
Forces behind the Supply Curve

In examining the forces determining the supply curve, the fundamental point to grasp is that producers supply commodities for profit and not for fun or charity. One major element underlying the supply curve is the *cost of production.* When production costs for a good are low relative to the market price, it is profitable for producers to supply a great deal. When production costs are high relative to price, firms produce little, switch to the production of other products, or may simply go out of business.

prices of inputs 投入要素的价格

technological advances 技术进步

Production costs are primarily determined by the *prices of inputs* and *technological advances.* The prices of inputs such as labor, energy, or machinery obviously have a very important influence on the cost of producing a given level of output. For example, when oil prices rose sharply in 2007, the increase raised the price of energy for manufacturers, increased their production costs, and lowered their supply. By contrast, as computer prices fell over the last three decades, businesses increasingly substituted computerized processes for other inputs, as for example in payroll or accounting operations; this increased supply.

An equally important determinant of production costs is *technological advances,* which consist of changes that lower the quantity of inputs needed to produce the same quantity of output. Such advances include everything from scientific breakthroughs to better application of existing technology or simply reorganization of the flow of work. For example, manufacturers have become much more efficient in recent years. It takes far fewer hours of labor to produce an automobile today than it did just 10 years ago. This advance enables car makers to produce more automobiles at the same cost. To give another example, if Internet commerce allows firms to compare more easily the prices of necessary inputs, that will lower the cost of production.

But production costs are not the only ingredient that goes into the supply curve. Supply is also influenced by the *prices of related goods,* particularly goods that are alternative outputs of the production process. If the price of one production substitute rises, the supply of another substitute will decrease. An interesting example occurred in U.S. farming. The government has raised the subsidy on automotive ethanol to reduce imports of foreign oil. Ethanol is today primarily made from corn. The increased demand for corn (a shift in the demand curve for corn) increased the corn price. As a result, farmers planted corn instead of soybeans. The net result was that the supply of soybeans declined and soybean prices rose. All of this occurred because of a subsidy to reduce oil imports.

Government policy also has an important impact on the supply curve. We just discussed the case of ethanol subsidies and corn production. Environmental and health considerations determine what technologies can be used, while taxes and minimum-wage laws can significantly affect input prices. Government trade policies have a major impact upon supply. For instance, when a free-trade agreement opens up the U.S. market to Mexican footwear, the total supply of footwear in the United States increases.

Finally, *special influences* affect the supply curve. The weather exerts an important influence on farming and on the ski industry. The computer industry has been marked by a keen spirit of innovation, which has led to a continuous flow of new products. Market structure will affect supply, and expectations about future prices often have an important impact upon supply decisions.

Table 3-4 highlights the important determinants of supply, using automobiles as an example.

供给的变动
Shifts in Supply

Businesses are constantly changing the mix of products and services they provide. What lies behind these changes in supply behavior?

When changes in factors other than a good's own price affect the quantity supplied, we call these changes shifts in supply. Supply increases (or decreases) when the amount supplied increases (or decreases) at each market price.

When automobile prices change, producers change their production and quantity supplied, but the supply and the supply curve do not shift. By contrast, when other influences affecting supply change, supply changes and the supply curve shifts.

We can illustrate a shift in supply for the automobile market. Supply would increase if the introduction of cost-saving computerized design and manufacturing reduced the labor required to produce cars, if autoworkers took a pay cut, if there were lower production costs in Japan, or if the government repealed environmental regulations on the

Factors affecting the supply curve	Example for automobiles
1. **Technology**	Computerized manufacturing lowers production costs and increases supply.
2. **Input prices**	A reduction in the wage paid to autoworkers lowers production costs and increases supply.
3. **Prices of related goods**	If truck prices fall, the supply of cars rises.
4. **Government policy**	Removing quotas and tariffs on imported automobiles increases total automobile supply.
5. **Special influences**	Internet shopping and auctions allow consumers to compare the prices of different dealers more easily and drives high-cost sellers out of business.

TABLE 3-4. Supply Is Affected by Production Costs and Other Factors ①

industry. Any of these elements would increase the supply of automobiles in the United States at each price. Figure 3-6 illustrates an increase in the supply of automobiles.

To test your understanding of supply shifts, think about the following: What would happen to the world supply curve for oil if a revolution in Saudi Arabia led to declining oil production? What would happen to the supply curve for clothing if tariffs were slapped on Chinese imports into the United States? What happens to the supply curve for computers if Intel introduces a new computer chip that dramatically increases computing speeds?

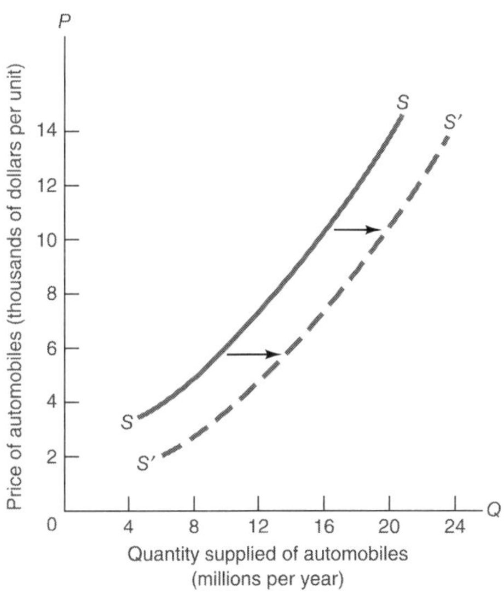

FIGURE 3-6. Increased Supply of Automobiles ②

As production costs fall, the supply of automobiles increases. At each price, producers will supply more automobiles, and the supply curve therefore shifts to the right. (What would happen to the supply curve if Congress were to put a restrictive quota on automobile imports?)

As you answer the questions above, make sure to keep in mind the difference between moving along a curve and a shift of the curve. Here that distinction applies to supply curves, whereas earlier we applied it to demand curves. Look back at the gasoline-price curve in Figure 3-1 on page 46. When the price of oil rose because of political disturbances in the 1970s, this led to an inward *shift of* the supply curve. When sales of gasoline declined in response to the higher price, that was a *movement along* the demand curve.

Does the history of computer prices and quantities shown in Figure 3-3 on page 49 look more like shifting supply or shifting demand? (Question 8 at the end of this chapter explores this issue further.)

How would you describe a rise in chicken production that was induced by a rise in chicken prices? What about the case of a rise in chicken production because of a fall in the price of chicken feed?

供给与需求的均衡

C. EQUILIBRIUM OF SUPPLY AND DEMAND

Up to this point we have been considering demand and supply in isolation. We know the amounts that are willingly bought and sold at each price. We have

① 表 3-4. 生产成本与其他因素影响下的供给

② 图 3-6. 汽车供给量的增加

seen that consumers demand different amounts of cornflakes, cars, and computers as a function of these goods' prices. Similarly, producers willingly supply different amounts of these and other goods depending on their prices. But how can we put both sides of the market together?

The answer is that supply and demand interact to produce an equilibrium price and quantity, or a market equilibrium. The *market equilibrium* comes at that price and quantity where the forces of supply and demand are in balance. At the equilibrium price, the amount that buyers want to buy is just equal to the amount that sellers want to sell. The reason we call this an equilibrium is that, when the forces of supply and demand are in balance, there is no reason for price to rise or fall, as long as other things remain unchanged.

Let us work through the cornflakes example in Table 3-5 to see how supply and demand determine a market equilibrium; the numbers in this table come from Tables 3-1 and 3-3. To find the market price and quantity, we find a price at which the amounts desired to be bought and sold just match. If we try a price of $5 per box, will it prevail for long? Clearly not. As row A in Table 3-5 shows, at $5 producers would like to sell 18 million boxes per year while demanders want to buy only 9. The amount supplied at $5 exceeds the amount demanded, and stocks of cornflakes pile up in supermarkets. Because too few consumers are chasing too many cornflakes, the price of cornflakes will tend to fall, as shown in column (5) of Table 3-5.

Say we try $2. Does that price clear the market? A quick look at row D shows that at $2 consumption exceeds production. Cornflakes begin to disappear from the stores at that price. As people scramble around to find their desired cornflakes, they will tend to bid up the price of cornflakes, as shown in column (5) of Table 3-5.

We could try other prices, but we can easily see that the equilibrium price is $3, or row C in Table 3-5. At $3, consumers' desired demand exactly equals producers' desired production, each of which is 12 units. Only at $3 will consumers and suppliers both be making consistent decisions.

A **market equilibrium** comes at the price at which quantity demanded equals quantity supplied. At that equilibrium, there is no tendency for the price to rise or fall. The equilibrium price is also called the **market-clearing price.** This denotes that all supply and demand orders are filled, the books are "cleared" of orders, and demanders and suppliers are satisfied. ①

供给曲线与需求曲线的均衡
EQUILIBRIUM WITH SUPPLY AND DEMAND CURVES

We often show the market equilibrium through a supply-and-demand diagram like the one in Figure 3-7; this figure combines the supply curve from Figure 3-5

Combining Demand and Supply for Cornflakes

	(1) Possible price ($ per box)	(2) Quantity demanded (millions of boxes per year)	(3) Quantity supplied (millions of boxes per year)	(4) State of market	(5) Pressure on price
A	5	9	18	Surplus	↓ Downward
B	4	10	16	Surplus	↓ Downward
C	3	12	12	Equilibrium	Neutral
D	2	15	7	Shortage	↑ Upward
E	1	20	0	Shortage	↑ Upward

TABLE 3-5. Equilibrium Price Comes Where Quantity Demanded Equals Quantity Supplied ②

The table shows the quantities supplied and demanded at different prices. Only at the equilibrium price of $3 per box does amount supplied equal amount demanded. At too low a price there is a shortage and price tends to rise. Too high a price produces a surplus, which will depress the price.

① 当需求量在一个特定的价格水平上等于供给量时就出现了**市场均衡**。在这样的均衡下，价格不会出现上下波动的趋势。这一均衡价格也叫做**市场出清价格**。这种现象意味着所有的供给与需求的订单均已完成，账面已经出清，供给者和需求者双方均得到了满足。

② 表 3-5. 供给量等于需求量时的均衡价格

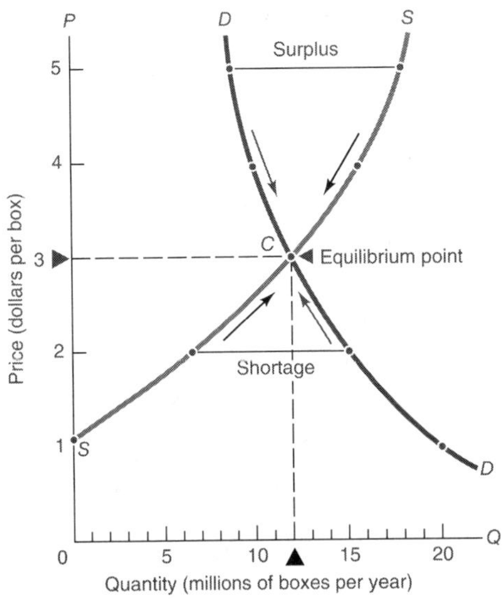

FIGURE 3-7. Market Equilibrium Comes at the ①
Intersection of Supply and Demand Curves

The market equilibrium price and quantity come at the intersection of the supply and demand curves. At a price of \$3, at point *C*, firms willingly supply what consumers willingly demand. When the price is too low (say, at \$2), quantity demanded exceeds quantity supplied, shortages occur, and the price is driven up to equilibrium. What occurs at a price of \$4?

with the demand curve from Figure 3-2. Combining the two graphs is possible because they are drawn with exactly the same variables and units on each axis.

We find the market equilibrium by looking for the price at which quantity demanded equals quantity supplied. *The equilibrium price comes at the intersec-* ②
tion of the supply and demand curves, at point C.

How do we know that the intersection of the supply and demand curves is the market equilibrium? Let us repeat our earlier experiment. Start with the initial high price of \$5 per box, shown at the top of the price axis in Figure 3-7. At that price, suppliers want to sell more than demanders want to buy. The result is a *surplus,* or excess of quantity supplied over quantity demanded, shown in the figure by the blue line labeled "Surplus." The arrows along the curves show the direction that price tends to move when a market is in surplus.

At a low price of \$2 per box, the market shows a *shortage,* or excess of quantity demanded over quantity supplied, here shown by the blue line labeled "Shortage." Under conditions of shortage, the competition among buyers for limited goods causes the price to rise, as shown in the figure by the arrows pointing upward.

We now see that the balance or equilibrium of supply and demand comes at point *C*, where the supply and demand curves intersect. At point *C*, where the price is \$3 per box and the quantity is 12 units, the quantities demanded and supplied are equal: there are no shortages or surpluses; there is no tendency for price to rise or fall. At point *C* and only at point *C*, the forces of supply and demand are in balance and the price has settled at a sustainable level.

The equilibrium price and quantity come where ③
the amount willingly supplied equals the amount willingly demanded. In a competitive market, this equilibrium is found at the intersection of the supply and demand curves. There are no shortages or surpluses at the equilibrium price.

供给或需求的移动对均衡的影响
Effect of a Shift in Supply or Demand

The analysis of the supply-and-demand apparatus can do much more than tell us about the equilibrium price and quantity. It can also be used to predict the impact of changes in economic conditions on prices and quantities. Let's change our example to the staff of life, bread. Suppose that a spell of bad weather raises the price of wheat, a key ingredient of bread. That shifts the supply curve for bread to the left. This is illustrated in Figure 3-8(*a*), where the bread supply curve has shifted from *SS* to *S′S′*. In contrast, the demand curve has not shifted because people's sandwich demand is unaffected by farming weather.

What happens in the bread market? The bad harvest causes profit-maximizing bakers to produce less bread at the old price, so quantity demanded exceeds quantity supplied. The price of bread therefore rises, encouraging production and thereby raising quantity supplied, while simultaneously discouraging consumption and lowering quantity demanded. The price continues to rise until, at the new equilibrium price, the amounts demanded and supplied are once again equal.

As Figure 3-8(*a*) shows, the new equilibrium is found at *E′*, the intersection of the new supply curve

① 图 3-7. 在供给曲线与需求曲线的交点，达到市场均衡

② 市场均衡出现在供给曲线与需求曲线的交点，即图中的 *C* 点。

③ 在愿意购买的数量和愿意供给的数量相等的情况下，就出现了均衡价格及均衡数量。在竞争性市场，这种均衡出现在供给和需求曲线的交点。在均衡价格水平上，商品的短缺或者过剩现象都不会发生。

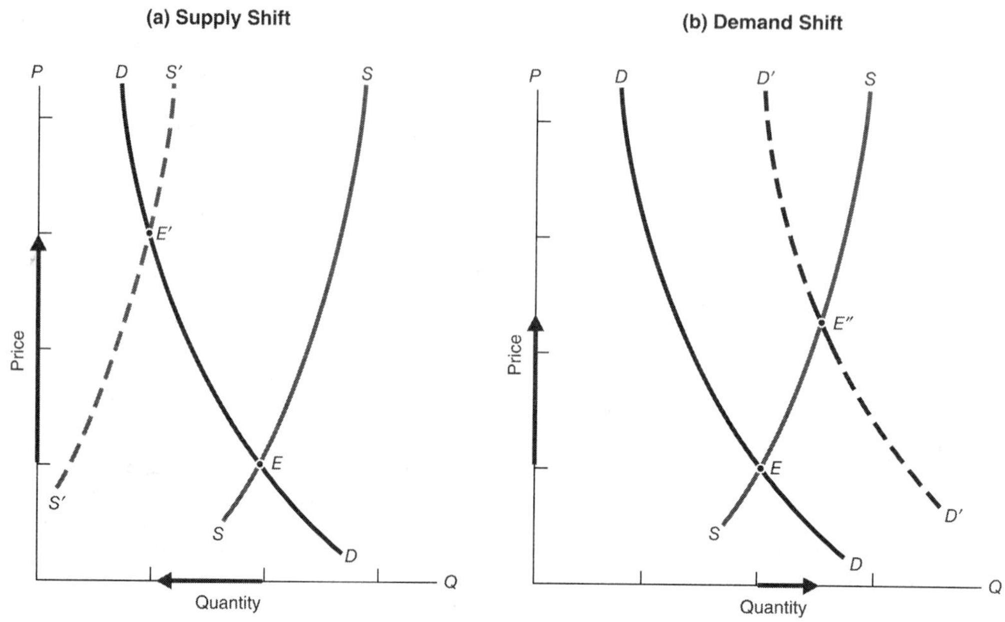

FIGURE 3-8. Shifts in Supply or Demand Change Equilibrium Price and Quantity ①

(**a**) If supply shifts leftward, a shortage will develop at the original price. Price will be bid up until quantities willingly bought and sold are equal, at new equilibrium E'. (**b**) A shift in the demand curve leads to excess demand. Price will be bid up as equilibrium price and quantity move upward to E''.

$S'S'$ and the original demand curve. Thus a bad harvest (or any leftward shift of the supply curve) raises prices and, by the law of downward-sloping demand, lowers quantity demanded.

Suppose that new baking technologies lower costs and therefore increase supply. That means the supply curve shifts down and to the right. Draw in a new $S'''S'''$ curve, along with the new equilibrium E'''. Why is the equilibrium price lower? Why is the equilibrium quantity higher?

We can also use our supply-and-demand apparatus to examine how changes in demand affect the market equilibrium. Suppose that there is a sharp increase in family incomes, so everyone wants to eat more bread. This is represented in Figure 3-8(b) as a "demand shift" in which, at every price, consumers demand a higher quantity of bread. The demand curve thus shifts *rightward* from DD to $D'D'$.

The demand shift produces a shortage of bread at the old price. A scramble for bread ensues. Prices are bid upward until supply and demand come back into balance at a higher price. Graphically, the increase in demand has changed the market equilibrium from E to E'' in Figure 3-8(b).

For both examples of shifts—a shift in supply and a shift in demand—a variable underlying the demand or supply curve has changed. In the case of supply, there might have been a change in technology or input prices. For the demand shift, one of the influences affecting consumer demand—incomes, population, the prices of related goods, or tastes—changed and thereby shifted the demand schedule (see Table 3-6).

When the elements underlying demand or supply change, this leads to shifts in demand or supply and to changes in the market equilibrium of price and quantity. ②

① 图 3-8. 供给曲线或需求曲线的位移改变了均衡价格和均衡数量

② 当影响需求和供给的因素发生变化时，需求和供给将发生变动，且价格和数量的市场均衡也将发生变化。

	Demand and supply shifts	Effect on price and quantity
If demand rises . . .	The demand curve shifts to the right, and . . .	Price ↑ Quantity ↑
If demand falls . . .	The demand curve shifts to the left, and . . .	Price ↓ Quantity ↓
If supply rises . . .	The supply curve shifts to the right, and . . .	Price ↓ Quantity ↑
If supply falls . . .	The supply curve shifts to the left, and . . .	Price ↑ Quantity ↓

TABLE 3-6. The Effect on Price and Quantity of Different Demand and Supply Shifts ①

解释价格和数量的变动

Interpreting Changes in Price and Quantity

An important issue that arises is how to interpret price and quantity changes. We sometimes hear, "Gasoline demand does not obey the law of downward-sloping demand. From 2003 to 2006 prices rose sharply [as shown in Figure 3-1], yet U.S. gasoline consumption went up rather than down. What do you economists say about that!"

We cannot provide a definitive explanation without a careful look at the forces affecting both supply and demand. But the most likely explanation for the paradox is that the rise in gasoline prices over this period was due to *shifts in demand* rather than *movements along the demand curve.* We know, for example, that the Chinese and Indian economies grew rapidly and their oil imports added to world demand. Moreover, the number of automobiles in the United States grew sharply, and the fuel efficiency of the fleet declined, increasing the U.S. demand for gasoline.

Economists deal with these sorts of questions all the time. When prices or quantities change in a market, does the situation reflect a change on the supply side or the demand side? Sometimes, in simple situations, looking at price and quantity simultaneously gives you a clue about whether it is the supply curve or the demand curve that has shifted. For example, a rise in the price of bread accompanied by a *decrease* in quantity suggests that the supply curve has shifted to the left (a decrease in supply). A rise in price accompanied by an *increase* in quantity indicates that the demand curve for bread has probably shifted to the right (an increase in demand).

Figure 3-9 illustrates the point. In both panel (*a*) and panel (*b*), quantity goes up. But in (*a*) the price rises, and in (*b*) the price falls. Figure 3-9(*a*) shows the case of an increase in demand, or a shift in the demand curve. As a result of the shift, the equilibrium quantity demanded increases from 10 to 15 units. The case of a movement along the demand curve is shown in Figure 3-9(*b*). In this case, a supply shift changes the market equilibrium from point *E* to point *E*″. As a result, the quantity demanded changes from 10 to 15 units. But demand does not change in this second case; rather, quantity demanded increases as consumers move along their demand curve from *E* to *E*″ in response to a price change.

Return to our example of the change in gasoline consumption from 2003 to 2006. Explain why such events are best explained by the changes in Figure 3-9(*a*). Explain why the law of downward-sloping demand is still alive in the gasoline market!

The Elusive Concept of Equilibrium ②

The notion of equilibrium is one of the most elusive concepts of economics. We are familiar with equilibrium in our everyday lives from seeing, for example, an orange sitting at the bottom of a bowl or a pendulum at rest. In economics, equilibrium means that the different forces operating on a market are in balance, so the resulting price and quantity reconcile the desires of purchasers and suppliers. Too low a price means that the forces are not in balance, that the forces attracting demand are greater than the forces attracting supply, so there is excess demand, or a shortage. We also

① 表 3-6. 需求和供给的不同移动对价格和数量的影响

② 难以捉摸的均衡概念

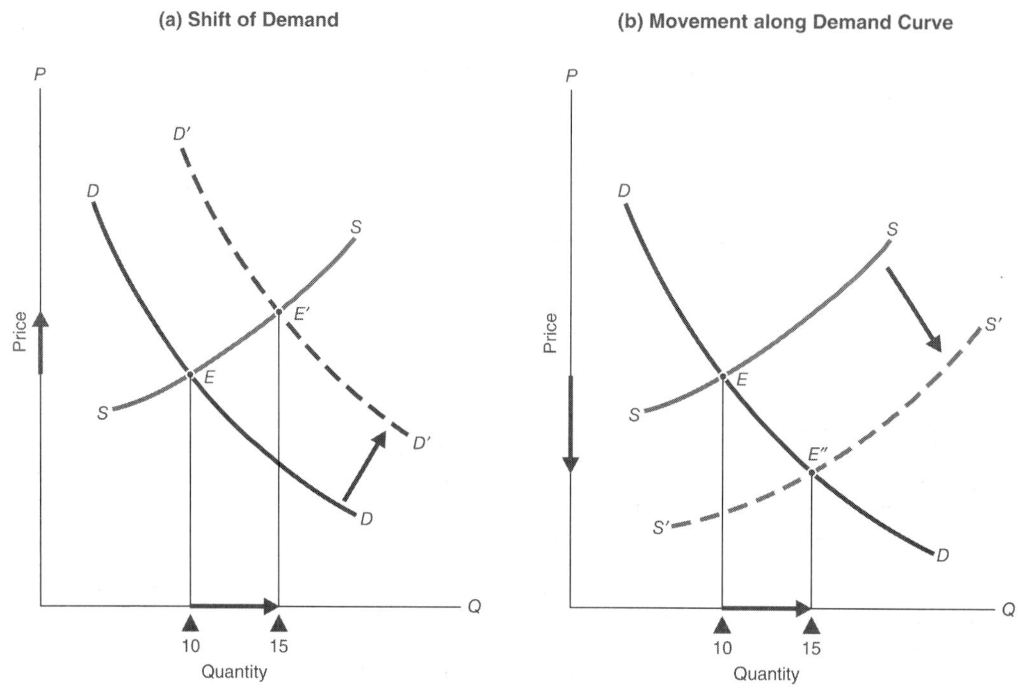

FIGURE 3-9. Shifts of and Movements along Curves ①

Start out with initial equilibrium at E and a quantity of 10 units. In (**a**), an increase in demand (i.e., a shift of the demand curve) produces a new equilibrium of 15 units at E'. In (**b**), a shift in supply results in a movement along the demand curve from E to E''.

know that a competitive market is a mechanism for producing equilibrium. If the price is too low, demanders will bid up the price to the equilibrium level.

The notion of equilibrium is tricky, however, as is seen by the statement of a leading pundit: "Don't lecture me about supply and demand equilibrium. The supply of oil is always equal to the demand for oil. You simply can't tell the difference." The pundit is right in an accounting sense. Clearly the oil sales recorded by the oil producers should be exactly equal to the oil purchases recorded by the oil consumers. But this bit of arithmetic cannot repeal the laws of supply and demand. More important, if we fail to understand the nature of economic equilibrium, we cannot hope to understand how different forces affect the marketplace. ②

In economics, we are interested in knowing the quantity of sales that will clear the market, that is, the equilibrium quantity. We also want to know the price at which consumers willingly buy what producers willingly sell. Only at this price will both buyers and sellers be satisfied with their decisions. Only at this price and quantity will there be no tendency for price and quantity to change.

Only by looking at the equilibrium of supply and demand can we hope to understand such paradoxes as the fact that immigration may not lower wages in the affected cities, that land taxes do not raise rents, and that bad harvests raise (yes, raise!) the incomes of farmers.

供给、需求和移民
Supply, Demand, and Immigration

A fascinating and important example of supply and demand, full of complexities, is the role of immigration in determining wages. If you ask people, they are likely to tell you that immigration into California or Florida surely lowers the wages of people in those

① 图 3-9. 沿曲线运动及曲线位移

② 然而，均衡这一概念本身就很微妙，正如一位权威的学者所言："别给我讲授什么供给和需求的均衡问题。石油的供给始终等于市场对石油的需求。你根本看不到两者之间的差别。"

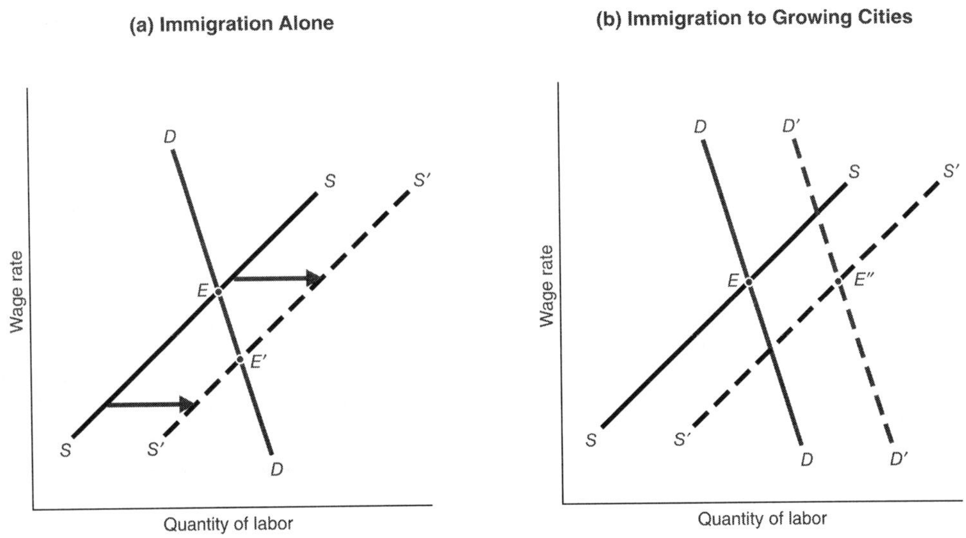

FIGURE 3-10. Impact of Immigration on Wages ①

In (**a**), new immigrants cause the supply curve for labor to shift from *SS* to *S′S′*, lowering equilibrium wages. But more often, immigrants go to cities with growing labor markets. Then, as shown in (**b**), the wage changes are small if the supply increase comes in labor markets with growing demand.

regions. It's just supply and demand. They might point to Figure 3-10(*a*), which shows a supply-and-demand analysis of immigration. According to this analysis, immigration into a region shifts the supply curve for labor to the right and pushes down wages.

Careful economic studies cast doubt on this simple reasoning. A survey of the evidence concludes:

> [The] effect of immigration on the labor market outcomes of natives is small. There is no evidence of economically significant reductions in native employment. Most empirical analysis . . . finds that a 10 percent increase in the fraction of immigrants in the population reduces native wages by at most 1 percent.[2]

How can we explain the small impact of immigration on wages? Labor economists emphasize the high geographic mobility of the American population. This means that new immigrants will quickly spread around the entire country. Once they arrive, immigrants may move to cities where they can get jobs—workers tend to move to those cities where the demand for labor is already rising because of a strong local economy.

This point is illustrated in Figure 3-10(*b*), where a shift in labor supply to *S′S′* is associated with a higher demand curve, *D′D′*. The new equilibrium wage at *E″* is the same as the original wage at *E*. Another factor is that native-born residents may move out when immigrants move in, so the total supply of labor is unchanged. This would leave the supply curve for labor in its original position and leave the wage unchanged.

Immigration is a good example for demonstrating the power of the simple tools of supply and demand.

通过价格配给
RATIONING BY PRICES

Let us now take stock of what the market mechanism accomplishes. By determining the equilibrium prices and quantities, the market allocates or rations out the scarce goods of the society among the possible

[2] Rachel M. Friedberg and Jennifer Hunt, "The Impact of Immigrants on Host Country Wages, Employment, and Growth," *Journal of Economic Perspectives*, Spring 1995, pp. 23–44. [2]

① 图 3-10. 移民对工资的影响

[2] 芮切尔・弗雷伯格（Rachel M. Friedberg），美国布朗大学（Brown University）经济系教授。杰尼弗・亨特（Jennifer Hunt），加拿大麦克基尔大学（McGill University）经济系教授。

Rationing by the purse
资金配给

uses. Who does the rationing? A planning board? Congress? The president? No. The marketplace, through the interaction of supply and demand, does the rationing. This is *rationing by the purse.*

What goods are produced? This is answered by the signals of market prices. High corn prices stimulate corn production, whereas falling computer prices stimulate a growing demand for computation. Those who have the most dollar votes have the greatest influence on what goods are produced.

For whom are goods produced? The power of the purse dictates the distribution of income and consumption. Those with higher incomes end up with larger houses, fancier cars, and longer vacations. When backed up by cash, the most urgently felt needs get fulfilled through the demand curve.

Even the *how* question is decided by supply and demand. When corn prices are high, farmers buy expensive tractors and more fertilizer and invest in irrigation systems. When oil prices are high, oil companies drill in deep offshore waters and employ novel seismic techniques to find oil.

With this introduction to supply and demand, ① we begin to see how desires for goods, as expressed through demands, interact with costs of goods, as reflected in supplies. Further study will deepen our understanding of these concepts and will show how these tools can be applied to other important areas. But even this first survey will serve as an indispensable tool for interpreting the economic world in which we live.

SUMMARY

1. The analysis of supply and demand shows how a market mechanism solves the three problems of *what, how,* and *for whom.* A market blends together demands and supplies. Demand comes from consumers who are spreading their dollar votes among available goods and services, while businesses supply the goods and services with the goal of maximizing their profits.

A. The Demand Schedule

2. A demand schedule shows the relationship between the quantity demanded and the price of a commodity, other things held constant. Such a demand schedule, depicted graphically by a demand curve, holds constant other things like family incomes, tastes, and the prices of other goods. Almost all commodities obey the *law of downward-sloping demand,* which holds that quantity demanded falls as a good's price rises. This law is represented by a downward-sloping demand curve.
3. Many influences lie behind the demand schedule for the market as a whole: average family incomes, population, the prices of related goods, tastes, and special influences. When these influences change, the demand curve will shift.

B. The Supply Schedule

4. The supply schedule (or supply curve) gives the relationship between the quantity of a good that producers desire to sell—other things constant—and that good's price. Quantity supplied generally responds positively to price, so the supply curve is upward-sloping.
5. Elements other than the good's price affect its supply. The most important influence is the commodity's production cost, determined by the state of technology and by input prices. Other elements in supply include the prices of related goods, government policies, and special influences.

C. Equilibrium of Supply and Demand

6. The equilibrium of supply and demand in a competitive market occurs when the forces of supply and demand are in balance. The equilibrium price is the price at which the quantity demanded just equals the quantity supplied. Graphically, we find the equilibrium at the intersection of the supply and demand curves. At a price above the equilibrium, producers want to supply more than consumers want to buy, which results in a surplus of goods and exerts downward pressure on price. Similarly, too low a price generates a shortage, and buyers will therefore tend to bid price upward to the equilibrium.
7. Shifts in the supply and demand curves change the equilibrium price and quantity. An increase in demand, which shifts the demand curve to the right, will increase both equilibrium price and quantity. An increase in supply, which shifts the supply curve to the right, will decrease price and increase quantity demanded.
8. To use supply-and-demand analysis correctly, we must (*a*) distinguish a change in demand or supply (which produces a shift of a curve) from a change in the

① 通过本章对供给与需求的介绍，我们开始认识到表现在需求当中的对商品的欲望，如何与反映在供给中的商品成本相互作用。进一步的学习将会加深我们对这些概念的理解，同时也将了解到这些工具是如何应用到其他重要领域的。虽然这仅仅是初步的学习，但它必将成为解释我们赖以生存的这个经济世界的不可或缺的工具。

quantity demanded or supplied (which represents a movement along a curve); (*b*) hold other things constant, which requires distinguishing the impact of a change in a commodity's price from the impact of changes in other influences; and (*c*) look always for the supply-and-demand equilibrium, which comes at the point where forces acting on price and quantity are in balance.

9. Competitively determined prices ration the limited supply of goods among those who demand them.

CONCEPTS FOR REVIEW

supply-and-demand analysis
demand schedule or curve, *DD*
law of downward-sloping demand
influences affecting demand curve
supply schedule or curve, *SS*
influences affecting supply curve
equilibrium price and quantity
shifts of supply and demand curves
all other things held constant
rationing by prices

FURTHER READING AND INTERNET WEBSITES

Further Reading

Supply-and-demand analysis is the single most important and useful tool in microeconomics. Supply-and-demand analysis was developed by the great British economist Alfred Marshall in *Principles of Economics,* 9th ed. (New York, Macmillan, [1890] 1961). To reinforce your understanding, you might look in textbooks on intermediate microeconomics. Two good references are Hal R. Varian, *Intermediate Microeconomics: A Modern Approach,* 6th ed. (Norton, New York, 2002), and Edwin Mansfield and Gary Yohe, *Microeconomics: Theory and Applications,* 10th ed. (Norton, New York, 2000).

A recent survey of the economic issues in immigration is in George Borjas, *Heaven's Door: Immigration Policy and the American Economy* (Princeton University Press, Princeton, N.J., 1999).

Websites

Websites in economics are proliferating rapidly, and it is hard to keep up with all the useful sites. A good place to start is always *rfe.org/*. A good starting point for multiple sites in economics is *rfe.org/OtherInt/MultSub/index.html,* and the Google search engine has its own economics site at *directory.google.com/Top/Science/Social_Sciences/Economics/*. Another useful starting point for Internet resources in economics can be found at *www.oswego.edu/~economic/econweb.htm*.

You can examine a recent study of the impact of immigration on American society from the National Academy of Sciences, *The New Americans* (1997), at *www.nap.edu*. This site provides free access to over 1000 studies from economics and the other social and natural sciences.

QUESTIONS FOR DISCUSSION

1. a. Define carefully what is meant by a demand schedule or curve. State the law of downward-sloping demand. Illustrate the law of downward-sloping demand with two cases from your own experience.
   b. Define the concept of a supply schedule or curve. Show that an increase in supply means a rightward and downward shift of the supply curve. Contrast this with the rightward and upward shift of the demand curve implied by an increase in demand.
2. What might increase the demand for hamburgers? What would increase the supply? What would inexpensive frozen pizzas do to the market equilibrium for hamburgers? To the wages of teenagers who work at McDonald's?
3. Explain why the price in competitive markets settles down at the equilibrium intersection of supply and demand. Explain what happens if the market price starts out too high or too low.

4. Explain why each of the following is *false:*
   a. A freeze in Brazil's coffee-growing region will lower the price of coffee.
   b. "Protecting" American textile manufacturers from Chinese clothing imports will lower clothing prices in the United States.
   c. The rapid increase in college tuitions will lower the demand for college.
   d. The war against drugs will lower the price of domestically produced marijuana.
5. The following are four laws of supply and demand. Fill in the blanks. Demonstrate each law with a supply-and-demand diagram.
   a. An increase in demand generally raises price and raises quantity demanded.
   b. A decrease in demand generally ________ price and ________ quantity demanded.
   c. An increase in supply generally lowers price and raises quantity demanded.
   d. A decrease in supply generally ________ price and ________ quantity demanded.
6. For each of the following, explain whether quantity demanded changes because of a demand shift or a price change, and draw a diagram to illustrate your answer:
   a. As a result of increased military spending, the price of Army boots rises.
   b. Fish prices fall after the pope allows Catholics to eat meat on Friday.
   c. An increase in gasoline taxes lowers the consumption of gasoline.
   d. After the Black Death struck Europe in the fourteenth century, wages rose.
7. Examine the graph for the price of gasoline in Figure 3-1, on page 46. Then, using a supply-and-demand diagram, illustrate the impact of each of the following on price and quantity demanded:
   a. Improvements in transportation lower the costs of importing oil into the United States in the 1960s.
   b. After the 1973 war, oil producers cut oil production sharply.
   c. After 1980, smaller automobiles get more miles per gallon.
   d. A record-breaking cold winter in 1995–1996 unexpectedly raises the demand for heating oil.
   e. Rapid economic growth in the early 2000s leads to a sharp upturn in oil prices.
8. Examine Figure 3-3 on page 49. Does the price-quantity relationship look more like a supply curve or a demand curve? Assuming that the demand curve was unchanged over this period, trace supply curves for 1965 and 2008 that would have generated the (P, Q) pairs for those years. Explain what forces might have led to the shift in the supply curve.
9. From the following data, plot the supply and demand curves and determine the equilibrium price and quantity:

Supply and Demand for Pizzas

Price ($ per pizza)	Quantity demanded (pizzas per semester)	Quantity supplied (pizzas per semester)
10	0	40
8	10	30
6	20	20
4	30	10
2	40	0
0	125	0

What would happen if the demand for pizzas tripled at each price? What would occur if the price were initially set at $4 per pizza?

PART TWO

Microeconomics: Supply, Demand, and Product Markets

微观经济学：供给、需求和产品市场

CHAPTER

4

Supply and Demand: Elasticity and Applications
供给和需求：弹性和应用

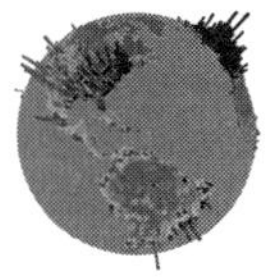

You cannot teach a parrot to be an economist simply by teaching it to say "supply" and "demand."

Anonymous

你可以调教一只鹦鹉模仿出"供给"与"需求"的声音，但却绝对不可能把它调教成一位经济学家。——**民间俗语**

We now move from our introductory survey to a detailed study of microeconomics—of the behavior of individual firms, consumers, and markets. Individual markets contain much of the grand sweep and drama of economic history and the controversies of economic policy. Within the confines of microeconomics we will study the reasons for the vast disparities in earnings between neurosurgeons and textile workers. Microeconomics is crucial to understanding why computer prices have fallen so rapidly and why the use of computers has expanded exponentially. We cannot hope to understand the bitter debates about health care or the minimum wage without applying the tools of supply and demand to these sectors. Even topics such as illegal drugs or crime and punishment are usefully illuminated by considering the way the demand for addictive substances differs from that for other commodities.

But understanding supply and demand requires more than simply parroting the words. A full mastery of microeconomic analysis means understanding the derivation of demand curves and supply curves, learning about different concepts of costs, and understanding how perfect competition differs from monopoly. All these and other key topics will be our subjects as we tour through the fascinating world of microeconomics.

需求和供给的价格弹性

A. PRICE ELASTICITY OF DEMAND AND SUPPLY

Supply and demand can often tell us whether certain forces increase or decrease quantities. But for these tools to be truly useful, we need to know *how much* supply and demand respond to changes in price. Some purchases, like those for vacation travel, are luxuries that are very sensitive to price changes. Others, like food or electricity, are necessities for which consumer quantities respond very little to price changes. The quantitative relationship between ①
price and quantity purchased is analyzed using the crucial concept of *elasticity*. We begin with a careful definition of this term and then use this new concept to analyze the microeconomic impacts of taxes and other types of government intervention.

需求的价格弹性
PRICE ELASTICITY OF DEMAND

Let's look first at the response of consumer demand to price changes:

The **price elasticity of demand** (sometimes sim- ②
ply called **price elasticity**) measures how much the quantity demanded of a good changes when its price

① 价格和购买量之间的定量关系可以用重要的弹性概念来进行分析。

② **需求的价格弹性**（有时简单地称之为**价格弹性**）所测量的是，当一种商品的价格发生变化时，该商品的需求量的变化大小。价格弹性的准确定义是需求量变化的百分比除以价格变化的百分比。

changes. The precise definition of price elasticity is the percentage change in quantity demanded divided by the percentage change in price.

Goods vary enormously in their price elasticity, or sensitivity to price changes. When the price elasticity of a good is high, we say that the good has "elastic" demand, which means that its quantity demanded responds greatly to price changes. When the price elasticity of a good is low, it is "inelastic" and its quantity demanded responds little to price changes.

Goods that have ready substitutes tend to have more elastic demand than those that have no substitutes. If all food or footwear prices were to rise 20 percent tomorrow, you would hardly expect people to stop eating or to go around barefoot, so food and footwear demands are price-inelastic. On the other hand, if mad-cow disease drives up the price of British beef, people can turn to beef from other countries or to lamb or poultry for their meat needs. Therefore, British beef shows a high price elasticity.

The length of time that people have to respond to price changes also plays a role. A good example is that of gasoline. Suppose you are driving across the country when the price of gasoline suddenly increases. Is it likely that you will sell your car and abandon your vacation? Not really. So in the short run, the demand for gasoline may be very inelastic.

In the long run, however, you can adjust your behavior to the higher price of gasoline. You can buy a smaller and more fuel-efficient car, ride a bicycle, take the train, move closer to work, or carpool with [1] other people. The ability to adjust consumption patterns implies that demand elasticities are generally higher in the long run than in the short run.

② 单个商品的需求价格弹性决定于需求的经济属性。当这种商品是奢侈品且有替代品，同时消费者也拥有更多的时间调整自己的行为时，这些奢侈品的价格弹性就会更高。相比之下，当这种商品是必需的且有很少的替代品，同时消费者没有太多的时间调整自己的行为时，这些必需品的价格弹性就会更低。

The price elasticities of demand for individual goods are determined by the economic characteristics of demand. Price elasticities tend to be higher when the goods are luxuries, when substitutes are available, and when consumers have more time to adjust their behavior. By contrast, elasticities are lower for necessities, for goods with few substitutes, and for the short run. ②

弹性的计算

Calculating Elasticities

The precise definition of price elasticity is the percentage change in quantity demanded divided by the percentage change in price. We use the symbol E_D to represent price elasticity, and for convenience we drop the minus signs, so elasticities are all positive.

We can calculate the coefficient of price elasticity numerically according to the following formula:

$$\text{Price elasticity of demand} = E_D = \frac{\text{percentage change in quantity demanded}}{\text{percentage change in price}}$$

Now we can be more precise about the different categories of price elasticity:

- When a 1 percent change in price calls forth more than a 1 percent change in quantity demanded, the good has **price-elastic demand.** For example, if a 1 percent increase in price yields a 5 percent decrease in quantity demanded, the commodity has a highly price-elastic demand. ③
- When a 1 percent change in price produces less than a 1 percent change in quantity demanded, the good has **price-inelastic demand.** This case occurs, for instance, when a 1 percent increase in price yields only a 0.2 percent decrease in demand. ④
- One important special case is **unit-elastic demand,** which occurs when the percentage change in quantity is exactly the same as the percentage change in price. In this case, a 1 percent increase in price yields a 1 percent decrease in demand. We will see later that this condition implies that total expenditures on the commodity (which equal $P \times Q$) stay the same even when the price changes. ⑤

We illustrate the calculation of elasticities with the example shown in Figure 4-1 and Table 4-1. To begin at point *A*, quantity demanded was 240 units at a price of 90. A price increase to 110 led consumers to reduce their purchases to 160 units, shown as point *B*.

Table 4-1 shows how we calculate price elasticity. The price increase is 20 percent, with the resulting quantity decrease being 40 percent. The price elasticity of demand is evidently $E_D = 40/20 = 2$. The price elasticity is greater than 1, and this good therefore has price-elastic demand in the region from *A* to *B*.

In practice, calculating elasticities is somewhat tricky, and we emphasize three key steps where you have to be especially careful:

1. Recall that we drop the minus signs from the numbers, thereby treating all percentage changes as *positive*. That means all elasticities are written as positive numbers, even though prices and

[1] Carpool：一种有利于改善交通拥堵，保护环境，并且还可节约税赋的合伙使用汽车的模式。具体做法为在内侧车道划出带有菱形标志的 HOV（High Occupancy Vehicle）专用快车道，与 vanpool 的共搭班车一起，杜绝单人驾驶机动车使用快车道的现象。

③ 当一种商品的价格发生一个百分点的变化导致了该商品需求量变化超过一个百分点时，该种商品就富有需求价格弹性。

④ 当一种商品的价格发生一个百分点的变化，导致该商品的需求量变化低于一个百分点时，该种商品就缺乏需求价格弹性。

⑤ 当需求量变化的百分数恰好等于价格变化的百分数时，就出现了单位需求价格弹性。

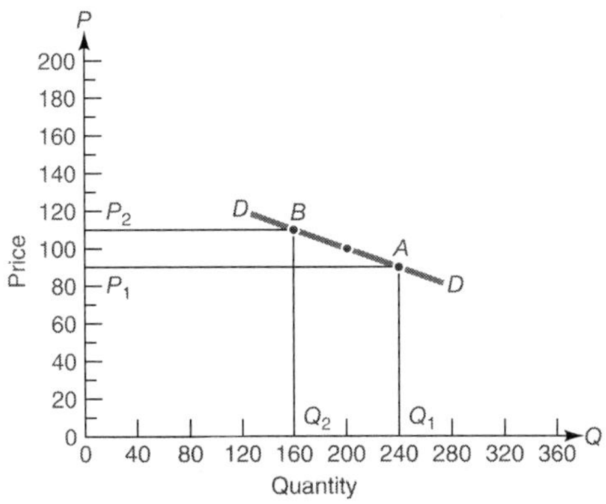

FIGURE 4-1. Elastic Demand Shows Large Quantity Response to Price Change ①

Market equilibrium is originally at point *A*. In response to a 20 percent price increase, quantity demanded declines 40 percent, to point *B*. Price elasticity is $E_D = 40/20 = 2$. Demand is therefore elastic in the region from *A* to *B*.

Case A: Price = 90 and quantity = 240

Case B: Price = 110 and quantity = 160

Percentage price change = $\Delta P/P = 20/100 = 20\%$

Percentage quantity change = $\Delta Q/Q = -80/200 = -40\%$

Price elasticity = $E_D = 40/20 = 2$

TABLE 4-1. Example of Good with Elastic Demand ②

Consider the situation where price is raised from 90 to 110. According to the demand curve, quantity demanded falls from 240 to 160. Price elasticity is the ratio of percentage change in quantity divided by percentage change in price. We drop the minus signs from the numbers so that all elasticities are positive.

quantities demanded move in opposite directions for downward-sloping demand curves.

2. Note that the definition of elasticity uses *percentage changes* in price and demand rather than absolute changes. This has the neat effect that a change in the units of measurement does not affect the elasticity. So whether we measure price in pennies or dollars, the price elasticity stays the same.
3. Note the use of *averaging* to calculate percentage changes in price and quantity. The formula for a percentage change is $\Delta P/P$. The value of ΔP in Table 4-1 is clearly 20 = 110 − 90. But it's not immediately clear what value we should use for *P* in the denominator. Is it the original value of 90, the final value of 110, or something in between?

   For very small percentage changes, such as from 100 to 99, it does not much matter whether we use 99 or 100 as the denominator. But for larger changes, the difference is significant. To avoid ambiguity, we will take the average price to be the base price for calculating price changes. In Table 4-1, we used the average of the two prices $[P = (90 + 110)/2 = 100]$ as the base or denominator in the elasticity formula. Similarly, we used the average quantity $[Q = (160 + 240)/2 = 200]$ as the base for measuring the percentage change in quantity. The exact formula for calculating elasticity is therefore

$$E_D = \frac{\Delta Q}{(Q_1 + Q_2)/2} \div \frac{\Delta P}{(P_1 + P_2)/2}$$

   where P_1 and Q_1 represent the original price and quantity and P_2 and Q_2 stand for the new price and quantity.

价格弹性图

Price Elasticity in Diagrams

It's possible to determine price elasticities in diagrams as well. Figure 4-2 illustrates the three cases of elasticities. In each case, price is cut in half and consumers change their quantity demanded from *A* to *B*.

In Figure 4-2(*a*), a halving of price has tripled quantity demanded. Like the example in Figure 4-1, this case shows price-elastic demand. In Figure 4-2(*c*), cutting price in half led to only a 50 percent increase in quantity demanded, so this is the case of price-inelastic demand. The borderline case of unit-elastic demand is shown in Figure 4-2(*b*); in this example, the doubling of quantity demanded exactly matches the halving of price.

Figure 4-3 displays the important polar extremes where the price elasticities are infinite and zero, or completely elastic and completely inelastic. Completely inelastic demands, or ones with zero elasticity, are ones where the quantity demanded responds not at all to price changes; such demand is seen to be a vertical demand curve. By contrast, when demand is infinitely elastic, a tiny change in price will lead to an

① 图 4-1. 富有弹性的需求表明需求量对价格变动的反应较大

② 表 4-1. 需求富有弹性的商品的案例

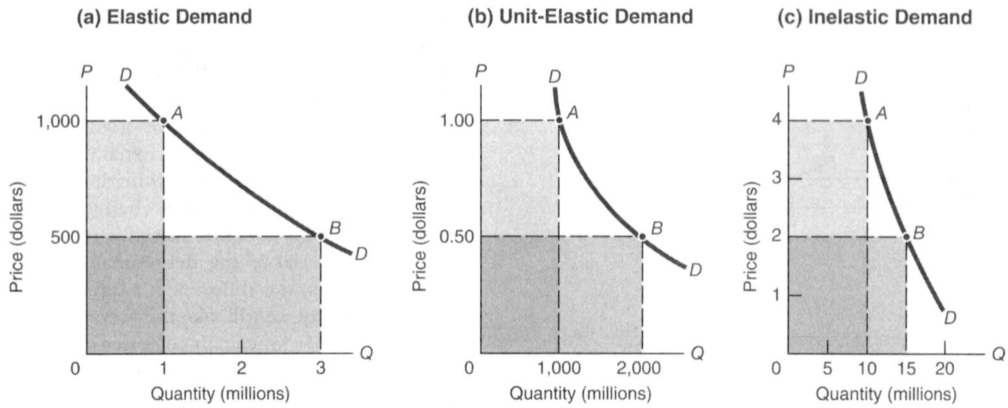

FIGURE 4-2. Price Elasticity of Demand Falls into Three Categories ①

indefinitely large change in quantity demanded, as in the horizontal demand curve in Figure 4-3.

计算弹性的捷径

A Shortcut for Calculating Elasticities

There is a simple rule for calculating the price elasticity of a demand curve:

> The elasticity of a straight line at a point is given ② by the ratio of the length of the line segment below the point to the length of the line segment above the point.

The procedure is shown in Figure 4-4. At the top of the line, a very small percentage price change induces a very large percentage quantity change, and the elasticity is therefore extremely large. Price

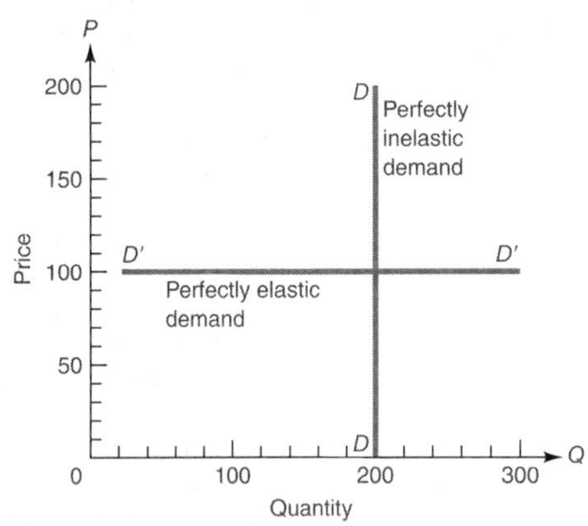

FIGURE 4-3. Perfectly Elastic and Inelastic Demands ③

Polar extremes of demand are vertical demand curves, which represent perfectly inelastic demand ($E_D = 0$), and horizontal demand curves, which show perfectly elastic demand ($E_D = \infty$).

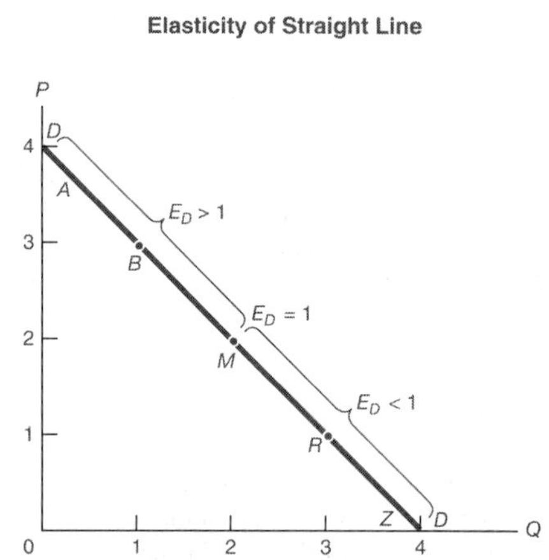

FIGURE 4-4. A Simple Rule for Calculating the Demand Elasticity ④

We can calculate the elasticity as the ratio of the lower segment to the upper segment at the demand point. For example, at point *B*, the lower segment is 3 times as long as the upper segment, so the price elasticity is 3.

---

① 图 4-2. 需求价格弹性的三种类型

② 直线上任何一点的需求弹性等于位于该点下方的线段长度与位于该点上方的线段长度之比。

③ 图 4-3. 完全富有需求价格弹性与完全缺乏需求价格弹性

④ 图 4-4. 需求弹性的简易计算法则

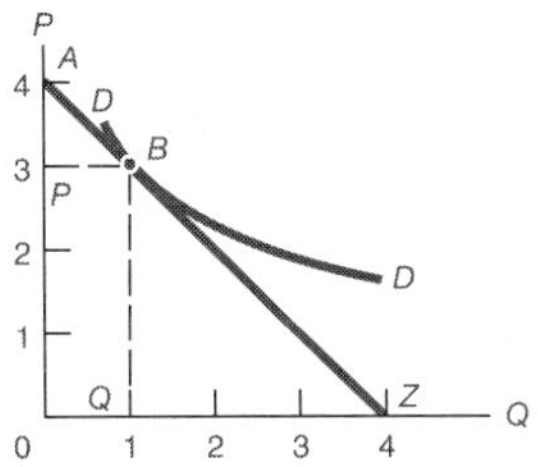

FIGURE 4-5. Calculating the Demand Elasticity for Curved Demand

To calculate the demand elasticity for a nonlinear demand curve, first draw a tangent line at the point. Then take the ratio of the length of the straight-line segment below the point to the length of the line segment above the point. Hence, at point *B* the elasticity can be calculated to be 3.

elasticity is relatively large when we are high up the linear *DD* curve. We use the rule to calculate the elasticity at point *B* in Figure 4-4. Calculate the ratio of the line segment *BZ* to the segment *AB*. Looking at the axes, we see that the ratio is 3. Therefore, price elasticity at point *B* is 3.

A similar calculation at point *R* shows that demand at that point is inelastic, with an elasticity of ⅓.

Finally, calculate elasticity at point *M*. Here, the ratio of the two line segments is one, so demand is unit-elastic at the midpoint *M*.

We can also use the rule to calculate the elasticity of a curved demand curve, as shown in Figure 4-5. For this case, you begin by drawing a line that is tangent to the point, and you then calculate the ratio of segments for the tangent line. This will provide the correct calculation of elasticity for the curved line. Use as an example point *B* in Figure 4-5. We have drawn a tangent straight line. A careful inspection will show that the ratio of the lower to upper segments of the straight line is 3. Therefore, the curved demand has an elasticity of 3 at point *B*.

弹性的代数计算

The Algebra of Elasticities

For the mathematically inclined, we can show the algebra of elasticities for straight-line (linear) demand curves. We begin with a demand curve, which is written as $Q = a - bP$. The demand elasticity at point (P_0, Q_0) is defined as $E_D = (\%\ \Delta Q)/(\%\ \Delta P) = (\Delta Q/Q_0)/(\Delta P/P_0) = (\Delta Q/\Delta P)(P_0/Q_0)$. This implies that the elasticity at point (P_0, Q_0) is

$$E_D = b(P_0/Q_0)$$

Note that the elasticity depends upon the slope of the demand curve, but it also depends upon the specific price and quantity pair. Question 11 at the end of this chapter provides examples that allow you to
① apply this formula.

弹性与斜率不同

Elasticity Is Not the Same as Slope

We must always remember not to confuse the elasticity of a curve with its slope. This distinction is easily seen when we examine the straight-line demand curves that are often found in illustrative examples.

What is the price elasticity of a straight-line demand curve? Surprisingly, along a straight-line demand curve, the price elasticity varies from zero to infinity! Table 4-2 gives a detailed set of elasticity calculations using the same technique as that in Table 4-1. This table shows that linear demand curves start out with high price elasticity, where price is high and quantity is low, and end up with low elasticity, where price is low and quantity is high.

This illustrates an important point. When you see a demand curve in a diagram, it is not true that a steep slope for the demand curve means inelastic demand or that a flat slope signifies elastic demand. The slope is not the same as the elasticity because the demand curve's slope depends upon the *changes* in *P* and *Q*, whereas the elasticity depends upon the *percentage changes* in *P* and *Q*. The only exceptions are the polar cases of completely elastic and inelastic demands.

We also illustrate the point in Figure 4-4. This straight-line demand curve has elastic demand in the top region and inelastic demand in the bottom region.

Finally, look at Figure 4-2(*b*). This demand curve is clearly not a straight line with constant slope. Yet it has a constant demand elasticity of $E_D = 1$ because the percentage change in price is equal everywhere to the percentage change in quantity.

Elasticities cannot be inferred by slope alone. ②
The general rule for elasticities is that the elasticity can be calculated as the ratio of the length of the straight-line or tangent segment below the demand point to the length of the segment above the point.

---

① 图 4-5. 计算需求曲线的需求弹性

② 需求弹性值并不能从单一的斜率推算出来。通常的方法是通过求得直线或者需求点切线下方线段的长度与该点上方线段的长度之比获得。

Numerical Calculation of Elasticity Coefficient

Q	ΔQ	P	ΔP	$\frac{Q_1+Q_2}{2}$	$\frac{P_1+P_2}{2}$	$E_D = \frac{\Delta Q}{(Q_1+Q_2)/2} \div \frac{\Delta P}{(P_1+P_2)/2}$	
0		6					
	10		2	5	5	$\frac{10}{5} \div \frac{2}{5} = 5$	(elastic)
10		4					
	10		2	15	3	$\frac{10}{15} \div \frac{2}{3} = 1$	(unit-elastic)
20		2					
	10		2	25	1	$\frac{10}{25} \div \frac{2}{1} = 0.2$	(inelastic)
30		0					

TABLE 4-2. Calculation of Price Elasticity along a Linear Demand Curve ①

ΔP denotes the change in price, i.e., $\Delta P = P_2 - P_1$, while $\Delta Q = Q_2 - Q_1$. To calculate numerical elasticity, the percentage change of price equals price change, ΔP, divided by average price $[(P_1 + P_2)/2]$; the percentage change in output is calculated as ΔQ divided by average quantity, $[(Q_1 + Q_2)/2]$. Treating all figures as positive numbers, the resulting ratio gives numerical price elasticity of demand, E_D. Note that for a straight line, elasticity is high at the top, low at the bottom, and exactly 1 in the middle.

弹性和收益
ELASTICITY AND REVENUE

Many businesses want to know whether raising prices will raise or lower revenues. This question is of strategic importance for businesses like airlines, baseball teams, and magazines, which must decide whether it is worthwhile to raise prices and whether the higher prices make up for lower demand. Let's look at the relationship between price elasticity and total revenue.

total revenue 总收益

Total revenue is by definition equal to price times quantity (or $P \times Q$). If consumers buy 5 units at \$3 each, total revenue is \$15. If you know the price elasticity of demand, you know what will happen to total revenue when price changes:

1. When demand is price-inelastic, a price decrease reduces total revenue. ②
2. When demand is price-elastic, a price decrease increases total revenue. ③
3. In the borderline case of unit-elastic demand, a price decrease leads to no change in total revenue. ④

Elasticity Air 弹性机票

The concept of price elasticity is widely used today as businesses attempt to separate customers into groups with different elasticities. This technique has been extensively pioneered by the airlines (see the box that follows). Another example is software companies, which have a wide range of different prices for their products in an attempt to exploit different elasticities. For example, if you are desperate about buying a new operating system immediately, your elasticity is low and the seller will profit from charging you a relatively high price. On the other hand, if you are not in a hurry for an upgrade, you can search around for the best price and your elasticity is high. In this case, the seller will try to find a way to make the sale by charging a relatively low price.

Fly the Financial Skies of "Elasticity Air" ⑤

Understanding demand elasticities is worth billions of dollars each year to U.S. airlines. Ideally, airlines would like to charge a relatively high price to business travelers, while charging leisure

① 表 4-2. 线性需求曲线的价格弹性计算
② 当需求缺乏价格弹性时，价格的降低会减少总收益。
③ 当需求具有价格弹性时，价格的降低会增加总收益。
④ 在需求具有单位价格弹性的临界状态下，价格的降低对总收益没有任何影响。
⑤ 弹性机票与航空公司的运营

passengers a low-enough price to fill up all their empty seats. That is a strategy for raising revenues and maximizing profits.

But if they charge low-elasticity business travelers one price and high-elasticity leisure passengers a lower price, the airlines have a big problem—keeping the two classes of passengers separate. How can they stop the low-elasticity business travelers from buying up the cheap tickets meant for the leisure travelers and not let high-elasticity leisure flyers take up seats that business passengers would have been willing to buy?

The airlines have solved their problem by engaging in "price discrimination" among their different customers in a way that exploits different price elasticities. **Price discrimination** is the practice of charging different prices for the same service to different customers. Airlines offer discount fares for travelers who plan ahead and who tend to stay longer. One way of separating the two groups is to offer discounted fares to people who stay over a Saturday night—a rule that discourages business travelers who want to get home for the weekend. Also, discounts are often unavailable at the last minute because many business trips are unplanned expeditions to handle an unforeseen crisis—another case of price-inelastic demand. Airlines have devised extremely sophisticated computer programs to manage their seat availability as a way of ensuring that their low-elasticity passengers cannot benefit from discount fares.

农作物大丰收背后的悖论

The Paradox of the Bumper Harvest

We can use elasticities to illustrate one of the most famous paradoxes of all economics: the paradox of the bumper harvest. Imagine that in a particular year nature smiles on farming. A cold winter kills off the pests; spring comes early for planting; there are no killing frosts; rains nurture the growing shoots; and a sunny October allows a record crop to come to market. At the end of the year, family Jones happily [1]
settles down to calculate its income for the year. The ②
Joneses are in for a major surprise: *The good weather and bumper crop have lowered their and other farmers' incomes.*

How can this be? The answer lies in the elasticity of demand for foodstuffs. The demands for basic food products such as wheat and corn tend to be inelastic; for these necessities, consumption changes very little in response to price. But this means farmers as a whole receive less total revenue when the harvest is good than when it is bad. The increase in supply arising from an abundant harvest tends to lower the price. But the lower price doesn't increase quantity demanded very much. The implication is that a low price elasticity of food means that large harvests (high Q) tend to be associated with low revenue (low $P \times Q$).

These ideas can be illustrated by referring back to Figure 4-2. We begin by showing how to measure revenue in the diagram itself. Total revenue is the product of price times quantity, $P \times Q$. Further, the area of a rectangle is always equal to the product of its base times its height. Therefore, total revenue at any point on a demand curve can be found by examining the area of the rectangle determined by the P and Q at that point.

price discrimination
价格歧视

Next, we can check the relationship between elasticity and revenue for the unit-elastic case in Figure 4-2(*b*). Note that the shaded revenue region ($P \times Q$) is \$1000 million for both points A and B. The shaded areas representing total revenue are the same because of offsetting changes in the Q base and the P height. This is what we would expect for the borderline case of unit-elastic demand.

We can also see that Figure 4-2(*a*) corresponds to elastic demand. In this figure, the revenue rectangle expands from \$1000 million to \$1500 million when price is halved. Since total revenue goes up when price is cut, demand is elastic.

In Figure 4-2(*c*) the revenue rectangle falls from \$40 million to \$30 million when price is halved, so demand is inelastic.

Which diagram illustrates the case of agriculture, where a bumper harvest means lower total revenues for farmers? Clearly it is Figure 4-2(*c*). Which represents the case of vacation travel, where a lower price could mean higher revenues? Surely Figure 4-2(*a*).

Table 4-3 shows the major points to remember about price elasticities.

Cigarette Taxes and Smoking

What is the impact of cigarette taxes on smoking? Some people say, "Cigarettes are so addictive that people will pay anything for their daily habit." Implicitly, when you say that the quantity demanded does not respond to price, you are saying

[1] Family Jones：北美著名的家族农场，位于康州西南部的舍尔顿小城。爱尔兰人菲利普·琼斯（Philip Jones 1821~1912）150 多年前从英国威尔士移民而来，购置 400 英亩土地建立家族农场经营至今。由于受丰收悖论的影响，琼斯家族的第六代已经将农场精心调整成为集奶牛饲养、圣诞树种植、草莓和蓝莓种植、葡萄酒酿造、菜篮子工程等多种经营的大型综合农场。目前，社会在拭目以待，即将接班的琼斯家族第七代将把 Family Jones 带向何方。

② 令琼斯一家百思不得其解的是，风调雨顺的年景和大好的收成却降低了他们家和其他农民的收入。

Value of demand elasticity	Description	Definition	Impact on revenues
Greater than one ($E_D > 1$)	Elastic demand	Percentage change in quantity demanded *greater* than percentage change in price	Revenues *increase* when price decreases
Equal to one ($E_D = 1$)	Unit-elastic demand	Percentage change in quantity demanded *equal* to percentage change in price	Revenues *unchanged* when price decreases
Less than one ($E_D < 1$)	Inelastic demand	Percentage change in quantity demanded *less* than percentage change in price	Revenues *decrease* when price decreases

TABLE 4-3. Elasticities: Summary of Crucial Concepts ①

that the price elasticity is zero. What does the evidence say about the price elasticity of cigarette consumption?

We can use a historical example to illustrate the issue. New Jersey doubled its cigarette tax from 40 cents to 80 cents per pack. The tax increased the average price of cigarettes from \$2.40 to \$2.80 per pack. Economists estimate that the effect of the price increase alone was a decrease in New Jersey's cigarette consumption from 52 million to 47.5 million packs.

Using the elasticity formula, you can calculate that the short-run price elasticity is 0.59. (Make sure you can get the same number.) Similar estimates come from more detailed statistical studies. The evidence indicates that the price elasticity of cigarettes is definitely not zero.

供给的价格弹性
PRICE ELASTICITY OF SUPPLY

Of course, consumption is not the only thing that changes when prices go up or down. Businesses also respond to price in their decisions about how much to produce. Economists define the price elasticity of supply as the responsiveness of the quantity supplied of a good to its market price.

More precisely, the **price elasticity of supply** is ② the percentage change in quantity supplied divided by the percentage change in price.

As with demand elasticities, there are polar extremes of high and low elasticities of supply. Suppose the amount supplied is completely fixed, as in the case of perishable fish brought to market to be sold at whatever price they will fetch. This is the limiting case of zero elasticity, or completely inelastic supply, which is a vertical supply curve.

At the other extreme, say that a tiny cut in price will cause the amount supplied to fall to zero, while the slightest rise in price will coax out an indefinitely large supply. Here, the ratio of the percentage change in quantity supplied to percentage change in price is extremely large and gives rise to a horizontal supply curve. This is the polar case of infinitely elastic supply.

Between these extremes, we call supply elastic or inelastic depending upon whether the percentage change in quantity is larger or smaller than the percentage change in price. In the borderline unit-elastic case, where price elasticity of supply equals 1, the percentage increase of quantity supplied is exactly equal to the percentage increase in price.

You can readily see that the definitions of price elasticities of supply are exactly the same as those for price elasticities of demand. The only difference is that for supply the quantity response to price is positive, while for demand the response is negative.

The exact definition of the price elasticity of supply, E_S, is as follows:

$$E_S = \frac{\text{percentage change in quantity supplied}}{\text{percentage change in price}}$$

Figure 4-6 displays three important cases of supply elasticity: (a) the vertical supply curve, showing completely inelastic supply; (c), the horizontal supply curve, displaying completely elastic supply; and (b), an intermediate case of a straight line, going

① 表 4-3. 弹性：关键概念小结

② 更为准确地讲，**供给的价格弹性**即供给量变化的百分比除以价格变化的百分比。

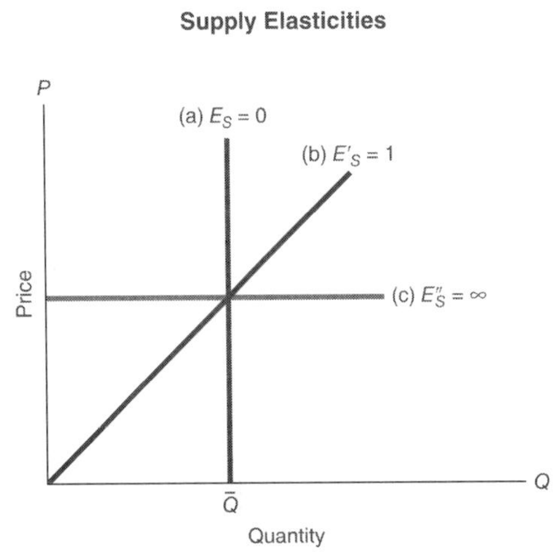

FIGURE 4-6. Supply Elasticity Depends upon Producer Response to Price ①

When supply is fixed, supply elasticity is zero, as in curve (a). Curve (c) displays an indefinitely large quantity response to price changes. Intermediate case (b) arises when the percentage quantity and price changes are equal.

through the origin, illustrating the borderline case of unit elasticity.[1]

What factors determine supply elasticity? The major factor influencing supply elasticity is the ease with which production in the industry can be increased. If all inputs can be readily found at going market prices, as is the case for the textile industry, then output can be greatly increased with little increase in price. This would indicate that supply elasticity is relatively large. On the other hand, if production capacity is severely limited, as is the case for gold mining, then even sharp increases in the price of gold will call forth but a small response in gold production; this would be inelastic supply.

Another important factor in supply elasticities ② is the time period under consideration. A given change in price tends to have a larger effect on amount supplied as the time for suppliers to respond increases. For very brief periods after a price increase, firms may be unable to increase their inputs of labor, materials, and capital, so supply may be very price-inelastic. However, as time passes and businesses can hire more labor, build new factories, and expand capacity, supply elasticities will become larger.

supply elasticities
供给弹性

We can use Figure 4-6 to illustrate how supply may change over time for the fishing case. Supply curve (a) might hold for fish on the day they are brought to market, where they are simply auctioned off for whatever they will bring. Curve (b) might hold for the intermediate run of a year or so, with the given stock of fishing boats and before new labor is attracted to the industry. Over the very long run, as new fishing boats are built, new labor is attracted, and new fish farms are constructed, the supply of fish might be very price-elastic, as in case (c) in Figure 4-6.

弹性在主要经济问题中的应用

B. APPLICATIONS TO MAJOR ECONOMIC ISSUES

Having laid the groundwork with our study of elasticities, we now show how these tools can assist our understanding of many of the basic economic trends and policy issues. We begin with one of the major transformations since the Industrial Revolution, the decline of agriculture. Next, we examine the implications of taxes on an industry, using the example of a gasoline tax. We then analyze the consequences of various types of government intervention in markets.

农业经济学
THE ECONOMICS OF AGRICULTURE

Our first application of supply-and-demand analysis comes from agriculture. The first part of this section lays out some of the economic fundamentals of the farm sector. Then we will use the theory of supply and demand to study the effects of government intervention in agricultural markets.

农业在长期相对衰落
Long-Run Relative Decline of Farming

③ Farming was once our largest single industry. A hundred years ago, half the American population lived and worked on farms, but that number has declined to less

[1] You can determine the elasticity of a supply curve that is not a straight line as follows: (*a*) Draw the straight line that lies tangent to the curve at a point, and (*b*) then measure the elasticity of that tangential straight line.

① 图 4-6. 供给弹性依赖生产商对价格的反应

② 供给弹性的另一个影响因素是观察中的时段长度。随着供给者反应时间增长，价格的既定变化趋向于对供给量产生更大影响。

③ 计算非线性供给曲线弹性的方法如下：(a) 过曲线上的一点作一条切线；(b) 测算出该切线的斜率。

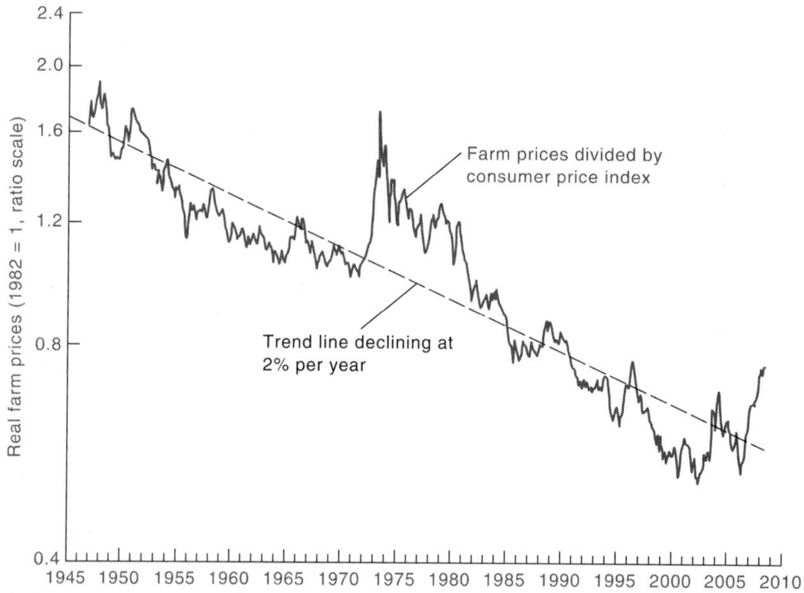

FIGURE 4-7. Prices of Basic Farm Products Have Declined Sharply ①

One of the major forces affecting the U.S. economy has been the decline in the relative ② prices of basic farm products—wheat, corn, soybeans, and the like. Over the past decades, farm prices have declined 2 percent per year relative to the general price level. The grain shortages since 2005 have slowed but not reversed the long slide in relative food prices. However, the recent upturn in food prices has contributed to inflation in most countries, and even to food riots in poor countries.

Source: Bureau of Labor Statistics.

than 3 percent of the workforce today. At the same time, prices for farm products have fallen relative to incomes and other prices in the economy. Figure 4-7 shows the steady decline of farm prices over the last half-century. While median family income has more than doubled, farm incomes have stagnated. Farm-state senators fret about the decline of the family farm.

A single diagram can explain the cause of the sagging trend in farm prices better than libraries of books and editorials. Figure 4-8 shows an initial equilibrium with high prices at point *E*. Observe what happens to agriculture as the years go by. Demand for food increases slowly because basic foods are necessities; the demand shift is consequently modest in comparison to growing average incomes.

What about supply? Although many people mistakenly think that farming is a backward business, statistical studies show that productivity (output per unit of input) has grown more rapidly in agriculture than in most other industries. Important advances include mechanization through tractors, combines, and cotton pickers; fertilization and irrigation; selective breeding; and development of genetically modified crops. All these innovations have vastly increased the productivity of agricultural inputs. Rapid productivity growth has increased supply greatly, as shown by the supply curve's shift from *SS* to *S′S′* in Figure 4-8.

What must happen at the new competitive equilibrium? Sharp increases in supply outpaced modest increases in demand, producing a downward trend in farm prices relative to other prices in the economy. And this is precisely what has happened in recent decades, as is seen in Figure 4-7.

① 图 4-7. 基本农产品价格的急剧下滑

② 基本农产品（诸如小麦、玉米、大豆等）价格的持续下滑已经成为影响美国经济的主要因素之一。在过去的几十年中，农产品的价格每年以相对于同期价格总水平 2% 的幅度下滑。虽然自 2005 年以来的粮食短缺状况适度减缓了下滑的速度，但并没有从根本上改变长期以来农产品相关价格持续下滑的态势。因此，近期粮食价格的攀升只是大多数国家的通货膨胀造成的，一些穷国因为粮食危机而爆发的骚乱也对此起了推波助澜的作用。

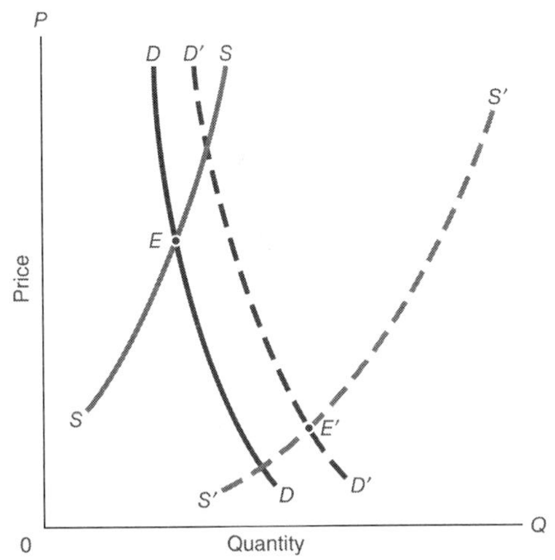

FIGURE 4-8. Agricultural Distress Results from Expanding Supply and Price-Inelastic Demand

Equilibrium at E represents conditions in the farm sector decades ago. Demand for farm products tends to grow more slowly than the impressive increase in supply generated by technological progress. Hence, competitive farm prices tend to fall. Moreover, with price-inelastic demand, farm incomes decline with increases in supply.

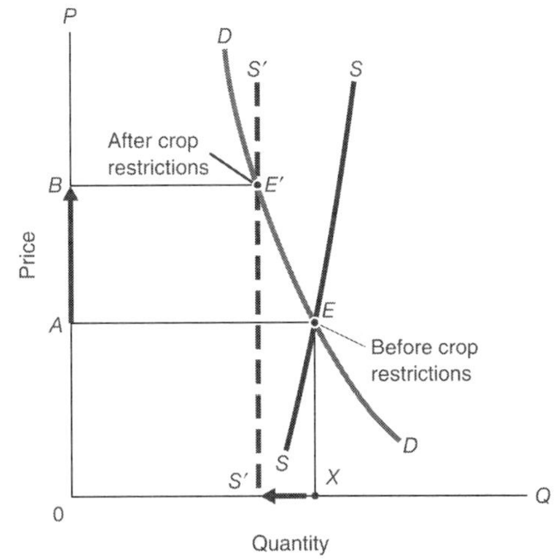

① **FIGURE 4-9. Crop-Restriction Programs Raise Both Price and Farm Income** ②

Before the crop restriction, the competitive market produces an equilibrium with low price at E. When government restricts production, the supply curve is shifted leftward to $S'S'$, moving the equilibrium to E' and raising price to B. Confirm that new revenue rectangle $0BE'S'$ is larger than original revenue rectangle $0AEX$—higher revenue being the result of inelastic demand.

Crop Restrictions. In response to falling incomes, farmers have often lobbied the federal government for economic assistance. Over the years, governments at home and abroad have taken many steps to help farmers. They have raised prices through price supports; they have curbed imports through tariffs and quotas; and they sometimes simply sent checks to farmers who agreed *not* to produce on their land.

How can *reducing production* actually *help* farmers? We can use the paradox of the bumper harvest to explain this result. Suppose the government requires every farmer to reduce production. As Figure 4-9 shows, this has the effect of shifting the supply curve up and to the left. Because the demand for food is inelastic, crop restrictions not only raise the price of crops but also tend to raise farmers' total revenues. Just as bumper harvests hurt farmers, crop restrictions raise farm incomes. Of course, consumers are hurt by the crop restrictions and higher prices—just as they would be if a flood or drought created a scarcity of food.

Restrictions on production are a typical example of government interference in individual markets. They often raise the income of one group at the expense of consumers. These policies are generally inefficient: the gain to farmers is less than the harm to consumers. ③

③ 限制生产是在单一产品市场中实施政府干预的典型案例。这些政策的结果通常是以增加消费者的消费成本来使一种特定产品的生产群体实现收入的增加。然而，这些政策总体上是无效的，农民所能增加的那一点收入比起对消费者产生的伤害是微不足道的。

税收对价格和数量的影响

IMPACT OF A TAX ON PRICE AND QUANTITY

Governments tax a wide variety of commodities—cigarettes, alcohol, imported goods, telephone services, and so on. We are often interested in determining who actually bears the burden of the tax, and here is where supply and demand are essential.

Take the example of gasoline taxes. In 2008, the average tax on gasoline in the United States was [4] around 50 cents per gallon. Many economists and environmentalists advocate much higher gasoline

① 图 4-8. 扩大供给和缺乏需求价格弹性共同导致农业的衰退

② 图 4-9. 限制种植计划使农产品价格和农民收入实现双增长

[4] 这一节是作者在微观经济学部分修改量最大的章节之一。实际上，美国的燃油税长期以来都维持在每加仑 50 美分左右。从 16 版以来，特别强调了巨大差别——欧洲国家平均每加仑征收 2~5 美元的税，借以抨击美国的能源消费战略。而本 19 版将此部分内容一并删除，只纵向讨论了美国自身的燃油税问题。纵然按书中所讨论的方案调到每加仑 1.80 美元，尚不及欧洲国家的最低限。更为有趣的是，本节第二段的例举还将本已长期执行的燃油税政策只微缩在了金融危机时期美国经济衰退不见底的 2008 年，令人不得不匪夷所思。更具讽刺意味的是，2008 年，美国政界和学术界提出所谓的未来第二次工业革命，即能源技术革命是美国面临以中国为代表的新兴国家严峻挑战的一年。

taxes for the United States. They point out that higher taxes would curb consumption, and thereby reduce global warming as well as lower our dependence on insecure foreign sources of oil. Some advocate raising gasoline taxes by $1 or $2 per gallon. What would be the impact of such a change?

For concreteness, suppose that the government decides to discourage oil consumption by levying a gasoline tax of $2 per gallon. Prudent legislators would of course be reluctant to raise gasoline taxes so sharply without a firm understanding of the consequences of such a move. They would want to know the incidence of the tax. *By* ***incidence*** *we mean* ① *the ultimate economic effect of a tax on the real incomes of producers and consumers.* Just because oil companies write a check for the taxes does not mean that the taxes in fact reduce their profits. By using supply and demand, we can analyze the exact incidence of the tax.

It could be that the burden of the tax is shifted forward to the consumers, which would occur if the retail price of gasoline goes up by the full $2 of the tax. Or perhaps consumers cut back so sharply on gasoline purchases that the burden of the tax is shifted back completely onto the oil companies. Where the actual impact lies between these extremes can be determined only from supply-and-demand analysis.

Figure 4-10 provides the answer. It shows the original pretax equilibrium at *E*, the intersection of the original *SS* and *DD* curves, at a gasoline price of $2 a gallon and total consumption of 100 billion gallons per year. We portray the imposition of a $2 tax in the retail market for gasoline as an upward shift of the supply curve, with the demand curve remaining unchanged. The demand curve does not shift because the quantity demanded at each retail price is unchanged by the gasoline-tax increase. Note that the demand curve for gasoline is relatively inelastic.

By contrast, the supply curve definitely does shift upward by $2. The reason is that producers are willing to sell a given quantity (say, 100 billion gallons) only if they receive the same *net* price as before. That is, at each quantity supplied, the market price must rise by exactly the amount of the tax. If producers had originally been willing to sell 80 billion gallons at $1.80 per gallon, they would still be willing to sell the same amount at a retail price of $3.80 (which, after subtracting the tax, yields the producers the same $1.80 per gallon).

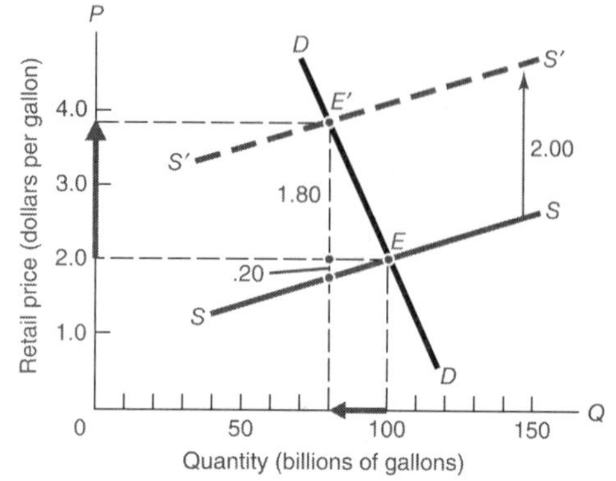

FIGURE 4-10. Gasoline Tax Falls on Both Consumer and Producer ②

What is the incidence of a tax? A $2 tax on gasoline shifts the supply curve up $2 everywhere, giving a new supply curve, *S'S'*, parallel to the original supply curve, *SS*. This new supply curve intersects *DD* at the new equilibrium, *E'*, where the price to consumers has risen 180 cents and the producers' price has fallen 20 cents. The green arrows show changes in *P* and *Q*. Note that consumers bear most of the burden of the tax.

What is the new equilibrium price? The answer is found at the intersection of the new supply and demand curves at *E'*, where *S'S'* and *DD* meet. Because of the supply shift, the retail price is higher. Also, the quantity supplied and demanded is reduced. If we read the graph carefully, we find that the new equilibrium price has risen from $2 to about $3.80. The new equilibrium output, at which supply and demand are in equilibrium, has fallen from 100 billion to about 80 billion gallons.

Who ultimately pays the tax? What is its incidence? Clearly the oil industry pays a small fraction, for it receives only $1.80 ($3.80 less the $2 tax) rather than $2. But the consumer bears most of the burden, with the retail price rising $1.80, because supply is relatively price-elastic whereas demand is relatively price-inelastic.

Subsidies. If taxes are used to discourage consumption of a commodity, subsidies are used to encourage

① 在此引入 **incidence** 一词，系指这一税种对生产商和消费者的实际收入所带来的最终的经济影响。

② 图 4-10. 由消费者和生产商共同承担的燃油税

production. One pervasive example of subsidies comes in agriculture. You can examine the impact of a subsidy in a market by shifting *down* the supply curve. The general rules for subsidies are exactly parallel to those for taxes.

General Rules on Tax Shifting. Gasoline is just a single example of how to analyze tax shifting. ① Using this apparatus, we can understand how cigarette taxes affect both the prices and the consumption of cigarettes; how taxes or tariffs on imports affect foreign trade; and how property taxes, social security taxes, and corporate-profit taxes affect land prices, wages, and interest rates.

The key issue in determining the incidence of a tax is the relative elasticities of supply and demand. If demand is inelastic relative to supply, as in the case of gasoline, most of the cost is shifted to consumers. By contrast, if supply is inelastic relative to demand, as is the case for land, then most of the tax is shifted to the suppliers. Here is the general rule for determining the incidence of a tax:

> The incidence of a tax denotes the impact of the tax on the incomes of producers and consumers. ② In general, the incidence depends upon the relative elasticities of demand and supply. (1) A tax is shifted *forward* to consumers if the *demand is inelastic* relative to supply. (2) A tax is shifted *backward* to producers if *supply is inelastic* relative to demand.

最低下限与最高上限
MINIMUM FLOORS AND MAXIMUM CEILINGS

Sometimes, rather than taxing or subsidizing a commodity, the government legislates maximum or minimum prices. History is full of examples. From biblical [3] days, governments have limited the interest rates that lenders can charge (so-called usury laws). In wartime, governments often impose wage and price controls to prevent spiraling inflation. During the energy crisis [4] of the 1970s, there were controls on gasoline prices. A few large cities, including New York, have rent controls on apartments.[2] Today, there are increasingly stringent limitations on the prices that doctors or hospitals can charge under federal health programs such as Medicare. Sometimes there are price floors, as in the case of the minimum wage.

These kinds of interferences with the laws of supply and demand are genuinely different from those in which the government imposes a tax and then lets the market act through supply and demand. Although political pressures always exist to keep prices down and wages up, experience has taught that sector-by-sector price and wage controls tend to create major economic distortions. Nevertheless, as Adam Smith well knew when he protested against mercantilist policies of an earlier age, most economic [5] systems are plagued by inefficiencies stemming from well-meaning but inexpert interferences with the mechanisms of supply and demand. Setting maximum or minimum prices in a market tends to produce surprising and sometimes perverse economic effects. Let's see why.

Two important examples of government intervention are the minimum wage and price controls on gasoline. These will illustrate the surprising side effects that can arise when governments interfere with market determination of price and quantity.

关于最低工资的争议
The Minimum-Wage Controversy

The minimum wage sets a minimum hourly rate that employers are allowed to pay workers. In the United States, the federal minimum wage began in 1938 when the government required that covered workers be paid at least 25 cents an hour. By 1947, the minimum wage was fully 65 percent of the average rate paid to manufacturing workers (see Figure 4-11). The most recent law increased the minimum wage to $7.25 per hour in 2009.

This is an issue that divides even the most eminent economists. For example, Nobel laureate Gary [6] Becker stated flatly, "Hike the minimum wage, and you put people out of work." Another group of Nobel ⑦ Prize winners countered, "We believe that the federal minimum wage can be increased by a moderate amount without significantly jeopardizing employment opportunities."

How can nonspecialists sort through the issues when the experts are so divided? How can we resolve these apparently contradictory statements? To begin with, we should recognize that statements on the

[2] See question 9 at the end of this chapter for an examination of rent controls.

[5] Mercantilist policies：重商主义政策。重商主义一词由亚当·斯密在《国富论》中提出并予以抨击。重商主义强调一个国家的国力来自贸易顺差，通过政府管制工、农、商，垄断对外贸易，抬高税率，掠夺殖民地的原料等手段来积累财富。

[6] 加里·贝克尔（Gary Becker），1930 年 12 月 2 日生于宾州中东部城市波茨维尔，1992 年诺贝尔经济学奖得主，当代西方最著名的经济学家之一，芝加哥学派的主要代表和新自由主义经济学派的重要成员。在几十年的研究和教学生涯中，他独树一帜地发动了一场以其开创或研究的新家庭经济学、人力资本理论、犯罪经济学等为主要内容的"贝克尔革命"。

---

① 税收转移的一般原则

② 税赋负担指出了税收对生产商和消费者的收入所带来的影响。总的来讲，影响程度取决于需求和供给的相关弹性：（1）如果需求相对于供给来讲缺乏弹性，则税赋向前向消费者转移；（2）如果供给相对于需求来讲缺乏弹性，则税赋向后向生产商转移。

[3] 从神权时代起，特指欧洲文艺复兴之前政教合一的社会。

[4] 在阿拉伯国家第四次中东战争失败后，其中的石油输出国收回石油标价权，猛然提高原油价格引起的能源危机。最终的结果是布雷顿森林体系（Bretton Woods System）的崩溃和随之而来的 1976 年生效的《牙买加体系》(Jamaica System)。随着黄金的非货币化，使美国成了这场危机实质上的受益者。

⑦ 而另几位诺奖得主却对此予以齐声反驳。

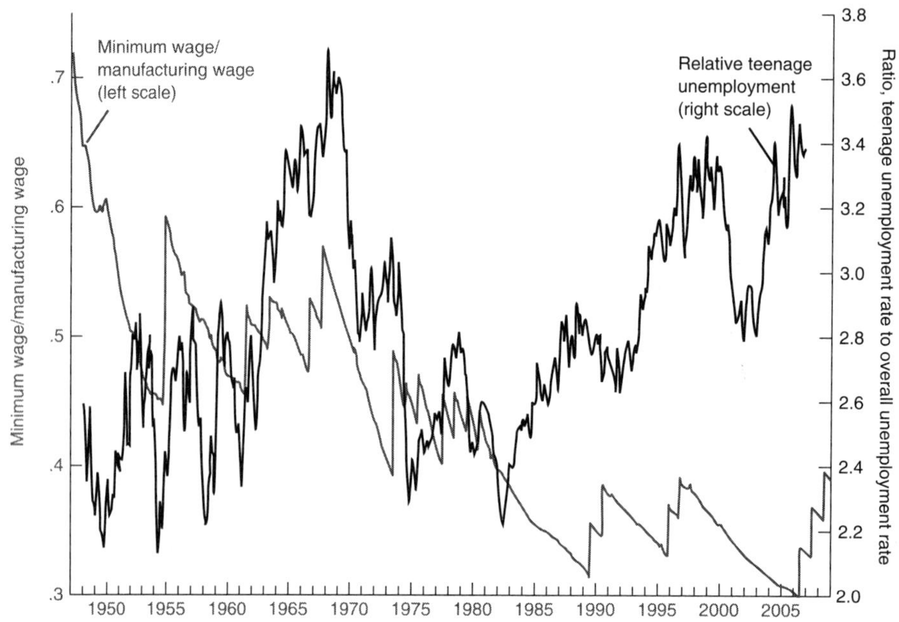

FIGURE 4-11. The Minimum Wage and Teenage Unemployment, 1947–2009 ① [2]

The green line shows the level of the minimum wage relative to average hourly earnings in manufacturing. Note how the minimum wage declined slowly relative to other wages over the last half-century. Additionally, the blue line shows the ratio of teenage unemployment to overall unemployment. Do you see any relationship between the two lines? What does this tell you about the minimum-wage controversy?

Source: Data are from the U.S. Department of Labor. Background on the minimum wage can be found at the Labor Department's website at *www.dol.gov/esa/minwage/q-a.htm.*

desirability of raising the minimum wage contain personal value judgments. Such statements might be informed by the best positive economics and still make different recommendations on important policy issues.

A cool-headed analysis indicates that the minimum-wage debate centers primarily on issues of interpretation rather than fundamental disagreements on empirical findings. Begin by looking at Figure 4-12, which depicts the market for unskilled workers. The figure shows how a minimum wage rate sets a floor for most jobs. As the minimum wage rises above the market-clearing equilibrium at *M,* the total number of jobs moves up the demand curve to *E,* so employment falls. The gap between labor supplied and labor demanded is shown as *U.* This represents the amount of unemployment.

Using supply and demand, we see that there is likely to be a rise in unemployment and a decrease in employment of low-skilled workers. But how large will these magnitudes be? And what will be the impact on the wage income of low-income workers? On these questions, we can look at the empirical evidence.

Most studies indicate that a 10 percent increase in the minimum wage would reduce employment of teenagers by between 1 and 3 percent. The impact on adult employment is even smaller. Some recent studies put the adult employment effects very close to zero, and one set of studies suggests that employment might even increase. So a careful reading of the

① 图 4-11. 1947-2009 年最低工资和青年失业状况

[2] Teenage unemployment：1985 年，联合国首次将青年界定为 15~24 岁的人群，Teenage unemployment 即指这个人群的失业状况，不宜按传统词典中的字面含义理解为 13~19 岁的“青少年”。

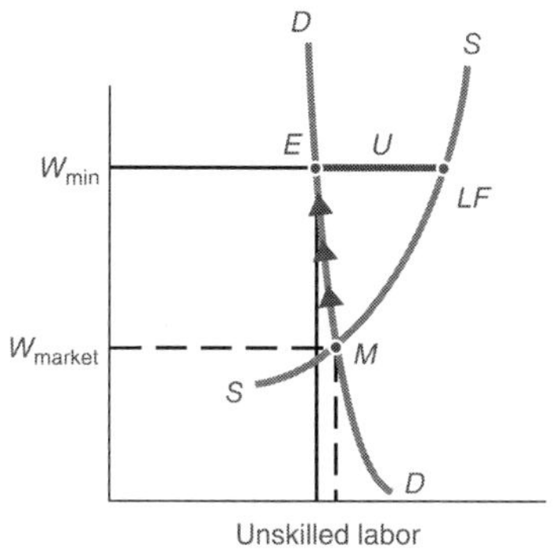

FIGURE 4-12. Effects of a Minimum Wage ①

Setting the minimum-wage floor at W_{min}, high above the free-market equilibrium rate at W_{market}, results in employment at *E*. Employment is reduced, as the arrows show, from *M* to *E*. Additionally, unemployment is *U*, which is the difference between labor supplied at *LF* and employment at *E*. If the demand curve is inelastic, increasing the minimum wage will increase the income of low-wage workers. To see this, shade in the rectangle of total wages before and after the minimum-wage increase.

quotations from the eminent economists indicates ②
that some economists consider small to be "insignificant" while others emphasize the existence of at least some job losses. Our example in Figure 4-12 shows a case where the *employment* decline (shown as the difference between *M* and *E*) is very small while the *unemployment* caused by the minimum wage (shown by the *U* line) is relatively large.

Figure 4-11 on page 78 shows the history of the minimum wage and teenage unemployment over the last half-century. With the declining power of the labor movement, the ratio of the minimum wage to the manufacturing wage declined from two-thirds in 1947 to around one-third in 2008. There was a slight upward trend in the relative unemployment rate of teenagers over this period. It is worth examining the pattern of changes to see whether you can detect an impact of the minimum wage on teenage unemployment.

Another factor in the debate relates to the impact of the minimum wage on incomes. Virtually every study concludes that the demand for low-wage workers is price-inelastic. The results we just cited indicate that the price elasticity is between 0.1 and 0.3. Given the elasticities just cited, a 10 percent increase in the minimum wage will increase the incomes of the affected groups by 7 to 9 percent. Figure 4-12 shows how the *incomes* of low-income workers rise despite the decline in their *total employment*. This can be seen by comparing the income rectangles under the equilibrium points *E* and *M*. (See question 8*e* at the end of this chapter.)

The impact on incomes is yet another reason why people may disagree about the minimum wage. Those who are particularly concerned about the welfare of low-income groups may feel that modest inefficiencies are a small price to pay for higher incomes. Others—who worry more about the cumulative costs of market interferences or about the impact of higher costs upon prices, profits, and international competitiveness—may hold that the inefficiencies are too high a price. Still others might believe that the minimum wage is an inefficient way to transfer buying power to low-income groups; they would prefer using direct income transfers or government wage subsidies rather than gumming up the wage system. How important are each of these three concerns to you? Depending upon your priorities, you might reach quite different conclusions on the advisability of increasing the minimum wage.

能源价格管制
Energy Price Controls

Another example of government interference comes when the government legislates a maximum price ceiling. This occurred in the United States in the 1970s, and the results were sobering. We return to our analysis of the gasoline market to see how price ceilings function.

a maximum price ceiling 价格上限

Let's set the scene. Suppose there is suddenly a ③
sharp rise in oil prices. This has occurred because of reduced cartel supply and booming demand, but it might also come about because of political disturbances in the Middle East due to war or revolution. Figure 3-1 on p. 46 showed the results of the interaction of supply and demand in oil markets.

Politicians, seeing the sudden jump in prices,
rise to denounce the situation. They claim that con- ④
sumers are being "gouged" by profiteering oil companies. They worry that the rising prices threaten to ignite an inflationary spiral in the cost of living. They fret about the impact of rising prices on the poor
and the elderly. They call upon the government to ⑤
"do something." In the face of rising prices, the U.S.

① 图 4-12. 最低工资的影响

② 因此，经过对一些著名经济学家所引用的数据进行仔细比对之后发现，他们中的一些人认为这些影响可以小到“可以忽略”的程度，而另外一些人则强调至少存在某种工作流失的情况。

③ 让我们来设想这样的一幕。

④ 他们宣称消费者正在遭受石油公司这些奸商们的“欺诈”。

⑤ 他们呼吁政府要“有所作为”。

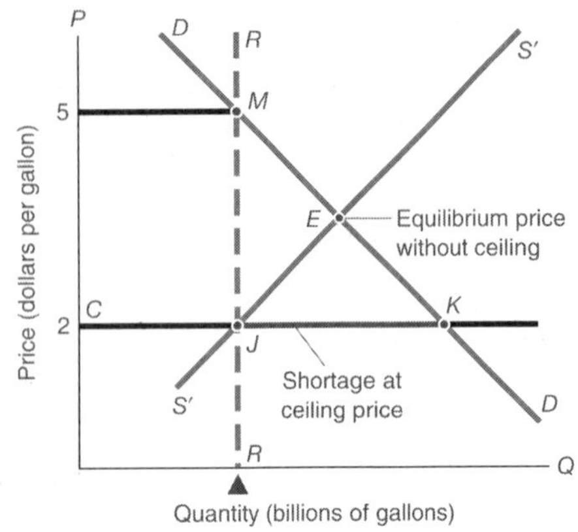

FIGURE 4-13. Price Controls Produce Shortages ① [2]

Without a legal price ceiling, price would rise to *E*. At the ceiling price of $2, supply and demand do not balance, and shortages break out. Some method of formal or informal rationing is needed to allocate the short supply and bring the actual demand down to supply at *RR*. If *CJ* ration coupons become marketable, this would imply a new supply curve of *RR*. At the ceiling price of $2, coupons would sell for $3, and the total price (coupons plus cash) would be $5.

government might be inclined to listen to these arguments and place a ceiling on oil prices, as it did from 1973 to 1981.

What are the effects of such a ceiling? Suppose the initial price of gasoline is $2 a gallon. Then, because of a drastic cut in oil supply, the market price of gasoline rises sharply. Now consider the gasoline market after the supply shock. In Figure 4-13, the post-shock equilibrium is given at point *E*. If the free market were allowed to operate, the market would clear with a price of perhaps $3.50. Consumers would complain but would willingly pay the higher price rather than go without fuel.

通过排队、配给券及资金进行配给

Rationing by the Queue, by Coupons, or by the Purse?

Enter the government, which passes a law setting the maximum price for gasoline at the old level of $2 a gallon. We can picture this legal maximum price as the ceiling-price line *CJK* in Figure 4-13.

At the legal ceiling price, quantities supplied and demanded do not match. The market does not "clear" because it is against the law for sellers to charge the equilibrium price. Consumers want more gasoline than producers are willing to supply at the controlled price. This is shown by the gap between *J* and *K*. There follows a period of frustration and shortage—a game of musical chairs in which somebody is left without gasoline when the pump runs dry.

The inadequate supply of gasoline must somehow be rationed. Initially, this may be done through a first-come, first-served approach. People wait in line—this is rationing by the "queue." Because people's time is valuable, the length of the line will serve as a kind of price that limits demand. We see rationing by the queue today in markets like health care, where the price of medical care is subsidized. This is a wasteful system because much valuable time is spent waiting in line just as a way of preventing prices from reaching equilibrium.

③ 有时，特别是在第二次世界大战期间，美国政府设计了一种更有效的非价格配给制度，此制度建立在合理分配或凭票配给的基础上。

Sometimes, particularly during large wars such as ③
World War II, governments design a more efficient system of nonprice rationing based on formal allocation or coupon rationing. Perhaps people get a gasoline ration that is distributed on the basis of the number of automobiles. Under coupon rationing, each customer must have a coupon as well as money to buy the goods—in effect, there are two kinds of money. When rationing is adopted, shortages disappear because demand is limited by the allocation of the coupons.

Just how do ration coupons change the supply-and-demand picture? In Figure 4-13, suppose the government hands out coupons corresponding to quantity *CJ*. Then, supply and the new demand balance at the ceiling price of $2.

Sometimes, the ration coupons will be marketable. Figure 4-13 shows a supply of coupons of *RR*. With this supply curve, the equilibrium price of gasoline is $5 per gallon, and the price of coupons is given by *JM*, or $3 per gallon. At this point, gasoline is once again a market commodity, where you pay $2 for the gasoline and $3 for a coupon. The price has indeed risen, but in an indirect way. Additionally, people with coupons have been given a new form of income in coupons. Note that because of the price control, quantity supplied is still at the old level, but the total price including coupons ($5) is actually

---

① 图 4-13. 价格管制造成的短缺

[2] 1973~1981 年的石油价格管制：美国政府从 1973 年 8 月开始对老油田生产的石油实行价格管制。同年 11 月 27 日，尼克松总统签署《紧急石油分配法案》（Emergency Petroleum Allocation Act），对原油产量采取“老油”和“新油”两级价格机制进行管制。1975 年 12 月 22 日生效的《能源政策与储备法案》（The Energy Policy and Conservation Act）再次提高了两类油的价格水平，但仍与国际油价每桶有 4~5 美元的差距。直至 1981 年 1 月 28 日，宣誓就职刚满一周的里根总统签署《解除石油价格和分配管制法案》（Petroleum Price and Allocation Decontrol Act），结束了对油价的控制，使美国国内油价首次与世界市场价格接轨。在管制期间，由于美国国内石油价格只相当于国际油价的一半，造成美国国内石油产量持续下降和勘探活动减少。同时，美国国内的低油价也变相鼓励了石油消费，使美国的石油消费量在 1978 年达到创纪录的水平。

higher than the original equilibrium price without rationing ($3.50).

All of this sounds complicated, and it is. History has shown that legal and illegal evasions of price controls grow over time. The inefficiencies eventually overwhelm whatever favorable impacts the controls might have on consumers. Particularly when there is room for ample substitution (i.e., when elasticities of supply or demand are high), price controls are costly, difficult to administer, and ineffective. Consequently, price controls on most goods are rarely used in most market economies.

There is a profound lesson here: Goods are always scarce. Society can never fulfill everyone's desires. In normal times, price itself rations the scarce supplies. When governments step in to interfere with supply and demand, prices no longer fill the role of rationers. Waste, inefficiency, and aggravation are likely companions of such interferences. ①

SUMMARY

A. Price Elasticity of Demand and Supply

1. Price elasticity of demand measures the quantitative response of demand to a change in price. Price elasticity of demand (E_D) is defined as the percentage change in quantity demanded divided by the percentage change in price. That is,

$$\text{Price elasticity of demand} = E_D = \frac{\text{percentage change in quantity demanded}}{\text{percentage change in price}}$$

In this calculation, the sign is taken to be positive, and P and Q are averages of old and new values.

2. We divide price elasticities into three categories: (*a*) Demand is elastic when the percentage change in quantity demanded exceeds the percentage change in price; that is, $E_D > 1$. (*b*) Demand is inelastic when the percentage change in quantity demanded is less than the percentage change in price; here, $E_D < 1$. (*c*) When the percentage change in quantity demanded exactly equals the percentage change in price, we have the borderline case of unit-elastic demand, where $E_D = 1$.
3. Price elasticity is a pure number, involving percentages; it should not be confused with slope.
4. The demand elasticity tells us about the impact of a price change on total revenue. A price reduction increases total revenue if demand is elastic; a price reduction decreases total revenue if demand is inelastic; in the unit-elastic case, a price change has no effect on total revenue.
5. Price elasticity of demand tends to be low for necessities like food and shelter and high for luxuries like snowmobiles and vacation air travel. Other factors affecting price elasticity are the extent to which a good has ready substitutes and the length of time that consumers have to adjust to price changes.
6. Price elasticity of supply measures the percentage change of output supplied by producers when the market price changes by a given percentage.

B. Applications to Major Economic Issues

7. One of the most fruitful arenas for application of supply-and-demand analysis is agriculture. Improvements in agricultural technology mean that supply increases greatly, while demand for food rises less than proportionately with income. Hence free-market prices for foodstuffs tend to fall. No wonder governments have adopted a variety of programs, like crop restrictions, to prop up farm incomes.
8. A commodity tax shifts the supply-and-demand equilibrium. The tax's incidence (or impact on incomes) will fall more heavily on consumers than on producers to the degree that the demand is inelastic relative to supply.
9. Governments occasionally interfere with the workings of competitive markets by setting maximum ceilings or minimum floors on prices. In such situations, quantity supplied need no longer equal quantity demanded; ceilings lead to excess demand, while floors lead to excess supply. Sometimes, the interference may raise the incomes of a particular group, as in the case of farmers or low-skilled workers. Often, distortions and inefficiencies result.

---

① 这里存在商品总是稀缺的这样一个深层次的问题。社会永远无法满足每一个人的欲望。多数情况下，价格本身起到了配给稀缺商品的作用。但当政府插手干预供给和需求时，价格即不再充当配给者的角色。这时，浪费、低效和短缺问题的加剧则势必成为这些干预行为的衍生物。

CONCEPTS FOR REVIEW

Elasticity Concepts

price elasticity of demand, supply
elastic, inelastic, unit-elastic demand
E_D = % change in Q/% change in P
determinants of elasticity
total revenue = $P \times Q$
relationship of elasticity and revenue change

Applications of Supply and Demand

incidence of a tax
distortions from price controls
rationing by price vs. rationing by the queue

FURTHER READING AND INTERNET WEBSITES

Further Reading

If you have a particular concept you want to review, such as elasticity, you can often look in an encyclopedia of economics, such as John Black, *Oxford Dictionary of Economics,* 2d ed. (Oxford, New York, 2002), or David W. Pearce, ed., *The MIT Dictionary of Modern Economics* (MIT Press, Cambridge, Mass., 1992). The most comprehensive encyclopedia, covering many advanced topics in seven volumes, is Steven N. Durlauf and Lawrence E. Blume, eds., *The New Palgrave Dictionary of Economics* (Macmillan, London, 2008), available in most libraries.

The minimum wage has generated a fierce debate among economists. A recent book by two labor economists presents evidence that the minimum wage has little effect on employment: David Card and Alan Krueger, *Myth and Measurement: The New Economics of the Minimum Wage* (Princeton University Press, Princeton, N.J., 1997).

Websites

There are currently no reliable online dictionaries for terms in economics. There are few good websites for understanding fundamental economic concepts like supply and demand or elasticities. The concise online encyclopedia of economics at *www.econlib.org/library/CEE.html* is generally reliable but covers only a small number of topics. Sometimes, the free site of the *Encyclopaedia Britannica* at *www.britannica.com* provides background or historical material. When all else fails, you can go to the online encyclopedia at *en.wikipedia.org/wiki/Main_Page,* but be warned that it is often unreliable. (For example, the 2008 definition of "price elasticity of demand" is close to incomprehensible.)

Current issues such as the minimum wage are often discussed in policy papers at the website of the Economic Policy Institute, a think tank focusing on economic issues of workers, at *www.epinet.org.*

QUESTIONS FOR DISCUSSION

1. "A good harvest will generally lower the income of farmers." Illustrate this proposition using a supply-and-demand diagram.
2. For each pair of commodities, state which you think is the more price-elastic and give your reasons: perfume and salt; penicillin and ice cream; automobiles and automobile tires; ice cream and chocolate ice cream.
3. "The price drops by 1 percent, causing the quantity demanded to rise by 2 percent. Demand is therefore elastic, with $E_D > 1$." If you change 2 to ½ in the first sentence, what two other changes will be required in the quotation?
4. Consider a competitive market for apartments. What would be the effect on the equilibrium output and price after the following changes (other things held equal)? In each case, explain your answer using supply and demand.
   a. A rise in the income of consumers
   b. A $10-per-month tax on apartment rentals
   c. A government edict saying apartments cannot rent for more than $200 per month
   d. A new construction technique allowing apartments to be built at half the cost
   e. A 20 percent increase in the wages of construction workers
5. Consider a proposal to raise the minimum wage by 10 percent. After reviewing the arguments in the chapter, estimate the impact upon employment and upon

the incomes of affected workers. Using the numbers you have derived, write a short essay explaining how *you* would decide if you had to make a recommendation on the minimum wage.

6. A conservative critic of government programs has written, "Governments know how to do one thing well. They know how to create shortages and surpluses." Explain this quotation using examples like the minimum wage or interest-rate ceilings. Show graphically that if the demand for unskilled workers is price-elastic, a minimum wage will decrease the total earnings (wage times quantity demanded of labor) of unskilled workers.
7. Consider what would happen if a tariff of $2000 were imposed on imported automobiles. Show the impact of this tariff on the supply and the demand, and on the equilibrium price and quantity, of American automobiles. Explain why American auto companies and autoworkers often support import restraints on automobiles.
8. Elasticity problems:
   a. The world demand for crude oil is estimated to have a short-run price elasticity of 0.05. If the initial price of oil were $100 per barrel, what would be the effect on oil price and quantity of an embargo that curbed world oil supply by 5 percent? (For this problem, assume that the oil-supply curve is completely inelastic.)
   b. To show that elasticities are independent of units, refer to Table 3-1. Calculate the elasticities between each demand pair. Change the price units from dollars to pennies; change the quantity units from millions of boxes to tons, using the conversion factor of 10,000 boxes to 1 ton. Then recalculate the elasticities in the first two rows. Explain why you get the same answer.
   c. Jack and Jill went up the hill to a gas station that does not display the prices. Jack says, "Give me $10 worth of gas." Jill says, "Give me 10 gallons of gas." What are the price elasticities of demand for gasoline of Jack and of Jill? Explain.
   d. Can you explain why farmers during a depression might approve of a government program requiring that pigs be killed and buried under the ground?
   e. Look at the impact of the minimum wage shown in Figure 4-12. Draw in the rectangles of total income with and without the minimum wage. Which is larger? Relate the impact of the minimum wage to the price elasticity of demand for unskilled workers.
9. No one likes to pay rent. Yet scarcities of land and urban housing often cause rents to soar in cities. In response to rising rents and hostility toward landlords, governments sometimes impose *rent controls*. These generally limit the increases on rent to a small year-to-year increase and can leave controlled rents far below free-market rents.
   a. Redraw Figure 4-13 to illustrate the impact of rent controls for apartments.
   b. What will be the effect of rent controls on the vacancy rate of apartments?
   c. What nonrent options might arise as a substitute for the higher rents?
   d. Explain the words of a European critic of rent controls: "Except for bombing, nothing is as efficient at destroying a city as rent controls." (*Hint:* What would happen to maintenance?)
10. Review the example of the New Jersey cigarette tax (p. 71). Using graph paper or a computer, draw supply and demand curves that will yield the prices and quantities before and after the tax. (Figure 4-10 shows the example for a gasoline tax.) For this example, assume that the supply curve is perfectly elastic. [*Extra credit:* A demand curve with constant price elasticity takes the form $Y = AP^{-e}$, where Y is quantity demanded, P is price, A is a scaling constant, and e is the (absolute value) of the price elasticity. Solve for the values of A and e which will give the correct demand curve for the prices and quantities in the New Jersey example.]
11. Review the algebra of demand elasticities on p. 69. Then assume that the demand curve takes the following form: $Q = 100 - 2P$.
   a. Calculate the elasticities at $P = 1$, 25, and 49.
   b. Explain why elasticity is different from slope using the formula.

CHAPTER

5 Demand and Consumer Behavior 需求和消费者行为

[1] 威廉·莎士比亚（William Shakespeare，1564.4.26~1616.4.23），英国诗人、剧作家，一生共创作 37 部戏剧、154 首十四行诗、两首长诗以及其他诗歌。《哈姆雷特》(*Hamlet, Prince of Denmark*)、《奥赛罗》(*Othello, the Moor of Venice*)、《李尔王》(*King Lear*) 和《麦克白》(*Macbeth*) 是著名的四大悲剧，创作于 1601~1607 年间。莎士比亚的戏剧与诗歌和莎氏后期的英王詹姆斯一世下令翻译并于 1611 年出版的《钦定圣经》(*King James Version of the Bible*，简称 KJV)，是西方现代文明的两大基石和取之不竭的思想源泉。

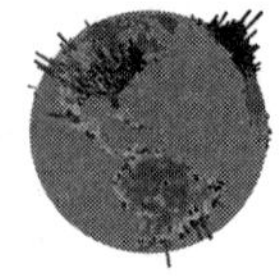

本段文字引自萨翁《李尔王》第二幕第四场中李尔王出场时的道白，此为该段道白的头两行。每行十个音节，莎氏习惯使用 Iambic Pentameter（抑扬格五步诗行，每步两个音节）。莎翁的戏剧基本使用这样的诗行，十四行诗则按其格律，全部为抑扬格五音步。

朱生豪先生的译文是国人公认的经典，先生对这两行的译文如下：

O, reason not the need: our basest beggars
Are in the poorest thing superfluous. [1]

Shakespeare,
King Lear

啊！不要跟我说什么需要不需要；最卑贱的乞丐，也有他的不值钱的身外之物；（接下注）

We make countless decisions every day about how to allocate our scarce money and time. Should we buy a pizza or a hamburger? Buy a new car or fix our old one? Spend our income today or save for future consumption? Should we eat breakfast or sleep late? As we balance competing demands and desires, we make the choices that define our lives.

The results of these individual choices are what underlie the demand curves and price elasticities that we met in earlier chapters. This chapter explores the basic principles of consumer choice and behavior. We shall see how patterns of market demand can be explained by the process of individuals' pursuing their most preferred bundle of consumption goods. We also will learn how to measure the benefits that each of us receives from participating in a market economy.

选择和效用理论 CHOICE AND UTILITY THEORY

In explaining consumer behavior, economics relies on the fundamental premise that people choose those goods and services they value most highly. To describe the way consumers choose among different consumption possibilities, economists a century ago developed the notion of *utility*. From the notion of utility, they were able to derive the demand curve and explain its properties.

What do we mean by "utility"? In a word, **utility** denotes satisfaction. More precisely, it refers to how consumers rank different goods and services. If basket A has higher utility than basket B for Smith, this ranking indicates that Smith prefers A over B. Often, it is convenient to think of utility as the subjective pleasure or usefulness that a person derives from consuming a good or service. But you should definitely resist the idea that utility is a psychological function or feeling that can be observed or measured. Rather, utility is a scientific construct that economists use to understand how rational consumers make decisions. We derive consumer demand functions from the assumption that people make decisions that give them the greatest satisfaction or utility.

In the theory of demand, we assume that people ② maximize their utility, which means that they choose the bundle of consumption goods that they most prefer.

边际效用和边际效用递减规律 *Marginal Utility and the Law of Diminishing Marginal Utility*

How does utility apply to the theory of demand? Say that consuming the first unit of ice cream gives you a certain level of satisfaction or utility. Now imagine consuming a second unit. Your total utility goes up

[1]（续）朱生豪（1912~1944），浙江嘉兴人，著名的莎士比亚戏剧翻译家和诗人，出生于一个破落的商人家庭，幼失父母，一生生活贫苦。1941 年日军进攻上海后，在被迫辗转流徙、贫病交加的逆境中，仍坚持翻译不止。先后共翻译莎士比亚戏剧 31 部，终因劳累过度患肺病于 1944 年 12 月 26 日的严寒中，在蜗居的阁楼斗室内伏案于尚未完成的莎氏戏剧译稿逝世，终年 32 岁。

② 在需求理论中，我们假定人们将最大化其效用，即人们总是选择自己最中意的一揽子消费品。

because the second unit of the good gives you some additional utility. What about adding a third and fourth unit of the same good? Eventually, if you eat enough ice cream, instead of adding to your satisfaction or utility, it makes you sick!

This leads us to the fundamental economic concept of marginal utility. When you eat an additional unit of ice cream, you will get some additional satisfaction or utility. The increment to your utility is called **marginal utility.**

marginal utility
边际效用

The expression "marginal" is a key term in economics and always means "additional" or "extra." Marginal utility denotes the additional utility you get from the consumption of an additional unit of a commodity. ①

One of the fundamental ideas behind demand theory is the **law of diminishing marginal utility.** This law states that the amount of extra or marginal utility declines as a person consumes more and more of a good.

law of diminishing marginal utility
边际效用递减规律

To understand this law, first remember that utility tends to increase as you consume more of a good. However, as you consume more and more, your total utility will grow at a slower and slower rate. This is the same thing as saying that your marginal utility (the extra utility added by the last unit consumed of a good) diminishes as more of a good is consumed.

The law of diminishing marginal utility states that, as the amount of a good consumed increases, the marginal utility of that good tends to decline. ②

(1) Quantity of a good consumed Q	(2) Total utility U	(3) Marginal utility MU
0	0	
		4
1	4	
		3
2	7	
		2
3	9	
		1
4	10	
		0
5	10	

TABLE 5-1. Utility Rises with Consumption ③

As we consume more of a good or service like pizza or concerts, total utility increases. The increment of utility from one unit to the next is the "marginal utility"—the extra utility added by the last extra unit consumed. By the law of diminishing marginal utility, the marginal utility falls with increasing levels of consumption.

效用的数字图表说明
A Numerical Example

We can illustrate utility numerically as in Table 5-1. The table shows in column (2) that total utility (U) enjoyed increases as consumption (Q) grows, but it increases at a decreasing rate. Column (3) measures marginal utility as the extra utility gained when 1 extra unit of the good is consumed. Thus when the individual consumes 2 units, the marginal utility is $7 - 4 = 3$ units of utility (call these units "utils").

Focus next on column (3). The fact that marginal utility declines with higher consumption illustrates the law of diminishing marginal utility.

Figure 5-1 on page 86 shows graphically the data on total utility and marginal utility from Table 5-1. In part (a), the blue blocks add up to the total utility at each level of consumption. In addition, the smooth blue curve shows the smoothed utility level for fractional units of consumption. It shows utility increasing, but at a decreasing rate. Figure 5-1(b) depicts marginal utilities. Each of the blue blocks of marginal utility is the same size as the corresponding block of total utility in (a). The straight blue line in (b) is the smoothed curve of marginal utility.

The law of diminishing marginal utility implies that the marginal utility (MU) curve in Figure 5-1(b) must slope downward. This is exactly equivalent to saying that the total utility curve in Figure 5-1(a) must look concave, like a dome.

Relationship of Total and Marginal Utility. Using Figure 5-1, we can easily see that the total utility of consuming a certain amount is equal to the sum of the marginal utilities up to that point. For example, assume that 3 units are consumed. Column (2) of Table 5-1 shows that the total utility is 9 units. In column (3) we see that the sum of the marginal utilities of the first 3 units is also $4 + 3 + 2 = 9$ units.

Examining Figure 5-1(b), we see that the total area under the marginal utility curve at a particular level of consumption—as measured either by blocks or by the area under the smooth MU curve—must

① "边际"一词是经济学的一条关键术语，通常指"新增"或"额外"之意。边际效用是指多消费一个单位的商品所新增的效用。

② 边际效用递减规律指随着消费的商品数量增加，该商品的边际效用趋于递减。

③ 表 5-1. 效用随消费量增加

[2] Utilitarianism：功利主义，亦称效益主义，属伦理学范畴，是道德哲学的理论之一，提倡追求“最大幸福”（maximum happiness），认为人应该做出能“最大善”（maximum goodness）的行为。所谓最大善，即依靠此行为所涉及的每个个体之苦乐感觉的总和。其中，每个个体都被视为具有相同分量，且快乐与痛苦是能够换算的，痛苦仅是“负的快乐”（negative happiness）。与一般伦理学学说之不同在于，功利主义不考虑一个人行为的动机与手段，仅考虑行为的结果对最大快乐值的影响。能增加最大快乐值的即是善，反之即为恶。

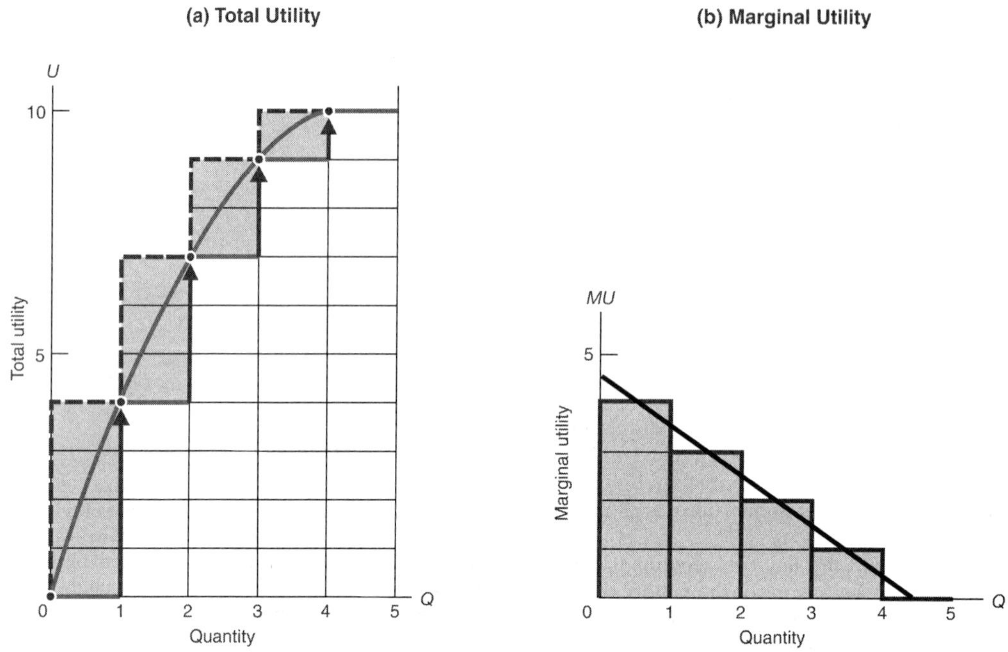

FIGURE 5-1. The Law of Diminishing Marginal Utility ① 图 5-1. 边际效用递减规律

Total utility in **(a)** rises with consumption, but it rises at a decreasing rate, showing diminishing marginal utility. This observation led early economists to formulate the law of downward-sloping demand.

The blue blocks show the extra utility added by each new unit. The fact that total utility increases at a decreasing rate is shown in **(b)** by the declining steps of marginal utility. If we make our units smaller, the steps in total utility are smoothed out and total utility becomes the smooth blue curve in **(a)**. Moreover, smoothed marginal utility, shown in **(b)** by the blue downward-sloping smooth curve, becomes indistinguishable from the slope of the smooth curve in **(a)**.

total utility
总效用

equal the height of the total utility curve shown for the same number of units in Figure 5-1(*a*).

Whether we examine this relationship using tables or graphs, we see that total utility is the sum of all the marginal utilities that were added from the beginning.

History of Utility Theory
Modern utility theory stems from *utilitari-* [2]
anism, which has been one of the major
currents of Western intellectual thought of
the last two centuries. The notion of utility arose soon
after 1700, as the basic ideas of mathematical probability
were being developed. Thus Daniel Bernoulli, a member [3]
of a brilliant Swiss family of mathematicians, observed in
1738 that people act as if the dollar they stand to gain in
a fair bet is worth less to them than the dollar they stand
to lose. This means that they are averse to risk and that
successive new dollars of wealth bring them smaller and
smaller increments of true utility.

An early introduction of the utility notion into the
social sciences was accomplished by the English philoso-
pher Jeremy Bentham (1748–1832). After studying legal [4]
theory, and under the influence of Adam Smith's doctrines,
Bentham turned to the study of the principles necessary

[4] 杰里米·本瑟姆（Jeremy Bentham，1748~1832），英国哲学家、经济学家、法学家，功利主义的创始人之一。本瑟姆认为人类的行为完全以快乐和痛苦为动机，人的本性是避苦趋乐，这既是道德原则，亦是立法原则。他将这一哲学思想贯穿于毕生所致力于的英国法律改革事业，是英国法律改革运动的先驱和领袖。

[3] 丹尼尔·伯努利（Daniel Bernoulli）1700 年 2 月 8 日生于荷兰，1782 年 3 月 17 日卒于瑞士巴塞尔，著名的伯努利家族中最杰出的数学家、物理学家、医学家，是数学物理方法的奠基人。伯努利家族是著名的瑞士数学家族，在 17~18 世纪，该家族代代相传，人才辈出，连续出现了十几位数学家，堪称神话。作者在这里所举案例即 1938 年丹尼尔经过仔细观察赌场的法罗牌游戏进行概率分析，得出了所谓“$(1/2)\times 2+(1/4)\times 4+(1/8)\times 8+(1/16)\times 16+\cdots=$ 无穷大！”的“伯努利效应”最大值公式。这个分析的核心思想即把钱和人们赋予钱的价值分开，主张任何财富的小幅度增长所带来的效用和之前拥有的财物数量成反比。伯努利当时由于与父亲的著作权纠纷被同是著名数学家的父亲约翰（John Bernoulli，1667~1748）赶出家门，到圣彼得堡工作。因此，“伯努利效应”系用俄文写成，utility 一词译自俄文，是伯努利的最大贡献之一。

for drawing up social legislation. He proposed that society should be organized on the "principle of utility," which he defined as the "property in any object . . . to produce pleasure, good or happiness or to prevent . . . pain, evil or unhappiness." All legislation, according to Bentham, should be designed on utilitarian principles, to promote "the greatest happiness of the greatest number." Among his other legislative proposals were quite modern-sounding ideas about crime and punishment in which he suggested that raising the "pain" to criminals by harsh punishments would deter crimes.

Bentham's views about utility seem familiar to many people today. But they were revolutionary 200 years ago because they emphasized that social and economic policies should be designed to achieve certain practical results, whereas legitimacy at that time was usually based on tradition, the divine right of kings, or religious doctrines. Today, many political thinkers defend their legislative proposals with utilitarian notions of what will make the largest number of people best off.

The next step in the development of utility theory came when the neoclassical economists—such as William Stanley Jevons (1835–1882)—extended Bentham's utility concept to explain consumer behavior. Jevons thought economic theory was a "calculus of pleasure and pain," and he developed the theory that rational people would base their consumption decisions on the extra or marginal utility of each good.

The ideas of Jevons and his coworkers led directly to the modern theories of ordinal utility and indifference curves developed by Vilfredo Pareto, John Hicks, R. G. D. Allen, Paul Samuelson, and others in which the Benthamite ideas of measurable cardinal utility are no longer needed.

需求曲线的衍生
DERIVATION OF DEMAND CURVES

等边际法则
The Equimarginal Principle

Having explained utility theory, we now apply that theory to explain consumer demand and to understand the nature of demand curves.

We assume that each consumer maximizes utility, which means that the consumer chooses the most preferred bundle of goods from what is available. We also assume that consumers have a certain income and face given market prices for goods.

What would be a sensible rule for choosing the preference bundle of goods in this situation? Certainly, I would not expect that the last egg brings the same marginal utility as the last pair of shoes, for shoes cost much more per unit than eggs. A satisfactory rule would be: If good A costs twice as much as good B, then buy good A only when its marginal utility is at least twice as great as good B's marginal utility.

This leads to the *equimarginal principle* that I should arrange my consumption so that the last dollar spent on each good is bringing me the same marginal utility.

Equimarginal principle: The fundamental condition of maximum satisfaction or utility is the equimarginal principle. It states that a consumer will achieve maximum satisfaction or utility when the marginal utility of the last dollar spent on a good is exactly the same as the marginal utility of the last dollar spent on any other good. ⑥

Why must this condition hold? If any one good gave more marginal utility per dollar, I would increase my utility by taking money away from other goods
① and spending more on that good—until the law of
[2] diminishing marginal utility drove its marginal utility per dollar down to equality with that of other goods. If any good gave less marginal utility per dollar than the common level, I would buy less of it until the marginal utility of the last dollar spent on it had risen back to the common level. The common marginal ⑦ utility per dollar of all commodities in consumer equilibrium is called the *marginal utility of income.* It
[3] measures the additional utility that would be gained
[4] if the consumer could enjoy an extra dollar's worth
[5] of consumption.

This fundamental condition of consumer equilibrium can be written in terms of the marginal utilities (*MU*s) and prices (*P*s) of the different goods in the following compact way:

$$\frac{MU_{\text{good 1}}}{P_1} = \frac{MU_{\text{good 2}}}{P_2} = \frac{MU_{\text{good 3}}}{P_3} = \cdots = MU \text{ per \$ of income}$$

为什么需求曲线向下倾斜
Why Demand Curves Slope Downward

Using the fundamental rule for consumer behavior, we can easily see why demand curves slope downward. For simplicity, hold the common marginal

[2] 威廉姆·斯坦利·杰文斯（William Stanley Jevons，1835~1882），著名的英国经济学家和逻辑学家，边际效用学派的创始人之一，数理经济学派早期代表人物。

[3] 维尔弗雷多·帕累托（Vilfredo Pareto，1848~1923），意大利经济学家、社会学家，经典精英理论的创始人，社会系统论的代表人物，对经济学、社会学和伦理学均做出了很多重要的贡献。帕累托因对意大利20%的人口拥有80%的财产的观察和分析而著名，即被后人概括的帕累托法则/分布（Pareto Principle，80/20法则，也称二八定律），就是著名的“关键的少数（vital few）和次要的多数（trivial many）”的分析方法，它被应用在自然科学和社会科学的很多领域。帕累托还提出了帕累托效率/最优、质量控制七工具之一的帕累托图表等概念，并用效用分析的方法（即后来通用的无差异曲线）帮助发展了个体经济学（*Individual Economics*）。同时，帕累托的理论还对墨索里尼的统治和意大利法西斯主义的发展起了推波助澜的作用。

[4] 约翰·希克斯（John Hicks，1904~1989），英国经济学家，1972年诺贝尔经济学奖得主，20世纪最重要和最具影响力的经济学家之一，一般均衡理论的创始人，IS/LM模型的设计者之一。希克斯爵士的主要贡献还包括微观经济学的消费者需求理论［需求补偿函数（*compensated demand function*），亦称 *Hicksian demand function*，即以他的名字命名］和福利经济学等。

① the neoclassical economists：新古典主义经济学家

[5] 罗伊·乔治·道格拉斯·艾伦（R. G. D. Allen：Sir Roy George Douglas Allen，1906~1983），英国司令勋章（CBE，Commander of the Order of the British Empire）爵士，不列颠学会（FBA, Fellow of the British Academy）会员，英国经济学家、数学家和统计学家；是使用数学方法解决经济学问题的先驱之一，局部弹性替代法（*partial elasticity of substitution*）的提出者。

⑥ **等边际法则**：最大程度满足或者效用最大化的根本条件是等边际法则。即指当消费者花费在某种商品上的最后一美元所得到的边际效用恰好与花费在任何其他商品上的最后一美元所得到的边际效用相同时，消费者所获得的满足感最大，或者说其效用达到最大化。

⑦ 在消费者的消费处于均衡状态时，用于所有商品消费的每一美元所得到的共同边际效用称作收入的边际效用。它衡量的是消费者追加一美元消费时，可以得到的额外的效用。

utility per dollar of income constant. Then increase the price of good 1. With no change in quantity consumed, the first ratio (i.e., $MU_{\text{good 1}}/P_1$) will be below the *MU* per dollar of all other goods. The consumer will therefore have to readjust the consumption of good 1. The consumer will do this by (*a*) lowering the consumption of good 1, thereby (*b*) raising the *MU* of good 1, until (*c*) at the new, reduced level of consumption of good 1, the new marginal utility per dollar spent on good 1 is again equal to the *MU* per dollar spent on other goods.

A higher price for a good reduces the consumer's ① desired consumption of that commodity; this shows why demand curves slope downward.

闲暇和时间的最优分配

Leisure and the Optimal Allocation of Time

[3] 温斯顿·丘吉尔（Winston Churchill），1940~1945 年及 1951~1955 年期间两度任英国首相，英国伟大的政治家和演说家，20 世纪最重要的政治领袖之一，带领英国获得第二次世界大战的胜利。同时也是多才多艺的画家、作家以及记者，历史上掌握英语单词词汇量最多的人之一，1953 年诺贝尔文学奖得主，2002 年被 BBC 评选为有史以来最伟大的英国人。本段话为丘吉尔于 1927 年担任英国下议院议员时写给时任英国首相斯坦利·鲍德温（Stanley Baldwin，1867~1947）的一封信中所讲。

A Spanish toast to a friend wishes "health, wealth, and the time to enjoy them." This saying captures the idea that we must allocate our time budgets in much the same way as we do our dollar budgets. Time is the great equalizer, for even the richest person has but 24 hours a day to "spend." Let's see how our earlier analysis of allocating scarce dollars applies to time.

Consider leisure, often defined as "time which one can spend as one pleases." Leisure brings out our personal eccentricities. The seventeenth-century philosopher Francis Bacon held that the purest of [2] human pleasures was gardening. The British statesman Winston Churchill wrote of his holiday: "I have [3] had a delightful month building a cottage and dictating a book: 200 bricks and 2000 words a day."

We can apply utility theory to the allocation of time as well as money. Suppose that, after satisfying all your obligations, you have 3 hours a day of free time and can devote it to gardening, laying bricks, or writing history. What is the best way to allocate your time? Let's ignore the possibility that time spent on some of these activities might be an investment that will enhance your earning power in the future. Rather, assume that these are all pure consumption or utility-yielding pursuits. The principles of consumer choice suggest that you will make the best use of your time when you equalize the marginal utilities of the last minute spent on each activity.

To take another example, suppose you want to maximize your knowledge in your courses but you have only a limited amount of time available. Should you study each subject for the same amount of time? Surely not. You may find that an equal study time for economics, history, and chemistry will not yield the same amount of knowledge in the last minute. If the last minute produces a greater marginal knowledge in chemistry than in history, you would raise your total knowledge by shifting additional minutes from history to chemistry, and so on, until the last minute yields the same incremental knowledge in each subject.

The same rule of maximum utility per hour can be applied to many different areas of life, including engaging in charitable activities, improving the environment, or losing weight. It is not merely a law of economics. It is a law of rational choice.

Are Consumers Wizards? The View from Behavioral Economics

All of this discussion makes it sound as if consumers are mathematical wizards who routinely make calculations of marginal utility to the tenth decimal place and solve complicated systems of equations in their everyday lives.

This unrealistic view is definitely not what we assume in economics. We know that most decisions are made in a routine and intuitive way. We may have Cheerios and [4] yogurt for breakfast every day because they are not too expensive, are easy to find in the store, and slake our morning hunger.

Rather, what we assume in consumer demand theory is that consumers are reasonably consistent in their tastes and actions. We expect that people do not flail around and make themselves miserable by constantly making mistakes. If most people act consistently most of the time, avoiding erratic changes in buying behavior and generally choosing their most preferred bundles, our theory of demand will provide a reasonably good approximation to the facts.

As always, however, we must be alert to situations where irrational or inconsistent behavior crops up. We know that people make mistakes. People sometimes buy useless gadgets or are bilked by unscrupulous sales pitches. A new area of research is *behavioral economics,* which recognizes that people have limited time and memory, that information is incomplete, and that patterns of irrational-looking behavior are persistent. This approach allows for the possibility that imperfect information, psychological biases, and costly decision making may lead to poor decisions.

---

① 一种商品的较高价格削弱了消费者对该种商品的消费欲望。这解释了需求曲线为什么向下倾斜。

[2] 弗兰西斯·培根（Francis Bacon，1561~1626），英国哲学家、作家。此段话的含义出自培根文集中《论园艺》（*Of Gardens*）篇。

[4] Cheerios：美国著名的早餐燕麦圈品牌，初名 *Cheeri Oats*，后更此名，以避与另一著名的食品厂商 *Quaker Oats Company* 共用 Oats 之嫌；它分别由通用食品公司（General Mills）设于明尼苏达州金色山谷和纽约布法罗的两家工厂生产和销售，并在英国、澳大利亚和新西兰等国家有大量的市场。2009 年，由于"连续食用六周可以降低 4% 的胆固醇"的不实广告用语被美国联邦食品药品署（FDA）以"未批准新药"予以处罚。

Behavioral economics explains why households save too little for retirement, why stock market bubbles occur, and how used-car markets behave when people's information is limited. A significant recent example illustrating behavioral principles came when millions of people took out "subprime mortgages" to buy homes in the 2000s. They did not read or could not understand the fine print, and as a result many people defaulted on their mortgages and lost their homes, triggering a major financial crisis and an economic downturn. It turns out that poor consumers were not the only people who could not read the fine print, however, for they were joined by banks, hedge-fund managers, bond-rating firms, and thousands of investors who bought assets that they did not understand.

Behavioral economics joined the mainstream in 2001 and 2002 when Nobel Prizes were awarded for economic research in this area. George Akerlof (University of California at Berkeley) was cited for developing a better understanding of the role of asymmetric information and the market for "lemons." Daniel Kahneman (Princeton University) and Vernon L. Smith (George Mason University) received the prize for "the analysis of human judgment and decision-making . . . and the empirical testing of predictions from economic theory by experimental economists."

效用理论的应用分析
Analytical Developments in Utility Theory

We pause here to provide an elaboration of some of the advanced issues behind the concept of utility and its application to demand theory. Economists today generally reject the notion of a cardinal (or measurable) utility that people feel or experience when consuming goods and services. Utility does not ring up like numbers on a gasoline pump.

Rather, what counts for modern demand theory is the principle of **ordinal utility.** Under this approach, consumers need to determine only their preference ranking of bundles of commodities. Ordinal utility asks, "Do I prefer a pastrami sandwich to a chocolate milk shake?" A statement such as "Bundle A is preferred to bundle B"—which does not require that we know how much A is preferred to B—is called ordinal, or dimensionless. Ordinal variables are ones that we can rank in order, but for which there is no measure of the quantitative difference between the situations. We might rank pictures in an exhibition by order of beauty without having a quantitative measure of beauty. Using only such ordinal preference rankings, we can establish firmly the general properties of market demand curves described in this chapter and in its appendix.

The discerning reader will wonder whether the equimarginal principle describing consumer equilibrium behavior implies cardinal utility. In fact, it does not; only ordinal measures are needed. An ordinal utility measure is one that we can stretch while always maintaining the same greater-than or less-than relationship (like measuring with a rubber band). Examine the marginal condition for consumer equilibrium. If the utility scale is stretched (say, by doubling or multiplying times 3.1415), you can see that all the numerators in the condition are changed by exactly the same amount, so the consumer equilibrium condition still holds.

[1] For certain special situations the concept of *cardinal,* or dimensional, utility is useful. An example of a cardinal measure comes when we say that the speed
[2] of a plane is six times that of a car. People's behav-
[3] ior under conditions of uncertainty is today analyzed using a cardinal concept of utility. This topic will be examined further when we review the economics of risk, uncertainty, and gambling in Chapter 11.

Our treatment of utility in the equimarginal principle assumed that goods can be divided into indefi-
[4] nitely small units. However, sometimes indivisibility of units is important and cannot be glossed over. Thus, Hondas cannot be divided into arbitrarily small portions the way juice can. Suppose I buy one Honda, but definitely not two. Then the additional utility of
[5] the first car is enough larger than the additional utility of the same number of dollars spent elsewhere to induce me to buy this first unit. The additional utility that the second Honda would bring is enough less to ensure I do not buy it. When indivisibility matters,
[6] our equality rule for equilibrium can be restated as an inequality rule.

另一种分析方法：替代效应和收入效应
AN ALTERNATIVE APPROACH: SUBSTITUTION EFFECT AND INCOME EFFECT

The concept of marginal utility has helped explain the fundamental law of downward-sloping demand. But over the last few decades, economists have developed an alternative approach to the analysis of demand—one that makes no mention of marginal utility. This alternative approach uses "indifference

behavioral economics
行为经济学

subprime mortgages
次级按揭贷款，即次揭

[1] 乔治·阿克尔洛夫（George Akerlof），1940年6月17日出生于康州的纽黑文，和迈克尔·斯宾斯（Michael Spence）、约瑟夫·斯蒂格利茨（Joseph Stiglitz）一起由于在"对信息不对称的市场进行的分析"领域所做出的重要贡献，分享了2001年诺贝尔经济学奖。著名的柠檬市场模型（注："柠檬"一词在美国俚语中表示次品或有缺陷的产品，如美国某些州的有缺陷汽车召回法即 *Lemon Laws*）是阿克尔洛夫做出的主要贡献，即卖方能向买方推销低质量商品等现象的存在是因为市场双方各自所掌握的不对称信息所造成的。

[2] 丹尼尔·卡内曼（Daniel Kahneman），以色列裔美国心理学家，1934年3月5日生于特拉维夫。他将心理学的综合洞察分析方法应用于经济学的研究，创立了行动经济学的研究学派，与弗农·史密斯（Vernon L. Smith）分享了2002年诺贝尔经济学奖。

[3] 弗农·史密斯（Vernon L. Smith），1927年1月1日出生于美国堪萨斯州的威奇托，实验经济学的奠基人，与丹尼尔·卡内曼分获了2002年诺贝尔经济学奖。史密斯设计和实践了一系列实验方法，即在可控的实验室条件下，模仿人们在市场上的相互行为和其他形式的相互影响的方法，有效地揭示了经济理论的发展，并给经济学实验确定了标准，证明了可选择性市场制度的重要性。

[4] 效用理论的应用分析
本节内容是作者一改16~18版，特别是17和18两版的内容框架，予以重点修订和新加的。这样的修订从另一个角度说明了效用理论在经济学中的重要性。

[5] Cardinal utility：基数效用，效用的大小可以用基数（1，2，3，……）来表示，可以计量并加总求和，故亦称可计量效用，与只在序数的层面上才有意义的序数效用相反。基数效用论（*Theory of Cardinal Utility*）即马歇尔（Alfred Marshall，1842~1924，近代英国著名的经济学家，新古典经济学派的创始人和标志性人物）的价值论（*Theory of Value*），是建立在效用可以直接计量的假设（假设效用量是可以计量，边际效用量随着物品数量的增加而递减）之上的边际效用学说，这一学说对西方经济学产生了深远的影响，是马歇尔创立新古典经济学的一个重要的理论来源，而新古典经济学则是现代西方经济学的基础。

[6] Ordinal utility：序数效用，效用作为一种心理现象无法计量，也不能加总求和，采用无差异曲线分析法，只能表示出满足程度的高低与顺序，用序数（第一，第二，第三，……）来表示，由英国经济学家、1972年诺贝尔经济学奖得主约翰·希克斯于1934年在其与罗伊·艾伦在《经济学杂志》（*Economica*）发表的著名文章《价值理论的重新审视》（*A Reconsideration of the Theory of Value*）中提出，它对基数效用起了补充和完善的作用。

curves," which are explained in the appendix to this chapter, to rigorously and consistently produce the major propositions about consumer behavior. This approach also helps explain the factors that tend to make the responsiveness of quantity demanded to price—the price elasticity of demand—large or small.

Indifference analysis asks about the substitution effect and the income effect of a change in price. By looking at these, we can see why the quantity demanded of a good declines as its price rises.

替代效应 Substitution Effect

The substitution effect is the most obvious factor for explaining downward-sloping demand curves. If the price of coffee goes up while other prices do not, then coffee has become relatively more expensive. When coffee becomes a more expensive beverage, less coffee and more tea or cola will be bought. Similarly, because sending electronic mail is cheaper and quicker than sending letters through the regular mail, people are increasingly relying on electronic mail for correspondence. More generally, the **substitution effect** says that when the price of a good rises, ① consumers will tend to substitute other goods for the more expensive good in order to satisfy their desires more inexpensively.

Consumers, then, behave the way businesses do when the rise in price of an input causes firms to substitute low-priced inputs for high-priced inputs. By this process of substitution, businesses can produce a given amount of output at the least total cost. Similarly, when consumers substitute less expensive goods for more expensive ones, they are buying a given amount of satisfaction at lower cost.

收入效应 Income Effect

A second impact of a price change comes through its effect on real income. The term *real income* means the actual quantity of goods that your money income can buy. When a price rises and money income is fixed, real income falls because the consumer cannot afford to buy the same quantity of goods as before. This produces the **income effect,** which is the change [2] in the quantity demanded that arises because a price change lowers consumer real incomes. Most goods respond positively to higher incomes, so the income effect will normally reinforce the substitution effect in producing a downward-sloping demand curve.

We can obtain a quantitative measure of the ③ income effect using a new concept, **income elasticity.** This term denotes the percentage change in quantity demanded divided by the percentage change in income, holding other things, such as prices, constant.

$$\text{Income elasticity} = \frac{\%\text{ change in quantity demanded}}{\%\text{ change in income}}$$

High income elasticities, such as those for airline travel or yachts, indicate that the demand for these goods rises rapidly as income increases. Low income elasticities, such as for potatoes or used furniture, denote a weak response of demand to increases in income.

Calculation of Income Elasticity

Suppose you are a city planner for Santa Fe, New Mexico, and you are concerned about the growth in the demand for water consumption by households in that arid region. You make inquiries and find the following data for 2000: The population is 62,000; the projected growth rate of the population is 20 percent per decade; per capita annual water consumption in 2000 was 1000 gallons; per capita incomes are projected to grow by 25 percent over the next decade; and the income elasticity of water use per capita is 0.50. You then estimate the water needs for 2010 (with unchanged prices) as

Water consumption in 2010

$$= \text{population in 2000} \times \text{population growth factor}$$
$$\times \text{ per capita water use}$$
$$\times [1 + (\text{income growth} \times \text{income elasticity})]$$
$$= 62{,}000 \times 1.2 \times 1000 \times (1 + 0.25 \times 0.50)$$
$$= 83{,}700{,}000$$

From these data, you project a growth in total household water use of 35 percent from 2000 to 2010.

Income and substitution effects combine to determine the major characteristics of demand curves of different commodities. Under some circumstances the resulting demand curve is very price-elastic, as where the consumer has been spending a good deal on the commodity and ready substitutes are available. In this case both the income and the

---

① 从更普遍的意义来讲，**替代效应**指的是当某种商品的价格上涨时，消费者倾向于用其他商品来替代较为昂贵的该种商品，从而以较为便宜的价格来满足自身的欲望。

[2] 这样的情况就导致了**收入效应**的发生，即由于价格的变化使得消费者的实际收入降低，从而引起需求量发生变化。

本版对 *income effect* 的定义较 16~18 版做了彻底的修订，更为简练和准确。

③ 我们可以引入**收入弹性**这一新的概念对收入效应进行量化测量。

substitution effects are strong and the quantity demanded responds strongly to a price increase.

But consider a commodity like salt, which requires only a small fraction of the consumer's budget. Salt is not easily replaceable by other items and is needed in small amounts to complement more important items. For salt, both income and substitution effects are small, and demand will tend to be price-inelastic.

从个人需求到市场需求
FROM INDIVIDUAL TO MARKET DEMAND

Having analyzed the principles underlying a single individual's demand for coffee or electronic mail, we next examine how the entire market demand derives from the individual demand. *The demand curve for a* ① *good for the entire market is obtained by summing up the quantities demanded by all the consumers.* Each consumer has a demand curve along which the quantity demanded can be plotted against the price; it generally slopes downward and to the right. If all consumers were exactly alike in their demands and if there were 1 million consumers, we could think of the market demand curve as a millionfold enlargement of each consumer's demand curve.

In fact, of course, people differ in their tastes. Some have high incomes, some low. Some greatly desire coffee; others prefer tea. To obtain the total market demand curve, we calculate the sum total of what all the different consumers consume at each price. We then plot that total amount as a point on the market demand curve. Alternatively, we might construct a numerical demand table by summing the quantities demanded by all individuals at each market price.

As a matter of convention, we label *individual* demand and supply curves with lowercase letters (*dd* and *ss*), while using uppercase letters (*DD* and *SS*) for the *market* demand and supply curves.

The market demand curve is the sum of individual demands at each price. Figure 5-2 shows how to add individual *dd* demand curves horizontally to get the market *DD* demand curve. ②

FIGURE 5-2. Market Demand Derived from Individual Demands ③

We add all individual consumers' demand curves to get the market demand curve. At each price, such as $5, we add quantities demanded by each person to get the market quantity demanded. The figure shows how, at a price of $5, we add horizontally Smith's 1 unit demanded to Brown's 2 units to get the market demand of 3 units.

① 把所有消费者对某种商品的需求量汇总在一起，就可以得到该种商品对于整个市场的需求曲线。

② 市场的需求曲线是在每一价格水平上的个体需求之和。图 5-2 说明了如何将个体的 *dd* 需求曲线依水平方向相加，就可以得到市场需求曲线 *DD*。

③ 图 5-2. 在个体需求的基础上推导而来的市场需求

需求的移动
Demand Shifts

We know that changes in the price of coffee affect the quantity of coffee demanded. We know this from budget studies, from historical experience, and from examining our own behavior. We discussed briefly in Chapter 3 some of the important nonprice determinants of demand. We now review the earlier discussion in light of our analysis of consumer behavior.

An increase in income tends to increase the amount we are willing to buy of most goods. Necessities tend to be less responsive than most goods to income changes, while luxuries tend to be more responsive to income. And there are a few anomalous goods, known as inferior goods, for which purchases may shrink as incomes increase because people can afford to replace them with other, more desirable goods. Soup bones, intercity bus travel, and black-and-white TVs are examples of inferior goods for many Americans today.

soup bones 煲汤的骨头

What does all this mean in terms of the demand curve? The demand curve shows how the quantity of a good demanded responds to a change in its own price. But the demand is also affected by the prices of other goods, by consumer incomes, and by special influences. The demand curve was drawn on the assumption that these other things were held constant. But what if these other things change? Then the whole demand curve will shift to the right or to the left.

Figure 5-3 illustrates changes in factors affecting demand. Given people's incomes and the prices for other goods, we can draw the demand curve for coffee as *DD*. Assume that price and quantity are at point *A*. Suppose that incomes rise while the prices of coffee and other goods are unchanged. Because coffee is a normal good with a positive income elasticity, people will increase their purchases of coffee. Hence the demand curve for coffee will shift to the right, say, to *D′D′*, with *A′* indicating the new quantity demanded of coffee. If incomes should fall, then we would expect a reduction in demand and in quantity bought. This downward shift we illustrate by *D″D″* and by *A″*.

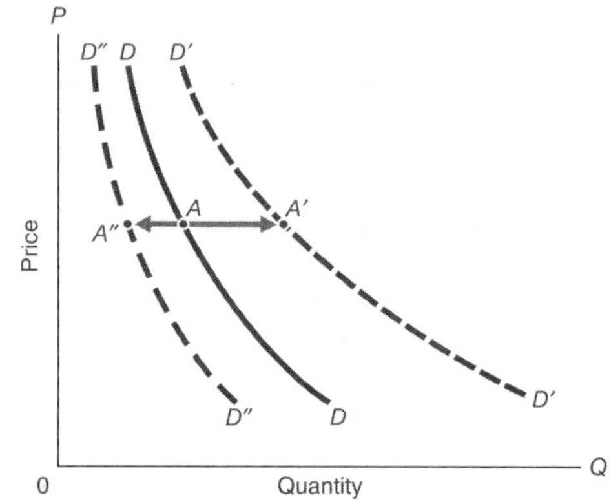

FIGURE 5-3. Demand Curve Shifts with Changes in Income or in Other Goods' Prices ①

As incomes increase, consumers generally want more of a good, thus increasing demand or shifting demand outward (explain why higher incomes shift *DD* to *D′D′*). Similarly, a rise in the price of a substitute good increases or shifts out the demand curve (e.g., from *DD* to *D′D′*). Explain why a decrease in income would generally shift demand to *D″D″*. Why would a decrease in chicken prices shift hamburger demand to *D″D″*?

替代品和互补品
Substitutes and Complements

Everyone knows that raising the price of beef will decrease the amount of beef demanded. We have seen that it will also affect the demand for other commodities. For example, a higher price for beef will increase the demand for substitutes like chicken. A higher beef price may lower the demand for goods like hamburger buns and ketchup that are used along with beef hamburgers. It will probably have little effect on the demand for economics textbooks.

We say, therefore, that beef and chicken are substitute products. Goods A and B are **substitutes** if an increase in the price of good A will increase the demand for substitute good B. Hamburgers and hamburger buns, or cars and gasoline, on the other hand, are complementary products; they are called **complements** because an increase in the price of good A causes a decrease in the demand for its complementary good B. In between are **independent goods,** such as beef and textbooks, for which a price change for one has no effect on the demand for the other. Try classifying the pairs turkey and cranberry sauce, oil and coal, college and textbooks, shoes and shoelaces, salt and shoelaces.

independent goods 独立品

Say Figure 5-3 represented the demand for beef. A fall in the price of chickens may well cause consumers to buy less beef; the beef demand curve would therefore shift to the left, say, to *D″D″*. But what if the price of hamburger buns were to fall? The resulting change on *DD*, if there is one, will be in the direction of increased beef purchases, a rightward shift of the demand curve.

① 图 5-3. 随着收入或者其他商品价格的变化而发生的需求曲线移动

Why do we see this difference in response? Because chicken is a substitute product for beef, while hamburger buns are complements to beef.

Review of key concepts: ①

- The **substitution effect** occurs when a higher price leads to substitution of other goods for the good whose price has risen.
- The **income effect** is the change in the quantity demanded of a good because the change in its price has the effect of changing a consumer's real income.
- **Income elasticity** is the percentage change in quantity demanded of a good divided by the percentage change in income.
- Goods are **substitutes** if an increase in the price of one increases the demand for the other.
- Goods are **complements** if an increase in the price of one decreases the demand for the other.
- Goods are **independent** if a price change for one has no effect on the demand for the other.

价格弹性和收入弹性的经验估计

Empirical Estimates of Price and Income Elasticities

For many economic applications, it is essential to have numerical estimates of price elasticities. For example, an automobile manufacturer will want to know the impact on sales of the higher car prices that result from installation of costly pollution-control equipment; a college needs to know the impact of higher tuition rates on student applications; and a publisher will calculate the impact of higher textbook prices on its sales. All these applications require a numerical estimate of price elasticity.

Similar decisions depend on income elasticities. A government planning its road or rail network will estimate the impact of rising incomes on automobile travel; the federal government must calculate the effect of higher incomes on energy consumption in designing policies for air pollution or global warming; in determining the necessary investments for generating capacity, electrical utilities require income elasticities for estimating electricity consumption.

Economists have developed useful statistical techniques for estimating price and income elasticities. The quantitative estimates are derived from market data on quantities demanded, prices, incomes, and other variables. Tables 5-2 and 5-3 show selected estimates of elasticities.

Commodity	Price elasticity
Tomatoes	4.60
Green peas	2.80
Legal gambling	1.90
Taxi service	1.24
Furniture	1.00
Movies	0.87
Shoes	0.70
Legal services	0.61
Medical insurance	0.31
Bus travel	0.20
Residential electricity	0.13

TABLE 5-2. Selected Estimates of Price Elasticities of Demand ②

Estimates of price elasticities of demand show a wide range of variation. Elasticities are generally high for goods for which ready substitutes are available, like tomatoes or peas. Low price elasticities exist for those goods like electricity which are essential to daily life and which have no close substitutes.

Source: Heinz Kohler, *Microeconomics: Theory and Applications* (Heath, Lexington, Mass., 1992).

Commodity	Income elasticity
Automobiles	2.46
Owner-occupied housing	1.49
Furniture	1.48
Books	1.44
Restaurant meals	1.40
Clothing	1.02
Physicians' services	0.75
Tobacco	0.64
Eggs	0.37
Margarine	−0.20
Pig products	−0.20
Flour	−0.36

TABLE 5-3. Income Elasticities for Selected Products ③

Income elasticities are high for luxuries, whose consumption grows rapidly relative to income. Negative income elasticities are found for "inferior goods," whose demand falls as income rises. Demand for many staple commodities, like clothing, grows proportionally with income.

Source: Heinz Kohler, *Microeconomics: Theory and Applications* (Heath, Lexington, Mass., 1992).

---

① **关键概念小结：**

- 当某种商品的价格上升以后，这种更高的价格就会导致其他商品来替代该种商品，这时**替代效应**发生。
- **收入效应**是由于某种商品价格的变化影响到消费者的实际收入发生变化之后，引起该商品的需求量发生的变化。
- **收入弹性**是某种商品需求量变化的百分比除以收入变化的百分比。
- 如果一种商品的价格上升导致另一种商品的需求增加，则这两种商品互为**替代品**。
- 如果一种商品的价格上升导致另一种商品的需求减少，则这两种商品为**互补品**。
- 如果一种商品价格的变化对另一种商品的需求没有任何影响，则这两种商品均为**独立品**。

② 表 5-2. 某些商品的需求价格弹性估算

③ 表 5-3. 某些商品的收入弹性

上瘾物品的经济学问题
THE ECONOMICS OF ADDICTION

In a free-market economy, the government generally lets people decide what to buy with their money. If some want to buy expensive cars while others want to buy expensive houses, we assume that they know what is best for them and that in the interests of personal freedom the government should respect their preferences.

merit goods 无害商品

demerit goods 有害商品

In some cases, but sparingly and with great hesitation, the government decides to overrule private adult decisions. These are cases of *merit goods,* whose consumption is thought intrinsically worthwhile, and the opposite, which are *demerit goods,* whose consumption is deemed harmful. For these goods, we recognize that some consumption activities have such serious effects that overriding individuals' private decisions may be desirable. Today, most societies provide for free public education and emergency health care; on the other hand, society also penalizes or forbids consumption of such harmful substances as cigarettes, alcohol, and heroin.

Among the most controversial areas of social policy are demerit goods involving addictions. An addiction is a pattern of compulsive and uncontrolled use of a substance. The heavy smoker or the heroin user may bitterly regret the acquired habit, but such habits are extremely difficult to break after they have become established. A regular user of cigarettes or heroin is much more likely to desire these substances than is a nonuser. Moreover, the demands for addictive substances are quite price-inelastic.

illegal drugs 非法毒品

The markets for addictive substances are big business. Consumer expenditures on tobacco products in 2007 were $95 billion, while total expenditures on alcoholic beverages were $155 billion. Numbers for illegal drugs involve guesswork, but recent estimates of spending on illegal drugs place the total at around $75 billion annually.

Consumption of these substances raises major public policy issues because addictive substances may injure users and often impose costs and harms on society. The harms to users include around 450,000 premature deaths annually, along with a wide variety of medical problems attributable to smoking; 10,000 highway fatalities a year attributed to alcohol; and failures in school, job, and family, along with high levels of AIDS, from intravenous heroin use. Harms to society include the predatory crime that addicts of high-price drugs engage in; the costs of providing subsidized medical care to those who consume drugs, cigarettes, or tobacco; the rapid spread of communicable diseases, especially AIDS and pneumonia; and the tendency of existing users to recruit new users.

One policy approach, often followed in the United States, is to prohibit the sale and use of addictive substances and to enforce prohibition with criminal sanctions. Economically, prohibition can be interpreted as a sharp upward shift in the supply curve. After the upward shift, the price of the addictive substance is much higher. During Prohibition (1920–1933), alcohol [1] prices were approximately 3 times higher than before. Estimates are that cocaine currently sells for at least 20 times its free-market price.

What is the effect of supply restrictions on the consumption of addictive substances? And how does the prohibition affect the injuries to self and to society? To answer these questions, we need to consider the nature of the demand for addictive substances. The evidence indicates that casual consumers of illegal drugs have cheap substitutes like alcohol and tobacco and thus will have relatively high price elasticity of demand. By contrast, hard-core users are often addicted to particular substances and have price-inelastic demands.

We can illustrate the market for addictive substances in Figure 5-4. The demand curve *DD* is extremely price-inelastic for established users. Now consider a policy of discouraging drug use. One approach, used for cigarettes, is to impose a large tax. As we saw in the previous chapter, this can be analyzed as an upward shift in the supply curve. A policy of prohibition such as is used for illegal substances has the same effect of shifting the supply curve from *SS* to *S′S′*.

Because demand is price-inelastic, quantity demanded will decline very little. At the higher price, total spending on drugs increases sharply. For illegal drugs, the required outlays may be so great that the user engages in predatory crime. The results, in the view of two economists who have studied the subject, are that "the market in illegal drugs promotes crime, destroys inner cities, spreads AIDS, corrupts law enforcement officials and politicians, produces and exacerbates poverty, and erodes the moral fabric of society."

A different case would arise for highly price-sensitive consumers such as casual users. For example,

---

[1] Prohibition（1920~1933）：在美国历史上被称为“贵族试验运动”的禁酒令。在戒酒运动的压力下，美国参议院于 1917 年 12 月 18 日提出关于禁酒的第 18 修正案，在经过 36 个州批准之后，于 1919 年 1 月 16 日获得通过，并于 1920 年 1 月 16 日生效，至 1933 年 12 月 23 日第 21 修正案批准，该禁酒令废止。在禁酒令期间，全美禁止生产、销售和运输烈性酒。

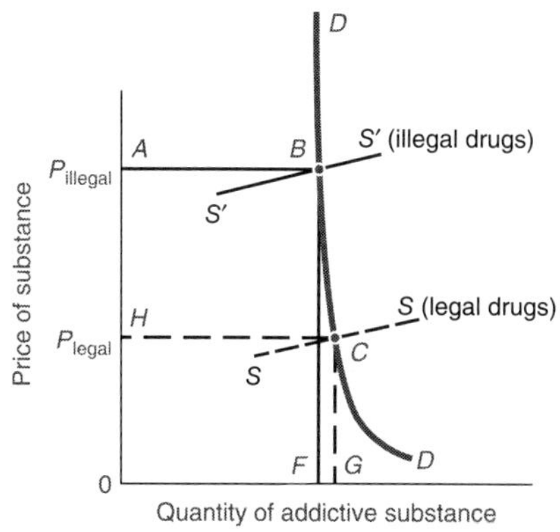

FIGURE 5-4. Market for Addictive Substances ①

The demand for addictive substances is price-inelastic for heavy smokers or hard-core users of drugs like heroin or cocaine. As a result, if prohibition or heavy taxation shifts supply from *SS* to *S′S′*, total spending on drugs will rise from 0*HCG* to 0*ABF*. For drugs that are highly price-inelastic, this implies that spending on drugs will rise when supply is restrained. What will happen to criminal activity after prohibition if a substantial fraction of the income of addicts is obtained by theft? Can you see why some people would argue for reduced drug enforcement or even decriminalization for addictive drugs?

a teenager might experiment with an addictive substance if it is affordable, while a high price (accompanied by low availability) would reduce the number of people who start down the road to addiction. In this case, supply restraints are likely to lower use sharply and to reduce spending on addictive substances. (See question 10 at the end of this chapter for further discussion.)

One of the major difficulties with regulating addictive substances comes because of the patterns of substitution among them. Many drugs appear to be close substitutes rather than complements. As a result, experts caution, raising the price of one substance may drive users to other harmful substances. For example, states that have criminal penalties for marijuana use tend to have higher teenage consumption of alcohol and tobacco.

Clearly, social policy toward addictive substances raises extremely complex issues. But the economic theory of demand provides some important insights into the impacts of alternative approaches. First, it suggests that raising the prices of harmful addictive substances can reduce the number of casual users who will be attracted into the market. Second, it cautions us that many of the negative consequences of illegal drugs result from the prohibition of addictive substances rather than from their consumption per se. Many thoughtful observers conclude with the paradoxical observation that the overall costs of addictive substances—to users, to other people, and to the ravaged inner cities in which the drug trade thrives—would be lower if government prohibitions were relaxed and the resources currently devoted to supply restrictions were instead put into treatment and counseling.

价值悖论
THE PARADOX OF VALUE

More than two centuries ago, in *The Wealth of Nations,* Adam Smith posed the paradox of value:

> Nothing is more useful than water; but it will scarce purchase anything. A diamond, on the contrary, has scarce any value in use; but a very great quantity of other goods may frequently be had in exchange for it. ②

In other words, how is it that water, which is essential to life, has little value, while diamonds, which are generally used for conspicuous consumption, command an exalted price?

Although this paradox troubled Adam Smith 200 years ago, we can imagine a dialogue between a probing student and a modern-day Adam Smith as follows:

Student: How can we resolve the paradox of value?

Modern Smith: The simplest answer is that the supply and demand curves for water intersect at a very low price, while the supply and demand for diamonds yield a very high equilibrium price.

Student: But you have always taught me to go behind the curves. Why do supply and demand for water intersect at such a low price and for diamonds at a high price?

Modern Smith: The answer is that diamonds are very scarce and the cost of getting extra ones is high, while water is relatively abundant and costs little in many areas of the world.

Student: But where is utility in this picture?

① 图 5-4. 上瘾商品市场

② 没有什么能比水更有用的物品了。但是，用水几乎购买不到任何东西。相反，钻石几乎没有任何使用价值，但却经常可以用它交换到巨大数量的其他物品［见亚当・斯密《国富论》第一篇第 4 章“论货币的起源与使用”（*An Inquiry into the Nature and Causes of the Wealth of Nations,* “Of the Origin and Use of Money”，Adam Smith, 1776）］。

Modern Smith: You are right that this answer still does not reconcile the cost information with the equally valid fact that the world's water is vastly more critical than the world's supply of diamonds. So, we need to add a second truth: The total utility from water consumption does not determine its price or demand. Rather, water's price is determined by its *marginal* utility, by the usefulness of the *last* glass of water. Because there is so much water, the last glass sells for very little. Even though the first few drops are worth life itself, the last few are needed only for watering the lawn or washing the car.

Student: Now I get it. The theory of economic value is easy to understand if you just remember that in economics the tail wags the dog. It is the tail of marginal utility that wags the dog of prices.

Modern Smith: Precisely! An immensely valuable commodity like water sells for next to nothing because its last drop is worth next to nothing.

We can restate this dialogue as follows: The more there is of a commodity, the less is the relative desirability of its last little unit. It is therefore clear why water has a low price and why an absolute necessity like air can become a free good. In both cases, it is the large quantities that pull the marginal utilities so far down and thus reduce the prices of these vital commodities.

消费者剩余
CONSUMER SURPLUS

The paradox of value emphasizes that the recorded monetary value of a good (measured by price times quantity) may be a misleading indicator of the total economic value of that good. The measured economic value of the air we breathe is zero, yet air's contribution to welfare is immeasurably large.

The gap between the total utility of a good and its total market value is called **consumer surplus.** The surplus arises because we "receive more than we pay for" as a result of the law of diminishing marginal utility. ①

We have consumer surplus basically because we pay the same amount for each unit of a commodity that we buy, from the first to the last. We pay the same price for each egg or glass of water. Thus we pay for *each* unit what the *last* unit is worth. But by our fundamental law of diminishing marginal utility, the earlier units are worth more to us than the last. Thus, we enjoy a surplus of utility on each of these earlier units.

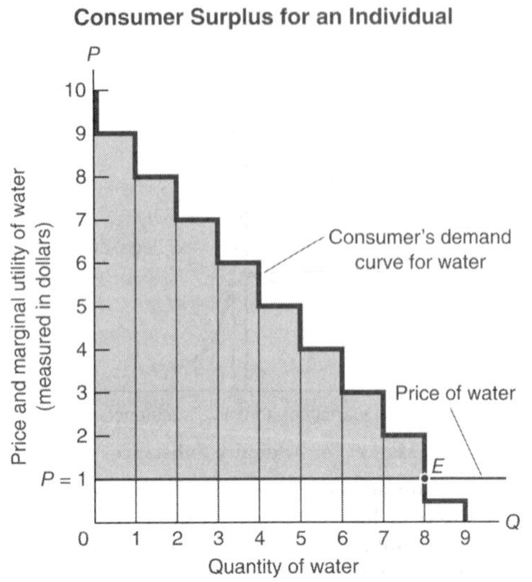

FIGURE 5-5. Because of Diminishing Marginal Utility, Consumer's Satisfaction Exceeds What Is Paid ②

The downward-sloping demand for water reflects the diminishing marginal utility of water. Note how much excess or surplus satisfaction occurs from the earlier units. Adding up all the blue surpluses ($8 of surplus on unit 1 + $7 of surplus on unit 2 + · · · + $1 of surplus on unit 8), we obtain the total consumer surplus of $36 on water purchases.

In the simplified case seen here, the area between the demand curve and the price line is the total consumer surplus.

Figure 5-5 illustrates the concept of consumer surplus in the case where money provides a firm measuring rod for utility. Here, an individual consumes water, which has a price of $1 per gallon. This is shown by the horizontal green line at $1 in Figure 5-5. The consumer considers how many gallon jugs to buy at that price. The first gallon is highly valuable, slaking extreme thirst, and the consumer is willing to pay $9 for it. But this first gallon costs only the market price of $1, so the consumer has gained a surplus of $8.

Consider the second gallon. This is worth $8 to the consumer, but again costs only $1, so the surplus is $7. And so on down to the ninth gallon, which is worth only 50 cents to the consumer, and so it is not bought. The consumer equilibrium comes at point *E*, where 8 gallons of water are bought at a price of $1 each.

But here we make an important discovery: Even though the consumer has paid only $8, the total

① 一种商品的总效用与其市场总价值之间的差额称为**消费者剩余**。即由于边际效用递减规律作用的结果，出现了“所得到的大于所支付的”的消费者剩余现象。

② 图 5-5. 由于边际效用递减规律的作用，消费者的满足度超过其支付

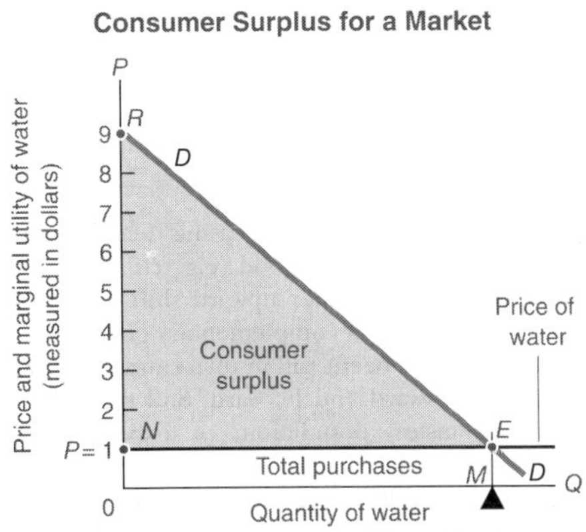

FIGURE 5-6. Total Consumer Surplus Is the Area under the Demand Curve and above the Price Line ①

The demand curve measures the amount consumers would pay for each unit consumed. Thus the total area under the demand curve (0*REM*) shows the total utility attached to the consumption of water. By subtracting the market cost of water to consumers (equal to 0*NEM*), we obtain the consumer surplus from water consumption as the blue triangle *NER*. This device is useful for measuring the benefits of public goods and the losses from monopolies and import tariffs.

value of the water is \$44. This is obtained by adding up each of the marginal utility columns (= \$9 + \$8 + · · · + \$2). Thus the consumer has gained a surplus of \$36 over the amount paid.

Figure 5-5 examines the case of a single consumer purchasing water. We can also apply the concept of consumer surplus to a market as a whole. The market demand curve in Figure 5-6 is the horizontal summation of the individual demand curves. The logic of the individual consumer surplus carries over to the market as a whole. The area of the market demand curve above the price line, shown as *NER* in Figure 5-6, represents the total consumer surplus.

Because consumers pay the price of the last unit for all units consumed, they enjoy a surplus of utility over cost. Consumer surplus measures the extra value that consumers receive above what they pay for a commodity. ②

消费者剩余的应用
Applications of Consumer Surplus

The concept of consumer surplus is useful in helping evaluate many government decisions. For example, how can the government decide on the value of building a new highway or of preserving a recreation site? Suppose a new highway has been proposed. Being free to all, it will bring in no revenue. The value to users will be found in time saved or in safer trips and can be measured by the individual consumer surplus. To avoid difficult issues of interpersonal utility comparisons, we assume that there are 10,000 users, all identical in every respect.

Suppose that each individual's consumer surplus is \$350 for the highway. The highway will raise consumer economic welfare if its total cost is less than \$3.5 million (10,000 × \$350). Economists use consumer surplus when they are performing a *cost-benefit analysis*, which attempts to determine the costs and benefits of a government program. Generally, an economist would recommend that a free road should be built if its total consumer surplus exceeds its costs. Similar analyses have been used for environmental questions such as whether to preserve wilderness areas for recreation or whether to require new pollution-abatement equipment.

The concept of consumer surplus also points to the enormous privilege enjoyed by citizens of modern societies. Each of us enjoys a vast array of enormously valuable goods that can be bought at low prices. This is a humbling thought. If you know someone who is bragging about his economic productivity, or explaining how high her real wages are, suggest a moment of reflection. If such people were transported with their specialized skills to an uninhabited desert island, how much would their wages buy? Indeed, without capital machinery, without the cooperation of others, and without the technological knowledge which each generation inherits from the past, how much could any of us produce? It is only too clear that all of us reap the benefits of an economic world we never made. As the great British sociologist L. T. Hobhouse said: [3]

> The organizer of industry who thinks that he has "made" himself and his business has found a whole social system ready to his hand in skilled workers, machinery, a market, peace and order—a vast apparatus and a pervasive atmosphere, the joint creation of millions of men and scores of generations. Take away the whole social factor and we [are] but . . . savages living on roots, berries, and vermin. ④

Now that we have surveyed the essentials of demand, we move on to costs and supply.

---

① 图 5-6. 总的消费者剩余即需求曲线与横轴的价格线之间的面积

② 由于消费者付清了最后一个单位的价格而购得所有单位的消费品之后，他们即可享受到所付成本之上的效用剩余。消费者剩余衡量的是其所购商品之外获得的额外价值。

[3] 霍布豪斯（L. T. Hobhouse，1864~1929），英国社会学家和哲学家。

④ 行业的组织者认为他已经靠所谓的“自身的奋斗”获得了成功，但同时也认识到是整个社会系统为他的企业提供了熟练工人、机器设备、市场、安全而有秩序的环境——这一庞大的渗透到每一个社会细胞的机构是千百万人经过几十代的努力共同创造出来的。离开这些社会因素，我们到现在还仍然是靠草根、野果和狩猎维生的野人……

SUMMARY

1. Market demands or demand curves are explained as stemming from the process of individuals' choosing their most preferred bundle of consumption goods and services.
2. Economists explain consumer demand by the concept of utility, which denotes the relative satisfaction that a consumer obtains from using different commodities. The additional satisfaction obtained from consuming an additional unit of a good is given the name *marginal utility*, where "marginal" means the extra or incremental utility. The law of diminishing marginal utility states that as the amount of a commodity consumed increases, the marginal utility of the last unit consumed tends to decrease.
3. Economists assume that consumers allocate their limited incomes so as to obtain the greatest satisfaction or utility. To maximize utility, a consumer must satisfy the *equimarginal principle* that the marginal utilities of the last dollar spent on each and every good must be equal.

   Only when the marginal utility per dollar is equal for apples, bacon, coffee, and everything else will the consumer attain the greatest satisfaction from a limited dollar income. But be careful to note that the marginal utility of a $50-per-ounce bottle of perfume is not equal to the marginal utility of a 50-cent glass of cola. Rather, their marginal utilities divided by price per unit are all equal in the consumer's optimal allocation. That is, their marginal utilities per last dollar, MU/P, are equalized.
4. Equal marginal utility or benefit per unit of resource is a fundamental rule of choice. Take any scarce resource, such as time. If you want to maximize the value or utility of that resource, make sure that the marginal benefit per unit of the resource is equalized in all uses.
5. The market demand curve for all consumers is derived by adding horizontally the separate demand curves of each consumer. A demand curve can shift for many reasons. For example, a rise in income will normally shift *DD* rightward, thus increasing demand; a rise in the price of a substitute good (e.g., chicken for beef) will also create a similar upward shift in demand; a rise in the price of a complementary good (e.g., hamburger buns for beef) will in turn cause the *DD* curve to shift downward and leftward. Still other factors—changing tastes, population, or expectations—can affect demand.
6. We can gain added insight into the factors that cause downward-sloping demand by separating the effect of a price rise into substitution and income effects. (*a*) The substitution effect occurs when a higher price leads to substitution of other goods to meet satisfactions; (*b*) the income effect means that a price increase lowers real income and thereby reduces the desired consumption of most commodities. For most goods, substitution and income effects of a price increase reinforce one another and lead to the law of downward-sloping demand. We measure the quantitative responsiveness of demand to income by the income elasticity, which is the percentage change in quantity demanded divided by the percentage change in income.
7. Remember that it is the tail of marginal utility that wags the market dog of prices. This point is emphasized by the concept of *consumer surplus*. We pay the same price for the last quart of milk as for the first. But, because of the law of diminishing marginal utility, marginal utilities of earlier units are greater than that of the last unit. This means that we would have been willing to pay more than the market price for each of the earlier units. The excess of total value over market value is called consumer surplus. Consumer surplus reflects the benefit we gain from being able to buy all units at the same low price. In simplified cases, we can measure consumer surplus as the area between the demand curve and the price line. It is a concept relevant for many public decisions—such as deciding when the community should incur the heavy expenses of a road or bridge or set aside land for a wilderness area.

CONCEPTS FOR REVIEW

utility, marginal utility
utilitarianism
law of diminishing marginal utility
demand shifts from income and other sources
ordinal utility
equimarginal principle: $MU_1/P_1 = MU_2/P_2 = \cdots = MU$ per \$ of income
market demand vs. individual demand
income elasticity
substitutes, complements, independent goods
substitution effect and income effect
merit goods, demerit goods
paradox of value
consumer surplus

FURTHER READING AND INTERNET WEBSITES

Further Reading

An advanced treatment of consumer theory can be found in intermediate textbooks; see the Further Reading section in Chapter 3 for some good sources.

Utilitarianism was introduced in Jeremy Bentham, *An Introduction to the Principles of Morals* (1789).

An interesting survey of psychology and economics is contained in Matthew Rabin, "Psychology and Economics," *Journal of Economic Literature,* March 1998, while serious students of the subject may want to read Colin Camerer, George Loewenstein, and Matthew Rabin, eds., *Advances in Behavioral Economics* (Princeton University Press, Princeton, N.J., 2003).

Consumers often need help in judging the utility of different products. Look at *Consumer Reports* for articles that attempt to rate products. They sometimes rank products as "Best Buys," which might mean the most utility per dollar of expenditure.

Jeffrey A. Miron and Jeffrey Zwiebel, "The Economic Case against Drug Prohibition," *Journal of Economic Perspectives,* Fall 1995, pp. 175–192, is an excellent nontechnical survey of the economics of drug prohibition.

Websites

Data on total personal consumption expenditures for the United States are provided at the website of the Bureau of Economic Analysis, *www.bea.doc.gov.* Data on family budgets are contained in Bureau of Labor Statistics, *Consumer Expenditures,* available at *www.bls.gov.*

Practical guides for consumers are provided at the government site *www.consumer.gov.* The organization Public Citizen lobbies in Washington "for safer drugs and medical devices, cleaner and safer energy sources, a cleaner environment, fair trade, and a more open and democratic government." Its website at *www.citizen.org* contains articles on many consumer, labor, and environmental issues.

You can read the Nobel lectures of laureates Akerlof, Kahneman, and Smith, with their views on behavioral economics, at *nobelprize.org/nobel_prizes/economics/laureates/.*

QUESTIONS FOR DISCUSSION

1. Explain the meaning of utility. What is the difference between total utility and marginal utility? Explain the law of diminishing marginal utility and give a numerical example.
2. Each week, Tom Wu buys two hamburgers at \$2 each, eight cokes at \$0.50 each, and eight slices of pizza at \$1 each, but he buys no hot dogs at \$1.50 each. What can you deduce about Tom's marginal utility for each of the four goods?
3. Which pairs of the following goods would you classify as complementary, substitute, or independent goods: beef, ketchup, lamb, cigarettes, gum, pork, radio, television, air travel, bus travel, taxis, and paperbacks? Illustrate the resulting shift in the demand curve for one good when the price of another good goes up. How would a change in income affect the demand curve for air travel? The demand curve for bus travel?

4. Why is it wrong to say, "Utility is maximized when the marginal utilities of all goods are exactly equal"? Correct the statement and explain.
5. Here is a way to think about consumer surplus as it applies to movies:
   a. How many movies did you watch last year?
   b. How much in total did you pay to watch movies last year?
   c. What is the *maximum* you would pay to see the movies you watched last year?
   d. Calculate **c** minus **b.** That is your consumer surplus from movies.
6. Consider the following table showing the utility of different numbers of days skied each year:

Number of days skied	Total utility ($)
0	0
1	70
2	110
3	146
4	176
5	196
6	196

   Construct a table showing the marginal utility for each day of skiing. Assuming that there are 1 million people with preferences shown in the table, draw the market demand curve for ski days. If lift tickets cost $40 per day, what are the equilibrium price and quantity of days skied?
7. For each of the commodities in Table 5-2, calculate the impact of a doubling of price on quantity demanded. Similarly, for the goods in Table 5-3, what would be the impact of a 50 percent increase in consumer incomes?
8. As you add together the identical demand curves of more and more people (in a way similar to the procedure in Figure 5-2), the market demand curve becomes flatter and flatter on the same scale. Does this fact indicate that the elasticity of demand is becoming larger and larger? Explain your answer carefully.
9. An interesting application of supply and demand to addictive substances compares alternative techniques for supply restriction. For this problem, assume that the demand for addictive substances is inelastic.
   a. One approach (used today for heroin and cocaine and for alcohol during Prohibition) is to reduce supply at the nation's borders. Show how this raises price and increases the total income of the suppliers in the drug industry.
   b. An alternative approach (followed today for tobacco and alcohol) is to tax the goods heavily. Using the tax apparatus developed in Chapter 4, show how this reduces the total income of the suppliers in the drug industry.
   c. Comment on the difference between the two approaches.
10. Demand may be price-elastic for casual users of drugs—ones who are not addicted or for whom substitute products are readily available. In this case, restrictions or price increases will have a significant impact on use. Draw a supply and demand diagram like Figure 5-4 where the demand curve is price-elastic. Show the effect of a steep tax on quantity demanded. Show that, because demand is price-elastic, total spending on drugs with restrictions will fall. Explain why this analysis would support the argument of those who would severely limit the availability of addictive substances.
11. Suppose you are very rich and very fat. Your doctor has advised you to limit your food intake to 2000 calories per day. What is your consumer equilibrium for food consumption?
12. *Numerical problem on consumer surplus:* Assume that the demand for travel over a bridge takes the form $Y = 1{,}000{,}000 - 50{,}000P$, where Y is the number of trips over the bridge and P is the bridge toll (in dollars).
   a. Calculate the consumer surplus if the bridge toll is $0, $1, and $20.
   b. Assume that the cost of the bridge is $1,800,000. Calculate the toll at which the bridge owner breaks even. What is the consumer surplus at the break-even toll?
   c. Assume that the cost of the bridge is $8 million. Explain why the bridge should be built even though there is no toll that will cover the cost.

Appendix 5

GEOMETRICAL ANALYSIS OF CONSUMER EQUILIBRIUM
附录 5　消费者均衡的几何分析

An alternative and more advanced approach to deriving demand curves uses the approach called indifference curves. This appendix derives the major conclusions of consumer behavior with this new tool.

无差异曲线
THE INDIFFERENCE CURVE

Start by assuming that you are a consumer who buys different combinations of two commodities, say, food and clothing, at a given set of prices. For each combination of the two goods, assume that you prefer one to the other or are indifferent between the pair. For example, when asked to choose between combination A of 1 unit of food and 6 units of clothing and combination B of 2 units of food and 3 of clothing, you might (1) prefer A to B, (2) prefer B to A, or (3) be indifferent between A and B.

Now suppose that A and B are equally good in your eyes—that you are indifferent as to which of them you receive. Let us consider some other combinations of goods about which you are likewise indifferent, as listed in the table for Figure 5A-1.

Figure 5A-1 shows these combinations diagrammatically. We measure units of clothing on one axis and units of food on the other. Each of our four combinations of goods is represented by its point, *A, B, C, D*. But these four are by no means the only combinations among which you are indifferent. Another batch, such as 1½ units of food and 4 of clothing, might be ranked as equal to *A, B, C,* or *D,* and there are many others not shown. The curved contour of Figure 5A-1, linking up the four points, is an **indifference curve.** The points on the curve rep- [1] resent consumption bundles among which the consumer is indifferent; all are equally desirable.

替代规律
Law of Substitution

Indifference curves are drawn as bowl-shaped, or convex to the origin. Hence, as you move downward and to the right along the curve—a movement that implies increasing the quantity of food and reducing the units of clothing—the curve becomes flatter. The curve is drawn in this way to illustrate a property that seems most often to hold true in reality and which we call the law of substitution:

The scarcer a good, the greater its relative substitution value; its marginal utility rises relative to the marginal utility of the good that has become plentiful. ②

Thus, in going from *A* to *B* in Figure 5A-1, you would swap 3 of your 6 clothing units for 1 extra food unit. But from *B* to *C,* you would sacrifice only 1 unit of your remaining clothing supply to obtain a third food unit—a 1-for-1 swap. For a fourth unit of food, you would sacrifice only ½ unit from your dwindling supply of clothing.

If we join the points *A* and *B* of Figure 5A-1, we find that the slope of the resulting line (neglecting its negative sign) has a value of 3. Join *B* and *C,* and the slope is 1; join *C* and *D,* and the slope is ½. These figures—3, 1, ½—are the *substitution ratios* (sometimes called the *marginal rates of substitution*) between the two goods. As the size of the movement along the curve becomes very small, the closer the substitution ratio comes to the actual slope of the indifference curve.

The slope of the indifference curve is the measure of the goods' relative marginal utilities, or of the substitution terms on which—for very small changes—the consumer would be willing to exchange a little less of one good in return for a little more of the other.

An indifference curve that is convex in the manner of Figure 5A-1 conforms to the law of substitution. As the amount of food you consume goes up—and the quantity of clothing goes down—food must become relatively cheaper in order for you to be persuaded to take a little extra food in exchange for a little sacrifice of clothing. The precise shape and slope of an indifference curve will, of course, vary from one consumer to the next, but the typical shape will take the form shown in Figures 5A-1 and 5A-2.

无差异曲线图
The Indifference Map

The table in Figure 5A-1 is one of an infinite number of possible tables. We could start with a more preferred consumption situation and list some of the different combinations that would bring the consumer this higher level of satisfaction. One such table might have begun with 2 food units and 7 clothing units;

[1] 无差异曲线是爱尔兰著名哲学家、政治家和经济学家埃奇沃思（Francis Ysidro Edgeworth，1845~1926）、帕累托以及若干当代经济学家在 20 世纪早期发展出来的。本书 16~18 版中的相关部分只提到了帕累托对该曲线所做出的贡献，论述欠妥，本版予以删除。此外，在 12 版之后的各版本对帕累托的介绍偏多，16~18 版有所减少，应该说 19 版有关对帕累托的修订内容更客观，更符合现代经济学发展的历史和现状。从这一点我们不难看出萨翁学术态度的严谨和求真精神。

② 一种商品越是稀缺，其相对的替代价值就越大。相对于充裕的商品，它的边际效用会上升。

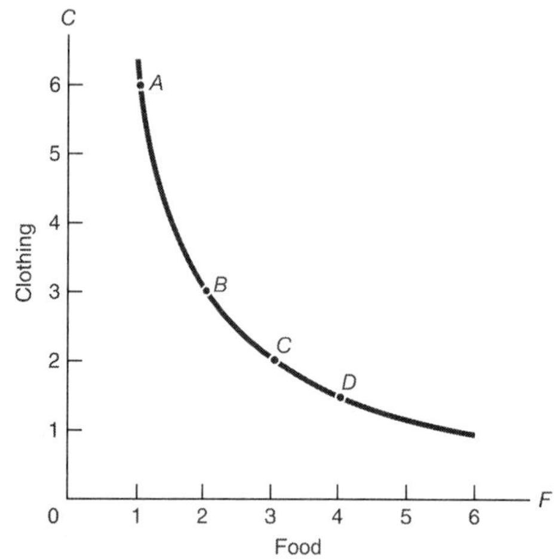

Indifference Combinations

	Food	Clothing
A	1	6
B	2	3
C	3	2
D	4	$1\frac{1}{2}$

FIGURE 5A-1. Indifference Curve for a Pair of Goods ①

Getting more of one good compensates for giving up some of the other. The consumer likes situation *A* exactly as much as *B, C,* or *D.* The food-clothing combinations that yield equal satisfaction are plotted as a smooth indifference curve. This is convex from below in accord with the law of substitution, which says that as you get more of a good, its substitution ratio, or the indifference curve's slope, diminishes.

another with 3 food units, 8 clothing units. Each table could be portrayed graphically, each with a corresponding indifference curve.

Figure 5A-2 shows four such curves; the curve from Figure 5A-1 is labeled U_3. This diagram is analogous to a geographic contour map. A person who walks along the path indicated by a particular height contour on such a map is neither climbing nor descending; similarly, the consumer who moves from one position to another along a single indifference curve enjoys neither increasing nor decreasing satisfaction from the change in consumption. Only a few of the possible indifference curves are shown in Figure 5A-2.

Note that as we increase both goods and thus move in a northeasterly direction across this map, we are crossing successive indifference curves; hence, we are reaching higher and higher levels of satisfaction (assuming that the consumer gets greater satisfaction from receiving increased quantities of both goods). Curve U_3 stands for a higher level of satisfaction than

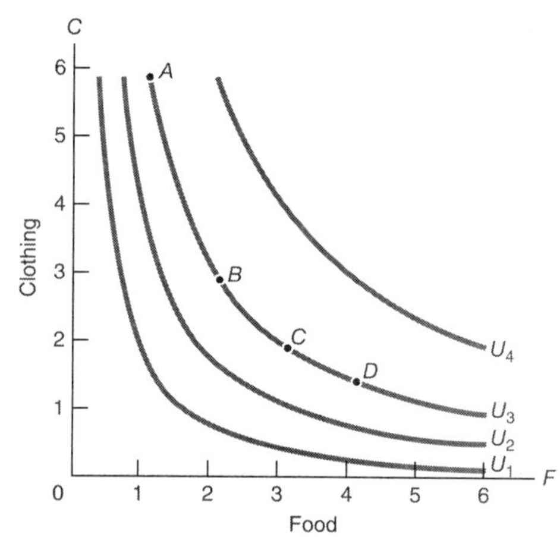

FIGURE 5A-2. A Family of Indifference Curves ②

The curves labeled U_1, U_2, U_3, and U_4 represent indifference curves. Which indifference curve is most preferred by the consumer?

① 图 5A-1. 一组商品的无差异曲线

② 图 5A-2. 一族无差异曲线

A Consumer's Budget Line

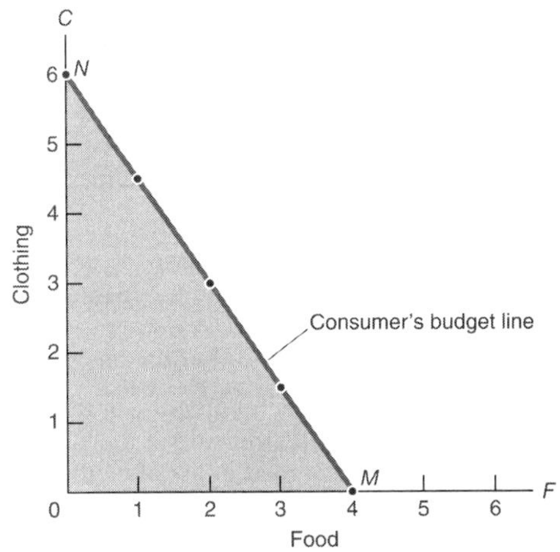

Alternative Consumption Possibilities

	Food	Clothing
M	4	0
	3	$1^1/_2$
	2	3
	1	$4^1/_2$
N	0	6

FIGURE 5A-3. Income Constrains Consumer Spending ①

The budget limit on expenditures can be seen in a numerical table. The total cost of each budget (reckoned as $\$1.50F + \$1C$) adds up to exactly \$6 of income. We can plot the budget constraint as a straight line whose absolute slope equals the P_F/P_C ratio. *NM* is the consumer's budget line. When income is \$6, with food and clothing prices \$1.50 and \$1, the consumer can choose any point on this budget line. (Why is its slope \$1.50/\$1 = $3/2$?)

U_2; U_4, for a higher level of satisfaction than U_3; and so forth.

预算线或预算约束

BUDGET LINE OR BUDGET CONSTRAINT

Now let us set a particular consumer's indifference map aside for a moment and give the consumer a fixed income. He has, say, \$6 per day to spend, and he is confronted with fixed prices for each food and clothing unit—\$1.50 for food, \$1 for clothing. It is clear that he could spend his money on any one of a variety of alternative combinations of food and clothing. At one extreme, he could buy 4 food units and no clothing; at the other, 6 clothing units and no food. The table with Figure 5A-3 illustrates some of the possible ways in which he could allocate his \$6.

Figure 5A-3 plots five of these possibilities. Note that all the points lie on a straight line, labeled *NM*. Moreover, any other attainable point, such as $3\frac{1}{3}$ food units and 1 clothing unit, lies on *NM*. The straight budget line *NM* sums up all the possible combinations of the two goods that would just exhaust the consumer's income.[1] The slope of *NM* (neglecting its sign) is $3/2$, which is the ratio of the food price to the clothing price. The meaning of the slope is that, given these prices, every time our consumer gives up 3 clothing units (thereby dropping down 3 vertical units on the diagram), he can gain 2 units of food (i.e., move right 2 horizontal units).

We call *NM* the consumer's **budget line** or **budget constraint.** budget line 预算线，即预算约束

[1] This is so because, if we designate quantities of food and clothing bought as *F* and *C*, respectively, total expenditure on food must be $\$1.50F$ and total expenditure on clothing, $\$1C$. If daily income and expenditure are \$6, the following equation must hold: $\$6 = \$1.50F + \$1C$. This is a linear equation, the equation of the budget line *NM*. Note:

$$\text{Arithmetic slope of } NM = \$1.50 \div \$1$$
$$= \text{price of food} \div \text{price of clothing}$$

① 图 5A-3. 消费支出受收入的制约

切点的均衡位置

THE EQUILIBRIUM POSITION OF TANGENCY

Now we are ready to put our two parts together. The axes of Figure 5A-3 are the same as those of Figures 5A-1 and 5A-2. We can superimpose the blue budget line *NM* upon this green consumer indifference map, as shown in Figure 5A-4. The consumer is free to move anywhere along *NM*. Positions to the right and above *NM* are not allowed because they require more than \$6 of income; positions to the left and below *NM* are irrelevant because the consumer is assumed to spend the full \$6.

Where will the consumer move? Obviously, to that point which yields the greatest satisfaction—that is, to the highest possible indifference curve—which in this case must be at the green point *B*. At *B*, the budget line just touches, but does not cross, the indifference curve U_3. At this point of tangency, where the budget line just kisses but does not cross an indifference contour, is found the highest utility contour the consumer can reach.

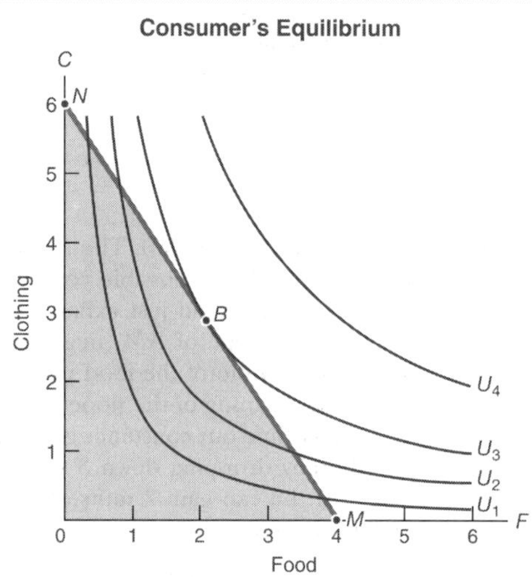

FIGURE 5A-4. Consumer's Most Preferred and Feasible Consumption Bundle Is Attained at *B* ①

We now combine the budget line and indifference contours in one diagram. The consumer reaches the highest indifference curve attainable with fixed income at point *B*, which is the tangency of the budget line with the highest indifference curve. At tangency point *B*, substitution ratio equals price ratio P_F/P_C. This means that all goods' marginal utilities are proportional to their prices, with the marginal utility of the last dollar spent on every good being equalized.

Geometrically, the consumer is at equilibrium where the slope of the budget line (which is equal to the ratio of food to clothing prices) is exactly equal to the slope of the indifference curve (which is equal to the ratio of the marginal utilities of the two goods).

Consumer equilibrium is attained at the point where the budget line is tangent to the highest indifference curve. At that point, the consumer's substitution ratio is just equal to the slope of the budget line. ②

Put differently, the substitution ratio, or the slope of the indifference curve, is the ratio of the marginal utility of food to the marginal utility of clothing. So our tangency condition is just another way of stating that the ratio of prices must be equal to the ratio of marginal utilities; in equilibrium, the consumer is getting the same marginal utility from the last penny spent on food as from the last penny spent on clothing. Therefore, we can derive the following equilibrium condition:

$$\frac{P_F}{P_C} = \text{substitution ratio} = \frac{MU_F}{MU_C}$$

This is exactly the same condition as we derived for utility theory in the main part of this chapter.

收入和价格的变化

CHANGES IN INCOME AND PRICE

Two important applications of indifference curves are frequently used to consider the effects of (*a*) a change in money income and (*b*) a change in the price of one of the two goods.

收入变化

Income Change

Assume, first, that the consumer's daily income is halved while the two prices remain unchanged. We could prepare another table, similar to the table for Figure 5A-3, showing the new consumption possibilities. Plotting these points on a diagram such as Figure 5A-5, we should find that the new budget line occupies the position *N′M′* in Figure 5A-5. The line has made a parallel shift inward.[2] The consumer is

[2] The equation of the new *N′M′* budget line is now \$3 = \$1.50*F* + \$1*C*.

① 图 5A-4. 消费者最偏好的并可行的消费组合在 B 点

② 在预算线与无差异曲线的切点达到消费均衡。在此点，消费者在该点的替代率正好等于预算线的斜率。

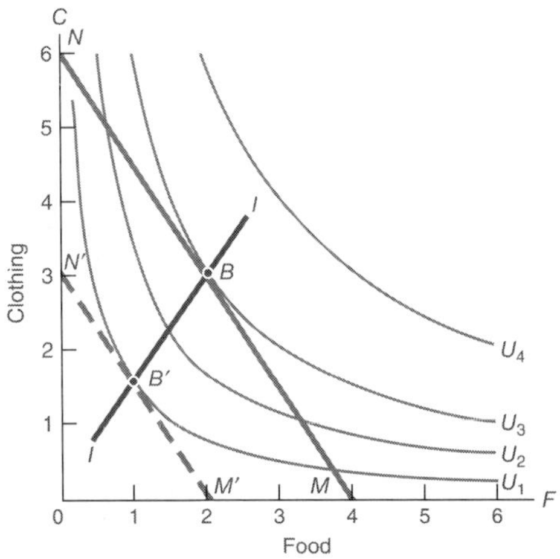

FIGURE 5A-5. Effect of Income Change on Equilibrium ①

An income change shifts the budget line in a parallel way. Thus, halving income to \$3 shifts *NM* to *N′M′*, moving equilibrium to *B′*. (Show what raising income to \$8 would do to equilibrium. Estimate where the new tangency point would come.)

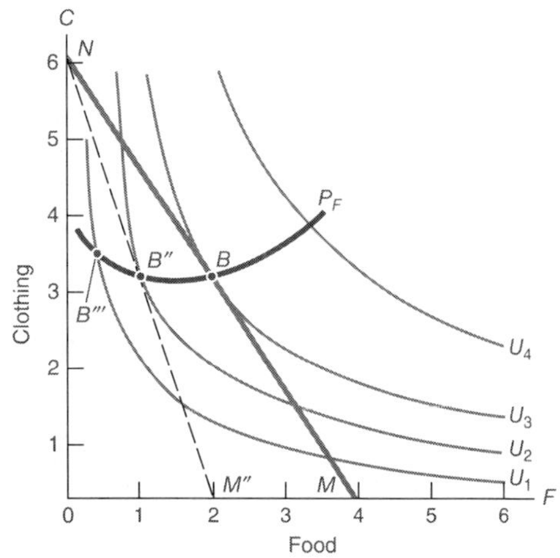

FIGURE 5A-6. Effect of Price Change on Equilibrium ②

A rise in the price of food makes the budget line pivot on *N*, rotating from *NM* to *NM″*. The new tangency equilibrium is at *B″*, where there is definitely less food consumed but clothing consumption may either go up or down.

now free to move only along this new (and lower) budget line; to maximize satisfaction, he will move to the highest attainable indifference curve, or to point *B′*. A tangency condition for consumer equilibrium applies here as before.

一种物品的价格变化
Single Price Change

Now return our consumer to his previous daily income of \$6, but assume that the price of food rises from \$1.50 to \$3 while the price of clothing is unchanged. Again we must examine the change in the budget line. This time we find that it has pivoted on point *N* and is now *NM″*, as illustrated in Figure 5A-6.[3]

The common sense of such a shift is clear. Since the price of clothing is unchanged, point *N* is just as available as it was before. But since the price of food has risen, point *M* (which represents 4 food units) is no longer attainable. With food costing \$3 per unit, only 2 units can now be bought with a daily income of \$6. So the new budget line still passes through *N*, but it must pivot at *N* and pass through *M″*, which is to the left of *M*.

Equilibrium is now at *B″*, and we have a new tangency point. Higher food price has definitely reduced food consumption, but clothing consumption may move in either direction. To clinch your understanding, work out the cases of an increase in income and a fall in the price of clothing or food.

推导需求曲线
DERIVING THE DEMAND CURVE

We are now in a position to derive the demand curve. Look carefully at Figure 5A-6. Note that as we increased the price of food from \$1.50 per unit to \$3 per unit, we kept other things constant. Tastes as represented by the indifference curves did not change, and money income and the price of clothing stayed constant. Therefore, we are in the ideal position to trace the demand curve for food. At a price of \$1.50, the consumer buys 2 units of food, shown as equilibrium point *B*. When the price rises to \$3 per unit, the food purchased is 1 unit, at equilibrium point

[3] The budget equation of *NM″* is now $\$6 = \$3F + \$1C$.

① 图 5A-5. 收入变化对均衡的影响
② 图 5A-6. 价格变化对均衡的影响

B''. If you draw in the budget line corresponding to a price of \$6 per unit of food, the equilibrium occurs at point B''', and food purchases are 0.45 unit.

Now plot the price of food against the purchases of food, again holding other things constant. You will have derived a neat downward-sloping demand curve from indifference curves. Note that we have ① done this without ever needing to mention the term "utility"—basing the derivation solely on measurable indifference curves.

SUMMARY TO APPENDIX

1. An indifference curve depicts the points of equally desirable consumption bundles. The indifference contour is usually drawn convex (or bowl-shaped) in accordance with the law of diminishing relative marginal utilities.
2. When a consumer has a fixed money income, all of which she spends, and is confronted with market prices of two goods, she is constrained to move along a straight line called the budget line or budget constraint. The line's slope will depend on the ratio of the two market prices; how far out it lies will depend on the size of her income.
3. The consumer will move along this budget line until reaching the highest attainable indifference curve. At this point, the budget line will touch, but not cross, an indifference curve. Hence, equilibrium is at the point of tangency, where the slope of the budget line (the ratio of the prices) exactly equals the slope of the indifference curve (the substitution ratio or the ratio of the marginal utilities of the two goods). This gives additional proof that, in equilibrium, marginal utilities are proportional to prices.
4. A fall in income will move the budget line inward in a parallel fashion, usually causing less of both goods to be bought. A change in the price of one good alone will, other things being constant, cause the budget line to pivot so as to change its slope. After a price or income change, the consumer will again attain a new tangency point of highest satisfaction. At every point of tangency, the marginal utility per dollar is equal for every good. By comparing the new and old equilibrium points, we trace the usual downward-sloping demand curve.

CONCEPTS FOR REVIEW

indifference curves
slope or substitution ratio
budget line or budget constraint

convexity of indifference curves and law of diminishing relative marginal utilities

optimal tangency condition:
P_F/P_C = substitution ratio
$= MU_F/MU_C$

QUESTIONS FOR DISCUSSION

1. Draw the indifference curves (*a*) between complementary goods like left shoes and right shoes and (*b*) between perfect substitutes like two bottles of cola sitting next to each other in a store.
2. Consider noodles and yachts. Draw a set of indifference curves and budget lines like those in Figure 5A-5 which show noodles as an inferior good and yachts as a "luxury" with an income elasticity greater than 1.

① 需要注意的是，我们对无差异曲线的推导仅仅是在可以比较的基础上做出的，我们并没有考虑效用概念。

CHAPTER

6

Production and Business Organization
生产和企业组织

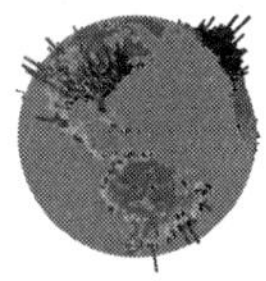

The business of America is business. [1]

Calvin Coolidge

美国人的主要任务就是如何赚全世界的钱。——卡尔文·柯立芝

Before we can eat our daily bread, someone must bake it. Similarly, the economy's ability to build cars, generate electricity, write computer programs, and deliver the multitude of goods and services that are in our gross domestic product depends upon our productive capacity. Productive capacity is deter- ②
mined by the size and quality of the labor force, by the quantity and quality of the capital stock, by the nation's technical knowledge along with the ability to use that knowledge, and by the nature of public and private institutions. Why are living standards high in North America? Low in tropical Africa? For answers, we should look to how well the machine of production is running.

Our goal is to understand how market forces determine the supply of goods and services. Over the next three chapters we will lay out the essential concepts of production, cost, and supply and show how they are linked. We first explore the fundamentals of production theory, showing how firms transform inputs into desirable outputs. Production theory also helps us understand why productivity and living standards have risen over time and how firms manage their internal activities.

生产理论和边际产量

A. THEORY OF PRODUCTION AND MARGINAL PRODUCTS

基本概念
BASIC CONCEPTS

A modern economy has an enormously varied set of productive activities. A farm takes fertilizer, seed, land, and labor and turns them into wheat or corn. Mod- ③
ern factories take inputs such as energy, raw materials, computerized machinery, and labor and use them to produce tractors, DVDs, or tubes of toothpaste. An airline takes airplanes, fuel, labor, and computerized reservation systems and provides passengers with the ability to travel quickly through its network of routes.

生产函数
The Production Function

We have spoken of inputs like land and labor and outputs like wheat and toothpaste. But if you have a fixed amount of inputs, how much output can you get? On any day, given the available technical knowledge, land, machinery, and so on, only a certain quantity of tractors or toothpaste can be obtained from a

[1] 卡尔文·柯立芝（Calvin Coolidge，1872~1933），美国第 30 任总统。由于哈定总统（Warren Gamaliel Harding，1865~1923，美国第 29 任总统）的突然去世，时任副总统的柯立芝接任，并于次年赢得大选，获得连任。这句话出自柯立芝总统连任后于 1925 年 1 月 17 日对美国报业协会（*American Society of Newspaper Editors*）所做的演讲，该段话的原文如下：

After all, the chief business of the American people is business. They are profoundly concerned with producing, buying, selling, investing and prospering in the world.

② 生产能力的大小决定于劳动力的规模和质量，股本的数量与质量，一个国家的科学技术水平和将科学技术转换为生产力的能力，以及公共部门和私人部门的性质。

③ 现代工厂投入诸如能源、原材料、数控机床和劳动等资源，并使用这些资源来生产拖拉机、DVD 光碟或牙膏等。

given amount of labor. The relationship between the ① amount of input required and the amount of output that can be obtained is called the *production function*.

The **production function** specifies the maximum ② output that can be produced with a given quantity of inputs. It is defined for a given state of engineering and technical knowledge.

An important example is the production function for generating electricity. Visualize it as a book with technical specifications for different kinds of plants. One page is for gas turbines, showing their inputs (initial capital cost, fuel consumption, and the amount of labor needed to run the turbine) and their outputs (amount of electricity generated). The next page shows inputs and outputs of coal-fired generating plants. Yet other pages describe nuclear power plants, solar power stations, and so forth. Taken together, they constitute the production function for electricity generation.

Note that our definition assumes that firms always strive to produce efficiently. In other words, they always attempt to produce the maximum level of output for a given dose of inputs.

Consider the humble task of ditchdigging. Outside our windows in America, we see a large and expensive tractor, driven by one person with another to supervise. This team can easily dig a trench 5 feet deep and 50 feet long in 2 hours. When we visit Africa, we see 50 laborers armed only with picks. The same trench might take an entire day. These two techniques—one capital-intensive and the other labor-intensive—are part of the production function for ditchdigging.

There are literally millions of different production functions—one for each and every product or service. Most of them are not written down but are in people's minds. In areas of the economy where technol- ③ ogy is changing rapidly, like computer software and biotechnology, production functions may become obsolete soon after they are used. And some, like the blueprints of a medical laboratory or cliff house, are [4] specially designed for a specific location and purpose and would be useless anywhere else. Nevertheless, the concept of a production function is a useful way of describing the productive capabilities of a firm.

总产量、平均产量和边际产量
Total, Average, and Marginal Product

Starting with a firm's production function, we can calculate three important production concepts: total, average, and marginal product. We begin by comput- ⑤ ing the total physical product, or **total product,** which designates the total amount of output produced, in physical units such as bushels of wheat or number of sneakers. Figure 6-1(*a*) on page 109 and column (2) of Table 6-1 on page 110 illustrate the concept of total product. For this example, they show how total product responds as the amount of labor applied is increased. The total product starts at zero for zero labor and then increases as additional units of labor are applied, reaching a maximum of 3900 units when 5 units of labor are used.

Once we know the total product, it is easy to derive an equally important concept, the marginal product. Recall that the term "marginal" means "extra."

The **marginal product** of an input is the extra out- ⑥ put produced by 1 additional unit of that input while other inputs are held constant.

For example, assume that we are holding land, machinery, and all other inputs constant. Then labor's marginal product is the extra output obtained by adding 1 unit of labor. The third column of Table 6-1 calculates the marginal product. The marginal product of labor starts at 2000 for the first unit of labor and then falls to only 100 units for the fifth unit. Marginal product calculations such as this are crucial for understanding how wages and other factor prices are determined.

The final concept is the **average product,** which ⑦ equals total output divided by total units of input. The fourth column of Table 6-1 shows the average product of labor as 2000 units per worker with one worker, 1500 units per worker with two workers, and so forth. In this example, average product falls through the entire range of increasing labor input.

Figure 6-1 plots the total and marginal products from Table 6-1. Study this figure to make sure you understand that the blocks of marginal products in (*b*) are related to the changes in the total product curve in (*a*).

边际收益递减规律
The Law of Diminishing Returns

Using production functions, we can understand one of the most famous laws in all economics, the law of diminishing returns:

Under the **law of diminishing returns,** a firm will get less and less extra output when it adds additional

③ 在诸如计算机软件和生物技术这样的经济领域，技术在日新月异地变化，某些生产函数在一经使用之后不久就很快过时。还有一些诸如医学实验室或者建在悬崖峭壁的海景酒店的设计图纸，则是在特定地点实现特定用途的个性化设计，换别的地方即毫无用处。

[4] Cliff house：著名的海景酒店品牌，1863 年建于风景秀美的旧金山中国海滩附近，以其连接过去与现在的旧金山历史而自居，以浪漫而温馨的环境著称于世，是旧金山的地标性建筑之一。近年来获奖无数，媒体口碑极佳。现在，全世界很多的此类型酒店都以加盟的形式与此联营，京郊的古崖居也可勉强译作 *the Ancient Cliff House*。

---

① 所需的投入量和所能达到的产出量之间的关系即称生产函数。

② **生产函数**指在既定的工程技术水平下，给定投入所能达到的最大产出。

⑤ 我们先从计算总的实物产量，即**总产量**开始。总产量指已经生产的以实际单位计量的产出总量，比如多少蒲式耳的小麦或者多少双运动鞋。

⑥ 一种投入的**边际产量**是在其他投入保持不变的情况下，每增加一个单位的该种投入所额外增加的产出量。

⑦ 最后一个概念是**平均产量**，它等于总产量除以总投入的单位数。

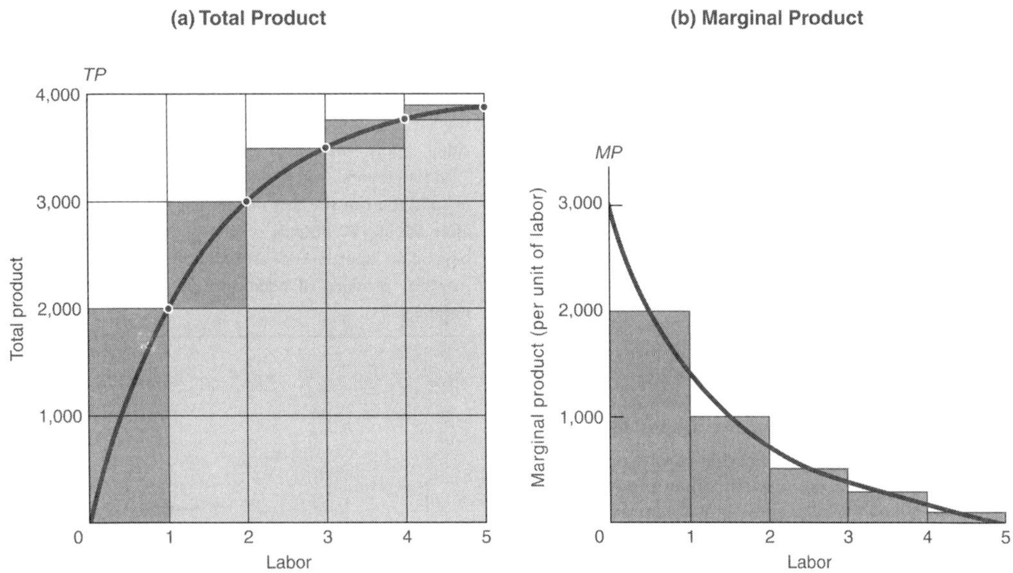

FIGURE 6-1. Marginal Product Is Derived from Total Product ①

Diagram **(a)** shows the total product curve rising as additional inputs of labor are added, holding other things constant. However, total product rises by smaller and smaller increments as additional units of labor are added (compare the increments of the first and the fifth worker). By smoothing between points, we get the green-colored total product curve.

Diagram **(b)** shows the declining steps of marginal product. Make sure you understand why each dark rectangle in **(b)** is equal to the equivalent dark rectangle in **(a)**. The area in **(b)** under the green-colored marginal product curve (or the sum of the dark rectangles) adds up to the total product in **(a)**.

units of an input while holding other inputs fixed. ② In other words, the marginal product of each unit of input will decline as the amount of that input increases, holding all other inputs constant.

The law of diminishing returns expresses a very basic relationship. As more of an input such as labor ③ is added to a fixed amount of land, machinery, and other inputs, the labor has less and less of the other factors to work with. The land gets more crowded, the machinery is overworked, and the marginal product of labor declines.

Table 6-1 illustrates the law of diminishing returns. Given fixed land and other inputs, we see that there is zero total output of corn with zero inputs of labor. When we add our first unit of labor to the same fixed amount of land, we observe that 2000 bushels of corn are produced.

In our next stage, with 2 units of labor and fixed land, output goes to 3000 bushels. Hence, the second unit of labor adds only 1000 bushels of additional output. The third unit of labor has an even lower marginal product than does the second, and the fourth unit adds even less. Table 6-1 thus illustrates the law of diminishing returns.

Figure 6-1 also illustrates the law of diminishing returns for labor. Here we see that the marginal product curve in (*b*) declines as labor inputs increase, which is the precise meaning of diminishing returns. In Figure 6-1(*a*), diminishing returns are seen as a concave or dome-shaped total product curve.

---

① 图 6-1. 由总产量推导边际产量

② 在**边际收益递减规律**的作用下，一家企业在保持其他投入不变的情况下，当某种投入的单位量增加时，其额外增加的产出将越来越少。换言之，在保持其他投入不变的情况下，当该种投入的量增加时，每一单位投入的边际产量将降低。

③ 像劳动这样的投入被更多地追加到固定数量的土地、机器设备以及其他投入要素上时，劳动对这些要素产生的作用就越来越小。

(1) Units of labor input	(2) Total product	(3) Marginal product	(4) Average product
0	0		
		2,000	
1	2,000		2,000
		1,000	
2	3,000		1,500
		500	
3	3,500		1,167
		300	
4	3,800		950
		100	
5	3,900		780

TABLE 6-1. Total, Marginal, and Average Product ①

The table shows the total product that can be produced for different inputs of labor when other inputs (capital, land, etc.) and the state of technical knowledge are unchanged. From total product, we can derive important concepts of marginal and average products.

What is true for labor is also true for any other input. We can interchange land and labor, now holding labor constant and varying land. We can calculate the marginal product of each input (labor, land, machinery, water, fertilizer, etc.), and the marginal product would apply to any output (wheat, corn, steel, soybeans, and so forth). We would find that other inputs also tend to show the law of diminishing returns.

Diminishing Returns in Farm Experiments

The law of diminishing returns is often observed in agriculture. As Farmer Tilly [2] adds more labor, the fields will be more thoroughly seeded and weeded, irrigation ditches will be neater, and scarecrows better oiled. At some point, however, the additional labor becomes less and less productive. The third hoeing of the field or the fourth oiling of the machinery adds little to output. Eventually, output grows very little as more people crowd onto the farm; too many tillers spoil the crop. ③

Agricultural experiments are one of the most important kinds of technological research. These techniques have been used for over a century to test different seeds, fertilizers, and other combinations of inputs in a successful effort to raise agricultural productivity. Figure 6-2 shows the results of an experiment in which different doses of phosphorus fertilizer were applied on two different plots, holding constant land area, nitrogen fertilizer, labor, and other inputs. Real-world experiments are complicated by "random errors"—in this case, due primarily to differences in soils. You can see that diminishing returns set in quickly after about 100 pounds of phosphorus per acre. Indeed, beyond an input level of around 300 pounds per acre, the marginal product of additional phosphorus fertilizer is negative.

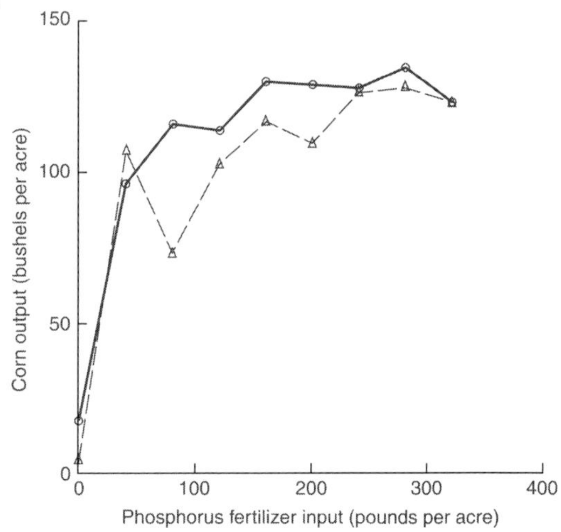

FIGURE 6-2. Diminishing Returns in Corn Production ④

Agricultural researchers experimented with different doses of phosphorus fertilizer on two different plots to estimate the production function for corn in western Iowa. In conducting the experiment, they were careful to hold constant other things such as nitrogen fertilizer, water, and labor inputs. Because of variations in soils and microclimate, even the most careful scientist cannot prevent some ⑤ random variation, which accounts for the jagged nature of the lines. If you fit a smooth curve to the data, you will see that the relationship displays diminishing returns for every dose and that marginal product becomes negative for a phosphate input of around 300.

Source: Earl O. Heady, John T. Pesek, and William G. Brown, *Crop Response Surfaces and Economic Optima in Fertilizer Use* (Agricultural Experiment Station, Iowa State College, Ames, Iowa, 1955), table A-15.

① 表 6-1. 总产量、边际产量和平均产量

[2] 法默·蒂莉（Farmer Tilly）：1810 年，17 岁的蒂莉·福斯特（Tilly Foster）在纽约州普特南县的东南小镇开了一家以自己名字命名的葡萄酒作坊，并逐渐扩大成综合性的农牧场。1864 年将作坊以 50 万美元出售，实现了葡萄酒的大规模生产。1943 年被纽约大商人 E. Benedict 收购成为以养马场为主、奶牛场为辅的著名农场。2002 年 10 月普特南县政府以 390 万美元收购为政府资产，用以保护城市的供水水源，并将其开辟为历史遗产予以保护，向公众开放。它至今仍然是纽约州乃至全美领先的综合性农牧场，在加拿大、英国、爱尔兰等国家均有 *Farmer Tilly*。

③ 最终，当更多的农工涌进该农场，太多的耕作反倒破坏了农作物的生长，导致产量增加甚微。

④ 图 6-2. 玉米生产的收益递减

⑤ 由于土壤和局部小气候的变化，使即便最精细的科学家也无法避免一些随机变化，这一点从曲线的锯齿形状就可以看出。

Diminishing returns are a key factor in explaining why many countries in Asia are so poor. Living standards in crowded Rwanda or Bangladesh are low because there are so many workers per acre of land and not because farmers are ignorant or fail to respond to economic incentives.

We can also use the example of studying to illustrate the law of diminishing returns. You might find that the first hour of studying economics on a given day is productive—you learn new laws and facts, insights and history. The second hour might find your attention wandering a bit, with less learned. The third hour might show that diminishing returns have set in with a vengeance, and by the next day the third hour is a blank in your memory. Does the law of diminishing returns suggest why the hours devoted to studying should be spread out rather than crammed into the day before exams?

The law of diminishing returns is a widely observed empirical regularity rather than a universal truth like the law of gravity. It has been found in numerous empirical studies, but exceptions have also been uncovered. Moreover, diminishing returns might not hold for all levels of production. The very first inputs of labor might actually show increasing marginal products, since a minimum amount of labor may be needed just to walk to the field and pick up a shovel. Notwithstanding these reservations, diminishing returns will prevail in most situations.

规模报酬
RETURNS TO SCALE

Diminishing returns and marginal products refer ① to the response of output to an increase of a *single* input when all other inputs are held constant. We saw that increasing labor while holding land constant would increase food output by ever-smaller increments.

But sometimes we are interested in the effect of increasing *all* inputs. For example, what would happen to wheat production if land, labor, water, and other inputs were increased by the same proportion? Or what would happen to the production of tractors if the quantities of labor, computers, robots, steel, and factory space were all doubled? These questions refer to the *returns to scale*, or the effects of scale increases of inputs on the quantity produced. Three important cases should be distinguished:

- **Constant returns to scale** denote a case where a change in all inputs leads to a proportional change in output. For example, if labor, land, capital, and other inputs are doubled, then under constant returns to scale output would also double. Many handicraft industries (such as haircutting in America or handloom operation in a developing country) show constant returns.
- **Increasing returns to scale** (also called **economies of scale**) arise when an increase in all inputs leads to a more-than-proportional increase in the level of output. For example, an engineer planning a small-scale chemical plant will generally find that increasing the inputs of labor, capital, and materials by 10 percent will increase the total output by more than 10 percent. Engineering studies have determined that many manufacturing processes enjoy modestly increasing returns to scale for plants up to the largest size used today.
- **Decreasing returns to scale** occur when a balanced increase of all inputs leads to a less-than-proportional increase in total output. In many processes, scaling up may eventually reach a point beyond which inefficiencies set in. These might arise because the costs of management or control become large. One case has occurred in electricity generation, where firms found that when plants grew too large, risks of plant failure grew too large. Many productive activities involving natural resources, such as growing wine grapes or providing clean drinking water to a city, show decreasing returns to scale.

constant returns to scale
规模报酬不变

increasing returns to scale (or economies of scale)
规模报酬递增，也称规模经济

decreasing returns to scale
规模报酬递减

Production shows increasing, decreasing, or ② constant returns to scale when a balanced increase in all inputs leads to a more-than-proportional, less-than-proportional, or just-proportional increase in output.

One of the common findings of engineers is that modern mass-production techniques require that factories be a certain minimum size. Chapter 2 explained that as output increases, firms may divide production into smaller steps, taking advantage of specialization and division of labor. In addition, large-scale production allows intensive use of specialized capital equipment, automation, and computerized

① 当所有的其他投入要素保持不变时，边际收益和产量的递减是产出对于单一投入要素增加的反应。

② 当所有投入要素都均衡地增加导致产出按比例增加、减少或者不变时，生产表现为规模报酬递增、递减或不变。

Production concept	Definition
Diminishing returns	Declining marginal product of an input, holding all other inputs constant
Returns to scale	Increase in output for balanced increase in all inputs is
Decreasing	. . . less than proportional
Constant	. . . proportional
Increasing	. . . more than proportional

TABLE 6-2. Important Production Concepts ①

This table shows succinctly the important production concepts.

design and manufacturing to perform simple and repetitive tasks quickly.

Information technologies often display strong economies of scale. A good example is Microsoft's Windows Vista operating system. Developing this program reportedly required $10 billion in research, development, beta-testing, and promotion. Yet the cost of adding Windows Vista to a new computer is very close to zero because doing so simply requires a
few seconds of computer time. We will see that strong ②
economies of scale often lead to firms with significant market power and sometimes pose major problems of public policy.

Table 6-2 summarizes the important concepts from this section.

短期和长期
SHORT RUN AND LONG RUN

Production requires not only labor and land but also time. Pipelines cannot be built overnight, and once built they last for decades. Farmers cannot change crops in midseason. It often takes a decade to plan, construct, test, and commission a large power plant. Moreover, once capital equipment has been put in the concrete form of a giant automobile assembly plant, the capital cannot be economically dismantled and moved to another location or transferred to another use.

To account for the role of time in production and costs, we distinguish between two different time periods. We define the **short run** as a period in which firms can adjust production by changing variable factors such as materials and labor but cannot change fixed factors such as capital. The **long run** is a period sufficiently long that all factors including capital can be adjusted.

To understand these concepts more clearly, consider the way the production of steel might respond to changes in demand. Say that Nippon Steel is operating its furnaces at 70 percent of capacity when an unexpected increase in the demand for steel occurs because of the need to rebuild from an earthquake in Japan or California. To adjust to the higher demand for steel, the firm can increase production by increasing worker overtime, hiring more workers, and operating its plants and machinery more intensively. The factors which are increased in the short run are called *variable* factors.

Suppose that the increase in steel demand persisted for an extended period of time, say, several years. Nippon Steel would examine its capital needs and decide that it should increase its productive capacity. More generally, it might examine all its *fixed* factors, those that cannot be changed in the short run because of physical conditions or legal contracts. The period of time over which all inputs, fixed and variable, can be adjusted is called the long run. In the long run, Nippon might add new and more efficient production processes, install a rail link or new computerized control system, or build a plant in Mexico. When all factors can be adjusted, the total amount of steel will be higher and the level of efficiency can increase.

Efficient production requires time as well as con- ③
ventional inputs like labor. We therefore distinguish between two different time periods in production and cost analysis. The short run is the period of time in which only some inputs, the variable inputs, can be adjusted. In the short run, fixed factors, such as plant and equipment, cannot be fully modified or adjusted. The long run is the period in which all factors employed by the firm, including capital, can be changed.

That Smells So Good!
The production processes of a modern market economy are extraordinarily complex. We can illustrate this with the lowly hamburger.

① 表6-2. 有关生产的重要概念

② 我们会发现，强大的规模经济常常造就具有市场控制力的企业，有时也会造成公共政策的主要难题。

③ 高效率的生产对时间有要求，同时也对劳动这样的传统投入要素提出了要求。为此，我们在生产和成本分析中区分两个不同的时间段。短期是指在该时间段里，只有某些投入要素，即可变投入要素可作调整；而在短期内的固定投入要素，如厂房和机器设备，则不能得到完全调整。长期指的是在该时间段里，企业所有已经投入的生产要素，包括资本，均可以变更。

As Americans spend more time in the workplace and less in the kitchen, their demand for prepared food has risen dramatically. TV dinners have replaced store-bought carrots and peas, while hamburgers bought at McDonald's now number in the billions. The move to processed foods has the undesirable property that the food—after being washed, sorted, sliced, blanched, frozen, thawed, and reheated—often loses most of its flavor. You want a hamburger to smell and taste like a hamburger, not like cooked cardboard.

This is where the "production of tastes and smells" enters. Companies like International Flavors and Fragrances (IFF) synthesize the flavor of potato chips, breakfast cereals, ice cream, cookies, and just about every other kind of processed food, along with the fragrance of many fine perfumes, soaps, and shampoos. If you read most food labels, you will discover that the food contains "natural ingredients" or "artificial ingredients"—such compounds as amyl acetate (banana flavor) or benzaldehyde (almond flavor).

But these unfamiliar chemicals can do amazing things. A food researcher recounts the following experience in the laboratories of IFF:

> [After dipping a paper fragrance-testing filter into each bottle from the lab,] I closed my eyes. Then I inhaled deeply, and one food after another was conjured from the glass bottles. I smelled fresh cherries, black olives, sautéed onions, and shrimp. [The] most remarkable creation took me by surprise. After closing my eyes, I suddenly smelled a grilled hamburger. The aroma was uncanny, almost miraculous. It smelled like someone in the room was flipping burgers on a hot grill. But when I opened my eyes, there was just a narrow strip of white paper.[1]

This story reminds us that "production" in a modern economy is much more than planting potatoes and casting steel. It sometimes involves disassembling things like chickens and potatoes into their tiny constituents, and then reconstituting them along with new synthesized tastes halfway around the world. Such complex production processes can be found in every sector, from pharmaceuticals that change our mood or help our blood flow more smoothly to financial instruments that take apart, repackage, and sell the streams of mortgage payments. And most of the time, we don't even know what exotic substances lie inside the simple (recycled) paper that wraps our $2 hamburger.

[1] Eric Schlosser, *Fast Food Nation* (Perennial Press, New York, [3] 2002), p. 129.

技术变革
TECHNOLOGICAL CHANGE

Economic history records that total output in the United States has grown more than tenfold over the last century. Part of that gain has come from increased inputs, such as labor and machinery. But much of the increase in output has come from technological change, which improves productivity and raises living standards.

Some examples of technological change are
① dramatic: wide-body jets that increased the num-
[2] ber of passenger-miles per unit of input by almost 50 percent; fiber optics that have lowered cost and improved reliability in telecommunications; and improvements in computer technologies that have increased computational power by more than 1000 times in three decades. Other forms of technological change are more subtle, as is the case when a firm adjusts its production process to reduce waste and increase output.

wide-body jets 宽体喷气式客机

We distinguish *process innovation,* which occurs when new engineering knowledge improves production techniques for existing products, from *product innovation,* whereby new or improved products are introduced in the marketplace. For example, a process innovation allows firms to produce more output with the same inputs or to produce the same output with fewer inputs. In other words, a process innovation is equivalent to a shift in the production function.

Figure 6-3 illustrates how technological change, in the form of a process innovation, would shift the total product curve. The lower line represents the feasible output, or production function, for a particular industry in the year 1995. Suppose that productivity, or output per unit of input, in this industry is rising at 4 percent per year. If we return to the same industry a decade later, we would likely see that changes in technical and engineering knowledge have led to a 48 percent improvement in output per unit of input $[(1 + .04)^{10} = 1.48]$.

Next, consider product innovations, which involve new and improved products. It is much more difficult to quantify the importance of product innovations, but they may be even more important in raising living standards than process innovations. Many of today's goods and services did not even exist 50 years ago. In producing this textbook, the authors used computer software, microprocessors, Internet

① 这里是“刺激人们味觉和嗅觉产品”走进生活的典型案例。

[2] International Flavors and Fragrances：国际香料香精公司，即 IFF，总部在纽约，在全球 30 多个国家和地区设有分支机构。

[3] *Fast Food Nation*：《快餐帝国》，2001 年的畅销书，2006 年由美国和英国联合拍摄成同名电影。该片由理查德·林克莱特（Richard Stuart Linklater，1960 年 7 月 30 日出生，著名的美国电影导演和剧作家）执导，剧本由林克莱特和原书作者埃里克·施洛瑟（Eric Schlooser，1959 年 8 月 17 日出生，著名的美国记者）共同改编。

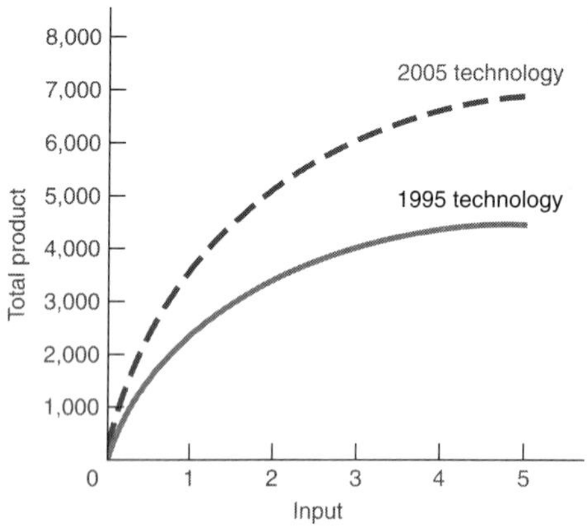

FIGURE 6-3. Technological Change Shifts Production Function Upward ①

The solid line represents maximum producible output for each level of inputs given the state of technical knowledge in 1995. As a result of improvements in computer technology and management practices, technological change shifts the production function upward, allowing much more output to be produced in 2005 for each level of inputs.

⑤ 在竞争性市场中，劣质产品终究会像尼安德特人那样消失。

[6] *Neanderthal* 指 35~60 万年前生活在欧洲和中亚西亚的穴居人，外延含义指极端守旧的人。

computer clusters 计算机集群

adoption externality 使用外部性

tippy 倾斜型的

sites, and databases that were not available a decade ago. Medicine, communications, and entertainment are other sectors where product innovations have been critical. The whole arena of the Internet, from ② e-commerce to e-mail, was not found even in science fiction literature 30 years ago. For fun, and to see this point, try to find any commodity or production process that has not changed since your grandparents [3] were your age!

Figure 6-3 shows the happy case of a technological advance. Is the opposite case—technological regress—possible? The answer is no for a well-functioning market economy. Inferior technologies are unprofitable and tend to be discarded in a market economy, while more productive technologies are introduced because they increase the profits of the innovating firms. To see this, suppose that someone invents an expensive new mousetrap that will never catch a mouse. No profit-oriented firm would produce such a device; and if a poorly managed firm decided to produce it, rational consumers who lived in mouse-infested houses would decline to buy it. Well-functioning markets innovate with better, not inferior, mousetraps.

When there are market failures, however, technological regress might occur. An unregulated company might introduce a socially wasteful process, say, dumping toxic wastes into a stream, because the wasteful process is more profitable. *But the economic* ④ *advantage of inferior technologies comes only because the social costs of pollution are not included in the firm's calculations of the costs of production.* If pollution costs were included in a firm's decisions, say by pollution taxes, the regressive process would no longer be profitable. In competitive markets, inferior products follow ⑤ Neanderthals into extinction. [6]

Networks

Many products have little use by themselves and generate value only when they are used in combination with other products. Such products are strongly complementary. An important case is a *network*, where different people are linked together through a particular medium. Types of networks include both those defined by physical linkages, such as telecommunication systems, electricity transmission networks, computer clusters, pipelines, and roads, and the indirect networks that occur when people use compatible systems (such as Windows operating systems) or speak the same language (such as English).

To understand the nature of networks, consider how far you could drive your car without a network of gas stations or how valuable your telephone or e-mail would be if no one else had telephones or computers.

Network markets are special because consumers derive benefits not simply from their own use of a good but also from the number of other consumers who adopt the good. This is known as an *adoption externality.* When I get a phone, everyone else with a phone can now communicate with me. Therefore, my joining this network leads to positive external effects for others. The network externality is the reason why many colleges provide universal e-mail for all their students and faculty—the value of e-mail is much higher when everyone participates. Figure 6-4 on page 115 illustrates how one individual's joining a network has an external benefit to others.

Economists have discovered many important features of network markets. First, network markets are "tippy," meaning that the equilibrium tips toward one or only a

---

① 图 6-3. 技术变革推动生产函数曲线上移

② 从电子商务到电子邮件的整个互联网“竞技场”，即便在 30 年前的科幻文学作品当中也还是一片空白。请注意，就这一点顺便开个玩笑，从你爷爷那代到现在，能否找出哪怕只有一种商品，或者任何一个生产工序还未曾变革？

[3] 这一段文字作者较 17~18 版做了两处小的改动，但效果却一大一小两个极端。一是 20 年修正成了 30 年，为其小；其大为萨翁的严谨和缜密思维精神之再现，将沿用 10 年之久的 *area* 改为 *arena*，为一大妙笔所在。Arena 一词源自拉丁文，在西方文化中有着太多的内涵和联想，其外延含义也颇深，甚至罗密欧与朱丽叶的爱情传说也源自于此。

④ 但这仅仅是由于污染问题所带来的社会成本未纳入企业的生产成本核算，才使得这些落后技术还能有其经济优势。

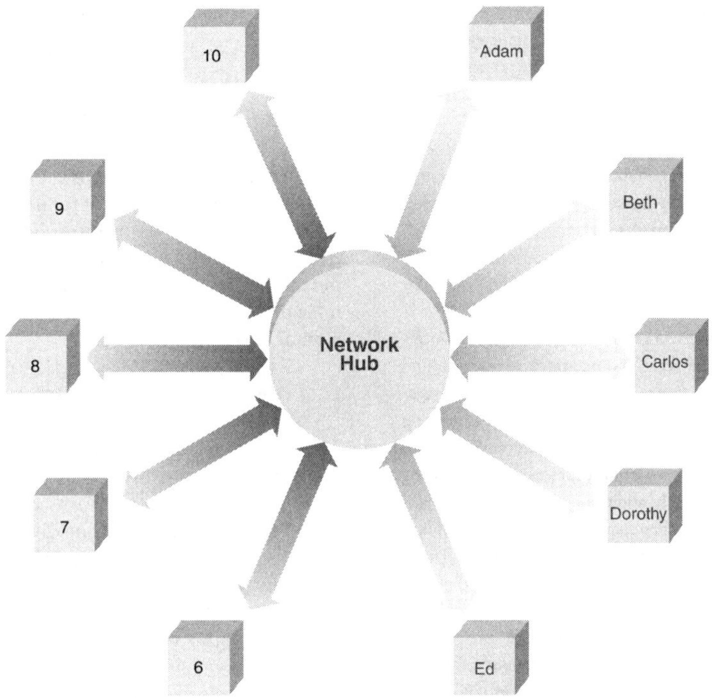

FIGURE 6-4. Value of Networking Increases as Membership Rises ①

Assume that each person derives a value of $1 for each additional person who is connected to a telephone or e-mail network. If Ed decides to join, he will get $4 of value from being connected to Adam, Beth, Carlos, and Dorothy. But there is an "adoption externality" because each of the four people already in the network gets $1 of additional value when Ed joins, for a total of $4 of external additional value.

These network effects make it difficult for networks to get started. To see this point, note that the second or third person who joins the network gets little value from joining. But when many people are in the network, each new member has a high value of joining because they are networked with a large number of people. (As an exercise, calculate the value of joining for the second and for the tenth people who join the network.)

few products. Because consumers dislike buying products ② that may turn out to be incompatible with dominant technologies, the equilibrium tends to gravitate to a single product which wins out over its rivals. One of the best-known examples is computer operating systems, where Microsoft Windows became the dominant system in part because consumers wanted to make sure that their computers could operate all the available software. (The important antitrust case involving Microsoft is discussed in Chapter 10.)

A second interesting feature is that "history matters" in network markets. A famous example is the QWERTY keyboard used with your computer. You might wonder why this particular configuration of keys, with its awkward placement of the letters, became the standard. The design of the QWERTY keyboard in the nineteenth century was [3] based on the concept of keeping frequently used keys (like "e" and "o") physically separated in order to prevent manual typewriters from jamming. By the time the technology for electronic typing evolved, tens of millions of people had

① 图 6-4. 网络的价值随着网络用户的增加而增加

② 因为消费者不喜欢购买那些与主流技术不兼容的产品，所以这样的均衡就会被吸引到那种彻底击败其对手的单一产品上来。

[3] QWERTY：即俗称的柯蒂键盘，1868 年由美国发明家、报业商人、政治家克里斯托弗·莱瑟姆·肖尔斯（Christopher Latham Sholes，1819~1890）设计，并于当年申请专利。

already learned to type on millions of typewriters. Replacing the QWERTY keyboard with a more efficient design would have been both expensive and difficult to coordinate. Thus, the placement of the letters remains unchanged on today's keyboards.

This example shows how an embedded network technology can be extremely stable. A similar example that worries many environmentalists is America's "wasteful" automobile culture, where the existing network of cars, roads, gasoline stations, and residential locations will be difficult to dislodge in favor of more environmentally friendly alternatives, like improved mass transit.

America's "wasteful" automobile culture 美国的"浪费型"汽车文化

improved mass transit 改进后的公共交通

Third, because networks involve a complicated interplay of economies of scale, expectations, dynamics, and tipping, they lead to a fascinating array of business strategies. The tippy nature of networks means that they tend to be "winner-take-all" markets with intense rivalry in the early stages and but a few competitors once the winning technology has emerged. In addition, network markets are often inertial, so once a product has a substantial lead, it may be very difficult for other products to catch up. These characteristics mean that companies often want to get an early lead on their rivals.

Suppose you are producing a network product. In order to build on your early lead, you might persuade users that you are number one by puffing up your sales; use "penetration pricing" by offering very low prices to early adopters; bundle your product with another popular product; or raise questions about your competitors' quality or staying power. Above all, you would probably invest heavily in advertising to shift out the demand curve for the product. If you are the fortunate winner, you will benefit from the economies of scale in the network and enjoy your monopoly profits. But don't take your dominant position for granted. Once your commanding lead is questioned, the virtuous cycle of market dominance can easily turn into the vicious cycle of market decline.

Networks raise important issues for public policy. Should government set standards to ensure competition? Should government regulate network industries? How should government antitrust policy treat monopolists like Microsoft that have been the fortunate winners in the network race but use anticompetitive tactics? These questions are on the minds of many public policymakers today.[2]

[2] See the Further Reading section at the end of this chapter.

生产率与总生产函数
PRODUCTIVITY AND THE AGGREGATE PRODUCTION FUNCTION

Productivity 生产率

One of the most important measures of economic performance is productivity. **Productivity** is a con- ②
cept measuring the ratio of total output to a weighted average of inputs. Two important variants are **labor productivity,** which calculates the amount of output per unit of labor, and **total factor productivity,** which measures output per unit of total inputs (typically of capital and labor).

规模经济和范围经济引起的生产率上升
Productivity Growth from Economies of Scale and Scope

① A central concept in economics is *productivity,* a term denoting the ratio of output to inputs. Economists typically look at two measures of productivity. Total factor productivity is output divided by an index of all inputs (labor, capital, materials, . . .), while labor productivity measures output per unit of labor (such
as hours worked). When output is growing faster ③
than inputs, this represents **productivity growth.**

Productivity grows because of technological advances such as the process and product innovations described above. Additionally, productivity grows because of economies of scale and scope.

Economies of scale and mass production have been important elements of productivity growth since the Industrial Revolution. Most production processes are many times larger than they were during the nineteenth century. A large ship in the mid-nineteenth century could carry 2000 tons of goods, while the largest supertankers today carry over 1 million tons of oil.

If increasing returns to scale prevail, the larger scale of inputs and production would lead to greater productivity. Suppose that, with no change in technology, the typical firm's inputs increased by 10 percent and that, because of economies of scale, output increased by 11 percent. Economies of scale would be responsible for a growth in total factor productivity of 1 percent.

A different kind of efficiency arises when there ④
are **economies of scope,** which occur when a number of different products can be produced more efficiently together than apart. A prominent example is seen for computer software. Software programs often incorporate additional features as they evolve. For

① Winner-take-all：赢者全拿 / 通吃

网络的倾斜性本质是，一旦有少数几家掌握了领先技术的竞争者脱颖而出，就能在该领域早期激烈竞争的态势下依循"赢者通吃"的规律而占领市场。

② **生产率**的定义是总产出与加权后的平均产出之比率。两个重要的变量是**劳动生产率**和**全要素生产率**；劳动生产率是每一单位劳动的产出量，全要素生产率是每单位总投入（特别是资本和劳动）的产出量。

③ **生产率增长**所代表的是产出的增长大于投入增长时的情况。

④ 当大量不同的产品集中生产的效率大于分别生产的效率时，就出现了**范围经济**，从而产生另外一种截然不同的效率。

example, when consumers buy software to prepare their federal income taxes, the CD-ROM usually contains several other modules, including a link to a Web page, government documents, and a tax preparation manual. This shows economies of scope because the different modules can be more inexpensively produced, packaged, and used together than separately. Economies of scope are like the specialization and division of labor that increase productivity as economies become larger and more diversified.

While increasing returns to scale and scope are potentially large in many sectors, at some point decreasing returns to scale and scope may take hold. As firms become larger and larger, the problems of management and coordination become increasingly difficult. In relentless pursuit of greater profits, a ① firm may find itself expanding into more geographic markets or product lines than it can effectively manage. A firm can have only one chief executive officer, one chief financial officer, and one board of directors. With less time to study each market and spend on each decision, top managers may become insulated from day-to-day production and begin to make mistakes. Like empires that have been stretched too thin, such firms find themselves vulnerable to invasion by smaller and more agile rivals.

总生产函数的经验估计
Empirical Estimates of the Aggregate Production Function

Now that we have examined the principles of produc- ② tion theory, we can apply these theories to measure how well the whole U.S. economy has performed in recent years. To do this, we need to look at *aggregate production functions*, which relate total output to the quantity of inputs (like labor, capital, and land). What have economic studies found? Here are a few of the important results:

- Total factor productivity has been increasing over the last century because of technological progress and higher levels of worker education and skill.
- The average rate of total productivity growth was slightly under 1½ percent per year since 1900.
- Over the twentieth century, labor productivity (output per hour worked) grew at an average rate of slightly more than 2 percent per year. From the early 1970s to the mid-1990s, however, all measures of productivity showed a marked slowdown in growth, and real wages and living standards consequently stagnated over this period. Since the mid-1990s, fueled largely by information technologies, there has been a marked upturn in productivity growth, with rates above the historical norm. (Figure 6-5 shows the historical trends.)
- The capital stock has been growing faster than the number of worker-hours. As a result, labor ④ has a growing quantity of capital goods to work with; hence, labor productivity and wages have tended to rise even faster than the 1½ percent per year attributable to total factor productivity growth alone.

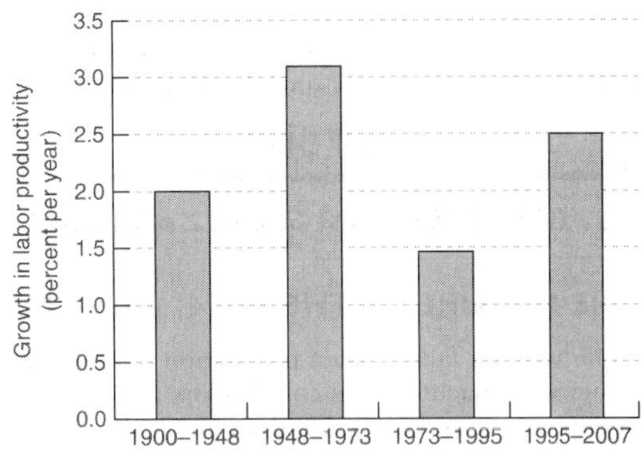

FIGURE 6-5. Growth in Labor Productivity ③

We see here the average growth in total productivity per hour worked during different periods. The last half-century had rapid growth after World War II, then a slowdown during the troubled 1970s and 1980s, and rapid growth during the period of rapid penetration of information technologies since 1995.

Source: Bureau of Labor Statistics and private scholars.

We end with a final word on the difficulties of measuring productivity growth accurately. Recent empirical studies suggest that we have seriously underestimated productivity growth in some areas. Studies of medical care, capital goods, consumer electronics, computers, and computer software indicate that our measuring rod for productivity is distorted. One particularly important shortcoming is the failure to account for the economic value of new and improved products. For example, when compact discs replaced "long-playing records," our measures of productivity did not include the improvement in

① 在不顾一切地追求更大利润的过程中，企业会发现其行为已经扩张至更大的市场地域，增加了更多的生产线，这一切已经超出了其有效管理的能力。

② 既然我们已经探讨了生产理论的原理，那么我们就能应用这些理论来评价美国经济在最近几年里整体运行的情况。

③ 图 6-5. 劳动生产率的增长

④ Worker-hour：工时，即每小时每人工或每人工小时

资本存量的增加一直高于工作时间的增长。其结果是，劳动使用的资本商品量持续增长。因此，劳动生产率与工资就形成了上升的态势，每年的上升速度甚至高于 1.5 个百分点，其原因完全是由于全要素生产率增长的结果。

durability and sound quality. Similarly, our economic accounts cannot accurately measure the contribution of the Internet to consumer economic welfare.

企业组织

B. BUSINESS ORGANIZATIONS

THE NATURE OF THE FIRM 企业的性质

So far we have talked about production functions as if they were machines that could be operated by anyone: put a pig in one end and a sausage comes out the other. In reality, almost all production is done by specialized organizations—the small, medium, and large businesses that dominate the landscape of modern economies. Why does production generally take place in firms rather than in our basements?

Firms or business enterprises exist for many reasons, but the most important is that *business firms are specialized organizations devoted to managing the process of production.* ① Among their important functions are exploiting economies of mass production, raising funds, and organizing factors of production.

economies of specialization 经济活动的专业化分工

In the first place, production is organized in firms because of *economies of specialization.* Efficient production requires specialized labor and machinery, coordinated production, and the division of production into many small operations. Consider a service such as a college education. This activity requires specialized personnel to teach economics and mathematics and Spanish, to produce the meals and housing services, to keep records, collect tuition, and pay the bills. We could hardly expect that a student could organize all these activities by herself. If there were no need for specialization and division of labor, we could each produce our own college education, surgical operations, electricity, and compact discs in our own backyard or buy them on the Internet. We obviously cannot perform such feats; efficiency generally requires large-scale production in businesses.

raising resources 筹集资金

A second function of firms is *raising resources* for large-scale production. Developing a new commercial aircraft costs billions of dollars or Euros; the research and development expenses for a new computer microprocessor are just as high. Where are such funds to come from? In the nineteenth century, businesses could often be financed by wealthy, risk-taking individuals. Today, in a private-enterprise economy, most funds for production must come from company profits or from money borrowed in financial markets. Indeed, efficient production by private enterprise would be virtually unthinkable if corporations could not raise billions of dollars each year for new projects.

manage and coordinate the production process 管理和协调生产过程

A third reason for the existence of firms is to *manage and coordinate the production process.* Once all the factors of production are engaged, someone has to monitor their daily activities to ensure that the job is being done effectively and honestly. The manager is the person who organizes production, introduces new ideas, products, or processes, makes the business decisions, and is held accountable for success or failure. Production cannot, after all, organize itself. Someone has to supervise the construction of a new factory, negotiate with labor unions, and purchase materials and supplies.

Take the case of a baseball team. How likely is it that 25 people would organize themselves into just the right combination of pitchers, catchers, and hitters, all in the right order and using the best strategy? If you were to purchase the franchise for a baseball team, you would have to rent a stadium, hire baseball players, negotiate with people for concessions, hire ushers, deal with unions, and sell tickets. This is the role of firms, to manage the production process, purchasing or renting land, capital, labor, and materials.

Business firms are specialized organizations devoted to managing the process of production. Production is organized in firms because efficiency generally requires large-scale production, the raising of significant financial resources, and careful management and coordination of ongoing activities. ② [3]

Production in the Firm or the Market?
If markets are such a powerful mechanism for efficiency, why does so much production take place within large organizations? A related question is, Why do some firms decide on an integrated production structure while others contract out a large fraction of their sales? For example, before 1982 AT&T was vertically and horizontally integrated, doing its own research [4]

---

① 企业是专业化管理生产过程的组织。

② 企业是管理生产过程的专业化组织。在企业内组织生产是因为效率一般要求规模化生产，筹集巨额资金，以及对正在进行的生产活动进行精细管理和协调。

[3] 本版的此段小结较此前的 16~18 版有一处比较重要的改动，将“monitoring”修改为“coordinate”。企业的性质由过去的“监控”变成“协调”，作者的良苦用心是与时代同步的。

[4] AT&T：美国电话电报公司（American Telephone & Telegraph Company，详见 36 页注 [1]）。

and development, designing and producing its own equipment, installing and renting telephones, and providing telephone service. By contrast, most personal computers are "produced" by assemblers who purchase the hard drives, circuits, monitors, and keyboards from outside vendors and package and sell them.

These central issues of industrial organization were [1] first raised by Ronald Coase in a pathbreaking study for which he was awarded the 1991 Nobel Prize.[3] This exciting area analyzes the comparative advantage of organizing production through the hierarchical control of firms as compared to the contractual relationships of the market.

Why might organizing through large firms be efficient? Perhaps the most important reason is the difficulty of ② designing "complete contracts" that cover all contingencies. [3] For example, suppose Snoozer Inc. thinks it has discovered a hot new drug to cure laziness. Should it do the research in its own laboratories or contract out to another com- [4] pany, WilyLabs, Inc.? The problem with contracting out is that there are all kinds of unforeseen contingencies that could affect the profitability of the drug. What would happen if the drug proves useful for other conditions? What if the patent, tax, or international-trade laws change? What if there is a patent-infringement suit?

Because of the contractual incompleteness, the com- ⑤ pany runs the risk of the *holdup problem*. Suppose that WilyLabs discovers that the antilaziness drug works only when taken with another drug that WilyLabs owns. WilyLabs goes to Snoozer and says, "Sorry, pal, but to get both drugs will cost you another $100 million." This is holdup with a vengeance. Fear of being held up in situations which involve relationship-specific investments and contractual incompleteness will lead Snoozer to do the research internally so that it can control the outcomes of its research.

⑥ The recent trend in many industries has been to move away from highly integrated firms by "outsourcing" or contracting out production. This has definitely been the trend in the computer industry since the days when IBM was almost as integrated as AT&T. Contracting out can function well in situations where, as in the PC industry, the components are standardized or "commoditized." Another example is Nike, which contracts out much of its production because the production process is standard and Nike's real value is tied to its design and trademark. In addition, new contractual forms, such as long-term contracts based on reputations, attempt to minimize holdup problems.

Those who study organizations point to the vital importance of large firms in promoting innovation and increasing productivity. In the nineteenth century, railroads not only brought wheat from farm to market but also introduced time zones. Indeed, the very notion of being "on time" first became crucial when being off schedule produced train wrecks. As the tragic story of centrally planned economies so clearly shows, without the organizational genius of the modern private-enterprise firm, all the land, labor, and capital can work for naught.

大企业、小企业和微型企业
BIG, SMALL, AND INFINITESIMAL BUSINESSES

Production in a market economy takes place in a wide variety of business organizations—from the tiniest individual proprietorships to the giant corporations that dominate economic life in a capitalist economy. There are currently around 30 million different businesses in America. The majority of these are tiny units owned by a single person—the individual proprietorship. Others are partnerships, owned by two or perhaps two hundred partners. The largest businesses tend to be corporations.

Tiny businesses predominate in numbers. But in sales and assets, in political and economic power, and in size of payroll and employment, the few hundred largest corporations dominate the economy.

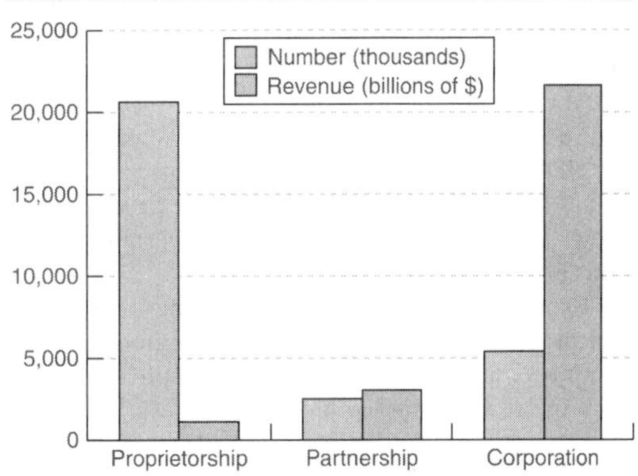

FIGURE 6-6. Number and Size of Different Business Forms, 2004 ⑦

Corporations are fewer in number but dominate the economy.

Source: Internal Revenue Service.

[1] 罗纳德·科斯（Ronald Coase），1910 年 12 月 29 日生于伦敦的威尔斯登，其主要学术成就为 1937 年发表的《企业的性质》（*The Nature of the Firm*）和 1960 年发表的《社会成本问题》（*The Problem of Social Cost*）两篇著名论文。科斯创造性地提出了交易成本的概念，来解释企业存在的原因与规模扩张的边界问题。著名的科斯定理探讨了运行和操作中的产权与交易成本及其外部性等涉及法律的经济学问题。1991 年获诺贝尔经济学奖。瑞典皇家科学院的颁奖辞是："For his discovery and clarification of the significance of transaction costs and property rights for the institutional structure and functioning of the economy"（其研究揭示和界定了交易成本在经济组织结构的产权和功能中的重要性），其学术文献对经济史的研究增加了新的推动力，使一门新的学科——《法律与经济学》，在经济学与法学的交叉地带应运而生。

[3] See the Further Reading section at the end of this chapter for examples of Coase's and related writings.

② complete contracts：完全契约

[3] Snoozer Inc.：一家专门生产宠物用品的美国供应商。

[4] WilyLabs Inc.：一家专为 CA 应用信息管理系统软件提供配套硬件服务器平台系统的美国供应商。

⑤ The holdup problem：被敲竹杠的问题

⑥ 近期在美国有一种趋势，许多行业采用外包或者利用使用承包出去的模式，放弃了过去高度集成化的公司组织生产模式。

⑦ 图 6-6. 2004 年不同企业的数量及其规模统计

Figure 6-6 shows the number and total revenue of the three major forms of economic organization in the United States.

独资经营
The Individual Proprietorship

mom-and-pop 夫妻店

At one end of the spectrum are the individual proprietorships, the classic small businesses often called "mom-and-pop" stores. A small store might do a few hundred dollars of business per day and barely provide a minimum wage for the owners' efforts.

These businesses are large in number but small in total sales. For most small businesses, a tremendous amount of personal effort is required. The self-employed often work 50 or 60 hours per week and take no vacations, yet the average lifetime of a small business is only a year. Still, some people will always want to start out on their own. Theirs may be the successful venture that gets bought out for millions of dollars.

合伙制
The Partnership

Often a business requires a combination of talents—say, lawyers or doctors specializing in different areas. Any two or more people can get together and form a partnership. Each agrees to provide a fraction of the work and capital and to share a percentage of the profits and losses.

unlimited liability 无限责任

Today, partnerships account for only a small fraction of total economic activity, as Figure 6-6 shows. Up to recently, partnerships were unattractive because they imposed *unlimited liability*. Under unlimited liability, ① partners are liable without limit for all debts contracted by the partnership. If you own 1 percent of the partnership and the business fails, you will be called upon to pay 1 percent of the bills. However, if your partners cannot pay, you may be called upon to pay all the debts, even if you must sell off your prized possessions to do so. Some states in the United States allow limited-liability partnerships for certain professions like law and architecture.

Except for a few sectors involving real estate and professionals, partnerships are cumbersome to administer and are less important than the corporate form of organization for most businesses.

公　司
The Corporation

The bulk of economic activity in an advanced market economy takes place in private corporations. Centuries ago, corporate charters were awarded by special acts of the monarch or legislature. The British East India Company was a privileged corporation and as such it practically ruled India for more than a century. In the nineteenth century, railroads often had to spend as much money on getting a charter through the legislature as on preparing their roadbeds. Over the past century, laws have been passed that allow almost anyone the privilege of forming a corporation for almost any purpose.

Today, a **corporation** is a form of business orga- ② nization chartered in one of the 50 states or abroad and owned by a number of individual stockholders. The corporation has a separate legal identity, and indeed is a legal "person" that may on its own behalf buy, sell, borrow money, produce goods and services, and enter into contracts. In addition, the corpora- ③ tion enjoys the right of *limited liability*, whereby each owner's investment and financial exposure in the corporation is strictly limited to a specified amount.

The central features of a modern corporation are the following:

- The ownership of a corporation is determined by the ownership of the company's common stock. If you own 10 percent of a corporation's shares, you have 10 percent of the ownership. Publicly owned corporations are valued on stock exchanges, like the New York Stock Exchange. It is in such stock markets that the titles to the largest corporations are traded and that much of the nation's risk capital is raised and invested.
- In principle, the shareholders control the companies they own. They collect dividends in proportion to the fraction of the shares they own, and they elect directors and vote on many important issues. But don't think that the shareholders have a significant role in running giant corporations. In practice, shareholders of giant corporations exercise virtually no control because they are too dispersed to overrule the entrenched managers.
- The corporation's managers and directors have the legal power to make decisions for the corporation. They decide what to produce and how to produce it. They negotiate with labor unions and decide whether to sell the firm if another firm wishes to take it over. When the newspaper announces that a firm has laid off 20,000 workers, this decision was made by the managers. The shareholders own the corporation, but the managers run it.

---

① 在无约束责任的机制下，合伙人对于合同中所规定的债务所承担的责任是没有约束的。

② 今天，**公司**是一种在美国的任何一个州或者海外注册的由众多的个人股东持股的企业组织形式。

③ 另外，公司享有有限责任的权利，所享权利与每一个持股人在公司的投资和资金量均严格地限制在一个特定的额度上。

Advantages and Disadvantages of Corporations. Corporations are the dominant form of organization in a market economy because they are an extremely efficient way to engage in business. A corporation is a legal person that can conduct business. Also, the corporation may have perpetual succession or existence, regardless of how many times the shares of stock
change hands. Corporations are hierarchical, with ①
the chief executive officer (CEO) exercising such power that they are sometimes called "autocratic" organizations. Managers can make decisions quickly, and often ruthlessly, which is in stark contrast to the way economic decisions are made by legislatures.

In addition, corporate stockholders enjoy limited liability, which protects them from incurring the debts or losses of the corporation beyond their initial contribution. If we buy $1000 worth of stock, we cannot lose more than our original investment.

Corporations face one major disadvantage: The government levies an extra tax on corporate profits. For an unincorporated business, any income after expenses is taxed as ordinary personal income. The large corporation is treated differently in that some of its income is doubly taxed—first as corporate profits and then as individual income on dividends.

Economists have criticized the corporation income tax as "double taxation" and have sometimes proposed integrating the corporate tax with the individual tax system. Under tax integration, corporate income is allocated to individuals and then taxed as individual income.

Sometimes, corporations undertake actions that provoke public outrage and government actions. In the late nineteenth century, corporations engaged in fraud, price fixing, and bribery, which led to enact-
ment of antitrust and securities-fraud legislation. In ③
the last few years, corporate scandals erupted when it was discovered that some companies engaged in massive accounting fraud and many corporate executives feathered their nests with huge bonuses and stock options. In private as in public life, power sometimes corrupts.

Efficient production often requires large-scale ④
enterprises, which need billions of dollars of invested capital. Corporations, with limited liability and a convenient management structure, can attract large supplies of private capital, produce a variety of related products, and pool investor risks.

所有权、控制和高管薪酬
Ownership, Control, and Executive Compensation

The operation of large corporations raises important issues of public policy. They control much of a market economy, yet they are not controlled by the public. Indeed, scholars have come to recognize that they are not really controlled by their owners. Let us review some of the issues here.

The first step in understanding large corporations is to realize that most large corporations are "publicly owned." Corporate shares can be bought by anyone, and ownership is spread among many
[2] investors. Take a company like IBM, which was worth about $170 billion in 2008. Tens of millions of people have a financial interest in IBM through their mutual funds or pension accounts. However, no single person owned even 0.1 percent of the total. Such dispersed ownership is typical of our large publicly owned corporations.

publicly owned
公众所有

Because the stock of large companies is so widely ⑤
dispersed, *ownership is typically divorced from control.* Individual owners cannot easily affect the actions of large corporations. And while the stockholders of a company do in principle elect its board of directors—a group of insiders and knowledgeable outsiders—it is the management that makes the major decisions about corporate strategy and day-to-day operations.

In some situations, there is no conflict of interest between management and stockholders. Higher profits benefit everyone. But one important potential conflict between managers and stockholders has caught people's attention—the question of executive compensation. Top managers are able to extract from their boards large salaries, stock options, expense accounts, bonuses, free apartments, expensive artwork, and generous retirement pensions at the stockholders' expense. Nobody is arguing that managers should work for the minimum wage, but executive pay in U.S. corporations has risen very rapidly in recent years. Some top executives at poorly performing companies—or even at companies like WorldCom or Enron which later went bankrupt—received salaries and bonuses totaling $100 million or more.

Figure 6-7 shows an arresting graph: the ratio of the average pay of the top executives in the largest firms to that of the average worker. That ratio rose

---

① 公司是分等级的，其首席执行官执行这些权利，所以这些公司有的时候称作“专制”组织。

[2] 这一段文字较 16~18 版进行了彻底的修订，语气更为强硬。

③ 过去几年，一些公司被发现卷入了大笔的会计欺诈案，许多公司的高管拿高额的红利和股票期权放入自己的腰包，丑闻频发。如同在公共部门一样，权力在私人部门也一样容易引起腐败。

④ 有效率的生产要求企业有很大的规模，这就需要达到几十亿美元的资本投资。具有有限责任并拥有合适的管理结构的公司就能够吸引大量私人资本的投入，生产各种相关产品并能够较好地分摊风险。

⑤ 由于大公司的股票持有者非常广泛和分散，所以这种所有权完全脱离了控制。

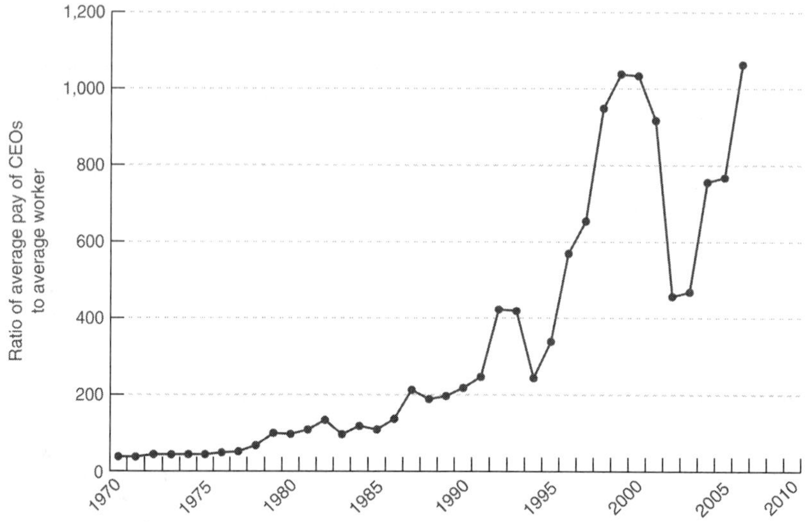

FIGURE 6-7. The Explosion in Executive Compensation ①

The figure shows the ratio of the average pay of the top 100 chief executive officers (CEOs) of U.S. corporations to the pay of the average U.S. worker. The ratio has risen from around 40 in 1970 to over 1000 in the mid-2000s. Many factors lie behind this explosive growth, but the most important is probably the ability of CEOs to manage the compensation process. [2]

Source: Thomas Piketty and Emmanuel Saez, data from their website at *elsa.berkeley.edu/~saez/*.

from a historical average of around 40 to more than 1000 in recent years. The rise in executive compensation has been part of the reason for the growth in income inequality in the United States. What is the reason for this increase? Why, economists ask, are American executives often paid 10 or 20 times more than are executives in comparable firms of other countries?

Research in this area has pointed to several reasons for the dramatic change. Defenders point to the great importance of managers in efficient capitalism, but this overlooks the role of marginal productivity in competitive markets. Defenders also argue that stock options, which have been the major source of increased executive pay, are efficient devices because they tie compensation to performance through stock prices.

Critics answer that the most important reason for the trend is the divorce of ownership from control. This is the symptom of a malady known as the *principal-agent problem,* wherein the incentives of the agents (the managers) are not appropriately aligned with the interests of the principal (the owners). Moreover, managers tend to hide the compensation procedures from stockholders, and so the owners never really have a vote on managerial compensation. Additionally, stock options may give incentives for management to distort the financial accounts as well as to produce sound profits.

The rising tide of executive compensation raises important questions about public policy. What are effective means of ensuring that compensation is efficient? Most economists are reluctant to have the government set any kind of pay standards. They would argue that a system of progressive taxation is the most evenhanded way to deal with income inequalities. Most agree that better information and more power to owners can also wring out the largest excesses.

① 图 6-7. 高管薪酬的暴涨

[2] 这段内容是作者在本版新加的，是萨翁对本次金融危机爆发的原因及其对公共政策带来的影响所作的深入分析和思考。

SUMMARY

A. Theory of Production and Marginal Products

1. The relationship between the quantity of output (such as wheat, steel, or automobiles) and the quantities of inputs (of labor, land, and capital) is called the production function. Total product is the total output produced. Average product equals total output divided by the total quantity of inputs. We can calculate the marginal product of a factor as the extra output added for each additional unit of input while holding all other inputs constant.
2. According to the law of diminishing returns, the marginal product of each input will generally decline as the amount of that input increases, when all other inputs are held constant.
3. The returns to scale reflect the impact on output of a balanced increase in all inputs. A technology in which doubling all inputs leads to an exact doubling of outputs displays constant returns to scale. When doubling inputs leads to less than double (more than double) the quantity of output, the situation is one of decreasing (increasing) returns to scale.
4. Because decisions take time to implement, and because capital and other factors are often very long-lived, the reaction of production may change over different time periods. The short run is a period in which variable factors, such as labor or material inputs, can be easily changed but fixed factors cannot. In the long run, the capital stock (a firm's machinery and factories) can depreciate and be replaced. In the long run, all inputs, fixed and variable, can be adjusted.
5. Technological change refers to a change in the underlying techniques of production, as occurs when a new product or process of production is invented or an old product or process is improved. In such situations, the same output is produced with fewer inputs or more output is produced with the same inputs. Technological change shifts the production function upward.
6. Attempts to measure an aggregate production function for the American economy tend to corroborate theories of production and marginal products. In the twentieth century, technological change increased the productivity of both labor and capital. Total factor productivity (measuring the ratio of total output to total inputs) grew at around 1½ percent per year over the twentieth century, although from the 1970s to the mid-1990s the rate of productivity growth slowed markedly and real wages stopped growing. But underestimating the importance of new and improved products may lead to a significant underestimate of productivity growth.

B. Business Organizations

7. Business firms are specialized organizations devoted to managing the process of production.
8. Firms come in many shapes and sizes—with some economic activity in tiny one-person proprietorships, some in partnerships, and the bulk in corporations. Each kind of enterprise has advantages and disadvantages. Small businesses are flexible, can market new products, and can disappear quickly. But they suffer from the fundamental disadvantage of being unable to accumulate large amounts of capital from a dispersed group of investors. Today's large corporation, granted limited liability by the state, is able to amass billions of dollars of capital by borrowing from banks, bondholders, and stock markets.
9. In a modern economy, business corporations produce most goods and services because economies of mass production necessitate that output be produced at high volumes, the technology of production requires much more capital than a single individual would willingly put at risk, and efficient production requires careful management and coordination of tasks by a centrally directed entity.
10. The modern corporation may involve divided incentives because of the divorce of ownership from control, which has produced the vast gulf between executive compensation and average wages.

CONCEPTS FOR REVIEW

inputs, outputs, production function
total, average, and marginal product
diminishing marginal product and the law of diminishing returns
constant, increasing, and decreasing returns to scale
short run vs. long run

technological change: process innovation, product innovation
Productivity:
    defined as output/input
    two versions: labor productivity, total factor productivity
aggregate production function
reasons for firms: scale economies, financial needs, management

major business forms: individual proprietorship, partnership, corporation
unlimited and limited liability
firm vs. market and the holdup problem
Divorce of ownership from control: principal-agent problem

FURTHER READING AND INTERNET WEBSITES

Further Reading

Ronald Coase's classic work is "The Nature of the Firm," *Economica,* November 1937. Students may enjoy a recent nontechnical survey of the field in the symposium "The Firm and Its Boundaries," *Journal of Economic Perspectives,* Fall 1998. For a thoughtful analysis of network effects, see the symposium in *Journal of Economic Perspectives,* Spring 1994. A fascinating study of networks and the new economy is contained in Chapter 7 in Carl Shapiro and Hal R. Varian, *Information Rules: A Strategic Guide to the Network Economy* (Harvard Business School Press, Cambridge, Mass., 1997).

For a recent survey of the issues and policies concerning executive compensation, see Gary Shorter and Marc Labonte, *The Economics of Corporate Executive Pay,* March 22, 2007, available at *digitalcommons.ilr.cornell.edu/crs/36/.* A discussion of the economic background on this subject is contained in a symposium in *The Journal of Economic Perspectives,* Fall 2003, particularly the article by Kevin Murphy and Brian Hall.

Trends in the income of top executives are shown in Thomas Piketty and Emmanuel Saez, "Income Inequality in the United States, 1913–1998," *Quarterly Journal of Economics,* 2003, pp. 1–39; that article and an updated version are available at *elsa.berkeley.edu/~saez/.*

Websites

One of the most interesting websites about networks is compiled by Hal R. Varian, dean of the School of Information Management and Systems at the University of California at Berkeley. This site, called "The Economics of the Internet, Information Goods, Intellectual Property and Related Issues," is at *www.sims.berkeley.edu/resources/infoecon.*

A specialized site on network economics maintained by Nicholas Economides of New York University is found at *raven.stern.nyu.edu/networks/site.html.*

QUESTIONS FOR DISCUSSION

1. Explain the concept of a production function. Describe the production function for hamburgers, computers, concerts, haircuts, and a college education.
2. Consider a production function of the following form: $X = 100L^{1/2}$, where X = output and L = input of labor (assuming other inputs are fixed).
    a. Construct a figure like Figure 6-1 and a table like Table 6-1 for inputs of $L = 0, 1, 2, 3,$ and 4.
    b. Explain whether this production function shows diminishing returns to labor. What values would the exponent need to take for this production function to exhibit increasing returns to labor?
3. The following table describes the actual production function for oil pipelines. Fill in the missing values for marginal products and average products:

(1)	(2)	(3)	(4)
	18-Inch Pipe		
Pumping horsepower	Total product (barrels per day)	Marginal product (barrels per day per hp)	Average product (barrels per day per hp)
10,000	86,000		____
		____	
20,000	114,000		____
		____	
30,000	134,000		____
		____	
40,000	150,000		____
		____	
50,000	164,000		____

4. Using the data in question 3, plot the production function of output against horsepower. On the same graph, plot the curves for average product and marginal product.
5. Suppose you are running the food concession at the athletic events for your college. You sell hot dogs, colas, and potato chips. What are your inputs of capital, labor, and materials? If the demand for hot dogs declines, what steps could you take to reduce output in the short run? In the long run?
6. An important distinction in economics is between shifts of the production function and movements along the production function. For the food concession in question 5, give an example of both a shift of and a movement along the hot-dog production function. Illustrate each with a graph of the relation between hot-dog production and labor employed.
7. Substitution occurs when firms replace one input for another, as when a farmer uses tractors rather than labor when wages rise. Consider the following changes in a firm's behavior. Which represent substitution of one factor for another with an unchanged technology, and which represent technological change? Illustrate each with a graphical production function.
   a. When the price of oil increases, a firm replaces an oil-fired plant with a gas-fired plant.
   b. A bookseller reduces its sales staff by 60 percent after it sets up an Internet outlet.
   c. Over the period 1970–2000, a typesetting firm decreases its employment of typesetters by 200 workers and increases its employment of computer operators by 100 workers.
   d. After a successful unionization drive for clerical workers, a college buys personal computers for its faculty and reduces its secretarial workforce.
8. Consider a firm that produces pizzas with capital and labor inputs. Define and contrast diminishing returns and decreasing returns to scale. Explain why it is possible to have diminishing returns for one input and constant returns to scale for both inputs.
9. Show that if the marginal product is always decreasing, the average product is always above the marginal product.
10. Review the example of a network shown in Figure 6-4. Assume that only one person can join the network each month, starting with Adam and proceeding clockwise.
    a. Construct a table showing the value to the joining person as well as the external value to others (i.e., the value to all others in the network) when an additional person joins. (*Hint:* The entries for Ed are \$4 and \$4.) Then calculate the total social value for each level of membership. Graph the relationship between the size of the network and the total social value. Explain why this shows increasing returns rather than diminishing returns.
    b. Assume that the cost of joining is \$4.50. Draw a graph which shows how membership changes over time if six people are in the network to begin with. Draw another one which shows what happens if there are initially three people in the network. What is the point at which the equilibrium "tips" toward universal membership?
    c. Suppose you are the sponsor of the network shown in Figure 6-4. What kind of pricing could you use to get the network started when there are only one or two members?

CHAPTER

7

Analysis of Costs

成本分析

[1] 弗兰克・奈特（Frank Knight，1885~1972），20 世纪美国经济学巨擘之一。1921 年出版的《风险、不确定性和利润》（*Risk, Uncertainty, and Profit*）一书通过对风险和不确定性的区分和论述建构了奈特不确定性（Knightian Uncertainty）的概念。本段文字引自该书第二编第 5 章的第 25 段，整个句子如下：

In so far as uncertainty is absent and competition obtains, it is clear that investment will distribute itself between the two fields and over all parts

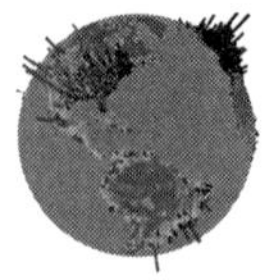

of each in such a way as constantly to equalize their net advantages. Which is to say (remembering that costs merely register competing attractions) that with uncertainty absent costs and values would be equal throughout the system; that is, there would be a perfect, profitless organization of production and exchange.

所以，这句话应该译作：

Costs merely register competing attractions. [1]

Frank Knight

Risk, Uncertainty, and Profit (1921)

成本仅仅是展示一下可持续竞争的吸引力而已。——弗兰克・奈特

Everywhere that production goes, costs follow close behind like a shadow. Firms must pay for their inputs: screws, solvents, software, sponges, secretaries, and statisticians. Profitable businesses are acutely aware of this simple fact as they determine their production strategies, since every dollar of unnecessary costs reduces the firm's profits by that same dollar.

But the role of costs goes far beyond influencing ②
production and profits. Costs affect input choices, investment decisions, and even the decision of whether to stay in business. Is it cheaper to hire a new worker or to pay overtime? To open a new factory or expand an old one? To invest in new machinery domestically or to outsource production abroad? Businesses want to choose those methods of production that are most efficient and produce output at the lowest cost.

This chapter is devoted to a thorough analysis of
cost. First we consider the full array of economic costs, ③
including the central notion of marginal costs. Then we examine how business accountants measure cost in practice. Finally, we look at the notion of opportunity cost, a broad concept that can be applied to a wide range of decisions. This comprehensive study of cost will lay the foundation for understanding the supply decisions of business firms.

成本的经济分析

A. ECONOMIC ANALYSIS OF COSTS

总成本：固定成本和可变成本
TOTAL COST: FIXED AND VARIABLE

Consider a firm that produces a quantity of output (denoted by q) using inputs of capital, labor, and materials. The firm's accountants have the task of calculating the total dollar costs incurred to produce output level q.

Table 7-1 on page 127 shows the total cost (TC) for each different level of output q. Looking at columns (1) and (4), we see that TC goes up as q goes up. This makes sense because it takes more labor and other inputs to produce more of a good; extra factors involve an extra money cost. It costs \$110 in all to produce 2 units, \$130 to produce 3 units, and so forth. In our discussion, we assume that the firm always produces output at the lowest possible cost.

固定成本
Fixed Cost

Columns (2) and (3) of Table 7-1 separate total cost into two components: total fixed cost (FC) and total variable cost (VC).

② 但是，成本的作用远远超越了对生产和利润的影响。它不仅影响投入的选择，投资决策，甚至还影响着企业是否继续经营的决策。

③ 首先，我们要全盘考虑各种经济成本问题，其中包括边际成本这一核心概念。

(1) Quantity q	(2) Fixed cost FC (\$)	(3) Variable cost VC (\$)	(4) Total cost TC (\$)
0	55	0	55
1	55	30	85
2	55	55	110
3	55	75	130
4	55	105	160
5	55	155	210
6	55	225	280

TABLE 7-1. Fixed, Variable, and Total Costs ①

The major elements of a firm's costs are its fixed costs (which do not vary at all when output changes) and its variable costs (which increase as output increases). Total costs are equal to fixed plus variable costs: $TC = FC + VC$.

Fixed costs are expenses that must be paid even ② if the firm produces zero output. Sometimes called "overhead" or "sunk costs," they consist of items such as rent for factory or office space, interest payments on debts, salaries of tenured faculty, and so forth. They are fixed because they do not change if output changes. For example, a law firm might have an office lease which runs for 10 years and remains an obligation even if the firm shrinks to half its previous size. Because FC is the amount that must be paid regardless of the level of output, it remains constant at \$55 in column (2).

可变成本
Variable Cost

Column (3) of Table 7-1 shows variable cost (VC). **Variable costs** do vary as output changes. Examples ③ include materials required to produce output (such as steel to produce automobiles), production workers to staff the assembly lines, power to operate factories, and so on. In a supermarket, checkout clerks are a variable cost, since managers can adjust the clerks' hours worked to match the number of shoppers coming through the store.

By definition, VC begins at zero when q is zero. VC is the part of TC that grows with output; indeed, the jump in TC between any two outputs is the same as the jump in VC.

Let us summarize these cost concepts:

Total cost represents the lowest total dollar ④ expense needed to produce each level of output q. TC rises as q rises.

Fixed cost represents the total dollar expense that is paid out even when no output is produced; fixed cost is unaffected by any variation in the quantity of output.

Variable cost represents expenses that vary with the level of output—such as raw materials, wages, and fuel—and includes all costs that are not fixed.

Always, by definition,

$$TC = FC + VC$$

Minimum Attainable Costs

Anyone who has managed a business knows that when we write down a cost schedule like the one in Table 7-1, we make the firm's job look altogether too simple. Much hard work lies behind Table 7-1. To attain the lowest level of costs, ⑤ the firm's managers have to make sure that they are paying the least possible amount for necessary materials, that the lowest-cost engineering techniques are incorporated into the factory layout, that employees are being honest, and that countless other decisions are made in the most economical fashion.

For example, suppose you are the owner of a baseball team. You have to negotiate salaries with players, choose managers, bargain with vendors, worry about electricity and other utility bills, consider how much insurance to buy, and deal with the 1001 other issues that are involved in running the team with minimum cost.

The total costs shown in Table 7-1 are the minimum costs that result from all these hours of managerial work.

边际成本的定义
DEFINITION OF MARGINAL COST

Marginal cost is one of the most important concepts in all of economics. **Marginal cost** (MC) denotes the ⑥ extra or additional cost of producing 1 extra unit of output. Say a firm is producing 1000 compact discs for a total cost of \$10,000. If the total cost of

---

① 表 7-1. 固定成本、可变成本和总成本

② **固定成本**指即使企业零产出也必须支付的费用。

③ **可变成本**指随产出的变化而变化的成本。

④ **总成本**表示生产每一产量水平 q 所对应的以美元计价的最低支出。总成本随 q 的增加而增加。

⑤ 为将成本降到最低，企业的管理者们必须确保他们为采购的材料支付尽可能低的价格，在满足设计要求的前提下采用最低成本的工程技术，还要相信员工对公司的一贯忠诚，这样，才能以最经济的方式做出无数的不同决策。

⑥ **边际成本**表示每多生产一个单位的产出所需增加的成本。

(1) Output q	(2) Total cost TC (\$)	(3) Marginal cost MC (\$)
0	55	
		30
1	85	
		25
2	110	
		20
3	130	
		___
4	160	
		50
5	210	

TABLE 7-2. Calculation of Marginal Cost ①

Once we know total cost, it is easy to calculate marginal cost. To calculate the MC of the fifth unit, we subtract the total cost of the 4 units from the total cost of the 5 units, i.e., $MC = \$210 - \$160 = \$50$. Fill in the blank for the marginal cost of the fourth unit.

producing 1001 discs is \$10,006, then the marginal cost of production is \$6 for the 1001st disc.

Sometimes, the marginal cost of producing an extra unit of output can be quite low. For an airline flying planes with empty seats, the added cost of another passenger is literally peanuts; no additional capital (planes) or labor (pilots and flight attendants) is necessary. In other cases, the marginal cost of another unit of output can be quite high. Consider an electric utility. Under normal circumstances, it can generate enough power using only its lowest-cost, most efficient plants. But on a hot summer day, when everyone's air conditioners are running and demand for electricity is high, the utility may be forced to turn on its old, high-cost, inefficient generators. This added electric power comes at a high marginal cost to the utility.

Table 7-2 uses the data from Table 7-1 to illustrate how we calculate marginal costs. The green-colored MC numbers in column (3) of Table 7-2 come from subtracting the TC in column (2) from the TC of the subsequent quantity. Thus the MC of the first unit is \$30(= \$85 − \$55); the marginal cost of the second unit is \$25(= \$110 − \$85); and so on.

Instead of getting MC from the TC column, we could get the MC figures by subtracting each VC number in column (3) of Table 7-1 from the VC in the row below it. Variable cost always grows exactly like total cost, the only difference being that VC must (by definition) start out from 0 rather than from the constant FC level. (Check that \$30 − \$0 = \$85 − \$55, and \$55 − \$30 = \$110 − \$85, and so on.)

The marginal cost of production is the additional cost incurred in producing 1 extra unit of output. ②

Marginal Cost in Diagrams. Figure 7-1 illustrates total cost and marginal cost. It shows that TC is related to MC in the same way that total product is related to marginal product or that total utility is related to marginal utility.

The Marginal Cost of Distributing Software

When the software company Microsoft decided to enter the market for Internet browsers, it did so by giving away its Internet Explorer browser, either as a stand-alone product or in combination with the Windows operating system. Its competitors complained that Microsoft was engaged in "predatory behavior." How could it give the browser software away and not lose money? ③

The answer lies in the unusual property of information technology (IT). According to IT specialist Hal Varian, IT "typically has the property that it is very costly to produce the first copy and very cheap to produce subsequent copies." In this case, while it cost Microsoft a great deal to develop Internet Explorer, the marginal cost of distributing an extra unit of the software was close to zero. That is, the cost to Microsoft of delivering 1,000,001 units was no more than the cost of 1,000,000 units. As long as the marginal cost was zero, Microsoft was not losing money by giving Internet Explorer away.

① 表 7-2. 边际成本的计算

② 生产的边际成本是指在追加生产一个单位的产出时所需要增加的成本。

③ 当软件业的巨头微软公司决定进入互联网的浏览器市场时，曾采用过一种免费分发的方式，即将该浏览器产品既作为一种独立的产品又与其视窗操作系统捆绑在一起赠送。微软的竞争对手们抱怨微软在进行一种“掠夺性的行为”。那么，微软公司是如何将浏览器软件免费赠送的同时又没有损失呢?

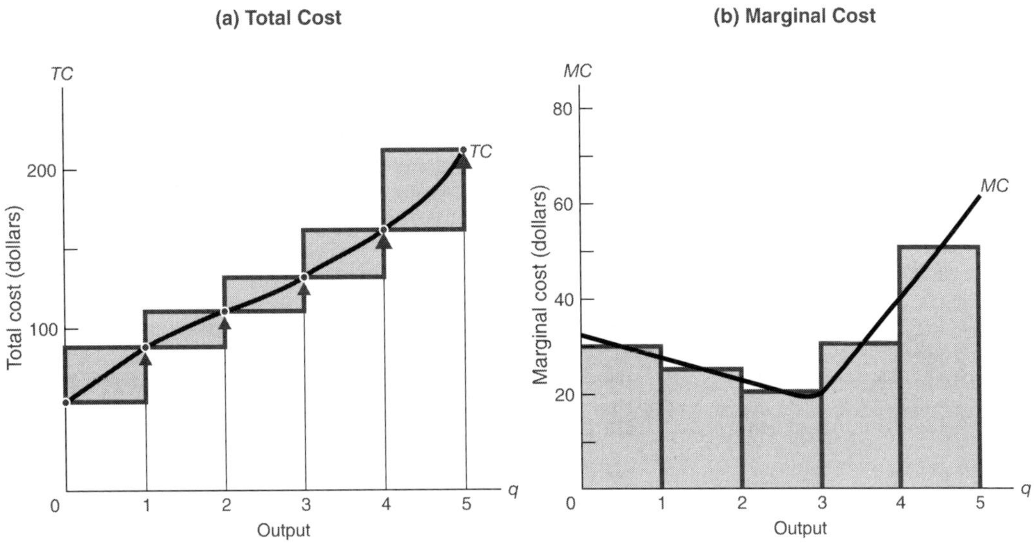

FIGURE 7-1. The Relationship between Total Cost and Marginal Cost ①

These graphs show the data from Table 7-2. Marginal cost in **(b)** is found by calculating the extra cost added in **(a)** for each unit increase in output. Thus to find the *MC* of producing the fifth unit, we subtract \$160 from \$210 to get *MC* of \$50. A smooth blue curve has been drawn through the points of *TC* in **(a)**, and the smooth blue *MC* curve in **(b)** links the discrete steps of *MC*.

平均成本
AVERAGE COST

We complete our catalog of the cost concepts with a discussion of different kinds of average or unit cost. Table 7-3 on page 130 expands the data of Tables 7-1 and 7-2 to include three new measures: average cost, average fixed cost, and average variable cost. ②

平均成本或单位成本
Average or Unit Cost

Average cost (*AC*) is a concept widely used in business; by comparing average cost with price or average revenue, businesses can determine whether or not they are making a profit. **Average cost** is the total cost divided by the total number of units produced, as shown in column (6) of Table 7-3. That is, ③

$$\text{Average cost} = \frac{\text{total cost}}{\text{output}} = \frac{TC}{q} = AC$$

In column(6), when only 1 unit is produced, average cost has to be the same as total cost, or \$85/1 = \$85. But for $q = 2$, $AC = TC/2 = \$110/2 = \$55$, as shown. Note that average cost falls lower and lower at first. (We shall see why in a moment.) *AC* reaches a minimum of \$40 at $q = 4$, and then slowly rises.

Figure 7-2 on page 131 plots the cost data shown in Table 7-3. Figure 7-2(*a*) depicts the total, fixed, and variable costs at different levels of output. Figure 7-2(*b*) shows the different average cost concepts, along with a smoothed marginal cost curve. Graph (*a*) shows how total cost moves with variable cost while fixed cost remains unchanged.

Now turn to graph (*b*). This plots the U-shaped *AC* curve and aligns *AC* right below the *TC* curve from which it is derived.

平均固定成本和平均可变成本
Average Fixed and Variable Costs

Just as we separated total cost into fixed and variable costs, we can also break average cost into fixed and variable components. **Average fixed cost** (*AFC*) is ④
defined as *FC/q*. Since total fixed cost is a constant, dividing it by an increasing output gives a steadily

① 图 7-1. 总成本与边际成本之间的关系

② 我们用讨论各种平均成本或者单位成本的方法就能理清所有关于成本的概念。

③ 平均成本是企业广泛使用的一个概念；通过平均成本与价格或者平均收益的比较，企业就能决定是否盈利。

④ **平均固定成本**的定义是固定成本与产出之比。

(1) Quantity q	(2) Fixed cost FC ($)	(3) Variable cost VC ($)	(4) Total cost $TC = FC + VC$ ($)	(5) Marginal cost per unit MC ($)	(6) Average cost per unit $AC = TC/q$ ($)	(7) Average fixed cost per unit $AFC = FC/q$ ($)	(8) Average variable cost per unit $AVC = VC/q$ ($)
0	55	0	55		Infinity	Infinity	Undefined
				30			
1	55	——	85		85	55	30
				25			
2	——	55	110		55	——	27½
				——			
3	55	75	130		43⅓	18⅓	25
				30			
4*	**55**	**105**	**160**	40*	**40***	**13¾**	**26¼**
				50			
5	55	155	210		42	11	——
				70			
6	55	225	280		46⅔	9⅙	37½

*Minimum level of average cost.

TABLE 7-3. All Cost Concepts Derive from Total Cost Schedule ①

We can derive all the different cost concepts from the *TC* in column (4). Columns (5) and (6) are the important ones to concentrate on: marginal cost is calculated by subtraction of adjacent rows of *TC* and is shown in green. The starred *MC* of 40 at an output of 4 is the smoothed *MC* from Fig. 7-2(*b*). In column (6), note the point of minimum cost of $40 on the U-shaped *AC* curve in Fig. 7-2(*b*). (Can you see why the starred *MC* equals the starred *AC* at the minimum? Also, calculate and fill in all the missing numbers.)

falling average fixed cost curve [see column (7) of Table 7-3]. In other words, as a firm sells more output, it can spread its overhead cost over more and more units. For example, a software firm may have a large staff of programmers to develop a new game. The number of copies sold does not directly affect how many programmers are necessary, thus making them a fixed cost. So if the program is a best-seller, the *AFC* of the programmers is low; if the program is a failure, the *AFC* is high.

The dashed blue *AFC* curve in Figure 7-2(*b*) is a hyperbola, approaching both axes: it drops lower and lower, approaching the horizontal axis as the constant *FC* gets spread over more and more units. If we allow fractional units of *q*, *AFC* starts infinitely high as finite *FC* is spread over ever tinier *q*.

Average variable cost (*AVC*) equals variable cost ② divided by output, or *AVC* = *VC*/*q*. As you can see in both Table 7-3 and Figure 7-2(*b*), for this example *AVC* first falls and then rises.

平均成本和边际成本之间的关系

The Relation between Average Cost and Marginal Cost

It is important to understand the link between average cost and marginal cost. We begin with three closely related rules: ③

1. When marginal cost is below average cost, it is pulling average cost down.
2. When *MC* is above *AC*, it is pulling up *AC*.
3. When *MC* just equals *AC*, *AC* is constant. At the bottom of a U-shaped *AC*, *MC* = *AC* = minimum *AC*.

To understand these rules, begin with the first one. If *MC* is below *AC*, this means that the last unit produced costs less than the average cost of all the previous units produced. This implies that the new *AC* (i.e., the *AC* including the last unit) must be less than the old *AC*, so *AC* must be falling.

We can illustrate this with an example. Looking at Table 7-3, we see that the *AC* of the first unit is 85.

① 表 7-3. 各种成本概念均源自总成本表

② **平均可变成本**等于可变成本除以产出。

③ 理解平均成本与边际成本之间的关联至关重要。我们从三条关系密切的规则入手：

1. 当边际成本低于平均成本时，平均成本将被边际成本拉低。
2. 当边际成本高于平均成本时，平均成本将被边际成本抬高。
3. 当边际成本等于平均成本时，平均成本保持不变。在 U 型平均成本曲线的底部，边际成本等于平均成本，即平均成本的最小值。

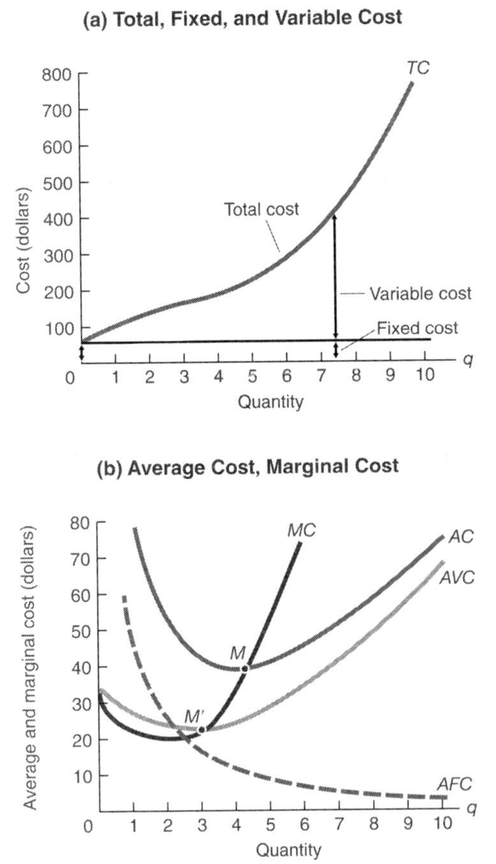

FIGURE 7-2. All Cost Curves Can Be Derived from the Total Cost Curve ①

(a) Total cost is made up of fixed cost and variable cost. **(b)** The green-colored curve of marginal cost falls and then rises, as indicated by the *MC* figures given in column (5) of Table 7-3. Note how *MC* intersects *AC* at its minimum.

q	*FC*	*VC*	*TC*	*MC*
3,998	55,000	104,920.03	159,920.03	
				39.98
3,999	55,000	104,960.01	159,960.01	
				39.99
4,000*	55,000	105,000.00	160,000.00	
				40.01
4,001	55,000	105,040.01	160,040.01	
				40.02
4,002	55,000	105,080.03	160,080.03	

*Production with minimum average cost.

TABLE 7-4. Take a Microscope to the *AC* and *MC* Calculations at the Minimum Point ②

This table magnifies the cost calculations around the minimum *AC* point. We assume for this calculation that the numbers in Table 7-3 are in thousands. Note how the marginal cost is a tiny bit below the minimum *AC* between 3999 and 4000 units and a tiny bit above it between 4000 and 4001 units.

The *MC* of the second unit is 25. This implies that the *AC* of the first 2 units is (85 + 25)/2 = 55. Because *MC* was below *AC*, this correctly implies that *AC* is falling.

The second rule is illustrated in Table 7-3 by the case of the sixth unit. The *AC* of 5 units is 42, and the *MC* between 5 and 6 units is 70. *MC* is pulling up *AC* as we see by the *AC* of the sixth unit, which is 46⅔.

The case of the fourth unit is a crucial one. At that level, note that *AC* is exactly equal to *MC* at a cost of 40. So the new *AC* is exactly equal to the old *AC* and is equal to *MC*. We illustrate the relationship in detail in Table 7-4, which focuses on the minimum *AC* level of production. For this table, we assume that the units in Table 7-3 are in thousands so that we can see tiny movements in output. See how *MC* is a tiny bit below *AC* when output is just below the minimum-*AC* point (and a tiny bit above *AC* when output is just above the minimum-*AC* point). If we were to increase the magnification further, we would come as close as we want to an exact equality of *MC* and *AC*.

You will improve your understanding of the relationship between *MC* and *AC* by studying Figure 7-2(*b*). Note that for the first 3 units, *MC* is below *AC*, and *AC* is therefore declining. At exactly 4 units, *AC* equals *MC*. Over 4 units, *MC* is above *AC* and pulling *AC* up. Graphically, that means the rising *MC* curve will intersect the *AC* curve precisely at its minimum point.

To summarize: In terms of our cost curves, if the ③ *MC* curve is below the *AC* curve, the *AC* curve must be falling. By contrast, if *MC* is above *AC*, *AC* is rising. Finally, when *MC* is just equal to *AC*, the *AC* curve is flat. The *AC* curve is always pierced at its minimum point by a rising *MC* curve.

① 图 7-2. 各种成本曲线均可以从总成本曲线导出
② 表 7-4. 平均成本和边际成本在最低点的计算
③ 小结：根据成本曲线，如果边际成本曲线低于平均成本曲线，那么平均成本曲线必然下降。与此相反，如果边际成本高于平均成本，平均成本曲线则上升。最终，当边际成本正好等于平均成本时，则平均成本曲线呈水平状态。平均成本曲线总是在它的最低点与上升的边际成本曲线相交。

Batting Averages to Illustrate *MC* and *AC* Rules

We can illustrate the *MC-AC* relationship using batting averages. Let *AB* be your lifetime batting average up to this year (your average) and *MB* be your batting average for this year (your marginal). For simplicity, we also assume that there are 100 "at bats" each year.

When your *MB* is below *AB*, it will pull the new *AB* down. For example, suppose that your lifetime batting average for your first 3 years was .300 and your batting average for your fourth year was .100. Your new lifetime average or *AB* at the end of your fourth year is .250. Similarly, if your *MB* in your fourth year is higher than your lifetime average for your first 3 years, your lifetime average will be pulled up. If your batting average in the fourth year is the same as your lifetime average for the first 3 years, your lifetime average will not change (i.e., if *MB* = *AB*, then the new *AB* is equal to the old *AB*).

生产与成本之间的联系

THE LINK BETWEEN PRODUCTION AND COSTS

What are the factors that determine the cost curves introduced above? The key elements are (1) factor prices and (2) the firm's production function.

Clearly the prices of inputs like labor and land are important ingredients of costs. Higher rents and higher wages mean higher costs, as any business manager will tell you. But costs also depend on the firm's technological opportunities. If technological improvements allow the firm to produce the same output with fewer inputs, the firm's costs will fall.

Indeed, if you know factor prices and the production function, you can calculate the cost curve. We can show the derivation of cost from production data and factor prices in the numerical example shown in Table 7-5. Suppose Farmer Smith rents 10 acres of land and can hire farm labor to produce wheat. Per period, land costs $5.5 per acre and labor costs $5 per worker. Using up-to-date farming methods, Smith can produce according to the production function shown in the first three columns of Table 7-5. In this example, land is a fixed cost (because Farmer Smith operates under a 10-year lease), while labor is a variable cost (because farmworkers can easily be hired and fired).

Using the production data and the input-cost data, for each level of output we calculate the total cost of production shown in column (6) of Table 7-5. As an example, consider the total cost of production for 3 tons of wheat. Using the given production function, Smith can produce this quantity with 10 acres of land and 15 farmhands. The total cost of producing 3 tons of wheat is (10 acres × $5.5 per acre) + (15 workers × $5 per worker) = $130. Similar calculations will give all the other total cost figures in column (6) of Table 7-5.

Note that these total costs are identical to the ones shown in Tables 7-1 through 7-3, so the other

(1) Output (tons of wheat)	(2) Land inputs (acres)	(3) Labor inputs (workers)	(4) Land rent ($ per acre)	(5) Labor wage ($ per worker)	(6) Total cost ($)
0	10	0	5.5	5	55
1	10	6	5.5	5	85
2	10	11	5.5	5	110
3	10	15	5.5	5	130
4	10	21	5.5	5	160
5	10	31	5.5	5	210
6	10	45	5.5	5	280

TABLE 7-5. Costs are Derived from Production Data and Input Costs ①

Farmer Smith rents 10 acres of wheatland and employs variable labor. According to the farming production function, careful use of labor and land allows the inputs and yields shown in columns (1) to (3) of the table. At input prices of $5.5 per acre and $5 per worker, we obtain Smith's cost of production shown in column (6). All other cost concepts (such as those shown in Table 7-3) can be calculated from the total cost data.

① 表 7-5. 由生产数据和投入成本推算出成本

cost concepts shown in the tables (i.e., *MC, FC, VC, AC, AFC,* and *AVC*) are also applicable to the production-cost example of Farmer Smith.

收益递减和 U 型成本曲线

Diminishing Returns and U-Shaped Cost Curves

Economists often draw cost curves like the letter "U" (the "U-shaped cost curves"). For a U-shaped cost curve, cost falls in the initial phase, reaches a minimum point, and finally begins to rise. Let's explore the reasons. Recall that Chapter 6's analysis of production distinguished two different time periods, the short run and the long run. The same concepts apply to costs as well:

- The *short run* is the period of time that is long enough to adjust variable inputs, such as materials and production labor, but too short to allow all inputs to be changed. In the short run, fixed or overhead factors such as plant and equipment cannot be fully modified or adjusted. Therefore, in the short run, labor and materials costs are typically variable costs, while capital costs are fixed. short run 短期
- In the *long run,* all inputs can be adjusted—including labor, materials, and capital. Hence, in the long run, all costs are variable and none are fixed.[1] long run 长期

Note that whether a particular cost is fixed or variable depends on the length of time we are considering. In the short run, for example, the number of planes that an airline owns is a fixed cost. But over the longer run, the airline can clearly control the size of its fleet by buying or selling planes. Indeed, there is an active market in used planes, making it relatively easy to dispose of unwanted planes. Typically, in the short run, we will consider capital to be the fixed cost and labor to be the variable cost. That is not always true (think of your college's tenured faculty), but generally labor inputs can be adjusted more easily than can capital.

Why is the cost curve U-shaped? Consider the short run in which capital is fixed but labor is variable. In such a situation, there are diminishing returns to the variable factor (labor) because each additional unit of labor has less capital to work with. As a result, the marginal cost of output will rise because the extra output produced by each extra labor unit is going down. In other words, diminishing returns to the variable factor will imply an increasing short-run marginal cost. This shows why diminishing returns lead to rising marginal costs.

Figure 7-3, which contains exactly the same data as Table 7-5, illustrates the point. It shows that the

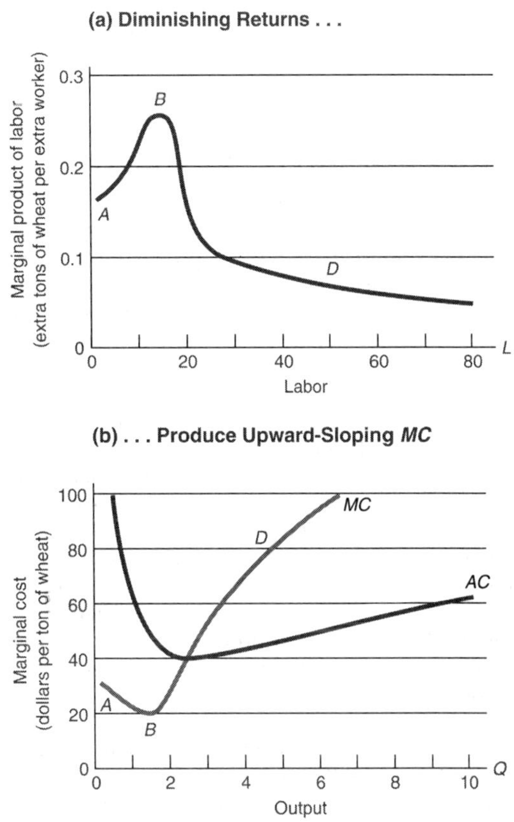

FIGURE 7-3. Diminishing Returns and U-Shaped Cost Curves ①

The U-shaped cost curves are based on diminishing returns in the short run. With fixed land and variable labor, the marginal product of labor in **(a)** first rises to the left of *B*, peaks at *B*, and then falls at *D* as diminishing returns to labor set in.

The cost curves in **(b)** are derived from the product curves and factor prices. Increasing and then diminishing marginal product of the variable factor gives U-shaped marginal and average cost curves.

[1] For a more complete discussion of the long and short runs, see Chapter 6.

① 图 7-3. 收益递减与 U 型成本曲线

region of increasing marginal product corresponds to falling marginal costs, while the region of diminishing returns implies rising marginal costs.

We can summarize the relationship between the productivity laws and the cost curves as follows:

In the short run, when factors such as capital are ① fixed, variable factors tend to show an initial phase of increasing marginal product followed by diminishing marginal product. The corresponding cost curves show an initial phase of declining marginal costs, followed by increasing *MC* after diminishing returns have set in.

企业的投入选择 CHOICE OF INPUTS BY THE FIRM

Marginal Products and the Least-Cost Rule 边际产量和最低成本法则

Every firm must decide *how* to produce its output. Should electricity be produced with oil or coal? Should cars be assembled in the United States or Mexico? Should classes be taught by faculty or graduate students? We now complete the link between production and cost by using the marginal product concept to illustrate how firms select the least-cost combinations of inputs.

In our analysis, we will rely on the fundamental assumption that *firms minimize their costs of production.* This cost-minimization assumption actually makes good sense not only for perfectly competitive firms but for monopolists or even nonprofit organizations like colleges or hospitals. It simply states that the firm should strive to produce its output at the lowest possible cost and thereby have the maximum amount of revenue left over for profits or for other objectives.

A simple example will illustrate how a firm might decide between different input combinations. Say a firm's engineers have calculated that the desired output level of 9 units could be produced with two possible options. In both cases, energy (E) costs $2 per unit, while labor (L) costs $5 per hour. Under option 1, the input mix is $E = 10$ and $L = 2$. Option 2 has $E = 4$ and $L = 5$. Which is the preferred option? At the market prices for inputs, total production costs for option 1 are ($2 × 10) + ($5 × 2) = $30, while total costs for option 2 are ($2 × 4) + ($5 × 5) = $33. Therefore, option 1 would be the preferred least-cost combination of inputs.

More generally, there are usually many possible input combinations, not just two. But we don't have to calculate the cost of every different combination of inputs in order to find the one which costs the least. Here's a simple way to find the least-cost combination: Start by calculating the marginal product of each input, as we did in Chapter 6. Then divide the marginal product of each input by its factor price. *This gives you the marginal product per dollar of input.* The cost-minimizing combination of inputs comes when the marginal product per dollar of input is equal for all inputs. That is, the marginal contribution to output of each dollar's worth of labor, of land, of oil, and so forth, must be just the same.

Following this reasoning, a firm will minimize its total cost of production when the marginal product per dollar of input is equalized for each factor of production. This is called the least-cost rule.

Least-cost rule: To produce a given level of output at least cost, a firm should buy inputs until it has equalized the marginal product per dollar spent on each input. This implies that ②

$$\frac{\text{Marginal product of } L}{\text{Price of } L} = \frac{\text{marginal product of } A}{\text{price of } A} = \cdots$$

This rule for firms is exactly analogous to what consumers do when they maximize utilities, as we saw in Chapter 5. In analyzing consumer choice, we saw that to maximize utility, consumers should buy goods so that the marginal utility per dollar spent on each consumer good is equalized for all commodities.

One way of understanding the least-cost rule is the following: Break each factor into packages worth $1 each. (In our earlier energy-labor example, $1 of labor would be ⅕ of an hour, while $1 of energy would be ½ unit.) Then the least-cost rule states that the marginal product of each dollar-unit of input must be equalized. If the marginal products per $1 of inputs were not equal, you could reduce the low-*MP*-per-dollar input and increase the high-*MP*-per-dollar input and produce the same output at lower cost.

A corollary of the least-cost rule is the substitution rule.

Substitution rule: If the price of one factor falls ③ while all other factor prices remain the same, firms

---

① 在短期内，像资本这样的要素固定不变时，可变要素趋向于在初始阶段边际产量递增和随后的阶段边际产量递减。相应的成本曲线表现为初始阶段边际成本递减，随后跟进的则是在收益递减之后发生的边际成本递增。

② **最低成本法则**：为了以最小的成本生产出既定数量的产出，企业应该买进各种投入要素，直到它等于花在每一投入要素上的每一美元的边际产量为止。

③ **替代法则**：如果一种要素的价格降低，而所有其他要素的价格保持不变，那么企业将通过使用时价较低的要素替代其他要素，直到花在投入要素上的每一美元的边际产量相等为止，即企业盈利。

will profit by substituting the now-cheaper factor for the other factors until the marginal products per dollar are equal for all inputs.

Let's take the case of labor (L). A fall in the price of labor will raise the ratio MP_L/P_L above the MP/P ratio for other inputs. Raising the employment of L lowers MP_L by the law of diminishing returns and therefore lowers MP_L/P_L. Lower price and MP of labor then bring the marginal product per dollar for labor back into equality with that ratio for other factors.

经济成本和企业会计

B. ECONOMIC COSTS AND BUSINESS ACCOUNTING

From General Motors down to the corner deli, businesses use more or less elaborate systems to keep track of their costs. [1] Many of the cost categories in business accounting look very similar to the concepts of economic cost we learned above. But there are some important differences between how businesses measure costs and how economists would do it. In this section we will lay out the rudiments of business accounting and point out the differences and similarities with economic costs.

收益表或损益表

THE INCOME STATEMENT, OR STATEMENT OF PROFIT AND LOSS

Let us start with a small company, called Hot Dog Ventures, Inc. As the name suggests, this company sells gourmet frankfurters in a small store. The operation consists of buying the materials (hot dogs, top-flight buns, expensive mustard, espresso coffee beans) and hiring people to prepare and sell the food. In addition, the company has taken out a loan of $100,000 for its cooking equipment and other restaurant furnishings, and it must pay rent on its store. The founders of Hot Dog Ventures have big aspirations, so they incorporated the business and issued common stock (see Chapter 6 on forms of business organization).

To determine whether Hot Dog Ventures is earning a profit, we must turn to the **income statement,** or—as many companies prefer to call it—the *statement of profit and loss,* shown in Table 7-6. This statement reports the following: (1) Hot Dog Ventures' revenues from sales in 2009, (2) the expenses to be charged against those sales, and (3) the net income, or profits remaining after expenses have been deducted. This gives the fundamental identity of the income statement:

Net income (or profit) =
total revenue − total expenses

This definition gives the famous "bottom line" ② of profits that firms want to maximize. And in many ways, business profits are close to an economist's definition of economic profits. Let's next examine the profit-and-loss statement in more detail, starting from the top. The first line gives the revenues, which were $250,000. Lines 2 through 9 represent the cost of different inputs into the production process. For example, the labor cost is the annual cost of employing labor, while rent is the annual cost of using the building. The selling and administrative ③ costs include the costs of advertising the product and running the back office, while miscellaneous operating costs include the cost of electricity.

The first three cost categories—materials, labor cost, and miscellaneous operating costs—basically correspond to the variable costs of the firm, or its *cost of goods sold.* The next three categories, lines 6 through 8, correspond to the firm's fixed costs, since in the short run they cannot be changed.

Line 8 shows a term we haven't seen before, *depreciation,* which relates to the cost of capital goods. Firms can either rent capital or own their capital goods. In the case of the building, which Hot Dog Ventures rented, we deducted the rent in item (7) of the income statement.

When the firm owns the capital good, the treatment is more complicated. Suppose the cooking equipment has an estimated useful lifetime of 10 years, at the end of which it is useless and worthless. In effect, some portion of the cooking equipment is "used up" in the productive process each year. We call the amount used up "depreciation," and calculate that amount as the cost of the capital input for that year. **Depreciation** ④ measures the annual cost of a capital input that a company actually owns itself.

The same reasoning would apply to any capital goods that a company owns. Trucks wear out, computers become obsolete, and buildings eventually begin to fall apart. For each of these, the company

② "bottom line"：报表底栏（即损益表底线的净收益）

③ 销售和管理成本包括产品的广告成本和内勤办公成本两项，而电费成本则计入杂项内。

④ 折旧衡量的是企业自身所实际拥有的资本投入的年平均成本。

income statement 收益表或损益表

statement of profit and loss 损益表

[1] General Motors：通用汽车公司，简称GM，前身是戴维·别克（David Dunbar Buick）创办的别克汽车公司（Buick Motorcar Co.），1904年被美国最大的马车制造商杜登客车公司（Durant-Dorn Carriage Co.）收购后业务逐年迅速扩大。1908年成立名为 *General Motors Corporation* 的汽车控股公司。从1931年起至2008年被日本丰田公司超越止，始终是全球汽车业的领导者。通用汽车公司的全球总部设在底特律，在全球的34个国家和地区与其战略合作伙伴生产各种汽车，销售遍及全球约140个国家和地区。从2007年8月9日开始爆发的金融危机使通用汽车公司深受其害，于2009年6月1日正式申请破产保护。2009年7月10日与美国政府签署文件，成功出售大部分优质资产以及4个核心品牌——雪佛兰（Chevrolet）、卡迪拉克（Cadillac）、别克（Buick）和GMC，并更名为 *General Motors Company* 的"新通用"。新通用由美国财政部控股60.8%，加拿大政府和安大略政府拥有11.7%的股份，UAW旗下一家医疗信托基金VEBA持有17.5%股份，剩下的10%则由债券持有人持有。公司的员工由宣布破产前的325 000人裁减到现在的235 000人。随着金融危机的深入，2010年新年伊始爆发的丰田汽车危机"召回门"事件实质上是美日两国争夺全球汽车业霸主地位及后金融危机时代美国力保其全球战略地位的重大政治事件之一。美国22家律师事务所于2月上旬联合组成诉讼团计划对日本丰田汽车公司提起"国家级诉讼"，指控丰田大规模召回行动使丰田车主蒙受巨额经济损失。美国30多个州的法院受理了丰田消费者的集体上诉，丰田汽车最终可能需为此付出逾20亿美元的代价。这一事件很快就在美国发酵，丰田公司2010年1月份在美国的汽车销量同比下降16%，自1999年以来该公司在美月销量首次跌破10万辆。而与此同时，美国本土汽车公司福特同比销量上升24%，通用同比上升15%，美国人在与日本丰田的博弈中首战告捷。

Income Statement of Hot Dog Ventures, Inc.
(January 1, 2009 to December 31, 2009)

(1)	**Net sales (after all discounts and rebates)**		**$250,000**
	Less cost of goods sold:		
(2)	Materials	$ 50,000	
(3)	Labor cost	90,000	
(4)	Miscellaneous operating costs (utilities, etc.)	10,000	
(5)	Less overhead costs:		
(6)	Selling and administrative costs	15,000	
(7)	Rent for building	5,000	
(8)	Depreciation	15,000	
(9)	Operating expenses	$185,000	185,000
(10)	Net operating income		$ 65,000
	Less:		
(11)	Interest charges on equipment loan		6,000
(12)	State and local taxes		4,000
(13)	Net income (or profit) before income taxes		$ 55,000
(14)	Less: Corporation income taxes		18,000
(15)	**Net income (or profit) after taxes**		**$ 37,000**
(16)	Less: Dividends paid on common stock		15,000
(17)	Addition to retained earnings		$ 22,000

TABLE 7-6. The Income Statement Shows Total Sales and Expenses for a Period of Time ①

would take a depreciation charge. There are a number of different formulas for calculating each year's depreciation, but each follows two major principles: (*a*) The total amount of depreciation over the asset's lifetime must equal the capital good's historical cost or purchase price; (*b*) the depreciation is taken in annual accounting charges over the asset's accounting lifetime, which is usually related to the actual economic lifetime of the asset. ②

We can now understand how depreciation would be charged for Hot Dog Ventures. The equipment is depreciated according to a 10-year lifetime, so the $150,000 of equipment has a depreciation charge of $15,000 per year (using the simplest "straight-line" method of depreciation). If Hot Dog Ventures owned its store, it would have to take a depreciation charge for the building as well.

Adding up all the costs so far gives us the operating expenses (line 9). The net operating income is net revenues minus operating expenses (line 1 minus line 9). Have we accounted for all the costs of production yet? Not quite. Line 11 includes the annual cost of interest on the $100,000 loan. This should be thought of as the cost of borrowing the financial capital. While this is a fixed cost, it is typically kept separate from the other fixed costs. State and local taxes, such as property taxes, are treated as another expense. Deducting lines 11 and 12 gives a total of $55,000 in profits before income taxes. How are these profits divided? Approximately $18,000 goes to the federal government in the form of corporate income taxes. That leaves a profit of $37,000 after taxes. Dividends of $15,000 on the common stock are paid, leaving $22,000 to be plowed back as retained earnings in the business. Again, note that profits are a residual of sales minus costs.

资产负债表
THE BALANCE SHEET

Business accounting is concerned with more than ③ the profits and losses that are the economic driving force. Business accounts also include the **balance sheet,** which is a picture of financial conditions on a given date. This statement records what a firm, person, or nation is worth at a given point in time. On one side of the balance sheet are the **assets** (valuable

① 表 7-6. 损益表反映一段时间内的总销售收入和总支出

② 每年的折旧核算有很多不同的计算公式，但每种计算方法均必须遵循两大原则：(a) 资产使用寿命周期的折旧总额必须等于该资本品的历史成本或购买价格；(b) 折旧费计入该资产会计寿命周期内（它通常与资产的实际经济寿命期相联系）的年度会计成本之中。

③ 企业会计不仅关注作为经济驱动力的利润收益和损失，还包括**资产负债表**——它是企业在某一既定日期的财务状况表。该表记录的是企业、个人或国家在某一既定的时间点上的价值所在。资产负债表的一边是**资产**（企业所拥有的有价值的财产和权利），另一边有两项——**负债**（企业所欠的资金或者债务）和**资产净值**（或净价值，等于总资产减去总负债的值）。

properties or rights owned by the firm). On the other side are two items, the **liabilities** (money or obligations owed by the firm) and **net worth** (or net value, equal to total assets minus total liabilities).

One important distinction between the income ① statement and the balance sheet is that between stocks and flows. A **stock** represents the level of a variable, such as the amount of water in a lake or, in this case, the dollar value of a firm. A **flow** variable represents the change per unit of time, like the flow of water in a river or the flow of revenue and expenses into and out of a firm. *The income statement measures the flows into and out of the firm, while the balance sheet measures the stocks of assets and liabilities at the end of the accounting year.*

The fundamental identity or balancing relationship of the balance sheet is that total assets are balanced by total liabilities plus the net worth of the firm to its owners:

Total assets = total liabilities + net worth

We can rearrange this relationship to find:

Net worth = assets − liabilities

Let us illustrate this by considering Table 7-7, which shows a simple balance sheet for Hot Dog Ventures, Inc. On the left are assets, and on the right are liabilities and net worth. A blank space has been deliberately left next to the retained earnings entry because the only correct entry compatible with our fundamental balance sheet identity is $200,000. *A balance sheet must always balance because net worth is a residual defined as assets minus liabilities.* Suppose one item on a balance sheet changes (such as an increase in assets); then there must be a corresponding change on the balance sheet to maintain balance (a decrease in assets, an increase in liabilities, or an increase in net worth).

To illustrate how net worth always balances, suppose that hot dogs valued at $40,000 have spoiled. Your accountant reports to you: "Total assets are down $40,000; liabilities remain unchanged. This means total net worth has decreased by $40,000, and I have no choice but to write net worth down from the previous $210,000 to only $170,000." That's how accountants keep score.

We summarize our analysis of accounting concepts as follows:

1. The income statement shows the flow of sales, ② cost, and revenue over the year or accounting period. It measures the flow of dollars into and out of the firm over a specified period of time.
2. The balance sheet indicates an instantaneous financial picture or snapshot. It is like a measure of the stock of water in a lake. The major items are assets, liabilities, and net worth.

Balance Sheet of Hot Dog Ventures, Inc. (December 31, 2009)

Assets		Liabilities and net worth	
		Liabilities	
Current assets:		Current liabilities:	
Cash	$ 20,000	Accounts payable	$ 20,000
Inventory	80,000	Notes payable	20,000
Fixed assets:		Long-term liabilities:	
Equipment	150,000	Bonds payable	100,000
Buildings	100,000		
		Net worth	
		Stockholders' equity:	
		Common stock	10,000
		Retained earnings	....
Total	**$350,000**	**Total**	**$350,000**

TABLE 7-7. The Balance Sheet Records the Stock of Assets and Liabilities, plus Net Worth, of a Firm at a Given Point in Time ③

① 损益表与资产负债表之间的一个重要区别存在于，存量和流量的区别。**存量**代表变量水平，比如湖内的水容量，如上表中所示的企业以美元核算的价值。**流量**表示单位时间内的变化，比如河中的水流量，或者像企业的收益流和支出流进出企业的变化情况。*损益表计量的是进出企业的流量，而资产负债表计量的是在会计年度结束时，资产和负债的存量。*

② 1. 损益表反映的是一年中或者会计期间内的销售额、成本和收益流量。它测量的是企业在一个特定的时间段内美元流进出的情况。

2. 资产负债表反映的是企业在任一时点的财务状况。它就像测量湖中水容量的计量表一样。其主要项目是资产、负债和资产净值。

③ 表 7-7. 资产负债表记录了企业在某一既定时间点上的资产、负债和资产净值的存量情况

会计惯例
Accounting Conventions

In examining the balance sheet in Table 7-7, you might well ask, How are the values of the different items measured? How do the accountants know that the equipment is worth $150,000?

The answer is that accountants use a set of agreed-upon rules or accounting conventions to answer most questions. The most important assumption used in a balance sheet is that the value placed on almost every item reflects its *historical cost.* This differs from the economist's concept of "value," as we will see in the next section. For example, the inventory of hot-dog buns is valued at the price that was paid for them. A newly purchased fixed asset—a piece of equipment or a building—is valued at its purchase price (this being the historical-cost convention). ① Older capital is valued at its purchase price minus accumulated depreciation, thus accounting for the gradual decline in usefulness of capital goods. Accountants use historical cost because it reflects an objective evaluation and is easily verified.

In Table 7-7 current assets are convertible into cash within a year, while fixed assets represent capital goods and land. Most of the specific items listed are self-explanatory. Cash consists of coins, currency, and money on deposit in the bank. Cash is the only asset whose value is exact rather than an estimate.

② On the liabilities side, accounts payable and notes payable are sums owed to others for goods bought or for borrowed funds. Bonds payable are long-term loans floated in the market. The last item on the balance sheet is net worth, which is also called "stockholders' equity." This has two components. The first is common stock, which represents what the stockholders originally contributed to the business. The second component is retained earnings. These are earnings reinvested in the business after the deduction of any distributions to shareholders, such as dividends. Recall from the income statement that Hot Dog Ventures had $22,000 of retained earnings for 2009. The net worth is the firm's assets less liabilities, when valued at historical cost. Confirm that net worth must equal $210,000 in Table 7-7.

财务欺诈
Financial Finagling

Now that we have reviewed the principles of accounting, we see that there is considerable judgment involved in determining the exact treatment of certain items. In the late 1990s, under pressure to produce rapidly growing earnings, many companies manipulated their accounts to show glowing results or to paper over losses. Some of the most egregious examples included pretending that capital assets were current revenues (Enron, Global [3] Crossing); capitalizing the outflow while recognizing the inflow as current revenues (Enron, Qwest); [4] increasing the salvage value of trucks over time (Waste Management); [5] increasing the value of the unused capacity of landfills even as they fill up (Waste Management); and reporting happy pro-forma numbers when the reality was unpleasant (Amazon.com, Yahoo, and Qualcomm, [6] among a crowd of other dot-coms dead or alive).

To see how an accounting fraud works, let's take the example of Enron. Enron started off as a genuinely profitable business which owned the largest interstate network of natural-gas pipelines. To continue its rapid growth, it turned to trading natural-gas futures, and then it leveraged its business model into other markets.

Along the way, however, its profits began to decline and it hid the declines from investors. You might well ask, How could a large, publicly owned company like Enron have fooled virtually all of the people most of the time until 2001?

Its success in hiding its failures rested on four complementary factors. First, when troubles arose, Enron began to exploit ambiguities in accounting principles, such as the ones described above. One example was a deal called "Project Braveheart" with Blockbuster Video. This deal projected future revenues over the next 20 years with a present value of $111 million, and Enron accounted for them as current revenues even though the projections were based on highly dubious assumptions.

Second, the firm elected not to report the details of many financial transactions—for example, it hid hundreds of partnerships from its stockholders. Third, the board of directors and outside auditors were passive and did not challenge or in some cases even inquire into some details of Enron's accounts. Finally, the investment community, such as the large mutual funds, exercised little deep independent analysis of Enron's numbers even though at its peak Enron absorbed $70 billion of investors' funds.

The Enron case is a reminder that financial markets, accounting firms, and investment managers ⑦ can be fooled into investing many billions of dollars

historical cost
历史成本

① 旧有资本的价值是由最初的购买价格减去累计折旧核定的，这就解释了资本品的使用价值逐渐降低的原因。

② 就负债方而言，应付账目与票据指由于购买物品或贷入资金所欠他人的款项之和。应付债券指在市场上自由流动的长期贷款。

[3] Enron：美国安然公司，曾是世界上最大的电力、天然气以及电信公司之一。由于持续多年精心策划的并已制度化和系统化的财务造假丑闻，其欧洲分公司和美国总部分别于 2001 年 11 月 30 日和 12 月 2 日申请破产保护，使资产和营业额均上千亿的巨无霸企业在几周内破产。
Global Crossing：美国环球光纤公司，1997 年创立并迅速上市，市值曾达 380 亿美元。随着网络经济泡沫的破灭，其财务丑闻几乎与安然公司的丑闻同时被披露，成为美国电信行业史上最大的破产案，也是美国历史上第四大破产案。

[4] Qwest：西部电讯公司，美国第三大电信运营商，业务遍及美国西部的 14 个州，先后在 1999~2001、2002、2005 和 2007 年因为财务丑闻以及股票的非法内线交易等受到美国证券交易委员会的处罚，涉案高层被起诉。

[5] Waste Management：美国最大的垃圾处理企业，总部设在休斯顿，1998 年因非法延长资产的折旧期以增加税后收益的财务丑闻致股价暴跌，1999 年受到美国证券交易委员会的处罚。

---

⑥ Amazon.com：亚马逊公司，美国最大的网络电子商务公司，总部设在华盛顿州的西雅图。亚马逊成立于 1995 年，由书籍的网上销售业务起家，逐步扩及到了 DVD、CD、电脑、软件、电视游戏、电子产品、衣服、家具等。
Yahoo：雅虎，美国著名的互联网门户网站和全球性互联网通信、商贸及媒体公司。是 20 世纪末互联网奇迹的创造者之一，为 24 个国家和地区提供搜索引擎、电邮、新闻等业务，为全球超过 5 亿的独立用户提供多元化的网络服务。
Qualcomm：高通公司，位于美国加州的圣迭戈，其业务涵盖了技术领先的 3G 芯片组、系统软件，开发工具和产品，技术许可的授予，BREW 应用开发平台，QChat、BREWChatVoIP 解决方案技术，QPoint 定位解决方案，Eudora 电子邮件软件，包括双向数据通信系统、无线咨询及网络管理服务等的全面无线解决方案，MediaFLO 系统和 GSM1x 技术等。该公司拥有所有 3000 多项 CDMA 及其他技术的专利及专利申请，这些标准已经被全球制定标准机构普遍采纳或建议采纳。

⑦ 安然案例所警示的是，企业内部的人一旦醉心于会计欺诈，金融市场、会计师事务所和投资管理者就能够被愚弄而掉进数十亿美元的投资陷阱之中。

when firm insiders engage in aggressive accounting and fraudulent practices. A larger set of issues arose in 2007–2008 when a trillion dollars of poorly designed mortgage-backed securities got sound credit ratings from bond-rating agencies, but agencies and investors had little understanding of the income streams behind these securities. The history of such accounting and financial finagling is a reminder of the importance of sound accounting practices and the need for vigilant oversight by government and nongovernment bodies.

机会成本

C. OPPORTUNITY COSTS

In this section we look at costs from yet another angle. Remember that one of the cardinal tenets of economics is that resources are scarce. That means every time we choose to use a resource one way, we've given up the opportunity to utilize it another way. That's easy to see in our own lives, where we must constantly decide what to do with our limited time and income. Should we go to a movie or study for next week's test? Should we travel to Mexico or buy [1] a car? Should we get postgraduate or professional training or begin work right after college?

In each of these cases, making a choice in effect costs us the opportunity to do something else. The value of the best alternative forgone is called the opportunity cost, which we met briefly in Chapter 1 and develop more thoroughly here. The dollar cost of going to a movie instead of studying is the price of a ticket, but the opportunity cost also includes the possibility of getting a higher grade on the exam. The ② opportunity costs of a decision include all its consequences, whether they reflect monetary transactions or not.

> Decisions have opportunity costs because choos- ③ ing one thing in a world of scarcity means giving up something else. The **opportunity cost** is the value of the most valuable good or service forgone.

One important example of opportunity cost is the cost of going to college. If you went to a public university in your state in 2008, the total costs of tuition, books, and travel averaged about $7000. Does this mean that $7000 was your opportunity cost of going to school? Definitely not! You must include as well the *opportunity cost of the time* spent studying and going to classes. A full-time job for a college-age high school graduate averaged $26,000 in 2008. If we add up both the actual expenses and the earnings forgone, we would find that the opportunity cost of college was $33,000 (equal to $7000 + $26,000) rather than $7000 per year.

the opportunity cost of time
时间的机会成本

Business decisions have opportunity costs, too. Do all opportunity costs show up on the profit-and-loss statement? Not necessarily. In general, business accounts include only transactions in which money actually changes hands. By contrast, the economist ④ always tries to "pierce the veil of money" to uncover the real consequences that lie behind the dollar flows and to measure the true *resource costs* of an activity. Economists therefore include all costs—whether they reflect monetary transactions or not.

There are several important opportunity costs that do not show up on income statements. For example, in many small businesses, the family may put in many unpaid hours, which are not included as accounting costs. Nor do business accounts include a capital charge for the owner's financial contributions. Nor do they include the cost of the environmental damage that occurs when a business dumps toxic wastes into a stream. But from an economic point of view, each of these is a genuine cost to the economy.

Let's illustrate the concept of opportunity cost by considering the owner of Hot Dog Ventures. The owner puts in 60 hours a week but earns no "wages." At the end of the year, as Table 7-6 showed, the firm earns a profit of $37,000—pretty good for a neophyte firm.

Hot Dog Ventures
热狗店

Or is it? The economist would insist that we should consider the value of a factor of production regardless of how the factor happens to be owned. We should count the owner's own labor as a cost even though the owner does not get paid directly but instead receives compensation in the form of profits. Because the owner has alternative opportunities for work, we must value the owner's labor in terms of the lost opportunities.

A careful examination might show that Hot Dog Ventures' owner could find a similar and equally interesting job working for someone else and earning $60,000. This represents the opportunity cost or earnings forgone because the owner decided to become the unpaid owner of a small business rather than the paid employee of another firm.

---

[1] 在墨西哥买车以价格便宜和手续简便著称，且各种税赋较低，分期购买零利率。

② 一项决策的机会成本包括了该决策所带来的所有后果，无论它们是否反映货币交易。

③ 决策有机会成本，因为在一个稀缺的世界里选择一种东西本身就意味着放弃其他的东西。**机会成本**就是放弃的最有价值的物品或者服务的价值所在。

④ 相比之下，经济学家们一直在尝试着"掀开货币的面纱"，来揭示隐藏在美元流幕后的真实结果，同时也在尝试去计量一项活动的真实资源成本。因此，无论这些成本是否反映货币交易，经济学家们都会把它们包括在内。

Therefore, the economist continues, let us calculate the true economic profits of the hot-dog firm. If we take the measured profits of $37,000 and subtract the $60,000 opportunity cost of the owner's labor, we find a net *loss* of $23,000. Hence, although the accountant might conclude that Hot Dog Ventures is economically viable, the economist would pronounce that the firm is an unprofitable loser.

What Was the Cost of the War in Iraq?

One of the most vexing questions facing Americans is to calculate how much the war in Iraq has cost. This issue involves questions of opportunity cost for the nation rather than for the firm, but the principles are similar. The Bush administration originally estimated that the war would be over quickly and that the costs would be around $50 billion. In reality, the war proved much longer and more expensive. According to a congressional report in 2008, the cumulative total spending on the campaigns in Iraq and Afghanistan was about $750 billion.

But economists Linda Bilmes and Joseph Stiglitz argue that even this large number underestimates the total because it does not take into account the entire opportunity cost of the war. One example of the understatement is that the pay of members of the military does not reflect the total costs to the nation because it underestimates costs in health care and other benefits. They write:

> When a young soldier is killed in Iraq or Afghanistan, his or her family will receive a U.S. government check for just $500,000 (combining life insurance with a "death gratuity")—far less than the typical amount paid by insurance companies for the death of a young person in a car accident. The "budgetary cost" of $500,000 is clearly only a fraction of the total cost society pays for the loss of life—and no one can ever really compensate the families. Moreover, disability pay seldom provides adequate compensation for wounded troops or their families. Indeed, in one out of five cases of seriously injured soldiers, someone in their family has to give up a job to take care of them.

Bilmes and Stiglitz also calculate that oil prices are higher because of the war, contributing to the increase in oil prices from $25 per barrel in 2003 to a peak of $155 a barrel in 2008.

When they add up all the opportunity costs through 2008, they conclude that the war in Iraq will cost the American people $3 trillion, or about $30,000 per household. While these numbers are subject to debate, they are a timely reminder of the difference between an accounting number and true economic or opportunity cost.

机会成本和市场
OPPORTUNITY COST AND MARKETS

At this point, however, you might well say: "Now I'm totally confused. First I learned that price is a good measure of true social cost in the marketplace. Now
[1] you tell me that opportunity cost is the right concept.
Can't you economists make up your minds?"

Actually, there is a simple explanation: *In well-* ②
functioning markets, when all costs are included, price equals opportunity cost. Assume that a commodity like wheat is bought and sold in a competitive market. If I bring my wheat to market, I will receive a number of bids from prospective buyers: $2.502, $2.498, and $2.501 per bushel. These represent the values of my wheat to, say, three different flour mills. I pick the highest—$2.502. The opportunity cost of this sale is the value of the best available alternative—that is, the second-highest bid, at $2.501—which is almost identical to the price that is accepted. As the market approaches perfect competition, the bids get closer and closer until, at the limit, the second-highest bid (which is our definition of opportunity cost) exactly
equals the highest bid (which is the price). In com- ③
petitive markets, numerous buyers compete for resources to the point where price is bid up to the best available alternative and is therefore equal to the opportunity cost.

Opportunity Cost outside Markets. The concept of opportunity cost is particularly crucial when you are analyzing transactions that take place outside markets. How do you measure the value of a road or a park? Of a health or safety regulation? Even the allocation of student time can be explained using opportunity cost.

- The notion of opportunity cost explains why students watch more TV the week after exams than the week before exams. Watching TV right before an exam has a high opportunity cost, for the alternative use of time (studying) has high value in improving grade performance and getting a good job. After exams, time has a lower opportunity cost.

---

[1] 伊拉克和阿富汗两场战争是布什政府留给奥巴马政府的两个烫手山芋，同时，这两场战争也是分析机会成本的极好案例。本部分内容全部为新加，这一点也印证了萨翁在本版自序中的中庸立场。

② 在机制完善的市场环境下，当所有的成本都包括在内时，价格就等于机会成本。

③ 在竞争的市场中，为数众多的买家为资源而相互竞价，从而使价格竞争到一个双方均满意的竞价点上，所以，这一点的价格就等于机会成本。

- Or take the case of a proposal to drill for oil off the California coast. A storm of complaints is heard. A defender of the program states, "We need that oil to protect us from insecure foreign sources who are holding us hostage. We have plenty of seawater to go around. This is just good economics for the nation." In fact, it might be poor economics because of the opportunity cost. If drilling leads to oil spills that spoil the beaches, it might reduce the recreational value of the ocean. That opportunity cost might not be easily measured, but it is every bit as real as the value of oil under the waters.

The Road Not Traveled. Opportunity cost, then, is a measure of what has been given up when we make a decision. Consider what Robert Frost had in mind [1] when he wrote,

> Two roads diverged in a wood, and I—
> I took the one less traveled by,
> And that has made all the difference.

What other road did Frost have in mind? An urban life? A life where he would not be able to write of roads and walls and birches? Imagine the immeasurable opportunity cost to all of us if Robert Frost had taken the road more traveled by.

But let us return from the poetic to the practical. The crucial point to grasp is this:

> Economic costs include, in addition to explicit money outlays, those opportunity costs incurred because resources can be used in alternative ways. ②

SUMMARY

A. Economic Analysis of Costs

1. Total cost (TC) can be broken down into fixed cost (FC) and variable cost (VC). Fixed costs are unaffected by any production decisions, while variable costs are incurred on items like labor or materials which increase as production levels rise.
2. Marginal cost (MC) is the extra total cost resulting from 1 extra unit of output. Average total cost (AC) is the sum of ever-declining average fixed cost (AFC) and average variable cost (AVC). Short-run average cost is generally represented by a U-shaped curve that is always intersected at its minimum point by the rising MC curve.
3. Useful rules to remember are

$$TC = FC + VC \quad AC = \frac{TC}{q} \quad AC = AFC + AVC$$

At the bottom of U-shaped AC, $MC = AC =$ minimum AC.

4. Costs and productivity are like mirror images. When the law of diminishing returns holds, the marginal product falls and the MC curve rises. When there is an initial stage of increasing returns, MC initially falls.
5. We can apply cost and production concepts to a firm's choice of the best combination of factors of production. Firms that desire to maximize profits will want to minimize the cost of producing a given level of output. In this case, the firm will follow the least-cost rule: different factors will be chosen so that the marginal product per dollar of input is equalized for all inputs. This implies that $MP_L/P_L = MP_A/P_A = \cdots$.

B. Economic Costs and Business Accounting

6. To understand accounting, the most important relationships are:
   a. The character of the income statement (or profit-and-loss statement); the residual nature of profits; and depreciation of fixed assets.
   b. The fundamental balance sheet relationship between assets, liabilities, and net worth; the breakdown of each of these into financial and fixed assets; and the residual nature of net worth.

C. Opportunity Costs

7. The economist's definition of costs is broader than the accountant's. Economic cost includes not only the obvious out-of-pocket purchases or monetary transactions but also more subtle opportunity costs, such as the return to labor supplied by the owner of a firm. These opportunity costs are tightly constrained by the bids and offers in competitive markets, so price is close to opportunity cost for marketed goods and services.
8. The most important application of opportunity cost arises for nonmarket goods—those like clean air or health or recreation—which may be highly valuable even though they are not bought and sold in markets.

---

[1] 罗伯特·弗罗斯特（Robert Frost，1874.3.26~1963.1.29），一位兼跨古典和现代的美国诗人，曾四次获得普利策诗歌奖（Pulitzer Prizes for Poetry）。其诗歌从乡村生活中汲取营养，作品既崇尚生活现实又富有神秘色彩。这三行诗节选自其发表于 1916 年的著名诗篇 *The Road Not Taken*（请注意，萨翁将"Taken"改为"Traveled"作为本小节的题目，意在强调经济活动的过程）第 4 节，也就是结尾节的结尾行，即该诗的着墨所在。本诗寓意颇深，似可理解为中西文化之本质区别所在，请参阅拙作文集《中国英语教育改革探思录》中所收的有关文章。该诗结构严谨，格式规范，全诗四节，每节五行，均为五步抑扬格的 abaab 结构（Iambic Pentameter）。

② 除了显性的货币支出外，经济学成本还包括由于资源可以改作它用而产生的那些机会成本。

CONCEPTS FOR REVIEW

Analysis of Costs

total costs: fixed and variable
marginal cost
least-cost rule:

$$\frac{MP_L}{P_L} = \frac{MP_A}{P_A} = \frac{MP_{\text{any factor}}}{P_{\text{any factor}}}$$

$TC = FC + VC$
$AC = TC/q = AFC + AVC$

Accounting Concepts

income statement (profit-and-loss statement): sales, cost, profits
depreciation
fundamental balance sheet identity
assets, liabilities, and net worth
stocks vs. flows
opportunity cost
cost concepts in economics and accounting

FURTHER READING AND INTERNET WEBSITES

Further Reading

Advanced treatment of cost and production theory can be found in intermediate textbooks. See the list provided in Chapter 3.

You can find interesting articles on business cost, production, and decision problems in magazines such as *Business Week, Fortune, Forbes,* and *The Economist.* An excellent nontechnical analysis of the Enron fraud is contained in Paul M. Healy and Krishna G. Palepu, "The Fall of Enron," *Journal of Economic Perspectives,* Spring 2003, pp. 3–26.

The quotation on the cost of war is from Linda J. Bilmes and Joseph E. Stiglitz, "The Iraq War Will Cost Us $3 Trillion, and Much More," *Washington Post,* March 9, 2008, p. B1. Their full study is Joseph E. Stiglitz and Linda J. Bilmes, *The Three Trillion Dollar War: The True Cost of the Iraq Conflict* (Norton, New York, 2008).

Websites

Good case studies on costs and production can be found in the business press. See the websites of the business magazines listed above, *www.businessweek.com, www.fortune.com, www.forbes.com,* and *www.economist.com.* Some of these sites require a fee or subscription.

Information about individual firms is filed with the Securities and Exchange Commission and can be found at *www.sec.gov/edgarhp.htm.*

QUESTIONS FOR DISCUSSION

1. During his major-league career from 1936 to 1960, Ted Williams had 7706 at bats and 2654 hits.
   a. What was his lifetime batting average?
   b. In his last year, 1960, Williams had 310 at bats and 98 hits. What was his lifetime batting average at the end of 1959? What was his batting average for 1960?
   c. Explain the relationship between his average for 1959 and the change of his lifetime average from 1959 to 1960. State how this illustrates the relationship between *MC* and *AC.*
2. To the $55 of fixed cost in Table 7-3, add $90 of additional *FC.* Now calculate a whole new table, with the same *VC* as before but new $FC = \$145$. What happens to *MC, AVC?* To *TC, AC, AFC?* Can you verify that minimum *AC* is now at $q^* = 5$ with $AC = \$60 = MC$?
3. Explain why *MC* cuts *AC* and *AVC* at their minimum values (i.e., the bottom of their U-shaped cost curves).
4. "Compulsory military service allows the government to fool itself and the people about the true cost of a big army." Compare the budget cost and the opportunity cost of a voluntary army (where army pay is high) with those of compulsory service (where pay is low). What does the concept of opportunity cost contribute to analyzing the quotation?
5. Consider the data in Table 7-8, which contains a situation similar to that in Table 7-5.
   a. Calculate the *TC, VC, FC, AC, AVC,* and *MC.* On a piece of graph paper, plot the *AC* and *MC* curves.
   b. Assume that the price of labor doubles. Calculate a new *AC* and *MC.* Plot the new curves and compare them with those in **a.**

(1) Output (tons of wheat)	(2) Land inputs (acres)	(3) Labor inputs (workers)	(4) Land rent ($ per acre)	(5) Labor wage ($ per worker)
0	15	0	12	5
1	15	6	12	5
2	15	11	12	5
3	15	15	12	5
4	15	21	12	5
5	15	31	12	5
6	15	45	12	5
7	15	63	12	5

TABLE 7-8.

c. Now assume that total factor productivity doubles (i.e., that the level of output doubles for each input combination). Repeat the exercise in **b.** Can you see two major factors that tend to affect a firm's cost curves?

6. Explain the fallacies in each of the following:
   a. Average costs are minimized when marginal costs are at their lowest point.
   b. Because fixed costs never change, average fixed cost is a constant for each level of output.
   c. Average cost is rising whenever marginal cost is rising.
   d. The opportunity cost of drilling for oil in Yosemite Park is zero because no firm produces anything there.
   e. A firm minimizes costs when it spends the same amount on each input.

7. In 2008, a fictitious software company named EconDisaster.com sold $7000 worth of a game called "Global Financial Meltdown." The company had salaries of $1000, rent of $500, and electricity use of $500, and it purchased a computer for $5000. The company uses straight-line depreciation with a lifetime of 5 years (this means that depreciation is calculated as the historical cost divided by the lifetime). It pays a corporation tax of 25 percent on profits and paid no dividends. Construct its income statement for 2008 based on Table 7-6.

8. Next, construct the balance sheet for EconDisaster.com for December 31, 2008. The company had no assets at the beginning of the year. The owners contributed $10,000 of start-up capital and obtained common stock. Net income and retained earnings can be calculated from question 7.

Appendix 7

PRODUCTION, COST THEORY, AND DECISIONS OF THE FIRM
附录 7　生产、成本理论和企业决策

The production theory described in Chapter 6 and the cost analysis of this chapter are among the fundamental building blocks of microeconomics. A thorough understanding of production and cost is necessary for an appreciation of how economic scarcity gets translated into prices in the marketplace. This appendix develops these concepts further and introduces the concept of an equal-product curve, or isoquant.

数值化的生产函数
A NUMERICAL PRODUCTION FUNCTION

Production theory and cost analysis have their roots ① in the concept of a production function, which shows the maximum amount of output that can be produced with various combinations of inputs. Table 7A-1 starts with a numerical example of a constant-returns-to-scale production function, showing the amount of inputs along the axes and the amount of output at the grid points of the table.

Land \ Labor	1	2	3	4	5	6
6	346	490	600	692	775	846
5	316	448	548	632	705	775
4	282	400	490	564	632	692
3	245	346	423	490	548	600
2	200	282	346	400	448	490
1	141	200	245	282	316	346

TABLE 7A-1. A Tabular Picture of a Production Function Relating Amount of Output to Varying Combinations of Labor and Land Inputs ②

When you have 3 land units and 2 labor units available, the engineer tells you the maximum obtainable output is 346 units. Note the different ways to produce 346. Do the same for 490. (The production function shown in the table is a special case of the Cobb-Douglas production function, one given by the formula $Q = 100\sqrt{2LA}$.)

Along the left-hand side are listed the varying amounts of land, going from 1 unit to 6 units. Along the bottom are listed amounts of labor, which also go from 1 to 6. Output corresponding to each land row and labor column is listed inside the table.

If we are interested in knowing exactly how much output there will be when 3 units of land and 2 units of labor are available, we count up 3 units of land and then go over 2 units of labor. The answer is seen to be 346 units of product. (Can you identify some other input combinations that will produce $q = 346$?) Similarly, we find that 3 units of land and 6 of labor produce 600 units of q. Remember that the production function shows the maximum output available given engineering skills and technical knowledge available at a particular time.

边际产量递减规律
THE LAW OF DIMINISHING MARGINAL PRODUCT

Table 7A-1 can nicely illustrate the law of diminishing returns. First, recall that the marginal product of labor is the extra production resulting from 1 additional unit of labor when land and other inputs are held constant. At any point in Table 7A-1, we can find the marginal product of labor by subtracting the output from the number on its right in the same row. Thus, when there are 2 units of land and 4 units of labor, the marginal product of an additional laborer would be 48, or 448 minus 400 in the second row.

By the "marginal product of land" we mean, of ③ course, the extra product resulting from 1 additional unit of land when labor is held constant. It is calculated by comparing adjacent items in a given column. Thus, when there are 2 units of land and 4 units of labor, the marginal product of land is shown in the fourth column as 490 – 400, or 90.

We can easily find the marginal product of each of our two factors by comparing adjacent entries in the vertical columns or horizontal rows of Table 7A-1.

Having defined the concept of marginal product of an input, we now can easily define the law of diminishing returns: *The law of diminishing returns*

① 生产理论与成本分析源自生产函数的概念。生产函数表示运用不同的投入要素组合生产出的最大产出量。

② 表 7A-1. 劳动与土地的不同投入要素组合与产出量关系的生产函数表

③ 当然，我们所讲的“土地的边际产量”指劳动这一要素在保持不变的情况下，追加一个单位的土地所额外增加的产量。

states that as we increase one input and hold other inputs constant, the marginal product of the varying input will, at least after some point, decline.

To illustrate this, hold land constant in Table 7A-1 by sticking to a given row—say, the row corresponding to land equal to 2 units. Now let labor increase from 1 to 2 units, from 2 to 3 units, and so forth. What happens to q at each step?

As labor goes from 1 to 2 units, the level of output increases from 200 to 282 units, or by 82 units. But the next dose of labor adds only 64 units, or 346 − 282. Diminishing returns have set in. Still further additions of a single unit of labor give us, respectively, only 54 extra units of output, 48 units, and finally 42 units. You can easily verify that the law holds for other rows and that the law holds when land is varied and labor held constant.

We can use this example to verify our intuitive justification of the law of diminishing returns—the assertion that the law holds because the fixed factor decreases relative to the variable factor. According to this explanation, each unit of the variable factor has less and less of the fixed factor to work with. So it is natural that extra product should drop off.

If this explanation is to hold water, output should ① increase proportionately when both factors are increased together. When labor increases from 1 to 2 and land simultaneously increases from 1 to 2, we should get the same increase in product as when both increase *simultaneously* from 2 to 3. This can be verified in Table 7A-1. In the first move we go from 141 to 282, and in the second move the product increases from 282 to 423, an equal jump of 141 units.

既定产量的最低成本要素组合 LEAST-COST FACTOR COMBINATION FOR A GIVEN OUTPUT

The numerical production function shows us the different ways to produce a given level of output. But which of the many possibilities should the firm use? If the desired level of output is $q = 346$, there are no less than four different combinations of land and labor, shown as A, B, C, and D in Table 7A-2.

As far as the engineer is concerned, each of these combinations is equally good at producing an output of 346 units. But the manager, interested in minimizing cost, wants to find the combination that costs the least.

	(1)	(2)	(3)	(4)
	Input Combinations		Total cost when $P_L = \$2$ $P_A = \$3$ (\$)	Total cost when $P_L = \$2$ $P_A = \$1$ (\$)
	Labor L	Land A		
A	1	6	20	____
B	2	3	13	7
C	3	2	12	____
D	6	1	15	____

TABLE 7A-2. Inputs and Costs of Producing a Given Level of Output ②

Assume that the firm has chosen 346 units of output. Then it can use any of the four choices of input combinations shown as A, B, C, and D. As the firm moves down the list, production becomes more labor-intensive and less land-intensive. Fill in the missing numbers.

The firm's choice among the different techniques will depend on input prices. When $P_L = \$2$ and $P_A = \$3$, verify that the cost-minimizing combination is C. Show that lowering the price of land from \$3 to \$1 leads the firm to choose a more land-intensive combination at B.

Let us suppose that the price of labor is \$2 and the price of land \$3. The total costs when input prices are at this level are shown in the third column of Table 7A-2. For combination A, the total labor and land cost will be \$20, equal to $(1 \times \$2) + (6 \times \$3)$. Costs at B, C, and D will be, respectively, \$13, \$12, and \$15. At the assumed input prices, C is the least costly way to produce the given output.

If either of the input prices changes, the equilibrium proportion of the inputs will also change so as ③ to use less of the input that has gone up most in price. (This is just like the substitution effect in Chapter 5's discussion of consumer demand.) As soon as input prices are known, the least-cost method of production can be found by calculating the costs of different input combinations.

等产量曲线 *Equal-Product Curves*

The commonsense numerical analysis of the way in which a firm will combine inputs to minimize costs can be made more vivid by the use of diagrams. We will take the diagrammatic approach by putting together two new curves, the equal-product curve and the equal-cost line.

---

① 如果这一解释的逻辑严密，那么当两种要素同时增加时，产量就应该相应地按比例增加。

② 表 7A-2. 生产一定产量的投入要素和成本

③ 如果两种投入要素的任意一种的价格发生变化，则投入品要素的均衡比例也将随之变化，进而导致价格已经攀升到最高点的投入要素的用量减少。

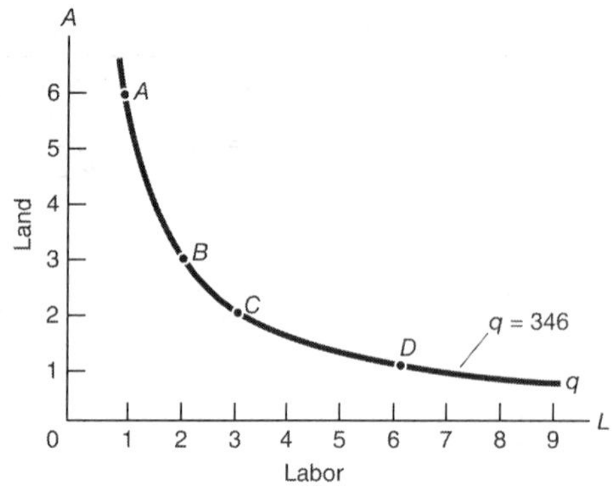

FIGURE 7A-1. Equal-Product Curve ①

All the points on the equal-product curve represent the different combinations of land and labor that can be used to produce the same 346 units of output.

Let's turn Table 7A-1 into a continuous curve by drawing a smooth curve through all the points that yield $q = 346$. This smooth curve, shown in Figure 7A-1, indicates all the different combinations of labor and land that yield an output of 346 units. This is called an **equal-product curve** or **isoquant** and is analogous to the consumer's indifference curve discussed in the appendix to Chapter 5. You should be able to draw on Figure 7A-1 the corresponding equal-product curve for output equal to 490 by getting the data from Table 7A-1. Indeed, an infinite number of such equal-product contour lines could be drawn in.

等成本线

Equal-Cost Lines

Given the price of labor and land, the firm can evaluate the total cost for points *A, B, C,* and *D* or for any other point on the equal-product curve. The firm will minimize its costs when it selects that point on its equal-product curve that has the lowest total cost.

An easy technique for finding the least-cost method of production is to construct **equal-cost lines.** This is done in Figure 7A-2, where the family of parallel straight lines represents a number of equal-cost curves when the price of labor is \$2 and the price of land \$3.

To find the total cost for any point, we simply ② read off the number appended to the equal-cost line going through that point. The lines are all straight and parallel because the firm is assumed to be able to buy all it wishes of either input at constant prices. The lines are somewhat flatter than 45° because the price of labor P_L is somewhat less than the price of land P_A. More precisely, we can always say that the arithmetic value of the slope of each equal-cost line must equal the ratio of the price of labor to that of land—in this case $P_L/P_A = 2/3$.

等产量曲线和等成本线的切点：最低成本

Equal-Product and Equal-Cost Contours: Least-Cost Tangency

Combining the equal-product and equal-cost lines, we can determine the optimal, or cost-minimizing, position of the firm. Recall that the optimal input combination comes at that point where the given output of $q = 346$ can be produced at least cost. To find such a point, simply superimpose the single green equal-product curve upon the family of blue equal-cost lines, as shown in Figure 7A-3. The firm will always keep moving along the green convex curve of Figure 7A-3 as long as it is able to cross over to lower cost lines. Its equilibrium will therefore be at *C*, where the equal-product curve touches (but does not cross) the lowest equal-cost line. This is a point of tangency, where the slope of the equal-product curve just matches the slope of an equal-cost line and the curves are just kissing.

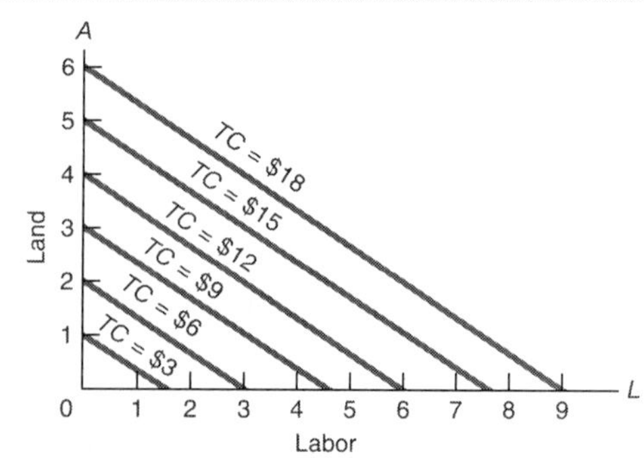

FIGURE 7A-2. Equal-Cost Lines ③

Every point on a given equal-cost line represents the same total cost. The lines are straight because factor prices are constant, and they all have a negative slope equal to the ratio of labor price to land price, \$2/\$3, and hence are parallel.

---

① 图 7A-1. 等产量曲线

② 要找到任何一点的总成本，我们只需要读出通过该点的等成本线上的相应数值即可。等成本线都是相互平行的直线，因为我们可以假设，企业有能力按照不变的价格购买所有它希望购买的任何一种投入要素。

③ 图 7A-2. 等成本线

Substituting Inputs to Minimize Cost of Production

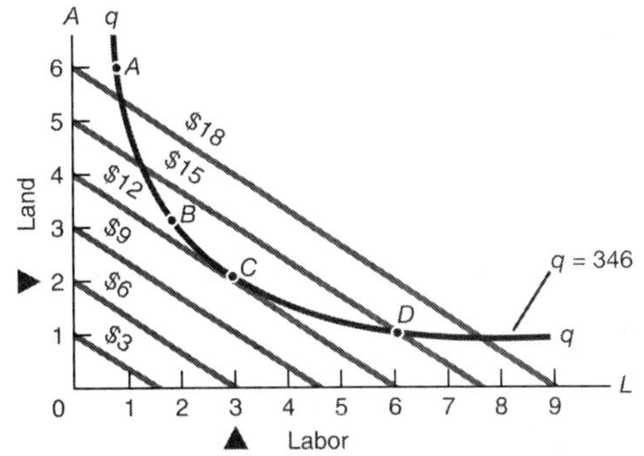

FIGURE 7A-3. Least-Cost Input Combination Comes at *C* ①

The firm desires to minimize its costs of producing a given output of 346. It thus seeks out the least expensive input combination along its green equal-product curve. It looks for the input combination that is on the lowest of the equal-cost lines. Where the equal-product curve touches (but does not cross) the lowest equal-cost line is the least-cost position. This tangency means that factor prices and marginal products are proportional, with equalized marginal products per dollar.

We already know that the slope of the equal-cost curves is P_L/P_A. But what is the slope of the equal-product curve? Recall from Chapter 1's appendix that the slope at a point of a curved line is the slope of the straight line tangent to the curve at the point in question. For the equal-product curve, this slope is a "substitution ratio" between the two factors. It depends upon the relative marginal products of the two factors of production, namely, MP_L/MP_A—just as the rate of substitution between two goods along a consumer's indifference curve was earlier shown to equal the ratio of the marginal utilities of the two goods (see the appendix to Chapter 5).

成本最小的条件

Least-Cost Conditions

Using our graphical apparatus, we have therefore derived the conditions under which a firm will minimize its costs of production:

1. The ratio of marginal products of any two inputs must equal the ratio of their factor prices:

$$\text{Substitution ratio} = \frac{\text{marginal product of labor}}{\text{marginal product of land}}$$

$$= \begin{matrix}\text{slope of}\\ \text{equal-product}\\ \text{curve}\end{matrix} = \frac{\text{price of labor}}{\text{price of land}}$$

2. We can also rewrite condition 1 in a different and illuminating way. From the last equation it follows that the marginal product per dollar received from the (last) dollar of expenditure must be the same for every productive input:

$$\frac{\text{Marginal product of } L}{\text{Price of } L} = \frac{\text{marginal product of } A}{\text{price of } A} = \cdots$$

But you should not be satisfied with abstract explanations. Always remember the commonsense ② economic explanation which shows how a firm will distribute its expenditure among inputs to equalize the marginal product per dollar of spending.

SUMMARY TO APPENDIX

1. A production-function table lists the output that can be produced for each labor column and each land row. Diminishing returns to one variable factor, when other factors are held fixed or constant, can be shown by calculating the decline of marginal products in any row or column.
2. An equal-product curve or isoquant depicts the alternative input combinations that produce the same level of output. The slope, or substitution ratio, along such an equal-product curve equals relative marginal products (e.g., MP_L/MP_A). Curves of equal total cost are parallel lines with slopes equal to factor-price ratios (P_L/P_A). Least-cost equilibrium comes at the tangency point, where an equal-product curve touches but does not cross the lowest *TC* curve. In least-cost equilibrium, marginal products are proportional to factor prices, with equalized marginal product per dollar spent on all factors (i.e., equalized MP_i/P_i).

① 图 7A-3. 在 C 点的成本最低的投入要素组合
② 应该始终牢记通常意义上的经济学解释，它说明了企业在各种投入要素上如何分配其支出，从而使支出每一美元所产生的边际产量相等。

CONCEPTS FOR REVIEW

equal-product curves, isoquants
parallel lines of equal TC
substitution ratio = MP_L/MP_A

P_L/P_A as the slope of parallel equal-TC lines

least-cost tangency condition:
$MP_L/MP_A = P_L/P_A$ or $MP_L/P_L = MP_A/P_A$

QUESTIONS FOR DISCUSSION

1. Show that raising labor's wage while holding land's rent constant will steepen the blue equal-cost lines and move tangency point C in Figure 7A-3 northwest toward B, with the now-cheaper input substituted for the input which is now more expensive. If we substitute capital for labor, restate the result. Should union leaders recognize this relationship?

2. What is the least-cost combination of inputs if the production function is given by Table 7A-1 and input prices are as shown in Figure 7A-3, where $q = 346$? What would be the least-cost ratio for the same input prices if output doubled to $q = 692$? What has happened to the "factor intensity," or land-labor ratio? Can you see why this result would hold for any output change under constant returns to scale?

CHAPTER

8

Analysis of Perfectly Competitive Markets

完全竞争市场分析

Cost of production would have no effect on competitive price if it could have none on supply. [1]

John Stuart Mill

生产成本若对供给不构成影响，则对物品本身的价值也不会构成影响。——约翰·斯图尔特·米尔

We have described how the market mechanism performs a kind of miracle every day, providing our daily necessities like bread and a vast array of high-quality goods and services without central control or direction. Exactly how does this market mechanism work?

The answer begins with the two sides to every market—supply and demand. These two components must be put together to understand how the market as a whole behaves. This first chapter ② on industrial organization analyzes the behavior of perfectly competitive markets; these are idealized markets in which firms and consumers are too small to affect the price. The first section shows how competitive firms behave, after which some special cases are examined. The chapter concludes by showing that a perfectly competitive industry will be efficient. After having surveyed the central case of perfect competition, we move on in the following chapters to other forms of market behavior, such as monopolies.

竞争企业的供给行为

A. SUPPLY BEHAVIOR OF THE COMPETITIVE FIRM

竞争企业的行为
BEHAVIOR OF A COMPETITIVE FIRM

We begin with an analysis of perfectly competitive firms. If you own such a firm, how much should you produce? How much wheat should Farmer Smith produce if wheat sells at $6 per bushel?

Our analysis of perfectly competitive firms relies ③ on two key assumptions. First, we will assume that our competitive firm *maximizes profits.* Second, we reiterate that perfect competition is a world of *atomistic firms who are price-takers.*

利润最大化
Profit Maximization

Profits are like the net earnings or take-home pay of a business. They represent the amount a firm can pay in dividends to the owners, reinvest in new plant

② 作为论述行业组织的开篇之章，本章旨在分析完全竞争环境下的市场行为。这些市场都是理想化的，企业和消费者在其中的作用甚至小到无法对价格产生影响。

③ 我们在分析完全竞争环境下的企业行为时，基于两个关键性的假设：第一，我们假设完全竞争的企业追求的是利润最大化。第二，我们重申，完全竞争市场是一个作为价格接受者的原子企业组成的世界。

[1] 约翰·斯图尔特·米尔（John Stuart Mill，1806.5.20~1873.5.8），曾被严复译作“穆勒”，英国著名的哲学家和经济学家，19 世纪极具影响力的古典自由主义思想家。本句话改编自米尔的代表性著作《政治经济学原理》（*The Principles of Political Economy*）第三编《分配》（Book 3: *Distribution*）的第 9 章《受生产成本支配的货币价值》（Chapter 9：*Of the Value of Money, as Dependent on Cost of Production*）的第三小节：

It is simply the law of demand and supply, which is acknowledged to be applicable to all commodities, and which, in the case of money as of most other things, is controlled, but not set aside, by the law of cost of production, since **cost of production would have no effect on value if it could have none on supply.**

“competitive price”的约定表述在米尔的著作中尚未发现，同时代的学者中只有恩格斯在其《资本论》第三卷和梵伯伦（Thorstein Veblen, 1857~1929）在《企业论》（*The Theory of Business Enterprise*）第 7 章以及哈伯森（J. A. Hobson, 1858~1940）在《劳动和财富：人类评价》（*Work and Wealth: A Human Valuation*）中提及，进入 20 世纪后才逐渐被经济学界广泛使用。

and equipment, or employ to make financial investments. All these activities increase the value of the firm to its owners.

Firms maximize profits because that maximizes the economic benefit to the owners of the firm. Allowing lower-than-maximum profits is like asking for a pay cut, which few business owners will voluntarily undertake.

Profit maximization requires the firm to manage its internal operations efficiently (prevent waste, encourage worker morale, choose efficient production processes, and so forth) and to make sound decisions in the marketplace (buy the correct quantity of inputs at least cost and choose the optimal level of output).

Because profits involve both costs and revenues, the firm must have a good grasp of its cost structure. Turn back to Table 7-3 in the previous chapter to make sure you are clear on the important concepts of total cost, average cost, and marginal cost.

完全竞争
Perfect Competition

Perfect competition is the world of *price-takers*. A perfectly competitive firm sells a *homogeneous product* (one identical to the product sold by others in the industry). The firm is so small relative to its market that it cannot affect the market price; it simply takes the price as given. When Farmer Smith sells a homogeneous product like wheat, she sells to a large pool of buyers at the market price of $6 per bushel. Just as consumers must generally accept the prices that are charged by Internet access providers or movie theaters, so must competitive firms accept the market prices of the wheat or oil that they produce.

We can depict a price-taking perfect competitor by examining the way demand looks to a perfectly competitive firm. Figure 8-1 shows the contrast between the industry demand curve (the *DD* curve) and the demand curve facing a single competitive firm (the *dd* curve). Because a competitive industry is populated by firms that are small relative to the market, the firm's segment of the demand curve is only a tiny segment of the industry's curve. Graphically, the com- ① petitive firm's portion of the demand curve is so small that, to the lilliputian eye of the perfect competitor, the firm's *dd* demand curve looks completely horizontal or infinitely elastic. Figure 8-1 illustrates how the elasticity of demand for a single competitor appears very much greater than that for the entire market.

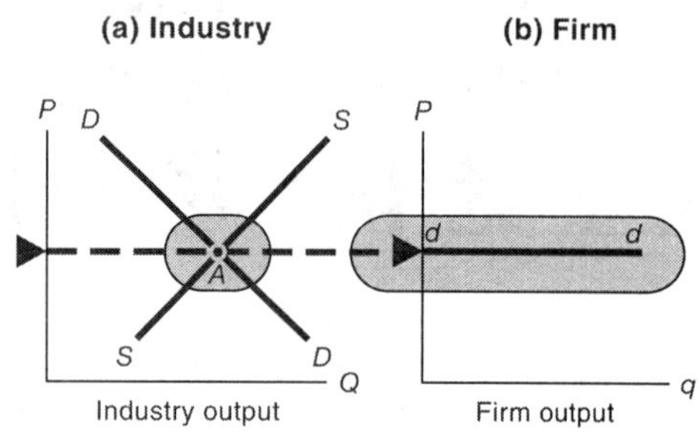

FIGURE 8-1. Demand Curve Is Completely Elastic for a Perfectly Competitive Firm ②

The industry demand curve on the left has inelastic demand at the market equilibrium at *A*. However, the demand curve for the perfectly competitive firm on the right is horizontal (i.e., completely elastic). The demand curve on the right is horizontal because a perfect competitor has such a small fraction of the market that it can sell all it wants at the market price.

Because competitive firms cannot affect the price, the price for each unit sold is the extra revenue that the firm will earn. For example, at a market price of $40 per unit, the competitive firm can sell all it wants at $40. If it decides to sell 101 units rather than 100 units, its revenue goes up by exactly $40.

Here are the major points to remember:

1. Under **perfect competition,** there are many small ③ firms, each producing an identical product and each too small to affect the market price.
2. The perfect competitor faces a completely horizontal demand (or *dd*) curve.
3. The extra revenue gained from each extra unit sold is therefore the market price.

边际成本等于价格时的竞争供给
Competitive Supply Where Marginal Cost Equals Price

Suppose *you* are managing Bob's oil operations and are responsible for setting the profit-maximizing output. How would you go about this task? Examine Table 8-1, which contains the same cost data as Tables 7-3 and 7-4 in the previous chapter. This table adds a further assumption that the market price of oil is $40 per unit.

---

① 如图所示，需求曲线上竞争企业所占的份额非常小，以至于从一个完全竞争者的角度看，该企业的 *dd* 需求曲线看上去是完全水平的或者是弹性无穷大的。

② 图 8-1. 一个完全竞争企业的需求曲线是完全富有弹性的

③ 1. 在**完全竞争**市场有许多的小企业，每一家企业都生产完全相似的产品，每家企业都小到根本无法对市场价格构成影响。
2. 完全竞争者面对的是一条完全水平的需求（或称 *dd*）曲线。
3. 从增加的每个单位销售量所获得的额外收益就是市场价格。

Supply Decision of Competitive Firm

(1) Quantity q	(2) Total cost TC (\$)	(3) Marginal cost per unit MC (\$)	(4) Average cost AC (\$)	(5) Price P (\$)	(6) Total revenue $TR = q \times P$ (\$)	(7) Profit $\pi = TR - TC$ (\$)
0	55,000					
1,000	85,000	27	85	40	40,000	−45,000
2,000	110,000	22	55	40	80,000	−30,000
3,000	130,000	21	43.33	40	120,000	−10,000
3,999	159,960.01	38.98	40.000+	40	159,960	−0.01
		39.99				
4,000	**160,000**	**40**	**40**	**40**	**160,000**	**0**
		40.01				
4,001	160,040.01	40.02	40.000+	40	160,040	−0.01
5,000	210,000	60	42	40	200,000	−10,000

TABLE 8-1. Profit Is Maximized at Production Level Where Marginal Cost Equals Price ①

The first four columns use the same cost data as that analyzed in Tables 7-3 and 7-4 of the previous chapter. Column (5) shows the price of \$40 that is received by the price-taking perfect competitor. Total revenue is price times quantity, while profit is total revenue less total cost.

This table shows that the maximum profit comes at that output where price equals *MC*. If output is raised above $q = 4000$, the additional revenue of \$40 per unit is less than the marginal cost, so profit is lowered. What happens to profit if output is raised when $q < 4000$?

You might take a guess and sell 3000 units. This yields total revenue of \$40 × 3000 = \$120,000, with total cost of \$130,000, so the firm incurs a loss of \$10,000. From economics, you have learned to think about *marginal* or incremental decisions. So you analyze the effect of selling an additional unit. The revenue from each unit is \$40, while the marginal cost at that volume is only \$21. This implies that the additional revenue outweighs the marginal cost of 1 more unit. So you analyze a production level of 4000 units. At this output, the firm has revenues of \$40 × 4000 = \$160,000 and costs of \$160,000, so profits are zero.

What would happen if you increase output to 5000 units? At this output, the firm has revenues of \$40 × 5000 = \$200,000 and costs of \$210,000. Now you're losing \$10,000 again. What went wrong? When ② you look at your accounts, you see that at the output level of 5000, the marginal cost is \$60. This is more than the market price of \$40, so you are losing \$20 (equal to price minus *MC*) on the last unit produced.

Now you see the light: *The maximum profit comes at* ③ *that output where marginal cost equals price.*

The reason underlying this proposition is that the competitive firm can always make additional profit as long as the price is greater than the marginal cost of the last unit. Total profit reaches its peak—is maximized—when there is no longer any extra profit to be earned by selling extra output. At the maximum-profit point, the last unit produced brings in an amount of revenue exactly equal to that unit's cost. What is that extra revenue? It is the price per unit. What is that extra cost? It is the marginal cost.

Let's test this rule by looking at Table 8-1. Starting at the profit-maximizing output of 4000 units, if

① 表 8-1. 在边际成本等于价格的产量水平下，利润达最大值

② 查一下账目你就会发现，在 5 000 个单位的产出水平下，边际成本为 60 美元。这高于 40 美元的市场价格，因此，你在生产完最后一个单位以后，将亏损 20 美元（即市场价格减去 *MC*）。

③ 现在你明白了一点：利润的最大值发生在边际成本等于价格的产出水平上。

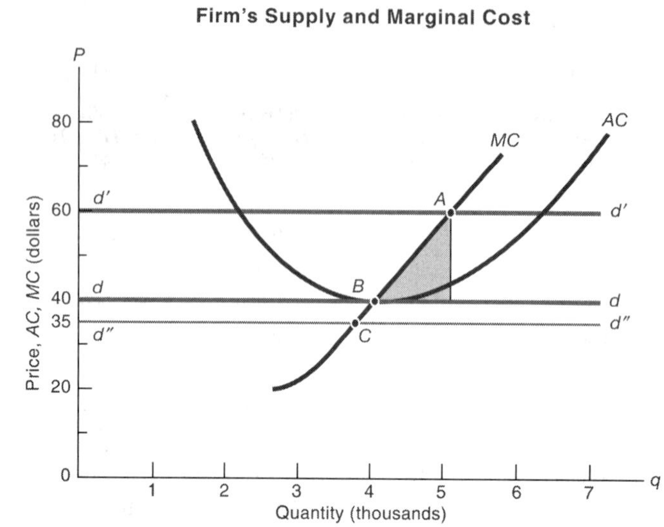

FIGURE 8-2. Firm's Supply Curve Is Its Rising Marginal Cost Curve ①

For a profit-maximizing competitive firm, the upward-sloping marginal cost (MC) curve is the firm's supply curve. For market price at $d'd'$, the firm will supply output at the intersection point at A. Explain why intersection points at B and C represent equilibria for prices at d and d'' respectively. The shaded blue region represents the loss from producing at A when price is $40.

[2] Bob：世界最大的从事原始证券、样张、手稿、华尔街藏品等礼品网上交易的公司，Bob 即 Best of Business 的缩写。

④ 在完全竞争市场，企业的供给原则，即当企业的产量位于边际成本等于价格的水平上时，该企业利润达到最大。

边际成本 = 价格 或 $MC=P$

Bob sells 1 more unit, that unit would bring a price [2] of $40 while the marginal cost of that unit is $40.01. So the firm would lose money on the 4001st unit. ③ Similarly, the firm would lose $0.01 if it produced 1 less unit. This shows that the firm's maximum-profit output comes at exactly $q = 4000$, where price equals marginal cost.

Rule for a firm's supply under perfect competition: A ④ firm will maximize profits when it produces at that level where marginal cost equals price:

$$\text{Marginal cost} = \text{price} \quad \text{or} \quad MC = P$$

Figure 8-2 shown above illustrates a firm's supply decision diagrammatically. When the market price of output is $40, the firm consults its cost data in Table 8-1 and finds that the production level corresponding to a marginal cost of $40 is 4000 units. Hence, at a market price of $40, the firm will wish to produce and sell 4000 units. We can find that ⑤ profit-maximizing amount in Figure 8-2 at the intersection of the price line at $40 and the MC curve at point B.

We designed this example so that at the profit- ⑥ maximizing output the firm has zero profits, with total revenues equal to total costs. Point B is the **zero-profit point,** the production level at which the firm makes zero economic profits; at the zero-profit point, price equals average cost, so revenues just cover costs.

What if the firm chooses the wrong output? Suppose the firm chooses output level A in Figure 8-2 when the market price is $40. It would be losing money because the last units have marginal cost above price. We can calculate the loss of profit if the firm mistakenly produces at A by the shaded blue triangle in Figure 8-2. This depicts the surplus of MC over price for production between B and A.

The general rule then is:

A profit-maximizing firm will set its output at that ⑦ level where marginal cost equals price. Diagrammatically, this means that a firm's marginal cost curve is also its supply curve.

总成本与停业条件

Total Cost and the Shutdown Condition

Our general rule for firm supply leaves open one possibility—that the price will be so low that the firm will want to shut down. Isn't it possible that at the $P = MC$ equilibrium, Bob may be losing a truckful of money and would want to shut down? In general, a firm will want to shut down in the short run when it can no longer cover its variable costs.

---

① 图 8-2. 企业的供给曲线是其边际成本曲线的上升部分

③ 所以，该企业在生产第 4 001 个单位时，有可能出现亏损。

⑤ 我们可以看到，图 8-2 中利润最大的产量值位于 MC 曲线上与 40 美元价格线相交的 B 点处。

⑥ 我们设计这个例子的目的就是要说明该企业在利润最大化时赚取的利润等于零。此时，总收益等于总成本。图示的 B 点即为**零利润点**，在这一点的产出水平上，该企业的经济利润为零。在零利润点，价格等于平均成本，所以收益正好弥补成本。

⑦ 一家利润最大化的企业会将其产量定在边际成本等于价格的水平上。用图示说明，这一水平意味着该企业的边际成本曲线也就是它的供给曲线。

For example, suppose the firm were faced with a market price of \$35, shown by the horizontal $d''d''$ line in Figure 8-2. At that price, *MC* equals price at point *C*, a point at which the price is actually less than the average cost of production. Would the firm want to keep producing even though it was incurring a loss?

The surprising answer is that the firm should *not* necessarily shut down if it is losing money. The firm should *minimize its losses*, which is the same thing as maximizing profits. Producing at point *C* would result in a loss of only \$20,000, whereas shutting down would involve losing \$55,000 (which is the fixed cost). The firm should therefore continue to produce.

To understand this point, remember that a firm must still cover its contractual commitments even when it produces nothing. In the short run, the firm must pay fixed costs such as interest to the bank, rentals on the oil rigs, and directors' salaries. The balance of the firm's costs are variable costs, such as those for materials, production workers, and fuel, which would have zero cost at zero production. It will be advanta- ①
geous to continue operations, with *P* at least as high as *MC*, as long as revenue covers variable costs.

The critically low market price at which revenues ②
just equal variable costs (or, equivalently, at which losses exactly equal fixed costs) is called the **shutdown point.** For prices above the shutdown point, the firm will produce along its marginal cost curve because, even though the firm might be losing money, it would lose more money by shutting down. For prices below the shutdown point, the firm will produce nothing at all because by shutting down the firm will lose only its fixed costs. This gives the shutdown rule:

> **Shutdown rule:** The shutdown point comes where ③
> revenues just cover variable costs or where losses are equal to fixed costs. When the price falls below average variable costs, the firm will maximize profits (minimize its losses) by shutting down.

Figure 8-3 shows the shutdown and zero-profit points for a firm. The zero-profit point comes where price is equal to *AC*, while the shutdown point comes where price is equal to *AVC*. Therefore, the firm's supply curve is the solid green line in Figure 8-3. It ④
first goes up the vertical axis to the price corresponding to the shutdown point; next jumps to the shutdown point at *M′*, where *P* equals the level of *AVC*; and then continues up the *MC* curve for prices above the shutdown price.

Zero-Profit and Shutdown Prices

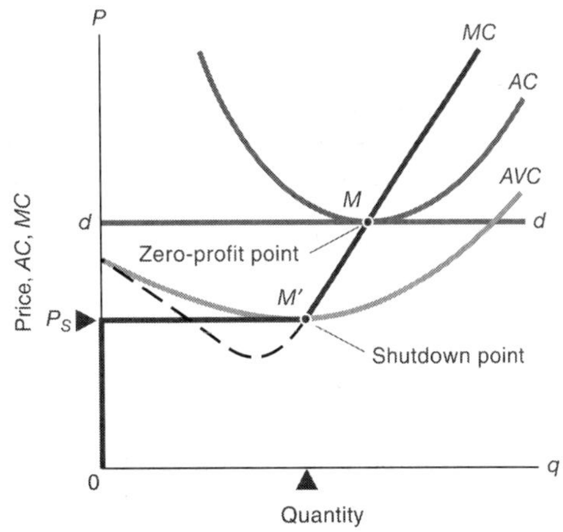

FIGURE 8-3. Firm's Supply Curve Travels Down the *MC* Curve to the Shutdown Point ⑤

The firm's supply curve corresponds to its *MC* curve as long as revenues exceed variable costs. Once price falls below P_s, the shutdown point, losses are greater than fixed costs, and the firm shuts down. Hence the solid green curve is the firm's supply curve.

The analysis of shutdown conditions leads to the surprising conclusion that profit-maximizing firms may in the short run continue to operate even though they are losing money. This condition will hold particularly for firms that are heavily indebted and therefore have high fixed costs (the airlines being a good example). For these firms, as long as losses are less than fixed costs, profits are maximized and losses are minimized when they pay the fixed costs and still continue to operate.

Unemployed Rigs in the Drilling Industry

A striking example of the shutdown rule at work was seen in the oil industry. New oil wells are drilled by "oil rigs." Each oil rig is like a little business, which can operate or shut down depending upon profitability. When a price war broke out among oil

Drilling Industry
石油钻井业

① 只要收益能与可变成本冲抵，那么在价格等于边际成本的情况下，继续生产将会是一个利好的决策。

② 在收益正好等于可变成本（或者同样的亏损正好等于固定成本）的情况下，所达到的临界的市场低价格点叫做**停业点**。

③ **停业原则**：企业的停业点出现在其收益正好弥补其可变成本，或者损失等于其固定成本时。当价格跌至平均可变成本之下时，企业就可通过停业的手段来使其利润最大化（即损失最小化）。

④ 这条线首先沿着纵轴上升到停业点对应的价格，然后跃到停业点 *M′* 处，此时的价格 *P* 等于 *AVC*，在此之后的价格将沿着 *MC* 曲线在高于停业点价格的基础上继续攀升。

⑤ 图 8-3. 企业的供给曲线沿 *MC* 曲线向下移动到停业点

producers in 1999, many shut down, and the number of rigs in operation in the United States declined to under 500. Had the oil fields run dry? Not at all. Rather, production was discouraged because the price of oil was so low. It was the profits, not the wells, that dried up.

What happened to drilling activity during the oil-price surge of the 2000s? From 2002 to 2008, when oil prices quadrupled, the number of rigs in operation went up by a factor of almost 4. In effect, as prices rose, these firms moved up along an upward-sloping *MC* supply curve similar to the one shown in Figure 8-3.

竞争行业的供给行为

B. SUPPLY BEHAVIOR IN COMPETITIVE INDUSTRIES

Our discussion up to now has concerned only the individual firm. But a competitive market comprises many firms, and we are interested in the behavior of all firms together, not just a single firm. How can we move from the one to the many? From Bob's operation to the entire oil industry?

加总所有企业的供给曲线得到市场供给曲线

SUMMING ALL FIRMS' SUPPLY CURVES TO GET MARKET SUPPLY

Suppose we are dealing with a competitive market for oil. At a given price, firm A will bring a given quantity of oil to market, firm B will bring another quantity, as will firms C, D, and so on. In each case, the quantity supplied will be determined by each firm's marginal costs. The *total* quantity brought to market at a given ① price will be the *sum* of the individual quantities that all firms supply at that price.[1]

This reasoning leads to the following relationship between individual and market supplies for a perfectly competitive industry:

The market supply curve for a good in a perfectly ② competitive market is obtained by adding horizontally the supply curves of all the individual producers of that good.

Figure 8-4 illustrates this rule for two firms. We obtain the industry's *SS* supply curve by horizontal addition at each price of the firms' individual supply

[1] Recall that the *DD* market demand curve is similarly obtained by horizontal summation of individual *dd* demand curves.

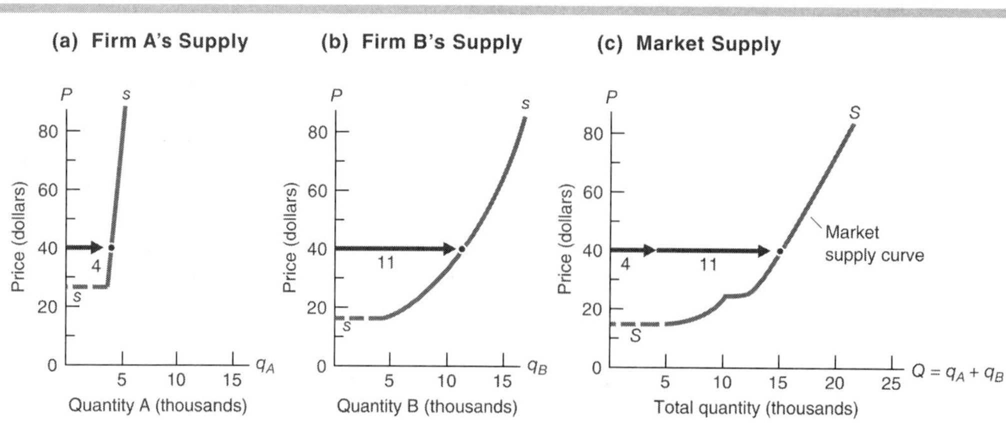

FIGURE 8-4. Add All Firms' Supply Curves to Derive Market Supply ③

The diagrams show how the market supply curve (*SS*) is derived from two individual supply curves (*ss*). We horizontally add quantities supplied by each firm at $40 to get total market supply at $40. This applies at each price and to any number of firms. If there are 1000 firms identical to firm A, the market supply curve would look like firm A's supply curve with a thousandfold change of horizontal scale.

① 在给定的价格下，市场供给总量将是在这一价格水平上所有企业各自供给量的总和。

② 在完全竞争市场，一种商品的市场供给曲线是将该种商品所有生产者的供给曲线按水平方向加总在一起获得。

③ 图 8-4. 将所有企业的供给曲线加总在一起得到的市场供给曲线

curves. At a price of \$40, firm A will supply 4000 units while firm B will supply 11,000 units. Therefore, the industry will supply a total of 15,000 units at a price of \$40. If there are 2 million rather than 2 firms, we would still derive industry output by adding all the 2 million individual-firm quantities at the going price. Horizontal addition of output at each price gives us the industry supply curve.

短期和长期均衡
SHORT-RUN AND LONG-RUN EQUILIBRIUM

Economists have observed that demand shifts pro- ① duce greater price adjustments and smaller quantity adjustments in the short run than they do in the long run. We can understand this observation by distinguishing two time periods for market equilibrium that correspond to different cost categories: (1) *short-run equilibrium,* when output changes must use the same fixed amount of capital, and (2) *long-run equilibrium,* when capital and all other factors are variable and there is free entry and exit of firms into and from the industry.

Entry and Exit of Firms

The birth (entry) and death (exit) of firms are important factors that affect the evolution of a market economy. Firms *enter* an industry either when they are newly formed or when an existing firm decides to start production in a new sector. Firms *exit* when they stop producing; they might leave voluntarily because a line of production is unprofitable, or they might go bankrupt if the entire firm cannot pay its bills. We say that there is *free entry and exit* when there are no barriers to entry or exit. Barriers to entry include such factors as government regulations or intellectual property rights (e.g., patents or software).

Many people are surprised by the large number of births and deaths of firms in a dynamic economy like the United States. For example, there were 6.5 million registered businesses at the beginning of 2003. In that year, 748,000 new businesses were born and 658,000 went out of business. The riskiest industry was Internet providers, where 30 percent of jobs were lost because of firm deaths in that year. The safest industry was colleges, where only 4 percent of jobs were lost by college closings.

Most firms exit quietly, but sometimes large firms have a noisy exit, as occurred when the telecommunications giant WorldCom, with \$104 billion of assets, went under because [2] of a massive accounting fraud. Although the smooth cost curves do not always capture the drama of entry and exit, the underlying logic of *P, MC,* and *AC* is a powerful force driving the growth and decline of major industries.

Let's illustrate the distinction between short-run and long-run equilibriums with an example. Consider the market for fresh fish supplied by a local fishing fleet. Suppose the demand for fish increases; this case is shown in Figure 8-5(*a*) as a shift from *DD* to *D′D′*. With higher prices, fishing captains will want to increase their catch. In the short run, they cannot build new boats, but they can hire extra crews and work longer hours. Increased inputs of variable factors will produce a greater quantity of fish along the *short-run supply curve* S_SS_S shown in Figure 8-5(*a*). The short-run supply curve intersects the new demand curve at *E′*, the point of short-run equilibrium.

The high prices lead to high profits, which in the long run coax out more shipbuilding and attract more sailors into the industry. Additionally, new firms may start up or enter the industry. This gives us the *long-run supply curve* S_LS_L in Figure 8-5(*b*) and the long-run equilibrium at *E″*. The intersection ③ of the long-run supply curve with the new demand curve yields the long-run equilibrium attained when all economic conditions (including the number of ships, shipyards, and firms) have adjusted to the new level of demand.

Long-Run Industry Supply. What is the shape of the long-run supply curve for an industry? Suppose that an industry has free entry of identical firms. If the identical firms use general inputs, such as unskilled labor, that can be attracted from the vast ocean of other uses without affecting the prices of those general inputs, we get the case of constant costs shown by the horizontal S_LS_L supply curve in Figure 8-6.

By contrast, suppose some of the inputs used in the industry are in relatively short supply—for example, fertile vineyard land for the wine industry or scarce beachfront properties for summer vacations. Then the supply curve for the wine or vacation industry must be upward-sloping, as shown by S_LS_L' in Figure 8-6.

---

① 经济学家们已经发现，需求的变化在短期内会比在长期内引发更大范围的价格调整和更小范围的产量调整。通过区别两个不同时期内与不同成本类别相对应的市场均衡，我们就可以理解这一发现：（1）当产出的变化必须使用同样固定数量的资本时，即出现短期均衡；（2）当资本和所有其他要素都是变化的，并且存在企业可以自由地从该行业进入和退出的机制时，即出现长期均衡。

[2] Worldcom：世通公司，一度是仅次于 AT&T 的一家美国通信公司，从 1999 年开始至 2002 年 5 月期间，采用少计可变成本并转计入固定资产、假造科目虚增收入等非法手段进行财务欺诈，2003 年破产。

③ 当所有的经济条件（包括船舶、船坞和企业的数量）都调整到新的需求水平之后，长期供给曲线与新的需求曲线相交即可达到长期均衡。

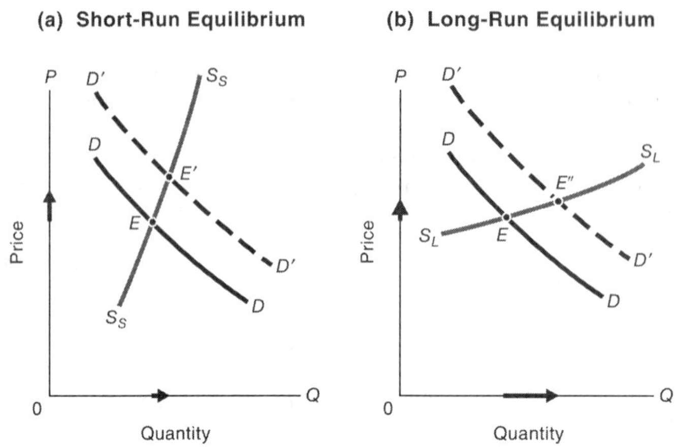

FIGURE 8-5. Effect of Increase in Demand on Price Varies in Different Time Periods ①

We distinguish between periods in which firms have time to make **(a)** adjustments in variable factors such as labor (short-run equilibrium) and **(b)** full adjustment of all factors, fixed as well as varying (long-run equilibrium). The longer the time for adjustments, the greater the elasticity of supply response and the smaller the rise in price.

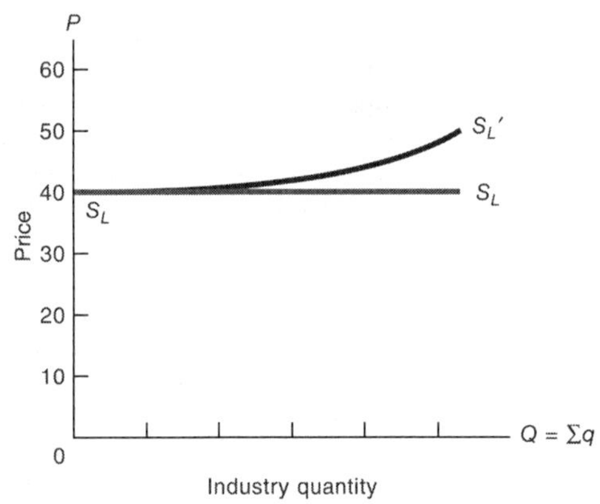

FIGURE 8-6. Long-Run Industry Supply Depends on Cost Conditions ②

With entry and exit free and any number of firms able to produce on identical, unchanged cost curves, the long-run S_LS_L curve will be horizontal at each firm's minimum average cost or zero-profit price. If the industry uses a specific factor, such as scarce beachfront property, the long-run supply curve must slope upward like S_LS_L', as higher production employs less well-suited inputs.

The long-run supply curve of industries using scarce factors rises because of diminishing returns. For example, take the case of the rare vineyard land. As firms apply increasing inputs of labor to fixed land, they receive smaller and smaller increments of wine-grape output. But each dose of labor costs the same in wages, so the *MC* of wine rises. This long-run rising *MC* means that the long-run supply curve must be rising.

竞争性行业的长期均衡

The Long Run for a Competitive Industry

Our analysis of zero-profit conditions showed that firms might stay in business for a time even though they are unprofitable. This situation is possible particularly for firms with high fixed capital costs. With this analysis we can understand why in business downturns many of America's largest companies, such as General Motors, stayed in business even though they were losing billions of dollars.

Such losses raise a troubling question: Is it possible that capitalism is heading toward "euthanasia of the capitalists," a situation where increased competition produces chronic losses? For this question, we ③

① 图 8-5. 需求增加对不同时期价格变化的影响
② 图 8-6. 行业的长期供给依赖于成本状况
③ 这样的亏损提出了一个令人烦恼的难题：资本主义是否有可能使所有的资本家走向“安乐死”，即竞争的加剧是否导致长期损失？

need to analyze the *long-run shutdown conditions.* We showed that firms shut down when they can no longer cover their variable costs. But in the long run, *all* costs are variable. A firm that is losing money can pay off its bonds, release its managers, and let its leases expire. In the long run, all commitments are once again options. Hence, in the long run firms will produce only when price is at or above the zero-profit condition where price equals average cost.

There is, then, a critical zero-profit point below ①
which long-run price cannot remain if firms are to stay in business. In other words, long-run price must cover out-of-pocket costs such as labor, materials, equipment, taxes, and other expenses, along with opportunity costs such as competitive return on the owner's invested capital. That means long-run price must be equal to or above total long-run average cost.

Take the case where price falls below this critical zero-profit level. Unprofitable firms will start leaving the industry. Since fewer firms are producing, the short-run market supply curve will shift to the left, and the price will therefore rise. Eventually, the price will rise enough so that the industry is no longer unprofitable. So, even though we produce very few horseshoes today compared to a century ago, horseshoe manufacturing will earn a zero long-run profit.

Consider the opposite case of a profitable industry such as developing computer games. At the beginning, the price starts above total long-run average cost, so firms are making positive economic profits. Now suppose entry into the industry is absolutely free in the long run, so any number of identical firms can come into the industry and produce at exactly the same costs as those firms already in the industry. In this situation, new firms are attracted by prospective profits, the short-run supply curve shifts to the right, and price falls. Eventually price falls to the zero-profit level, so it is no longer profitable for other firms to enter the industry. Thus, even though computer games might be a thriving industry, it would earn a zero long-run profit.

The conclusion is that in the long run, the price ②
in a competitive industry will tend toward the critical point where revenues just cover full competitive costs. Below this critical long-run price, firms would leave the industry until price returns to long-run average cost. Above this long-run price, new firms would enter the industry, thereby forcing market price back down to the long-run equilibrium price where all competitive costs are just covered.

Zero-profit long-run equilibrium: In a competitive ③
industry populated by identical firms with free entry and exit, the long-run equilibrium condition is that price equals marginal cost equals the minimum long-run average cost for each identical firm:

$$P = MC = \text{minimum long-run } AC = \text{zero-profit price}$$

This is the long-run **zero-economic-profit** condition.

We have reached a surprising conclusion about the long-run profitability of competitive capitalism. The forces of competition tend to push firms and industries toward a zero-profit long-run state. In the long run, competitive firms will earn the normal return on their investment, but no more. Profitable industries tend to attract entry of new firms, thereby driving down prices and reducing profits toward zero. By contrast, firms in unprofitable industries leave to seek better profit opportunities; prices
and profits then tend to rise. *The long-run equilibrium* ④
in a perfectly competitive industry is therefore one with no economic profits.

竞争市场的特殊情况

C. SPECIAL CASES OF COMPETITIVE MARKETS

This section probes more deeply into supply-and-demand analysis. We first consider certain general propositions about competitive markets and then continue with some special cases.

一般原则
GENERAL RULES

We analyzed above the impact of demand and supply shifts in competitive markets. These findings apply to virtually any competitive market, whether it is for codfish, brown coal, Douglas fir, Japanese yen, IBM stock, or petroleum. Are there any general rules? The propositions that follow investigate the impact of shifts in supply or demand upon the price and
quantity bought and sold. Remember always that by ⑤
a shift in demand or supply we mean a shift of the demand or supply curve or schedule, not a movement along the curve.

---

① 如果有些企业计划长期致力于某一产业，则长期的价格绝不能停留在既有的临界状态的零利润点之下。

② 据此我们可以得出这样的一个结论：在长期内，一个竞争性行业的价格将走向临界点，收益在这一点正好弥补全部的竞争成本。

③ 长期零利润均衡：在进出机制自由、由相似企业构成的竞争性行业，其长期均衡条件是价格等于边际成本，又等于每家企业长期平均成本的最小值，即

$$P=MC=\text{长期内 } AC \text{ 的最小值} = \text{零利润价格}$$

这就是长期内**零经济利润**的条件。

④ 在完全竞争的行业里，长期均衡是一种没有经济利润的状态。

⑤ 必须始终牢记的是，我们所讲的需求或者供给的变动是指需求或者供给曲线（或表）的移动，而不是沿曲线的运动。

Demand rule: (*a*) Generally, an increase in demand for a commodity (the supply curve being unchanged) will raise the price of the commodity. (*b*) For most commodities, an increase in demand will also increase the quantity demanded. A decrease in demand will have the opposite effects. ①

Supply rule: (*c*) An increase in supply of a commodity (the demand curve being constant) will generally lower the price and increase the quantity bought and sold. (*d*) A decrease in supply has the opposite effects. ②

These two rules of supply and demand summarize the qualitative effects of shifts in supply and demand. But the quantitative effects on price and quantity depend upon the exact shapes of the supply and demand curves. In the cases that follow, we will see the response for a number of important cost and supply situations.

成本不变

Constant Cost

Production of many manufacturing items, such as textiles, can be expanded by merely duplicating factories, machinery, and labor. Producing 200,000 shirts per day simply requires that we do the same thing as we did when we were manufacturing 100,000 per day but on a doubled scale. In addition, assume that the textile industry uses land, labor, and other inputs in the same proportions as the rest of the economy.

In this case the long-run supply curve *SS* in Figure 8-7 is a horizontal line at the constant level of unit costs. A rise in demand from *DD* to *D′D′* will shift the new intersection point to *E′*, raising *Q* but leaving *P* the same. ③

成本递增，收益递减

Increasing Costs and Diminishing Returns

The last section discussed industries, such as for wine or beach properties, where a product uses an input in limited supply. In the case of wine vineyards, good sites are limited in number. The annual output of wine can be increased to some extent by adding more labor to each acre of land. But the law of diminishing returns will eventually operate if variable factors of production, such as labor, are added to fixed amounts of a factor such as land. ④

As a result of diminishing returns, the marginal cost of producing wine increases as wine production rises. Figure 8-8 shows the rising supply curve *SS*. How will price be affected by an increase in demand? The figure shows that higher demand will increase the price of this good even in the long run with identical firms and free entry and exit.

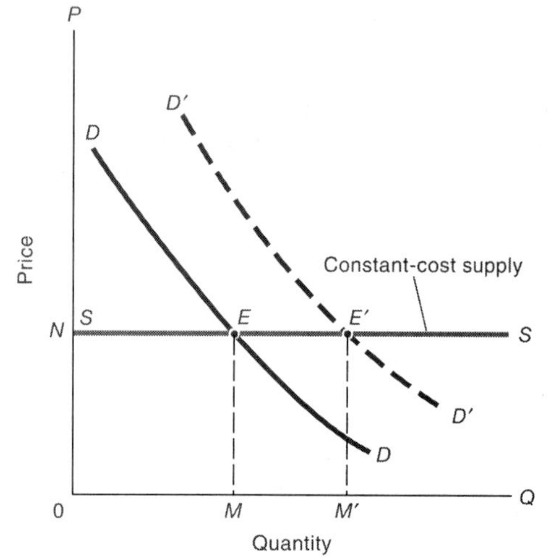

FIGURE 8-7. Constant-Cost Case ⑤

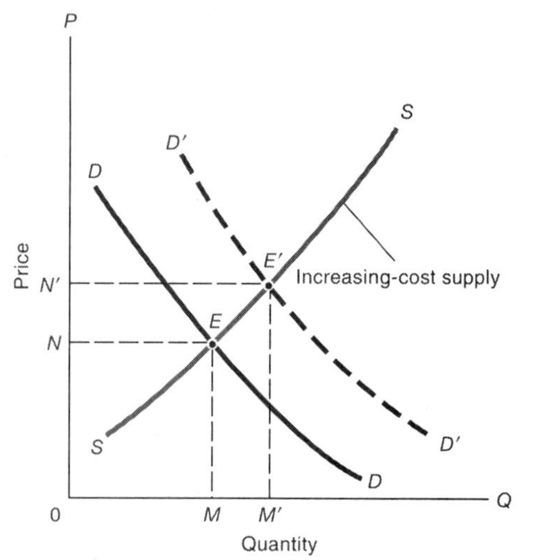

FIGURE 8-8. Increasing-Cost Case ⑥

---

① 需求法则：(a) 通常情况下，一种商品在需求上的增加（供给曲线保持不变）将会抬高该商品的价格；(b) 对大多数商品来讲，在需求上的增加也将导致需求量的增加，而在需求上的减少将会产生相反的效果。

② 供给法则：(c) 一种商品在供给上的增加（需求曲线保持不变）通常情况下都会导致价格的下降和买卖数量的上升；(d) 在供给上的减少所产生的效果刚好相反。

③ 在这一案例中，如图 8-7 所示，长期供给曲线 *SS* 是一条在不变的单位成本水平上的水平线。从 *DD* 到 *D′D′* 的需求上升将移动到新的交点 *E′*，*Q* 提高了，但 *P* 保持不变。

④ 葡萄酒的年产量某种程度上可以通过在每英亩土地上投入更多的劳动而得到提高。

⑤ 图 8-7. 成本不变的情况

⑥ 图 8-8. 成本增加的情况

固定供给与经济租金

Fixed Supply and Economic Rent

Some goods or productive factors are completely fixed in amount, regardless of price. There is only one *Mona Lisa* by da Vinci. Nature's original endow- [1] ment of land can be taken as fixed in amount. Raising the price offered for land cannot create an additional corner at 57th Street and Fifth Avenue [2] in New York City. Raising the pay of top managers is unlikely to change their effort. When the quantity ③ supplied is constant at every price, the payment for the use of such a factor of production is called **rent** or **pure economic rent.**

When supply is independent of price, the supply curve is vertical in the relevant region. Land will continue to contribute to production no matter what its price. Figure 8-9 shows the case of land, for which a higher price cannot coax out any increase in output.

An increase in the demand for a fixed factor will affect only the price. Quantity supplied is unchanged.

When a tax is placed upon the fixed commodity, the tax is completely paid by (or "shifted" back to) the supplier (say, the landowner). The supplier absorbs ④ the entire tax out of economic rent. The consumer buys exactly as much of the good or service as before and at no higher price.

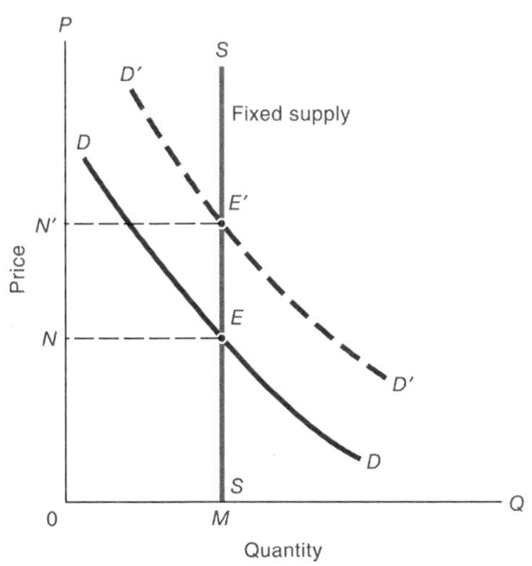

FIGURE 8-9. Factors with Fixed Supply Earn Rent ⑤

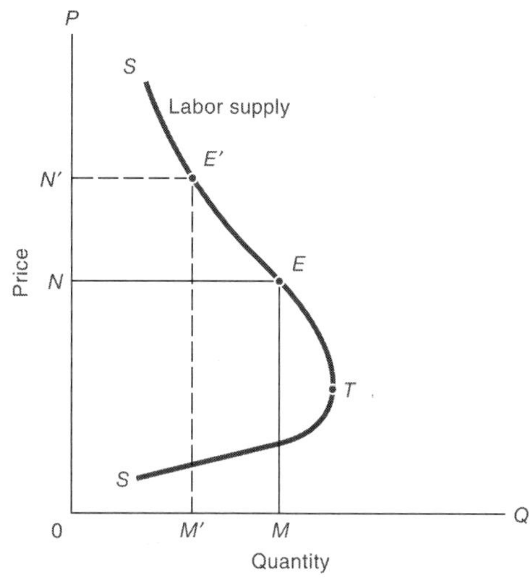

FIGURE 8-10. Backward-Bending Supply Curve ⑥

向后弯曲的供给曲线

Backward-Bending Supply Curve

Firms in poor countries sometimes found that when they raised wages, the local workers worked fewer hours. When the wage was doubled, instead of continuing to work 6 days a week, the workers might work 3 days and go fishing for the other 3 days. The same has been observed in high-income countries. As ⑦ improved technology raises real wages, people feel that they want to take part of their higher earnings in the form of more leisure and early retirement. Chapter 5 described income and substitution effects, which explain why a supply curve might *bend backward.*

Figure 8-10 shows what a supply curve for labor might look like. At first the labor supplied rises as higher wages coax out more labor. But beyond point *T*, higher wages lead people to work fewer hours and to take more leisure. An increase in demand raises the price of labor, as was stated in the demand rule at the beginning of this section. But note why we were cautious to add "for most commodities" to demand rule (*b*), for now the increase in demand decreases the quantity of labor supplied.

供给的移动

Shifts in Supply

All the above discussions dealt with a shift in demand and no shift in supply. To analyze the supply rule,

---

[1] 达芬奇的著名油画《蒙娜丽莎》，藏巴黎卢浮宫。

[2] 57th Street and Fifth Avenue in New York City：均位于纽约曼哈顿的中心区，第五大道是中央大街，第 57 大街有近 20 家顶级名牌旗舰店以及数家豪华酒店。

③ 当供给量在每一价格水平上都保持不变时，对所使用的这样一种生产要素产生的支付称作**租金**或者**纯经济租金**。

④ 供给方使用其经济租金来承担所有的税赋。消费者对商品和服务的购买力与以前没有任何变化，也没有支付更高的价格。

⑤ 图 8-9. 供给不变的要素赚取租金的情况

⑥ 图 8-10. 向后弯曲的供给曲线

⑦ 当通过技术进步来提高实际工资时，人们觉得他们需要以更多的休闲和提早退休的方式来得到更高的收益。

① (*c'*) 当需求缺乏弹性时，增加供给将使 *P* 大幅下降。(*d'*) 当需求缺乏弹性时，增加供给将使 *Q* 大幅下降。

② 在全面分析了竞争性市场的基本运作之后，让我们看一下市场的表现。充满竞争的市场在满足人们的需要方面是否值得高度褒奖？

[3] **帕累托效率**：（有时只称**效率**。有关帕累托的详细信息请参阅本书 87 页注疏部分，16~18 版在本节的引言部分作了说明，而在紧跟其后的定义中称其为 *Allocative efficiency*，本版采纳了当前经济学界普遍使用的 *Pareto efficiency*，更为通用。）当任何可能的生产重组或者分配在没有使其他人的状况变坏的条件下，都不能使任何一个人的状况变好，那么就达到了帕累托效率。在配置效率的条件下，只有通过降低其他人的效用才能增加某个人的满意度或者效用。

we must now shift supply, keeping demand constant. If the law of downward-sloping demand is valid, increased supply must decrease price and increase quantity demanded. You should draw your own supply and demand curves and verify the following quantitative corollaries of the supply rule:

(*c'*) An increased supply will decrease *P* most when ①
demand is inelastic.

(*d'*) An increased supply will increase *Q* least when demand is inelastic.

What are commonsense reasons for these rules? Illustrate with cases of elastic demand for autos and of inelastic demand for electricity.

竞争市场的效率和公平

D. EFFICIENCY AND EQUITY OF COMPETITIVE MARKETS

对市场机制的评价
EVALUATING THE MARKET MECHANISM

One of the remarkable features of the last decade has been the "rediscovery of the market." Many countries have abandoned the heavy-handed interventionism of government command and regulation for the decentralized coordination of the invisible hand. Having reviewed the basic operation of com- ②
petitive markets, let's ask how well they perform. Do they deserve high grades for satisfying people's economic needs? Is society getting many guns and much butter for a given amount of inputs? Or does the butter melt on the way to the store, while the guns have crooked barrels? We will provide an overview of the efficiency of competitive markets in this chapter.

效率的概念
The Concept of Efficiency

Efficiency is one of the central concepts in all of economics. In a general sense, an economy is efficient when it provides its consumers with the most desired set of goods and services, given the resources and technology of the economy.[2] A more precise definition uses the concept of *Pareto efficiency* (alternatively called *allocative efficiency, Pareto optimality,* or sometimes simply *efficiency*).

Pareto efficiency (or sometimes just **efficiency**) [3]
occurs when no possible reorganization of production or distribution can make anyone better off without making someone else worse off. Under conditions of allocative efficiency, one person's satisfaction or utility can be increased only by lowering someone else's utility.

We can think of the concept of efficiency intuitively in terms of the production-possibility frontier. An economy is clearly inefficient if it is inside the *PPF*. If we move out to the *PPF*, no one need suffer a decline in utility. At a minimum, an efficient economy is on its *PPF*. But efficiency goes further and requires not only that the right mix of goods be produced but also that these goods be allocated among consumers to maximize consumer satisfactions.

竞争性均衡的效率
Efficiency of Competitive Equilibrium

One of the most important results in all economics is that the allocation of resources by perfectly competitive markets is efficient. This important result assumes that all markets are perfectly competitive and that there are no externalities like pollution or imperfect information. In this section, we use a simplified example to illustrate the general principles underlying the efficiency of competitive markets.

Consider an idealized situation where all individuals are identical. Further assume: (*a*) Each person works at growing food. As people increase their work and cut back on their leisure hours, each additional hour of sweaty labor becomes increasingly tiresome. (*b*) Each extra unit of food consumed brings diminished marginal utility (*MU*).[3] (*c*) Because food production takes place on fixed plots of land, by the law of diminishing returns each extra minute of work brings less and less extra food.

Figure 8-11 shows supply and demand for our simplified competitive economy. When we sum

---

[2] Economic efficiency is different from engineering efficiency, ④
and sometimes it will be economical to use a production method that is *less* efficient from an engineering point of view. For example, physics shows that more energy can be converted to electricity if combustion occurs at 2500°C than at 1000°C. Yet the higher temperature might require exotic metals and designs and cost more. So the lower temperature would be economically efficient even though the higher temperature would have higher thermodynamic efficiency.

[3] To keep matters at their simplest, we measure welfare in fixed ⑤
"utils" of leisure time (or "disutils" of sweaty labor time). We further assume that each hour of forgone leisure has a constant marginal utility, so all utilities and costs are reckoned in these leisure-labor units.

---

④ 经济学意义上的效率与工程学意义上的效率不同，有时我们还将借代工程学上的意义来描述经济学意义上的生产方法缺乏效率的问题。比如，从物理学意义上讲来，加热到 2500℃ 时所产生的热能比加热到 1000℃ 时可以转化为更多的电能。然而，更高的温度则可能需要更多的稀有金属、更复杂的设计和更高的成本。因此，即使更高的温度可能会产生更高的热动力学意义上的效率，但较低的温度从经济学的意义上来讲，应该是有效率的。

⑤ 为了将复杂的问题尽可能地简单化，我们用闲暇时间的"效用度"（"util" 是 "utility" 的缩写，常用于计算机编程语言中表示与数据库有关的杂项，后在经济学意义上引伸指为测量需要而引入的虚拟数值，注疏者译此。其反义词 "disutils" 指重体力劳动的"非效用度"）来计量福利。我们做一个进一步的假设——放弃的每个小时的闲暇所产生的边际效用不变，这样就可以计算出用"效用度"和"非效用度"表示的所有效用和成本。

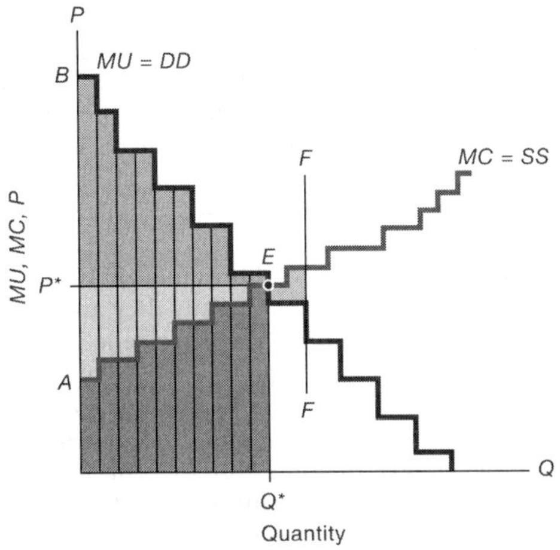

FIGURE 8-11. At Competitive Equilibrium Point *E*, the Marginal Costs and Utilities of Food Are Exactly Balanced ①

Many identical farmer-consumers bring their food to market. The *MC* = *SS* curve adds together the individual marginal cost curves, while the *MU* = *DD* curve is the horizontal sum of consumer valuations of food. At competitive market equilibrium *E*, the utility gain from the last unit of food equals the utility cost (in terms of forgone leisure).

The figure also illustrates economic surplus. The cost of producing food is shown by the dark blue slices. The light-colored green slices above the *SS* curve and below the price line add up to the "producer surplus." The dark-colored green slices under *DD* and above the price line are the "consumer surplus." The sum of the consumer and producer surpluses is "economic surplus." At the competitive equilibrium at *E*, economic surplus is maximized. Verify that production at *FF* lowers total surplus.

horizontally the identical supply curves of our identical farmers, we get the upward-stepping *MC* curve. As we saw earlier in this chapter, the *MC* curve is also the industry's supply curve, so the figure shows *MC* = *SS*. Also, the demand curve is the horizontal summation of the identical individuals' marginal utility (or demand-for-food) curves; it is represented by the downward-stepping *MU* = *DD* curve for food in Figure 8-11.

The intersection of the *SS* and *DD* curves shows the competitive equilibrium for food. At point *E*, farmers supply exactly what consumers want to purchase at the equilibrium market price. Each person ② will be working up to the critical point where the declining marginal-utility-of-consuming-food curve intersects the rising marginal-cost-of-growing-food curve.

Figure 8-11 shows a new concept, **economic surplus,** which is the green area between the supply and demand curves at the equilibrium. The eco- ③ nomic surplus is the sum of the consumer surplus that we met in Chapter 5, which is the area between the demand curve and the price line, and the **producer surplus,** which is the area between the price line and the *SS* curve. The producer surplus includes the rent and profits to firms and owners of specialized inputs in the industry and indicates the excess of revenues over cost of production. The economic surplus is the welfare or net utility gain from production and consumption of a good; it is equal to the consumer surplus plus the producer surplus.

A careful analysis of the competitive equilibrium will show that it maximizes the economic surplus available in that industry. For this reason, it is economically efficient. At the competitive equilibrium at ④ point *E* in Figure 8-11, the representative consumer will have higher utility or economic surplus than would be possible with any other feasible allocation of resources.

Another way of seeing the efficiency of the competitive equilibrium is by comparing the economic effect of a small change from the equilibrium at *E*. As the following three-step process shows, if *MU* = *P* = *MC*, then the allocation is efficient.

1. *P* = *MU*. Consumers choose food purchases up to the amount where *P* = *MU*. As a result, every person is gaining *P* utils of satisfaction from the last unit of food consumed. (Utils of satisfaction are measured in terms of the constant marginal utility of leisure, as discussed in footnote 3.)
2. *P* = *MC*. As producers, each person is supplying food up to the point where the price of food exactly equals the *MC* of the last unit of food supplied (the *MC* here being the cost in terms of the forgone leisure needed to produce the last unit of food). The price then is the utils of leisure-time satisfaction lost because of working to grow that last unit of food.
3. Putting these two equations together, we see that *MU* = *MC*. This means that the utils gained from the last unit of food consumed exactly equal the

① 图 8-11. 在竞争性的均衡点 *E*，粮食的边际成本和边际效用刚好平衡

② 每一个人都竭力地达到这个临界点，在这一点上，递减的食品消费边际效用曲线与递增的粮食种植边际成本曲线相交。

③ 经济剩余指的是在第 5 章中我们所谈到的消费者剩余的总和。消费者剩余是需求曲线与价格线之间的区域；**生产者剩余**则是价格线与 *SS* 曲线之间的区域。生产者剩余包括行业内所有企业和特殊投入所有者的租金及利润，即抵扣生产成本之后的超额收益部分。经济剩余指生产和消费某种物品的福利或净效用，它等于消费者剩余加生产者剩余之和。

④ 图 8-11 中位于 *E* 点的竞争性均衡表明，具有代表性的消费者将会获得比可能使用其他任何可行性资源配置方案更高的效用或者经济剩余。

leisure utils lost from the time needed to produce that last unit of food. *It is exactly this condition—that the marginal gain to society from the last unit consumed equals the marginal cost to society of that last unit produced—which guarantees that a competitive equilibrium is efficient.* ①

众多消费者和市场的均衡

Equilibrium with Many Consumers and Markets

Let us now turn from our simple parable about identical farmer-consumers to an economy populated by millions of different firms, hundreds of millions of people, and countless commodities. Can a perfectly competitive economy still be efficient in this more complex world?

The answer is "yes," or better yet, "yes, if . . ." Efficiency requires some stringent conditions that are addressed in later chapters. These include having reasonably well-informed consumers, perfectly competitive producers, and no externalities like pollution or incomplete knowledge. For such economies, ② a system of perfectly competitive markets will earn the economist's gold star of Pareto efficiency.

Figure 8-12 illustrates how a competitive system brings about a balance between utility and cost for a single commodity with nonidentical firms and consumers. On the left, we add horizontally the demand curves for all consumers to get the market curve *DD* in the middle. On the right, we add all the different *MC* curves to get the industry *SS* curve in the middle.

At the competitive equilibrium at point *E*, consumers on the left get the quantity they are willing to purchase of the good at the price reflecting efficient social *MC*. On the right, the market price also allocates production efficiently among firms. The ③ blue area under *SS* in the middle represents the minimized sum of the blue cost areas on the right. Each firm is setting its output so that $MC = P$. Production efficiency is achieved because there is no reorganization of production that would allow the same level of industry output to be produced at lower cost.

Many Goods. Our economy produces not only food but also clothing, movies, and many other

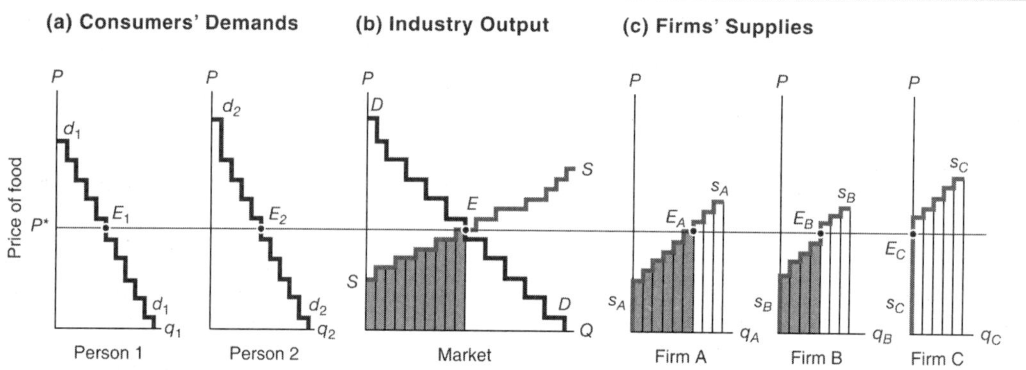

FIGURE 8-12. Competitive Market Integrates Consumers' Demands and Producers' Costs ④

(a) Individual demands are shown on the left. We add the consumers' *dd* curves horizontally to obtain the market demand *DD* curve in the middle.

(b) The market brings together all consumer demands and firm supplies to reach market equilibrium at *E*. The horizontal price-of-food line shows where each consumer on the left and each producer on the right reach equilibrium. At P^*, see how each consumer's *MU* is equated to each firm's *MC*, leading to allocative efficiency.

(c) For each competitive firm, profits are maximized when the supply curve is given by the rising *MC* curve. The blue area depicts each firm's cost of producing the amount at *E*. At prices equal to marginal cost, the industry produces output at the least total cost.

① 它完全符合这一条件：社会从最后一单位的消费中所得到的边际效用量等于其生产最后一单位的产品的边际成本，这就确保了竞争性均衡是有效率的。

② 对于这些经济状态来讲，完全竞争的市场体系将达到经济学家理想中的帕累托效率。

③ 图中 *SS* 线下方的蓝色区域代表了右图中蓝色区域所表示的成本总和的最小值。

④ 图 8-12. 竞争性市场将消费者的需求和生产者的成本结合在一起

commodities. How does our analysis apply when consumers must choose among many products?

The principles are exactly the same, but now we recall one further condition: Utility-maximizing consumers spread their dollars among different goods until the marginal utility of the last dollar is equalized for each good consumed. In this case, as long as the ideal conditions are met, a competitive economy is efficient with a multitude of goods and factors of production.

In other words, a perfectly competitive economy ① is efficient when marginal private cost equals marginal social cost and when both equal marginal utility. Each industry must balance *MC* and *MU*. For example, if movies have 2 times the *MC* of hamburgers, the *P* and the *MU* of movies must also be twice those of hamburgers. Only then will the *MU*s, which are equal to the *P*s, be equal to the *MC*s. By equating price and marginal cost, competition guarantees that an economy can attain allocative efficiency.

The perfectly competitive market is a device for ② synthesizing (*a*) the willingness of consumers possessing dollar votes to pay for goods with (*b*) the marginal costs of those goods as represented by firms' supply. Under certain conditions, competition guarantees efficiency, in which no consumer's utility can be raised without lowering another consumer's utility. This is true even in a world of many factors and products.

边际成本是效率的标杆
Marginal Cost as a Benchmark for Efficiency

This chapter has shown the importance of marginal cost in attaining an efficient allocation of resources. But the importance of marginal cost extends far beyond perfect competition. Using marginal cost to achieve productive efficiency holds for any society or organization trying to make the most effective use of its resources—whether that entity is a capitalist or socialist economy, a profit-maximizing or nonprofit organization, a university or a church, or even a family.

The essential role of marginal cost is this: Sup- ③ pose you have an objective that can be reached using several approaches, each of which is costly. In deciding how much of each approach to use, always do so by equating the marginal cost among the different approaches. Only when marginal costs are equalized can we squeeze the maximum from our scarce resources.

The use of marginal cost as a benchmark for efficient resource allocation is applicable not just to profit-maximizing firms but to all economic problems, indeed to all problems involving scarcity. Suppose that you have been charged with solving a critical environmental problem, such as global warming. You will soon find that marginal cost will be crucial to attaining your environmental objectives most efficiently. By ensuring that the marginal costs of reducing greenhouse-gas emissions are equalized in every industry and in every corner of the world, you can guarantee that your environmental objectives are being reached at the lowest possible costs.

Marginal cost is a fundamental concept for ④ efficiency. For any goal-oriented organization, efficiency requires that the marginal cost of attaining the goal should be equal in every activity. In a market, an industry will produce its output at minimum total cost only when each firm's *MC* is equal to a common price.

④ 边际成本对效率而言是一个极其重要的概念。对于任何目标导向型的组织来讲，效率要求达到目标的边际成本应该在每项经济活动中都相等。在市场环境下，只有当每家企业的 *MC* 都等值于同一个价格时，一个行业才能以最小的总成本来生产其产品。

限　制
QUALIFICATIONS

We have now seen the essence of the invisible hand—the remarkable efficiency properties of competitive markets. But we must quickly qualify the analysis by pointing to shortcomings of the market.

There are two important areas where markets fail to achieve a social optimum. First, markets may be inefficient in situations where pollution or other externalities are present or when there is imperfect competition or information. Second, the distribution of incomes under competitive markets, even when it is efficient, may not be socially desirable or acceptable. We will review both of these points in later chapters, but it will be useful to describe each of these shortcomings briefly here.

市场失灵
Market Failures

What are the market failures which spoil the idyllic ⑤ picture assumed in our discussion of efficient markets? The important ones are imperfect competition, externalities, and imperfect information.

⑤ 哪些市场失灵破坏了我们讨论的有效率的市场环境中所设想的田园牧歌般的意境？其中最重要的就是不完全性竞争、外部性和不完全信息。

Imperfect Competition. When a firm has market power in a particular market (say it has a monopoly

① 换句话说，当个人的边际成本等于社会的边际成本，并且两者均等于边际效用时，完全竞争的经济就是有效率的。

② 完全竞争性的市场是一种将（a）持有货币选票的消费者购买产品的意愿和（b）用企业的供给所代表的那些商品的边际成本结合起来的机制。在这样的环境之下，竞争为效率提供了保障，置身其中，在不降低其他消费者效用的情况下，就不可能增加任何一个消费者的效用。这在多种要素和产品的环境中也完全适用。

③ 边际成本的关键作用是：假设你有一个可以用几种方法而达到的目标，每一种方法的成本都很高。在决定所使用的每一种方法所花费的成本时，总是要在不同的方法中将边际成本等值化处理来进行。只有将边际成本等值化，我们才能将稀缺资源的利用尽可能地最大化。（这一节从题目到内容都做了彻底的修订。）

because of a patented drug or a local electricity franchise), the firm can raise the price of its product above its marginal cost. Consumers buy less of such goods than they would under perfect competition, and consumer satisfaction is reduced. This kind of reduction of consumer satisfaction is typical of the inefficiencies created by imperfect competition.

Externalities. Externalities are another important market failure. Recall that externalities arise when some of the side effects of production or consumption are not included in market prices. For example, a power company might pump sulfurous fumes into the air, causing damage to neighboring homes and to people's health. If the power company does not pay for the harmful impacts, pollution will be inefficiently high and consumer welfare will suffer.

Not all externalities are harmful. Some are beneficial, such as the externalities that come from knowledge-generating activities. For example, when Chester Carlson invented xerography, he [1] became a millionaire; but he still received only a tiny fraction of the benefits when the world's secretaries and students were relieved of billions of hours of drudgery. Another positive externality arises from public-health programs, such as inoculation against smallpox, cholera, or typhoid; an inoculation protects not only the inoculated person but also others whom that person might otherwise have infected.

Imperfect Information. A third important market failure is imperfect information. The invisible-hand theory assumes that buyers and sellers have complete information about the goods and services they buy and sell. Firms are assumed to know about all the production functions for operating in their industry. Consumers are presumed to know about the quality and prices of goods—such as whether the financial statements of firms are accurate and whether the drugs they use are safe and efficacious.

Clearly, reality is far from this idealized world. The critical question is, How damaging are departures from perfect information? In some cases, the loss of efficiency is slight. I will hardly be greatly disadvantaged if I buy a chocolate ice cream that is slightly too sweet or if I don't know the exact temperature of the beer that flows from the tap. In other cases, the loss is severe. Take the case of steel mogul Eben Byers, who a century ago took Radithor, sold as a cure-all, to relieve his ailments. Later analysis showed that Radithor was actually distilled water laced with radium. Byers died a hideous death when his jaw and other bones disintegrated. This kind of invisible hand we don't need.

One of the important tasks of the government ② is to identify those areas where informational deficiencies are economically significant—such as in finance—and then to find appropriate remedies. [3]

市场有优点，也有缺点

Two Cheers for the Market, but Not Three

We have seen that markets have remarkable efficiency properties. But can we therefore conclude that laissez-faire capitalism produces the greatest happiness of the greatest numbers? Does the market necessarily result in the fairest possible use of resources? The answers are no and no.

People are not equally endowed with purchasing power. A system of prices and markets may be one in which a few people have most of the income and wealth. They may have inherited scarce land or oil properties or manage a big corporation or a profitable hedge fund. Some are very poor through no fault of their own, while others are very rich through no virtue of their own. So the weighting of dollar votes, which lie behind the individual demand curves, may be unfair.

An economy with great inequality is not necessarily inefficient. The economy might be squeezing a large quantity of guns and butter from its resources. But the rich few may be eating the butter and feeding it to their cats, while the guns are mainly protecting the butter of the rich.

A society does not live on efficiency alone. A society may choose to alter market outcomes to improve the equity or fairness of the distribution of income and wealth. Nations may levy progressive taxes on those with high incomes and wealth and use the proceeds to finance food, schools, and health care for the poor. But there are vexing questions here. How much should the rich be taxed? What programs will best benefit the poor? Should immigrants be included in the benefit programs? Should capital be taxed at the same rate as labor? Should the nonworking poor get government help?

---

[1] 切斯特·卡尔森（Chester Carlson，1906.2.8~1968.9.18），美国物理学家和发明家，瞬间电子复印术的发明者，后改名为静电复印术——由施乐公司于1959年购买并迅速商业化至今。

② 政府的重要任务之一是确认哪些领域会像金融业一样，因为信息缺失导致经济上的严重后果，然后找到补救的办法。

[3] 此前的版本均举毒品业的例子，因为金融危机的原因，本版改为金融业。

There are no scientifically correct answers to ① these questions. Positive economics cannot say how much governments should intervene to correct the inequalities and inefficiencies of the marketplace. These normative questions are appropriately answered through political debate and fair elections. But economics can offer valuable insights into the merit of alternative interventions so that the goals of a modern society can be achieved in the most effective manner.

SUMMARY

A. Supply Behavior of the Competitive Firm

1. A perfectly competitive firm sells a homogeneous product and is too small to affect the market price. Competitive firms are assumed to maximize their profits. To maximize profits, the competitive firm will choose that output level at which price equals the marginal cost of production, that is, $P = MC$. Diagrammatically, the competitive firm's equilibrium will come where the rising *MC* supply curve intersects its horizontal demand curve.
2. Variable costs must be taken into consideration in determining a firm's short-run shutdown point. Below the shutdown point, the firm loses more than its fixed costs. It will therefore produce nothing when price falls below the shutdown price.
3. A competitive industry's long-run supply curve, $S_L S_L$, must take into account the entry of new firms and the exodus of old ones. In the long run, all of a firm's commitments expire. It will stay in business only if price is at least as high as long-run average costs. These costs include out-of-pocket payments to labor, lenders, material suppliers, or landlords and opportunity costs, such as returns on the property assets owned by the firm.

B. Supply Behavior in Competitive Industries

4. Each firm's rising *MC* curve is its supply curve. To obtain the supply curve of a group of competitive firms, we add horizontally their separate supply curves. The supply curve of the industry hence represents the marginal cost curve for the competitive industry as a whole.
5. Because firms can adjust production over time, we distinguish two different time periods: (*a*) short-run equilibrium, when variable factors like labor can change but fixed factors like capital and the number of firms cannot, and (*b*) long-run equilibrium, when the numbers of firms and plants, and all other conditions, adjust completely to the new demand conditions.
6. In the long run, when firms are free to enter and leave the industry and no one firm has any particular advantage of skill or location, competition will eliminate any excess profits earned by existing firms in the industry. So, just as free exit implies that price cannot fall below the zero-profit point, free entry implies that price cannot exceed long-run average cost in long-run equilibrium.
7. When an industry can expand its production without pushing up the prices of its factors of production, the resulting long-run supply curve will be horizontal. When an industry uses factors specific to it, such as scarce beachfront property, its long-run supply curve will slope upward.

C. Special Cases of Competitive Markets

8. Recall the general rules that apply to competitive supply and demand: Under the demand rule, an increase in the demand for a commodity (the supply curve being unchanged) will generally raise the price of the commodity and also increase the quantity demanded. A decrease in demand will have the opposite effects.

   Under the supply rule, an increase in the supply of a commodity (the demand curve being constant) will generally lower the price and increase the quantity sold. A decrease in supply has the opposite effects.
9. Important special cases include constant and increasing costs, completely inelastic supply (which produces economic rents), and backward-bending supply. These special cases will explain many important phenomena found in markets.

D. Efficiency and Equity of Competitive Markets

10. The analysis of competitive markets sheds light on the efficient organization of a society. Allocative or Pareto efficiency occurs when there is no way of reorganizing production and distribution such that everyone's satisfaction can be improved.
11. Under ideal conditions, a competitive economy attains allocative efficiency. Efficiency requires that all firms are perfect competitors and that there are no externalities like pollution or imperfect information. Efficiency implies that economic surplus is maximized, where economic surplus equals consumer surplus plus producer surplus.
12. Efficiency comes because (*a*) when consumers maximize satisfaction, the marginal utility (in terms of leisure) just equals the price; (*b*) when competitive

① 以上这些问题均找不到科学正确的答案。实证经济学也无法解答政府应该采取多么强有力的干预措施来矫正市场中的不公平和低效率。这些规范经济学方面的问题，可适当地通过政治辩论和公正的选举来寻求答案。但经济学能够对各种政府干预的优点提供有价值的见解，所以，现代社会的目标可以最有效的方式达到。

producers supply goods, they choose output so that marginal cost just equals price; (*c*) since $MU = P$ and $MC = P$, it follows that $MU = MC$.

13. There are exacting limits on the social optimality of competitive markets.
    a. Pareto efficiency requires perfect competition, complete information, and no externalities. When all three conditions are met, this will lead to the important efficiency condition:

    Price ratio = marginal cost ratio = marginal utility ratio

    b. The most perfectly competitive markets may not produce a fair distribution of income and consumption. Societies may therefore decide to modify the laissez-faire market outcomes. Economics has the important role of analyzing the relative costs and benefits of alternative kinds of interventions.
14. Marginal cost is a fundamental concept for attaining any goal, not just for profits. Efficiency requires that the marginal cost of attaining the goal be equal in every activity.

CONCEPTS FOR REVIEW

Competitive Supply

$P = MC$ as maximum-profit condition
firm's *ss* supply curve and its MC curve
zero-profit condition, where $P = MC = AC$
shutdown point, where $P = MC = AVC$
summing individual *ss* curves to get industry *SS*
short-run and long-run equilibrium
long-run zero-profit condition
producer surplus + consumer surplus = economic surplus
efficiency = maximizing economic surplus

Efficiency and Equity

allocative efficiency, Pareto efficiency
conditions for allocative efficiency: $MU = P = MC$
efficiency of competitive markets
efficiency vs. equity

FURTHER READING AND INTERNET WEBSITES

Further Reading

The efficiency of perfect competition is one of the major findings of microeconomics. Advanced books in microeconomics, such as those listed in Chapter 4, can give insights into the basic findings.

Nobel Prizes in economics were awarded to Kenneth Arrow, John Hicks, and Gerard Debreu for their contributions to developing the theory of perfect competition and its relationship to economic efficiency. Their essays surveying the field are highly useful and are contained in Assar Lindbeck, *Nobel Lectures in Economics* (University of Stockholm, 1992). See also the Nobel website listed below for the Nobel citations for these economists.

Websites

For the citations of Arrow, Hicks, and Debreu, look at the website *www.nobel.se/economics/index.html* to read about the importance of their contributions and how they relate to economics.

QUESTIONS FOR DISCUSSION

1. Explain why each of the following statements about profit-maximizing competitive firms is incorrect. Restate each one correctly.
    a. A competitive firm will produce output up to the point where price equals average variable cost.
    b. A firm's shutdown point comes where price is less than minimum average cost.
    c. A firm's supply curve depends only on its marginal cost. Any other cost concept is irrelevant for supply decisions.

d. The $P = MC$ rule for competitive industries holds for upward-sloping, horizontal, and downward-sloping *MC* curves.
e. The competitive firm sets price equal to marginal cost.

2. Suppose you are a perfectly competitive firm producing computer memory chips. Your production capacity is 1000 units per year. Your marginal cost is $10 per chip up to capacity. You have a fixed cost of $10,000 if production is positive and $0 if you shut down. What are your profit-maximizing levels of production and profit if the market price is (*a*) $5 per chip, (*b*) $15 per chip, and (*c*) $25 per chip? For case (*b*), explain why production is positive even though profits are negative.
3. One of the most important rules of economics, business, and life is the *sunk-cost principle*, "Let bygones be bygones." This means that sunk costs (which are bygone in the sense that they are unrecoverably lost) should be ignored when decisions are being made. Only future costs, involving marginal and variable costs, should count in making rational decisions.

   To see this, consider the following: We can calculate fixed costs in Table 8-1 as the cost level when output is 0. What are fixed costs? What is the profit-maximizing level of output for the firm in Table 8-1 if price is $40 while fixed costs are $0? $55,000? $100,000? $1,000,000,000? Minus $30,000? Explain the implication for a firm trying to decide whether to shut down.
4. Examine the cost data shown in Table 8-1. Calculate the supply decision of a profit-maximizing competitive firm when price is $21, $40, and $60. What would the level of total profit be for each of the three prices? What would happen to the exit or entry of identical firms in the long run at each of the three prices?
5. Using the cost data shown in Table 8-1, calculate the price elasticity of supply between $P = 40$ and $P = 40.02$ for the individual firm. Assume that there are 2000 identical firms, and construct a table showing the industry supply schedule. What is the industry price elasticity of supply between $P = 40$ and $P = 40.02$?
6. Examine Figure 8-12 to see that competitive firm C is not producing at all. Explain the reason why the profit-maximizing output level for firm C is at $q_c = 0$. What would happen to total industry cost of production if firm C produced 1 unit while firm B produced 1 less unit than the competitive output level?

   Say that firm C is a mom-and-pop grocery store. Why would chain grocery stores A and B drive C out of business? How do you feel about keeping C in business? What would be the economic impact of legislation that divided the market into three equal parts between the mom-and-pop store and chain stores A and B?
7. Often, consumer demand for a commodity will depend upon the use of durable goods, such as housing or transportation. In such a case, demand will show a time-varying pattern of response similar to that of supply. A good example is gasoline. In the short run the stock of automobiles is fixed, while in the long run consumers can buy new automobiles or bicycles.

   What is the relationship between the time period and the price elasticity of demand for gasoline? Sketch the short-run and long-run demand curves for gasoline. Show the impact of a decline in the supply of gasoline in both periods. Describe the impact of an oil shortage on the price of gasoline and the quantity demanded in both the long run and the short run. State two new rules of demand, (*c*) and (*d*), parallel to the rules of supply (*c*) and (*d*) discussed in the General Rules portion of Section C above, that relate the impact of a shift in supply on price and quantity in the long run and the short run.
8. Interpret this dialogue:

   A: "How can competitive profits be zero in the long run? Who will work for nothing?"

   B: "It is only *excess* profits that are wiped out by competition. Managers get paid for their work; owners get a normal return on capital in competitive long-run equilibrium—no more, no less."
9. Consider three firms which are emitting sulfur into the California air. We will call supply the units of pollution control or reduction. Each firm has a cost-of-reduction schedule, and we will say that these schedules are given by the *MC* curves of firms A, B, and C in Figure 8-12.
   a. Interpret the "market" supply or *MC* schedule for reducing sulfur emissions, shown in the middle of Figure 8-12.
   b. Say that the pollution-control authority decides to seek 10 units of pollution control. What is the efficient allocation of pollution control across the three firms?
   c. Say that the pollution-control authority decides to have the first two firms produce 5 units each of pollution control. What is the additional cost?
   d. Say that the pollution-control authority decides upon a "pollution charge" to reduce pollution to 10 units. Can you identify what the appropriate charge would be using Figure 8-12? Can you say how each firm would respond? Would the pollution reduction be efficient?
   e. Explain the importance of marginal cost in the efficient reduction of pollution in this case.
10. In any competitive market, such as illustrated in Figure 8-11, the area above the market price line and below the *DD* curve is consumer surplus (see the discussion in Chapter 5). The area above the *SS* curve

and below the price line is producer surplus and equals profits plus rent to the firms in the industry or owners of specialized inputs to the industry. The sum of the producer and consumer surpluses is economic surplus and measures the net contribution of that good to utility above the cost of production.

Can you find any reorganization of production that would increase the economic surplus in Figure 8-11 as compared to the competitive equilibrium at point E? If the answer is no, then the equilibrium is allocationally efficient (or Pareto efficient). Define allocational efficiency; then answer the question and explain your answer.

CHAPTER

Imperfect Competition and Monopoly 9

不完全竞争及垄断

[1] 约翰·理查德·希克斯（John Richard Hicks，1904~1989），英国经济学家，在微观经济学、宏观经济学、经济学方法论，以及经济史学方面卓有成就。1972 年与美国经济学家肯尼斯·约瑟夫·阿罗（Kenneth J. Arrow，1921~，

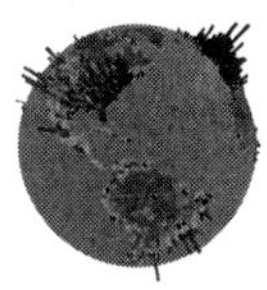

详见 p309 注 [3]）一起获诺贝尔经济学奖。本段文字引自 *Annual Survey of Economic Theory: The Theory of Monopoly, Econometrica, Volume 3,* Number 1, Jan., 1935, p. 8，拟译如下：

The best of all monopoly profits is a quiet life. [1]

J. R. Hicks

所有垄断性利润的最佳形态是一种风平浪静的市场环境。——希克斯

quiet
市场的清淡萧条
life
存在的形态

Perfect competition is an idealized market of atomistic firms who are price-takers. In fact, while they are easily analyzed, such firms are hard to find. When you buy your car from Ford or Toyota, your hamburgers [2] from McDonald's or Wendy's, or your computer from [3] Dell or Apple, you are dealing with firms large enough [4] to affect the market price. Indeed, most markets in the economy are dominated by a handful of large firms, often only two or three. Welcome to the world you live in, the world of imperfect competition.

不完全竞争的模式

A. PATTERNS OF IMPERFECT COMPETITION

We shall see that for a given technology, prices are higher and outputs are lower under imperfect competition than under perfect competition. But imperfect competitors have virtues along with these vices. Large firms exploit economies of large-scale pro- ⑤ duction and are responsible for much of the innovation that propels long-term economic growth. If you understand how imperfectly competitive markets work, you will have a much deeper understanding of modern industrial economies.

Recall that a perfectly competitive market is one in which no firm is large enough to affect the market price. By this strict definition, few markets in the U.S. economy are perfectly competitive. Think of the following: aircraft, aluminum, automobiles, computer software, breakfast cereals, chewing gum, cigarettes, electricity distribution, refrigerators, and wheat. How many of these are sold in perfectly competitive markets? Certainly not aircraft, aluminum, or automobiles. Until World War II there was only one aluminum company, Alcoa. Even today, the four largest U.S. firms produce three-quarters of U.S. aluminum output. The world commercial-aircraft market is dominated by only two firms, Boeing and Airbus. In the automotive industry, too, the top five automakers (including Toyota and Honda) have almost 80 percent of the U.S. car and light-truck market. The software industry shows rapid innovation, yet for most individual software applications, from tax accounting to gaming, a few firms have most of the sales.

What about breakfast cereals, chewing gum, cigarettes, and refrigerators? These markets are dominated even more completely by a relatively small number of companies. Nor does the retail market in electricity meet the definition of perfect competition. In most localities, a single company distributes all the electricity used by the population. Very few of us will find it economical to build a windmill to generate our own power!

Looking at the list above, you will find that only wheat falls within our strict definition of perfect

⑤ 大型企业采用了大规模生产的经济模式，承担了绝大部分技术创新的责任，从而推动了经济的长期发展。

[6] Alcoa：美铝投资有限公司，全球铝业的领军企业。

[7] Honda：本田技研工业株式会社，日本第二大汽车生产企业，世界最大的摩托车和小功率内燃机制造商。

[2] Ford：福特汽车公司（Ford Motor Company），美国三大汽车公司之一。
Toyota：丰田自动车株式会社（Toyota Motor Corporation），世界最大的汽车制造商。

[3] McDonald's：麦当劳公司，全球最大的快餐连锁企业。
Wendy's：温迪快餐（Wendy's Old Fashioned Hamburgers），美国第三大快餐连锁集团。

[4] Dell：戴尔电脑股份有限公司，以戴尔直销模式享誉业界。这种商业模式消除了中间商，减少了不必要的成本和时间，从而有能力为消费者提供有竞争力的价格。
Apple：苹果股份有限公司，2007.1.9 前称苹果电脑（Apple Computer），在高科技企业界以创新立业著称。

competition. All the other goods, from autos to cigarettes, fail the competitive test for a simple reason: Some of the firms in the industry can affect the market price by changing the quantity they sell. To put it another way, they have *some* control over the price of their output.

不完全竞争的定义
Definition of Imperfect Competition

If a firm can affect the market price of its output, the firm is classified as an imperfect competitor.

Imperfect competition prevails in an industry ① whenever individual sellers can affect the price of their output. The major kinds of imperfect competition are monopoly, oligopoly, and monopolistic competition.

Imperfect competition does not imply that a firm has absolute control over the price of its product. Take the cola market, where Coca-Cola and Pepsi [2] together have the major share of the market, and imperfect competition clearly prevails. If the average price of other producers' sodas in the market is 75 cents, Pepsi may be able to set the price of a can at 70 or 80 cents and still remain a viable firm. The firm could hardly set the price at $40 or 5 cents a can because at those prices it would go out of business. We see, then, that an imperfect competitor has some but not complete discretion over its prices.

Moreover, the amount of discretion over price will differ from industry to industry. In some imperfectly competitive industries, the degree of monopoly power is very small. In the retail computer business, for example, more than a few percent difference in price will usually have a significant effect upon a firm's sales. In the market for computer operating systems, by contrast, Microsoft has a virtual monopoly and has great discretion about the price of its Windows software. ③

Graphical Depiction. Figure 9-1 shows graphically the difference between the demand curves faced by perfectly and imperfectly competitive firms. Figure 9-1(*a*) reminds us that a perfect competitor faces a horizontal demand curve, indicating that it can sell all it wants at the going market price. An imperfect competitor, in contrast, faces a downward-sloping demand curve. Figure 9-1(*b*) shows that if an imperfectly competitive firm increases its sales, it will definitely depress the market price of its output as it moves down its *dd* demand curve.

Another way of seeing the difference between perfect and imperfect competition is by considering

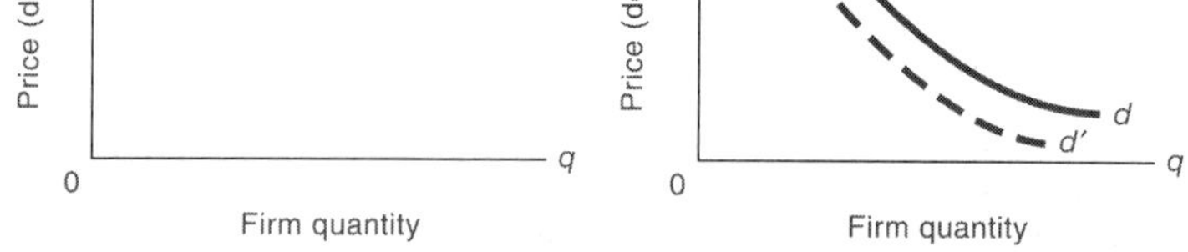

FIGURE 9-1. Acid Test for Imperfect Competition Is Downward Tilt of Firm's Demand Curve ④

(a) The perfectly competitive firm can sell all it wants along its horizontal *dd* curve without depressing the market price. **(b)** But the imperfect competitor will find that its demand curve slopes downward as higher price drives sales down. And unless it is a sheltered monopolist, a cut in its rivals' prices will appreciably shift its own demand curve leftward to *d′d′*.

---

① 当个别生产销售商无论在任何时候都能影响其产品价格时，我们即定义该行业存在**不完全竞争**。不完全竞争的主要种类为垄断、寡头和垄断竞争。

[2] Coco-Cola：可口可乐公司。
Pepsi：百事可乐公司。

③ 与之相反的是，在计算机的操作系统市场，微软公司具有事实上的垄断地位，并且就视窗软件的价格拥有巨大的决定权。

④ 图 9-1. 对不完全竞争的严格检验是企业的需求曲线的向下倾斜程度

the price elasticity of demand. For a perfect competitor, demand is perfectly elastic; for an imperfect competitor, demand has a finite elasticity. As an exercise in use of the elasticity formulas, calculate the elasticities for the perfect competitor in Figure 9-1(a) and the imperfect competitor at point B in 9-1(b). ①

The fact that the demand curves of imperfect competitors slope down has an important implication: Imperfect competitors are *price-makers* not *price-takers*. They must decide on the price of their product, while perfect competitors take the price as given. ②

形形色色的不完全竞争者
VARIETIES OF IMPERFECT COMPETITORS

A modern industrial economy like the United States is a jungle populated with many species of imperfect competition. The dynamics of the personal computer industry, driven by rapid improvements in technology, are different from the patterns of competition in the not-so-lively funeral industry. ③ Nevertheless, much can be learned about an industry by paying careful attention to its market structure, particularly the number and size of sellers and how much of the market the largest sellers control. Economists classify imperfectly competitive markets into three different market structures.

垄 断
Monopoly

At one pole of the competitive spectrum is the perfect competitor, which is one firm among a vast multitude of firms. At the other pole is the **monopoly,** which is a single seller with complete control over an industry. ④ (The word comes from the Greek words *mono* for "one" and *polist* for "seller.") [5] A monopolist is the only firm producing in its industry, and there is no industry producing a close substitute. Moreover, for now we assume that the monopolist must sell everything at the same price—there is no price discrimination.

True monopolies are rare today. Most monopolies persist because of some form of government regulation or protection. For example, a pharmaceutical company that discovers a new wonder drug may be granted a patent, which gives it monopoly control over that drug for a number of years. Another important example of monopoly is a franchised local utility, such as the firm that provides your household water. In such cases there is truly a single seller of a service with no close substitutes. One of the few examples of a monopoly without government license is Microsoft Windows, which has succeeded in maintaining its monopoly through large investments in research and development, rapid innovation, network economies, and tough (and sometimes illegal) tactics against its competitors.

But even monopolists must always be looking over their shoulders for potential competitors. The pharmaceutical company will find that a rival will produce a similar drug; telephone companies that were monopolists a decade ago now must reckon with cellular telephones; Bill Gates worries that some small firm is waiting in the wings to unseat Microsoft's monopolistic position. *In the long run, no monopoly is completely secure from attack by competitors.*

寡 头
Oligopoly

The term **oligopoly** means "few sellers." Few, in this context, can be a number as small as 2 or as large as 10 or 15 firms. The important feature of oligopoly is that each individual firm can affect the market price. ⑥ In the airline industry, the decision of a single airline to lower fares can set off a price war which brings down the fares charged by all its competitors.

⑥ 寡头的重要特征是每家企业都可以影响市场价格。

Oligopolistic industries are common in the U.S. economy, especially in the manufacturing, transportation, and communications sectors. For example, there are only a few car makers, even though the automobile industry sells many different models. The same is true in the market for household appliances: stores are filled with many different models of refrigerators and dishwashers, all made by a handful of companies. You might be surprised to know that the breakfast cereal industry is an oligopoly dominated by a few firms even though there seem to be endless varieties of cereals.

垄断竞争
Monopolistic Competition

The final category we examine is **monopolistic competition.** ⑦ In this situation, a large number of sellers produce differentiated products. This market structure resembles perfect competition in that there are many sellers, none of whom has a large share of the market. It differs from perfect competition in that the products sold by different firms are not identical. **Differentiated products** are ones whose important characteristics vary. Personal computers, for example, have differing characteristics such as speed, memory, hard disk, modem, size, and weight. Because computers are differentiated, they can sell at slightly different prices.

⑦ 我们所讨论的最后一种不完全竞争是**垄断竞争**。在这一环境中有为数众多的生产商，各自生产有差异的产品。这一市场结构类似于完全竞争市场，因为市场上有大量卖家，但没有一家卖家拥有太大的市场份额。这不同于完全竞争市场，因为在这一市场中不同企业销售的产品是不同的。**差异化的产品**系指产品的重要特征各异。

---

① 对于一个完全竞争者来讲，需求是完全具有弹性的；然而对于一个不完全竞争者而言，需求的弹性是有限的。

② 实际情况是，不完全竞争者的需求曲线向下倾斜是一个重要的暗示：不完全竞争者是*价格的制定者*而不是*价格的接受者*。他们必须就其产品的价格做出决定，而完全竞争者则要接受这一既定的价格。

③ 受技术快速发展驱动的个人电脑业发展的动力，与不那么富有活力的殡葬业有着截然不同的竞争模式。

④ 在竞争的图谱上，一端是完全的竞争者，即众多企业中的一家。另一端是**垄断**，一家对本行业有完全控制能力的单一卖家。

[5] 垄断一词源自希腊语 *mono* 和 *polist*，*mono* 是英文中“一”的意思；*polist* 是英文中“卖家”的意思。

The classic case of monopolistic competition is the retail gasoline market. You may go to the local Shell station, even though it charges slightly more, because it is on your way to work. But if the price at Shell rises more than a few pennies above the competition, you might switch to the Merit station a short distance away.

This example illustrates the importance of location in product differentiation. It takes time to go to the bank or the grocery store, and the amount of time needed to reach different stores will affect our shopping choices. The *whole price* of a good includes not ① just its dollar price but also the opportunity cost of search, travel time, and other non-dollar costs. Because the whole prices of local goods are lower than those in faraway places, people generally tend to shop close to home or to work. This consideration also explains why large shopping complexes are so popular: they allow people to buy a wide variety of goods while economizing on shopping time. Today, shopping on the Internet is increasingly important because, even when shipping costs are added, the time required to buy the good online can be very low compared to getting in your car or walking to a shop.

Product quality is an increasingly important part of product differentiation today. Goods differ in their characteristics as well as their prices. Most personal computers can run the same software, and there are many manufacturers. Yet the personal computer industry is a monopolistically competitive industry, because computers differ in speed, size, memory, repair services, and ancillaries like CDs, DVDs, Internet connections, and sound systems. Indeed, a whole batch of monopolistically competitive computer magazines is devoted to explaining the differences among the computers produced by the monopolistically competitive computer manufacturers!

Internet connections 互联网接入服务

sound systems 音响系统

Competition vs. Rivalry
When studying oligopolies, it is important to recognize that imperfect competition is not the same as no competition. Indeed, ② some of the most vigorous rivalries in the

Types of Market Structures

Structure	Number of producers and degree of product differentiation	Part of economy where prevalent	Firm's degree of control over price	Methods of marketing
Perfect competition	Many producers; identical products	Financial markets and agricultural products	None	Market exchange or auction
Imperfect competition				
Monopolistic competition	Many producers; many real or perceived differences in product	Retail trade (pizzas, beer, . . .), personal computers		
Oligopoly	Few producers; little or no difference in product	Steel, chemicals, . . .	Some	Advertising and quality rivalry; administered prices
	Few producers; products are differentiated	Cars, word-processing software, . . .		
Monopoly	Single producer; product without close substitutes	Franchise monopolies (electricity, water); Microsoft Windows; patented drugs	Considerable	Advertising

TABLE 9-1. Alternative Market Structures ③

Most industries are imperfectly competitive. Here are the major features of different market structures.

① 一种商品的总价格不仅包括了该商品的美元价格，同时也包括了搜寻商品、耗费时间的机会成本以及其他非美元成本。

② 实际上，在特定的经济体中竞争最为激烈的某个行业的市场，只有为数不多的几家企业参与竞争。

③ 表 9-1. 各种市场结构

economy occur in markets where there are but a few firms. Just look at the cutthroat competition in the airline industry, where two or three airlines may fly a particular route but still engage in periodic fare wars.

How can we distinguish the rivalry of oligopolists from perfect competition? Rivalry encompasses a wide variety of behavior to increase profits and market share. It includes advertising to shift out the demand curve, price cuts to attract business, and research to improve product quality or develop new products. Perfect competition says nothing about rivalry but simply means that no single firm in the industry can affect the market price.

Table 9-1 on page 172 gives a picture of the various possible categories of imperfect and perfect competition. This table is an important summary of the different kinds of market structures and warrants careful study.

市场不完全竞争的根源
SOURCES OF MARKET IMPERFECTIONS

Why do some industries display near-perfect competition while others are dominated by a handful of large firms? Most cases of imperfect competition can be traced to two principal causes. First, industries tend to have fewer sellers when there are significant economies of large-scale production and decreasing costs. Under these conditions, large firms can simply produce more cheaply and then undersell small firms, which cannot survive.

Second, markets tend toward imperfect competition when there are "barriers to entry" that make it difficult for new competitors to enter an industry. In some cases, the barriers may arise from government laws or regulations which limit the number of competitors. In other cases, there may be economic factors that make it expensive for a new competitor to break into a market. We will examine both sources of imperfect competition.

成本与市场的不完全性
Costs and Market Imperfection

The technology and cost structure of an industry help determine how many firms that industry can support and how big they will be. The key is whether there are economies of scale in an industry. If there are economies of scale, a firm can decrease its average costs by expanding its output, at least up to a point. That means bigger firms will have a cost advantage over smaller firms.

When economies of scale prevail, one or a few firms will expand their outputs to the point where they produce most of the industry's total output. The industry then becomes imperfectly competitive. Perhaps a single monopolist will dominate the industry; a more likely outcome is that a few large sellers will control most of the industry's output; or there might be a large number of firms, each with slightly different products. Whatever the outcome, we must inevitably find some kind of imperfect competition instead of the atomistic perfect competition of price-taking firms.

We can see how the relationship between the size of the market and the scale economies helps determine the market structure. There are three interesting cases, illustrated in Figure 9-2.

1. To understand further how costs may determine market structure, let's first look at a case which is favorable for perfect competition. Figure 9-2(*a*) shows an industry where the point of minimum average cost is reached at a level of output that is tiny relative to the market. As a result, this industry can support the large number of efficiently operating firms that are needed for perfect competition. Figure 9-2(*a*) illustrates the cost curves in the perfectly competitive farm industry. ①
2. An intermediate case is an industry with economies of scale that are large relative to the size of the industry. Numerous detailed econometric and engineering studies confirm that many nonagricultural industries show declining average long-run costs. For example, Table 9-2 shows the results of a study of six U.S. industries. For these cases, the point of minimum average cost occurs at a large fraction of industry output. ②

   Now consider Figure 9-2(*b*), which shows an industry where firms have minimum average costs at a sizable fraction of the market. The industry demand curve allows only a small number of firms to coexist at the point of minimum average cost. Such a cost structure will lead to oligopoly. Most manufacturing industries in the United States—including steel, automobiles, cement, and oil—have a demand and cost structure similar to the one in Figure 9-2(*b*). These industries will tend to be oligopolistic, since they can support only a few large producers. ③
3. A final important case is natural monopoly. A **natural monopoly** is a market in which the ④

---

① 为了进一步了解成本如何决定市场结构的问题，让我们先看一个有助于完全竞争的案例。

② 一个中性的案例是与行业规模大范围关联、具有规模经济的某一种产业。

③ 现在，我们来分析一下图 9-2（b），它所展现的是某一种行业在一个具有相当规模的市场中，各企业的平均成本最小。该行业的需求曲线只允许一定数量的企业在平均成本处于最小值的这一点上共存。这样的一种成本结构必然导致几家寡头企业的垄断。美国的绝大多数制造业，其中包括钢铁、汽车、水泥以及石油，都有与图 9-2（b）中的某条曲线类似的需求曲线与成本结构。这些行业趋向于寡头垄断，因为它们只容忍屈指可数的几家生产者存在。

④ 最后一个非常重要的例子是自然垄断。**自然垄断**是指在市场中该行业中只能容纳一家企业有效率地进行生产。

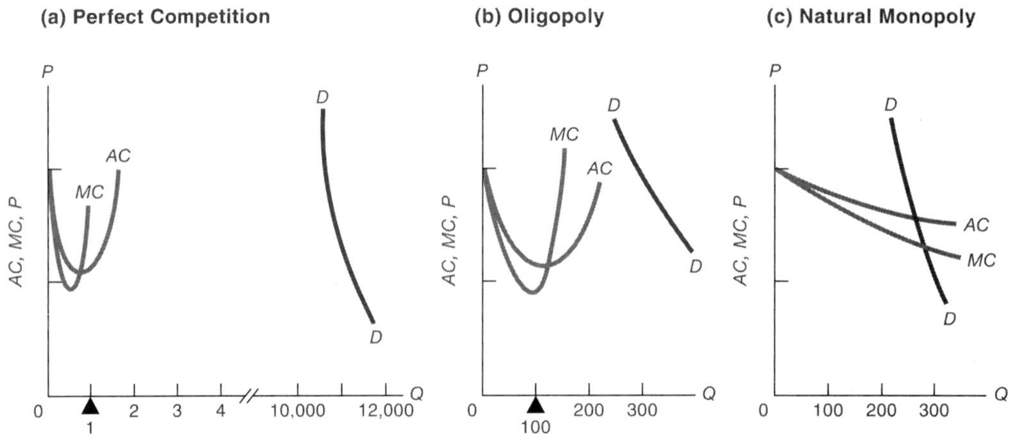

FIGURE 9-2. Market Structure Depends on Relative Cost and Demand Factors ①

Cost and demand conditions affect market structures. In perfectly competitive (**a**), total ② industry demand *DD* is so vast relative to the efficient scale of a single seller that the market allows viable coexistence of numerous perfect competitors. In (**b**), costs turn up at a higher level of output relative to total industry demand *DD*. Coexistence of numerous perfect competitors is impossible, and oligopoly will emerge. When costs fall rapidly and indefinitely, as in the case of natural monopoly in (**c**), one firm can expand to monopolize the industry.

Industry	(1) Share of U.S. output needed by a single firm to exploit economies of scale (%)	(2) Actual average market share of each of the top three firms (%)	(3) Reasons for economies of large-scale operations
Beer brewing	10–14	13	Need to create a national brand image and to coordinate investment
Cigarettes	6–12	23	Advertising and image differentiation
Glass bottles	4–6	22	Need for central engineering and design staff
Cement	2	7	Need to spread risk and raise capital
Refrigerators	14–20	21	Marketing requirements and length of production runs
Petroleum	4–6	8	Need to spread risk on crude-oil ventures and coordinate investment

TABLE 9-2. Industrial Competition Is Based on Cost Conditions ③

This study examined the impact of cost conditions on concentration patterns. Column (1) ④ shows the estimate of the point where the long-run average cost curve begins to turn up, as a share of industry output. Compare this with the average market share of each of the top three firms in column (2).

Source: F. M. Scherer and David Ross, *Industrial Market Structure and Economic Performance*, 3d ed. (Houghton Mifflin, Boston, 1990).

① 图 9-2. 市场结构取决于相对成本与需求因素

② 如图（a）所示，在完全竞争的环境下，行业的总需求 *DD* 相对于单一生产销售商的规模效率而言非常巨大，从而使为数众多的完全竞争企业在该市场中得以共存。

③ 表 9-2. 以成本为基本条件的行业竞争

④ 本项研究分析了成本条件对于集中模式的影响。

industry's output can be efficiently produced only by a single firm. This occurs when the technology exhibits significant economies of scale over the entire range of demand. Figure 9-2(*c*) shows the cost curves of a natural monopolist. With perpetual increasing returns to scale, average and marginal costs fall forever. As output grows, the firm can charge lower and lower prices and still make a profit, since its average cost is falling. Peaceful competitive coexistence of thousands of perfect competitors will be impossible because one large firm is so much more efficient than a collection of small firms.

Some important examples of natural monopolies are the local distribution in telephone, electricity, gas, and water as well as long-distance links in railroads, highways, and electrical transmission. Many of the most important natural monopolies are "network industries" (see the discussion in Chapter 6).

Technological advances, however, can undermine natural monopolies. Most of the U.S. ①
population is now served by at least two cellular telephone networks, which use radio waves instead of wires and are undermining the old natural monopoly of the telephone companies. We see a similar trend today in cable TV as competitors invade these natural monopolies and are turning them into hotly contested oligopolies.

进入壁垒

Barriers to Entry

Although cost differences are the most important factor behind market structures, barriers to entry can also prevent effective competition. **Barriers to** ②
entry are factors that make it hard for new firms to enter an industry. When barriers are high, an industry may have few firms and limited pressure to compete. Economies of scale act as one common type of barrier to entry, but there are others, including legal restrictions, high cost of entry, advertising, and product differentiation.

Legal Restrictions. Governments sometimes restrict competition in certain industries. Important legal restrictions include patents, entry restrictions, and foreign-trade tariffs and quotas. A *patent* is granted to an inventor to allow temporary exclusive use (or monopoly) of the product or process that is patented. For example, pharmaceutical companies are often granted valuable patents on new drugs in which they have invested hundreds of millions of research-and-development dollars. Patents are one of the few forms of government-granted monopolies that are generally approved of by economists. Governments grant patent monopolies to encourage inventive activity. Without the prospect of monopoly patent protection, a company or a sole inventor might be unwilling to devote time and resources to research and development. The temporarily high monopoly ③
price and the resulting inefficiency is the price society pays for the invention.

Governments also impose *entry restrictions* on ④
many industries. Typically, utilities, such as telephone, electricity distribution, and water, are given *franchise monopolies* to serve an area. In these cases, the firm gets an exclusive right to provide a service, and in return the firm agrees to limit its prices and provide universal service in its region even when some customers might be unprofitable.

Free trade is often controversial, as we will see in the chapter on that subject. But one factor that will surprise most people is how important international trade is to promoting vigorous competition.

Historians who study the tariff have written, "The ⑤
tariff is the mother of trusts." (See question 10 at the end of this chapter for an analysis of this subject.) This is because government-imposed *import restrictions* have the effect of keeping out foreign competitors. It could very well be that a single country's market for [6]
a product is only big enough to support two or three firms in an industry, while the world market is big enough to support a large number of firms.

We can see the effect of restricting foreign competition in terms of Figure 9-2. Suppose a small country like Belgium or Benin decides that only *its* national airlines should provide airline service in the country. It is unlikely that such tiny airlines could have an efficient fleet of airplanes, reservation and repair systems, and Internet support. Service to Belgium and Benin would be poor, and prices would be high. What has happened is that the protectionist policy has changed the industry structure from Figure 9-2(*b*) to 9-2(*c*).

When markets are broadened by abolishing tariffs in a large free-trade area, vigorous and effective competition is encouraged and monopolies tend to lose their power. One of the most dramatic examples

⑤ 研究关税的历史学家们曾经这样写道："关税是行业托拉斯之母。"

[6] *The tariff is the mother of trusts.* 出自时任《穆迪》(*Moody's Magazine*)主编的拜伦·霍尔特(Byron W. Holt)于1899年11月23日发表的《硼砂业简史》(*A Brief History of the Borax Industry*)一文，原文如下：

Our borax tariff is, therefore, the real mother of this great world trust.

---

① 绝大多数美国民众至少可以享有两种以上的蜂窝式移动电话网的服务，这种服务用无线电波取代了有线网络，并且正在削弱着电话公司长期以来的自然垄断地位。

② **进入壁垒**系指阻碍新企业进入一个行业的因素。

③ 暂时的垄断高价及其所导致的低效率是商业社会为发明创造支付的价格。

④ 政府也在许多行业实施了准入限制。比如电信、供电、供水这样一些典型的公共事业行业，就由政府赋予在当地的特许垄断经营权。

of increased competition has come in the European Union, which has lowered tariffs among member countries steadily over the last three decades and has benefited from larger markets for firms and lower concentration of industry.

High Cost of Entry. In addition to legally imposed barriers to entry, there are economic barriers as well. In some industries the price of entry simply may be very high. Take the commercial-aircraft industry, for example. The high cost of designing and testing new airplanes serves to discourage potential entrants into the market. It is likely that only two companies—Boeing and Airbus—can afford the $10 to $20 billion that the next generation of aircraft will cost to develop.

In addition, companies build up intangible forms of investment, and such investments might be very expensive for any potential new entrant to match. Consider the software industry. Once a spreadsheet ①
program (like Excel) or a word-processing program (like Microsoft Word) has achieved wide acceptability, potential competitors find it difficult to make inroads into the market. Users, having learned one program, are reluctant to switch to another. Consequently, in order to get people to try a new program, any potential entrant will need to run a big promotional campaign, which would be expensive and may still result in failure to produce a profitable product. (Recall our discussion of network effects in Chapter 6.)

Advertising and Product Differentiation. Sometimes it is possible for companies to create barriers to entry for potential rivals by using advertising and product differentiation. Advertising can create product awareness and loyalty to well-known brands. For example, Pepsi and Coca-Cola spend hundreds of millions of dollars per year advertising their brands, which makes it very expensive for any potential rivals to enter the cola market.

In addition, product differentiation can impose a barrier to entry and increase the market power of producers. In many industries—such as breakfast cereals, automobiles, household appliances, and cigarettes—it is common for a small number of manufacturers to produce a vast array of different brands, models, and products. In part, the variety appeals to the widest range of consumers. But the enormous number of differentiated products also serves to discourage potential competitors. The demands for each of the individual differentiated products will be so small that they will not be able to support a large number of firms operating at the bottom of their U-shaped cost curves. The result is that perfect competition's *DD* curve in Figure 9-2(*a*) contracts so far to the left that it becomes like the demand curves of oligopoly or monopoly shown in Figure 9-2(*b*) and (*c*). Hence, differentiation, like tariffs, produces greater concentration and more imperfect competition.

Branding and Differentiated Products

One important part of modern business strategy is to establish a brand. Suppose, for example, that all the Coca-Cola factories were to collapse in an earthquake. What would happen to the value of Coca-Cola's stock price? Would it go to zero?

The answer, according to finance specialists, is that, even with no tangible assets, Coca-Cola would still be worth about $67 billion. This is the company's *brand value*. A product's brand involves the perception of taste and quality in the minds of consumers. Brand value is established when a firm has a product that is seen as better, more reliable, or tastier than other products, branded or nonbranded.

In a world of differentiated products, some firms earn fancy profits because of the value of their brands. The following table shows recent estimates of the top 10 brands:

Rank	Brand	Brand value, 2006 ($, billion)
1	Coca-Cola	67
2	Microsoft	60
3	IBM	56
4	GE	49
5	Intel	32
6	Nokia	30
7	Toyota	28
8	Disney	28
9	McDonald's	27
10	Mercedes-Benz	22

Source: *BusinessWeek*, available on the Internet at *http://www.businessweek.com/*.

Thus, for Coca-Cola, the market value of the firm was ②
$67 billion more than would be justified by its plant,

---

① 像 Excel 这样的电子表格软件和 Word 这样的文字处理软件一旦获得广泛的接受之后，潜在的竞争对手们就会发现开拓进入这个市场是很困难的。

② 因此，对于可口可乐公司而言，该公司的市场价值比起其厂房、生产设备以及其他资产所达到的作价要高出 670 亿美元之巨。

equipment, and other assets. How do firms establish and maintain brand value? First, they usually have an innovative product, such as a new drink, a cute cartoon mouse, or a high-quality automobile. Second, they maintain their brand value by heavy advertising, even associating a deadly product like Marlboro cigarettes (brand rank 14) with a good-looking cowboy in a romantic sunset with beautiful horses. Third, they protect their brands using intellectual property rights such as patents and copyrights. In one sense, brand value is the residue of past innovative activity.

垄断行为

B. MONOPOLY BEHAVIOR

We begin our survey of the behavior of imperfect competitors with an analysis of the polar case of monopoly. We need a new concept, marginal revenue, which will have wide applications for other market structures as well. The major conclusion will be that monopolistic practices lead to inefficiently high prices and low outputs and therefore reduce consumer welfare.

边际收益的概念

THE CONCEPT OF MARGINAL REVENUE

价格、数量和总收益

Price, Quantity, and Total Revenue

Suppose that you have a monopoly on a new kind of computer game called *Monopolia*. You wish to maximize your profits. What price should you charge, and what output level should you produce?

To answer these questions, we need a new concept, *marginal revenue* (or *MR*). From the firm's demand curve, we know the relationship between price (P) and quantity sold (q). These are shown in columns (1) and (2) of Table 9-3 and as the blue demand curve (dd) for the monopolist in Figure 9-3(a).

We next calculate the total revenue at each sales level by multiplying price times quantity. Column (3) of Table 9-3 shows how to calculate the **total revenue** (TR), which is simply $P \times q$. Thus 0 units bring in TR of 0; 1 unit brings in $TR = \$180 \times 1 = \$180$; 2 units bring in $\$160 \times 2 = \$320$; and so forth.

In this example of a straight-line or linear ① demand curve, total revenue at first rises with output, since the reduction in P needed to sell the extra q is moderate in this upper, elastic range of the demand curve. But when we reach the midpoint of the straight-line demand curve, TR reaches its maximum. This comes at $q = 5$, $P = \$100$, with $TR = \$500$. Increasing q beyond this point brings the firm into the inelastic demand region. For inelastic demand, ② reducing price increases sales less than proportionally, so total revenue falls. Figure 9-3(b) shows TR to be dome-shaped, rising from zero at a very high price to a maximum of \$500 and then falling to zero as price approaches zero.

How could you find the price at which revenues are maximized? You would see in Table 9-3 that TR is maximized when $q = 5$ and $P = 100$. This is the point where the demand elasticity is exactly 1.

Note that the price per unit can be called *average revenue* (AR) to distinguish it from total revenue. Hence, we get $P = AR$ by dividing TR by q (just as we earlier got AC by dividing TC by q). Verify that if column (3) had been written down before column (2), we could have filled in column (2) by division.

边际收益和价格

Marginal Revenue and Price

The final new concept is marginal revenue. **Marginal** ③ **revenue** (MR) is the change in revenue that is generated by an additional unit of sales. MR can be either positive or negative.

Table 9-3 shows marginal revenue in column (4). MR is calculated by subtracting the total revenues of adjacent outputs. When we subtract the TR we get by selling q units from the TR we get by selling $q + 1$ units, the difference is extra revenue or MR. Thus, from $q = 0$ to $q = 1$, we get $MR = \$180 - \$0$. From $q = 1$ to $q = 2$, MR is $\$320 - \$180 = \$140$.

MR is positive until we arrive at $q = 5$ and negative from then on. What does the strange notion of negative marginal revenue mean? That the firm is paying people to take its goods? Not at all. Negative ④ MR means that in order to sell additional units, the firm must decrease its price on earlier units so much that its total revenues decline.

For example, when the firm sells 5 units, it gets

$$TR\ (5\ \text{units}) = 5 \times \$100 = \$500$$

Now say the firm wishes to sell an additional unit of output. Because it is an imperfect competitor, it can increase sales only by lowering price. So to sell 6 units, it lowers the price from \$100 to \$80. It gets

---

① 在这一直线或者线性需求曲线的例子中，总收益在起始阶段会随产量的增加而上升，这是因为在这条需求曲线上部富有弹性的区间，售出更多的 q 而需要降低的 P 是适中的。

② 由于需求缺乏弹性，降低售价并没有同比增加销售量，从而使总收益出现下滑。

③ **边际收益**（MR）系指多增加一个单位的销售所引起的收益的变化，其值可为负值，也可以为正值。

④ 负的边际收益系指为了售出更多单位的产品，企业必须大幅降低售出价格，这样总收益才出现下滑。

Total and Marginal Revenue

(1) Quantity q	(2) Price $P = AR = TR/q$ ($)	(3) Total revenue $TR = P \times q$ ($)	(4) Marginal revenue MR ($)
0	200	0	
			+180
1	180	180	
			+140
2	160	320	
			+100
3	140	420	
			+60
4	120	480	+40
			+20
5	100	500	
			———
6	80	480	
			−60
7	60	———	
			−100
8	40	320	
			−140
9	———	180	
			−180
10	0	0	

TABLE 9-3. Marginal Revenue Is Derived from Demand Schedule ①

Total revenue (TR) in column (3) comes from multiplying P by q. To get marginal revenue ② (MR), we increase q by a unit and calculate the change in total revenue. MR is less than P because of the lost revenue from lowering the price on previous units to sell another unit of q. Note that MR is positive when demand is elastic. But after demand turns inelastic, MR becomes negative even though price is still positive.

\$80 of revenue from the sixth unit, but it gets only 5 × \$80 on the first 5 units, yielding

$$TR(6 \text{ units}) = (5 \times \$80) + (1 \times \$80)$$
$$= \$400 + \$80 = \$480$$

Marginal revenue between 5 and 6 units is \$480 − \$500 = −\$20. The necessary price reduction on the first 5 units was so large that, even after adding in the sale of the sixth unit, total revenue fell. This is what happens when MR is negative. To test your understanding, fill in the blanks in columns (2) to (4) of Table 9-3.

Note that even though MR is negative, AR, or price, is still positive. Do not confuse marginal revenue with average revenue or price. Table 9-3 shows

① 表 9-3. 从需求表推算边际收益值

② MR 值小于 P 值的原因在于，多售出 1 单位 P 就会低于以前各单位的价格，这样会带来收益损失。

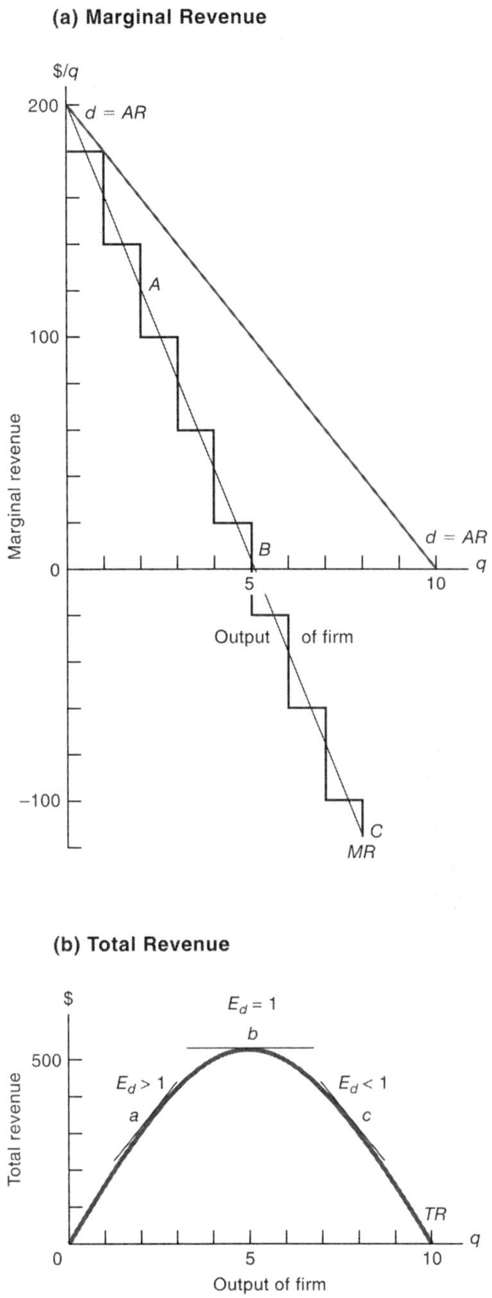

FIGURE 9-3. Marginal Revenue Curve Comes from Demand Curve ①

(a) The steps show the increments of total revenue from each extra unit of output. *MR* falls below *P* from the beginning. *MR* becomes negative when *dd* turns inelastic. Smoothing the incremental steps of *MR* gives the smooth, thin green *MR* curve, which in the case of straight line *dd* will always have twice as steep a slope as *dd*.

(b) Total revenue is dome-shaped—rising from zero where $q = 0$ to a maximum (where *dd* has unitary elasticity) and then falling back to zero where $P = 0$. If we graph *TR* as a smooth blue line in (*b*), this gives smoothed green *MR* in (*a*).

Source: Table 9-3.

that they are different. In addition, Figure 9-3(*a*) plots the demand (*AR*) curve and the marginal revenue (*MR*) curve. Scrutinize Figure 9-3(*a*) to see that the plotted green steps of *MR* definitely lie below the blue *dd* curve of *AR*. In fact, *MR* turns negative ② when *AR* is halfway down toward zero.

弹性和边际收益

Elasticity and Marginal Revenue

What is the relationship between the price elasticity of demand and marginal revenue? Marginal rev- ③ enue is positive when demand is elastic, zero when demand is unit-elastic, and negative when demand is inelastic.

This result is an important implication of the definition of elasticity that we used in Chapter 4. Recall that demand is elastic when a price decrease leads to a revenue increase. In such a situation, a price decrease raises output demanded so much that revenues rise, so marginal revenue is positive. For example, in Table 9-3, as price falls in the elastic region from $P = \$180$ to $P = \$100$, output demanded rises sufficiently to raise total revenue, and marginal revenue is positive.

What happens when demand is unit-elastic? A percentage price cut then just matches the percentage output increase, and marginal revenue is therefore zero. Can you see why marginal revenue is always negative in the inelastic range? Why is the marginal revenue for the perfect competitor's infinitely elastic demand curve always positive?

Table 9-4 shows the important elasticity relationships. Make sure you understand them and can apply them.

---

① 图 9-3. 源自需求曲线的边际收益曲线

② 事实上，当 *AR* 中途向零点以下移动时，*MR* 即变为负值。

③ 当需求富有弹性时，边际收益为正值；当需求为单位弹性时，边际收益为零；当需求缺乏弹性时，边际收益为负值。

If demand is	Relation of q and P	Effect of q on TR	Value of marginal revenue (MR)
Elastic ($E_D > 1$)	% change q > % change P	Higher q raises TR	$MR > 0$
Unit-elastic ($E_D = 1$)	% change q = % change P	Higher q leaves TR unchanged	$MR = 0$
Inelastic ($E_D < 1$)	% change q < % change P	Higher q lowers TR	$MR < 0$

TABLE 9-4. Relationships of Demand Elasticity, Output, Price, Revenue, and Marginal Revenue ①

② 1. 边际收益（MR）是在增加一个单位的销售产生的收益变化。
2. 价格 = 平均收益（$P=AR$）
3. 当需求曲线向下倾斜时，$P > MR = P$ − 此前全部单位售出之后所减少的收益。
4. 当需求富有弹性时，边际收益为正值；当需求为单位弹性时，边际收益为零；当需求缺乏弹性时，边际收益为负值。
5. 对于完全竞争者而言，$P=MR=AR$。

Here are the key points to remember:

1. *Marginal revenue* (MR) is the change in revenue that is generated by an additional unit of sales. ②
2. Price = average revenue ($P = AR$).
3. With downward-sloping demand,
   $P > MR$
   $= P -$ reduced revenue on all previous units.
4. Marginal revenue is positive when demand is elastic, zero when demand is unit-elastic, and negative when demand is inelastic.
5. For perfect competitors, $P = MR = AR$.

利润最大化的条件
PROFIT-MAXIMIZING CONDITIONS

Now return to the question of how a monopolist should set its quantity and price if it wants to maximize profits. By definition, total profit equals total revenue minus total costs; in symbols, $TP = TR - TC = (P \times q) - TC$. We will show that *maximum profit will occur when output is at that level where the firm's marginal revenue is equal to its marginal cost.* ③

One way to determine this maximum-profit condition is by using a table of costs and revenues, such as Table 9-5. To find the profit-maximizing quantity and price, compute total profit in column (5). This column tells us that the monopolist's best quantity, which is 4 units, requires a price of $120 per unit. This produces a total revenue of $480, and, after subtracting total costs of $250, we calculate total profit to be $230. A glance shows that no other price-output combination has as high a level of total profit.

We get more insight using a second approach, which is to compare marginal revenue in column (6) with marginal cost in column (7). As long as each additional unit of output provides more revenue than it costs, the firm's profit will increase as output increases. So the firm should continue to increase its output as long as MR is greater than MC. ④

On the other hand, suppose that MR is less than MC at a given output. This means that increasing output lowers profits, so the firm should cut back on output. Clearly, the best-profit point comes where marginal revenue exactly equals marginal cost. The rule for finding maximum profit is therefore:

> The maximum-profit price (P^*) and quantity (q^*) of a monopolist come where the firm's marginal revenue equals its marginal cost: ⑤
>
> $MR = MC$, at the maximum-profit P^* and q^*

These examples show the logic of the $MC = MR$ rule for maximizing profits, but we always want to understand the intuition behind the rules. Look for a moment at Table 9-5 and suppose that the monopolist is producing $q = 2$. At that point, its MR for producing 1 full additional unit is +$100, while its MC is $20. Thus, if it produced 1 additional unit, the firm would make additional profits of $MR - MC = \$100 - \$20 = \$80$. Indeed, column (5) of Table 9-5 shows that the extra profit gained by moving from 2 to 3 units is exactly $80. ⑥

Thus, when MR exceeds MC, additional profits can be made by increasing output; when MC exceeds MR, additional profits can be made by decreasing q. Only when $MR = MC$ can the firm maximize profits, because there are no additional profits to be made by changing its output level.

垄断均衡图示
Monopoly Equilibrium in Graphs

Figure 9-4 shows the monopoly equilibrium. Part (*a*) combines the firm's cost and revenue curves. The maximum-profit point comes at that output where MC equals MR, which is given at their intersection at E. The monopoly equilibrium, or maximum-profit point, is at an output of $q^* = 4$. To find the profit-maximizing price, we run vertically up from E to the

① 表 9-4. 需求弹性、产量、价格、收益以及边际收益之间的关系

③ 我们在此所要说明的是，当企业的边际收益等于其边际成本时所达到的产量，即实现利润最大化。

④ 只要每增加 1 个单位的产量所产生的收益大于其成本，企业的利润就会随产量的增加而增加。

⑤ 一家垄断企业在边际收益等于其边际成本时，该企业实现利润最大化时的价格（P^*）与产量（q^*）：当 $MR=MC$ 时，达到利润最大值时的 P^* 和 q^*

⑥ 这些例子说明了利润最大化时 $MC=MR$ 法则的逻辑关系，但是，我们始终要理解法则背后需要凭借直觉去感知的知识。

Summary of Firm's Maximum Profit

(1) Quantity q	(2) Price P ($)	(3) Total revenue TR ($)	(4) Total cost TC ($)	(5) Total profit TP ($)	(6) Marginal revenue MR ($)	(7) Marginal cost MC ($)	
0	200	0	145	−145			
					+180	30	$MR > MC$
1	180	180	175	+5			
					+140	25	
2	160	320	200	+120			
					+100	20	
3	140	420	220	+200			
					+60	30	
4*	**120***	**480**	**250**	**+230**	+40	40	$MR = MC$
					+20	50	
5	100	500	300	+200			
					−20	70	
6	80	480	370	+110			
					−60	90	
7	60	420	460	−40			
					−100	110	$MR < MC$
8	40	320	570	−250			

*Maximum-profit equilibrium.

TABLE 9-5. Equating Marginal Cost to Marginal Revenue Gives Firm's Maximum-Profit q and P ①

Total and marginal costs of production are now brought together with total and marginal revenues. The maximum-profit condition is where $MR = MC$, with $q^* = 4$, $P^* = \$120$, and maximum $TP = \$230 = (\$120 \times 4) - \$250$.

dd curve at *G*, where $P^* = \$120$. The fact that average revenue at *G* lies above average cost at *F* guarantees a positive profit. The actual amount of profit is given by the green area in Figure 9-4(*a*).

The same story is told in part (*b*) with curves of total revenue, cost, and profit. Total revenue is dome-shaped. Total cost is ever rising. The vertical difference between them is total profit, which begins negative and ends negative. In between, *TP* is positive, reaching its maximum of \$230 at $q^* = 4$.

We add one further important geometric point. *The slope of a total value is a marginal value.* (You can refresh your memory on this by looking at page 22 in Chapter 1's appendix.) So look at point *G* in Figure 9-4(*b*). If you carefully calculate the slope at that point, you will see that it is \$40 per unit. This means that every unit of additional output produces \$40 of additional revenue, which is just the definition of *MR*. So the slope of the *TR* curve is *MR*. Similarly, the slope of the *TC* curve is *MC*. Note that at $q = 4$, *MC* is also \$40 per unit. At $q = 4$, marginal cost and marginal revenue are equal. At that point total profit ② (*TP*) reaches its maximum, and an additional unit adds exactly equal amounts to costs and revenues.

① 表 9-5. 边际成本等于边际收益使企业获得最大利润的 q 和 P

② 在那一点上，总利润（*TP*）达到了最大值，在增加了另外一个单位的产量之后正好等于成本和收益的总和。在利润最大化时的产量水平上，*TR* 与 *TC* 的斜率（即图中的 *MR* 与 *MC*）相互平行，因此相等。

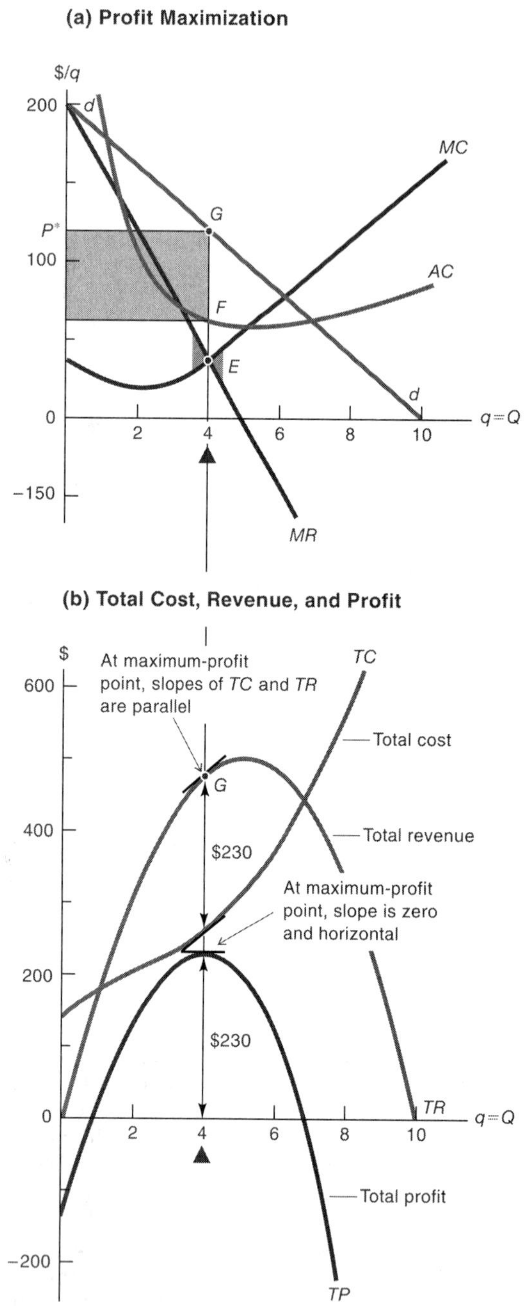

FIGURE 9-4. Profit-Maximizing Equilibrium Can Be Shown Using Either Total or Marginal Curves ①

(a) At *E*, where *MC* intersects *MR*, the monopolist gets maximum profits. Price is on the demand curve at *G*, above *E*. Since *P* is above *AC*, the maximized profit is a positive profit. (Can you explain why the blue triangles of shading on either side of *E* show the reduction in total profit that would come from a departure from *MR* = *MC*?)

Panel **(b)** tells the same story of maximizing profit as does **(a)**, but it uses total concepts rather than marginal concepts. The *TR* curve shows the total revenue, while the *TC* curve shows total cost. Total profit is equal to *TR* minus *TC*, shown geometrically as the vertical distance from *TR* to *TC*. The slope of each curve is that curve's marginal value (e.g., *MR* is the slope of *TR*). At the maximum profit, *TR* and *TC* are parallel and therefore have equal slopes, *MR* = *MC*.

At the maximum-profit output, the blue slopes of *TR* and *TC* (which are *MR* and *MC*) are parallel and therefore equal.

A monopolist will maximize its profits by setting output at the level where *MC* = *MR*. Because the monopolist has a downward-sloping demand curve, this means that $P > MR$. Because price is above ②
marginal cost for a profit-maximizing monopolist, the monopolist reduces output below the level that would be found in a perfectly competitive industry.

完全竞争是不完全竞争的一个极端情况

Perfect Competition as a Polar Case of Imperfect Competition

Although we have applied the *MC* = *MR* rule to monopolists that desire to maximize profits, this rule is actually applicable far beyond the present analysis. A little thought shows that the *MC* = *MR* rule applies with equal validity to a profit-maximizing perfect competitor. We can see this in two steps:

1. MR *for a perfect competitor.* What is *MR* for a perfect competitor? For a perfect competitor, the sale of extra units will never depress price, and the "lost revenue on all previous *q*" is therefore equal to zero. Price and marginal revenue are identical for perfect competitors.

   Under perfect competition, price equals ③
   average revenue equals marginal revenue (*P* = *AR* = *MR*). A perfect competitor's *dd* curve and its *MR* curve coincide as horizontal lines.

---

① 图 9-4. 利润最大化时的均衡既可以使用总量的曲线，也可以使用边际的曲线来说明

② 对于一个追求利润最大化的垄断者来讲，由于其价格高于边际成本，所以垄断者会将其产量降低到完全竞争行业的水平。

③ 在完全竞争的环境中，价格即等于平均收益也等于边际收益（*P*=*AR*=*MR*）。一个完全竞争者的 *dd* 曲线与其 *MR* 曲线重合为相同的水平线。

2. MR = P = MC *for a perfect competitor.* In addition, we can see that the logic of profit maximization for monopolists applies equally well to perfect competitors, but the result is a little different. Economic logic shows that profits are maximized at that output level where *MC* equals *MR*. But by step 1 above, for a perfect competitor, *MR* equals *P*. Therefore, the *MR* = *MC* profit-maximization condition becomes the special case of *P* = *MC* that we derived in the last chapter for a perfect competitor:

> Because a perfect competitor can sell all it wants at the market price, *MR* = *P* = *MC* at the maximum-profit level of output. ①

You can see this result visually by redrawing Figure 9-4(*a*). If the graph applied to a perfect competitor, the *dd* curve would be horizontal at the market price, and it would coincide with the *MR* curve. The profit-maximizing *MR* = *MC* intersection would also come at *P* = *MC*. We see then how the general rule for profit maximization applies to perfect as well as imperfect competitors.

边际原则：让过去成为过去
THE MARGINAL PRINCIPLE: LET BYGONES BE BYGONES

We close this chapter with a more general point about the use of marginal analysis in economics. While economic theory will not necessarily make you fabulously wealthy, it does introduce you to some new ways of thinking about costs and benefits. *One of the most important lessons of economics is that you should look at the marginal costs and marginal benefits of decisions and ignore past or sunk costs.* We might put this as follows: ②

> Let bygones be bygones. Don't look backward. Don't cry over spilt milk or moan about yesterday's losses. Make a hard-headed calculation of the extra costs you'll incur by any decision, and weigh these against its extra advantages. Make a decision based on marginal costs and marginal benefits. ③

This is the **marginal principle,** which means that people will maximize their incomes or profits or satisfactions by counting only the marginal costs and marginal benefits of a decision. There are countless situations in which the marginal principle applies. We have just seen that the marginal principle of equating marginal cost and marginal revenue is the rule for profit maximization by firms. ④

损失规避和边际原则
Loss Aversion and the Marginal Principle

An interesting application is the behavior of people who are selling their houses. Behavioral economists have observed that people often resist selling their house for less than the dollar purchase price even in the face of steep declines in local housing prices.

For example, suppose you bought your house in San Jose for $250,000 in 2005 and wanted to sell it in 2008. Because of the decline in housing prices, comparable houses sold for $200,000 in 2008. As was the case for millions of people in the last few years, you are faced with a nominal dollar loss.

Studies show that you might well set the price at your purchase price of $250,000 and wait for several months without a single serious offer. This is what behavioral economists call "loss aversion," meaning that people resist taking a loss even though it is costly to hold on to an asset. This behavior has been verified in housing markets, where people subject to a loss set higher asking prices and wait longer for sales.

Economists counsel against this kind of behavior. It would be better to observe the marginal principle. Forget about what you paid for your house. Just get the best price you can.

Monopolists of the Gilded Age

Economic abstractions sometimes hide the human drama of monopoly, so we close this section by recounting one of the most colorful periods of American business history. Because of changing laws and customs, monopolists in today's America bear little resemblance to the brilliant, unscrupulous, and often dishonest robber barons of the Gilded Age (1870–1914).[6] Legendary figures like Rockefeller, Gould, Vanderbilt, Frick, Carnegie, Rothschild, and Morgan were driven to create entire industries like railroads or oil, provide their finance, develop the western frontier, destroy their competitors, and pass on fabulous fortunes to their heirs. ⑤

The last three decades of nineteenth-century America experienced robust economic growth lubricated by tremendous graft and corruption. Daniel Drew was a cattle rustler, horse trader, and railroader who mastered the trick of "watering the stock." This practice involved depriving his cattle of water until they reached the slaughterhouse; he then induced a great thirst with salt and allowed the beasts to engorge themselves on water just before being weighed. Later, tycoons would "water their stock" by inflating the value of their securities.[7]

[6] The Gilded Age：出自马克·吐温（Mark Twin，1835~1910）和华纳（Charles Dudley Warner，1829 ~1900）于1873年联合出版的小说《镀金年代，今天的故事》（*The Gilded Age: A Tale of Today*）。
Rockefeller：约翰·洛克菲勒（John D. Rockefeller，1839.7.8~1937.5.23），美国实业家、超级资本家，美孚石油公司（Mobil Oil Company，1911年成立Standard Oil Company，即标准石油公司，1999年与Exxon合并，成立Exxon Mobil Corporation，即埃克森美孚公司）的创办人。其个人资产如果转换为2006年的美元，将达到今天的世界首富盖茨的数倍。
Gould：杰伊·古尔德（Jay Gould，1836~1892），美国著名的投机家和金融家，曾于1867年成功地从范德比尔特家族手中夺得伊利铁路（Erie Railroad）的控制权，与其合伙人詹姆斯·菲斯克（James Fisk，1834-1872）一起掀起了1869年的金融危机，试图垄断当时的黄金市场。
Vanderbilt：考捏列斯·范德比尔特（Cornelius Vanderbilt，1794~1877），美国铁路大亨，著名的范德比尔特大学（Vanderbilt University）的创始人。其子威廉·亨利·范德比尔特（William Henry Vanderbilt，1821~1885），著名的美国商人，在其父的基础上成就并绵延数代至今的显赫的范德比尔特家族。
Frick：亨利·克莱·弗里克（Henry Clay Frick，1849~1919），著名的美国实业家，煤炭和钢铁大亨。
Carnegie：安德鲁·卡内基（Andrew Carnegie，1835~1919），苏格兰出生的美国实业家和慈善家，钢铁大亨。
Rothschild：罗斯柴尔德，著名的德国银行世家，包括法兰克福银行的创始人迈耶·罗斯柴尔德（Meyer A. Rothschild，1743~1812），他的两个儿子萨洛蒙（Salomon，1774-1855）和内森·迈耶（Nathan Mayer，1774~1836），将分行开遍了欧洲各国。
Morgan：约翰·皮尔庞特·摩根（John Pierpont Morgan，1837~1913），著名的美国金融家和慈善家，铁路和钢铁大亨。

[7] Daniel Drew：丹尼尔·德鲁（1797~1879），著名的美国金融家，曾通过操纵股票价格的非法手段夺取铁路的控制权。
Cattle rustler：特指德鲁本人，因其发明牛的“灌水术”（watering the stock）骗术以增加肉牛的重量而被冠名。后来企业界的大亨们操纵本公司股票价格的骗术也被借称为“股票灌水术”（watering their stock）.

---

① 由于完全竞争者可以按照市场价格出售其所有想要出售的产品，所以在利润最大化的产量水平时 MR=P=MC。

② 经济学所要告诫人们的最重要的一点是，应该高度地关注决策的边际成本和边际获益，同时忽略掉过去或者沉没的成本。

③ 让过去的事情真正成为过去。不要回头看，不要为已经洒掉的牛奶哭泣，也不要为昨天的损失哀愁。精心地测算出你做出任何决策时所要承受的额外成本，并把它们与你所要获得的利益相权衡，而后根据边际成本和边际获益做出你的决策。

④ 这就是**边际原则**，它指的是人们仅仅通过核算决策的边际成本和边际获益就可以将他们的收入、利润或者满意度最大化。

⑤ 经济学的抽象性有时掩饰了人类社会垄断现象的戏剧效果，因此，我们通过对美国经济史上最丰富多彩的一段时期做一个回顾，来结束本节的内容。由于法律环境和习俗的不断变化，今天美国社会的垄断者们与镀金年代（1870~1914）那些才华横溢、不择手段，并且常常与欺诈和残酷剥削集于一身的企业大亨们比较起来，几乎没有多少相似之处。

The railroaders of the American frontier west were among the most unscrupulous entrepreneurs on record. The transcontinental railroads were funded with vast federal land grants, aided by bribes and stock gifts to numerous members of Congress and the cabinet. Shortly after the Civil War, the wily railroader Jay Gould attempted to corner the entire gold supply of the United States, and with it the nation's money supply. Gould later promoted his railroad by describing the route of his northern line—snowbound much of the year—as a tropical paradise, filled with orange groves, banana plantations, and monkeys. By century's end, all the bribes, land grants, watered stock, and fantastic promises had led to the greatest rail system in the world.

The story of John D. Rockefeller epitomizes the nineteenth-century monopolist. Rockefeller saw visions of riches in the fledgling oil industry and began to organize oil refineries. He was a meticulous manager and sought to bring "order" to the quarrelsome wildcatters. He bought up competitors and consolidated his hold on the industry by persuading the railroads to give him deep and secret rebates and supply information about his competitors. When competitors stepped out of line, Rockefeller's railroads refused to ship their oil and even dumped it on the ground. By 1878, John D. controlled 95 percent of the pipelines and oil refineries in the United States. Prices were raised and stabilized, ruinous competition was ended, and monopoly was achieved.

Rockefeller devised an ingenious new device to ensure control over his alliance. This was the "trust," in which the stockholders turned their shares over to "trustees" who would then manage the industry to maximize its profits. Other industries imitated the Standard Oil Trust, and soon trusts were set up in kerosene, sugar, whiskey, lead, salt, and steel.

These practices so upset agrarians and populists that the nation soon passed antitrust laws (see Chapter 10). In 1910, the Standard Oil Corporation was dissolved in the first great victory by the Progressives against "Big Business." Ironically, Rockefeller actually profited from the breakup because the price of Standard Oil shares soared when they were offered to the public.

Great monopolies produced great wealth. Whereas the United States had three millionaires in 1861, there were 4000 of them by 1900 ($1 million at the turn of the century is equivalent to about $100 million in today's dollars).

Great wealth in turn begot conspicuous consumption (a term introduced into economics by Thorstein Veblen in [1] *The Theory of the Leisure Class,* 1899). Like European popes and aristocrats of an earlier era, American tycoons wanted to transform their fortunes into lasting monuments. The wealth was spent in constructing princely palaces such as the "Marble House," which can still be seen in Newport, Rhode Island; in buying vast art collections, which form the core of the great American museums like New York's Metropolitan Museum of Art; and in launching foundations and universities such as those named after Stanford, Carnegie, Mellon, and Rockefeller. Long after their pri- [2] ③ vate monopolies were broken up by the government or overtaken by competitors, and long after their wealth was largely dissipated by heirs and overtaken by later generations of entrepreneurs, the philanthropic legacy of the robber barons continues to shape American arts, science, and education.[1]

[1] See the Further Reading section for books on this topic.

SUMMARY

A. Patterns of Imperfect Competition

1. Most market structures today fall somewhere on a spectrum between perfect competition and pure monopoly. Under imperfect competition, a firm has some control over its price, a fact seen as a downward-sloping demand curve for the firm's output.
2. Important kinds of market structures are (*a*) monopoly, where a single firm produces all the output in a given industry; (*b*) oligopoly, where a few sellers of a similar or differentiated product supply the industry; (*c*) monopolistic competition, where a large number of small firms supply related but somewhat differentiated products; and (*d*) perfect competition, where a large number of small firms supply an identical product. In the first three cases, firms in the industry face downward-sloping demand curves.
3. Economies of scale, or decreasing average costs, are the major source of imperfect competition. When

[1] Thorstein Veblen：索尔斯坦·邦德·凡勃伦（Thorstein Bunde Veblen，1857~1929），美国经济学家，其代表作《休闲阶级论》（*The Theory of the Leisure Class*，1899）论述了商品供给和赚钱之间的根本性冲突，提出了"炫耀性消费"（conspicuous consumption）的概念。

[2] Mellon：安德鲁·威廉·梅隆（Andrew William Mellon，1855~1937），美国金融家和政客，曾于1921~1932年任美国财政部长。

③ 在他们的私人垄断王国，由于政府或者被竞争对手取代等原因而破落之后的很长时间里，或者，在他们的财富被后继子孙大规模地挥霍，同时又被后来一代又一代的企业家们所接管的时间的长河中，这些披着绅士外衣的强盗们的慈善壮举对美国艺术、科学和教育的影响与时间同在。

firms can lower costs by expanding their output, perfect competition is destroyed because a few companies can produce the industry's output most efficiently. When the minimum efficient size of plants is large relative to the national or regional market, cost conditions produce imperfect competition.

4. In addition to declining costs, other forces leading to imperfect competition are barriers to entry in the form of legal restrictions (such as patents or government regulation), high entry costs, advertising, and product differentiation.

B. Monopoly Behavior

5. We can easily derive a firm's total revenue curve from its demand curve. From the schedule or curve of total revenue, we can then derive marginal revenue, which denotes the change in revenue resulting from an additional unit of sales. For the imperfect competitor, marginal revenue is less than price because of the lost revenue on all previous units of output that will result when the firm is forced to drop its price in order to sell an extra unit of output. That is, with demand sloping downward,

$$P = AR > MR = P - \text{lost revenue on all previous } q$$

6. Recall Table 9-4's rules relating demand elasticity, price and quantity, total revenue, and marginal revenue.
7. A monopolist will find its maximum-profit position where $MR = MC$, that is, where the last unit it sells brings in extra revenue just equal to its extra cost. This same $MR = MC$ result can be shown graphically by the intersection of the MR and MC curves or by the equality of the slopes of the total revenue and total cost curves. In any case, *marginal revenue = marginal cost* must always hold at the equilibrium position of maximum profit.
8. For perfect competitors, marginal revenue equals price. Therefore, the profit-maximizing output for a perfect competitor comes where $MC = P$.
9. Economic reasoning leads to the important *marginal principle*. In making decisions, count marginal future advantages and disadvantages, and disregard sunk costs that have already been paid. Be wary of loss aversion.

CONCEPTS FOR REVIEW

Patterns of Imperfect Competition

perfect vs. imperfect competition
monopoly, oligopoly, monopolistic competition
product differentiation
barriers to entry (government and economic)

Marginal Revenue and Monopoly

marginal (or extra) revenue, MR
$MR = MC$ as the condition for maximizing profits
$MR = P$, $P = MC$, for perfect competitors
natural monopoly
the marginal principle

FURTHER READING AND INTERNET WEBSITES

Further Reading

The theory of monopoly was developed by Alfred Marshall around 1890; see his *Principles of Economics,* 9th ed. (Macmillan, New York, 1961).

An excellent review of monopoly and industrial organization is F. M. Scherer and David Ross, *Industrial Market Structure and Economic Performance,* 3rd ed. (Houghton Mifflin, Boston, 1990).

The Gilded Age period gave birth to "yellow journalism" in the United States and fostered many muckraking histories, such as Matthew Josephson, *The Robber Barons* (Harcourt Brace, New York, 1934). A more balanced recent account is Ron Chernow, *Titan: The Life of John D. Rockefeller, Sr.* (Random House, New York, 1998).

For a study of loss aversion in the housing market, see David Genesove and Christopher Mayer, "Loss Aversion and Seller Behavior: Evidence from the Housing Market," *Quarterly Journal of Economics,* 2001. The foundation of this theory is in Amos Tversky and Daniel Kahneman, "Loss Aversion in Riskless Choice: A Reference-Dependent Model," *Quarterly Journal of Economics,* 1991.

Websites

An important legal case over the last decade has concerned whether Microsoft had a monopoly on PC operating systems. This is thoroughly discussed in the "Findings of Fact" of the Microsoft antitrust case by Judge Thomas Penfield Jackson (November 5, 1999). His opinion and further developments can be found at *www.microsoft.com/presspass/legalnews.asp.*

QUESTIONS FOR DISCUSSION

1. Suppose a monopolist owns a mineral spring. Answer and demonstrate each of the following:
   a. Assume that the cost of production is zero. What is the elasticity of demand at the profit-maximizing quantity?
   b. Assume that the *MC* of production is always $1 per unit. What is the elasticity of demand at the profit-maximizing quantity?
2. Explain why each of the following statements is false. For each, write the correct statement.
   a. A monopolist maximizes profits when $MC = P$.
   b. The higher the price elasticity, the higher is a monopolist's price above its *MC*.
   c. Monopolists ignore the marginal principle.
   d. Monopolists will maximize sales. They will therefore produce more than perfect competitors and their price will be lower.
3. What is *MR*'s numerical value when *dd* has unitary elasticity? Explain.
4. In his opinion on the Microsoft antitrust case, Judge Jackson wrote: "[T]hree main facts indicate that Microsoft enjoys monopoly power. First, Microsoft's share of the market for Intel-compatible PC operating systems is extremely large and stable. Second, Microsoft's dominant market share is protected by a high barrier to entry. Third, and largely as a result of that barrier, Microsoft's customers lack a commercially viable alternative to Windows." (See the website reference, section 34, in this chapter's Further Readings.) Why are these elements related to monopoly? Are all three necessary? If not, which ones are crucial? Explain your reasoning.
5. Estimate the numerical price elasticities of demand at points *A* and *B* in Figure 9-1. (*Hint:* You may want to review the rule for calculating elasticities in Figure 4-5.)
6. Redraw Figure 9-4(*a*) for a perfect competitor. Why is *dd* horizontal? Explain why the horizontal *dd* curve coincides with *MR*. Then proceed to find the profit-maximizing *MR* and *MC* intersection. Why does this yield the competitive condition $MC = P$? Now redraw Figure 9-4(*b*) for a perfect competitor. Show that the slopes of *TR* and *TC* must still match at the maximum-profit equilibrium point for a perfect competitor.
7. Banana Computer Company has fixed costs of production of $100,000, while each unit costs $600 of labor and $400 of materials and fuel. At a price of $3000, consumers would buy no Banana computers, but for each $10 reduction in price, sales of Banana computers increase by 1000 units. Calculate marginal cost and marginal revenue for Banana Computer, and determine its monopoly price and quantity.
8. Show that a profit-maximizing monopolist will never operate in the price-inelastic region of its demand curve.
9. Explain the error in the following statement: "A firm out to maximize its profits will always charge the highest price that the traffic will bear." State the correct result, and use the concept of marginal revenue to explain the difference between the correct and the erroneous statements.
10. Recall from pp. 183–184 how trusts were organized to monopolize industries like oil and steel. Explain the saying, "The tariff is the mother of trusts." Use Figure 9-2 to illustrate your analysis. Use the same diagram to explain why lowering tariffs and other trade barriers reduces monopoly power.
11. *For students who like calculus:* You can show the condition for profit maximization easily using calculus. Define $TP(q)$ = total profits, $TC(q)$ = total costs, and $TR(q)$ = total revenues. Marginal this-or-that is the derivative of this-or-that with respect to output, so $dTR/dq = TR'(q) = MR$ = marginal revenue.
    a. Explain why $TP = TR - TC$.
    b. Show that a maximum of the profit function comes where $TC'(q) = TR'(q)$. Interpret this finding.

CHAPTER 10

Competition among the Few
几个竞争者之间的竞争

[1] Akshay R. Rao：阿克萨伊·拉奥，明尼苏达州卡尔森管理学院副教授。

Mark E. Bergen：马克·伯根，明尼苏达州卡尔森管理学院副教授。

Scott Davis：斯科特·戴维斯，加利福尼亚市场战略和决策咨询公司创始人和老板。

American Airlines：美洲航空公司，2008 年之前系全球第一大航空公司。

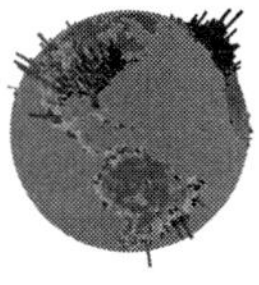

Northwest Airlines：美国西北航空公司，2008 年 4 月与美国达美航空公司（Delta Airlines）合并，超越了美洲航空公司。

三人合作撰写的《如何应战价格战？》（*How to Fight a Price War*）一文发表于《哈佛经济评论》（*Harvard Business Review*）2000 年 3-4 月期第 15 页，是近十年来经济学界著名的论文之一。本段文字为该文的第二自然段的后半部分，前半段为：

Creating low-price appeal is often the goal, but the result of one retaliatory price slashing after another is often a precipitous decline in industry profits.

全段译文如底注。（接下）

Look at the airline price wars of 1992. When American Airlines, Northwest Airlines, and other U.S. carriers went toe-to-toe in matching and exceeding one another's reduced fares, the result was record volumes of air travel—and record losses. Some estimates suggest that the overall losses suffered by the industry that year exceed the combined profits for the entire industry from its inception.

Akshay R. Rao, Mark E. Bergen, and Scott Davis [1]
"How to Fight a Price War"

Earlier chapters analyzed the market structures of perfect competition and complete monopoly. If ② you look out the window at the American economy, however, you will see that such polar cases are rare. Most industries lie between these two extremes and are populated by a small number of firms competing with each other.

What are the key features of these intermediate types of imperfect competitors? How do they set their prices and outputs? To answer these questions, we look closely at what happens under oligopoly and monopolistic competition, paying special attention to the role of concentration and strategic interaction. We then introduce the elements of game theory, which is an important tool for understanding how people and businesses interact in strategic situations. The final section reviews the different public policies used to combat monopolistic abuses, focusing on regulation and antitrust laws.

不完全竞争者的行为

A. BEHAVIOR OF IMPERFECT COMPETITORS

Look back at Table 9-1, which shows the following kinds of market structures: (1) *Perfect competition* is found when a large number of firms produce an identical product. (2) *Monopolistic competition* occurs when a large number of firms produce slightly differentiated products. (3) *Oligopoly* is an intermediate form of imperfect competition in which an industry is dominated by a few firms. (4) *Monopoly* is the most concentrated market structure, in which a single firm produces the entire output of an industry.

How do we measure the power of firms in an industry to control price and output? How do the different species behave? We begin with these issues.

[1]（接上注）创造低价经常是目标性的诉求点，但是，一波压倒一波猛跌的报复性价格的竞争结果常常导致行业利润的陡然下滑。让我们回过头来再关注一下 1992 年在航空业界发生的价格战。当时，美洲航空公司、美国西北航空公司和其他的美国航空公司在竞争中针锋相对，竞相压低票价，结果同时创下了航空业运输量的新高和亏损量的新记录。一些估计表明，当年美国航空业全行业所遭受的全部损失超过了美国航空业自开创以来所赚利润的总和。

Toe-to-toe：始于太平洋战争时期的 1942 年，意为“针锋相对”，“短兵相接”。

本章内容作者进行了大范围的修订，章首所引用的名言也用此段置换了沿用三版（16~18 版）的美洲航空公司和布兰尼夫航空公司（Braniff Airlines，由于竞争的激烈、油价飙升和盲目扩张等原因于 1982 年停业）老板之间谈话的录音记录稿。本章的题目也由 *Oligopoly and Monopolistic Competition*（寡头与垄断竞争）改为现题目。

② 然而，如果你透过窗户看一下美国的经济就会发现，这样极端的案例是很少见的。大多数行业都介于这两个极端案例之间，由为数不多的相互竞争的小企业构成。

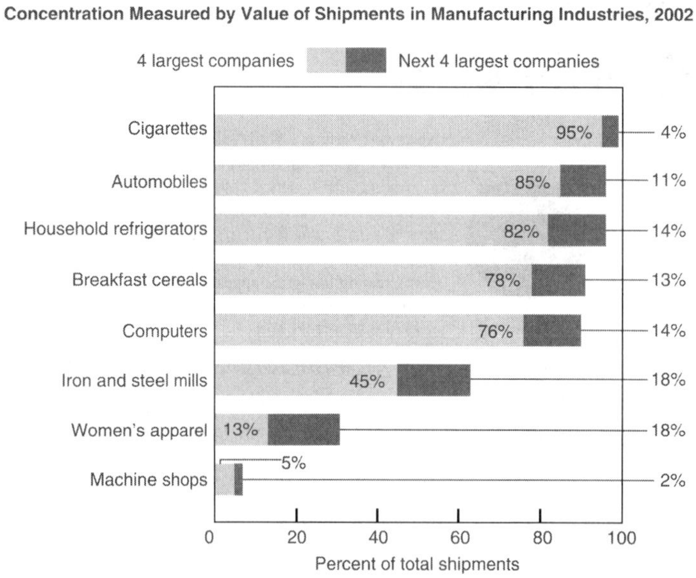

FIGURE 10-1. Concentration Ratios Are Quantitative Measures of Market Power ①

For refrigerators, automobiles, and many other industries, a few firms produce most of the domestic output. Compare this with the ideal of perfect competition, in which each firm is too small to affect the market price.

Source: U.S. Bureau of the Census, 2002 data.

市场力量的衡量

Measures of Market Power

In many situations—such as deciding whether the government should intervene in a market or whether a firm has abused its monopoly position—economists need a quantitative measure of the extent of a firm's market power. **Market power** signifies the degree of ② control that a single firm or a small number of firms have over the price and production decisions in an industry.

The most common measure of market power is the *concentration ratio* for an industry, illustrated in Figure 10-1. The **four-firm concentration ratio** ③ measures the fraction of the market or industry accounted for by the four largest firms. Similarly, the eight-firm concentration ratio is the percent of the market taken by the top eight firms. The market is customarily measured by domestic sales, shipments, or output. In a pure monopoly, the four-firm and eight-firm concentration ratios would be 100 percent because one firm produces 100 percent of the output; under perfect competition, both ratios would be close to zero because even the largest firms produce only a tiny fraction of industry output.

③ 图中所示的**四企业集中度**计量的是最大的四家企业在市场或行业中所占的份额。同理，八企业集中度是指排名前八位的企业所占的市场份额比例，均以百分数表示。

Many economists believe that traditional concentration ratios do not adequately measure market power. An alternative, which better captures the ④
role of dominant firms, is the **Herfindahl-Hirschman Index (HHI).** This is calculated by summing the [5]
squares of each participant's market share. Perfect competition would have an HHI of near zero because each firm produces only a small percentage of the total output, while complete monopoly would have an HHI of 10,000 because one firm produces 100 percent of the output ($100^2 = 10,000$). (For the formula and an example, see question 2 at the end of this chapter.)

Warning on Concentration Measures

Although concentration measures are ⑥
widely used, they are often misleading because of international competition and competition from closely related industries. Conventional concentration measures such as those shown in Figure 10-1 exclude imports and include only domestic production. Because foreign

① 图 10-1. 市场力量的定量分析——集中度

② **市场力量**表示在某一行业中，一家或者少数几家企业对价格和生产决策的控制程度。

④ **赫芬达尔—赫希曼指数（HHI）**是一种可以取代集中度从而更好地表示具有行业统治地位企业所扮演角色的方法，它通过将每一家参与企业所占市场份额的平方，经过加总后获得。

[5] Herfindahl—Hirschman：分别为美国经济学家 Orris C. Herfindahl 和德国裔美国经济学家 Albert O. Hirschman。

⑥ 虽然集中度指标得到了广泛的使用，但由于存在国际性的竞争以及密切相关的产业间的竞争，经常在误导使用者。

competition is very intense in the manufacturing sector, the actual market power of domestic firms is much smaller than is indicated by measures of market power based solely on domestic production. For example, the conventional concentration measures shown in Figure 10-1 indicate that the top four U.S. automotive firms had 85 percent of the U.S. market. If we include imports as well, however, these top four U.S. firms had only 43 percent of the U.S. market.

In addition to ignoring international competition, traditional concentration measures ignore the impact of competition from other, related industries. For example, concentration ratios have historically been calculated for a narrow industry definition, such as "wired telecommunications carriers." Sometimes, however, strong competition comes from other quarters. For example, cellular telephones are a major threat to traditional wired telephone service even though the two are produced by different industries. Even though the four-firm concentration ratio for wired carriers alone is 60 percent, the four-firm ratio for all telecommunications carriers is only 46 percent, so the definition of a market can strongly influence the calculation of the concentration ratios.

In the end, some measure of market power is essential for many legal purposes, such as aspects of antitrust law, examined later in this chapter. A careful delineation of the market to include all the relevant competitors can be helpful in determining whether monopolistic abuses are in fact a real threat.

不完全竞争的实质
THE NATURE OF IMPERFECT COMPETITION

In analyzing the determinants of concentration, economists have found that three major factors are at work in imperfectly competitive markets. These factors are economies of scale, barriers to entry, and strategic interaction (the first two were analyzed in the previous chapter, and the third is the subject of detailed examination in the next section):

- *Costs.* When the minimum efficient size of operation for a firm occurs at a sizable fraction of industry output, only a few firms can profitably survive and oligopoly is likely to result. ①
- *Barriers to competition.* When there are large economies of scale or government restrictions to entry, these will limit the number of competitors in an industry.
- *Strategic interaction.* When only a few firms operate in a market, they will soon recognize their interdependence. **Strategic interaction,** which is a genuinely new feature of oligopoly that has inspired the field of game theory, occurs when each firm's business depends upon the behavior of its rivals.

Why are economists particularly concerned about industries characterized by imperfect competition? The answer is that such industries behave in certain ways that are inimical to the public interest. For example, imperfect competition generally leads to prices that are above marginal costs. Sometimes, without the spur of competition, the quality of service deteriorates. Both high prices and poor quality are undesirable outcomes.

As a result of high prices, oligopolistic industries often (but not always) have supernormal profits. The profitability of the highly concentrated tobacco and pharmaceutical industries has been the target of political attacks on numerous occasions. Careful studies show, however, that concentrated industries tend to have only slightly higher rates of profit than unconcentrated ones.

Historically, one of the major defenses of imperfect competition has been that large firms are responsible for most of the research and development (R&D) and innovation in a modern economy. There is certainly some truth in this idea, for highly concentrated industries sometimes have high levels of R&D spending per dollar of sales as they try to achieve a technological edge over their rivals. At the same time, individuals and small firms have produced many of the greatest technological breakthroughs. We review the economics of innovation in Chapter 11.

不完全竞争理论
THEORIES OF IMPERFECT COMPETITION

While the concentration of an industry is important, it does not tell the whole story. Indeed, to explain ② the behavior of imperfect competitors, economists have developed a field called *industrial organization.* We cannot cover this vast area here. Instead, we will focus on three of the most important cases of imperfect competition—collusive oligopoly, monopolistic competition, and small-number oligopoly.

---

① • *成本*：对于一家企业来讲，当其最低效益的经营规模占该行业产量的份额达到一个相当大的比例时，只有寥寥无几的几家企业有能力获利而得以生存，其结局就很可能形成寡头。

• *竞争壁垒*：如果存在大的规模经济或者有政府的准入限制时，那么行业内竞争对手的数量就必然非常有限。

• *策略互动*：当市场中只有少数几家企业经营时，它们必然会很快地认识到相互之间的依存性。**策略互动**是寡头的一个新特征，当每一家企业的业务都依赖于其竞争对手们的经营活动时，策略互动就会发生，这种特征引发了对博弈论领域的研究。

② 为便于解释不完全竞争者的行为，经济学家们已经开拓了一个称为*产业组织*的研究领域。

勾结寡头
Collusive Oligopoly

The degree of imperfect competition in a market is influenced not just by the number and size of firms but by their behavior. When only a few firms operate in a market, they see what their rivals are doing and react. For example, if there are two airlines operating along the same route and one raises its fare, the other must decide whether to match the increase or to stay with the lower fare, undercutting its rival. *Strategic interaction* is a term that describes how each ① firm's business strategy depends upon its rivals' business behavior.

When there are only a small number of firms ② in a market, they have a choice between *cooperative* and *noncooperative* behavior. Firms act noncooperatively when they act on their own without any explicit or implicit agreements with other firms. That's what produces price wars. Firms operate in a cooperative mode when they try to minimize competition. When firms in an oligopoly actively cooperate with each other, they engage in **collusion.** This term denotes a situation in which two or more firms jointly set their prices or outputs, divide the market among themselves, or make other business decisions jointly.

② 当市场中只有少数几家企业时，每一家企业都需在合作性和非合作性的行为之间进行选择。其单独做出的选择如果没有与其他企业达成的任何公开或者私下的协议为前提，即是非合作性的。价格战遂由此引发。当企业间试图将相互间的竞争降低到最低限度时，企业就在以合作的模式经营。当寡头企业积极地彼此合作时，它们就形成了**共谋**。这一术语指两家以上的企业共同制定价格以及产量的状况，它将市场在几家企业间瓜分，或者它们共同制定其他的商业决策。

During the early years of American capitalism, before the passage of effective antitrust laws, oligopolists often merged or formed a trust or cartel (recall Chapter 9's discussion of trusts, page 184). A **cartel** ③ is an organization of independent firms, producing similar products, that work together to raise prices and restrict output. Today, with only a few exceptions, it is strictly illegal in the United States and most other market economies for companies to collude by jointly setting prices or dividing markets.

Nonetheless, firms are often tempted to engage in tacit collusion, which occurs when they refrain from competition without explicit agreements. When firms tacitly collude, they often quote identical high prices, pushing up profits and decreasing the risk of doing business. In recent years, sellers of online music, diamonds, and kosher Passover products have been investigated for price fixing, while private universities, art dealers, airlines, and the telephone industry have been accused of collusive behavior.

The rewards for successful collusion can be great. Consider an industry where four firms have tired of ruinous price wars. They agree to charge the same price and share the market. They form a **collusive** ④ **oligopoly** and set a price which maximizes their joint profits. By joining together, the four firms in effect become a monopolist.

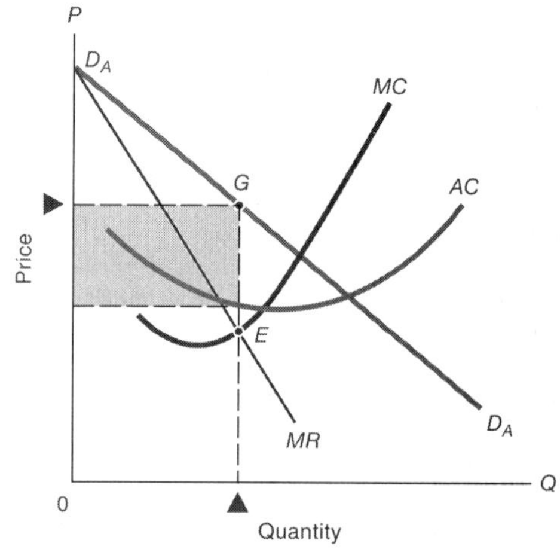

FIGURE 10-2. Collusive Oligopoly Looks Much Like Monopoly ⑤

After experience with disastrous price wars, firms will ⑥ surely recognize that each price cut is canceled by competitors' price cuts. So oligopolist A may estimate its demand curve D_AD_A by assuming that others will be charging similar prices. When firms collude to set a jointly profit-maximizing price, the price will be very close to that of a single monopolist. Can you see why profits are equal to the blue rectangle?

Figure 10-2 illustrates oligopolist A's situation, where there are four firms with identical cost and demand curves. We have drawn A's demand curve, D_AD_A, assuming that the other three firms always charge the same price as firm A.

The maximum-profit equilibrium for the collusive oligopolist is shown in Figure 10-2 at point *E*, the intersection of the firm's *MC* and *MR* curves. Here, the appropriate demand curve is D_AD_A. The optimal ⑦ price for the collusive oligopolist is shown at point *G* on D_AD_A, above point *E*. This price is identical to the monopoly price: it is above marginal cost and earns each of the colluding oligopolists a handsome monopoly profit.

When oligopolists collude to maximize their ⑧ joint profits, taking into account their mutual

---

① *策略互动*是一个专用术语，指的是每家企业的经营策略对其竞争对手商业行为的依赖性。

③ **卡特尔**系指生产类似产品，共同抬高价格、限制产量的若干独立企业形成的组织。

④ 这些企业形成了**勾结寡头**，并制定能将它们的共同利润最大化的价格。

⑤ 图 10-2. 共谋寡头看上去很像垄断

⑥ 经过了灾难性价格战的历练，各企业必然会认识到每一次降低价格都会被竞争对象同样的举措所抵消。

⑦ 上图中的 D_AD_A 是一条合适的需求曲线。对于共谋寡头，其最优的价格出现在 D_AD_A 曲线上位于 E 点正上方的 G 点。这一价格与垄断价格相似，即高于边际成本，并且使得每一家寡头企业都赢得了可观的垄断性利润。

⑧ 如果寡头们通过共谋来将它们共同的利润最大化，考虑到彼此之间相互的依赖性，它们必然会对价格和产量实施垄断，以获得垄断利润。

interdependence, they will produce the monopoly output and price and earn the monopoly profit.

Although many oligopolists would be delighted to earn such high profits, in reality many obstacles hinder effective collusion. First, collusion is illegal. Second, firms may "cheat" on the agreement by cutting their price to selected customers, thereby increasing their market share. Clandestine price cutting is particularly likely in markets where prices are secret, where goods are differentiated, where there is more than a handful of firms, or where the technology is changing rapidly. Third, the growth of international trade means that many companies face intensive competition from foreign firms as well as from domestic companies.

Indeed, experience shows that running a successful cartel is a difficult business, whether the collusion is explicit or tacit.

A long-running thriller in this area is the story of the international oil cartel known as the Organization of Petroleum Exporting Countries, or OPEC. OPEC is an international organization which sets production quotas for its members, which include Saudi Arabia, Iran, and Algeria. Its stated goal is "to secure fair and stable prices for petroleum producers; an efficient, economic and regular supply of petroleum to consuming nations; and a fair return on capital to those investing in the industry." Its critics claim it is really a collusive monopolist attempting to maximize the profits of producing countries.

OPEC became a household name in 1973, when it reduced production sharply and oil prices skyrocketed. But a successful cartel requires that members set a low production quota and maintain discipline. Every few years, price competition breaks out when some OPEC countries ignore their quotas. This happened in a spectacular way in 1986, when Saudi Arabia drove oil prices from $28 per barrel down to below $10.

Another problem faced by OPEC is that it must negotiate production quotas rather than prices. This leads to high levels of price volatility because demand is unpredictable and highly price-inelastic in the short run. Oil producers became rich in the 2000s as prices soared, but the cartel had little control over actual events.

The airline industry is another example of a market with a history of repeated—and failed—attempts at collusion. It would seem a natural candidate for collusion. There are only a few major airlines, and on many routes there are only one or two rivals. But just look back to the quote at the beginning of the chapter, which describes one of the recent price wars in the United States. Airline bankruptcy is so frequent that some airlines spend more time bankrupt than solvent. Indeed, the evidence shows that ① the only time an airline can charge supernormal fares is when it has a near-monopoly on all flights to a city.

垄断竞争

Monopolistic Competition

At the other end of the spectrum from collusive oli- ② gopolies is **monopolistic competition.** Monopolistic competition resembles perfect competition in three ways: there are many buyers and sellers, entry and exit are easy, and firms take other firms' prices as given. The distinction is that products are identical under perfect competition, while under monopolistic competition they are differentiated.

OPEC 石油输出国组织

Monopolistic competition is very common—just scan the shelves at any supermarket and you'll see a dizzying array of different brands of breakfast cereals, shampoos, and frozen foods. Within each product group, products or services are different, but close enough to compete with each other. Here are some other examples of monopolistic competition: There may be several grocery stores in a neighborhood, each carrying the same goods but at different locations. Gas stations, too, all sell the same product, but they compete on the basis of location and brand name. The several hundred magazines on a newsstand rack are monopolistic competitors, as are the 50 or so competing brands of personal computers. The list is endless.

The important point to recognize is that each seller has some freedom to raise or lower prices because of product differentiation (in contrast to perfect competition, where sellers are price-takers). Product differentiation leads to a downward slope in each seller's demand curve.

Figure 10-3 might represent a monopolistically competitive computer magazine which is in short-run equilibrium with a price at *G*. The firm's *dd* demand curve shows the relationship between sales and its price when other magazine prices are unchanged; its demand curve slopes downward since this magazine is a little different from everyone else's because

---

① 事实证明，在一家航空公司近乎垄断了飞往一个城市的所有航线的情况下，惟一的结局就是这家航空公司会把票价定得异乎寻常得高。

② 共谋寡头的另一个极端即**垄断竞争**。垄断竞争在三个方面与完全竞争类似；买家和卖家众多、进入和退出机制宽松；以及各企业都将其他企业的价格视为既定的价格。两者之间的区别在于在完全竞争环境下的产品是相同的，而在垄断竞争环境下，产品是差异化的。

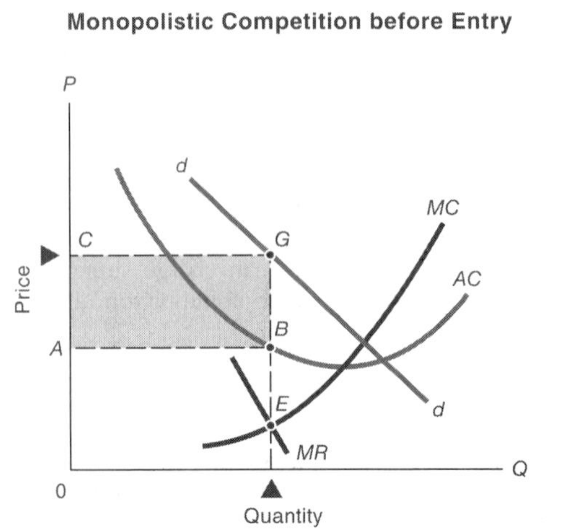

FIGURE 10-3. Monopolistic Competitors Produce Many Similar Goods ①

Under monopolistic competition, numerous small firms sell differentiated products and therefore have downward-sloping demand. Each firm takes its competitors' prices as given. Equilibrium has $MR = MC$ at E, and price is at G. Because price is above AC, the firm is earning a profit, area $ABGC$.

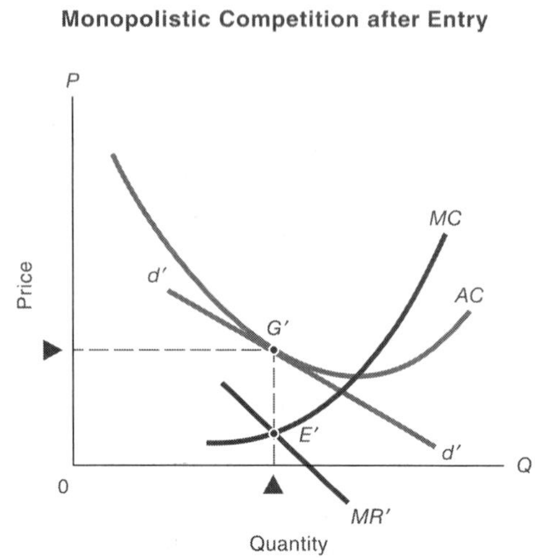

FIGURE 10-4. Free Entry of Numerous Monopolistic Competitors Wipes Out Profit ④

The typical seller's original profitable *dd* curve in Figure 10-3 will be shifted downward and leftward to $d'd'$ by the entry of new rivals. Entry ceases only when each seller has been forced into a long-run, no-profit tangency such as at G'. At ⑤ long-run equilibrium, price remains above MC, and each producer is on the left-hand declining branch of its long-run AC curve.

of its special focus. The profit-maximizing price is at G. Because price at G is above average cost, the firm is making a handsome profit represented by area $ABGC$.

But our magazine has no monopoly on writers or ② newsprint or insights on computers. Firms can enter the industry by hiring an editor, having a bright new idea and logo, locating a printer, and hiring workers. Since the computer magazine industry is profitable, entrepreneurs bring new computer magazines into the market. With their introduction, the demand curve for the products of existing monopolistically competitive computer magazines shifts leftward as the new magazines nibble away at our magazine's market.

The ultimate outcome is that computer magazines will continue to enter the market until all economic profits (including the appropriate opportunity costs for owners' time, talent, and contributed capital) have been beaten down to zero. Figure 10-4 shows the final long-run equilibrium for the typical seller.

In equilibrium, the demand is reduced or shifted to the left until the new $d'd'$ demand curve just touches (but never goes above) the firm's AC curve. Point G' is a long-run equilibrium for the industry because profits are zero and no one is tempted to enter or forced to exit the industry.

This analysis is well illustrated by the personal computer industry. Originally, such computer manufacturers as Apple and Compaq made big profits. [6] But the personal computer industry turned out to have low barriers to entry, and numerous small firms entered the market. Today, there are dozens of firms,
[3] each with a small share of the computer market but no economic profits to show for its efforts.

The monopolistic competition model provides ⑦ an important insight into American capitalism: The rate of profit will in the long run be zero in this kind of imperfectly competitive industry as firms enter with new differentiated products.

② 但是，我们的杂志并没有对作者、报刊以及对计算机行业深度观察分析形成垄断。企业只要聘用好编辑、拥有崭新的观点和形象、找好印刷厂商、雇佣好工作人员，就可以进入这个行业。由于计算机类的杂志利润比较可观，所以会有企业家们将新的计算机类杂志投放市场。随着这些杂志的进入，并一点一滴地蚕食掉我们杂志的市场份额，已存在的处于垄断竞争状态的计算机类杂志的需求曲线就会向左移动。

[3] 16~18 版中的本段内容列举的均是垂钓类杂志的例子，本版的修订更贴近了当今国际社会的现状，更具现实性。

---

① 图 10-3. 垄断竞争生产许多类似的产品

④ 图 10-4. 众多垄断竞争者的自由进入冲抵了我们的利润

⑤ 在长期均衡下，价格始终高于 MC，同时，每一家生产商均处于其长期 AC 曲线左端的下降部分。

[6] Compaq：Compaq Computer Corporation，康柏计算机公司，始建于 1982 年，曾经是全球最大的个人计算机供应商，2002 年被惠普以 250 亿美元并购，产品均以 Hewlett-Packard Compaq 这一新的品牌投放。

⑦ 垄断竞争的模式给我们提供了一个深入思考美国式资本主义的素材，即随着投放新的差异化产品的企业进入，处于这种不完全竞争环境下的产业，其长期的利润率将为零。

In the long-run equilibrium for monopolistic ① competition, prices are above marginal costs but economic profits have been driven down to zero.

Critics of capitalism argue that monopolistic competition is inherently inefficient. They point to an excessive number of trivially different products that lead to wasteful duplication and expense. To understand the reasoning, look back at the long-run equilibrium price at G' in Figure 10-4. At that point, price is above marginal cost and output is reduced below the ideal competitive level.

This economic critique of monopolistic competition has considerable appeal: It takes real ingenuity to demonstrate the gains to human welfare from adding Apple Cinnamon Cheerios to Honey Nut Cheerios and Whole Grain Cheerios. It is hard to see the reason for gasoline stations on every corner of an intersection.

But there is logic to the differentiated goods and ② services produced by a modern market economy. The great variety of products fills many niches in consumer tastes and needs. Reducing the number of monopolistic competitors might lower consumer welfare because it would reduce the diversity of available products. People will pay a premium to be free to choose among various options.

寡头之间的竞争
Rivalry among the Few

For our third example of imperfect competition, we turn back to markets in which only a few firms compete. This time, instead of focusing on collusion, we consider the fascinating case where firms have a strategic interaction with each other. Strategic interaction is found in any market which has relatively few competitors. Like a tennis player trying to outguess her opponent, each business must ask how its rivals will react to changes in key business decisions. If GE introduces a new model of refrigerator, what [3] will Whirlpool, its principal rival, do? If American Airlines lowers its transcontinental fares, how will United react? [4]

Consider as an example the market for air shuttle services between New York and Washington, currently served by Delta and US Airways. This mar- ⑤ ket is called a **duopoly** because industry output is produced by only two firms. Suppose that Delta has determined that if it cuts fares 10 percent, its profits will rise as long as US Airways does not match its cut [6] but its profits will fall if US Airways does match its price cut. If they cannot collude, Delta must make an educated guess as to how US Airways will respond to its price moves. Its best approach would be to ⑦ estimate how US Airways would react to each of its actions and then to maximize profits *with strategic interaction recognized.* This analysis is the province of game theory, discussed in Section B of this chapter.

⑦ 其最好的方法是估计全美航空公司对其每一项举措的反应，然后应用已被证明有效的策略互动来实现利润最大化。

Similar strategic interactions are found in many large industries: in television, in automobiles, even in economics textbooks. Unlike the simple approaches of monopoly and perfect competition, it turns out that there is no simple theory to explain how oligopolists behave. Different cost and demand structures, different industries, even different managerial temperaments will lead to different strategic interactions and to different pricing strategies. Sometimes, the best behavior is to introduce some randomness into the response simply to keep the opposition off balance.

Competition among the few introduces a com- ⑧ pletely new feature into economic life: It forces firms to take into account competitors' reactions to price and output decisions and brings strategic considerations into their markets.

⑧ 少数企业之间的相互竞争将一种全新的特征引入到了经济生活之中，它迫使企业考虑竞争对手对价格和产量决策的反应，同时引发对市场的战略性思考。

价格歧视
PRICE DISCRIMINATION

When firms have market power, they can sometimes increase their profits through price discrimination. **Price discrimination** occurs when the same ⑨ product is sold to different consumers for different prices.

⑨ **价格歧视**系指同样的产品以不同的价格卖给不同的消费者。

Consider the following example: You run a company selling a successful personal-finance program called MyMoney. Your marketing manager comes in and says:

> Look, boss. Our market research shows that our buyers fall into two categories: (1) our current customers, who are locked into MyMoney because they keep their financial records using our program, and (2) potential new buyers who have been using other programs. Why don't we raise our price, but give a ⑩ rebate to new customers who are willing to switch from our competitors? I've run the numbers. If we raise our price from $20 to $30 but give a $15 rebate for people who have been using other financial programs, we will make a bundle.

⑩ 我们在对有意愿投向我们竞争对手的新客户给予折扣的同时，为何不能对老客户提高价格？我算了一笔账。如果我们将价格从20美元提高到30美元的同时，给予一直在使用其他财务软件的客户15美元的折扣，我们就可以赚到一大笔的利润。

---

① 在垄断竞争的长期均衡下，价格高于边际成本，但经济利润已经猛跌到零。

② 但是，由现代市场经济所生产出来的差异产品和服务是合乎逻辑的。丰富多样的产品满足了消费者各种各样的品位和需求。垄断竞争者数量的减少降低了消费者的福利。这是因为它降低了已有产品的多样性。人们愿意在不同选择中通过支付较高的价格来自由地选择商品。

[3] GE：General Electric Company，通用电气公司，全球最大的有能力提供多元化服务的公司，从飞机发动机、发电设备、金融服务、医疗造影、电视节目到塑料等领域均能提供高质量和高科技含量的产品。

[4] United：United Airlines, Inc.，美国联合航空公司，其重要基地为芝加哥奥黑尔国际机场。

⑤ 由于该行业的产品只由两家公司提供，所以，这一市场被称作**双头垄断市场**。

[6] US Airways：美国合众航空公司，台湾译作全美航空公司，美国第六大航空公司。

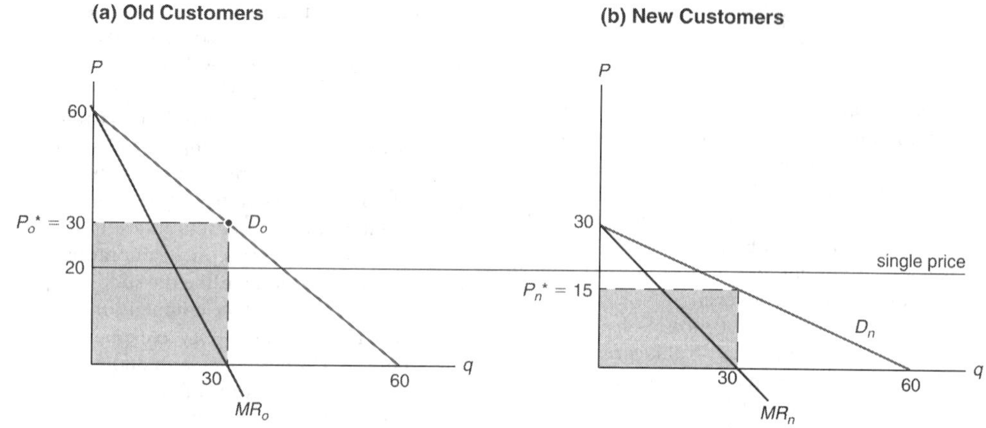

① 图 10-5. 企业可以通过价格歧视手段来增加利润

FIGURE 10-5. Firms Can Increase Their Profits through Price Discrimination ①

You are a profit-maximizing monopoly seller of computer software with zero marginal cost. Your market contains established customers in **(a)** and new customers in **(b)**. Old customers have more inelastic demand because of the high costs of switching to other programs.

If you must set a single price, you will maximize profits at a price of \$20 and earn profits of \$1200. But suppose you can segment your market between locked-in current users and reluctant new buyers. This would increase your profits to (\$30 × 30) + (\$15 × 30) = \$1350.

② 你或许为这样的谏言感到好奇。经济顾问为你勾画出了如图 5 所示的需求曲线。她的研究表明，你的老客户比起你的潜在新客户来讲，具有更小的价格弹性，这是因为新的客户必须要实质性地支付转移成本。如果你的折扣计划能够发挥作用，并且成功地细分了市场，那么上述一组数字显示，你的利润将从 1 200 美元上升到 1 350 美元。

You are intrigued by the suggestion. Your house ② economist constructs the demand curves in Figure 10-5. Her research indicates that your old customers have more price-inelastic demand than your potential new customers because new customers must pay substantial switching costs. If your rebate program works and you succeed in segmenting the market, the numbers show that your profits will rise from \$1200 to \$1350. (To make sure you understand the analysis, use the data shown in Figure 10-5 to estimate the monopoly price and profits if you set a single monopoly price and if you price-discriminate between the two markets.)

Price discrimination is widely used today, particularly with goods that are not easily transferred from the low-priced market to the high-priced market. Here are some examples:

- Identical textbooks are sold at lower prices in ③ Europe than in the United States. What prevents wholesalers from purchasing large quantities abroad and undercutting the domestic market? A protectionist import quota prohibits the practice. However, as an individual, you might well reduce the costs of your books by buying them abroad through online bookstores.
- Airlines are the masters of price discrimina- ④ tion (review our discussion of "Elasticity Air" in Chapter 4). They segment the market by pricing tickets differently for those who travel in peak or off-peak times, for those who are business or pleasure travelers, and for those who are willing to stand by. This allows them to fill their planes without eroding revenues.
- Local utilities often use "two-part prices" (some- ⑤ times called nonlinear prices) to recover some of their overhead costs. If you look at your telephone or electricity bill, it will generally have a "connection" price and a "per-unit" price of service. Because connection is much more price-inelastic than the per-unit price, such two-part pricing allows sellers to lower their per-unit prices and increase the total quantity sold.
- Firms engaged in international trade often ⑥ find that foreign demand is more elastic than domestic demand. They will therefore sell at

③ 同样的教科书在欧洲的售价就要比在美国的售价便宜很多。是什么原因阻止了批发商大量地从国外进口，从而降低国内市场的价格？是贸易保护主义进口配额在作祟。

④ 航空公司都是使用价格歧视手段的行家里手（请参阅第 4 章中关于"弹性机票"的讨论）。它们通过给那些高峰或者非高峰时段的不同旅客、商务人士和普通游客，以及专事等候廉价机票的旅客定不同的票价细分航空市场。这样就使它们在不影响利润的前提下保证了航班的上座率。

⑤ 地方性的公用事业常常使用"双轨制的价格"（有时叫做非线性价格）来弥补某些行政成本。

⑥ 从事国际贸易的企业常常会发现，国际市场的需求比国内的需求更富有弹性。因此，在国际市场上它们以低于国内市场的价格销售。这样的市场行为称作"倾销"，有的时候是被国际贸易协定所禁止的。

lower prices abroad than at home. This practice is called "dumping" and is sometimes banned under international-trade agreements.

- Sometimes a company will actually *degrade* its top- ①
of-the-line product to make a less capable product, which it will then sell at a discounted price to capture a low-price market. For example, IBM inserted special commands to slow down its laser printer from 10 pages per minute to 5 pages per minute so that it could sell the slow model at a lower price without cutting into sales of its top model.

What are the economic effects of price discrimination? Surprisingly, they often improve economic welfare. To understand this point, recall that monopolists raise their price and lower their sales to increase profits. In doing so, they may capture the market for eager buyers but lose the market for reluctant buyers. By charging different prices for those willing to ②
pay high prices (who get charged high prices) and those willing to pay only lower prices (who may sit in the middle seats or get a degraded product, but at a lower price), the monopolist can increase both its profits and consumer satisfactions.[1]

博弈论

B. GAME THEORY

Strategic thinking is the art of outdoing an adversary, knowing that the adversary is trying to do the same to you.

Avinash Dixit and Barry Nalebuff,
Thinking Strategically (1991)

Economic life is full of situations in which people or firms or countries compete for profits or dominance. The oligopolies that we analyzed in the previous section sometimes break out into economic warfare. Such rivalry was seen in the last century when Vanderbilt and Drew repeatedly cut shipping rates on their parallel railroads. In recent years, airlines would occasionally launch price wars to attract customers and sometimes end up ruining everyone (see this chapter's introductory quote). But airlines learned that they needed to think and act strategically. Before an airline cuts its fares, it needs to consider how its rivals will react, and how it should then react to that reaction, and so on.

Once decisions reach the stage of thinking about ④
what your opponent is thinking, and how you would then react, you are in the world of *game theory*. This is the analysis of situations involving two or more interacting decision makers who have conflicting objectives. Consider the following findings of game theorists in the area of imperfect competition:

- As the number of noncooperative oligopolists ⑤
becomes large, the industry price and quantity tend toward the perfectly competitive outcome.
- If firms succeed in colluding, the market price and quantity will be close to those generated by a monopoly.
- Experiments suggest that as the number of firms increases, collusive agreements become more difficult to police and the frequency of cheating and noncooperative behavior increases.
- In many situations, there is no stable equilibrium for an oligopolistic market. Strategic interplay may lead to unstable outcomes as firms threaten, bluff, start price wars, punish weak opponents, signal their intentions, or simply exit from the market.

[3] **Game theory** analyzes the ways in which two or more players choose strategies that jointly affect each other. This theory, which sounds frivolous, is in fact fraught with significance and was largely developed
by John von Neumann (1903–1957), a Hungarian- [6]
born mathematical genius. Game theory has been used by economists to study the interaction of oligopolists, union-management disputes, countries' trade policies, international environmental agreements, reputations, and a host of other topics.

Game theory offers insights for politics and warfare, as well as for everyday life. For example, game theory suggests that in some circumstances a carefully chosen random pattern of behavior may be the best strategy. Inspections to catch illegal drugs or weapons should sometimes search randomly rather than
predictably. Likewise, you should occasionally bluff ⑦
at poker, not simply to win a pot with a weak hand but also to ensure that other players do not drop out

[1] For an example of how perfect price discrimination improves efficiency, see question 3 at the end of this chapter.

[3] 博弈论这一节在此前的16~18版中均与"不确定性"问题合在一起作为单独的第11章出现。本版因应了金融危机的教训，将第10章中惯有的B节"创新与信息"内容基本删除。同时，将原在第11章中重点讨论的"博弈论"问题提前，在本章中结合18版出版后5年来全球经济和政治局势的发展，将原有内容和数据做了大量的修订和更新，进行了更为详尽的论述。C节的标题"不完全竞争中的损益问题"（*A Balance Sheet on Imperfect Competition*）也因应形势，改成了"公共政策与市场力量的搏击"（*Public Policies to Combat Market Power*）。

Avinash Dixit：阿维纳什·迪克西特，印度裔的美国经济学家，1944年出生于孟买。

Barry Nalebuff：巴里·奈勒波夫，1958年出生，耶鲁大学管理学院教授。

本段文字出自两人合著的《策略性思考》（*Thinking Strategically*）一书前言中的第一段，该书的副标题是《商业和政治活动以及日常生活中的竞争艺术》（*The Competitive Edge in Business, Politics and Everyday Life*）。

纵观全段上下文，试译如下：

策略性思考是一门克敌制胜的艺术，要知道对手也在设法运用同样的方法来对付你。

⑦ 同理，一个人在牌桌上也偶尔需要一点策略，这不仅仅是为手拿一付弱牌赢得一局而已，而且是为在手拿一手好牌下了大赌注之后，要确保其他的牌手中途辍牌。在本节中我们将就博弈论中的某些主要概念展开来进行讨论。

① 有时公司会降低其顶级产品的级别来生产删掉了某些功能的产品，这样的结果就可以以折扣后的价格来占领低端市场。

② 通过对那些愿意支付高价格的消费者（支付高价格的顾客）和愿意支付低价格的消费者（或支付中等价格，或者购买降低了级别的产品，但必须是低价格）制定不同的价格，垄断者既提高了消费者的满意度又增加了利润。

④ 只要对对手所想了如指掌，并随之思考如何做出反应的时候，你就进入了博弈论的领域。这就是对形势——涉及两个以上决策者的互动，他们有相互冲突的目标——的分析。

⑤
- 随着非合作寡头数量变得庞大起来，该行业的价格和产量趋向于呈现完全竞争的态势。
- 如果各企业成功地达成了共谋，市场价格和产量就会接近垄断状态的水平。
- 实践表明，随着企业数量的增加，共谋协议会变得越来越困难，欺诈和非合作行为也会增加。
- 在大多数情况下，寡头市场不会存在稳定均衡。同时，由于企业间的威胁、欺诈、发动价格战、伤害比自己弱的竞争对手、暗示自己的意图，以及轻易地退出市场等策略互动导致出现极不稳定的结果。

[6] John von Neumann：约翰·冯·诺伊曼，匈牙利出生的美国籍犹太数学家，现代电子计算机和博弈论之父，在量子力学以及几乎所有数学领域都做出过重大贡献。

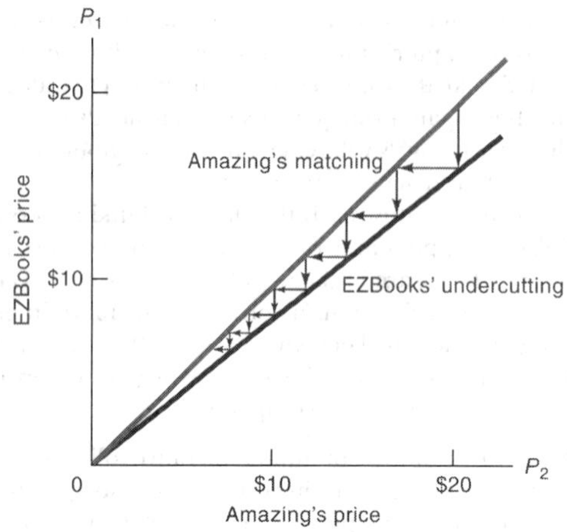

FIGURE 10-6. What Happens When Two Firms Insist on Undercutting Each Other? ①

Trace through the steps by which dynamic price cutting leads to ever-lower prices for two rivals.

when you bet high on a good hand. We will sketch out some of the major concepts of game theory in this section.

定价策略

Thinking about Price Setting

② 让我们先从分析动态的竞相降价开始。假设你是已成立的 Amazing.com 公司的老板，该公司信奉“我们绝不以低于市价售出。”但是，当你打开浏览器会发现，一家网上书店的新锐 EZBooks.com 公司的广告词竟也类似：“所售图书，一律九折”。（Amazing.com 和 EZBooks.com 均为通过互联网销售图书与影像类产品的公司。）

Let's begin by analyzing the dynamics of price ② cutting. You are the head of an established firm, Amazing.com, whose motto is "We will not be undersold." You open your browser and discover that EZBooks.com, an upstart Internet bookseller, has an advertisement that says, "We sell for 10 percent less." Figure 10-6 shows the dynamics. The vertical arrows show EZBooks' price cuts; the horizontal arrows show Amazing's responding strategy of matching each price cut.

By tracing through the pattern of reaction and counterreaction, you can see that this kind of rivalry will end in mutual ruin at a zero price. Why? Because the only price compatible with both strategies is a price of zero: 90 percent of zero is zero.

Finally, it dawns on the two firms: When one firm cuts its price, the other firm will match the price cut. Only if the firms are shortsighted will they think that they can undercut each other for long. Soon each begins to ask, What will my rival do if I cut my price, or raise my price, or leave it alone? *Once you begin* ③ *to consider how others will react to your actions, you have entered the realm of game theory.*

基本概念

BASIC CONCEPTS

We will illustrate the basic concepts of game theory ④ by analyzing a **duopoly price game.** A duopoly is a market which is served by only two firms. For simplicity, we assume that each firm has the same cost and demand structure. Further, each firm can choose whether to charge its normal price or lower its price below marginal costs and try to drive its rival into bankruptcy and then capture the entire market. The novel element in the duopoly game is that the firm's profits will depend on its rival's strategy as well as on its own.

A useful tool for representing the interaction ⑤ between two firms or people is a two-way **payoff table.** A payoff table is a means of showing the strategies and the payoffs of a game between two players. Figure 10-7 shows the payoffs in the duopoly price game for our two companies. In the payoff table, a firm can choose between the strategies listed in its rows or columns. For example, EZBooks can choose between its two columns and Amazing can choose between its two rows. In this example, each firm decides whether to charge its normal price or to start a price war by choosing a lower price.

Combining the two decisions of each duopolist gives four possible outcomes, which are shown in the four cells of the table. Cell A, at the upper left, shows the outcome when both firms choose the normal price; D is the outcome when both choose to conduct a price war; and B and C result when one firm has a normal price and one a war price.

The numbers inside the cells show the **payoffs** of the two firms, that is, the profits earned by each firm for each of the four outcomes. The number in the lower left shows the payoff to the player on the left (Amazing); the entry in the upper right shows the payoff to the player at the top (EZBooks). Because the firms are identical, the payoffs are mirror images.

其他策略

Alternative Strategies

Now that we have described the basic structure of a game, we next consider the behavior of the players. The new element in game theory is analyzing ⑥ not only your own actions but also the interaction

---

① 图 10-6. 两家企业竞相降价时出现的情况

③ 一旦你开始思考他人会如何就你的行动做出反应时，你就已经进入了博弈论的领地。

④ 我们将通过对**双头垄断的价格博弈**的分析来阐明博弈论的基本概念。双头垄断指的是只有两家企业为市场提供服务的市场。

⑤ 代表两家企业或者个人互动的有用工具是双向**损益表**。这是一种表示参与博弈的双方之间策略互动和相互支付状况的手段。

⑥ 博弈论中的新元素是不仅要分析己方的行为，而且要分析自己的目标、行为与竞争对手目标、行为的互动。试图瞒骗你的竞争对手的过程中，你要始终记得你的竞争对手也在试图瞒骗你。

A Price War

Amazing's price	EZBooks' price: Normal price*	EZBooks' price: Price war
Normal price*	A† $10 $10	B −$100 −$10
Price war	C −$10 −$100	D −$50 −$50

* Dominant strategy
† Dominant equilibrium

FIGURE 10-7. A Payoff Table for a Price War ①

The payoff table shows the payoffs associated with different strategies. Amazing has a choice between two strategies, shown as its two rows; EZBooks can choose between its two strategies, shown as two columns. The entries in the cells show the profits for the two players. For example, in cell C, Amazing plays "price war" and EZBooks plays "normal price." The result is that Amazing has green profit of −$100 while EZBooks has blue profit of −$10. Thinking through the best strategies for each player leads to the dominant equilibrium in cell A.

between your goals and moves and those of your opponent. But in trying to outwit your opponent, you must always remember that your opponent is trying to outwit you.

The guiding philosophy in game theory is the following: Pick your strategy by asking what makes most sense for you assuming that your opponents are analyzing your strategy and doing what is best for them. ②

Let's apply this maxim to the duopoly example. First, note that our two firms have the highest joint profits in outcome A. Each firm earns $10 when both follow a normal-price strategy. At the other extreme is the price war, where each cuts its price and runs a big loss.

In between are two interesting strategies where only one firm engages in the price war. In outcome C, for example, EZBooks follows a normal-price strategy while Amazing engages in a price war. Amazing takes most of the market but loses a great deal of money because it is selling below cost; EZBooks is actually better off selling at a normal price rather than responding.

Dominant Strategy. In considering possible strategies, the simplest case is that of a **dominant strategy.** ③ This situation arises when one player has a single best strategy *no matter what strategy the other player follows.*

In our price-war game, for example, consider the options open to Amazing. If EZBooks conducts business as usual with a normal price, Amazing will get $10 of profit if it plays the normal price and will lose $100 if it declares economic war. On the other hand, if EZBooks starts a war, Amazing will lose $10 if it follows the normal price but will lose even more if it also engages in economic warfare. You can see that the same reasoning holds for EZBooks. Therefore, ④ no matter what strategy the other firm follows, each firm's best strategy is to have the normal price. *Charging the normal price is a dominant strategy for both firms in this particular price-war game.*

④ 因此，无论其他企业跟进的是何种策略，每一家企业的最佳决策都应该是按照正常的价格销售。在此类特殊的价格战的博弈中，正常价格对于参与博弈的两家企业是占优策略。

When both (or all) players have a dominant strategy, we say that the outcome is a **dominant equilibrium.** ⑤ We can see that in Figure 10-7, outcome A is a dominant equilibrium because it arises from a situation where both firms are playing their dominant strategies.

Nash Equilibrium. Most interesting situations do not ⑥ have a dominant equilibrium, and we must therefore look further. We can use our duopoly example to

① 图 10-7. 价格战的损益表
② 博弈论的指导思想是：通过不时地提醒自己，假想竞争对手正在分析我方策略并采取了最有利于他们的行为，那么我们如何做才是最合理的，此为上策。
③ **占优策略**：在考虑可能的策略时，最简单方法即所谓的**占优策略**决策法。无论另一方采取什么样的策略，一方都有惟一一个最佳策略，就是占优策略。
⑤ 当参与博弈的双方（或者所有参与博弈的各方）有占优策略时，我们说最后的结果是实现**占优策略均衡**。
⑥ **纳什均衡**：大多数有意思的博弈局面都没有占优策略均衡，为此，我们必须要做进一步的研究。上面所举的双头垄断的例子就是一个可以探讨的案例。我们把它称作**敌对博弈**。在这一案例中，每一家企业都在考虑是按照正常价格来定价，还是将其价格提高到垄断价格水平，从而尽可能地赚取垄断利润。

The Rivalry Game

Amazing's price	EZBooks' price: High price	EZBooks' price: Normal price*
High price	A $200 / $100	B $150 / −$20
Normal price*	C −$30 / $150	D* $10 / $10

* Nash equilibrium

FIGURE 10-8. Should a Duopolist Try the Monopoly Price? ①

In the rivalry game, each firm can earn $10 by staying at its normal price. If both raise price to the high monopoly level, their joint profits will be maximized. However, each firm's temptation to "cheat" and raise its profits by lowering price ensures that the normal-price Nash equilibrium will prevail in the absence of collusion.

explore this case. In this example, which we call the *rivalry game,* each firm considers whether to charge its normal price or to raise its price toward the monopoly price and try to earn monopoly profits.

The rivalry game is shown in Figure 10-8. The firms can stay at their normal-price equilibrium, which we found in the price-war game. Or they can raise their price in the hopes of earning monopoly profits. Our two firms have the highest *joint* profits in cell A; here they earn a total of $300 when each follows a high-price strategy. Situation A would surely come about if the firms could collude and set the monopoly price. At the other extreme is the competitive-style strategy of the normal price, where each rival has profits of $10.

In between are two interesting strategies where one firm chooses a normal-price and one a high-price strategy. In cell C, for example, EZBooks follows a high-price strategy but Amazing undercuts. Amazing takes most of the market and has the highest profit of any situation, while EZBooks actually loses money. In cell B, Amazing gambles on high price, but EZBooks' normal price means a loss for Amazing.

Amazing has a dominant strategy in this new game. It will always have a higher profit by choosing a normal price. On the other hand, the best strategy for EZBooks depends upon what Amazing does. EZBooks would want to play normal if Amazing plays normal and would want to play high if Amazing plays high.

This leaves EZBooks with a dilemma: Should it play high and hope that Amazing will follow suit? Or play safe? Here is where game theory becomes useful. EZBooks should choose its strategy by first putting itself in Amazing's shoes. By doing so, EZBooks will find that Amazing should play normal regardless of what EZBooks does because playing normal is Amazing's dominant strategy. EZBooks should assume that Amazing will follow its best strategy and play normal, which therefore means that EZBooks should play normal. *This illustrates the basic* ② *rule of game theory: You should choose your strategy based on the assumption that your opponents will act in their own best interest.*

The approach we have described is a deep con- ③ cept known as the **Nash equilibrium,** named after [4] mathematician John Nash, who won a Nobel Prize for his discovery. In a Nash equilibrium, no player can gain anything by changing his own strategy, given the other player's strategy. The Nash equilibrium is also sometimes called the **noncooperative equilibrium** because each party chooses the strategy which is best for himself—without collusion or cooperation and without regard for the welfare of society or any other party.

Let us take a simple example: Assume that other people drive on the right-hand side of the road. What is your best strategy? Clearly, unless you are suicidal, you should also drive on the right-hand side. Moreover, a situation where everyone drives on the right-hand side is a Nash equilibrium: as long as everybody else is driving on the right-hand side, it will not be in anybody's interest to start driving on the left-hand side.

[Here is a technical definition of the Nash equilibrium for the advanced student: Suppose

[4] 约翰·福布斯·纳什（John Nash），1928年生，美国数学家，博弈论大师，1994年与另外两位博弈论学者约翰·豪尔沙尼（John Harsanyi，1920~2000）和莱因哈德·塞尔腾（Reinhard Selten，1930~）共同获得了当年的诺贝尔经济学奖。2005年6月1日，纳什应邀出席《诺贝尔经济学奖得主北京论坛》。在故宫东侧菖蒲河公园内的东苑戏楼闭幕以及隆重的晚宴结束之后，纳什婉拒了主办方安排的专车，像一个普普通通的北京老人，踽踽独行地走出了东苑戏楼，在菖蒲河公园到南河沿大街的暮色中渐渐远去。这似乎应该是电影《美丽心灵》（*A Beautiful Mind*，2002年获奥斯卡最佳影片奖，纳什的传记艺术片）结尾的一组特写镜头。这就是约翰·纳什。

① 图10-8. 双头垄断者应该寻求垄断价格吗？

② 这说明了博弈论的基本法则：你应该基于竞争对手会按照自身利益最大化的假设选择你的策略。

③ 我们所讨论的这一方法是一个深奥的概念，即著名的**纳什均衡**，它以数学家约翰·纳什的名字命名。约翰·纳什也因这一发现而获诺贝尔经济学奖。在纳什均衡中，在给定其他参与者策略的条件下，没有参与者能够通过改变自己的策略而获益。由于参与各方都选择对自身而言最优的策略——没有共谋或合作，也不考虑社会福利或任何其他方。因此，纳什均衡有时也被称为**非合作均衡**。

that player A picks strategy S_A* while player B picks strategy S_B*. The pair of strategies (S_A*, S_B*) is a Nash equilibrium if neither player can find a better strategy to play assuming that the other player sticks to his original strategy. This discussion focuses on two-person games, but the analysis, and particularly the important Nash equilibrium, can be usefully extended to many-person or "*n*-person" games.]

You should verify that the starred strategies in Figure 10-8 constitute a Nash equilibrium. That is, neither player can improve its payoffs from the (normal, normal) equilibrium as long as the other doesn't change its strategy. Verify that the dominant equilibrium shown in Figure 10-7 is also a Nash equilibrium.

The Nash equilibrium (also called the noncooperative equilibrium) is one of the most important concepts of game theory and is widely used in economics and the other social sciences. Suppose that each player in a game has chosen a best strategy (the one with the highest payoff) *assuming* that all the other players keep their strategies unchanged. An outcome where all players follow this strategy is called a Nash equilibrium. Game theorists have shown that a competitive equilibrium is a Nash equilibrium. ①

博弈无处不在

Games, Games, Everywhere . . .

The insights of game theory pervade economics, the social sciences, business, and everyday life. In economics, for example, game theory can help explain trade wars as well as price wars.

Game theory can also suggest why foreign competition may lead to greater price competition. What happens when Chinese or Japanese firms enter a U.S. market where domestic firms had tacitly colluded on a strategy that led to high oligopolistic prices? The foreign firms may "refuse to play the game." They did not agree to the rules, so they may cut prices to increase their share of the market. Collusion among the domestic firms may break down because they must lower prices to compete effectively with the foreign firms.

A key feature in many games is the attempt on behalf of players to build *credibility*. You are credible if you can be expected to keep your promises and carry out your threats. But you cannot gain credibility simply by making promises. Credibility must be consistent with the incentives of the game.

How can you gain credibility? Here are some examples: Central banks earn reputations for being tough on inflation by adopting politically unpopular policies. Even greater credibility comes when the central bank is independent of the elected branches. Businesses make credible promises by writing contracts that inflict penalties if they do not perform as promised. A more perilous strategy is for an army to burn its bridges behind it. Because there is no retreat, the threat that they will fight to the death is a credible one.

The short discussion here provides a tiny peek at the vast terrain of game theory. This area has been enormously useful in helping economists and other social scientists think about situations where small numbers of people are well informed and try to outwit each other. Students who go on in economics, business, management, and even national security will find that using game theory can help them think strategically.

公共政策对市场的削弱

C. PUBLIC POLICIES TO COMBAT MARKET POWER

Economic analysis shows that monopolies produce economic waste. How significant are these inefficiencies? What can public policy do to reduce monopolistic harms? We address these two questions in this final section.

不完全竞争的经济成本

ECONOMIC COSTS OF IMPERFECT COMPETITION

物价上涨与产出降低的成本

The Cost of Inflated Prices and Reduced Output

Our analysis has shown how imperfect competitors reduce output and raise prices, thereby producing less (and charging more) than would be forthcoming in a perfectly competitive industry. This can be seen most clearly for monopoly, which is the most extreme version of imperfect competition. To see ②
how and why monopoly keeps output too low, imagine that all other industries are efficiently organized. In such a world, price is the correct economic standard or measure of scarcity; price measures both the marginal utility of consumption to households and the marginal cost of production to firms.

credibility
信用，信誉

① 纳什均衡（也称非合作性均衡）是博弈论最重要的概念之一，它在经济学和其他社会科学领域有着极其广泛的应用。在一场博弈中，假设参与博弈的每一方在其余各方均保持策略不变的前提下，选择了最佳策略（该决策有最高的收益）。这种所有博弈方全部跟随这一策略的结果就叫做纳什均衡。博弈理论家已证明，竞争均衡即纳什均衡。

② 为了弄明白垄断是如何将产量保持在极低的水平，以及垄断为什么将产量保持在极低的水平，需要假设所有的其他产业均是有效组织的。在这样的环境中，价格是正确的经济标准，或者稀缺指标；家庭消费的边际效用也衡量了企业生产的边际成本。

Now Monopoly Inc. enters the picture. A monopolist is not a wicked firm—it doesn't rob people or force its goods down consumers' throats. Rather, Monopoly Inc. exploits the fact that it is the sole seller and raises its price above marginal cost (i.e., $P > MC$). Since $P = MC$ is necessary for economic efficiency, the marginal value of the good to consumers is therefore above its marginal cost. The same is true for oligopoly and monopolistic competition, as long as companies hold prices above marginal cost.

[1] 不完全竞争的静态成本（本节在16~18版的题目只单一地介绍了对不完全竞争带来损失的测量，即将 *Measuring the Waste from* 改为 *The Static Costs of*，系作者对金融危机的反思。）

不完全竞争的静态成本

The Static Costs of Imperfect Competition

We can depict the efficiency losses from imperfect competition by using a simplified version of our monopoly diagram, here shown in Figure 10-9.

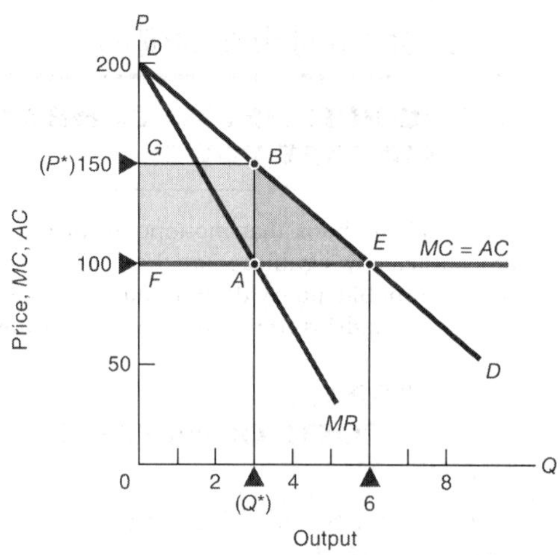

② 图 10-9. 由于垄断者限制产量而导致的经济浪费

FIGURE 10-9. Monopolists Cause Economic Waste by Restricting Output ②

Monopolists make their output scarce and thereby drive up price and increase profits. If the industry were competitive, equilibrium would be at point *E*, where economic surplus is maximized.

At the monopolist's output at point *B* (with $Q = 3$ and $P = 150$), price is above *MC*, and consumer surplus is lost. Adding together all the consumer-surplus losses between $Q = 3$ and $Q = 6$ leads to economic waste from monopoly equal to the blue shaded area *ABE*. In addition, the monopolist has monopoly profits (that would have been consumer surplus) given by the green shaded region *GBAF*.

If the industry were perfectly competitive, the equilibrium would be reached at point *E*, where $P = MC$. Under universal perfect competition, this industry's quantity would be 6 with a price of 100.

Now consider the impact of monopoly. The monopoly might be created by a foreign-trade tariff or quota, by a labor union which monopolizes the supply of labor, or by a patent on a new product. The monopolist would set its *MC* equal to *MR* (not to industry *P*), displacing the equilibrium to
[1] the lower $Q = 3$ and the higher $P = 150$ in Figure 10-9. The area *GBAF* is the monopolist's profit, which compares with a zero-profit competitive equilibrium.

The inefficiency loss from monopoly is some- ③
times called **deadweight loss.** This term refers to the loss of economic welfare arising from distortions in prices and output such as those due to monopoly, as well as those due to taxation, tariffs, or quotas. Consumers might enjoy a great deal of consumer surplus if a new anti-pain drug is sold at marginal cost; however, if a firm monopolizes the product, consumers will lose more surplus than the monopolist will gain. That net loss in economic welfare is called deadweight loss.

We can picture the deadweight loss from a monopoly diagrammatically in Figure 10-9. Point *E* is the efficient level of production at which $P = MC$. For each unit that the monopolist reduces output below *E*, the efficiency loss is the vertical distance
between the demand curve and the *MC* curve. The ④
total deadweight loss from the monopolist's output restriction is the sum of all such losses, represented by the blue triangle *ABE*.

The technique of measuring the costs of market imperfections by "little triangles" of deadweight loss, such as the one in Figure 10-9, can be applied to most situations where output and price deviate from the competitive levels.

This cost calculation is sometimes called the ⑤
"static cost" of monopoly. It is static because it assumes that the technology for producing output is unchanging. Some economists believe that imperfect competitors may have "dynamic benefits" if they generate more rapid technological change than do perfectly competitive markets. We will return to this question in the next chapter's discussion of innovation.

③ 垄断所带来的无效损失有时被称作**无谓损失**。这一术语系指由于垄断以及税收、关税配额等原因造成的价格和产量的扭曲而带来的经济福利方面的损失。如果一种新镇痛药以边际成本价格出售，消费者就可以享受到大量的消费者剩余。然而，如果有一家企业垄断了该产品，则消费者在剩余上所遭受的损失将远远超过该垄断企业之所得。这种在经济福利方面所遭受的净损失就叫做无谓损失。

④ 由垄断者限制产量所造成的总的无谓损失是所有这些损失之和，即图中三角形 *ABE* 所表示的面积。

⑤ 这样计算出来的成本有时叫做垄断的“静态成本”。这里所讲静态的假设前提是，生产产品的技术不会发生变化。有的经济学家认为，如果参与不完全竞争者比起完全竞争状态的市场环境以更快的速度进行技术更新，则他们可以获得动态收益。我们将在下一章关于创新的讨论中再进一步探讨这个问题。

不完全竞争的公共政策
Public Policies on Imperfect Competition

How can nations reduce the harmful effects of monopolistic practices? Three approaches are often recommended by economists and legal scholars:

1. Historically, the first tool used by governments ① to control monopolistic practices was economic regulation. As this practice has evolved over the last century, economic regulation now allows specialized regulatory agencies to oversee the prices, outputs, entry, and exit of firms in regulated industries such as public utilities and transportation. It is, in effect, limited government control without government ownership.
2. The major method now used for combating ② excessive market power is the use of antitrust policy. Antitrust policies are laws that prohibit certain kinds of behavior (such as firms' joining together to fix prices) or curb certain market structures (such as pure monopolies and highly concentrated oligopolies).
3. More generally, anticompetitive abuses can be ③ avoided by encouraging competition wherever possible. There are many government policies that can promote vigorous rivalry even among large firms. It is particularly crucial to reduce barriers to entry in all industries. That means encouraging small businesses and not walling off domestic markets from foreign competition.

We will review the first two approaches in the balance of this chapter.

对经济活动的干预
REGULATING ECONOMIC ACTIVITY

Economic regulation of American industry goes back more than a century. The first federal regulation applied to transportation, with the Interstate [4] Commerce Commission (ICC) in 1887. The ICC was designed as much to prevent price wars and to guarantee service to small towns as it was to control monopoly. Later, federal regulation spread to banks in 1913, to electric power in 1920, and to communications, securities markets, labor, trucking, and air travel during the 1930s.

Economic regulation involves the control of prices, entry and exit conditions, and standards of service. Such regulation is most important in industries that are natural monopolies. (Recall that a natural monopoly occurs when the industry's output can be efficiently produced only by a single firm.) Prominent examples of industries regulated today include public utilities (electricity, natural gas, and water) and telecommunications (telephone, radio, cable TV, and more generally the electromagnetic spectrum). The financial industry has been regulated since the 1930s, with strict rules specifying what banks, brokerage firms, and insurance companies can and cannot do. Since 1977, many economic regulations have been loosened or lifted, such as those on the airlines, trucking, and securities firms.

为什么干预产业
Why Regulate Industry?

Regulation restrains the unfettered market power of firms. What are the reasons why governments might choose to override the decisions made in the marketplace? The first reason is to *prevent abuses of market power* by monopolies or oligopolies. A second major reason is to *remedy informational failures*, such as those which occur when consumers have inadequate information. A third reason is to *correct externalities* like pollution. The third of these reasons pertains to social regulation and is examined in the chapter on environmental economics; we review the first two reasons in this section. ⑤

⑤ 首要的原因是防止垄断或者寡头滥用市场力量。第二个主要原因是弥补信息失灵，诸如由于消费者拥有不完全信息而出现的信息失灵。第三个原因是纠正诸如污染的外部性。

遏制市场力量
Containing Market Power

The traditional view is that regulatory measures should be taken to reduce excessive market power. More specifically, governments should regulate industries where there are too few firms to ensure vigorous rivalry, particularly in the extreme case of natural monopoly.

We know from our discussion of declining costs in earlier chapters that pervasive economies of scale are inconsistent with perfect competition; we will find oligopoly or monopoly in such cases. But the point here is even more extreme: *When there are such powerful economies of scale or scope that only one firm can survive, we have a natural monopoly.* ⑥

⑥ 当有强大的规模经济或范围经济，以致只有一家企业幸存时，我们就有了自然垄断。

Why do governments sometimes regulate natural monopolies? They do so because a natural monopolist, enjoying a large cost advantage over its potential competitors and facing price-inelastic demand, can jack up its price sharply, obtain enormous monopoly profits, and create major economic inefficiencies. Hence, regulation allows society to enjoy the benefits

---

① 历史上，政府用来控制垄断行为的首要工具就是经济管制。

② 现在，政府用来抑制市场力量过大的主要办法是使用反托拉斯政策。

③ 从更为一般的意义上讲，通过在任何可能的环境中鼓励竞争的办法就可以避免反竞争措施的滥用。

[4] Interstate Commerce Commission（ICC）：州际商务委员会，美国历史上主要的商务委员会之一，1887 年依据由时任美国总统的格罗弗・克利夫兰（Stephen Grover Cleveland，1837~1908，美国历史上惟一两次任期不相连的总统，1885~1889 的第 22 任和 1893~1897 的第 24 任总统）签署的州际商务法案（Inters-tate Commerce Act of 1887）成立，1995 年撤销，保留功能移交陆上运输委员会（Surface Transportation Board）。

of a natural monopoly while preventing the superhigh prices that might result if it were unregulated. A typical example is local water distribution. The cost of gathering water, building a water-distribution system, and piping water into every home is sufficiently large that it would not pay to have more than one firm provide local water service. This is a natural monopoly. Under economic regulation, a government agency would provide a franchise to a company in a particular region. That company would agree to provide water to all households in that region. The government would review and approve the prices and other terms that the company would then present to its customers.

Another kind of natural monopoly, particularly prevalent in network industries, arises from the requirement for standardization and coordination through the system for efficient operation. Railroads need standard track gauges, electrical transmission requires load balancing, and communications systems require standard codes so that different parts can "talk" to each other.

In earlier times, regulation was justified on the dubious grounds that it was needed to prevent cutthroat or destructive competition. This was one argument for continued control over railroads, trucks, airlines, and buses, as well as for regulation of the level of agricultural production. Economists today have little sympathy for this argument. After all, competition will increase efficiency, and ruinously low prices are exactly what an efficient market system *should* produce. ①

弥补信息失灵

Remedying Information Failures

Consumers often have inadequate information about products in the absence of regulation. For example, testing pharmaceutical drugs is expensive and scientifically complex. The government regulates drugs by allowing only the sale of those drugs which are proved "safe and efficacious." Government also prohibits false and misleading advertising. In both cases, the government is attempting to correct for the market's failure to provide information efficiently on its own.

One area where regulating the provision of information is particularly critical is financial markets. When people buy stocks or bonds of private companies, they are placing their fortunes in the hands of people about whom they know next to nothing. Before buying shares of ZYX.com, I will examine their financial statements to determine what their sales, earnings, and dividends have been. But how can I know exactly how they measure earnings? How can I be sure that they are reporting this information honestly?

This is where government regulation of financial markets steps in. Most regulations of the financial industry serve the purpose of improving the quantity and quality of information so that markets can work better. When a company sells stocks or bonds in the United States, it is required to issue copious documentation of its current financial condition and future prospects. Companies' books must be certified by independent auditors.

Occasionally, particularly in times of speculative frenzies, companies will bend or even break the rules. This happened on a large scale in the late 1990s and early 2000s, particularly in communications and many "high-tech" firms. When these illegal practices were made public, Congress passed a ② [3]
new law in 2002; this law made it illegal to lie to an auditor, established an independent board to oversee accountants, and provided new oversight powers to the Securities and Exchange Commission (SEC). Some argue that this kind of law should be welcomed by honest businesses; tough reporting standards are beneficial to financial markets because they reduce informational asymmetries between buyers and sellers, promote trust, and encourage financial investment.

Stanford's John McMillan uses an interesting [4]
analogy to describe the role of government regulation. Sports are contests in which individuals and teams strive to defeat opponents with all their strength. But the participants must adhere to a set of extremely detailed rules; moreover, referees keep an eagle eye on players to make sure that they obey the rules, with appropriately scaled penalties for infractions. Without carefully crafted rules, a game would turn into a bloody brawl. Similarly, government regulations, along with a strong legal system, are necessary in a modern economy to ensure that overzealous competitors do not monopolize, pollute, defraud, mislead, maim, or otherwise mistreat workers and consumers. This sports analogy reminds us that the government still has an important role to play in monitoring the economy and setting the rules of the road.

[4] 约翰·麦克米伦（John McMillan，1951~2007），新西兰裔的美国经济学家，斯坦福大学教授，56岁时因患癌症英年早逝，生前对中国等新兴经济体以及中国的国有企业做了深入的研究，发表过许多关于中国经济的论文。在《市场演进的故事》（*Reinventing the Bazaar: A Natural History of Markets*）一书中以其与生俱来的讲故事的能力，将复杂的市场设计理论用荷兰阿斯米尔每日壮观的鲜花拍卖、印度的骆驼贸易、日本东京的筑地海产市场等一个个鲜活的故事娓娓道来。

① 总而言之，竞争会提高效率，而灾难性的低价格也的确是一个高效的市场机制的产物。

② 国会在2002年通过了一项新的法案，该法案规定了对审计师撒谎属违法行为，并同时成立了一家独立的机构对会计师的业务实施监督，还赋予证券交易委员会新的监管权。

[3] 此处所谓“新的法案”即2002年7月30日布什总统签署的《萨班斯—奥克斯利法案》（Sarbanes-Oxley Act），是美国国会根据安然公司、世通公司等因财务欺诈事件破产暴露出来的公司和证券监管问题所立的监管法规，简称《SOX法案》或《索克思法案》。

反垄断法与经济意义

ANTITRUST LAW AND ECONOMICS

A second important government tool for promoting ① competition is antitrust law. The purpose of antitrust policies is to provide consumers with the economic benefits of vigorous competition. Antitrust laws attack anticompetitive abuses in two different ways: First, they prohibit certain kinds of *business conduct,* such as price fixing, that restrain competitive forces. Second, they restrict some *market structures,* such as monopolies, that are considered most likely to restrain trade and abuse their economic power in other ways. The framework for antitrust policy was set by a few key legislative statutes and by more than a century of court decisions.

框架条例

The Framework Statutes

Antitrust law is like a huge forest that has grown from a handful of seeds. The statutes on which the law is based are so concise and straightforward that they can be quoted in Table 10-1; it is astounding how much law has grown from so few words.

Sherman Act (1890). Monopolies had long been illegal under the common law, based on custom and past judicial decisions. But the body of laws proved ineffective against the mergers, cartels, and trusts that swept through the American economy in the 1880s. (Reread the section on the monopolists of the Gilded Age in Chapter 9 to get a flavor of the cutthroat tactics of that era.)

In 1890, populist sentiments led to the passage of the Sherman Act, which is the cornerstone of American antitrust law. Section 1 of the Sherman Act prohibits contracts, combinations, and conspiracies "in restraint of trade." Section 2 prohibits "monopolizing" and conspiracies to monopolize. Neither the statute nor the accompanying discussion contained any clear notion about the exact meaning

[2] Sherman Act (1890)：③ 全称为谢尔曼反托拉斯法（Sherman Antitrust Act）1890 年修订案，1890 年获国会通过，以起草人——时任参议院金融委员会主席的俄亥俄州共和党参议员约翰·谢尔曼（John Sherman, 1823~1900）的名字命名。

③ 在过去的很长一段时期里，在以习俗和以往的司法判决为基础的普通法系里，垄断始终被认为是违法的。但有关的法条在处理 19 世纪 80 年代席卷美国经济的企业兼并、卡特尔和托拉斯等经济行为时却被证明毫无效力。

[4] Clayton Antitrust Act (1914, as amended)：克莱顿反托拉斯法（1914 年修订案），常缩写为 Clayton Act (1914)，美国国会于 1914 年通过的第二部反托拉斯法，系对谢尔曼法的补充。由当时的阿拉巴马州共和党众议员亨利·⑥ 克莱顿（Henry De Lamar Clayton，187~1929）起草并以他的名字命名。

The Antitrust Laws

Sherman Antitrust Act (1890, as amended)

§1. Every contract, combination in the form of trust or otherwise, or conspiracy, in restraint of trade or commerce among the several States, or with foreign nations, is declared to be illegal.

§2. Every person who shall monopolize, or attempt to monopolize, or combine or conspire with any other person or persons, to monopolize any part of the trade or commerce among the several States, or with foreign nations, shall be deemed guilty of a felony. . . .

Clayton Antitrust Act (1914, as amended)

§2. It shall be unlawful . . . to discriminate in price between different purchasers of commodities of like grade and quality . . . where the effect of such discrimination may be substantially to lessen competition or tend to create a monopoly in any line of commerce. . . . *Provided,* That nothing herein contained shall prevent differentials which make only due allowance for differences in the cost. . . .

§3. That it shall be unlawful for any person . . . to lease or make a sale or contract . . . on the condition, agreement, or understanding that the lessee or purchaser thereof shall not use or deal in the . . . commodities of a competitor . . . where the effect . . . may be to substantially lessen competition or tend to create a monopoly in any line of commerce.

§7. No [corporation] . . . shall acquire . . . the whole or any part . . . of another [corporation] . . . where . . . the effect of such an acquisition may be substantially to lessen competition, or to tend to create a monopoly.

Federal Trade Commission Act (1914, as amended) [5]

§5. Unfair methods of competition . . . and unfair or deceptive acts or practices . . . are declared unlawful.

TABLE 10-1. American Antitrust Law Is Based on a Handful of Statutes

The Sherman, Clayton, and Federal Trade Commission Acts laid the foundation for American antitrust law. Interpretation of these acts has fleshed out modern antitrust doctrines.

① 政府用来鼓励竞争的第二个重要工具是反托拉斯法，其立法的目的通过有活力的竞争给消费者提供经济利益。反托拉斯法在两个不同的方面纠正了反竞争的不良行为：第一，它们禁止某种商业行为，诸如限制竞争力的限价。第二，它们限制某些市场结构，比如垄断，因为这些机构被认为是最有可能在其他方面滥用其经济职权来限制贸易。

[5] Federal Trade Commission Act (1914, as amended)：联邦贸易委员会法（1914 年修订案），常缩写为 FTC Act（1914），美国联邦贸易委员会成立的立法依据，并规定了该会的权力、责任以及其他主管事项。该法是一个“口袋法”（catchall act），被视为所有其他反托拉斯法乃至其他经济立法的补充。美国联邦贸易委员会由总统任命的民主和共和两党的 5 名成员组成，任期 7 年。

⑥ 表 10-1. 美国反托拉斯法依据的几个法案

of monopoly or which actions were prohibited. The meaning was fleshed out in later case law.

Clayton Act (1914). The Clayton Act was passed to clarify and strengthen the Sherman Act. It outlawed *tying contracts* (in which a customer is forced to buy product B if she wants product A); it ruled *price discrimination* and exclusive dealings illegal; it banned *interlocking directorates* (in which some people would be directors of more than one firm in the same industry) and *mergers* formed by acquiring common stock of competitors. These practices were not illegal *per se* (meaning "in itself") but only when they might substantially lessen competition. The Clayton Act emphasized prevention as well as punishment.

per se
从自身角度来讲

bid rigging
操纵投标

Another important element of the Clayton Act was that it specifically provided antitrust immunity to labor unions.

Federal Trade Commission Acts. In 1914 the Federal Trade Commission (FTC) was established to prohibit "unfair methods of competition" and to warn against anticompetitive mergers. In 1938, the FTC was also empowered to ban false and deceptive advertising. To enforce its powers, the FTC can investigate firms, hold hearings, and issue cease-and-desist orders.

price discrimination
价格歧视

反垄断法的基本问题：行为和结构
BASIC ISSUES IN ANTITRUST LAW: CONDUCT AND STRUCTURE

tying contracts
捆绑性合同

While the basic antitrust statutes are straightforward, it is not easy in practice to decide how to apply them to specific situations of industry conduct or market structure. Actual law has evolved through an interaction of economic theory and case law.

ruinously low prices
灾难性的低价格

One key issue that arises in many cases is, What is the relevant market? For example, what is the "telephone" industry in Albuquerque, New Mexico? Is it all information industries, or only telecommunications, or only wired telecommunications, or wired phones in all of New Mexico, or just in some specific zip code? In recent U.S. cases, the market has been defined to include products which are reasonably close substitutes. If the price of land-line telephone service goes up and people switch to cell-phone service in significant numbers, then these two products would be considered to be in the same industry. If by contrast few people buy more newspapers when the price of phone service increases, then newspapers are not in the telephone market.

非法行为
Illegal Conduct

Some of the earliest antitrust decisions concerned illegal behavior. The courts have ruled that certain kinds of collusive behavior are illegal per se; there is simply no defense that will justify these actions. The offenders cannot defend themselves by pointing to some worthy objective (such as product quality) or mitigating circumstance (such as low profits).

The most important class of per se illegal conduct is agreements among competing firms to fix prices. Even the severest critic of antitrust policy can find no redeeming virtue in price fixing. Two other practices are illegal in all cases:

- *Bid rigging,* in which different firms agree to set their bids so that one firm will win the auction, usually at an inflated price, is always illegal.
- *Market allocation schemes,* in which competitors [1] divide up markets by territory or by customers, are anticompetitive and hence illegal per se.

Many other practices are less clear-cut and require some consideration of the particular circumstances:

- *Price discrimination,* in which a firm sells the same product to different customers at different prices, is unpopular but generally not illegal. (Recall the discussion of price discrimination earlier in this chapter.) To be illegal, the discrimination must not be based on differing production costs, and it must injure competition.
- *Tying contracts,* in which a firm will sell product A only if the purchaser buys product B, are generally illegal only if the seller has high levels of market power.
- What about *ruinously low prices?* Suppose that because of Wal-Mart's efficient operations and [2] low prices, Pop's grocery store goes out of business. Is this illegal? The answer is no. Unless Wal-Mart did something else illegal, simply driving its competitors bankrupt because of its superior efficiency is not illegal.

Note that the practices on this list relate to a firm's *conduct.* It is the acts themselves that are illegal, not the structure of the industry in which the acts take place. Perhaps the most celebrated example is the great electric-equipment conspiracy. In 1961, the electric-equipment industry was found guilty of collusive price agreements. Executives of the largest companies— ③ such as GE and Westinghouse—conspired to raise

[1] Market Allocation Schemes：也称 Division of Market，市场划分

[2] Wal-Mart：沃尔玛百货投资有限公司，以 Walmart 注册，美国大型的全球平价连锁店，2008 年"福布斯世界 500 强"中最大的上市公司。

③ 像通用电气和西屋这些最大的跨国公司的老总们合谋抬高价格，一个个犹如间谍小说中的人物，在守猎用的小屋中秘密协商，互用代码联系，甚至互通电话都躲在公共电话亭进行。结果导致这些公司同意向其消费者赔偿由于过高的索价所带来的损失，有些高层则因违反反托拉斯法而被捕入狱。

prices and covered their tracks like characters in a spy novel by meeting in hunting lodges, using code names, and making telephone calls from phone booths. The companies agreed to pay extensive damages to their customers for overcharges, and some executives were jailed for their antitrust violations.

结构：大的不好吗

Structure: Is Bigness Badness? [1]

The most visible antitrust cases concern the structure of industries rather than the conduct of companies. These cases consist of attempts to break up or limit the conduct of dominant firms.

The first surge of antitrust activity under the Sherman Act focused on dismantling existing monopolies. In 1911, the Supreme Court ordered that the American Tobacco Company [2] and Standard Oil [3] be broken up into many separate companies. In condemning these flagrant monopolies, the Supreme Court enunciated the important "rule of reason." Only *unreasonable* restraints of trade (mergers, agreements, and the like) came within the scope of the Sherman Act and were considered illegal.

The rule-of-reason doctrine virtually nullified the antitrust laws' attack on monopolistic mergers, as shown by the *U.S. Steel case* (1920). [4] J. P. Morgan had put this giant together by merger, and at its peak it controlled 60 percent of the market. But the Supreme Court held that pure size or monopoly by itself was no offense. In that period, as they do today, the cases that shaped the economic landscape focused on illegal monopoly structures more than anticompetitive conduct.

In recent years, two important cases have set the ground rules for monopolistic structure and behavior. In the *AT&T case,* [5] the Department of Justice filed a far-reaching suit. For most of the twentieth century, the American Telephone and Telegraph (AT&T, sometimes called the Bell System) was a vertically and horizontally integrated regulated monopoly supplier of telecommunications services. In 1974, the Department of Justice filed an antitrust suit, contending that AT&T had monopolized the regulated long-distance market by anticompetitive means, such as preventing MCI [6] and other carriers from connecting to the local markets, and had monopolized the telecommunications-equipment market by refusing to purchase equipment from non-Bell suppliers.

Faced with the prospect of losing the antitrust suit, the company settled in a consent decree in 1982. The local Bell operating companies were divested (legally separated) from AT&T and were regrouped into seven large regional telephone holding companies. AT&T retained its long-distance operations as well as Bell Labs [7] (the research organization) and Western Electric [8] (the equipment manufacturer). The net effect was an 80 percent reduction in the size and sales of the Bell System.

The dismantling of the Bell System set off a breathtaking revolution in the telecommunications industry. New technologies are changing the telecommunications landscape: cellular phone systems are eating away at the natural monopoly of Alexander Graham Bell's [9] wire-based system; telephone companies are joining forces to bring television signals into homes; fiber-optic lines are beginning to function as data superhighways, carrying vast amounts of data around the country and the world; the Internet is linking people and places together in ways that were unimagined a decade ago. One clear lesson of the breakup of the Bell System is that monopoly is not necessary for rapid technological change.

The most recent major antitrust case involved the giant software company *Microsoft.* In 1998, the federal government and 19 states lodged a far-reaching suit alleging that Microsoft had illegally maintained its dominant position in the market for operating systems and had used that dominance to leverage itself into other markets, such as the Internet browser market. The government claimed that "Microsoft has engaged in a broad pattern of unlawful conduct with the purpose and effect of thwarting emerging threats to its powerful and well-entrenched operating system monopoly." Although a monopoly acquired by fair means is legal, acting to stifle competition is illegal.

In his "Findings of Fact," Judge Jackson declared that Microsoft was a monopoly that had controlled more than 90 percent of the market share for PC operating systems since 1990 and that Microsoft had abused its market power and caused "consumer harm by distorting competition." Judge [10] Jackson found that Microsoft had violated Sections 1 and 2 of the Sherman Act. He found that "Microsoft maintained its monopoly power by anticompetitive means, attempted to monopolize the Web browser market, and violated the Sherman Act by unlawfully tying its Web browser to its operating system."

---

[1] Is Bigness Badness?：系 Big is bad 之说，与 Small is beautiful（详见本书 Preface 中的注疏）相对，其源头 Big Bad 源自美国从 1997 年至 2003 年播送近六年之久的电视连续剧《吸血鬼猎人巴菲》（*Buffy the Vampire Slayer*），用以代表每年播出的电视剧中的反面角色。

[2] American Tobacco Company：美国烟草公司，1890 年创立，曾是 1896 年道琼斯工业指数 12 家发起公司之一。在这一时期，像标准石油公司（Standard Oil）在石油行业一样，美国烟草公司在烟草业内大肆扩张，到 1907 年启动反托拉斯法为止，共兼并了 200 多家对手。1911 年，其在英美烟草公司（British American Tobacco，即 BAT）的股权被联邦最高法院裁定拍卖，拆分为包括该公司名称在内的四家新公司。上世纪 70 和 80 年代，将业务扩展到了除烟草之外的很多领域，遂在 1986 年更名为“美国品牌”（American Brands）的控股公司，而后又更名为“财富品牌”（Fortune Brands），美国烟草公司成为其麾下的子公司，并开始逐渐地将拥有的烟草品牌出售给了长期以来的竞争对手们。

[3] Standard Oil：标准石油公司，曾是洛克菲勒与他的合伙人在 1863 年创立的石油提炼公司。1868 年成为当时世界上最大的炼油公司，遂开始大肆并购，至 1878 年已经垄断了全美 90% 的炼油业。1911 年被联邦最高法院裁定违法垄断，将其支解为 37 家新公司。

[4] U.S. Steel case (1920)：1920 年联邦最高法院对美国钢铁公司（United States Steel Corporation）垄断一案的裁定，即该公司虽占有 60% 市场份额的垄断地位，但其采用的是价格领导制，并对同行内的小企业提供了价格保护，因此被判不违法。

J. P. Morgan：J. P. 摩根公司，19 世纪早期为英国的一家商业银行，由摩根（John Pierpont Morgan，1837~1913）的父亲在伦敦创立。在 19 世纪末 20 世纪初期，公司对包括美国钢铁、通用电气以及美国电话电报公司等知名企业最初的创立及融资起了重大作用。该公司与大通银行（Chase Manhattan Bank）和富林明集团（Robert Fleming & Co.）合并为摩根大通公司（JPMorgan Chase & Co.），系全球历史最长、规模最大的金融服务集团之一。

[5] AT&T case：曾经是全球最大电信企业的 AT&T，近 20 多年来曾先后数次被联邦最高法院裁定拆分。1984 年被一分为八；1995 年主动一分为三，将贝尔实验室（Bell Labs）和计算机公司（NCR）予以剥离；2000 年又宣布一分为四。从竞争意义上来讲，AT&T 被动与主动的拆分成就了当今电信的新时代。所以，AT&T 的案例已经没有列具体年份的必要。

[6] MCI：美国微波通信公司，1963 年创立，1968 年开始进入电信运营市场并坚持对 AT&T 进行反垄断诉讼，1980 年胜诉。这一胜诉直接导致了 1984 年 AT&T 的拆分，并给其带来了巨大利益。上世纪 80 年代末，MCI 迎来了其发展的黄金时期，一度跃居美国第二大电信公司，1997 年被世通公司斥巨资并购。

[7] Bell Labs：贝尔实验室，最早可追溯到 1884 年由美国贝尔电话公司创建的设计部，1925 年 AT&T 收购了西方电子的研究部后正式成立至今，随 AT&T 辗转，现属法国阿尔卡特朗讯公司。

[8] Western Electric：美国西方电子公司，从 1881 年至 1995 年一百多年间始终是 AT&T 的设备制造商，于 1925 年将其研究部的 50% 股权售予 AT&T，成立了贝尔电话实验室股份公司。

[9] Alexander Graham Bell：亚历山大·格雷厄姆·贝尔（1847~1922），英国裔的美国发明家和企业家，贝尔电话公司的创建者，被誉为“电话之父”。

[10] Judge Jackson：贾奇·杰克逊，前华盛顿哥伦比亚特区地方法院法官。在从 1994 年起美国司法部起诉微软公司视窗操作系统垄断、从事反竞争行为以及网络浏览器捆绑搭售等案例中，杰克逊法官将微软公司一分为二的判决被哥伦比亚特区上诉法院宣判无效，并随后被清除出该案的审理，从而成为该案实际上的输家。2004 年，上诉法院同意微软公司的反托拉斯案和解。

The Department of Justice proposed the radical step of separating Microsoft along functional lines. This "divestiture" would require a separation of Microsoft into two separate, independent companies. One company ("WinCo") would own Microsoft's Windows and other operating-system businesses, and the other ("AppCo") would own the applications and other businesses. Judge Jackson accepted the Department of Justice's remedy recommendation with no modifications.

But then the case took a bizarre twist when it turned out that Judge Jackson had been holding private heart-to-heart discussions with journalists even as he was trying the case. He was chastised for his unethical conduct and removed from the case. Shortly thereafter, the Bush administration decided it would not seek to separate Microsoft but would settle for "conduct" remedies. These measures would restrict Microsoft's conduct through steps such as prohibiting contractual tying and discriminatory pricing as well as ensuring the interoperability of Windows with non-Windows software. After extensive further hearings, the case was settled in November 2002 with Microsoft intact but under the watchful eye of the government and the courts.

反垄断法与效率

Antitrust Laws and Efficiency

Economic and legal views toward regulation and antitrust have changed dramatically over the last three decades. Increasingly, economic regulation and antitrust laws are aimed toward the goal of improving economic efficiency rather than combating businesses simply because they are big or profitable.

What has prompted the changing attitude toward antitrust policy? First, economists found that concentrated industries sometimes had outstanding performance. That is, while concentrated industries might have static inefficiencies, these were more than outweighed by their dynamic efficiencies. Consider Intel, Microsoft, and Boeing. They have had substantial market shares, but they have also been highly innovative and commercially successful.

A second thrust of the new approach to regulation and antitrust arose from new findings on the nature of competition. Considering both experimental evidence and observation, many economists believe that intense rivalry will spring up even in oligopolistic markets as long as collusion is strictly prohibited. Indeed, in the words of Richard Posner, formerly a law professor and currently a federal judge,

> The only truly unilateral acts by which firms can get or keep monopoly power are practices like committing fraud on the Patent Office or blowing up a competitor's plant, and fraud and force are in general adequately punished under other statutes. ①

In this view, the only valid purpose of the antitrust laws should be to replace existing statutes with a simple prohibition against *agreements*—explicit or tacit—that unreasonably restrict competition.

A final reason for the reduced activism in antitrust has been growing globalization in many concentrated industries. As more foreign firms gain a foothold in the American economy, they tend to compete vigorously for a share of the market and often upset established sales patterns and pricing practices as they do so. For example, when the U.S. sales of Japanese automakers increased, the cozy coexistence of the Big Three American auto firms dissolved. Many economists believe that the threat of foreign competition is a much more powerful tool for enforcing market discipline than are antitrust laws.

---

① 企业为达到或者保持其垄断地位而惟一可以真正采取的单方面行为是诸如欺骗专利局或者炸掉竞争对手的厂房，但是，根据其他的法规，欺骗和暴力行为在通常情况下都足以受到严惩。

SUMMARY

A. Behavior of Imperfect Competitors

1. Recall the four major market structures: (*a*) *Perfect competition* is found when no firm is large enough to affect the market price. (*b*) *Monopolistic competition* occurs when a large number of firms produce slightly differentiated products. (*c*) *Oligopoly* is an intermediate form of imperfect competition in which an industry is dominated by a few firms. (*d*) *Monopoly* comes when a single firm produces the entire output of an industry.
2. Measures of concentration are designed to indicate the degree of market power in an imperfectly competitive industry. Industries which are more concentrated tend to have higher levels of R&D expenditures, but on average their profitability is not higher.
3. High barriers to entry and complete collusion can lead to collusive oligopoly. This market structure produces a price and quantity relation similar to that under monopoly.
4. Another common structure is the monopolistic competition that characterizes many retail industries. Here we see many small firms, with only slight differences in the characteristics of their products (such as different locations of gasoline stations or different types of breakfast cereals). Product differentiation leads each firm to face a downward-sloping demand curve as each firm is free to set its own prices. In the long run, free entry extinguishes profits as these industries show an equilibrium in which their *AC* curves are tangent to their demand curves. In this tangency equilibrium, prices are above marginal costs, but the industry exhibits greater diversity of quality and service than would occur under perfect competition.
5. A final situation recognizes the strategic interplay that is present when an industry has but a handful of firms. When a small number of firms compete in a market, they must recognize their strategic interactions. Competition among the few introduces a completely new feature into economic life: It forces firms to take into account competitors' reactions to price and output decisions and brings strategic considerations into these markets.
6. Price discrimination occurs when the same product is sold to different consumers at different prices. This practice often occurs when sellers can segment their market into different groups.

B. Game Theory

7. Economic life contains many situations with strategic interaction among firms, households, governments, or others. Game theory analyzes the way that two or more parties, who interact in an arena such as a market, choose actions or strategies that jointly affect all participants.
8. The basic structure of a game includes the players, who have different possible actions or strategies, and the payoffs, which describe the various possible profits or other benefits that the players might obtain under each outcome. The key new concept is the payoff table of a game, which displays information about the strategies and the payoffs or profits of the different players for all possible outcomes.
9. The key to choosing strategies in game theory is for players to think about their opponent's goals as well as their own, never forgetting that the other side is doing the same. When playing a game in economics or any other field, assume that your opponent will choose his or her best option. Then pick your strategy to maximize your benefit, always assuming that your opponent is similarly analyzing your options.
10. Sometimes a dominant strategy is available—one that is best no matter what the opposition does. More often, we find a Nash equilibrium (or noncooperative equilibrium), in which no player can improve his or her payoff as long as the other player's strategy remains unchanged.

C. Public Policies to Combat Market Power

11. Monopoly power often leads to economic inefficiency when prices rise above marginal cost, costs are bloated by lack of competitive pressure, and product quality deteriorates.
12. Economic regulation involves the control of prices, production, entry and exit conditions, and standards of service in a particular industry. The normative view of economic regulation is that government intervention is appropriate when there are major market failures. These include excess market power in an industry, an inadequate supply of information for consumers and workers, and externalities such as pollution. The strongest case for economic regulation comes in regard to natural monopolies. Natural monopoly occurs when average costs are falling for every level of output, so the most efficient

organization of the industry requires production by a single firm.

13. Antitrust policy, prohibiting anticompetitive conduct and preventing monopolistic structures, is the primary way that public policy limits abuses of market power by large firms. This policy grew out of legislation like the Sherman Act (1890) and the Clayton Act (1914). The primary purposes of antitrust policy are (*a*) to prohibit anticompetitive activities (which include agreements to fix prices or divide up territories, price discrimination, and tie-in agreements) and (*b*) to break up illegal monopoly structures. In today's legal theory, such structures are those that have excessive market power (a large share of the market) and also engage in anticompetitive acts.
14. Legal antitrust policy has been significantly influenced by economic thinking during the last three decades. As a result, antitrust policy now focuses almost exclusively on improving efficiency and ignores earlier populist concerns with bigness itself.

CONCEPTS FOR REVIEW

Models of Imperfect Competition

concentration: concentration ratios, HHI
market power
strategic interaction
tacit and explicit collusion
imperfect competition:
- collusive oligopoly
- monopolistic competition
- small-number oligopoly

no-profit equilibrium in monopolistic competition
inefficiency of $P > MC$

Game Theory

players, strategies, payoffs
payoff table
dominant strategy and equilibrium
Nash or noncooperative equilibrium

Policies for Imperfect Competition

deadweight losses
reasons for regulation:
- market power
- externalities
- information failures

Antitrust Policy

Sherman, Clayton, and FTC Acts
natural monopoly
per se prohibitions vs. the "rule of reason"
efficiency-oriented antitrust policy

FURTHER READING AND INTERNET WEBSITES

Further Reading

An excellent review of industrial organization is Dennis W. Carlton and Jeffrey M. Perloff, *Modern Industrial Organization* (Addison-Wesley, New York, 2005).

Game theory was developed in 1944 by John von Neumann and Oscar Morgenstern and published in *Theory of Games and Economic Behavior* (Princeton University Press, Princeton, N.J., 1980). An entertaining review of game theory by two leading microeconomists is Avinash K. Dixit and Barry J. Nalebuff, *Thinking Strategically: The Competitive Edge in Business, Politics, and Everyday* (Norton, New York, 1993). A nontechnical biography of John Nash by journalist Silvia Nasar, *A Beautiful Mind: A Biography of John Forbes Nash Jr.* (Touchstone Books, New York, 1999), is a vivid history of game theory and of one of its most brilliant theorists.

Law and economics advanced greatly under the influence of scholars like Richard Posner, now a circuit court judge. His book, *Antitrust Law: An Economic Perspective* (University of Chicago Press, 1976), is a classic.

Websites

Game theorists have set up a number of sites. See particularly those by David Levine of UCLA at *levine.sscnet.ucla.edu* and Al Roth of Harvard at *www.economics.harvard.edu/~aroth/alroth.html*.

OPEC has its site at *www.opec.org*. This site makes interesting reading from the point of view of oil producers, many of which are Arab countries.

Data and methods pertaining to concentration ratios can be found in a Bureau of the Census publication at *www.census.gov/epcd/www/concentration.html*.

An excellent website with links to many issues on antitrust is *www.antitrust.org*. The homepage for the Antitrust Division of the Department of Justice, at *www.usdoj.gov/atr/public/div_stats/211491.htm*, contains an overview of antitrust issues.

QUESTIONS FOR DISCUSSION

1. Review collusive oligopoly and monopolistic competition, which are two theories of imperfect competition discussed in this chapter. Draw up a table that compares perfect competition, monopoly, and the two theories with respect to the following characteristics: (*a*) number of firms; (*b*) extent of collusion; (*c*) price vs. marginal cost; (*d*) price vs. long-run average cost; (*e*) efficiency.
2. Consider an industry whose firms have the following sales:

Firm	Sales
Appel Computer	1000
Banana Computer	800
Cumquat Computer	600
Dellta Computer	400
Endive Computer	300
Fettucini Computer	200
Grapefruit Computer	150
Hamburger Computer	100
InstantCoffee Computer	50
Jasmine Computer	1

The Herfindahl-Hirschman Index (HHI) is defined as

$$\text{HHI} = (\text{market share of firm 1 in }\%)^2 + (\text{market share of firm 2 in }\%)^2 + \cdots + (\text{market share of last firm in }\%)^2$$

   a. Calculate the four-firm and six-firm concentration ratios for the computer industry.
   b. Calculate the HHI for the industry.
   c. Suppose that Appel Computer and Banana Computer were to merge with no change in the sales of any of the different computers. Calculate the new HHI.
3. "Perfect price discrimination" occurs when each consumer is charged his or her maximum price for the product. When this happens, the monopolist is able to capture the entire consumer surplus. Draw a demand curve for each of six consumers and compare (*a*) the situation in which all consumers face a single price with (*b*) a market under perfect price discrimination. Explain the paradoxical result that perfect price discrimination removes the inefficiency of monopoly.
4. The government decides to tax a monopolist at a constant rate of $\$x$ per unit. Show the impact upon output and price. Is the post-tax equilibrium closer to or further from the ideal equilibrium of $P = MC$?
5. Show that a profit-maximizing, unregulated monopolist will never operate in the price-inelastic region of its demand curve. Show how regulation can force the monopolist into the inelastic portion of its demand curve. What will be the impact of an increase in the regulated price of a monopolist upon revenues and profits when it is operating on (*a*) the elastic portion of the demand curve, (*b*) the inelastic portion of the demand curve, and (*c*) the unit-elastic portion of the demand curve?
6. Make a list of the industries that you feel are candidates for the title "natural monopoly." Then review the different strategies for intervention to prevent exercise of monopoly power. What would you do about each industry on your list?
7. Firms often lobby for tariffs or quotas to provide relief from import competition.
   a. Suppose that the monopolist shown in Figure 10-9 has a foreign competitor that will supply output perfectly elastically at a price slightly above the monopolist's $AC = MC$ but below P. Show the impact of the foreign competitor's entry into the market.
   b. What would be the effect on the price and quantity if a prohibitive tariff were levied on the foreign good? (A prohibitive tariff is one that is so high as to effectively wall out all imports.) What would be the effect of a small tariff? Use your analysis to explain the statement, "The tariff is the mother of monopoly."
8. Explain in words and with the use of diagrams why a monopolistic equilibrium leads to economic inefficiency relative to a perfectly competitive equilibrium. Why is the condition $MC = P = MU$ of Chapter 8 critical for this analysis?
9. Consider the *prisoner's dilemma*, one of the most famous of all games. Molly and Knuckles are partners in crime. The district attorney interviews each separately, saying, "I have enough on both of you to send you to jail for a year. But I'll make a deal with you: If you *alone* confess, you'll get off with a 3-month sentence, while your partner will serve 10 years. If you *both* confess, you'll both get 5 years." What should Molly do? Should she confess and hope to get a short sentence? Three months are preferable to the year she would get if she remains silent. But wait. There is an even better reason for confessing. Suppose Molly doesn't confess and, unbeknownst to her, Knuckles does confess. Molly stands to get 10 years! It's clearly better in this situation for Molly to confess and get

5 years rather than 10 years. Construct a payoff table like that in Figure 10-8. Show that each player has a dominant strategy, which is to confess, and both therefore end up with long prison terms. Then show what would happen if they could make binding commitments not to confess.

10. In his Findings of Fact in the Microsoft case, Judge Jackson wrote: "It is indicative of monopoly power that Microsoft felt that it had substantial discretion in setting the price of its Windows 98 upgrade product (the operating system product it sells to existing users of Windows 95). A Microsoft study from November 1997 reveals that the company could have charged $49 for an upgrade to Windows 98—there is no reason to believe that the $49 price would have been unprofitable—but the study identifies $89 as the revenue-maximizing price. Microsoft thus opted for the higher price." Explain why these facts would indicate that Microsoft is not a perfect competitor. What further information would be needed to prove Microsoft was a monopoly?

11. In long-run equilibrium, both perfectly competitive and monopolistically competitive markets achieve a tangency between the firm's *dd* demand curve and its *AC* average cost curve. Figure 10-4 shows the tangency for a monopolistic competitor, while Figure 10-10 displays the tangency for a perfect competitor. Discuss the similarities and differences in the two situations with respect to:
    a. The elasticity of the demand curve for the firm's product
    b. The extent of divergence between price and marginal cost
    c. Profits
    d. Economic efficiency

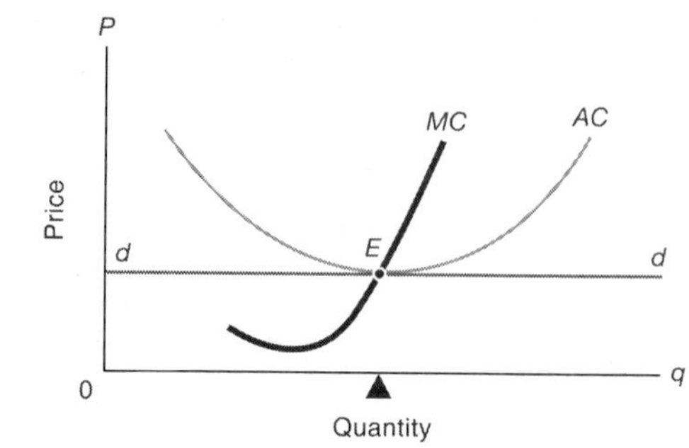

FIGURE 10-10. Perfect Competition

12. Reread the history of OPEC. Draw a set of supply and demand curves in which supply is completely price-inelastic. Show that a cartel that sets a quantity target (the inelastic supply curve) will experience more volatile prices if demand is price-inelastic than if demand is price-elastic when (*a*) the demand curve shifts horizontally by a certain quantity (such as would occur with an unanticipated demand shock) or (*b*) there is a shift in the supply curve (say, due to cheating by a cartel member).

CHAPTER

11

Economics of Uncertainty
不确定性经济学

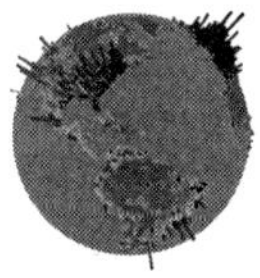

Pearls lie not on the seashore. If thou desirest one, thou must dive for it. [1]

Chinese proverb

Life is full of uncertainties. Suppose that you are in the oil business. You might be in charge of a joint venture in Siberia. What obstacles would you face? You would face major risks that plague oil producers everywhere—the risks of a price plunge, of embargoes, or of an attack on your tankers by some hostile regime. Added to these are the uncertainties of operating in uncharted terrain: you are unfamiliar with the geological formations, with the routes for getting the oil to the market, with the success rate on drilling wells, and with the skills of the local workforce.

In addition to these uncertainties are the political risks, along with the problems that arise from from occasional wars and from corrupt elements in a country where bribes are common and the rule of law is insecure. And your partners may turn out to be unscrupulous fellows who take advantage of their local knowledge to get more than their fair share.

The economic issues in your joint venture present complexities that are not captured in our elementary theories. Many of these issues involve *risk, uncertainty,* and *information.* Our oil company must deal with the ② uncertainties of drilling, of volatile prices, and of shifting markets. Likewise, households must contend with uncertainty about future wages or employment and about the return on their investments in education or in financial assets. Additionally, some people suffer from misfortunes such as devastating hurricanes, earthquakes, or illnesses. The first section of this chapter discusses the fundamental economics of uncertainty.

How do individuals and societies cope with uncertainties? One important approach is through insurance. The second section deals with the fundamentals of insurance, including the important concept of social insurance. The third section applies the concept of social insurance to health care, which is a growing political and social dilemma in the United States. We conclude with an examination of the economics of information and apply this to the rise of the Internet.

No study of the realities of economic life is complete without a thorough study of the fascinating questions involved in decision making under uncertainty and the economics of information.

风险和不确定性经济学

A. ECONOMICS OF RISK AND UNCERTAINTY

Our analysis of markets presumed that costs and demands were known for certain. In reality, business life is teeming with risk and uncertainty. We described

[1] 全句的含义研判应该是成语“不入虎穴，焉得虎子”的意译。“thou”和“desirest”系早期现代英语用法，大致可以看出是从 13 世纪马可·波罗（Marco Polo, 1254~1324）游历中国起至 17 世纪初期之前的文艺复兴时期，即莎士比亚时代西方传教士的译作。西方流行的“Chinese proverb”有不少是那个时期的传教士介绍到欧洲的。约半个世纪之后，17 世纪英国著名的桂冠诗人（*Poet Laureate*）约翰·德莱顿（John Dryden，1631~1700）于 1678 年发表的长诗《博爱》（*All for Love*）中曾有类似的诗句，似可判断受其影响（五步抑扬格，在莎士比亚的剧本和 14 行诗中普遍使用）。

② 我们的石油公司必须要处理钻探、波动的价格以及市场动荡中的各种不确定性因素。同样，居家生活也必须应对未来的工资走势和就业的不确定性问题，以及教育或者金融资产投资的回报等问题。

the uncertainties involved in a joint venture for oil in Siberia, but these problems are not confined to the oil business. Virtually all firms face uncertainties about their output and input prices. They may find that their markets are shrinking because of a recession or that credit is hard to find in a financial crisis. Furthermore, the behavior of their competitors cannot be forecast in advance. The essence of business is ① to invest now in order to make profits in the future, in effect putting fortunes up as hostage to future uncertainties. Economic life is a risky business.

Modern economics has developed useful tools to incorporate uncertainty into the analysis of business and household behavior. This section examines the role of markets in spreading risks over space and time and analyzes the theory of individual behavior under uncertainty. These topics are but a brief glimpse into the fascinating world of risk and uncertainty in economic life.

投机：资产与商品的跨时空调配
SPECULATION: SHIPPING ASSETS OR GOODS ACROSS SPACE AND TIME

We begin by considering the role of speculative markets. **Speculation** involves buying and selling in order ② to make profits from fluctuations in prices. A speculator wants to buy low and sell high. The item might be grain, oil, eggs, stocks, or foreign currencies. Speculators do not buy these items for their own sake. The ③ last thing they want is to see the egg truck show up at their door. Rather, they make a profit from price changes.

Many people think of speculation as a slightly sinister activity, particularly when it arises from accounting frauds and inside information. But speculation can be beneficial to society. The economic function of speculators is to "move" goods from periods of abundance to periods of scarcity. Even though speculators may never see a barrel of oil or a Brazilian bond, they can help even out the price and yield differences of these items among regions or over time. They do this by buying when goods are abundant and prices are low and selling when goods are scarce and prices are high, and this indeed can improve a market's efficiency.

套利和价格地理格局
Arbitrage and Geographic Price Patterns

The simplest case is one in which speculative activity reduces or eliminates regional price differences by buying and selling the same commodity. This activity is called **arbitrage,** which is the purchase of a good or asset in one market for immediate resale in another market in order to profit from a price discrepancy.

Let's say that the price of wheat is 50 cents per bushel higher in Chicago than in Kansas City. Further, suppose that the costs of insurance and transportation are 10 cents per bushel. An *arbitrager* (someone engaged in arbitrage) can purchase wheat in Kansas City, ship it to Chicago, and make a profit of 40 cents per bushel. As a result of market arbitrage, the differential will be reduced so that the price difference between Chicago and Kansas City can never exceed 10 cents per bushel. *As a result of* ④ *arbitrage, the price difference between markets will generally be less than the cost of moving the good from one market to the other.*

The frenzied activities of arbitragers—talking on the phone simultaneously to several brokers in several markets, searching out price differentials, trying to eke out a tiny profit every time they can buy low and sell high—tend to align the prices of identical products in different markets. Once again, we see the invisible hand at work—the lure of profit acts to smooth out price differentials across markets and make markets function more efficiently.

不同时间的投机和价格行为
Speculation and Price Behavior over Time

Forces of speculation will tend to establish definite patterns of prices over time as well as over space. But ⑤ the difficulties of predicting the future make this pattern less than perfect: we have an equilibrium that is constantly being disturbed but is always in the process of reforming itself—rather like a lake's surface under the play of the winds.

Consider the simplest case of a crop like corn that is harvested once a year and can be stored for future use. To avoid shortages, the crop must last for the entire year. Since no one passes a law regulating the storage of corn, how does the market bring about an efficient pattern of pricing and use over the year? The equilibrium is set by the activities of speculators trying to make a profit.

A well-informed corn speculator realizes that if all the corn is thrown on the market immediately after the autumn harvest, it will fetch a very low price because there will be a glut on the market. Several

---

① 企业的本质即现在投资，未来获利，从实质上来讲，财富的积累就好像是为了应对明天的不确定性。经济生活就是一桩冒险的交易。

② **投机**即是买卖双方从不断波动的价格中找准机会赚取利益的行为。投机者要的就是低价买进，然后再高价卖出。

③ 他们最不愿意看到的事情就是卖鸡蛋的卡车开到了自家门口。他们愿意看到的是，从变化的价格中谋利。

④ 由于套利交易的结果，市场之间的价格差异通常低于将商品从一个市场转移到另外一个市场的成本。

⑤ 但是，由于预测未来的重重困难，使得这样的价格范式仍不完善。它不断地受到干扰，却又始终处于重新构建的过程，一定程度上像风吹涟漪的湖面，保持了一种均衡的态势。

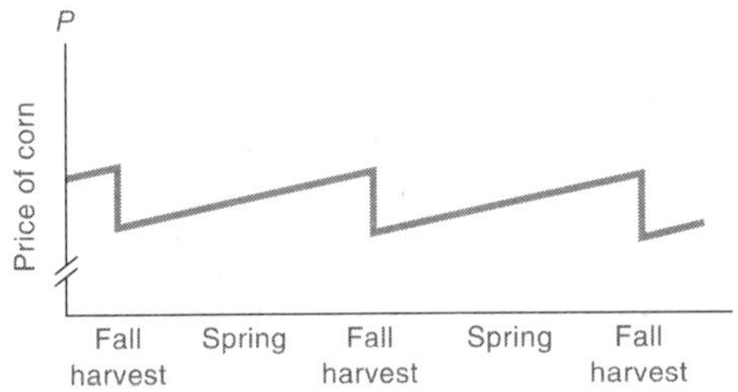

FIGURE 11-1. Speculators Even Out the Price of a Commodity over Time ①

When a good is stored, the expected price rise must match holding costs. In equilibrium, price is lowest at harvest time, rising gently with accumulated storage, insurance, and interest costs until the next harvest. This flexible pattern tends to even out consumption over the seasons. Otherwise, a harvest glut would cause very low autumn price and sky-high spring price.

months later, when corn is running short, the price will tend to skyrocket. In this case, speculators can make a profit by (1) purchasing some of the autumn crop while it is cheap, (2) putting it into storage, and (3) selling it later when the price has risen.

As a result of the speculative activities, the autumn price increases, the spring supply of corn increases, and the spring price declines. The process of speculative buying and selling tends to even out the supply, and therefore the price, over the year. Figure 11-1 shows the behavior of prices over an idealized yearly cycle.

Interestingly, if there is brisk competition among speculators, none of them will make excess profits. The returns to speculators will include the interest ② on invested capital, the appropriate earnings for their time, and a risk premium to compensate them for the noninsurable risks that they bear.

Speculation reveals the invisible-hand principle ③ at work. By evening out supplies and prices, speculation actually increases economic efficiency. By moving goods over time from periods of abundance to periods of scarcity, the speculator is buying where the price and marginal utility of the good are low and selling where the price and marginal utility are high. By pursuing their private interests (profits), speculators are at the same time increasing the public interest (total utility).

通过套期保值分摊风险

Shedding Risks through Hedging

One important function of speculative markets is to allow people to shed risks through hedging. **Hedging** ④ consists of reducing the risk involved in owning an asset or commodity by making an offsetting sale of that asset. Let's see how it works. Consider someone who owns a corn warehouse. She buys 2 million bushels of Kansas corn in the fall, stores it for 6 months, and sells it in the spring at a 10-cents-per-bushel profit, just covering her costs.

The problem is that corn prices tend to fluctuate. If the price of corn rises, she makes a large windfall gain. But if the price falls sharply, the decrease could completely wipe out her profits. How can the warehouse owner make a living storing only corn while avoiding the risks of corn-price fluctuations?

She can avoid the corn-price risk by *hedging her investments.* The owner hedges by selling the corn the moment it is bought rather than waiting until it is shipped 6 months later. Upon buying 2 million bushels of corn in September, she sells the corn immediately for delivery in the future at an agreed-upon price that will just yield a 10-cents-per-bushel storage cost. She thereby protects herself against all corn-price risk. *Hedging allows businesses to insulate themselves from the risk of price changes.*

⑤ 在9月份买进200万蒲式耳的玉米以后，她就立即以期货交易的形式将其卖出——以议定的价格在未来交割，恰好能得到每蒲式耳10美分的存储费用。因此，她使自己先承受了所有的玉米价格风险。对冲交易允许企业免遭价格变动引起的风险。

投机的经济影响

The Economic Impacts of Speculation

But who buys the corn, and why? Someone agrees to buy the warehouse owner's corn now for future delivery. This buyer might be a baker who has a contract to sell bread in 6 months and wants to lock in the price. Or perhaps an ethanol plant needs corn for next year's production. Or the buyer might be a group of investors who believe that corn prices will rise and that they will therefore make a supernormal return on their investment. Someone, somewhere, and at the right price, has an economic incentive to take on the risk of corn-price fluctuations.

Speculative markets serve to improve the price ⑥ and allocation patterns across space and time as well as to help transfer risks. If we look behind the veil of money, we see that ideal speculation reallocates goods from times of feast (when prices are low) to times of famine (when prices are high).

⑥ 投机市场不仅在时间和空间上改善了价格和配置方式，还有助于转移风险。如果掀开其面纱深入地分析一下，我们会发现，理想的对冲交易实现了商品从其丰盛期（价格低）向贫乏期（价格高）的重新配置。

Our discussion has suggested that ideal speculative markets can increase economic efficiency. Let's see how. Say that identical consumers have utility

---

① 图11-1. 投机者对季节性商品价格的平衡作用

② 投机者的收益包括所投入资本的利息所得，按时间计算的应得报酬，再加上补偿其所承担的不可抗风险而给予的风险补贴。

③ 投机行为揭示了看不见的手的市场法则所起的作用。通过平衡供给与价格，投机行为实际上提高了经济效率。通过将商品从丰富时期向短缺时期的跨季节流动，投机者在该商品价格和边际效用处于低位时购进，在价格和边际效用位于高位时售出。投机者以这样的方式在追求其自身利益（利润）的同时，也将使公共利益（总效用）得以提高。

④ **对冲交易**是通过对所拥有的一种资产或者商品做一笔补偿性的交易来降低风险的商业行为。

schedules in which satisfaction in one year is independent of that in every other year. Now suppose that in the first of 2 years there is a big crop—say, 3 units per person—while the second year has a small crop of only 1 unit per person. If this crop deficiency could be foreseen perfectly, how should the consumption of the 2-year, 4-unit total be spread over the 2 years? Neglecting storage, interest, and insurance costs, *total utility and economic efficiency for the 2 years together will be maximized only when consumption is equal in each year.* ①

Why is uniform consumption better than any other division of the available total? Because of the law of diminishing marginal utility. This is how we might reason: "Suppose I consume more in the first year than in the second. My marginal utility (*MU*) in the first year will be low, while it will be high in the second year. So if I carry some crop over from the first to the second year, I will be moving consumption from low-*MU* times to high-*MU* times. When consumption levels are equalized, *MU*s will be equal and I will be maximizing my total utility."

A graph can illuminate this argument. If we measure utility in dollars, with each dollar always denoting the same marginal utility, the demand curves for the risky commodity would look just like the marginal utility schedule of Figure 5-1 on page 85. The two curves of Figure 11-2(*a*) show what would happen with no carryover and with unequal consumption. Here, price is determined first at A_1, where higher S_1S_1 intersects *DD,* and second at A_2, where the lower supply S_2S_2 intersects *DD.* Total utility of the blue shaded areas would add up to only (4 + 3 + 2) + 4, or $13.

But with optimal carryover of 1 unit to the second year, as shown in Figure 11-2(*b*), *P*s and *Q*s will be equalized at E_1 and E_2, and the total utility of the shaded areas will add up to (4 + 3) + (4 + 3), or $14 per person. A little analysis can show that the gain in utility of $1 is measured by Figure 11-2(*b*)'s dark green block, which represents the excess of the second unit's marginal utility over that of the third. This shows why the equality of marginal utilities, which is achieved by ideal speculation, is optimal.

While this discussion has focused on commodities, most speculation today involves financial assets such as stocks, bonds, mortgages, and foreign exchange. Every day, literally trillions of dollars of assets change hands as people speculate, hedge, and invest their

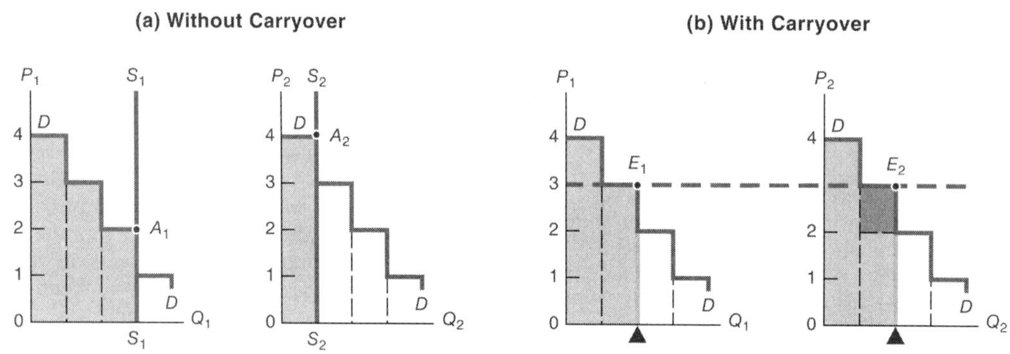

FIGURE 11-2. Speculative Storage Can Improve Efficiency ②

The blue areas measure total utility enjoyed each year. Carrying 1 unit to the second year equalizes *Q* and also *P* and *MU* and increases total utility by the amount of the dark green block.

This diagram will apply equally well to a number of situations. It could be labeled "**(a)** Without Arbitrage across Regional Markets" and "**(b)** With Arbitrage across Markets." We can also use this diagram to illustrate risk aversion if we label it "**(a)** With a Risky Gamble" and "**(b)** Without a Risky Gamble." Insurance then serves to move people from **(a)** to **(b)** by spreading the risks across many independent potential gambles.

① 如果忽略了仓储、利息和保险成本，则只有当每一年的消费量相等时，两年中的总效用和经济效益合计起来，才会达到最大值。

② 图 11-2. 投机性的仓储可以改善效率

funds. The general principles underlying financial ① speculation, hedging, and arbitrage are exactly the same as those outlined here, although the stakes are even higher.

Ideal speculation serves the important func- ② tion of reducing undesired variations in consumption. In a world where individuals are averse to risk, speculation can increase total utility and allocational efficiency.

风险和不确定性
RISK AND UNCERTAINTY

What are people's attitudes toward risk? Why do people try to insulate themselves from many important risks? How can market institutions like insurance help individuals avoid major risks? Why do markets fail to provide insurance in some circumstances? We turn now to these issues.

Whenever you drive a car, own a house, join the army, or invest in the stock market, you are risking life, limb, or fortune. People generally want to avoid major risks to their income, consumption, and health. When people avoid risks, they are *risk-averse.*

A person is **risk-averse** when the pain from losing ③ a given amount of income is greater in magnitude than the pleasure from gaining the same amount of income.

For example, suppose that we are offered a risky coin flip in which we will win $1000 if the coin comes up heads and lose $1000 if the coin comes up tails. This bet has an *expected value* of 0 (equal to a probability of ½ times $1000 plus a probability of ½ times − $1000). A bet which has a zero expected value is called a fair bet. If we turn down all fair bets, we are risk-averse.

In terms of the utility concept that we analyzed in Chapter 5, risk aversion is the same as *diminishing marginal utility of income.* Being risk-averse implies that the gain in utility achieved by getting an extra amount of income is less than the loss in utility from losing the same amount of income. For a fair bet (such as flipping a coin for $1000), the expected dollar value is zero. But in terms of utility, the expected utility value is negative because the utility you stand to win is less than the utility you stand to lose.

Figure 11-2 illustrates the concept of risk aversion. Say that situation (*b*) is the initial position, in which you have equal amounts of consumption in states 1 and 2, consuming 2 units in both states. Someone comes to you and says, "Let's flip a coin for 1 unit." This person is in effect offering you the chance to move to situation (*a*), where you would have 3 units of consumption if the coin came up heads and 1 unit if tails. By careful calculation, you see that if you refuse the bet and stay in situation (*b*), the expected value of utility is 7 utils (= ½ × 7 utils + ½ × 7 utils), whereas if you accept the bet, the expected value of utility is 6½ utils (= ½ × 9 utils + ½ × 4 utils). This example shows that if you are risk-averse, with diminishing marginal utility, you will avoid actions that increase uncertainty without some expectation of gain.

Say that I am a corn farmer. While I clearly must contend with the weather, I prefer to avoid corn-price risks. Suppose that there are two equally likely outcomes with prices of $3 and $5 per bushel, so the expected value of the corn price is $4 per bushel. Unless I can shed the price risk, I am forced into a lottery where I must sell my 10,000-bushel crop for either $30,000 or $50,000 depending upon the flip of the corn-price coin.

Because I am risk-averse, I would prefer a sure thing to such a lottery. The prospect of losing $10,000 is more painful than the prospect of gaining $10,000 is pleasant. If my income is cut to $30,000, I will have to cut back on important spending, such as replacing an aging tractor. On the other hand, the extra $10,000 might be less critical, going toward luxuries like a winter vacation. I therefore decide to hedge my price risk by selling my corn for the expected-value price of $4 per bushel.

People are generally risk-averse, preferring a sure ④ thing to uncertain levels of consumption: people prefer outcomes with less uncertainty and the same average values. For this reason, activities that reduce the uncertainties of consumption lead to improvements in economic welfare.

The Troubling Rise in Gambling

Gambling has historically been a "vice" that was—along with illegal drugs, commercial sex, alcohol, and tobacco—discouraged by the state. Attitudes about such activities ebb and flow. Over the last two decades, attitudes toward gambling

---

① 虽然金融性的投机、对冲以及套利的交易活动所涉及的金融资产额更高，但其所遵循的潜在一般性原理与上述实物性交易活动没什么区别。

② 理想的投机对于减少形形色色不受欢迎的变异性消费的不利变化具有重要作用。在一个风险厌恶的世界里，投机可以增加总效用和提高分配效率。

③ 当一个人由于损失了一笔特定额度的收入之后所遭受的痛苦，大于其得到一笔同等额度的收入时所带来的喜悦时，这个人就是一个**风险厌恶者**。

④ 通常，人们都是风险厌恶型的人——相对于消费的不确定性水平，更喜欢确定的事情：人们偏好不确定性较小的结果或者相同的平均值。因此，降低消费不确定性的活动可以改善经济福利。

became permissive as those toward drugs and tobacco hardened. Overall, gambling has been one of the fastest-growing sectors of the (legal) economy.

Gambling is a different animal from speculation. While ideal speculative activity increases economic welfare, gambling raises serious economic issues. To begin with, aside from recreational value, gambling does not create goods and services. In the language of game theory, described in the previous chapter, gambling is a "negative-sum game" for the players—the customers are (almost) sure to lose in the long run because the house takes a cut of all bets. In addition, by its very nature, gambling increases income inequality. People who sit down to the gambling table with the same amount of money go away with widely different amounts. A gambler's family must expect to be on top of the world one week only to be living on crumbs and remorse when luck changes. Some observers also believe that gambling has adverse social impacts. These include addiction to gambling, neighborhood crime, political corruption, and infiltration of gambling by organized crime.

Given the substantial economic case against gambling, how can we understand the recent trend to legalize gambling and operate government lotteries? One reason is that when states are starved for tax revenues, they look under every tree for new sources; they rationalize lotteries and casinos as a way to channel private vices to the public interest by skimming off some of the revenues to finance public projects. In addition, legal gambling may drive out illegal numbers rackets and take some of the profitability out of organized crime. Notwithstanding these rationales, many observers raise questions about an activity in which the state profits by promoting irrational behavior among those who can least afford it.

保险经济学

B. THE ECONOMICS OF INSURANCE

Most people would like to avoid the risks of losing life, limb, and house. But risks cannot simply be buried. When a house burns down, when someone is hurt in an automobile accident, or when a hurricane destroys New Orleans—someone, somewhere, must bear the cost.

Markets handle risks by **risk spreading.** This pro- ③
cess takes risks that would be large for one person and spreads them around so that they are but small risks for a large number of people. The major form of risk spreading is **insurance,** which is a kind of gambling in reverse.

For example, in buying fire insurance on a house, homeowners seem to be betting with the insurance company that the house will burn down. If it does not, the owners forfeit the small premium charge. If it does burn down, the company must reimburse the owners for the loss at an agreed-upon rate. What is true of fire insurance is equally true of life, accident, automobile, or any other kind of insurance.

The insurance company is spreading risks by pooling many different risks: it may insure millions of houses or lives or cars. The advantage for the insurance company is that what is unpredictable for one individual is highly predictable for a population. Say that the Inland Fire Insurance Company insures 1 million homes, each worth \$100,000. The chance that a house will burn down is 1 in 1000 per year. The expected value of losses to Inland is then .001 × \$100,000 = \$100 per house per year. Inland charges
① each homeowner \$100 plus another \$100 for administration and for reserves.

Each homeowner is faced with the choice between the *certain* loss of \$200 for each year or the *possible* 1-in-1000 catastrophic loss of \$100,000. Because of risk aversion, the household will choose to buy insur-
[2] ance that costs more than the expected value of the household's loss in order to avoid the small chance of a catastrophic loss. Insurance companies can set a premium that will earn the company a profit and at the same time produce a gain in expected utility of individuals. Where does the economic gain come from? It arises from the law of diminishing marginal utility.

Insurance breaks large risks into small pieces and ④
then sells these smaller pieces in return for a small risk premium. Although insurance appears to be just another form of gambling, it actually has the opposite effect. Whereas nature deals us risks, insurance helps reduce individual risks by spreading them out.

资本市场与风险分担
Capital Markets and Risk Sharing

Another form of risk sharing takes place in the capital markets because the financial ownership of *physical* capital can be spread among many owners through the vehicle of corporate *financial* ownership.

① 一个重要的原因是，当国家为税收所困时，将会饥不择食地渴望找到新的财源。政府令博彩业合理化，使一些隐蔽性的丑恶行为也能为公共利益服务，将部分收益有效地投资于公共项目。此外，合法的赌博活动可以有效地遏制非法的政策赌戏活动，并且能获得相当数量的的有组织的犯罪活动的收益。尽管政府的这些举措具有充分的合理性，但仍然有许多的观察家们对此提出质疑。他们指出，政府是在那些支付能力极低的人群中通过推广如此非理性的行为来敛财。

[2] Numbers rac-kets 亦作 numbers game 和 numbers pool，一种非法的赌博游戏，通常使用当日报纸刊发的金融类文章和表格中的最后三个数字下赌，赌额一般较小。因此，此种赌博亦称为政策赌戏(*policy game*)。

③ 市场通过**风险分散**来进行风险管理。这样的过程所承担的风险对于个人来讲是很大的，应该将其分散。这样，很大的风险就化解成了由为数众多的人来分担若干小的风险。这种风险分散的主要形式就是**保险业**，反过来看，保险本身就是一种赌博。

④ 所谓保险就是将各种大的风险分解成一个个小的风险，然后再将其进一步分解成更小单位的风险后出售，以得到小额风险溢价。虽然保险看上去仅是另外一种赌博的形式，但其所起的作用正好相反。虽然我们所生存的自然环境存在着各种各样的风险，但保险业通过分散机制有助于将一个个单一的风险予以降低。

Take the example of investment to develop a new commercial aircraft. A completely new design, including research and development, might require $5 billion of investment spread over 10 years. Yet there is no guarantee that the plane will find a large-enough commercial market to repay the invested funds. Few people have the wealth or inclination to undertake such a risky venture.

Market economies accomplish this task through publicly owned corporations. A company like Boeing is owned by millions of people, none of whom owns a major portion of the shares. In a hypothetical case, divide Boeing's ownership equally among 10 million individuals. Then the $5 billion investment becomes $500 per person, which is a risk that many would be willing to bear if the returns on Boeing stock appear attractive.

By spreading the ownership of risky investments among a multitude of owners, capital markets can spread risks and encourage much larger investments and risks than would be tolerable for individual owners. ①

信息的市场失灵
MARKET FAILURES IN INFORMATION

Our analysis up to now has assumed that investors and consumers are well informed about the risks they face and that speculative and insurance markets function efficiently. In reality, markets involving risk and uncertainty are plagued by market failures. Two of the major failures are adverse selection and moral hazard. When these are present, markets may give ② the wrong signals, incentives may get distorted, and sometimes markets may simply not exist. Because of market failures, governments may decide to step in and offer social insurance.

道德风险与逆向选择
Moral Hazard and Adverse Selection

While insurance is a useful device for reducing risks, sometimes insurance is not available. The reason is that efficient insurance markets can thrive only under limited conditions.

What are the conditions for efficient insurance markets? First, there must be a large number of insurable events. Only then will companies be able ③ to spread the risks so that what is a large risk to an individual will become a small risk to many people.

Moreover, the events must be statistically independent. No prudent insurance company would sell all its fire-insurance policies in the same building or sell only hurricane insurance in Miami. Insurance companies try to diversify their coverage among many independent risks.

Additionally, there must be sufficient experience regarding such events so that insurance companies can reliably estimate the losses. For example, after the September 11 terrorist attacks, private terrorism insurance was canceled because insurance companies could not get reliable estimates of the chances of future attacks (see question 3 at the end of this chapter).

Finally, the insurance must be relatively free of moral hazard. **Moral hazard** is at work when insurance increases risky behavior and thereby changes the probability of loss. In many situations moral hazard is unimportant. Few people will risk death because they have a generous life-insurance policy. In some areas, moral hazard is severe. Studies indicate that the presence of insurance increases the amount of cosmetic surgery, and most medical-insurance policies consequently exclude this procedure.

④ 最后，保险业必须相对地摆脱道德风险。当保险增加了冒险性行为，并因此改变了损失的概率，**道德风险**就开始发生作用。

When these ideal conditions are met—when there are many outcomes, all more or less independent, and when the probabilities can be accurately gauged and are not contaminated by moral hazard—private insurance markets can function efficiently.

⑤ 当上述这些理想化的条件均得以满足时，即投保众多时，所有的投保之间或多或少地具备独立性；所有的随机事件均可以做出准确的评估，并不受道德风险破坏时，个人保险市场就可以高效地运转。

Sometimes, private insurance is limited or expensive because of adverse selection. **Adverse selection** ⑥ arises when the people with the highest risk are also those who are most likely to buy the insurance. Adverse selection can lead to a market where only the people with the highest risks are insured, or even to a situation where there is no market at all.

A good example occurs when a company is offering life insurance to a population made up of smokers and nonsmokers. Suppose the company cannot determine whether a person is a smoker, or perhaps there is a government policy which says that companies cannot differentiate among people on the basis of their personal behavior. However, people know their smoking habits. We see here the phenomenon of asymmetric information between buyer and seller. **Asymmetric information** occurs when buyers and ⑦ sellers have different information on important facts, such as a person's health status or the quality of a good being sold.

---

① 通过将风险投资分散到众多的所有者中，资本市场就可以分散风险，从而可以鼓励和吸引比个体所有者能够承受的更大的投资。

② 当这些迹象出现之后，市场就有可能发出错误的信号，激励机制会被扭曲，甚至有的时候市场的机制会出现完全不复存在的状况。由于市场失灵，所以政府决定介入，并提供社会保险。

③ 只有这样，保险公司才有能力去分散风险，使得对个体来讲是巨大的风险变成对许多人来讲的小风险。

⑥ 当最有可能遭遇高风险的人同时也是那些最有可能购买保险的人时，就会发生**逆向选择**现象。

⑦ 当买家和卖家就重要的事实（如一个人的健康状况或正在出售的商品的质量）有不同的信息时，就会出现**信息不对称**的现象。

Suppose that the company starts by setting a price based on the average mortality rate of the population. At this price, many smokers buy the insurance, but most nonsmokers do not. This means that people have sorted themselves unfavorably for the company—there is adverse selection. Soon the data begin to come in, and the company learns that its experience is much worse than it had forecast.

What happens next might be that the company raises the premiums on its insurance. As the price rises, more of the nonsmokers drop out, and the experience becomes even worse. Perhaps the price rises so high that even the smokers stop buying insurance. In the worst case, the market just dries up completely.

We see that the policy of uniform market pricing has led to adverse selection—raising the cost, limiting the coverage, and producing an incomplete market. Another example is the market for "lemons" such as used cars, where only the worst cars are sold, and the prices of used cars in equilibrium are reduced. Such market failures are particularly severe when there is asymmetric information between buyers and sellers.

Would You Invest in a Company for Grade Insurance?

A friend of yours proposes the following scheme: He wants you to invest in a start-up company called G-Insure.com, which offers grade insurance for students. In return for a modest premium, the company promises to compensate students for 100 percent of the income loss from poor grades. This seems like a good idea because income risks are very large for most people.

On reflection, can you see why G-Insure.com is almost sure to be a bad idea? The reason is that grades depend too much on individual effort and the market would therefore be infected with moral hazard and adverse selection. Students would be tempted to study less (moral hazard), and students who expected to have lower grades would be more prone to buy grade insurance (adverse selection). These problems might even produce a "missing market"—one in which supply and demand intersect at a zero level of grade insurance. So the company will either have no business or lose piles of money.

社会保险
SOCIAL INSURANCE

When market failures are so severe that the private ①
market cannot provide coverage in an effective manner, governments turn to **social insurance.** This consists of mandatory programs, with broad or universal coverage, funded by taxes or fees. These programs are insurance because they cover risky situations such as unemployment, illness, or low incomes during retirement. The taxing and regulatory powers of the government, plus the ability to prevent adverse selection through universal coverage, can make government insurance a welfare-improving measure. The rationale for social insurance was explained as follows by the distinguished public-policy economist Martin Feldstein:[1] [2]

> There are two distinct reasons for providing social insurance. Both reflect the asymmetry of information. The first is that asymmetric information weakens the functioning of private insurance markets. The second is the inability of the government to distinguish between those who are poor in old age or when unemployed because of bad luck or an irrational lack of foresight from those who are intentionally "gaming" the system by not saving in order to receive transfer payments.

The key point is that social insurance is provided when the requirements of private insurance are not met. Perhaps the risks are not independent, as when many people simultaneously become unemployed in a recession. Perhaps adverse selection is serious, as when people choose to buy catastrophic health insurance soon after they learn they have a terrible disease. Perhaps the risks cannot be easily evaluated, as in the case of insurance against terrorist attacks. In each of these cases, the private market functioned poorly or not at all, so the government stepped in with social insurance.

Let's spend a moment on the example of unemployment insurance. This is an example of a private market that cannot function because so many of the requirements for private insurance are violated: moral hazard is high (people may decide to become unemployed if benefits are generous); there is severe adverse selection (those who often lose jobs are more likely to participate); spells of unemployment are not independent (they tend to occur together

[1] See the reference in this chapter's Further Reading section.

---

① 当市场失灵的程度严重到个人保险市场无法以行之有效的方式提供所应覆盖的保险项目时，政府就要转向**社会保险**。社会保险由税收或者土地出让的收入建立，由各种强制性的保险项目构成，有广阔或者普遍性的覆盖面。

[2] Martin Feldstein：马丁·费尔德斯坦，1939年生于纽约，犹太裔美国经济学家，供给学派经济学之父，著名的逆效合作理论提出者，最具实力的与伯南克竞逐美联储主席的人选，里根政府时期曾任经济顾问委员会主席，奥巴马政府经济复苏顾问委员会委员。

during business-cycle recessions); and business cycles are unpredictable, so the risks cannot be accurately measured. At the same time, some countries feel that people should have a safety net under them should they lose their job. As a result, governments generally step in to provide unemployment insurance.

The next section discusses the important case of government-provided health care, which for many countries is the largest program of social insurance.

Social insurance is provided by governments when private insurance markets cannot function effectively and society believes that individuals should have a social safety net for the most severe risks such as unemployment, illness, and low incomes. ①

卫生保健：问题不会消失

C. HEALTH CARE: THE PROBLEM THAT WON'T GO AWAY

Health care is the single largest government program of the U.S. federal government. For 2008, expenditures on health care totaled close to $700 billion—larger even than the military budget. Most of this spending was on the social insurance program called Medicare, which provides subsidized health care for the elderly. The balance was health care for the poor, the disabled, and veterans. ②

The U.S. health-care system is controversial both because it is expensive and because a large number of people are not covered by insurance or other programs. Health-care spending rose from 4 percent of national output (GDP) in 1940 to 7 percent in 1970 and reached 16 percent in 2008. Yet almost 16 percent of the nonelderly population has no coverage. This has been called the problem that can't be solved and won't go away.

医疗保健经济学

THE ECONOMICS OF MEDICAL CARE

Why has health care been so controversial? In the United States, the health-care system is a partnership between the market system and the government. In recent years, this system has produced some remarkable accomplishments. Many terrible diseases, such as smallpox and polio, have been eradicated. Life expectancy—one of the key indexes of health—has improved more in developing countries since 1900 than it did during the entire prior span of recorded history. Advances in medical technology—from arthroscopic knee surgery to sophisticated anticancer drugs—have enabled more people to live pain-free and productive lives. ③

Even with these great achievements, major health problems remain unsolved in the United States: Infant mortality is higher than in many countries with lower incomes; many Americans are without health insurance coverage; great disparities in care exist between the rich and the poor; and communicable diseases like AIDS and tuberculosis are spreading.

The issue that most concerns the public, the business community, and political leaders is the exploding cost of health care. Virtually everyone agrees that the U.S. health system has contributed greatly to the nation's health, but many worry that it is becoming unaffordable.

卫生保健的特殊经济特点

Special Economic Features of Health Care

The health-care system in the United States has three characteristics that have contributed to the rapid growth of the health-care sector in recent years: a high income elasticity, rapid technological advance, and the increasing insulation of consumers from prices. ④

Health care has a high income elasticity, indicating that ensuring a long and fit life becomes increasingly important as people are able to pay for other essential needs. Goods with high income elasticities, other things held constant, tend to take a growing share of consumer income as income rises.

Health care has enjoyed rapid improvements in medical technology over the last century. Advances in fundamental biomedical knowledge, discovery and use of a wide variety of vaccines and pharmaceuticals, progress in understanding the spread of communicable diseases, and increasing public awareness of the role of individual behavior in areas such as smoking, drinking, and driving—all these have contributed to the remarkable improvement in the health of Americans. The new and improved technologies have created new markets and stimulated spending in the health-care sector.

Additionally, spending on health care has risen rapidly because of the increased subsidization of

[5] Health-care：本节内容为本版新加。开头的两段文字简要介绍了美国作为惟一的超级大国，是发达国家中惟一没有实行全民医保的尴尬现状。2010 年 3 月 21 日深夜，奥巴马竭力推行的健保案（Health Care Program）在美国国会众议院终于以 219 票对 212 票的 7 票优势惊险通过，从而使其成为继罗斯福总统 1935 年的《社会保障法》（Social security Act）、约翰逊总统 1965 年实行医疗保险法案（Medicare）后，在国民医疗和健康事业方面创造历史的总统。

① 当个人保险市场无法有效地运转时，全社会都认为每一个人都应该享有一个社会安全网络，以抵御诸如失业、疾病和低收入等最严重的风险。这时，社会保险由政府来提供。

② 医疗费用是美国联邦政府最大的政府支出。2008 年，医疗的总支出接近 7 000 亿美元，这一支出甚至超出了当年的国防预算。其中的绝大部分支出花在了称作医疗保险的社会保险项目上，该项目为老年人提供医疗补贴。其余部分用来为穷人、残疾人以及退伍军人提供医疗保障。

③ 在美国，医疗体系是一种介于市场体系和政府行为之间的合作关系。

④ 美国医疗体系有三个特征：很高的收入弹性；医疗技术突飞猛进；以及消费者逐渐地不再受价格的影响。这三者对近年来医保事业的飞速发展贡献良多。

medical care over recent decades. Health-care coverage in the United States is largely provided by employers as a tax-free fringe benefit. Tax-free status is, in effect, a government subsidy. In 1960, 60 percent of medical expenses were paid directly by consumers; by 2007, only 15 percent of medical expenses were paid out of pocket. This phenomenon is sometimes called the "third-party payment effect" to indicate that when a third party pays the bill, the consumer often ignores the cost.

All these forces (high income elasticity, the development of new technologies, and the increasing scope of third-party payments) contribute to the rapid growth of expenditures on medical care. ①

社会保险计划中的卫生保健

Health Care as a Social Insurance Program

Why is health care a social insurance program? Three reasons are cited by experts on health-care economics:

1. Many parts of the health-care system, such as the prevention of communicable diseases and the development of basic science, are *public goods* that the market will not provide efficiently. Eradication of smallpox benefited billions of potential victims, yet no firm could collect even a small fraction of the benefits of the eradication program. When one person stops smoking because of knowledge of its dangers, or when another person uses condoms after learning how AIDS is transmitted, these activities are no less valuable to others. This syndrome will lead to underinvestment in public health improvements by the market. ②
2. A second set of market failures arises because of the failure of private insurance markets. One significant reason for this failure is the presence of *asymmetric information* among patients, doctors, and insurance companies. Medical conditions are often isolated occurrences for patients, so such asymmetric information between doctors and patients means that patients may be completely dependent upon doctors' recommendations regarding the appropriate level of health care. Sometimes, as when patients are wheeled into the emergency room, they may be incapacitated and unable to choose treatment strategies for themselves, so demand depends even more upon the recommendations of the suppliers. Special protection must be given to ensure that consumers do not unwittingly purchase unnecessary, poor-quality, or high-cost services. ③

   There are also informational asymmetries between the patient and the insurance provider. People may know more about their medical condition than do insurance companies. Low-risk individuals may choose not to buy health insurance. This leads to *adverse selection*, which increases the average riskiness of the group and subsequently increases the cost for those who do participate. It is not surprising that healthy people in their twenties are those most likely to be uninsured.
3. A third concern of government policy is *equity*—to provide a minimum standard of medical care for all. In part, good health care is increasingly viewed as a basic right in wealthy countries. But good health care is also a good social investment. Inadequate health care is particularly harmful for poor people not only because they tend to be sicker than wealthier individuals but also because their incomes are almost entirely derived from their labor. A healthier population is a more productive population because healthier people have higher earnings and require less medical care. ④

   Inadequate health care is most costly for children. The medical condition of poor and minority children in the United States has in some dimensions actually worsened in recent years. Sick children are handicapped from the start: they are less likely to attend school, perform more poorly when they do attend, are more likely to drop out, and are less likely to get good jobs with high pay when they grow up. No country can prosper when a significant fraction of its children have inadequate medical care.

医疗护理分配

Rationing Health Care

Whether or not a country provides equal health care for all its residents, health care must be rationed because supply is limited. Until we get to the point where every symptom of every hypochondriac can be extensively examined, probed, and treated, it will be necessary to leave some perceived medical need unsatisfied. There is no choice but to ration health care. ⑤

However, it is not obvious *how* we are to ration such a good. Most goods and services are rationed

---

① 所有这些力量（高收入弹性、新技术的发展以及第三方支付范围的扩大）加速了医疗保险费用的飞速增长。

② 医疗体系的许多内容，诸如传染病预防和基础科学研究，都属于市场无法有效提供的公共产品。

③ 由于私人保险市场的失灵，导致二级市场出现失灵。造成这种问题出现的重要原因是病人、医生以及保险公司三者之间的信息不对称。

④ 政府政策所要关注的第三个问题是所提供的最低医疗保障对所有公民来讲是否公平。在部分富裕国家中，良好的医疗保障正逐渐被视为公民的基本权利，但良好的医疗保障也是一项很好的社会投资。

⑤ 一个国家无论是否能给它的居民提供公平的医疗保障，都必须是限量供应的，因为供给是有限的。

by the purse. Prices ration out the limited supply of fancy cars and mansions, as well as the not-so-fancy food and shoes, to those who most want and can afford them. In many areas of health care, by contrast, we do not allow prices to ration out services to the highest bidders. For example, we do not auction off liver transplants or blood or emergency-room access to the highest bidder. Rather, we desire that these goods be allocated equitably.

The subsidization of health care leads to shortages, and demand for the good must therefore be limited in some other way. This phenomenon is known as *nonprice rationing*. Many of us have experienced this kind of rationing when we wait in line for a good or service. When price is not allowed to rise to balance supply and demand, some other mechanism must be found to "clear the market."

Figure 11-3 illustrates nonprice rationing in the medical market. Suppose that there are only Q_0 units of medical care available with a consumer demand

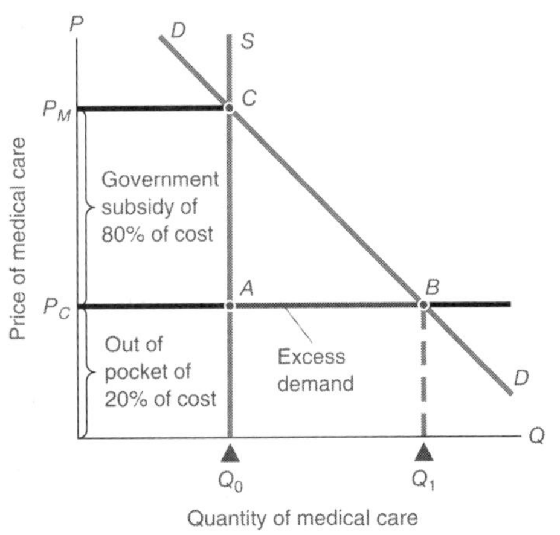

① **FIGURE 11-3. Free Health Care Leads to Nonprice Rationing**

When governments provide free or subsidized access to medical care, some way must be found to ration out the limited services. In the example of a government subsidy, when the quantity demanded exceeds the quantity supplied, the excess demand *AB* must be choked off by some mechanism other than price. Most often, people must wait for nonemergency services, sometimes for hours, sometimes for months.

function of *DD*. The market-clearing price would come at *C*, where quantities supplied and demanded are equal. However, because the consumer pays only 20 percent of the costs out of pocket, the quantity demanded is Q_1. The *AB* segment is unsatisfied demand, which is subject to nonprice rationing; the greater the subsidy, the more nonprice rationing must be used.

Health care is an economic commodity like ② shoes and gasoline. Physicians' services, nursing care, hospitalization, and other services are limited in supply. The demands of consumers—summing up the critical, the reasonable, the marginal, and the nonsensical—outstrip the available resources. But the resources must somehow be rationed out. Rationing of health care according to dollar votes is unacceptable because it does too much damage to the public health, leaves crucial demands unmet, and impoverishes many. What should be the scope of the market, and what nonmarket mechanism should be used where the market is supplanted? These questions are the crux of the great debate about medical care.

[3] Dollar vote：美元选票，经济学中的一种类比术语，用来说明消费者购买性选择行为刺激厂家继续生产和市场继续供给的现象，即对一种特定产品所支付的每一美元可以被认为是投向该种产品的一张"美元选票"。

创新与信息

D. INNOVATION AND INFORMATION

One of the most important topics in economics is the economics of information. Information includes things as varied as e-mails, songs, new vaccines, and even the textbook you are reading. Information is a very different kind of commodity from things like pizza and shoes because information is expensive to produce but cheap to reproduce. Because of the unusual nature of information, it is subject to market failures, so we need to develop different kinds of public policies to regulate it—the law of "intellectual property."

熊波特的激进式创新
Schumpeter's Radical Innovation

We set the stage for our discussion by returning to the economics of imperfect competition that we discussed in the previous two chapters. We learned that imperfect competitors set prices too high, earn supernormal profits, and neglect product quality.

This dismal view of monopoly was challenged by one of the great economists of the last century,

① 图 11-3. 免费的医疗保障导致非价格配给

② 医疗是像鞋子或者汽油一样的经济商品。医生所提供的服务、护士所给予的护理、住院治疗以及其他的医疗服务在供给的意义上都是有限的。就消费者的需求而言，危重型的、合理型的、边缘型的以及荒谬型的统统加在一起，已经远远地超过了现有的医疗资源。但在某种程度上，这些资源又必须合理地配给出去。根据美元选票来配给医疗服务是令人无法接受的，因为这损害了公共健康，使关键需求得不到满足，并使很多人的境况恶化。市场所应覆盖的范围是什么？那些不能被市场化的地方所应采取的非市场机制又是什么？这一系列的问题都是争论不休的医疗保障问题的关键症结所在。

Joseph Schumpeter. He argued that the essence of economic development is innovation and that monopolists are in fact the wellsprings of innovation in a capitalist economy.

Joseph Schumpeter: Economist as Romantic

Born in the Austrian Empire, Joseph Schumpeter (1883–1950), a legendary scholar whose research ranged widely in the social sciences, led a flamboyant private life.

He began studying law, economics, and politics at the University of Vienna—then one of the world centers of economics and the home of the "Austrian School" that today reveres laissez-faire capitalism. As a professor, he was often the champion of his students. Six months into his teaching career, he charged into the library and scolded the librarian for not allowing his students to have free use of the books. After trading insults, the librarian challenged Schumpeter to a duel. Schumpeter won by nicking the librarian on the shoulder, and his students thereupon had unlimited access to the library.

In between dueling, insulting the stodgy faculty by showing up at faculty meetings in riding pants, and carousing, Schumpeter devoted himself to introducing economic theory to the European continent, founding the Econometric Society, and traveling to England and America. He later moved to Harvard University, where he eventually became embittered as the theories of his great rival, John Maynard Keynes, swept the profession.

Schumpeter's writings covered much of economics, sociology, and history, but his first love was economic theory. Schumpeter's early classic, *The Theory of Economic Development* (1911), broke with the traditional static analysis of its time by emphasizing the importance of the entrepreneur or innovator, the person who introduces "new combinations" in the form of new products or methods of organization. Innovations result in temporary supernormal profits, which are eventually eroded away by imitations. Ever the romantic, Schumpeter saw in the entrepreneur the hero of capitalism, the person of "superior qualities of intellect and will," motivated by the will to conquer and the joy of creation.

His magisterial *History of Economic Analysis* (published posthumously in 1954) is a superb survey of the emergence of modern economics. His "popular" book, *Capitalism, Socialism, and Democracy* (1942), laid out his startling hypothesis on the technological superiority of monopoly and developed the theory of competitive democracy, which later grew into public-choice theory. (See question 7 at the end of this chapter.) He ominously predicted that capitalism would wither away because of disenchantment among the elites. Were he alive today, he might well join in the conservative complaint that the welfare state drains the economic vitality from the market economy.

信息经济学
The Economics of Information

Modern economics emphasizes the special problems ①
involved in the **economics of information.** Information is a fundamentally different commodity from normal goods. Because information is costly to produce but cheap to reproduce, markets in information are subject to severe market failures.

Consider the production of a software program, such as Windows Vista. Developing this program took several years and cost Microsoft many billions of dollars. Yet you can purchase a legal copy for about \$220 or buy an illegal pirated copy for \$5. The same phenomenon is at work in pharmaceuticals, entertainment, and other areas where much of the value of a good comes from the information it contains. In each of these areas, the research and development on the product may be an expensive process that takes years. But once the information is recorded on paper, in a computer, or on a compact disc, it can be reproduced and used by a second person essentially for free.

The inability of firms to capture the full mon- ②
etary value of their inventions is called **inappropriability.** Inventions are not fully appropriable because other firms may imitate or pirate an invention, in which case the other firms may derive some of the benefits of the inventive investments; sometimes, imitators may drive down the price of the new product, in which case consumers would get some of the rewards. Case studies have found that the *social return* to invention (the value of an invention to all consumers and producers) is many times the appropriable *private return* to the inventor (the monetary value of the invention to the inventor).

Information is expensive to produce but cheap ③
to reproduce. To the extent that the rewards to invention are inappropriable, we would expect private research and development to be underfunded, with the most significant underinvestment in basic

---

① 现代经济学强调涉及**信息经济学**的特殊问题。从根本上来讲，信息是一种与正常品截然不同的商品。因为信息本身的生产成本很高，但复制的成本却非常低，所以，信息市场的失灵问题通常非常严重。

② 企业不可能将自身发明所拥有的货币价值全部占有的现象被称为**不可分拨性**。

③ 信息的生产成本很高，但复制成本很低。就一定程度而言，对发明的奖励具有不可分拨性，因此，我们预期，由于信息的不可分拨性，私人研发资金不足，尤其在基础研究领域投资不足。研究成果的不可分拨性和社会的高收益使绝大多数政府对于健康和科学领域的基础研究都给予补贴，并对其他的创新行为提供了特别的激励。

research because that is the least appropriable kind of information. The inappropriability and high social return on research lead most governments to subsidize basic research in the fields of health and science and to provide special incentives for other creative activities.

知识产权

Intellectual Property Rights

Governments have long recognized that creative activities need special support because the rewards for producing valuable information are reduced by imitation. The U.S. Constitution authorizes Congress "to promote the Progress of Science and useful Arts, by securing, for limited Times, to Authors and Inventors, the exclusive Right to their respective Writings and Discoveries." Thus special laws governing ① patents, copyrights, business and trade secrets, and electronic media create **intellectual property rights.** The purpose is to give the owner special protection against the material's being copied and used by others without compensation to the owner or original creator.

The earliest intellectual property right was the ② **patent,** under which the U.S. government creates an exclusive use (in effect, a limited monopoly) over a "novel, nonobvious, and useful" invention for a limited period, currently set at 20 years. Similarly, copyright laws provide legal protection against unauthorized copying of original works in different media such as text, music, video, art, software, and other information goods.

Why would governments actually encourage monopolies? In effect, patents and copyrights grant property rights to inventors over books, music, and ideas. By allowing inventors to have exclusive use of their intellectual property, the government increases the degree of appropriability and thereby increases the incentives for people to invent useful new products, write books, compose songs, and write computer software. A patent also requires disclosure of the technological details of the invention, which encourages further invention and lawful imitation. Examples of successful patents include those on the cotton gin, the telephone, the Xerox machine, and many profitable drugs.

互联网的困境

The Dilemma of the Internet

Inventions that improve communications are hardly limited to the modern age. But the rapid growth of electronic storage, access, and transmission of information highlights the dilemma of providing incentives for creating new information. Many new information technologies have large up-front or sunk costs but virtually zero marginal costs. With the low cost of electronic information systems like the Internet, it is technologically possible to make large amounts of information available to everyone, everywhere, at close to zero marginal cost. Perfect competition cannot survive here because a price equal to a zero marginal cost will yield zero revenues and therefore no viable firms.

The economics of the information economy highlights the conflict between efficiency and incentives. On the one hand, all information might be provided free of charge—free economics textbooks, free movies, free songs. Free provision of information looks economically efficient because the price would thereby be equal to the marginal cost, which is zero. But a zero price on intellectual property would destroy the profits and therefore reduce the incentives to produce new books, movies, and songs because creators would reap little return from their creative activity. Society has struggled with this dilemma in the past. But with the costs of reproduction and transmission so much lower for electronic information than for traditional information, finding sensible public policies and enforcing intellectual property rights is becoming ever more difficult.

Experts emphasize that intellectual property laws are often hard to enforce, especially when they apply across national borders. The United States has a long-running trade dispute charging that some country condone the illegal copying of American movies, musical recordings, and software.

In a world increasingly devoted to developing new ③ knowledge—much of it intangible, like music, movies, patents, new drugs, and software—governments must find a middle ground in intellectual property rights. If intellectual property rights are too strong, this will lead to high prices and monopoly losses, while too weak intellectual property laws will discourage invention and innovation.

---

① 因此，政府制定了特别法案，用以指导和管理专利、版权、商业和贸易机密以及电子传媒，这就产生了**知识产权**。

② 最早的知识产权是**专利权**，在该法案的保护下，美国政府营造了一个排它性的使用环境（即在有效期内的有限垄断），就“新颖、神奇和实用”的发明设定了受保护期限，现在为 20 年。

③ 在一个新知识不断日新月异的世界中，有许许多多像音乐、电影、专利、新药物、软件等的无形资产，政府必须在这些知识产权领域找到一个适中的立场。如果知识产权的保护过度，则会导致高价格和垄断性损失，但是，过弱的知识产权保护法将严重地阻碍发明和创新。

SUMMARY

A. Economics of Risk and Uncertainty

1. Economic life is full of uncertainty. Consumers face uncertain incomes and employment patterns as well as the threat of catastrophic losses; businesses have uncertain costs, and their revenues contain uncertainties about price and production.
2. In well-functioning markets, arbitrage, speculation, and insurance help smooth out the unavoidable risks. Speculators are people who buy and sell assets or commodities with an eye to making profits on price differentials across markets. They move goods across regions from low-price to high-price markets, across time from periods of abundance to periods of scarcity, and even across uncertain states of nature to periods when chance makes goods scarce.
3. The profit-seeking action of speculators and arbitragers tends to create certain equilibrium patterns of price over space, time, and risks. These market equilibria are zero-profit outcomes where the marginal costs and marginal utilities in different regions, times, or uncertain states of nature are in balance. To the extent that speculators moderate price and consumption instability, they are part of the invisible-hand mechanism that performs the socially useful function of reallocating goods from feast times (when prices are low) to famine times (when prices are high).
4. Speculative markets allow individuals to hedge against unwelcome risks. The economic principle of risk aversion, which derives from diminishing marginal utility, implies that individuals will not accept risky situations with zero expected value. Risk aversion implies that people will buy insurance to reduce the potentially disastrous declines in utility from fire, death, or other calamities.

B. The Economics of Insurance

5. Insurance and risk spreading tend to stabilize consumption in different states of nature. Insurance takes large individual risks and spreads them so broadly that they become acceptable to a large number of individuals. Insurance is beneficial because, by helping to equalize consumption across different uncertain states, it raises the expected level of utility.
6. The conditions necessary for the operation of efficient insurance markets are stringent: there must be large numbers of independent events and little chance of moral hazard or adverse selection. When market failures such as adverse selection arise, prices may be distorted or markets may simply not exist.
7. If private insurance markets fail, the government may step in to provide social insurance. Social insurance is provided by governments when private insurance markets cannot function effectively and society believes that individuals should have a social safety net for major risks such as unemployment, illness, and low incomes. Even in the most laissez-faire of advanced market economies today, governments insure against unemployment and health risks in old age.

C. Health Care: The Problem That Won't Go Away

8. Health care is the largest social insurance program. The health-care market is characterized by multiple market failures that lead governments to intervene. Health-care systems have major externalities. Additionally, the asymmetric information between doctors and patients leads to uncertainties about the appropriate treatment and level of care, and the asymmetry between patients and insurance companies leads to adverse selection in the purchase of insurance. Finally, because health care is so important to human welfare and to labor productivity, most governments strive to provide a minimum standard of health care to the population.
9. When the government subsidizes health care and attempts to provide universal coverage, there will be excess demand for medical services. One of the challenges is to develop efficient and equitable mechanisms of nonprice rationing.

D. Innovation and Information

10. Schumpeter emphasized the importance of the innovator, who introduces "new combinations" in the form of new products and new methods of organization and is rewarded by temporary entrepreneurial profits.
11. Today, the economics of information emphasizes the difficulties involved in the efficient production and distribution of new and improved knowledge. Information is different from ordinary goods because it is expensive to produce but cheap to reproduce. The inability of firms to capture the full monetary value of their inventions is called inappropriability. To increase appropriability, governments create intellectual property rights governing patents, copyrights, trade secrets, and electronic media. The growth of electronic information systems like the Internet has increased the dilemma of how to efficiently price information services.

CONCEPTS FOR REVIEW

Risk, Uncertainty, and Insurance

arbitrage leading to regional equalization of prices
ideal seasonal price pattern
speculation, arbitrage, hedging
risk aversion and diminishing marginal utility
consumption stability vs. instability
insurance and risk spreading
moral hazard, adverse selection
social insurance
nonprice rationing

Economics of Information

information economics
inappropriability, protection of intellectual property rights, dilemma of efficient production of knowledge
market failure in information

FURTHER READING AND INTERNET WEBSITES

Further Reading

The concept of social insurance was described by Martin Feldstein in "Rethinking Social Insurance," *American Economic Review,* March 2005 and available at *www.nber.org/feldstein/aeajan8.pdf.*

For an analysis of gambling, see William R. Eadington, "The Economics of Casino Gambling," *Journal of Economic Perspectives,* Summer 1999.

The Schumpeterian hypothesis was developed in Joseph Schumpeter, *Capitalism, Socialism, and Democracy* (Harper & Row, New York, 1942).

Many of the economic, business, and policy issues involved in the new information economy are covered in a nontechnical book by two eminent economists, Carl Shapiro and Hal R. Varian, *Information Rules* (Harvard Business School Press, Cambridge, Mass., 1998). A discussion of the economics of the Internet is contained in Jeffrey K. MacKie-Mason and Hal Varian, "Economic FAQs about the Internet," *Journal of Economic Perspectives,* Summer 1994, p. 92.

A discussion by the U.S. government of infringement of intellectual property rights can be found at *www.ustr.gov/Document_Library/Reports_Publications/Section_Index.html.*

Websites

One of the most interesting websites about the Internet and intellectual property rights is compiled by Hal R. Varian, chief economist of Google and former dean of the School of Information Management and Systems at the University of California at Berkeley. This site, called "The Economics of the Internet, Information Goods, Intellectual Property and Related Issues," is at *www.sims.berkeley.edu/resources/infoecon.*

Information on the American health-care system is usefully compiled by the National Center on Health Statistics at *www.cdc.gov/nchs/.*

QUESTIONS FOR DISCUSSION

1. Suppose a friend offers to flip a fair coin, with you paying your friend $100 if it comes up heads and your friend paying you $100 if it comes up tails. Explain why the expected dollar value is $0. Then explain why the expected utility value is negative if you are risk-averse.
2. Consider the example of grade insurance (see page 218). Suppose that with a grade-insurance policy, students would be compensated $5000 a year for each point that their grade point average fell below the top grade (the resulting number might be an estimate of the impact of grades on future earnings). Explain why the presence of grade insurance would produce moral hazard and adverse selection. Why would moral hazard and adverse selection make insurance companies reluctant to sell grade insurance? Are you surprised that you cannot buy grade insurance?
3. After the terrorist attacks of September 11, 2001, most insurance companies canceled their insurance coverage for terrorism. According to President Bush, "More than $15 billion in real estate transactions have been canceled or put on hold because owners and investors could not obtain the insurance protection they need."

As a result, the federal government stepped in to provide coverage for up to $90 billion in claims. Using the principles of insurance, explain why insurance companies might decline to insure property against terrorist attacks. Explain whether or not you think the federal program is an appropriate form of social insurance.

4. In the early nineteenth century, little of the nation's agricultural output was sold in markets, and transportation costs were very high. What would you expect to have been the degree of price variation across regions as compared with that of today?
5. Assume that a firm is making a risky investment (say, spending $2 billion developing a competitor to Windows). Can you see how the diversified ownership of this firm could allow near-perfect risk spreading on the software investment?
6. Health insurance companies sometimes do not allow new participants to be covered on "existing conditions," or preexisting illnesses. Explain why this policy might alleviate problems of adverse selection.
7. Joseph Schumpeter wrote as follows:

> The modern standard of life of the masses evolved during the period of relatively unfettered "big business." If we list the items that enter the modern workman's budget and, from 1899 on, observe the course of their prices, we cannot fail to be struck by the rate of the advance which, considering the spectacular improvement in qualities, seems to have been greater and not smaller than it ever was before. Nor is this all. As soon as we inquire into the individual items in which progress was most conspicuous, the trail leads not to the doors of those firms that work under conditions of comparatively free competition but precisely to the doors of the large concerns—which, as in the case of agricultural machinery, also account for much of the progress in the competitive sector—and a shocking suspicion dawns upon us that big business may have had more to do with creating that standard of life than keeping it down. (*Capitalism, Socialism, and Democracy*)

   Use this passage to describe the tradeoff between "static" monopoly inefficiencies and "dynamic" efficiencies of technological change.

8. Long-term care for the elderly involves helping individuals with activities (such as bathing, dressing, and toileting) that they cannot perform for themselves. How were these needs taken care of a century ago? Explain why moral hazard and adverse selection make long-term-care insurance so expensive today that few people choose to buy it.
9. Economic studies have found that the private rate of return on inventions is typically as low as one-third of the social return. Explain this finding in terms of the economics of innovation.

PART THREE

Factor Markets: Labor, Land, and Capital

要素市场：劳动、土地和资本

CHAPTER

12

How Markets Determine Incomes

市场如何决定收入

[1] F. Scott Fitzgerald：弗朗西斯・斯科特・菲茨杰拉德（1896~1940），著名的美国小说家，“迷惘一代”的代表人物之一。1925 年，代表作《了不起的盖茨比》（*The Great Gatsby*）的出版，确立了其在美国文学史上的地位。《了不起的盖茨比》通过描写主人公盖茨比的悲剧，揭示了“美国梦”的幻灭。

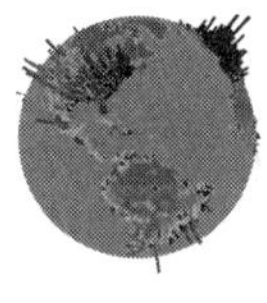

Ernest Hemingway：欧内斯特・海明威（1899~1961），蜚声世界文坛的美国小说家，1954 年诺贝尔文学奖获得者，“新闻体”小说的创始人，“迷惘一代”的主要代表人物。“迷惘一代”出自美国作家和诗人格特鲁德・斯坦（Gertrude Stein，1874~1946）在沙龙上的一次谈话，海明威将其附于其著名小说《太阳照样升起》（*The Sun Also Rises*）的扉页，原文为：“*You are all a lost generation.*”。中国读者熟悉的海明威的著名小说还有：

《永别了，武器》（*A Farewell to Arms*），1929；

《丧钟为谁而鸣》（*For Whom the Bell Tolls*），1940；

《老人与海》（*The Old Man and the Sea*），1952；等。

1961 年 7 月 2 日，海明威用心爱的猎枪结束了自己波澜壮阔的一生。

本书所引用的海明威与菲茨杰拉德之间的这一段对话实质上是海明威本人一次错误的引用，出自海明威与爱尔兰文学批评家玛丽・卡罗（Mary Colum，1884~1957）一次邂逅后有关菲茨杰拉德未完成小说的谈话，原文如下：

Hemingway: I am getting to know the rich.

Colum: I think you'll find the only difference between the rich and other people is that the rich have more money.

You know, Ernest, the rich are different from us. [1]

F. Scott Fitzgerald

Yes, I know. They have more money than we do.

Ernest Hemingway

收入与财富

A. INCOME AND WEALTH

Earlier chapters have surveyed the output and prices of goods and services produced by tiny farms and giant corporations. But the vast array of products that we enjoy do not simply gush from the earth—they are produced by workers who are equipped with machines, which are housed in factories, which are sitting on land. These inputs into the productive process earn factor incomes—wages, profits, interest, and rents. The time has come to understand the determination of factor prices along with the forces that affect the distribution of income among the population.

America is a land of extremes of income and wealth. If you are one of the 400 richest Americans, you are likely to be a 60-year-old white male with a degree from a top university and a net worth of about \$4 billion. This tiny sliver of American society owns about 3 percent of the total wealth of the country. In the past, you made your fortune in manufacturing or real estate, but recent billionaires come largely from information technology and finance. Your ②
voyage to the top was as much the product of birth as of brains, for your family probably gave you a head start with an expensive education, but there are more self-made men and women today than there were a decade ago.

At the other extreme are forgotten people who never make the cover of *Forbes* or *People* magazine. Listen to the story of Robert Clark, homeless and unemployed. A roofer and Vietnam veteran, he came to Miami from Detroit looking for work. He slept on the city streets on a piece of cardboard covered by a stolen sheet. Every day he and other homeless men crept out of the culverts into the daylight to work for temporary-employment firms. These firms charged clients \$8 to \$10 an hour, paid the men the minimum wage, and then took most of the money back for transportation and tools. Clark's pay stub showed earnings of \$31.28 for 31 hours of work.

How can we understand these extremes of income and wealth? Why are some people paid \$10 million a year, while others net only \$1 an hour? Why is real estate in Tokyo or Manhattan worth thousands of dollars a square foot, while land in the desert may sell for but a few dollars an acre? And what is the source of the billions of dollars of profits earned by giant enterprises like Microsoft and General Electric?

Questions about the distribution of income are among the most controversial in all economics.

[1]（续）菲茨杰拉德这句话的全文出自其 1926 年发表的短篇小说《阔少》（*The Rich Boy*）的第三段：“Let me tell you about the very rich. *They are different from you and me.* They possess and enjoy early, and it does something to them, makes them soft, where we are hard, cynical where we are trustful, in a way that, unless you were born rich, it is very difficult to understand.”

② 在你的人生旅程中能否步入社会名流的行列与你的出生和智商密切相关，如果你的家庭有能力给你提供昂贵的受教育机会，就使你有一个领先的起点。但是，与十年前相比，今天有更多的男女是靠自我奋斗获得了成功。

Some people argue that high incomes are the unfair ① result of past inheritance and luck while poverty stems from discrimination and lack of opportunity. Others believe that people get what they deserve and that interfering with the market distribution of income would injure an economy's efficiency and make everyone worse off. Government programs in America today reflect an uneasy consensus that incomes should be largely determined by market earnings but the government should provide a social safety net to catch the deserving poor who fall below some minimum standard of living.

收 入
INCOME

In measuring the economic status of a person or a nation, the two yardsticks most often used are income and wealth. **Income** refers to the flow of wages, inter- ② est payments, dividends, and other things of value accruing during a period of time (usually a year). The aggregate of all incomes is *national income*, the components of which are shown in Table 12-1. The biggest share of national income goes to labor, either as wages or salaries or as fringe benefits. The remainder goes to the different types of *property income:* rent, net interest, corporate profits, and proprietors' income. This last category basically includes the returns to the owners of small businesses.[1]

The earnings in a market economy are distributed ③ to the owners of the economy's factors of production in the form of wages, profits, rent, and interest.

要素收入和个人收入
Factor Incomes vs. Personal Incomes

It is important to understand the distinction between factor incomes and personal incomes. Table 12-1 reports the distribution of factor incomes—the division between labor and property incomes. But the same person may own many different factors of production. For example, someone might receive a salary, earn interest on money in a savings account, get dividends from shares in a mutual fund, and collect rent on a real-estate investment. In economic lan- ④ guage, we observe that a person's market income is

[1] Economists and accountants often measure "income" in different ways. We studied accounting measures of income and wealth in Chapter 7.

Type of income	Amount ($, billion)	Share of total (%)	Examples
Labor income:			
Wages and salaries	6,356	51.8	Autoworker's wages; teacher's salary
Benefits and other labor income	1,457	11.9	Company contribution to pension fund
Property income:			
Proprietors' income	1,056	8.6	Barber's earnings; lawyer's share of partnership net income
Rental income	40	0.3	Landlord's rent from apartments after expenses and depreciation
Corporate profits	1,642	13.4	Microsoft's profits
Net interest	664	5.4	Interest paid on savings account
Taxes on production and other	1,056	8.6	
Total	**12,271**	**100.0**	

TABLE 12-1. Division of National Income, 2007 ⑤

National income includes all the incomes paid to factors of production. Almost three-quarters consists of wages and other kinds of compensation of labor, while the rest is divided among rents, corporate profits, and the incomes of proprietors.

Source: U.S. Department of Commerce, Bureau of Economic Analysis, at the Web page *www.bea.gov.*

① 有些人认为，高收入只不过是过去财产继承以及运气降临的不公平的结果，而贫穷则是缺乏机遇所致。而另有一些人则坚信，人们得到的即是他们应得的，对市场分配机制的人为干预会损伤一个经济体的效率，还会使每一个人的境况恶化。

② **收入**系指一段时间内（通常为一年）工资、利息收益、股息以及应计的其他有价物品的流入。

③ 市场经济中的收入以工资、利润、租金和利息的形式向经济体中各生产要素的所有者进行分配。

④ 在经济学语汇里，我们所观察到的一个人的市场收入是其出售的生产要素的数量乘以其所得工资或者每一种要素的价格的结果。

⑤ 表 12-1. 2007 年度国民收入分配表

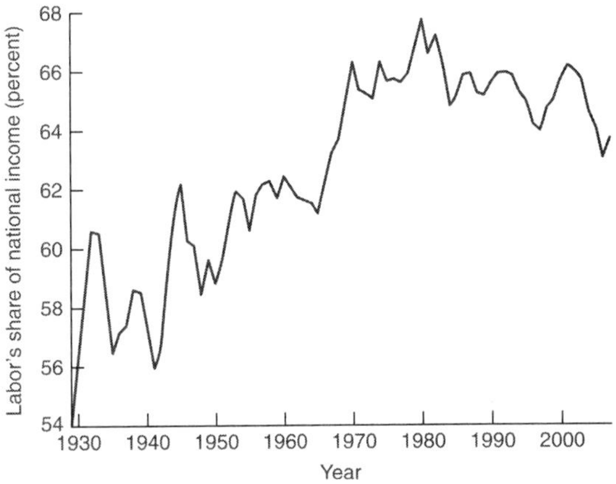

FIGURE 12-1. The Share of Labor in National Income ①

The share of labor income increased gradually until 1970. Since then, it has been remarkably stable at around two-thirds of national income. The remainder of income is distributed among rents, interest, corporate profits, and proprietors' income and miscellaneous items like production taxes.

simply the quantities of factors of production sold by that person times the wage or price of each factor.

About two-thirds of national income goes to labor, while the rest is distributed as some form of returns to property. The last quarter-century has been a turbulent one. What has been the impact of energy shortages, the computer revolution, globalization, corporate downsizing, and the financial turmoil of recent years on labor's share of the total income pie? Looking at Figure 12-1, we can see that the share of national income going to labor has changed very little since 1970. This is one of the remarkable features of the income distribution in the United States.

政府的角色
Role of Government

How does government fit into this picture? Governments at every level form the largest source of wages, rents, and interest payments. The results of government purchases are included in the payments to factors of production shown in Table 12-1.

Yet government also has a direct role in incomes that does not show up in Table 12-1. To begin with, the government collects a sizable share of national income through taxation and other levies. In 2008 about 30 percent of gross domestic product was collected by federal, state, and local governments as various types of taxes, including personal income taxes, corporate-profit taxes, and social security taxes.

But what governments tax, they also spend or give away. Governments at all levels provide ②
incomes in the form of **transfer payments,** which are payments by governments to individuals that are not made in return for current goods or services. The biggest single category of transfer payments is social security for older Americans, but transfer payments also include unemployment insurance, farm subsidies, and welfare payments. Whereas Americans derived almost none of their incomes from governments in 1929, fully 15 percent of personal incomes in 2008 came from government transfer payments.

Personal income equals market income plus ③
transfer payments. Most market income comes from wages and salaries; a small, affluent minority derives its market income from earnings on property. The major component of government transfers is social security payments to the elderly.

财　富
WEALTH

We see that some income comes from interest or dividends on holdings of bonds or stocks. This brings us to the second important economic concept: **Wealth** ④
consists of the net dollar value of assets owned at a given point in time. Note that wealth is a *stock* (like the volume of a lake) while income is a *flow* per unit of time (like the flow of a stream). A household's wealth

① 图 12-1. 劳动收入在国民收入中的份额

② 各级政府以**转移支付**的形式向社会发放收入，这是由政府向个体提供的支付，它不需要用商品或服务加以回报。

③ 个人的收入等于市场收入与转移支付的和。市场收入的绝大部分来自工资和薪金，极少数富人的市场收入来自其财产的收益。政府转移支付的主要部分是为老年人支付的社会保险。

④ **财富**是指在既定的时点上所拥有的资产的美元净值。请注意，这里所讲的财富是一个存量的概念（如某一湖泊的库容量），而收入是每一单位时间内的流量（如某一条河的流量）。

Distribution of Assets of All Families as Percentage of All Assets, 1989–2004

	Percentage of Total Assets		
	1989	1995	2004
Financial:			
Bank deposits and similar	9.4	7.7	6.2
Bonds	3.1	2.3	1.9
Stocks	6.2	10.4	11.5
Retirement accounts	6.6	10.3	11.4
Other	5.3	6.0	4.7
Tangible and other assets:			
Own home	31.9	30.0	32.3
Other real estate and property	13.4	10.0	11.1
Vehicles	3.9	4.5	3.3
Business equity	18.6	17.2	16.7
Other	1.7	1.5	1.0
	Thousands of 2004 Dollars		
Family net worth:			
Median	68.9	70.8	93.1
Average	272.3	260.8	448.2

TABLE 12-2. Trends in Wealth of American Households ①

Households own tangible assets (such as houses and cars) as well as financial assets (such as savings accounts and stocks). The largest single asset for most Americans continues to be the family home. The median wealth is much smaller than the average, reflecting the great inequality of wealth holding. [2]

Source: Federal Reserve Board, Survey of Consumer Finances, available in *Federal Reserve Bulletin or at www.federalreserve.gov/Pubs/oss/oss2/2004/bull0206.pdf.*

includes its tangible items (houses, cars and other consumer durable goods, and land) and its financial holdings (such as cash, savings accounts, bonds, and stocks). All items that are of value are called *assets,* while those that are owed are called *liabilities.* The difference between total assets and total liabilities is called wealth or *net worth.*

Table 12-2 presents a breakdown of the asset holdings of Americans from 1989 to 2004. The single most important asset of most households is the family home: 68 percent of families own houses, as compared with 55 percent a generation ago. Most households own a modest amount of financial wealth in savings accounts, and about one-fifth directly own corporate stocks. But it turns out that a large proportion of the nation's financial wealth is concentrated in the hands of a small fraction of the population. ③ About one-third of all wealth is owned by the richest 1 percent of American households.

边际生产率决定投入的价格

B. INPUT PRICING BY MARGINAL PRODUCTIVITY

The **theory of income distribution** (or **distribution theory**) studies how incomes are determined in a market economy. ④ People are often puzzled by the vast differences in incomes of different families. Are they caused by differences in talents? By monopoly power? By government intervention? Why is Bill Gates worth $60 billion while half of American black families have net worth less than $20 thousand? Why

① 表 12-2. 美国家庭所拥财富的变化趋势。

[2] 此处文字由 16 版的 *Tangible and Financial Assets of Households* 到 17~18 版的 *Trends in Assets Owned by American Families*，再到本版的标题，反映了作者对家庭财产定位的变化，*Wealth* 更为客观，更符合美国当前的财富结构。

③ 上表表明，美国全国的金融资产中的大部分集中掌握在少数人手中。

④ **收入分配理论**（或称**分配理论**）所研究的是在市场经济中收入如何决定的问题。

are land prices so much higher in the city than in the desert?

Our first answer to these questions is that the ① distribution theory is a special case of the theory of prices. Wages are the price of labor; rents are the price for using land; and so forth. Moreover, the prices of factors of production are primarily set by the interaction between supply and demand for different factors—just as the prices of goods are largely determined by the supply and demand for goods.

But pointing to supply and demand is just the first step on the road to understanding income distribution in a competitive market economy. We will see that the key to incomes lies in the *marginal products* of different factors of production. In this section, we will see that wages are determined by the value of the *marginal product of labor,* or what is known as the marginal revenue product of labor. The same holds for other factors of production as well. We first discuss this new concept and then show how it solves the puzzle of how incomes are determined.

要素需求的性质
THE NATURE OF FACTOR DEMANDS

The demand for factors differs from that for con- ② sumption goods in two important respects: (1) Factor demands are derived demands, and (2) factor demands are interdependent demands.

要素需求是派生需求
Demands for Factors Are Derived Demands

Let's consider the demand for office space by a firm which produces computer software. A software company will rent office space for its programmers, customer service representatives, and other workers. Similarly, other companies like pizza shops or banks will need space for their activities. In each region, there will be a downward-sloping demand curve for office space linking the rental being charged by landlords to the amount of office space desired by companies—the lower the price, the more space companies will want to rent.

But there is an essential difference between ordinary demands by consumers and the demand by firms for inputs. Consumers demand final goods like computer games or pizzas because of the direct enjoyment or utility these consumption goods provide. By contrast, a business does not pay for inputs like office space because they yield direct satisfaction. Rather, it buys inputs because of the production and revenue that it can gain from employment of those factors.

Satisfactions are in the picture for inputs—but at one stage removed. The satisfaction that consumers get from playing computer games determines how many games the software company can sell, how many clerks it needs, and how much office space it must rent. The more successful its software, the greater its demand for office space. An accurate analysis of the demand for inputs must, therefore, recognize that consumer demands do *ultimately* determine business demands for office space.

This analysis is not limited to office space. Consumer demands determine the demand for all inputs, including farmland, oil, and pizza ovens. Can you see how the demand for professors of economics is ultimately determined by the demand for economics courses by students?

The firm's demand for inputs is derived indirectly ③ from the consumer demand for its final product.

Economists therefore speak of the demand for ④ productive factors as a **derived demand.** This means that when firms demand an input, they do so because that input permits them to produce a good which consumers desire now or in the future. Figure 12-2 on page 234 shows how the demand for a given input, such as fertile cornland, must be regarded as being derived from the consumer demand curve for corn. In the same way, the demand for office space is derived from the consumer demand for software and all the other products and services provided by the companies that rent office space.

要素需求相互依赖
Demands for Factors Are Interdependent

Production is a team effort. A chain saw by itself is useless for cutting down a tree. A worker with empty hands is equally worthless. Together, the worker and the saw can cut the tree very nicely. In other words, the productivity of one factor, such as labor, depends upon the amount of other factors available to work with.

Therefore, it is generally impossible to say how much output has been created by a single input taken by itself. Asking which factor is more important is like asking whether a mother or a father is more essential in producing a baby.

---

① 对于上述这些问题，我们的回答首先是，分配理论是价格理论中的一个特殊案例。

② 要素需求与对消费商品的需求有两点不同：(1) 要素需求是衍生需求；(2) 要素需求是相互依赖的需求。

③ 企业对投入的需求是从消费者对其最终产品的消费需求中间接地衍生出来的。

④ 因此，经济学家们在谈到生产要素的需求时把它当作**派生需求**。其含义在于，当企业对某种投入有需求时，即是因为投入可使企业生产出消费者在现在或者是未来所需要的商品。

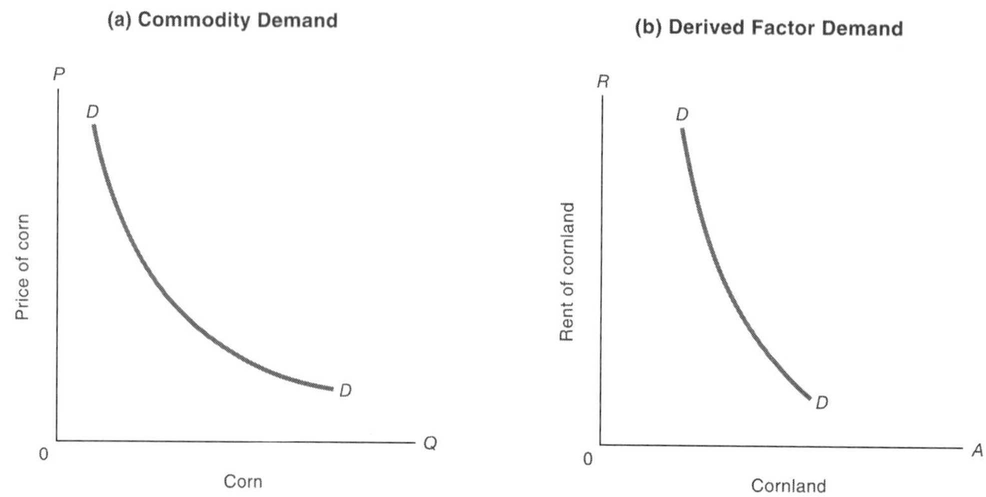

FIGURE 12-2. Demand for Factors Is Derived from Demand for Goods They Produce ①

The green curve of derived demand for cornland comes from the blue curve of commodity demand for corn. Shift the blue curve out, and out goes the green curve. If the blue commodity curve becomes more inelastic, the same tends to happen to the green input demand curve.

It is the *interdependence* of productivities of land, ② labor, and capital that makes the distribution of income a complex topic. Suppose that you were in charge of determining the income distribution of a country. If land had by itself produced so much, and labor had by itself produced so much, and machinery had by itself produced the rest, distribution would be easy. Moreover, under supply and demand, if each factor produced a certain amount by itself, it could enjoy the undivided fruits of its own work.

But reread the above paragraph and underline such words as "by itself." They refer to a fantasy world of independent productivities which simply does not exist in reality. When an omelette is produced by chef's labor and chicken's eggs and cow's butter and land's natural gas, how can you unscramble the separate contributions of each input?

To find the answer, we must look to the interaction of marginal productivities and factor supplies—both of which determine the competitive prices and quantities of factors of production.

Review of Production Theory

Before showing the relationship between factor prices and marginal products, we will review the essentials of Chapter 6's production theory.

The theory of production begins with the notion of the *production function*. The production function indicates the maximum amount of output that can be produced, with a given state of technical knowledge, for each combination of factor inputs. The production-function concept provides a rigorous definition of marginal product. Recall that the *marginal product* of an input is the extra product or output added by 1 extra unit of that input while other inputs are held constant.[2] The first three columns

[2] Note that the marginal product of a factor is expressed in *physical* units of product per unit of additional input. So economists sometimes use the term "marginal physical product" rather than "marginal product," particularly when they want to avoid any possible confusion with a concept we will soon encounter called "marginal revenue product." For brevity, we will skip the word "physical" and abbreviate marginal product as *MP*.

① 图 12-2. 企业对产品生产的需求派生出对要素的需求

② 正是由于土地、劳动和资本在生产活动中的相互依赖关系，致使收入的分配问题变得非常复杂。

Marginal Revenue Product

(1) Unit of labor (workers)	(2) Total product (bushels)	(3) Marginal product of labor (bushels per worker)	(4) Price of output ($ per bushel)	(5) Marginal revenue product of labor ($ per worker)
0	0			
		20,000	3	60,000
1	20,000			
		10,000	3	30,000
2	30,000			
		5,000	3	15,000
3	35,000			
		3,000	3	9,000
4	38,000			
		1,000	3	3,000
5	39,000			

TABLE 12-3. Calculation of Marginal Revenue Product for Perfectly Competitive Firm ①

The marginal product of labor is shown in column (3). Marginal revenue product of labor shows how much additional revenue the firm receives when an additional unit of labor is employed. It equals the marginal product in column (3) times the competitive output price in column (4).

of Table 12-3 provide a review of the way marginal products are calculated.

As a final element of review, recall the *law of diminishing returns*. Column (3) of Table 12-3 shows that each successive unit of labor has a declining marginal product. "Declining marginal product" is another name for diminishing returns. Moreover, we can interchange land for labor, varying the amount of land while holding constant labor and other inputs, and we would generally observe the law of diminishing returns at work for land as well as for labor.

分配理论和边际收益产量

DISTRIBUTION THEORY AND MARGINAL REVENUE PRODUCT

The fundamental point about distribution theory ② is that *the demands for the various factors of production are derived from the revenues that each factor yields on its marginal product.* Before showing this result, we begin by defining some new terms.

边际收益产量

Marginal Revenue Product

We can use the tools of production theory to devise a key concept, *marginal revenue product (MRP)*. Suppose we are operating a giant shirt factory. We know how many shirts each additional worker produces. But the firm wants to maximize profits measured in dollars, for it pays salaries and dividends with money, not with shirts. We therefore need a concept that measures the additional *dollars* each additional unit of input produces. Economists give the name "marginal rev- ③ enue product" to the money value of the additional output generated by an extra unit of input.

The **marginal revenue product** of input A is the ④ additional revenue produced by an additional unit of input A.

① 表 12-3. 完全竞争企业边际收益产量的计算

② 有关分配理论的基本的观点是，对各种生产要素的需求是从依赖于边际产量的每一种要素的全部生产收益中派生而来的。

③ 经济学家们将增加每一个单位的投入所产生的额外产出的货币价值命名为"边际收益产量"。

④ 投入 A 的**边际收益产量**是每追加一个单位的投入 A 所产生的额外收益。

Perfectly Competitive Case. It is easy to calculate marginal revenue product when product markets are perfectly competitive. In this case, each unit of the worker's marginal product (MP_L) can be sold at the competitive output price (P). Moreover, since we are considering perfect competition, the output price is unaffected by the firm's output, and price therefore equals marginal revenue (MR). ① If we have an MP_L of 10,000 bushels and a price and MR of \$3, the dollar value of the output produced by the last worker—the marginal revenue product of labor (MRP_L)—is \$30,000 (equal to 10,000 × \$3). This is shown in column (5) of Table 12-3. Hence, under perfect competition, each worker is worth to the firm the dollar value of the last worker's marginal product; the value of each acre of land is the marginal product of land times the output price; and so forth for each factor.

Table 12-3 provides the essential linkage between production theory and factor demand theory; it should be studied carefully. The first three columns show the inputs, output, and marginal product of labor. Multiplying the MP in column (3) by the price in column (4), we derive the marginal revenue product of labor (in dollars per worker) in column (5). It is this last column which is critical for determining the demand for labor, as we will see later in this chapter. Once we know the wage rate, we can calculate the demand for labor from column (5).

Imperfect Competition. What happens in the case of imperfect competition, where the individual firm's demand curve is downward-sloping? Here, the marginal revenue received from each extra unit of output sold is less than the price because the firm must lower its price on previous units to sell an additional unit. Each unit of marginal product will be worth $MR < P$ to the firm. ②

To continue our previous example, say that the MR is \$2 while the price is \$3. Then the MRP of the second worker in Table 12-3 would be \$20,000 (equal to the MP_L of 10,000 × the MR of \$2), rather than the \$30,000 of the competitive case.

To summarize:

> Marginal revenue product represents the additional revenue a firm earns from using an additional unit of an input, with other inputs held constant. It is calculated as the marginal product of the input multiplied by the marginal revenue obtained from selling an extra unit of output. This holds for labor (L), land (A), and other inputs. In symbols: ③
>
> $$\text{Marginal revenue product of labor } (MRP_L) = MR \times MP_L$$
>
> $$\text{Marginal revenue product of land } (MRP_A) = MR \times MP_A$$
>
> and so forth.
>
> Under conditions of perfect competition, because $P = MR$, this implies:
>
> $$\text{Marginal revenue product } (MRP_i) = P \times MP_i$$
>
> for each input.

生产要素的需求
THE DEMAND FOR FACTORS OF PRODUCTION

Having analyzed the underlying concepts, we now show how profit-maximizing firms decide upon the optimal combination of inputs, which allows us to derive the demand for inputs.

追求利润最大化的厂商的要素需求
Factor Demands for Profit-Maximizing Firms

What determines the demand for any factor of production? We can answer this question by analyzing how a profit-oriented firm chooses its optimal combination of inputs.

Imagine that you are a profit-maximizing farmer. In your area, you can hire all the farmhands you want at \$20,000 per worker. Your accountant hands you a spreadsheet with the data in Table 12-3. How would you proceed?

You could try out different possibilities. If you hire one worker, the additional revenue (the MRP) is \$60,000 while the marginal cost of the worker is \$20,000, so your extra profit is \$40,000. A second worker gives you an MRP of \$30,000 for an additional profit of \$10,000. The third worker produces extra output yielding revenue of only \$15,000 but costs \$20,000; hence, it is not profitable to hire the third worker. Table 12-3 shows that the maximum profit is earned by hiring two workers.

By using this reasoning, we can derive the rule for choosing the optimal combination of inputs:

> To maximize profits, firms should add inputs up to the point where the marginal revenue product of ④

---

① 此外，由于我们在此讨论的是完全竞争的案例，产品的价格可以免受该企业产量的影响，因此此时的价格等于边际收益（MR）。

② 从每一个所售出的额外单位的产品中所获得的边际收益低于价格，因为该企业必须在此前所售产品数量的基础上施行降低价格的措施来出售额外单位的产品。

③ 边际收益产量表示在其他投入保持不变的情况下，企业从一个单位的额外投入中所赚得的额外收益。这一收益是投入后的边际产量乘以从出售一个单位的额外产量中所获得的边际收益的结果。

④ 要想达到利润的最大化，企业就应该将投入增加到所投入的边际收益产量等于边际成本，或投入的价格为止。

the input equals the marginal cost or price of the input.

For perfectly competitive factor markets, the rule is even simpler. Recall that under perfect competition the marginal revenue product equals price times marginal product ($MRP = P \times MP$).

The profit-maximizing combination of inputs for a perfectly competitive firm comes when the marginal product times the output price equals the price of the input: ①

$$\text{Marginal product of labor} \times \text{output price} = \text{price of labor} = \text{wage rate}$$

$$\text{Marginal product of land} \times \text{output price} = \text{price of land} = \text{rent}$$

and so forth.

We can understand this rule by the following reasoning: Say that each kind of input is bundled into little packages each worth \$1—packages of \$1 worth of labor, \$1 worth of land, and so forth. To maximize profits, firms will purchase inputs up to that point where each little \$1 package produces output which is worth just \$1. In other words, each \$1 input package will produce *MP* units of corn so that the $MP \times P$ just equals \$1. The *MRP* of the \$1 units is then exactly \$1 under profit maximization. ②

Least-Cost Rule. We can restate the condition much more generally in a way that applies to both perfect and imperfect competition in product markets (as long as factor markets are competitive). Reorganizing the basic conditions shown above, profit maximization implies: ③

$$\frac{\text{Marginal product of labor}}{\text{Price of labor}} = \frac{\text{marginal product of land}}{\text{price of land}} = \cdots = \frac{1}{\text{marginal revenue}}$$

Suppose that you own a cable television monopoly. If you want to maximize profits, you will want to choose the best combination of workers, land easements for your cables, trucks, and testing equipment to minimize costs. If a month's truck rental costs \$8000 while monthly labor costs per worker are \$800, costs are minimized when the marginal products *per dollar of input* are the same. Since trucks cost 10 times as much as labor, truck *MP* must be 10 times labor *MP*.

Least-cost rule: Costs are minimized when the marginal product per dollar of input is equalized for each input. This holds for both perfect and imperfect competitors in product markets. ④

边际收益产量和要素需求

Marginal Revenue Product and the Demand for Factors

Having derived the *MRP* for different factors, we can now understand the demand for factors of production. We just saw that a profit-maximizing firm would choose input quantities such that the price of each input equaled the *MRP* of that input. This means that from the *MRP* schedule for an input, we can immediately determine the relationship between the price of the input and the quantity demanded of that input. This relationship is what we call the input demand curve.

Glance back at Table 12-3 on page 235. This table shows in the last column the *MRP* of labor for our corn farm. By the profit-maximizing condition, we know that at a wage of \$60,000 the firm would choose 1 unit of labor; at a \$30,000 wage, 2 units of labor would be sought; and so forth.

The *MRP* schedule for each input gives the demand schedule of the firm for that input. ⑤ 每一种投入的边际收益产量（*MRP*）表均可以推算出企业对该投入的需求表。

We have used this result in Figure 12-3 to draw a labor demand curve for our corn farm using the data shown in Table 12-3. We have in addition drawn a smooth curve through the individual points to show how the demand curve would appear if fractional units of labor could be purchased.

From Firm to Market Demand. The final step in determining the demand for labor and other factors is the aggregation of the demand curves for different firms. As with all demand curves, the competitive-market demand curve is the *horizontal summation of the demand curves of all the firms.* Hence, if there were 1000 identical firms, then the market demand for labor would be exactly like that in Figure 12-3 except the horizontal axis would have each entry multiplied by 1000. We see, then, that the competitive demand ⑥ 如果所有的需求曲线均已齐备，将它们进行水平加总之后，就可以得到竞争市场的需求曲线。

① 对于一家完全竞争企业来讲，当其边际产量乘以该产品的价格等于其所投入的价格时，其综合成果即实现了利润的最大化。

② 为了实现利润的最大化，企业对投入的采购直到每一美元的投入组合生产出刚好价值一美元的产品为止。

③ **最低成本法则**：我们以更广泛的方式来重述这一条件——既适用于完全竞争，也适用于不完全竞争产品市场（只要要素市场是竞争性的）。

④ **最低成本法则**：在每一美元投入的边际产量等于每一笔投入时，成本可实现最小化。这一点对于完全竞争的产品市场和非完全竞争的产品市场同样适用。

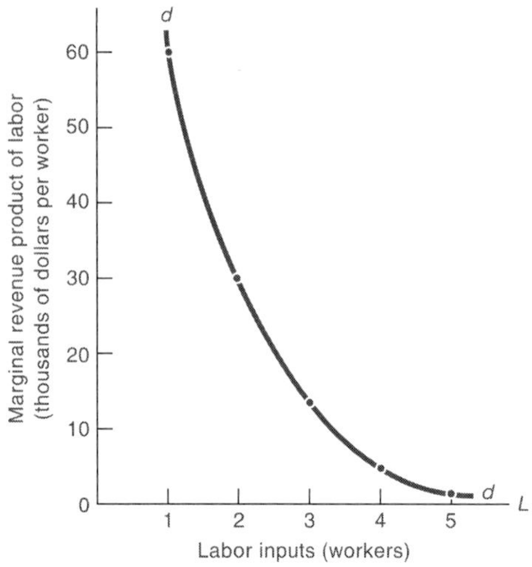

FIGURE 12-3. Demand for Inputs Derived through Marginal Revenue Products ①

The demand for labor is derived from the marginal revenue product of labor. This figure uses the data for the competitive firm displayed in Table 12-3.

for factors of production is determined by the sum of the demands of all the firms at each marginal revenue product.

Substitution Rule. A corollary of the least-cost rule ② is the **substitution rule:** If the price of one factor rises while other factor prices remain fixed, the firm will profit from substituting more of the other inputs for the more expensive factor. A rise in labor's price, P_L, will reduce MP_L/P_L. Firms will respond by reducing employment and increasing land use until equality of marginal products per dollar of input is restored—thus lowering the amount of needed L and increasing the demand for land acres. A rise in land's price alone will, by the same ③ logic, cause labor to be substituted for more expensive land. Like the least-cost rule, the substitution rule and the derived demand for factors apply to both perfect and imperfect competition in product markets.

生产要素的供给
SUPPLY OF FACTORS OF PRODUCTION

A complete analysis of the determination of factor prices and of incomes must combine both the demand for inputs just described and the supplies of different factors. The general principles of supply vary from input to input, and this topic will be explored in depth in the following chapters. At this point we provide a few introductory comments.

In a market economy, most factors of production are privately owned. People "own" their labor ④ in the sense that they control its use; but this crucial "human capital" can today only be rented, not sold. Capital and land are generally privately owned by households and by businesses.

Decisions about *labor* supply are determined by many economic and noneconomic factors. The important determinants of labor supply are the price of labor (i.e., the wage rate) and demographic factors, such as age, gender, education, and family structure. The quantity of *land* and other natural resources is determined by geology and cannot be significantly changed, although the quality of land is affected by conservation, settlement patterns, and improvements. The supply of *capital* depends upon past investments made by businesses, households, and governments. In the short run, the stock of capital is fixed like land, but in the long run the supply of capital reacts to economic factors such as risks, taxes, and rates of return.

Can we say anything about the elasticity of supply of inputs? Actually, the supply curve may slope positively or be vertical and might even have a negative slope. For most factors, we would expect that the supply responds positively to the factor's price in the long run; in this case, the supply curve would slope upward and to the right. The *total* supply of land is usually thought to be unaffected by price, and in this case the *total* supply of land will be perfectly inelastic, with a vertical supply curve. In some special cases, when the return to the factor increases, owners may supply less of the factor to the market. For example, if people feel they can afford to work fewer hours when wages rise, the supply curve for labor might bend backward at high wage rates, rather than slope upward.

---

① 图 12-3. 边际收益产量派生的投入需求

② **替代法则**是最低成本法则的一个推论：如果一种要素的价格在其他要素的价格保持不变的情况下上升，企业将更多地从使用其他要素来取代此种涨价后的要素中获利。

③ 同样的道理，土地价格的单独上涨将使企业求助于使用更多的劳动，来替代更为昂贵的土地。

④ 就这种意义来讲，人们“拥有”自己的劳动系指他们控制了劳动的使用。但是，此种至关重要的“人力资本”现在只允许租借，不允许出售。资本和土地在通常情况下，都是家族和企业的私有财产。

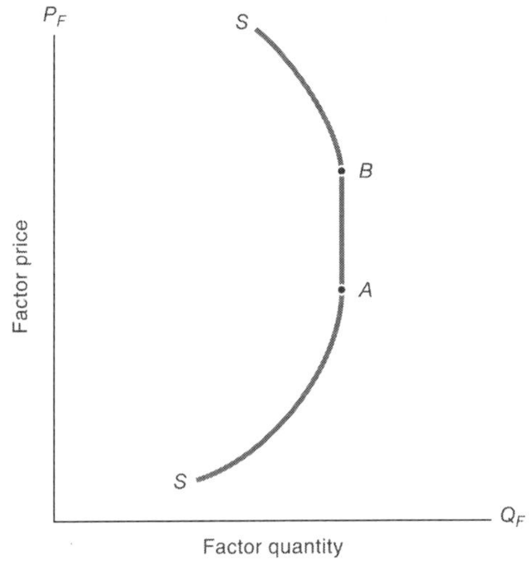

FIGURE 12-4. Supply Curve for Factors of Production ①

Supplies of factors of production depend upon characteristics of the factors and the preferences of their owners. Generally, supplies will respond positively to price, as in the region below *A*. For factors that are fixed in supply, like land, the supply curve will be perfectly inelastic, as from *A* to *B*. In special cases where a higher price of the factor increases the income of its owner greatly, as with labor or oil, the supply curve may bend backward, as in the region above *B*.

The different possible elasticities for the supply of factors are illustrated by the *SS* supply curve shown in Figure 12-4.

供给和需求决定要素价格 DETERMINATION OF FACTOR PRICES BY SUPPLY AND DEMAND

A full analysis of the distribution of income must combine the supply of and demand for factors of production. Earlier parts of this section provided the underpinnings for analysis of demand and gave a brief description of supply. We showed that, for given factor prices, profit-maximizing firms would choose input combinations according to their marginal revenue products. As the price of land falls, each farmer would substitute land for other inputs such as labor, machinery, and fertilizer. Each farmer therefore would show a demand for cornland inputs like that in Figure 12-2(*b*).

How do we obtain the *market demand* for inputs (whether cornland, unskilled labor, or computers)? We add together the individual demands of each of the firms. Thus at a given price of land, we add together all the demands for land of all the firms at that price; and we do the same at every price of land. In other words, *we add horizontally the demand curves for land of all the individual firms to obtain the market demand curve for land.* ② We follow the same procedure for any input, summing up all the derived demands of all the businesses to get the market demand for each input. And in each case, the derived demand for the input is based on the marginal revenue product of the input under consideration.[3] Figure 12-5 shows a general demand curve for a factor of production as the *DD* curve.

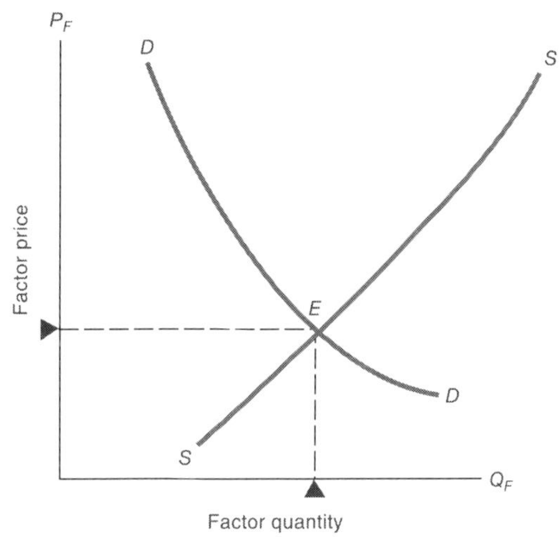

FIGURE 12-5. Factor Supply and Derived Demand Interact to Determine Factor Prices and Income Distribution ③

Factor prices and quantities are determined by the interaction of factor supply and demand.

[3] Note that this process of adding factor demand curves horizontally is exactly the same procedure that we followed in obtaining market demand curves for goods in Chapter 5.

① 图 12-4. 生产要素的供给曲线

② 换言之，我们把所有单个企业对土地的需求曲线按水平方向加总，就可以得到土地的市场需求曲线。

③ 图 12-5. 要素供给与衍生需求的相互作用决定要素价格与收入分配

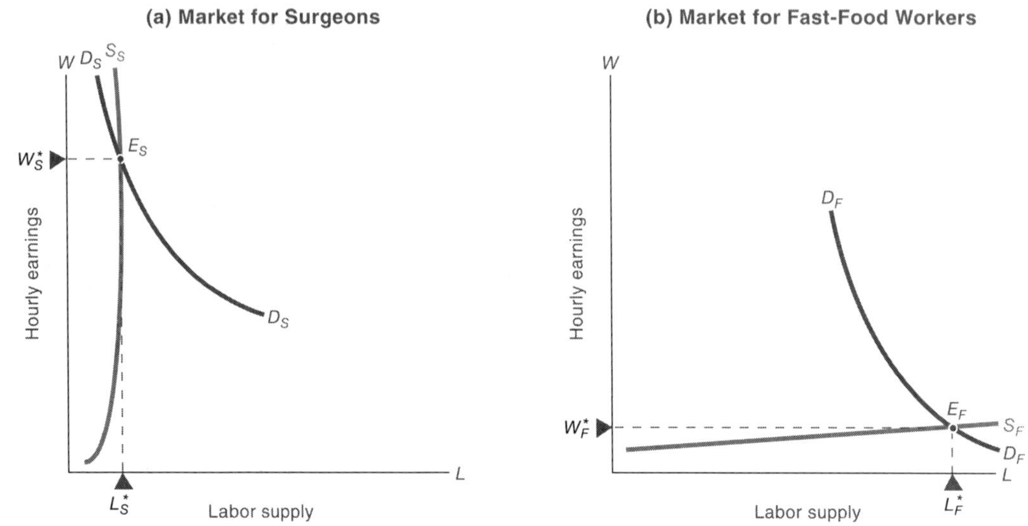

FIGURE 12-6. The Markets for Surgeons and Fast-Food Workers ①

In (a), we see the impact of a limited supply of surgeons: small output and high earnings per surgeon. What would be the effect on total earnings of surgeons and on the price of an operation if an aging population increased the demand for surgeons?

In (b), open entry and low skill requirements imply a highly elastic supply of fast-food workers. Wages are beaten down and employment is high. What would be the effect on wages and employment if more teenagers looked for jobs?

How do we find the overall market equilibrium? ② *The equilibrium price of the input in a competitive market comes at that level where the quantities supplied and demanded are equal.* This is illustrated in Figure 12-5, where the derived demand curve for a factor intersects its supply curve at point *E*. Only at this price will the amount that owners of the factor willingly supply just balance the amount that the buyers willingly purchase.

The Wages of Slicers and Flippers

We can apply these concepts to two factor markets to see why disparities in incomes are so high. Figure 12-6 shows the markets for two kinds of labor—surgeons and fast-food workers. The supply of surgeons is severely limited by the need for medical licensing and the length and cost of education and training. Demand for surgery is growing rapidly, along with other health-care services. The result is that surgeons earn $300,000 a year on average. Moreover, an increase in demand will result in a sharp increase in earnings, with little increase in the number of surgeons.

At the other end of the earnings scale are fast-food workers. These jobs have no skill or educational requirements and are open to virtually everyone. The supply of food workers is highly elastic. As the demand for fast foods increased in recent years, employment grew sharply. Because of the ease of entry into this market, the average full-time fast-food employee was near the bottom of the earnings pyramid at $19,000 a year. What is the reason for the vast difference in earning power of surgeons and hamburger flippers? It is mainly the quality of labor, not the quantity of hours.

The Rich and the Rest

If you are one of the richest Americans, you might have $50 million of interest, dividends, and other property income, while the median household earns less than

① 图 12-6. 外科医生与快餐业工人的市场

② 我们如何才能找到整个市场的均衡呢？在竞争性的市场环境中，投入的均衡价格系指供给量等于需求量时的价格水平。

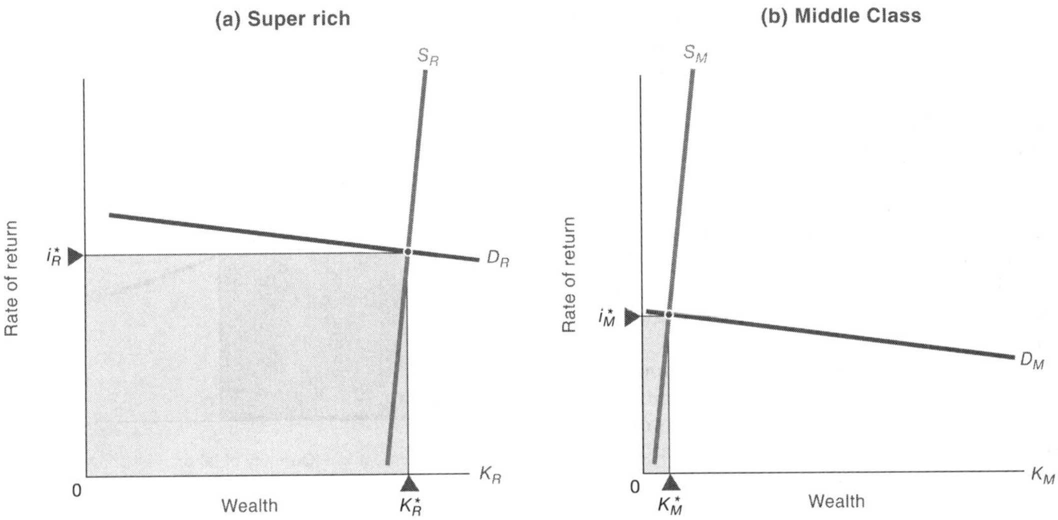

FIGURE 12-7. Differences in Total Returns to Wealth ①

This figure shows the demand and supply for wealth held by the super rich and the middle class. The horizontal axis shows the total wealth, while the vertical axis shows the rate of return on wealth. The shaded region is $r \times W$, or total income earned on wealth. Why is the shaded rectangle of the rich so much larger than that of the middle class? The reason is primarily that the wealth of the rich (K_R) is so much larger than that of the middle class (K_M).

$1000 a year on its financial wealth. Figure 12-7 explains this difference. The rate of return on stocks or bonds is not that much higher for the richest than for the middle class.

Rather, the rich have a much bigger wealth base on which to earn. The shaded rectangles in Figure 12-7 show the capital earnings of the two groups. Make sure you understand that it is the amount of wealth rather than the rate of return that makes the rectangle of the top wealth holders so large.

These two examples show how factor prices and individual incomes are determined by underlying market forces. ② Supply and demand operate to create high returns to factors that have either limited supply or high demand as reflected in high marginal revenue product. If a factor such as surgeons becomes scarcer—say, because training requirements are tightened—the price of this factor will rise and surgeons will enjoy higher incomes. ③ However, if demand decreases in some field like psychiatry—perhaps because insurance companies decide to cut back on psychiatric coverage, or because close substitutes like social workers and psychologists lure away patients, or because people rely more heavily on medications than on therapy—the lower demand will produce a fall in psychiatrists' incomes. Competition giveth, but competition also taketh away. [4]

国民收入的分配

THE DISTRIBUTION OF NATIONAL INCOME

With our new understanding of marginal-productivity theory, we can now come back to the question raised at the beginning of the chapter. In a world of intense competition, how do markets allocate national income among the many factors of production?

This section develops the neoclassical theory of factor-income distribution. ⑤ It can be applied to competitive markets for any number of final products and factor inputs. But it is most easily grasped if we consider a simplified world with only one product in

[4] *Competition giveth, but competition also taketh away*：源自英语中常讲的所谓引自圣经的名言 *The Lord giveth and the Lord taketh away*，系中古英语版本。本书前文也有类似的表述手法。*Giveth* 和 *taketh* 系中古英语（Middle English，以 1066 年诺曼底公爵征服英格兰建立诺曼底王朝始，至文艺复兴兴盛期开始，即约 1400 年止）的用法。权威的《钦定圣经》（*The Holy Bible of King James Version*）中《旧约》（*The Books of the Old Testament*）的《约伯记》（*Book of Job*）篇第一章第 21 节中的原文为：……the LORD gave, and the LORD hath taken away; ……《钦定圣经》的英文与莎士比亚剧本中的英文一样，属于早期现代英文。此处的文字有点类似现代中文的表达中半文半白的修辞手法，以求画龙点睛的效果。整句含义相当于成语“成也萧何，败也萧何”。参照本句的句式结构，译为“成也竞争，败也竞争”，可谓贴切。

① 图 12-7. 财富总收益的差异

② 供给和需求给有限供给或高需求的要素创造了高回报，这反映在高边际收益产品上。

③ 然而，如果像精神病科这样一些领域的需求减少，其原因可能是保险公司削减了医疗保险对精神病的承保范围；或者是因为关闭了像社工组织这样的替代性资源，使得心理医生吸引走了一些病人；还有可能因为过重地依赖药物治疗而忽略了心理疏导，从而导致对心理医生的需求降低，使心理医生的收入下滑。真可谓成也竞争，败也竞争。

⑤ 这一理论可以应用在任意产量的最终产品及其相应的要素投入量的竞争市场中。

which all accounts are kept in "real" units, that is, in terms of goods. The goods could be corn or a basket of different goods and services, but we will call it *Q*. Moreover, by setting the price equal to 1, we can conduct the entire discussion in real terms, with the value of output being *Q* and with the wage rate being the real wage in terms of goods or *Q*. In this situation, a production function tells how much *Q* is produced for each quantity of labor-hours, *L*, and for each quantity of acres of homogeneous land, *A*. Note that because $P = 1$, under perfect competition $MRP = MP \times P = MP \times 1 = MP$. The wage is therefore equal to MP_L.

The analysis in the neoclassical model is as follows: A first worker has a large marginal product because there is so much land to work with. Worker 2 has a slightly smaller marginal product. But the two workers are alike, so they must get exactly the same wage. The puzzle is, which wage? The *MP* of worker 1, or that of worker 2, or the average of the two?

Under perfect competition, the answer is clear: Landlords will not hire a worker if the market wage exceeds that worker's marginal product. So competi- ①
tion will ensure that *all* the workers receive a wage rate equal to the marginal product of the last worker.

But now there is a surplus of total output over the wage bill because earlier workers had higher *MP*s than the last worker. What happens to the excess *MP*s produced by all the earlier workers? The excess stays with the landlords as their residual earnings, which we will later call *rent*. Why, you might ask, do the landlords, who may be sitting on their yachts thousands of miles away, earn anything on the land? The reason is that each ②
landowner is a participant in the competitive market for land and rents the land for its best price. Just as workers compete with each other for jobs, landowners compete with each other for for workers. We see in this competitive world no labor unions keeping wages up, no landowners' conspiracy exploiting workers, and indeed no particular fairness in the wages and rents earned—we see just the operation of supply and demand.

We have therefore determined the total wages paid to labor. Figure 12-8 shows that the marginal product curve of labor gives the demand curve of all employers in terms of real wages. Labor-supply factors determine the supply of labor (shown as *SS*). The equilibrium wage comes at *E*. The total wages paid to labor are given by $W \times L$ (for example, if

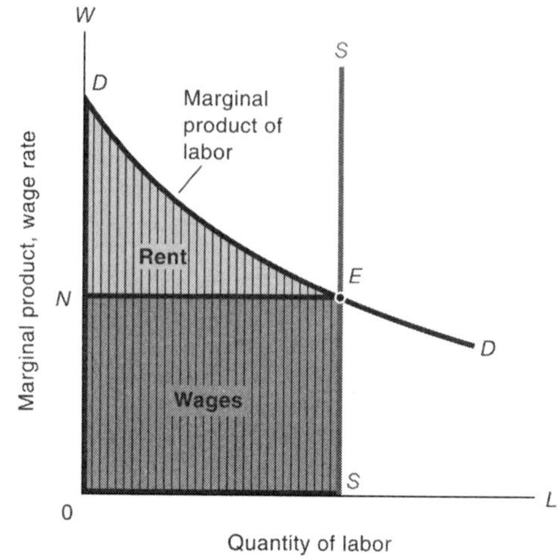

FIGURE 12-8. Marginal Product Principles Determine Factor Distribution of Income ③

Each vertical slice represents the marginal product of that unit of labor. Total national output *ODES* is found by adding all the vertical slices of *MP* up to the total supply of labor at *S*.

The distribution of output is determined by marginal product principles. Total wages are the lower rectangle (equal to the wage rate *0N* times the quantity of labor *0S*). Land rents get the residual upper triangle *NDE*.

$W = 5$ and $L = 1$ million, total wages = 5 million); this is shown by the dark rectangle, *0SEN*.

Surprisingly, we can also calculate the rent income of land. The light green rent triangle *NDE* in Figure 12-8 measures all the surplus output which was produced but was not paid out in wages. The size of the rent triangle is determined by how much the *MP* of labor declines as additional labor is added—that is, by the extent of diminishing returns. If there are only a few high-quality acres, additional units of labor will show sharp diminishing returns and rent's share will be large. If, by contrast, there is a great ④
deal of homogeneous frontier land just waiting to be cleared, there will be little diminishing returns and land's rent triangle will be very small.

We have drawn Figure 12-8 so that labor's wages are about 3 times larger than property's rents. This 3-to-1 relationship reflects the fact that labor earnings constitute about three-quarters of national income.

---

① 这样，竞争的结果就确保所有工人都能享受到与最后一位受雇工人的边际产量相等的同等水平的工资。

② 其原因是每一位土地所有者都是竞争性土地市场的参与者，都要为其出租的地块索要一个最好的价格。

③ 图 12-8. 边际产量原则决定收入的要素分配

④ 与此形成对照的是，如果在边远地区有大量等待出售的同类型土地，收益则很难递减，图中土地租金的三角形会变得很小。

The marginal-productivity theory described here is widely used in economics. An important application is to the impact of immigration on wages and profits, which is examined in question 8 at the end of this chapter.

多种投入要素的边际生产率理论
Marginal-Productivity Theory with Many Inputs

The marginal-productivity theory is a great step forward in understanding the pricing of different inputs. Note additionally that the positions of land and labor could be reversed to get a complete theory of distribution. To switch the roles of labor and land, add successive units of variable land to fixed labor. Calculate each successive acre's marginal product.

Then draw a demand curve showing how many acres labor owners will demand of land at each rent rate. In the new version of Figure 12-8 that you draw, find a new E' point of equilibrium. Identify land's rectangle of rent as determined by rent times quantity of land. Identify labor's residual wage triangle. Finally, note the complete symmetry of the factors. This new graph shows that we should think of the distributive shares of each and every factor of production as being simultaneously determined by their interdependent marginal products.

That is not all. Instead of labor and land, suppose the only two factors were labor and some versatile capital goods. Suppose a smooth production function relates Q to labor and capital with the same general properties as in Figure 12-8. In this case, you can redraw Figure 12-8 and get an identical picture of income distribution between labor and capital. Indeed, we can perform the same operation for three, four, or any number of factors.

In competitive markets, the demand for inputs is ① determined by the marginal products of factors. In the simplified case where factors are paid in terms of the single output, we get

Wage = marginal product of labor

Rent = marginal product of land

and so forth for any factor. This distributes 100 percent of output, no more and no less, among all the factors of production.

We see, then, that the aggregate theory of the distribution of income is compatible with the competitive pricing of any number of goods produced by any number of factors. This simple but powerful theory shows how the distribution of income is related to productivity in a competitive market economy.

收入分配中是否也存在看不见的手
AN INVISIBLE HAND FOR INCOMES?

We have now sketched how a perfectly competitive economy distributes national product among the different inputs in a simplified world.

People naturally ask, Are incomes under market capitalism fair and just? In one sense, this is like asking whether animals get their fair shares of food in the jungle. Just as the battles of the jungle distribute ② food without regard to right or wrong, so does a competitive market distribute wages and profits according to productivity rather than ethics.

Is there an invisible hand in the marketplace that ensures that the most deserving people will obtain their just rewards? Or that those who toil long hours or nights and weekends or in tedious or dangerous work will receive a decent standard of living? Or that those who work in developing countries will get a comfortable living standard?

In reality, competitive markets do not guarantee that income and consumption will necessarily go to the neediest or most deserving. Laissez-faire competition might lead to great inequality, to malnourished children who grow up to raise more malnourished children, and to the perpetuation of inequality of incomes and wealth for generations. There is no economic law that ensures that the poor countries of Africa will catch up to the rich countries of North America. The rich may get healthier and richer as the poor get sicker and poorer. In a market economy, the distribution of income and consumption reflects not only hard work, ingenuity, and cunning but also factors such as race, gender, location, health, and luck.

While the market can work wonders in producing ③ a growing array of goods and services in an efficient manner, there is no invisible hand which ensures that a laissez-faire economy will produce a fair and equitable distribution of income and property.

Now that we are armed with the general principles underlying the pricing of factors of production and the determination of the distribution of income, we can turn to a detailed discussion of the special features in the three major factor markets—land, labor, and capital.

---

① 在竞争性的市场中，对投入要素的需求是由要素的边际产量所决定的。简化的案例中，根据单一产量进行要素支付，我们就可以得到上面原文中的计算公式。

② 正如丛林中弱肉强食的食物分配无对错可言一样，竞争性市场的工资和利润是依据生产率的高低而不是道德标准来进行分配的。

③ 当市场有效地生产出日益丰富的商品和服务的过程中，不断地创造奇迹时，那只可以保证自由主义经济会构建出公正和公平的收入和财产分配机制的看不见的手，是不复存在的。

SUMMARY

A. Income and Wealth

1. Distribution theory is concerned with the basic question of *for whom* economic goods are to be produced. In examining how the different factors of production—land, labor, and capital—get priced in the market, distribution theory considers how supplies and demands for these factors are linked and how they determine all kinds of wages, rents, interest rates, and profits.
2. Income refers to the total receipts or cash earned by a person or household during a given time period (usually a year). Income consists of labor earnings, property income, and government transfer payments.
3. National income consists of the labor earnings and property income generated by the economy in a year. Government takes a share of that national income in the form of taxes and gives back part of what it collects as transfer payments. The post-tax personal income of an individual includes the returns on all the factors of production—labor and property—that the individual owns, plus transfer payments from the government, less taxes.
4. Wealth consists of the net dollar value of assets owned at a given point in time. Wealth is a stock, while income is a flow per unit of time. A household's wealth includes its tangible items such as houses and its financial holdings such as bonds. Items that are of value are called assets, while those that are owed are called liabilities. The difference between total assets and total liabilities is called wealth or net worth.

B. Input Pricing by Marginal Productivity

5. To understand the pricing of different factors of production, we must analyze the theory of production and the derived demand for factors. The demand for inputs is a derived demand: we demand pizza ovens not for their own sake but for the pizzas that they can produce for consumers. Factor demand curves are derived from demand curves for final products. An upward shift in the final demand curve causes a similar upward shift in the derived factor demand curve; greater inelasticity in commodity demand produces greater inelasticity of derived factor demand.
6. We met in earlier chapters the concepts of the production function and marginal products. The demand for a factor is drawn from its marginal revenue product (*MRP*), which is defined as the extra revenue earned from employing an extra unit of a factor. In any market, *MRP* of a factor equals the marginal revenue earned by the sale of an additional unit of the product times the marginal product of the factor ($MRP = MR \times MP$). For competitive firms, because price equals marginal revenue, this simplifies to $MRP = P \times MP$.
7. A firm maximizes profits (and minimizes costs) when it sets the *MRP* of each factor equal to that factor's marginal cost, which is the factor's price. This can be stated equivalently as a condition in which the *MRP* per dollar of input is equalized for each input. This must hold in equilibrium because a profit-maximizing employer will hire any factor up to the point where the factor's marginal product will return in dollars of marginal revenue just what the factor costs.
8. To obtain the market demand for a factor, we add horizontally all firms' demand curves. This, along with the particular factor's own supply curve, determines the supply-and-demand equilibrium. At the market price for the factor of production, the amounts demanded and supplied will be exactly equal—only at equilibrium will the factor price have no tendency to change.
9. The marginal-productivity theory of income distribution analyzes the way total national income gets distributed among the different factors. Competition of numerous landowners and laborers drives factor prices to equal their marginal products. That process will allocate exactly 100 percent of the product. Any factor, not just labor alone, can be the varying factor. Because each unit of the factor gets paid only the *MP* of the last unit hired, there is a residual surplus of output left over from the *MP*s of early inputs. This residual is exactly equal to the incomes of the other factors under marginal productivity pricing. Hence, the marginal-productivity theory of distribution, though simplified, is a logically complete picture of the distribution of income under perfect competition.
10. Even though a competitive economy may squeeze the maximum amount of bread out of its available resources, one major reservation about a market economy remains. We have no reason to think that incomes will be fairly distributed under laissez-faire capitalism. Market incomes might produce acceptable differences or enormous disparities in income and wealth that persist for generations.

CONCEPTS FOR REVIEW

income distribution
income (flow), wealth (stock)
national income
transfer payments
personal income
marginal product, marginal revenue product, derived demand

marginal revenue product of input i $= MRP_i = MR \times MP_i = P \times MP_i$ for competitive firm
neoclassical theory of income distribution
MP rectangle, residual rent triangle

factor demands under competition: $MP_i \times P =$ factor price$_i$, which gives least-cost rule:

$$\frac{MP_L}{P_L} = \frac{MP_A}{P_A} = \cdots = \frac{1}{\text{marginal revenue}}$$

fairness of market incomes

FURTHER READING AND INTERNET WEBSITES

Further Reading

The neoclassical theory of income distribution was developed by one of the pioneers of American economics, John Bates Clark. You can get a flavor of his major ideas in *The Distribution of Wealth: A Theory of Wages, Interest and Profits* (1899) in an online publication at *www.econlib.org/library/Clark/clkDWO.html*.

Websites

Information on the distribution of income is gathered by the Census Bureau at *www.census.gov/hhes/www/income.html*. The most comprehensive data on the population is gathered in the decennial census, available at *www.census.gov*.

If you want to examine data on income dynamics, an exemplary site for data is that on the Panel Study on Income Dynamics at *www.isr.umich.edu/src/psid*.

The most comprehensive data on the wealth of Americans is collected by the Federal Reserve Board; see *www.federalreserve.gov/PUBS/oss/oss2/scfindex.html*.

QUESTIONS FOR DISCUSSION

1. For each of the following factors, name the final output for which the item is a derived demand: wheatland, gasoline, barber, machine tool for basketballs, wine press, economics textbook.
2. Table 12-4 shows the basic numbers for production of pizzas, holding other factors constant.
   a. Fill in the blanks in columns (3) and (5).
   b. Construct a diagram like that in Figure 12-3 which shows the marginal revenue product of pizza workers and labor inputs.
   c. If the wage of pizza workers is \$30 per worker, how many workers will be employed?
   d. Assume that the price of pizzas doubles. Draw the new *MRP* curve. Estimate the impact on the employment of pizza workers, assuming there are no other changes.
3. Over the last century, hours of work per lifetime have declined about 50 percent while real earnings have increased by a factor of 8. Assuming that the main change was an increase in the marginal-productivity-of-labor schedule, draw supply-and-demand diagrams for labor in 1900 and 2000 that will explain this trend. In your diagrams, put the number of hours worked per lifetime on the horizontal axis and the real wage rate

Marginal Revenue Product

(1) Unit of labor (workers)	(2) Total product (pizzas)	(3) Marginal product of labor (pizzas per worker)	(4) Price of output ($ per pizza)	(5) Marginal revenue product of labor ($ per worker)
0	0			
		___	5	___
1	30			
		___	5	___
2	50			
		___	5	___
3	60			
		___	5	___
4	65			
		___	5	___
5	68			
		___	5	___
6	68			

TABLE 12-4.

on the vertical axis. What key factor about the supply of labor must you invoke to explain this historical trend?

4. Why is each of the following incorrect? State the correct proposition.
   a. Marginal revenue product is calculated as total revenue earned per worker.
   b. Distribution theory is simple. You simply figure out how much each factor produces and then give the factor its share of output.
   c. Under competition, workers get paid the total output produced minus the costs of raw materials.
5. Figure 12-1 shows that the share of labor in national income changed little from 1970 to 2007 even though total incomes (GDP) rose by a factor of three. Draw a set of economywide curves like those in Figure 12-8 which can explain these two facts.
6. Labor leaders used to say, "Without any labor there is no product. Hence labor deserves *all* the product." Apologists for capital would reply, "Take away all capital goods, and labor scratches a bare pittance from the earth; practically all the product belongs to capital."

   Analyze the flaws in these arguments. If you were to accept the arguments, show that they would allocate 200 or 300 percent of output to two or three factors, whereas only 100 percent can be allocated. How does the neoclassical marginal-productivity theory resolve this dispute?
7. Draw the supply and demand curves for the oil market. Now suppose that a workable electric car shifts demand away from oil. Draw the new demand curve and the new equilibrium. Describe the outcome in terms of the price of oil, the quantity consumed, and the total income of the oil producers.
8. We can use the neoclassical theory of distribution to analyze the impact of immigration on the distribution of total national income. Assume that there are two factors, homogeneous labor and capital, with returns being wages and profits. Look at Figure 12-9, which has the same variables as Figure 12-8. We begin with initial supply curve *S* and at equilibrium point *A*.

   Now assume that there is a large increase in labor supply due to immigration, shifting the supply-of-labor curve from *S* to *S*′, as shown by the arrow. Assume that all other inputs are unchanged. Answer the following:
   a. Describe and draw the new equilibrium after the immigration.
   b. Explain what will happen to the wage rate.

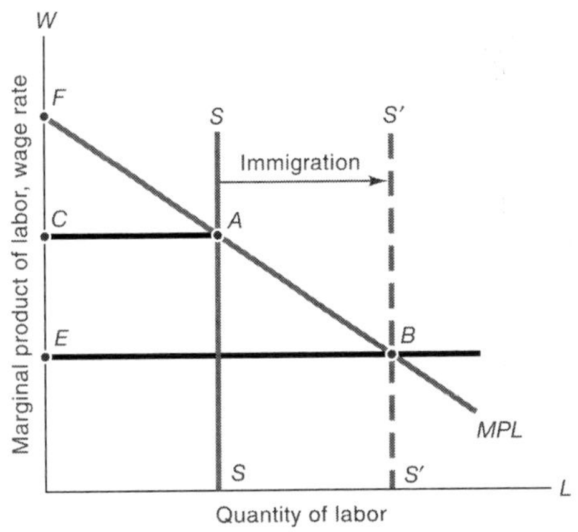

FIGURE 12-9.

c. Explain what happens to total profits and to the rate of profit (profits per unit of capital).

d. Explain why you cannot tell what will happen to total wages or to the share of labor income in total national income.

e. Note that this question looks at the impact of immigration on total national income. This analysis appears to differ from Chapter 3's supply-and-demand analysis of the impact of immigration on different cities. Explain the reason why immigration from Mexico to the United States will affect overall wages in the United States in this example, while immigration will not affect wage differentials between Miami and Detroit in the Chapter 3 example.

9. In the marginal-productivity theory shown in Figure 12-8, let land rather than labor be the varying input. Draw a new figure and explain the theory with this new diagram. What is the residual factor?

CHAPTER

13

The Labor Market
劳动市场

[1] *Work is the curse of drinking class.* 并非出自王尔德（见 45 页注）的著作，而是英国裔的美国作家弗兰克·哈里斯（Frank Harris, 1856~1931）1916 年为王尔德写的传记《奥斯卡·王尔德：生平与自白》（*Oscar Wilde: His Life and Confessions*）中第 116 页记述作者在与王尔德的一次餐叙中王尔德所讲的一句话，原文如下：
"Just as work is the curse of the drinking classes of this country," he said laughing, "so education is the curse of the acting classes."

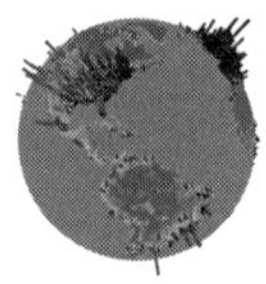

所以，根据以上文字及王尔德的文风和思想，这句话翻译如下。

Class：原文为复数，意为有良好教育背景的上流社会阶层。

Work is the curse of the drinking class. [1]

Oscar Wilde

所谓工作只不过是上流社会酒桌上的咒语而已。——奥斯卡·王尔德

Labor is more than an abstract factor of production. Workers are people who want good jobs with high wages so that they can buy the things they need and want. This chapter explores how wages are set in a market economy. The first section reviews the supply of labor and the determination of wages under competitive conditions. This is followed by a discussion of some of the noncompetitive elements of labor markets, including labor unions and the thorny problem of labor market discrimination.

工资决定的基本理论

A. FUNDAMENTALS OF WAGE DETERMINATION

一般工资水平
THE GENERAL WAGE LEVEL

In analyzing labor earnings, economists tend to ②
look at the average **real wage,** which represents the purchasing power of an hour's work, or the money wages divided by the cost of living.[1] By that measure, American workers today are far better off than they were 100 years ago. Figure 13-1 on page 249 shows the ③
real average hourly wage, or the dollar wage adjusted for inflation, along with the average hours of work.

The same powerful gains for workers are found virtually everywhere. Across Western Europe, Japan, and the rapidly industrializing countries of East Asia, there has definitely been a steady, long-term improvement in the average worker's ability to buy food, clothing, and housing, as well as in the health and longevity of the population. In Europe and the United States, these gains began in earnest in the early 1800s, with the advent of the technological and social changes associated with the Industrial Revolution. Before that time real wages meandered up and down, with few long-term gains.

That is not to say that the Industrial Revolution was an unmitigated benefit to workers, especially in the laissez-faire days of the 1800s. In point of fact, a ④
Dickens novel could hardly do justice to the dismal [5]
conditions of child labor, workplace dangers, and poor sanitation in factories of the early nineteenth century. A workweek of 84 hours was the prevailing rule, with time out for breakfast and sometimes supper. A good deal of work could be squeezed out of a 6-year-old child, and if a woman lost two fingers in a loom, she still had eight left.

Was it a mistake for people to leave the farms for the rigors of the factory? Probably not. Economic

[1] In this chapter, we will generally use the term "wages" as a shorthand expression for wages, salaries, and other forms of compensation.

③ 图 13-1 表示了每小时的实际平均所得，或者说是在扣除通货膨胀因素之后，以平均劳动时长所体现的美元工资。

do justice to
对某事的短暂满足

④ 事实上，一部狄更斯的小说根本无法给童工凄惨的生活、危险的工作环境，以及 19 世纪早期工厂里严重匮乏的卫生条件，带来哪怕是稍纵即逝的一丝改善。

② 经济学家们在对劳动所得进行分析的时候，往往关注于**实际的平均工资**，即劳动一个小时所能获得的购买力，或者除以生活成本之后的货币工资。

[5] 查尔斯·狄更斯（Charles Dickens, 1812~1870），19 世纪英国现实主义文学的主要代表，被马克思誉为"英国杰出的小说家"。出生于海军小职员家庭，10 岁时全家被迫迁入负债者监狱，11 岁承担起繁重的家务劳动，并在皮鞋油作坊当童工，15 岁入律师事务所当学徒，之后升任民事诉讼法庭书记员，接着又担任报社派驻议会的记者，靠刻苦自学和艰辛劳动成为知名作家。主要作品有《匹克威克外传》（*The Posthumous Papers of the Pickwick Club*，1836）、《雾都孤儿》（*Oliver Twist*，1838）、《老古玩店》（*The Old Curiosity Shop*，1841）、《大卫·科波菲尔德》（*David Copperfield*，1850）、《艰难时世》（*Hard Times*，1854）、《双城记》（*A Tale of Two Cities*，1859）、《远大前程》（*Great Expectations*，1861）、《我们共同的朋友》（*Our Mutual Friend*，1865）等等。

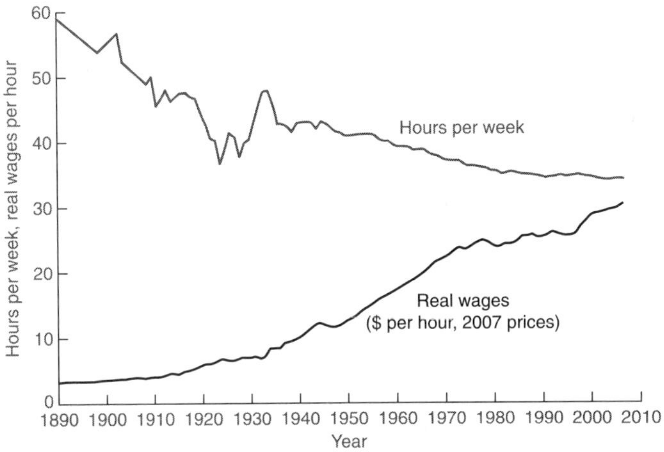

FIGURE 13-1. Wages Have Improved as Hours of Work Have Declined ①

With advancing technology and improved capital goods, American workers enjoy higher wages while working fewer hours. These are the fruits of long-term economic growth.

capital goods 必需的资本

historians emphasize that even with the demanding conditions in the factories, living standards were nevertheless greatly improved over those in the earlier centuries of agrarian feudalism. The Industrial Revolution was a giant step forward for the working class, not a step back. The idyllic picture of the healthful, ② jolly countryside peopled by stout yeomen and happy peasantry is a historical myth unsupported by statistical research.

对劳动的需求
DEMAND FOR LABOR

边际生产率差异
Marginal Productivity Differences

We begin our examination of the general wage level by examining the factors underlying the demand for labor. The basic tools were provided in the previous chapter, where we saw that the demand for a factor of production reflects the marginal productivity of that input.

Figure 13-2 illustrates the marginal-productivity theory. Holding technology and other inputs constant, there exists a relationship between the quantity of labor inputs and the amount of output. By the law ③ of diminishing returns, each additional unit of labor input will add a smaller and smaller slab of output. In the example shown in Figure 13-2, at 10 units of labor, the competitively determined general wage level will be $20 per unit.

But probe deeper and ask what lies behind marginal product. To begin with, the marginal ④

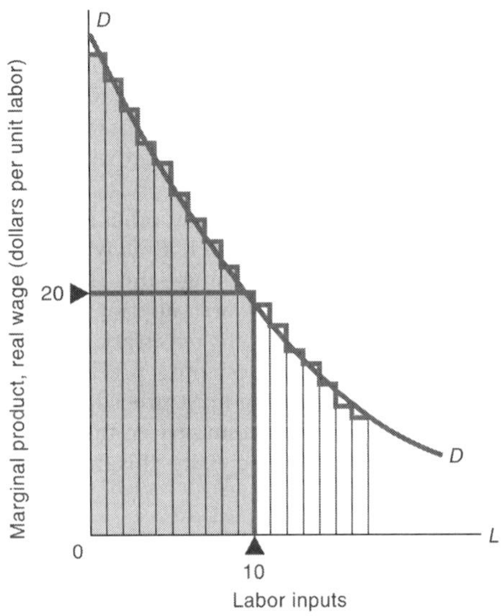

FIGURE 13-2. Demand for Labor Reflects Marginal Productivity ⑤

The demand for labor is determined by its marginal productivity in producing national output. The light blue vertical slices represent the extra output produced by the first, second, . . . unit of labor. The competitively determined general wage level at 10 units of labor is $20 per unit, equal to the marginal productivity of the tenth unit. The labor demand curve shifts up and out over time with capital accumulation, technological advance, and improvements in labor quality.

---

① 图 13-1. 工资随着工作时间的减少而提高

② 那些壮硕的自给自足的农户以及陶醉于此的农民们，生活在空气清新、充满鸟语花香的乡间，这样的田园诗画是虚构的历史故事，统计研究对此无法予以证实。

③ 根据边际收益递减规律，每追加一个单位的劳动投入所产生的以条形图所表示的产出增量就会越来越少。

④ 首先，如果工人可以得到更多或更好的必需的资本支持，其劳动的边际生产率就会提高。

⑤ 图 13-2. 对劳动的需求反映了边际生产率

productivity of labor will rise if workers have more or better capital goods to work with. Compare the productivity of a ditchdigger using a bulldozer with that of a similar digger using a hand shovel, or the communications capabilities of medieval messengers with modern e-mail. Second, marginal productivity of better-trained or better-educated workers will generally be higher than that of workers with less "human capital."

These reasons explain why wages and living standards rose so much during the twentieth century. Wages are high in the United States and other industrial countries because these nations have accumulated substantial capital stocks: dense networks of roads, rails, and communications; substantial amounts of plant and equipment for each worker; and adequate inventories of spare parts. Even more important are the vast improvements in technologies compared to those of an earlier era. We have seen lightbulbs replace oil lamps, airplanes replace horses, xerography replace quill and ink, computers replace abacuses, and Internet commerce invade traditional ways of doing business. Just imagine how productive the average American would be today with the technologies of 1900.

The quality of labor inputs is another factor determining the general wage level. By any measure—literacy, education, or training—the skills of the American workforce today are superior to those of 1900. Years of education are necessary to produce an engineer capable of designing precision equipment. A decade of training must precede the ability ① to perform successful brain surgery. As the workforce increases its education and skills, this increases the productivity of labor.

国际比较

International Comparisons

The same reasoning explains why wage levels differ so dramatically across the world. Look at Table 13-1, which shows average wages plus benefits in manufacturing industries for eight countries. Note that hourly wages in the United States are lower than those in Europe but almost 20 times higher than in China.

What accounts for the enormous differences? ② It's not that governments in China and Mexico are suppressing wage increases, though government policies do have some impact on the minimum wage and other aspects of the labor market. Rather, real wages differ among countries primarily because of the operation of the supply and demand for labor. Look at Figure 13-3. Suppose that Figure 13-3(*a*) represents the state of affairs in the United States while Figure 13-3(*b*) describes Mexico. In Figure 13-3(*a*), the supply of U.S. workers is shown by the supply curve, $S_{US}S_{US}$, while the demand for workers is represented by $D_{US}D_{US}$. The equilibrium wage will settle at the level shown at E_{US}. If the wage were lower than E_{US}, shortages of labor would occur and employers would bid up wages to E_{US}, restoring the equilibrium. Similar forces determine E_M, the Mexican wage.

We see that the Mexican wage is lower than the U.S. wage principally because the Mexican demand curve for labor is far lower as a result of the low marginal productivity of labor in Mexico. The most important factor lies in the quality of the workforce. The average education level in Mexico falls far short of the American standard, with a substantial fraction of the population illiterate. Additionally, compared to the United States, a country like Mexico has much less capital to work with: many of the roads are unpaved, few computers and fax machines are

Region	Wages and fringe benefits in manufacturing, 2006 ($ per hour)
Germany	34.21
Italy	25.07
United States	23.82
Japan	20.20
The Republic of Korea	14.72
Mexico	2.75
China	1.37
Philippines	1.07

TABLE 13-1. General Wage Levels Vary Enormously across Countries ③

Western European nations, Japan, and the United States are high-wage countries, while China's hourly wages are a tiny fraction of American levels. General wage levels are determined by supply and demand for labor, but other factors such as capital, education levels, technology levels, and civil strife have a major impact on supply and demand curves.

Source: U.S. Bureau of Labor Statistics at *ftp://ftp.bls.gov/pub/special.requests/ForeignLabor/ichccpwsuppt02.txt* and estimates by the authors. Note these estimates use market exchange rates and not purchasing-power-parity exchange rates.

① 只有经过 10 年以上的专业训练才能具备掌刀脑部手术的能力。随着劳动力受教育水平的提高和技能的增强，劳动生产率也随之提升。

② 是什么原因导致出现了如此巨大的差异？虽然中国和墨西哥政府所实施的政策确实对最低工资和劳动力市场的其他方面产生了作用，但这些国家的政府并没有压制工资水平的增长。

③ 表 13-1. 各国普通工资水平的巨大差异

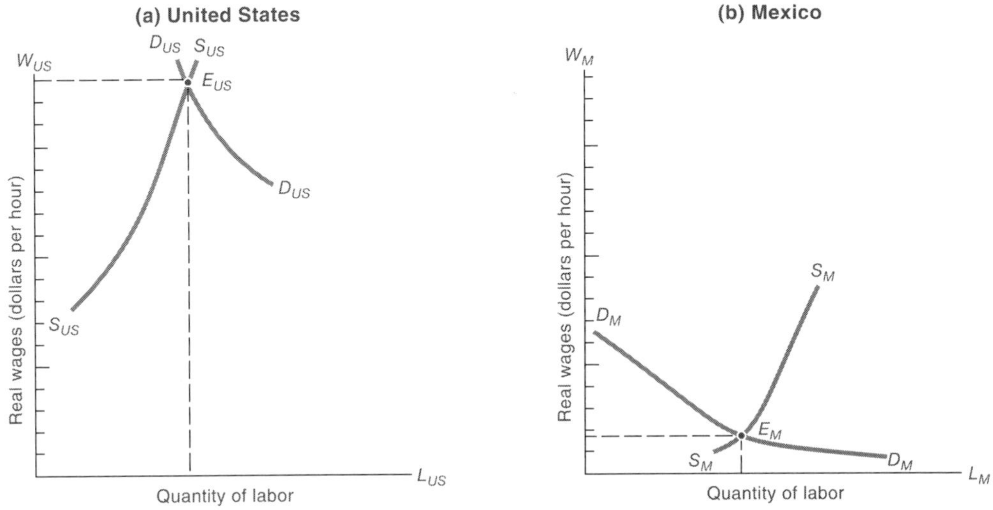

FIGURE 13-3. Favorable Resources, Skills, Management, Capital, and Technology Explain ① High U.S. Wages

Supply and demand determine a higher competitive wage in the United States than in Mexico. The major forces leading to high U.S. wages are a better-educated and more skilled workforce, a larger stock of capital per worker, and modern technologies.

in use, and much of the equipment is old or poorly maintained. All these factors make labor's marginal productivity low and tend to reduce wages.

This analysis can also help explain why wages have risen rapidly in East Asian regions such as Hong Kong and Taiwan of China as well as The Republic of Korea. These economies are devoting a sizable share of their outputs to educating their populations, investing in new capital goods, and importing the latest productive technologies. The *MP* and *DD* curves for these regions have shifted greatly upward and to the right. As a result, real wages have doubled over the last 20 years in these regions, while wages have stagnated in relatively closed regions which invest less in education, public health, and tangible capital.

劳动的供给
THE SUPPLY OF LABOR

供给的决定因素
Determinants of Supply

So far we have focused on the demand side of the labor market. Now we turn to the supply side. *Labor supply* refers to the number of hours that the ② population desires to work in gainful activities. The three key elements for labor supply are hours per worker, labor-force participation, and immigration.

labor-force participation 劳动力就业

Hours Worked. While some people have jobs with flexible hours, most Americans work between 35 and 40 hours a week, without much leeway to increase or cut back their weekly hours. However, most people do have a great deal of control over how many hours they work over the course of their lifetimes. They may decide to go to college, to retire early, or to work part-time rather than full-time—all of these can reduce the number of total lifetime hours worked. On the other hand, the decision to take on a second job will increase the lifetime hours worked.

Suppose that wages rise. Will that increase or decrease the lifetime hours of work? Look at the supply curve of labor in Figure 13-4. Note how the supply curve rises at first; then at the critical point *C*, it begins to bend back. How can we explain why higher wages may first increase and then decrease the quantity of labor supplied?

① 图 13-3. 导致美国工资居高的资源、技能、管理、资本和技术

② 劳动供给指的是人们所欲从事的可以获得预期所得的劳动的小时数。它的三个关键因素是每个劳动者的工作时间、劳动力的就业形势，以及移民状况。

FIGURE 13-4. As Wages Rise, Workers May Work Fewer Hours ①

Above the critical point *C*, raising the wage rate reduces the amount of labor supplied as the income effect outweighs the substitution effect. Why? Because at higher wages workers can afford more leisure even though each extra hour of leisure costs more in wages forgone.

Put yourself in the shoes of a worker who has just been offered higher hourly rates and is free to choose the number of hours to be worked. You are tugged in two different directions. On one side is the *substitution effect.* (Chapter 5 explained that the substitution effect operates when people consume more of, or substitute in favor of, a good whose relative price falls and consume less of a good whose relative price increases.) Because each hour of work is now ② better paid, each hour of leisure has become more expensive; you thus have an incentive to substitute extra work for leisure.

But acting against the substitution effect is the *income effect.* With the higher wage, your income is higher. With a higher income, you will want to buy more goods and services, and, in addition, you will want more leisure time. You can afford to take longer vacations or to retire earlier than you otherwise would.

Which will be more powerful, the substitution effect or the income effect? There is no single correct answer; it depends upon the individual. In the case shown in Figure 13-4, for all wage rates below point *C*, labor supplied increases with a higher wage: the substitution effect outweighs the income effect. But from point *C* upward, the income effect outweighs the substitution effect, and labor supplied declines as wage rates climb higher.

Labor-Force Participation. One of the most dramatic developments in recent decades has been the sharp influx of women into the workforce. The labor-force participation rate of women (i.e., the fraction of women over 15 employed or actively looking for jobs) has jumped from 34 percent in 1950 to 60 percent today. In part this can be explained by rising real wages, which have made working more attractive for women. However, a change of this magnitude cannot be explained by economic factors alone. To under- ③ stand such a significant alteration in working patterns, one must look outside economics to changing social attitudes toward the role of women as mothers, homemakers, and workers.

Immigration. The role of immigration in the labor-force supply has always been important in the United States. Whereas only 5 percent of the U.S. population was foreign-born in 1970, by 2008 that number had risen to 12 percent.

The flow of legal immigrants is controlled by an intricate quota system which favors skilled workers and their families, as well as close relatives of U.S. citizens and permanent residents. In addition, there are special quotas for political refugees. Most immigrants today are undocumented ("illegal") people who enter the United States looking for better economic opportunities. In recent years, the biggest groups of legal immigrants have come from places like Mexico, the Philippines, Vietnam, and some of the Central American and Caribbean countries.

The major change in immigration in recent decades has been a change in the characteristics of immigrants. In the 1950s, Germany and Canada were the major sources, while in the 1980s and 1990s Mexico and the Philippines were the dominant sources. As a result, recent immigrants have been relatively less skilled and less educated than those of an earlier age.

From the point of view of labor supply, the over- ④ all effect of recent immigration has been an increase

---

① 图 13-4. 随着工资增长，工人的工作时间减少

② 由于每小时的劳动所得有了大幅度的提高，使得每小时所能享受到的闲暇变得更加昂贵起来。这样你就有动力，牺牲闲暇时间去从事额外的工作。

③ 为了很好地理解就业形式如此显著的变化，就必须透过经济学，去观察女性作为母亲、家庭主妇以及劳动者等多重角色变化中的社会形态。

④ 从劳动供给的角度分析，近年来全美移民问题的总体效应相对于熟练型技工而言，非熟练型劳工的供给始终处于上升的态势。

in the supply of low-skilled workers in the United States relative to high-skilled workers. Studies have estimated that this change in supply has contributed to the decline in the wages of less educated groups relative to the college-educated.

实证发现
Empirical Findings

Theory does not tell us whether the labor supply of a group will react positively or negatively to a wage change. Will an income-tax increase on high-income workers—which reduces their after-tax wages—cause them to reduce their work hours? Will subsidizing the wages of the working poor reduce or increase their hours worked? These vital questions must be ① considered by policymakers as they weigh issues of equity and efficiency. We often need to know the exact shape or elasticity of the labor supply curve.

Table 13-2 presents a summary of numerous studies of the subject. This survey shows that the labor supply curve for adult males appears to be slightly backward-bending, while the responses of other demographic groups look more like a conventional upward-sloping supply curve. For the population as a whole, labor supply appears to respond very little to changes in real wages.

工资差异
WAGE DIFFERENTIALS

While analysis of the general wage level is important for comparing different countries and times, we often want to understand *wage differentials*. In practice, wage rates differ enormously. The average wage ② is as hard to define as the average person. A hedge-fund manager may earn $400 million a year, while a hedge-fund janitor may earn $400 a week. A doctor may earn 20 times more than a lifeguard even though both are saving lives.

There are major differences in earnings among broad industry groups, as is shown in Table 13-3. Sectors with small firms such as farming, retail trade, or private households tend to pay low wages, while the larger firms in manufacturing pay twice as much. But

Labor-Supply Patterns

Group of workers	Labor-Force Participation Rate (% of population) 1960	2007	Response of labor supply to increase in real wages
Adult males (25 to 54 years)	97	91	Supply curve found to be backward-bending in most studies. Income effect dominates substitution effect. Elasticities are around –0.1 for prime-age males.
Adult females (25 to 54 years)	43	76	Females generally have shown significant positive labor-supply elasticities.
Teenagers	48	40	Teenage response is highly variable.
Seniors (65 and older)	21	16	Seniors have been responsive to relative generosity of retirement programs relative to wages.
Entire population (16 and over)	60	66	Elasticity of total labor supply is close to zero, with income effects balancing out substitution effects. Estimated labor-supply elasticity for entire population is in the range from 0.0 to 0.2.

TABLE 13-2. Empirical Estimates of Labor-Supply Responses ③

Economists have devoted careful study to the response of labor supply to real wages. For prime-age males (the quaint term used to designate males between 25 and 54), the supply curve is backward-bending (that is, the elasticity is negative), while teenagers and adult females generally respond positively to wages. For the economy as a whole, the labor supply curve is close to completely inelastic or vertical.

Source: U.S. Department of Labor, *Employment and Earnings*, March 2008.

① 政策制定者在权衡公平与效率的问题时，这些至关重要的问题必须予以考虑。

② 对平均工资的定义就像定义一个普通的常人一样困难。

③ 表 13-2. 实证评估劳动供给的反应

Compensation by Industry

Industry	Average earnings per full-time employee, 2006* ($ per year)
All industries	**47,000**
Farms	30,400
Mining	79,200
Manufacturing	52,300
Retail trade	29,400
Finance and insurance	82,800
Securities and related	205,600
Accommodation and food services	20,800
Food services	18,900

* Total compensation per full-time equivalent worker.

TABLE 13-3. Earnings Vary by Industry ①

Average annual wages and salaries in broad industry groups range from a high of $82,800 in finance to a low of $20,800 in accommodation and food services. In narrow industry groups, earnings vary enormously between security analysts and food-service workers.

Source: U.S. Bureau of Economic Analysis at *www.bea.gov*, Table 6.6D in the complete NIPA tables.

within major sectors there are large variations that depend on worker skills and market conditions—fast-food workers make much less than doctors even though they all provide services.

How can we explain these wage differentials? Let's consider first a *perfectly competitive labor market*, one in which there are large numbers of workers and employers, none of which has the power to affect wage rates appreciably. Few labor markets are perfectly competitive in reality, but some (such as a large city's market for teenage workers or clerical workers) approach the competitive concept reasonably closely. If all jobs and all people are identical in a perfectly competitive labor market, competition will cause the hourly wage rates to be exactly equal. No employer ② would pay more for the work of one person than for that person's identical twin or for another person who possessed identical skills.

This means that to explain the pervasive wage differences across industries or individuals, we must look to either differences in jobs, differences in people, or imperfect competition in labor markets.

工种之间的差异：补偿性工资差异

Differences in Jobs: Compensating Wage Differentials

Some of the tremendous wage differentials observed in everyday life arise because of differences in the quality of jobs. Jobs differ in their attractiveness; hence wages may have to be raised to coax people into the less attractive jobs.

Wage differentials that serve to compensate for the ③ relative attractiveness, or nonmonetary differences, among jobs are called **compensating differentials.**

Window washers must be paid more than janitors because of the risks of climbing skyscrapers. Workers often receive 5 percent extra pay on the 4 P.M. to midnight "swing shift" and 10 percent extra pay for the midnight to 8 A.M. "graveyard shift." For hours beyond 40 per week or for holiday and weekend work, 1½ to 2 times the base hourly pay is customary. Jobs that ④ involve hard physical labor, tedium, low social prestige, irregular employment, seasonal layoff, or physical risk all tend to be less attractive. No wonder, then, that companies must pay $50,000 to $80,000 a year to recruit people to work at dangerous and lonely jobs on offshore oil platforms or in northern Alaska. Similarly, for jobs that are especially pleasant or psychologically rewarding, such as those of park rangers and the clergy, pay levels tend to be modest.

To test whether a given difference in pay between two jobs is a compensating differential, ask people who are well qualified for both jobs: "Would you take the higher-paying job in preference to the lower?" If they are not eager to take the higher-paying job, the pay difference is probably a compensating differential that reflects the nonmonetary differences between the jobs.

补偿性工资的差异：劳动质量

Differences in People: Labor Quality

We have just seen that some wage differentials serve to compensate for the differing degrees of attractiveness of different jobs. But look around you. Garbage collectors make much less than lawyers, yet surely the legal life has higher prestige and much more pleasant working conditions. We see countless examples of high-paying jobs that are more pleasant than low-paying work. We must look to factors beyond compensating differentials to explain the reason for most wage differences.

One key to wage disparities lies in the qualitative ⑤ differences among people. A biologist might classify

---

① 表 13-3. 不同行业间的工资差异

② 任何雇主都不会为同为其雇员的孪生兄弟中的任一位，或者是具备同等技能的另一位雇员，就同样的工作支付更高的工资。

③ 为补偿不同岗位的适度吸引力或非货币因素的差别而制定的工资级差机制称作**补偿性差异**。

④ 像高强度体力劳动、单调枯燥的劳动、社会地位低下的工作、非固定职业、季节性失业以及危险性职业等都属于缺乏吸引力的岗位。

⑤ 导致工资差异的关键原因之一是从业者参差不齐的职业素养。生物学家会把我们所有的人归类为智人种群中的成员，但人事官员却会坚持认为，从业者个体能力的巨大差异对企业生产贡献良多。

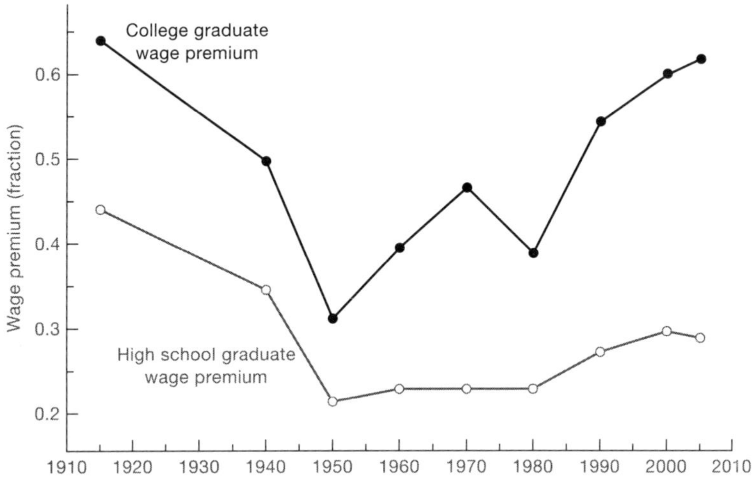

FIGURE 13-5. Relative Income Gains Have Been Dramatic for College Graduates ①

The education premium for college and high school has increased sharply in recent years. The college premium shows the income advantage of college graduates relative to high school graduates, while the high school premium shows the advantage relative to those who complete eighth grade. Note how sharply the college premium grew after 1980.

Source: Claudia Goldin and Lawrence F. Katz, *The Race between Education and Technology* (Harvard University Press, Cambridge, Mass., 2008).

all of us as members of the species *Homo sapiens,* but a personnel officer would insist that people differ enormously in their abilities to contribute to a firm's output.

While many of the differences in labor quality are determined by noneconomic factors, the decision to accumulate **human capital** can be evaluated economically. The term "human capital" refers to ② the stock of useful and valuable skills and knowledge accumulated by people in the process of their education and training. Doctors, lawyers, and engineers invest many years in their formal education and on-the-job training. They spend large sums on tuition and wages forgone and often work long hours. Part of the high salaries of these professionals should be viewed as a return on their investment in human capital—a return on the education that makes these highly trained workers a very special kind of labor.

Economic studies of incomes and education show that human capital is a good investment on average. Figure 13-5 shows the ratio of the hourly earnings of college graduates to those of high school graduates. Relative earnings rose sharply after 1980 as the "price of skill" rose.

Should You Invest in Human Capital?

Students may be surprised to learn that every day in college is an investment in human capital. When students go to college, each year they pay thousands of dollars in tuition and earnings forgone. This cost is just as much an investment as buying a bond or a house.

Does college actually pay off? The evidence suggests that it pays off smartly for the average graduate. Look at Figure 13-5. Suppose that the total investment in college is \$200,000 and that a high school graduate earns \$40,000 per year. If the college premium is 60 percent, this says that a college graduate would earn \$64,000 per year. This represents a \$24,000 return on the investment, or around 12 percent per year. While this would not hold for

① 图 13-5. 大学毕业生相对工资收入水平呈现出的戏剧性变化

② "人力资本"这一术语是指，人们在接受教育和培训的过程中，所累积的实用而有价值的技能和知识，所能转换成的资本总额。

everyone, it does suggest why students are working hard to get into good colleges.

Why has the college premium risen so sharply? More and more, in today's service economy, companies are processing information rather than raw materials. In the information economy, the skills learned in college are a prerequisite for a high-paying job. A high school dropout is generally at a severe disadvantage in the job market. Even ①
if you have to borrow for your education, put off years of gainful employment, live away from home, and pay for rent and books, your lifetime earnings in the occupations that are open only to college graduates will probably more than compensate you for the costs.

Often, people point to the role of luck in determining economic circumstances. But, as Louis Pasteur remarked, "Chance favors the prepared mind." In a world of rapidly changing technologies, education prepares people to understand and profit from new circumstances.

人们的差异：独特个体的“租金”

Differences in People: The "Rents" of Unique Individuals

For the lucky few, fame has lifted incomes to astronomical levels. Software guru Bill Gates, investment [2]
wizard Warren Buffett, basketball star Shaquille [3]
O'Neal, and even economists who consult for busi- [4]
ness can earn fabulous sums for their services.

These extremely talented people have a particular skill that is highly valued in today's economy. Outside their special field, they might earn but a small fraction of their high incomes. Moreover, their labor supply is unlikely to respond perceptibly to wages that are 20 or even 50 percent higher or lower. Econ- ⑤
omists refer to the excess of these wages above those of the next-best available occupation as a pure economic rent; these earnings are logically equivalent to the rents earned by fixed land.

Some economists have suggested that technological changes are making it easier for a small number of top individuals to serve a larger share of the market. The "winners" in athletics, entertainment, and finance far outdistance the runners-up in the race for compensation. Top entertainers or athletes can now give a single performance that reaches a billion people via television and recordings—something that was not possible just a few years ago. If this trend continues, and labor rents rise further, the income gap between the winners and the runners-up may widen even further in the years ahead.

分割的市场和非竞争性群体

Segmented Markets and Noncompeting Groups

Even in a perfectly competitive world where people could move easily from one occupation to another, substantial wage differentials would appear. These differences would be necessary to reflect differences in the costs of education and training or in the unattractiveness of certain occupations or to indicate rewards for unique talents.

But even after taking into account all these reasons for wage differentials, we still find a large disparity in wage rates. The major reason for the remaining difference is that labor markets are segmented into *noncompeting groups.*

A moment's thought will suggest that, instead of being a single factor of production, labor is many different, but closely related, factors of production. Doctors and economists, for example, are noncompeting groups because it is difficult and costly for a member of one profession to enter into the other. Just as there are many different kinds of houses, each ⑥
commanding a different price, so are there many different occupations and skills that compete only in a general way. Once we recognize the existence of many different submarkets of the labor market, we can see why wages may differ greatly among groups.

Why is the labor market divided into so many noncompeting groups? The major reason is that, for the professions like law and medicine, it takes a large investment of time and money to become proficient. If coal mining declines because of environmental restrictions, the miners can hardly hope to land jobs teaching environmental economics overnight. Once people specialize in a particular occupation, they become part of a particular labor submarket. They are thereby subject to the supply and demand for that skill and will find that their own labor earnings rise and fall depending upon events in that occupation and industry. Because of this segmentation, the wages for one occupation can diverge substantially from the wages in other areas.

The job choice of new immigrants is a classic case of noncompeting groups. Rather than just answering random classified ads, new immigrants from a particular country tend to cluster in certain occupations. For example, in many cities, such as Los Angeles and New York, a large number of grocery stores tend to be owned by Koreans. The reason is that the Koreans can get advice and support from friends and relatives

---

① 即使你不得不以举债的方式来接受教育，将收入颇丰的就业推迟数年，独自离乡背井，并且还得承担房租和书费，但你一生中在那些只有大学毕业生才有可能获得的职业上所赚取的收入，将很可能大大超过对你所付出的这一切成本的补偿。

[2] 比尔·盖茨（Bill Gates），英文全名为 William Henry Bill Gates III，1955 年 10 月 28 日出生于西雅图。美国企业家、软件工程师、慈善家、微软公司董事长。1995 年到 2007 年连续 13 年蝉联《福布斯》全球亿万富翁排行榜榜首。2008 年 6 月 27 日宣布正式退出微软公司，并把 580 亿美元个人财产捐给与妻子于 2000 年创办的盖茨基金会（Bill & Melinda Gates Foundation）。《福布斯》杂志 2009 年 3 月 12 日公布全球富豪排名，比尔·盖茨又以 400 亿美元资产重登榜首。

⑤ 经济学家们将那些超过其在次优职业中获得的额外报酬，称之为纯粹的经济租金。这些收益在逻辑上等于不动产的土地资源出租后获得的租金。

⑥ 就像现实中如果有很多栋不同种类的房产，每一栋都可标定一个不同的价格一样，不同的职业和技能同样仅以这样的方式竞争。

[3] 沃伦·巴菲特（Warren Buffet），1930 年 8 月 30 日出生于美国内布拉斯加州的奥马哈市（Omaha, Nebraska）。美国投资家，企业家，慈善家，被称为“奥马哈股神”。目前拥有约 620 亿美元的净资产。根据《福布斯》杂志公布的 2008 年度全球富豪榜，他已经超过卡洛斯·斯利姆·埃卢（Carlos Slim Helú，1940 年 1 月 28 日出生于墨西哥城，电信业大亨，拉丁美洲最富有的人）和比尔·盖茨成为全球首富。可口可乐及其股票为巴菲特钟爱之“上帝之泉”，其办公室的饮料冷藏柜里始终装满了灌装的可乐。2009 年 10 月 27 日，BBC 播发了其著名主持人、经济学家伊万·大卫两天之前对巴菲特的专访，有两件轶事值得我们思考。一是巴菲特又一次特别提到了可口可乐，并以之待客。二是巴菲特特意将其案头的“韦氏”大词典（国外上流社会公认的权威工具书，某种程度上是一种深厚修养和上流社会重要的身份佐证）给了一个特写镜头，以示其自誉为哲学家背后的严谨。

[4] 沙奎尔·奥尼尔（Shaquille O'Neal），1972 年 3 月 6 日出生，身高 2.16m，体重超过 147 公斤，但却能像短跑运动员一样冲刺，能像跳高运动员一样腾起，还可以像举重运动员一样在两三个人的重压下跳起扣篮，被誉为篮球运动百年史上出现的最庞大的“大力神”，获 1996 亚特兰大奥运会金牌。球场之外的奥尼尔还是一位摇滚歌手和影视演员，出版了自己的数张歌曲专集，出演了《火爆教头》（*Blue Chips*）、《精灵也疯狂》（*Kazaam*）等数部影片。

Summary of Competitive Wage Determination

Labor situation	Wage result
1. People are all alike—jobs are all alike.	No wage differentials
2. People are all alike—jobs differ in attractiveness.	Compensating wage differentials
3. People differ, but each type of labor is in unchangeable supply (noncompeting groups).	Wage differentials that reflect supply and demand for segmented markets
4. People differ, but there is some mobility among groups (partially competing groups).	General-equilibrium pattern of wage differentials as determined by general demand and supply (includes 1 through 3 as special cases)

TABLE 13-4. Market Wage Structure Shows Great Variety of Patterns under Competition ①

who also own grocery stores. As immigrants get more experience and education in the United States and become fluent in English, their job choice widens and they become part of the overall labor supply.

In addition, the theory of noncompeting groups helps us understand labor market discrimination. We will see in the next section of this chapter that much discrimination arises because workers are separated by gender, race, or other personal characteristics into noncompeting groups as a result of custom, law, or prejudice. ②

While the theory of noncompeting groups highlights an important aspect of labor markets, we must recognize that in the longer run entry and exit will reduce differentials. It is true that copper miners are unlikely to become computer programmers when computers and fiber optics displace rotary dials and copper wires. Consequently, we may see wage differentials arise between the two kinds of labor. But in the longer run, as more young people study computer science rather than go to work in copper mines, competition will tend to reduce the differentials of these noncompeting groups.

Table 13-4 summarizes the different forces at work in determining wage rates in competitive conditions.

劳工市场的问题与政策

B. LABOR MARKET ISSUES AND POLICIES

Our survey has up to now examined the case of competitive labor markets. In reality, distortions prevent the operation of perfect competition in labor markets. One source of imperfect competition is labor unions. Unions represent a significant, although shrinking, fraction of workers. A second facet of labor markets is discrimination—also less important than in earlier decades, but still an issue to consider. Yet another factor acting on labor markets is government policies. By setting minimum wages (discussed in Chapter 4), encouraging or discouraging unions, or outlawing discrimination, governments have a powerful effect on labor markets.

工会组织的经济意义

THE ECONOMICS OF LABOR UNIONS

Sixteen million Americans, or 12 percent of wage and salary workers, belonged to labor unions in 2007. Unions definitely have market power and sometimes serve as monopoly suppliers of labor. Unions negotiate collective-bargaining agreements which specify who can fill different jobs, how much workers will be paid, and what the work rules are. ③ And unions can decide to go on strike—withdraw their labor supply completely and even cause a factory to shut down—in order to win a better deal from an employer. The study of unions is an important part of understanding the dynamics of labor markets.

The wages and fringe benefits of unionized workers are determined by **collective bargaining.** ④ This is the process of negotiation between representatives of firms and of workers for the purpose of establishing mutually agreeable conditions of employment. The centerpiece is the *economic package.* This includes the basic wage rates for different job categories, along with the rules for holidays and coffee breaks. ⑤

① 表13-4. 在竞争环境下，市场工资结构多样化非常显著

② 此外，非竞争性群体的理论有助于我们理解劳动力市场的歧视问题。

③ 工会通过谈判协商签署协议，明确不同岗位的人员要求、必须要支付的报酬，以及劳动规章内容。

④ 工会组织成员的工资和福利是通过**集体协商**的方式决定的。

⑤ 其核心内容是一揽子经济协议。它包括了不同工作岗位类别的基本工资，同时也包括了有关休假和工间休息的具体规章。

[3] Fair Labor Standards Act (1938)：《公平劳动标准法案》，是罗斯福"新政"的一部重要法律。罗斯福总统于1937年5月提交国会，1938年6月25日获得通过。罗斯福称赞其为除《社会保障法》（*Social Security Law*）之外，最有远见的一项保护工人利益的法案。

[4] National Labor Relations (or Wagner) Act of 1935：《国家劳工关系法》（瓦格纳法），以提案人民主党参议员罗伯特·瓦格纳（Robert Ferdinand Wagner，1877~1953）的名字命名，1935年7月获国会通过。该法案确认了劳工享有自发组织、建立和参加工会，并通过自己选出的代表以集体协商的形式进行劳资谈判等权利，以及有关非法行为的界定等。还依据该法案成立了第三方机构国家劳工关系委员会（national labor relations board，NLRB）负责该法案的有效执行。

In addition, the agreement contains provisions for fringe benefits such as a pension plan, coverage for health care, and similar items.

A second important issue is *work rules*. These concern work assignments and tasks, job security, and workloads. Particularly in declining industries, the staffing requirements are a major issue because the demand for labor is falling. In the railroad industry, for example, there were decades of disputes about the number of people needed to run a train.

Collective bargaining is a complicated business, a matter of give-and-take. Much effort is spent negotiating purely economic issues, dividing the pie between wages and profits. Sometimes agreements get hung ① up on issues of management prerogatives, such as the ability to reassign workers or change work rules. In the end, both workers and management have a large stake in ensuring that workers are satisfied and productive on their jobs.

政府和集体协议
Government and Collective Bargaining

The legal framework is an important determinant of economic organization. Two hundred years ago, when labor first tried to organize in England and America, common-law doctrines against "conspiracy in restraint of trade" were used to block unions. In the early 1900s, unions and their members were convicted by courts, fined, jailed, and harassed by various injunctive procedures. The Supreme Court repeatedly struck down acts designed to improve working conditions for women and children and other reform legislation on hours and wages.

It was only after the pendulum swung toward ② support of unions and collective bargaining that the explosive growth of unions began. A major landmark was the Clayton Act (1914), designed to remove labor from antitrust prosecution. The Fair Labor [3] Standards Act (1938) barred child labor, called for time-and-a-half pay for weekly hours over 40, and set a federal minimum wage for most nonfarm workers.

The most important labor legislation of all was the National Labor Relations (or Wagner) Act of [4] 1935. This law stated: "Employees shall have the right to . . . join . . . labor organizations, to bargain collectively . . . , and to engage in concerted activities." Spurred by pro-labor legislation, union membership rose from less than one-tenth of the labor force in the 1920s to one-quarter of the workforce by the end of World War II. The decline of American unions began in the early 1970s. In essence, the monopoly power of unions was eroded by the deregulation of many industries, increased international competition, and a less favorable government attitude toward unions.

工会如何提高工资
HOW UNIONS RAISE WAGES

How can labor unions raise the wages and improve the working conditions of their members? *Unions gain* ⑤ *market power by obtaining a legal monopoly on the provision of labor services to a particular firm or industry.* Using this monopoly, they compel firms to provide wages, benefits, and working conditions that are above the competitive level. For example, if nonunion plumbers earn $20 per hour in Alabama, a union might bargain with a large construction firm to set the wage at $30 per hour for that firm's plumbers.

Such an agreement is, however, valuable to the union only if the firm's access to alternative labor supplies can be restricted. Hence, under a typical ⑥ collective-bargaining agreement, firms agree not to hire nonunion plumbers, not to contract out plumbing services, and not to subcontract to nonunion firms. Each of these provisions helps prevent erosion of the union's monopoly on the supply of plumbers to the firm. In some industries, like steel and auto manufacturing unions will try to unionize the entire industry so that firm A's unionized workers need not compete with firm B's nonunion workers. All these steps are necessary to protect high union wage rates.

Figure 13-6 shows the impact of agreed-upon high standard wages. Here, the union forces employers to pay wages at the standard rate shown by the horizontal line *rr*. The equilibrium is at E', where *rr* intersects the employers' demand curve. Note that the union has not directly reduced supply when it sets high standard wage rates. Rather, at the high wage rates, employment is limited by the firms' demand for labor. The number of workers who seek employment exceeds the demand by the segment $E'F$. These excess workers might be unemployed and waiting for vacancies in the high-paying union sector, or they might become discouraged and look for jobs in other sectors. The workers from E' to F ⑦ are as effectively excluded from jobs as they would be if the union had directly limited entry.

The need to prevent nonunion competition also explains many of the political goals of the national

---

① 有时，协议会因为涉及资方的特权而被搁置，诸如有关资方有权重新调配工人或者修改劳动规章等。

② 只是由于钟摆效应的缘故，对工会和集体协商机制的支持的一边倒，工会组织才开始蓬勃发展起来。

⑤ 工会通过对某一特定的企业或者产业提供劳工服务的合法垄断，获得了市场力量。

⑥ 受制于典型的集体协商机制，企业承诺不雇佣那些没有参加工会组织的管道工，不对外签约管道维修业务，也不向没有成立工会组织的企业转包合同。

⑦ 实际上，图中从 E' 至 F 两点之间的所有工人均处于失业状态，其结果与将他们拒之于工会大门之外如出一辙。

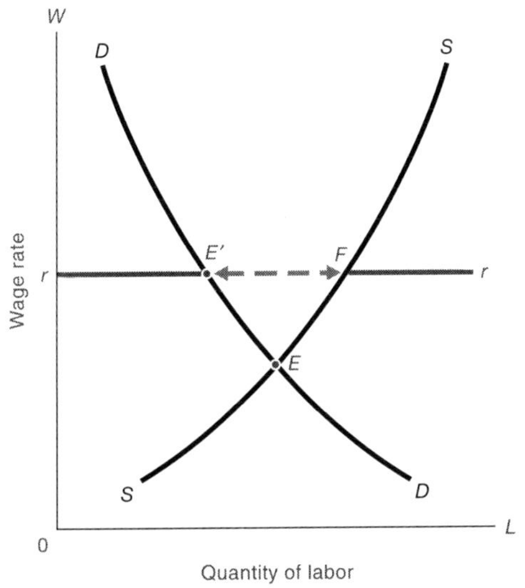

FIGURE 13-6. Unions Set High Standard Wage and Limit Employment ①

Raising the standard wage to *rr* increases wages and decreases the employment in the unionized labor market. Because of supply and demand imbalance, workers from *E′* to *F* cannot find employment in this market.

If unions push real wages too high for an entire economy, firms will demand *E′* while workers will supply *F*. Thus the blue arrow from *E′* to *F* represents the amount of classical unemployment. This source of unemployment is particularly important when a country cannot affect its price level or exchange rate, and it differs from the unemployment caused by insufficient aggregate demand.

labor movement. It explains why unions want to limit immigration; why unions support protectionist legislation to limit imports of foreign goods, which are goods made by workers who are not members of American unions; why quasi unions like medical associations fight to restrict the practice of medicine by other groups; and why unions sometimes oppose deregulation in industries such as trucking, communications, and airlines.

集体协议在理论上的含糊之处
Theoretical Indeterminacy of Collective Bargaining

In most collective-bargaining negotiations, the workers press for higher wages while management holds out for lower compensation costs. This is a situa- ②
tion known as *bilateral monopoly*—where there is but one buyer and one seller. The outcome of bilateral monopoly cannot be predicted by economic forces of costs and demands alone; it depends as well on psychology, politics, and countless other intangible factors.

对工资和就业的影响
EFFECTS ON WAGES AND EMPLOYMENT

The advocates of labor unions claim that unions have raised real wages and have benefited workers. Critics argue that the result of raising wages is high unemployment, inflation, and distorted resource allocation. What are the facts?

工会化提高了工资吗
Has Unionization Raised Wages?

Let's start by reviewing the effects of unions on relative wages. If we look at all private industrial workers in 2006, union workers had average hourly earnings about 15 percent above those of nonunion workers. However, this raw number does not reflect the fact that the skill, educational, and industrial composition of union workers differs from that of nonunion workers.

Taking into account worker differences, economists have concluded that union workers receive on average a 10 to 15 percent wage differential over nonunion workers. The differential ranges from a negligible amount for hotel workers and barbers to 25 to 30 percent higher earnings for skilled construction workers or coal miners. The pattern of results suggests that where unions can effectively monopolize labor supply and control entry, they will be most effective in raising wages. There is some evidence that the impact of unions on wages has declined in recent years.

Overall Impacts. Let us assume that unions can in fact raise the wages of their members above competitive levels. Would this lead to an increase in the average wage of the entire economy? Economists who study this question conclude that the answer is no. They find that unions redistribute income from non- ③
union labor to union labor. Put differently, if unions succeed in raising their wages above competitive levels, their gains come at the expense of the wages of nonunion workers.

---

① 图 13-6. 工会制定的高工资标准限制了就业

② 这是一种众所周知的双边垄断——参与方的买家和卖家各自仅有一家。

③ 他们发现，工会是将工资从非工会成员向工会成员进行再分配。所不同的是，如果工会将这部分成员的工资成功地提高到具有竞争力的水平以上，那么结果却是以非工会成员工资的损失为代价换来的。

This analysis is supported by empirical evidence showing that the share of national income going to labor has changed little over the last six decades. Once cyclical influences are removed, we can see no appreciable impact of unionization on the share of wages in the United States (see Figure 12-1 on page 231). Moreover, the evidence from heavily unionized European countries suggests that when unions succeed in raising money wage rates, they sometimes trigger an inflationary wage-price spiral with little or no permanent effect upon real wages.

工会与古典失业
Unions and Classical Unemployment

If unions do not affect overall real wage levels, this suggests that their impact lies primarily upon relative wages. That is, wages in unionized industries would rise relative to those in nonunionized industries. Moreover, employment would tend to be reduced in unionized industries and expanded in nonunionized industries.

When powerful unions raise real wages to arti- ① ficially high levels, the result is an excess supply of labor that is called *classical unemployment.* This case is also illustrated by Figure 13-6. Assume that unions raise wages above the market-clearing wage at E to a higher real wage at rr. Then, if the supply of and demand for labor in general are unchanged, the arrow between E' and F will represent the number of workers who want to work at wage rr but cannot find work. This is called classical unemployment because it results from real wages that are above competitive levels.

Economists often contrast classical unemploy- ② ment with the unemployment that occurs in business cycles, often called Keynesian unemployment, which results from insufficient aggregate demand. The effects of too high real wages were seen after the economic unification of Germany in 1990. The economic union fixed East German wages at a level estimated to be at least twice as high as could be justified by labor's marginal revenue product. The result was a sharp decline in employment in eastern Germany after unification.

This analysis suggests that when an economy gets locked into real wages that are too high, high levels of unemployment may result. The unemployment ③ will not respond to the traditional macroeconomic policy of increasing aggregate spending but, rather, will require remedies that lower real wages.

Declining Unionism in the United States

One of the major trends in American labor markets has been the gradual erosion of labor unions since World War II. Whereas unions had organized one-quarter of the labor force in 1955, the fraction has fallen sharply since 1980. The share of unionized workers in manufacturing has shrunk dramatically in the last two decades; only in the public sector are unions still a powerful force.

One of the reasons for the decline in unions is the waning power of the strike, which is the ultimate threat in collective bargaining. In the 1970s U.S. labor unions used that weapon regularly, averaging almost 300 strikes per year. More recently, though, strikes have become relatively uncommon; in fact, they have virtually disappeared from the American labor market. The reason for the decline is that strikes have often backfired on workers. In 1981, the striking air-traffic controllers were all fired by President Reagan. When the professional football players went on strike in 1987, they were forced back to work when the football owners put on the games with replacement players. In 1992, workers striking at Caterpillar Inc., a huge maker [4] of heavy equipment, had to end their 6-month strike when Caterpillar threatened to fill their jobs with permanent replacements. The inability to hurt firms through strikes has led to a significant weakening in the overall power of labor unions in the previous two decades.

You might wonder if the declining power of unions will reduce labor compensation. Economists generally hold that a decline in union power will lower the relative wages of union workers rather than lower the overall share of labor. Look back at Figure 12-1 to examine the share of labor in national income. Can you determine any effect of the declining power of unions after 1980 on labor's share? Most economists believe not.

歧 视
DISCRIMINATION

Racial, ethnic, and gender discrimination has been a pervasive feature of human societies since the beginning of recorded history. At one extreme, seen before the Civil War in the United States, black slaves were considered property, had virtually no rights, and were often treated harshly. In other times or places, such as in the United States during the segregation period or under apartheid in South Africa until the 1990s, blacks were segregated in housing

---

① 当势力强大的工会组织人为地将实际工资大幅度地提高以后，所导致的结果是劳动力供给的过剩，即古典失业。

② 经济学家们经常将这种古典失业与商业周期中出现的失业，即通常所讲的凯恩斯失业现象相比较，凯恩斯所定义的失业是总需求不足造成的。在 1990 年德国统一之后，过高的实际工资所带来的后果表现得淋漓尽致。德国经济的统一将东德的工资水平固定在边际收益产量基础上的合理工资水平的至少两倍。结果导致了东德的就业状况在统一之后急剧恶化。

③ 这样的失业对于传统的旨在增加总支出的宏观经济政策来讲不会产生任何影响，但降低实际工资水平却是可行的弥补举措。

[4] Caterpillar Inc.：卡特彼勒公司，全球最大的工程机械生产厂家之一，在纽约证券交易所的代码为 CAT。旗下的卡特彼勒（苏州）有限公司于 2010 年 1 月 25 日在苏州市正式落成。

and transportation and faced prohibitions against interracial marriage and the most desirable forms of employment. Even today, in an era when discrimina-① tion is illegal, subtle forms of informal, premarket, criminal-justice, and statistical discrimination continue to produce disparate outcomes between men and women and particularly among different racial and ethnic groups.

Those who study or experience discrimination know that it extends far beyond the marketplace. Our discussion is limited to economic discrimination, focusing primarily on employment. We want to know why group differences persist decades after discrimination became illegal. We need to understand the sources of the differences between the wages of different groups. Why do African-American and Hispanic citizens in the United States continue to have a measurably lower level of income and wealth than other groups? Why are women excluded from many of the best jobs in business? These are troubling questions that need answers.

歧视的经济学分析
ECONOMIC ANALYSIS OF DISCRIMINATION

歧视的定义
Definition of Discrimination

When economic differences arise because of irrelevant personal characteristics such as race, gender, sexual orientation, or religion, we call this **discrimination.** Discrimination typically involves either (*a*) disparate treatment of people on the basis of personal characteristics or (*b*) practices (such as tests) that have an "adverse impact" on certain groups.

Economists who first began to study discrimination, like the University of Chicago's Gary Becker, realized that a fundamental puzzle arises: If two groups of workers have equivalent productivity, but one has lower wages, why don't competitive profit-maximizing firms hire the low-wage workers and increase their profits? For example, suppose that a group of managers in a competitive market decides to pay blue-eyed workers more than equally productive brown-eyed workers. Nondiscriminating firms ② could enter the market, undercut the costs and prices of the discriminating firms by hiring mainly brown-eyed workers, and drive the discriminating firms out of business. Thus, even if some employers are biased against a group of workers, their bias should not be sufficient to reduce that group's income. Becker's analysis suggests, therefore, that forces other than pure discriminating attitudes are necessary to maintain income disparities between equivalent groups.

排他性歧视
Discrimination by Exclusion

The most pervasive form of discrimination is to exclude certain groups from employment or housing. The history of black Americans illustrates how social processes depressed their wages and social status. After slavery was abolished, the black population of the American south fell into a caste system of peonage under "Jim Crow" legislation. Even though [3] legally free and subject to the laws of supply and demand, black workers had earnings far below those of whites. Why? Because they had inferior schooling and were excluded from the best jobs by trade unions, local laws, and customs. They were consequently shunted into menial, low-skilled occupations that were effectively noncompeting groups. Employment segregation allowed discrimination to persist for decades.

Supply and demand can illustrate how exclusion lowers the incomes of groups that are targets of discrimination. Under discrimination, certain jobs are reserved for the privileged group, as is depicted in Figure 13-7(*a*). In this labor market, the supply of privileged workers is shown by S_pS_p, while the demand for such labor is depicted as D_pD_p. Equilibrium wages occur at the high level shown at E_p.

Meanwhile, Figure 13-7(*b*) shows what is happening for minority workers, who, because they live in areas with poor schools and cannot afford private education, do not receive training for the high-paying jobs. With low levels of skills, they take low-skill jobs and have low marginal revenue products, so their wages are depressed to the low-wage equilibrium at E_m.

Note the difference between the two markets. Because minorities are excluded from good jobs, market forces have decreed that they earn much lower wages than the privileged workers. Someone might even argue that minorities "deserve" lower wages because their competitive marginal revenue products are lower. But this rationalization over- ④ looks the root of the wage differential, which is that wage differences arose because certain groups were excluded from the good jobs by their inability to obtain education and training and by the force of custom, law, or collusion.

---

① 即便在今天，歧视被视为是非法的，那些非正规、上市销售之前、刑事司法以及统计歧视现象的种种微妙表现形式，仍然在男性和女性之间做出截然不同的结局，这一现象在不同种族和民族群体中表现更为突出。

② 通过主要雇佣黑色眼睛的工人，来降低存在歧视的企业所制定的成本与价格，非歧视性企业得以进入市场，从而将这些存在歧视的企业在本行业排挤出局。

[3] "Jim Crow" legislation :《吉姆・克劳法》，1876~1965年期间美国歧视黑人的州的地方性法律，被《1964民权法案》和《1965选举权法案》废除。Jim Crow指黑人，含贬义。

④ 但是，这种近乎合理的行为忽略了产生工资差异的根本原因，即工资差异产生的根源是某些群体由于没有能力获得良好的教育和职业培训，以及由于风俗、法律或者合谋等势力所使，被排斥在好的工作之外。

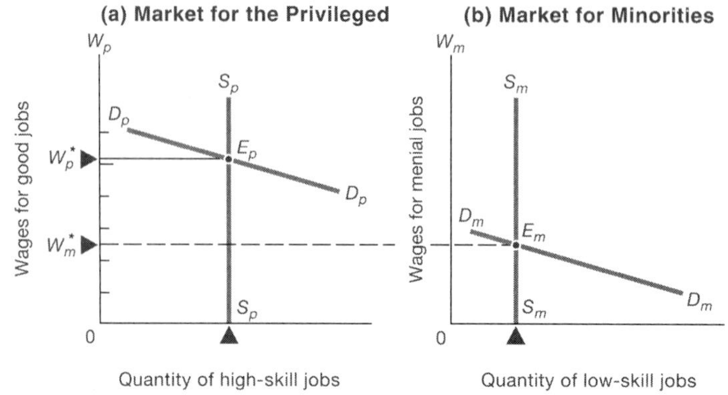

FIGURE 13-7. Discrimination by Exclusion Lowers the Wage Rates of Excluded Minorities ①

Discrimination is often enforced by excluding certain groups from privileged jobs. If minorities are excluded from good jobs in market **(a),** they must work in inferior jobs in **(b).** The privileged group enjoys high wage rates at E_p, while minorities earn low wage rates at E_m in market **(b)**.

歧视的偏好

Taste for Discrimination

The exclusion example still raises the issue of why some profit-maximizing firms do not evade the laws or customs to undercut their competitors. One explanation proposed by Becker was that either firms or their customers have a "taste for discrimination." Perhaps some managers do not like hiring black workers; maybe salespersons are prejudiced and don't want to sell to Hispanic customers. Critics complain that this approach is tautological, in essence saying, "Things are the way they are because people ③ like them that way."

[2] Hispanic：拉丁文为 Hispanicus，源自古代对伊比利亚半岛的拉丁文称谓"Hispania"。该半岛位于欧洲西南部，被西班牙和葡萄牙占领，故指与西班牙或葡萄牙相关联的语言、文化和人等，在全球的官方和非官方的语境中被广泛使用。

统计性歧视

Statistical Discrimination

One of the most interesting variants of discrimination occurs because of the interplay between incomplete information and perverse incentives. This is known as **statistical discrimination,** in which individuals are treated on the basis of the average behavior of members of the group to which they belong rather than on the basis of their personal characteristics.

One common example arises when an employer ④ screens employees on the basis of their college. The employer may have observed that people who graduate from better schools are *on average* more productive; in addition, grade point averages are often difficult to compare because of differences in grading standards. Employers therefore often hire people on the basis of their college rather than of their grades. A more careful screening process would show that there are many highly qualified workers from the less well-known schools. We see here a common form of statistical discrimination based on average quality of schooling.

[2] Statistical discrimination leads to economic ⑤ inefficiencies because it reinforces stereotypes and reduces the incentives of individual members of a group to develop skills and experience. Consider someone who goes to a little-known school. She knows that she will be largely judged by the quality of her schooling credentials. The grade point average, the difficulty of the courses taken, her actual knowledge, and her on-the-job experience may be ignored. The result is that, when subject to statistical discrimination, individuals have greatly reduced incentives to invest in activities that will improve their skills and make them better workers.

Statistical discrimination is particularly pernicious when it involves race, gender, or ethnic groups. If employers treat all black youths as "unproductive" because of average experience with hiring black youths, then gifted individuals not only will

---

① 图 13-7. 排他性歧视降低了被排斥在外的少数族群的工资水平

③ 批评家们抨击这是一种赘冗之说，其实质在道明："事情之所以成为事情，只因为人们想要它们成为事情。"

④ 一个极为普通的案例是，当雇主在筛选雇员时，常以他们就读的大学为基本要求。作为雇主，可能已经注意到从名牌大学毕业的人平均来讲能创造更多的价值。另外，各校的绩点分（grade point averages，GPA）标准不一，通常情况下很难对毕业生的能力差异给予界定。

⑤ 由于统计性歧视强化了人们本来的成见，减少了对某一群体中个体成员增强技能和知识的激励，从而导致经济效率低下。

be treated as the average worker but will have little incentive to upgrade their skills.

Statistical discrimination is seen in many areas ① of society. Life insurance and automobile insurance generally average the risks of people who are careful with those who live dangerously; this tends to reduce the incentive to behave cautiously and leads to a decrease in the average amount of caution in the population. Women were traditionally excluded from quantitatively oriented professions like engineering; as a result, women were more likely to choose humanities and social sciences for their majors and their careers, thereby reinforcing the stereotype that women were uninterested in engineering.

Statistical discrimination not only stereotypes ② individuals on the basis of group characteristics; it also reduces the incentives of individuals to make investments in education and training and thereby tends to reinforce the original stereotype.

对妇女的经济歧视
ECONOMIC DISCRIMINATION AGAINST WOMEN

The largest group to suffer from economic discrimination is women. A generation ago, women earned about 70 percent of the wages of men. Part of this was due to differences in education, job experience, and other factors. Today, the gender gap has shrunk sharply. Most of the remaining difference is the "family gap"—a wage penalty against women with children.

What lay behind the income differentials between men and women? The causes are complex, grounded in social customs and expectations, statistical discrimination, and economic factors such as education and work experience. In general, women are not paid less than men for the same job. Rather, the lower pay of women arose because women were excluded from certain high-paying professions, such as engineering, construction, and coal mining. In addition, women tended to interrupt their careers to have children and perform household duties, and this continues to persist in the family gap. Also, economic inequality of the sexes was maintained because, until recently, few women were elected to the boards of directors of large corporations, to senior partnerships in major law firms, or to tenured professorships in top universities.

经验证据
EMPIRICAL EVIDENCE

Having analyzed the mechanisms by which discrimination is enforced, let us next examine empirical evidence on earnings differentials. On average, women and minorities earn less than do white men. For example, women who worked full-time had earnings equal to 60 percent of men's earnings in 1967. By 2007, that number had risen to 80 percent.

Labor economists emphasize that earnings differentials are not the same as discrimination. Wage differentials often reflect differences in skill and productivity. Many Hispanic workers, particularly immigrants, have historically received less education than have native whites; women customarily spend more time out of the labor force than do men. Since both education and continuing work experience are linked to higher pay, it is not surprising that some earnings differentials exist.

How much of the earnings differentials is due to discrimination rather than productivity differences? Here are some recent findings:

- For women, the extent of discrimination has declined markedly in recent years. Statisticians have uncovered a family gap, which refers to the fact that women who leave the labor force to care for children have an earnings penalty. Aside from the family gap, women appear to have approximately the same earnings as equally qualified men.
- The gap between African-Americans and whites was extremely large for most of American history. However, African-American workers made major progress in the first seven decades of the twentieth century. Data from the 1990s indicate that African-Americans suffer a 5 to 15 percent loss in earnings due to labor market discrimination.
- One of the major encouraging trends is the crumbling of barriers to employment of women and minorities in highly paid professions. In the period from 1950 to 2000, the fraction of women and minorities employed as physicians, engineers, lawyers, and economists has grown sharply. This is particularly striking for women in professional schools. The proportion of women in law schools increased from 4 percent in 1963 to 44 percent in 2006, while for medical schools the proportion rose from 5 percent in 1960 to almost 50 percent in 2006. We see similar trends in other occupations that were once traditionally tied to gender or race.

---

① 统计性歧视散见于社会的各个领域。人寿保险和机动车保险是要谨慎行事的人平均分担那些习惯于莽撞冒险的人随时可能有的风险。这倾向于降低对谨慎行事的激励，导致人群中做事谨慎的人的平均数大幅减少。

② 统计性歧视不仅将以群体性特征为基础的个体模式化，同时还减弱了个体在教育和培训方面的投资动力，从而导致原始性陈规陋习的进一步增强。

减少劳工市场的歧视

REDUCING LABOR MARKET DISCRIMINATION

Over the last half-century, government has taken numerous measures to end discriminatory practices. The major steps were legal landmarks, such as the Civil Rights Act of 1964 (which outlaws employment [1] discrimination based on race, color, religion, sex, or national origin) and the Equal Pay Act of 1963 [2] (which requires that employers pay men and women equally for the same work).

Such laws helped dismantle the most blatant discriminatory practices, but more subtle barriers remain. To counter them, more aggressive and controversial ③ policies have been introduced, including measures such as *affirmative action*. This requires that employers show they are taking extra steps to locate and hire underrepresented groups. Studies indicate that this approach has had a positive effect on the hiring and wages of women and minorities. Affirmative ④ action has, however, been widely criticized in recent years as representing "reverse discrimination," and some states have banned its use in employment and education.

不平坦的进步

Uneven Progress

Discrimination is a complex social and economic ⑤ process. It was enforced by laws that denied disadvantaged groups equal access to jobs, housing, and education. Even after equality under law was established, separation of races and sexes perpetuated social and economic stratification.

The progress in narrowing the earnings gaps among different groups slowed over the last three decades. The disintegration of the traditional nuclear family, cuts in government social programs, harsh drug laws and imprisonment rates, a backlash against many antidiscrimination programs, and the declining relative wages of the unskilled have led to declining living standards for many minority groups. Progress is uneven, and substantial differences in incomes, wealth, and jobs persist.

[1] Civil Rights Act of 1964：1964 年 7 月 2 日，时任美国总统的约翰逊签署并颁布了《1964 美国民权法案》，这是美国立法史上里程碑性的法案之一。美国的种族隔离以及种族、肤色、宗教、性别和国别歧视制度自此在法律上正式废止。从某种意义上来讲，此法案的颁布起源于抗美援朝战争。战争结束后，美军的黑人战俘将“不分种族肤色，人人平等”的志愿军优待战俘政策的火种带回美国，潜移默化地促成了上世纪 60 年代美国黑人如火如荼的反歧视、争平等的民权运动。

SUMMARY

A. Fundamentals of Wage Determination

1. The demand for labor, as for any factor of production, is determined by labor's marginal product. Therefore, a country's general wage level tends to be higher when its workers are better trained and educated, when it has more and better capital to work with, and when it uses more advanced production techniques.
2. For a given population, the supply of labor depends on three key factors: population size, average number of hours worked, and labor-force participation. For the United States, immigration has been a major source of new workers in recent years, increasing the proportion of relatively unskilled workers.
3. As wages rise, there are two opposite effects on the supply of labor. The substitution effect tempts each worker to work longer because of the higher pay for each hour of work. The income effect operates in the opposite direction because higher wages mean that workers can now afford more leisure time along with other good things of life. At some critical wage, the supply curve may bend backward. The labor supply of very gifted, unique people is quite inelastic: their wages are largely pure economic rent.
4. Under perfect competition, if all people and jobs were identical, there would be no wage differentials. But once we drop unrealistic assumptions concerning the uniformity of people and jobs, we find substantial wage differentials even in a perfectly competitive labor market. Compensating wage differentials, which compensate for nonmonetary differences in the quality of jobs, explain some of the differentials. Differences in the quality of labor explain many of the other differentials. In addition, the labor market is made up of innumerable categories of noncompeting and partially competing groups.

B. Labor Market Issues and Policies

5. Labor unions occupy an important but diminishing role in the American economy, in terms of both membership and influence. Management and labor representatives meet together in collective bargaining to negotiate a contract. Such agreements typically contain provisions for wages, fringe benefits, and work rules. Unions affect wages by bargaining for standard rates. However, in order to raise real wages above prevailing market-determined levels, unions must prevent entry or competition from nonunion workers.

[2] Equal Pay Act of 1963：肯尼迪遇刺半年前（1963 年 6 月 10 日）签署的《1963 同酬法案》，是其竞选总统时提出的《新边疆》（New Frontier）施政方针之一，它废止了美国妇女和少数族裔同工不同酬的歧视制度。

③ 为了反对这些歧视陋习，政府实施了更为强势和有争议性的政策，其中包括反歧视行动这样的举措。

④ 然而，这样的反歧视行动近年来被广泛地批评为“变相歧视”的代表，导致一些州在就业和教育领域禁止使用。

⑤ 歧视是一种复杂的社会和经济行为，历来被弱势群体在就业、住房和教育等领域享有同等权利的法律所强化。即便平等权利已被立法，但种族隔离和性别歧视在社会和经济的层级结构中有着长期存在的历史渊源。

6. While unions may raise the wages of their members above those of non-union workers, they probably do not increase a country's real wages or labor's share of national income. They are likely to increase unemployment among union members who would prefer to wait for recall from layoff of their high-paid jobs rather than move or take low-paying jobs in other industries. And in a nation with inflexible prices, real wages that are too high may induce classical unemployment.
7. By an accident of history, a tiny minority of white males in the world has enjoyed the greatest affluence. Even more than a century after the abolition of slavery, inequality of opportunity and economic, racial, and gender discrimination continue to lead to loss of income by underprivileged groups.
8. There are many sources of discrimination. One important mechanism is the establishment and maintenance of noncompeting groups. In addition, statistical discrimination occurs when individuals are treated on the basis of the average behavior of members of the group to which they belong. This subtle form of discrimination stereotypes individuals on the basis of group characteristics, reduces the incentives of individuals to engage in self-improvement, and thereby reinforces the original stereotype.
9. Many steps have been taken to reduce labor market discrimination over the last half-century. Early approaches focused on outlawing discriminatory practices, while later steps mandated policies such as affirmative action.

CONCEPTS FOR REVIEW

Wage Determination under Perfect Competition

elements in demand for labor:
- labor quality
- technology
- quality of other inputs

elements in supply of labor:
- hours
- labor-force participation
- immigration

income effect vs. substitution effect
compensating differentials in wages
rent element in wages
segmented markets and non-competing groups

Labor Market Issues

collective bargaining
unions as monopolies
classical unemployment
discrimination
earnings differentials: quality differences vs. discrimination
statistical discrimination
antidiscrimination policies

FURTHER READING AND INTERNET WEBSITES

Further Reading

The elements of the theory of human capital are given in Gary S. Becker, *Human Capital: A Theoretical and Empirical Analysis, with Special Reference to Education,* 3rd ed. (University of Chicago Press, 1993).

Labor economics is an active area. Many important topics are covered in advanced surveys, such as Ronald G. Ehrenberg and Robert S. Smith, *Modern Labor Economics: Theory and Public Policy,* 9th ed. (Addison-Wesley, Reading, Mass., 2005).

An excellent overview of the economics of discrimination is contained in the symposium on discrimination in product, credit, and labor markets in *Journal of Economic Perspectives,* Spring 1998.

An important source on the impact of immigration is George Borjas, Richard Freeman, and Lawrence Katz, "How Much Do Immigration and Trade Affect Labor Market Outcomes?" *Brookings Papers on Economic Activity,* vol. 1, 1997, pp. 1–90.

Websites

Analysis of the labor market data for the United States comes from the Bureau of Labor Statistics, at *www.bls.gov.* This site also has an online version of *The Monthly Labor Review,* which is an excellent source for studies about wages and employment.

An excellent review of trends in labor markets with special reference to new technologies and discrimination is in *Economic Report of the President, 2000,* chap. 4, "Work and Learning in the 21st Century," available online at *w3.access.gpo.gov/eop/.*

For an international perspective, visit the site of the International Labour Organization at *www.ilo.org.* If you want a detailed reading list on labor economics, visit the MIT open course website at *ocw.mit.edu/OcwWeb/Economics/14-64Spring-2006/Readings/index.htm.*

QUESTIONS FOR DISCUSSION

1. What steps could be taken to break down the segmented markets shown in Figure 13-7?
2. Explain, both in words and with a supply-and-demand diagram, the impact of each of the following upon the wages and employment in the affected labor market:
   a. *Upon union bricklayers:* The bricklayers' union negotiated a lower standard work rule, from 60 bricks per hour to 50 bricks per hour.
   b. *Upon airline pilots:* After the deregulation of the airlines, nonunion airlines increased their market share by 20 percent.
   c. *Upon M.D.s:* Many states began to allow nurses to assume more of physicians' responsibilities.
   d. *Upon American autoworkers:* Japan agreed to limit its exports of automobiles to the United States.
3. Explain what would happen to wage differentials as a result of each of the following:
   a. An increase in the cost of going to college
   b. Free migration among the nations of Europe
   c. Introduction of free public education into a country where education had previously been private and expensive
   d. Through technological change, a large increase in the number of people reached by popular sports and entertainment programs
4. Discrimination occurs when disadvantaged groups like women or African-Americans are segmented into low-wage markets. Explain how each of the following practices, which prevailed in some cases until recently, helped perpetuate discriminatory labor market segmentation:
   a. Many state schools would not allow women to major in engineering.
   b. Many top colleges would not admit women.
   c. Nonwhites and whites received schooling in separate school systems.
   d. Elite social clubs would not admit women, African-Americans, or Catholics.
   e. Employers refused to hire workers who had attended inner-city schools because the average productivities of workers from those schools were low.
5. Recent immigration has increased the number of low-skilled workers with little impact upon the supply of highly trained workers. A recent study by George Borjas, Richard Freeman, and Lawrence Katz estimated that the wages of high school dropouts declined by 4 percent relative to the wages of college graduates in the 1980s as a result of immigration and trade.
   a. To see the impact of *immigration,* turn back to Figure 12-6 in the previous chapter. Redraw the diagrams, labeling part (*a*) "Market for Skilled Workers" and part (*b*) "Market for Unskilled Workers." Then let immigration shift the supply of unskilled labor to the right while leaving the supply of skilled workers unchanged. What would happen to the relative wages of the skilled and unskilled and to the relative levels of employment as a result of immigration?
   b. Next analyze the impact of *international trade* on wages and employment. Suppose that globalization increases the demand for domestic skilled workers in (*a*) while reducing the demand for domestic unskilled workers in (*b*). Show that this would tend to increase the inequality between skilled and unskilled workers.
6. People often worry that high tax rates would reduce the supply of labor. Consider the impact of higher taxes with a backward-bending supply curve as follows: Define the before-tax wage as W, the post-tax wage as W_p, and the tax rate as t. Explain the relationship $W_p = (1 - t)W$. Draw up a table showing the before-tax and post-tax wages when the before-tax wage is \$20 per hour for tax rates of 0, 15, 25, and 40 percent.

   Now turn to Figure 13-4. For the regions above and below point *C*, show the impact of a lower tax rate upon the supply curve. In your table, show the relationship between the tax rate and the government's tax revenues.

CHAPTER

14

Land, Natural Resources, and the Environment

土地、自然资源和环境

[1] 威尔·罗杰斯（Will Rogers，1879~1935），印第安人后裔，著名的美国牛仔，幽默喜剧和杂剧演员、电影演员，杰出的社会评论家，上世纪二三十年代美国著名的社会名流。这段话出自1930年4月13日罗杰斯关于房地产业的一段著名评论，原文为：" ...out here I had been putting what little money I had in Ocean Frontage，for the sole reason that there was only so much of it and no more, and that they weren't making any more..."。这段文字常被人们诠释性地引用为："Put your money in land, because they aren't making any more of it."。萨缪尔森在此处依然习惯性地为其所用，拟译为：

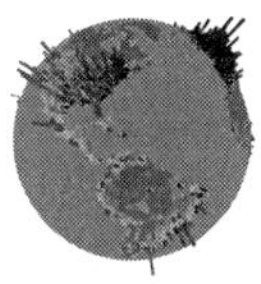

Land is a good investment: they ain't making it no more.

Will Rogers [1]

投资土地乃上佳之策：因为土地投资者根本无法使土地再生出土地来。

本章是本版修订量最大的章节。在第18版之前的几个版本中，本章讨论的均是"土地与资本"问题。17版只在小范围内对16版做了少量修订，比如，上述引用罗杰斯的名言在16版时是作为该章A节"土地及出租"第一段中的引语出现，17版起即置于章首，作为全章的点睛之笔。18版基本保持了17版的原貌。为适应当前全球局势的最新发展，作者将之前这几个版本中第18章"环境保护"的大部分内容修订后移至本章——一揽子讨论"土地、自然资源和环境"的问题。

If you look at any economic process, you will see that it is powered by a specialized combination of the three fundamental factors of production: land, labor, and capital. In Chapter 1, we learned that land and natural resources provide the footing and fuel for our economy; that durable capital goods and intangibles are produced partners in the production process; and that human labor tills the soil, operates the capital stock, and manages the production processes.

Earlier chapters surveyed both the economic theory of pricing and the marginal productivities of factors, as well as the role of labor in the economy. The present chapter continues the study of the factors of production by looking at the workings of the markets for land, natural resources, and the environment. We will start by looking at the markets for land and natural resources, which are nonproduced factors. We then turn to the vital area of environmental economics. This topic covers an important market failure and some proposed remedies and discusses the topic of global warming.

自然资源的经济学问题

A. THE ECONOMICS OF NATURAL RESOURCES

When sentient humans first evolved hundreds of thousands of years ago, their economies were based on hunting, fishing, and gathering, with a rich natural environment but little capital beyond a few sharp sticks and stones. Today, we generally take for granted the bounty of clean air, plentiful water, and unspoiled land. But what is the threat to humanity if we do not respect the limits of our natural environment?

At one pole is an environmentalist philosophy of confines and perils. In this view, human activities threaten to poison our soils, deplete our natural resources, disrupt the intricate web of natural ecosystems, and trigger disastrous climate change. The environmentalist point of view is well expressed in the bleak warning from the distinguished Harvard biologist E. O. Wilson: [2]

> Environmentalism . . . sees humanity as a biological species tightly dependent on the natural world. . . . Many of Earth's vital resources are about to be exhausted, its atmospheric chemistry is deteriorating, and human populations have already grown dangerously large. Natural ecosystems, the wellsprings of a healthful environment, are being irreversibly degraded. . . . I am radical enough to take seriously the question heard with increasing frequency: Is humanity suicidal? ③

Believers in this dismal picture argue that humans must practice "sustainable" economic growth and learn to live within the limitations of our scarce natural resources or we will suffer dire and irreparable consequences.

[2] 爱德华·威尔逊（E. O. Wilson），1929年生于阿拉巴马州的伯明翰，哈佛大学生物学教授，著名的蚁类学家、生物社会学家和博物学家，《知识融通论》（*Consilience*）和《生命亲近学》（*Biophilio*）以及《生态管理保护论》（*The Conservationist*）的作者。两度获普利策奖，被《时代》杂志评为当代美国最具影响力的25位人物之一。

③ 环境保护论把人类视为一种依赖自然世界的生物物种。地球上的许多重要资源正在枯竭，大气层的化学性质在加剧恶化，而人口的数量却已膨胀到了危险规模。大自然的生态系统，这些构建健康生存环境的所有渊源，正在不可逆转地恶化……面对日益频繁地摆到人类面前的严酷现实，心绪难抑，一个严重的问题在责问自己：人类是不是要灭亡？

At the other pole are "cornucopians," or technological optimists, who believe that we are far from exhausting either natural resources or the capabilities of technology. In this optimistic view, we can look forward to continued economic growth and rising living standards, and human ingenuity can cope with any resource limits or environmental problems. If oil runs out, there is plenty of coal. If that doesn't pan out, then rising energy prices will induce innovation on solar, wind, and nuclear power. Cornucopians view technology, economic growth, and market forces as the saviors, not the villains. One of the most prominent of the technological optimists was Julian [1] Simon, who wrote:

> ② Ask an average roomful of people if our environment is becoming dirtier or cleaner, and most will say "dirtier." The irrefutable facts are that the air in the U.S. (and in other rich countries) is safer to breathe now than in decades past. The quantities of pollutants have been declining, especially particulates which are the main pollutant. Concerning water, the proportion of monitoring sites in the U.S. with water of good drinkability has increased since the data began in 1961. Our environment is increasingly healthy, with every prospect that this trend will continue.

Generally, mainstream economists tend to lie between the environmentalist and the cornucopian extremes. They recognize that humans have been drawing upon the earth's resources for ages. Economists tend to emphasize that *efficient management of the economy requires proper pricing of natural and environmental resources.* ③ In this chapter we will survey the concepts involved in the pricing of scarce natural resources and the management of the environment.

资源种类
RESOURCE CATEGORIES

What are the important natural resources? They include land, water, and the atmosphere. The land gives us food and wine from fertile soils, as well as oil and other minerals from the earth's mantle. Our waters give us fish, recreation, and a remarkably efficient medium for transportation. The precious atmosphere yields breathable air, beautiful sunsets, and flying space for airplanes. Natural resources (including land) are a set of factors of production, just like labor and capital. They are factors of production because we derive output or satisfaction from their services.

Economists make two major distinctions in analyzing natural resources. The most important is whether the resource is appropriable or inappropriable. A commodity is called **appropriable** when firms or consumers can capture its full economic value. Appropriable natural resources include land (whose fertility can be captured by the farmer who sells wheat or wine produced on the land), mineral resources like oil and gas (where the owner can sell the value of the mineral deposit), and trees (where the owner can sell the land or the trees to the highest bidder). In a well-functioning competitive market, appropriable natural resources would be efficiently priced and allocated. ④

On the other hand, a resource is **inappropriable** when some of the costs and benefits associated with its use do not accrue to its owner. In other words, inappropriable resources are ones involving externalities. (Recall that *externalities* are those activities in which production or consumption imposes uncompensated costs or benefits on other parties.) ⑤

Examples of inappropriable resources are found in every corner of the globe. Consider, for instance, the depletion of stocks of many important fish, such as whales, tuna, herring, and sturgeon. A school of tuna can provide not only food for the dinner table but also stock for breeding future generations of tuna. Yet the breeding potential is not reflected in the market price of fish. Consequently, when a fishing boat pulls out a yellowtail tuna, it does not compensate society for the depletion of future breeding potential. This is why unregulated fisheries often tend to be overfished.

This leads to a central result in the economics of natural resources and the environment:

> When markets do not capture all the costs and benefits of using natural resources, and externalities are therefore present, markets give the wrong signals and prices are distorted. Markets generally produce too much of goods that generate negative externalities and too little of goods that produce positive externalities. ⑥

Techniques used for managing resources depend on whether the resources are renewable or nonrenewable. A **nonrenewable resource** is one whose supply is essentially fixed. Important examples are the fossil fuels, which were laid down millions of years ago and are not renewable on the time scale of ⑦

---

[1] 朱利安·西蒙（Julian Simon，1932~1998），马里兰大学工商管理学教授，一生著述颇丰，尤以关于人口、自然资源和移民问题的著述著称。生前长期担任华盛顿特区著名的自由派智囊机构——加图研究所的高级研究员。

② 如果你对满屋子的人提一个关于我们的生存环境是越来越好，还是越来越坏的问题，大多数人肯定会说“越来越坏”。但是，不容置疑的事实是，美国（包括其他发达国家）现在的大气环境，比几十年以前已经安全了许多。各种污染物的排放量在持续减少，特别是作为大气中主要污染物的悬浮微粒。关于水质的问题，全美对优质可饮用水的监测数据显示，达到高标准饮用水的水源自1961年开始记录以来，已经有所增加。我们的环境在向健康的方向发展，所有迹象表明，这一趋势将继续下去。

③ 经济学家们普遍强调，经济的有效管理需要对自然和环境资源进行正确的定价。

④ 经济学家们在分析自然资源时，做了两种重要的区分。最重要的一种区分是资源是专用的，还是非专用的。当企业或者消费者可以占有一件物品的全部经济价值时，这件物品就具有**可专用性**。

⑤ 另一方面，当与资源的使用相关联的所有成本和收益中的一部分，对其拥有者来讲无法自然增加时，资源是**非专用的**。换句话说，那些非专用的资源都具有外部性。

⑥ 当市场无法获得使用自然资源的所有成本和收益，且其外部性又存在时，市场就会发出错误的信号，价格就会出现扭曲。市场生产的商品通常会出现过剩，催生负的外部性，而商品严重匮乏时，呈现正的外部性。

⑦ 资源管理所使用的技术，取决于资源是否可以再生。对于**不可再生的资源**，其供给从本质上讲是固定不变的。

human civilizations, and nonfuel mineral resources, such as copper, silver, gold, stone, and sand.

By contrast, **renewable resources** are ones whose ① services are replenished regularly. If properly managed, these can yield useful services indefinitely. Solar energy, agricultural land, river water, forests, and fisheries are among the most important categories of renewable resources.

The principles of efficient management of these two classes of resources present quite different challenges. Efficient use of a nonrenewable resource entails the distribution of a finite quantity of the resource over time: Should we use our low-cost natural gas in this generation or save it for the future? By contrast, prudent use of renewable resources involves ensuring that the flow of services is efficiently maintained through, for example, appropriate forest management, protection of fish breeding grounds, and regulation of pollution entering rivers and lakes.

This chapter considers the economics of natural resources. We begin this section by focusing on land. We want to understand the principles underlying the pricing of a fixed resource. In Section B, we turn to the economics of the environment, which involves the important public-policy questions relevant to protecting the quality of our air, water, and land from pollution, as well as global issues such as climate change.

固定数量的土地和租金
FIXED LAND AND RENTS

The single most valuable natural resource is land. Under law, ownership of "land" consists of a bundle of rights and obligations such as the rights to occupy, to cultivate, to deny access, and to build. Unless you ② are planning to run your company from a balloon, land is an essential factor of production for any business. The unusual feature of land is that its quantity is fixed and completely unresponsive to price.[1]

作为固定要素收益的租金
Rent as Return to Fixed Factors

The price of such a fixed factor is called **rent** or **pure** ③ **economic rent.** Economists apply the term "rent" not only to land but also to any other factor that is fixed in supply. If you pay Alex Rodriguez $30 million per year to play for your baseball team, that money would be considered rent for the use of that unique factor.

Rent is calculated as dollars per unit of the fixed factor per unit of time. The rent on land in the Arizona desert might be $0.50 per acre per year, while that in midtown New York or Tokyo might be $1 million per acre per year. Always remember that the word "rent" is used in a special and specific way in economics to denote payments made to factors in fixed supply. Everyday usage of the word often includes other meanings, such as payment for the use of an apartment or building.

> Rent (or pure economic rent) is payment for the ④ use of factors of production that are fixed in supply.

Market Equilibrium. The supply curve for land is completely inelastic—that is, vertical—because the supply of land is fixed. In Figure 14-1, the demand

market equilibrium
市场均衡

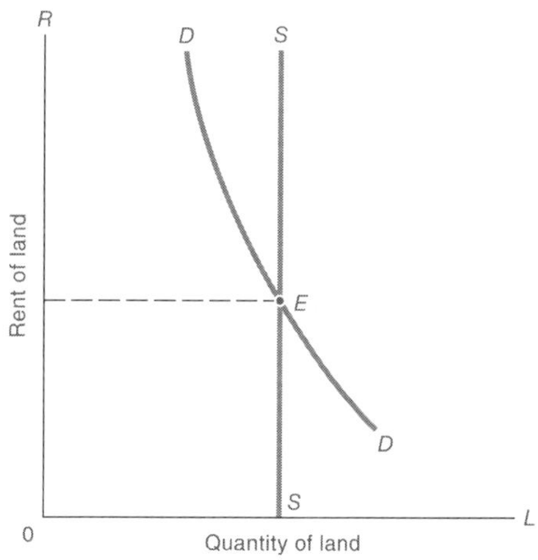

FIGURE 14-1. Fixed Land Must Work for Whatever It Can Earn ⑤

Perfectly inelastic supply characterizes the case of rent, sometimes also called pure economic rent. We run up the *SS* curve to the factor demand curve to determine rent. Aside from land, we can apply rent considerations to gold mines, 7-foot-tall basketball players, and anything else in fixed supply.

[1] This statement must be qualified by the possibility that swamps can be drained and in some cases land can be "produced" by filling shallow bays with landfill. The land area of Boston tripled from 1630 to 1900. Also, land can be used for different purposes, and much agricultural land has been converted to urban land around the world.

① 相比之下，**可再生资源**是那些通常可以不断使用的资源。

② 对于任何企业来讲，土地永远是最重要的生产要素，除非你计划把你的公司开进气球里去。土地的这一非同寻常的特点体现在，其总量永远是固定不变的，对价格是完全迟钝的。

③ 体现在这一固定要素上的价格称为**租金**或者**纯经济租金**。经济学家们赋予"租金"的定义不仅对土地而言，同时也包括在供给上固定不变的其他任何要素。

④ 租金（或称经济租金）是为使用供给固定的生产要素而支付的价格。

⑤ 图 14-1. 使用总量固定的土地必须以获利为目的。

and supply curves intersect at the equilibrium point *E*. It is toward this factor price that the rent of land must tend. Why?

If rent were above the equilibrium, the amount of land demanded by all firms would be less than the fixed supply. Some landowners would be unable to rent their land and would have to offer their land for less and thus bid down its rent. By similar reasoning, the rent could not long remain below the equilibrium. Only at a competitive price where the total amount of land demanded exactly equals the fixed supply will the market be in equilibrium.

Suppose the land can be used only to grow corn. If the demand for corn rises, the demand curve for corn land will shift up and to the right, and the rent will rise. This leads to an important point about land: The price of corn land is high because the price of corn is high. This is a fine example of *derived demand,* which ① signifies that the demand for the factor is derived from the demand for the product produced by the factor.

Because the supply of land is inelastic, land will ② always work for whatever it can earn. Thus the value of the land derives entirely from the value of the product, and not vice versa.

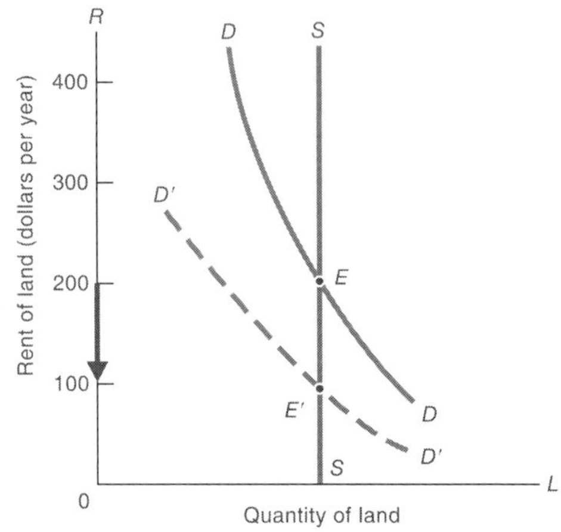

FIGURE 14-2. Tax on Fixed Land Is Shifted Back to Landowners, with Government Skimming Off Pure Economic Rent ③

A tax on fixed land leaves prices paid by users unchanged at *E* but reduces rent retained by landowners to *E′*. This provides the rationale for Henry George's single-tax movement, which aimed to capture for society the increased land values without distorting the allocation of resources.

对土地征税
Taxing Land

The fact that the supply of land is fixed has a very important consequence. Consider the land market in Figure 14-2. Suppose the government introduces a 50 percent tax on all land rents, taking care to ensure that there is no tax on buildings or improvements.

After the tax, the total demand for the land's services will not have changed. At a price (*including* tax) of $200 in Figure 14-2, people will continue to demand the entire fixed supply of land. Hence, with land fixed in supply, the market rent on land services (including the tax) will be unchanged and must be at the original market equilibrium at point *E*.

What will happen to the rent received by the landowners? Demand and quantity supplied are unchanged, so the market price will be unaffected by the tax. Therefore, the tax must be completely paid out of the landowner's income.

The situation can be visualized in Figure 14-2. What the farmer pays and what the landlord receives are now two quite different things. As far as the landlords are concerned, once the government steps in to take its 50 percent share, the effect is just the same as it would be if the net demand to the owners had shifted down from *DD* to *D′D′*. Landowners' equilibrium return after taxes is now only *E′*. *The entire tax* ④ *has been shifted backward onto the owners of the factor in perfectly inelastic supply.*

Landowners will surely complain. But under perfect competition there is nothing they can do about it, since they cannot alter the total supply and the land must work for whatever it can get. Half a loaf is better than none.

You might at this point wonder about the effects of such a tax on economic efficiency. The striking result ⑤ is that *a tax on rent will lead to no distortions or economic inefficiencies.* This surprising result comes because a tax on pure economic rent does not change anyone's economic behavior. Demanders are unaffected because their price is unchanged. The behavior of suppliers is unaffected because the supply of land is fixed and cannot react. Hence, the economy operates after the tax exactly as it did before the tax—with no distortions or inefficiencies arising as a result of the land tax.

---

① 这是一个派生需求的上佳案例。它说明，对要素的需求是从要素本身所生产的产品的需求派生出来的。

② 因为土地供给是缺乏弹性的，所以，土地使用总以获利为目的。因此，土地的价值完全由产品的价值派生而来，反之则不然。

③ 图 14-2. 对固定数量的土地征税，由土地所有者承担，政府则坐收纯经济租金。

④ 全部税收由完全无弹性供给的要素承担。

⑤ 引人注目的结果是，对租金征税绝不会使经济发生畸变，也不可能使经济出现无效率。

A tax on pure economic rent will lead to no distortions or inefficiencies. ①

Henry George's Single-Tax Movement

The theory of pure economic rent was the basis for the single-tax movement of the late 1800s. At the time, America's population was expanding rapidly as people migrated here from all over the world. With the growth in population and the expansion of railroads into the American West, land rents soared, creating handsome profits for those who were lucky or farsighted enough to buy land early. ②

Why, some people asked, should landowners be permitted to receive these "unearned land increments"? Henry George (1839–1897), a journalist who thought a great deal about economics, crystallized these sentiments in his best-selling book *Progress and Poverty* (1879). He called for financing government principally through property taxes on land, while cutting or eliminating all other taxes on capital, labor, and the improvements on the land. George believed that such a "single tax" could improve the distribution of income without harming the productivity of the economy.

While the U.S. economy obviously never went very far toward the single-tax ideal, many of George's ideas were picked up by subsequent generations of economists. In the 1920s, the English economist Frank Ramsey extended George's approach by analyzing the efficiency of different kinds of taxes. This led to the development of efficient or Ramsey tax theory. This analysis shows that taxes are least distortionary if levied on sectors whose supplies or demands are highly price-inelastic. ③

The reasoning behind Ramsey taxes is essentially the same as that shown in Figure 14-2. If a commodity is highly inelastic in supply or demand, a tax on that sector will have very little impact on production and consumption, and the resulting distortion will be relatively small.

环境经济学

B. ENVIRONMENTAL ECONOMICS

In the introductory section of this chapter, we read about some of the controversies surrounding environmental problems. A stern warning from environmentalists Paul R. Ehrlich and Ann H. Ehrlich [4] in 2008 illustrates these concerns:

> Our species has already plucked the low-hanging resource fruit and converted the richest lands to human uses. To support [population growth], metals will have to be won from ever-poorer ores, while oil, natural gas, and water will need to be obtained from ever-deeper wells and transported further. So-called "marginal" lands, often the last strongholds of the biodiversity on which we all depend for essential ecosystem services, increasingly will be converted into yet more crops to feed people, livestock, or SUVs. . . . Climate change is a major threat, even if it may not be the greatest environmental problem. Land-use change, toxification of the planet, increased probability of vast epidemics, or conflicts over scarce resources, involving, possibly, use of nuclear weapons—all population-related—may prove more menacing. [5]

While many technological optimists believe that such concerns are exaggerated, our task is to understand the *economic forces underlying environmental degradation*. This section explores the nature of environmental externalities, describes why they produce economic inefficiencies, and analyzes potential remedies. ⑥

外部性
EXTERNALITIES

Recall that an *externality* is an activity that imposes involuntary costs or benefits on others, or an activity whose effects are not completely reflected in its market price.

Externalities come in many guises: Some are positive, while others are negative. When a firm dumps toxic wastes into a stream, doing so may kill fish and plants and reduce the stream's recreational value. This is a negative or harmful externality because the firm does not compensate people for the damages imposed on the stream. If you discover a new flu vaccine, the benefits will extend to many people who are not vaccinated because they are less likely to be exposed to the flu. This is a positive or beneficial externality.

Some externalities have pervasive effects, while others have smaller spillover components. When a carrier of bubonic plague entered a town during the Middle Ages, [7] an entire population could be felled by the Black Death. On the other hand, when you eat an onion at a football stadium on a windy day, the external impacts are hardly noticeable. ⑧

---

[4] 埃里奇夫妇（Paul R. Ehrlich and Ann H. Ehrlich），两人于1954年结婚，育有一女。保罗·拉尔夫·埃里奇，1932年出生，美国当代著名的生物学家和教育家，斯坦福大学生物保护中心主任，著名的也是极具争议的《人口爆炸》（Population Bomb）一书的作者，"西蒙—埃里奇赌局"（Simon-Ehrlich Wager，两人于1980年对未来10年铜、铬、镍、锡、钨等常规金属资源的价格走势所下的赌注）的输家。安·豪兰·埃里奇，1933年出生，著名的环境保护活动家，埃里奇事业的得力助手和合著者。

[5] 本段文字为埃里奇夫妇与著名环境保护作家比尔·麦克吉本（Bill McKibben，*The End of Nature* 的作者）在2008年2月1日的一次谈话中的一段。

我们人类早已将那些易于开采的资源几乎采伐殆尽，同时也把那些最肥沃的土地派作他用。为了支撑日益膨胀的人口压力，各种金属材料将不得不从曾经被遗弃的贫矿中提炼。与此同时，石油、天然气和水则需要从曾经望深莫叹的更深的井中开采，并运到更远的地方。我们赖以生存的具有生物多样性的最后一块根据地——所谓的"贫瘠"的土地，正被越来越多地转化为耕地，以生产更多的粮食来满足人、生畜，或者越野车……气候变暖是当今的主要威胁，即便它尚不太可能成为最严重的环境问题。土地用途的转变；我们赖以生存和繁衍的这颗星球，已经由于化合物的滥用而导致其肌肤在急剧恶化，其大规模扩散的可能性已经日益严峻；资源稀缺引起的冲突可能会引发核战争——所有这一切都与人口的膨胀问题有着紧密的关联，并且都有可能见证更为险恶的结局。

① 对纯经济租金征税绝不会导致经济发生畸变，也不可能出现经济无效率。

② 随着人口的增长和铁路延伸至美国的西部，土地的租金也随之飙升起来，同时也为那些幸运或者有远见的、早就购买土地的人带来了可观的收益。

③ 这一分析表明，如果被征对象的供给或者需求是缺乏弹性的，那么所征税收的扭曲最小。

⑥ 当许许多多笃信科学技术的人们确信，这样的担忧只是在杞人忧天时，摆在我们眼前的任务就是要把潜伏在环境恶化之下的经济推力彻底搞清楚。

[7] Middle Ages：中世纪，指欧洲历史上从公元476年西罗马帝国灭亡始，至14世纪中叶文艺复兴在意大利兴起时止的千年，为史学界"三段断代说"中承接"古希腊罗马时期"（Classical）和文艺复兴开始至今的"现代时期"（Modern）的"中世纪"（Medieval）。英语语言的历史也与此同步，分为"古英语"（Old English），"中古英语"（Middle English），和"现代英语"（Modern English，文艺复兴时期的英文，或称莎士比亚时期的英文为"早期现代英语"，即 Early Modern English）。

Black Death：14世纪蔓延欧亚两洲的黑死病，即鼠疫。它是人类历史上最惨烈的传染病之一，1348~1350年间在欧洲达到高峰，导致欧洲大陆30%~60%的人死亡。

⑧ 在欧洲中世纪，当黑死病病菌的携带者进城之后，城里几乎所有的居民都有可能被这一致命的鼠疫所传染。而另一方面，在一个狂风大作的日子，如果哪位在足球场上咀嚼葱头，其外在的影响则很难被人察觉。

公共物品和私人物品
Public vs. Private Goods

A polar case of an externality is a *public good,* which is a commodity that can be provided to everyone as easily as it can be provided to one person.

The case par excellence of a public good is national defense. Nothing is more vital to a society than its security. But national defense, as an economic good, differs completely from a *private good* like bread. Ten loaves of bread can be divided up in many ways among individuals, and what I eat cannot be eaten by others. But national defense, once provided, affects everyone equally. It matters not at all whether you are hawk or dove, old or young, ignorant or learned—you will receive the same amount of national security from the Army as does every other resident of the country.

Note therefore the stark contrast: The decision to ①
provide a certain level of a public good like national
defense will lead to a number of batallions, air- [2]
planes, and tanks to protect each of us. By contrast, the decision to consume a private good like bread is an individual act. You can eat four slices, or two, or none; the decision is purely your own and does not commit anyone else to a particular amount of bread consumption.

The example of national defense is a dramatic and extreme case of a public good. But when you think of a smallpox vaccine, the Hubble telescope, clean drinking water, or many similar government projects, you generally find elements of public goods involved. In summary:

> **Public goods** are ones whose benefits are indivis- ③
> ibly spread among the entire community, whether or not individuals desire to consume the public good. **Private goods,** by contrast, are ones that can be divided up and provided separately to different individuals, with no external benefits or costs to others. Efficient provision of public goods often requires government action, while private goods can be efficiently allocated by private markets.

Global Public Goods

Perhaps the thorniest of all market failures are global public goods. These are externalities whose impacts are indivisibly spread across the entire globe. Important examples are actions to slow global warming (considered later in this chapter), measures to prevent ozone depletion, or discoveries to prevent a global pandemic of avian flu. Global public goods pose particular problems because there are no effective market or political mechanisms available to allocate them efficiently. Markets routinely fail because individuals do not have appropriate incentives to produce these goods, while national governments cannot capture all the benefits of their investments in global public goods.

Why do global public goods differ from other goods? If a terrible storm destroys much of America's corn crop, the price system will guide farmers and consumers to equilibrate needs and availabilities. If America's public road system needs modernization, voters will lobby the government to develop an efficient transportation system. But if problems arise concerning global public goods, such as global warming or antibiotic resistance, neither market participants nor national governments have appropriate incentives to find an efficient outcome. The marginal cost of investments to any individual or nation is much less than the global marginal benefits, and underinvestment is the certain outcome.

外部性造成的市场低效率
MARKET INEFFICIENCY WITH EXTERNALITIES

Abraham Lincoln said that government should "do [4]
for the people what needs to be done, but which they cannot, by individual effort, do at all, or do so well, for themselves." Pollution control satisfies this guideline since the market mechanism does not provide an adequate check on polluters. Firms will not voluntarily restrict emissions of noxious chemicals, nor will they always abstain from dumping toxic wastes into landfills. Pollution control is therefore generally
held to be a legitimate government function. ⑤

对低效率的分析
Analysis of Inefficiency

Why do externalities like pollution lead to economic inefficiency? Take a hypothetical coal-burning elec-
tric utility. Dirty Light & Power generates an exter- [6]
nality by spewing out tons of noxious sulfur dioxide fumes. Some of the sulfur harms the utility, requiring more frequent repainting and raising the firm's medical bills. But most of the damage is "external" to the firm, harming vegetation and buildings and causing various kinds of respiratory ailments and even premature death in people.

① 因此，上述讨论所要表明的强烈对比是：对于提供一定水平的像国防这样的公共产品，其决策包括组建大量成建制的作战营、生产各式作战飞机和坦克用以保卫我们每一个公民。

[2] batallion：亦拼作 battalion，因 *Batallion War* 等网络游戏而风靡。在 18 版前均使用传统的"submarines"（潜艇）和"cruise missiles"（巡航导弹，本版中被 air planes 取代），94 岁的萨翁依然与网络一代同步。

③ **公共产品**（亦译作"公共物品"、"公共品"）是指那些无论公民个体是否去消费它们，但却惠及全社会所有组成部分的产品。与此形成鲜明对比的是，**私人物品**是指那些可供逐一分割，以供不同个体所需，同时对他人既没有外部性收益，也不产生成本的物品。公共产品的有效供给通常需要政府行为，而私人物品则可以由私人市场有效地分配。

[4] 亚伯拉罕·林肯（Abraham Lincoln，1809~1865），美国共和党政治家，1861 年 3 月 4 日 ~1865 年 4 月 15 日任美国第 16 任总统，与乔治·华盛顿、富兰克林·罗斯福并列为美国历史上最伟大的三位总统，也是美国历史上首名遇刺身亡的总统。在任期间领导了美国南北战争，维护了美国统一，颁布了《解放黑奴宣言》，被《泰晤士报》评为最伟大的美国总统。

⑤ 林肯总统曾经指出，政府应该"为人民做那些需要政府去做的任何事情，这些惠及大众的事情仅仅凭借个体的努力是无法完成的，或者是根本做不好的。"控制污染的问题就符合这样的指导方针，市场机制对排污者无法实施有效的监管。

[6] Dirty Light & Power：常是一些反思煤电污染的摄影绘画作品的名字，此处是作者虚拟的一家"黑色照明热电厂"，乌克兰著名美女流行歌手尤莉娅著名专辑的主打歌曲也取名 *Dirty Light*。

Dirty Light & Power must decide how much to reduce its pollution, but it also has to answer to its profit-oriented shareholders. With no pollution cleanup, its workers, plant, and profits will suffer. Cleaning up every last particle, on the other hand, will be very costly. Such a complete cleanup would cost so much that Dirty Light & Power could not hope to survive in the marketplace.

The managers therefore decide to clean up ① just to the point where profits are maximized. This requires that the benefits to the firm from additional abatement ("marginal private benefits") be equal to the cost of additional cleanup ("marginal cost of abatement"). Careful economic and engineering calculations might show that the firm's private interests are maximized when abatement is set at 50 tons. At that level, the marginal private benefits equal the marginal costs of $10 per ton. Put differently, when Dirty Light & Power produces electricity in a least-cost manner, weighing only private costs and benefits, it will abate only 50 tons and pollute 350 tons.

Suppose, however, that a team of environmental scientists and economists is asked to examine the overall benefits of abatement to society rather than only the benefits to Dirty Light & Power. In examining the total impacts, the auditors find that the *marginal social benefits* of pollution control—including improved health and increased property values in neighboring regions—are 10 times the marginal private benefits. The impact from each extra ton on Dirty Light & Power is $10, but the rest of society suffers an additional impact of $90 per ton of external costs. Why doesn't Dirty Light & Power include the $90 of additional social benefits in its calculations? The $90 is excluded because these benefits are external to the firm and have no effect on its profits.

We now see how pollution and other externalities lead to inefficient economic outcomes: In an unregulated environment, firms will determine their most profitable pollution levels by equating the marginal private benefit from abatement with the marginal private cost of abatement. When the pollution spillovers are significant, the private equilibrium will produce inefficiently high levels of pollution and too little cleanup activity.

Socially Efficient Pollution. Given that private decisions on pollution control are inefficient, is there a better solution? In general, economists look to determine the socially efficient level of pollution by balancing social costs and benefits. More precisely, ② *efficiency requires that the marginal social benefits from abatement equal the marginal social costs of abatement.*

How might an efficient level of pollution be determined? Economists recommend an approach known as *cost-benefit analysis,* in which efficient emissions are set by balancing the marginal costs of an action against the marginal benefits of that action. In the case of Dirty Light & Power, suppose that experts study the cost data for abatement and environmental damage. They determine that marginal social costs and marginal social benefits are equalized when the amount of abatement is increased from 50 tons to 250 tons. At the efficient pollution rate, they find that the marginal costs of abatement are $40 per ton, while the marginal social benefits from the last unit removed are also $40 per ton.

The resulting level of pollution is *socially efficient* because such an emissions rate maximizes the net social value of production. Only at this level of pollution would the marginal social cost of abatement equal the marginal social benefit. Here again, as in many areas, we determine the most efficient outcome by equating the marginal costs and benefits of an activity.

Cost-benefit analysis will show why extreme "no-risk" or "zero-discharge" policies are generally wasteful. Reducing pollution to zero would generally impose astronomically high cleanup costs, while the marginal benefits of reducing the last few grams of pollution may be quite modest. In some cases, it may even be impossible to continue to produce with zero emissions, so a no-risk philosophy might require closing down the computer industry or banning all vehicular traffic. Generally, economic efficiency calls for a compromise, balancing the extra value of the industry's output against the extra damage from pollution.

> An unregulated market economy will generate lev- ③
> els of pollution (or other externalities) at which the marginal private benefit of abatement equals the marginal private cost of abatement. Efficiency requires that the marginal social benefit of abatement equals the marginal social cost of abatement. In an unregulated economy, there will be too little abatement and too much pollution.

---

① 这样，该厂的管理者就可以在保证利润最大化的前提下，制定出控制污染的措施。这要求将从额外减少的污染排放中所获得的收益（"自有的边际收益"），等于额外的污染控制举措中所付出的成本（"减少污染排放的边际成本"）。

② 更为确切地讲，效率要求从减少污染排放中获得的边际社会收益等于减少污染排放中所付出的边际社会成本。

③ 没有制约的市场经济必定导致不同程度的污染（或其他外部性），在这种情况下，减少污染所产生的自有边际收益等于减少污染所需的自有边际成本。效率则要求减少污染所能获得的边际社会收益等于减少污染需要付出的边际社会成本。在一个没有制约的经济体中，必然存在极其严重的污染问题，而减少污染的可能性则几乎为零。

对危害的评估

Valuing Damages

One of the major difficulties involved in setting efficient environmental policies arises because of the need to estimate the benefits of pollution control and other policies. In cases where pollution affects only marketed goods and services, the measurement is relatively straightforward. If a warmer climate reduces wheat yields, we can measure the damage by the change in the net value of the wheat. Similarly, if a new road requires tearing down someone's house, we can calculate the market value of a replacement dwelling.

Unfortunately, many types of environmental damage are extremely difficult to value. A classic ① example was the proposal to ban logging across much of the Pacific Northwest [2] in order to preserve the habitat of the spotted owl. That would cost thousands of logging jobs and raise lumber prices. How should we value the benefits in terms of the continued existence of the spotted owl? Or, to take another example, the *Exxon Valdez* oil spill [3] in Prince William Sound, Alaska, damaged beaches and killed wildlife. How much is the life of a sea otter worth?

Economists have developed several approaches for estimating impacts, such as those on owls and otters, that do not show up directly in market prices. The most reliable techniques examine the impact ④ of environmental damage on different activities and then put market-derived values on those activities. For example, in estimating the impact of emissions of sulfur dioxide, environmental economists first estimate the impact of higher emissions on health, and they then place a dollar value on health changes using either survey techniques or estimates that are revealed by people's actual behavior.

Some of the most difficult cases occur in situations that involve ecosystems and the survival of different species. How much should society pay to ensure that the spotted owl survives? Most people will never see a spotted owl, just as they will never see a whooping crane or actually visit Prince William Sound. They may nevertheless place a value on these natural resources. Some environmental economists use a technique called *contingent valuation*, which involves asking people how much they would be willing to pay in a hypothetical situation, say, to keep some natural resource undamaged. This technique will yield answers, but these answers have not always proved to be reliable.

Few would doubt that a healthy and clean environment ⑤ has a high value, but placing reliable values on the environment, particularly on the nonmarket components, has proved a difficult business.

对污染的图形分析

Graphical Analysis of Pollution

We can illustrate these points with the help of Figure 14-3. The upward-sloping market *MC* curve ⑥ is the marginal cost of abatement. The downward-sloping curves are the marginal benefits of reducing pollution, with the upper, solid *MSB* line being the marginal social benefit from less pollution while the lower, dashed *MPB* line is the marginal private benefit of abatement to the polluter.

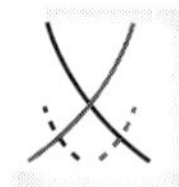

Caution on Graphing Pollution

In analyzing pollution, it is useful to think of pollution control or abatement as a "good." In the graphs, we therefore measure marginal costs and benefits on the vertical axis and the abatement or pollution removed on the horizontal axis. The trick here is to remember that because pollution removal is a good, it is measured positively on the horizontal axis. You can also think of pollution as measured negatively from the far-right point of 400. So abatement of zero is pollution of 400, while abatement of 400 means zero pollution.

The unregulated market solution comes at point *I*, where the marginal private costs and benefits are equated. At this point, only 50 tons are removed, and the marginal private costs and benefits are \$10 per ton. But the unregulated market solution is inefficient. We can see this by performing an experiment that increases abatement by 10 tons; this is represented by the thin slice to the right of point *I*. For this additional removal, the marginal benefits are given by the total area of the slice under the *MSB* curve, while the marginal costs are given by the area of the slice under the *MC* curve. The net benefits are that part of the slice shown by the shaded area between the two curves.

The efficient level of pollution comes at point *E*, where marginal social benefits are equated to marginal costs of abatement. At that point, both *MSB* and *MC* are equal to \$40 per ton. Also, because *MSB* ⑦ and *MC* are equal, the experiment of increasing

① 一个经典的案例是，在太平洋西北部，为保护斑点猫头鹰的栖息地而禁止伐木的提案。

[2] Pacific Northwest：指北美大陆西北部至太平洋东岸的广大地区，包括华盛顿州、俄勒冈州、爱达荷州和加拿大的大不列颠哥伦比亚省，通常也将阿拉斯加州的东南部、蒙塔纳州西部和加州北部包括在内。

[3] *Exxon Valdez Oil Spill*：瓦尔迪兹（*Valdez*）是阿拉斯加南部毗邻威廉王子海湾（Prince William Sound）的最大港口，此处指埃克森美孚石油公司以此港命名的瓦尔迪兹号油轮。1989 年 3 月 24 日，该油轮在威廉王子海湾触礁，多达 75 万桶原油泄漏于此，成为此前人类历史上最严重的人为造成的环境灾难之一。2010 年 4 月 20 日，美国路易斯安那州沿岸英国石油公司的一座石油钻井平台爆炸起火后，连续数月无法制止的漏油事故打破了这个记录，即著名的墨西哥湾漏油事件。

④ 最为可靠的措施是密切跟踪环境灾难对人类的不同活动带来的冲击，然后核算出这些冲击所折合的市场价值。

⑤ 很少有人会对一个有益于健康的清洁环境所具有的高价值产生怀疑。但是，对环境所能带来的真实价值，特别是基于一切非市场因素的真实价值，业已证明是一件极其困难的事情。

⑥ 向上倾斜的 *MC* 曲线表示的是减少污染所付出的边际成本。向下倾斜的两条曲线表示通过控制污染所能获得的边际效益。向上的实线 *MSB* 表示的是减少污染所带来的边际社会收益，向下的虚线 *MPB* 表示的则是对于污染者而言，减少污染所能获得的自有边际收益。

⑦ 同时，由于在 *E* 点 *MSB* 和 *MC* 相等，通过逐渐控制污染的排放量（极少量）将证明，两条曲线之间没有差别，所以从控制污染的额外举措中无法获得任何净收益。

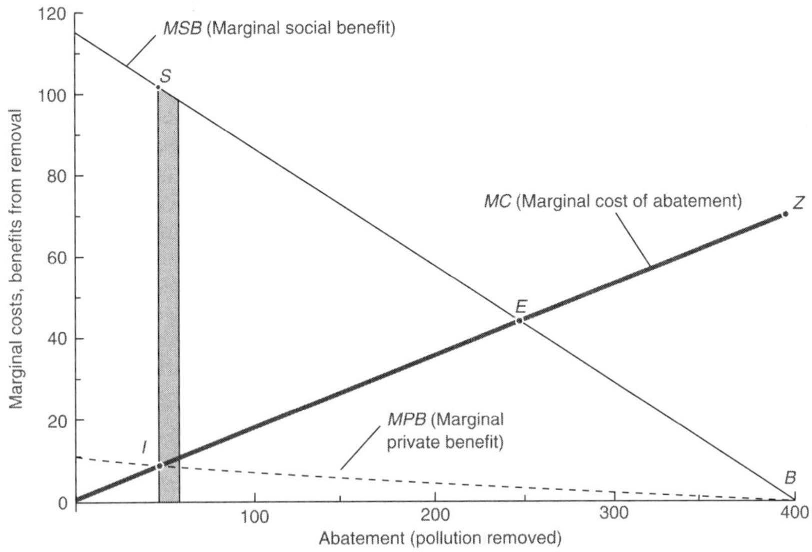

FIGURE 14-3. Inefficiency from Externalities ①

When marginal social benefit (*MSB*) diverges from marginal private benefit (*MPB*), markets will generate unregulated equilibrium at *I*, with too little abatement or pollution cleanup. Efficient cleanup comes at *E*, where *MSB* equals *MC*.

abatement by a tiny amount will find that there is no difference between the curves, so there is no net benefit from additional pollution control. We can also measure the net benefits of the efficient solution relative to the unregulated market by taking all the little slices of net benefit from the shaded slice to point *E*. This calculation shows that the area *ISE* represents the gains from efficient removal of pollutants.

制止外部性的政策
POLICIES TO CORRECT EXTERNALITIES

What are the weapons that can be used to combat inefficiencies arising from externalities? The most visible activities are government antipollution programs that use either direct controls or financial incentives to induce firms to correct externalities. More subtle ② approaches use enhanced property rights to give the private sector the instruments for negotiating efficient solutions. We survey these approaches in this section.

政府计划
Government Programs

Direct Controls. For almost all pollution, as well as ③ other health and safety externalities, governments rely on direct regulatory controls; these are often called *social regulations*. For example, the 1970 Clean [4] Air Act reduced allowable emissions of three major pollutants by 90 percent. In 1977, utilities were told to reduce sulfur emissions at new plants by 90 percent. In a series of regulations, firms were told they must phase out ozone-depleting chemicals. And so it goes with regulation.

direct controls 直接控制

How does the government enforce a pollution regulation? To continue our example of Dirty Light & Power, the state Department of Environmental Protection might tell Dirty Light & Power to increase its abatement to 250 tons of pollution. Under *command-and-control regulations,* the regulator ⑤ would simply order the firm to comply, giving detailed instructions on what pollution-control technology to use and where to apply it. There would be little scope for novel approaches or tradeoffs within the

① 图 14-3. 外部性所导致的无效率

② 更为微妙的举措是通过强化产权的立法，赋予私人部门通过协商找到有效解决污染的权利。

③ 对于几乎所有的污染问题，以及其他健康和安全的外部性问题，政府依靠直接监管加以控制。这就是通常所讲的社会管制。

[4] The 1970 Clean Air Act：美国政府于 1970 年颁布的《国家环境政策法》，是由政府执行的强制性的大气环境标准。

⑤ 在命令—控制型规制下，监管者会以简单的行政命令，责成企业执行，同时就污染控制技术的使用和具体实施细则给予详细的规范。

firm or across firms. *If* standards are appropriately set—a very big "if"—the outcome might approach the efficient pollution level described in the previous part of this section.

While it is possible that the regulator might choose a combination of pollution-control edicts that guarantees economic efficiency, in practice that is not very likely. Indeed, much pollution control suffers from extensive inefficiencies. For example, pollution regulations are often set without comparisons of marginal costs and marginal benefits, and without such comparisons there is no way to determine the most efficient level of pollution control.

In addition, standards are inherently a very blunt tool. Efficient pollution reduction requires that the marginal cost of pollution be equalized across all sources of pollution. Command-and-control regulations generally do not allow differentiation across firms, regions, or industries. Hence, regulations are usually the same for large firms and small firms, for cities and rural areas, and for high-polluting and low-polluting industries. Even though firm A might be able to reduce a ton of pollution at a tiny fraction of the cost to firm B, both firms will be required to meet the same standard; nor will there be any incentives for the low-cost firm to reduce pollution beyond the standard even though it would be economical to do just that. Study after study has confirmed that our environmental goals have proved unnecessarily costly when we use command-and-control regulation.

market solution
利用市场机制的解决方案

Market Solution: Emissions Fees. In order to avoid some of the pitfalls of direct controls, many economists have suggested that environmental policy rely instead on market-type regulations. One approach is the use of *emissions fees,* which would require that firms pay a tax on their pollution equal to the amount of external damage it causes. If Dirty Light & Power were imposing external marginal costs of $35 per ton on the surrounding community, the appropriate emissions charge would be $35 per ton. This is in effect *internalizing* the externality by making the firm pay the social costs of its activities. In calculating its private costs, Dirty Light & Power would find ①
that, at point *E* in Figure 14-3, an additional ton of pollution would cost $5 of internal costs to the firm plus $35 in emissions fees, for an overall marginal cost of $40 per ton of pollution. By equating the new marginal *private* benefit (private benefit plus emissions fee) with the marginal abatement cost, the firm would set its abatement at the efficient level. *If* ②
the emissions fee were correctly calculated—another big "if"—profit-minded firms would be led as if by a mended invisible hand to the efficient point where marginal social costs and marginal social benefits of pollution are equal.

The alternative approaches are shown graphically in Figure 14-4, which is similar to Figure 14-3. With the direct-control approach, the government instructs the firm to remove 250 tons of pollutants (or to emit no more than 150 tons). This would, in effect, place the standard at the heavy vertical line. If the standard were set at the right level, the firm would undertake the socially efficient level of abatement. Hence, with efficient regulation, the firm will choose point *E*, where *MSB* equals *MC*.

We can also see how emissions fees would operate. Suppose that the government levies a fee of $35 per ton of pollution. Including the fee, the marginal private benefit of abatement would

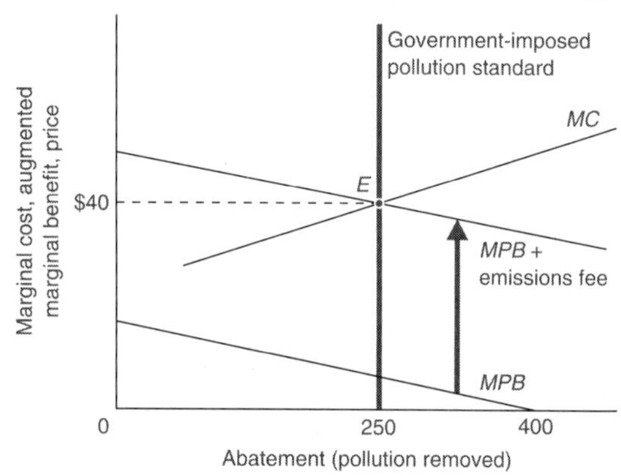

FIGURE 14-4. Pollution Standards and Emissions Fees ③

When government sets the pollution limitation at 150 tons, or requires removal of 250 tons, this standard will lead to efficient pollution at point *E*.

The same result can be achieved with pollution fees of $35 per ton. The $5 *MPB* plus the emissions fee gives a total marginal benefit of $40 at an abatement of 250 tons. Hence the augmented marginal benefit curve (*MPB* + emissions fee) equals *MC* at the efficient level, *E*.

---

① 黑色照明热电厂在对自身的自有成本进行测算之后会发现，在图 14-3 中的 E 点处，一吨额外的污染排放量就要消耗掉 5 美元的公司内部成本，还需要缴纳 35 美元的排污费，这就意味着每排放一吨的污染物，就要支付 40 美元的总边际成本。

② 一个大胆的假设——如果排污费是经过精确的计算出来的，那么以利润最大化为目标的企业就像被一只施以魔力的看不见的手所牵引，直接达至效率点。在这一点上，污染所付出的边际社会成本恰好等于它能获得的边际社会效益。

③ 图 14-4. 污染排放标准与排污费

rise from \$5 to \$40 per ton. We show this as the augmented marginal-private-benefit schedule in Figure 14-4. Faced with the new incentives, the firm would choose efficient point E in Figure 14-4.

Market Solution: Tradeable Emissions Permits. A new approach that does not require the government to legislate taxes is the use of tradeable emissions permits. With this approach, instead of telling firms that they must pay \$$x$ per unit of pollution and then allowing firms to choose the level of pollution, the government chooses the level of pollution and allocates the appropriate number of permits. The price of permits, which represents the level of the emissions fee, is then set by supply and demand in the market for permits. Assuming that firms know their costs of production and abatement, the tradeable-permits approach has the same outcome as the emissions-fee approach.

tradeable emissions permits 可供交易的排放许可证机制

Economic Innovations: Trading Pollution Permits

Most environmental regulations use a command-and-control approach that limits the emissions from individual sources, such as power plants or automobiles. This approach cannot cap overall emissions. More important, it virtually guarantees that the overall program is inefficient because it does not satisfy the condition that emissions from all sources must have equal marginal costs of abatement.

In 1990, the United States introduced a radical new approach to environmental control in its program on control of sulfur dioxide, which is one of the most harmful environmental pollutants. Under the 1990 Clean Air Act ① amendments, the government allocates a limited number of pollution permits. The total number of tons permitted for the country has been gradually reduced since 1990. The innovative aspect of the plan is that the permits are freely tradeable. Electric utilities receive pollution permits and are allowed to buy and sell them with each other just like pork bellies or wheat. Those firms which can reduce their sulfur emissions most cheaply do so and sell their permits to pollute; other firms which need additional permits for new plants or have no leeway to reduce emissions find it economical to buy permits rather than install expensive antipollution equipment or shut down.

Environmental economists believe that the enhanced ② incentives allow the ambitious targets to be met at a much lower cost than would be paid under traditional command-and-control regulation. Studies by economist Tom Tietenberg of Colby College in Maine have determined that the traditional approaches cost 2 to 10 times as much as would cost-effective regulations like emissions trading.

The behavior of this market has produced a big surprise. Originally, the government projected that permits in the early years would sell for around \$300 per ton of sulfur dioxide. But in practice, the market price in the early years fell to below \$100 per ton. One reason for the success was that the program gave strong incentives for firms to innovate, and firms found that low-sulfur coal could be used much more easily and cheaply than had earlier been anticipated. This important experiment has given powerful support to economists who argue for market-based approaches to environmental policy.

自主模式
Private Approaches

It is generally thought that some form of government intervention in the market is necessary to overcome the market failures associated with pollution and other externalities. In some cases, however, strong property rights can substitute for government regulations or taxes.

One private-sector approach relies upon *liability laws* rather than upon direct government regulations. Under this approach, the legal system makes ③ the generator of externalities legally liable for any damages caused to other persons. In effect, by imposing an appropriate liability system, the externality is internalized.

liability laws 民事责任法

In some areas, this doctrine is well established. For example, in most states, if you are injured by a negligent driver, you can sue for damages. Or if you are injured or become ill from a defective product, the company can be sued for product liability.

While liability rules are in principle an attractive means of internalizing the nonmarket costs of production, they are quite limited in practice. They usually involve high litigation costs, which add an additional cost to the original externality. In addition, many damages cannot be litigated because of incomplete property rights (such as those involving

---

① The 1990 Clean Air Act：1990 年颁布的《国家环境政策法修正案》

② 环境经济学家认为，相比于传统的命令—控制型规制，通过强化激励可以更低的成本达到雄心勃勃的目标。

③ 在这种模式下，此种法律制度使外部性的发生方承担起了对他人造成任何伤害的法律责任。事实上，通过恰当的责任承担机制，外部性就有效地被内在化了。

clean air) or because of the large number of companies that contribute to the externality (as in the case of chemicals flowing into a stream).

A second private approach relies upon strong property rights and *negotiations among parties*. This approach was developed by the University of Chicago's Ronald Coase, who showed that voluntary negotiations among the affected parties can sometimes lead to an efficient outcome.

For example, suppose that I am a farmer using fertilizers that flow downstream and kill many of the fish in your ponds. Further, suppose that you cannot sue me for killing your fish. If your fish business is sufficiently profitable, you may try to get me to reduce my fertilizer use. In other words, if there is a net profit to be made from reorganizing our joint operations, we have a powerful incentive to get together and agree on the efficient level of fertilizer runoff. Moreover, this incentive would exist without any government antipollution program.

When property rights are well defined and trans- ①
action costs are low, particularly when there are few affected parties, strong liability laws or negotiation can sometimes operate to produce an efficient resolution in the presence of externalities.

气候变化：放缓还是加快

CLIMATE CHANGE: TO SLOW OR NOT TO SLOW [2]

Of all the environmental issues, none is so worrisome to scientists as the threat of global warming from the greenhouse effect. Climatologists and other scientists warn that the accumulation of gases like carbon dioxide (CO_2), largely produced by the combustion of fossil fuels, is likely to lead to global warming and other significant climatic changes over the next century. On the basis of climate models, scientists project that if current trends continue, the earth may warm 4° to 8° Fahrenheit over the next
century. This would take the earth's climate out of ③
the range experienced during the entire period of human civilization.

The greenhouse effect is the granddaddy of public-good problems; actions today will affect the climate for all people in all countries for centuries to
come. The costs of reducing CO_2 emissions come in ④
the near term as countries cut back their use of fossil fuels by conserving energy and using alternative energy sources (solar energy or perhaps nuclear power), plant trees, and take other measures. In the short run, that means we will have to accept more-expensive energy, lower living standards, and lower consumption levels. The benefits of emissions reductions will come many years in the future, when lower emissions reduce future climate-induced damages—with less disruption to agriculture, seacoasts, and ecosystems.

Economists have begun to study the economic impacts of climate change in order to understand how nations might undertake sensible strategies. Economic studies indicate that the market economies in advanced countries like the United States are likely to be relatively insulated from climate change in the coming decades. The major impacts are likely to be in agriculture, forests, and fisheries, along with unmanaged ecosystems such as coral reefs.

An efficient strategy for containing climate change requires weighing the marginal costs of reducing carbon-dioxide (CO_2) emissions against the marginal benefits. Figure 14-5 shows schematically the marginal costs of reductions as *MC* and the marginal social benefits as *MSB*. The vertical axis measures costs and benefits in dollars, while the horizontal axis

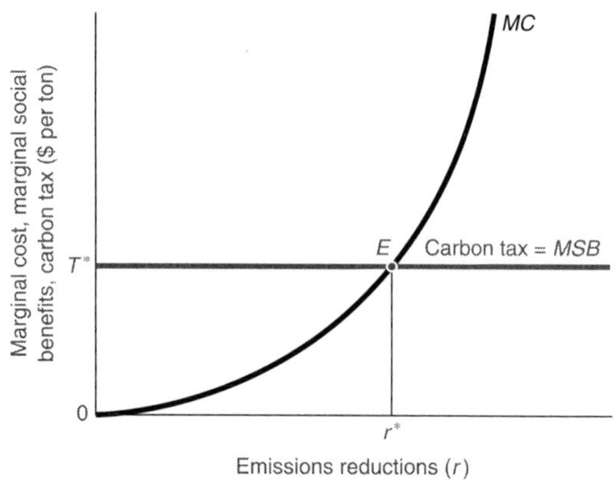

FIGURE 14-5. Carbon Taxes Can Slow Harmful Climate Change ⑤

Slowing climate change efficiently requires setting carbon taxes at T^* or limiting carbon dioxide emissions to r^*. Such measures would equate marginal costs of emissions reductions with marginal benefits of reducing damages from climate change.

---

① 在产权明晰，交易成本很低的情况下，特别是只有少数几家当事方的情况下，通过强有力的民事责任法或者通过协商，可以有效地解决外部性问题。

[2] To Slow or Not to Slow：源自莎士比亚经典悲剧《哈姆雷特》中第三幕第一场哈姆雷特著名独白的第一行："*To be, or not to be; that is the question*"。

③ 在整个人类文明史上将有可能出现从来没有经历过的气候。

④ 各国通过节约能源、使用替代能源（太阳能或者更多地发展核能）、植树造林，以及其他措施，减少了矿石的使用量，从而可在近期降低二氧化碳的排放成本。

⑤ 图 14-5. 碳排放税的征收可以减缓有害的气候变化

measures reduction of carbon-dioxide emissions. Point E in the graph represents the efficient point at which marginal abatement costs equal marginal social benefits from slowing climate change. This is the point which maximizes the net economic benefits of emissions reductions. By contrast, the pure-market solution would come with emissions reductions at 0, where MSB is far above the zero MC. An extreme environmentalist solution, which attempts to reduce emissions to zero, would come at the right-hand edge of the graph, where MC far exceeds MSB.

How can point E, the efficient level of CO_2 reduction, be achieved? Since CO_2 emissions come from burning carbon-containing fuels, some have suggested a "carbon tax" on the carbon content of fuels. Fuels which contain more carbon, like coal, would be taxed more heavily than low-carbon fuels such as natural gas. Economists have developed models that estimate efficient paths for carbon taxes—ones that balance the economic costs of higher taxes with the benefits of reduced damages from global warming. These models can serve as a guide to policymakers in the design of policies to combat global warming. Figure 14-5 shows that if the carbon tax is set at the appropriate level, this would induce the efficient level of emissions reductions.

Global Public Goods and the Kyoto Protocol

We discussed the problem of global public goods earlier in this chapter. Nations deal with global public goods through international agreements like treaties. These are designed to move from an inefficient noncooperative outcome to an efficient cooperative solution to the pollution game. But reaching efficient agreements often proves difficult. Measures to slow global warming provide a useful example. Although scientists have raised alarms about climate change for more than three decades, there were no major international agreements on climate change until the Framework Convention on Climate Change (FCCC) in 1992. The FCCC contained provisions in which high-income countries agreed to nonbinding commitments to limit the emissions of greenhouse gases like CO_2.

When voluntary measures were ineffective, countries negotiated the 1997 Kyoto Protocol on climate change. Under the protocol, high-income countries along with formerly socialist countries agreed to *binding commitments* to reduce by 2010 their total emissions of greenhouse gases by 5 percent (relative to 1990 levels). Each country was allocated a specific target. Based on both economic theory and the experience of the U.S. sulfur dioxide trading program (discussed above), the Kyoto Protocol included a provision for emissions trading among countries. The protocol got off to a shaky start when the Bush administration withdrew the United States from participation in 2001.

Economists have undertaken detailed analyses of the alternative approaches available to tackle the issues involved in global warming. One conclusion of such studies is that it is critical to make sure that market participants face the full costs of their actions. Currently, the climate-change externality is not "internalized" in most countries because CO_2 emissions have a zero price. Without the appropriate price signals, it is unrealistic to think that the millions of firms and billions of consumers will make decisions that reduce the use of carbon fuels. Economic studies also indicate that global participation—not just the participation of high-income countries—is critical to slow-
ing climate change in an economical fashion. By excluding ③
energy-intensive developing countries like China and India from reduction requirements, the cost of meeting the global emissions goal is increased greatly relative to a cost-effective global agreement.

The first round of the Kyoto Protocol went into effect in 2008, but it covers only the period through 2012. Many who are concerned about the future of the globe are looking to see whether the new Obama administration in the United States will join the effort and whether an efficient long-term solution can be designed, implemented, and enforced.

争议和污染，争辩和计算
Quarrel and Pollute, or Reason and Compute?

We have seen that many environmentalists are asking gloomy questions about the future of humanity. Having surveyed the field, what should we conclude? Depending on one's perspective, it is easy to become either optimistic or pessimistic about our ability to understand and cope with the threats to our environment. On the one hand, it is true that we are moving into uncharted waters, depleting many resources while altering others in an irreversible manner, and gambling with our world in more ways than we real-
[1] ize. Humans seem just as quarrelsome today as they
② were at the dawn of recorded history, and they have

[1] Kyoto Protocol：《京都议定书》，是《联合国气候变化框架公约》(*United Nations Framework Convention on Climate Change*，UNFCCC）的补充条款，全称为《联合国气候变化框架公约的京都议定书》，由联合国气候变化框架公约参加国于 1997 年 12 月在日本京都经三次会议制定。克林顿政府签署，遭国会反对；小布什政府退出，使美国成为八大工业国中惟一拒绝执行《京都议定书》的国家。正如本部分内容的最后一段所述，全世界都在看奥巴马政府能否兑现承诺。

② 在这一协议的约束下，高收入国家同意与前社会主义国家做出具有约束力的承诺——在 2010 年之前，将温室气体的总排放量减少 5%（相当于 1990 年的水平）。每一个国家都分配了具体的目标。

③ 由于排除了像中国和印度这样的能源消耗型的发展中国家所应履行的减排义务，实现全球排放目标的所需成本相对于成本效率型的全球性协议来讲，将大大增加。

devised weapons that are awesomely effective at avenging their grudges. At the same time, our powers of observation and analysis are also orders of magnitude more formidable.

① What will prevail in this race between our tendencies to quarrel and pollute and our powers to reason and compute? Are there enough resources to allow the poor to enjoy the consumption standards of today's high-income countries, or will today's rich pull the ladder up behind them? There are no final answers to these deep questions. But economists believe that one central answer is to employ market mechanisms to provide incentives to reduce pollution and other harmful side effects of economic growth. Wise decisions along with appropriate incentives will help to ensure that *Homo sapiens* can not only survive but also thrive for a long time to come.

SUMMARY

A. The Economics of Natural Resources

1. Natural resources are nonrenewable when they cannot regenerate quickly and are therefore essentially fixed in supply. Resources are renewable when their services are replenished regularly and they can, if properly managed, yield useful services indefinitely.
2. Natural resources are appropriable when firms or consumers can capture the full benefits of their services; examples include vineyards and oil fields. Natural resources are inappropriable when their total costs or benefits do not accrue to the owners; in other words, they involve externalities.
3. The return to fixed factors like land is called pure economic rent, or rent, for short. Since the supply curve for land is vertical and completely inelastic, the rent will be price-determined rather than price-determining.
4. A factor like land that is inelastically supplied will continue to work the same amount even though its factor reward is reduced. For this reason, Henry George pointed out that rent is in the nature of a surplus rather than a reward necessary to coax out the factor's effort. This provides the basis for his single-tax proposal to tax the unearned increment of land value, which raises tax revenues without raising prices to consumers or distorting production. Modern tax theory extends George's insight by showing that inefficiencies are minimized by taxing goods that are relatively inelastic in supply or demand because such taxes lead to relatively small distortions in behavior.

B. Environmental Economics

5. Environmental problems arise because of externalities that stem from production or consumption. An externality is an activity that imposes involuntary costs or benefits on others and whose effects are not completely reflected in market prices.
6. The polar extreme of an externality is the case of public goods, like national defense, where all consumers in a group share equally in the consumption of the good and cannot be excluded. Public health, inventions, parks, and dams also possess public-good properties. These contrast with private goods, like bread, which can be divided and provided to a single individual.
7. An unregulated market economy will produce too much pollution and too little abatement. Unregulated firms decide on abatement and other public goods by comparing the marginal *private* benefits of abatement with the marginal costs. But efficiency requires that the marginal *social* benefits of abatement equal the marginal costs.
8. Economists emphasize that the efficient management of externalities requires the proper pricing of natural and environmental resources. This involves ensuring that market participants face the full social costs of their activities.
9. There are different approaches through which governments can take steps to internalize or correct the inefficiencies arising from externalities. Alternatives include decentralized or private solutions (such as negotiations or legal liability rules) and government-imposed approaches (such as pollution-emission standards or emissions taxes). Experience indicates that no single approach will fit every circumstance, but many economists believe that greater use of market-oriented approaches would improve the efficiency of regulatory systems.
10. Global public goods present the thorniest problems because they cannot easily be solved by either markets or national governments. Nations must work together to devise new tools to forge international agreements when issues such as global warming threaten our ecosystem and our standards of living.

---

① 一边为污染问题争吵不休，一边为核算的能力而辩论，在双方之间激烈的竞赛中，究竟哪一方将有能力胜出？能有足够的资源让穷人也能享受到今天高收入国家国民的消费标准吗？或者，今天的富人能在他们的身后为自己竖好向上攀登的阶梯吗？对于这样一些深层次的问题，根本找不到最终的答案。但是，经济学家们确信，首要的解决办法是引入市场机制来推出各种激励措施，以减少污染和经济增长带来的其他负面作用。只要我们做出明智的决定，并配套适当的激励措施，就能保证现代人不仅能够继续生存繁衍，并且能够迎来长期的繁荣与昌盛。

CONCEPTS FOR REVIEW

Land and Natural Resources

renewable vs. nonrenewable resources
appropriable vs. inappropriable resources
rent, pure economic rent
inelastic supply of land
taxation of fixed factors

Environmental Economics

externalities and public goods
private vs. public goods
inefficiency of externalities
internal vs. external costs, social vs. private benefits
remedies for externalities: standards, taxes, liability, bargaining
tradeable emissions permits
global public goods

FURTHER READING AND INTERNET WEBSITES

Further Reading

Environmental economics is a rapidly growing field. You can explore advanced topics in a textbook such as Thomas H. Tietenberg, *Environmental Economics and Policy,* 7th ed. (Addison-Wesley, New York, 2006). An excellent book of readings is Robert Stavins, ed., *Economics of the Environment: Selected Readings,* 5th ed. (Norton, New York, 2005).

The quote from Wilson is from Edward O. Wilson, "Is Humanity Suicidal?" *New York Times Magazine,* May 30, 1993, p. 27. The quotation from Julian Simon is from *Scarcity or Abundance? A Debate on the Environment* (Norton, New York, 1994), available at *www.juliansimon.com/writings/Norton/NORTON01.txt.* The quotation from Ehrlich and Ehrlich is from *The New York Review of Books,* February 14, 2008.

Websites

One of the best websites on resources and the environment is maintained by the nonprofit organization Resources for the Future at *www.rff.org.* You can consult this site for information on a wide range of issues.

Energy data are available at the Energy Information Agency's comprehensive site at *www.eia.doe.gov.*

You can learn more about environmental policy at the U.S. Environmental Protection Agency's website at *www.epa.gov.* International environmental policy is found at the United Nations Environmental Program's site at *www.unep.org.* Information on the Kyoto Protocol and other programs to address climate change can be found at *www.ipcc.ch* and *www.unfccc.de.*

QUESTIONS FOR DISCUSSION

1. What is the difference between renewable and nonrenewable resources? Give examples of each.
2. What is meant by an inappropriable natural resource? Provide an example and explain why the market allocation of this resource is inefficient. What would be your preferred way to improve the market outcome?
3. Define "pure economic rent."
   a. Show that an increase in the supply of a rent-earning factor will depress its rent and lower the prices of the goods that use it.
   b. Explain the following statement from rent theory: "It is not true that the price of corn is high because the price of corn land is high. Rather, the reverse is closer to the truth: the price of corn land is high because the price of corn is high." Illustrate with a diagram.
   c. Consider the quotation in **b.** Why is this correct for the market as a whole but incorrect for the individual farmer? Explain the fallacy of composition that is at work here.
4. Assume that the supply curve for top baseball players is perfectly inelastic with respect to their salaries.
   a. Explain what completely inelastic supply means in terms of number of games played.
   b. Next assume that because of television, the demand for the services of major-league baseball

players increases. What would happen to their salaries? What would happen to their batting averages (other things held constant)? Does this theory fit historical trends?

5. Explain why a tax on land rent is efficient. Compare a tax on the land with a tax on the houses on the land.
6. "Local public goods" are ones that mainly benefit the residents of a specific town or state—such as beaches or schools open only to town residents. Is there any reason to think that towns might act competitively to provide the correct amount of local public goods to their residents? If so, does this suggest an economic theory of "fiscal federalism" whereby local public goods should be locally supplied?
7. Decide whether each of the following externalities is serious enough to warrant collective action. If so, which of the four remedies considered in this chapter would be most efficient?
   a. Steel mills emitting sulfur oxides into the Birmingham air
   b. Smoking by people in restaurants
   c. Smoking by students without roommates in their own rooms
   d. Driving by persons under the influence of alcohol
   e. Driving by persons under age 21 under the influence of alcohol
8. Get your classmates together to do a contingent-valuation analysis on the value of the following: Prohibiting drilling in all wilderness areas in the United States; preventing the extinction of spotted owls for another 10,000 years; ensuring that there are at least 1 million spotted owls in existence for another 10,000 years; reducing the chance of dying in an automobile accident from 1 in 1000 to 1 in 2000 per year. How reliable do you think this technique is for gathering information about people's preferences?
9. Don Fullerton and Robert Stavins argue that the following are myths about how economists think about the environment (see Chapter 1 in the Stavins book in the Further Reading section). For each, explain why it is a myth and what the correct approach is:
   a. Economists believe that the market solves all environmental problems.
   b. Economists always recommend market solutions to environmental problems.
   c. Economists always use market prices to evaluate environmental issues.
   d. Economists are concerned only with efficiency and never with income distribution.
10. **Advanced problem:** Global public goods pose special problems because no single nation can capture all the benefits of its own pollution-control efforts. To see this, redraw Figure 14-5, labeling it "Emissions Reduction for the United States." Label all the curves with "US" to indicate that they refer to costs and benefits for the United States alone. Next, draw a new *MSB* curve which is 3 times higher than the MSB_{US} at every point to indicate that the benefits to the world are 3 times higher than those to the United States alone. Consider the "nationalistic" equilibrium at *E* where the United States maximizes its own net benefits from abatement. Can you see why this is inefficient from the point of view of the entire globe? (*Hint:* The reasoning is analogous to that in Figure 14-3.)

    Consider this issue from the point of view of game theory. The Nash equilibrium would occur when each country chose the nationalistic equilibrium you have just analyzed. Describe why this is analogous to the inefficient Nash equilibrium described in Chapter 10—only here the players are nations rather than firms. Now consider the cooperative game in which nations get together to find the efficient equilibrium. Describe the efficient equilibrium in terms of global *MC* and *MSB* curves. Can you see why the efficient equilibrium would require a uniform carbon tax in each country?

CHAPTER 15

Capital, Interest, and Profits
资本、利息和利润

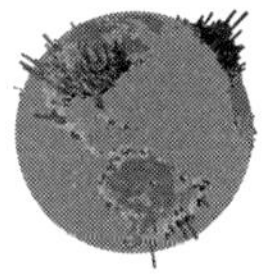

[1] 本章是在第16~18版《土地与资本》一章中的“B节”《资本与利息》的基础上，经过全新的修订和改写，并将原属宏观经济学部分《金融市场与货币的特殊形态》一章中的相关内容平移至此而形成的。需要说明的是，这两章基本上在每一版都是修订量最大的章节。本版对这两章的修订，是作者对2008年爆发的金融危机所进行的深刻反思，是一位94岁的耄耋老翁与时俱进的精神所在。因此，本章理所当然地成为19版中崭新而亮丽的章节之一。原“B节”开头的谚语也置换在了本章的开头。

这句话源自家喻户晓的常用英文谚语“Have one’s cake and eat it too”。最早的版本出现在16世纪中叶的文艺复兴时期（见1989年出版的《牛津英语词典》，第二版），1812年被第一次固定下来，成为现在通用的形式。其含义为“You can’t eat your cake and have it too”，即“一个人不能把两头的好处全占尽”，相当于汉语成语“脚踏两只船”之意。萨翁在此依然延续了其一贯的“为我所用”风格，用“：”引出了作者的“醉翁之意”。“：”在此是画龙点睛的一笔，“Lend it out at interest”则是“have”和“eat”两者必选其一之外的最佳解决方案，即本章的核心思想所在。而所署的“Anonymous”拟为“A proverb”。所以，译文应当如上。

You can have your cake and eat it too: Lend it out at interest.

Anonymous [1]

鱼和熊掌两者兼得：借出去吃利息乃上策。

The United States is a “capitalist” economy. By this we mean that most of the country’s capital and other assets are privately owned. In 2008, the net stock of capital in the United States was more than $150,000 per capita, of which 67 percent was owned by private corporations, 14 percent by individuals, and 19 percent by governments. Moreover, the ownership of the nation’s wealth was highly concentrated in the portfolios of the richest Americans. Under capitalism, individuals and private firms do most of the saving, own most of the wealth, and get most of the profits on these investments.

This chapter is devoted to the study of capital. We begin with a discussion of the basic concepts in capital theory. These include the notion of “roundaboutness” and different measures of the rate of return on investment. Then we will turn to the crucial questions of the supply and demand for capital. This overview will give us a much deeper understanding of some of the key features of a private market economy.

利息和资本的基本概念
A. BASIC CONCEPTS OF INTEREST AND CAPITAL

什么是资本
What Is Capital?

We begin with a brief summary of the important concepts of capital and finance developed in this chapter. **Capital** consists of those durable produced ② items that are in turn used as productive inputs for further production. Some capital might last for only a few years, while others might last for a century or more. But the essential property of capital is that it is both an input and an output.

In an earlier era, capital consisted primarily of tangible assets. Three important categories of tangible capital are structures (such as factories and homes), equipment (such as consumer durable goods like automobiles and producer durable equipment like machine tools and trucks), and inventories (such as cars in dealers’ lots).

Today, intangible capital is increasingly important. Examples include software (such as computer operating systems), patents (such as the ones on microprocessors), and brand names (such as Coca-Cola). Robert Hall of Stanford calls this “e-capital” [3] to distinguish between traditional tangible capital and increasingly important intellectual capital. ④

投资的价格和租金
Prices and Rentals on Investments

Capital is bought and sold in capital markets. For example, Boeing sells aircraft to airlines; the airlines then use these specialized capital goods along with software, skilled labor, land, and other inputs to produce and sell air travel.

Most capital is owned by the firms that use it. Some capital, however, is rented out by its owners.

---

② **资本**是由生产出来的各种耐用品构成的，这些耐用品反过来又作为生产性的投入，以供进一步生产所需。

[3] Robert Hall：罗伯特·霍尔，生于1943年，2010年当选美国经济学会（American Economic Association）主席，斯坦福大学教授，应用经济学家，对总体经济和各种特定市场中出现的就业、竞争、经济政策及技术等问题有深入的研究。著名的经济学教科书《经济学：原理与应用》（*Economics: Principles and Applications*）的作者之一，另一位作者为马克·利伯曼（Marc Lieberman，纽约大学经济系教授）。

④ 斯坦福大学的罗伯特·霍尔称之为“电子资本”，以区别于传统的有形资本与重要性日益凸显的知识资本。

② 这一数量称之为**投资回报率**。以固定利率作为回报的金融资产，其所得即被称作**利率**。从经济学角度讲，投资的利率或者回报是指借入或者贷出资金的价格。

[3]"投资回报率"在之前的相关版本中均为资本收益率（the rate of return on capital），本版中的这一最新表述凸显了作者强化了资本、资本品与投资三者之间的微妙区别，应该说是作者对本次金融危机深刻反思的结果。在18版之前的相关版本中，"资本"与"资本品"是同一概念的两种表述，基本没有区别，如前文有关资本定义的论述在之前的几个相关版本中均为"capital (or capital goods)"。本版后文关于三者之间关系的相关论述，其实在之前的几个相关版本中的《资本的基本理论》一节中均已基本厘清，本版中未做大的修订。

Payments for the temporary use of capital goods are called rentals. An apartment that is owned by Ms. Landlord might be rented out for a year to a student, and the monthly payment of $800 per month would constitute a rental. We distinguish *rent* on fixed factors like land from *rentals* on durable factors like capital.

资本和金融资产

Capital vs. Financial Assets

Individuals and businesses own a mix of different kinds of assets. One class is the productive input capital that we just discussed—items like computers, automobiles, and houses that are used to produce other goods and services. But we must distinguish ①
these tangible assets from *financial assets,* which are essentially pieces of paper or electronic records. More precisely, financial assets are monetary claims by one party against another party. An important example is a mortgage, which is a claim against a homeowner for monthly payments of interest and principal; these payments will repay the original loan that helped finance the purchase of the house.

Often, as in the case of a mortgage, a tangible asset will lie behind (or serve as collateral for) a financial asset. In other cases, such as student loans, a financial asset may derive its value from a promise to pay based on the future earning power of an individual.

It is clear that tangible assets are an essential part of an economy because they increase the productivity of other factors. But what function do financial assets serve? These assets are crucial because of the mismatch between savers and investors. Students need money to pay for college, but they do not currently have the earnings or the savings necessary to pay the bills. Older people, who are working and saving for retirement, may have income in excess of their expenditures and can provide the savings. A vast financial system of banks, mutual funds, insurance companies, and pension funds—often supplemented by government loans and guarantees—serves to channel the funds of those who are saving to those who are investing. Without this financial system, it would not be possible for firms to make the huge investments needed to develop new products, for people to buy houses before they had saved the entire housing price, or for students to go to college without first saving the large sums necessary.

投资回报率

The Rate of Return on Investments

Suppose that you own some capital and rent it out or that you have some cash and lend it to a bank or to a small business. Or perhaps you want to take out a mortgage to buy a house. You will naturally want to know what you will pay to borrow or how much you will earn by lending. This amount is called the **rate** ②
of return on investments. In the special case of the [3]
return on fixed-interest financial assets, these earnings are called the **interest rate.** From an economic point of view, interest rates or returns on investments are the price of borrowing or lending money. The returns will vary greatly depending upon the maturity, risk, tax status, and other attributes of the investment.

We will devote considerable space in this chapter to understanding these concepts. The following summary highlights the major ideas:

1. Capital consists of durable produced items that ④
are in turn used as productive inputs for the production of other goods. Capital consists of both tangible and intangible assets.
2. Capital is bought and sold in capital markets. Payments for the temporary use of capital goods are called rentals.
3. We must distinguish financial assets, which are essentially pieces of paper deriving their value from ownership of other tangible or intangible assets.
4. The rate of return on investments, and the special case of the interest rate, is the price for borrowing and lending funds. We usually calculate rates of return on the funds using units of percent per year.

收益率和利率

RATES OF RETURN AND INTEREST RATES

We now examine in greater detail the major concepts in capital and financial theory. We begin with the definition of a rate of return on investments, which is the most general concept. We then apply these definitions to financial assets.

资本收益率

Rate of Return on Capital

One of the most important tasks of any economy is to allocate its capital across different possible investments. Should a country devote its investment resources to heavy manufacturing like steel or to

---

① 但是，我们必须将这些有形资产与金融资产区分开来，从材质上讲，它们只不过是一片片的纸，或者是一些用电子技术所做的记录。更准确一点讲，金融资产是一方对另一方主张的货币额。

④ 1. 资本由生产出来的耐用品组成，这些耐用品反过来又作为生产其他物品的生产性投入。资本分为有形资产和无形资产两部分。
2. 资本在资本市场进行买卖。对资本品短期使用所需的支付称为租金。
3. 我们必须将金融资产与有形资产和无形资产的所有权严格区别开来，金融资产从本质上讲，只不过是描述其价值的纸片。
4. 投资的回报率，作为利率的特别案例，是指借入和贷出资金的价格。通常情况下，我们对这些租金回报利率的计算以年度核计，用百分数表示。

information technologies like the Internet? Should Intel build a $4 billion factory to produce the next generation of microprocessors? These questions involve costly investments—laying out money today to obtain a return in the future.

In deciding upon the best investment, we need a ①
measure for the yield or return. One important measure is the **rate of return on investment,** which denotes the net dollar return per year for every dollar of invested capital.

Let's consider the example of a rental car company. Ugly Duckling Rental Company buys a used car for $20,000 and rents it out. After subtracting all expenses (revenues less expenses such as wages, office supplies, and energy costs) and assuming no change in the car's price, Ugly Duckling earns a net rental of $2400 each year. The rate of return is 12 percent per year (12% = $2400/$20,000). Note that the rate of return is a pure or unitless number per unit of time. That is, the rate of return has the dimensions of (dollars per period)/(dollars), and it is usually calculated with units of percent per year.

These concepts are useful for comparing investments. Suppose you are considering investments in rental cars, oil wells, apartments, education, and so forth. How can you decide which investment to make?

One useful approach is to compare the rates of return on the different investments. For each possibility, calculate the dollar cost of the capital good. Then estimate the net annual dollar receipts or rentals yielded by the asset. The ratio of the annual net rental to the dollar cost is the rate of return on investment, which tells you how much money you get back for every dollar invested, measured as dollars per year per dollar of investment or percent per year.

> The rate of return on investment is the annual net ②
> return (rentals less expenses) per dollar of invested capital. It is a pure or unitless number—percent per year.

Of Wine, Trees, and Drills. Here are some examples of rates of return on investments:

- I buy a plot of land for $100,000 and sell it a year later for $110,000. If there are no other expenses, the rate of return on this investment is $10,000 per year/$100,000, or 10 percent per year.
- I plant a pine tree with a labor cost of $100. At the end of 25 years, the grown tree sells for $430. The rate of return on this capital project is then 330 percent per quarter-century, which, as a calculator will show you, is equivalent to a return of 6 percent per year. That is, $\$100 \times (1.06)^{25} = \$430$.
- I buy a $20,000 piece of oil-drilling equipment. For 10 years it earns annual rentals of $30,000, but I also incur annual expenses of $26,000 for fuel, insurance, and maintenance. The $4000 net return covers interest and repays the principal of $20,000 over 10 years. What is the rate of return here? Statistical tables show that the rate of return is 15 percent per year.

金融资产和利率
Financial Assets and Interest Rates

For the case of financial assets, we use a different set of terms when measuring the rate of return. When you buy a bond or put money in your savings account, the financial yield on this investment is called the *interest rate*. For example, if you bought a 1-year bond in 2008, you would have earned a yield of around 3 percent per year. This means that if you bought a $1000 bond on January 1, 2008, you would have $1030 on January 1, 2009.

You will usually see interest rates quoted in percent per year. This is the interest that would be paid if the sum were borrowed (or loaned) for an entire year; for shorter or longer periods, the interest payment is adjusted accordingly.

资产的现值
THE PRESENT VALUE OF ASSETS

Most assets will produce a stream of rentals or
receipts over time. If you own an apartment building, ③
for example, you will collect rental payments over the life of the building, much as the owner of a fruit orchard will pick fruit from the trees each year.

Suppose you become weary of tending the building and decide to sell it. To set a fair price for the building, you would need to determine the value today of the entire stream of future income. The value of that stream is called the present value of the capital asset.

> The **present value** is the dollar value today of a ④
> stream of future income. It is measured by calculating how much money invested today would be needed, at the going interest rate, to generate the asset's future stream of receipts.

---

① **投资回报率**是一个重要的计量指标，它表示所投入资本中的每一美元在每一年度的美元净收益。

② 投资回报率是指所投的每一美元资本的年度净收益（即减去支出之后的租金收入）。它是以年度百分数计量的纯数字或者没有单位的数字。

③ 举例来讲，假设一个人拥有一栋公寓楼，那么，在该栋建筑的使用年限内，他将能收取租金。这一点与果园的园主每年从果树上收获果实的例子极为相似。

④ **现值**指的是未来收入流在当下用美元核计的价值。它是根据利率的走势，核算出当前需要投入的资金量在未来所能创造出的收入流。

Let's start with a very simple example. Say that someone offers to sell you a bottle of wine that matures in exactly 1 year and can then be sold for exactly \$11. Assuming the market interest rate is 10 percent per year, what is the present value of the wine—that is, how much should you pay for the wine today? Pay exactly \$10, because \$10 invested today at the market interest rate of 10 percent will be worth \$11 in 1 year. So the present value of next year's \$11 wine is today \$10.

永久资产的现值

Present Value for Perpetuities

We discuss the first way of calculating present value ① by examining the case of a *perpetuity,* which is an asset like land that lasts forever and pays $\$N$ each year from now to eternity. We are seeking the present value (V) if the interest rate is i percent per year, where the present value is the amount of money invested today that would yield exactly $\$N$ each year. This is simply

$$V = \frac{\$N}{i}$$

where V = present value of the land (\$)
$\$N$ = perpetual annual receipts (\$ per year)
i = interest rate in decimal terms (e.g., 0.05, or $\frac{5}{100}$ per year)

This says that if the interest rate is always 5 percent per year, an asset yielding a constant stream of income will sell for exactly 20 (= 1 ÷ $\frac{5}{100}$) times its annual income. In this case, what would be the present value of a perpetuity yielding \$100 every year? At a 5 percent interest rate its present value would be \$2000 (= \$100 ÷ 0.05).

The formula for perpetuities can also be used to value stocks. Suppose that a share of Spring Water Co. is expected to pay a dividend of \$1 every year into the indefinite future and that the discount rate on stocks is 5 percent per year. Then the stock price should be $P = \$1/0.05 = \$20$ per share. (These numbers are corrected for inflation, so the numerator is "real dividends" and the denominator is a "real interest rate" or a "real discount rate," defined below).

现值的一般公式

General Formula for Present Value

Having seen the simple case of the perpetuity, we move to the general case of the present value of an asset with an income stream that varies over time. The main thing to remember about present value is that future payments are worth less than current payments and they are therefore *discounted* relative to the present. Future payments are worth less than current payments just as distant objects look smaller than nearby ones. The interest rate produces a similar shrinking of time perspective.

Let's take a fantastic example.[1] Say that someone proposes to pay \$100 million to your heirs in 100 years. How much should you pay for this today? ② According to the general rule for present value, to figure out the value today of $\$P$ payable t years from now, ask yourself how much must be invested today to grow into $\$P$ at the end of t years. Say the interest rate is 6 percent per annum. Applying this each year to the growing amount, a principal amount of $\$V$ grows in t years to $\$V \times (1 + 0.06)^t$. Hence, we need only invert this expression to find present value: the present value of $\$P$ payable t years from now is today $\$P/(1 + 0.06)^t$. Using this formula, we determine that the present value of \$100 million paid in 100 years is \$294,723.

In most cases, there are several terms in an asset's stream of income. In present-value calculations, each dollar must stand on its own feet. First, evaluate the ③ present value of each part of the stream of future receipts, giving due allowance for the discounting required by its payment date. Then simply add together all these separate present values. This summation will give you the asset's present value.

The exact formula for present value (V) is the following:

$$V = \frac{N_1}{1+i} + \frac{N_2}{(1+i)^2} + \cdots + \frac{N_t}{(1+i)^t} + \cdots$$

In this equation, i is the one-period market interest rate (assumed constant). Further, N_1 is the net receipts (positive or negative) in period 1, N_2 the net receipts in period 2, N_t the net receipts in period t, and so forth. Then the stream of payments (N_1, N_2, . . . , N_t, . . .) will have the present value, V, given by the formula.

For example, assume that the interest rate is 10 percent per year and that I am to receive \$1100

[1] Question 9 at the end of this chapter asks about the real life example of the present value of the real estate of Manhattan when it was purchased by the Dutch.

① 我们在此通过永久资产来讨论计算现值的第一种方法。永久资产指的是像土地一样可以永远存续，并且从现在开始每年要支付 N 美元，直到永远。

② 让我们幻想一个极端的例子（见 300 页的问题 9）。假设有人建议你 100 年之后，给你的财产继承人一亿美元。那么，你今天应该为此支付多少美元？

③ 首先要评估出每一部分未来收入流的现值，在扣除掉支付期内必付的利息之后，所应支付的额度。然后，将这些分门别类的现值简单地加在一起即可。其相加后的结果即你所需要的该资产的现值。

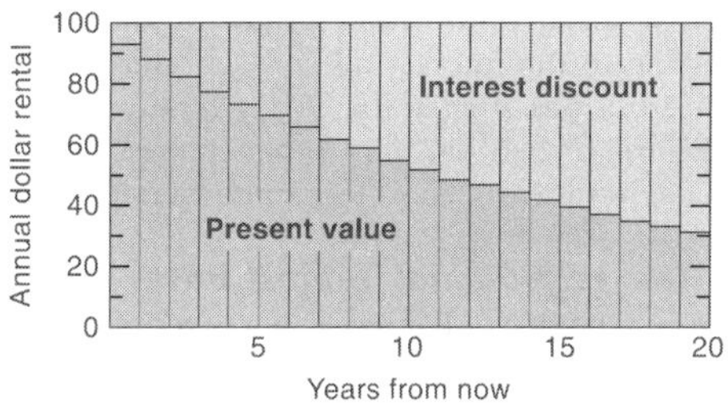

FIGURE 15-1. Present Value of an Asset ①

The lower, green area shows the present value of a machine giving net annual rentals of $100 for 20 years with an interest rate of 6 percent per year. The upper, blue area has been discounted away. Explain why raising the interest rate increases the blue area and therefore depresses the market price of an asset.

next year and $2662 in 3 years. The present value of this stream is

$$V = \frac{1100}{(1.10)^1} + \frac{2662}{(1.10)^3} = 3000$$

Figure 15-1 shows graphically the calculation of present value for a machine that earns steady net annual rentals of $100 over a 20-year period and has no scrap value at the end. Its present value is not $2000 but only $1157. Note how much the later dollar earnings are scaled down or discounted because of our time perspective. The total area remaining after discounting (the blue shaded area) represents the machine's total present value—the value today of the stream of all future incomes.

使现值最大化
Acting to Maximize Present Value

The present-value formula tells us how to calculate the value of any asset once we know the future earnings. But note that an asset's future receipts usually depend on business decisions: Shall we use a truck 8 or 9 years? Overhaul it once a month or once a year? Replace it with a cheap, nondurable truck or an expensive, durable one?

There is one rule that gives correct answers to all investment decisions: Calculate the present value resulting from each possible decision. Then always act so as to maximize present value. In this way you will have more wealth to spend whenever and however you like. ②

Interest Rates and Asset Prices

When interest rates rise, many asset prices fall. For example, if the Federal Reserve unexpectedly tightens monetary policy and raises interest rates, you will generally read that bond and stock prices fall. We can understand the reason for this pattern using the concept of present value.

Our previous discussion showed that the present value of an asset will depend on both the stream of future returns and the interest rate. As interest rates change, so will the present value and therefore the market value of an asset. Here are some examples:

- Begin with a 1-year bond and an initial interest rate of 5 percent per year. If the bond returns $1000 one year from now, then its current present value is $1000/1.05 = $952.38. Now suppose that the interest rate rises to 10 percent per year. Then the present value of the bond would be only $1000/1.1 = $909.09. The price of the asset declined as the interest rate increased.
- Take the case of a perpetuity that yields $100 per year. At an interest rate of 5 percent per year, the perpetuity has a present value of $100/0.05 = $2000. Now if the interest rate rises to 10 percent per year, the value falls by half to only $1000.

We can now see that asset prices tend to move inversely with interest rates because their present value decreases as the interest rate increases. Note as well that the prices of longer-term assets tend to change more than do the prices of shorter-term assets. This occurs because more of the return is in the future, and the prices of long-term assets are therefore affected more by the changing interest rate.

The dependence of asset prices on interest rates is a general property of financial assets. The prices of stocks, bonds, real estate, and many other long-lived assets will decline as interest rates rise.

利率的神秘世界
THE MYSTERIOUS WORLD OF INTEREST RATES

Textbooks often speak of "*the* interest rate" as if there were only one, but in fact today's complex financial system has a vast array of interest rates. If you look at *The Wall Street Journal*, you will see page after page of [4] financial interest rates. Interest rates depend mainly on the characteristics of the loan or of the borrower. Let us review the major differences.

---

① 图 15-1. 资产的现值

② 有一个规则可以给所有的投资决策提供正确的答案：把每一个可能的决策所产生的结果的现值计算出来，然后尽量使现值最大化。这样，你就可以拥有更多的财富以供其随时随地按照自己的意愿充分地予以支配。

[4] *The Wall Street Journal*：《华尔街日报》，是全美乃至全球影响力最大的平面媒体之一，侧重金融、商业领域的报道。1889 年由道琼斯公司（Dow Jones & Company）创办，2007 年被新闻集团（News Corporation）并购，成为默多克新闻帝国旗下的又一媒体王国。

[3] The Federal Reserve：美国联邦储备局，即简称的"美联储"，英文全称为 The Federal Reserve System，常缩写为"Fed"。该系统根据《联邦储备法》（Federal Reserve Act）于 1913 年成立，负责履行美国中央银行的职责，它由核心机构联邦储备委员会（The Board of Governors of The Federal Reserve System）和另外两个主要机构联邦公开市场委员会（The Federal Open Market Committee），以及遍布全美 12 个储备区的联邦储备银行（Federal Reserve Banks）组成。美联储的成立还应该追溯到美国开国元勋亚历山大·汉密尔顿（Alexan-der Hamilton，1757~1804，美国第一任财政部长，美国宪法的起草人之一）。在美国开国之初，汉密尔顿顶着来自以杰斐逊（Thomas Jefferson，1743~1826，美国开国元勋之一，第三任总统，独立宣言的主要起草人）等人为首的众多反对者的巨大压力，于 1791 年 2 月 25 日经国会特许，华盛顿总统亲自签署成立了履行中央银行职责的第一美国银行（First Bank of the United States），并设计和创建了全民信用体系，使美国的国家机器得以从建国之初就能够较为健康有效地运行。同时，也使汉密尔顿和杰斐逊与华盛顿一道各司其责，成为美国开国和建国的真正伟人。

Loans differ in their *term* or *maturity*—the length of time until they must be paid off. The shortest loans are overnight. Short-term securities are for periods up to a year. Companies often issue bonds that have maturities of 10 to 30 years, and mortgages are up to 30 years in maturity. Longer-term securities generally command a higher interest rate than do short-term ones because lenders are willing to sacrifice quick access to their funds only if they can increase their yield.

Loans also vary in terms of *risk*. Some loans are virtually riskless, while others are highly speculative. Investors require that a premium be paid when they invest in risky ventures. The safest assets in the world ① are the securities of the U.S. government. These bonds are backed by the full faith, credit, and taxing powers of the government. Intermediate in risk are borrowings of creditworthy corporations, states, and localities. Risky investments, which bear a significant chance of default or nonpayment, include those of companies close to bankruptcy, cities with shrinking tax bases, or countries like Argentina with large overseas debts and unstable political systems.

[2] Victorian mansion：维多利亚风格的庄园。维多利亚风格是19世纪英国鼎盛时期，即所谓的“日不落帝国”时期，维多利亚女王在位期间（1837~1901年）形成的艺术复辟的风格。在建筑上将文艺复兴、罗曼、都铎、伊丽莎白时期以及意大利的风格经过重新演绎之后加入了更多的现代元素；室内设计则大胆地使用色彩，强调色彩的强烈对比和绚丽的效果，黑、白、灰等中性色与褐色、金色等搭配凸显豪华和大气的品位，至今仍是高档星级酒店和豪华住宅常采用的风格。维多利亚风格是人类追求自然和装饰的唯美视觉效果最大化的产物和具体体现。

The U.S. government pays what is called the “riskless” interest rate; over the last two decades this has ranged from 0 to 15 percent per year for short-term bonds. Riskier securities might pay 1, 2, or even 10 percent per year more than the riskless rate; this premium reflects the amount necessary to compensate the lender for losses in case of default.

Assets vary in their liquidity. An asset is said to be *liquid* if it can be converted into cash quickly and with little loss in value. Most marketable securities, including common stocks and corporate and government bonds, can be turned into cash quickly for close to their current value. Illiquid assets include unique assets for which no well-established market exists. For example, if you own the only Victorian mansion in a [2] small town, you might find it difficult to sell the asset quickly or at a price near its realistic market value—your house is an illiquid asset. Because of the higher risk and the difficulty of realizing the asset values quickly, illiquid assets or loans require higher interest rates than do liquid, riskless ones.

When these three factors (along with other considerations such as tax status and administrative costs) are considered, it is not surprising that we see so many different financial assets and so many different interest rates. Figure 15-2 and Table 15-1 show the behavior of a few important interest rates over the last five decades. In the discussion that follows, when we speak of “the interest rate,” we are generally referring to the interest rate on short-term government securities, such as the 90-day Treasury-bill rate. As Figure 15-2 shows, most other interest rates rise and fall in step with short-term interest rates.

实际利率和名义利率

Real vs. Nominal Interest Rates

Interest is paid in dollar terms, not in terms of houses or cars or goods in general. The *nominal interest rate* ③ measures the yield in dollars per year per dollar invested. But dollars can become distorted yardsticks. The prices of houses, cars, and goods in general change from year to year—these days prices generally rise due to inflation. Put differently, the interest rate on dollars does not measure what a lender really earns in terms of goods and services. Let us say that you lend \$100 today at 5 percent-per-year interest. You would get back \$105 at the end of a year. But because prices changed over the year, you would not be able to obtain the same quantity of goods that you could have bought at the beginning of the year if you had \$105.

Clearly, we need another concept that measures the return on investments in terms of real goods and services rather than the return in terms of dollars. This alternative concept is the *real interest rate,* ④ which measures the quantity of goods we get tomorrow for goods forgone today. The real interest rate is obtained by correcting nominal or dollar interest rates for the rate of inflation.

The **nominal interest rate** (sometimes also called ⑤ the *money interest rate*) is the interest rate on money in terms of money. When you read about interest rates in the newspaper, or examine the interest rates in Figure 15-2, you are looking at nominal interest rates; they give the dollar return per dollar of investment.

In contrast, the **real interest rate** is corrected for ⑥ inflation and is calculated as the nominal interest rate minus the rate of inflation. As an example, suppose the nominal interest rate is 8 percent per year and the inflation rate is 3 percent per year; we can calculate the real interest rate as $8 - 3 = 5$ percent per year.

To take a simple example, suppose that you live in an economy where the only product is bread. Further suppose that the price of bread in the first period is \$1 per loaf and that bread inflation is 3 percent per year. If you lend \$100 at 8 percent-per-year interest, you will have \$108 at the end of the year. However, because of inflation, next year you will get

---

① 世界上最安全的资产当属美国政府发行的证券。

③ 名义利率计量的是投资的每一美元在每一年中所获得的以美元为单位的收益。但作为计量标准的美元自身也有发生扭曲的可能。

④ 这一替代概念即实际利率，它用来计量那些在今天被我们所摒弃但在将来可供使用的物品的数量。

⑤ **名义利率**（有时也称作货币利率）是用货币表示的以货币为基础的利率。

⑥ 相比之下，由于名义利率减去通货膨胀率即实际利率，所以，通货膨胀可以对**名义利率**加以矫正。

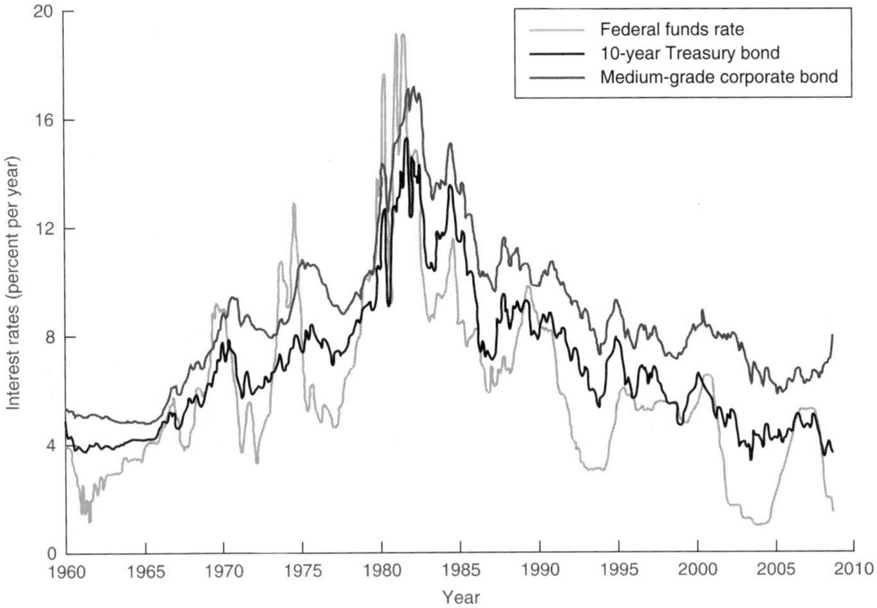

FIGURE 15-2. Most Interest Rates Move Together ①

This graph shows the major interest rates in the U.S. economy. The lowest rate is generally ② the federal funds rate, set by the Federal Reserve in its monetary policy. Longer-term and riskier interest rates are usually higher than safe and short-term rates.

Source: Federal Reserve System, available at *www.federalreserve.gov/releases/*.

Asset class	Period	Nominal rate of return (% per year)	Real rate of return (% per year)
Government securities:			
3 month	1960–2008	5.2	1.0
10 year	1960–2008	6.9	2.7
Corporate bonds:			
Safe (Aaa rated)	1960–2008	7.7	3.4
Risky (Baa rated)	1960–2008	8.7	4.4
Corporate equities	1960–2008	9.9	5.6
Consumer loans:			
Mortgages (fixed rate)	1971–2008	9.2	4.9
Credit cards	1972–2008	16.4	11.8
New-car loans	1972–2008	10.4	6.0

TABLE 15-1. Interest Rates on Major Financial Assets ③

Safe government securities have the lowest yields. Note that consumers pay a substantial ④ penalty on credit-card debt (students beware!). The real interest rates are corrected for inflation. Note that Aaa bonds are the safest type of corporate security, while Baa securities have significant risks of bankruptcy.

Source: Federal Reserve Board, available at *www.federalreserve.gov/releases/*, and Department of Commerce.

① 图 15-2. 大多数利率的走势趋于统一

② 本图表示美国经济生活中的主要利率。联邦基金的利率一般最低，因为它是美联储依据其货币政策制定的。长期的、风险较高的利率通常都高于安全的、短期的利率。

③ 表 15-1. 主要金融资产的利率

④ 安全性高的政府证券收益最低。消费者特别需要注意的是，信用卡透支所要承受的代价高昂的惩罚（学生尤其要小心！）。实际利率为通货膨胀所矫正。请注意，Aaa 级债券是公司债券中最安全的，而 Baa 级证券则有显著的破产风险。

back only 105 (and not 108) loaves of bread. The real (or bread) rate of interest is 8 − 3 = 5 percent.[2]

During inflationary periods, we must use real ① interest rates, not nominal or money interest rates, to calculate the yield on investments in terms of goods earned per year on goods invested. The real interest rate is approximately equal to the nominal interest rate minus the rate of inflation.

[2] The exact algebra of real interest rates is as follows: Let π be the inflation rate, i the nominal interest rate, and r the real interest rate. If you invest \$1 today, you get $\$(1 + i)$ back in 1 year. However, prices have risen, so you need $\$(1 + \pi)$ in 1 year to buy the same amount of goods that you could buy with \$1 today. Instead of buying 1 unit of goods today, you can therefore buy $(1 + r)$ units tomorrow, where $(1 + r) = (1 + i)/(1 + \pi)$. For small values of i and π, $r = i - \pi$.

The World's Safest Investment

U.S. Treasury bonds are generally considered a riskless investment. Their one [2]
shortcoming is that they pay a fixed-dollar interest rate. This means that if inflation heats up, the real interest rate could easily turn negative.

In 1997, the U.S. government fixed this problem by introducing Treasury inflation-protected securities (TIPS). [3]
TIPS have their interest and principal tied to inflation, so they pay a constant real interest rate over their lifetime.

This is how these special bonds work: Each year the principal value is adjusted by the increase in the consumer price index (CPI). Let's take a specific example: In [4]
January 2000, the Treasury issued a 4¼ percent 10-year inflation-protected bond. Between January 2000 and June 2003, the CPI increased by 12 percent. Therefore, the same

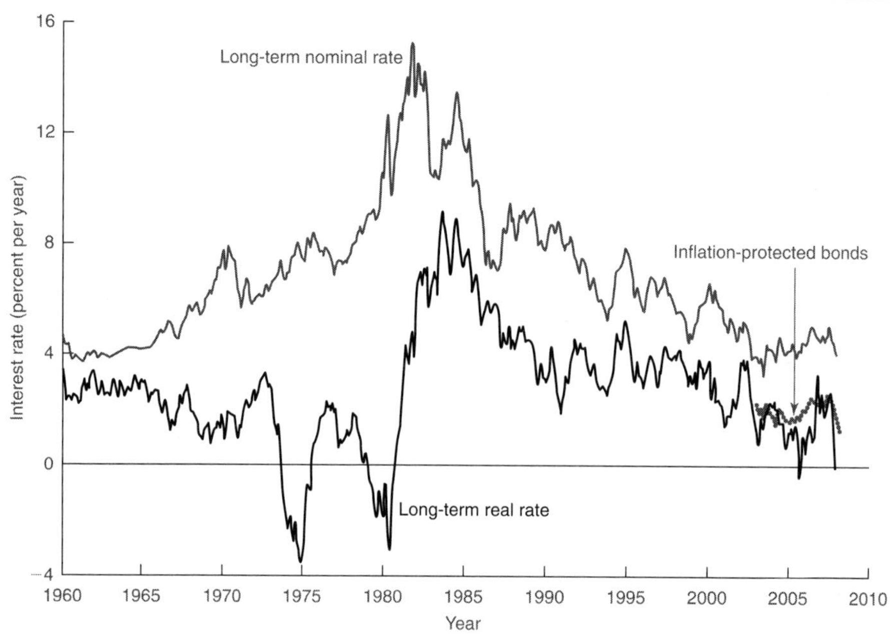

FIGURE 15-3. Nominal vs. Real Interest Rates ⑤

The long green line shows the nominal interest rate on long-term Treasury bonds. The blue line shows the "calculated" real interest rate, equal to the nominal interest rate minus the realized inflation rate over the previous year. Note that real interest rates drifted downward until 1980. After 1980, however, real interest rates moved up sharply. The short green line since 2003 shows the real interest rate on long-term inflation-indexed securities.

Source: Federal Reserve Board, Department of Labor.

① 在通货膨胀发生期间，我们必须使用实际利率，而不是名义利率或者货币利率来计算每年投资在商品上以所产生收益的商品为核算形式的投资回报。实际利率约等于名义利率减去通货膨胀率的差。

[2] U.S. Treasury bonds：美国的长期国债。

[3] TIPS（Treasury inflation-protected securities）：通货膨胀保值债券，是美国财政部发行的与消费者价格指数挂钩的债券，1997 年首次发行，规模为 70 亿美元。

[4] CPI（consumer price index）：消费者价格指数，是与居民生活有关的产品及劳务价格的变动指标，通常作为观察通货膨胀水平的重要手段，具有滞后性的特点。

⑤ 图 15-3. 名义利率与实际利率

\$1000 bond bought in 2000 would be valued at \$1120 in June 2003. If the Treasury made an interest payment in June 2003, it would be 4¼ percent of \$1120, instead of 4¼ percent of \$1000 as would be the case for a standard bond. Let's further suppose that inflation averaged 3 percent per year from 2000 to 2010. This means that the principal value of the bond upon redemption would be \$1343.92 [= \$1000 × $(1.3)^{10}$], instead of the \$1000 for a conventional bond.

As long as people expect that there will be inflation in the coming years, the interest rate on TIPS will be less than that on standard Treasury bonds. For example, in April 2008, standard 10-year Treasury bonds had a nominal yield of 3.6 percent, while 10-year TIPS had a real yield of 1.2 percent. This indicates that the average investor expected 10-year inflation to average 3.6 − 1.2 = 2.4 percent per year.

The difference between nominal and real interest rates on long-term bonds is illustrated in Figure 15-3. The upper line shows the nominal interest rate, while the long lower line shows the calculated real interest rate. In addition, the short green segment that begins in 2003 shows the real interest rate on TIPS. This figure shows that the rise in nominal interest rates from 1960 to 1980 was purely illusory, for nominal interest rates were just keeping up with inflation during those years. After 1980, however, real interest rates rose sharply and remained high for a decade. The data on TIPS show that the real interest rate declined sharply during the credit crisis of 2007–2008.

① Economists have long been enthusiasts of indexed bonds. Such bonds can be bought by pensioners who wish to guarantee that their retirement incomes will not be eroded away by inflation. Similarly, parents who wish to save for their children's education can sock away some of their savings knowing that their investment will keep up with the general price level. Even monetary-policy makers find value in indexed bonds, for the difference between the interest on conventional bonds and that on TIPS gives an indication of what is happening to expected inflation. The main puzzle for many economists is why it took the government so long to introduce this important innovation.

资本、利润和利率理论

B. THE THEORY OF CAPITAL, PROFITS, AND INTEREST

Now that we have surveyed the major concepts, we turn to an analysis of the *theory of capital and interest*. This theory explains how the supply and demand for capital determines returns such as real interest rates and profits.

基本资本理论
BASIC CAPITAL THEORY

Roundaboutness 迂回性

In Chapter 2, we noted that investment in capital goods involves indirect or *roundabout* production. Instead of catching fish with our hands, we find it ultimately more worthwhile first to build boats and make nets—and then to use the boats and nets to catch many more fish than we could by hand.

Put differently, investment in capital goods ② involves forgoing present consumption to increase future consumption. Consuming less today frees labor for making nets to catch many more fish tomorrow. In the most general sense, capital is productive because by forgoing consumption today we get more consumption in the future.

To see this, imagine two islands that are exactly alike. Each has the same amount of labor and natural resources. Island A uses these primary factors directly to produce consumption goods like food and clothing; it uses no produced capital goods at all. By contrast, thrifty Island B sacrifices current consumption and uses its resources and labor to produce capital goods, such as plows, shovels, and looms. After this temporary sacrifice of current consumption, B ends up with a large stock of capital goods.

Figure 15-4 shows the way that Island B forges ahead of A. For each island, measure the amount of consumption that can be enjoyed while maintaining the existing capital stock. Because of its thrift, Island B, using roundabout, capital-intensive methods of production, will enjoy more future consumption than Island A. Island B gets more than 100 units of future-consumption goods for its initial sacrifice of 100 units of present consumption.

sock away 把钱存放在安全的地方以备未来使用

By sacrificing current consumption and building ③ capital goods today, societies can increase their consumption in the future.

收益递减和资本需求
Diminishing Returns and the Demand for Capital

What happens when a nation sacrifices more and more of its consumption for capital accumulation and production becomes more and more roundabout or indirect? We would expect the law of diminishing

① 长期以来，经济学家们对与物价指数挂钩的债券始终抱有极大的热情。那些领取退休金，并且希望自己的退休金收入不因通货膨胀而缩水的人，可以购买这样的债券。同理，那些为孩子的教育做储蓄性投资的父母，可以把他们的部分积蓄存放在安全的地方。因为他们懂得，他们的这种投资将跟上物价水平。甚至货币政策的制订者们也都发现了这种与物价指数挂钩的债券的价值，因为这种通货膨胀保值债券与常规债券之间的不同利率，可以对预期的通货膨胀情况提供预警。对广大经济学家们来讲，主要的困惑是，政府为什么花这么长时间引入这样一项重要的创新。

② 换言之，对资本品的投资涉及到为了增加未来的消费而放弃当前消费的问题。

③ 今天，通过牺牲当前的消费来生产资本品，未来，各社会群体的消费量就得以增加。

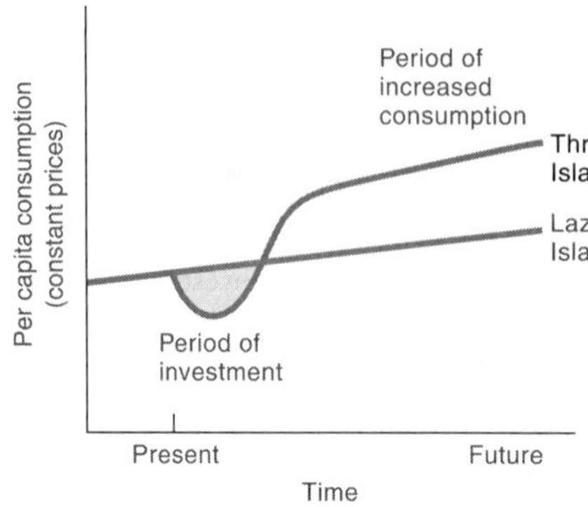

FIGURE 15-4. Investments Today Yield Consumption Tomorrow ①

Two islands begin with equal endowments of labor and natural resources. Lazy Island A invests nothing and shows a modest growth in per capita consumption. Thrifty Island B devotes an initial period to investment, forgoing consumption, and then enjoys the harvest of much higher consumption in the future.

returns to set in. Let's take the example of computers. The first computers were expensive and used intensively. Four decades ago, scientists would eke every last hour of time from an expensive mainframe computer that had less power than today's personal computer. By 2009, the nation's stock of computers had millions of times more computational and storage capacity. Therefore, the marginal product of ② computer power—the value of the last calculation or the last byte of storage—had diminished greatly as computer inputs increased relative to labor, land, and other capital. More generally, as capital accumulates, diminishing returns set in and the rate of return on the investments tends to fall.

Surprisingly, the rate of return on capital has not fallen markedly over the course of the last two centuries, even though our capital stocks have grown manyfold. Rates of return have remained high because innovation and technological change have created profitable new opportunities as rapidly as past investment has annihilated them. Even though computers are thousands of times more powerful than they were a few years ago, new applications in every corner of society from medical diagnostics to Internet commerce continue to make investments in computers profitable.

Irving Fisher: Economist as Crusader

Irving Fisher (1867–1947) was a multifaceted genius and crusader. His pioneering [3] economic research ranged from fundamental theoretical studies on utility and capital theory to practical investigations into business cycles, index numbers, and monetary reform.

Among his fundamental contributions was the development of a complete theory of capital and interest in *The Nature of Capital and Income* (1906) and *The Theory of Interest* (1907). Fisher described the interplay between the interest rate and innumerable other elements of the economy. Yet the basic determinants of the interest rate, ④ Fisher showed, were two fundamental pillars: impatience as reflected in "time discounting" and investment opportunity [5] as reflected in the "marginal rate of return over cost." It was Fisher who uncovered the deep relationship between interest and capital and the economy, as described in this summary from *The Theory of Interest:*

> The truth is that the rate of interest is not a narrow phenomenon applying only to a few business contracts, but permeates all economic relations. It is the link which binds man to the future and by which he makes all his far-reaching decisions. It enters into the price of securities, land, and capital goods generally, as well as into rent, wages, and the value of all "interactions." It affects profoundly the distribution of wealth. In short, upon its accurate adjustment depend the equitable terms of all exchange and distribution. ⑥

Fisher always aimed at research that could be empirically applied. His philosophy is embodied in the Econometric Society, which he helped found, whose constitution trumpeted a science which would lead to "the advancement of economic theory in its relation to statistics and mathematics [and] the unification of the theoretical-quantitative and the empirical-quantitative approach."

In addition to research on pure economics, Fisher was a habitual crusader. He lobbied for a "compensated dollar" as a substitute for the gold standard. After he contracted tuberculosis, he became an impassioned advocate for improved health and developed 15 rules of personal hygiene. These included a strong advocacy of Prohibition and idiosyncracies such as chewing 100 times before swallowing. It is said that with no alcohol and much chewing, dinner parties at the Fishers were not the liveliest gatherings in New Haven.

Fisher's most famous forecast came in 1929 when he argued that the stock market had achieved a "permanent plateau of prosperity." He put his money behind his

① 图 8-4. 今天的投资产生明天的消费

② 因此，当计算机的输入存储能力相对于劳动、土地和其他资本增加之后，计算机性能的边际产品，即末端计算能力或者终端存储能量的价值，早已大幅度地缩水。

④ 然而，费希尔指出，利率的基本决定因素是两个重要支柱：以“价格贴现”为表现形式的焦急心态和以“超越成本之外的边际收益”为表现形式的投资机会。

⑥ 事实上，利率的问题绝不仅仅是几份商业合约中一项需要精确核算的内容，同时还渗透在商业关系中的所有环节。它是把人们与他们的未来绑定在一起的纽带，一个人可以使用这条纽带制定出远期决策。一般情况下，利率会渗透进证券、土地、资本品以及租金、工资和所有价值“互动”的价格机制中。它深刻地影响着财富的分配问题。一句话，所有的交换和分配活动中每一环节的公平都依赖于利率来实现精准的调节。

[3] 欧文·费希尔（Irving Fisher，1867~1947），耶鲁大学教授。美国最早的新古典经济学家之一，第一位美国数理经济学家，其主要贡献是使经济学变成了一门更精密的科学。已故的诺贝尔经济学奖得主米尔顿·弗里德曼（Milton Friedman，1912~2006）在1994年出版的《货币史话》（*Money Mischief: Episodes in Monetary History*）一书中，深情地赞誉欧文·费希尔是“美国本土培养的最伟大的经济学家”。分别于1906年和1907年出版的《资本与收入》（*The Nature of Capital and Income*）与《利息论》（*The Theory of Interest*）是其学术思想的两部代表作。

[5] time discounting：商业用语，买卖成交付账之前的价格折扣，“time”意为“即时贴现”，“-ing”强调讨价的过程，故译“价格贴现”为宜。

forecast, and his substantial wealth was wiped out in the Great Depression.

Even though Fisher's financial acumen has been questioned, his legacy in economics has grown steadily, and he is generally regarded as the greatest American economist of all time.

利率决定和资本收益
Determination of Interest and the Return on Capital

We can use the classical theory of capital to understand the determination of the rate of interest. Households *supply* funds for investment by abstaining from consumption and accumulating savings over time. At the same time, businesses *demand* capital goods to combine with labor, land, and other inputs. In the end, a firm's demand for capital is driven by its desire to make profits by producing goods.

Or, as Irving Fisher put the matter a century ago:

> The quantity of capital and the rate of return on capital are determined by the interaction between (1) people's *impatience* to consume now rather than accumulate more capital goods for future consumption (perhaps for old-age retirement or for that proverbial rainy day); and (2) *investment opportunities* that yield higher or lower returns to such accumulated capital. ①

To understand interest rates and the return on capital, consider an idealized case of a closed economy with perfect competition and without risk or inflation. In deciding whether to invest, a profit-maximizing firm will always compare its cost of borrowing funds with the rate of return on capital. If the rate of return is higher than the market interest rate at which the firm can borrow funds, it will undertake the investment. If the interest rate is higher than the rate of return on investment, the firm will not invest.

Where will this process end? Eventually, firms will undertake all investments whose rates of return are higher than the market interest rate. Equilibrium is then reached when the amount of investment that firms are willing to undertake at a given interest rate just equals the savings which that interest rate calls forth.

In a competitive economy without risk or inflation, the competitive rate of return on capital would be equal to the market interest rate. The market interest rate serves two functions: It rations out society's scarce supply of capital goods for the uses that have the highest rates of return, and it induces people to sacrifice current consumption in order to increase the stock of capital. ②

资本收益的图形分析
Graphical Analysis of the Return on Capital

We can illustrate capital theory by concentrating on a simple case in which all physical capital goods are alike. In addition, assume that the economy is in a steady state with no population growth or technological change.

In Figure 15-5, *DD* shows the demand curve for the stock of capital; it plots the relationship between the quantity of capital demanded and the rate of return on capital. Recall from Chapter 12 that the demand for a factor like capital is a derived demand—the demand comes from the *marginal product of capital,* which is the extra output yielded by additions to the capital stock.

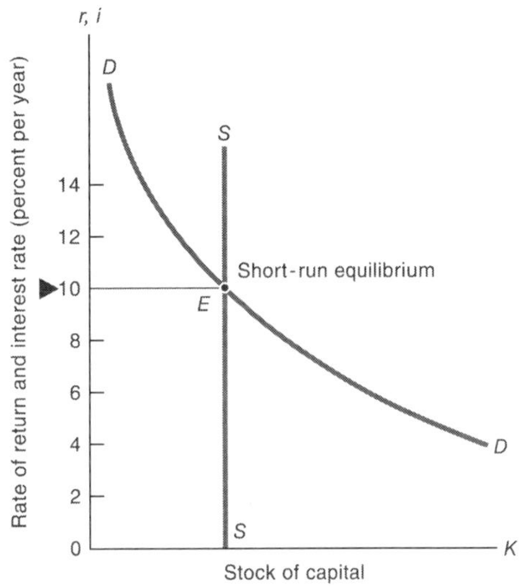

FIGURE 15-5. Short-Run Determination of Interest and Returns ③

In the short run, the economy has inherited a given stock of capital from the past, shown as the vertical *SS* supply-of-capital schedule. The intersection of the short-run supply curve with the demand-for-capital schedule determines the short-run return on capital, and the short-run real interest rate, at 10 percent per year.

---

① 资本投入量及其收益率由以下两个因素的相互作用决定：(1)人们对当前消费所持的焦急心态淹没了为未来消费所需累积的更多的资本品投资（或许是因为年迈退休的缘故，或者是谚语所讲的未雨绸缪心态的警示）；(2)所累积的资本投资能带来高于或是低于预期收益的各种投资机会。

② 在没有风险和通货膨胀的竞争性经济体中，有竞争力的资本收益率应该等于市场利率。这里的市场利率有两个作用：将社会上稀缺的资本品供应配发给具有最高收益率的所有用途中去；它引导人们牺牲当前的消费以增加资本的存量。

③ 图 8-5. 利息及收益的短期决策

The law of diminishing returns can be seen in ① the fact that the demand-for-capital curve in Figure 15-5 is downward-sloping. When capital is very scarce, the most profitable projects have a very high rate of return. Gradually, as the community exploits all the high-yield projects by accumulating capital, with total labor and land fixed, diminishing returns to capital set in. The community must then invest in lower-yield projects as it moves down the demand-for-capital curve.

Short-Run Equilibrium. We can now see how supply and demand interact. In Figure 15-5, past investments have produced a given stock of capital, shown as the vertical short-run supply curve, *SS*. Firms will demand capital goods in a manner shown by the downward-sloping demand curve, *DD*.

At the intersection of supply and demand, at point *E*, the amount of capital is just rationed out to the demanding firms. At this short-run equilibrium, firms are willing to pay 10 percent a year to borrow funds to buy capital goods. At that point, the lenders of funds are satisfied to receive exactly 10 percent a year on their supplies of capital.

Thus, in our simple, riskless world, the rate of re- ② turn on capital exactly equals the market interest rate. Any higher interest rate would find firms unwilling to borrow for their investments; any lower interest rate would find firms clamoring for the too scarce capital. Only at the equilibrium interest rate of 10 percent are supply and demand equilibrated. (Recall that these are *real* interest rates because there is no inflation.)

But the equilibrium at *E* is sustained only for the short run: At this high interest rate, people desire to accumulate more wealth, that is, to continue saving and investing. This means that the capital stock increases. However, because of the law of diminishing returns, the rate of return and the interest rate move downward. As capital increases—while other things ③ such as labor, land, and technical knowledge remain unchanged—the rate of return on the increased stock of capital goods falls to ever-lower levels.

This process is shown graphically in Figure 15-6. Note that capital formation is taking place at point *E*.

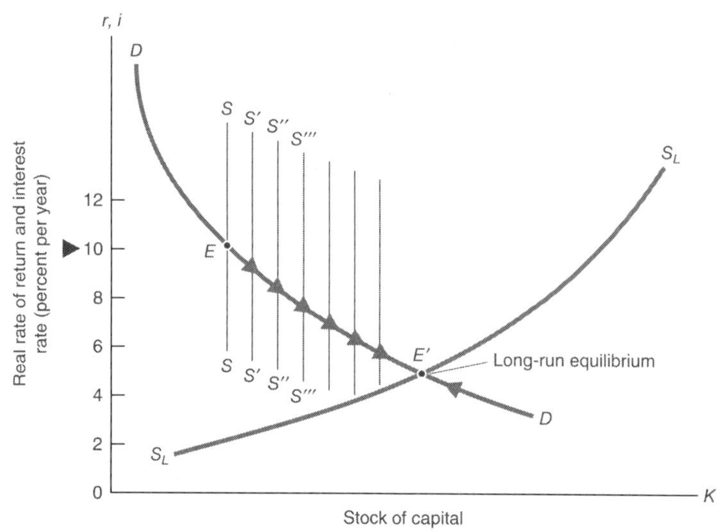

FIGURE 15-6. Long-Run Equilibration of the Supply and Demand for Capital ④

In the long run, society accumulates capital, so the supply curve is no longer vertical. As pictured here, the supply of capital and wealth is responsive to higher interest rates. At the original short-run equilibrium at *E* there is net investment, so the economy moves down the *DD* demand curve as shown by the blue arrows. Long-run equilibrium comes at *E*′, where net saving ceases.

---

① 从收益递减规律可以看出图 15-5 中的资本需求曲线是向右下方倾斜的，这是个不争的事实。

② 这样，在简单又无风险的世界中，资本的收益率恰好等于市场利率。任何更高的利率都会导致企业不愿借款进行投资的结局。而任何更低的利率又会促使企业向过于稀缺的资本发难。只有当利率位于 10% 的均衡点时，供给和需求才处于平衡状态。（请记住，这就是实际利率，前提是通货膨胀没有发生。）

③ 在诸如劳动、土地、技术知识等保持不变的情况下，随着资本的增加，增加后的资本品存量所产生的收益率就会降至新低。

④ 图 15-6. 资本供求关系的长期均衡

So each year, the capital stock is a little higher as net investment occurs. As time passes, the community moves slowly down the *DD* curve as shown by the blue arrows in Figure 15-6. You can actually see a series of very thin short-run supply-of-capital curves in the figure—S, S', S'', S''', ... These curves show how the short-run supply of capital increases with capital accumulation.

Long-Run Equilibrium. The eventual equilibrium is shown at E' in Figure 15-6; this is where the long-run supply of capital (shown as S_LS_L) intersects with the demand for capital. In long-run equilibrium, ① the real interest rate settles at that level where the quantity of capital that firms desire to hold just matches the value of wealth that people want to own. At the long-run equilibrium, net saving stops, net capital accumulation is zero, and the capital stock is no longer growing.

Would investment gradually decline to zero as all investment opportunities are exhausted? Some economists (such as Joseph Schumpeter) have likened [2] the investment process to a plucked violin string: In a world of unchanging technology, the string gradually comes to rest as capital accumulation drives down returns on capital. But before the economy has settled into a steady state, an outside event or invention comes along to pluck the string and set the forces of investment in motion again.

The long-run equilibrium stock of capital comes ③ at that real interest rate where the value of assets that people want to hold exactly matches the amount of capital that firms want for production.

利润作为资本回报
PROFITS AS A RETURN TO CAPITAL

Now that we have examined the determinants of the return to capital, we turn to an analysis of profits. In addition to discussing wages, interest, and rent, economists often talk about a fourth category of income called *profits.* What are profits? How do they differ from interest and the returns on capital more generally?

申报利润统计
Reported Profit Statistics

Before we present the economic concepts, we begin with the measures used in accounting. Accountants ④ define profits as the difference between total revenues and total costs. To calculate profits, accountants start with total revenues and subtract all expenses (wages, salaries, rents, materials, interest, excise taxes, and the rest). The leftover residual is called profits.

It is important in analyzing profits, however, to ⑤ distinguish between *accounting profits* and *economic profits.* Accounting profits (also called business income or business earnings) are the residual income measured in financial statements by accountants. Economic profits are the earnings after all costs—both money and implicit or opportunity costs—are subtracted. These concepts of profits differ because accounting profits omit some implicit returns. The opportunity costs of factors owned by firms are called *implicit returns.*

For example, most businesses own much of their capital, and there is no accounting charge for the opportunity cost or implicit return on owned capital. Accounting profits therefore include an implicit return on the capital owned by firms. In large corporations, economic profits would equal business profits minus an implicit return on the capital owned by the firm along with any other costs not fully compensated at market prices. Economic profits are generally smaller than business profits.

利润的决定因素
Determinants of Profits

What determines the rate of profit in a market economy? Profits are in fact a combination of different ⑥ elements, including implicit returns on owners' capital, rewards for risk-bearing and innovational profits.

Profits as Implicit Returns. Much of reported business profits is primarily the return to the owners of the firm for the factors of production, including capital and labor provided by the owners. For example, some profits are the return on the personal work provided by the owners of the firm—such as the doctor or the lawyer who works in a small professional corporation. Another part is the rent return on the land owned by the firm. In large corporations, most profits represent the opportunity costs of invested capital.

Thus some of what is ordinarily called profit is ⑦ really nothing but "implicit rentals," "implicit rent," and "implicit wages," which are the earnings on factors that the firm itself owns.

---

① 在长期的均衡状态下，实际利率就会稳定在企业期望持有的资本量正好与人们所要拥有的财富价值相匹配的水平上。在长期均衡状态的水平上，净储蓄停止，净资本积累归零，资本的存量不再上升。

[2] 约瑟夫·熊彼特（Joseph Schumpeter，1883~1950），奥地利学者，被誉为“最伟大的经济思想家”，详见p40注[3]。

③ 资本存量的长期均衡出现在当人们期望持有的财产价值正好与企业生产所需要的资本量相匹配时的实际利率水平上。

④ 会计师们将利润定义为总收入与总成本之间的差额。

⑤ 重要的是在分析利润时，要想尽办法将会计利润与经济利润严格区别开来。

⑥ 实际上，利润就是各种不同利润组成部分的组合，其中包括资本所有者的隐性收益，承担风险所应得的回报，以及创新所产生的利润。

⑦ 这样，通常情况下我们所称之的某笔利润实际上只不过是“隐性租费”、“隐性租金”以及“隐性工资”，它们是企业自身所拥有的要素的收益。

Profits as Rewards for Risk-Bearing. Profits also include a reward for the riskiness of the relevant investments. Most businesses must incur a risk of default, which occurs when a loan or investment cannot be paid, perhaps because the borrower went bankrupt. In addition, there are many insurable risks, such as those for fires or hurricanes, which can be covered through the purchase of insurance. A further concern is the uninsurable or systematic risk of investments. A company may have a high degree ① of sensitivity to business cycles, which means that its earnings fluctuate a great deal when aggregate output goes up or down. All of these risks must either be insured against or earn a risk premium in profits.

Profits as Reward for Innovation. A third kind of profits consists of the returns to innovation and invention. A growing economy is constantly producing new goods and services—from telephones in the nineteenth century to automobiles early in the twentieth century to computer software in the present era. These new products are the result of research, development, and marketing. We call the person who brings a new prod- ② uct or process to market an *innovator* or *entrepreneur.*

What do we mean by "innovators"? Innovators are people who have the vision, originality, and daring to introduce new ideas. Our economy has been revolutionized by the discoveries of great inventors like Alexander Graham Bell (telephone), Jack Kilby [3] (integrated circuit), and Kary Mullis (polymerase chain reaction).

Every successful innovation creates a temporary pool of monopoly. We can identify innovational profits (sometimes called Schumpeterian profits) as the [4] temporary excess return to innovators and entrepreneurs. These profit earnings are temporary and are soon competed away by rivals and imitators. But just as one source of innovational profits disappears, another is being born. An economy will generate this type of profits as long as it innovates.

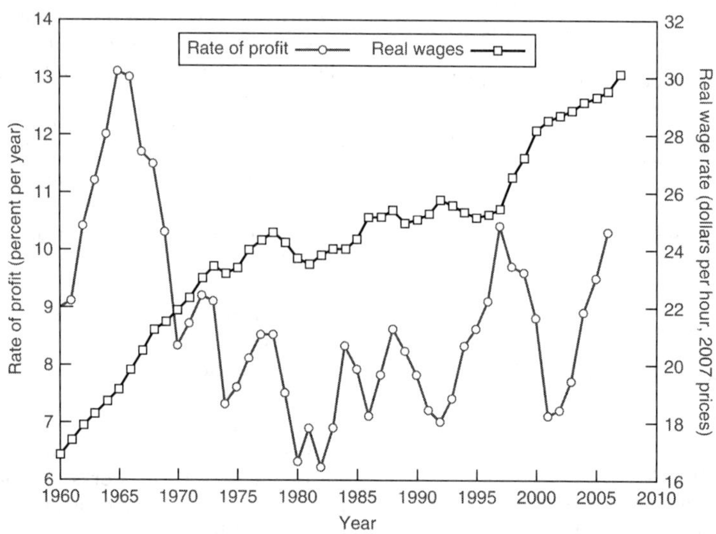

FIGURE 15-7. Trends in Wages and Rate of Profit in the United States ⑤

How have the returns to labor and capital varied in recent years? Average real wages have continued to grow. After peaking in the mid-1960s, the pretax rate of profit on American business capital fell sharply and then meandered around over the last three decades, with an average of around 8 percent per year.

Source: U.S. Departments of Commerce and Labor.

① 一家公司可能对商业周期有高度的敏感性，这就意味着其收益在总产出上升或下降时有大幅波动。所有这些风险必须通过投保或者在利润中赚出风险溢价来规避。

② 我们将那些把新产品或者新的生产工艺引入市场的人称为发明家或者企业家。

[3] 亚历山大·格雷厄姆·贝尔（Alexander Graham Bell，1847~1922），英裔的美国发明家和企业家，贝尔电话公司的创建者，被誉为"电话之父"。杰克·基尔比（Jack Kilby，1923~2005），由于1958年在德州仪器（Texas Instruments，TI）供职时发明集成电路而获2000年诺贝尔物理学奖，同时也是手持计算器和热敏打印机的发明者。

[4] Schumpeterian profits：熊彼特利润，也译作舒彼特利润，是熊彼特"创造性破坏"（creative destruction）理论的内容之一，即只有在创新发展的模式下，才能产生真正的利润的思想，也称作"创新性利润"。

⑤ 图 15-7. 美国工资与利润率的走势图

Corporate profits are the most volatile component of national income. The rights to earn corporate profits—represented by the ownership of corporate stocks or equities—must therefore provide a significant premium to attract risk-averse investors. This excess return on equities above that on risk-free investments is called the *equity premium.* Empirical studies suggest that the equity premium averaged around 5 percent per year over the twentieth century (see Table 15-1 on page 289).

Profits are a residual income item, equal to ①
total revenues minus total costs. Profits contain elements of implicit returns (such as return on owners' capital), return for risk-bearing, and innovational profits.

劳动和资本收益的经验证据
Empirical Evidence on Returns to Labor and Capital

We close with a look at the actual trends in the return ②
to labor and capital in the United States over the last four decades, as illustrated in Figure 15-7. Real wages (which are average hourly earnings corrected for movements in the consumer price index) grew steadily. The pretax rate of profit on capital declined from its peak in the mid-1960s and has averaged around 8 percent per year for the last three decades.

SUMMARY

A. Basic Concepts of Interest and Capital

1. Recall the major concepts:
   - *Capital:* durable produced items used for further production
   - *Rentals:* net annual dollar returns on capital goods
   - *Rate of return on investment:* net annual receipts on capital divided by dollar value of capital (measured as percent per year)
   - *Interest rate:* yield on financial assets, measured as percent per year
   - *Real interest rate:* yield on funds corrected for inflation, also measured as percent per year
   - *Present value:* value today of an asset's stream of future returns
2. Interest rates are the rate of return on financial assets, measured in percent per year. People willingly pay interest because borrowed funds allow them to buy goods and services to satisfy current consumption needs or make profitable investments.
3. We observe a wide variety of interest rates. These rates vary because of many factors such as the term or maturity of loans, the risk and liquidity of investments, and the tax treatment of the interest.
4. Nominal or money interest rates generally rise during inflationary periods, reflecting the fact that the purchasing power of money declines as prices rise. To calculate the interest yield in terms of real goods and services, we use the real interest rate, which equals the nominal interest rate minus the rate of inflation.
5. Assets generate streams of income in future periods. By calculating the present value of the asset, we can convert the stream of future returns into a single value today. This is done by asking what sum today will generate the total value of all future returns when invested at the market interest rate.
6. The exact present-value formula is as follows: Each dollar payable t years from now has a present value (V) of $\$1/(1+i)^t$. So for any net-receipt stream ($N_1, N_2, \ldots, N_t$), where N_t is the dollar value of receipts t years in the future, we have

$$V = \frac{N_1}{1+i} + \frac{N_2}{(1+i)^2} + \cdots + \frac{N_t}{(1+i)^t} + \cdots$$

B. The Theory of Capital, Profits, and Interest

7. A third factor of production is capital, a produced durable item that is used in further production. In the most general sense, investing in capital represents deferred consumption. By postponing consumption today and instead producing buildings or equipment, society increases consumption in the future. It is an economic fact that roundabout production yields a positive rate of return.
8. Interest is a device that serves two functions in the economy: As a motivating device, it provides an incentive for people to save and accumulate wealth. As a rationing device, interest allows society to select only those investment projects with the highest rates of

① 利润是一个剩余收入项目，它等于总收入减去总成本的差额。利润的组成包括隐性收益（如资本拥有者的收益）、承担风险所应得的回报以及创新所产生的利润。

② 正如图 15-7 所示，我们在过去的 40 多年美国劳动和资本收益的实际走势的基础上做一个小结。实际工资水平（根据消费者价格指数的波动情况矫正之后的平均每小时所得）获得了平稳的增长。资本的税前利润率从 20 世纪 60 年代的中期冲顶之后开始下滑，在过去的 30 年间，平均每年保持在 8% 左右的水平。

return. However, as more and more capital is accumulated, and as the law of diminishing returns sets in, the rate of return on capital and the interest rate will be beaten down by competition. Falling interest rates are a signal to society to adopt more capital-intensive projects with lower rates of return.

9. Saving and investing involve waiting for future consumption rather than consuming today. Such thrift interacts with the net productivity of capital to determine interest rates, the rate of return on capital, and the capital stock. The funds or financial assets needed to purchase capital are provided by households that are willing to sacrifice consumption today in return for larger consumption tomorrow. The demand for capital comes from firms that have a variety of roundabout investment projects. In long-run equilibrium, the interest rate is thus determined by the interaction between the net productivity of capital and the willingness of households to sacrifice consumption today for consumption tomorrow.

10. Profits are revenues minus costs. Remember that economic profits differ from those measured by accountants. Economics distinguishes between three categories of profits: (*a*) An important source is profits as implicit returns. Firms generally own many of their own nonlabor factors of production—capital, natural resources, and patents. In these cases, the implicit return on owned inputs is part of the profits. (*b*) Another source of profits is uninsured or uninsurable risk, particularly that associated with the business cycle. (*c*) Finally, innovational profits will be earned by entrepreneurs who introduce new products or innovations.

CONCEPTS FOR REVIEW

capital, capital goods
tangible assets vs. financial assets
rentals, rate of return on capital,
    interest rate, profits
present value
interest rate, real and nominal
interest-rate premiums due to
    maturity, risk, illiquidity

inflation-indexed bonds
investment as abstaining from current
    consumption
present value
twin elements in interest
    determination:
    returns to roundaboutness
    impatience

elements of profits:
    implicit returns
    risk
    innovation

FURTHER READING AND INTERNET WEBSITES

Further Reading

The foundations of capital theory were laid by Irving Fisher, *The Theory of Interest* (Macmillan, New York, 1930). You can pursue advanced topics in finance theory in an intermediate textbook such as Lawrence S. Ritter, William L. Silber, and Gregory F. Udell, *Principles of Money, Banking, and Financial Markets,* 11th ed. (Addison Wesley Longman, New York, 2003). The standard reference on U.S. monetary history is Milton Friedman and Anna Jacobson Schwartz, *Monetary History of the United States 1867–1960* (Princeton University Press, Princeton, N.J., 1963).

Modern capital and finance theories are very popular subjects and are often covered in the macroeconomics part of an introductory course or in special courses. A good book on the subject is Burton Malkiel, *A Random Walk down Wall Street* (Norton, New York, 2003). A recent book surveying financial history and theory and arguing that the stock market was extraordinarily overvalued in the bull market of 1981–2000 is Robert Shiller, *Irrational Exuberance,* 2nd ed. (Princeton University Press, Princeton, N.J., 2005). A recent summary of evidence on the efficient-market theory by Burton Malkiel and

Robert Shiller is found in *Journal of Economic Perspectives*, Winter 2003.

Websites

Data on financial markets are plentiful. See *finance.yahoo.com* for an entry point into stock and bond markets as well as information on individual companies. Also see *www.bloomberg.com* for up-to-date financial information.

Data on financial markets are also produced by the Federal Reserve System at *www.federalreserve.gov.*

QUESTIONS FOR DISCUSSION

1. Calculate the present value of each of the following income streams, where I_t = the income t years in the future and i is the constant interest rate in percent per year. Round to two decimal points where the numbers are not integers.
   a. $I_0 = 10, I_1 = 110, I_3 = 133.1; i = 10.$
   b. $I_0 = 17, I_1 = 21, I_2 = 33.08, I_3 = 23.15; i = 5.$
   c. $I_0 = 0, I_1 = 12, I_2 = 12, I_3 = 12, \ldots; i = 5.$
2. Contrast the following four returns on durable assets: (*a*) rent on land, (*b*) rental of a capital good, (*c*) rate of return on a capital good, and (*d*) real interest rate. Give an example of each.
3. Interest-rate problems (which may require a calculator):
   a. You invest $2000 at an interest rate of 13.5 percent per year. What is your total balance after 6 months?
   b. Interest is said to be "compounded" when you earn interest on whatever interest has already been paid; most interest rates quoted today are compounded. If you invest $10,000 for 3 years at a compound annual interest rate of 10 percent, what is the total value of the investment at the end of each year?
   c. Consider the following data: The consumer price index in 1977 was 60.6, and in 1981 it was 90.9. Interest rates on government securities in 1978 through 1981 (in percent per year) were 7.2, 10.0, 11.5, and 14.0. Calculate the average nominal and real interest rates for the 4-year period 1978–1981.
   d. Treasury bills (T-bills) are usually sold on a discounted basis; that is, a 90-day T-bill for $10,000 would sell today at a price such that collecting $10,000 at maturity would produce the market interest rate. If the market interest rate is 6.6 percent per year, what would be the price on a 90-day $10,000 T-bill?
4. Present-value questions:
   a. Consider the 1-year bond in the discussion of present value. Calculate the present value of the bond if the interest rate is 1, 5, 10, and 20 percent.
   b. What is the value of a perpetuity yielding $16 per year at interest rates of 1, 5, 10, and 20 percent per year?
   c. Compare the answers to **a** and **b.** Which asset is more sensitive to interest-rate changes? Quantify the difference.
5. Using the supply-and-demand analysis of interest, explain how each of the following would affect interest rates in capital theory:
   a. An innovation that increased the marginal product of capital at each level of capital
   b. A decrease in the desired wealth holdings of households
   c. A 50 percent tax on the return on capital (in the short run and the long run)
6. Looking back to Figures 15-5 and 15-6, review how the economy moved from the short-run equilibrium interest rate at 10 percent per year to the long-run equilibrium. Now explain what would occur in both the long run and the short run if innovations shift up the demand-for-capital curve. What would happen if the government debt became very large and a large part of people's supply of capital was siphoned off to holdings of government debt? Draw new figures for both cases.
7. Explain the rule for calculating the present discounted value of a perpetual income stream. At a 5 percent interest rate, what is the worth of a perpetuity paying $100 per year? Paying $200 per year? Paying $$N$ per year? At 10 or 8 percent, what is the worth of a perpetuity paying $100 per year? What does doubling the interest rate do to the capitalized value of a perpetuity—say, a perpetual bond?
8. Recall the algebraic formula for a convergent geometric progression:

$$1 + K + K^2 + \cdots = \frac{1}{1 - K}$$

for any fraction K less than 1. If you set $K = 1/(1 + i)$, can you verify the present-value formula for a permanent income stream, $V = \$N/i$? Provide an alternative proof using common sense. What would be the value of a lottery that paid you and your heirs $5000 per year forever, assuming an interest rate of 6 percent per year?

9. The value of land in Manhattan was around $150 billion in 2008. Imagine that it is 1626 and you are the economic adviser to the Dutch when they are considering whether to buy Manhattan from the Manhasset Indians. Further, assume that the relevant interest rate for calculating the present value is 4 percent per year. Would you advise the Dutch that a purchase price of $24 is a good deal or not? How would your answer change if the interest rate were 6 percent? 8 percent? (*Hint:* For each interest rate, calculate the present value in 1626 of the land value as of 2008. Then compare that with the purchase price in 1626. For this example, simplify by assuming that the owners collect no rents on the land. As an advanced further question, assume that the rent equals 2 percent of the value of the land each year.)

10. An increase in interest rates will generally lower the prices of assets. To see this, calculate the present value of the following two assets at interest rates of 5 percent, 10 percent, and 20 percent per year:
    a. A perpetuity yielding $100 per year
    b. A Christmas tree that will sell for $50 one year from now

    Explain why the price of the long-lived asset is more sensitive to interest-rate changes than the price of the short-lived asset.

PART FOUR

Applications of Economic Principles

经济学原理的应用

CHAPTER

16

Government Taxation and Expenditure

政府的税收和支出

[1] 约瑟夫·熊彼特（Joseph Schumpeter，1883~1950），匈牙利裔的奥地利学者（详见 p40 注[3]），被誉为“最伟大的经济思想家”。这段文字摘自熊彼特《资本主义经济学和社会学》（*The Economics and Sociology of Capitalism, Princeton University Press*, 1991）一书第 101 页，即第一章《征税国家的危机》（*The Crisis of the Tax State*）第二节《财政社会学》（*Fiscal Sociology*）中冗长的第一段的结尾文字。原文如下：

The spirit of a people, its cultural level, its social structure, the deeds its policy may prepare—all this and more is written in its fiscal history, stripped of all phrases. He who knows how to listen to its messenger here discerns the thunder of world history more clearly than anywhere else.

我们可以发现，除“stripped of all phrases.”用省略号被省略之外，萨缪尔森只字未改地引用了熊彼特的原文，实属难得。

①

The spirit of a people, its cultural level, its social structure, the deeds its policy may prepare, all this and more is written in its fiscal history. . . . He who knows how to listen to its messenger here discerns the thunder of world history more clearly than anywhere else.

Joseph Schumpeter [1]

一个民族的精神风貌、文化水平、社会结构以及施政水平助其成功所铺就的道路，加上其他诸多因素，均记录在它的财政历史中，……（省略部分为：华而不实的语言均被排除在外）。那些懂得如何去倾听其民族信使所承载的历史的人，此时比在任何别的地方，都能更加清楚地洞悉到文明社会的呐喊。

When we look at a market economy—providing all sorts of products from apples and boats to X-ray machines and zithers—it would be tempting to think that markets require little more than skilled workers and lots of capital. But history has shown that markets cannot work effectively alone. At a minimum, ② an efficient market economy needs police to ensure physical security, an independent judicial system to enforce contracts, regulatory mechanisms to prevent monopolistic abuses and lethal pollution, schools to educate the young, and a public health system to ward off communicable diseases. Exactly where to draw the line between government and private activities is a difficult and controversial question, and people today debate the appropriate role of government in education, health care, and income support.

As economists, we want to go beyond the partisan debates and analyze the functions of government—government's comparative advantage in the mixed economy. The present chapter examines the role of government in an advanced economy. What are the appropriate goals for economic policy in a market economy, and what instruments are available to carry them out? What principles underlie an efficient tax system? Understanding the answers to these questions is key to developing sound public policies.

政府对经济的控制

A. GOVERNMENT CONTROL OF THE ECONOMY

Debates about the role of government often take place on bumper stickers, with rallying cries such as "No new taxes" or "Balance the budget." These simplistic phrases cannot capture the serious business of government economic policy. Say the populace decides that it wants to devote more resources to improving public health; or that more resources should be devoted to educating the young; or that unemployment in a deep recession should be reduced. A market economy cannot automatically solve these problems. Each of these objectives can be met if and only if the government changes its taxes, spending, or regulations. The thunder of world history is heard ③ in fiscal policy because taxing and spending are such powerful instruments for social change.

② 在最低限度，一个有效的市场的经济体需要警察来确保社会的平安，需要独立的司法系统来保障各种契约的强制履行，需要各种监管机制来防止垄断的滥用和致命的污染，需要学校来教育青少年，还需要公共的卫生体系来杜绝传染病的爆发。

③ 有史以来，人类社会发出的呐喊均清晰地记录在财政政策里，这是因为税收政策和政府的支出是推动社会变革的强有力的工具。

政府的政策工具

THE TOOLS OF GOVERNMENT POLICY

In a modern economy, no sphere of economic life is ① untouched by the government. We can identify three major instruments or tools that government uses to influence private economic activity:

1. *Taxes* on incomes and goods and services. These ② reduce private income, thereby reducing private expenditures (on automobiles or restaurant food) and providing resources for public expenditures (on missiles and school lunches). The tax system also serves to discourage certain activities by taxing them more heavily (such as smoking cigarettes) while encouraging other activities by taxing them lightly or even subsidizing them (such as health care).
2. *Expenditures* on certain goods or services (such ③ as roads, education, or police protection), along with *transfer payments* (like social security and food stamps) that provide resources to individuals.
3. *Regulations* or controls that direct people to per- ④ form or refrain from certain economic activities. Examples include rules that limit the amount firms can pollute, or that divide up the radio spectrum, or that mandate testing the safety of new drugs.

政府规模的变动趋势

Trends in the Size of Government

For more than a century, national income and production have been rising in all economies. At the same time, in most countries, government expenditures have been rising even faster than the overall economy. Each period of emergency—depression, war, or concern over social problems such as poverty or pollution—expanded the activity of government. After the crisis passed, government controls and spending never returned to their previous levels.

Before World War I, the combined federal, state, and local government expenditures or taxation amounted to little more than one-tenth of the entire U.S. national income. The war effort during World War II compelled government to consume about half the nation's greatly expanded total output. By 2007, expenditures of all levels of government in the United States ran around 33 percent of GDP.

Figure 16-1 shows the trend in taxes and expenditures for all levels of government in the United

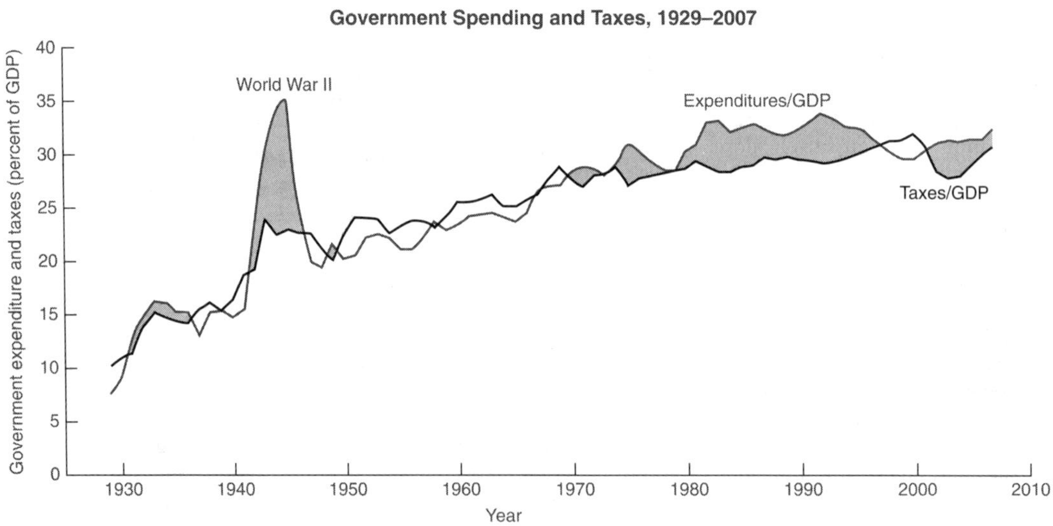

FIGURE 16-1. Government's Share of the Economy Has Grown Sharply ⑤

Government expenditures include spending on goods, services, and transfers at the federal, state, and local levels. Note how spending grew rapidly during wartime but did not return to prewar levels afterward. The difference between spending and taxes is the government deficit or surplus.

Source: U.S. Department of Commerce.

① 在一个现代经济体中，社会经济生活已经没有不被政府影响的任何环节。

② 对收入、商品和服务征税。

③ 商品和服务的支出（如道路、教育和安保系统），以及为个体提供不同资源的转移支付（像社会保障和社会救济）。

④ 指导民众从事或者禁止某些经济活动的规章或控制。

⑤ 图 16-1. 政府支出在整个经济中所占的份额保持着快速增长之势

States. The rising curves indicate that the shares of government taxes and spending have grown steadily upward over recent decades.

Government's expansion has not occurred without opposition; each new spending and tax program provoked a fierce reaction. For example, when social ① security was first introduced in 1935, opponents denounced it as an ominous sign of socialism. But with the passage of time, political attitudes evolve. The "socialistic" social security system is today defended by politicians of all stripes as an essential part of the "social contract" between the generations. The radical doctrines of one era become accepted gospel of the next.

Figure 16-2 shows how government spending as a percentage of GDP varies among countries. High-income countries tend to tax and spend a larger fraction of GDP than do poor countries. Can we discern a pattern among wealthy countries? Within the high-income countries, no simple law relating tax burdens and the citizenry's well-being can do justice to the true diversity of the fiscal facts of nations. For example, financing for education and health care, two of the largest components of government spending, is organized very differently across countries.

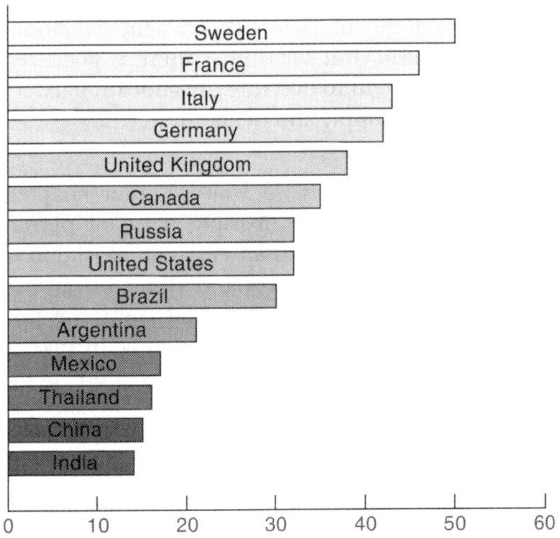

FIGURE 16-2. Government Taxation Is Highest in Rich Countries ②

Governments of poor countries tax and spend relatively little of national income. With affluence come greater demands for public goods and redistributional taxation to aid low-income families. ③

Source: United Nations for period 2000–2002, at *unpan1.un.org/intradoc/groups/public/documents/un/unpan014052.pdf.*

Figures 16-1 and 16-2 show the total expenditures of governments. Such expenditures include purchases of goods and services (like missiles and education) as well as transfer payments (like social security payments and interest on the government debt). Purchases of goods and services are called "exhaustive" because they make a direct claim upon the production of a country; transfer payments, by contrast, increase people's income and allow individuals to purchase goods and services but do not directly reduce the quantity of goods and services available for private consumption and investment.

政府对经济的控制和管制增加

The Growth of Government Controls and Regulation

In addition to the growth in spending and taxing, there has also been a vast expansion in the laws and regulations governing economic affairs.

Nineteenth-century America came as close ④ as any economy has come to being a pure laissez-faire society—the system that the British historian Thomas Carlyle labeled "anarchy plus the constable." [5] This philosophy permitted people great personal freedom to pursue their economic ambitions and produced a century of rapid material progress. But critics saw many flaws in this laissez-faire idyll. Historians record periodic business crises, extremes of poverty and inequality, deep-seated racial discrimination, and poisoning of water, land, and air by pollution. Muckrakers and progressives called for a bridle on capitalism so that the people could steer this wayward beast in more humane directions.

Beginning in the 1890s, the United States gradually turned away from the belief that "government governs best which governs least." [6] Presidents Theodore Roosevelt, Woodrow Wilson, Franklin Roosevelt, and Lyndon Johnson—in the face of strenuous opposition—pushed out the boundaries of federal control over the economy, devising new regulatory and fiscal tools to combat the economic ailments of their time.

① 例如，当社会保障制度于1935年刚刚开始实施的时候，反对者们就公开站出来指责它是社会主义的不祥之兆。但是，随着时间的推移，不同的政治立场均在发生着变化。"社会主义的"社会保障系统已经是今天各派政客共同捍卫的跨越代际的"社会契约"中最基本的组成部分。这些曾经的激进教条几乎已经成为普世的福音。

② 图16-2.政府税收最高的国家在富国

③ 穷国政府的税收和支出相较于国民收入来讲所占比重很小。由于公共品需求的大幅度增加，以税收二次分配的形式帮助低收入家庭的力度也随之加大。

④ 19世纪的美国像历史上任何已经进入完全自由放任的经济体一样，几乎是一个纯粹自由化的社会，这就是英国历史学家托马斯·卡莱尔所标榜的"无政府加街头警察"的社会体制。

[5] 托马斯·卡莱尔（Thomas Carlyle，1795~1881），苏格兰历史学家、评论家和讽刺作家。"anarchy plus the constable"（无政府加警察）的原文为"Anarchy plus a street-constable"，见《卡莱尔文选》（*A Carlyle Reader, Random House, Inc., 1969; Cambridge University Press*, 1984）437页。据此，上述译文笔者加"街头"二字更贴近卡莱尔原意，也与本部分内容相符，请读者谅知。

[6] 这段文字虽然和汤姆斯·杰弗逊的建国思想完全合拍，但却不是出自杰弗逊之笔。它最早出自1837年出版的《美国杂志与民主评论》（The United States Magazine and Democratic Review）中的编者按，原文为："That government is best which governs least"。

西奥多·罗斯福（Theodore Roosevelt，1858~1919），第26任美国总统。美国历史上最伟大的总统之一，其公共福利高于个人财产的改革指导思想对20世纪美国的迅速崛起影响深远，并因成功地调停了日俄战争而于1906年成为美国历史上第一位获得诺贝尔和平奖的美国人。美国历史上，共有包括老罗斯福在内的威尔逊（1919）、卡特（2002）、奥巴马（2009）四位总统和戈尔（2007）副总统在位或卸任后获诺贝尔和平奖。

伍德罗·威尔逊（Woodrow Wilson，1856~1924），第28任美国总统，继罗斯福后，成为"进步年代"（Progressive Era）的旗手，曾任普林斯顿大学校长8年，是美国历史上"学术地位最高"的总统。在第一任期内，力主通过了《联邦储备法》（Federal Reserve Act）、《联邦贸易委员会》（Federal Trade Commission）、《克莱顿反托拉斯法》（The Clayton Antitrust Act）、《联邦农场贷款法》（The Federal Farm Loan Act），以及通过新的收入所得税法在联邦一级开征收入所得税等一系列法案。在第一次世界大战的最后阶段，由于其为避免世界再遭战火提出的《14点和平原则》（*Fourteen Points*）和在筹建国际联盟以及拟定凡尔赛和约中所起的主导作用，而于1919年成为美国历史上第二位获得诺贝尔和平奖的总统。今天的奥巴马和当年的威尔逊无论在个性和执政风格以及执政环境上，有着很多相似之处。所以，不少舆论认为，奥巴马很可能成为美国历史上第二个威尔逊式的满怀超级理想主义的总统。

富兰克林·罗斯福（Franklin Roosevelt，1882~1945），美国历史上唯一连任四届（1933~1945，第四届未任满）的总统。罗斯福在20世纪的经济大萧条和第二次世界大战中扮演了重要的角色，被学界评为美国历史上最伟大的三位总统之一，同华盛顿和林肯齐名。美国第26任总统西奥多·罗斯福是富兰克林·罗斯福的远房堂叔，故称"小罗斯福"总统。与肯尼迪总统的"JFK"以及约翰逊总统的LBJ一起，享有"FDR"这样亲切的缩写式昵称。

林登·约翰逊（Lyndon Johnson，1908~1973），肯尼迪总统被刺后入主白宫，出任第36届美国总统。在任期间由于提出了"伟大社会"（Great Society）、"向贫穷宣战"（War on Poverty）的施政纲领，通过了老年医疗保健制度、医疗补助制度，不遗余力地推行民权法案等，因此在1964年的总统大选中大获全胜。但是，约翰逊的这一美国梦的追寻，也人为地制造了一个大政府的缺憾，违背了美国"管制最少的政府即最好的政府"（即"government governs best which governs least"）的建国思想。如果没有其在任期间越南战争的错误政策，约翰逊无疑会成为美国历史上伟大的总统之一。

Constitutional powers of government were interpreted broadly and used to “secure the public interest” and to “police” the economic system. In 1887, the [1]
federal Interstate Commerce Commission (ICC) was established to regulate rail traffic across state boundaries. Soon afterward, the Sherman Antitrust Act and other laws were aimed against monopolistic combinations in “restraint of trade.”

During the 1930s, a whole set of industries came ②
under *economic regulation,* in which government sets the prices, conditions of exit and entry, and safety standards. Regulated industries since that time have included the airlines, trucking, and barge and water traffic; electric, gas, and telephone utilities; financial markets; and oil and natural gas, as well as pipelines.

In addition to regulating the prices and standards of business, the nation attempted to protect health and safety through increasingly stringent *social regulation.* Following the revelations of the muckraking era of the early 1900s, pure food and drug acts were passed. During the 1960s and 1970s, Congress passed a series of acts that regulated mine safety and then worker safety more generally; regulated air and water pollution; authorized safety standards for automobiles and consumer products; and regulated strip mining, nuclear power, and toxic wastes.

Over the last three decades, the growth in government programs slowed. Economists argued persuasively that many economic regulations were impeding competition and keeping prices up rather than down. In the area of social regulations, economists have ③
emphasized the need to ensure that the marginal benefits of regulations exceed their marginal costs. Today, “entitlement programs” (programs available to everyone who meets certain well-defined eligibility criteria), such as pensions and health care, are now the major spending programs for most high-income countries.

Still, there is no likelihood of a return to the laissez-faire era. Government programs have changed the very nature of capitalism. Private property is less and less wholly private. Free enterprise has become progressively less free. Irreversible evolution is part of history.

[1] the federal Interstate Commerce Commission:(联邦)州际商业委员会。
the Sherman Antitrust:谢尔曼反托拉斯法。

② 在20世纪30年代，整个美国的产业界都在经济管制之下，政府限定价格、制定市场准入和退出的条件以及安全标准等。

③ 在社会管制领域，经济学家们始终强调一个需要注意的问题，即确保管制的边际收益要大于管制的边际成本。

政府的职能
THE FUNCTIONS OF GOVERNMENT

We are beginning to get a picture of how government directs and interacts with the economy. What are the appropriate economic goals for government action in a modern mixed economy? Let’s examine the four major functions:

1. Improving economic efficiency ④
2. Reducing economic inequality
3. Stabilizing the economy through macroeconomic policies
4. Conducting international economic policy

提高经济效率
Improving Economic Efficiency

A central economic purpose of government is to assist ⑤
in the socially desirable allocation of resources. This is the *microeconomic* side of government policy; it concentrates on the *what* and *how* of economic life. Microeconomic policies differ among countries according to customs and political philosophies. Some countries emphasize a hands-off, laissez-faire approach, leaving most decisions to the market. Other countries lean toward heavy government regulation, or even public ownership of businesses, in which production decisions are made by government planners.

The United States is fundamentally a market economy. On any microeconomic issue, most people presume that the market will solve the economic problem at hand. But sometimes there is good reason for government to override the allocational decisions of market supply and demand.

The Limits of the Invisible Hand. Earlier chapters have explained how the invisible hand of perfect competition would lead to an efficient allocation of resources. But this invisible-hand result holds only under limited conditions. All goods must be produced efficiently by perfectly competitive firms. All goods must be private goods like loaves of bread, the total of which can be cut up into separate slices of consumption for different individuals. There can be no externalities like air pollution. Consumers and firms must be fully informed about the prices and characteristics of the goods they buy and sell.

If all these idealized conditions were met, the invisible hand could provide perfectly efficient production and distribution of national output, and there would be no need for government intervention to promote efficiency.

Yet even in this ideal case, if there were to be a ⑥
division of labor among people and regions, and if a price mechanism were to work, government would

---

④ 1. 提高经济效率
2. 减少经济的不公平现象
3. 通过宏观经济政策保持经济的稳定
4. 管控国际经济的政策

⑤ 政府的核心经济目标是给社会按其意愿配置资源提供助力。这就是政府政策的微观方面。它关注于经济生活中生产什么和如何生产的问题。

⑥ 然而，即便按照这样理想的案例，假设在民众中和各地区间有可能进行劳动分工，价格机制也可以奏效，那么政府就将扮演一个很重要的角色。为确保契约的履行，杜绝欺诈和暴力行为，免受盗窃和抵御外敌入侵，以及依法保护物权等，法庭和警察部队也应该是必需的。

have an important role. Courts and police forces would be needed to ensure fulfillment of contracts, nonfraudulent and nonviolent behavior, freedom from theft and external aggression, and the legislated rights of property.

Inescapable Interdependencies. Laissez-faire with minimal government intervention might be a good system if the idealized conditions listed above were truly present. In reality, each and every one of the idealized conditions enumerated above is violated to some extent in all human societies. Unregulated factories do tend to pollute the air, water, and land. When contagious diseases threaten to break out, private markets have little incentive to develop effective public-health programs. Consumers are sometimes poorly informed about the characteristics of the goods they buy. The market is not ideal. There are market failures.

In other words, government often deploys its weapons to correct significant market failures, of which the most important are the following:

- *The breakdown of perfect competition.* When monop- ① olies or oligopolies collude to fix prices or drive firms out of business, government may apply antitrust policies or regulations.
- *Externalities and public goods.* The unregulated market may produce too much air pollution and too little investment in public health or basic science. Government can use its influence to control harmful externalities or to fund programs in science and public health. Government can levy taxes on activities which impose external public costs (such as cigarette smoking), or it can subsidize activities which are socially beneficial (such as education or prenatal health care).
- *Imperfect information.* Unregulated markets tend to provide too little information for consumers to make well-informed decisions. In an earlier era, hucksters hawked snake oil remedies that might just as easily kill you as cure you. This led to food and drug regulations requiring that pharmaceutical companies provide extensive data on the safety and efficacy of new drugs before they can be sold. The government also requires that companies provide information on energy efficiency of major household appliances like refrigerators and water heaters. In addition, government may use its spending power to collect and provide needed information itself, as it does with automobile crash-and-safety data.

Clearly, there is much on the agenda of possible allocational problems for government to handle.

减少经济不公平
Reducing Economic Inequality

Even when the invisible hand is marvelously efficient, it may at the same time produce a very unequal distribution of income. Under laissez-faire, people end up rich or poor depending on where they were born, on their inherited wealth, on their talents and efforts, on their luck in finding oil, and on their gender or the color of their skin. To some people, the distri- ② bution of income arising from unregulated competition looks as arbitrary as the Darwinian distribution of food and plunder in the jungle.

In the poorest societies, there is little excess income to take from the better-off and provide to the unfortunate. However, as a nation becomes wealthier, it can devote more resources to provide basic necessities and social insurance for all of its residents. These activities are the role of the "welfare state"—in which governments provide a minimum living standard to all—which is surveyed in detail in the next chapter. The welfare states of North America and Western Europe now devote a significant share of their revenues to maintaining minimum standards of health, nutrition, and income.

Income redistribution is usually accomplished through taxation and spending policies. Most wealthy countries now rule that children shall not go hungry because of the economic circumstances of their parents; that the poor shall not die because of insufficient money for needed medical care; that the young shall receive free public education; and that the old shall live out their years with a minimum level of income. In the United States, these government activities are provided primarily by transfer programs, such as food stamps, Medicaid, and social security. [3]

But attitudes about redistribution evolve as well. With rising tax burdens and government budget deficits, along with rising costs of income-support programs, taxpayers increasingly resist redistributive programs and progressive taxation.

通过宏观政策稳定经济
Stabilizing the Economy through Macroeconomic Policies

Early capitalism was prone to financial panics and bouts of inflation and depression. Today government

---

① • 打破完全竞争。当垄断或者寡头合谋绑定物价或者将别的厂商逐出市场时，政府就应该启动反托拉斯法或者实施管制。

② 对某些人来讲，来源于非管制竞争环境中的收入分配，就好像丛林中弱肉强食的达尔文进化论法则一样，是反复无常的。

[3] Food stamps：政府发放给低收入者的食物券，系约翰逊总统在 1964 年启动的“向贫穷宣战”(War on Poverty) 中的具体项目之一，其余的《基础教育争先》(Head Start)、《职业发展》(Work Study)、老年医疗保健制度和医疗补助制度等都是后来的历届总统不得不跟进的施政内容。约翰逊总统的“向贫穷宣战”是在力促国会在同年通过了《税收法案，1964》(Revenue Act of 1964) 和《经济振兴法案》(Economic Opportunity Act) 的背景下大力实施的。

has the responsibility of preventing calamitous business depressions by the proper use of monetary and fiscal policy, as well as regulation of the financial system. In addition, government tries to smooth out the ① ups and downs of the business cycle, in order to avoid either large-scale unemployment at the bottom of the cycle or high inflation at the top of the cycle. More recently, government has become concerned with finding economic policies which boost long-term economic growth. These questions are considered at length in the chapters on macroeconomics.

① 此外，政府还必须竭尽全力地平抑商业周期的大起大落，以避免周期中的低谷导致大规模的失业，或者在处于峰值状态时的通货膨胀率出现过高的情况。现在，政府已经越来越关注于推进经济长期增长的经济政策的探索和制定。

执行国际经济政策
Conducting International Economic Policy

As we will see in Chapter 18's review of international trade, the United States has become increasingly linked to the global economy in recent years. Government now plays a critical role representing the interests of the nation on the international stage and negotiating beneficial agreements with other countries on a wide range of issues. We can group the international issues of economic policy into four main areas:

- *Reducing trade barriers.* An important part of eco- ② nomic policy involves harmonizing laws and reducing trade barriers so as to encourage fruitful international specialization and division of labor. In recent years, nations have negotiated a series of trade agreements to lower tariffs and other trade barriers on agricultural products, manufactured goods, and services.

  Such agreements are often contentious. They sometimes harm certain groups, as when removing textile tariffs reduces employment in that industry. In addition, international agreements may require giving up national sovereignty as the price of raising incomes. Suppose that one country's laws protect intellectual property rights, such as patents and copyrights, while another country's laws allow free copying of books, videos, and software. Whose laws shall prevail?
- *Conducting assistance programs.* Rich nations have ③ numerous programs designed to improve the lot of the poor in other countries. These involve direct foreign aid, disaster and technical assistance, the establishment of institutions like the World Bank to give low-interest-rate loans to poor countries, and concessionary terms on exports to poor nations.
- *Coordinating macroeconomic policies.* Nations have ④ seen that fiscal and monetary policies of other nations affect inflation, unemployment, and financial conditions at home. The international monetary system cannot manage itself; establishing a smoothly functioning exchange-rate system is a prerequisite for efficient international trade. When the American credit crisis ⑤ erupted in 2008, it quickly spread to Europe and threatened several European banks. Central banks needed to act in a coordinated fashion to ensure that a bank failure, or even the fear of failure, in one country did not spread like wildfire to the entire international financial system. Particularly in tightly integrated regions, like Western Europe, countries work to coordinate their fiscal, monetary, and exchange-rate policies, or even adopt a common currency, so that inflation, unemployment, or financial crises in one country do not spill over to hurt the entire area.
- *Protecting the global environment.* The most recent ⑥ facet of international economic policy is to work with other nations to protect the global environment in cases where several countries contribute to or are affected by spillovers. The most active areas historically have been protecting fisheries and water quality in rivers. When the Antarctic ozone hole threatened public health, countries reached an agreement to limit the use of ozone-depleting chemicals. Other treaties are designed to reduce the threats of deforestation, global warming, and species extinction. Clearly, international environmental problems can be resolved only through the cooperation of many nations.

Even the staunchest conservatives agree that government has a major role to play in representing the national interest in the anarchy of nations.

公共选择理论
PUBLIC-CHOICE THEORY

For the most part, our analysis has concentrated on the *normative* theory of government—on the appropriate policies that the government *should follow* to increase the welfare of the population. But econo- ⑦ mists are not starry-eyed about the government any more than they are about the market. Governments

---

② 减少贸易壁垒。

③ 实施援助计划。

④ 把控好宏观经济政策。

⑤ 2008 年美国的信用危机爆发之后，很快就蔓延到了欧洲，欧洲的几家银行受到了严重威胁。各国中央银行以协调一致的方式采取行动，以便确保没有一家银行出现破产，或者尽可能地缓解破产所引起的恐慌，从而使在一个国家发生的危机不至于像野火一样波及到整个国际金融系统。

⑥ 保护好全球环境。

⑦ 但是，经济学家们对政府的不乐观如同对市场的不乐观一样。政府很可能做出糟糕的决策，或者将很好的计划执行得一无是处。正如有市场失灵（如垄断和污染）一样，也会有“政府失灵”——政府的干预措施均会错失宝贵的时机，收入也会以人们所不愿意看到的方式进行再分配。

can make bad decisions or carry out good ideas badly. Indeed, just as there are market failures such as monopoly and pollution, so are there "government failures" in which government interventions lead to waste or redistribute income in an undesirable fashion.

These issues are the domain of **public-choice** ①
theory, which is the branch of economics and political science that studies the way that governments make decisions. Public-choice theory examines the way different voting mechanisms can function and shows that there are no ideal mechanisms to sum up individual preferences into social choices. This approach also analyzes government failures, which arise when state actions fail to improve economic efficiency or when the government redistributes income unfairly. Public-choice theory points to issues such as the short time horizons of elected representatives, the lack of a hard budget constraint, and the role of money in financing elections as sources of government failures. A careful study of government failures is crucial for understanding the limitations of government and ensuring that government programs are not excessively intrusive or wasteful.

The Economics of Politics

Economists focus most of their analysis on the workings of the marketplace. But serious economists have also pondered the government's role in society. Joseph Schumpeter pioneered public-choice theory in *Capitalism, Socialism, and Democracy* (1942), and Kenneth Arrow's Nobel Prize–winning study on social choice brought rigor to this field. The landmark study by Anthony Downs, *An Economic Theory of Democracy* (1957), sketched a powerful new theory which held that politicians choose economic policies in order to be reelected. Downs showed that this theory implies that political parties would move toward the center of the political spectrum because of electoral competition.

Among the most important applications of public-choice theory were those to economic regulation. George Stigler argued that regulatory agencies have been "captured" by the regulated and often served the industries they regulated more than consumers. Studies by James Buchanan and Gordon Tullock in *The Calculus of Consent* (1959) defended checks and balances and advocated the use of unanimity in political decisions, arguing that unanimous decisions do not coerce anyone. Public-choice economics has been applied to such areas as farm policy and the courts, and it formed the theoretical basis for a proposed constitutional amendment to balance the budget.

政府支出

B. GOVERNMENT EXPENDITURES

Nowhere can the changes in government's role be seen more clearly than in the area of government spending. Look back at Figure 16-1 on page 304. It shows the share of national output going to government spending, which includes things like purchases of goods, salaries of government workers, social security and other transfers, and interest on the government debt. You can see that government's share rose for most of the twentieth century, with temporary bulges during wartime, but it has leveled off in recent years.

财政联邦制

FISCAL FEDERALISM

While we have been referring to government as if it were a single entity, in fact Americans face three levels of government: federal, state, and local. This reflects a division of fiscal responsibilities among
[2] the different levels of government—a system known
[3] as *fiscal federalism.* The boundaries are not always
clear-cut, but in general the federal government
[4] directs activities that concern the entire nation—
paying for defense, space exploration, and foreign affairs. Local governments educate children, police streets, and remove garbage. States build highways, run university systems, and administer welfare programs.

The total U.S. spending at the different levels of government is shown in Table 16-1. The dominance
[5] of the federal role is a comparatively recent phenomenon. Before the twentieth century, local government was by far the most important of the three
[6] levels. The federal government did little more than
[7] support the military, pay interest on the national

---

① 这些问题都属于**公共选择理论**的范畴。公共选择理论是研究政府决策方式的经济学和政治学的分支之一。公共选择理论研究不同选举机制的运作方式，并证明没有任何理想的选举机制可以将个体的选择意向汇总成社会的选择。这一方法也分析了政府失灵。当国家行为无法改善经济效率，或者政府的收入再分配有失公平时，政府的功能就会失灵。

[2]《资本主义、社会主义与民主》(*Capitalism, Socialism, and Democracy*)，是熊彼特最家喻户晓的著作，于1942年出版。该书从讨论马克思关于资本主义必定由社会主义取代的思想开始，借代"创造性毁灭"的思想，总结出了否定马克思取代学说的预言，提出了关于资本主义制度必定由自身力量实现涅槃而重生的著名理论。本书第16页第一自然段的《阅读建议》中还提到了熊彼特的另一本代表著作《经济分析史》(*History of Economic Analysis*)。见p40注[3]。

[3] 肯尼斯·阿罗（Kenneth Arrow，1921~），美国经济学家，因在一般均衡理论方面的突出贡献与约翰·希克斯（John Hicks，1904~1989）共同荣获1972年诺贝尔经济学奖，时年51岁，创下诺贝尔经济学奖得主最年轻者的记录。阿罗在社会选择、风险决策、微观经济学、组织经济学、不确定性经济学、信息经济学、福利经济学、保险经济学、沟通经济学和政治民主理论等方面均卓有成就，被认为是战后新古典经济学的开创者之一。

[4] 安东尼·唐斯（Anthony Downs，1930~），著名的公共政策和公共管理学者，美国布热津斯研究院高级研究员，《民主经济学》(*An Economic Theory of Democracy*，1957）和《行政管理》(*Inside Bureaucr-acy*，1967）是唐斯最有影响的两部经典著作。

[5] 乔治·施蒂格勒（George Stigler，1911~1991），美国经济学家，信息经济学和管制经济学的创始人，1982年诺贝尔经济学奖得主，与弗里德曼一起，是芝加哥经济学派的领军双雄。

[6] 詹姆斯·布坎南（James Buchanan，1919~），美国经济学家，由于其在公共选择理论的突出贡献获1986年度的诺贝尔经济学奖。与第15任美国总统詹姆斯·布坎南（1791~1868，任期1857~1861）同名，经济学家布坎南常使用其全名James McGill Buchanan以示区别。

[7] 戈登·塔洛克（Gordon Tullock，1922~），国际上最重要的公共选择经济学家之一，将经济学的理性分析方法引入政治决策过程是其毕生致力的研究，其他研究领域包括国家起源理论、官僚主义、独裁、民主和法庭内部的决策行为等等，著名的法学和经济学教授，2003年获诺贝尔经济学奖候选人提名。

《同意的算计》(*The Calculus of Consent*)，布坎南和塔洛克合著的经典，是公共选择学派的奠基性著作。

Level of government	Total expenditures, 2007 ($, billion)	Percent of total
All levels	4,429	100.0
Federal	2,515	56.8
State	857	19.3
Local	1,058	23.9

① 表 16-1. 联邦、各州和地方政府的常态支出

TABLE 16-1. Federal, State, and Local Government Current Expenditures

In the early days of the Republic, most spending was at the state and local levels. Today, more than half of total government outlays are federal.

Source: U.S. Bureau of Economic Analysis.

debt, and finance a few public works. Most of its tax collection came from liquor and tobacco excises and
② import tariffs. But two world wars and the rise of the welfare state, with transfer programs such as social security and Medicare, increased spending gradually. The advent of the national income tax in 1913 provided a source of funds that no state or locality could match.

② 但是，随着社会和医疗保障等一些转移支付计划的实施，两次世界大战和福利国家的兴起逐步增加了政府支出。1913 年出台的国民收入税为此提供了资金来源，这些资金是任何州政府和地方政府都无力承受的。

To understand fiscal federalism, economists emphasize that spending decisions should be allocated among the levels of government according to the spillovers from government programs. In general, localities are responsible for *local public goods,* activities whose benefits are largely confined to local residents. Since libraries are used by townspeople and streetlights illuminate city roads, decisions about these goods are appropriately made by local residents. Many federal functions involve *national public goods,* which provide benefits to all the nation's citizens. For example, an AIDS vaccine would benefit people from every state, not just those living near the laboratory where it is discovered. What about global concerns such as protecting the ozone layer or slowing global warming? These are *global public goods* because they transcend the boundaries of individual countries.

An efficient system of fiscal federalism takes into account the way the benefits of public programs spill over political boundaries. The most efficient arrangement is to locate the tax and spending decisions so that the beneficiaries of programs pay the taxes and can weigh the tradeoffs. ③

联邦支出

Federal Expenditures

Let's look now at the different levels of government. The U.S. government is the world's biggest enterprise. It buys more automobiles and steel, meets a bigger payroll, and handles more money than any other organization anywhere. The numbers involved in federal finance are astronomical—in the billions and trillions of dollars. The federal budget expen-
① ditures for 2009 are projected to be $3107 billion, or $3.1 trillion; this enormous number amounts to roughly $27,000 for each American household.

Table 16-2 lists the major categories of federal expenditure for fiscal year 2009. (The federal fiscal year 2009 covers October 1, 2008, through September 30, 2009.)

The most rapidly expanding items in the last three decades have been entitlement programs, which provide benefits or payments to any persons who meet certain eligibility requirements set down by law. The major entitlements are social security (old-age, survivors, and disability insurance), health programs (including Medicare for those over 65 and Medicaid for indigent families), and income-security programs (including subsidies for food and unemployment insurance). In fact, virtually the entire growth in federal spending in recent years can be accounted for by entitlement programs, which increased from 28 percent of the budget in 1960 to 60 percent in 2009.

州政府和地方政府的支出

State and Local Expenditures

Although the battles over the federal budget com- ④
mand the headlines, state and local units provide many of the essential functions in today's economy. Figure 16-3 illustrates the way states and localities spend their money. By far the largest item is education because most of the nation's children are educated in schools financed primarily by local governments. By attempting to equalize the educational resources available to every child, public education helps level out the otherwise great disparities in economic opportunity.

In recent years, the fastest-growing categories of spending for states and localities have been health care and prisons. In the last two decades, the number of prisoners in state prisons tripled, as the United States fought a war on crime partly by using longer prison sentences, especially for drug offenders. At the same time, state and local governments were forced to absorb their share of rising health-care costs.

③ 有效的财政联邦制系统高度重视公共事业项目的收益超出行政边界的方式。最有效的对策应该是配置税收和支出决策，这样，这些项目的受益者们就能纳税并权衡利弊。

④ 尽管关于联邦预算的争论占据了各媒体的头条，但在当今的经济生活中，州和地方政府机构还是提供了许多基础功能。图 16-3 即描绘了州及地方政府的支出。迄今为止，教育是最大的一头，因为全美的绝大多数孩子是在主要由地方政府财政支持的学校里接受教育的。通过尽力地让每一个孩子都能享受到平等的教育资源，就能使公共教育以另一种方式，在抚平经济机会的巨大差异中提供一点帮助。

Federal Expenditures, Fiscal Year 2009

Description	Expenditures ($, billion)	Percent of total
Total expenditures	**3,107.4**	**100.0**
National defense	675.1	21.7
Social security	649.3	20.9
Medicare	413.3	13.3
Income security	401.7	12.9
Health	299.4	9.6
Net interest	260.2	8.4
Veterans benefits and services	91.9	3.0
Education, training, employment, and social services	88.3	2.8
Transportation	83.9	2.7
Administration of justice	51.1	1.6
International affairs	38.0	1.2
Natural resources and environment	35.5	1.1
General science, space and technology	29.2	0.9
Community and regional development	23.3	0.8
General government	21.5	0.7
Agriculture	19.1	0.6
Commerce and housing credit	4.2	0.1
Energy	3.1	0.1

TABLE 16-2. Federal Spending Is Dominated by Defense and Entitlement Programs ①

About one-fifth of federal spending is for defense or pensions due to past wars. More than half of spending today is for rapidly growing entitlement programs—income security, social security, and health. Note how small is the traditional cost of government.

Source: Office of Management and Budget, Budget of the U.S. Government, Fiscal Year 2009, available at *www.whitehouse.gov/omb/budget/fy2009/hist.html.*

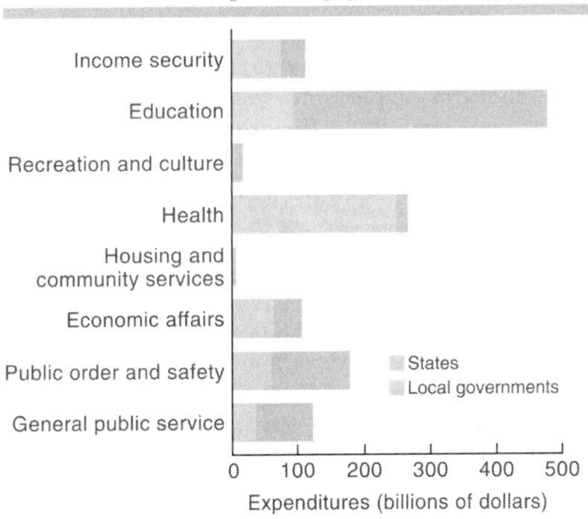

FIGURE 16-3. Distribution of Spending by State and Local Governments, 2006

State and local programs include providing education, financing hospitals, and maintaining the streets. Education and health take an increasing fraction of state and local spending.

Source: Bureau of Economic Analysis.

文化和技术影响
CULTURAL AND TECHNOLOGICAL IMPACTS

Government programs have subtle impacts on the country beyond the dollar spending. The federal ② government has changed the landscape through the interstate highway system. By making automotive [3] travel much faster, this vast network lowered transportation costs, displaced the railroads, and brought goods to every corner of the country. It also helped accelerate urban sprawl and the growth of the suburban culture.

The government has put the United States on the map in many areas of science and technology. Government support gave a powerful start to the electronics industries. The development of the transistor by Bell Labs, for example, was partially funded by the U.S. military, anxious for better radar and communications. Today's computer and airplane industries were boosted in their early years by strong government support. The Internet was

① 表 16-2. 国防和福利项目是联邦政府最主要的支出

② 联邦政府通过建设州际高速公路网彻底改变了美国的景观。汽车的行驶速度大大加快之后，这一庞大的高速公路网系统降低了运输成本，取代了铁路，并将商品带到了全美的每一个角落。同时，它也促使城市的加速外延和乡村文化的发展。

[3] Interstate highway system：全名 Dwight D. Eisenhower National System of Interstate and Defense Highways，美国的州际高速公路网。正如其全名所示，是艾森豪威尔总统（1890~1969，1953~1961 在任）在任期间启动（1956），历时 50 年（2006）建成的，全长 75 440 公里，只有约 8 000 公里象征性地收取很少的过路费，其余约 90% 全部免费。建设资金的 90% 由联邦财政支付，相关州政府只负担剩余的 10%。该公路网是迄今全世界最长的高速公路系统，也是人类历史上最大的公共工程。

developed by the Department of Defense to create a network that would continue to function in the event of nuclear war.

The government today plays an especially important role in basic science. Of all the basic research in the United States, 85 percent is funded by the government or by nonprofit institutions like universities. Often, if you follow a successful invention upstream to its source, you will find that government subsidized the inventor's education and supported basic university research. Economic studies indicate that these funds were well spent, moreover, for the social rates of return to research and development exceed the returns on investments in most other areas.

税收的经济学问题

C. ECONOMIC ASPECTS OF TAXATION

Taxes are what we pay for a civilized society. ①

Justice Oliver Wendell Holmes [2]

① 纳税是我们为文明社会所做的补偿。

[2] 霍姆斯大法官（Justice Oliver Wendell Holmes，1841~1935），1902~1932 年在联邦最高法院长期担任助理大法官，是美国历史上著名的大法官之一。1932 年在 90 高龄时从大法官的位置上退休，创造了美国最高法院历史上最年长法官的记录。本句话是 1904 年霍姆斯在一次演讲中所讲，见 *Compania General De Tabacos De Filipinas v. Collector of Internal Revenue*, U. S. 87，100 第 275 页（1927）。

Governments must pay for their programs. The funds come mainly from taxes, and any shortfall is a deficit that is borrowed from the public.

But in economics we always need to pierce the veil of monetary flows to understand the flow of real resources. ③ Behind the dollar flows of taxes, what the government really needs is the economy's scarce land, labor, and capital. When a nation goes to war, people argue about how to finance the military spending. But in reality, what really happens is that people are diverted from their civilian jobs, airplanes transport troops rather than tourists, and oil goes to airplanes rather than cars. When the government gives out a grant for biotechnology research, its decision really means that a piece of land that might have been used for an office building is now being used for a laboratory.

In taxing, government is in reality deciding how ④ to draw the required resources from the nation's households and businesses for public purposes. The money raised through taxation is the vehicle by which real resources are transferred from private goods to collective goods.

税收原则
PRINCIPLES OF TAXATION

受益原则和支付能力原则
Benefit vs. Ability-to-Pay Principles

Once the government has decided to collect some amount of taxes, it has many possible taxes available to it. It can tax income, tax profits, or tax sales. It can tax the rich or tax the poor, tax the old or tax the young. Are there any guidelines that can help construct a fair and efficient tax system?

Indeed there are. Economists and political philosophers have proposed two major principles for organizing a tax system:

- The **benefit principle,** which holds that individuals ⑤ should be taxed in proportion to the benefit they receive from government programs. Just as people pay private goods like dollars in proportion to their consumption of private goods like bread, a person's taxes should be related to his or her use of collective goods like public roads or parks.
- The **ability-to-pay principle,** which states that the ⑥ amount of taxes people pay should relate to their income or wealth. The higher the wealth or income, the higher the taxes. Usually tax systems organized on the ability-to-pay principle are also *redistributive,* meaning that they raise funds from higher-income people to increase the incomes and consumption of poorer groups.

For instance, if the construction of a new bridge is funded by tolls on the bridge, that's a reflection of the benefit principle, since you pay for the bridge only if you use it. But if the bridge were funded out of income-tax collections, that would be an example of the ability-to-pay principle.

横向公平和纵向公平原则
Horizontal and Vertical Equity

Whether they are organized along benefit or ability-to-pay lines, most modern tax systems attempt to incorporate modern views about fairness or equity. One important principle is that of **horizontal equity,** ⑦ which states that those who are essentially equal should be taxed equally.

The notion of equal treatment of equals has deep roots in Western political philosophy. If you and I are alike in every way except the color of our eyes, all principles of taxation would hold that we should pay equal taxes. In the case of benefit taxation, if we receive exactly the same services from the highways or parks, the principle of horizontal equity states that

③ 然而，在经济学中，我们在任何时候都有必要揭开货币流通的面纱，以便很好地了解实际资源的流动情况。

④ 征税的过程，实际上就是决定如何从全国所有家庭和企业手中吸纳所需资源，用于公共目标。通过税收所筹集的资金是一种媒介，实际所需的资源就可以通过它由私人物品转化为供集体使用的公共物品。

⑤ **受益原则**所强调的是不同个体都应该就他们从政府项目中所获得的收益按比例纳税。

⑥ **支付能力原则**则主张人们纳税的数额应该与他们的收入或者财富有关。

⑦ **横向公平**所强调的一项重要原则是，那些在基本要素上均等的人，其纳税的额度也应该相同。

we should therefore pay equal taxes. Or if a tax system follows the ability-to-pay approach, horizontal equity dictates that people who have equal incomes should pay the same taxes.

A more controversial principle is **vertical equity,** ① which concerns the tax treatment of people with different levels of income. Abstract philosophical principles provide little guidance in resolving the issues of fairness here. Imagine that A and B are alike in every respect except that B has 10 times the property and income of A. Does that mean that B should pay the same absolute tax dollars as A for government services such as police protection? Or that B should pay the same percentage of income in taxes? Or, since the police spend more time protecting the property of well-to-do B, is it perhaps fair for B to pay a larger fraction of income in taxes?

Be warned that general and abstract principles cannot determine the tax structure for a nation. When Ronald Reagan campaigned for lower taxes, he did so because he thought high taxes were unfair to those who had worked hard and saved for the future. A decade later, Bill Clinton said, "We now have real [2] fairness in the tax code with over 80 percent of the new tax burden being borne by those who make over $200,000 a year." What looks fair to the goose seems ③ foul to the gander.

Horizontal equity is the principle that equals ④ should be treated equally. Vertical equity holds that people in unequal circumstances should be treated unequally and fairly, but there is no consensus on exactly how vertical equity should be applied.

税收的实用主义折中
Pragmatic Compromises in Taxation

How have societies resolved these thorny philosophical questions? Governments have generally adopted pragmatic solutions that are only partially based on benefit and ability-to-pay approaches. Political representatives know that taxes are highly unpopular. After all, the cry of "taxation with- ⑤ out representation" helped launch the American [6] Revolution. Modern tax systems are an uneasy compromise between lofty principles and political pragmatism. As the canny French finance minister Colbert wrote three centuries ago, "Raising [7] taxes is like plucking a goose: you want to get the maximum number of feathers with the minimum amount of hiss."

What practices have emerged? Often, public services primarily benefit recognizable groups, and those groups have no claim for special treatment by virtue of their average incomes or other characteristics. In such cases, modern governments generally rely on benefit taxes.

Thus, local roads are usually paid for by local residents. "User fees" are charged for water and sewage treatment, which are treated like private goods. Taxes collected on gasoline may be devoted (or "earmarked") to roads.

Progressive and Regressive Taxes. Benefit taxes are a declining fraction of government revenues. Today, advanced countries rely heavily on **progressive income taxes.** With progressive taxes, a family with $50,000 of income is taxed more than one with $20,000 of income. Not only does the higher-income family pay a larger income tax, but it in fact pays a higher fraction of its income.

This progressive tax is in contrast to a strictly **proportional tax,** in which all taxpayers pay exactly the same proportion of income. A **regressive tax** takes a larger fraction of income in taxes from poor families than it does from rich families.

A tax is called *proportional, progressive,* or *regressive* ⑧ depending on whether it takes from high-income people the same fraction of income, a larger fraction of income, or a smaller fraction of income than it takes from low-income people.

The different kinds of taxes are illustrated in Figure 16-4. What are some examples? A personal income tax that is graduated to take more and more out of each extra dollar of income is progressive. Economists have found, by contrast, that the cigarette tax is regressive. The reason is that the number of cigarettes purchased rises less rapidly than income. For example, some studies have determined that the income elasticity of cigarette use is around 0.6. This means that a 10 percent increase in income leads to a 6 percent increase in expenditures on cigarettes, and also to a 6 percent increase in cigarette taxes. Thus, high-income groups pay a smaller fraction of their income in cigarette taxes than do low-income groups.

Direct and Indirect Taxes. Taxes are classified as direct or indirect. **Indirect taxes** are ones that are levied on goods and services and thus only "indirectly"

⑤ 最终，还是“不让派代表，坚决不纳税”的呐喊引爆了美国革命。

[6] “taxation without representation” 最早被正式引用当追溯到1750年波士顿西部老教堂（Old West Church）的著名牧师马修（Jonathan Mayhew，1720~1766）所做的一次布道中，独立战争前后在最早独立的13个州中是家喻户晓的口号，克林顿、小布什等在竞选期间均多次引用这个口号与自己关于税收政策的施政目标相联系，原文应为“No taxation without representation”。

[7] 科尔伯特（Colbert，1619~1683），路易十四国王（1665~1683）的财政大臣。萨缪尔森在此引用的科尔伯特的这段话的原文为：“The art of taxation consists in so plucking the goose as to obtain the largest possible amount of feathers with the smallest possible amount of hissing.”

⑧ 被称为比例税、累进税和累退税的税种，分别依据高收入者的纳税额度占其收入的比例是等于、大于还是小于低收入者的纳税额度占其收入的比例。

① **纵向公平**是一项关于处理不同收入水平的人纳税问题的原则，这是一项颇具争议的原则。抽象的哲学原理在解决这里的公平性问题时几乎不能提供任何指导。

[2] 比尔·克林顿（Bill Clinton，1946~），美国第42任总统，任期1993~2001。其夫人希拉里·克林顿（Hillary Rodham Clinton，1947~）现任奥巴马政府国务卿。上任不久即通过《综合预算调整法，1993》（*Omnibus Budget Reconciliation Act of 1993*），为1500万低收入家庭和90%的小企业减税，提高了占总人口1.2%的最富裕的人的税赋，是其任期内重要的政绩之一，即这段话中所讲的超过80%的税收由年薪超过$200 000美元的人承担。

③ 配在雄鹅身上看上去很美的东西，配在雌鹅身上就会丑陋无比。“橘生淮南为橘，生于淮北则为枳”，即为此意。

④ 横向公平是平等的各方都应该享受到平等待遇的原则。纵向公平则强调的是经济状况不同的人，出于公平，所享受的待遇应该与其经济条件相匹配，但就纵向公平原则如何付诸实施的问题，始终没有达成共识。

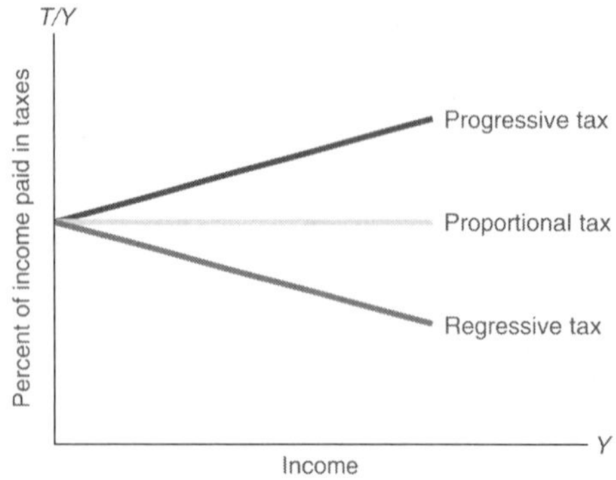

FIGURE 16-4. Progressive, Proportional, and Regressive Taxes ①

Taxes are progressive if they take a larger fraction of income as income rises; proportional if they are a constant fraction of income; and regressive if they place a larger relative burden on low-income families than on high-income families.

Federal Tax Receipts, Fiscal Year 2009

	Receipts (% of total)
Progressive:	
Individual income taxes	46.6
Estate and gift taxes	1.0
Corporate income taxes	12.6
Proportional:	
Payroll taxes	35.2
Regressive:	
Excise taxes	2.6
Customs duties	1.1
Other taxes and receipts	1.0
Total	**100.0**

TABLE 16-3. Income and Payroll Taxes Are the Main Federal Revenue Sources ③

Progressive taxes are still the leading source of federal revenues, but proportional payroll taxes are closing fast. Regressive consumption taxes have declined sharply at the federal level.

Source: See Table 16-2.

on individuals. Examples are excise and sales taxes, cigarette and gasoline taxes, tariffs on imports, and property taxes. By contrast, **direct taxes** are levied ② directly upon individuals or firms. Examples of direct taxes are personal income taxes, social security or other payroll taxes, and inheritance and gift taxes. Direct taxes have the advantage of being easier to tailor to fit personal circumstances, such as size of family, income, age, and more generally the ability to pay. By contrast, indirect taxes have the advantage of being easier to collect, since they can be levied at the retail or wholesale level.

联邦税
FEDERAL TAXATION

Let us now try to understand the principles by which the federal system of taxation is organized. Table 16-3 provides an overview of the major taxes collected by the federal government and shows whether they are progressive, proportional, or regressive.

个人所得税
The Individual Income Tax

Our discussion begins with the individual income tax, which is the most complex part of the tax system. The income tax is a direct tax, and it is the tax which most clearly reflects the ability-to-pay principle.

The individual income tax arrived late in our nation's history. The Constitution forbade any [4] direct tax that was not apportioned among the states according to population. This was changed in 1913, when the Sixteenth Amendment to the Constitu- [5] tion provided that "Congress shall have power to lay and collect taxes on income, from whatever source derived."

How does the federal income tax work? The principle is simple, although the forms are complicated. You start by calculating your income; you next subtract certain expenses, deductions, and exemptions to obtain taxable income. You then calculate your taxes on the basis of your taxable income.

Suppose you have just graduated from college and take a job in California with a salary of $60,000 in 2009. Table 16-4 shows a calculation of the total direct tax payments that you should expect. It will be worthwhile going line by line to understand the different items.

Line 1 begins with your salary. The first set of taxes is social insurance taxes. We will postpone our

① 图 16-4. 累进税、比例税和累退税

② 相比而言，各种**直接税**都是直接向个人或企业征收。直接税的例子如个人所得税、社会保障或者其他种类的工资税、遗产税和赠予税。

③ 表 16-3. 所得税和工资税是联邦税收的主要来源

[4] The Constitution：美国宪法，依据此宪法，美国建立了三权分立的立法、两院制的国会，以及总统领导的政府。

[5] The Sixteenth Amendment of the Constitution：宪法第 16 修正案。

1	Annual salary	$60,000
2	Social security taxes:	
3	Pension	3,720
4	Medicare	870
5	Federal adjusted gross income = (1)	60,000
6	Less:	
7	Personal exemption	3,500
8	Standard deduction	5,450
9	Federal taxable income = (5) − (7) − (8)	51,050
10	Income tax:	
11	Federal	9,106
12	State (California)	2,672
13	Total taxes = (3) + (4) + (11) + (12)	16,368
14	Income after tax = (1) − (13)	43,632
15	Tax rate	
16	Average = (13)/(1)	27.3%
17	Marginal*	42.0%

*Marginal tax rate is the additional total taxes per additional dollar of income. This would be calculated by repeating all the lines for an additional $1000 of income and then dividing the extra number of dollars of taxes by 1000.

TABLE 16-4. Calculation of Individual Income Taxes, 2009 ①

The table shows an illustrative calculation of total taxes for a single worker living in California in 2009. The worker has a total salary of $60,000. Social security taxes are for future social security benefits and pay health benefits for current retired workers. Income taxes are levied by the federal government and most states.

The average tax rate is 27.3 percent. Economists focus on the marginal tax rate, which is the additional tax per additional dollar of income. For our worker, the marginal tax rate is calculated to be 42 percent.

Source: Internal Revenue Service and State of California (preliminary tax tables).

discussion of these to the next section. Line 5 shows ② your *adjusted gross income*—that is, total wages, interest, dividends, and other income earned. If you were single, you would have a *personal exemption* of $3500. If you do not own a house, you are likely to take the *standard deduction* of $5450. Subtracting both of these yields your *federal taxable income* of $51,050.

Next, you go to the tax tables. These currently show a tax of $9106 on this income. You would also have taxes due to the state, $2672 in this case.

Adding up all the taxes, you find you owe $16,368. This represents 27.3 percent of your income. This ③ is called the **effective** or **average tax rate,** which is equal to total taxes divided by total income.

The last row introduces an important new concept. The **marginal tax rate** is the extra tax that is ④ paid per dollar of additional income. We have met the term "marginal" before, and it always means "extra." If you were to earn an additional $1000 of income, you would pay an additional $420 in taxes. This means that your marginal tax rate is $420/$1000, or 42 percent. The marginal tax rate is a critical tool for tax analysis because people and companies tend to respond to their marginal tax rates, not their average tax rates. Moreover, when marginal tax rates are extremely high, incentives to work are dulled and effort may significantly decrease.

The marginal tax rate is a central concept of tax ⑤ analysis. It refers to the extra tax paid per dollar of extra income and is particularly important for understanding the incentive effects of taxation.

Figure 16-5 shows the estimated marginal tax rate for households with incomes up to $100,000. Low-income households have a "negative income tax," because they receive an earned-income tax credit.

The notion of marginal tax rates is extremely important in modern economics. Remember the

② 第5行列出的是调整后的总收入，即全部工资、利息、红利，以及其他收入所得。如果此人单身，还应该有资格享受3 500美元的免税额度。如果此人还没有住房，那么就能按照扣除标准再享受5 450美元的免税。减去这两项之后，这个人联邦应纳税收入为51 050美元。

① 表16-4. 2009年个人所得税的计算

③ 这就是所称的**有效税率**，亦称**平均税率**，它等于总纳税额除以总收入的值。

④ **边际税率**是每多增加一美元的收入所额外缴纳的税额。“边际”一词我们之前已经作过讨论，始终表示“外加”的意思。如果一个人可以挣到一笔1 000美元的额外收入，他额外所应缴纳的税额是420美元。其含义为，这个人的边际税率是420美元除以1 000美元，即42%。

⑤ 边际税率是税收分析中的核心概念。它指的是，每一美元的额外收入所额外缴纳的税额，这一点对理解税收的激励作用至关重要。

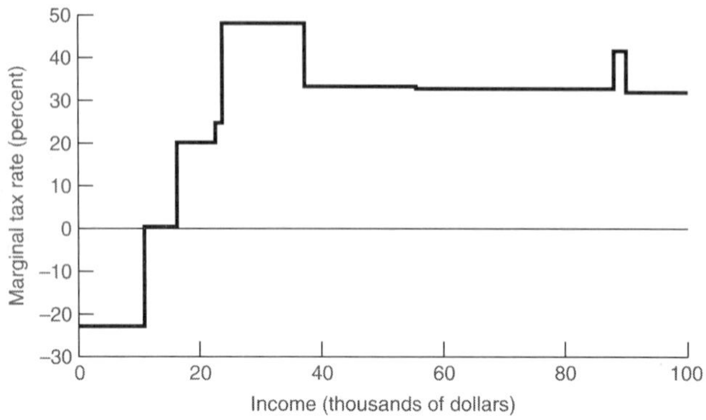

FIGURE 16-5. Marginal Tax Rate of U.S. Households by Income Category, 2005 ①

The marginal tax rate is the extra tax that is paid per dollar of additional income. The figure shows the estimated marginal tax rates of households in 2005. These include social insurance as well as federal and average state taxes. Because of the earned-income tax credit, low-income workers get a tax rebate—this is a "negative income tax" on wages. Note that the marginal tax rates in this figure differ from those in Table 16-4 because California has relatively high taxes and because the CBO uses different assumptions about exemptions and deductions.

Source: Congressional Budget Office, *Effective Marginal Tax Rates on Labor Income*, November 2005, available at *www.cbo.gov*.

marginal principle. People should be concerned only ② with the extra costs or benefits that occur. They should "let bygones be bygones." Under this principle, the major effect of any tax on incentives comes from the marginal tax rate.

The Flat Tax
统一税

Radical Tax Reform: The Flat Tax

The individual income tax is a powerful engine for raising revenues. But it has become enormously complex over the century since its introduction. Moreover, it is full of loopholes or "tax preferences" that provide benefits to particular forms of income or expenditure and even to individual groups of taxpayers. For example, expenditures on mortgage interest and medical care are deductible from income—they are, in effect, subsidized spending.

Economists have campaigned tirelessly for a more streamlined tax system—one that *broadens* the tax base, and thus raises revenues by eliminating unnecessary tax breaks, and can therefore *lower marginal tax rates*. One of the most radical and innovative proposals for fundamental tax reform is the *flat tax*, which was developed in detail by Stanford's Robert Hall and Alvin Rabushka.[1] Their proposal [3]
incorporates the following major features (see question 9 at the end of this chapter for an example):

- It taxes consumption rather than income. As we will discuss later in this chapter, taxing consumption serves to increase the incentive to save and can help boost the declining national savings rate.
- It integrates the corporate income tax with the individual income tax. This removes one of the major distortions in the U.S. tax code.
- It eliminates virtually all loopholes and tax preferences. Gone are subsidies for medical care, owner-occupied homes, and charitable contributions.
- It provides a basic exemption of around $20,000 per family and then imposes a constant marginal tax rate of 19 percent above that level.

The economic effects of a flat tax would be far-reaching. Heavily taxed entities such as corporations would find their taxes lowered and would experience a major capital

[1] *The Flat Tax*, rev. ed. Hoover Institute Press, Palo Alto, Calif., 2007.

① 图 16-5. 2005 年度美国家庭税种的边际税率

② 边际税率是当代经济学中极其重要的概念，一定要牢记边际原则。人们应该只关心所发生的新增成本或者新增收益即可。过去的事就尽可能地让它成为过去。牢记这一原则，任何激励性税收的主要作用都可以从边际税率上体现出来。

let bygones be bygones：尽可能让过去的事真正成为过去。

[3] 罗伯特·霍尔（Robert Hall），斯坦福大学胡佛研究院高级研究员，应用经济学教授，2010 年刚刚当选美国经济学会理事长（President of the American Economic Association）。

阿尔温·拉布什卡（Alvin Rabushka），斯坦福大学胡佛研究院高级研究员，研究领域涵盖美国及全球税制，环太平洋国家、以色列和中东转型国家的经济发展等。《统一税》（*The Flat Tax: Hoover Institution Press*）是霍尔及其同事合作的力作。

gain. High-income wage earners would find their taxes cut in half. At the same time, the amount of owner-occupied housing and medical expenditures would shrink and charitable giving would drop sharply.

Hall and Rabushka emphasize above all the importance of reducing the marginal tax rates. They argue that the flat tax would "give an enormous boost to the U.S. economy by dramatically improving incentives to work, save, invest, and take entrepreneurial risks. The flat tax would save taxpayers hundreds of billions in direct and indirect compliance costs."

The plan's critics point out that it would lead to a major redistribution of income to high-income people at the expense of low- and middle-income households. The losers will question whether the rich, whose share has risen dramatically over the last three decades, deserve yet another windfall. We see here yet another example of the tradeoff between fairness and efficiency that runs through many of the most controversial economic policy issues.

社会保险税
Social Insurance Taxes

Virtually all industries now come under the Social Security Act. Workers receive retirement benefits that depend on their earnings history and past social security taxes. The social insurance program also funds a disability program and health insurance for the poor and elderly.

To pay for these benefits, employees and employers are charged a *payroll tax*. As shown in Table 16-4, in 2008, this consisted of a total of 15.3 percent of all wage income below a ceiling of $102,000 a year per person, along with a payroll tax of 2.9 percent of annual wage income above $102,000. The tax is split equally between employer and employee.

Table 16-3 shows the payroll tax as a proportional tax because it taxes a fixed fraction of employment earnings. The tax incidence is more complicated, however, because the payroll tax includes only labor earnings (which makes it regressive) and finances retirement most generously for low-income people (which makes it progressive).

公司税
Corporation Taxes

The federal government collects a wide variety of other taxes, some of which are shown in Table 16-3. The *corporate income tax* is a tax on the profits of corporations.

The corporation income tax has been heavily criticized by some economists. Critics oppose the tax, arguing that corporations are but legal fictions and should not be taxed. By taxing first corporate ③
profits and then the dividends paid by corporations
① and received by individuals, the government subjects corporations to double taxation.

消费税
Consumption Taxes

While the United States relies heavily on income taxes, a radically different approach is consumption
② taxes, which are taxes on purchases of goods and services rather than on income. The rationale is that people should be penalized for what they *use* rather than what they *produce*. Sales taxes are the most familiar example of consumption taxes. The United States has no national sales tax, although there are a number of *federal excise taxes* on specific commodities such as cigarettes, alcohol, and gasoline. Sales and excise taxes are generally regressive because they consume a larger fraction of the income of poor families than of high-income families.

Many have argued that the United States should rely more heavily on sales or consumption taxes. One tax, widely used outside the United States, is the *value-added tax,* or VAT. The VAT is like a sales tax, but ④
it collects taxes at each stage of production. Thus, if a VAT were levied on bread, it would be collected from the farmer for wheat production, from the miller for flour production, from the baker at the dough stage, and from the grocer at the delivered-loaf stage.

The advocates of consumption taxes argue that the country is currently saving and investing less than is necessary for future needs and that by substituting consumption taxes for income taxes, the national savings rate would increase. Critics of consumption taxes respond that such a change is undesirable because sales taxes are more regressive than today's income tax. The *flat tax,* discussed earlier, is actually equivalent to a highly simplified system of personal consumption taxation (see question 9 below).

州和地方税
STATE AND LOCAL TAXES

Under the U.S. system of fiscal federalism, state and local governments rely on a very different set of taxes than does the federal government. Figure 16-6 illustrates the main sources of funds that finance state and local expenditures.

---

① 他们强调，统一税通过改善就业、储蓄、投资，以及企业的风险承担能力，从而大大推进美国经济的发展。统一税直接和间接地考虑了纳税人的纳税成本，从而为纳税人节约了亿万美元。

② 对此方案持批评态度的人指出，统一税的开征有可能以中低收入家庭为高收入家庭埋单的形式，导致大量收入的再次分配。

③ 通过首先对公司利润征税，然后分别向公司派发和个人股东所接收的红利分别征税，政府实际上是向公司进行了双重课税。

④ VAT，即 *value-added tax*：增值税。

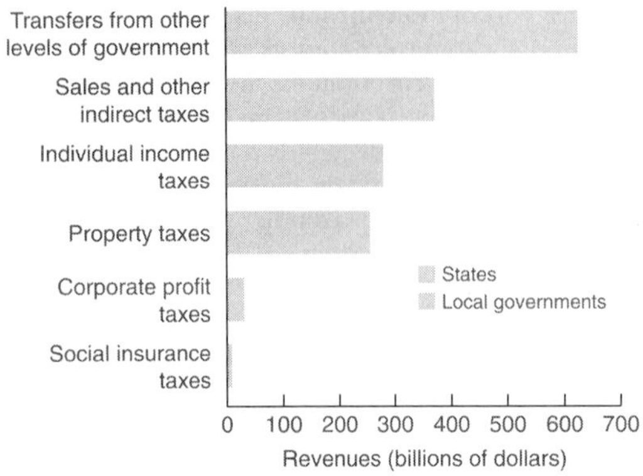

FIGURE 16-6. States and Localities Rely on Transfers and Indirect Taxes ①

Cities rely heavily on property taxes because houses and land cannot easily flee to the suburbs to avoid a city's tax. States get most revenues from sales and income taxes.

Source: Bureau of Economic Analysis.

财产税
Property Tax

The *property tax* is levied primarily on real estate—land and buildings. Each locality sets an annual tax rate which is levied on the assessed value of the land and structures. In many localities, the assessed value may be much smaller than the true market value. The property tax accounts for about 30 percent of the total revenues of state and local finance. Figure 16-6 shows that localities are the main recipient of property taxes.

Because about one-fourth of property values are from land, the property tax has elements of a capital tax and elements of a Henry George–type land tax. [2] Economists believe that the land component of the property tax has little distortion, while the capital component will drive investment from high-tax central cities out to the low-tax suburbs.

其他税收
Other Taxes

Most other state and local taxes are closely related to the analogous federal taxes. States get most of their ③ revenues from *general sales taxes* on goods and services. Each purchase at the department store or restaurant incurs a percentage tax (food and other necessities are exempt in some states). States tax the net income of corporations. Forty-three states imitate the federal government, on a much smaller scale, by taxing individuals according to the size of their incomes.

There are other miscellaneous revenues. Many ④ states levy "highway user taxes" on gasoline. A growing source of revenue is lotteries and legalized gambling, in which the states benefit from encouraging people to impoverish themselves.

税收体系的效率和公平
EFFICIENCY AND FAIRNESS IN THE TAX SYSTEM

有效税收的目标
The Goal of Efficient Taxation

In recent years, economists have focused increasingly ⑤ on the efficiency of different tax systems. The first point to recall here is that efficiency depends primarily on the marginal tax rates faced by taxpayers. Look back at Figure 16-5 to recall how the marginal tax rates differ across income groups.

Taxes on Labor Income. How do high marginal tax rates affect economic behavior? In the area of labor supply, the impacts are mixed. As we saw in Chap- ⑥ ter 13, the impact of tax rates on hours worked is unclear because the income and substitution effects of wage changes work in opposite directions. As a result of progressive taxes, some people may choose more leisure over more work. Other people may work harder in order to make their millions. Many high-income doctors, artists, celebrities, and business executives, who enjoy their jobs and the sense of power or accomplishment that they bring, will work as hard for $800,000 after tax as for $1,000,000 after tax.

Figure 16-7 shows how an increase in the tax rate on labor will affect labor supply; note the paradox that hours worked may actually decline after a tax-rate cut if the labor supply curve is backward-bending.

Taxes on Capital Income. In the area of saving and investment, taxes are likely to have major effects on amounts supplied and efficiency. When taxes are high in one sector, resources will flow into more lightly taxed areas. For example, because corporate profits are double-taxed, people's savings will flow out of the corporate sector and into lightly taxed sectors. If risky investments are taxed unfavorably, investors may prefer safer investments.

Impacts of Globalization. With increased openness of economies, countries need to ensure that mobile factors of production like capital or highly skilled workers are not lured away to low-tax countries. This

[2] Henry George-type land tax：亨利·乔治型土地税，即著名的“单一土地税”（single tax on land）。亨利·乔治（Henry George，1839~1897），美国作家、政治家和政治经济学家，是对“土地价值税”即“单一土地税”最具影响力的经济学家和政治家。经济学家们确信，财产税中有关土地内容的部分几乎不存在任何曲解，而关于资本的部分必将促使投资从高税收的中心城市撤出，并向低税收的郊区转移。

---

① 图 16-6. 各州和各地方政府对转移支付和间接税的依赖

③ 各州政府的绝大部分收入来自对商品和服务征收的一般销售税。

④ 各州政府还有其他各种各样的收入来源。许多州依赖于附加在燃油上的“高速公路使用税”。

⑤ 近年来，经济学家们已经把注意力越来越多地关注于不同税制的效率问题。这里所要特别提醒的第一点是，效率首先是依赖于纳税人所直接面对的边际税率。

⑥ 正如在第 13 章中所讨论的问题，我们尚不明白各种税率对工时有何影响，因为收入以及工资变化产生的替代影响总在相反的方向起作用。

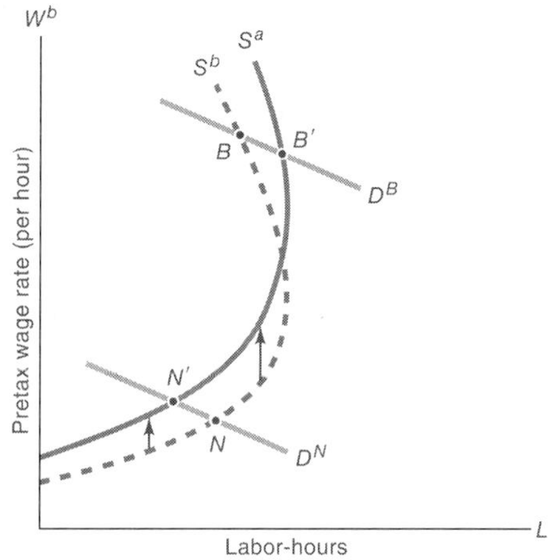

FIGURE 16-7. Response of Work to Taxes Depends on Shape of Supply Curve ①

Supply and demand plots labor supplied against pretax wage. Before-tax supply curve of labor (S^b) shifts vertically upward to after-tax supply (S^a) after imposition of a 25 percent income tax on labor earnings. If demand for labor intersects supply in the normal region at bottom, we see an expected decline in labor supplied from N to N'. If the labor supply is backward-bending, as at top, the labor supplied actually rises with the tax increase, going from B to B'.

concern is particularly important for company taxes, for companies can easily move their headquarters to some island tax haven.

效率和公平

Efficiency vs. Fairness

Economists have long been concerned with the impact of taxes on economic efficiency. Recall from Chapter 14 that Henry George argued that a tax on land will have little impact on efficiency because the supply of land is completely inelastic. The modern theory of efficient taxation puts forth the *Ramsey tax* [2] *rule*, which states that the government should levy the heaviest taxes on those inputs and outputs that are most price-inelastic in supply or demand.[2] The ratio- ③ nale for the Ramsey tax rule is that if a commodity is very price-inelastic in supply or demand, a tax on the commodity will have little impact upon consumption and production. In some circumstances, Ramsey taxes may constitute a way of raising revenues with a minimum loss of economic efficiency.

But economies and politics do not run on efficiency alone. While stiff taxation of land rents or food might be efficient, many would think them unfair. A sober reminder of the dilemma was the proposal to introduce a poll tax in Britain in 1990. A *poll tax* is a *lump-sum tax*, or a fixed tax per person. The advantage [4] of this tax is that, like a land tax, it would induce no inefficiencies. After all, people are unlikely to decamp to Russia or commit hari-kari to avoid the tax, so the economic distortions would arguably be minimal.

Alas, the British government underestimated the extent to which the populace felt this tax to be unfair. The poll tax is highly regressive because it places a much higher proportional burden on low-income people than on high-income people. Criticism of the poll tax played a key role in bringing down the Thatcher government after 11 years in power. This illustrates clearly the difficult choice between efficiency and fairness in taxes and other areas of economic policy.

Taxing "Bads" rather than "Goods": Green Taxes

While economists have rarely advocated ⑤ poll taxes, they have favored an approach wherein the tax system would weigh more heavily on "bads" than on "goods." The main source of inefficiency is that taxes generally tax "goods"—economic activities like working, investing in capital, saving, or taking risk—and thereby discourage these activities. An alternative approach is to tax "bads." Traditional taxes on bads include "sin taxes": taxes on alcohol, cigarettes, and other substances that have harmful health effects.

A new approach to taxation is to tax pollution and other undesirable externalities; such taxes are called *green taxes* because they are designed to help the environment as well as to raise revenues. Say that the nation decides to help slow global warming by levying a "carbon tax," which is a tax on carbon-dioxide emissions from power plants and other sources. By standard economic reasoning we know that the tax will lead firms to lower their carbon-dioxide emissions, thereby improving the environment. In addition, this green tax will provide revenues, which the government can use either to finance its activities or to reduce

[2] Recall Chapter 14's discussion of Henry George's single tax and the extension to efficient or Ramsey taxes.

① 图 16-7. 劳动对各种税收的反应取决于供给曲线的形状

[2] *Ramsey*：弗兰克·拉姆齐（Frank Ramsey，1903~1930），著名的英国数学家，27 岁时因患严重的黄疸英年早逝。24 岁发表拉姆齐法则，开创了最优商品税领域研究的先河。

③ 拉姆齐税收法则的基本原理是，如果一种产品在供给或者需求上缺乏价格弹性，那么对该种产品征税几乎对消费和生产没有任何影响。

[4] *Lump-sum tax*：也叫 Poll tax，一种“定额税”，即无论纳税实体的情况发生何种变化，其纳税总额保持不变。这种税收的优点在于，它像土地税一样，不会带来任何低效率。毕竟，人们不太可能拔营撤寨逃往俄罗斯，也不可能切腹自尽以逃避纳税，所以，其对经济产生的负面影响虽然有待证明，但应该是最低的。

⑤ 经济学家们始终很少鼓吹征收人头税，他们所钟情的是一种税收系统，在这种系统中，可以对“劣品”而非“益品”课以重税。

tax rates on beneficial activities like working or saving. So green taxes are doubly effective: the state gets revenue, and the environment is improved because the taxes discourage harmful externalities.

最后的话 FINAL WORD

Our introductory survey of government's role in the economy is a sobering reminder of the responsibilities and shortcomings of collective action. On the one hand, governments must defend their borders, stabilize their economies, protect the public health, and regulate pollution. On the other hand, policies often reflect primarily the attempt to redistribute income from consumers to politically powerful interest groups.

Does this mean we should abandon the visible hand of government for the invisible hand of markets? Economics cannot answer such deep political questions. But economics can examine the strengths ① and weaknesses of both collective and market choices, and point to mechanisms (such as green taxes or subsidies to research and development) by which a mended invisible hand may be more efficient and fair than the extremes of either pure laissez-faire or unbridled bureaucratic rulemaking.

SUMMARY

A. Government Control of the Economy

1. The economic role of government has increased sharply over the last century. The government influences and controls private economic activity by using taxes, expenditures, and direct regulation.
2. A modern welfare state performs four economic functions: (*a*) It remedies market failures; (*b*) it redistributes income and resources; (*c*) it establishes fiscal and monetary policies to stabilize the business cycle and promote long-term economic growth; and (*d*) it manages international economic affairs.
3. Public-choice theory analyzes how governments actually behave. Just as the invisible hand can break down, so there are government failures, in which government interventions lead to waste or redistribute income in an undesirable fashion.

B. Government Expenditures

4. The American system of public finance is one of fiscal federalism. The federal government concentrates its spending on issues of national concern—on national public goods like defense and space exploration. States and localities generally focus on local public goods—those whose benefits are largely confined within state or city boundaries.
5. Government spending and taxation today take approximately one-third of total national output. Of this total, about 55 percent is spent at the federal level, and the balance is divided between state and local governments. Only a small fraction of government outlays is devoted to traditional functions like police and the courts.

C. Economic Aspects of Taxation

6. Notions of "benefits" and "ability to pay" are two principal theories of taxation. A tax is progressive, proportional, or regressive as it takes a larger, equal, or smaller fraction of income from rich families than it does from poor families. Direct and progressive taxes on incomes are in contrast to indirect and regressive sales and excise taxes.
7. More than half of federal revenues come from personal and corporate income taxes. The rest comes from taxes on payrolls or consumption goods. Local governments raise most of their revenue from property taxes, while sales taxes are most important for states.
8. The individual income tax is levied on "income from whatever source derived," less certain exemptions and deductions. The marginal tax rate, denoting the fraction paid in taxes for every dollar of additional income, is the key to determining the impact of taxes on incentives to work and save.
9. The fastest-growing federal tax is the payroll tax, used to finance social security. This is an "earmarked" levy, with funds going to provide public pensions and health and disability benefits. Because there are visible benefits at the end of the stream of payments, the payroll tax has elements of a benefit tax.
10. Economists point to the Ramsey tax rule, which emphasizes that efficiency will be promoted when taxes are levied more heavily on those activities that are relatively price-inelastic. A new approach is green taxes, which levy fees on environmental externalities, reducing harmful activities while raising revenues that would otherwise be imposed on goods or productive inputs. But in all taxes, equity and political acceptability are severe constraints.

① 经济学无法回答如此深奥的政治问题。但是，经济学能够探讨集体选择和市场选择的优缺点，并指明合适的机制（比如绿色税收，或者研究开发的资助经费）应该是一种经过修正的“看不见的手”。这样的机制比起纯粹的自由市场环境，或者不受约束的由官僚制定游戏规则的机制会更为有效和公平。

CONCEPTS FOR REVIEW

Functions of Government

three tools of government economic control:
- taxes
- expenditures
- regulation

market failures vs. government failures
public-choice theory

four functions of government:
- efficiency
- distribution
- stabilization
- international representation

Government Expenditures and Taxation

fiscal federalism and local vs. national public goods
economic impact of government spending
benefit and ability-to-pay principles
horizontal and vertical equity
direct and indirect taxes
entitlement programs
progressive, proportional, and regressive taxes
Ramsey and green taxes

FURTHER READING AND INTERNET WEBSITES

Further Reading

An excellent review of tax issues is contained in the symposium on tax reform in *Journal of Economic Perspectives*, Summer 1987. The classic study of the flat tax referred to in the text is also online, at *www.hoover.org/publications/books/3602666.html*.

Websites

Data on government budget and tax trends can be found at government sites. For example, overall trends are presented by the Bureau of Economic Analysis at *www.bea.gov*. Budget information for the federal government comes from the Office of Management and Budget at *www.whitehouse.gov/omb*.

The Internal Revenue Service (IRS) has a lively site with a plethora of tax statistics at *www.irs.gov* and *www.irs.gov/taxstats/index.html*.

Two organizations which study taxation and have good websites are the National Tax Association at *www.ntanet.org* and the Brookings Institution at *www.brookings.org*. Policy papers by a British research institute that focuses on social security and taxation can be found at *www.ifs.org.uk*.

QUESTIONS FOR DISCUSSION

1. Recall Justice Oliver Wendell Holmes's statement, "Taxes are what we pay for a civilized society." Interpret this statement, remembering that in economics we always need to pierce the veil of monetary flows to understand the flow of real resources.
2. In considering whether you want a pure laissez-faire economy or government regulation, discuss whether there should be government controls over prostitution, addictive drugs, heart transplants, assault weapons, and alcohol. Discuss the relative advantages of high taxes and prohibition for such goods (recall the discussion of drug prohibition in Chapter 5).
3. Critics of the U.S. tax system argue that it harms incentives to work, save, and innovate and therefore reduces long-run economic growth. Can you see why "green taxes" might promote economic efficiency and economic growth? Consider, for example, taxes on sulfur or carbon-dioxide emissions or on leaky oil tankers. Construct a list of taxes that you think would increase efficiency, and compare their effects with the effects of taxes on labor or capital income.
4. Tax economists often speak of lump-sum taxes, which are levied on individuals without regard to their economic activity. Lump-sum taxes are efficient because they impose zero marginal tax rates on all inputs and outputs.

   Assume that the government imposes a lump-sum tax of $200 on each individual. Show the effect of this on the supply and demand for labor in a graph. Does the marginal revenue product of labor still equal the wage in equilibrium?

In a lifetime framework, the dynamic equivalent of a lump-sum tax is an "endowment tax," which would tax individuals on the basis of their potential labor incomes. Would you favor such a change? Describe some of the difficulties in implementing an endowment tax.

5. Make a list of different federal taxes in order of their progressiveness. If the federal government were to trade in income taxes for consumption or sales taxes, what would be the effect in terms of overall progressiveness of the tax system?
6. Some public goods are local, spilling out to residents of small areas; others are national, benefiting an entire nation; some are global, affecting all nations. A private good is one whose spillover is negligible. Give some examples of purely private goods and of local, national, and global public goods or externalities. For each, indicate the level of government that could design relevant policies most efficiently, and suggest one or two appropriate government actions that could solve the externality.
7. Recall from our discussion of tax incidence that the incidence of a tax refers to its ultimate economic burden and to its total effect on prices, outputs, and other economic magnitudes. Below are some incidence questions that can be answered using supply and demand. Use graphs to explain your answers.
   a. In the 1993 Budget Act, Congress raised federal gasoline taxes by 4.3 cents a gallon. Assuming the wholesale price of gasoline is determined in world markets, what is the relative impact of the tax on American producers and consumers?
   b. Social insurance taxes are generally levied on labor earnings. What is their incidence if labor supply is perfectly inelastic? If labor supply is backward-bending?
   c. Assume that firms must earn a given post-tax rate of return on investment, where the return is determined in world capital markets. What is the incidence of a tax on corporate income in a small open economy?
8. An interesting question involves the *Laffer curve*, named for California economist and sometime senatorial candidate Arthur Laffer. In Figure 16-8, the Laffer curve shows how revenues rise as *tax rates* are increased, reach a maximum at point *L*, and then decline to zero at a 100 percent tax rate as activity is completely discouraged. The exact shape of the Laffer curve for different taxes is highly controversial.

   A common mistake in discussing taxes is the post hoc fallacy (see Chapter 1's discussion of this). Proponents of lower taxes often invoke the Laffer curve in their arguments. They point to tax cuts of the 1960s to suggest that the economy is to the right of the peak of Mt. Laffer, say, at *B*. They say, in effect, "After the Kennedy-Johnson tax cuts of 1964, federal revenues actually rose from $110 billion in 1963 to $133 billion in 1966. Therefore, cutting taxes raises revenues." Explain why this does not prove that the economy was to the right of *L*. Further explain why this is an example of the post hoc fallacy. Give a correct analysis.

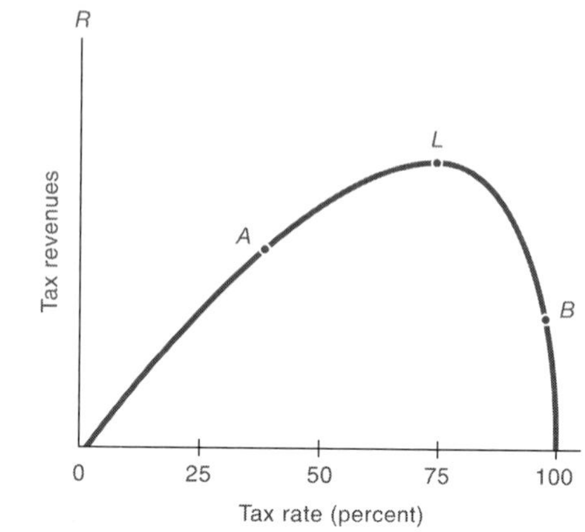

FIGURE 16-8. The Laffer Curve

9. Under the flat tax, all personal and corporate income is taxed only once at a low fixed rate. Table 16-5 shows how such a flat tax might work. Compare the average and marginal tax rates of the flat tax with the tax schedule shown in Table 16-4 in the text. List advantages and disadvantages of both. Which is more progressive?

(1) Adjusted gross income ($)	(2) Deductions and exemptions ($)	(3) Taxable income ($)	(4) Individual income tax ($)
5,000	20,000	0	0
10,000	20,000	0	0
20,000	20,000	0	0
50,000	20,000	30,000	6,000
100,000	20,000	80,000	16,000
1,000,000	20,000	980,000	196,000

TABLE 16-5.

CHAPTER

17

Efficiency vs. Equality: The Big Tradeoff
效率与公平的平衡

[1] 阿瑟·奥肯（Arthur Okun，1928~1980），美国经济学家，1961 年之后长期担任肯尼迪和约翰逊两任总统的经济顾问委员会委员，1968 年被任命为该委员会主席。奥肯对于经济学的突出贡献是分析了失业率与 GNP 之间的线性变化关系，总结出了著名的《奥肯定理》（*Okun's Law*），即失业率每下降 1%，实际 GNP 将上升 3%。奥肯的研究是基于从二战开始至 1960 年间美国政府公布的详细的官方统计数据分析出来的，尤其在失业率居于 3%~7.5% 时更为准确。本段话出自布热津斯研究院于 1975 年出版的奥肯的经典著作《公平与效率，重大的抉择》（*Equality and Efficiency, the Big Tradeoff*; The Brookings Institute, 1975）第一章《美元与权利》（Chapter One：Rights and Dollars）第二页。译文如下：

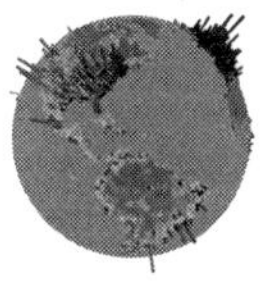

[The conflict] between equality and efficiency [is] our biggest socioeconomic tradeoff, and it plagues us in dozens of dimensions of social policy. We can't have our cake of market efficiency and share it equally.

Arthur Okun (1975) [1]

公平与效率之间的矛盾，是社会经济学中最大的需要平衡的问题，在社会政策的广域范围内始终在困扰着我们，使我们既不能高效率地生产市场这块蛋糕，更无法公平地将它予以分配。

——阿瑟·奥肯（1975）

② About a century ago, many Western governments began to intervene in the marketplace and introduce a social safety net as a bulwark against socialist pressures—this new conception of society was called the "welfare state." Attitudes toward the welfare state evolved gradually into the mixed market economy found today in the democracies of Europe and North America. In these countries, the market is responsible for production and pricing of most goods and services, while governments manage the economy and provide a safety net for the poor, unemployed, and aged.

One of the most controversial aspects of government policy involves policies toward the poor. Should families have guaranteed incomes? Or perhaps just minimum levels of food, shelter, and health care? Should taxation be progressive, redistributing incomes from the rich to the poor? Or should taxation be aimed primarily at promoting economic growth and efficiency?

Surprisingly, these questions have been just as contentious as societies have become richer. You might think that as a country becomes more prosperous, it would devote a larger share of its income to programs helping the needy at home and abroad. This has not always proved to be the case. As tax burdens have risen over the last half-century, tax revolts have sparked reductions in tax rates. People are also increasingly aware that attempts to equalize incomes can harm incentives and efficiency. Today, people ask: How much of the economic pie must be sacrificed in order to divide it more equally? How should we redesign income-support programs to retain the objective of reducing want and inequality without bankrupting the nation?

The purpose of this chapter is to examine the distribution of income along with the dilemmas of policies designed to reduce inequality. These issues are among the most controversial economic questions of today. Remember the first chapter suggestion that ③
economics best serves the public interest in using cool heads to inform warm hearts. This chapter surveys the trends in inequality and the relative merits of different approaches and indicates how cool-headed economic analysis can help promote both fairness and continued growth of the mixed economy.

不平等的根源

A. THE SOURCES OF INEQUALITY

To measure the inequality of control over economic resources, we need to concern ourselves with both income and wealth differences. Recall that by **personal**

② 大约在一个世纪以前，许多西方国家的政府开始对市场进行干预，并且推行网络化的社会安全体系作为屏障来应对来自社会主义国家的压力，这种崭新的社会概念就是所谓的“福利国家”。

③ 必须牢牢记住第 1 章中所讲的：经济学是最能用冷静的头脑和满腔热忱为公共利益服务的。在本章中，将对不同方法的相对优势和各种不公平的倾向进行综合分析，指出冷静的经济学分析是如何使混合型的经济体从公平和持续增长两个方面发挥助力和推动作用的。

income we mean the total receipts or cash earned by ① a person or household during a given time period (usually a year). The major components of personal income are labor earnings, property income (such as rents, interest, and dividends), and government transfer payments. **Disposable personal income** con- ② sists of personal income less any taxes paid. **Wealth** or "net worth" consists of the dollar value of financial and tangible assets minus the amount of money owed to banks and other creditors. You can refresh your memory about the major sources of income and wealth by reviewing Tables 12-1 and 12-2 (look at pages 230 and 232).

收入和财富的分配
THE DISTRIBUTION OF INCOME AND WEALTH

Statistics show that in 2006 the median income of American families was $48,200—this means that half of all families received less than this figure while half received more. This number concerns the *distribution of income*, which shows the variability or dispersion of incomes. To understand the income distribution, consider the following experiment: Suppose one person from each household writes down the yearly income of his or her household on an index card. We can then sort these cards into *income classes*. Some of the cards go into the lowest 20 percent, the group with an average income of $11,551. Some go into the next class. A few go into the top 5 percent of households, those with an average income of $362,514.

The actual income distribution of American households in 2006 is shown in Table 17-1. Column (1) shows the different income-class fifths, or quintiles, plus the top 5 percent of households. Column (2) shows the average income in each income class. Column (3) shows the percentage of the households in each income class, while column (4) shows the percentage of total national income that goes to the households in an income class.

Table 17-1 enables us to see at a glance the wide range of incomes in the U.S. economy. Half of the population makes less than $50,000 per year. As you move up the distribution, the number of people gets smaller and smaller. If we made an income pyramid out of building blocks, with each layer portraying $500 of income, the peak would be far higher than Mount Everest, but most people would be within a few feet of the ground.

如何在收入等级间计量不平等程度
How to Measure Inequality among Income Classes

How can we measure the degree of income inequality? At one pole, if incomes were absolutely equally distributed, there would be no difference between the lowest 20 percent and the highest 20 percent of the population: each quintile would receive exactly 20 percent of the nation's income. That's what absolute equality means.

The reality is very different. In 2006, the lowest fifth, with 20 percent of the households, earned less than 4 percent of the total income. Meanwhile the

(1) Income class of households	(2) Average	(3) Percentage of all households in this class	(4) Percentage of total income received by households in this class
Lowest fifth	$11,551	20	3.4
Second fifth	$29,442	20	8.7
Third fifth	$49,968	20	14.8
Fourth fifth	$79,111	20	23.4
Highest fifth	$169,971	20	49.7
Top 5 percent	$362,514	5	21.2

TABLE 17-1. **Distribution of Money Incomes of American Households, 2006** ③

How was total income distributed among households in 2006? We group households into the fifth (or quintile) with the lowest income, the fifth with the second-lowest income, and so on.

Source: U.S. Bureau of the Census, Current Population Report, *Income, Poverty, and Health Insurance Coverage in the United States: 2007*, available at *www.census.gov/hhes/www/income/income.html*.

---

① 我们所指的**个人收入**是一个人或者一个家庭在给定的时间段（通常为一年）内所挣的全部现金或票证收入。

② **个人可支配收入**的构成是个人收入减去所有缴纳的税赋之后的余额。**财富**或"净价值"则由金融与有形资产之和减去所欠银行和其他信用机构的总额之后以美元为单位的价值。

③ 表 17-1. 2006 年美国家庭货币收入的分布情况

situation is reversed for the top 5 percent of households, which get 21 percent of the income.

We can show the degree of inequality in a diagram ① known as the **Lorenz curve,** a widely used device for analyzing income and wealth inequality. Figure 17-1 is a Lorenz curve showing the amount of inequality listed in the columns of Table 17-2; that is, it contrasts the patterns of (1) absolute equality, (2) absolute inequality, and (3) actual 2006 American inequality.

Absolute equality is depicted by the numbers in column (4) of Table 17-2. When they are plotted, these become the diagonal 45° dashed green line of Figure 17-1's Lorenz diagram.

At the other extreme, we have the hypothetical case of absolute inequality, where one person has all the income. Absolute inequality is shown in column (5) of Table 17-2 and by the lowest curve on the Lorenz diagram—the dashed, right-angled blue line.

Any actual income distribution, such as that for 2006, will fall between the extremes of absolute equality and absolute inequality. The green-colored column (6) in Table 17-2 presents the data derived from the first two columns in a form suitable for plotting as an actual Lorenz curve. This actual Lorenz curve appears in Figure 17-1 as the solid green intermediate curve. The shaded area indicates the deviation from absolute equality, hence giving us a measure of the degree of inequality of income distribution.

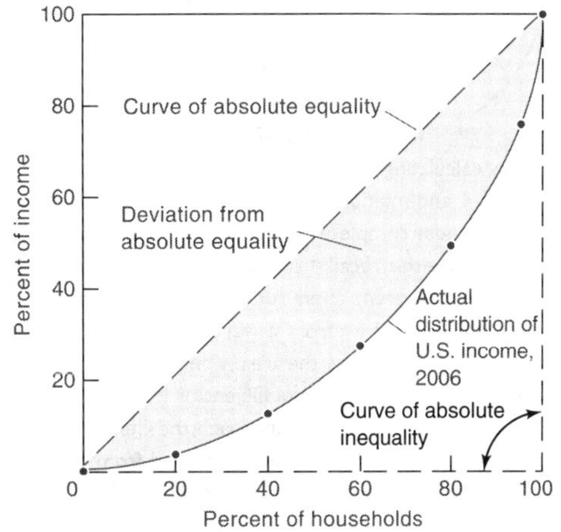

FIGURE 17-1. Lorenz Curve Shows Income Inequality ②

By plotting the figures from Table 17-2's column (6), we ③ see that the solid green actual-distribution-of-income curve lies between the two extremes of absolute equality and absolute inequality. The shaded area of this Lorenz curve (as a percentage of the triangle's area) measures the relative inequality of income. (How would the curve have looked back in the roaring 1920s when inequality was greater? In an egalitarian Utopia where all have equal inheritances and opportunities?)

(1) Income class of households	(2) Percentage of total income received by households in this class	(3) Percentage of households in this class and lower ones	(4) Percentage of Income Received by This Class and Lower Ones: Absolute equality	(5) Absolute inequality	(6) Actual distribution
Lowest fifth	3.4	20	**20**	**0**	3.4
Second fifth	8.7	40	**40**	**0**	12.1
Third fifth	14.8	60	**60**	**0**	26.9
Fourth fifth	23.4	80	**80**	**0**	50.3
Highest fifth	49.7	100	**100**	**100**	100.0

TABLE 17-2. Actual and Polar Cases of Inequality ④

By cumulating the income shares of each quintile shown in column (2), we can compare in column (6) the actual distribution with polar extremes of complete inequality and equality.

Source: Table 19-1.

① 我们可以将不公平的程度用著名的**洛伦兹曲线**来表示，该曲线广泛应用于收入和财富不公平状况的分析中。

② 图 17-1. 洛伦兹曲线所表示的收入不公平情况

③ 我们将表 17-2 中第 6 列的数据绘入本图就可以连成一条介于绝对公平和绝对不公平之间的实际收入分布曲线的灰色线。图中我们所看到的洛伦兹曲线的阴影部分（即三角形面积的百分位数）测量出的是收入的相对不公平状况。（在不公平现象更为严重的 20 世纪 20 年代，我们回过头去看当时动荡的社会，能绘出一条怎样的曲线？在所有人都享有同样的遗产和机会的人人平等的乌托邦社会又会是怎样？）

④ 表 17-2. 实际情况与不公平的极端案例

The Gini Coefficient

Economists often need to calculate quantitative measures of inequality. One useful measure is the *Gini coefficient*. This is measured by calculating the shaded area in the Lorenz curve of Figure 17-1 and multiplying it by 2. The Gini coefficient is equal to 1 under complete inequality and 0 under complete equality. To see this, recall that a society with equal incomes would have the Lorenz curve run along the 45° line, so the shaded area would be zero. Conversely, when the Lorenz curve runs along the axes, the area is one-half, which, when multiplied by 2, gives a Gini coefficient of 1.

Using the Gini coefficient approach, the Census Bureau calculates that inequality was little changed from 1967 to 1980 (the Gini coefficient rose from .399 to .403) but then rose steadily from 1980 to 2006 (from .403 to .469).

President T. Roosevelt
老罗斯福总统

财富的分配
Distribution of Wealth

One major source of the inequality of income is inequality of ownership of *wealth*, which is the net ownership of financial claims and tangible property. Those who are fabulously wealthy—whether because of inheritance, skill, or luck—enjoy incomes far above ②

② 那些拥有巨额财富的人，无论他们的财富是由于继承遗产、过人的技能还是运气等原因，对收入的享有程度远高于那些一般家庭的收入总额。而那些没有财富的人每天都得面对捉襟见肘的收入难题。

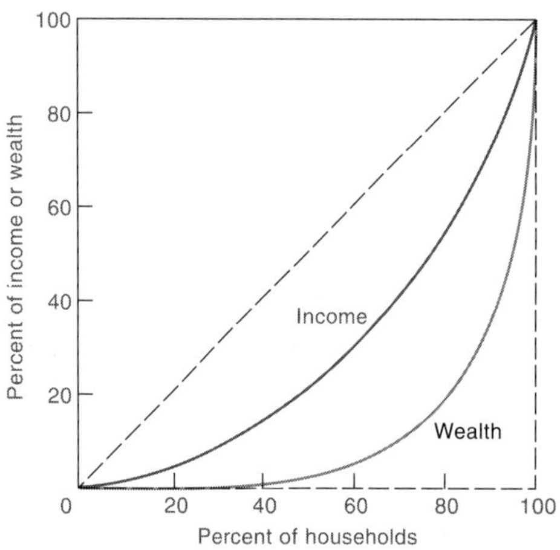

FIGURE 17-2. Inequality of Wealth Is Greater Than for Income ③

Holdings of wealth tend to be more concentrated than annual incomes.

Source: For income, see Table 17-1. Source for wealth is Federal Reserve Board, *Survey of Consumer Finances, 2004*, available at *www.federalreserve.gov/Pubs/oss/oss2/2004/scf2004home_modify.html.*

③ 图 17-2. 财富分布的不公平远大于收入分配的不公

④ 在市场经济中，财富分布不公平的情况远大于收入分配的不公。

the amount earned by the average household. Those
[1] without wealth begin with an income handicap.

In market economies, wealth is much more ④ unequally distributed than is income, as Figure 17-2 shows. In the United States, the top 10 percent of households in 2004 owned 70 percent of wealth, and the top 1 percent of the households owned around 35 percent of all wealth.

Societies are ambivalent about large wealth holdings. A century ago, President T. Roosevelt criticized "malefactors of great wealth" and introduced sharply progressive income and inheritance taxes. A century later, conservatives attempted to abolish all inheritance and gift taxes, labeling them as "death taxes."

国家间的不平等
Inequality across Countries

Countries show quite different income distributions depending upon their economic and social structures. Table 17-3 shows the inequality of different countries as measured by the ratio of the income of

	Ratio of income of top 10% to income of bottom 10%
Japan	4.5
Czech Republic	5.2
Sweden	6.2
Germany	6.9
The Republic of Korea	7.8
France	9.0
Spain	9.0
Canada	10.0
Italy	11.7
Australia	12.7
United Kingdom	13.6
United States	15.7
South Africa	31.9
Argentina	38.9
Brazil	67.0
Namibia	129.0

TABLE 17-3. Comparative Inequality in Different Countries ⑤

This shows the ratio of the income of the top 10 percent of the population to the income of the bottom 10 percent. Inequality differs greatly across countries. Japan and Western Europe have the least inequality, while South American countries show the greatest.

Source: World Bank, *World Development Indicators*, 2005, available at *devdata.worldbank.org/wdi2005/index2.htm.*

[1] Gini Coefficient：基尼系数，是意大利经济学家基尼（Corrado Gini，1884~1965）根据洛伦茨曲线所定义的判断收入分配公平程度的指标于 1922 年提出的，数值在 0 和 1 之间，是国际上用来综合考察居民内部收入分配差异状况的一个重要分析指标。按照联合国有关组织规定：低于 0.2 表示收入绝对平均；0.2~0.3 表示比较平均；0.3~0.4 表示相对合理；0.4~0.5 表示收入差距较大；0.5 以上表示收入差距悬殊。通常把 0.4 作为收入分配差距的“警戒线”，根据黄金分割律，其准确值应为 0.382。一般发达国家在 0.24 到 0.36 之间，美国偏高，为 0.4。中国大陆基尼系数在 2010 年超过 0.5，比 2004 年国家统计局公布的 0.47 又高出 0.03。

⑤ 表 17-3. 不同国家不公平情况比较

the top 10 percent to that of the bottom 10 percent of the income distribution. Market-oriented countries like the United States tend to have the most unequal income distributions among the high-income countries. The welfare states of western Europe tend to have the least inequality. The sources of high inequality in the United States are discussed later in this chapter.

The experience of developing countries shows an interesting relationship. Inequality begins to rise as countries begin to industrialize, after which inequality then declines. The greatest extremes of inequality occur in middle-income countries, particularly Latin American countries like Brazil and Argentina.

美国的贫穷问题
POVERTY IN AMERICA

"You will always have the poor with you," accord- [1]
ing to the Scriptures. Poverty is indeed an enduring concern in the United States and in the wider world. Before we can analyze antipoverty programs, we must examine the definition of poverty.

Scriptures 指《圣经》

The Elusive Concept of Poverty

The word "poverty" means different things to different people. Clearly, poverty is a condition in which people have inadequate incomes, but it is hard to draw an exact line between the poor and the nonpoor. Economists have therefore devised certain techniques which provide the official definition of poverty.

Poverty was officially defined in the 1960s in the United States as an income insufficient to buy basic food, clothing, shelter, and other necessities. This was calculated from family budgets and double-checked by examining the fraction of incomes that was spent on food. Since that time, the poverty budget has been updated by the government's consumer price index to reflect changes in the cost of living. According to the standard definition, the subsistence cost of living for a family of four was $21,200 in 2008. This figure represents the "poverty line" or demarcation between poor and nonpoor families. The poverty line also varies by family size.

While an exact figure for measuring poverty is helpful, scholars recognize that "poverty" is a relative term. The notion of a subsistence budget includes subjective questions of taste and social convention. Housing that is today considered substandard often includes household appliances and plumbing that were unavailable to the millionaires and robber barons of an earlier age.

Because of shortcomings in the current definition, a panel of experts of the National Academy of Sciences recommended that the definition of poverty be changed to reflect *relative-income status*. The panel recommended that a family be considered poor if its consumption is less than 50 percent of the median family's consumption of food, clothing, and housing. Poverty in the relative-income sense would decline when inequality decreased; poverty would be unchanged if the economy prospered with no change
in the distribution of income and consumption. In this ②
new world, a rising tide would lift all boats but not change the fraction of the population considered poor. This new approach is being weighed carefully by the government.

谁是穷人
Who Are the Poor?

Poverty hits some groups harder than others. Table 17-4 shows the incidence of poverty in different groups for 2006. Whites have lower poverty rates than blacks and Hispanics. The elderly no longer have above-average poverty.

Poverty in Major Groups, 2006

Population group	Percentage of group in poverty
Total population	12.3
By racial and ethnic group:	
White (non-Hispanic)	8.2
Black	24.3
Hispanic	20.6
By age:	
Under 18 years	17.4
18 to 64 years	10.8
65 years and over	9.4
By type of family:	
Married couple	5.7
Female householder, no husband present	30.5
Male householder, no wife present	13.8

TABLE 17-4. Incidence of Poverty in Different Groups, 2006 ③

Whites and married couples have lower-than-average poverty rates. Blacks, Hispanics, and female-headed households have above-average poverty rates.

Source: U.S. Bureau of the Census, *Poverty in the United States: 2006*, CPS 2007 Annual Social and Economic Supplement, downloaded from *pubdb3.census.gov/macro/032007/pov/toc.htm*.

[1] "You will always have the poor with you," 出自新约圣经开篇《圣马修》, 第 26 章 11 款, 原文为:

For ye have the poor always with you; but me ye have not always. (The Holy Bible, King James Version, 即《钦定圣经》)

权威的《钦定圣经》1611 年出版, 属于早期现代英文,个别地方仍留有中世纪英文的痕迹。此处"ye"是主格, 单数主格的 "you" 为 "thou", 单数宾格的 "you" 为 "thee"。现代英语版本 (Today' s English Version) 的 *Good News Bible* (United Bible Societies, 1976) 翻译的现代英语为: You will always have poor people with you, but you will not always have me.

② 在这个新的社会环境中, 发展的大潮也会让所有的船只水涨船高, 但却无法改变人口中被认为是穷人的存在。这一新的举措正在政府的天平中小心翼翼地增加砝码。

③ 表 17-4. 2006 年不同人群中的贫困发生率

Perhaps the most troubling trend is that single-parent families headed by women are an increasingly large share of the poor population. In 1959, about 18 percent of poor families were headed by women raising children alone. By 2006, the poverty rate of that group was 30 percent. Social scientists worry that children in single-parent families will receive inadequate nutrition and education and will find it difficult to escape from poverty when they are adults.

Why are so many female-headed and minority families poor? What is the role of discrimination? Experienced observers conclude that blatant racial or gender discrimination in which firms simply pay minorities or women less is vanishing today. Yet the relative poverty of women and blacks continues at a high rate. How can we reconcile these two apparently contradictory trends? The major factor at work is the increasing gap between earnings of highly educated and skilled workers and those of unskilled and less educated workers. Over the last 25 years, the wage differential between these two groups has grown sharply. The growing wage gap has hit minority groups particularly hard.

谁是富人
Who Are the Rich?

At the other extreme are the high earners. Many of the top earners get primarily *property income,* which consists of income on assets like stocks, bonds, and real estate. A generation ago, many of the richest Americans got their wealth through inheritances. Today, entrepreneurship is a much more important road to riches. Most of the richest people in America got that way by taking risks and creating profitable new businesses, such as computer software companies, television networks, and retail chains. The people who invented new products or services or organized the companies that brought them to market got rich on the "Schumpeterian profits" from these innovations. This group of wealthy individuals includes folk heroes like Bill Gates (head of software [1] giant Microsoft), the Waltons (founders of Wal-Mart), [2] and Warren Buffett (investment guru). In an earlier [3] era, the rich lived on stocks, bonds, and land rents.

[2] 沃顿家族（The Waltons）。Samuel Moore Walton，或 Sam Walton（1918~1992），沃尔玛和山姆巨型连锁超市的创始人，与其七个孩子一道，在大萧条时期和随后的第二次世界大战期间，开创了家族的奇迹至今。

Another major change among top earners is that wages (including proprietorships) today account for 85 percent of the income of the top 1 percent, whereas that share was only about 50 percent at the beginning of the twentieth century. The high earners are increasingly working in finance and business. What single profession makes the most money? In recent years, it has been investment bankers and specialists working in financial markets. The average earnings in the securities industry in 2006 was $206,000 for all workers, and the top managers and analysts make many times that amount.

Why are there such vast differences in compensation among jobs? Some of the differences come from investments in human capital, such as the years of training needed to become a top doctor. Abilities also play a role, for example, in limiting jobs in finance to those who have a deep appreciation of the decimal point. Some jobs pay more because they are dangerous or unpleasant (recall the discussion of compensating differentials in Chapter 13). Moreover, when the supply of labor is limited in an occupation (say, because of union restrictions or professional licensing rules), the supply restrictions drive up the wages and salaries of that occupation.

不平等的变化趋势
Trends in Inequality

The inequality of income in the United States has gone through a complete cycle over the last century. The history of inequality in the United States is shown in Figure 17-3. This shows the ratio of the incomes received by the top fifth of families to those received by the bottom fifth. We can see three distinct periods: falling inequality until World War II, stable shares until the 1970s, and then rising inequality over the last three decades. We see that the ratio of upper- to lower-group incomes has almost doubled. Also, examine the income shares of the four top groups, shown in Figure 17-4. The most striking trend is the very top 0.1 percent of the income pyramid. The 133 thousand families in that group had an average income of $6.3 million in 2006.

Diminishing Inequality. Inequality peaked in 1929 and then declined sharply in the Great Depression [4] as stock prices reduced capital income of the upper groups. The long postwar boom brought prosperity to the middle-class workers, and the share of top income groups declined to its trough in the late 1960s. The share of total income going to the poorest fifth of families rose from 3.8 percent to about 5 percent between 1929 and 1975.

Why did inequality narrow over this period? Inequality declined in part because of the narrowing of wage inequality. With increasing education of

---

[1] 比尔·盖茨（Bill Gates，1955~），美国企业家、软件工程师、慈善家、微软公司董事长。详见 p256 注[2]。

[3] 沃伦·巴菲特（Warren Buffett，1930~），美国投资家、企业家、慈善家。详见 p256 注 [3]。

[4] The Great Depression：指上世纪30年代的大萧条时期，萨翁在 17 版的前言中将上世纪的前 50 年用它来定义（笔者译为"危机四伏时期"），后 50 年则相应地定义为"伟大的和平时期"（the Great Peace）。这是迄今为止国际学术界对上世纪 100 年符合"长波论"的科学断代，但在此后的 18 版即予删除（见本书前言部分笔者对此的注疏内容）。因此，本书的 17 版在学术上由于这个断代说和对美国网络经济泡沫破灭（2001 年 3 月正式出版）的反思，更有其独特的价值所在。有关论文详见笔者《中国英语教育改革探思录》（现代教育出版社，2009.5）一书。

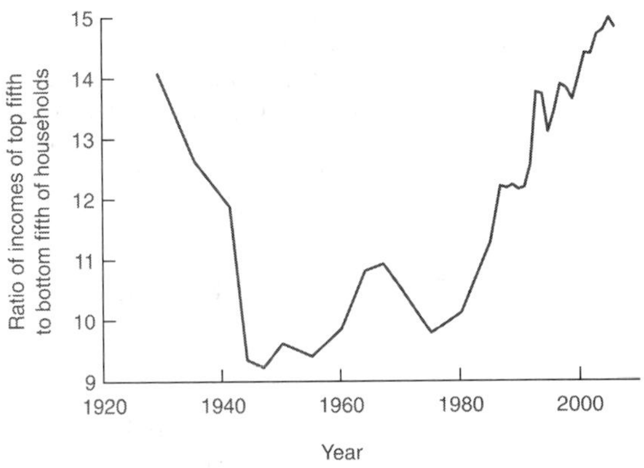

FIGURE 17-3. Trends in Inequality in the United States, 1929–2006 ①

A useful measure of inequality is the ratio of the incomes of the top fifth of the population to those of the bottom fifth. The share of top incomes declined after 1929 with the stock market collapse of the 1930s, the low unemployment and reduced barriers to women and minorities during World War II, and the migration from the farm to the city. Since 1980, income inequality has grown sharply with higher immigration and decline of wages of the unskilled. ②

Source: U.S. Bureau of the Census, with historical series spliced together by authors.

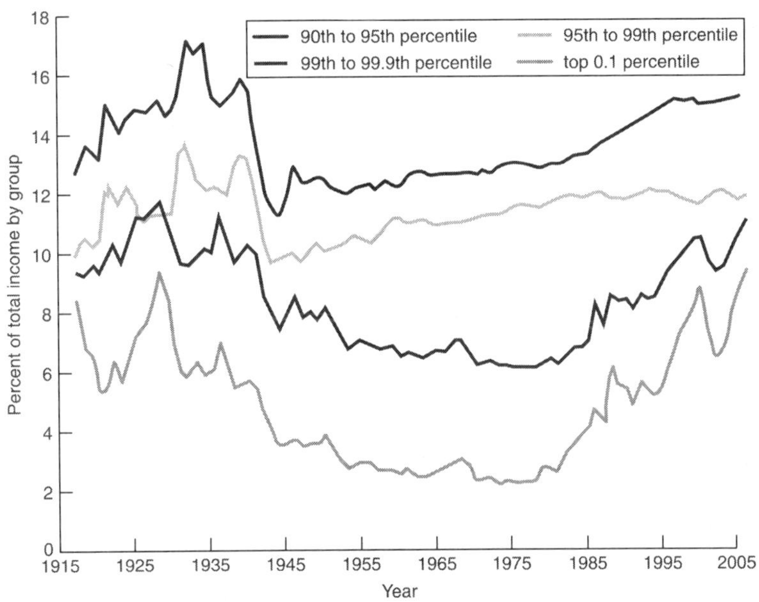

FIGURE 17-4. Income Shares of Top Income Groups, United States, 1917–2006 ③

Inequality fell over most of the twentieth century and then began to rise around 1970. The most dramatic gains were in the very top group—the top 0.1 percent of households. Their share rose from 2 percent of income in 1975 to over 9 percent in the latest year. ④

Source: The methods were developed in Thomas Piketty and Emmanuel Saez, "Income Inequality in the United States, 1913–1998," *Quarterly Journal of Economics*, 2003. The data here are from their update of March 2008, downloaded from *elsa.berkeley.edu/~saez/*.

① 图 17-3. 1929~2006 年美国不公平情况的走势

② 对不公平现象非常有用的测评数据是收入最高的前五类人群的收入总额与收入最低的后五类人群的收入总额的比值。

③ 图 17-4. 1917~2006 年美国最富有的人群的收入份额走势

④ 在 20 世纪的大部分时间不公平情况在下降，然后从 1970 年左右开始上升。最具戏剧性的受益者竟然是处于全美家庭总数最顶端仅占 0.1% 的最富有的家庭。他们在全民总收入中所占比例从 1975 年的 2% 一路攀升到最近几年的 9%。

lower-income groups and unionization of the workforce, the wage gap declined. Government policies ①
like social security made a big difference for the elderly population, while programs like cash assistance and food stamps for the indigent and unemployment insurance boosted the incomes of other low-income groups. Our progressive income-tax system, which taxed high incomes more heavily than low incomes, tended to reduce the degree of inequality.

Widening Gaps. In the last quarter-century, several of these trends have reversed themselves. The share of total income going to the bottom quintile declined sharply in the 1980s, sinking from 5.4 percent in 1975 to 3.4 percent in 2006. Average real incomes for families in the bottom fifth are well below their peak. Although the incomes of the poor stagnated during the last quarter-century, the share of income going to the richest Americans soared.

Why did inequality rise in recent decades? After years of intensive debate on this question, a tentative verdict has been proposed in a recent survey by Robert J. Gordon and Ian Dew-Becker. Their con- [2]
clusions are:

- Virtually none of the rising inequality came from changes in the overall share of labor in national income. That share has been virtually unchanged since 1970.
- The decline of trade unions contributed slightly to increased inequality for men.
- The impact of foreign trade on relative wages appears minimal, while immigration appears to have adversely affected foreign-born workers who are close "substitutes" for immigrants.
- Technological change appears primarily to have depressed the relative wages of the middle-income groups while boosting the incomes of complementary highly skilled workers and having little effect on unskilled service-sector workers.
- The very top of the income distribution has increased its share sharply because of three phenomena. First, the pay of superstars has risen as technology has increased the audience of athletes and entertainers. Second, the incomes of top professionals, particularly in finance, have increased with the increased globalization of the U.S. economy. Third, they endorse the idea that the separation of ownership from control has allowed "the outsized gains in CEO pay."

This concludes our description of the measurement and sources of inequality. In the next section, we turn to an analysis of government programs to combat poverty and reduce inequality. High-income ③
democracies everywhere are rethinking these programs as they redefine the role of the state.

反贫穷政策

B. ANTIPOVERTY POLICIES

All societies take steps to provide for their poor citizens. But what is given to the poor must come from other groups, and that is undoubtedly the major point of resistance to redistributive programs. In addition, economists worry about the impact of redistribution upon the efficiency and morale of a country. In this section, we review the rise of the welfare state, consider the costs of income redistribution, and survey the current system of income maintenance.

福利国家的崛起
The Rise of the Welfare State

The early classical economists believed the distribution of income was unalterable. They argued that ④
attempts to alleviate poverty by government interventions in the economy were foolish endeavors that would simply end up reducing total national income. This view was contested by the English economist and philosopher John Stuart Mill. While cautioning [5]
against interferences with the market mechanism, he argued eloquently that government policies could reduce inequality.

A half-century later, at the end of the nineteenth century, political leaders in Western Europe took steps that marked a historic turning point in the economic role of government. Bismarck in Germany, [6]
Gladstone and Disraeli in Britain, followed by [7]
Franklin Roosevelt in the United States introduced a new concept of government responsibility for the welfare of the populace.

This marked the rise of the **welfare state,** in which ⑧
government takes steps to protect individuals against specified contingencies and to guarantee people a minimum standard of living.

Important welfare-state programs include public pensions, accident and sickness insurance, unemployment insurance, health insurance, food and housing

① 诸如社会保障这样的政府政策，已使老年人的生活大获改观；与此同时，给那些贫困人口和领取失业保险的人发放现金补助和食物券的措施也使其他低收入群体的收入得以增加。

[2] 罗伯特·戈登（Robert J. Gordon），美国西北大学社会学教授，出生于经济学家世家，父母和兄长都是著名的经济学家。其关于生产力、增长、失业和航空经济学等经济问题的著作享有盛名。伊恩·迪尤－贝克尔（Ian Dew-Becker），哈佛大学经济学院在读博士，著名的青年经济学者，关于不公平、生产力、失业、通货膨胀等经济热点问题的著述颇丰。

③ 每一个高收入的民主国家在它们重新定义国家的角色时，都需要对这些政策加以反思。

④ 他们强调，在该经济中，政府试图减轻贫困的任何举措，只不过是有可能以降低国民总收入为结局的愚蠢行为。

[5] 约翰·斯图尔特·米尔（John Stuart Mill，1806~1873），著名的英国哲学家和经济学家，19世纪极具影响力的古典自由主义思想家。详见p149注[1]。

[6] 奥托·冯·俾斯麦（Otto Von Bismarck，1815~1898），普鲁士宰相兼外交大臣、"铁血宰相"，普鲁士德国容克资产阶级最著名的政治家和外交家，"自上而下统一德国"（踢出奥地利）的代表人物。

[7] 威廉·尤尔特·格兰德斯通（William Ewart Gladstone，1809~1898），英国自由派政治家，在长达60年之久的政治生涯中，曾四次出任首相（1868~1874, 1880~1885, 1886年2~7月，以及1892~1894），四次出任财政大臣（1853~1855、1859~1866、1873~1874和1880~1882）。在最后一次任首相期间，80多岁高龄的格兰德斯通虽然听力和视力均老年性衰退，但依然精力充沛，创下英国历史之最。
本杰明·迪斯雷利（Benjamin Disraeli，1804~1881），犹太裔英国保守派政治家，在英国政府供职长达30年之久，两次出任首相（1868年2月~12月，1874~1880），在英国当代保守党的创建过程中扮演了极其重要的吹鼓手的角色，是英国历史上第一位也是迄今仅有的一位犹太裔首相。

⑧ 这一点标志着**福利国家**的兴起。在这些国家中，政府采取各种措施来保护公民免受各种特殊的意外事故，以保证人们的最低生活标准。

programs, family allowances, and income supplements for certain groups of people. These policies were introduced gradually from 1880 through to the modern era. The welfare state came late to the United States, being introduced in the New Deal of the 1930s with [1] unemployment insurance and social security. Medical care for the aged and the poor was added in the 1960s. In 1996 the federal government turned back the clock by removing the guarantee of a minimum income. The debate over redistribution never ends.

再分配的成本
THE COSTS OF REDISTRIBUTION

One of the goals of a modern mixed economy is to provide a safety net for those who are temporarily or permanently unable to provide adequate incomes for themselves. One reason for these policies is to promote greater equality.

What are the different concepts of equality? To begin with, democratic societies affirm the principle of equality of *political rights*—generally including the right to vote, the right to trial by jury, and the right to free speech and association. In the 1960s, liberal philosophers espoused the view that people should also have equal *economic opportunity*. In other words, all people should play by the same rules on a level playing field. All should have equal access to the best schools, training, and jobs. Then discrimination on the basis of race or gender or religion would disappear. Many steps were taken to promote greater [2] equality, but inequalities of opportunity have proved very stubborn.

A third, and the most far-reaching, ideal is equality of *economic outcomes*. In this utopia, people would have the same consumption whether they were smart or dull, eager or lazy, lucky or unfortunate. Wages would be the same for doctor and nurse, lawyer and secretary. "From each according to his abilities, to each according to his needs" was Karl Marx's formulation of this philosophy.

Today, even the most radical socialist recognizes [3] that some differences in economic outcome are necessary if the economy is to function efficiently. Without some differential reward for different kinds of work, how can we ensure that people will do the unpleasant as well as the enjoyable work, that they will work on dangerous offshore oil derricks as well as in beautiful parks? Insisting on equality of outcomes would severely hamper the functioning of the economy.

The Leaky Bucket

In taking steps to redistribute income from the rich to the poor, governments may harm economic efficiency and reduce the amount of national income available to distribute. On the other hand, if equality is a social good, it is one worth paying for.

The question of how much we are willing to pay in reduced efficiency for greater equity was addressed by Arthur Okun in his "leaky bucket" experiment. He noted that if we value equality, we would approve when a dollar is taken in a bucket from the very rich and given to the very poor. But, he continued, suppose the bucket of redistribution has a leak in it. Suppose only a fraction—maybe only one-half—of each dollar paid by the rich in taxes actually reaches the poor. Then redistribution in the name of equity has been at the expense of economic efficiency.[1]

Okun presented a fundamental dilemma. Redistributional measures like the progressive income tax, analyzed in Chapter 16, will reduce real output by reducing incentives to work and save. As a nation considers its income-distribution policies, it will want to weigh the benefit of greater equality against the impact of these policies on total national income.

再分配成本的图形分析
Redistribution Costs in Diagrams

We can illustrate Okun's point by using the income-possibility curve of Figure 17-5. This graph shows the incomes available to different groups when government programs redistribute income.

We begin by dividing the population in half; the real income of the lower half is measured on the vertical axis of Figure 17-5, while the income of the upper half is measured on the horizontal axis. At point *A*, which is the pre-redistribution point, no taxes are levied and no transfers are given, so people simply live with their market incomes. In a competitive economy, point *A* will be efficient and the no-redistribution policy maximizes total national income.

However, at laissez-faire point *A*, the upper-income group receives substantially more income than the lower half. People might strive for greater equality by tax and transfer programs, hoping to move toward the point of equal incomes at *E*. If such

[1] Arthur M. Okun, *Equality and Efficiency: The Big Tradeoff* (Brookings Institution, Washington, D.C., 1975).

[1] New Deal：罗斯福新政，特指 1933~1938 年在罗斯福总统的第一任期内，经国会通过，为应对大萧条而采取的一系列刺激经济的措施，即历史学家们称之为"3Rs"的"救济"（relief）、"复兴"（recovery）和"改革"（reform）。

[2] 尽管政府采取了多种措施来推进公平，但机会的种种不公平始终是非常难以撼动的。

[3] 今天，即便是最为激进的社会主义者也认识到，如果要使该国的经济有效地运行，那么探索一些不同的经济出路是必要的。

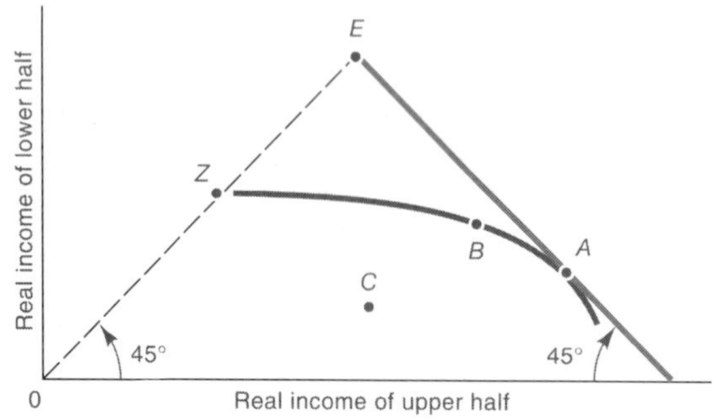

FIGURE 17-5. Redistributing Income May Harm Economic Efficiency ①

Point A marks the most efficient outcome, with maximal national output. If society could redistribute with no loss ② of efficiency, the economy would move toward point E. Because redistributive programs generally create distortions and efficiency losses, the path of redistribution might move along the green line ABZ. Society must ③ decide how much efficiency to sacrifice to gain greater equality. Why would everyone want to avoid redistributional programs that take the economy from point B to point C?

steps could be taken without reducing national output, the economy would move along the blue line from A toward E. The slope of the AE line is –45°, reflecting the assumption about efficiency that the redistributive bucket has no leaks, so every dollar taken from the upper half increases the income of the lower half by exactly \$1. Along the –45° line, total national income is constant, indicating that redistributional programs have no impact upon the total national income.

Most redistributive programs do affect efficiency. If a country redistributes income by imposing high tax rates on the wealthiest people, their saving and work effort may be reduced or misdirected, with a resulting lower total national output. They may spend more money on tax lawyers or invest less in high-yielding but risky innovations. Also, if society puts a guaranteed floor beneath the incomes of the poor, the sting of poverty will be reduced and the poor may work less. All these reactions to redistributive programs reduce the total size of real national income.

In terms of Okun's experiment, we might find that for every \$100 of taxation on the rich, the income of the poor increased by only \$50, with the rest dissipated because of reduced effort or administrative costs. The bucket of redistribution has developed a leak. Costly redistribution is shown by the ABZ curve in Figure 17-5. Here, the hypothetical frontier of real incomes bends away from the –45° line because taxes and transfers produce inefficiencies.

The experience of countries exemplifi es how attempts to equalize incomes by expropriating property from the rich can end up hurting everyone. By prohibiting private ownership of businesses, socialist governments reduced the inequalities that arise from large property incomes. But the reduced incentives for work, investment, and innovation crippled this radical experiment of "to each according to his needs" and impoverished entire countries. By 1990, comparisons of living standards in East and West had convinced many socialist countries that private ownership of business would benefit the living standards of workers as well as capitalists.

漏洞有多大
How Big Are the Leaks?

Okun characterized our redistributive system of taxes and transfers as a leaky bucket. But just how big are the leaks in the American economy? Is the country closer to Figure 17-5's point A, where the leaks are negligible? Or to B, where they are substantial? Or to Z, where the redistributive bucket is in fact a sieve? To find the answer, we must examine the major inefficiencies induced by high tax rates and by generous income-support programs: administrative costs, damage to work and saving incentives, and socioeconomic costs.

- The government must hire tax collectors to raise revenues and social security accountants to disburse them. These are clear inefficiencies or regrettable necessities, but they are small: the Internal Revenue Service spends only half a [4] penny on administrative costs for each dollar of collected revenues.
- As the tax collector's bite grows larger and larger, might I not become discouraged and end up working less? Tax rates might conceivably be so high that total revenues are actually lower

① 图 17-5. 收入再分配对经济效率的损害

② 如果社会有可能在不牺牲效率的同时进行再分配，则经济就会移向 E 点。

③ 社会必须决定要牺牲更少效率才能获得更大的公平。为什么每一个人都试图避免使经济从 E 点掉到 C 点的再分配计划呢？

[4] Internal Revenue Service：美国国内收入署，负责收缴税收和税法的强制执行。

than they would be at more modest tax rates. Empirical evidence, however, suggests that the damage of taxes on work effort is limited. For ① a few groups, the labor supply curve may actually be backward-bending, indicating that a tax on wages might increase rather than decrease work effort. Most studies find that taxes have only a small impact on labor effort for middle-income and high-income workers. However, there may well be substantial impacts of the tax and transfer system on the behavior of poor people.

- Perhaps the most important potential leakage from the revenue bucket is the savings component. Some believe that current government programs discourage saving and investment. Some economic studies indicate that by taxing income rather than consumption, total saving is reduced. Additionally, economists worry that the nation's saving rate has declined sharply because of generous social programs—especially social security and Medicare—that reduce the need for people to save for old age and health contingencies.
- Some claim that the leaks cannot be found in ② the cost statistics of the economist; instead, the costs of equality are seen in attitudes rather than in dollars. Are people so turned off by the prospect of high taxes that they turn on to drugs and idleness? Is the welfare system leading to a permanent underclass, a society of people who are trapped in a culture of dependency?
- Some people criticize the entire notion of costly redistribution, arguing as follows: Poverty is rooted in malnourishment in the early years, broken families, illiteracy at home, poor education, and lack of job training. Poverty begets poverty; the vicious cycle of malnutrition, poor education, drug dependency, low productivity, and low incomes leads to yet another generation of poor families. These analysts contend that enhanced programs to provide health care and adequate food for poor families will increase productivity and efficiency rather than decrease output. By breaking the vicious cycle of poverty ③ today, we will be raising the skills, human capital, and productivity of the children of poverty tomorrow.

把所有的漏洞加总

Adding Up the Leaks

When all the leaks are added up, how big are they? Okun argued that the leaks are small, particularly when funds for redistributive programs are drawn from the tap of a broad-based income tax. Others disagree strenuously, pointing to high marginal tax rates and overly generous transfer programs as confusing and destructive of economic efficiency.

What is the reality? While much research has been undertaken on the cost of redistribution, the truth has proved elusive. A cautious verdict is that there are but modest losses to economic efficiency from redistributional programs of the kind used in the United States today. For many people, the efficiency costs of redistribution are a reasonable price to pay for reducing the economic and human costs of poverty in malnutrition, poor health, lost job skills, and human misery. But countries whose welfare-state policies have gone far beyond those in the United States see major inefficiencies. Egalitarian countries like Sweden and the Netherlands, which provided cradle-to-grave protection for their citizens, found declining labor-force participation, growing unemployment, and rising budget deficits. These countries have taken steps to reduce the burden of the welfare state.

Countries need to design their policies carefully to avoid the extremes of unacceptable inequality or great inefficiency.

反贫穷政策：计划与批评
ANTIPOVERTY POLICIES: PROGRAMS AND CRITICISMS

All societies provide for their aged, their young, and their sick. Sometimes, the support comes from families or religious organizations. Over most of the last century, central governments have increasingly assumed the responsibility for providing income support for the poor and needy. Yet, as governments have assumed larger responsibilities for more people, the fiscal burdens of transfer programs have grown steadily. Today, most high-income countries face ④ the prospect of rising tax burdens to finance health and retirement programs as well as income-support programs for poor families. This rising tax burden has provoked a sharp backlash against "welfare programs," particularly in the United States. Let's review the major antipoverty programs and recent reforms.

---

① 对很多群体来讲，劳动供给的曲线实质上是向后弯曲的，这表明，对工资征税有可能增加而不是降低劳动的努力程度。

② 有些人断言，经济学家们在成本统计的过程中绝不可能发现这些漏洞。相反，公平的成本所体现的是态度问题，而不是金钱问题。

③ 今天，我们只有通过打破贫穷的恶性循环，才能在明天提高劳动技能、增加人力资本，以及提高处于贫困中的孩子们的生产率。

④ 今天，绝大多数高收入国家都面临着增加税收，以为医疗保健、退休金以及对贫困家庭实施收入资助计划募集资金。

收入保障计划
Income-Security Programs

What are the major income-security programs today? Let's look briefly at a few of the programs that have been established in the United States.

Most income-security programs are targeted at the elderly rather than the poor. The major programs are social security, which is a contributory federal retirement program, and Medicare, which is a subsidized health program for those over 65 years old. These two programs are the largest transfer programs in the United States and in most other high-income countries.

Programs specifically targeted to poor households are a patchwork quilt of federal, state, and local programs. Some of these are cash assistance. Others subsidize particular goods or services, such as the food-stamps program or Medicaid, which provides poor families with free health care. Most of the programs targeted to poor families have shrunk sharply over the last two decades.

The most controversial program was cash assistance to poor parents with small children. This program was drastically reformed in 1996, and we will discuss the reform below.

How much do all federal programs add up to in terms of budget expenditures? All federal poverty programs today amount to 20 percent of the total federal budget.

贫穷的激励问题
Incentive Problems of the Poor

One of the major obstacles faced by poor families is that the rules in most welfare programs severely reduce the incentives of low-income adults to seek work. If a poor person on welfare gets a job, the government will trim back food stamps, income-support payments, and rent subsidies, and the person might even lose medical benefits. We might say that poor people face high marginal "tax rates" (or, more accurately, "benefit-reduction rates") because welfare benefits are sharply reduced as earnings rise. ①

福利改革斗争
THE BATTLE OVER WELFARE REFORM

The traditional welfare system has few defenders. Some want to dismantle it; others, to strengthen it. Some wish to devolve responsibility for income support to states, localities, or families; others, to broaden the federal role. These disparate approaches reflect disparate views of poverty and lead to strikingly different policy proposals.

贫穷的两种观点
Two Views of Poverty

Social scientists put forth a wide variety of proposals to cure or alleviate poverty. The different approaches often reflect differing views of the roots of poverty. Proponents of strong government action ② see poverty as the result of social and economic conditions over which the poor have little control. They stress malnutrition, poor schools, broken families, discrimination, lack of job opportunities, and a dangerous environment as central determinants of the fate of the poor. If you hold this view, you might well believe that government bears a responsibility to alleviate poverty—either by providing income to the poor or by correcting the conditions that produce poverty.

A second view holds that poverty grows out of maladaptive individual behavior—behavior that is the responsibility of individuals and is properly cured by the poor themselves. In earlier centuries, laissez-faire apologists held that the poor were shiftless, lazy, or drunk; as a charity worker wrote almost a century ago, "Want of employment . . . is, as often as not, [caused by] drink." Sometimes the government itself is blamed for breeding dependency on government programs that squelch individual initiative. Critics who hold these views advocate that the government should cut back on welfare programs so that people will develop their own resources.

The poverty debate was succinctly summarized by the eminent social scientist William Wilson: [3]

> Liberals have traditionally emphasized how the plight of disadvantaged groups can be related to the problems of the broader society, including problems of discrimination and social class subordination. . . . Conservatives, in contrast, have traditionally stressed the importance of different group values and competitive resources in accounting for the experiences of the disadvantaged.[2]

Much of today's debate can be better understood if these two views and their implications are factored into the political equation.

[2] William Julius Wilson, "Cycles of Deprivation and the Underclass Debate," *Social Service Review,* December 1985, pp. 541–559.

① 如果一个享受福利津贴的穷人得到了一份工作，政府就会消减他的食物券、收入资助款以及租房补贴，甚至有失去医保津贴的可能。

② 那些极力主张强化政府行为的人，将贫困问题看作是社会和经济地位作用的结果，穷人对此几乎没有多少掌控的能力。他们强调指出，营养不良、缺少学校教育、家庭破裂、各种歧视、缺乏工作机会和生活环境险恶是决定其贫穷命运的关键因素。

[3] 威廉 · 朱利斯 · 威尔逊（William Wilson，1935~），美国社会学家，1972~1996 年任芝加哥大学教授，1996 年至今任哈佛大学教授，是哈佛大学校务委员会授予的该校最杰出的 22 位教授之一。

今天美国的收入支持计划

Income-Support Programs in the United States Today

Most high-income countries provide guaranteed income supplements for poor families with children, and that model was followed by the United States until 1996. At that time, the country took a radically different approach to increasing incomes of the poor. First, the government augmented a program to supplement wages of working families. Second, it fundamentally altered cash assistance programs, abolishing a federal entitlement for poor families.

所得税抵免

The Earned-Income Tax Credit

The wage supplement program is called the *earned-income tax credit* or *EITC.* [1] This credit applies to labor incomes and is in effect a wage supplement. In 2008, the EITC provided a supplement to wage income of as much as 40 percent, up to a maximum of $4824 for a family with two children. A single father or mother would receive some credit for an income up to around $39,000 of wages. It is known as a "refundable" credit because it is actually paid to an individual when the individual owes no taxes. ②

What is the difference between a traditional cash-assistance program and the earned-income tax credit? Cash assistance provides a minimum benefit for poor families and then reduces the benefit as market income increases. The earned-income tax credit, by contrast, gives nothing to those who do not work and supplements the earnings of those who do work. The philosophy of the EITC in essence is, "Those who do not work shall not get government dollars."

1996 年的美国福利改革

The 1996 U.S. Welfare Reform

From the 1930s until 1996, poor families could also benefit from a federal cash-assistance program known as Aid to Families with Dependent Children. This was an *entitlement program,* meaning that anyone who met certain qualifications could receive the benefits as a matter of law.

President Bill Clinton had run on a platform of "reforming welfare as we know it." In 1996, he teamed up with a Republican Congress and completely changed the rules for cash assistance. The old ③ program was replaced by the Temporary Assistance for Needy Families (TANF) program, which removed the federal entitlement to cash benefits and turned the program over to the 50 states.

The major provisions of the new program were the following:

- The primary responsibility for the income support of poor people was turned over to state and local governments. This replaced the earlier system in which the federal government picked up most of the costs of income support.
- The entitlement for federal cash assistance under TANF was removed.
- Each family is subject to a lifetime limit of 5 years of benefits under the federally supported program. After 5 years, TANF funds can no longer be used to support the family, even if it moves to a new state or has been off the welfare rolls for a number of years.
- Adults in the program must engage in work activities after 2 years of benefits.
- Legal immigrants may be excluded from TANF benefits.
- Other major low-income-support programs were largely unchanged.

Appraisal. The 1996 welfare reform was a major change in social policy. One aspect is the effect on *labor markets.* To the extent that the loss of benefits forces people to seek work, this will increase the supply of relatively uneducated and unskilled labor. This increased supply will tend to lower wages of the lowest-paid workers and increase income inequality. (This effect operates much the same way that the sharp increase in immigration has contributed to lowering of wages of the unskilled in the last three decades.) If the equilibrium wages of some workers are driven down below the minimum wage, this may also lead to an increase in the unemployment rate of these groups.

One important feature of the new law, emphasized by social and economic conservatives, was the *transfer of responsibility* for income support for poor families to the states. ④ The idea behind this change was that states would reverse the century-long trend of increasing generosity of welfare programs. Critics of this transfer believed that placing decision-making responsibility in the states would give strong incentives for states to trim welfare benefits to reduce the costs and the fiscal burden of the low-income population. This has been called a "race to the bottom" in which the equilibrium is for states to have the

---

[1] The earned-income tax credit：收入所得税抵免，缩写为 EITC。

② 这就是众所周知的“返还”的抵免政策，因为当一个人没有欠税时，他就可以实实在在地拿到这笔抵免的支付。

③ 旧有的法案已经被《贫困家庭临时援助法案》(即 TANF) 所取代。这项新的行动法案将原先以联邦政府名义发放的现金补贴权全部移交给了 50 个州的政府执行。

④ 正如社会学和经济学界的保守派学者所强调的，这项新法案的一个重要的特征，是对全美各州的贫困家庭发放收入补贴的责任转移。

lowest-possible benefits and drive low-income households elsewhere.

The *impacts* of the expanded EITC and 1996 welfare reform have surprised most analysts. Among the major impacts have been the following:

- The fall in welfare caseloads has been unprecedented, widespread, and continuous. From 1995 to 2008, the number of households on welfare has fallen by more than 70 percent. While a decline was expected, its size and duration were surprising.
- There was a large increase in the labor-force participation rate of single women with young children. The combination of economic incentives and a strong labor market was successful in pushing women off welfare and into jobs.

21 世纪经济政策
ECONOMIC POLICY FOR THE 21ST CENTURY

How should government's role in the economy be redefined? We close with three final reflections:

1. We have examined the key economic functions of the government. The government combats market failures, redistributes income, stabilizes the economy, manages international affairs, and promotes long-term economic growth. Each of these is essential. No serious person today advo- ①
cates shutting down the government. No one today proposes to allow nuclear dumping, to let poor orphans starve in the streets, to privatize the central bank, or to open the borders to all flows of people and drugs. The question is not whether government should regulate the economy but how and where it should intervene.
2. While government plays a central role in a civilized society, we must constantly reassess the mission and instruments of government policy. Governments have a monopoly on political power, and this imposes a special responsibility for government to operate efficiently. Every public dollar spent on wasteful programs could be used for promoting scientific research or alleviating hunger. Every inefficient tax reduces people's consumption opportunities, whether for food or education or housing. The central premise of economics is ②
that resources are scarce—and this applies to the government as well as to the private sector.
3. While economics can analyze the major public-policy controversies, it cannot have the final word. For underlying all public-policy debates ③
are normative assumptions and value judgments about what is just and fair. What an economist does, therefore, is try very hard to keep positive science cleanly separated from normative judgments—to draw a line between the economic calculations of the head and the human feelings of the heart. But keeping description separate from prescription does not mean that the professional economist is a bloodless computer. Economists are as divided in their political philosophies as is the rest of the population. Conservative econo- ④
mists argue strenuously for reducing the scope of government and ending programs to redistribute income. Liberal economists are just as passionate in advocating reducing poverty or using macroeconomic policies to combat unemployment. Economic science cannot say which political point of view is right or wrong. But it can arm us for the great debate.

SUMMARY

A. The Sources of Inequality

1. In the previous century, the classical economists believed that inequality was a universal constant, unchangeable by public policy. This view does not stand up to scrutiny. Poverty made a glacial retreat over the early part of the twentieth century, and absolute incomes for those in the bottom part of the income distribution rose sharply. Since around 1980, this trend has reversed, and inequality has increased.
2. The Lorenz curve is a convenient device for measuring the spreads or inequalities of income distribution. It shows what percentage of total income goes to the poorest 1 percent of the population, to the poorest 10 percent, to the poorest 95 percent, and so forth.

---

① 今天，没有任何一个严肃认真的公民会鼓吹废除政府。没有人会赞同核废料随处弃置，让可怜的孤儿在街头挨饿，让中央银行私有化，或者赞同开放边境全部让人和各种毒品流入。问题不是政府是否应该对经济实施管制，而是如何干预、在何处进行干预的问题。

② 经济学的重要假设是资源是稀缺的，这一点对政府，同时也对私人部门适用。

③ 所有这些关于公共政策辩论的基础是规范假设和关于公平和公正的价值判断。

④ 保守派的经济学家坚持认为，必须减少政府的职权范围，终结收入的再分配计划。而自由派的经济学家们则满怀激情地主张减少贫困，或者运用宏观经济政策与失业作斗争。经济学并不能就这些政治观点下对还是错的结论，但却可以把我们的头脑武装起来，投入到这场伟大的辩论中去。

The Gini coefficient is a quantitative measure of inequality.

3. Poverty is essentially a relative notion. In the United States, poverty was defined in terms of the adequacy of incomes in the early 1960s. By this standard of measured income, little progress in reducing inequality has been made in the last decade.
4. Income inequality declined markedly over most of the twentieth century. Then, beginning around 1975, the gap between rich and poor began to widen. The largest income gains have gone to the very top of the income distribution, to the richest 0.1 percent of people. Analysts believe that the "rich man's crash" of 2007–2009 will narrow income gaps at the very top. Wealth is even more unequally distributed than is income, both in the United States and in other capitalist economies.

B. Antipoverty Policies

5. Political philosophers write of three types of equality: (*a*) equality of political rights, such as the right to vote; (*b*) equality of opportunity, providing equal access to jobs, education, and other social systems; and (*c*) equality of outcomes, whereby people are guaranteed equal incomes or consumptions. Whereas the first two types of equality are increasingly accepted in most advanced democracies like the United States, equality of outcomes is generally rejected as impractical and too harmful to economic efficiency.
6. Equality has costs as well as benefits; the costs show up as drains from Okun's "leaky bucket." That is, attempts to reduce income inequality by progressive taxation or transfer payments may harm economic incentives to work or save and may thereby reduce the size of national output.
7. Major programs to alleviate poverty are welfare payments, food stamps, Medicaid, and a group of smaller or less targeted programs. As a whole, these programs are criticized because they impose high benefit-reduction rates (or marginal "tax" rates) on low-income families when families begin to earn wages or other income.

CONCEPTS FOR REVIEW

trends of income distribution
Lorenz curve of income and wealth
Gini coefficient
poverty
welfare state
Okun's "leaky bucket"
equality: political, of opportunity, of outcomes
equality vs. efficiency
income-possibility curve: ideal and realistic cases

FURTHER READING AND INTERNET WEBSITES

Further Reading

An influential book on equality versus efficiency is Arthur Okun, *Equality and Efficiency: The Big Tradeoff* (Brookings Institution, Washington, D.C., 1975).

For a nontechnical review of issues in health-care reform, see the symposium in *Journal of Economic Perspectives*, Summer 1994.

Websites

The Census Department collects poverty data. See *www.census.gov/hhes/www/poverty.html*. For information on welfare and poverty, see *www.welfareinfo.org*. The site *www.doleta.gov* describes the results of welfare reform from the perspective of individuals.

The Urban Institute (*www.urban.org*) and the Joint Center for Poverty Research (*www.jcpr.org*) are organizations devoted to analyzing trends in poverty and income distribution.

QUESTIONS FOR DISCUSSION

1. Let each member of the class anonymously write down on a card an estimate of his or her family's annual income. From these, draw up a frequency table showing the distribution of incomes. What is the median income? The mean income?
2. What effect would the following have on the Lorenz curve of after-tax incomes? (Assume that the taxes are spent by the government on a representative slice of GDP.)
   a. A proportional income tax (i.e., one taxing all incomes at the same rate)
   b. A progressive income tax (i.e., one taxing high incomes more heavily than low incomes)
   c. A sharp increase in taxes on cigarettes and food

   Draw four Lorenz curves to illustrate the original income distribution and the income distribution after each of the three tax categories.
3. Review Okun's leaky bucket experiment. Get a group together and have each member of the group write down on a piece of paper how large a leak should be tolerated when government transfers $100 from the top income quintile to the bottom income quintile. Do you think it should be 99 percent? Or 50 percent? Or zero? Each person should write a short justification of the maximum number. Tabulate the results and then discuss the differences.
4. Consider two ways of supplementing the income of the poor: (*a*) cash assistance (say, $500 per month) and (*b*) categorical benefits such as subsidized food or medical care. List the pros and cons of using each strategy. Can you explain why the United States tends to use mainly strategy (*b*)? Do you agree with this decision?
5. In a country called Econoland, there are 10 people. Their incomes (in thousands) are $3, $6, $2, $8, $4, $9, $1, $5, $7, and $5. Construct a table of income quintiles like Table 17-2. Plot a Lorenz curve. Calculate the Gini coefficient defined in Section A.
6. People continue to argue about what form assistance for the poor should take. One school says, "Give people money and let them buy health services and the foods they need." The other school says, "If you give money to the poor, they may spend it on beer and drugs. Your dollar goes further in alleviating malnourishment and disease if you provide the services "in kind" (meaning by directly providing the good or service rather than providing money to buy the good or service.) The dollar that you earn may be yours to spend, but society's income-support dollar is a dollar that society has the right to channel directly to its targets."

   The argument of the first school might rest on demand theory: Let each household decide how to maximize its utility on a limited budget. Chapter 5 shows why this argument might be right. But what if the parents' utility includes mainly beer and lottery tickets and no milk or clothing for the children? Might you agree with the second view? From your own personal experience and reading, which of these two arguments would you endorse? Explain your reasoning.

International Trade [1]
国际贸易

CHAPTER
18

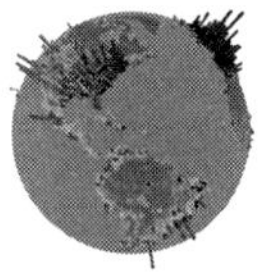

TO THE CHAMBER OF DEPUTIES:
We are subject to the intolerable competition of a foreign rival, who enjoys such superior facilities for the production of light that he can inundate our national market at reduced price. This rival is no other than the sun. Our petition is to pass a law shutting up all windows, openings, and fissures through which the light of the sun is used to penetrate our dwellings, to the prejudice of the profitable manufacture we have been enabled to bestow on the country. Signed: The Candle Makers

F. Bastiat [2]

致参众两院：
我们正在遭受一场无法忍受的与国外对手的竞争。这个对手沉醉于自己生产光明的超级设备中，以至于完全有能力以刻意低廉的价格席卷我们的国内市场。这个对手就是太阳。为此，我们请求通过一项法令，关闭所有太阳光可以穿透我们住所的窗户、通道和缝隙，以使我们长期以来尽心竭力地为国家谋福祉的产业免受侵害。

签字：蜡烛制造商

——F. 巴斯夏

国际贸易实质

A. THE NATURE OF INTERNATIONAL TRADE

As we go about our daily lives, it is easy to overlook the importance of international trade. America ships enormous volumes of food, airplanes, computers, and machinery to other countries; and in return we get vast quantities of oil, footwear, cars, coffee, and other goods and services. While Americans pride themselves on their ingenuity, it is sobering to realize how many of our products—including gunpowder, classical music, clocks, railroads, penicillin, and radar—arose from the inventions of long-forgotten people in faraway places.

What are the economic forces that lie behind international trade? Simply put, trade promotes specialization, and specialization increases productivity. Over the long run, increased trade and higher productivity raise living standards for all nations. Gradually, countries have realized that opening up their economies to the global trading system is the most secure road to prosperity.

This chapter extends our analysis by examining the principles governing *international trade*, through which nations export and import goods, services, and capital. International economics involves many of the most controversial questions of the day. Should the nation be concerned that so many of its consumer goods are made abroad? Do we gain from free trade, or should we tighten up the rules on trading with Mexico and China? Are workers hurt in competition with "cheap foreign labor"? How should the principles governing trade be extended to intellectual property rights, such as patents and copyrights? The economic stakes are high in finding sound answers to these questions.

[1] 这一章在近几个版本（特别是 12~18 版）中都是修订量最大的章节之一，版版不同。2008 年，诺贝尔经济学奖得主保罗·克鲁格曼（Paul Krugman, 1953~）的得奖原因之一就是由于其在国际贸易的数学模型方面所做的开创性贡献。特别需要指出的是，两个"保罗"（萨缪尔森和克鲁格曼同名不同姓）是诺贝尔经济学奖得主中为数不多的哲学思维缜密、文字功底堪称语言大师的人之一。克鲁格曼长期担任《纽约时报》的专栏作家，不仅多产，而且经常有语惊四座的专栏文章面世。所以，这一章在本版冠以《国际贸易》不能不说与克鲁格曼有关（另请参阅本书由笔者所撰的《注疏者序》）。

[2] 弗雷德里克·巴斯夏（F. Bastiat，1801~1850），法国古典自由主义思想家，政治经济学家，一生著述颇丰。本段文字的英文出处见《医保政治学，政策与法律》（*Journal of Health Politics, Policy and Law*），第 5 卷，第 4 期 588 页，杜克大学医疗管理系 1981 年出版（Vol.5, No.4, 1981, the Dept. of Health Administration, Duke University）。

国际贸易与国内贸易

International vs. Domestic Trade

In a deep economic sense, trade is trade, whether it involves people within the same nation or people in different countries. There are, however, three important differences between domestic and international trade, and these have important practical and economic consequences:

1. *Expanded trading opportunities.* The major advantage of international trade is that it expands the scope of trade. If people were forced to consume only what they produced at home, the world would be poorer on both the material and the spiritual planes. Canadians could drink no wine, Americans could eat no bananas, and most of the world would be without jazz and Hollywood movies. ①
2. *Sovereign nations.* Trading across frontiers involves people and firms living in different nations. Each nation is a sovereign entity which regulates the flow of people, goods, and finance crossing its borders. This contrasts with domestic trade, where there is a single currency, where trade and money flow freely within the borders, and where people can migrate easily to seek new opportunities. Countries sometimes build barriers to international trade, using tariffs or quotas, to "protect" affected workers or firms from foreign competition. ②
3. *International finance.* Most nations have their own currencies. I want to pay for a Japanese car in U.S. dollars, while Toyota wants to be paid in Japanese yen. Dollars are translated into yen by the foreign exchange rate, which is the relative price of different currencies. The international financial system must ensure a smooth flow and exchange of dollars, yen, and other currencies—or else risk a breakdown in trade. The financial aspects of international trade are analyzed in the chapters on macroeconomics. ③

International Trade in Goods and Services, 2007 (billions of dollars)	Exports	Imports
Goods	**1,149**	**1,965**
Food and beverages	84	50
Industrial supplies	316	269
Capital goods	446	284
Motor vehicles	121	204
Consumer goods	146	308
Other goods	36	49
Services	**479**	**372**
Travel	97	76
Passenger fares	25	29
Other transportation	52	67
Royalties and license fees	71	28
Other private services	217	135
Military sales and government	17	37
Total goods and services	**1,628**	**2,337**

TABLE 18-1. International Trade in Goods and Services ④

The United States exports a wide array of goods and services from food to intellectual property. In 2007, U.S. imports exceeded exports by around $700 billion. The United States exports primarily specialized capital goods like machinery. At the same time, it imports many other manufactured goods, like cars and cameras, because other countries specialize in different market niches and enjoy economies of scale.

Source: U.S. Bureau of Economic Analysis, available at *www.bea.gov/international/*.

对外贸易趋势

Trends in Foreign Trade

What are the major components of international trade for the United States? Table 18-1 shows the composition of U.S. foreign trade for 2007. The bulk of trade is in goods, particularly manufactured goods, although trade in services has increased rapidly. The data reveal that the United States exports surprisingly large amounts of primary commodities (such as food) and imports large quantities of sophisticated, capital-intensive manufactured goods (like automobiles and computer parts). Moreover, we find a great deal of two-way, or intra-industry, trade. Within a particular ⑤ industry, the United States exports and imports at the same time because a high degree of product differentiation means that different countries tend to have niches in different parts of a market.

商品和服务的国际贸易原因

THE REASONS FOR INTERNATIONAL TRADE IN GOODS AND SERVICES

What are the economic factors that lie behind the patterns of international trade? Nations find it bene- ⑥ ficial to participate in international trade for several

① 拓展贸易机会。
② 国家主权与贸易。
③ 国际金融与贸易。
④ 表 18-1. 商品和服务形式的国际贸易
⑤ 在一个特定的行业之内，由于产品差异性很高的缘故，美国在同一时间的出口和进口就意味着在不同的市场，不同的国家都想找到自身产品的生存空间。
⑥ 各国都发现，参与到国际贸易之中，是一件很有利的事情。其原因有生产环境的多样性、不同国家之间偏好的差异性，以及大规模生产可以降低成本。

reasons: diversity in the conditions of production, differences in tastes among nations, and decreasing costs of large-scale production.

自然资源的多样性
Diversity in Natural Resources

Trade may take place because of the diversity in productive possibilities among countries. In part, these differences reflect endowments of natural resources. One country may be blessed with a supply of petroleum, while another may have a large amount of fertile land. Or a mountainous country may generate large amounts of hydroelectric power which it sells to its neighbors, while a country with deep-water harbors may become a shipping center.

偏好不同
Differences in Tastes

A second reason for trade lies in preferences. Even if the conditions of production were identical in all regions, countries might engage in trade if their tastes for goods were different.

For example, suppose that Norway and Sweden both produce fish from the sea and meat from the land in about the same amounts but the Swedes have a great fondness for meat while the Norwegians are partial to fish. A mutually beneficial export of meat from Norway and fish from Sweden would take place. Both countries would gain from this trade; the sum of human happiness is increased, just as when Jack Sprat trades fat meat for his wife's lean.

成本不同
Differences in Costs

Perhaps the most important reason for trade is differences among countries in production costs. We see vast differences in labor costs among nations. In 2006, for example, China's hourly wage of $1 was about one-thirtieth of that in Western Europe. Companies looking to compete effectively strive to find those parts of the production chain that can profitably be located in China to use unskilled Chinese workers. When an iPod or mobile phone is labeled "Made in China," that probably means that it was assembled in China, while the design, patents, marketing, and hard drives were produced in other countries.

An important feature in today's world is that some companies or countries enjoy economies of scale; that is, they tend to have lower average costs of production as the volume of output expands. So when a particular country gets a head start in producing a particular product, it can become the high-volume, low-cost producer. The economies of scale ①
give it a significant cost and technological advantage over other countries, which find it cheaper to buy from the leading producer than to make the product themselves.

Large-scale production is an important advantage in industries with major research-and-development expenses. As the leading aircraft maker in the world, Boeing can spread the enormous cost of designing, developing, and testing a new plane over a large sales volume. That means it can sell planes at a lower price than competitors with a smaller volume. Boeing's only real competitor, Airbus, got off the ground through large subsidies from several European countries to cover its research-and-development costs.

The example of decreasing cost helps explain the important phenomenon of extensive intra-industry trade shown in Table 18-1. Why is it that the United States both imports and exports computers and related equipment? Consider a company such as Intel, which produces high-end semiconductors. Intel has facilities in the United States as well as in China, Malaysia, and the Philippines, and the company often ships products manufactured in one country to be assembled and tested in another country. Similar patterns of intra-industry specialization are seen with cars, steel, textiles, and many other manufactured products.

国际间的比较优势
B. COMPARATIVE ADVANTAGE AMONG NATIONS

比较优势原则
THE PRINCIPLE OF COMPARATIVE ADVANTAGE

It is only common sense that countries will produce and export goods for which they are uniquely qualified. But there is a deeper principle underlying *all* trade—in a family, within a nation, and among nations—that goes beyond common sense. The *prin-* ②
ciple of comparative advantage holds that a country can benefit from trade even if it is absolutely more efficient (or absolutely less efficient) than other countries in the production of every good. Indeed, trade according to comparative advantage provides mutual benefits to all countries.

---

① 规模经济给许多国家带来了巨大的成本和技术优势，它们发现，从一流的厂商那里购买，比自己组织生产要便宜很多。

② 比较优势原则所强调的是，即便一个国家自身在每一种产品上的生产效率比起别的国家都占有绝对的优势（或者绝对地处于劣势），它也可以从国际贸易中获利。不容置疑，在比较原则基础上开展的国家贸易给所有国家提供了一个共同获益的机会。

似乎有悖常识

Uncommon Sense

Take a world in which there are only two goods, computers and clothing. Suppose that the United States has higher output per worker (or per unit of input) than the rest of the world in making both computers and clothing. But suppose the United States is relatively more efficient in the production of computers than it is in clothing. For example, it might be 50 percent more productive in computers and 10 percent more productive in clothing than other countries. In this case, it would benefit the United States to export that good in which it is relatively more efficient (computers) and import that good in which it is relatively less efficient (clothing).

Or consider a poor country like Mali. How could impoverished Mali, whose workers use handlooms and have productivity that is only a fraction of that of workers in industrialized countries, hope to export any of its textiles? Surprisingly, according to the principle of comparative advantage, Mali can benefit by exporting the goods in which it is *relatively* more efficient (like textiles) and importing those goods which it produces *relatively* less efficiently (like turbines and automobiles).

① 比较优势原则强调的是，如果每一个国家都专业地生产并出口其以相对低廉的成本生产出的产品，各国必定会从中获利。反过来讲，每一个国家所需要的商品如果由自己组织生产时成本相对很高的话，改为进口则获利良多。

The **principle of comparative advantage** holds ① that each country will benefit if it specializes in the production and export of those goods that it can produce at relatively low cost. Conversely, each country will benefit if it imports those goods which it produces at relatively high cost.

This simple principle provides the unshakable basis for international trade.

李嘉图的比较优势分析

Ricardo's Analysis of Comparative Advantage

Let us illustrate the fundamental principles of international trade by considering America and Europe two centuries ago. If labor (or resources, more generally) is absolutely more productive in America than in Europe, does this mean that America will import nothing? And is it economically wise for Europe to "protect" its markets with tariffs or quotas?

These questions were first answered in 1817 by the English economist David Ricardo, who showed [2] that international specialization benefits a nation. He called this result the law of comparative advantage.

For simplicity, Ricardo worked with only two regions and only two goods, and he chose to measure all production costs in terms of labor-hours. We will follow his lead here, analyzing food and clothing for Europe and America.[1]

American and European Labor Requirements for Production

Product	Necessary Labor for Production (labor-hours) In America	In Europe
1 unit of food	1	3
1 unit of clothing	2	4

TABLE 18-2. Comparative Advantage Depends Only on Relative Costs ③

In a hypothetical example, America has lower labor costs in both food and clothing. American labor productivity is between 2 and 3 times Europe's (twice in clothing, thrice in food).

Table 18-2 shows the illustrative data. In America, it takes 1 hour of labor to produce a unit of food, while a unit of clothing requires 2 hours of labor. In Europe the cost is 3 hours of labor for food and 4 hours of labor for clothing. We see that America has *absolute advantage* in both goods, for it can produce either one with greater absolute efficiency than can Europe. However, America has *comparative advantage* in food, while Europe has *comparative advantage* in clothing. The reason is that food is *relatively inexpensive* in America compared to Europe, while clothing is *relatively inexpensive* in Europe compared to America.

From these facts, Ricardo proved that both regions will benefit if they specialize in their areas of comparative advantage—that is, if America specializes in the production of food while Europe specializes in the production of clothing. In this situation, America will export food to pay for European clothing, while Europe will export clothing to pay for American food.

To analyze the effects of trade, we must measure the amounts of food and clothing that can be produced and consumed in each region (1) if there is no international trade and (2) if there is free trade with each region specializing in its area of comparative advantage.

[1] An analysis of comparative advantage with many countries and many commodities is presented later in this chapter.

[2] 戴维·李嘉图（David Ricardo，1772~1823），英国资产阶级古典政治经济学的主要代表之一，是最有影响力的古典经济学家。李嘉图早期的职业是证券经纪人，后受亚当·斯密《国富论》一书的影响，激发了他对经济学研究的兴趣，其主要的经济学代表作是1817年完成的《政治经济学及税赋原理》（*Principles of Political Economy and Taxation*）。书中论述了货币流通量的规律、对外贸易中的比较优势学说等。李嘉图只关注经济范畴中的数量关系，很难在价值规律基础上说明资本和劳动的交换、等量资本获等量利润等，是资本主义制度忠实的卫道士。李嘉图自负有加，坚持认为在英国，能看懂自己著作的人不会超过25人。

③ 表 18-2. 比较优势只取决于相对成本

Before Trade. Start by examining what occurs in the absence of any international trade, say, because all trade is illegal or because of a prohibitive tariff. Table 18-2 shows the real wage of the American ① worker for an hour's work as 1 unit of food or ½ unit of clothing. The European worker earns only ⅓ unit of food or ¼ unit of clothing per hour of work.

Clearly, if perfect competition prevails in each isolated region, the prices of food and clothing will be different in the two places because of the difference in production costs. In America, clothing will ② be 2 times as expensive as food because it takes twice as much labor to produce a unit of clothing as it does to produce a unit of food. In Europe, clothing will be only ⅘ as expensive as food.

After Trade. Now suppose that all tariffs are repealed and free trade is allowed. For simplicity, further assume that there are no transportation costs. What is the flow of goods when trade is opened up? Clothing is relatively more expensive in America (with a price ratio of 2 as compared to ⅘), and food is relatively more expensive in Europe (with a price ratio of ¾ as compared to ½). Given these relative prices, and with no tariffs or transportation costs, food will soon be shipped from America to Europe and clothing from Europe to America.

As European clothing penetrates the American market, American clothiers will find prices falling and profits shrinking, and they will begin to shut down their factories. By contrast, European farmers will find that the prices of foodstuffs begin to fall when American products hit the European markets; they will suffer losses, some will go bankrupt, and resources will be withdrawn from farming.

After all the adjustments to international trade have taken place, the prices of clothing and food must be equalized in Europe and America (just as the water in two connecting pipes must come to a common level once you remove the barrier between them). Without further knowledge about the exact supplies and demands, we cannot know the exact level to which prices will move. But we do ③ know that the relative prices of food and clothing must lie somewhere between the European price ratio (which is ¾ for the ratio of food to clothing prices) and the American price ratio (which is ½). Let us say that the final ratio is ⅔, so 2 units of clothing trade for 3 units of food. For simplicity, we measure prices in American dollars and assume that the free-trade price of food is $2 per unit, which means that the free-trade price of clothing must be $3 per unit.

With free trade, the regions have shifted their productive activities. America has withdrawn resources from clothing in favor of food, while Europe has contracted its farm sector and expanded its clothing manufacture. *Under free trade, countries shift production toward their areas of comparative advantage.*

贸易的经济收益

The Economic Gains from Trade

What are the economic effects of opening up the two regions to international trade? America as a whole benefits from the fact that imported clothing costs less than clothing produced at home. Likewise, Europe benefits by specializing in clothing and consuming food that is less expensive than domestically produced food.

We can most easily reckon the gains from trade by calculating the effect of trade upon the real wages of workers. Real wages are measured by the quantity of goods that a worker can buy with an hour's pay. Using Table 18-2, we can see that the real wages after trade will be greater than the real wages before trade for workers in both Europe *and* America. For simplicity, assume that each worker buys 1 unit of clothing and 1 unit of food. Before trade, this bundle of goods costs an American worker 3 hours of work and a European worker 7 hours of work.

After trade has opened up, the price of clothing is $3 per unit while the price of food is $2 per unit. An American worker must still work 1 hour to buy a unit of food, because food is domestically produced; but at the price ratio of 2 to 3, the American worker need work only 1½ hours to produce enough to buy 1 unit of European clothing. Therefore the bundle of goods costs the American worker 2½ hours of work when trade is allowed—this represents an increase of 20 percent in the real wage of the American worker.

For European workers, a unit of clothing will still cost 4 hours of labor in a free-trade situation. To obtain a unit of food, however, the European worker need produce only ⅔ of a unit of clothing (which requires ⅔ × 4 hours of labor) and then trade that ⅔ clothing unit for 1 unit of American food. The total European labor needed to obtain the bundle of consumption is then 4 + 2⅔ = 6⅔, which represents an

---

① 表 18-2 列出了美国工人工作一小时的实际工资，即生产一个单位的食品和半个单位的服装的小时工资。

② 在美国，由于每生产一个单位的服装所需的劳动是每生产一个单位食品的两倍，所以，服装的销售价格是食品的两倍。

③ 但是，我们确实明白，食品和服装的相对价格某种程度上必定会居于欧洲价格比率（其食品和服装的价格比率为 3/4）和美国的价格比率（其为 1/2）之间。

[2] 乔治·布什（G. W. Bush，1946~），刚卸任的43届美国总统，即“小布什”。

[3] 格雷格·曼昆（Greg Mankiw，1958~），美国宏观经济学家，2003~2005年任布什总统经济顾问委员会主任，被康涅狄格大学经济系的专业评估机构IDEAS评为全球最有影响力的经济学家之一。曼昆本人编著的经济学教材《经济学原理》(*Principles of Economics*，目前最新版本为2009年的第5版）是一本专门为学生编的教科书，通俗易懂，广受好评。某种程度上，萨缪尔森的《经济学》教材是历时60年、哲思深邃的“经济哲学”（特别是本版，绝版的第19版，以及第1、12、17版等），是一部永远的古典交响乐，曼昆的《经济学原理》是一首甜美的流行轻音乐。或者，正如本段结尾萨缪尔森引用目前美国政界、经济学界精英们经常挂在嘴边的口头禅，曼昆的经济学教材就像是一部“爱丽丝梦游经济学仙境”（Alice in Wonderland economics）的美丽童话。

[4] Alice in Wonderland：《爱丽丝梦游仙境》，全名为*Alice's Adventures in Wonder-land*，常缩写为*Alice in Wonderland*，是英国作家查尔斯·勒特威奇·道奇森（Charles Lutwidge Dodgson，1832~1898）以笔名刘易斯·卡罗尔（Lewis Carroll）于1865年出版的一部享誉世界的经典儿童文学作品。

increase in real wages of about 5 percent over the no-trade situation.

When countries concentrate on their areas of comparative advantage under free trade, each country is better off. Compared to a no-trade situation, workers in each region can obtain a larger quantity of consumer goods for the same amount of work when they specialize in their areas of comparative advantage and trade their own production for goods in which they have a relative disadvantage. ①

作为另一种贸易的外包
Outsourcing as Another Kind of Trade

Recently, Americans have become concerned about outsourcing (sometimes also called “offshoring”). What exactly is the issue here? *Outsourcing* refers to locating services or production processes abroad. Prominent examples are telemarketing, medical diagnostics, publishing, web development, and engineering. These differ from the more conventional international trade in goods because they relate to services that were expensive to locate in foreign countries in an earlier era, whereas today, with rapid and low-cost communication, such processes can be economically located where costs are lower. Just as low-cost ocean shipping made possible greater international trade in grains in the nineteenth century, low-cost communication makes it possible to have Indian architects work on designs for New York firms today.

Many economists respond to outsourcing by arguing that it is just an extension of the principle of comparative advantage to more sectors. For example, when he was G. W. Bush's chief economist, Greg [2] Mankiw stated, “I think outsourcing is a growing phe- [3] nomenon, but it's something that we should realize is probably a plus for the economy in the long run.” His comment ignited a firestorm of controversy among both Republicans and Democrats, and one political figure called it “Alice in Wonderland economics.” [4]

Most economists tend to agree with Mankiw that outsourcing is another example of comparative advantage at work. But there are policy consequences for governments. A careful analysis by Princeton economist (and adviser to Democratic presidents) Alan Blinder suggested the following advice for the [5] country, and perhaps also for today's students:

> Rich countries such as the United States will have to reorganize the nature of work to exploit their big advantage in non-tradable services: they are close to where the money is. That will mean, in part, specializing more in the delivery of services where personal presence is either imperative or highly beneficial. Thus, the U.S. work force of the future will likely have more divorce lawyers and fewer attorneys who write routine contracts, more internists and fewer radiologists, more salespeople and fewer typists. The market system is very good at making adjustments like these, even massive ones. It has done so before and will do so again. But it takes time and can move in unpredictable ways.

比较优势的图形分析
GRAPHICAL ANALYSIS OF COMPARATIVE ADVANTAGE

We can use the production-possibility frontier (*PPF*) to expand our analysis of comparative advantage. We will continue with the simple numerical example developed in this chapter, but the theory is equally valid in a competitive world with many different inputs.

美国如果没有贸易
America without Trade

Chapter 1 introduced the *PPF*, which shows the combinations of commodities that can be produced with a society's given resources and technology. Using the production data shown in Table 18-2, and assuming that both Europe and America have 600 units of labor, we can easily derive each region's *PPF*. The table that accompanies Figure 18-1 shows the possible levels of food and clothing that America can produce with its inputs and technology. Figure 18-1 plots the production possibilities; the green line *DA* shows America's *PPF*. The *PPF* has a slope of −½, which represents the terms on which food and clothing can be substituted in production. In competitive markets with no international trade, the price ratio of food to clothing will also be one-half.

So far we have concentrated on production and ignored consumption. Note that if America is isolated from all international trade, it can consume only what it produces. Say that, for the incomes and demands in the marketplace, point *B* in Figure 18-1 marks America's production and consumption in the absence of trade. Without trade, America produces and consumes 400 units of food and 100 units of clothing.

We can do exactly the same thing for Europe. But Europe's *PPF* will look different from America's

① 在自由贸易的大背景下，当各国都在将各自的注意力集中于自身占有比较优势的领域时，每个国家都会从中大为受益。与没有贸易的情况相比较，当该国或该地区的工人在自己拥有比较优势的领域从事专业化的生产，并且用自己所生产的商品通过贸易去获得自己在生产上处于相对劣势的商品时，这些生产工人就能够在付出同样劳动量的前提下，得到更大数量的消费品。

[5] 阿兰·布莱德（Alan Blinder，1945~），美国经济学家，普林斯顿大学经济系经济学与公共事务教授，《纽约时报》、《华盛顿邮报》、《华尔街日报》专栏作家；被康涅狄格大学经济系的专业评估机构IDEAS评为全球最有影响力的经济学家之一。1993~1994年任克林顿总统经济顾问委员会委员，1994~1996年任美联储副主席。与威廉·鲍莫尔（William Baumol，1922~，纽约大学和普林斯顿大学经济学教授，著名经济学家）合著的经济学教材《经济学、原理与政策》（*Economics, Principles and Policy*，在2009年刚刚出版第11版的基础上又在2010年8月出该版的最新修订本）享有很高的声誉。每一章均以政策和现实中的疑难案例开头，采用“问题或政策导向”的方式展开论述，全彩印刷，是典型的当代“冷教育”（Cool Education，详见笔者《中国英语教育改革探思录》一书）环境下吸引读者眼球的时尚做法。

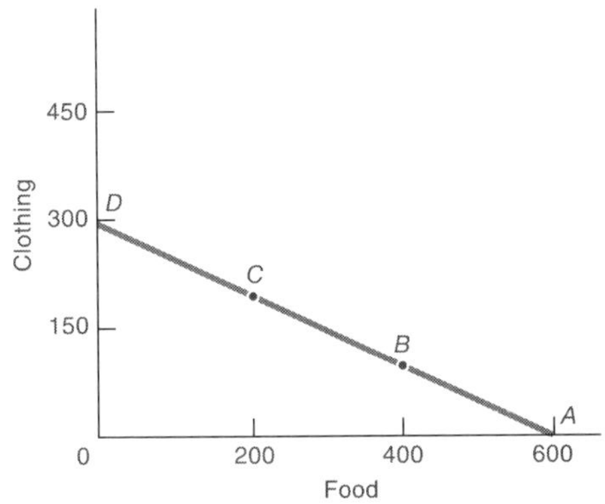

America's Production-Possibility Schedule
(1-to-2 constant-cost ratio)

Possibilities	Food (units)	Clothing (units)
A	600	0
B	400	100
C	200	200
D	0	300

FIGURE 18-1. American Production Data ①

The constant-cost line *DA* represents America's domestic production-possibility frontier. America will produce and consume at *B* in the absence of trade.

because Europe has different efficiencies in producing food and clothing. Europe's price ratio is ¾, reflecting the relative cost of food and clothing in that region.

贸易开放
Opening Up to Trade

Now allow trade between the two regions. Food can be exchanged for clothing at some price ratio. We call ② the ratio of export prices to import prices the **terms of trade.** To indicate the trading possibilities, we put the two *PPF*s together in Figure 18-2. America's green *PPF* shows its domestic production possibilities, while Europe's blue *PPF* shows the terms on which it can domestically substitute food and clothing. Note that Europe's *PPF* is drawn closer to the origin than America's because Europe has lower productivities in both industries; it has an absolute disadvantage in the production of both food and clothing.

Europe need not be discouraged by its absolute disadvantage, however, for it is the difference in relative productivities or comparative advantage that makes trade beneficial. The gains from trade are illustrated by the outer lines in Figure 18-2. If America could trade at Europe's pretrade relative prices, it could produce 600 units of food and move northwest along the outer blue line in Figure 18-2(*a*)—where the blue line represents the price ratio or terms of trade that are generated by Europe's *PPF*. Similarly, if Europe could trade at America's pretrade prices, Europe could specialize in clothing and move southeast along the green line in Figure 18-2(*b*)—where the green line is America's pretrade price ratio.

This leads to an important and surprising conclusion: Small countries have the most to gain from international trade. Small countries affect world prices the least and therefore can trade at world prices that are very different from domestic prices. Additionally, countries that are very different from ③ other countries gain most, while large countries have the least to gain. (These points are raised in question 3 at the end of this chapter.)

Equilibrium Price Ratio. Once trade opens up, some set of prices must hold in the world marketplace depending upon the overall market supplies and demands. Without further information we cannot specify the exact price ratio, but we can determine what the price range will be. The prices must lie somewhere between the prices of the two regions. That is, we know that the relative price of food to clothing must lie somewhere in the range between ½ and ¾.

The final price ratio will depend upon the relative demands for food and clothing. If food were very much in demand, the food price would be relatively high. If food demand were so high that Europe produced food as well as clothing, the price ratio would be that of Europe's pretrade relative prices, or ¾. On the other hand, if clothing demand were so strong that America produced clothing as well as food, the terms of trade would equal America's pretrade price ratio of ½. If each region specializes completely in the area of its comparative advantage, with Europe producing only clothing and America producing only food, the price ratio will lie somewhere between ½ and ¾. The exact ratio will depend on the strength of demand.

Assume now that the demands are such that the ④ final price ratio is ⅔, with 3 units of food selling for

---

① 图 18-1. 美国的生产数据

② 我们把出口价格和进口价格之间的比率称为**贸易条件**。为了说明贸易可能性，我们把图 18-2 中的两条生产可能性边界 *PPFs* 放在一起。美国的 *PPF* 线表示的是国内的生产可能性边界，欧洲的 *PPF* 线则表示的是在其内部食物和服装之间的替代条件。请注意，欧洲的 *PPF* 线与美国的 *PPF* 线相比较更接近原点，这是因为欧洲在这两个产业有较低的生产率，因此，在食物和服装的生产上欧洲都处在绝对劣势的地位。

③ 另外还可以看出，那些与传统经济强国截然不同的国家获得了最大的好处，而这些从前的大国却收益甚微。

④ 我们现在做一个这样的需求假设：以销售三个单位的食物换取两个单位的服装，即最终的价格比率是 2/3。

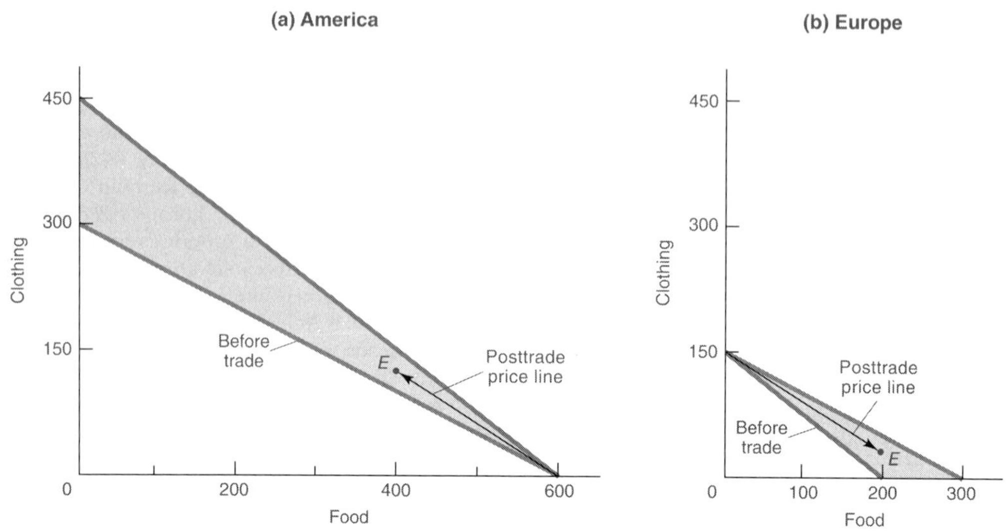

FIGURE 18-2. Comparative Advantage Illustrated ①

Through trade, both Europe and America improve their available consumption. If no trade is allowed, each region must be satisfied with its own production. It is therefore limited to its production-possibility curve, shown for each region as the line marked "Before trade." After borders are opened and competition equalizes the relative prices of the two goods, the relative-price line will be as shown by the arrows. If each region is faced with prices given by the arrows, can you see why its consumption possibilities must improve?

2 units of clothing. With this price ratio, each region will then specialize—America in food and Europe in clothing—and export some of its production to pay for imports at the world price ratio of ⅔.

Figure 18-2 illustrates how trade will take place. Each region will face a consumption-possibility curve according to which it can produce, trade, and consume. *The consumption-possibility curve begins at the region's point of complete specialization and then runs out at the world price ratio of ⅔.* ② Figure 18-2(*a*) shows America's consumption possibilities as a thin blue arrow with a slope of −⅔ coming out of its complete-specialization point at 600 units of food and no clothing. Similarly, Europe's posttrade consumption possibilities are shown in Figure 18-2(*b*) by the blue arrow running southeast from its point of complete specialization with a slope of −⅔.

The final outcome is shown by the points *E* in Figure 18-2. At this free-trade equilibrium, Europe specializes in producing clothing and America specializes in producing food. Europe exports 133⅓ units of clothing for 200 units of America's food. Both regions are able to consume more than they could produce alone; both regions have benefited from international trade.

Figure 18-3 illustrates the benefits of trade for America. The green inner line shows the *PPF*, while the blue outer line shows the consumption possibilities at the world price ratio of ⅔. The green arrows show the amounts exported and imported. America ends up at point *B*′. Through trade it moves along ③ the blue line *D′A* just as if a fruitful new invention had pushed out its *PPF*.

The lessons of this analysis are summarized in Figure 18-4. This figure shows the *world* production possibility frontier. The world *PPF* represents the max- ④ imum output that can be obtained from the world's resources when goods are produced in the most efficient manner—that is, with the most efficient division of labor and regional specialization.

① 图 18-2. 比较优势图解

② 消费可能性曲线从该地区完全专业化生产的分界点开始移动，至 2/3 的世界价格比率处止。

③ 通过贸易它沿 *D′A* 线移动，就好像一项成果累累的新发明早已将生产可能性边界 *PPF* 外推。

④ 世界的生产可能性边界 *PPF* 代表了最大产出，即当产品以最有效的方式生产时，最为有效的劳动力和地区专业化生产分工就可以从世界资源的利用中获得最大产出。

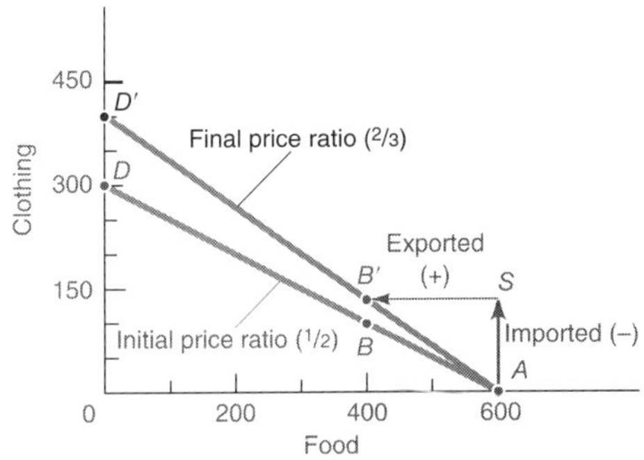

FIGURE 18-3. America before and after Trade ①

Free trade expands the consumption options of America. The green line *DA* represents America's production-possibility curve; the blue line *D′A* is the new consumption-possibility curve when America is able to trade freely at the price ratio of ⅔ and, in consequence, to specialize completely in the production of food (at *A*). The green arrows from *S* to *B′* and *A* to *S* show the amounts exported (+) and imported (−) by America. As a result of free trade, America ends up at *B′*, with more of both goods available than would be the case if it consumed only what it produced along *DA*.

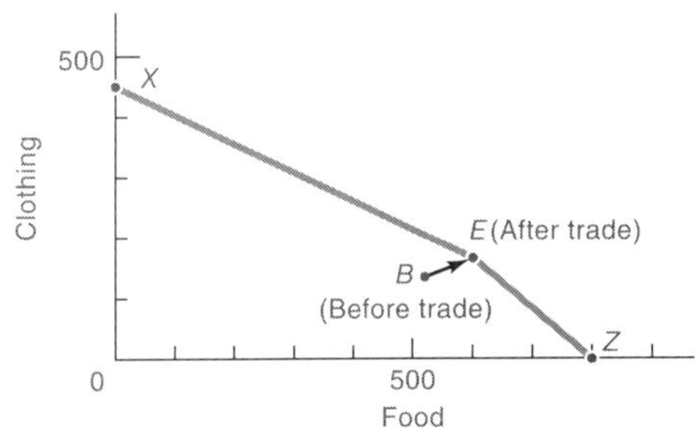

FIGURE 18-4. Free Trade Allows the World to Move to Its Production-Possibility Frontier ②

We show here the effect of free trade from the viewpoint of the world as a whole. Before trade is allowed, each region is on its own national *PPF*. Because the no-trade equilibrium is inefficient, the world is inside its *PPF* at point *B*.

Free trade allows each region to specialize in the goods in which it has comparative advantage. As a result of efficient specialization, the world moves out to the efficiency frontier at point *E*.

The world *PPF* is built up from the two regional *PPF*s in Figure 18-2 by determining the maximum level of world output that can be obtained from the individual regional *PPF*s. For example, the maximum quantity of food that can be produced (with no clothing production) is seen in Figure 18-2 to be 600 units in America and 200 units in Europe, for a world maximum of 800 units. This same point (800 food, 0 clothing) is then plotted in the world *PPF* in Figure 18-4. Additionally, we can plot the point (0 food, 450 clothing) in the world *PPF* by inspection of the regional *PPF*s. All the individual points in between can be constructed by a careful calculation of the maximum world outputs that can be produced if the two regions are efficiently specializing in the two goods.

Before opening up borders to trade, the world is at point *B*. This is an inefficient point—inside the world *PPF*—because regions have different levels of relative efficiency in different goods. After opening the borders to trade, the world moves to the free-trade equilibrium at *E*, where countries are specializing in their areas of comparative advantage.

Free trade in competitive markets allows the world to move to the frontier of its production-possibility curve. ③

扩展到多种商品和多个国家
EXTENSIONS TO MANY COMMODITIES AND COUNTRIES

The world of international trade consists of more than two regions and two commodities. However, the principles we explained above are essentially unchanged in realistic situations.

多种商品
Many Commodities

When two regions or countries produce many commodities at constant costs, the goods can be arranged in order according to the comparative advantage or cost of each. For example, the commodities might be microprocessors, computers, aircraft, automobiles, wine, and croissants—all arranged in the comparative-advantage sequence shown in Figure 18-5. As you can see from the figure, of all the commodities, microprocessors are least expensive in America relative to the costs in Europe. Europe has its greatest comparative advantage in croissants. Two decades ago, America was dominant in the commercial-aircraft market, but

① 图 18-3. 贸易前后的美国
② 图 18-4. 贸易自由化可以让世界移至其生产可能性边界
③ 竞争市场的自由贸易允许世界移至其生产可能性曲线的边界。

FIGURE 18-5. With Many Commodities, There Is a Spectrum of Comparative Advantages ①

Europe has now gained a substantial market share, so aircraft have been moving right on the line.

We can be virtually certain that the introduction of trade will cause America to produce and export microprocessors, while Europe will produce and export croissants. But where will the dividing line fall? Between aircraft and automobiles? Or wine and croissants? Or will the dividing line fall on one of the commodities rather than between them? Perhaps automobiles will be produced in both places.

You will not be surprised to find that the answer depends upon the demands and supplies of the different goods. We can think of the commodities as beads ②
arranged on a string according to their comparative advantage; the strength of supply and demand will determine where the dividing line between American and European production will fall. An increased demand for microprocessors and computers, for example, would tend to raise the relative prices of American goods. This shift might lead America to specialize so much more in areas of its comparative advantage that it would no longer be profitable to produce in areas of comparative disadvantage, like automobiles.

多个国家
Many Countries

What about the case of many countries? Introducing many countries need not change our analysis. As far as a single country is concerned, all the other nations can be lumped together into one group as "the rest of the world." The advantages of trade have no special relationship to national boundaries. The principles already developed apply between groups of countries and, indeed, between regions within the same country. In fact, they are just as applicable to trade between our northern and southern states as to trade between the United States and Canada.

三角贸易和多边贸易
Triangular and Multilateral Trade

With many countries brought into the picture, it will ③
generally be beneficial to engage in *triangular* or *multilateral trade* with many other countries. Bilateral trade between two countries is generally unbalanced.

Consider the simple example of triangular trade flows presented in Figure 18-6, where the arrows show the direction of exports. America buys consumer electronics from Japan, Japan buys oil and primary commodities from developing countries, and developing countries buy computers from America. In reality, trade patterns are more complex than this triangular example.

限制条件和结论
QUALIFICATIONS AND CONCLUSIONS

We have now completed our look at the elegant theory of comparative advantage. Its conclusions apply for any number of countries and commodities. Moreover, it can be generalized to handle many inputs, changing factor proportions, and diminishing returns. But we cannot conclude without noting two important qualifications to this elegant theory:

1. *Classical assumptions.* From a theoretical point of ④
view, the major defect of comparative-advantage theory lies in its classical assumptions. This theory assumes a smoothly working competitive economy. But trade might lead to worsening environmental problems if there are local or global public goods (see Chapter 14 for a further discussion). Moreover, inefficiencies might arise in the presence of inflexible prices and wages, business cycles, and involuntary unemployment. When there are macroeconomic or microeconomic

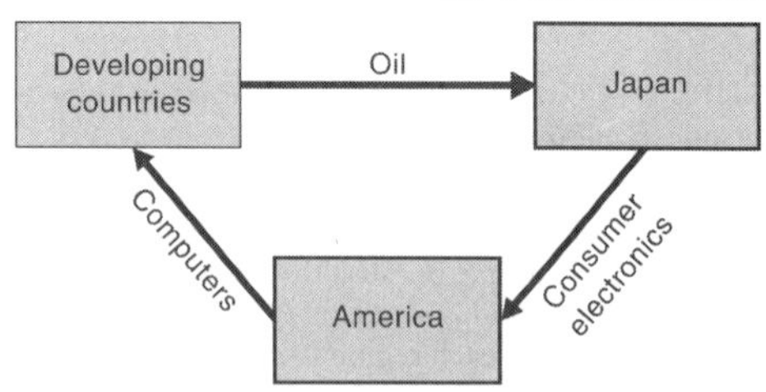

FIGURE 18-6. Triangular Trade Benefits All ⑤

In reality, international trade, like domestic trade, is many-sided.

---

① 图 18-5. 多种商品的比较优势图谱

② 我们可以把这些商品按照它们的比较优势，把它们设想为串在一条绳子上的珠子。供给与需求之间孰强孰弱的角力将决定出美国生产和欧洲生产的分界线。

③ 如图所示，在与他国的三边或者多边贸易中，多国都是受益方。而两国之间的双边贸易通常则是不平衡的。

④ 古典假定。

⑤ 图 18-6. 三角贸易对各方都有利

market failures, trade might well push a nation *inside* its *PPF*. When the economy is in depression or the price system malfunctions because of environmental or other reasons, we cannot be sure that countries will gain from trade.

Given these reservations, there can be little wonder that the theory of comparative advantage sells at a big discount during business downturns. In the Great Depression of the 1930s, as unemployment soared and real outputs fell, nations built high tariff walls at their borders and the volume of foreign trade shrank sharply. Additionally, during the prosperous 1990s, free trade was increasingly attacked by environmental advocates, who saw it as a means of allowing companies to dump pollutants in oceans or in countries with lax regulations. Environmentalists were among the leading critics of the latest attempts to promote freer trade (see the section "Negotiating Free Trade" at the end of this chapter).

2. *Income distribution.* A second proviso concerns the impact on particular people, sectors, or factors of production. We showed above that opening a country to trade will raise a country's national income. The country can consume more of all goods and services than would be possible if the borders were sealed to trade.

But this does not mean that *everyone* will benefit from trade, as shown by the Stolper-Samuelson [1] theorem. We can illustrate this theorem using an example. Suppose that America has a relatively skilled labor force, while China has a relatively unskilled labor force. Moreover, suppose that skilled labor is used more heavily in aircraft, while unskilled labor is used more heavily in clothing. Now move from a situation of no trade to a situation of free trade. As in the example, we would expect that America will export aircraft and import clothing. The price of aircraft in America would rise, and the price of clothing would fall.

The interesting point is the impact on labor. As a result of the shift in domestic production, the demand for unskilled labor falls because of the decline in clothing prices and production, while the demand for skilled labor rises because of the rise in aircraft prices and production. In a world of flexible wages, this leads to a decline in the wages of unskilled labor and a rise in the wages of skilled labor in America. More generally, free trade tends to increase the prices of factors that are intensive in exports and to reduce the prices of factors that are intensive in imports. (In a world with inflexible wages, it may lead to unemployment of unskilled workers, as our discussion of macroeconomics shows.)

Recent studies indicate that unskilled workers in high-income countries have suffered reductions in real wages in the last three decades because of the increased imports of goods from low-wage developing countries. Wage losses occur because imports ② of goods like clothing are produced by unskilled workers in developing countries. In a sense, these workers are close substitutes for the unskilled workers in the clothing industry of high-income countries. The increased international trade in clothing reduces the prices of clothing, and that tends to reduce the wages of unskilled workers in high-income countries.

The theory of comparative advantage shows that other sectors will gain more than the injured sectors will lose. Moreover, over long periods of time, those displaced from low-wage sectors eventually gravitate to higher-wage jobs. But those who are temporarily injured by international trade are genuinely harmed and are vocal advocates for protection and trade barriers.

Notwithstanding its limitations, the theory of ③ comparative advantage is one of the deepest truths in all of economics. Nations that disregard comparative advantage pay a heavy price in terms of their living standards and economic growth.

③ 尽管存在其自身的局限性，但是，比较优势的理论依然是所有经济学理论中最深奥的真理之一。那些忽视比较优势的国家，会为该国的生活水平和经济增长付出沉重的代价。

贸易保护主义

C. PROTECTIONISM

Go back to the beginning of this chapter and reread the "Petition of the Candle Makers," written by the French economist Frederic Bastiat to satirize solemn proposals to protect domestic goods from imports. Today, people often regard foreign competition with suspicion, and campaigns to "Buy American" sound patriotic.

Yet economists since the time of Adam Smith have marched to a different drummer. Economists generally believe that free trade promotes a mutually beneficial division of labor among nations; free and open trade allows *each* nation to expand its production and consumption possibilities, raising the

[1] Stolper-Samuelson theorem：斯托尔珀—萨缪尔森定理，简称SS定理，1941年由斯托尔帕（Wolfgang Stolper，1912~2002，美国经济学家）和萨缪尔森合作完成的论文《保护主义与实际工资》(*Protection and Real Wages*，见 *Review of Economic Studies* 第9期58~73页）中提出关于关税对国内生产要素价格或国内收入分配影响的经济学理论。

② 工资降低是因为像服装这样的进口商品是由发展中国家的非熟练工人生产的。某种意义上讲，这些工人几近于替代了高收入国家从事服装业的非熟练工人。这种发生在服装业领域高速增长的国际贸易降低了服装的价格，并且导致高收入国家非熟练工人的工资走低。

world's living standard. Protectionism prevents the ① forces of comparative advantage from working to maximum advantage.

This section reviews the economic arguments about protectionism.

贸易和关税的供求分析
SUPPLY-AND-DEMAND ANALYSIS OF TRADE AND TARIFFS

自由贸易和无贸易
Free Trade vs. No Trade

The theory of comparative advantage can be illuminated through the analysis of supply and demand for goods in foreign trade. Consider the clothing market in America. Assume, for simplicity, that America is a small part of the market and therefore cannot affect the world price of clothing. (This assumption will allow us to analyze supply and demand very easily; the more realistic case in which a country can affect world prices will be considered later in this chapter.)

Figure 18-7 shows the supply and demand curves for clothing in America. The demand curve of American consumers is drawn as *DD* and the domestic supply curve of American firms as *SS*. We assume that the price of clothing is determined in the world market and is equal to $4 per unit. Although transactions in ② international trade are carried out in different currencies, for now we can simplify by converting the foreign supply schedule into a dollar supply curve by using the current exchange rate.

No-Trade Equilibrium. Suppose that transportation costs or tariffs for clothing were prohibitive (say, $100 per unit of clothing). Where would the no-trade equilibrium lie? In this case, the American market for clothing would be at the intersection of *domestic*

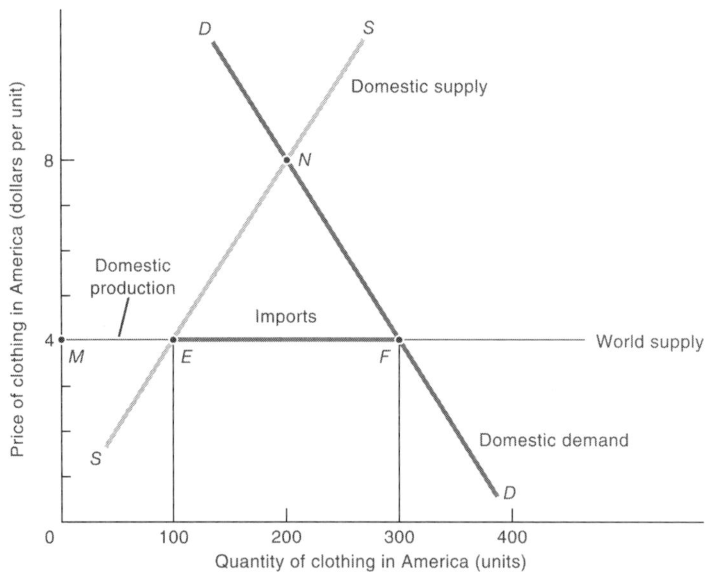

FIGURE 18-7. American Production, Imports, and Consumption under Free Trade ③

We see here the free-trade equilibrium in the market for clothing. America has a comparative disadvantage in clothing. Therefore, at the no-trade equilibrium at *N*, America's price would be $8, while the world price is $4.

Assuming that American demand does not affect the world price of $4 per unit, the free-trade equilibrium comes when America produces *ME* (100 units) and imports the difference between domestic demand and domestic supply, shown as *EF* (or 200 units).

---

① 但是，贸易保护主义却严重阻碍了比较优势发挥其最大作用。

② 虽然国际贸易的交易活动是以不同的货币来完成的，但我们却可以依据当前的汇率进行简化——把国外的供给清单转变为以美元为计价单位的供给曲线。

③ 图 18-7. 在自由贸易的环境下美国的生产、进口和消费

supply and demand, shown at point *N* in Figure 18-7. At this no-trade point, prices would be relatively high at $8 per unit, and domestic producers would be meeting all the demand.

Free Trade. Now open the American clothing market to international trade. In the absence of transport costs, tariffs, and quotas, the price in America must be equal to the world price. Why? Because if the American price were above the Chinese price, sharp-eyed entrepreneurs would buy where clothing was cheap (China) and sell where clothing was expensive (America); China would therefore export clothing to America. Once trade flows fully adjusted to supplies and demands, the price in America would equal the world price level. (In a world with transportation and tariff costs, the price in America would equal the world price adjusted for these costs.)

Figure 18-7 illustrates how prices, quantities, and trade flows will be determined under free trade in our clothing example. The horizontal line at $4 represents the supply curve for imports; it is horizontal, or perfectly price-elastic, because American demand is assumed to be too small to affect the world price of clothing.

Once trade opens up, imports flow into America, lowering the price of clothing to the world price of $4 per unit. At that level, domestic producers will supply the amount *ME*, or 100 units, while at that price consumers will want to buy 300 units. The difference, shown by the heavy line *EF*, is the amount of clothing imports. Who decided that we would import just this amount of clothing and that domestic producers would supply only 100 units? A Chinese planning agency? A cartel of clothing firms? No, the amount of trade was determined by supply and demand.

Moreover, the level of prices in the no-trade equilibrium determined the direction of the trade flows. America's no-trade prices were higher than China's, so goods flowed into America. Remember this rule: *Under* ① *free trade, indeed in markets generally, goods flow uphill from low-price regions to high-price regions.* When markets are opened to free trade, clothing flows uphill from the lower-price Chinese market to the higher-price American market until the price levels are equalized.

贸易壁垒

Trade Barriers

For centuries, governments have used tariffs and quotas to raise revenues and influence the development of individual industries. Since the eighteenth ② century—when the British Parliament attempted to impose tariffs on tea, sugar, and other commodities on its American colonies—tariff policy has proved fertile soil for revolution and political struggle.

We can use supply-and-demand analysis to understand the economic effects of tariffs and quotas. To ③ begin with, note that a **tariff** is a tax levied on imports. A **quota** is a limit on the quantity of imports. The United States has quotas on many products, including textiles, watches, and cheeses.

Table 18-3 shows the average tariff rates for major countries in 2003. Note that tariffs vary widely for different goods in most countries. It would take deep study to understand why tariffs on imports of horses are zero while those on asses are 6.8 percent of value in the United States. On the other hand, it does not ④ take much study to understand why textiles and steel have tight quotas or high tariffs, because these are industries with political clout in Congress or the White House.

Country or region	**Average tariff rate, 2003 (%)**
Hong Kong (China)	0.0
Switzerland	0.0
Japan	3.3
United States	3.9
Canada	4.2
European Union	4.4
Russia	11.3
China	12.0
Mexico	17.3
Pakistan	17.2
India	33.0
Iran	30.0
Average of major groups:	
Low-income countries	5.9
Middle-income countries	14.1

TABLE 18-3. Average Tariff Rates, 2003 ⑤

Tariff rates vary widely among regions. The United States and regions like Singapore and Hong Kong (China) have low tariff rates today, although there are exceptions such as for textiles and steel. Countries like India continues to maintain protectionist trade barriers.

Source: World Trade Organization and government organizations.

① 在自由贸易的环境下，市场中的商品实际上都是由低价地区向高价地区流动。

② 从 18 世纪英国议会试图开始向北美殖民地出产的茶叶、蔗糖和其他商品征收关税以来，关税政策就已经被证明是一块培植革命和政治斗争的沃土。

③ 首先请注意，**关税**是对进口商品课征的一种税种。**配额**是对进口商品数量的一种限制措施。美国政府对许多商品实行配额管理，其中包括纺织品、手表和奶酪等。

④ 另一方面，并不需要做更多的研究就可以明白，为什么纺织品和钢铁有紧张的配额和高关税，原因就是这些行业背后都有国会或白宫政治势力的干预。

⑤ 表 18-3. 2003 年各国和各关税区平均关税率

Prohibitive Tariff. The easiest case to analyze is a *prohibitive tariff*—one that is so high that it chokes off all imports. Looking back at Figure 18-7, what would happen if the tariff on clothing were more than \$4 per unit (that is, more than the difference between America's no-trade price of \$8 and the world price of \$4)? This would be a prohibitive tariff, shutting off all clothing trade. Any importer who buys clothing at the world price of \$4 would sell it in America at the no-trade price of \$8. But this price would not cover the cost of the good plus the tariff. Prohibitive tariffs thus kill off all trade.

Nonprohibitive Tariff. Lower tariffs (less than \$4 per unit of clothing) would injure but not kill off trade. Figure 18-8 shows the equilibrium in the clothing market with a \$2 tariff. Again assuming no transportation costs, a \$2 tariff means that foreign clothing will sell in America for \$6 per unit (equal to the \$4 world price plus the \$2 tariff).

The equilibrium result of a \$2 tariff is that domestic consumption (or quantity demanded) is lowered from 300 units in the free-trade equilibrium to 250 units after the tariff is imposed, the amount of domestic production is raised by 50 units, and the quantity of imports is lowered by 100 units. This example summarizes the economic impact of tariffs:

A tariff will tend to raise price, lower the amounts ① consumed and imported, and raise domestic production of the covered good.

Quotas. Quotas have the same qualitative effect as tariffs. A prohibitive quota (one that prevents all imports) is equivalent to a prohibitive tariff. The price and quantity would move back to the no-trade equilibrium at *N* in Figure 18-8. A less stringent quota might limit imports to 100 clothing units; this quota would equal the heavy line *HJ* in Figure 18-8. A quota of 100 units would lead to the same equilibrium price and output as did the \$2 tariff.

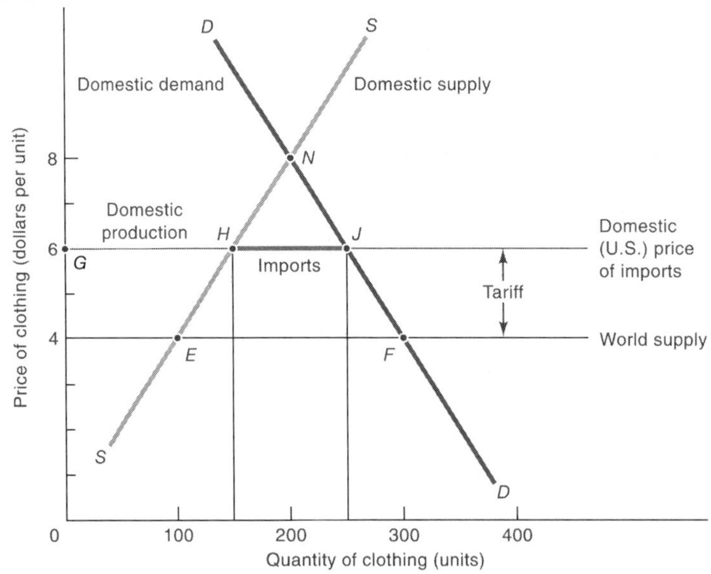

FIGURE 18-8. Effect of a Tariff ②

A tariff lowers imports and consumption and raises domestic production and price. Starting ③ from the free-trade equilibrium in Fig. 18-7, America now puts a \$2 tariff on clothing imports. The price of Chinese clothing imports rises to \$6 (including the tariff).

The market price rises from \$4 to \$6, so the total amount demanded falls. Imports shrink from 200 to 100 units, while domestic production rises from 100 to 150 units.

① 关税的作用是提高销售价格，降低消费以及进口的数量，以提高国内对相关课税商品的生产。

② 图 18-8. 关税效应

③ 关税的征收降低了进口和消费量，并且提高了国内产量和销售价格。

Although there is no essential difference between tariffs and quotas, some subtle differences do exist. A tariff gives revenue to the government, perhaps allowing other taxes to be reduced and thereby offsetting some of the harm done to consumers in the importing country. A quota, on the other hand, puts ① the profit from the resulting price difference into the pocket of the importers or exporters lucky enough to get a permit or import license. They can afford to use the proceeds to wine, dine, or even bribe the officials who give out import licenses.

Because of these differences, economists generally regard tariffs as the lesser evil. However, if a gov- ② ernment is determined to impose quotas, it should auction off the scarce import-quota licenses. An auction will ensure that the government rather than the importer gets the revenue from the scarce right to import; in addition, the bureaucracy will not be tempted to allocate quota rights by bribery, friendship, or nepotism.

Transportation Costs. What of transportation costs? The cost of moving bulky and perishable goods has the same effect as tariffs, reducing the extent of beneficial regional specialization. For example, if it costs $2 per unit to transport clothing from China to the United States, the supply-and-demand equilibrium would look just like Figure 18-8, with the American price $2 above the Chinese price.

But there is one difference between protection and transportation costs: Transport costs are imposed by nature—by oceans, mountains, and rivers—whereas restrictive tariffs are squarely the responsibility of nations. Indeed, one economist called tariffs "negative railroads." Imposing a tariff has the same economic impact as throwing sand in the engines of vessels that transport goods to our shores from other lands.

关税的经济成本
The Economic Costs of Tariffs

What happens when America puts a tariff on clothing, such as the $2 tariff shown in Figure 18-8? There are three effects: (1) The domestic producers, operating under a price umbrella provided by the tariff, can expand production; (2) consumers are faced with higher prices and therefore reduce their consumption; and (3) the government gains tariff revenue.

Tariffs create economic inefficiencies. When tar- ③ iffs are imposed, the economic loss to consumers exceeds the revenue gained by the government plus the extra profits earned by producers.

Diagrammatic Analysis. Figure 18-9 shows the economic cost of a tariff. The supply and demand curves are identical to those in Figure 18-8, but three areas are highlighted. (1) Area *B* is the tariff revenue collected by the government. It is equal to the amount of the tariff times the units of imports and totals $200. (2) The tariff raises the price in domestic markets from $4 to $6, and producers increase their output to 150. Hence total profits rise by $250, shown by area *LEHM* and equal to $200 on old units plus an additional $50 on the 50 new units. (3) Finally, note that a tariff imposes a heavy cost on consumers. The total consumer-surplus loss is given by area *LMJF* and is equal to $550.

The overall social impact is, then, a gain to producers of $250, a gain to the government of $200, and a loss to consumers of $550. The net social cost (counting each of these dollars equally) is therefore $100. We can reckon this as equal to the sum of *A* and *C*. The interpretation of these areas is important:

- Area *A* is the net loss that comes because domestic production is more costly than foreign production. When the domestic price rises, businesses are thereby induced to increase the use of relatively costly domestic capacity. They produce output up to the point where the marginal cost is $6 per unit instead of up to $4 per unit under free trade. Firms reopen inefficient old factories or work existing factories extra shifts. From an economic point of view, these plants have a comparative disadvantage because the new clothing produced by these factories could be produced more cheaply abroad. The new social cost of this inefficient production is area *A*, equal to $50.
- In addition, there is a net loss to the country from the higher price, shown by area *C*. This is the loss in consumer surplus that cannot be offset by business profits or tariff revenue. This area represents the economic cost incurred when consumers shift their purchases from low-cost imports to high-cost domestic goods. This area is also equal to $50.

Hence, the total social loss from the tariff is $100, calculated either way.

---

① 另一个角度讲，配额是将使用这一手段带来的价格差异所产生的利润，放进进口商或者出口商的口袋里，使他们能够足够幸运地获得进口许可证。

② 但是，如果政府决定要设置配额，就应该对稀缺的进口配额许可进行公开拍卖。

③ 关税的征收会酿成经济的无效率。关税政策一出台，对消费者造成的经济损失就会超越政府获得的收入加上厂商所挣的额外利润之和。

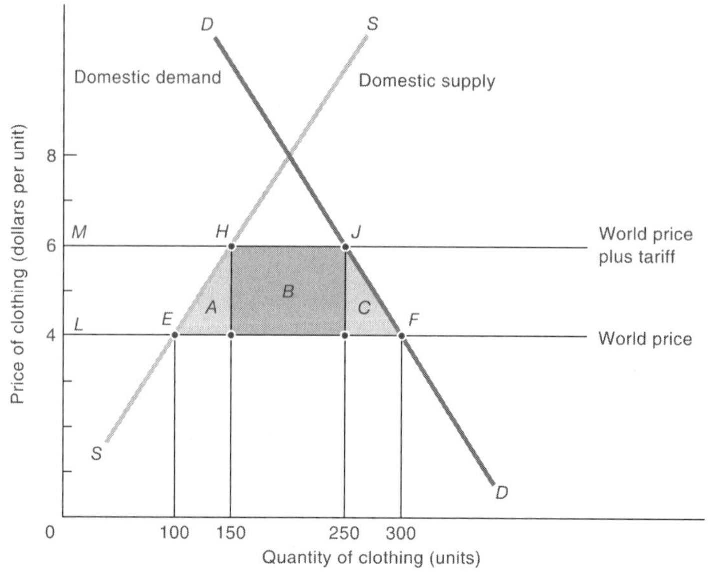

FIGURE 18-9. Economic Cost of a Tariff ①

Imposing a tariff raises revenues and leads to inefficiency. We see the impact of the tariff as three effects. Rectangle *B* is the tariff revenue gained by the government. Triangle *A* is the excess cost of production by firms producing under the umbrella of the tariff. Triangle *C* is the net loss in consumer surplus from the inefficiently high price. Areas *A* and *C* are the irreducible inefficiencies caused by the tariff.

Figure 18-9 illustrates one feature that is important in understanding the politics and history of tariffs. When a tariff is imposed, part of the economic impact comes because tariffs redistribute income from consumers to the protected domestic producers and workers. In the example shown in Figure 18-9, areas *A* and *C* represent efficiency losses from inefficiently high domestic production and inefficiently low consumption, respectively. Under the simplifying assumptions used above, the efficiency losses sum up to \$100. The redistribution involved is much larger, ② however, equaling \$200 raised in tariff revenues levied upon consumers of the commodity plus \$250 in higher profits. Consumers will be unhappy about the higher product cost, while domestic producers and workers in those firms will benefit. We can see why battles over import restrictions generally center more on the redistributive gains and losses than on the issues of economic efficiency.

Imposing a tariff has three effects: It encourages inefficiently high domestic production; it raises prices, thus inducing consumers to reduce their purchases of the tariffed good below efficient levels; and it raises revenues for the government. Only the first two of these necessarily impose efficiency costs on the economy. ③

The Cost of Textile Protection

Let's flesh out this analysis by examining the effects of a particular tariff, one on clothing. Today, tariffs on imported textiles and apparel are among the highest levied by the United States. How do these high tariffs affect consumers and producers?

To begin with, the tariffs raise domestic clothing prices. Because of the higher prices, many factories, which would otherwise be bankrupt in the face of a declining comparative advantage in textiles, remain open. They are just barely

① 图 18-9. 关税的经济成本

② 但是，涉及到的再分配金额则更大，等于在商品消费者身上征收的关税收入 200 美元，另加厂商的新增利润 250 美元。消费者对更高的产品成本极为不满，而国内相关企业中的制造商和生产工人从中受益。我们可以看出，为什么进口限制的争论一般更容易集中在再分配的损益上，而不是集中在经济效率的问题上。

③ 征收关税有三个作用：它能鼓励产能很高但效率很低的国内生产；它能提高价格，以促使消费者减少对那些低于效率水平的关税商品的购买；它能够增加政府的收入。但这其中的头两项，却不可避免地给经济增加了各种效率成本。

profitable, but they manage to eke out enough sales to continue domestic production. Domestic employment in textiles exceeds the free-trade situation, although—because of pressure from foreign competition—textile wages are among the lowest of any manufacturing industry.

From an economic point of view, the nation is wasting resources in textiles. These workers, materials, and capital would be more productively used in other sectors—perhaps in aircraft or financial services or Internet commerce. The nation's productive potential is lower because it keeps factors of production working in an industry in which it has lost its comparative advantage.

Consumers, of course, pay for this protection of the textile industry with higher prices. They get less satisfaction from their incomes than they would if they could buy textiles from The Republic of Korea, China, or Indonesia at prices that exclude the high tariffs. Consumers are induced to cut back on their clothing purchases, channeling funds into food, transportation, and recreation, whose relative prices are lowered by the tariffs.

Finally, the government gets revenues from tariffs on textiles. These revenues can be used to buy public goods or to reduce other taxes, so (unlike the consumer loss or the productive inefficiency) this effect is not a real social burden.

保护主义经济学
THE ECONOMICS OF PROTECTIONISM

Having examined the impact of tariffs on prices and quantities, we now turn to an analysis of the arguments for and against protectionism. The arguments for tariff or quota protection against the competition of foreign imports take many different forms. Here are the main categories: (1) noneconomic arguments that suggest it is desirable to sacrifice economic welfare in order to subsidize other national objectives, (2) arguments that are based on a misunderstanding of economic logic, and (3) analyses that rely on market power or macroeconomic imperfections.

非经济目标
Noneconomic Goals

If you are ever on a debating team given the assignment of defending free trade, you will strengthen ① your case at the beginning by conceding that there is more to life than economic welfare. A nation surely should not sacrifice its liberty, culture, and human rights for a few dollars of extra income.

The U.S. semiconductor industry provides a useful example here. In the 1980s, the Defense Department claimed that without an independent semiconductor industry, the military would become excessively dependent on Japanese and other foreign suppliers for chips to use in high-technology weaponry. This led to an agreement to protect the industry. Economists were skeptical about the value of this approach. Their argument did not question the goal of national security. Rather, it focused on the efficiency of the means of achieving the desired result. They thought that protection was more expensive than a policy targeting the domestic industry, perhaps a program to buy a minimum number of high-quality chips. [2]

National security is not the only noneconomic goal in trade policy. Countries may desire to preserve their cultural traditions or environmental conditions. France argued that its citizens need to be protected from "uncivilized" American movies. The fear is that the French film industry could be drowned by the new wave of stunt-filled, high-budget Hollywood thrillers. As a result, France has maintained strict quotas on the number of U.S. movies and television shows that can be imported.

站不住脚的关税观
Unsound Grounds for Tariffs

Mercantilism. To Abraham Lincoln has been attributed the remark, "I don't know much about the tariff. I do know that when I buy a coat from England, I have the coat and England has the money. But when I buy a coat in America, I have the coat and America has the money."

This reasoning represents an age-old fallacy typical of the so-called mercantilist writers of the seventeenth and eighteenth centuries. They considered a country fortunate which sold more goods than it bought, because such a "favorable" balance of trade meant that gold would flow into the country to pay for its export surplus.

The mercantilist argument confuses means and ends. Accumulating gold or other monies will not improve a country's living standard. Money is worthwhile not for its own sake but for what it will buy from other countries. Most economists today therefore reject the idea that raising tariffs to run a trade surplus will improve a country's economic welfare.

Tariffs for Special Interests. The single most important source of pressure for protective tariffs is powerful

---

① 如果你是辩论队中的一名辩手，为自由贸易辩护，那么辩论一开始，你就要采取以退为守的办法——说明经济福利仅仅是生活中微不足道的内容来强调你的观点。

[2] U.S. semiconductor industry：核心半导体元器件的生产和研发，从上世纪 80 年代以来一直是美国国防部密切关注并严格管控的问题。1965 年，英特尔公司的创始人戈登·摩尔（Gordon Moore, 1929~）所预言的每隔 18 年半导体芯片的运算速度增加一倍，价格随之减少一倍（即著名的摩尔定律，*Moore's Law*），一直被不断证明至世纪之交。随着全球化步伐的加快，从 20 世纪 80 年代开始，美国的半导体元器件生产开始向亚洲转移，遂开始引起美国军方的高度关注和严格管制。进入新世纪之后，随着摩尔定律被全球化大潮所带来的巨大市场所打破，美国国防部的忧心和管控更为加剧，时至今日。

special-interest groups. Firms and workers know very well that a tariff on their particular products will help *them* even if it imposes costs on others. Adam Smith understood this point well when he wrote:

> To expect freedom of trade is as absurd as to expect ① Utopia. Not only the prejudices of the public, but what is much more unconquerable, the private interests of many individuals, irresistibly oppose it. [2]

If free trade is so beneficial to the nation as a ③ whole, why do the proponents of protectionism continue to wield such a disproportionate influence on legislatures? The few who benefit gain much from specific protection and therefore devote large sums to lobbying politicians. By contrast, individual consumers are only slightly affected by the tariff on one product; because losses are small and widespread, individuals have little incentive to spend resources expressing an opinion on every tariff case. A century ago, outright bribery was used to buy the votes necessary to pass tariff legislation. Today, powerful political action committees (PACs), financed by labor or business, round up lawyers and drum up support for tariffs or quotas on textiles, lumber, steel, sugar, and other goods.

If political votes were cast in proportion to total economic benefit, nations would legislate most tariffs out of existence. But each dollar of economic interests does not get proportional representation. It is much harder to persuade consumers about the benefits of free trade than it is to organize a few companies or labor unions to argue against "cheap Chinese labor." In every country, the special interests of protected firms and workers are the tireless enemies of free trade.

A dramatic case is the U.S. quota on sugar, which benefits a few producers while costing American consumers over $1 billion a year. The average consumer is probably unaware that the sugar quota costs about a penny a day per person, so there is little incentive to lobby for free trade in sugar.

Competition from Cheap Foreign Labor. Of all the arguments for protection, the most persistent is that free trade exposes U.S. workers to competition from low-wage foreign labor. The only way to preserve high U.S. wages, so the argument goes, is to protect domestic workers by keeping out or putting high tariffs on goods produced in low-wage countries. An extreme version of this contention is that under free trade U.S. wages would decline to the low level of foreign wages. This point was trumpeted by presidential candidate Ross Perot during the debates over the [4] North American Free Trade Agreement (NAFTA) [5] when he argued:

> Philosophically, [NAFTA] is wonderful, but realistically it will be bad for our country. ⑥ That thing is going to create a giant sucking sound in the United States at a time when we need jobs coming in, not jobs going out. Mexican wages will come up to $7½ an hour and our wages will come down to $7½ an hour.

This argument sounds plausible, but it is all ⑦ wrong because it ignores the principle of comparative advantage. The reason American workers have higher wages is that they are on average more productive. If America's wage is 5 times that in Mexico, it is because the marginal product of American workers is on average 5 times that of Mexican workers. Trade flows according to comparative advantage, not wage rates or absolute advantage.

Having shown that the nation gains from importing the goods produced by "cheap foreign labor" in which it has a comparative disadvantage, we should not ignore the impacts that trade may have on particular firms and workers. Remember the Stolper-Samuelson theorem explained above. If America has a comparative disadvantage in industries like textiles or toys, and these industries are intensive in unskilled labor, reducing trade barriers will tend to reduce the wages of unskilled labor in America. There may also be temporary effects on workers whose wages drop while they look for alternative jobs. The difficulties of displaced workers will be greater when the overall economy is depressed or when the local labor markets have high unemployment. Over the long run, labor markets will reallocate workers from declining to advancing industries, but the transition may be costly for many people.

In summary:

> The cheap-foreign-labor argument is flawed because it ignores the theory of comparative advantage. A country will benefit from trade even though its wages are far above those of its trading partners. High wages come from high efficiency, not from tariff protection.

① 对自由贸易的期待其实像幻想构建乌托邦一样荒唐。不仅公众会对此持有偏见，而且几乎无法控制的因素是，许许多多个体的私人利益，以及不可遏制的反对力量。

[2] 本段文字出自亚当·斯密《国富论》(*An Inquiry into the Nature and Causes of the Wealth of Nations*, Book IV, Chapter II, 43, London: Methuen & Co., Ltd., 1904, 5th edition）第四编第二章第 43 自然段，原文如下：

To expect, indeed, that the freedom of trade should ever be entirely restored in Great Britain is as absurd as to expect that an Oceana or Utopia should ever be established in it. Not only the prejudices of the public, but what is much more unconquerable, the private interests of many individuals, irresistibly oppose it.

③ 如果自由贸易对整个国家来讲是有益的，那为什么贸易保护主义的支持者持续地对立法者施加影响呢?

---

[4] 罗斯·佩罗（Ross Perot，1930~），美国商人，1992 和 1996 两年曾参选美国总统。

[5]《北美自由贸易协定》，由美国、加拿大和墨西哥于 1992 年 8 月 12 日签署 1994 年 1 月 1 日正式生效，是世界最大的自由贸易集团。

⑥ 按道理讲，北美自由贸易协定是很好的，但从现实角度来思考，它对我们国家极为不利。它带来的问题是，在此时的美国，我们需要的是工作流入而不是流出，这个协定却在发出“巨大的吞食声”。墨西哥工人的平均工资将因此涨到每小时 7.5 美元，而美国工人平均每小时的工资将跌到 7.5 美元的水平。

注：2009 年美国产业工人的最低工资标准已经涨到每小时 7.25 美元（见本书 77 页），与此仅差 25 美分。

⑦ 这一观点听起来似乎有道理，但它是错的，因为它忽略了比较优势原则。美国工人有更高工资的原因是，平均来说他们的生产效率更高。

Retaliatory Tariffs. While many people would agree that a world of free trade would be the best of all possible worlds, they note that this is not the world we live in. They reason, "As long as other countries impose import restrictions or otherwise discriminate against our products, we have no choice but to play the protection game in self-defense. We'll go along with free trade only as long as it is fair trade. But we insist on a level playing field." On several occasions in the 1990s, the United States went to the brink of trade wars with Japan and China, threatening high tariffs if the other country did not stop some objectionable trade practice.

Those who advocate this approach argue that it can beat down the walls of protectionism in other countries. This rationale was described in an analysis of protection in the *Economic Report of the President:*

> Intervention in international trade . . . even though ① costly to the U.S. economy in the short run, may, however, be justified if it serves the strategic purpose of increasing the cost of interventionist policies by foreign governments. Thus, there is a potential role for carefully targeted measures . . . aimed at convincing other countries to reduce their trade distortions.

While potentially valid, this argument should be used with great caution. Just as threatening war leads to armed conflict as often as to arms control, protectionist bluffs may end up hurting the bluffer as well as the opponent. Historical studies show that retaliatory tariffs usually lead other nations to raise their tariffs still higher and are rarely an effective bargaining chip for multilateral tariff reduction.

Import Relief. In the United States and other countries, firms and workers that are injured by foreign competition attempt to get protection in the form of tariffs or quotas. Today, relatively little direct tariff business is conducted on the floor of Congress. Congress realized that tariff politics was too hot to handle and has set up specialized agencies to investigate and rule on complaints. Generally, a petition for relief is analyzed by the U.S. Department of Commerce and the U.S. International Trade Commission. Relief measures include the following actions:

- The *escape clause* was popular in earlier periods. It ② allows temporary import relief (tariffs, quotas, or export quotas negotiated with other countries) when an industry has been "injured" by imports. Injury occurs when the output, employment, and profits in a domestic industry have fallen while imports have risen.
- *Antidumping tariffs* are levied when foreign coun- ③ tries sell in the United States at prices below average costs or at prices lower than those in the home market. When dumping is found, a "dumping duty" is placed on the imported good.
- *Countervailing duties* are imposed to offset the cost ④ advantage for imports that arises when foreigners subsidize exports to the United States. They have become the most popular form of import relief and have been pursued in hundreds of cases.

What is the justification for such measures? Import relief sounds reasonable, but it actually is completely counter to the theory of comparative advantage. That theory says that an industry which cannot compete with foreign firms ought to be injured by imports. *From an economic vantage point, less productive* ⑤ *industries are actually being killed off by the competition of more productive domestic industries.*

This sounds ruthless indeed. No industry willingly dies. No region gladly undergoes conversion to new industries. Often the shift from old to new industries involves considerable unemployment and hardship. The weak industry and region feel they are being singled out to carry the burden of progress.

可能符合逻辑的贸易保护观点
Potentially Valid Arguments for Protection

Finally, we can consider three arguments for protection that may have true economic merit:

- Tariffs may shift the terms of trade in a country's favor.
- Temporary tariff protection for an "infant industry" with growth potential may be efficient in the long run.
- A tariff may under certain conditions help reduce unemployment.

The Terms-of-Trade or Optimal-Tariff Argument. One valid argument for imposing tariffs is that doing so will shift the terms of trade in a country's favor and against foreign countries. The phrase *terms of trade* refers to the ratio of export prices to import prices. The idea is that when a large country levies tariffs on its imports, the reduced demand for the good in world markets will lower the equilibrium price and thereby reduce the pretariff cost of the

---

① 即使短期内美国的经济会付出一定的代价，但如果外国政府实施干预政策的成本猛增，就是变相地为美国的战略目标服务，那么这点代价就是值得的。因此，对于这些精心策划过的措施（旨在使其他国家确信这会减少它们自身的贸易扭曲）来讲，它还扮演了幕后英雄的角色。

② 例外条款

③ 反倾销税

④ 反补贴税（抵消性关税）

⑤ 从经济优势的观点分析，生产效率不高的产业实际上正在面临因国内生产率高的产业的竞争而被踢出局的危险。

good to the country. Such a change will improve the country's terms of trade and increase domestic real income. The set of tariffs that maximizes domestic real income is called the *optimal tariff.*

The terms-of-trade argument goes back over 150 years to the free-trade proponent John Stuart [1] Mill. It is the only argument for tariffs that is valid under conditions of full employment and perfect competition. Suppose that the U.S. imposes an "optimal" tariff on imported oil. The tariff will increase the price of domestic oil and will reduce the world demand for oil. The world market price of oil will therefore be bid down. So part of the tariff actually falls on the oil producer. (We can see that a very small country could not use this argument, since it cannot affect world prices.)

Have we not therefore found a theoretically secure argument for tariffs? The answer would be yes if we could forget that this is a "begger-thy-neighbor" [2] policy and could ignore the reactions of other countries. But other countries are likely to react. After all, if the United States were to impose an optimal tariff of 30 percent on its imports, why should the European Union and Japan not put 30 or 40 percent tariffs on their imports? In the end, as every country ③ calculated and imposed its own nationalistic optimal tariff, the overall level of tariffs might spiral upward in the tariff version of an arms race.

Ultimately, such a situation would surely not represent an improvement of either world or individual economic welfare. When all countries impose optimal tariffs, it is likely that *everyone's* economic welfare will decline as the impediments to free trade become larger. All countries are likely to benefit if all countries abolish trade barriers.

Tariffs for Infant Industries. In his famous *Report on Manufactures* (1791), Alexander Hamilton proposed to encourage the growth of manufacturing by protecting "infant industries" from foreign competition. According to this doctrine, which received the cautious support of free-trade economists like John Stuart Mill and Alfred Marshall, there are lines of [4] production in which a country could have a comparative advantage if only they could get started.

Such infant industries would not be able to survive the rough treatment by larger bullies in the global marketplace. With some temporary nurturing, however, they might grow up to enjoy economies of mass production, a pool of skilled labor, inventions well adapted to the local economy, and the technological efficiency typical of many mature industries. Although protection will raise prices to the consumer at first, the mature industry would become so efficient that cost and price would actually fall. A tariff is justified if the benefit to consumers at that later date would be more than enough to make up for the higher prices during the period of protection.

This argument must be weighed cautiously. Historical studies have turned up some genuine cases of protected infant industries that grew up to stand on their own feet. And studies of successful newly industrialized countries (such as Singapore) show that they have often protected their manufacturing industries from imports during the early stages of industrialization. But subsidies will be a more efficient. cient and transparent way of nurturing young indus-
In fact, the history of tariffs reveals many cases like ⑤
steel, sugar, and textiles in which perpetually protected infants have not shed their diapers after these many years.

Brazil's Tragic Protection of Its Computer Industry

Brazil offers a striking example of the pitfalls of protectionism. In 1984, Brazil passed a law actually banning most foreign computers. The idea was to provide a protected environment in which Brazil's own infant computer industry could develop. The law was vigorously enforced by special "computer police" who would search corporate offices and classrooms looking for illegal imported computers.

The results were startling. Technologically, Brazilian-made computers were years behind the fast-moving world market, and consumers paid 2 or 3 times the world price—when they could get them at all. At the same time, because Brazilian computers were so expensive, they could not compete on the world market, so Brazilian computer companies could not take advantage of economies of scale by selling to other countries. The high price of computers hurt competitiveness in the rest of the economy as well. "We are effectively very backward because of this senseless nationalism," said Zelia Cardoso de Mello, Brazil's [6] economy minister in 1990. "The computer problem effectively blocked Brazilian industry from modernizing."

The combination of pressure from Brazilian consumers and businesses and U.S. demands for open markets

---

[2] "begger-thy-neighbor"：课本中的begger为罕见的拼读错误，应为beggar。beggar作动词，指"使别人变穷"之意；thy为早期现代英文之前的用法，相当于现代英语your的单数含义。故这个短语的译文应为"使邻居变穷"，正好与中国的"睦邻、富邻"政策相悖。

③ 总之，当每一个国家都仔细地核算并设置了对自己国家最优的关税时，关税的总水平就有可能螺旋式攀升，这就完全变成了关税版本的军备竞赛。

[4] 艾尔弗雷德·马歇尔（Alfred Marshall，1842~1924），新古典学派的创始人，19世纪末和20世纪初英国经济学界最重要的人物，在剑桥大学建立了世界上第一个经济学系，使经济学从仅仅是人文和历史学科的一门必修课发展成为一门独立的学科。1881年出版的《经济学原理》（*Principles of Economics*）是其主要的代表作。此书将以本书的注疏模式，与斯密的《国富论》、凯恩斯的《通论》等一起，已经列入出版计划，由本人独立完成它们的注疏版本，以期在数百年之后，以崛起中的中国学人的视觉重新审视西方的经典，准确地理解这些经典中所承载的人文史迹。本书的16、61、185页对马歇尔均有提及，请予参阅。另见p89注[5]。

[1] 约翰·斯图尔特·米尔（John Stuart Mill，1806~1873），著名的英国哲学家和经济学家，19世纪极具影响力的古典自由主义思想家。详见p149注[1]。

⑤ 事实上，关税的历史也给我们揭示了许多像钢铁、蔗糖和纺织品等产业的案例，在这些案例中，即便它们作为"幼稚产业"多年以来备受呵护，但至今仍然无法摆脱被呵护的"幼稚"。

[6] 齐利亚·卡多索·德·梅洛（Zelia Cardoso de Mello，1953~），1990~1991任巴西经济部长，1995年移居美国，1998年后在哥伦比亚大学做访问学者。其主要著作《卡洛的行动计划》（*Plano Collor*），是一部论述经济改革和抑制通货膨胀的文集。"Collor"是梅洛任部长期间的巴西总统费尔南多·卡洛·德·梅洛（Fernando Collor de Mello，1949~），他1990年上任，1992年为免受弹劾，辞去总统职务。在任期间推行贸易自由化和私有化的"空前革命"，是典型的南美激进派改革者。两人虽然同姓，但无亲缘关系。

forced Brazil to drop the ban on imported computers in 1992. Within a year, electronics stores in São Paulo and Rio de Janeiro were filled with imported laptop computers, laser printers, and cellular telephones, and Brazilian companies could begin to exploit the computer revolution. Each country and each generation learns anew the lessons of comparative advantage.

Tariffs and Unemployment. Historically, a powerful motive for protection has been the desire to increase employment during a period of recession or stagnation. Protection creates jobs by raising the price of imports and diverting demand toward domestic production; Figure 18-8 demonstrates this effect. As domestic demand increases, firms will hire more workers and unemployment will fall. This too is a beggar-thy-neighbor policy, for it raises domestic demand at the expense of output and employment in other countries.

However, while economic protection may raise employment, it does not constitute an effective program to pursue high employment, efficiency, and stable prices. Macroeconomic analysis shows that there are better ways of reducing unemployment than by imposing import protection. By the appropriate use of monetary and fiscal policy, a country can increase output and lower unemployment. Moreover, the use of general macroeconomic policies will allow workers displaced from low-productivity jobs in industries losing their comparative advantage to move to high-productivity jobs in industries enjoying a comparative advantage. ①

This lesson was amply demonstrated in the 1990s. From 1991 to 1999, the United States created 16 million net new jobs while maintaining open markets and low tariffs; its trade deficit increased sharply during this period. By contrast, the countries of Europe created virtually no new jobs while moving toward a position of trade surpluses.

Tariffs and import protection are an inefficient way to create jobs or to lower unemployment. A more effective way to increase productive employment is through domestic monetary and fiscal policy. ②

其他贸易壁垒

Other Barriers to Trade

While this chapter has mainly spoken of tariffs, most points apply equally well to any other impediments to trade. Quotas have much the same effects as tariffs, for they prevent the comparative advantages of different countries from determining prices and outputs in the marketplace. In recent years, countries have negotiated quotas with other countries. The United States, for example, forced Japan to put "voluntary" export quotas on automobiles and negotiated similar export quotas on televisions, shoes, and steel. ③

We should also mention the so-called nontariff barriers (or NTBs). These consist of informal restrictions or regulations that make it difficult for countries to sell their goods in foreign markets. For example, American firms complained that Japanese regulations shut them out of the telecommunications, tobacco, and construction industries. ④

How important are the nontariff barriers relative to tariffs? Economic studies indicate that nontariff barriers were actually more important than tariffs during the 1960s; in recent years, they have effectively doubled the protection found in the tariff codes. In a sense, nontariff barriers have been substitutes for more conventional tariffs as the latter have been reduced.

多边贸易谈判

MULTILATERAL TRADE NEGOTIATIONS

Given the tug-of-war between the economic benefits of free trade and the political appeal of protection, which force has prevailed? The history of U.S. tariffs, shown in Figure 18-10, has been bumpy. For most of American history, the United States was a high-tariff nation. The pinnacle of protectionism came after the infamous Smoot-Hawley tariff of 1930, which was [5] opposed by virtually every American economist yet sailed through Congress.

The trade barriers erected during the Great Depression helped raise prices and exacerbated economic distress. In the trade wars of the 1930s, countries attempted to raise employment and output by raising trade barriers at the expense of their neighbors. Nations soon learned that at the end of the tariff-retaliation game, all were losers. ⑥

自由贸易谈判

Negotiating Free Trade

At the end of World War II, the international community established a number of institutions to promote peace and economic prosperity through cooperative policies.

[5] Smoot-Hawley tariff of 1930:《斯穆特—霍利关税法案》,也称《1930关税法案》,由1929年开始的经济大萧条催生的贸易保护主义法案，对国际贸易产生了破坏性的影响。威利斯·霍利（Willis Hawley, 1864~1941），1907~1933年间一直代表共和党在众议院任众议员；里德·斯穆特（Reed Smoot, 1862~1941）长期任参议院参议员，著名的后期圣徒（The Church of Jesus Christ of latter-day saint，美国基督教新教摩门教徒）领袖，美国现任驻华大使洪博培（Jon Meade Huntsman, Jr. 1960~）即为该摩门教传教士。两人同年去世。

① 然而，虽然经济保护可以提高就业，但它还不足以成为追求高就业、高效率和价格稳定的有效举措。

② 对于创造就业机会和降低失业率来讲，征收关税和实施进口保护的政策都是一种于事无补之举。一种增加生产性就业的更为有效的举措是通过国内的货币政策和财政政策的杠杆作用来实现。

③ 配额的作用在很大程度上与关税的作用相同，因为它们阻碍了不同国家之间发挥比较优势去决定市场中的价格和产量。

④ 在此我们也应该提一下所谓的非关税壁垒（即NTBs）。

⑥ 在大萧条时期，美国建立的贸易壁垒加剧了物价的飞涨，使经济危机进一步恶化。

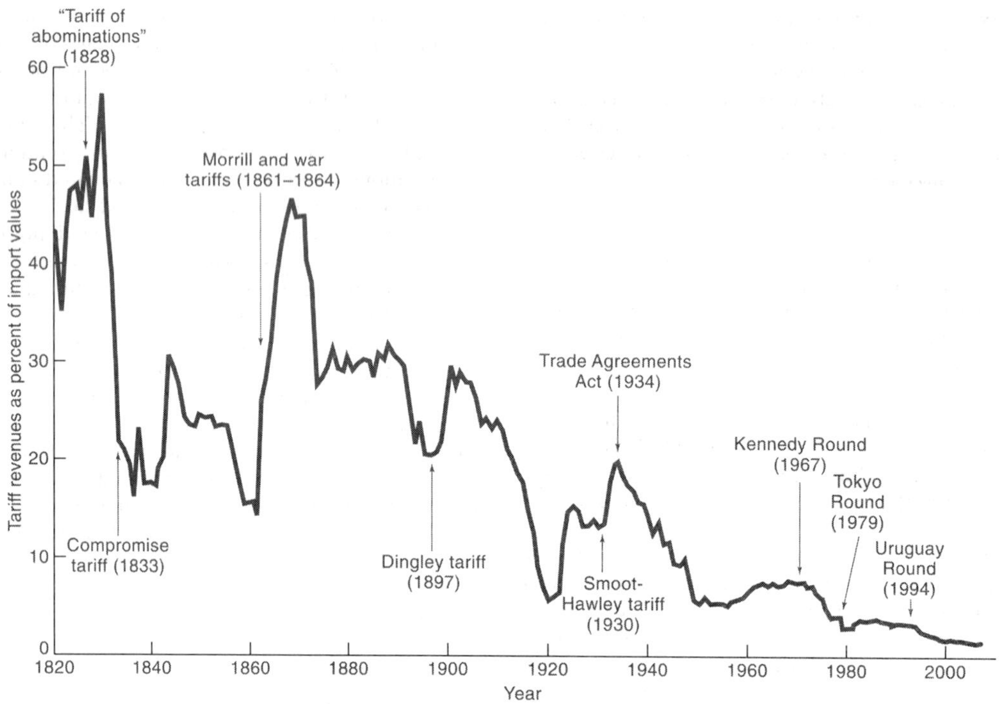

FIGURE 18-10. America Was Historically a High-Tariff Nation ①

Tariffs were high for most of our nation's history, but trade negotiations since the 1930s have lowered tariffs significantly.

Multilateral Agreements. One of the most successful multilateral agreements was the General Agreement on Tariffs and Trade (GATT). Its provisions were incorporated into the World Trade Organization (WTO) at the beginning of 1995. Their charters ② speak of raising living standards through "substantial reduction of tariffs and other barriers to trade and the elimination of discriminatory treatment in international commerce." As of 2008, the WTO had 153 member countries, which accounted for 90 percent of international trade.

Among the principles underlying the WTO are (1) countries should work to lower trade barriers; (2) all trade barriers should be applied on a nondiscriminatory basis across nations (i.e., all nations should enjoy "most-favored-nation" status); (3) when a country increases its tariffs above agreed-upon levels, it must compensate its trading partners for the economic injury; and (4) trade conflicts should be settled by consultations and arbitration.

Multilateral trade negotiations successfully lowered trade barriers in the half-century following World War II. The latest successful negotiations were the Uruguay Round, which included 123 countries and [3] was completed in 1994. In 2001, countries launched a new round in Doha, Qatar. Among the items on the agenda are agriculture, intellectual property rights, and the environment. The new negotiations have been controversial both among developing countries, which believe that the rich countries are protecting agriculture too heavily, and among antiglobalization groups, which argue that growing trade is hurting the environment. In the face of deep divisions, the Doha Round has made no progress as of 2008.

① 图 18-10. 历史上美国曾经是一个高关税国家

② 其宪章宣称生活水平的提高必须通过“实质性地降低关税和其他贸易壁垒，以及消除国际商业活动中的歧视性行为”等举措来实现。

[3] Uruguay Round，Doha Round：“乌拉圭回合”、“多哈回合”均为世贸谈判中的艰难回合。正如本页的最后一句所示，到 2008 年止，面对严重的分歧局面，多哈回合谈判毫无进展。

Regional Approaches. Over the last few years, governments have taken a number of steps to promote free trade or to broaden regional markets. Among the most important were the following.

The most controversial proposal for lowering trade barriers was the North American Free Trade Agreement (NAFTA), which was hotly debated and passed by Congress by a close vote in 1993. Mexico is the third-largest trading partner of the United States, and most U.S.-Mexico trade is in manufactured goods. NAFTA not only allows goods to pass tariff-free across the borders but also liberalizes regulations on investments by the United States and Canada in Mexico. Proponents of the plan argued that it would allow a more efficient pattern of specialization and would enable U.S. firms to compete more effectively against firms in other countries; opponents, particularly labor groups, argued that it would increase the supply of goods produced by low-skilled labor and thereby depress the wages of workers in the affected industries.

Economists caution, however, that regional trading agreements like NAFTA can cause inefficiency if they exclude potential trading countries. They point to the stagnation in the Caribbean countries, which were excluded from the free-trade provisions of NAFTA, as a cautionary example of the dangers of the regional approach.

The most far-reaching trade accord has been the movement toward a single market among the major European countries. Since World War II, the nations ①
of the European Union (EU) have developed a common market with minimal barriers to international trade or movement of factors of production. The first step involved eliminating all internal tariff and regulatory barriers to trade and labor and capital flows. The most recent step was the introduction of a common currency (the Euro) for most of the members of the EU. European unification is one of history's most eloquent tributes to the power of an idea—the idea that free and open trade promotes economic efficiency and technological advance.

评 价

Appraisal

After World War II, policymakers around the world believed firmly that free trade was essential for world prosperity. These convictions translated into several successful agreements to lower tariffs, as Figure 18-10 shows. The free-trade philosophy of economists and market-oriented policymakers has been severely tested by periods of high unemployment, by exchange-rate disturbances, and recently by antiglobalization forces. Nevertheless, most countries have continued the trend toward increased openness and outward orientation.

Economic studies generally show that countries ②
have benefited from lower trade barriers as trade flows and living standards have grown. But the struggle to preserve open markets is constantly tested as the political and economic environment changes.

SUMMARY

A. The Nature of International Trade

1. Specialization, division of labor, and trade increase productivity and consumption possibilities. The gains from trade hold among nations as well as within a nation. Engaging in international exchange is more efficient than relying only on domestic production. International trade differs from domestic trade because it broadens the market, because trade takes place among sovereign nations, and because countries usually have their own monies which must be converted using foreign exchange rates.
2. Diversity is the fundamental reason that nations engage in international trade. Within this general principle, we see that trade occurs (*a*) because of differences in the conditions of production, (*b*) because of decreasing costs (or economies of scale), and (*c*) because of diversity in tastes.

B. Comparative Advantage among Nations

3. Recall that trade occurs because of differences in the conditions of production or diversity in tastes. The foundation of international trade is the Ricardian principle of comparative advantage. The principle of comparative advantage holds that each country will benefit if it specializes in the production and export of those goods that it can produce at relatively low cost.

① 自第二次大战以来，欧盟的所有成员国以设置最小的贸易壁垒或加强生产要素流动的方式，开发共同市场。

② 经济学的研究普遍证明，随着贸易流动和生活水平的提高，各国都从降低贸易壁垒当中受益匪浅。但是，为维护市场的开放而付出的艰苦努力，随全球政治和经济环境的持续变化而不断地经受着考验。

Conversely, each country will also benefit if it imports those goods which it produces at relatively high cost. This principle holds even if one region is absolutely more or less productive than another in all commodities. As long as there are differences in *relative* or *comparative* efficiencies among countries, every country must enjoy a comparative advantage or a comparative disadvantage in the production of some goods.

4. The law of comparative advantage predicts more than just the geographic pattern of specialization and the direction of trade. It also demonstrates that countries are made better off and that real wages (or, more generally, total national income) are improved by trade and the resulting enlarged world production. Quotas and tariffs, designed to "protect" workers or industries, will lower a nation's total income and consumption possibilities.
5. Even with many goods or many countries, the same principles of comparative advantage apply. With many commodities, we can arrange products along a continuum of comparative advantage, from relatively more efficient to relatively less efficient. With many countries, trade may be triangular or multilateral, with countries having large bilateral (or two-sided) surpluses or deficits with other individual countries.

C. Protectionism

6. Completely free trade equalizes prices of tradeable goods at home with those in world markets. Under trade, goods flow uphill from low-price to high-price markets.
7. A tariff raises the domestic prices of imported goods, leading to a decline in consumption and imports along with an increase in domestic production. Quotas have very similar effects and may, in addition, lower government revenues.
8. A tariff causes economic waste. The economy suffers losses from decreased domestic consumption and from the wasting of resources on goods lacking comparative advantage. The losses generally exceed government revenues from the tariff.
9. Most arguments for tariffs simply rationalize special benefits to particular pressure groups and cannot withstand economic analysis. Three arguments that can stand up to careful scrutiny are the following: (*a*) The terms-of-trade or optimal tariff can in principle raise the real income of a large country at the expense of its trading partners. (*b*) In a situation of less-than-full employment, tariffs might push an economy toward fuller employment, but monetary or fiscal policies could attain the same employment goal with fewer inefficiencies than this beggar-thy-neighbor policy. (*c*) Sometimes, infant industries may need temporary protection in order to realize their true long-run comparative advantages.
10. The principle of comparative advantage must be qualified if markets malfunction because of unemployment or exchange-market disturbances. Moreover, individual sectors or factors may be injured by trade if imports lower their returns. Opening up to trade may hurt the factors that are most embodied in imported goods.

CONCEPTS FOR REVIEW

Principles of International Trade

absolute and comparative advantage (or disadvantage)
principle of comparative advantage
economic gains from trade
triangular and multilateral trade
world vs. national *PPF*s
consumption vs. production possibilities with trade
Stolper-Samuelson theorem

Economics of Protectionism

price equilibrium with and without trade
tariff, quota, nontariff barriers
effects of tariffs on price, imports, and domestic production
mercantilist, cheap-foreign-labor, and retaliatory arguments
the optimal tariff, unemployment, and infant-industry exceptions

FURTHER READING AND INTERNET WEBSITES

Further Reading

The theory of comparative advantage was discovered and discussed by David Ricardo in *Principles of Political Economy and Taxation* (1819, various publishers). This is online at several sites, including *www.econlib.org/library/Ricardo/ricP.html.* A classic review of the debate about free trade is Jagdish Bhagwati, *Protectionism* (MIT Press, Cambridge, Mass., 1990). Some of the best popular writing on international economics is found in *The Economist,* which is also available at *www.economist.com.*

Mankiw's remarks on outsourcing, as well as some reactions, can be found at *www.cnn.com/2004/US/02/12/bush.outsourcing/.* Blinder's article, "Offshoring: The Next Industrial Revolution?" appeared in *Foreign Affairs,* March–April 2006, and is available at *www.foreignaffairs.org/.*

Websites

The World Bank (*www.worldbank.org*) has information on its programs and publications at its site, as does the International Monetary Fund, or IMF (*www.imf.org*). The United Nations website has links to most international institutions and their databases (*www.unsystem.org*). Another good source of information about high-income countries is the Organisation for Economic Cooperation and Development, or OECD (*www.oecd.org*). U.S. trade data are available at *www.census.gov.*

You can find information on many countries through their statistical offices. A compendium of national agencies is available at *www.census.gov/main/www/stat_int.html.*

One of the best sources for policy writing on international economics is *www.iie.com/homepage.htm,* the website of the Peterson Institute for International Economics.

QUESTIONS FOR DISCUSSION

1. State whether or not each of the following is correct and explain your reasoning. If the quotation is incorrect, provide a corrected statement.
   a. "We Mexicans can never compete profitably with the Northern colossus. Her factories are too efficient, she has too many computers and machine tools, and her engineering skills are too advanced. We need tariffs, or we can export nothing!"
   b. "If American workers are subjected to the unbridled competition of cheap Mexican labor, our real wages must necessarily fall drastically."
   c. "The principle of comparative advantage applies equally well to families, cities, and states as it does to nations and continents."
   d. The quotation from Ross Perot on page 356.
2. Reconstruct Figure 18-1 and its accompanying table to show the production data for Europe; assume that Europe has 600 units of labor and that labor productivities are those given in Table 18-2.
3. What if the data in Table 18-2 changed from (1, 2; 3, 4) to (1, 2; 2, 4)? Show that all trade is killed off. Use this to explain the adage *"Vive la différence!"* (freely translated as "Let diversity thrive!"). Why do the largest gains in trade flow to small countries whose pretrade prices are very different from prevailing world prices?
4. *Follow-up to question 3:* Suppose that the data in Table 18-2 pertain to a newly industrialized country (NIC) and America. What are the gains from trade between the two countries? Now suppose that NIC adopts American technology and has production possibilities identical to those in the American column of Table 18-2. What will happen to international trade? What will happen to NIC's living standards and real wages? What will happen to America's living standards? Is there a lesson here for the impact of converging economies on trade and welfare?
5. A U.S. senator wrote the following: "Trade is supposed to raise the incomes of all nations involved—or at least that is what Adam Smith and David Ricardo taught us. If our economic decline has been caused by the economic growth of our competitors, then these philosophers—and the entire discipline of economics they founded—have been taking us on a 200-year ride."

   Explain why the first sentence is correct. Also explain why the second sentence does not follow from the first. Can you give an example of how economic growth of Country J could lower the standard of living in Country A? (*Hint:* The answer to question 4 will help uncover the fallacy in the quotation.)
6. Modern protectionists have used the following arguments for protecting domestic industries against foreign competition:
   a. In some situations, a country can improve its standard of living by imposing protection if no one else retaliates.
   b. Wages in China are a tiny fraction of those in the United States. Unless we limit the imports of Chinese manufactures, we face a future in which our trade deficit continues to rise under the onslaught of competition from low-wage workers.
   c. A country might be willing to accept a small drop in its living standard to preserve certain industries that it deems necessary for national security, such as supercomputers or oil, by protecting them from foreign competition.
   d. *For those who have studied macroeconomics:* If inflexible wages and prices or an inappropriate exchange rate leads to recession and high unemployment,

tariffs might increase output and lower the unemployment rate.

In each case, relate the argument to one of the traditional defenses of protectionism. State the conditions under which it is valid, and decide whether you agree with it.

7. The United States has had quotas on steel, shipping, automobiles, textiles, and many other products. Economists estimate that by auctioning off the quota rights, the Treasury would gain at least $10 billion annually. Use Figure 18-9 to analyze the economics of quotas as follows: Assume that the government imposes a quota of 100 on imports, allocating the quota rights to importing countries on the basis of last year's imports. What would be the equilibrium price and quantity of clothing? What would be the efficiency losses from quotas? Who would get revenue rectangle *B*? What would be the effect of auctioning off the quota rights?

PART FIVE

Macroeconomics: Economic Growth and Business Cycles

宏观经济学：经济增长与商业周期

CHAPTER

19

Overview of Macroeconomics

宏观经济学概述

[2] 詹姆斯·托宾（James Tobin，1918~2002），美国最杰出的凯恩斯学派经济学家，长期供职于美国国家经济顾问委员会和美联储。“为表彰他对金融市场及其与支出决策、就业、产量和价格机制的关联分析”而被授予1981年诺贝尔经济学奖；其理论解释了金融市场对民众消费和投资决策的作用机理。托宾与本书的第二作者诺德豪斯同是耶鲁大学的货币金融学教授，两人曾于1972年为美国国家经济研究院（The National Bureau of Economic Research，NBER）合编《经济研究》第96期《回顾与展望:经济增长》（*Economic Research: Retrospect and Prospect: Economic Growth* Vol. 5，No. 96）；1973年又共同撰写著名的《经济增长过时了吗》（*Is Growth Obsolete?*），发表在NBER当年出版的论文集《经济测量及社会功能》（*The Measurement of Economic and Social Performance*，1973，Milton Moss，ed.，pp509-564）。

这段文字出自其自选文集《国家经济政策》（*National Economic Policy*）。该书收录了托宾针对国会、政府机构和政界那些非经济学专业领袖们写的咨询文稿。

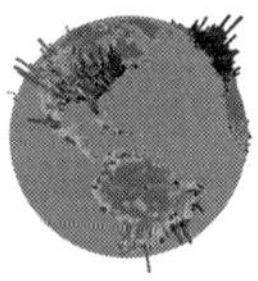

The whole purpose of the economy is production of goods or services for consumption now or in the future. I think the burden of proof should always be on those who would produce less rather than more, on those who would leave idle people or machines or land that could be used. It is amazing how many reasons can be found to justify such waste: fear of inflation, balance-of-payments deficits, unbalanced budgets, excessive national debt, loss of confidence in the dollar. ①

James Tobin, [2]
National Economic Policy

Are jobs plentiful or hard to find? Are real wages and living standards growing rapidly, or are consumers struggling to make ends meet as price inflation reduces real wages? Is there a period of financial exuberance with stock prices rising rapidly? Or is the central bank using monetary policy to fight off the effects of falling housing prices and a financial crisis? What are the impacts of globalization and foreign trade on domestic employment and output? These questions are central to macroeconomics, which is the subject of the following chapters.

Macroeconomics is the study of the behavior of the economy as a whole. It examines the forces that affect firms, consumers, and workers in the aggregate. It contrasts with **microeconomics,** which studies individual prices, quantities, and markets. ③

Two central themes will run through our survey of macroeconomics:

- The short-term fluctuations in output, employment, financial conditions, and prices that we call the *business cycle*
- The longer-term trends in output and living standards known as *economic growth*

The development of macroeconomics was one of the major breakthroughs of twentieth-century economics, leading to a much better understanding of how to combat periodic economic crises and how to stimulate long-term economic growth. In response to the Great Depression, John Maynard Keynes developed his revolutionary theory, which helped explain the forces producing economic fluctuations and suggested how governments can

---

① 一国经济的全部目的就是为现在或将来的消费提供商品或服务。在我看来，证明这一点的责任应该交给那些宁愿少生产而不愿多生产的人，以及让有可能派作用场的人力、机器设备或者土地闲置起来的那些人。然而，令人惊奇的是，有很多理由可以证明这种浪费是合理的：担忧通货膨胀、收支赤字、预算失衡、过重的国家债务，以及对美元信心的丧失。

③ **宏观经济学**是将经济行为作为一个整体来进行研究的科学。研究对象为，总体上影响企业、消费者和劳动者的各种作用力。而**微观经济学**则截然不同，所研究的对象为单个价格、产量以及市场。

control the worst excesses of the business cycle. At the same time, economists have endeavored to understand the mechanics of long-term economic growth.

Macroeconomic issues dominated the U.S. political and economic agenda for much of the last century. In the 1930s, when production, employment, and prices collapsed in the United States and across much of the industrial world, economists and political leaders wrestled with the calamity of the Great Depression. During the Vietnam War in the 1960s and the energy crises [1]
of the 1970s, the burning issue was "stagflation," a combination of slow growth and rising prices. The 1990s witnessed a period of rapid growth, falling unemployment, and stable prices—years when everything went right, labeled by some as "the fabulous decade." Then asset-market bubbles burst twice in the first decade of the 2000s. The first shock was a sharp decline in the prices of technology stocks in 2000, and this was followed by a sharp decline in housing prices after 2007. The 2007–2009 housing-price decline produced a profound financial crisis and led to a deep and long recession.

Sometimes, macroeconomic failures raise life-and-death questions for countries and even for ideologies. The communist leaders of the former Soviet [2]
Union proclaimed that they would overtake the West ③
economically. History proved that to be a hollow promise, as Russia, a country teeming with natural resources and military might, was unable to produce adequate butter for its citizens along with the guns for its imperial armies. Eventually, macroeconomic failures brought down the communist regimes of the Soviet Union and Eastern Europe and convinced people of the economic superiority of private markets as the best approach to encouraging rapid economic growth.

This chapter will serve as an introduction to mac- ④
roeconomics. It presents the major concepts and shows how they apply to key historical and policy questions of recent years. But this introduction is only a first course to whet the appetite. Not until you have mastered all the chapters in Parts Five through Seven can you fully enjoy the rich macroeconomic banquet that has been a source of both inspiration for economic policy and continued controversy among macroeconomists.

宏观经济学的主要概念

A. KEY CONCEPTS OF MACROECONOMICS

宏观经济学的诞生
THE BIRTH OF MACROECONOMICS

The 1930s marked the first stirrings of the science of macroeconomics, founded by John Maynard [5]
Keynes as he tried to understand the economic mechanism that produced the Great Depression. After World War II, reflecting both the increasing influence of Keynesian views and the fear of another depression, the U.S. Congress formally proclaimed federal responsibility for macroeconomic performance. It enacted the landmark Employment Act [6]
of 1946, which stated:

> The Congress hereby declares that it is the continuing ⑦
> policy and responsibility of the federal government to use all practicable means consistent with its needs and obligations . . . to promote maximum employment, production, and purchasing power.

For the first time, Congress affirmed the government's role in promoting output growth, fostering employment, and maintaining price stability. The Employment Act usefully frames the three central questions of macroeconomics:

1. *Why do output and employment sometimes fall, and* ⑧
how can unemployment be reduced? All market economies show patterns of expansion and contraction known as *business cycles.* The latest business-cycle recession in the United States occurred after a severe financial-market crisis that began in 2007. Housing and stock prices fell sharply, and banks tightened credit and lending. As a result, output and employment fell sharply. Political leaders around the world used the tools of monetary and fiscal policy to reduce unemployment and stimulate economic activity.

   From time to time countries experience high unemployment that persists for long periods, sometimes as long as a decade. Such a period occurred in the United States during the Great Depression, which began in 1929. In the following years, unemployment rose to almost one-quarter of the workforce, while industrial production fell by one-half. One of the deepest

[1] Vietnam War：越南战争，泛指法国人的越南战争、美国人的越南战争、越南内战等。此处由后面的“in the 1960s”所定义，即国人所称的“抗美援越”战争。从1961年5月肯尼迪总统派遣一支美国国防军特种部队进驻越南共和国（即“南越”）起，至1973年1月27日在巴黎签署《关于在越南结束战争、恢复和平的协定》（巴黎和平条约）止，在这11年零8个月里，美国投入兵力50万人以上，军费开支约2 500亿美元，阵亡官兵约50 000名。中国政府全力支持了这场抗美援越战争，提供了几乎全部的作战物资，在越南民主共和国共计派出了32万余人的二线作战部队，作战兵力最多时达到17万人，并帮助越南空军组建和培训了空军人员。中国政府先后给越南提供了价值近200亿美元的无偿援助，足够装备200万陆海空军的武器弹药，援助越南建设了上百个生产企业和修配厂，支援了修建铁路的全部铁轨、机车和车厢以及3亿斤大米、200万吨汽油、3 000千米以上的油管等物资。自1964年到1969年，中国政府还向越南政府提供了1.8亿美元的现汇，1970年到1973年，中越双方共签定经济、军事物资援助计划八项，中国向越南提供90亿元的经济、军事援助。1974年中国又向越南提供了25亿元的援助，其中包括1.3亿美元的现汇。这一切，迫使美国在战争期间始终未敢逾越北纬17度线，与朝鲜战争一起，为中国的国际地位和国内的建设赢得了所需的战略空间和格局。

[2] The former Soviet Union：前苏联（Union of Socialist Soviet Republics，USSR），全称为苏维埃社会主义共和国联盟，成立于1922年12月30日，1991年12月26日解体。国土占东欧的大部分，以及几乎整个中亚和北亚，面积曾达22 402 200平方公里。

③ 前苏联的共产党领袖们声称，他们会在经济上全面地超越西方。历史证明，这只是一句空喊的愿景而已。因为，拥有丰富的自然资源和强大军事力量的俄国，在有能力为其帝国军队提供大炮的同时，却没有能力为其国民生产足量的黄油。

④ 本章的内容只是第一道“开胃菜”。只有将第二编至第四编所有章节的内容全部掌握之后，才有可能尽情地享用宏观经济学的盛宴大餐。这道大餐自始至终既是经济政策的灵感源泉，又是宏观经济学家们喋喋不休的论战领域。

[5] John Maynard Keynes：J. M. 凯恩斯（1883~1946），英国经济学家，开创了经济学的“凯恩斯革命”，现代西方经济学最有影响的经济学家之一，被誉为上世纪30年代经济大萧条的终结者，他创立的宏观经济学被称为20世纪人类知识界的三大革命之一。《就业、利率及货币通论》（*General Theory of Employment, Interest and Money*，简称《通论》）是其革命性的代表作。

[6] Employment Act of 1946：《1946年就业法案》，以联邦立法的形式，明确规定了保障经济平稳运行、抑制通货膨胀和降低失业水平是联邦政府的职责。该法案是在蒙大拿州民主党参议员James Murray提交国会的《完全就业法案》（*Full Employment Bill of 1945*）的基础上修订通过的，源于二次大战胜利前夕，美国举国上下担忧有可能卷土重来的大萧条和严重的失业。

⑦ 国会据此宣称，这是一项连续性的政策。联邦政府有责任施行一切可行的与需求和义务相一致的措施……以促进就业水平、生产力和购买力的最大化。

⑧ 产出和就业水平为什么有时会下降？如何才能减少失业？

and most prolonged economic downturns of the modern era came in Japan, which experienced declining prices and was unable to shake off high unemployment and slow economic growth after 1990.

Macroeconomics studies the sources of persistent unemployment and high inflation. Having considered the symptoms, macroeconomists suggest possible remedies, such as using monetary policy to alter interest rates and credit conditions or using fiscal instruments such as taxes and spending. The lives and fortunes of millions of people depend upon whether economists find correct diagnoses for major macroeconomic ailments—and upon whether governments apply the right medicine at the right time.

2. *What are the sources of price inflation, and how can it be kept under control?* ① A market economy uses [2] prices as a yardstick to measure economic values and conduct business. When prices are rising—a phenomenon we call *inflation*—the price yardstick loses its value. During periods of high inflation, people may get confused about relative prices and make mistakes in their spending and investment decisions. Tax burdens may rise. Households on fixed incomes find that inflation is eating away at their real incomes.

   Macroeconomic policy has increasingly emphasized low and stable inflation as a key goal. Many countries set "inflation targets" for their economic policy, with targets often being in the range from 1 to 3 percent per year. Except for brief spikes, the United States has succeeded in containing inflation over the last two decades, with an average inflation rate of 3 percent per year for the consumer price index. Many countries have not been so successful. Formerly socialist countries like Russia and many Latin American and developing countries experienced inflation rates of 50, 100, or 1000 percent per year in the last two decades. The inflationary record in the last few years was in troubled Zimbabwe, where inflation was around 20,000,000 percent per year in 2008. A chicken that cost 10 thousand Zimbabwean dollars at the beginning of the year would cost 10 trillion Zimbabwean dollars at the end! Why was the United States able to contain the inflationary tiger, while Zimbabwe failed to do so? Macroeconomics can suggest the proper role of monetary and fiscal policies, of exchange-rate systems, and of an independent central bank in containing inflation.

3. *How can a nation increase its rate of economic growth?* ③ The single most important goal of macroeconomics concerns a nation's long-term economic growth. This refers to the growth in the per capita output of a country. Such growth is the central factor in determining the growth in real wages and living standards. Most countries of North America and Western Europe have enjoyed rapid economic growth for two centuries, and residents in these countries have high average incomes. Over the last five decades, Asian countries such as Japan, South Korea produced dramatic gains in living standards for their peoples. China's growth has similarly been outstanding in recent years. A few countries, particularly those of sub-Saharan Africa, have [4] suffered declining per capita output and living standards.

   Nations want to know the ingredients in a successful growth recipe. Economic historians have found that the key factors in long-term economic growth include reliance on well-regulated private markets for most economic activity, stable macroeconomic policy, high rates of saving and investment, openness to international trade, and accountable and noncorrupt governing institutions.

All economies face inevitable tradeoffs among these goals. Increasing the rate of growth of output over the long run may require greater investment in education and capital, but higher investment requires lower current consumption of items like food, clothing, and recreation. Additionally, policymakers are ⑤ sometimes forced to rein in the economy through macroeconomic policies when it grows too fast in order to prevent rising inflation or when financial conditions exhibit irrational exuberance.

There are no magic formulas for ensuring low and stable inflation, high employment, and rapid growth. Macroeconomists have vigorous debates about both the goals and the appropriate policies for reaching the goals. But sound macroeconomic policies are essential if a country wishes to achieve its economic objectives in the most effective manner.

---

① 通货膨胀的源头是什么？怎样才能控制它？

[2] 此处“price inflation”为作者严谨的表述，中文“通货膨胀”尚欠严谨，如20世纪二三十年代通货膨胀期间的物价并没有完全上涨。

③ 一个国家如何才能提高其经济增长率？

[4] sub-Saharan Africa，指撒哈拉以南的非洲地区，以与属于阿拉伯世界的北非六国（苏丹、埃及、利比亚、突尼斯、阿尔及利亚、摩洛哥，通常还包括大西洋中的葡属马德拉群岛以及亚速尔群岛）相区隔。

⑤ 除此之外，在经济增速过快或者金融环境凸现非理性繁荣的情况下，政策的制定者们往往出台宏观经济政策，以抑制日益上升的通货膨胀势头。

[1] The Patron Saint 将 John Maynard Keynes 赋予了具有宗教色彩的“保护神”的崇高地位。萨缪尔森在本书的14版之前尚未给予凯恩斯如此高的评价。在本次金融危机大背景下，更突显萨缪尔森对凯恩斯历史地位的褒奖。

[2] a world-famous economics journal，即 *The Economic Journal*（《经济学杂志》），1891年创刊，英国皇家经济学会（Royal Economic Society）会刊，年出八期，是经济学界权威杂志，同时也是经济学界历史最长的杂志之一，凯恩斯于1911~1946年期间期担任该杂志主编。学界普遍认为，是凯恩斯的突出贡献奠定了该杂志在国际学术界的权威地位。

⑤ *The General Theory of Employment, Interest, and Money*，《就业、利息与货币通论》，凯恩斯革命性的代表作。

⑥ 对一个经济体总产出所作的最全面的测量是**国内生产总值**（GDP）。

---

[1] The Patron Saint of Macroeconomics

Every discussion of macroeconomic policy must begin with John Maynard Keynes. Keynes (1883–1946) was a many-sided genius who won eminence in the fields of mathematics, philosophy, and literature. In addition, he found time to run a large insurance company, advise the British treasury, help govern the Bank
[2] of England, edit a world-famous economics journal, collect modern art and rare books, start a repertory theater, and marry a leading Russian ballerina. He was also an investor who knew how to make money by shrewd speculation, both
[3] for himself and for his college, King's College, Cambridge.

His principal contribution, however, was his invention of a new way of looking at macroeconomics and macro-
④ economic policy. Before Keynes, most economists and policymakers accepted the highs and lows of business cycles as being as inevitable as the tides. These long-held views left them helpless in the face of the Great Depression of the 1930s. But Keynes took an enormous intellectual leap in
⑤ his 1936 book, *The General Theory of Employment, Interest, and Money*. He made a twofold argument: First, he argued that it is possible for high unemployment and underutilized capacity to persist in market economies. In addition, he argued that government fiscal and monetary policies can affect output and thereby reduce unemployment and shorten economic downturns.

These propositions had an explosive impact when Keynes first introduced them, engendering much controversy and dispute. In the years after World War II, Keynesian economics came to dominate macroeconomics and government policy. Since then, new developments incorporating supply factors, expectations, and alternative views of wage and price dynamics have undermined the earlier Keynesian consensus. While few economists now believe that government action can eliminate business cycles, as Keynesian economics once seemed to promise, neither economics nor economic policy has been the same since Keynes's great discovery.

宏观经济学的研究目标及其工具
OBJECTIVES AND INSTRUMENTS OF MACROECONOMICS

Having surveyed the principal issues of macroeconomics, we now turn to a discussion of the major goals and instruments of macroeconomic policy. How do economists evaluate the success of an economy's overall performance? What are the tools that governments can use to pursue their economic goals? Table 19-1 lists the major objectives and instruments of macroeconomic policy.

Objectives
Output:
High level and rapid growth of output
Employment:
High level of employment with low involuntary unemployment
Stable prices
Instruments
Monetary policy:
Buying and selling bonds, regulating financial institutions
Fiscal policy:
Government expenditures
Taxation

TABLE 19-1. Goals and Instruments of Macroeconomic Policy

The top part of the table displays the major goals of macroeconomic policy. The lower half shows the major instruments or policy measures available to modern economies. Policymakers change the instruments of policy to affect the pace and direction of economic activity.

经济成就的测量
Measuring Economic Success

The major macroeconomic goals are a high level and rapid growth of output, low unemployment, and stable prices. We will use this section both to define the major macroeconomic terms and to discuss their importance. A more detailed treatment of the data of macroeconomics is postponed to the next chapter. Some key data are provided in the appendix to this chapter.

Output. The ultimate objective of economic activity is to provide the goods and services that the population desires. What could be more important for an economy than to produce ample shelter, food, education, and recreation for its people?

The most comprehensive measure of the total ⑥
output in an economy is the **gross domestic product** (GDP). GDP is the measure of the market value of all

---

[3] his college, King's College, Cambridge，剑桥大学国王学院。凯恩斯的父亲老凯恩斯（John Neville Keynes，1852~1949，享97岁高寿，晚凯恩斯三年去逝）曾是19世纪中期剑桥大学的经济学家和伦理学讲师，规范经济学和实证经济学理论的创始人。凯恩斯即出生于此。幼年的凯恩斯耳边常听着祖母的教导：“因为你出生在剑桥，所以生来就聪明。”凯恩斯1902从伊顿公学毕业考入国王学院，用两年的时间获得一等学士学位，被著名新古典学派经济学家马歇尔选中和极力挽留，21岁即走上剑桥大学国王学院的讲台，以研究生的身份非正式地讲授经济学课程，并将兴趣投注于哲学研究，两年后赴英国政府的“印度办”（India Office）供职。所以，这里的“his”意指凯恩斯出生、成长和受教育的地方，是萨缪尔森对本段文字的点睛之笔。

④ 凯恩斯之前，大多数经济学家和政策的制定者都认为，商业周期的高峰和低谷，犹如潮汐的自然现象，不可避免。

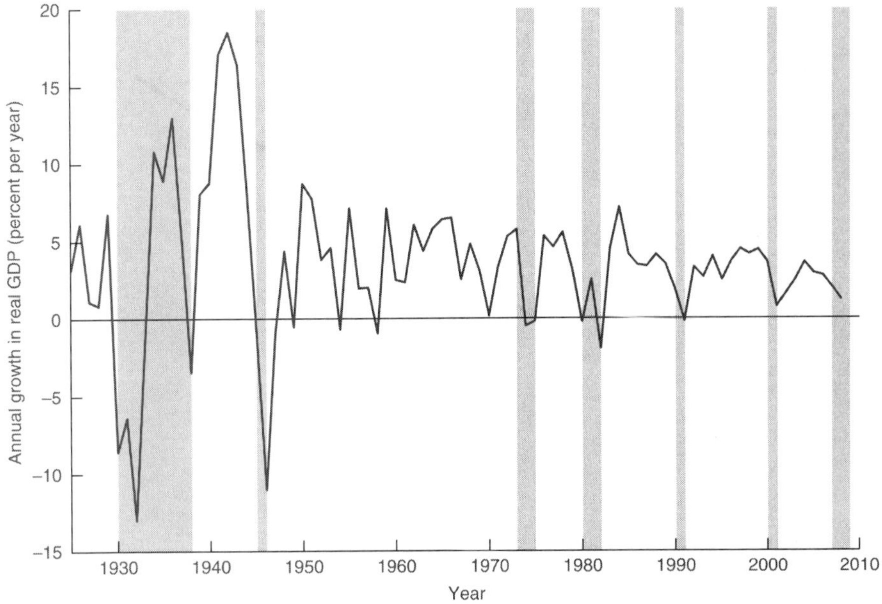

FIGURE 19-1. Growth Rate of U.S. Real Gross Domestic Product, 1929–2008

Real GDP is the most comprehensive measure of an economy's output. This figure shows the rate of growth from one year to the next. Note the string of negative growth rates in the Great Depression of the 1930s. Also, we see the Great Moderation of the last few years, in which output was less volatile than in earlier periods.

Source: U.S. Bureau of Economic Analysis at *www.bea.gov*. Shaded regions are major economic downturns.

final goods and services—beer, cars, rock concerts, donkey rides, and so on—produced in a country during a year. There are two ways to measure GDP. *Nominal GDP* is measured in actual market prices. *Real GDP* is calculated in constant or invariant prices (where we measure the number of cars times the prices of cars in a given year such as 2000).

Real GDP is the most closely watched measure ① of output; it serves as the carefully monitored pulse of a nation's economy. Figure 19-1 shows the growth rate of real GDP in the United States since 1929. The growth rate is defined as

$$\% \text{ growth rate of real GDP in year } t = 100 \times \frac{\text{GDP}_t - \text{GDP}_{t-1}}{\text{GDP}_{t-1}}$$

For example, real GDP in 2006 was $11,294.8 billion and in 2007 was $11,523.9 billion (both in 2000 prices). A calculator will show that the growth of real GDP in 2007 was 2.0 percent over the year. It is worthwhile making sure you can replicate this calculation. Note the sharp economic decline during the Great Depression of the 1930s, the boom during World War II, and the recessions in 1974, 1982, 1991, and 2008.

Despite the short-term fluctuations seen in busi- ②
ness cycles, advanced economies generally exhibit a steady long-term growth in real GDP and an improvement in living standards; this process is known as *economic growth*. The American economy has proved itself a powerful engine of progress over a period of more than a century, as shown by the growth in potential output.

Potential GDP represents the maximum sus- ③
tainable level of output that the economy can produce. When an economy is operating at its

① 实际 GDP 是衡量经济体总产出最近似的测量指标，它用于监测一国经济的脉搏。

② 尽管在发达经济体存在商业周期中的短期波动，但在总体上，实际 GDP 呈现稳定的长期增长，以及生活水平提高的态势。这一过程被称为经济增长。

③ **潜在 GDP** 指的是经济体能够生产的最大可持续产出水平。

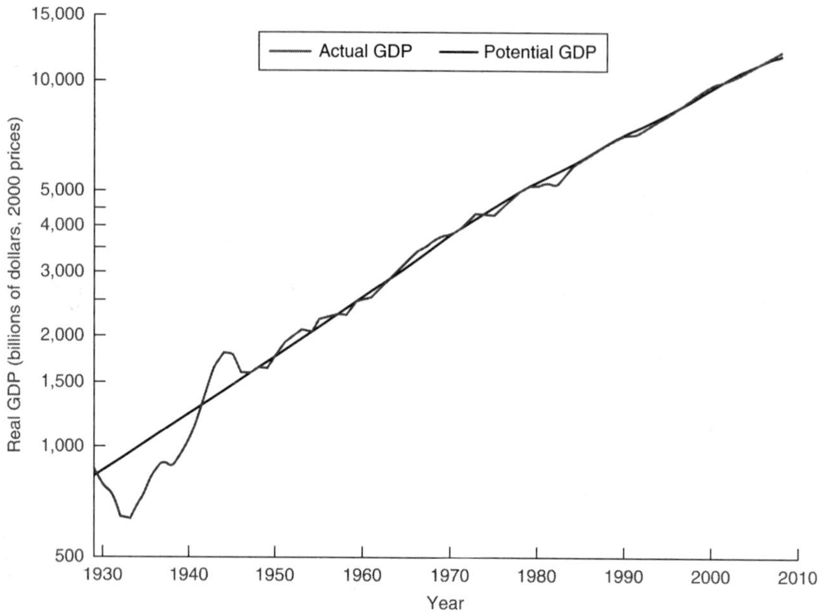

FIGURE 19-2. Actual and Potential GDP in the United States

Business cycles occur when actual output departs from its potential. The smooth blue line shows potential or trend output over the period 1929–2008. Potential output has grown about 3.4 percent annually. Note the large gap between actual and potential output during the Great Depression of the 1930s.

Source: U.S. Bureau of Economic Analysis, Congressional Budget Office, and authors' estimates. Note that actual GDP is directly estimated from underlying data while potential output is an analytical concept derived from actual GDP and unemployment data.

potential, there are high levels of utilization of the labor force and the capital stock. When output rises above potential output, price inflation tends to rise, while a below-potential level of output leads to high unemployment.

Potential output is determined by the economy's productive capacity, which depends upon the inputs available (capital, labor, land, etc.) and the economy's technological efficiency. Potential GDP tends to grow steadily because inputs like labor and capital and the level of technology change quite slowly over time. By ① contrast, actual GDP is subject to large business-cycle swings if spending patterns change sharply.

During business downturns, actual GDP falls below its potential, and unemployment rises. In 1982, for example, the U.S. economy produced about $400 billion less than its potential output. This represented $5000 lost per family during a single year. A *recession* is a period of significant decline in total output, income, and employment, usually lasting more than a few months and marked by widespread contractions in many sectors of the economy. A severe ② and protracted downturn is called a *depression*. Output can be temporarily above its potential during booms and wartime as capacity limits are strained, but the high utilization rates may bring rising inflation and are usually brought to an end by monetary or fiscal policy.

Figure 19-2 shows the estimated potential and actual output for the period 1929–2008. Note how large the gap between actual and potential output was during the Great Depression of the 1930s.

① 反之，如果支出的模式急剧地变化，实际 GDP 就会随着商业周期出现大的波动。

② 严重而持续的经济低迷则被称为萧条。在经济的急剧增长期或战争期间，产能的极限被扭伸，产出可以在短期内超过其潜在水平。但是，高设备使用率有可能引发持续攀高的通货膨胀，并且通常要出台货币或者财政政策来加以抑制。

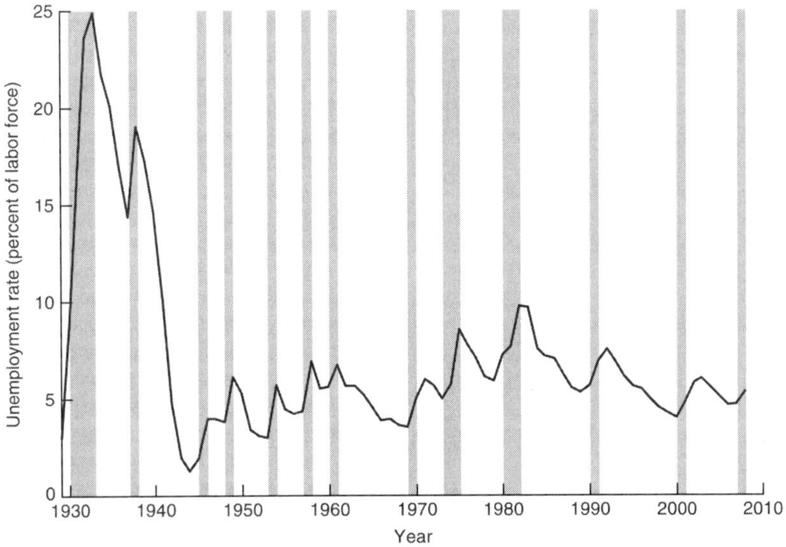

FIGURE 19-3. Unemployment Rises in Recessions, Falls during Expansions

The unemployment rate measures the fraction of the labor force that is looking for work but cannot find work. Unemployment rises in business-cycle downturns and falls during expansions. Shaded regions are NBER recessions.

Source: U.S. Bureau of Labor Statistics at *www.bea.gov.*

High Employment, Low Unemployment. Of all the macroeconomic indicators, employment and unemployment are most directly felt by individuals. People want to be able to get high-paying jobs without searching or waiting too long, and they want to have job security and good benefits. In macroeconomic terms, these are the objectives of *high employment,* which is the counterpart of *low unemployment.* Figure 19-3 shows trends in unemployment over the last eight decades. The **unemployment rate** on the ① vertical axis is the percentage of the labor force that is unemployed. The labor force includes all employed persons and those unemployed individuals who are seeking jobs. It excludes those without work who are not looking for jobs.

The unemployment rate tends to reflect the state of the business cycle: when output is falling, the demand for labor falls and the unemployment rate rises. Unemployment reached epidemic proportions ② in the Great Depression of the 1930s, when as much as one-quarter of the workforce was idled. Since World War II, unemployment in the United States has fluctuated but has avoided the high rates associated with depressions.

Price Stability. The third macroeconomic objective is *price stability.* This is defined as a low and stable inflation rate.

To track prices, government statisticians construct **price indexes,** or measures of the overall price level. An important example is the **consumer price index** (CPI), which measures the trend in the average price of goods and services bought by consumers. We will generally denote the overall price level by the letter P.

Economists measure price stability by looking at ③ **inflation,** or the **rate of inflation.** The inflation rate is the percentage change in the overall level of prices from one year to the next. For example, the CPI was 201.6 in 2006 and 207.3 in 2007. The inflation-rate calculation is just like the growth-rate calculation above:

$$\text{Rate of inflation in year } t = 100 \times \frac{P_t - P_{t-1}}{P_{t-1}}$$

① 纵轴上表示的**失业率**系指没有被雇佣的劳动力的百分比。劳动力包括了所有受雇佣人员和正在找工作的失业个体，那些没有工作但又不准备找工作的人除外。

② 在 20 世纪 30 年代的大萧条时期，有高达 1/4 的劳动力被闲置，失业呈现愈演愈烈的态势。第二次世界大战以来，美国的失业状况始终处在波动之中，但却避免了与萧条所伴随的高失业率现象。

③ 经济学家们通过关注**通货膨胀**或者**通货膨胀率**来衡量价格的稳定性。

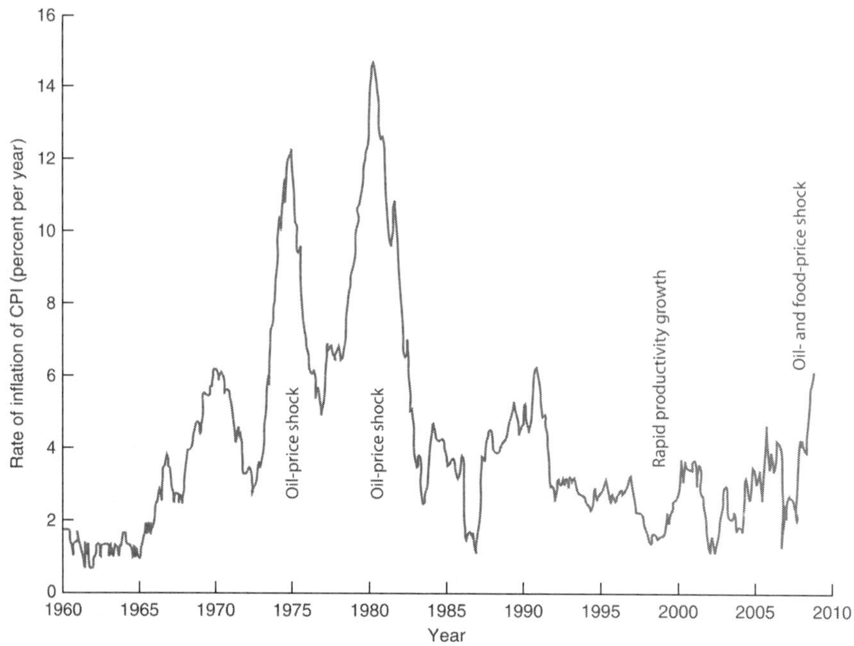

FIGURE 19-4. U.S. Consumer Price Inflation, 1960–2008

The rate of inflation measures the rate of change of prices from one year to the next; here we see the rate of inflation as measured by the consumer price index (CPI). Most inflationary episodes have been associated with shocks to oil or food prices. Note that inflation has moved in a narrow corridor since the mid-1980s.

Source: U.S. Bureau of Labor Statistics. Data show rate of inflation from 12 months earlier.

We thus calculate the inflation rate for 2007 as

$$\text{Rate of inflation in 2007} = 100 \times \frac{207.3 - 201.6}{201.6} = 2.8\% \text{ per year}$$

Figure 19-4 shows the inflation rate for the CPI from 1960 to 2008. Since the end of the inflationary period in the early 1980s, inflation has averaged 3 percent per year through 2008.

A *deflation* occurs when prices decline (which ① means that the rate of inflation is negative). At the other extreme is a *hyperinflation*, a rise in the price level of a thousand or a million percent a year. In such situations, as in Weimar Germany in the 1920s, [2] Brazil in the 1980s, Russia in the 1990s, or Zimbabwe in recent years, prices are virtually meaningless and the price system breaks down.

Price stability is important because a smoothly functioning market system requires that prices accurately convey information about relative scarcities. History has shown that high inflation imposes many costs—some visible and some hidden—on an economy. With high inflation, taxes become highly variable, the real values of people's pensions are eroded, and people spend real resources to avoid depreciating rubles or pesos. But declining prices (deflation) are also costly. Hence, most nations seek ③ the golden mean of slowly rising prices as the best way of encouraging the price system to function efficiently.

---

① 当价格下滑时，即出现通货紧缩现象（意味着通货膨胀率为负）。极端情况下会出现恶性通货膨胀，即一年中价格飞涨了 1 000%，甚至 1 000 000%。

[2] Weimar Germany，魏玛德国，1919 年德国国民议会在其文化中心小城魏玛制订了第一部共和宪法，即魏玛宪法，成立了魏玛共和国，其短暂的 14 年历史经历了西方民主史上最严重的经济危机。

Brazil in the 1980s，20 世纪 70 年代初期的能源危机使外债累累的巴西雪上加霜，导致 80 年代初期和后期出现经济停滞和空前衰退。

Russia in the 1990s，1991 年苏联解体，俄罗斯开始实施休克疗法来进行经济改革，导致经济濒于崩溃。

Zimbabwe in recent years，恶性通货膨胀目前正在津巴布韦肆虐，按 2008 年 7 月的官方统计，通胀率达 231 000 000%。

③ 因此，大多数国家都在寻找一条通过缓慢提高价格来促进经济繁荣的中间道路，作为刺激价格机制有效运转的最佳途径。

To summarize:

The goals of macroeconomic policy are: ①

1. A high and growing level of national output
2. High employment with low unemployment
3. A stable or gently rising price level

宏观经济政策的工具
The Tools of Macroeconomic Policy

Put yourself in the shoes of the chief economist ② advising the government. Unemployment is rising and GDP is falling. Or perhaps the burst of a speculative bubble in housing prices has led to massive defaults, banking losses, and a credit crunch. Or your country has a balance-of-payments crisis, with a large trade deficit and a foreign-exchange rate that is in free fall. What policies will help reduce inflation or unemployment, speed economic growth, or correct a trade imbalance?

Governments have certain instruments that they can use to affect macroeconomic activity. A *policy instrument* is an economic variable under the control of government that can affect one or more of the macroeconomic goals. By changing monetary, fiscal, and other policies, governments can avoid the worst excesses of the business cycle or increase the growth rate of potential output. The major instruments of macroeconomic policy are listed in the bottom half of Table 19-1.

Fiscal Policy. **Fiscal policy** denotes the use of taxes ③ and government expenditures. *Government expenditures* come in two distinct forms. First there are government purchases. These comprise spending on goods and services—purchases of tanks, construction of roads, salaries for judges, and so forth. In addi- ④ tion, there are government transfer payments, which increase the incomes of targeted groups such as the elderly or the unemployed. Government spending determines the relative size of the public and private sectors, that is, how much of our GDP is consumed collectively rather than privately. From a macroeconomic perspective, government expenditures also affect the overall level of spending in the economy and thereby influence the level of GDP.

The other part of fiscal policy, *taxation,* affects the overall economy in two ways. To begin with, taxes affect people's incomes. By leaving households ⑤ with more or less disposable or spendable income, taxes affect the amount people spend on goods and services as well as the amount of private saving. Private consumption and saving have important effects on investment and output in the short and long run.

In addition, taxes affect the prices of goods and factors of production and thereby affect incentives and behavior. The United States has often ⑥ employed special tax provisions (such as an investment tax credit or accelerated depreciation) as ways of increasing investment and boosting economic growth. Many provisions of the tax code have an important impact on economic activity through their effect on the incentives to work and to save.

Monetary Policy. The second major instrument of ⑦ macroeconomic policy is **monetary policy,** which the government conducts through managing the nation's money, credit, and banking system. You may have read how our central bank, the Federal Reserve System, affects the economy by determining short-term interest rates. How does the Federal Reserve or any other central bank actually accomplish this? It does so primarily by setting short-run interest-rate targets and through buying and selling government securities to attain those targets. Through its operations, the Federal Reserve influences many financial and economic variables, such as interest rates, stock prices, housing prices, and foreign exchange rates. These financial variables affect spending on investment, particularly in housing, business investment, consumer durables, and exports and imports.

Historically, the Fed has raised interest rates when inflation threatened to rise too high. This led to reduced investment and consumption, causing a decline in GDP and lower inflation. In the most recent slowdown, which started in 2007, the Fed acted quickly to lower interest rates, provide credit, and extend its lending facilities outside traditional banking institutions.

The central bank is a key macroeconomic institution for every country. Japan, Britain, Russia, and the countries of the European Union all have powerful central banks. In an "open economy"—that is, one whose borders are open to goods, services, and financial flows—the exchange-rate system is also a central part of monetary policy.

Monetary policy is the tool that countries most often rely on to stabilize the business cycle, although it becomes less potent in deep recessions. The exact way that central banks can affect economic activity

---

① 宏观经济政策的目标是：
1. 处于高位的不断增长的国民产出水平。
2. 低失业，同时实现高就业。
3. 稳定或者缓慢上升的价格水平。

② 假设你站在为政府提供建议的首席经济学家的立场。

③ **财政政策：财政政策**系指税收以及政府支出的使用。

④ 此外，还有政府的转移支付，以增加诸如老年人或者失业者这样的目标群体的收入。

⑤ 通过增加或减少家庭可支配收入，税收就可以影响人们在物品和服务的支出量以及私人储蓄额。

⑥ 美国常常应用特殊的税赋条款（如投资税抵免或加速折旧），作为增加投资和推动经济增长的手段。

⑦ **货币政策：**宏观经济政策的第二个主要工具是**货币政策**，政府通过对本国货币、信贷以及银行系统的管理来实施货币政策。

will be thoroughly analyzed in the chapters on monetary policy.

Summary:

A nation has two major kinds of policies that can ①
be used to pursue its macroeconomic goals—fiscal policy and monetary policy.

1. Fiscal policy consists of government expenditure and taxation. Government expenditure influences the relative size of collective spending and private consumption. Taxation subtracts from incomes, reduces private spending, and affects private saving. In addition, it affects investment and potential output. Fiscal policy is primarily used to affect long-term economic growth through its impact on national saving and investment; it is also used to stimulate spending in deep or sharp recessions.
2. Monetary policy, conducted by the central bank, determines short-run interest rates. It thereby affects credit conditions, including asset prices such as stock and bond prices and exchange rates. Changes in interest rates, along with other financial conditions, affect spending in sectors such as business investment, housing, and foreign trade. Monetary policy has an important effect on both actual GDP and potential GDP.

国际联系
INTERNATIONAL LINKAGES

No nation is an island unto itself. Nations increasingly participate in the world economy and are linked together through trade and finance—this is the phenomenon called *globalization*. As the costs of transportation and communication have declined, international linkages have become tighter than they were a generation ago. International trade has replaced empire-building and military conquest as the surest road to national wealth and influence.

The trade linkages of imports and exports of goods and services are seen when the United States imports cars from Japan or exports computers to
Mexico. Financial linkages come in activities such ②
as foreigners' buying U.S. bonds for their sovereign debt funds or Americans' diversifying their pension funds with emerging-market stocks.

Nations keep a close watch on their international transactions. One particularly important measure is the *balance on current account*. This represents the numerical difference between the value of exports and the value of imports, along with some other adjustments. (The current account is closely related to *net exports*, which is the difference between the value of exports and the value of imports of goods and services.) When exports exceed imports, the difference is a surplus, while a negative balance is a deficit. In 2007, exports totaled \$2463 billion, while total imports and net transfers were \$3194 billion; the difference was the U.S. current-account deficit of \$731 billion.

For most of the twentieth century, the United States had a surplus in its foreign trade, exporting more than it imported. But trading patterns changed dramatically in the last quarter-century. As saving in the United States declined and foreign saving increased, a substantial part of foreign saving flowed to the United States. The counterpart of foreigners saving in the United States was that the current account turned sharply to deficit. As foreign investment in the nation increased, the United States by 2008 owed on balance around \$2½ trillion to foreigners. Some economists worry that the large foreign debt poses major risks for the United States—risks that we will analyze in later chapters.

As economies become more closely linked, international economic policy becomes more important, particularly in small open economies. But remember that international trade and finance are not ends in
themselves. Rather, international exchange serves ③
the ultimate goal of improving living standards.

The major areas of concern are trade policies and international financial management. *Trade policies* consist of tariffs, quotas, and other regulations that restrict or encourage imports and exports. Most trade policies have little effect on short-run macroeconomic performance, but from time to time, as was the case in the 1930s, restrictions on international trade are so severe that they cause major economic dislocations, inflations, or recessions.

A second set of policies is *international financial management*. A country's international trade is influenced by its foreign exchange rate, which represents the price of its own currency in terms of the currencies of other nations. Foreign exchange systems are an integral part of monetary policy. In small open economies, managing the exchange rate is the single most important macroeconomic policy.

The international economy is an intricate web of ④
trading and financial connections among countries.

---

① 一个国家主要使用两种经济政策来实现其宏观经济目标：财政政策与货币政策。

1. 财政政策由政府支出与税收两部分组成。政府支出影响着集体支出和私人消费的相关规模。从收入中所征的税收，减少了私人支出，并进而影响了私人储蓄。此外，它也会影响到投资和潜在产出。财政政策主要通过其对国民储蓄和投资施加的影响来对经济的长期增长发挥作用；同时，也对已陷入严重衰退中的经济产生刺激支出的作用。
2. 中央银行实施的货币政策决定了短期利率，以期对包括诸如股票、债券以及汇率的资产价格在内的信贷条件施加影响。利率以及伴随而来的金融环境的变化同样影响到商业投资、不动产以及对外贸易等领域的支出水平。货币政策对实际 GDP 和潜在 GDP 均有极其重要的影响。

② 别的国家在为其主权债务基金购买美国国债，或者美国购买新兴市场国家的股票使其养老基金多元化的种种国家间的金融交易活动，构建了国际金融联系。

③ 更确切一点讲，国际间交往活动符合提高人民生活水平的终极目标。

④ 国际经济是一个国家间贸易和金融联系的错综复杂的网络。当国际经济体系平稳运行时，助推经济快速增长；当国际贸易体系崩溃，全世界的生产和收入都会饱受其害。所以，各国在制定自己国家高产出、高就业和稳定价格的目标时，都要充分考虑贸易政策和国际金融政策的影响。

When the international economic system runs smoothly, it contributes to rapid economic growth; when trading systems break down, production and incomes suffer throughout the world. Countries therefore consider the impacts of trade policies and international financial policies on their domestic objectives of high output, high employment, and price stability.

总供给和总需求

B. AGGREGATE SUPPLY AND DEMAND

The economic history of nations can be seen in their macroeconomic performance. Economists have developed aggregate supply-and-demand analysis to help explain the major trends in output and prices. We begin by explaining this important tool of macroeconomics and then use it to understand some important historical events.

宏观经济体内部的总供给与总需求
INSIDE THE MACROECONOMY: AGGREGATE SUPPLY AND DEMAND

总供给与总需求的定义
Definitions of Aggregate Supply and Demand

How do different forces interact to determine overall economic activity? Figure 19-5 shows the relationships among the different variables inside the macroeconomy. It separates variables into two categories: those affecting aggregate supply and those affecting aggregate demand. While the division is ① simplified, dividing variables into these two categories helps us understand what determines the levels of output, prices, and unemployment.

The lower part of Figure 19-5 shows the forces affecting aggregate supply. **Aggregate supply** refers ② to the total quantity of goods and services that the nation's businesses willingly produce and sell in a given period. Aggregate supply (often written *AS*) depends upon the price level, the productive capacity of the economy, and the level of costs.

In general, businesses would like to sell everything they can produce at high prices. Under some circumstances, prices and spending levels may be depressed, so businesses might find they have excess capacity. Under other conditions, such as during a wartime boom, factories may be operating at capacity as businesses scramble to produce enough to meet all their orders.

We see, then, that aggregate supply depends on the price level that businesses can charge as well as on the economy's capacity or potential output. Potential output in turn is determined by the avail- ③ ability of productive inputs (labor and capital being the most important) and the managerial and technical efficiency with which those inputs are combined.

National output and the overall price level are ④ determined by the twin blades of the scissors of aggregate supply and demand. The second blade is **aggregate demand,** which refers to the total amount that different sectors in the economy willingly spend in a given period. Aggregate demand (often written *AD*) equals total spending on goods and services. It depends on the level of prices, as well as on monetary policy, fiscal policy, and other factors.

The components of aggregate demand include *consumption* (the cars, food, and other consumption goods bought by consumers); *investment* (construction of houses and factories as well as business equipment); *government purchases* (such as spending on teachers and missiles); and *net exports* (the difference between exports and imports). Aggregate demand is affected by the prices at which the goods are offered, by exogenous forces like wars and weather, and by government policies.

Using both blades of the scissors of aggregate supply and demand, we achieve the resulting equilibrium, as is shown in the right-hand circle of Figure 19-5. National output and the price level settle at that level where demanders willingly buy what businesses willingly sell. The resulting output and price level determine employment, unemployment, and international trade.

总供给和总需求曲线
Aggregate Supply and Demand Curves

Aggregate supply and demand curves are often used to help analyze macroeconomic conditions. Recall that in Chapter 3 we used market supply and demand curves to analyze the prices and quantities of individual products. An analogous graphical apparatus can help us understand how monetary policy or technological change acts through aggregate supply and demand to determine national output and the price level.

---

① 这样的划分不仅使问题简化，同时，将变量分成这样的两种类型有助于我们理解产出、价格和失业水平的决定因素。

② **总供给**系指在一给定时段内，该国企业自愿生产和出售的物品和服务的总和。

③ 反过来，潜在产出水平取决于生产性投入要素的可获得程度（最重要的是劳动力和资本），以及整合这些投入要素的管理和技术效率。

④ 国民产出与价格总水平是由总供给和总需求这把剪刀的两个刀刃共同决定的。**总需求**扮演着第二刀刃的角色，指的是在一给定时段内，该经济体的不同部门愿意支出的总量。

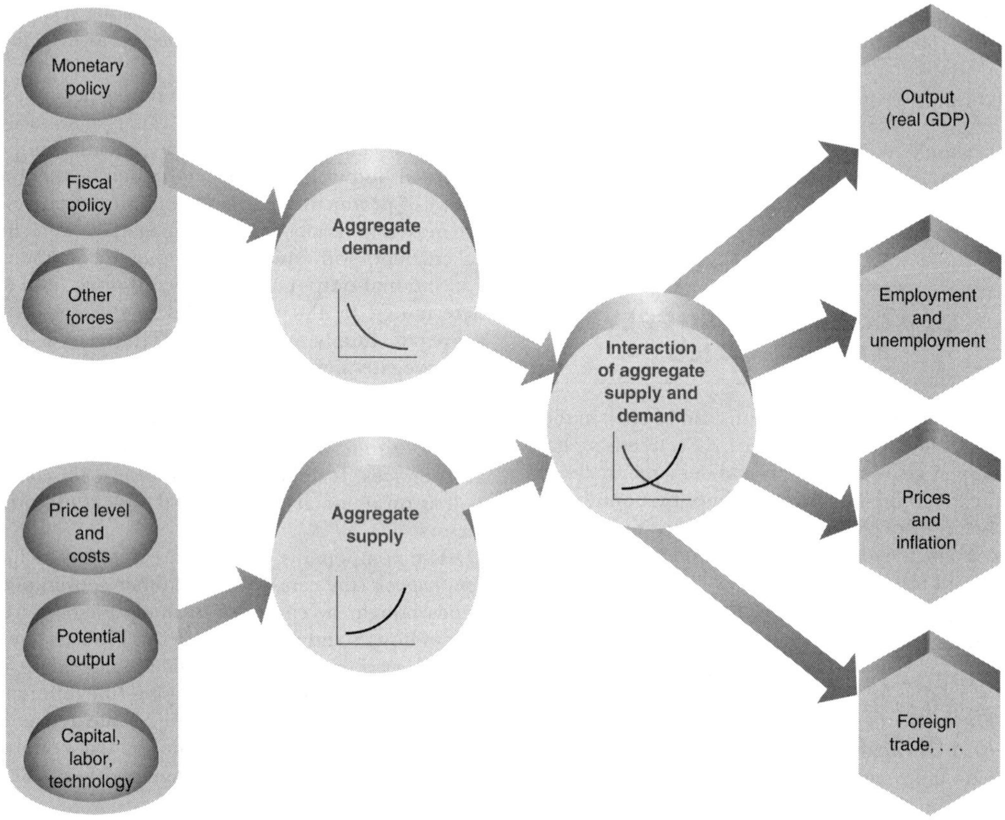

FIGURE 19-5. Aggregate Supply and Demand Determine the Major Macroeconomic Variables

This key diagram shows the major factors affecting overall economic activity. On the left are the major variables determining aggregate supply and demand; these include policy variables, like monetary and fiscal policies, along with stocks of capital and labor. In the center, aggregate supply and demand interact. The chief outcomes are shown on the right in hexagons: output, employment, the price level, and international trade. ①

Figure 19-6 shows the aggregate supply and demand schedules for the output of an entire economy. On the horizontal axis is the total output (real GDP) of the economy. On the vertical axis is the overall price level (as measured by the "price of GDP"). We use the symbol Q for real output and P for the price level.

The downward-sloping curve is the **aggregate demand schedule,** or *AD* curve. It represents what everyone in the economy—consumers, businesses, foreigners, and governments—would buy at different aggregate price levels (with other factors affecting aggregate demand held constant). From the curve, we see that at an overall price level of 150, total spending would be \$3000 billion (per year). If the price level rises to 200, total spending would fall to \$2300 billion.

The upward-sloping curve is the **aggregate supply schedule,** or *AS* curve. This curve represents the

① 在中间部分，总供给与总需求相互影响。右侧的四个六边形表示主要结果：产出、就业、价格水平和国际贸易。

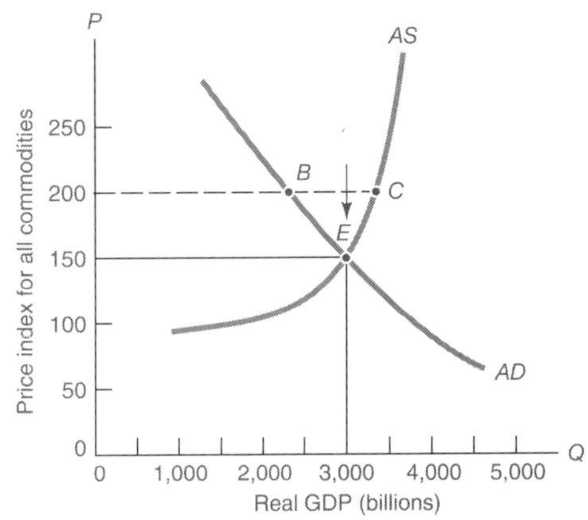

FIGURE 19-6. Aggregate Price and Output Are Determined by the Interaction of Aggregate Supply and Demand

The *AD* curve represents the quantity of total spending at different price levels, with other factors held constant. The *AS* curve shows what firms will produce and sell at different price levels, other things equal.

National output and the overall price level are determined at the intersection of the aggregate demand and supply curves, at point *E*. This equilibrium occurs at an overall price level where firms willingly produce and sell what consumers and other demanders willingly buy.

quantity of goods and services that businesses are willing to produce and sell at each price level (with other determinants of aggregate supply held constant). According to the curve, businesses will want to sell \$3000 billion at a price level of 150; they will want to sell a higher quantity, \$3300 billion, if prices rise to 200. As the level of total output demanded rises, businesses will want to sell more goods and services at a higher price level.

Warning on *AS* and *AD* Curves

Before proceeding, here is one important word of caution: Do not confuse the macroeconomic *AD* and *AS* curves with the microeconomic *DD* and *SS* curves. The microeconomic supply and demand curves show the quantities and prices of individual commodities, with such things as national income and other goods' prices held as given. By contrast, the aggregate supply and demand curves show the determination of total output and the overall price level, with such things as the money supply, fiscal policy, and the capital stock held constant.

Aggregate supply and demand explain how *total taxes* affect aggregate demand, national output, and the overall price level. Microeconomic supply and demand might consider the way increases in *gasoline taxes* affect purchases of gasoline, holding income constant. The two sets of curves have a superficial resemblance, but they explain very different phenomena.

Note as well that we have drawn the *AS* curve as upward-sloping and the *AD* curve as downward-sloping. We explain the reasons for these slopes in later chapters.

Macroeconomic Equilibrium. We now see how aggregate output and the price level adjust or equilibrate to bring aggregate supply and aggregate demand into balance. That is, we use the *AS* and *AD* concepts to see how *equilibrium values of price and quantity* are determined or to find the *P* and *Q* that satisfy the buyers and sellers all taken together. For the *AS* and *AD* curves shown in Figure 19-6, the overall economy is in equilibrium at point *E*. Only at that point, where the level of output is $Q = 3000$ and $P = 150$, are spenders and sellers satisfied. Only at point *E* are demanders willing to buy exactly the amount that businesses are willing to produce and sell.

How does the economy reach its equilibrium? Indeed, what do we mean by equilibrium? A ①
macroeconomic equilibrium is a combination of overall price and quantity at which all buyers and sellers are satisfied with their overall purchases, sales, and prices.

Figure 19-6 illustrates the concept. If the price level were higher than equilibrium, say, at $P = 200$, businesses would want to sell more than purchasers would want to buy; businesses would desire to sell quantity *C*, while buyers would want to purchase only amount *B*. Goods would pile up on the shelves as firms produced more than consumers bought. Because of the excess aggregate supply of goods, firms would cut production and shave their prices. The overall price level would begin to decline or rise less rapidly. As the price level declined from ②
its original too high level, the gap between desired total spending and desired total sales would narrow. Eventually, prices would decline to the point where overall demand and production were in balance. At the macroeconomic equilibrium, there would be

① **宏观经济均衡**系指全部买家和卖家均对购买量、销售量和价格满意的情况下，数量和价格的总体组合。

② 当价格水平从最初过高的水平下降时，期望的总支出与期望的总销售量之间的差异就会缩小。

neither excess supply nor excess demand—and no pressure to change the overall price level.

宏观经济史：1900~2008
MACROECONOMIC HISTORY: 1900–2008

We can use the aggregate supply-and-demand apparatus to analyze recent American macroeconomic history. We focus on the economic expansion during the Vietnam War, the deep recession caused by [1] the monetary contraction of the early 1980s, and the phenomenal record of economic growth during the twentieth century. This chapter's appendix also provides data on major macroeconomic variables.

Wartime Boom. The American economy entered the 1960s having experienced multiple recessions (see Figure 19-3). President John Kennedy brought [2] Keynesian economics to Washington. His economic advisers recommended expansionary policies, and Congress enacted measures to stimulate the economy, particularly cuts in personal and corporate taxes in 1963 and 1964. GDP grew rapidly during this period, unemployment declined, and inflation was contained. By 1965, the economy was at its potential output.

Unfortunately, the government underestimated the magnitude of the buildup for the Vietnam War; defense spending grew by 55 percent from 1965 to 1968. Even when it became clear that a major inflationary boom was under way, President Johnson post- [3] poned painful fiscal steps to slow the economy. Tax ④ increases and civilian expenditure cuts came only in 1968, which was too late to prevent inflationary pressures from overheating the economy. The Federal Reserve accommodated the expansion with rapid money growth and low interest rates. As a result, the economy grew very rapidly over the period 1966–1970. Under the pressure of low unemployment and high factory utilization, inflation began to rise, inaugurating the "Great Inflation" that lasted from 1966 [5] through 1981.

Figure 19-7 illustrates the events of this period. The tax cuts and defense expenditures shifted the aggregate demand curve to the right from *AD* to *AD′*, with the equilibrium shifting from *E* to *E′*. Output and employment rose sharply, and inflation rose as output exceeded capacity limits. Economists learned that it was easier to stimulate the economy than to persuade policymakers to raise taxes to slow the economy when inflation threatened. This lesson led many to question the wisdom of using fiscal policies to stabilize the economy.

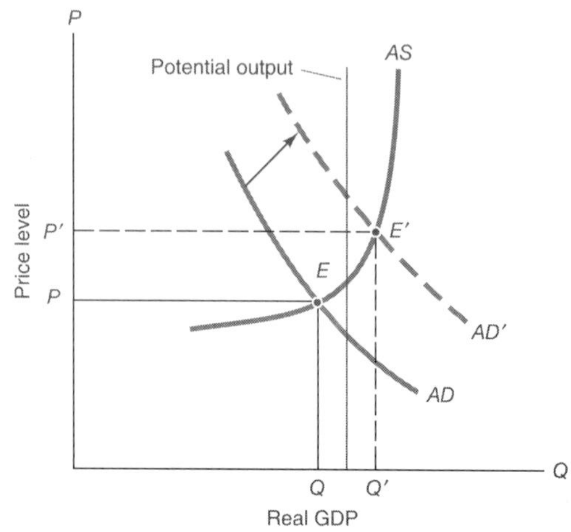

FIGURE 19-7. Wartime Boom Is Propelled by Increasing Aggregate Demand

During wartime, increased military spending increases aggregate spending, moving aggregate demand from *AD* to *AD′*, with equilibrium output increasing from *E* to *E′*. When output rises far above potential output, the price level moves up sharply from *P* to *P′*, and wartime inflation ensues.

Tight Money, 1979–1982. The 1970s were a time ⑥ of troubles, with rising oil prices, grain shortages, a sharp increase in import prices, union militancy, and accelerating wages. Price inflation became embedded in the U.S. and many other economies. As Figure 19-4 on page 374 shows, inflation rose to double-digit levels in the 1978–1980 period.

Double-digit inflation was unacceptable. In response, the Federal Reserve, under the leader- [7] ship of economist Paul Volcker, prescribed the [8] strong medicine of tight money to slow the inflation. Interest rates rose sharply in 1979 and 1980, the stock market fell, and credit was hard to find. The Fed's tight-money policy slowed spending by

[1] 见第368页[1]。

[2] John Kennedy，约翰·肯尼迪（1917~1963），美国第35任总统，著名的肯尼迪家族成员。47岁（1961年）入主白宫，1963年11月22日，在得克萨斯州达拉斯市遇刺身亡。全名John Fitzgerald Kennedy，常缩写为JFK（二战时的罗斯福总统也享有此殊荣，缩写为FDR）。详见xi页。

[3] Johnson全名Lyndon Baines Johnson，林登·贝恩斯·约翰逊（1908~1973），美国第36任总统（更详细的注疏请参阅笔者序）。这一节所论述的***Wartime Boom*（战时繁荣）**问题实际上是对约翰逊总统"伟大的社会"思想的冷思考。该思想集中体现在约翰逊总统1964年5月22日在密西根大学所作的著名演讲：《伟大的社会》（*The Great Society*）。其中一句话"美国社会在你们的手上不仅有机会走向富裕和强大，而且有机会建成一个伟大的社会"（For in your time we have the opportunity to move not only toward the rich society and the powerful society, but upward to the Great Society）被广为流传。萨翁在本段的结尾借用"Great Inflation"予以批评。

[7] Federal Reserve，美国联邦储备系统，简称Fed，履行美国中央银行的职责，主要由联邦储备委员会（Federal Reserve Board）、联邦储备银行（Federal Reserve Banks）及联邦公开市场委员会（Federal Open Market Committee）等机构组成。

④ 增加税收和削减国民支出的措施仅在1968年推出，它对于缓解经济过热现象所带来的的通货膨胀压力，已经为时已晚。

[5] Great Inflation，"伟大的通货膨胀"，出自卡耐基梅隆大学泰珀商学院（Tepper School of Business）著名政治经济学教授Allan H. Meltzer 2005年4月发表在《圣路易评论·联邦储备银行》（*Federal Reserve Bank of St. Louis Review*）的一篇著名论文《伟大的通货膨胀的起源》（*Origins of the Great Inflation*）。该文将约翰逊总统所吹捧的"伟大的社会"的1965s~1980s定义为*The Great Inflation*，定位为20世纪后半叶重要的货币改革事件。这一事件摧毁了固定汇率的布雷顿森林体系，重创了储蓄银行业，并利用对美国债券业课以重税的手段，强制性地对收入和财富实施了二次分配。这一政策所产生的政治影响也是极其深远的。

⑥ **货币紧缩，1979~1982。**20世纪70年代是一个麻烦叠加的年代，石油价格飞涨，粮食短缺，进口价格飙升，工会滋事，工资加速上涨。

[8] Paul Volcker，保罗·沃克尔，美国经济学家，被誉为"伟大的通货膨胀"的终结者。卡特和里根时期出任美联储主席（1979~1987），2009.2~2011.1出任奥巴马的"经济顾问委员会"主席。

consumers and businesses. Particularly hard-hit were interest-sensitive components of aggregate demand. After 1979, housing construction, automobile purchases, business investment, and net exports declined sharply.

We can picture how tight money reduced aggregate demand in Figure 19-7 simply by reversing the arrow. That is, tight monetary policy reduced spending and produced a leftward and downward shift of the aggregate demand curve—exactly the opposite of the effect of the tax cuts and defense buildup during the 1960s.

The effects of the tight money were twofold. First, output moved below its potential and unemployment rose sharply (see Figure 19-3 on page 373). Second, tight money and high unemployment produced a dramatic decline in inflation, from an average of 12 percent per year in the 1978–1980 period to an average of around 4 percent per year in the subsequent period (see Figure 19-4). Tight monetary policies succeeded in bringing an end to the Great Inflation, but the nation paid through higher unemployment and lower output during the period of tight money.

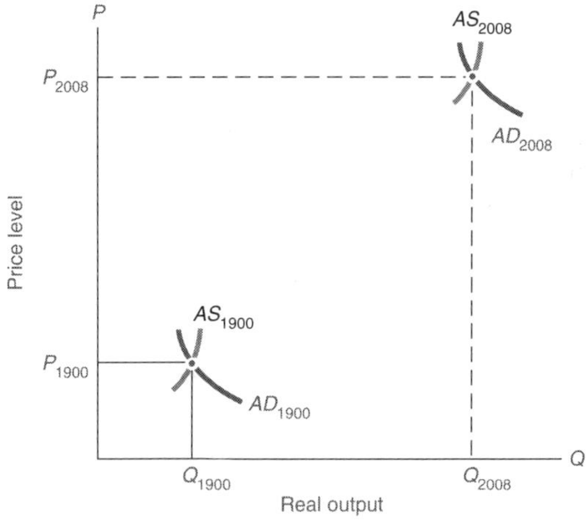

FIGURE 19-8. Growth in Potential Output Determines Long-Run Economic Performance

Over the twentieth century, increases in labor, capital, and efficiency led to a vast increase in the economy's productive potential, shifting aggregate supply far to the right. In the long run, aggregate supply is the primary determinant of output growth.

The Growth Century. The final act in our macroeconomic drama concerns the growth of output and prices over the entire period since 1900. Output has grown by a factor of 34 since the beginning of the twentieth century. How can we explain this phenomenal increase?

A careful look at American economic growth reveals that the growth rate during the twentieth century averaged 3⅓ percent per year. Part of this growth was due to growth in the scale of production as inputs of capital, labor, and even land grew sharply over this period. Just as important were improvements in efficiency due to new products (such as automobiles) and new processes (such as electronic computing). Other, less visible factors also contributed to economic growth, such as improved management techniques and improved services (including such innovations as the assembly line and overnight delivery).

Many economists believe that the measured ① growth understates true growth because our official statistics tend to miss the contribution to living standards from new products and improvements in product quality. For example, with the introduction of the indoor toilet, millions of people no longer had to struggle through the winter snows to relieve themselves in outhouses, yet this increased comfort never showed up in measured gross domestic product.

How can we picture the tremendous rise in output in our *AS-AD* apparatus? Figure 19-8 shows the way. The increase in inputs and improvements in efficiency led to a massive rightward shift of the *AS* curve from AS_{1900} to AS_{2008}. Production costs also increased sharply. For example, average earnings rose from \$0.15 per hour in 1900 to over \$30 per hour in 2008. These cost increases shifted the *AS* curve upward. The overall effect, then, was the increase in both output and prices shown in Figure 19-8.

宏观经济政策的作用
The Role of Macroeconomic Policy

Macroeconomic policy played a central role in the ② improved business-cycle conditions of the last half-century. The discovery and application of macroeconomics, along with a good appreciation of the role and limitations of monetary and fiscal policy, reduced business-cycle volatility and led to the

① 许多经济学家认为，对经济增长的评价低估了真实的增长水平，这是因为官方的统计数字往往遗漏了新产品和产品质量的改进对提高生活水平所做的贡献。

② 过去半个世纪改善的商业周期状况，归功于宏观经济政策在其中所发挥的重要作用。宏观经济学的问世与应用，以及对货币和财政政策的作用和局限性的深入理解，降低了商业周期的波动性，起到了“伟大的调节”作用。

Great Moderation. The application of fiscal policy, [1] and especially monetary policy, helped lower unemployment and ensured largely stable prices over the last two decades. When the United States faced a major shock to its financial system in 2007–2009, central bankers remembered *and understood* the lessons of the Great Depression. They knew that financial fears are contagious, that bank collapses can lead to bank runs, and that instability breeds more instability. Knowledge of macroeconomic history and theory, and the intervention of the central bank as a lender of last resort, can cushion a banking shock and prevent bank crises from turning into deep depressions.

There is no miracle cure for macroeconomic ② shocks, however. When a steep decline in output and employment hit the United States in 2007–2009, monetary and fiscal policies were launched to soften the blow, but they could not completely offset it. Up to now, the knowledge is available to prevent depressions, but not to banish recessions.

SUMMARY

A. Key Concepts of Macroeconomics

1. Macroeconomics is the study of the behavior of the entire economy: It analyzes long-run growth as well as the cyclical movements in total output, unemployment and inflation, and international trade and finance. This contrasts with microeconomics, which studies the behavior of individual markets, prices, and outputs.
2. The United States proclaimed its macroeconomic goals in the Employment Act of 1946, which declared that federal policy was "to promote maximum employment, production, and purchasing power." Since then, the nation's priorities among these three goals have shifted. But all market economies still face three central macroeconomic questions: (*a*) Why do output and employment sometimes fall, and how can unemployment be reduced? (*b*) What are the sources of price inflation, and how can it be kept under control? (*c*) How can a nation increase its rate of economic growth?
3. In addition to these perplexing questions is the hard fact that there are inevitable conflicts or tradeoffs among these goals: Rapid growth in future living standards may mean reducing consumption today, and curbing inflation may involve a temporary period of high unemployment.
4. Economists evaluate the success of an economy's overall performance by how well it attains these objectives: (*a*) high levels and rapid growth of output (measured by real gross domestic product) and consumption; (*b*) a low unemployment rate and high employment, with an ample supply of good jobs; (*c*) low and stable inflation.
5. Before the science of macroeconomics was developed, countries tended to drift around in the shifting macroeconomic currents without a rudder. Today, there are numerous instruments with which governments can steer the economy: (*a*) Fiscal policy (government spending and taxation) helps determine the allocation of resources between private and collective goods, affects people's incomes and consumption, and provides incentives for investment and other economic decisions. (*b*) Monetary policy—particularly the setting of short-term interest rates by the central bank—affects all interest rates, asset prices, credit conditions, and exchange rates. The most heavily affected sectors are housing, business investment, consumer durables, and net exports.
6. The nation is but a small part of an increasingly integrated global economy in which countries are linked together through trade of goods and services and through financial flows. A smoothly running international economic system contributes to rapid economic growth, but the international economy can throw sand in the engine of growth when trade flows are interrupted or the international financial mechanism breaks down. Dealing with international trade and finance is high on the agenda of all countries.

B. Aggregate Supply and Demand

7. The central concepts for understanding the determination of national output and the price level are aggregate supply (*AS*) and aggregate demand (*AD*). Aggregate demand consists of the total spending in an economy by households, businesses, governments, and foreigners. It represents the total output that would be willingly bought at each price level, given the monetary and fiscal policies and other factors affecting demand. Aggregate supply describes how much output businesses would willingly produce and sell given prices, costs, and market conditions.

---

[1] Great Moderation，“伟大的调节”，特指 20 世纪 80 年代中期发达国家通过制度性变革和结构改革遏制商业周期的波动，由哈佛大学教授 James Stock 和普林斯顿大学教授 Mark Watsond 在发表的论文 *Has the Business Cycle Changed and Why?* 中首度提出，由美联储现任主席伯南克于 2004 年 2 月 20 日在美国东部经济学会（Eastern Economic Association）年会所作的 *The Great Moderation* 演讲而被广泛接受。

② 然而，没有任何灵丹妙药可以医治宏观经济震荡。在 2007~2009 年间，当产出和就业的急剧下滑重创美国经济时，各种货币和财政政策的出台平缓了这场风暴，但却无法彻底抵御。迄今为止，我们对宏观经济的研究成果，可以有效地防止经济大萧条的出现，但对面临的经济衰退却束手无策。

8. *AS* and *AD* curves have the same shapes as the familiar supply and demand curves analyzed in microeconomics. But beware of potential confusions of microeconomic and aggregate supply and demand.
9. The overall macroeconomic equilibrium, determining both aggregate price and output, comes where the *AS* and *AD* curves intersect. At the equilibrium price level, purchasers willingly buy what businesses willingly sell. Equilibrium output can depart from full employment or potential output.
10. Recent American history shows an irregular cycle of aggregate demand and supply shocks and policy reactions. In the mid-1960s, war-bloated deficits plus easy money led to a rapid increase in aggregate demand. The result was a sharp upturn in prices and inflation. At the end of the 1970s, economic policymakers reacted to the rising inflation by tightening monetary policy and raising interest rates. The result lowered spending on interest-sensitive demands such as housing, investment, and net exports. Since the mid-1980s, the U.S. economy has experienced a period of low inflation and infrequent and, until recently, mild recessions.
11. Over the long run, the growth of potential output increased aggregate supply enormously and led to steady growth in output and living standards.

CONCEPTS FOR REVIEW

Major Macroeconomic Concepts

macroeconomics vs. microeconomics
gross domestic product (GDP), actual and potential
employment, unemployment, unemployment rate
inflation, deflation
consumer price index (CPI)
net exports
fiscal policy (government expenditures, taxation)
monetary policy

Aggregate Supply and Demand

aggregate supply, aggregate demand
AS curve, *AD* curve
equilibrium of *AS* and *AD*
sources of long-run economic growth

FURTHER READING AND INTERNET WEBSITES

Further Reading

The great classic of macroeconomics is John Maynard Keynes, *The General Theory of Employment, Interest, and Money* (Harcourt, New York, first published in 1935). Keynes was one of the most graceful writers among economists. An online edition of *The General Theory* is available at *www.marxists.org/reference/subject/economics/keynes/general-theory/*.

There are many good intermediate textbooks on macroeconomics. You may consult these when you want to dig more deeply into specific topics.

Websites

Macroeconomic issues are a central theme of analysis in *Economic Report of the President*. Various years are available online at *www.access.gpo.gov/eop*. Another good source on macroeconomic issues is the Congressional Budget Office, which issues periodic reports on the economy and the state of the budget at *www.cbo.gov*.

Research organizations often contain excellent online discussions of current macroeconomic issues. See especially the websites of the Brookings Institution, *www.brookings.org*, and the American Enterprise Institute, *www.aei.org*.

Some excellent blogs containing macroeconomics are the following: A blog of leading European and some American economists contains much interesting economic commentary at *www.voxeu.org;* the *International Herald Tribune* has a fine group of expert writers at *blogs.iht.com/tribtalk/business/globalization*.

QUESTIONS FOR DISCUSSION

1. What are the major objectives of macroeconomics? Write a brief definition of each of these objectives. Explain carefully why each objective is important.
2. Using the data from the appendix to this chapter, calculate the following:
   a. The inflation rate in 1981 and 2007
   b. The growth rate of real GDP in 1982 and 1984
   c. The average inflation rate from 1970 to 1980 and from 2000 to 2007
   d. The average growth rate of real GDP from 1929 to 2008

   {*Hint:* The formulas in the text give the technique for calculating 1-year growth rates. Growth rates for multiple years use the following formula:

$$g_t^{(n)} = 100 \times \left[\left(\frac{X_t}{X_{t-n}}\right)^{1/n} - 1\right]$$

   where $g_t^{(n)}$ is the average annual growth rate of the variable X for the n years between year $(t - n)$ and year t. For example, assume that the CPI in $(t - 2)$ is 100.0 while the CPI in year t is 106.09. Then the average rate of inflation is $100 \times \left[\left(\frac{106.09}{100.0}\right)^{1/2} - 1\right] = 3$ percent per year.}
3. What would be the effect of each of the following on aggregate demand or on aggregate supply, as indicated (always holding other things constant)?
   a. A large cut in personal and business taxes (on *AD*)
   b. An arms-reduction agreement reducing defense spending (on *AD*)
   c. An increase in potential output (on *AS*)
   d. A monetary loosening that lowers interest rates (on *AD*)
4. For each of the events listed in question 3, use the *AS-AD* apparatus to show the effect on output and on the overall price level.
5. Put yourself in the shoes of an economic policymaker. The economy is in equilibrium with $P = 100$ and $Q = 3000$ = potential GDP. You refuse to "accommodate" inflation; that is, you want to keep prices absolutely stable at $P = 100$, no matter what happens to output. You can use monetary and fiscal policies to affect aggregate demand, but you cannot affect aggregate supply in the short run. How would you respond to:
   a. A surprise increase in investment spending
   b. A sharp food-price increase following catastrophic flooding of the Mississippi River
   c. A productivity decline that reduces potential output
   d. A sharp decrease in net exports that followed a deep depression in East Asia
6. In 1981–1983, the Reagan administration implemented a fiscal policy that reduced taxes and increased government spending.
   a. Explain why this policy would tend to increase aggregate demand. Show the impact on output and prices assuming only an *AD* shift.
   b. The supply-side school holds that tax cuts would affect aggregate supply mainly by increasing potential output. Assuming that the Reagan fiscal measures affected *AS* as well as *AD*, show the impact on output and the price level. Explain why the impact of the Reagan fiscal policies on output is unambiguous while the impact on prices is unclear.
7. The Clinton economic package as passed by Congress in 1993 had the effect of tightening fiscal policy by raising taxes and lowering spending. Show the effect of this policy (*a*) assuming that there is no counteracting monetary policy and (*b*) assuming that monetary policy completely neutralized the impact on GDP and that the lower deficit leads to higher investment and higher growth of potential output.
8. The United States experienced a major economic downturn in the early 1980s. Consider the data on real GDP and the price level in Table 19-2.
   a. For the years 1981 to 1985, calculate the rate of growth of real GDP and the rate of inflation. Can you determine in which year there was a steep business downturn or recession?
   b. In an *AS-AD* diagram like Figure 19-6 (page 379), draw a set of *AS* and *AD* curves that trace out the price and output equilibria shown in the table. How would you explain the recession that you have identified?

Year	Real GDP ($, billion, 2000 prices)	Price level* (2000 = 100)
1980	5,161.7	54.1
1981	5,291.7	59.1
1982	5,189.3	62.7
1983	5,423.8	65.2
1984	5,813.6	67.7
1985	6,053.7	69.7

*Note that the price index shown is the price index for GDP, which measures the price trend for all components of GDP.

TABLE 19-2.

Appendix 19

MACROECONOMIC DATA FOR THE UNITED STATES
美国宏观经济数据

Year	Nominal GDP ($, billion)	Real GDP, 2000 prices ($, billion)	Unemployment rate (%)	CPI 1982–1984 = 100	Inflation rate (CPI) (% per year)	Federal budget surplus (+) or deficit (−) ($, billion)	Net exports ($, billion)
1929	103.6	865.2	3.2	17.1	0.0	1.0	0.4
1933	56.4	635.5	24.9	13.0	−5.2	−0.9	0.1
1939	92.2	950.7	17.2	13.9	−1.4	−2.1	0.8
1945	223.1	1,786.3	1.9	18.0	2.2	−29.0	−0.8
1948	269.2	1,643.2	3.8	24.0	7.4	3.6	5.5
1950	293.8	1,777.2	5.2	24.1	1.1	5.5	0.7
1960	526.4	2,501.8	5.5	29.6	1.5	7.2	4.2
1970	1,038.5	3,771.9	5.0	38.8	5.7	−15.2	4.0
1971	1,127.1	3,898.7	6.0	40.5	4.1	−28.4	0.6
1972	1,238.3	4,104.9	5.6	41.8	3.2	−24.4	−3.4
1973	1,382.7	4,341.4	4.9	44.4	6.1	−11.3	4.1
1974	1,500.0	4,319.5	5.6	49.3	10.4	−13.8	−0.8
1975	1,638.3	4,311.2	8.5	53.8	8.7	−69.0	16.0
1976	1,825.3	4,540.9	7.7	56.9	5.6	−51.7	−1.6
1977	2,030.9	4,750.6	7.1	60.6	6.3	−44.1	−23.1
1978	2,294.7	5,015.0	6.1	65.2	7.4	−26.5	−25.4
1979	2,563.3	5,173.5	5.9	72.6	10.7	−11.3	−22.5
1980	2,789.5	5,161.7	7.2	82.4	12.7	−53.6	−13.1
1981	3,128.4	5,291.7	7.6	90.9	9.9	−53.3	−12.5
1982	3,255.0	5,189.3	9.7	96.5	6.0	−131.9	−20.0
1983	3,536.7	5,423.8	9.6	99.6	3.1	−173.0	−51.7
1984	3,933.2	5,813.6	7.5	103.9	4.3	−168.1	−102.7
1985	4,220.3	6,053.8	7.2	107.6	3.5	−175.0	−115.2
1986	4,462.8	6,263.6	7.0	109.7	1.9	−190.8	−132.7
1987	4,739.5	6,475.1	6.2	113.6	3.5	−145.0	−145.2
1988	5,103.8	6,742.7	5.5	118.3	4.0	−134.5	−110.4
1989	5,484.4	6,981.4	5.3	123.9	4.7	−130.1	−88.2
1990	5,803.1	7,112.5	5.6	130.7	5.3	−172.0	−78.0
1991	5,995.9	7,100.5	6.9	136.2	4.1	−213.7	−27.5
1992	6,337.7	7,336.6	7.5	140.3	3.0	−297.4	−33.2
1993	6,657.4	7,532.7	6.9	144.5	2.9	−273.5	−65.0
1994	7,072.2	7,835.5	6.1	148.2	2.6	−212.3	−93.6
1995	7,397.7	8,031.7	5.6	152.4	2.8	−197.0	−91.4
1996	7,816.9	8,328.9	5.4	156.9	2.9	−141.8	−96.2
1997	8,304.3	8,703.5	4.9	160.5	2.3	−55.8	−101.6
1998	8,747.0	9,066.9	4.5	163.0	1.5	38.8	−159.9
1999	9,268.4	9,470.4	4.2	166.6	2.2	103.6	−260.5
2000	9,817.0	9,817.0	4.0	172.2	3.3	189.5	−379.5
2001	10,128.0	9,890.7	4.7	177.0	2.8	46.7	−367.0
2002	10,469.6	10,048.9	5.8	179.9	1.6	−247.9	−424.4
2003	10,960.8	10,301.1	6.0	184.0	2.3	−372.1	−499.4
2004	11,685.9	10,675.7	5.5	188.9	2.6	−370.6	−615.4
2005	12,433.9	11,003.5	5.1	195.3	3.3	−318.3	−714.6
2006	13,194.7	11,319.4	4.6	201.6	3.2	−220.0	−762.0
2007	13,807.6	11,523.9	4.6	207.3	2.8	−399.4	−707.8
2008	14,304.4	11,666.0	5.8	215.2	4.1	−456.5	−727.9

TABLE 19A-1.

Table 19A-1 contains some of the major macroeconomic data discussed in this chapter. Major data can be obtained through government websites at *www.fedstats.gov*, *www.bea.gov*, or *www.bls.gov*.

CHAPTER

20 Measuring Economic Activity 经济活动的测量

When you can measure what you are speaking about, and express it in numbers, you know something about it; when you cannot measure it, when you cannot express it in numbers, your knowledge is of a meager and unsatisfactory kind; it may be the beginning of knowledge, but you have scarcely, in your thoughts, advanced to the stage of science. ②

Lord Kelvin [1]

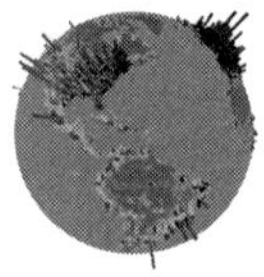

[1] 开尔文男爵（Lord Kelvin），原名威廉·汤姆森（1824~1907）。由于在热力学和电磁学领域成就卓著，于1866年被封爵。1892年被加封“First Baron”（一等男爵）后，遂改名“Kelvin”，意为“武士加朋友”，以彰显自己凯尔特人的高贵血统，100多年来均被习惯性地冠以“Lord Kelvin”。英国功绩勋章和维多利亚大十字勋章获得者，曾任枢密院顾问官、皇家学会会长和爱丁堡皇家科学院院长等要职。

本段文字出自其1891~1894年期间先后出版的三卷本《公共演讲集》（*Popular Lectures and Addresses*）中的第一卷《电气测量单位》（*Electrical Units of Measurement*），原文为：

In physical science the first essential step in the direction of learning any subject is to find principles of numerical reckoning and practicable methods for measuring some quality connected with it. I often say that when you can measure what you are speaking about, and express it in numbers, you know something about it; but when you cannot measure it, when you cannot express it in numbers, your knowledge is of a meager and unsatisfactory kind; it may be the beginning of knowledge, but you have scarcely in your thoughts advanced to the state of Science, whatever the matter may be.

② 当你能对你所谈到的内容进行测量，并能用数字表达时，你才能真正对其掌握。当你无法对其进行测量，更无法用数字加以表达时，你的认知就是肤浅的，也是差强人意的。尽管你所做的这一切有可能是认知的开始，但就你的思想而言，还几乎没有发展到科学认知的阶段。

The single most important concept in macroeconomics is the gross domestic product (GDP), which measures the total value of goods and services produced in a country during a year. GDP is part of the *national income and product accounts* (or *national accounts*), which are a body of statistics that enables policymakers to determine whether the economy is contracting or expanding and whether a severe recession or inflation threatens. When economists want to determine the level of economic development of a country, they look at its GDP per capita.

While the GDP and the rest of the national accounts may seem to be arcane concepts, they are truly among the great inventions of modern times. Much as a satellite in space can survey the weather ③ across an entire continent, so can the GDP give an overall picture of the state of the economy. In this chapter, we explain how economists measure GDP and other major macroeconomic indicators.

国内生产总值：经济绩效的尺度
GROSS DOMESTIC PRODUCT: THE YARDSTICK OF AN ECONOMY'S PERFORMANCE

What is the *gross domestic product*? GDP is the name we give to the total market value of the final goods and services produced within a nation during a given year. It is the figure you get when you apply ④ the measuring rod of money to the diverse goods and services—from apples to zithers—that a country produces with its land, labor, and capital resources. GDP equals the total production of consumption and investment goods, government purchases, and net exports to other lands.

The gross domestic product (GDP) is the most ⑤ comprehensive measure of a nation's total output of goods and services. It is the sum of the dollar values of consumption (C), gross investment (I), government purchases of goods and services (G), and

③ 这一点，与空间卫星可以俯瞰整个大陆以通盘监测大气状况极为相似，GDP可以对该国经济的总体运行状况做一通盘的描述。

④ 当你用货币这一标尺来测量一个国家使用自身的土地、劳动及资本等资源来生产从诸如苹果到西撒拉琴的各种物品和服务时，你就对该国有了一个概括的了解。

⑤ 国内生产总值（GDP）是对一个国家物品与服务总产出量最综合的测量。它是一个国家在一年内消费（C）、总投资（I）、政府购买的物品与服务（G）以及净出口（X）以美元为计价单位的总和。

net exports (X) produced within a nation during a given year.

In symbols:

$$GDP = C + I + G + X$$

GDP is used for many purposes, but the most important one is to measure the overall performance of an economy. If you were to ask an economic historian what happened during the Great Depression, the best short answer would be:

> Between 1929 and 1933, GDP fell from $104 billion to $56 billion. This sharp decline in the dollar value of goods and services produced by the American economy caused high unemployment, hardship, a steep stock market decline, bankruptcies, bank failures, riots, and political turmoil.

Similarly, if you were to ask a macroeconomist about the second half of the twentieth century, she might reply:

> The second half of the twentieth century was a unique economic period. During those years, the affluent regions of the North—consisting of Japan, the United [1]
> States, and Western Europe—experienced the most rapid growth of output per capita in recorded history. From the end of World War II until 2000, for example, real GDP per capita in the United States expanded by almost 250 percent.

We now discuss the elements of the national income and product accounts. We start by showing different ways of measuring GDP and distinguishing real from nominal GDP. We then analyze the major components of GDP. We conclude with a discussion of the measurement of the general price level and the rate of inflation.

国民产值的两种测量方法：产品流量法和收入流量法

Two Measures of National Product: Goods Flow and Earnings Flow

How do economists actually measure GDP? One of the major surprises is that we can measure GDP in two entirely independent ways. As Figure 20-1 shows, ②
GDP can be measured either as a flow of products or as a sum of earnings.

To demonstrate the different ways of measuring GDP, we begin by considering an oversimplified world in which there is no government, no foreign trade, and no investment. For the moment, our little economy produces only *consumption goods,* which are items that are purchased by households to satisfy their wants. (Important note: Our first example is oversimplified to show the basic ideas. In the realistic examples that follow, we will add investment, government, and the foreign sector.)

Flow-of-Product Approach. Each year the public consumes a wide variety of final goods and services: goods such as apples, computer software, and blue jeans; services such as health care and haircuts. We include only *final goods*—goods ultimately bought and used by consumers. Households spend their incomes for these consumer goods, as is shown in the upper loop of Figure 20-1. Add together all the consumption dollars spent on these final goods, and you will arrive at this simplified economy's total GDP.

Thus, in our simple economy, you can easily ③
calculate national income or product as the sum of the annual flow of final goods and services: (price of blue jeans × number of blue jeans) plus (price of apples × number of apples) and so forth for all other final goods. The gross domestic product is defined as the total money value of the flow of final products produced by the nation.

National accountants use market prices as weights in valuing different commodities because market prices reflect the relative economic value of diverse goods and services. That is, the relative prices of different goods reflect how much consumers value their last (or marginal) units of consumption of these goods.

Earnings or Income Approach. The second and equivalent way to calculate GDP is the income accounts (also called the earnings or cost approach). Look at the lower loop in Figure 20-1. Through it flow all the costs of doing business; these costs include the wages paid to labor, the rents paid to land, the profits paid to capital, and so forth. But these business costs are also the earnings that households receive from firms. By measuring the annual flow of these earnings or incomes, statisticians will again arrive at the GDP.

Hence, a second way to calculate GDP is as the total of factor earnings (wages, interest, rents, and

---

[1] the North：富国集团，因最富的国家基本在北半球而得名，与 the South 相对。

② 如图 20-1 所示，GDP 既可用产品的流量来测量，也可用收入的总和来测量。

③ 这样，在简化的经济中，就可以很容易地将最终物品和服务的年度总流量加总起来，计算出国民收入或国民产值：(牛仔裤的价格 × 牛仔裤的总量）加（苹果的价格 × 苹果的总量）……，直至将所有的最终产品全部加总在内。

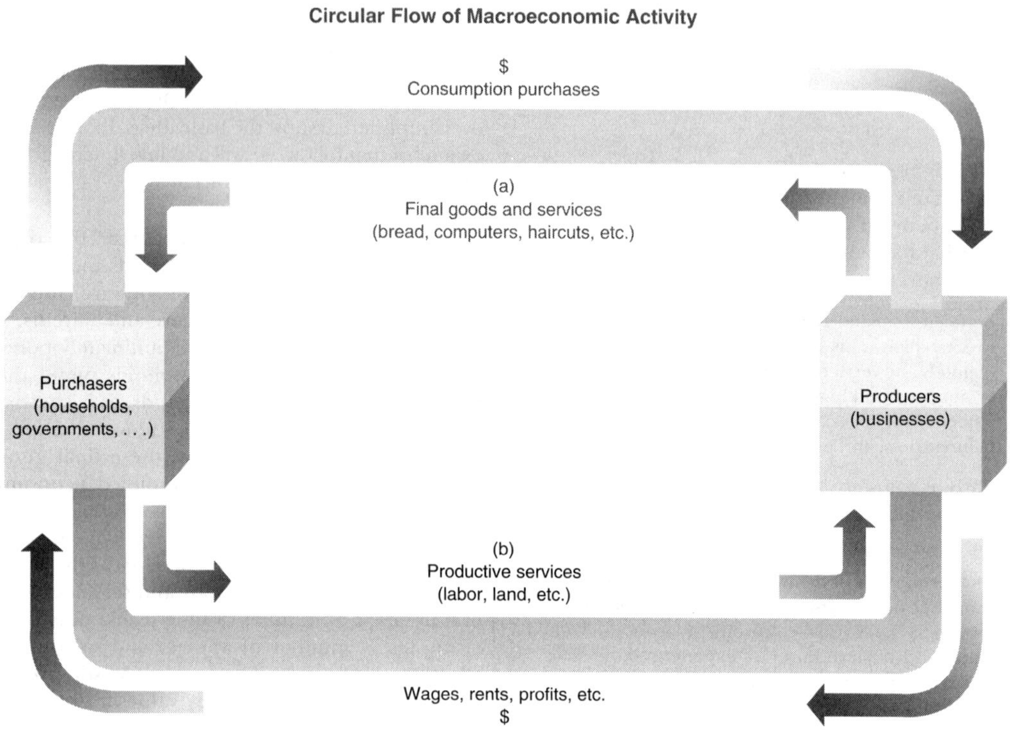

FIGURE 20-1. Gross Domestic Product Can Be Measured Either as (*a*) a Flow of Final Products or, Equivalently, as (*b*) a Flow of Earnings or Incomes

In the upper loop, purchasers buy final goods and services. The total dollar flow of their spending each year is one measure of gross domestic product. The lower loop measures the annual flow of costs of output: the earnings that businesses pay out in wages, rent, interest, dividends, and profits.

The two measures of GDP must always be identical. Note that this figure is the macroeconomic counterpart of Fig. 2-1, which presented the circular flow of supply and demand.

profits) that are the costs of producing society's final products.

Equivalence of the Two Approaches. Now we have calculated GDP by the upper-loop flow-of-product approach and by the lower-loop earnings-flow approach. Which is the better approach? The surprise is that *they are exactly the same.*

We can see why the product and earnings approaches are identical by examining a simple barbershop economy. Say the barbers have no expenses other than labor. If they sell 10 haircuts at $8 each, GDP is $80. But the barbers' earnings (in wages and profits) are also exactly $80. Hence, the GDP here ① is identical whether measured as a flow of products ($80 worth of haircuts) or as a flow of costs and incomes ($80 worth of wages and profits).

In fact, the two approaches are identical because we have included "profits" in the lower loop along with other incomes. What exactly is profit? Profit is what remains from the sale of a product after you have paid the other factor costs—wages, interest, and rents. It

① 所以，无论以产品流量（价值 80 美元的美发费用）作为测量手段，还是以成本和收入流量（80 美元的工资和利润）作为测量手段，这里所讲的 GDP 都是一样的。

(a) Income Statement of Typical Farm

Output in Farming		Earnings	
Sales of goods (corn, apples, etc.)	**$1,000**	**Costs of production:**	
		Wages	$ 800
		Rents	100
		Interest	25
		Profits (residual)	75
Total	$1,000	Total	$1,000

(b) National Product Account (millions of dollars)

Upper-Loop Flow of Product		Lower-Loop Flow of Earnings	
Final output (10 × 1,000)	**$10,000**	**Costs or earnings:**	
		Wages (10 × 800)	$ 8,000
		Rents (10 × 100)	1,000
		Interest (10 × 25)	250
		Profits (10 × 75)	750
GDP total	**$10,000**	**GDP total**	**$10,000**

TABLE 20-1. Construction of National Product Accounts from Business Accounts

Part **(a)** shows the income statement of a typical farm. The left side shows the value of production, while the right side shows the farm's costs. Part **(b)** then adds up or aggregates the 10 million identical farms to obtain total GDP. Note that GDP from the product side exactly equals GDP from the earnings side.

is the residual that adjusts automatically to make the lower loop's costs or earnings exactly match the upper loop's value of goods and services.

To sum up:

GDP, or gross domestic product, can be measured in two different ways: (1) as the flow of spending on final products, or (2) as the total costs or incomes of inputs. Both approaches yield exactly the same measure of GDP. ①

源于企业账户的国民账户

National Accounts Derived from Business Accounts

You might wonder where on earth economists find all the data for the national accounts. In practice, government economists draw on a wide array of sources, including surveys, income-tax returns, retail-sales statistics, and employment data.

The most important source of data is business accounts. An *account* for a firm or nation is a numerical record of all flows (outputs, costs, etc.) during a given period. We can show the relationship between business accounts and national accounts by constructing the accounts for an economy made up only of farms. The top half of Table 20-1 shows the results of a year's farming operations for a single, typical farm. We put sales of final products on the left-hand side and the various costs of production on the right. The bottom half of Table 20-1 shows how to construct the GDP accounts for our simple agrarian economy in which all final products are produced on 10 million identical farms. The national accounts simply add together or *aggregate* the outputs and costs of the 10 million identical farms to get the two different measures of GDP.

"重复计算"问题

The Problem of "Double Counting"

We defined GDP as the total production of final goods and services. A *final product* is one that is produced and sold for consumption or investment. GDP excludes *intermediate goods*—goods that are used up to produce other goods. GDP therefore includes

① GDP，即国内生产总值，可用两种不同的方法来测量：（1）以最终产品为基准的支出流量；（2）各种投入要素的总成本或总收入。GDP 的这两种测量方法计算出的最终结果正好相等。

bread but not flour, and home computers but not computer chips.

For the flow-of-product calculation of GDP, excluding intermediate products poses no major complications. We simply include the bread and home computers in GDP but avoid including the flour and yeast that went into the bread or the chips and plastic that went into the computers. If you look again at the upper loop in Figure 20-1, you will see that bread and computers appear in the flow of products, but you will not find any flour or computer chips. ①

What has happened to products like flour and computer chips? They are intermediate products and are simply cycling around inside the block marked "Producers." If they are not bought by consumers, they never show up as final products in GDP. ②

"Value Added" in the Lower Loop. A new statistician who is being trained to make GDP measurements might be puzzled, saying:

> I can see that, if you are careful, your upper-loop product approach to GDP will avoid including intermediate products. But aren't you in some trouble when you use the lower-loop cost or earnings approach?
>
> After all, when we gather income statements from the accounts of firms, won't we pick up what grain merchants pay to wheat farmers, what bakers pay to grain merchants, and what grocers pay to bakers? Won't this result in double counting or even triple counting of items going through several productive stages?

These are good questions, but there is an ingenious technique that resolves the problem. In making lower-loop earnings measurements, statisticians are very careful to include in GDP only a firm's value added. **Value added** is the difference between a firm's sales and its purchases of materials and services from other firms.

In other words, in calculating the GDP earnings or value added by a firm, the statistician includes all costs except for payments made to other businesses. Hence business costs in the form of wages, salaries, interest payments, and dividends are included in value added, but purchases of wheat or steel or electricity are excluded from value added. Why are all the purchases from other firms excluded from value added to obtain GDP? Because those purchases will get properly counted in GDP in the values added by other firms. ③

Table 20-2 uses the stages of bread production to illustrate how careful adherence to the value-added approach enables us to subtract purchases of intermediate goods that show up in the income statements ④

Bread Receipts, Costs, and Value Added (cents per loaf)

Stage of production	(1) Sales receipts	(2) *Less:* Cost of intermediate products		(3) Value added (wages, profits, etc.) (3) = (1) − (2)
Wheat	23	0	=	23
Flour	53	23	=	30
Baked dough	110	53	=	57
Final product: bread	190	110	=	80
Total	376	186		190 (sum of value added)

TABLE 20-2. GDP Sums Up Value Added at Each Production Stage

To avoid double counting of intermediate products, we calculate value added at each stage of production. This involves subtracting all the costs of materials and intermediate products bought from other businesses from total sales. Note that every blue intermediate-product item both appears in column (1) and is subtracted in the next stage of production in column (2). (By how much would we overestimate GDP if we counted all receipts, not just value added? The overestimate would be 186 cents per loaf.)

① 采用产品流量来计算 GDP 时，排除中间产品并不复杂。我们可以简单地只将面包和家用计算机计入 GDP 中，但不包括生产面包用的面粉和发酵粉，以及生产计算机用的蕊片和塑胶制品。

② 那么，像面粉与电脑芯片这样的产品究竟到哪里去了？很简单，作为中间产品，在“生产者”的方框内循环流动。这些产品如果不被消费者所购买，就不可能作为最终产品在 GDP 中表现出来。

③ 换句话说，在计算 GDP 中所含的企业收入或附加值时，统计人员计入了所有成本，扣除了对其他企业的支付。

④ 表 20-2 列出了面包生产过程中的所有环节，以说明小心谨慎地使用附加值法，可使我们从列出农场主、面粉商、面包生产商和杂货店的损益表中扣除购买中间产品的支出。

of farmers, millers, bakers, and grocers. The final calculation shows the desired equality between (1) final sales of bread and (2) total earnings, calculated as the sum of all values added in all the different stages of bread production.

Value-added approach: To avoid double counting, ① we take care to include only final goods in GDP and to exclude the intermediate goods that are used up in making the final goods. By measuring the value added at each stage, taking care to subtract expenditures on the intermediate goods bought from other firms, the lower-loop earnings approach properly avoids all double counting and records wages, interest, rents, and profits exactly one time.

国民账户的测量细节

DETAILS OF THE NATIONAL ACCOUNTS

Now that we have an overview of the national income and product accounts, we will proceed, in the rest of this chapter, on a whirlwind tour of the various sectors. Before we start on the journey, look at Table 20-3 to get an idea of where we are going. This table shows a summary set of accounts for both the product and the income sides. If you understand the structure of the table and the definitions of the terms in it, you will be well on your way to understanding GDP and its family of components.

实际 GDP 与名义 GDP：用价格指数“紧缩”GDP

Real vs. Nominal GDP: "Deflating" GDP by a Price Index

We define GDP as the dollar value of goods and services. In measuring the dollar value, we use the measuring rod of *market prices* for the different goods and services. But prices change over time, as inflation generally sends prices upward year after year. Who would ② want to measure things with a rubber yardstick—one that stretches in your hands from day to day—rather than a rigid and invariant yardstick?

The problem of changing prices is one of the problems economists have to solve when they use money as their measuring rod. Clearly, we want a measure of the nation's output and income that uses an invariant yardstick. Economists can replace the elastic yardstick with a reliable one by removing the price-increase component so as to create a real or quantity index of national output.

Here is the basic idea: We can measure the GDP for a particular year using the actual market prices of that year; this gives us the **nominal GDP,** or GDP at current prices. But we are usually more interested in determining what has happened to the **real GDP,** which is an index of the volume or quantity of goods and services produced. Real GDP is calculated by tracking the volume or quantity of production after removing the influence of changing prices or inflation. Hence, nominal GDP is calculated using changing prices, while real GDP represents the change in the volume of total output after price changes are removed.

Product Approach	Earnings Approach
Components of gross domestic product:	**Earnings or income approach to gross domestic product:**
Consumption (C)	Compensation of labor (wages, salaries, and supplements)
+ Gross private domestic investment (I)	+ Corporate profits
+ Government purchases (G)	+ Other property income (rent, interest, proprietors' income)
+ Net exports (X)	+ Depreciation
	+ Net production taxes
Equals: Gross domestic product	**Equals: Gross domestic product**

TABLE 20-3. Overview of the National Income and Product Accounts

This table presents the major components of the two sides of the national accounts. The left side shows the components of the product approach (or upper loop); the symbols C, I, G, and X are often used to represent these four items of GDP. The right side shows the components of the earnings or income approach (or lower loop). Each approach will ultimately add up to exactly the same GDP.

① 附加值法：为避免重复计算，我们小心地只将最终产品计入 GDP，把生产最终产品时消耗的中间产品排除在外。通过对每一环节附加值的核算，认真仔细地扣除从其他厂商购买中间产品的支出，环形图下部所示的收入法能恰当地避免所有的重复计算，准确地将工资、利息、租金和利润一次性计入。

② 有谁愿意使用一条橡皮绳作测量工具（整天在人们的手中伸来缩去），而不去使用一把固定不变的刚性标尺呢？

Date	(1) Nominal GDP (current $, billion)	(2) Index number of prices (GDP deflator, 1929 = 1)	(3) Real GDP ($, billion, 1929 prices) $(3)=\frac{(1)}{(2)}$
1929	104	1.00	$\frac{104}{1.00} = 104$
1933	56	0.74	$\frac{56}{0.74} = 76$

TABLE 20-4. Real (or Inflation-Corrected) GDP Is Obtained by Dividing Nominal GDP by the GDP Deflator

Using the price index of column (2), we deflate column (1) to get real GDP in column (3). (Riddle: Can you show that 1929's real GDP was $77 billion in terms of 1933 prices? *Hint:* With 1933 as a base of 1, 1929's price index is 1.35.)

The difference between nominal GDP and real ① GDP is the **price of GDP,** sometimes called the **GDP deflator.**

A simple example will illustrate the general idea. Say that a country produces 1000 bushels of corn in year 1 and 1010 bushels in year 2. The price of a bushel is $1 in year 1 and $2 in year 2. We can calculate nominal GDP (PQ) as $1 × 1000 = $1000 in year 1 and $2 × 1010 = $2020 in year 2. Nominal GDP therefore grew by 102 percent between the two years.

But the actual amount of output did not grow anywhere near that rapidly. To find real output, we need to consider what happened to prices. One common approach is to use the first year as the base year. The *base year* is the year in which we measure prices. We can, for index purposes, set the price index for the first year (the base year) at $P_1 = 1$. This means that output will be measured in prices of the base year. From the data in the previous paragraph, we see that the GDP deflator is $P_2 = \$2/\$1 = 2$ in year 2. Real GDP (Q) is equal to nominal GDP (PQ) divided by the GDP deflator (P). Hence real GDP was equal to $1000/1 = $1000 in year 1 and $2020/2 = $1010 in year 2. Thus the growth in real GDP, which cor- ② rects for the change in prices, is 1 percent and equals the growth in the output of corn, as it should.

A 1929–1933 comparison will illustrate the deflation process for an actual historical episode. Table 20-4 gives nominal GDP figures of $104 billion for 1929 and $56 billion for 1933. This represents a 46 percent drop in nominal GDP from 1929 to 1933. But the government estimates that prices on average dropped about 26 percent over this period. If we choose 1929 as our base year, with the GDP deflator of 1 in that year, this means that the 1933 price index was 0.74. So our $56 billion of GDP in 1933 was really worth much more than half the $104 billion GDP of 1929. Table 20-4 shows that, in terms of 1929 prices, or dollars of 1929 purchasing power, real GDP fell to $76 billion. Hence, part of the near-halving shown by the nominal GDP was due to the rapidly declining price level, or deflation, during the Great Depression.

The green line in Figure 20-2 shows the growth of nominal GDP since 1929, expressed in the actual dollars and prices that were current in each historical year. Then, for comparison, the real GDP, expressed in 2000 dollars, is shown in blue. Clearly, much of the increase in nominal GDP over the last eight decades was due to inflation in the price units of our money yardstick.

Table 20-4 shows the simplest way of calculating real GDP and the GDP deflator. Sometimes these calculations give misleading results, particularly when the relative prices and quantities of important goods are changing rapidly. For example, over the last three decades, computer prices have been falling very sharply while the quantity of computers produced has risen rapidly (we return to this issue in our discussion of price indexes below).

① 名义 GDP 与实际 GDP 之间的差异即 **GDP 的价格指数**，有时也称之为 **GDP 紧缩指数**。

② 这样，价格变化因素在经过校正之后，实际 GDP 的增长幅度为 1%，正好等于玉米的增产幅度，与期望值相同。

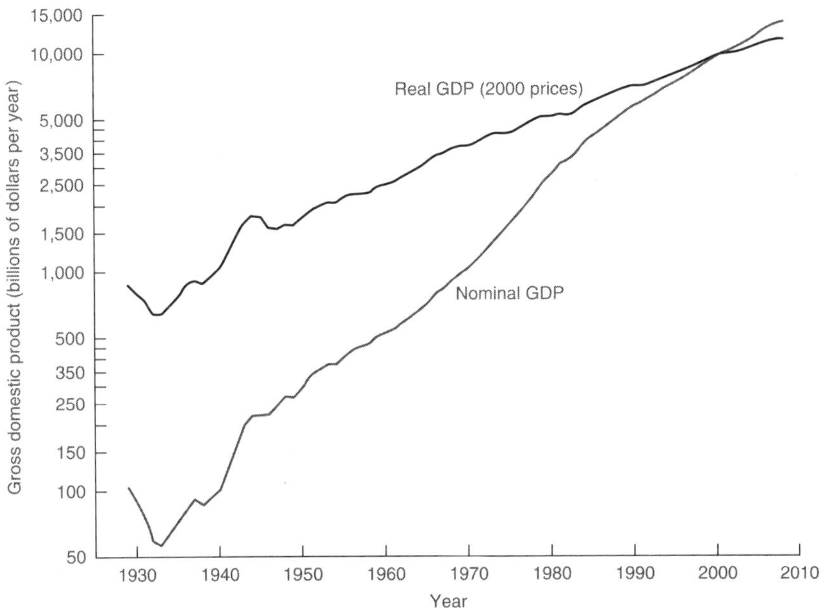

FIGURE 20-2. Nominal GDP Grows Faster than Real GDP because of Price Inflation

The rise in nominal GDP exaggerates the rise in output. Why? Because growth in nominal GDP includes increases in prices as well as growth in output. To obtain an accurate measure of real output, we must correct GDP for price changes.

Source: U.S. Bureau of Economic Analysis.

When relative prices of different goods are changing very rapidly, using prices of a fixed year will give a misleading estimate of real GDP growth. To correct for this bias, statisticians use a procedure known as *chain weighting*. Instead of the relative weights on each good being kept fixed (say, by the use of weights for a given year, like 1990), the weights of the different goods and services change each year to reflect the changes in spending patterns in the economy. Today, the official U.S. government measures of real GDP and the GDP price index rely upon chain weights. The technical names for these constructs are "real GDP in chained dollars" and the "chain-type price index for GDP." As a shorthand, we generally refer to these as real GDP and the GDP price index.

Further Details on Chain Weights. The details of using chain weights are somewhat involved, but we can get the basic idea using a simple example. The ① calculation of chain weights involves linking the output or price series together by multiplying the growth rates from one period to another. An example for a haircut economy will show how this works. Say that the value of the haircuts was \$300 in 2003. Further suppose that the quantity of haircuts increased by 1 percent from 2003 to 2004 and by 2 percent from 2004 to 2005. The value of real GDP (in chained 2003 dollars) would be \$300 in 2003, then \$300 × 1.01 = \$303 in 2004, and then \$303 × 1.02 = \$309.06 in 2005. With many different goods and services, we ② would add together the growth rates of the different components of apples, bananas, catamarans, and so on, and weight the growth rates by the expenditure or output shares of the different goods.

To summarize:

Nominal GDP (*PQ*) represents the total money ③ value of final goods and services produced in a given year, where the values are expressed in terms of the

① 连锁权重系数的计算，需要将某一时期到下一时期之间的增长率连乘，将产出系列或价格系列连接起来。

② 在处理种类繁多的物品和服务时，我们所要做的只是将苹果、香蕉、游艇等各种不同部分的增长率加总在一起，然后以不同商品的支出或者产出份额作为增长率的权重。

③ 名义 GDP（*PQ*）表示给定年度中所生产出的最终产品和服务的货币价值总量，其价值总量以各自年度的市场价格表示。实际 GDP（*Q*）剔除了名义 GDP 中价格指数的变化，以物品和服务的数量来计算。

market prices of each year. Real GDP (Q) removes price changes from nominal GDP and calculates GDP in terms of the quantities of goods and services. The following equations provide the link between nominal GDP, real GDP, and the GDP price index:

$$Q = \text{real GDP} = \frac{\text{nominal GDP}}{\text{GDP price index}} = \frac{PQ}{P}$$

To correct for rapidly changing relative prices, the ① U.S. national accounts use chain weights to construct real GDP and price indexes.

消 费

Consumption

The first important part of GDP is consumption, or "personal consumption expenditures." Consumption is by far the largest component of GDP, equaling about two-thirds of the total in recent years. Figure 20-3 shows the fraction of GDP devoted to ② consumption over the last eight decades. Consumption expenditures are divided into three categories: durable goods such as automobiles, nondurable goods such as food, and services such as medical care. The most rapidly growing sector is services.

投资与资本的形成

Investment and Capital Formation

So far, our analysis has banished all capital. In real life, however, nations devote part of their output to production of capital—durable items that increase future production. Increasing capital requires the sacrifice of current consumption to increase future consumption. Instead of eating more pizza now, people build new pizza ovens to make it possible to produce more pizza for future consumption.

In the accounts, **investment** consists of the additions to the nation's capital stock of buildings, equipment, software, and inventories during a year. The ③

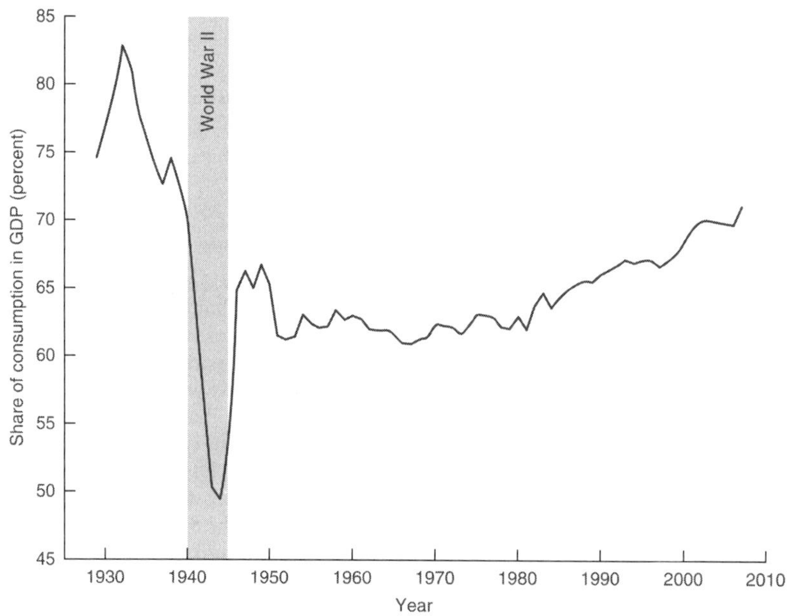

FIGURE 20-3. Share of Consumption in National Output Has Risen Recently

The share of consumption in total GDP rose during the Great Depression as investment prospects soured, then shrank sharply during World War II when the war effort displaced civilian needs. In recent years, consumption has grown more rapidly than total output as the national saving rate and government purchases have declined.

Source: U.S. Bureau of Economic Analysis.

① 为了校正快速变化的相对价格，美国的国民账户采用连锁权重系数来构建实际 GDP 和价格指数。

② 图 20-3 列出了过去八个十年期间，在 GDP 中消费所占比例的变化。消费支出分为三类：像汽车这样的耐用品、像食品这样的非耐用品，以及像医疗保健这样的服务。其中，服务部门增长的速度最快。

③ 账户中的**投资**这一项，由该国一年中不动产、设备、软件产品及存货等资本存量的增加部分构成。国民账户主要包括了有形资本（如建筑物和计算机设备），忽略了绝大多数无形资本（诸如研发或教育费用）。

national accounts include mainly tangible capital (such as buildings and computers) and omit most intangible capital (such as research-and-development or educational expenses).

Real Investment versus Financial Investment

Economists define "investment" (or sometimes *real investment*) as production of durable capital goods. In common usage, "investment" often denotes using money to buy General Motors stock or to open a savings account. For clarity, economists call this *financial investment*. Try not to confuse these two different uses of the word "investment."

If I take $1000 from my safe and buy some stocks, this is not what macroeconomists call investment. I have simply exchanged one financial asset for another. Investment takes place when a durable capital good is produced.

How does investment fit into the national accounts? Economic statisticians recognize that if people are using part of society's production for capital formation, such outputs must be included in the upper-loop flow of GDP. Investments represent additions to the stock of durable capital that increase production possibilities in the future. So we must modify our original definition to read:

> Gross domestic product is the sum of all final ② products. Along with consumption goods and services, we must also include gross investment.

Net vs. Gross Investment. Our revised definition includes "gross investment" along with consumption. What does the word "gross" mean in this context? It indicates that investment includes all investment goods produced. Gross investment is not adjusted for **depreciation,** which measures the amount of capital that has been used up in a year. Thus gross investment includes all the machines, factories, and houses built during a year—even though some were produced simply to replace old capital goods that burned down or were thrown on the scrap heap.

If you want to get a measure of the increase in society's capital, gross investment is not a sensible measure. Because it does not subtract depreciation, gross investment is too large a number—too gross.

An analogy to population will make clear the importance of considering depreciation. If you want to measure the increase in the size of the population, you cannot simply count the number of births, for this would clearly exaggerate the net change in population. To get population growth, you must also subtract the number of deaths.

The same point holds for capital. To find the net increase in capital, you must start with gross investment and subtract the deaths of capital in the form ① of depreciation, or the amount of capital used up.

Thus to estimate the increase in the capital stock ③ we measure *net investment*. Net investment is always births of capital (gross investment) less deaths of capital (capital depreciation):

> Net investment equals gross investment minus ④ depreciation.

政府采购
Government Purchases

Some of our national output is purchased by federal, state, and local governments, and these purchases are clearly part of our GDP. Some government purchases are consumption-type goods (like food for the military), while some are investment-type items (such as schools or roads). In measuring government's contribution to GDP, we simply add all these government purchases to the flow of private consumption, private investment, and, as we will see later, net exports.

Hence, all the government payroll expenditures on its employees plus the costs of goods it buys from private industry (lasers, roads, and airplanes) are included in this third category of flow of products, called "government consumption expenditures and gross investment." This category equals the contribution of federal, state, and local governments to GDP.

Exclusion of Transfer Payments. Does this mean that every dollar of government expenditure is included in GDP? Definitely not. GDP includes only government purchases; it excludes spending on transfer payments.

Government **transfer payments** are payments to ⑤ individuals that are not made in exchange for goods or services supplied. Examples of government transfers include unemployment insurance, veterans' benefits, and old-age or disability payments. These

---

① General Motors：通用汽车。

② 国内生产总值是所有最终产品的加总之和。除消费品和服务之外，我们还必须将投资总额也统计在内。

③ 由此，为估计资本存量的增量，我们必须测量净投资。在任何情况下，净投资始终等于新投入的资本（总投资）减去已经死亡的资本（资本折旧）。

④ 净投资等于总投资减去折旧。

⑤ 政府**转移支付**系指政府对个体的支付，它不是通过商品交换与服务供给来完成的。

payments meet important social purposes. But they are not purchases of current goods or services, and they are therefore omitted from GDP.

Thus if you teach in the local public school and receive a salary from the government, your salary is a factor payment and your services are included in GDP. If you receive a social security benefit as a retired worker, that payment is a transfer payment and is excluded from GDP. Similarly, government interest payments are treated as transfers and are excluded from GDP.

Finally, do not confuse the way the national ① accounts measure government spending on goods and services (G) with the official government budget. When the Treasury measures its expenditures, it includes purchases of goods and services (G) *plus* transfers.

Taxes. In using the flow-of-product approach to compute GDP, we need not worry about how the government finances its spending. It does not matter whether the government pays for its goods and services by taxing, by printing money, or by borrowing. Wherever the dollars come from, the statistician computes the governmental component of GDP as the actual cost to the government of the goods and services.

But while it is fine to ignore taxes in the flow-of-product approach, we must account for taxes in the earnings or cost approach to GDP. Consider wages, for example. Part of my wage is turned over to the government through personal income taxes. These direct taxes definitely do get included in the wage component of business expenses, and the same holds for direct taxes (personal or corporate) on interest, rent, and profits.

Or consider the sales tax and other indirect taxes that manufacturers and retailers have to pay on a loaf of bread (or on the wheat, flour, and dough stages). Suppose these indirect taxes total 10 cents per loaf, and suppose wages, profit, and other value-added items cost the bread industry 90 cents. What will the bread sell for in the product approach? For 90 cents? Surely not. The bread will sell for $1, equal to 90 cents of factor costs plus 10 cents of indirect taxes.

Thus the cost approach to GDP includes both indirect and direct taxes as elements of the cost of producing final output.

净出口
Net Exports

The United States is an open economy engaged in importing and exporting goods and services. The last component of GDP—and an increasingly important one in recent years—is **net exports,** the difference between exports and imports of goods and services.

How do we draw the line between our GDP and other countries' GDPs? The U.S. GDP represents all goods and services produced within the boundaries of the United States. Production differs from sales in the United States in two respects. First, some of our production (Iowa wheat and Boeing aircraft) is bought by foreigners and shipped abroad, and these items constitute our *exports.* Second, some of what we consume at home (Mexican oil and Japanese cars) is produced abroad, and such items are American *imports.*

A Numerical Example. We can use a simple farming economy to understand how the national accounts work. Suppose that Agrovia produces 100 bushels of corn and 7 bushels are imported. Of these, 87 bushels are consumed (in C), 10 go for government purchases to feed the army (as G), and 6 go into domestic investment as increases in inventories (I). In addition, 4 bushels are exported, so net exports (X) are 4 − 7, or minus 3.

What, then, is the composition of the GDP of Agrovia? It is the following:

$$\begin{aligned} \text{GDP} &= 87 \text{ of } C + 10 \text{ of } G + 6 \text{ of } I - 3 \text{ of } X \\ &= 100 \text{ bushels} \end{aligned}$$

国内生产总值、国内生产净值和国民生产总值
Gross Domestic Product, Net Domestic Product, and Gross National Product

Although GDP is the most widely used measure of national output in the United States, two other concepts are frequently cited: net domestic product and gross national product.

Recall that GDP includes *gross* investment, which is net investment plus depreciation. A little thought ② suggests that including depreciation is rather like including wheat as well as bread. A better measure would include only *net* investment in total output. By subtracting depreciation from GDP we obtain **net domestic product** (NDP). If NDP is a sounder measure of a nation's output than GDP, why do national accountants focus on GDP? They do so because

① 归根结底，测量政府在商品与服务的支出（G）时，绝不能与政府的官方预算混淆在一起。当财政部对政府支出总额进行核算时，包括商品与服务的支出（G）加上政府的转移支付。

② 略经思考就会发现，计入折旧的方法与将小麦计入的同时也将面包包括在内如出一辙。

1. **GDP from the product side is the sum of four major components:**
   - Personal consumption expenditures on goods and services (C)
   - Gross private domestic investment (I)
   - Government consumption expenditures and gross investment (G)
   - Net exports of goods and services (X), or exports minus imports
2. **GDP from the cost side is the sum of the following major components:**
   - Compensation (wages, salaries, and supplements)
   - Property income (corporate profits, proprietors' incomes, interest, and rents)
   - Production taxes and depreciation of capital

   (Remember to use the value-added technique to prevent double counting of intermediate goods bought from other firms.)
3. **The product and cost measures of GDP are identical** (by adherence to the rules of value-added bookkeeping and the definition of profit as a residual).
4. **Net domestic product (NDP) equals GDP minus depreciation.**

TABLE 20-5. Key Concepts of the National Income and Product Accounts

depreciation is somewhat difficult to estimate, whereas gross investment can be estimated fairly accurately.

An alternative measure of national output, widely used until recently, is **gross national product** (GNP). What is the difference between GNP and GDP? GNP is the total output produced with labor ① or capital *owned by U.S. residents,* while GDP is the output produced with labor and capital *located inside the United States.*

For example, some of the U.S. GDP is produced in Honda plants that are owned by Japanese corporations operating in the U.S. The profits from these plants are included in U.S. GDP but not in U.S. GNP because Honda is a Japanese company. Similarly, when an American economist flies to Japan to give a paid lecture on baseball economics, payment for that lecture would be included in Japanese GDP and in American GNP. For the United States, GDP is very close to GNP, but these may differ substantially for very open economies.

To summarize:

Net domestic product (NDP) equals the total ② final output produced within a nation during a year, where output includes net investment, or gross investment less depreciation:

$$\text{NDP} = \text{GDP} - \text{depreciation}$$

Gross national product (GNP) is the total final ③ output produced with inputs owned by the residents of a country during a year.

Table 20-5 provides a comprehensive definition of important components of GDP.

GDP 和 NDP：数据观察
GDP and NDP: A Look at Numbers

Armed with an understanding of the concepts, we can turn to look at the actual data in the important Table 20-6.

Flow-of-Product Approach. Look first at the left side of Table 20-6. It gives the upper-loop, flow-of-product approach to GDP. Each of the four major components appears there, along with the dollar total for each component for 2007. Of these, C and G and their obvious subclassifications require little discussion.

Gross private domestic investment does require one comment. Its total ($2130 billion) includes all new business investment, residential construction, and increase in inventory of goods. This gross total is the amount before a subtraction for depreciation of capital. After subtracting $1721 billion of depreciation from gross investment, we obtain $410 billion of net investment.

Finally, note the large negative entry for net exports, −$708 billion. This negative entry represents the fact that in 2007 the United States imported $708 billion more in goods and services than it exported.

Adding up the four components on the left gives the total GDP of $13,808 billion. This is the harvest

① 国民生产总值（GNP）系指用美国国民所拥有的劳动和资本生产的总产出量，而国内生产总值（GDP）则是只用美国境内的劳动和资本生产的总产出量。

② 国内生产净值（NDP）等于一个国家在一年内所生产的最终产出量，这里所讲的产出包括净投资，即总投资减去折旧。

③ 国民生产总值（GNP）系指用一国全体居民拥有的投入要素在一年内所生产的最终产出总量。

Gross Domestic Product, 2007
(billions of current dollars)

Production Approach			**Earnings or Cost Approach**	
1. Personal consumption expenditures		9,710	1. Compensation of employees	7,812
Durable goods	1,083		2. Proprietors' income	1,056
Nondurable goods	2,833		3. Rental income	40
Services	5,794		4. Net interest	664
2. Gross private domestic investment		2,130	5. Corporate profits (with adjustments)	1,642
Fixed investment			6. Depreciation	1,721
Nonresidential	1,504		7. Production taxes, statistical discrepancy, and miscellaneous	872
Residential	630			
Change in private inventories	−4			
3. Net exports of goods and services		−708		
Exports	1,662			
Imports	2,370			
4. Government consumption expenditures and gross investment		2,675		
Federal	979			
State and local	1,696			
Gross domestic product		13,808	**Gross domestic product**	13,808

TABLE 20-6. The Two Ways of Looking at the GDP Accounts, in Actual Numbers

The left side measures flow of products (at market prices). The right side measures flow of costs (factor earnings and depreciation).

Source: U.S. Bureau of Economic Analysis.

we have been working for: the money measure of the American economy's overall performance for 2007.

Flow-of-Cost Approach. Now turn to the right-hand side of the table, which gives the lower-loop, flow-of-cost approach. Here we have all *costs of production* plus *taxes* and *depreciation.*

Compensation of employees represents wages, salaries, and other employee supplements. Net interest is a similar item.

Rent income of persons includes rents received by landlords. In addition, if you own your own home, you are treated as *paying rent to yourself.* This is one of many "imputations" (or derived data) in the national accounts. It makes sense if we really ① want to measure the housing services the American people are enjoying and do not want the estimate to change when people decide to own a home rather than rent one.

Production taxes are included as a separate item ② along with some small adjustments, including the inevitable "statistical discrepancy," which reflects the fact that the officials never have every bit of needed data.[1]

Depreciation on capital goods that were used up must appear as an expense in GDP, just like other expenses. Profit is a residual—what is left over after all other costs have been subtracted from total sales. There are two kinds of profits: profit of corporations and net earnings of unincorporated enterprises.

Income of unincorporated enterprises consists of earnings of partnerships and single-ownership businesses. This includes much farm and professional

[1] Statisticians work with incomplete reports and fill in data gaps by estimation. Just as measurements in a chemistry lab differ from the ideal, so do errors creep into both upper- and lower-loop GDP estimates. These are balanced by an item called the "statistical discrepancy." Along with the civil servants who are heads of units called "Wages," "Interest," and so forth, there actually used to be someone with the title "Head of the Statistical Discrepancy." If data were perfect, that individual would have been out of a job.

① 如果我们真要测量美国人民享受的住房服务，又不想估计决定拥有住房而非租房所带来的变化，这种估算方法就有了意义。

② 企业的生产税与某些小的调整（包括不可避免的统计误差）一起，单列为一项。统计误差反映出的事实是，官方从来就没有完全掌握过所需的统计数据。

income. Finally, corporate profits before taxes are shown.

On the right side, the flow-of-cost approach gives us the same $13,808 billion of GDP as does the flow-of-product approach. The right and left sides do agree.

从 GDP 到可支配收入

From GDP to Disposable Income

The basic GDP accounts are of interest not only for themselves but also because of their importance for understanding how consumers and businesses behave. Some further distinctions will help illuminate the way the nation's books are kept.

National Income. To help us understand the division of total income among the different factors of production, we construct data on *national income (NI)*. *NI* represents the total incomes received by labor, capital, and land. It is constructed by subtracting depreciation from GDP. National income equals total compensation of labor, rental income, net interest, income of proprietors, and corporate profits. ①

The relationship between GDP and national income is shown in the first two bars of Figure 20-4. The left-hand bar shows GDP, while the second bar shows the subtractions required to obtain *NI*.

From GDP to National Income to Disposable Income

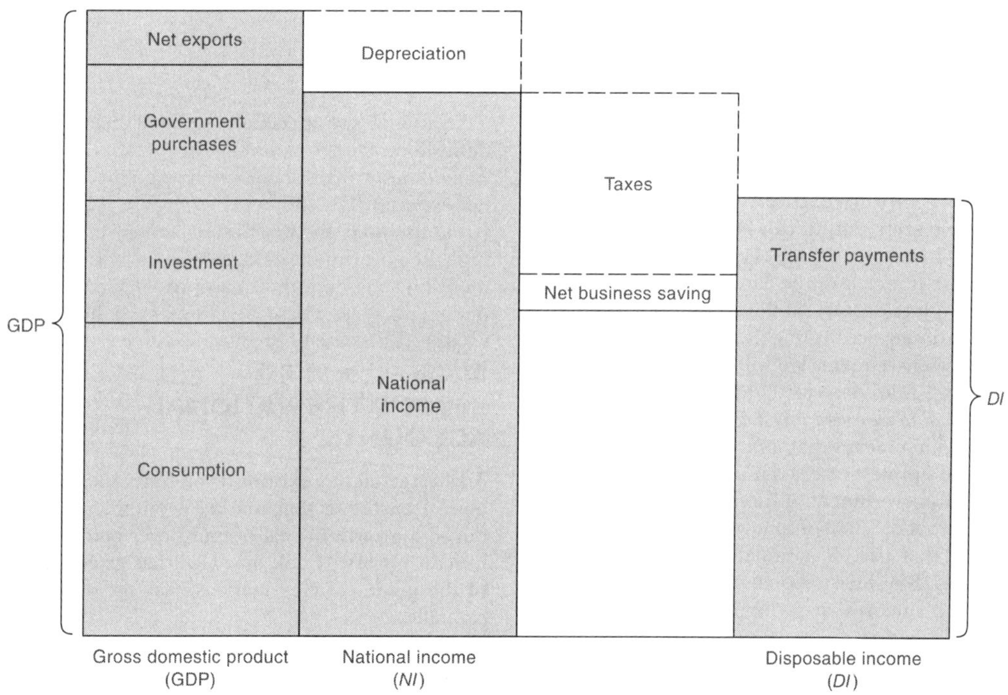

FIGURE 20-4. Starting with GDP, We Can Calculate National Income (*NI*) and Disposable Personal Income (*DI*)

Important income concepts are (1) GDP, which is total gross income to all factors; (2) national income, which is the sum of factor incomes and is obtained by subtracting depreciation from GDP; and (3) disposable personal income, which measures the total incomes of the household sector, including transfer payments but subtracting taxes.

① 为帮助我们理解总收入在不同的生产要素中的分配情况，我们建构了国民收入（*NI*）这一数据。

Disposable Income. A second important concept asks, How many dollars per year do households actually have available to spend? The concept of disposable personal income (usually called **disposable income,** or *DI*) answers this question. To get disposable income, you calculate the market and transfer incomes received by households and subtract personal taxes. ①

Figure 20-4 shows the calculation of *DI.* We begin with national income in the second bar. We then subtract all taxes and further subtract net business saving. (Net business saving is profits after depreciation less dividends.) Finally, we add back the transfer payments that households receive from governments. This constitutes *DI,* shown as the right-hand bar in Figure 20-4. Disposable income is what actually gets into the hands of consumers to dispose of as they please. (This discussion omits some minor items such as the statistical discrepancy and net foreign factor incomes that are usually close to zero.) ②

As we will see in the next chapters, *DI* is what people divide between (1) consumption spending and (2) personal saving. ③

储蓄与投资
Saving and Investment

As we have seen, output can be either consumed or invested. Investment is an essential economic activity because it increases the capital stock available for future production. One of the most important points about national accounting is the identity between saving and investment. We will show that, under the accounting rules described above, *measured saving is exactly equal to measured investment.* This equality is an *identity,* which means that it must hold by definition.

In the simplest case, assume for the moment that there is no government or foreign sector. Investment is that part of national output which is not consumed. Saving is that part of national income which is not consumed. But since national income and output are equal, this means that saving equals investment. In symbols:

$$I = \text{product-approach GDP minus } C$$
$$S = \text{earnings-approach GDP minus } C$$

However, both approaches always give the same measure of GDP, so

$I = S$: the identity between measured saving and investment

That is the simplest case. We also need to consider the complete case which brings businesses, government, and net exports into the picture. On the saving side, *total* or *national saving* (S^T) is composed of *private saving* by households and businesses (S^P) along with *government saving* (S^G). Government saving equals the government's budget surplus or the difference between tax revenues and expenditures.

On the investment side, total or *national investment* (I^T) starts with *gross private domestic investment* (I) but also adds *net foreign investment,* which is approximately the same as net exports (X). Hence, the complete saving-investment identity is given by[2]

$$\text{National investment} = \text{private investment} + \text{net exports}$$
$$= \text{private saving} + \text{government saving} = \text{national saving}$$

or

$$I^T = I + X = S^P + S^G = S^T$$

National saving equals national investment by definition. The components of investment are private domestic investment and foreign investment (or net exports). The sources of saving are private saving (by households and businesses) and government saving (the government budget surplus). Private investment plus net exports equals private saving plus the budget surplus. These identities must hold always, whatever the state of the business cycle. ④

国民账户之外的问题
BEYOND THE NATIONAL ACCOUNTS

Advocates of the existing economic and social system often argue that market economies have produced a growth in real output never before seen in human history. "Look how GDP has grown because of the genius of free markets," say the admirers of capitalism.

But critics point out the deficiencies of GDP. GDP includes many questionable entries and omits many

[2] For this discussion, we consider only private investment and therefore treat all government purchases as consumption. In most national accounts today, government purchases are divided between consumption and tangible investments. If we include government investment, then this amount will add to both national investment and the government surplus.

① 个人的可支配收入（通常称为**可支配收入**，*DI*）概念回答了这个问题。将家庭收到的市场收入和转移支付相加，再减去个人所得税，即可支配收入。

② 可支配收入系指消费者手中实际所能得到的可供自己随意支配的收入。（这一讨论，省略了某些小项，诸如通常情况下接近于零的统计误差和净外国要素收入。）

③ 正如下面的章节中我们所要讨论的，人们将 *DI* 分为：（1）消费支出；（2）个人储蓄。

④ 从上式可以看出，国民投资含国内个人投资和对外投资（即净出口）两个部分，与国民储蓄相等。储蓄的来源是个人储蓄（包括家庭和企业）和政府储蓄（政府的预算盈余）。个人投资和净出口之和等于个人储蓄与政府预算盈余之和。无论商业周期如何变化，这些等式必须始终恒等。

valuable economic activities. As one dissenter said, "Don't speak to me of all your production and your dollars, your gross domestic product. To me, GDP stands for gross domestic pollution!"

What are we to think? Isn't it true that GDP includes government production of bombs and missiles along with salaries paid to prison guards? Doesn't an increase in crime boost sales of home alarms, which adds to the GDP? Doesn't cutting our irreplaceable redwoods show up as a positive output in our national accounts? Doesn't GDP fail to account for environmental degradation such as acid rain and global warming?

In recent years, economists have begun developing new measures to correct the major defects of the standard GDP numbers and better reflect the true satisfaction-producing outputs of our economy. The new approaches attempt to extend the boundar- ① ies of the traditional accounts by including important nonmarket activities as well as correcting for harmful activities that are included as part of national output. Let's consider some of the omitted pluses and minuses.

Omitted Nonmarket Activities. Recall that the standard accounts include primarily market activities. Much useful economic activity takes place outside the market. For example, college students are investing in human capital. The national accounts record ② the tuition, but they omit the opportunity costs of earnings forgone. Studies indicate that inclusion of [3] nonmarket investments in education and other areas would more than double the national saving rate.

Similarly, many household activities produce valuable "near-market" goods and services such as meals, laundering, and child-care services. Recent estimates of the value of unpaid household work indicate that it might be half as large as total market consumption. Perhaps the largest omission from the market accounts is the value of leisure time. On ④ average, Americans spend as much of their time on utility-producing leisure activities as they do on money-producing work activities. Yet the value of leisure time is excluded from our official national statistics.

You might wonder about the underground economy, which covers a wide variety of market activities that are not reported to the government. These include activities like gambling, prostitution, drug dealing, work done by illegal immigrants, bartering of services, and smuggling. Actually, much underground activity is intentionally excluded because national output excludes illegal activities—these are by social consensus "bads" and not "goods." A swelling cocaine trade will not enter into GDP. For legal but unre- ⑤ ported activities, like unreported tips, the Commerce Department makes estimates on the basis of surveys and audits by the Internal Revenue Service.

Omitted Environmental Damage. In addition to omitting activities, sometimes GDP omits some of the harmful side effects of economic activity. An important example is the omission of environmental damages. For example, suppose the residents of Suburbia buy 10 million kilowatt-hours of electricity to cool their houses, paying Utility Co. 10 cents per kilowatt-hour. That $1 million covers the labor costs, plant costs, and fuel costs. But suppose the company damages the neighborhood with pollution in the process of producing electricity. It incurs no monetary costs for this externality. Our measure of output should not only add in the value of the electricity (which GDP does) but also subtract the environmental damage caused by the pollution (which GDP does not).

Suppose that in addition to 10 cents of direct costs, there are 2 cents per kilowatt-hour of environmental damages to human health. These are the "external costs" of pollution not paid by Utility Co., and they total $200,000. To correct for this hidden cost in a set of augmented accounts, we should subtract $200,000 of "pollution bads" from the $1,000,000 flow of "electricity goods." In fact, government statisticians do *not* subtract pollution costs in the economic accounts.

Economists have made considerable progress in developing *augmented national accounts*, which are designed to include activities beyond the traditional definitions of the national accounts. The general principle of augmented accounting is to include as much of economic activity as is feasible, whether or not that activity takes place in the market. Examples of augmented accounts include estimates of the value of research and development, nonmarket investments in human capital, the value of unpaid production in the home, the value of forests, and the value of leisure time. Economists are even developing accounts for the damages from air pollution

---

① 这些新的方法，通过将重要的非市场行为，以及作为国民产出部分的那些需要校正的有害行为统计在内，试图将传统账户的边界予以扩展。让我们在此讨论一下那些被忽略的某些加减掉的项目。

② 国民账户记录了学费，却忽略了所舍弃收入的机会成本。

[3] earnings forgone，劳动经济法术语，指所付成本在不付前提下的总收入。

④ 平均来讲，美国人花在创造效用的休闲活动时间，与他们赚钱的工作时间相当。

⑤ 至于像小费这样的不需申报的合法行为，商务部只能在参考国内税收总署公布的调查和审计数据的基础上予以估算。

and global warming. When these further accounts are completed, we will have a more comprehensive financial picture of the economy.

But be warned that even the most refined economic accounts still measure only economic activity. They do not attempt to—indeed, cannot—measure the ultimate satisfactions, pleasures, or pains of people in their everyday lives. This point was eloquently put by Robert Kennedy in one of his last [1] speeches:

[1] 罗伯特·肯尼迪（Robert Kennedy，1925~1968），肯尼迪总统的弟弟和政治顾问，曾任司法部长，著名的美国政治家和演说家。1968年6月6日凌晨，在刚刚赢得加州民主党总统候选人预选之后，于洛杉矶的国宾酒店遭枪击身亡。同其兄的遇刺身亡事件一样，至今仍存悬疑。同时，也与其兄一样，享有RFK（F为其教名Francis的第一个字母）的缩写姓名尊称。

> The gross national product does not allow for the health of our children, the quality of their education, or the joy of their play. It does not include the beauty of our poetry or the strength of our marriages; the intelligence of our public debate or the integrity of our public officials. It measures neither our wit nor our courage; neither our wisdom nor our learning; neither our compassion nor our devotion to our country.

价格指数与通货膨胀
PRICE INDEXES AND INFLATION

This chapter has up to now focused on measuring national output and its components. But people today worry about overall price trends, that is to say, about inflation. What do these terms mean?

Let us begin with a careful definition:

A **price index** (with symbol P) is a measure of the ② average level of prices. **Inflation** (with symbol π, or "pi") denotes a rise in the general level of prices. The **rate of inflation** is defined as the rate of change of the general price level and is measured as follows:

$$\text{Rate of inflation in year } t = \pi_t = 100 \times \frac{P_t - P_{t-1}}{P_{t-1}}$$

Most periods in recent history have been ones of positive inflation. The opposite of inflation is **deflation,** ③ which occurs when the general price level is falling. Deflations have been rare in the last half-century. In the United States, the last time consumer prices actually fell from one year to the next was 1955. Sustained deflations, in which prices fall steadily over a period of several years, are associated with depressions, such as those that occurred in the United States in the 1890s and the 1930s. More recently, Japan experienced a deflation over much of the last two decades as its economy suffered a prolonged recession.

价格指数
Price Indexes

When newspapers tell us "Inflation is rising," they are really reporting the movement of a price index. A price index is a weighted average of the price of a basket of goods and services. In constructing price indexes, economists weight individual prices by the economic importance of each good. The most important price indexes are the consumer price index, the GDP price index, and the producer price index.

The Consumer Price Index (CPI). The most widely used measure of the overall price level is the consumer price index, also known as the CPI, calculated by the U.S. Bureau of Labor Statistics (BLS). The CPI is a measure of the average price paid by urban consumers for a market basket of consumer goods and services. Each month, government statisticians record the prices of around 80,000 goods and services for more than 200 major categories. The prices are then arranged into the following eight major groups, listed with some examples:

- Food and beverages (breakfast cereal, milk, and snacks)
- Housing (rent of primary residence, owner's equivalent rent, bedroom furniture)
- Apparel (shirts and sweaters, jewelry)
- Transportation (new vehicles, gasoline, motor vehicle insurance)
- Medical care (prescription drugs, physicians' services, eyeglasses)
- Recreation (televisions, sports equipment, admissions)
- Education and communication (college tuition, computer software)
- Other goods and services (haircuts, funeral expenses)

How are the different prices weighted in constructing price indexes? It would clearly be silly merely to add up the different prices or to weight them by their mass or volume. Rather, a price index is constructed by *weighting each price according to the economic importance of the commodity in question.*

In the case of the traditional CPI, each item is ④ assigned a fixed weight proportional to its relative importance in consumer expenditure budgets; the weight for each item is proportional to the total spending by consumers on that item as determined by a survey of consumer expenditures in the

---

② **价格指数**（以大写字母 P 表示）衡量的是价格的平均水平。**通货膨胀**（用希腊字母 π 或"pi"表示）表示整体价格水平的上升。**通货膨胀率**则定义为整体价格水平的变化率，可用下式求得。

③ 与通货膨胀相反的是**通货紧缩**，在整体价格水平下降时发生。在上世纪后半叶，通货紧缩很少发生。

④ 在计算传统的CPI时，对应于消费者各项支出预算的相对重要性，给每一项支出均分配了一个固定的权重；每一项的权重，均与消费者在该项的总支出成比例，权重由对消费者在2005~2006年度支出的调查数据决定。

2005–2006 period. As of 2008, housing-related costs were the single biggest category in the CPI, taking up more than 42 percent of consumer spending budgets. By comparison, the cost of new cars and other motor vehicles accounts for only 7 percent of the CPI's consumer expenditure budgets.

Calculating the CPI

It is worth spending a moment on the exact technique that is used to calculate CPI changes. The formula in the text is correct, but we need to explain how the formula works when there are many goods and services. The change in the overall CPI is the weighted average of the change of the components:

% change in CPI in period t

$$= 100 \times \left\{ \sum_{\text{All items}} [\text{weight of good } i \text{ in } (t-1)] \times [\%\text{ change in the price of good } i \text{ from } (t-1) \text{ to } t] \right\}$$

To take a concrete example, the following table shows the actual price-change and relative-importance data:

Expenditure category	Relative importance, December 2007 (%)	Percentage change over the last year
Food and beverages	14.9	4.4
Housing	42.4	3.0
Apparel	3.7	-1.4
Transportation	17.7	8.2
Medical care	6.2	4.6
Recreation	5.6	1.3
Education and communication	6.1	3.0
Other goods and services	3.3	3.2
All items	**100.0**	**4.0**

The rate of inflation over the period from March 2007 to March 2008 is seen to be 4.0 percent per year. (Question 9 at the end of this chapter examines this calculation further.)

This example captures the essence of how the traditional CPI measures inflation. The only difference between this simplified calculation and the actual ones is that the CPI contains many more commodities and regions. Otherwise, the procedure is exactly the same.

GDP Price Index. Another widely used price index is the *GDP price index* (also sometimes referred to as the GDP deflator), which we met earlier in this chapter. The GDP price index is the price of all goods ① and services produced in the country (consumption, investment, government purchases, and net exports) rather than of a single component (such as consumption). This index also differs from the traditional CPI because it is a chain-weighted index that takes into account the changing shares of different goods (see the discussion of chain weights on page 393). In addition, there are price indexes for components of GDP, such as for investment goods, computers, personal consumption, and so forth, and these are sometimes used to supplement the CPI.

The Producer Price Index (PPI). This index, dating from 1890, is the oldest continuous statistical series published by the BLS. It measures the level of prices [2] at the wholesale or producer stage. It is based on over 8000 commodity prices, including prices of foods, manufactured products, and mining products. The fixed weights used to calculate the PPI are the net sales of each commodity. Because of its great detail, this index is widely used by businesses.

Getting the Prices Right

Measuring prices accurately is one of the central issues of empirical economics. Price indexes affect not only obvious things like the inflation rate. They also are embedded in measures of real output and productivity. And through government policies, they affect monetary policy, taxes, government transfer programs like social security, and many private contracts.

The purpose of the consumer price index is to measure the cost of living. You might be surprised to learn that this is a difficult task. Some problems are intrinsic to price indexes. One issue is the *index-number problem,* which involves how the different prices are weighted or averaged. Recall that the traditional CPI uses a fixed weight for each good. As a result, the cost of living is

---

① GDP价格指数是一个国家生产的全部商品和服务（消费、投资、政府采购，以及净出口）的价格，并非某个构成部分（如消费）的价格。同时，它也不同于传统的CPI，因为它是一个连锁权重指数，将不同商品所占份额的变化均考虑在内。除此之外，GDP的各组成部分，如投资品、计算机和个人消费等等，均有各自的价格指数，有时，用于补充CPI。

[2] BLS，美国政府劳工统计局（U.S. Bureau of Labor Statistics）的缩写。

[3] Arthur Okun，阿瑟·奥肯（1928~1980），耶鲁大学经济学教授，1968~1969 年间任约翰逊总统的经济顾问委员会主席，发现了周期波动中经济增长率和失业率之间经验关系的奥肯定律（Okun's Law）。

④ 个人的成功无法保证一个家庭的幸福，以小比大，一个国家的繁荣同样无法确保社会的幸福，这并不让人意外。GDP 的增长根本无法平缓一场不受欢迎且不可能取胜的战争所引发的紧张局势，无法面对长期以来由于种族歧视引发的良知拷问，无法抵御火山喷发似的性道德堕落，无法阻止年轻一代对其独立性的史无前例的索求。即便如此，相比较而言，繁荣经济依然是我们有望成功实现众多愿景的先决条件。

overestimated compared to the situation where consumers substitute relatively inexpensive for relatively expensive goods.

The case of energy prices can illustrate the problem. When gasoline prices rise sharply, people tend to reduce their gasoline purchases, buy smaller cars, and travel less. Yet the CPI assumes that they buy the same quantity of gasoline even though gasoline prices may have doubled. The overall rise in the cost of living is thereby exaggerated. Statisticians have devised ways of minimizing such index-number problems by using different weighting approaches, such as adjusting the weights as expenditures change, but government statisticians are just beginning to experiment with these newer approaches for the CPI.

A more important problem arises because of the difficulty of adjusting price indexes to capture the contribution of *new and improved goods and services*. An example will illustrate this problem. In recent years, consumers have benefited from compact fluorescent lightbulbs; these lightbulbs deliver light at approximately one-fourth the cost of the older, incandescent bulbs. Yet none of the price indexes incorporate the quality improvement. Similarly, as CDs and MP3s replaced long-playing records, as cable TV with hundreds of channels replaced the older technology with a few fuzzy channels, as air travel replaced rail or road travel, and in thousands of other improved goods and services, the price indexes did not reflect the improved quality.

Recent studies indicate that if quality change had been properly incorporated into price indexes, the CPI would have risen less rapidly in recent years. This problem is especially acute for medical care. In this sector, reported prices have risen sharply in the last two decades. Yet we have no adequate measure of the quality of medical care, and the CPI completely ignores the introduction of new products, such as pharmaceuticals which replace intrusive and expensive surgery.

A panel of distinguished economists led by Stanford's Michael Boskin examined this issue and estimated that the upward bias in the CPI was slightly more than 1 percent per year. This is a small number with large implications. It indicates that our real-output numbers may have been *underestimated* by the same amount. If the CPI bias carries through to the GDP deflator, then the growth in output per hour worked in the United States would be understated by around 1 percent per year.

This finding also implies that cost-of-living adjustments (which are used for social security benefits and the tax system) have overcompensated people for changes in the cost of living. The bias would have substantial effects on overall taxes and benefits over a period of many years. Price indexes are not just abstruse concepts of interest only to a handful of technicians. Proper construction of price and output indexes affects our government budgets, our retirement programs, and even the way we assess our national economic performance.

In response to its own research and to its critics, the BLS has undertaken a major overhaul of the CPI. The most ① important innovation was the publication starting in 2002 of a "chained consumer price index" that augments the fixed-weight price index with a changing-weight system (like the chain weights used in the GDP accounts discussed on page 393 above) that accounts for consumer substitution. Over the decade since it was published, the chain CPI did indeed rise more slowly than the traditional CPI. It appears that critics were correct that the traditional CPI overstates inflation, although the size of the overstatement is likely to be less than the large number estimated by the Boskin Commission.[3] [2]

国民账户简评
ACCOUNTING ASSESSMENT

This chapter has examined the way economists measure national output and the overall price level. Having reviewed the measurement of national output and analyzed the shortcomings of the GDP, what should we conclude about the adequacy of our measures? Do they capture the major trends? Are they adequate measures of overall social welfare? The answer was aptly stated in a review by Arthur Okun: [3]

> It should be no surprise that national prosperity ④
> does not guarantee a happy society, any more than personal prosperity ensures a happy family. No growth of GDP can counter the tensions arising from an unpopular and unsuccessful war, a long overdue self-confrontation with conscience on racial injustice, a volcanic eruption of sexual mores, and an unprecedented assertion of independence by the young. Still, prosperity . . . is a precondition for success in achieving many of our aspirations.[4]

[3] See this chapter's Further Reading section for a symposium on CPI design.

[4] *The Political Economy of Prosperity* (Norton, New York, 1970), p. 124.

① 其中最重要的一项创新是从 2002 年开始公布的“消费者连锁价格指数”。它将固定的价格权重指数使用一个可变权重（比如在前面 91 页所讨论的在 GDP 账户中采用的连锁权重方法）方法予以补充，这样，就可以对消费者的替代行为予以解释。在其公布十年来，消费者连锁价格指数相比传统的 CPI，增长缓慢。它清楚地表明，有关传统的 CPI 高估通货膨胀的批评是完全正确的，尽管高估的幅度低于波斯金委员会估计的数字。

[2] Boskin Commission，全称为 Advisory Commission to Study the Consumer Price Index，1995 年由美国国会授命，专门研究 CPI 可能出现的计算偏差，由斯坦福大学胡佛研究院经济学教授 Michael Boskin（1945~）任主席，故简称波斯金委员会。

SUMMARY

1. The national income and product accounts contain the major measures of income and product for a country. The gross domestic product (GDP) is the most comprehensive measure of a nation's production of goods and services. It comprises the dollar value of consumption (C), gross private domestic investment (I), government purchases (G), and net exports (X) produced within a nation during a given year. Recall the formula:

$$\text{GDP} = C + I + G + X$$

This will sometimes be simplified by combining private domestic investment and net exports into total gross national investment ($I^T = I + X$):

$$\text{GDP} = C + I^T + G$$

2. We can match the upper-loop, flow-of-product measurement of GDP with the lower-loop, flow-of-cost measurement, as shown in Figure 20-1. The flow-of-cost approach uses factor earnings and carefully computes value added to eliminate double counting of intermediate products. And after summing up all (before-tax) wage, interest, rent, depreciation, and profit income, it adds to this total all indirect tax costs of business. GDP does not include transfer items such as social security benefits.
3. By use of a price index, we can "deflate" nominal GDP (GDP in current dollars) to arrive at a more accurate measure of real GDP (GDP expressed in dollars of some base year's purchasing power). Use of such a price index corrects for the "rubber yardstick" implied by changing levels of prices.
4. Net investment is positive when the nation is producing more capital goods than are currently being used up in the form of depreciation. Since depreciation is hard to estimate accurately, statisticians have more confidence in their measures of gross investment than in those of net investment.
5. National income and disposable income are two additional official measurements. Disposable income (DI) is what people actually have left—after all tax payments, corporate saving of undistributed profits, and transfer adjustments have been made—to spend on consumption or to save.
6. Using the rules of the national accounts, measured saving must exactly equal measured investment. This is easily seen in a hypothetical economy with nothing but households. In a complete economy, *private saving and government surplus equal domestic investment plus net foreign investment.* The identity between saving and investment is just that: saving must equal investment no matter whether the economy is in boom or recession, war or peace. It is a consequence of the definitions of national income accounting.
7. Gross domestic product and even net domestic product are imperfect measures of genuine economic welfare. In recent years, statisticians have started correcting for nonmarket activities such as unpaid work at home and environmental externalities.
8. Inflation occurs when the general level of prices is rising (and deflation occurs when it is falling). We measure the overall price level and rate of inflation using price indexes—weighted averages of the prices of thousands of individual products. The most important price index is the consumer price index (CPI), which traditionally measured the cost of a fixed market basket of consumer goods and services relative to the cost of that bundle during a particular base year. Recent studies indicate that the CPI trend has a major upward bias because of index-number problems and omission of new and improved goods, and the government has undertaken steps to correct some of this bias.
9. Recall the useful formulas from this and the prior chapter:
   a. For calculating single-period growth of GDP:

   Growth of real GDP in year t

$$= 100 \times \frac{\text{GDP}_t - \text{GDP}_{t-1}}{\text{GDP}_{t-1}}$$

   b. For calculating inflation with a single good:

$$\text{Rate of inflation in year } t = \pi_t = 100 \times \frac{P_t - P_{t-1}}{P_{t-1}}$$

   c. Multiyear growth rate:

   Growth from $(t - n)$ to t:

$$g_t^{(n)} = 100 \times \left[\left(\frac{X_t}{X_{t-n}}\right)^{1/n} - 1\right]$$

   d. For calculating the CPI with multiple goods:

   % change in CPI

$$= 100 \times \left[\sum_{\text{All items}} (\text{weight}_i) \times (\%\text{ change } p_i)\right]$$

CONCEPTS FOR REVIEW

national income and product accounts (national accounts)
real and nominal GDP
GDP deflator
GDP = $C + I + G + X$
net investment = gross investment − depreciation
GDP in two equivalent views:
  product (upper loop)
  earnings (lower loop)

intermediate goods, value added
NDP = GDP − depreciation
government transfers
disposable income (DI)
investment-saving identity:
  $I = S$
  $I^T = I + X = S^P + S^G = S^T$
inflation, deflation

price index:
  CPI
  GDP price index
  PPI
growth-rate formulas

FURTHER READING AND INTERNET WEBSITES

Further Reading

A magnificent compilation of historical data on the United States is Susan Carter et al., *Historical Statistics of the United States: Millennial Edition* (Cambridge, 2006). This is available online from many college websites at *hsus.cambridge.org/HSUSWeb/HSUSEntryServlet.* A review of the issues involving measuring the consumer price index is contained in "Symposium on the CPI," *Journal of Economic Perspectives,* Winter 1998.

Robert Kennedy's remarks are from "Recapturing America's Moral Vision," March 18, 1968, in *RFK: Collected Speeches* (Viking Press, New York, 1993).

Websites

The premium site for the U.S. national income and product accounts is maintained by the Bureau of Economic Analysis (BEA) at *www.bea.gov.* This site also contains issues of *The Survey of Current Business,* which discusses recent economic trends.

A comprehensive launching pad for government data in many areas is "FRED," assembled by the Federal Reserve Bank of St. Louis at *research.stlouisfed.org/fred2.* The best single statistical source for data on the United States is *The Statistical Abstract of the United States,* published annually. It is available online at *www.census.gov/compendia/statab/.* Many important data sets can be found at *www.economagic.com/.*

A recent review of alternative approaches to augmented and environmental accounting is contained in a report by the National Academy of Sciences in William Nordhaus and Edward Kokkelenberg, eds., *Nature's Numbers: Expanding the National Accounts to Include the Environment* (National Academy Press, Washington, D.C., 1999), available at *www.nap.edu.*

QUESTIONS FOR DISCUSSION

1. Define carefully the following and give an example of each:
   a. Consumption
   b. Gross private domestic investment
   c. Government consumption and investment purchases (in GDP)
   d. Government transfer payments (not in GDP)
   e. Exports
2. You sometimes hear, "You can't add apples and oranges." Show that we can and do add apples and oranges in the national accounts. Explain how.
3. Examine the data in the appendix to Chapter 19. Locate the figures for nominal and real GDP for 2006 and 2007. Calculate the GDP deflator. What were the rates of growth of nominal GDP and real GDP for 2007? What was the rate of inflation (as measured by

the GDP deflator) for 2007? Compare the rate of inflation using the GDP deflator with that using the CPI.

4. Robinson Crusoe produces upper-loop product of \$1000. He pays \$750 in wages, \$125 in interest, and \$75 in rent. What must his profit be? If three-fourths of Crusoe's output is consumed and the rest invested, calculate Crusoeland's GDP with both the product and the income approaches and show that they must agree exactly.

5. Here are some brain teasers. Can you see why the following are not counted in U.S. GDP?
   a. The gourmet meals produced by a fine home chef
   b. The purchase of a plot of land
   c. The purchase of an original Rembrandt painting
   d. The value I get in 2009 from playing a 2005 compact disc
   e. Damage to houses and crops from pollution emitted by electric utilities
   f. Profits earned by IBM on production in a British factory

6. Consider the country of Agrovia, whose GDP is discussed in "A Numerical Example" on page 396. Construct a set of national accounts like that in Table 20-6 assuming that wheat costs \$5 per bushel, there is no depreciation, wages are three-fourths of national output, indirect business taxes are used to finance 100 percent of government spending, and the balance of income goes as rent income to farmers.

7. Review the discussion of bias in the CPI. Explain why failure to consider the quality improvement of a new good leads to an upward bias in the trend of the CPI. Pick a good you are familiar with. Explain how its quality has changed and why it might be difficult for a price index to capture the increase in quality.

8. In recent decades, women have worked more hours in paid jobs and fewer hours in unpaid housework.
   a. How would this increase in work hours affect GDP?
   b. Explain why this increase in measured GDP will overstate the true increase in output. Also explain how a set of augmented national accounts which includes home production would treat this change from nonmarket work to market work.
   c. Explain the paradox, "When a person marries his or her gardener, GDP goes down."

9. Examine the price-change numbers shown in the example on page 403.
   a. Use the formula to calculate the increase in the CPI from March 2007 to March 2008 to two decimal places. Verify that the number shown in the table is correct to a single decimal place.
   b. The level of the CPI in March 2007 was 205.10. Calculate the CPI for March 2008.

10. Robert Kennedy's remarks about the shortcomings of measures of national output also contained the following: "The Gross National Product includes air pollution and advertising for cigarettes, and ambulances to clear our highways of carnage. It counts special locks for our doors, and jails for the people who break them. GNP includes the destruction of the redwoods and the death of Lake Superior." List ways that the accounts can be redesigned to incorporate these effects.

CHAPTER

21 Consumption and Investment 消费与投资

[1] 查尔斯·狄更斯（Charles Dickens，1812~1870），19 世纪英国现实主义文学的主要代表，被马克思誉为“英国杰出的小说家”。他出生于海军小职员家庭，10 岁时全家被迫迁入负债者监狱，11 岁承担起繁重的家务劳动，曾在鞋油作坊当童工，15 岁入律师事务所当学徒，之后升任民事诉讼法庭书记员，接着又担任报社派驻议会的记者，靠刻苦自学和艰辛劳动成为知名作家。主要作品有《匹克威克外传》（*The Posthumous Papers of the Pickwick Club*，1836）、《雾都孤儿》（*Oliver Twist*，1838）、《老古玩店》（*The Old Curiosity Shop*，1841）、《大卫·科波菲尔》（*David Copperfield*，1850）、《艰难时世》（*Hard Times*，1854）、《双城记》（*A Tale of Two Cities*，1859）、《远大前程》（*Great Expectations*，1861）、《我们共同的朋友》（*Our Mutual Friend*，1865）等等。其中，半自传体长篇小说《大卫·科波菲尔》被托尔斯泰誉为“最好的一部英国小说”，是狄更斯耗费心血最多、[接下]

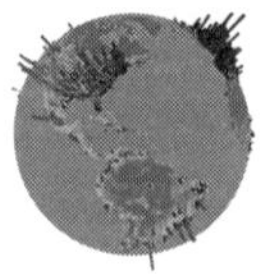

Micawber's equation:
Income 20 pounds; expenditure 19 pounds, 19 shillings and sixpence = happiness.
Income 20 pounds; annual expenditure 20 pounds and sixpence = misery.

Charles Dickens [1]
David Copperfield

本段译为：
米考伯幸福等式：
年收入 20 镑 − 年支出 19 镑 19 先令 6 便士 =6 便士 = 幸福。
年收入 20 镑 − 年支出 20 镑 6 便士 =−6 便士 = 痛苦。

② 如果消费快速增长，则总支出或总需求就会增加，短期内，将带动产出和就业的提高。20 世纪 90 年代末期美国经济的繁荣，很大程度上就是由消费支出的快速增长驱动的。但是，当美国的消费者勒紧了裤腰带之后，这便成为促成 2007~2009 年经济衰退的原因之一。

The major components of national output are consumption and investment. Naturally, nations want high levels of consumption—items such as housing, food, education, and recreation. The purpose of the economy is, after all, to transform inputs like labor and capital into consumption.

But saving and investment—that part of output that is not consumed—also play a central role in a nation's economic performance. Nations that save and invest large fractions of their incomes tend to have rapid growth of output, income, and wages; this pattern characterized the United States in the nineteenth century, Japan in the twentieth century, and the miracle economies of East Asia in recent decades. By contrast, nations that consume most of their incomes, like many poor countries in Africa and Latin America, have obsolete capital, low educational standards, and backward techniques; they experience low rates of growth of productivity and real wages. High consumption relative to income spells low investment and slow growth; high saving leads to high investment and rapid growth.

The interaction between spending and income plays quite a different role during business-cycle expansions and contractions. When consumption ② grows rapidly, this increases total spending or aggregate demand, raising output and employment in the short run. America's economic boom of the late 1990s was largely fueled by rapid growth in consumer spending, but when American consumers tightened their belts, this contributed to the recession of 2007–2009.

Because consumption and investment are so central to macroeconomics, we devote this chapter to them.

消费与储蓄
A. CONSUMPTION AND SAVING

This section considers consumption and saving behavior, beginning with individual spending patterns and then looking at aggregate consumption behavior. Recall from Chapter 20 that *consumption* (or, more precisely, personal consumption expenditures) is expenditures by households on final goods and services. *Saving* is that part of personal disposable income that is not consumed.

Consumption is the largest single component of GDP, constituting 70 percent of total spending over the last decade. What are the major elements of consumption? Among the most important categories

[1]（接上）篇幅最长，同时也是他最喜爱的一部最重要著作。小说通过大卫悲欢离合的一生，多层次地刻画了一个善良纯洁、奋发向上，最终实现了生活幸福和谐的丰满的人物形象。Micawber 是大卫刚到伦敦时的房东，一位喜好卖弄学问、得乐且乐、浑身酸腐气、总是屈尊就教的人物，梦想着有一天时来运转，由此演绎出 Micawberish（米考伯式的）一词，形容那些思无远虑而想入非非的乐天派。原文为：Annual income twenty pounds, annual expenditure nineteen pounds nineteen and six, result happiness. Annual income twenty pounds, annual expenditure twenty pounds ought and six, result misery.（注：与现行 New Pound 币制的 1 新镑等于 100 便士不同，这里的先令和便士均为 1971 年以前英国的币制，1 镑 =20 先令，1 先令 =12 便士。）

Category of consumption	Value of consumption ($, billion, 2007)		Percent of total
Durable goods		**1,083**	11.2%
Motor vehicles and parts	440		
Furniture and household equipment	415		
Other	227		
Nondurable goods		**2,833**	29.2%
Food	1,329		
Clothing and shoes	374		
Energy goods	367		
Other	763		
Services		**5,794**	59.7%
Housing	1,461		
Household operation	526		
Transportation	357		
Medical care	1,681		
Recreation	403		
Other	1,366		
Total personal consumption expenditures		**9,710**	**100.0%**

TABLE 21-1. The Major Components of Consumption

We divide consumption into three categories: durable goods, nondurable goods, and services. The service sector is growing in importance as basic needs for food are met and as health, recreation, and education claim a larger part of family budgets.

Source: U.S. Bureau of Economic Analysis, available at *www.bea.gov.*

are housing, motor vehicles, food, and medical care. Table 21-1 displays the major elements, broken down into the three main categories of durable goods, nondurable goods, and services. The items themselves ① are familiar, but their relative importance, particularly the increasing importance of services, is worth a moment's study.

预算支出模式
Budgetary Expenditure Patterns

How do the patterns of consumption spending differ across different households in the United States? No two families spend their disposable incomes in exactly the same way. Yet statistics show that there is a predictable regularity in the way people allocate their expenditures among food, clothing, and other major items. The thousands of budgetary ② investigations of household spending patterns show remarkable agreement on the general, qualitative patterns of behavior.[1] Figure 21-1 on page 410 tells the story.

Poor families must spend their incomes largely on the necessities of life: food and shelter. As income increases, expenditure on many food items goes up. People eat more and eat better. There are, however, ③ limits to the extra money people will spend on food when their incomes rise. Consequently, the proportion of total spending devoted to food declines as income increases.

Expenditure on clothing, recreation, and automobiles increases more than proportionately to after-tax

[1] The spending patterns shown in Fig. 21-1 are called "Engel's Laws," after the nineteenth-century Prussian statistician Ernst Engel. The average behavior of consumption expenditure does change fairly regularly with income. But averages do not tell the whole story. Within each income class, there is a considerable spread of consumption around the average.

① 这些项目本身都是大家熟悉的，但他们的相对重要程度，尤其对于日益增长的服务的重要性而言，值得在此稍费笔墨予以探讨。

② 对家庭预算的支出模式所作的数千次调查结果表明，这些行为模式在总体特性上均具有显著的一致性。

③ 然而，在收入增加的同时，人们花在食品上的额外支出却是有限的。其结果是，随着收入的增加，食品支出对总支出所做贡献的比例呈下降趋势。

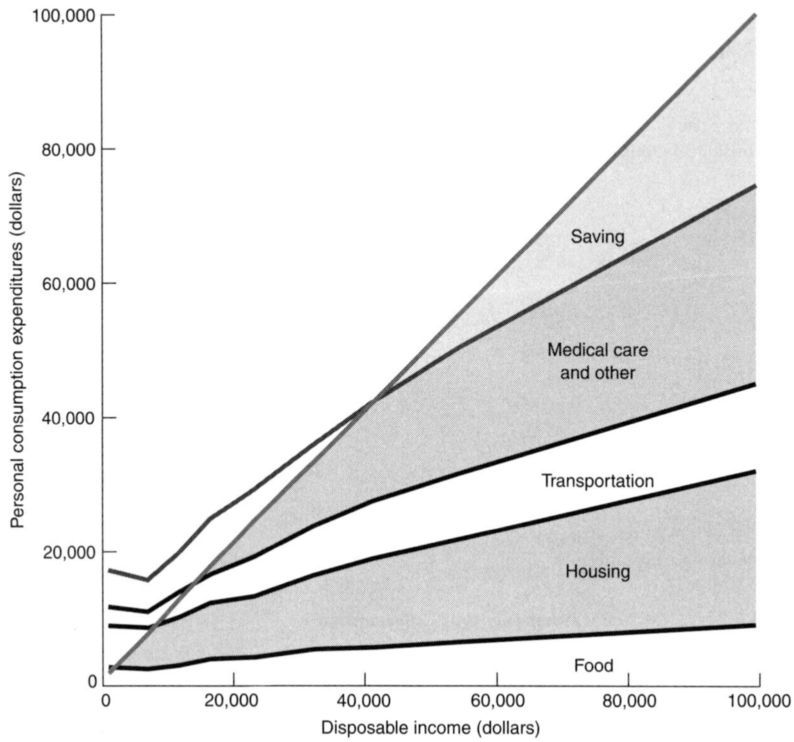

FIGURE 21-1. Family Budget Expenditures Show Regular Patterns

Surveys verify the importance of disposable income as a determinant of consumption expenditures. Notice the drop in food as a percentage of income as incomes rise. Note also that saving is negative at low incomes but rises substantially at high incomes.

Source: U.S. Department of Labor, *Consumer Expenditure Surveys, 1998*, available on the Internet at *www.bls.gov/csxstnd.htm.*

income, until high incomes are reached. Spending on luxury items increases in greater proportion than income. Finally, as we look across families, note that ① saving rises rapidly as income increases. Saving is the greatest luxury of all.

The Evolution of Consumption in the Twentieth Century

Continual changes in technology, incomes, and social forces have led to dramatic changes in U.S. consumption patterns over time. In 1918, American households on average spent 41 percent of their incomes on food and drink. By comparison, households now spend only about 14 percent on these items. What lies behind this striking decline? The major factor is that spending on food tends to grow more slowly than incomes. Similarly, spending on apparel has fallen from 18 percent of household income at the beginning of the twentieth century to only 4 percent today.

What are the "luxury goods" that Americans are spending more on? One big item is transportation. In 1918, Americans spent only 1 percent of their incomes on vehicles—but of course Henry Ford didn't sell his first Model T until 1908. Today, there are 1.2 cars for every licensed driver in the United States. It is not surprising that

① 最后，我们在对不同家庭所做的观察进行比对之后注意到，储蓄是随着收入的增加而快速上升的。因此，储蓄就成了所有支出项目中最大的奢侈品。

11 cents out of every dollar of spending goes for automotive transportation expenses. What about recreation and entertainment? Households now lay out large sums for televisions, cellular phones, and digital video recorders, items that did not exist 75 years ago. Housing services take ① about the same fraction of expenditures—15 percent of the total. However, those dollars today can buy a much larger house packed with consumer durables that make housework less of a chore.

Over the last decade, the biggest increase in consumption spending has been for health care. Surprisingly, consum- ② ers' out-of-pocket expenses for health care take about the same share of the *household* budget as they did in the early part of the twentieth century. The major increase has come as governments pay for an ever-larger fraction of health care.

消费、收入及储蓄 CONSUMPTION, INCOME, AND SAVING

Income, consumption, and saving are all closely ③ linked. More precisely, **personal saving** is that part of disposable income that is not consumed; saving equals income minus consumption.

The relationship between income, consumption, and saving for the United States in 2007 is shown in Table 21-2. Begin with personal income (composed, as Chapter 20 showed, of wages, fringe benefits, interest, rents, dividends, transfer payments, and so forth). In 2007, 12.8 percent of personal income went to personal taxes. This left $10,171 billion of **personal disposable income.** Household outlays for consumption (including interest) amounted to 99.4 percent of disposable income, leaving $57 billion as personal saving. The last item in the table shows the important ④ **personal saving rate.** This is equal to personal saving as a percent of disposable income—a tiny 0.6 percent in 2007.

Economic studies have shown that income is the primary determinant of consumption and saving. Rich ⑤ people save more than poor people, both absolutely and as a percent of income. The very poor are unable to save at all. Instead, as long as they can borrow or draw down their wealth, they tend to dissave. That is, they tend to spend more than they earn, reducing their accumulated savings or going deeper into debt.

Table 21-3 contains illustrative data on disposable income, saving, and consumption drawn from budget studies on American households. The first column shows seven different levels of disposable income. Column (2) indicates saving at each level of income, and the third column indicates consumption spending at each level of income.

The *break-even point*—where the representative household neither saves nor dissaves but consumes all its income—comes at $25,000. Below the

Item	Amount, 2007 ($, billion)
Personal income	11,663
Less: Personal taxes	1,493
Equals: Disposable personal income	10,171
Less: Personal outlays (consumption and interest)	10,113
Equals: Personal saving	57.4
Memo: Personal saving as percent of disposable personal income	0.6

TABLE 21-2. Saving Equals Disposable Income Less Consumption

Source: U.S. Bureau of Economic Analysis, available at *www.bea.gov.*

	(1) Disposable income ($)	(2) Net saving (+) or dissaving (−) ($)	(3) Consumption ($)
A	24,000	−200	24,200
B	25,000	0	25,000
C	26,000	200	25,800
D	27,000	400	26,600
E	28,000	600	27,400
F	29,000	800	28,200
G	30,000	1,000	29,000

TABLE 21-3. Consumption and Saving Are Primarily Determined by Income

Consumption and saving rise with disposable income. The break-even point at which people have zero saving is shown here at $25,000. How much of each extra dollar of income do people devote to extra consumption at this income level? How much to extra saving? (Answer: 80 cents and 20 cents, respectively, when we compare row B and row C.)

---

① 住房支出比例与此大致相同，即总支出的 15%。这些钱放在今天，可以买下一套更大的房子，还配有可以大大减轻家务劳动的耐用消费品。

② 令人吃惊的是，当今消费者对医疗保健的现金支出在家庭预算中所占的比例，与 20 世纪早期相当。医疗保健支出的比例越来越大，是因为其增长的大部分来自政府。

③ 收入、消费与储蓄三者紧密地链接在一起。更确切地讲，**个人储蓄**就是可支配收入中没有用于消费的那一部分，即收入减去消费所得的差额。

④ 表中所示的最后一项是重要的**个人储蓄率**，其值等于个人储蓄与其可支配收入的百分比，2007 年为微不足道的 0.6%。

⑤ 富人无论储蓄额的绝对值，还是所占收入的百分比，均超过了穷人。赤贫者根本就没有能力储蓄分文。相反，只要能借到或者是花光其财富，不惜动用储蓄金。也就是说，他们习惯于支出大于收入的生活，不断地消耗积蓄，或者更深地陷入债务之中。

break-even point, say, at \$24,000, the household actually consumes more than its income; it dissaves (see the −\$200 item). Above \$25,000 it begins to show positive saving [see the +\$200 and other positive items in column (2)].

Column (3) shows the consumption spending for each income level. Since each dollar of income is divided between the part consumed and the remaining part saved, columns (3) and (2) are not independent; they must always exactly add up to column (1).

To understand the way consumption affects national output, we need to introduce some new tools. We need to understand how each dollar of additional income is divided between additional saving and additional consumption. This relationship is shown by:

- The consumption function, relating consumption and income ①
- Its twin, the saving function, relating saving and income ②

消费函数
The Consumption Function

One of the most important relationships in all macroeconomics is the **consumption function.** The consumption function shows the relationship between the level of consumption expenditures and the level of disposable personal income. This concept, introduced by Keynes, is based on the hypothesis that there is a stable empirical relationship between consumption and income. ③

We can see the consumption function most vividly in the form of a graph. Figure 21-2 plots the seven levels of income listed in Table 21-3. Disposable income [column (1) of Table 21-3] is placed on the horizontal axis, and consumption [column (3)] is on the vertical axis. Each of the income-consumption ④

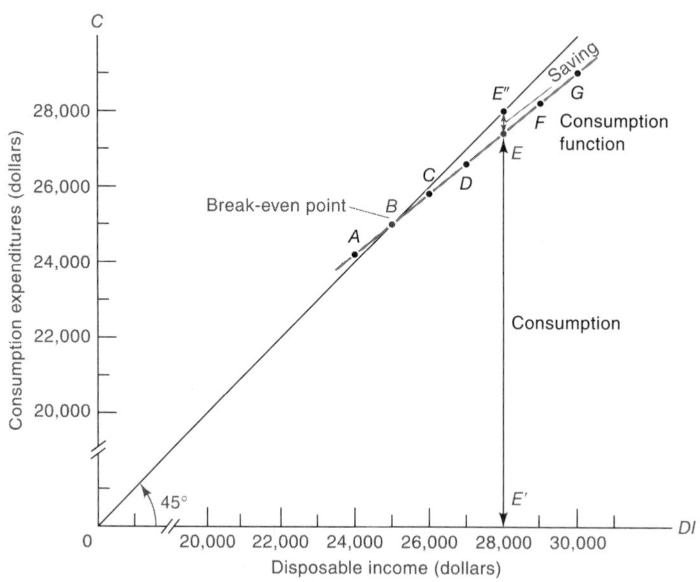

FIGURE 21-2. A Plot of the Consumption Function

The curve through *A, B, C,…, G* is the consumption function. The horizontal axis depicts the level of disposable income (*DI*). For each level of *DI*, the consumption function shows the dollar level of consumption (*C*) for the household. Note that consumption rises with increases in *DI*. The 45° line helps locate the break-even point and helps our eye measure net saving.

Source: Table 21-3.

① 消费函数与消费和收入相关联。
② 与消费函数相对应的是储蓄函数，其与储蓄和收入相关联。
③ 在宏观经济学范畴内，**消费函数**是最重要的关系之一。消费函数表示消费支出水平与个人可支配收入水平之间的关系。这一概念由凯恩斯提出，所基于的假设是消费和收入之间存在稳定的经验关系。
④ 收入与消费的每一个组合都使用一个点表示，然后将所有的点用一条平滑的曲线连接起来。

combinations is represented by a single point, and the points are then connected by a smooth curve.

The relationship between consumption and income shown in Figure 21-2 is called the consumption function. ①

The "Break-Even" Point. To understand the figure, it is helpful to look at the 45° line drawn northeast from the origin. Because the vertical and horizontal axes have exactly the same scale, the 45° line has a very special property. At any point on the 45° line, the distance up from the horizontal axis (consumption) exactly equals the distance across from the vertical axis (disposable income). You can use your eyes or a ruler to verify this fact.

The 45° line tells us immediately whether consumption spending is equal to, greater than, or less than the level of disposable income. The point where the consumption schedule intersects the 45° line is the **break-even point**—it is the level of disposable income at which households just break even. ②

This break-even point is at B in Figure 21-2. Here, consumption expenditures exactly equal disposable income; the household is neither a borrower nor a saver. To the right of point B, the consumption function lies below the 45° line. The relationship between income and consumption can be seen by examining the thin blue line from E' to E in Figure 21-2. At an income of $28,000, the level of consumption is $27,400 (see Table 21-3). We can see that consumption is less than income by the fact that the consumption function lies below the 45° line at point E.

What a household is not spending, it must be saving. The 45° line enables us to find how much the household is saving. Net saving is measured by the vertical distance from the consumption function up to the 45° line, as shown by the EE'' saving arrow in green.

The 45° line tells us that to the left of point B the household is spending more than its income. The excess of consumption over income is "dissaving" and is measured by the vertical distance between the consumption function and the 45° line.

To review:

At any point on the 45° line, consumption exactly equals income and the household has zero saving. When the consumption function lies above the 45° line, the household is dissaving. When the consumption function lies below the 45° line, the household has positive saving. The amount of dissaving or saving is always measured by the vertical distance between the consumption function and the 45° line. ③

储蓄函数
The Saving Function

The **saving function** shows the relationship between the level of saving and income. This is shown graphically in Figure 21-3. Again we show disposable income on the horizontal axis; but now saving, whether negative or positive in amount, is on the vertical axis.

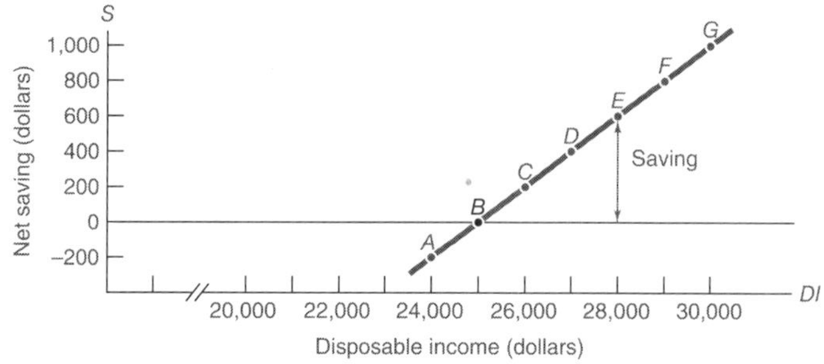

FIGURE 21-3. The Saving Function Is the Mirror Image of the Consumption Function

This saving schedule is derived by subtracting consumption from income. Graphically, the saving function is obtained by subtracting vertically the consumption function from the 45° line in Fig. 21-2. Note that the break-even point B is at the same $25,000 income level as in Fig. 21-2.

① 图 21-2 所示的消费与收入之间的关系称作消费函数。

② 这条 45º 线直观地告诉我们，消费支出究竟是等于、大于还是小于可支配收入水平。消费曲线与这条 45º 线的交点即**收支相抵点**，该点表示家庭收支相抵时的可支配收入水平。

③ 在这条 45º 线上的任何一点，消费都恰好等于收入，即家庭的储蓄为零。当消费函数值位于 45º 线上方时，家庭储蓄为负。当消费函数位于 45º 线下方时，家庭储蓄为正。任何情况下，负储蓄或者正储蓄额均以消费函数与 45º 线之间的垂直距离来衡量。

This saving function comes directly from Figure 21-2. It is the vertical distance between the 45° line and the consumption function. For example, at point *A* in Figure 21-2, we see that the household's saving is negative because the consumption function lies above the 45° line. Figure 21-3 shows this dissaving directly—the saving function is below the zero-saving line at point *A*. Similarly, positive saving occurs to the right of point *B* because the saving function is above the zero-saving line.

边际消费倾向

The Marginal Propensity to Consume

Modern macroeconomics attaches much importance to the response of consumption to changes in income. This concept is called the marginal propensity to consume, or *MPC*. ①

The **marginal propensity to consume** is the extra amount that people consume when they receive an extra dollar of disposable income. ②

The word "marginal" is used throughout economics to mean extra or additional. For example, "marginal cost" means the additional cost of producing an extra unit of output. "Propensity to consume" designates the desired level of consumption. The *MPC* is therefore the additional or extra consumption that results from an extra dollar of disposable income. ③

Table 21-4 rearranges Table 21-3's data in a more convenient form. First, verify its similarity to Table 21-3. Then, look at columns (1) and (2) to see how consumption expenditure goes up with higher levels of income.

Column (3) shows how we compute the marginal propensity to consume. From B to C, income rises by \$1000, going from \$25,000 to \$26,000. How much does consumption rise? Consumption grows from \$25,000 to \$25,800, an increase of \$800. The extra consumption is therefore 0.80 of the extra income. Out of each extra dollar of income, 80 cents goes to consumption and 20 cents goes to saving.

The example shown here is a linear consumption function—one in which the *MPC* is constant. You can verify that the *MPC* is everywhere 0.80. In reality, ④

	(1) Disposable income (after taxes) (\$)	(2) Consumption expenditure (\$)	(3) Marginal propensity to consume *MPC*	(4) Net saving (\$) (4) = (1) − (2)	(5) Marginal propensity to save *MPS*
A	24,000	24,200		−200	
			800/1,000 = 0.80		200/1,000 = 0.20
B	25,000	25,000		0	
			800/1,000 = 0.80		200/1,000 = 0.20
C	26,000	25,800		200	
			800/1,000 = 0.80		200/1,000 = 0.20
D	27,000	26,600		400	
			800/1,000 = 0.80		200/1,000 = 0.20
E	28,000	27,400		600	
			800/1,000 = 0.80		200/1,000 = 0.20
F	29,000	28,200		800	
			800/1,000 = 0.80		200/1,000 = 0.20
G	30,000	29,000		1,000	

TABLE 21-4. The Marginal Propensities to Consume and to Save

Each dollar of disposable income not consumed is saved. Each extra dollar of disposable income goes either into extra consumption or into extra saving. Combining these facts allows us to calculate the marginal propensity to consume (*MPC*) and the marginal propensity to save (*MPS*).

① 现代的宏观经济学认为，消费对于收入变化的反应具有十分重要的意义。这一概念即称为边际消费倾向（*MPC*）。

② **边际消费倾向**系指人们的可支配收入每增加一美元时所增加的消费额。

③ "边际"是整个经济学中广泛使用的一个词，用以表示"额外"或者"附加"之意。比如，"边际成本"系指额外生产一个单位的产出所需增加的成本。"消费倾向"表示所期望的消费水平。所以，边际消费倾向用来表示每增加一美元的可支配收入所带来的新增或者额外的消费。

④ 实际上，消费函数不可能呈现确切的线性关系，但这是我们所期待的合理的近似值。

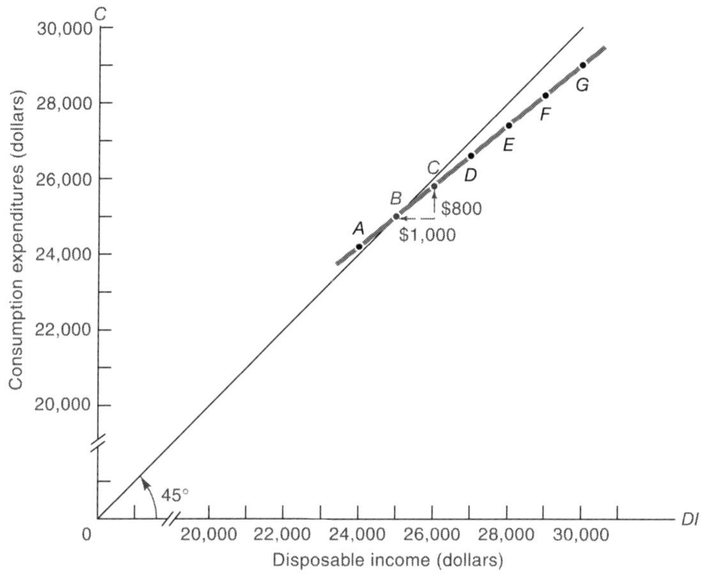

FIGURE 21-4. The Slope of the Consumption Function Is Its *MPC*

To calculate the marginal propensity to consume (*MPC*), we measure the slope of the consumption function by forming a right triangle and relating height to base. From point *B* to point *C*, the increase in consumption is \$800 while the change in disposable income is \$1000. The slope, equal to the change in *C* divided by the change in *DI*, gives the *MPC*. If the consumption function is everywhere upward-sloping, what does this imply about the *MPC*? If the line is a straight line, with a constant slope, what does this imply about the *MPC*?

consumption functions are unlikely to be exactly linear, but this is a reasonable approximation for our purposes.

Marginal Propensity to Consume as Geometrical Slope. We now know how to calculate the *MPC* from data on income and consumption. Figure 21-4 shows how we can calculate the *MPC* graphically. Near points *B* and *C* a little right triangle is drawn. As income increases by \$1000 from point *B* to point *C*, the amount of consumption rises by \$800. The *MPC* in this range is therefore \$800/\$1000 = 0.80. But, as the appendix to Chapter 1 showed, the numerical slope of a line is "the rise over the run."[2] We can therefore see that the slope of the consumption function is the same as the marginal propensity to consume.

The slope of the consumption function, which measures the change in consumption per dollar change in disposable income, is the marginal propensity to consume. ①

边际储蓄倾向

The Marginal Propensity to Save

Along with the marginal propensity to consume goes its mirror image, the marginal propensity to save, or *MPS*. The **marginal propensity to save** is defined as the fraction of an extra dollar of disposable income that goes to extra saving. ②

Why are *MPC* and *MPS* related like mirror images? Recall that disposable income equals consumption plus saving. This implies that each extra dollar of disposable income must be divided between

[2] For curved lines, we calculate the slope as the slope of the tangent line at a point.

① 消费函数的斜率，测量的是可支配收入中每变化一美元时所带来的消费变化，即边际消费倾向。

② 与边际消费倾向相伴并存的，是其镜像的边际储蓄倾向（*MPS*）。**边际储蓄倾向**定义为，每增加一美元的可支配收入被用来增加储蓄的部分。

extra consumption and extra saving. Thus if *MPC* is 0.80, then *MPS* must be 0.20. (What would *MPS* be if *MPC* were 0.6? Or 0.99?) Comparing columns (3) and (5) of Table 21-4 confirms that at any income level, *MPC* and *MPS* must always add up to exactly 1, no more and no less. $MPS + MPC = 1$, always and everywhere.

定义汇总
Brief Review of Definitions

Let's review briefly the main definitions we have learned:

1. The *consumption function* relates the level of consumption to the level of disposable income. ①
2. The *saving function* relates saving to disposable income. Because what is saved equals what is not consumed, saving and consumption schedules are mirror images.
3. The *marginal propensity to consume (MPC)* is the amount of extra consumption generated by an extra dollar of disposable income. Graphically, it is given by the slope of the consumption function.
4. The *marginal propensity to save (MPS)* is the extra saving generated by an extra dollar of disposable income. Graphically, this is the slope of the saving schedule.
5. Because the part of each dollar of disposable income that is not consumed is necessarily saved, $MPS \equiv 1 - MPC$.

国民消费行为
NATIONAL CONSUMPTION BEHAVIOR

Up to now we have examined the budget patterns and consumption behavior of typical families at different incomes. Let's now consider consumption for the entire nation. This transition from household behavior to national trends exemplifies the methodology of macroeconomics: We begin by examining economic activity on the individual level and then add up or aggregate the totality of individuals to study the way the overall economy operates.

Why are we interested in national consumption trends? Consumption behavior is crucial for understanding both short-term business cycles and long-term economic growth. In the short run, consumption is a major component of aggregate spending. When consumption changes sharply, the change is likely to affect output and employment through its impact on aggregate demand. This mechanism will be described in the chapters on Keynesian macroeconomics.

Additionally, consumption behavior is crucial because what is not consumed—that is, what is saved—is available for investment in new capital goods, and capital serves as a driving force behind long-term economic growth. *Consumption and saving behavior are key to understanding economic growth and business cycles.*

消费的决定因素
Determinants of Consumption

We begin by analyzing the major forces that affect consumer spending. What factors in a nation's ②
life and livelihood set the pace of its consumption outlays?

Disposable Income. Figure 21-5 shows how closely consumption followed current disposable income over the period 1970–2008. When *DI* declines in recessions, consumption usually follows the decline. Increases in *DI*, say, following tax cuts, stimulate consumption growth. The effects of the large cuts in personal taxes in 1981–1983 can be seen in the growth of *DI* and *C*.

Permanent Income and the Life-Cycle Model of Consumption. The simplest theory of consumption uses only the current year's income to predict consumption expenditures. Consider the following examples, which suggest why other factors might also be important:

> If bad weather destroys a crop, farmers will draw upon their previous savings to finance consumption.
> Similarly, law-school students borrow for consumption purposes while in school because they expect that their postgraduate incomes will be much higher than their meager student earnings.

In both these circumstances, people are in effect ③
asking, "Given my current and future income, how much can I consume today without incurring excessive debts?"

Careful studies show that consumers generally choose their consumption levels with an eye to both current income and long-run income prospects. In order to understand how consumption depends

---

① 1. 消费函数与消费水平和可支配收入的水平相关联。
2. 储蓄函数与储蓄和可支配收入相关联。由于所储蓄的等于未被消费的，所以储蓄曲线与消费曲线之间形成了互为镜像的关系。
3. 边际消费倾向（*MPC*）是每增加一美元的可支配收入所驱动的消费增加量，在图形上，可以用消费函数的斜率表示。
4. 边际储蓄倾向（*MPS*）是每增加一美元的可支配收入所驱动的储蓄增加量，在图形上，可以用储蓄曲线的斜率来表示。
5. 因为每增加一美元可支配收入中的未消费部分必然变成了储蓄，所以：$MPS \equiv 1-MPC$。

② 在一国的国计民生中，哪些因素在决定消费支出的数量？

③ 在这两种情况下，人们总是在问一个实质性问题："就我当前和未来的收入，在不增加债务的情况下，眼下我能消费多少？"

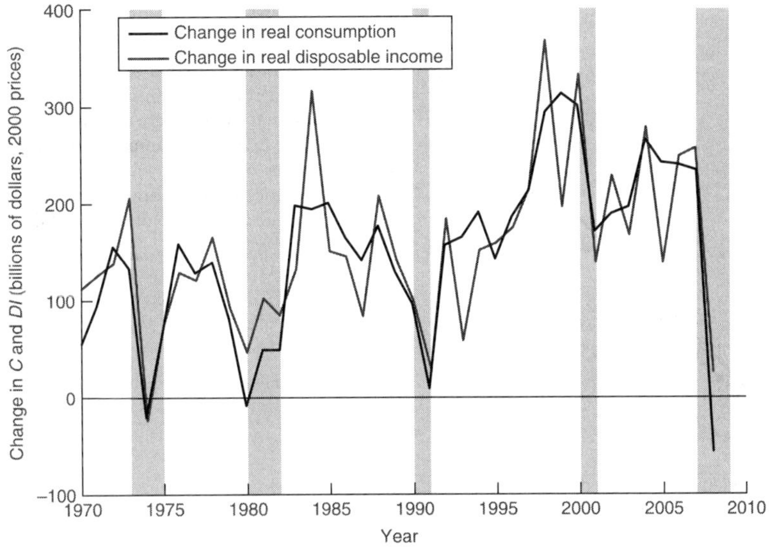

Shaded regions are NBER recessions.

FIGURE 21-5. Changes in Consumption and Disposable Income, 1970–2008

Note how changes in consumption track changes in disposable income. Macroeconomists can forecast consumption accurately based on the historical consumption function. Recessions usually produce declines in consumption as income declines.

Source: U.S. Bureau of Economic Analysis. Real disposable income is calculated using the price index for personal consumption expenditures.

on long-term income trends, economists have developed the permanent-income theory and the life-cycle hypothesis.

Permanent income is the trend level of income—that is, income after removing temporary or transient influences due to windfall gains or losses. According to the permanent-income theory, consumption responds primarily to permanent income. This approach implies that consumers do not respond equally to all income shocks. If a change in income appears permanent (such as being promoted to a secure and high-paying job), people are likely to consume a large fraction of the increase in income. On the other hand, if the income change is clearly transitory (for example, if it arises from a one-time bonus or a good harvest), a significant fraction of the additional income may be saved.

The *life-cycle hypothesis* assumes that people save in order to smooth their consumption over their lifetime. One important objective is to have an adequate retirement income. Hence, people tend to save while ① working so as to build up a nest egg for retirement and then spend out of their accumulated savings in their twilight years. One implication of the life-cycle hypothesis is that a program like social security, which provides a generous income supplement for retirement, will reduce saving by middle-aged workers since they no longer need to save as much for retirement.

Wealth and Other Influences. A further important determinant of the amount of consumption is wealth. Consider two consumers, each earning $50,000 per year. One has $200,000 in the bank, while the other has no savings at all. The first person may consume part of wealth, while the second has no wealth to draw down. The fact that higher wealth leads to higher consumption is called the *wealth effect.*

Wealth usually changes slowly from year to year. However, when wealth rises or declines sharply, this

① 因此，人们倾向于在工作期间储蓄，为退休之后的生活储备养老之需，以求在晚年将这些储备消耗殆尽。

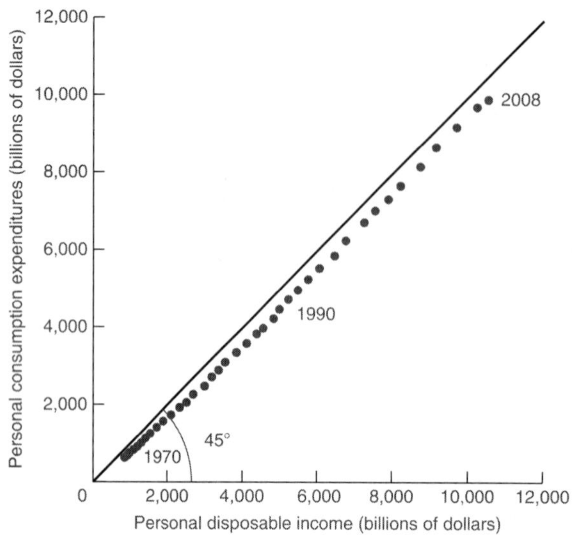

FIGURE 21-6. A Consumption Function for the United States, 1970–2008

The figure shows a scatter plot of personal disposable income and consumption. We have drawn a 45° line that shows where consumption exactly equals *DI*. Next, draw a consumption-function line through the points. Make sure you understand why the slope of the line you have drawn is the *MPC*. Can you verify that the *MPC* slope of the fitted line is close to 0.96?

Source: U.S. Bureau of Economic Analysis.

may lead to major changes in consumption spending. One important historical case was the stock market crash in 1929, when fortunes collapsed and paper-rich capitalists became paupers overnight. Economic historians believe that the sharp decline in wealth after the 1929 stock market crash reduced consumption spending and contributed to the depth of the Great Depression.

Over the last decade, the rise and decline of housing prices had a marked effect on consumption. From 2000 to 2006, the total value of household real estate rose over $7000 billion (about $70,000 per household). Many households refinanced their homes, took out home equity loans, or dipped into their savings. This is one of the reasons for the decline in the saving rate in recent years, as we will see shortly.

However, what went up then went down. By early 2009, the average price of residential houses had declined almost 30 percent from the peak in 2006. The wealth effect from declining housing values was a drag on consumer spending during this period.

国民消费函数
The National Consumption Function

Having reviewed the theory of consumption behavior, we conclude that the determinants are complex, including disposable income, wealth, and expectations of future income. We can plot the simplest consumption function in Figure 21-6. The scatter diagram shows data for the period 1970–2008, with each point representing the level of consumption and disposable income for a given year.

In addition, you might draw a line in Figure 21-6 through the scatter points and label it "Fitted consumption function." This fitted consumption function shows how closely consumption has followed disposable income over the period shown. In fact, economic historians have found that a close relationship between disposable income and consumption holds back to the nineteenth century. ①

The Declining Personal Saving Rate
Although consumption behavior tends to be stable over time, the personal saving rate dropped sharply in the United States over the last three decades. The personal saving rate as measured in the national accounts averaged around 8 percent of personal disposable income over most of the twentieth century. Starting about 1980, however, it began to decline and is now close to zero. (See Figure 21-7.) ②

① 事实上，经济史学家们已经发现，可支配收入和消费之间的密切关系可追溯到 19 世纪。

② 在 20 世纪的绝大部分时间里，依照国民账户的统计，个人储蓄率大约是个人可支配收入中的 8%。

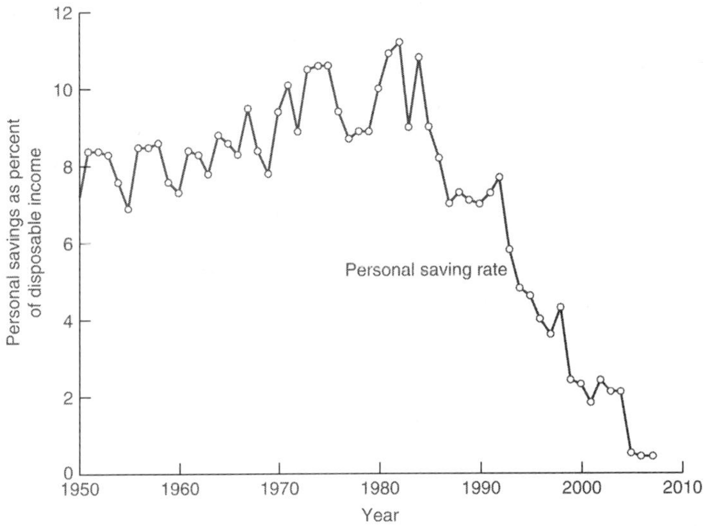

FIGURE 21-7. Personal Saving Rate Has Declined

After rising slowly over the postwar period, the personal saving rate took a sharp nosedive after 1980.

Source: U.S. Bureau of Economic Analysis.

This drop alarmed many economists because, over the long run, the growth in a nation's capital stock is largely determined by its national saving rate. National saving is composed of private and government saving. A high-saving nation has a rapidly growing capital stock and enjoys a rapid growth in its potential output. When a nation's saving rate is low, its equipment and factories become obsolete and its infrastructure begins to rot away. (This discussion abstracts away from borrowing abroad, but that cannot be a substantial fraction of income forever.)

What were the reasons for the sharp decline in the personal saving rate? This is a controversial question today, but economists point to the following potential causes:

- *Social security.* Some economists argued that the social security system has removed some of the need for private saving. In earlier times, as the life-cycle model of consumption suggests, a household would save during working years to build up a nest egg for retirement. ① When the government collects social security taxes and pays out social security benefits, people have less need to save for retirement. Other income-support systems have a similar effect, reducing the need to save for a rainy day. Disaster insurance for farmers, unemployment insurance for workers, and medical care for the poor and elderly all reduce the precautionary motive for people to save.
- *Financial markets.* For most of economic history, financial markets had numerous imperfections. People found it hard to borrow funds for worthwhile purposes, whether to buy a house, finance an education, or start a business. As financial markets developed, often with the help of the government, new loan instruments allowed people to borrow more easily. One example is the proliferation of credit cards, which encourage people to borrow (even though the interest rates are quite high). A generation ago, it would be difficult to borrow more than $1000 unless a person had substantial assets. Today, credit-card solicitations arrive daily in the mail. It is not unusual to receive multiple promotions offering credit lines of $5,000 or more in a single week!

  Perhaps the biggest and ultimately most troublesome source of finance was the "subprime" mortgages that proliferated in the early 2000s. These were loans at as much as 100 percent of the value of a house, sometimes to people with no documented income. When housing prices declined, literally hundreds of billions of dollars of these loans were in default, and investors worldwide took huge losses.
- *The rapid growth in paper wealth.* Part of the decline in personal saving in the 1990–2007 period was caused by the rapid increase in personal wealth. First, the ②

① 早年，正如消费的生命周期模型所揭示的那样，家庭会在工作期间积累一笔储备金以便为退休之后养老所用。

② 账面财富快速增长。在1990~2007年期间，个人储蓄中的部分下降是由个人财富的迅猛增加所致。首先，股票市场繁荣，其次，住房价格飞涨。经济学家们估算，到2000年代后期，仅财富效应就可能使个人储蓄率下降三个百分点。

stock market boomed, and then housing prices took off. Economists calculate that the wealth effect alone might have contributed to a decline in the personal saving rate of 3 percentage points by the late 2000s.

测量储蓄的其他方法
Alternative Measures of Saving

You might at this point ask, "If people are saving so little, why are there so many rich people?" This question raises an important point about measuring personal saving. Saving looks different to the household than to the nation as a whole. This is so because ① saving as measured in the national income and product accounts is not the same as that measured by accountants or in balance sheets. The *national-accounts measure of saving* is the difference between disposable income (excluding capital gains) and consumption. The *balance-sheet measure of saving* calculates the change in real net worth (that is, assets less liabilities, corrected for inflation) from one year to the next; this measure includes real capital gains.

If we examine the balance-sheet savings rate for the decade from 1997 to 2007—the viewpoint from the dining room table, so to speak—the savings rate was relatively high. Average household net worth over this period in 2007 prices rose from $157,000 to $191,000. The change in net worth was 17 percent of disposable income. So the balance-sheet saving rate was 17 percent, while the national-account saving rate shown in Figure 21-7 was 2 percent.

Does this alternative view mean that we can breathe a sigh of relief? Probably not. The reason is that the high saving over the last decade was largely an increase in "paper wealth." A rise in stock prices or the prices of existing assets like housing does not necessarily reflect the productivity or "real wealth" of the economy. Although people feel richer when asset prices rise in a speculative bubble, the economy cannot produce more cars, computers, food, or housing. Indeed, if everyone wanted to sell their houses, they would find that prices would fall and they could not convert their paper wealth into consumption.

Hence, economists are justified in worrying ② about the decline in the national-accounts saving rate. While consumers may *feel* richer because of a booming stock or housing market, an economy is *actually* richer only when its productive tangible and intangible assets increase.

投　资
B. INVESTMENT

The second major component of private spending, after consumption, is investment. Investment plays two roles in macroeconomics. First, because it is a large and volatile component of spending, investment often leads to changes in aggregate demand and affects the business cycle. In addition, investment leads to capital accumulation. Adding to the stock of buildings and equipment increases the nation's potential output and promotes economic growth in the long run.

Thus investment plays a dual role, affecting short-run output through its impact on aggregate demand and influencing long-run output growth through the impact of capital formation on potential output and aggregate supply.

The Meaning of "Investment" in Economics
Remember that macroeconomists use the term "investment" or "real investment" to mean additions to the stock of productive assets or capital goods like computers or trucks. When Amazon.com builds a new warehouse or when the Smiths build a new house, these activities represent investment.

Many people speak of "investing" when buying a piece of land, an old security, or any title to property. In economics, these purchases are really financial transactions or "financial investments," because what one person is buying, someone else is selling, and the net effect is zero. There is investment only when real capital is produced.

投资的决定因素
DETERMINANTS OF INVESTMENT

In this discussion, we focus on *gross private domestic investment*, or *I*. This is the domestic component of national investment. Recall, however, that *I* is but one component of total social investment, which also includes foreign investment, government investment, and intangible investments in human capital and improved knowledge.

The major types of gross private domestic investment are the building of residential structures; investment in business fixed equipment, software, and structures; and additions to inventory. In this discussion, we focus on business investment, but the principles apply to investments by other sectors as well.

① 这的确是因为，作为统计在国民收入和产品账户中的储蓄，与会计师们在资产负债表中所作的核算并不一样。国民账户中对储蓄的测量，是可支配收入（资本所得除外）与消费之差。资产负债表中对储蓄的测量，计算的是从一年到下一年度的实际净资产（即资产减去负债，校正后的通货膨胀）的变化。这一测量包括实际资本收益。

② 因此，经济学家们对国民账户中储蓄率的下降表示担忧不无道理。由于股票或者住房市场繁荣，消费者有可能感觉变得更富有了，但是，经济体只在生产的有形和无形资产增加时，才能确实变得更加富裕。

Why do businesses invest? Ultimately, businesses buy capital goods when they expect that this action will earn them a profit—that is, will bring them revenues greater than the costs of the investment. This simple statement contains the three elements essential to understanding investment: revenues, costs, and expectations.

收 入
Revenues

An investment will bring the firm additional revenue if it helps the firm sell more product. This suggests that the overall level of output (or GDP) will be an important determinant of investment. When factories are lying idle, firms have relatively little need for new factories, so investment is low. More generally, investment depends upon the revenues that will be generated by the state of overall economic activity. Most studies find that investment is very sensitive to the business cycle.

成 本
Costs

A second important determinant of the level of investment is the costs of investing. Because investment goods last many years, reckoning the costs of investment is somewhat more complicated than doing so for other commodities like coal or wheat. For durable goods, the cost of capital includes not only the price of the capital good but also the interest rate that borrowers pay to finance the capital as well as the taxes that firms pay on their incomes.

To understand this point, note that investors often raise the funds for buying capital goods by borrowing (say, through a mortgage or in the bond market). What is the cost of borrowing? It is the *interest rate* on borrowed funds. Recall that the interest rate is the price paid for borrowing money for a period of time; for example, you might have to pay 8 percent to borrow $1000 for a year. In the case of a family buying a house, the interest rate is the mortgage interest rate.

Additionally, taxes can have a major effect on investment. One important tax is the federal corporation income tax. This tax takes up to 35 cents of the ① last dollar of corporate profits, thereby discouraging investment in the corporate sector. Sometimes, the government gives tax breaks to particular activities or sectors. For example, the government encourages home ownership by allowing homeowners to deduct real-estate taxes and mortgage interest from their taxable income.

预 期
Expectations

Additionally, profit expectations and business confidence are central to investment decisions. Investment is a gamble on the future. This means that business investments require a weighing of certain present costs with uncertain future profits. If businesses are concerned that political conditions in Russia are unstable, they will be reluctant to invest there. Conversely, if businesses believe that Internet commerce is the key to riches, they will invest heavily in that sector.

However, economists also realize that emotions weigh in the balance, that some investments are moved as much by intuition as by spreadsheets. This point was emphasized by J. M. Keynes as one of the reasons for the instability of a market economy:

> Even apart from the instability due to speculation, ② there is the instability due to the characteristic of human nature that a large proportion of our positive activities depend on spontaneous optimism rather than mathematical expectations, whether moral or hedonistic or economic. Most, probably, of our decisions to do something positive, the full consequences of which will be drawn out over many days to come, can only be taken as the result of *animal spirits*—a spontaneous urge to action rather than inaction, and not as the outcome of a weighted average of quantitative benefits multiplied by quantitative probabilities.

Thus, investment decisions hang by a thread on ③ expectations and forecasts. But accurate forecasting is difficult. Businesses spend much energy analyzing investments and trying to narrow the uncertainties about their investments.

We can sum up our review of the forces lying behind investment decisions as follows:

> Businesses invest to earn profits. Because capital ④ goods last many years, investment decisions depend on (1) the level of output produced by the new investments, (2) the interest rates and taxes that influence the costs of the investment, and (3) business expectations about the state of the economy.

投资需求曲线
THE INVESTMENT DEMAND CURVE

In analyzing the determinants of investment, we focus particularly on the relationship between interest rates and investment. This linkage is crucial because interest rates (influenced by central banks) are the

③ 这样预期和预测的投资决策命悬一线。准确地做出预测着实是一件非常困难的事情。企业需要投入大量的精力来做投资分析，力图压低投资决策的不确定性。

④ 企业投资的目的是为了赢利。由于资本品要延续多年，投资的决策就必须取决于（1）由新的投资所拉动的产出水平；（2）影响投资成本的利率和税收；（3）企业对经济状况的预期。

① 这一税种从公司每最后一美元的利润中征收35美分，因此抑制了公司投资。有的时候，政府对某些特殊的活动或者特定领域给予税收上的优惠。比如，为鼓励购房，政府允许民众从应纳税收入中扣除不动产税和抵押贷款利息。

② 即便将投机导致的不稳定性排除，人性本身特点所带来的不稳定性依然存在。人类的大部分积极行为，都依赖于自发的乐观主义，而非数学推导，无论这些活动是道德的、享乐主义的，还是经济的。大多数情况下，我们决意要做的积极的事，仅可认为是动物精神所致，而其全部后果必须经过很长时间才能得以显现。这种动物精神是一种自发的冲动所驱使的有为之举，而非惰性使然，也不是使用权重后的平均收益量乘以定量概率的结果。

major instrument by which governments influence investment. To show the relationship between interest rates and investment, economists use a schedule called the **investment demand curve.** ①

Consider a simplified economy where firms can invest in different projects: A, B, C, and so forth, up to H. These investments are so durable (like power plants or buildings) that we can ignore the need for replacement. Further, they yield a constant stream of net income each year, and there is no inflation. Table 21-5 shows the financial data on each of the investment projects.

Consider project A. This project costs $1 million. It has a very high return—$1500 per year of revenues per $1000 invested (this is a rate of return of 150 percent per year). Columns (4) and (5) show the cost of investment. For simplicity, assume that the investment is financed purely by borrowing at the market interest rate, here taken alternately as 10 percent per year in column (4) and 5 percent in column (5).

Thus at a 10 percent annual interest rate, the cost of borrowing $1000 is $100 a year, as is shown in all entries of column (4); at a 5 percent interest rate, the borrowing cost is $50 per $1000 borrowed per year.

Finally, the last two columns show the *annual net profit* from each investment. For lucrative project A, the net annual profit is $1400 a year per $1000 invested at a 10 percent interest rate. Project H loses money.

To review our findings: In choosing among investment projects, firms compare the annual revenues from an investment with the annual cost of capital, which depends upon the interest rate. The difference between annual revenue and annual cost is the annual net profit. When annual net profit is positive, the investment makes money, while a negative net profit denotes that the investment loses money.

Look again at Table 21-5 and examine the last column, showing annual net profit at a 5 percent interest rate. Note that at this interest rate, investment

(1)	(2)	(3)	(4)	(5)	(6)	(7)
			Cost per $1,000 Borrowed at Annual Interest Rate of:		Annual Net Profit per $1,000 Borrowed at Annual Interest Rate of:	
Project	Total investment in project ($, million)	Annual revenues per $1,000 invested ($)	10% ($)	5% ($)	10% ($) (6) = (3) − (4)	5% ($) (7) = (3) − (5)
A	1	1,500	100	50	1,400	1,450
B	4	220	100	50	120	170
C	10	160	100	50	60	110
D	10	130	100	50	30	80
E	5	110	100	50	10	60
F	15	90	100	50	−10	40
G	10	60	100	50	−40	10
H	20	40	100	50	−60	−10

TABLE 21-5. The Profitability of Investment Depends on the Interest Rate

The economy has eight investment projects, ranked in order of return. Column (2) shows the investment in each project. Column (3) calculates the perpetual return each year per $1000 invested. Columns (4) and (5) then show the cost of the project, assuming all funds are borrowed, at interest rates of 10 and 5 percent; this is shown per $1000 borrowed.

The last two columns calculate the annual net profit per $1000 invested in the project. If net profit is positive, profit-maximizing firms will undertake the investment; if negative, the investment project will be rejected.

Note how the cutoff between profitable and unprofitable investments moves as the interest rate rises. (Where would the cutoff be if the interest rate rose to 15 percent per year?)

① 经济学家们使用**投资需求曲线**来验证利率与投资两者之间的关系。

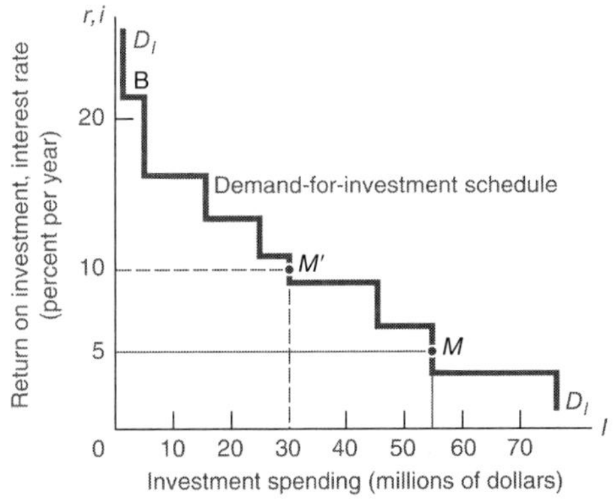

FIGURE 21-8. Investment Depends upon Interest Rate

The downward-stepping demand-for-investment schedule plots the amount that businesses would invest at each interest rate, as calculated from the data in Table 21-5. Each step represents a lump of investment: project A has such a high rate of return that it is off the figure; the highest visible step is project B, shown at the upper left. At each interest rate, all investments that have positive net profit will be undertaken.

projects A through G would be profitable. We would thus expect profit-maximizing firms to invest in all seven projects, which [from column (2)] total up to $55 million in investment. Thus at a 5 percent interest rate, investment demand would be $55 million.

However, suppose that the interest rate rises to 10 percent. Then the cost of financing these investments would double. We see from column (6) that investment projects F and G become unprofitable at an interest rate of 10 percent; investment demand would fall to $30 million.

We show the results of this analysis in Figure 21-8. This figure shows the *demand-for-investment schedule*, which is here a downward-sloping step function of the interest rate. This schedule shows the amount of investment that would be undertaken at each interest rate; it is obtained by adding up all the investments that would be profitable at each level of the interest rate.

Hence, if the market interest rate is 5 percent, the desired level of investment will occur at point *M*, which shows investment of $55 million. At this interest rate, projects A through G are undertaken. If interest rates were to rise to 10 percent, projects F and G would be squeezed out; in this situation, investment demand would lie at point *M′* with total investment of $30 million.[3]

投资需求曲线的移动
Shifts in the Investment Demand Curve

We have seen how interest rates affect the level of investment. Investment is affected by other forces as well. For example, an increase in the GDP will shift the investment demand curve out, as shown in Figure 21-9(*a*) on the next page.

An increase in business taxation would depress investment. Say that the government taxes away half the net yield in column (3) of Table 21-5, with interest costs in columns (4) and (5) not being deductible. The net profits in columns (6) and (7) would therefore decline. [Verify that at a 10 percent interest rate, a 50 percent tax on column (3) would raise the cutoff to between projects B and C, and the demand for investment would decline to $5 million.] The case of a tax increase on investment income is shown in Figure 21-9(*b*).

We can also see how expectations enter the picture from a historical example. In the late 1990s, investors became infatuated with the Internet and the "new economy." They poured money into now-defunct companies on the basis of wild projections. Some seasoned investors even succumbed to the "animal spirits," as, for example, when Time Warner [1]
paid $180 billion for the online company AOL. Figure 21-9(*c*) illustrates how a bout of business optimism would shift out the investment demand schedule in the 1990s. When the technology-stock bubble burst in 2000, the demand for investment in software and equipment fell sharply as well, and the curve in Figure 21-9(*c*) shifted sharply back to the left. These are but two examples of how expectations ②
can have powerful effects on investment.

After learning about the factors affecting investment, you will not be surprised to discover that investment is the most volatile component of spending. Investment behaves unpredictably because it depends on such uncertain factors as the success or failure of new and untried products, changes in tax rates and interest rates, political attitudes and

[3] We will later see that when prices are changing, it is appropriate to use a real interest rate, which represents the nominal or money interest rate corrected for inflation.

[1] Time Warner，时代华纳，美国大型传媒公司，业务横跨出版、电影、电视和互联网等产业，旗下有CNN、HBO、《时代周刊》、《美国在线》(*AOL*)等约20个著名品牌，对中国传媒市场的投资也异常活跃。

② 单就这两个案例即可见预期对投资的影响何其强大。

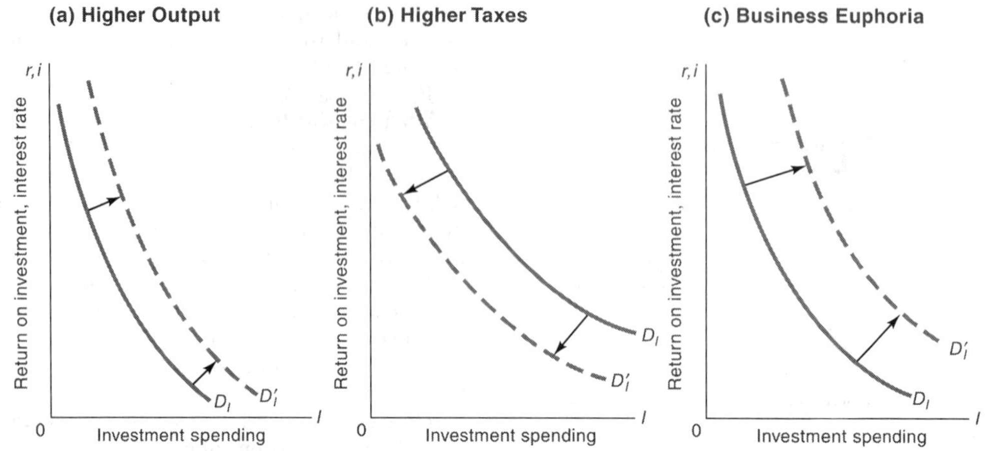

FIGURE 21-9. Shifts in Investment Demand Function

In the demand-for-investment (D_I) schedule, the arrows show the impact of **(a)** a higher level of GDP, **(b)** higher taxes on capital income, and **(c)** a burst of business euphoria.

approaches to stabilizing the economy, and similar changeable events of economic life. *In virtually every* ① *business cycle, investment fluctuations have been the driving force behind boom or bust.*

总需求理论
ON TO THE THEORY OF AGGREGATE DEMAND

We have now completed our introduction to the basic concepts of macroeconomics. We have examined the determinants of consumption and investment and seen how they can fluctuate from year to year, sometimes quite sharply.

At this point, macroeconomics branches into two major subjects—business cycles and economic growth. We begin our survey in the next chapter with business cycles, which concern the short-term fluctuations in output, employment, and prices. Modern business-cycle theories rely primarily on the ② Keynesian approach. This analysis shows the impact of financial shocks and changes in investment, government spending and taxation, and foreign trade. These shocks are amplified through induced consumption effects and determine aggregate demand. We will learn that the wise application of government fiscal and monetary policies can reduce the severity of recessions and inflation, but also that poor policies can amplify shocks. The theories of consumption and investment surveyed in this chapter will be the major players in our business-cycle drama.

SUMMARY

A. Consumption and Saving

1. Disposable income is an important determinant of consumption and saving. The consumption function is the schedule relating total consumption to total disposable income. Because each dollar of disposable income is either saved or consumed, the saving function is the other side or mirror image of the consumption function.

① 几乎在每一个商业周期中，投资的波动始终是经济繁荣或者萧条背后的驱动力量。

② 现代商业周期理论主要基于凯恩斯理论。这一分析说明了金融动荡以及投资、政府支出、税收和对外贸易的变化所带来的影响。

2. Recall the major features of consumption and saving functions:
   a. The consumption (or saving) function relates the level of consumption (or saving) to the level of disposable income.
   b. The marginal propensity to consume (*MPC*) is the amount of extra consumption generated by an extra dollar of disposable income.
   c. The marginal propensity to save (*MPS*) is the extra saving generated by an extra dollar of disposable income.
   d. Graphically, the *MPC* and the *MPS* are the slopes of the consumption and saving schedules, respectively.
   e. $MPS \equiv 1 - MPC$.
3. Adding together individual consumption functions gives us the national consumption function. In simplest form, it shows total consumption expenditures as a function of disposable income. Other variables, such as permanent income or long-term income trends as well as wealth, also have a significant impact on consumption patterns.
4. The personal saving rate has declined sharply in the last three decades. To explain this decline, economists point to social security and government health programs, changes in financial markets, and wealth effects. Declining saving hurts the economy because personal saving is a major component of national saving and investment. While people feel richer because of the booming stock market, the nation's true wealth increases only when its productive tangible and intangible assets increase.

B. Investment

5. The second major component of spending is gross private domestic investment in housing, plant, software, and equipment. Firms invest to earn profits. The major economic forces that determine investment are therefore the revenues produced by investment (primarily influenced by the state of the business cycle), the cost of investment (determined by interest rates and tax policy), and the state of expectations about the future. Because it depends on highly unpredictable future events, investment is the most volatile component of aggregate spending.
6. An important relationship is the investment demand schedule, which connects the level of investment spending to the interest rate. Because the profitability of investment varies inversely with the interest rate, which affects the cost of capital, we can derive a downward-sloping investment demand curve. As the interest rate declines, more investment projects become profitable.

CONCEPTS FOR REVIEW

Consumption and Saving

disposable income, consumption, saving
consumption and saving functions
personal saving rates
marginal propensity to consume (*MPC*)
marginal propensity to save (*MPS*)
$MPC + MPS \equiv 1$
break-even point
45° line
determinants of consumption:
- current disposable income
- permanent income
- wealth
- life-cycle effect

Investment

determinants of investment:
- revenues
- costs
- expectations

role of interest rates in *I*
investment demand function
animal spirits

FURTHER READING AND INTERNET WEBSITES

Further Reading

Economists have studied consumer expenditure patterns in order to improve predictions and aid economic policy. One of the most influential studies is Milton Friedman, *The Theory of the Consumption Function* (University of Chicago Press, 1957). A historical overview by an economic historian is Stanley Lebergott, *Pursuing Happiness: American Consumers in the Twentieth Century* (Princeton University Press, Princeton, N.J., 1993).

Firms devote much management time to deciding about investment strategies. A good survey can be found in Richard A. Brealey, Stewart C. Myers, and Franklin Allen,

Principles of Corporate Finance (McGraw-Hill, New York, 2009).

Websites

Data on total personal consumption expenditures for the United States are provided at the website of the Bureau of Economic Analysis, *www.bea.gov.*

Data on family budgets are contained in Bureau of Labor Statistics, "Consumer Expenditures," available at *www.bls.gov.*

Data and analysis of investment for the U.S. economy are provided by the Bureau of Economic Analysis at *www.bea.gov.*

Milton Friedman and Franco Modigliani made major contributions to our understanding of the consumption function. Visit the Nobel website at *nobelprize.org/nobel_prizes/economics* to read about the importance of their contributions to macroeconomics.

QUESTIONS FOR DISCUSSION

1. Summarize the budget patterns for food, clothing, luxuries and saving.
2. In working with the consumption function and the investment demand schedule, we need to distinguish between shifts of and movements along these schedules.
   a. Define carefully for both curves changes that would lead to shifts of and those that would produce movements along the schedules.
   b. For the following, explain verbally and show in a diagram whether they are shifts of or movements along the consumption function: increase in disposable income, decrease in wealth, fall in stock prices.
   c. For the following, explain in words and show in a diagram whether they are shifts of or movements along the investment demand curve: expectation of a decline in output next year, rise of interest rates, increase in taxes on profits.
3. Exactly how were the *MPC* and *MPS* in Table 21-4 computed? Illustrate by calculating *MPC* and *MPS* between points *A* and *B*. Explain why it must always be true that $MPC + MPS \equiv 1$.
4. I consume all my income at every level of income. Draw my consumption and saving functions. What are my *MPC* and *MPS*?
5. Estimate your income, consumption, and saving for last year. If you dissaved (consumed more than your income), how did you finance your dissaving? Estimate the composition of your consumption in terms of each of the major categories listed in Table 21-1.
6. "Along the consumption function, income changes more than consumption." What does this imply for the *MPC* and *MPS*?
7. "Changes in disposable income lead to movements along the consumption function; changes in wealth or other factors lead to a shift of the consumption function." Explain this statement with an illustration of each case.
8. What would be the effects of the following on the investment demand function illustrated in Table 21-5 and Figure 21-8?
   a. A doubling of the annual revenues per $1000 invested shown in column (3)
   b. A rise in interest rates to 15 percent per year
   c. The addition of a ninth project with data in the first three columns of (J, 10, 70)
   d. A 50 percent tax on net profits shown in columns (6) and (7)
9. Using the augmented investment demand schedule from question 8(**c**) and assuming that the interest rate is 10 percent, calculate the level of investment for cases **a** through **d** in question 8.
10. **Advanced problem:** According to the life-cycle model, people consume each year an amount that depends upon their *lifetime* income rather than upon their current income. Assume that you expect to receive future income (in constant dollars) according to the schedule in Table 21-6.
    a. Assume that there is no interest paid on savings. You have no initial savings. Further assume that you want to "smooth" your consumption (enjoying equal consumption each year) because of diminishing extra satisfaction from extra consumption. Derive your best consumption trajectory for the 5 years, and write the figures in column (3). Then calculate your saving and enter the amounts in column (4); put your end-of-period wealth, or cumulative saving, for each year into column (5). What is your average saving rate in the first 4 years?
    b. Next, assume that a government social security program taxes you $2000 in each of your working

(1) Year	(2) Income ($)	(3) Consumption ($)	(4) Saving ($)	(5) Cumulative saving (end of year) ($)
1	30,000	______	______	______
2	30,000	______	______	______
3	25,000	______	______	______
4	15,000	______	______	______
5*	0	______	______	0

*Retired.

TABLE 21-6.

years and provides you with an $8000 pension in year 5. If you still desire to smooth consumption, calculate your revised saving plan. How has the social security program affected your consumption? What is the effect on your average saving rate in the first 4 years? Can you see why some economists claim that social security can lower saving?

CHAPTER

22

Business Cycles and Aggregate Demand

商业周期与总需求

[1] 威廉·莎士比亚（William Shakespeare，1564~1616），英国诗人、剧作家，一生共创作 37 部戏剧、154 首十四行诗、2 首长诗以及其他诗歌等。以《哈姆雷特》（*Hamlet, Prince of Denmark*）、《奥赛罗》（*Othello, the Moor of Venice*）、《李尔王》（*King Lear*）和《麦克白》（*Macbeth*）四大悲剧为代表的悲剧 12 部，《裘力斯·凯撒》（创作于 1599 年，全名：*The Tragedy of Julius Caesar*）是其中的一部，四大悲剧的奠基性作品。莎士比亚的戏剧与诗歌，以及莎氏后期英王詹姆斯一世下令翻译并于 1611 年出版的《钦定圣经》（*King James Version of the Bible*，简称 KJV），是西方现代文明的两大基石和取之不竭的思想源泉。

本段文字引自该剧第一幕第二场中 Cassius（凯撒叛党中的煽动者）对

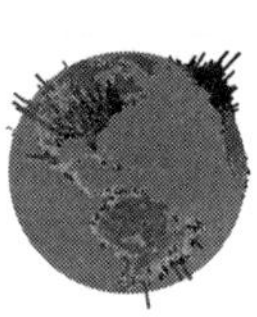

Brutus（本剧实际上的主角，以为罗马万民谋福祉之名，对凯撒百般谄媚，致其失去警觉而予刺死；此举不得罗马民心，终战败自刎。）讲的一段话，这一句完整的原文为：

(Men at some time are masters of their fates:)
The fault, dear Brutus, is not in our stars,
But in ourselves, that we are underlings.

The fault, dear Brutus, is not in our stars—but in ourselves.

William Shakespeare [1]
Julius Caesar

朱生豪先生的译文为：

（人们有时可以支配他们自己的命运；）要是我们受制于人，亲爱的勃鲁托斯，那错处并不在我们的命运，而在我们自己。

朱生豪（1912~1944），浙江嘉兴人，著名的莎士比亚戏剧翻译家和诗人，出生于一个破落的商人家庭，幼失父母，一生生活贫苦。1941 年日军进攻上海后，在被迫辗转流徙、贫病交加的逆境中，仍坚持翻译，先后共翻译莎士比亚戏剧 31 部，终因劳累过度于 1944 年逝世，终年 32 岁。先生所译的 31 部莎士比亚戏剧是国人公认的经典。

The American economy has been subject to business ② cycles since the early days of the Republic. Sometimes, business conditions are healthy, with rapidly growing employment, factories working overtime, and robust profits. The "fabulous 1990s" was such a period for [3] the American economy. The economy grew rapidly; employment and capacity utilization were exceptionally high, and unemployment was low. Yet, unlike the case in earlier long expansions, inflation remained low throughout the 1990s.

Such periods of prosperity often come to an unhappy end. In the nineteenth and early twentieth centuries, and again in 2007–2009, financial crises turned into waves of contagious pessimism, businesses failed, credit conditions tightened, and a downturn in the banking and financial sectors rippled through the rest of the economy. During business downturns, jobs are hard to find, factories are idle, and profits are low. These downturns are usually short and mild, as was the case in the recession that began in March 2001 and ended in November 2001. From time to time the contraction may persist for a decade and cause widespread economic hardships, as during the 1930s in the Great Depression of the 1930s or in Japan in the 1990s. [4]

These short-term fluctuations in economic activity, known as *business cycles,* are the central topic of this chapter. Understanding business cycles has proved to be one of the most enduring issues in all of macroeconomics. What causes business fluctuations? How can government policies reduce their virulence? Economists were largely unable to answer these questions until the 1930s, when the revolutionary macroeconomic theories of John Maynard Keynes highlighted the importance of the forces of aggregate demand in determining business cycles. Keynesian economics emphasizes that ⑤ *changes in aggregate demand can have powerful impacts on the overall levels of output, employment, and prices in the short run.*

This chapter describes the basic features of the business cycle and presents the simplest theories of output determination. The structure of this chapter is as follows:

- We begin with a description of the key elements of the business cycle.
- We then summarize the basics of aggregate demand and show how the modern business cycle fits into that framework.
- Next, we develop the multiplier model—the simplest Keynesian example of a model of aggregate demand.
- We close with an application of the multiplier model to the question of the impact of fiscal policy on output.

---

② 从建国早期开始，美国经济始终处于商业周期中。

[3] fabulous 1990s，有的学者称作"The Fabulous Decade"，拟译作"鼓噪的十年"，指美国经济结构急剧变化的十年，即金融市场受互联网泡沫驱动极度膨胀而工资收入远远滞后的十年。

[4] Japan in the 1990s，也称作"A Lost Decade"，指日本经济受美国经济左右而低迷、徘徊，以致下滑的十年，拟译作"失落的十年"。

⑤ 凯恩斯主义经济学强调的是，总需求的变化会在短期内对产出、就业和价格总水平产生强有力的影响。

什么是商业周期

A. WHAT ARE BUSINESS CYCLES?

Economic history shows that no economy grows in a smooth and even pattern. A country may enjoy sev- ①
eral years of economic expansion and prosperity, with rapid increases in stock prices (as in the 1990s) or housing prices (as in the early 2000s). Then, the irrational exuberance may flip over to irrational pessimism as, during the 2007–2009 period, lenders stop issuing mortgages or car loans on favorable terms, banks slow their lending to businesses, and spending declines. Consequently, national output falls, unemployment rises, and profits and real incomes decline.

Eventually the bottom is reached and recovery begins. The recovery may be incomplete, or it may ②
be so strong as to lead to a new boom. Prosperity may mean a long, sustained period of brisk demand, plentiful jobs, and rising living standards. Or it may be marked by a quick, inflationary flare-up in prices and speculation, followed by another slump.

Upward and downward movements in output, inflation, interest rates, and employment form the business cycle that characterizes all market economies.

商业周期的特点
FEATURES OF THE BUSINESS CYCLE

What exactly do we mean by "business cycles"?

Business cycles are economywide fluctuations in ③
total national output, income, and employment, usually lasting for a period of 2 to 10 years, marked by widespread expansion or contraction in most sectors of the economy.

Economists typically divide business cycles into two main phases: *recession* and *expansion*. Peaks and troughs mark the turning points of the cycle. Figure 22-1 shows the successive phases of the business cycle. The downturn of a business cycle is called a recession. A ④
recession is a recurring period of decline in total output, income, and employment, usually lasting from 6 to 12 months and marked by contractions in many sectors of the economy. A recession that is large in both scale and duration is called a **depression.**

The semiofficial judge of the timing of contractions and expansions is the National Bureau [5]
of Economic Research (NBER), a private research organization. The NBER defines a recession as "a significant decline in economic activity spread across the economy, lasting more than a few months, normally visible in real GDP, real income, employment,

[5] National Bureau of Economic Research，国家经济研究局（NBER），美国最大规模的经济研究机构，成立于1920年，是一个非营利的无党派分歧的私人研究机构。成员中包括许多诺贝尔经济学奖得主。它对经济衰退期的起始和终结的研究有很高的权威性。

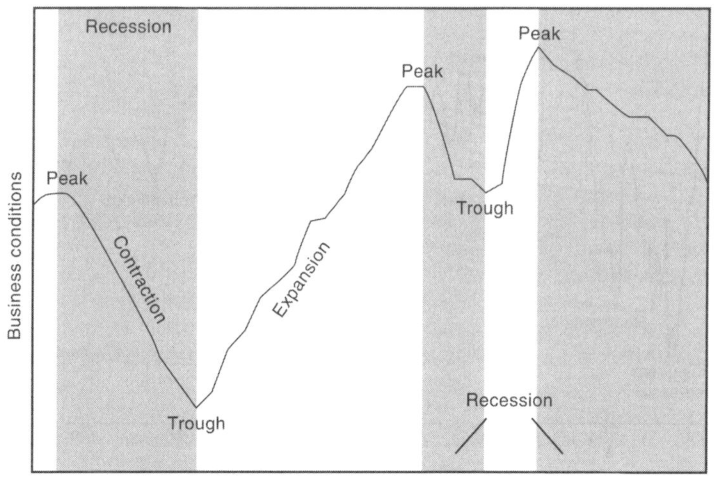

FIGURE 22-1. A Business Cycle, like the Year, Has Its Seasons

Business cycles are the irregular expansions and contractions in economic activity. (These are the actual monthly data on industrial production for a recent business-cycle period.)

① 一个国家会在几年中享受经济的扩张和繁荣（比如20世纪90年代），以及随之而来的股票价格和楼市价格的快速增长（比如21世纪初）。

② 经济可能不会完全复苏，也有可能强劲得足以启动新一轮经济繁荣。

③ **商业周期**系指国民总产出、总收入和总就业的整体波动，通常需要持续2~10年的时间，它以大多数经济部门的扩张或者紧缩为标志。

④ **衰退**是指总产出、总收入和总就业再一次出现的持续下滑期，通常延续6~12个月的时间，它以经济体中许多部门的紧缩为标志。持续时间长且规模大的衰退称作**萧条**。

① 虽然每一个商业周期各异，但常具有“家族”相似性。如果一位可信的经济预言家预测衰退即将发生的话，你预期会出现什么样的典型现象？

③ 通常情况下，就业情况会在衰退的早期出现急剧滑坡，但其复苏却常常滞后。这就是我们常讲的“无就业复苏”。

industrial production, and wholesale-retail sales." (See "Websites" at the end of this chapter for further information on dating of recessions.)

An alternative definition sometimes used is that a recession occurs when real GDP has declined for two consecutive calendar quarters. (Question 12 at the end of the chapter reviews the difference between the two definitions.)

Although we call these short-term fluctuations "cycles," the actual pattern is irregular. No two business cycles are quite the same. No exact formula, such as might apply to the revolutions of the planets or the swings of a pendulum, can be used to predict the duration and timing of business cycles. Rather, business cycles more closely resemble the irregular fluctuations of the weather. Figure 22-2 shows the American business cycles throughout recent history. Here you can see that business cycles are like mountain ranges, with some valleys that are deep and broad, as in the Great Depression, and others that are shallow and narrow, as in the recession of 1991.

While individual business cycles are not identical, ①
they often share a family similarity. If a reliable economic forecaster announces that a recession is about to arrive, what are the typical phenomena that you should expect? The following are a few of the *customary characteristics* of a recession:

- Investment usually falls sharply in recessions. Housing has generally been the first to decline, either because of a financial crisis or because the Federal Reserve has raised interest rates to slow [2]
inflation. Consumer purchases often decline sharply as well. As businesses slow production lines, real GDP falls.
- Employment usually falls sharply in the early stages ③
of a recession. It sometimes is slow to recover in what are often called "jobless recoveries."

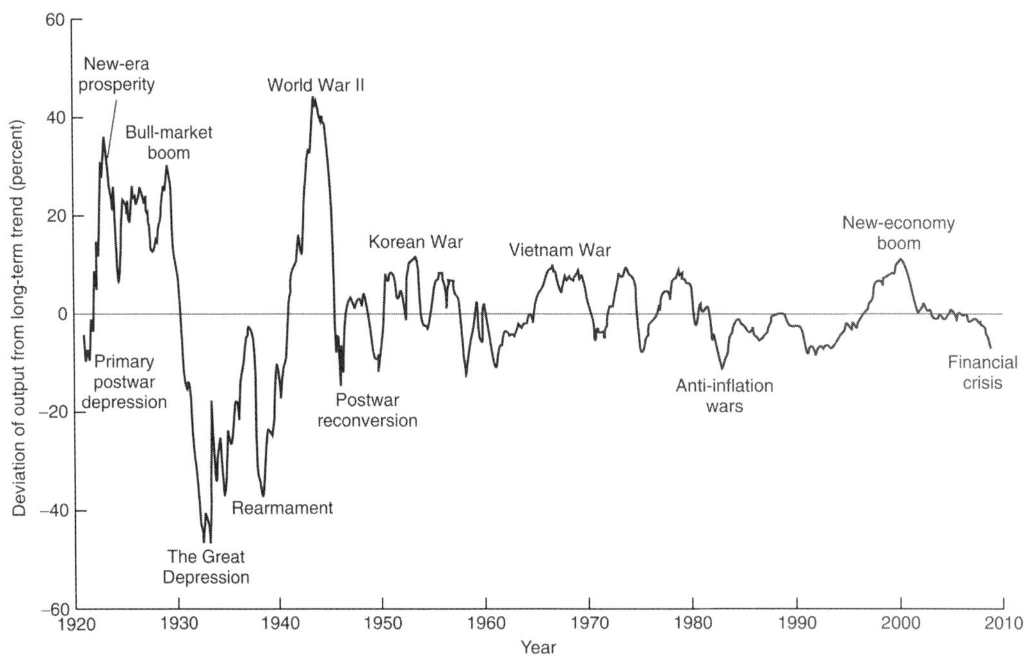

FIGURE 22-2. Business Activity since 1919

Industrial production has fluctuated irregularly around its long-run trend. Can you detect a more stable economy in recent years?

Source: Federal Reserve Board, detrended by authors.

[2] the Federal Reserve，美国联邦储备局，简称“美联储”，英文全称为 The Federal Reserve System，常缩写为“Fed”。该系统根据《联邦储备法》于 1913 年成立，负责履行美国中央银行的职责，由核心机构联邦储备委员会和另外两个主要机构——联邦公开市场委员会以及遍布全美 12 个储备区的联邦储备银行组成。美联储的成立还应该追溯到美国开国元勋亚历山大·汉密尔顿（Alexander Hamilton，1757~1804，美国第一任财政部长，美国宪法的起草人之一）。在美国开国之初，汉密尔顿顶着来自以杰弗逊（Thomas Jefferson，1743~1826，美国第三任总统，开国元勋之一，独立宣言的主要起草人）等人为首的众多反对者的巨大压力，于 1791 年 2 月 25 日经国会特许、华盛顿总统亲自签署成立了履行中央银行职责的第一美国银行，并设计和创建了全民信用体系，使美国的国家机器得以从建国之初就能够较为健康有效地运行。同时，也使汉密尔顿和杰弗逊与华盛顿一道各司其责，成为美国开国和建国的真正伟人。

- As output falls, inflation slows and the demand for crude materials declines, and materials' prices tumble. Wages and the prices of services are unlikely to face a similar decline, but they tend to rise less rapidly in economic downturns.
- Business profits fall sharply in recessions. In anticipation of this, common-stock prices usually fall as investors sniff the scent of a business downturn. ①
- Generally, as business conditions deteriorate and employment falls, the Federal Reserve begins to lower short-term interest rates to stimulate investment, and other interest rates decline as well.

商业周期理论
BUSINESS-CYCLE THEORIES

Exogenous vs. Internal Cycles. Over the years, macroeconomists have engaged in vigorous debates about the reasons for business fluctuations. Some think they are caused by monetary fluctuations, others by productivity shocks, and still others by changes in exogenous spending. ②

There is certainly no end to possible explanations, but it is useful to classify the different theories into two categories: exogenous and internal. The *exogenous* theories find the sources of the business cycle in the fluctuations of factors outside the economic system—in wars, revolutions, and elections; in oil prices, gold discoveries, and population migrations; in discoveries of new lands and resources; in scientific breakthroughs and technological innovations; even in sunspots, climate change, and the weather.

An example of an exogenous cycle was the outbreak of World War II. When Germany and Japan launched wars on Europe and the United States, this led to a rapid military buildup, large increases in spending, and an increase in aggregate demand that propelled the United States out of the Great Depression. Here we saw an exogenous event—a major war—that led to a huge increase in military spending and to the biggest economic expansion of the twentieth century. (We will examine this episode later in this chapter.) ③

By contrast, the *internal* theories look for mechanisms within the economic system itself. In this approach, every expansion breeds recession and contraction, and every contraction breeds revival and expansion. Many business cycles in U.S. economic history were internal cycles that originated in the financial sector. It is for this reason that we devote much of our attention to monetary and financial economics. ④

金融危机与商业周期
Financial Crises and Business Cycles

One common feature of capitalism around the world is the speculative booms and busts that occurred frequently in the nineteenth century, produced the upheaval of the Great Depression, and reappeared in the United States several times over the last two decades. Below are some important examples.

Panics of Early Capitalism. The nineteenth century witnessed frenzies of investment speculation—notably in canals, land, and railroads. Inevitably, "animal spirits" would take over. Railroads would be overbuilt, land prices would rise too high, and people would take on too much debt. Bankruptcy would lead to bank failures, a run on the banks, and a banking crisis. Output and prices would fall sharply in the panic. Eventually, after the worst excesses were wrung out, the economy would begin to expand again.

Hyperinflation. Sometimes, an overheated economy leads to high inflation, or even hyperinflation. Hyperinflation occurs when prices rise at 100 percent or more *per month.* The most famous hyperinflation in history occurred in Germany in 1923. The government was unable to meet its financial obligations through taxing and borrowing, so it turned to the monetary printing press. By the end of 1923, currency was printed with more and more digits, and the largest banknote in circulation was for 25 billion marks! Central banks today are vigilant in their defense against even the most moderate inflation.

[5] Germany in 1923，两次世界大战期间德国发生的恶性通货膨胀，在1923年这一年最为严重，物价飞涨，政府裁员1/3。

The New-Economy Bubble. The classic pattern of speculative boom was seen again in the late 1990s. The phenomenal pattern of growth and innovation in the "new-economy" sectors—including software, the Internet, and the newly invented dot.com companies—produced a speculative boom in new-economy stocks. Companies sold online dating services, gave away free electronic birthday cards, and issued stock for Flooz.com, which sold a worthless digital currency. College students dropped out of school to become instant millionaires (or so they dreamed). All of this spurred real investment in computers, software, and telecommunications. Investment in information-processing equipment rose by 70 percent from 1995 to 2000, representing one-fifth of the entire rise in real GDP during this period.

[6] Flooz.com，20世纪90年代后半期的互联网泡沫期，纽约一位滑稽演员表演的系列电视广告，系一个俄罗斯犯罪团伙所为，2001年被FBI通报。

---

① 企业的利润在衰退期内急剧地下滑。由于预期到这一点，普通股票的价格通常都会随之下跌，就好像投资者嗅出了经济低迷的气味一样。

② 长期以来，宏观经济学家关于商业周期起因的争论始终喋喋不休。

③ 这里我们看到的是一起外部事件，一场导致美国军费支出大幅增加的大规模战争，进而刺激了美国经济在20世纪最大程度的扩张。

④ 所不同的是，内因理论关注经济体系自身的运行机制问题。该理论认为，每一次经济扩张，都孕育着经济衰退和紧缩，而每一次紧缩又都孕育着复苏和扩张。美国经济史上的许多次商业周期，都是源自金融部门的内部周期。

Eventually, investors became skeptical about the fundamental value of many of these firms. Losses piled up on top of losses. The urge to buy the stocks before prices rose higher was replaced by the panicky desire to sell before they collapsed. The stock price of a typical new-economy company fell from $100 per share to pennies by 2003. Many such companies went bankrupt. College dropouts went back to school wiser but seldom richer.

The changed expectations about the new economy and the resulting stock market decline contributed to the recession and slow growth in the 2000–2002 period. Investment in information-processing equipment fell by 10 percent, and investment in computers fell by twice as much. The impressive innovations of the new economy have become a staple feature of modern technology, but, with a few exceptions, investors have little or no profits to show for their efforts.

The Housing Bubble. Less than a decade later, another ① financial crisis erupted, and this was again the result of rapid innovation. But in this case, the innovation was the process of financial "securitization." This occurs when a financial instrument, such as a simple home mortgage, is sliced and diced, repackaged, and then sold on securities markets. While securitization itself was not a new phenomenon, the scope of packaging and repackaging grew sharply. Rating agencies failed to provide accurate ratings of the riskiness of these new securities, and many people bought them thinking they were as good as gold. The worst examples were "subprime mortgages," mortgages provided to people for the entire value of a house on the basis of little or no documentation of their income and job status. By early 2007, the total value of these new securities was over $1 trillion.

All went well as long as housing prices were rising, as they did starting in 1995. But then in 2006 the housing bubble burst—echoing the end of the speculative dot.com stock-market bubble from a decade earlier. Many of the new securities lost value. It turned out they were not top-grade AAA securities but junk bonds. As banks and other financial institutions suffered large losses, they began to tighten credit, reduce loans, and cut back sharply on new mortgages. Risk premiums rose sharply.

The Federal Reserve took steps to ease monetary conditions—lowering interest rates and extending credit—but it was flying against powerful headwinds. As the value of stocks fell more sharply than at any time in a century, many financial institutions were on the verge of bankruptcy. Many of the large investment banking firms disappeared. The Federal Reserve and U.S. Treasury loaned massive amounts of federal money and bailed out several financial firms. Yet, even with the strong countercyclical activities, the economy went into a deep recession at the end of 2007.

You begin to see the theme running through all these events. The next few chapters survey our economic theories to explain them.

总需求与商业周期

B. AGGREGATE DEMAND AND BUSINESS CYCLES

We have now begun to understand the short-term changes in output, employment, and prices that characterize business fluctuations in market economies. Most explanations of business cycles rely upon the theory of aggregate demand. This section explains *AD* theory in greater detail.

总需求理论
THE THEORY OF AGGREGATE DEMAND

What are the major components of aggregate demand? How do they interact with aggregate supply to determine output and prices? Exactly how do short-run fluctuations in *AD* affect GDP? We first examine aggregate demand in more detail in order to get a better understanding of the forces driving the economy. Then, in the following sections, we derive the simplest model of aggregate demand: the multiplier model.

Aggregate demand (or *AD*) is the total or aggregate quantity of output that is willingly bought at a given level of prices, other things held constant. *AD* is the desired spending in all product sectors: consumption, private domestic investment, government purchases of goods and services, and net exports. It has four components: ②

1. *Consumption.* As we saw in the last chapter, consumption (*C*) is primarily determined by

① 相隔不到十年，一场金融危机再次席卷而来，这次又是快速创新的结果。所不同的是，这次是金融产品“证券化”过程的创新。这种创新是将某个金融产品，如住房抵押，在被块状切割并细分后再包装，然后在证券市场上出售。

② **总需求**（*AD*）系指在其他条件保持不变的前提下，人们愿意以某一给定价格购买的产出总量。总需求是所有生产部门（消费、国内私人投资、政府对商品和服务的购买和净出口）愿意支出的总量。

disposable income, which is personal income less taxes. Other factors affecting consumption are longer-term trends in income, household wealth, and the aggregate price level. Aggregate ① demand analysis focuses on the determinants of *real* consumption (that is, nominal or dollar consumption divided by the price index for consumption).

2. *Investment.* Investment (I) spending includes purchases of buildings, software, and equipment and accumulation of inventories. Our analysis in Chapter 21 showed that the major determinants of investment are the level of output, the cost of capital (as determined by tax policies along with interest rates and other financial conditions), and expectations about the future. The major channel by which economic policy can affect investment is monetary policy.
3. *Government purchases.* A third component of aggregate demand is government purchases of goods and services (G). This includes the purchases of goods like tanks and school books, as well as the services of judges and public-school teachers. Unlike private consumption and investment, this component of aggregate demand is determined directly by the government's spending decisions; when the Pentagon buys a new fighter aircraft, this output directly adds to the GDP.
4. *Net exports.* A final component of aggregate demand is net exports (X), which equal the value of exports minus the value of imports. Imports are determined by domestic income and output, by the ratio of domestic to foreign prices, and by the foreign exchange rate of the dollar. Exports (which are imports of other countries) are the mirror image of imports, and they are determined by foreign incomes and outputs, by relative prices, and by foreign exchange rates. Net exports, then, will be determined by domestic and foreign outputs, relative prices, and exchange rates.

Figure 22-3 shows the *AD* curve and its four major components. At price level *P*, we can read the levels of consumption, investment, government purchases, and net exports, which sum to GDP, or *Q*. The sum of the four spending streams at that price level is aggregate spending, or aggregate demand, at that price level.

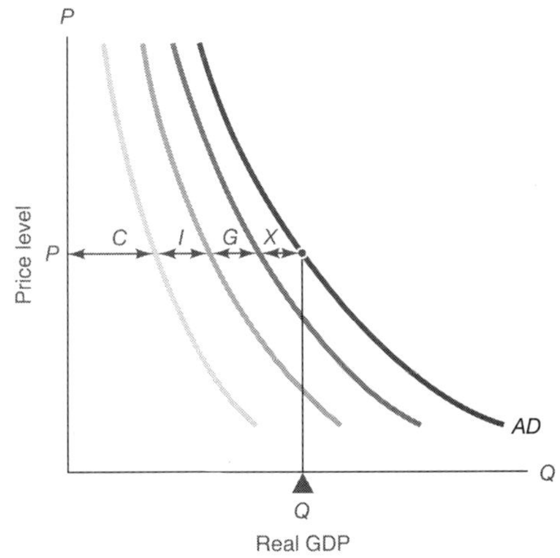

FIGURE 22-3. Components of Aggregate Demand

Aggregate demand (AD) consists of four components—consumption (C), domestic private investment (I), government spending on goods and services (G), and net exports (X).

Aggregate demand shifts when there are changes in macroeconomic policies (such as monetary-policy changes or changes in government expenditures or tax rates) or when exogenous events change spending (as would be the case with changes in foreign output, affecting X, or in business confidence, affecting I).

向下倾斜的总需求曲线
THE DOWNWARD-SLOPING AGGREGATE DEMAND CURVE

One important point you should notice is that the aggregate demand curve in Figure 22-3 slopes downward. This means that, holding other things constant, the level of real spending declines as the overall price level in the economy rises.

What is the reason for the downward slope? The basic reason is that there are some elements of income or wealth that do not rise when the price level rises. For example, some items of personal ② income might be set in nominal dollar terms—some government transfer payments, the minimum wage, and company pensions are examples. When the price level goes up, therefore, real disposable income falls, leading to a decline in real consumption expenditures.

---

① 总需求分析关注实际消费（即名义消费量或者货币消费量除以消费价格指数）的决定因素。

② 例如，有些个人收入项目就是以名义货币定义的，政府转移支付、最低工资以及企业养老金均是这样的例子。当价格水平上升之后，实际的可支配收入水平就会随之下滑，从而导致实际消费支出水平的下降。

In addition, some elements of wealth may be fixed in nominal terms. Examples here would be holdings of money and bonds, which usually contain promises to pay a certain number of dollars in a given period. If the price level rises, therefore, the real value of ① wealth declines, and this would again lead to lower levels of real consumption.

We illustrate the impact of a higher price level graphically in Figure 22-4(*a*) on page 436. Say that the economy is in equilibrium at point *B*, with a price level of 100 and a real GDP of $3000 billion. Next assume that prices rise by 50 percent, so the price index *P* rises from 100 to 150. Suppose that at that higher price level, real spending declines because of lower real disposable income. Total real spending declines to $2000 billion, shown at point *C*. We see here how higher prices have reduced real spending.

To summarize:

The *AD* curve slopes downward. This downward ② slope implies that real spending declines as the price level rises, other things held constant. Real spending declines with a higher price level primarily because of the effect of higher prices on real incomes and real wealth.

总需求的移动

Shifts in Aggregate Demand

We have seen that total spending in the economy tends to decline as the price level rises, holding other things constant. But those other things do in fact tend to change, thereby producing changes in aggregate demand. What are the key determinants of changes in aggregate demand?

We can separate the determinants of *AD* into two categories, as shown in Table 22-1. One set includes

Variable	Impact on aggregate demand
	Policy Variables
Monetary policy	Monetary expansion may lower interest rates and loosen credit conditions, inducing higher levels of investment and consumption of durable goods. In an open economy, monetary policy also affects the exchange rate and net exports.
Fiscal policy	Increases in government purchases of goods and services directly increase spending; tax reductions or increases in transfers raise disposable income and induce higher consumption. Tax incentives like an investment tax credit can induce higher spending in a particular sector.
	Exogenous Variables
Foreign output	Output growth abroad leads to an increase in net exports.
Asset values	Rise in stock market increases household wealth and thereby increases consumption; also, higher stock prices lower the cost of capital and thereby increase business investment.
Advances in technology	Technological advances can open up new opportunities for business investment. Important examples have been the railroad, the automobile, and computers.
Other	Defeat of a socialist government stimulates foreign investment; peace breaks out, with an increase in world oil production, and lowers oil prices; good weather leads to lower food prices.

TABLE 22-1. Many Factors Can Increase Aggregate Demand and Shift out the *AD* Curve

The aggregate demand curve relates total spending to the price level. But numerous other influences affect aggregate demand—some policy variables, others exogenous factors. The table lists changes that would tend to increase aggregate demand and shift out the *AD* curve.

① 如果价格水平上升，则财富的实际价值就会下降，从而导致实际消费水平的再一次降低。

② 总需求曲线是向下倾斜的。向下倾斜指在其他条件保持不变的条件下，在价格水平上升时，实际支出会随之下降。由于价格水平的攀升而导致的实际支出的下降，主要是因为更高的价格对实际收入和实际财富施加的影响造成的。

the macroeconomic *policy variables*, which are under government control. These are monetary policy (steps by which the central bank can affect interest rates and other financial conditions) and fiscal policy (taxes and government expenditures). Table 22-1 illustrates how these government policies can affect different components of aggregate demand.

The second set includes *exogenous variables*, or variables that are determined outside the *AS-AD* framework. As Table 22-1 shows, some of these vari- ①
ables (such as wars or revolutions) are outside the scope of macroeconomic analysis proper, some (such as foreign economic activity) are outside the control of domestic policy, and others (such as the stock market) have significant independent movement.

What are the effects of changes in the variables lying behind the *AD* curve? Consider the economic effects of a sharp increase in military spending, such as took place in World War II. The additional costs of the war included pay for the troops, purchases of ammunition and equipment, and costs of transportation. The effect of these purchases was an increase in *G*. Unless some other component of spending decreased to offset the increase in *G*, the total *AD* curve would shift out and to the right as *G* increased. Similarly, a radical new innovation that increased the profitability of new investment, or an increase in consumer wealth because of higher housing prices, would lead to an increase in aggregate demand and an outward shift of the *AD* curve.

Figure 22-4(*b*) on page 436 shows how the changes in the variables listed in Table 22-1 would affect the *AD* curve. To test your understanding, construct a similar table showing forces that would tend to decrease aggregate demand (see question 2 at the end of the chapter).

Two Reminders

We pause for two important reminders.

1. We first emphasize the difference ②
between macroeconomic and microeconomic demand curves. Recall from our study of supply and demand that the microeconomic demand curve has the price of an individual commodity on the vertical axis and production of that commodity on the horizontal axis, with all other prices and total consumer incomes held constant.

In the aggregate demand curve, the general price level is on the vertical axis, while total output and incomes vary along the horizontal axis. By contrast, total incomes and output are held constant for the microeconomic demand curve.

Finally, the negative slope of the microeconomic demand curve occurs because consumers substitute other goods for the good in question when its price rises. If the price of meat rises, the quantity demanded falls because consumers tend to substitute bread and potatoes for meat, using more of the relatively inexpensive commodities and less of the relatively expensive one.

The aggregate demand curve is downward-sloping for completely different reasons: Total spending falls when the overall price level rises because consumer real incomes and real wealth fall, reducing consumption, and interest rates rise, reducing investment spending.

2. Remember also the important distinction between ③
the *movement along* a curve and the *shift of* a curve. Figure 22-4(*a*) shows a case of movement along the aggregate demand curve. This might occur when higher oil prices reduce real disposable income. Figure 22-4(*b*) shows a shift of the aggregate demand curve. This might occur because of a sharp increase in war spending. Always keep this distinction in mind as you analyze a particular policy or shock.

商业周期与总需求
Business Cycles and Aggregate Demand

One important source of business fluctuations is shocks to aggregate demand. A typical case is illustrated in Figure 22-5 on page 436, which shows how a decline in aggregate demand lowers output. Say that the economy begins in short-run equilibrium at point *B*. Then, perhaps because of a financial panic or a tax increase, the aggregate demand curve shifts leftward to *AD*′. If there is no change in aggregate supply, the economy will reach a new equilibrium at point *C*. Note that output declines from *Q* to *Q*′. In addition, prices are now lower than they were at the previous equilibrium, and the rate of inflation falls.

The case of an economic expansion is just the opposite. Suppose that a war leads to a sharp increase in government spending. As a result, the *AD* curve would shift to the right, output and employment would increase, and prices and inflation would rise.

Business-cycle fluctuations in output, employ- ④
ment, and prices are often caused by shifts in aggregate demand. These occur as consumers, businesses,

① 如表 7-1 所示，这类变量中有的（诸如战争或者革命）完全超出了宏观经济分析的范畴，有的（如外国的经济活动）超出了国内政策的控制范围，还有的（如股票市场）则具有显著的独立变动性。

② 我们首先强调的是宏观经济学的需求曲线和微观经济学的需求曲线之间的区别。回顾一下我们对供给和需求的讨论，微观经济学中的需求曲线以纵轴表示单个商品的价格，以横轴来表示该种商品的产量，前提是，其他所有商品的价格和消费者的总收入保持不变。

③ 此外需要记住的是，沿曲线的运动和曲线自身的移动之间的显著区别。

④ 商业周期在产出、就业和价格上的波动，常常是总需求的变化所致。这些变化的产生，是由于消费者、企业或者政府相对于该经济体的生产能力，在总支出上发生了变化。当总需求的这些变化导致经济急剧下滑时，该经济体即陷入了衰退甚至萧条之中。经济活动的急剧升温则会引发通货膨胀。

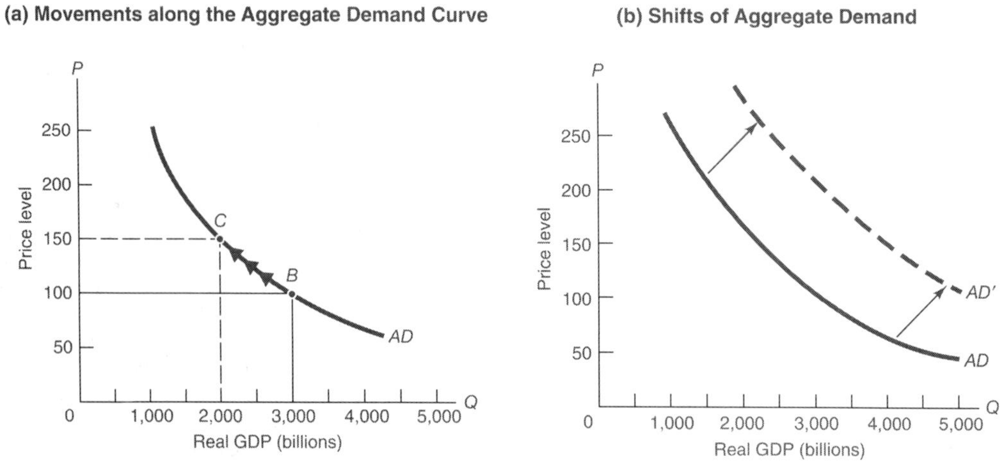

FIGURE 22-4. Movement along vs. Shifts of the Aggregate Demand Curve

In (**a**), a higher price level with given nominal money incomes lowers real disposable income; this leads to higher interest rates and declining spending on interest-sensitive investment and consumption. This illustrates a *movement along* the *AD* curve from *B* to *C* when other things are held constant.

In (**b**), other things are no longer constant. Changes in variables underlying *AD*—such as the money supply, tax policy, or military spending—lead to changes in total spending at a given price level. This leads to a *shift of* the *AD* curve.

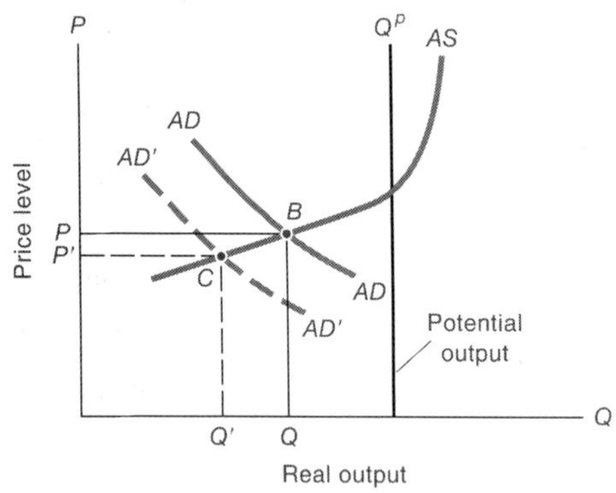

FIGURE 22-5. A Decline in Aggregate Demand Leads to an Economic Downturn

A downward shift in the *AD* curve along a relatively flat and unchanging *AS* curve leads to lower levels of output. Note that as a result of the leftward shift in the *AD* curve, actual output declines relative to potential output and makes a recession worse.

or governments change total spending relative to the economy's productive capacity. When these shifts in aggregate demand lead to sharp business downturns, the economy suffers recessions or even depressions. A sharp upturn in economic activity can lead to inflation.

商业周期可否避免
Is the Business Cycle Avoidable?

The history of business cycles in the United States shows a remarkable trend toward greater stability in the last quarter-century (look back at Figure 22-2). The period through 1940 witnessed numerous crises and depressions—prolonged, cumulative slumps
like those of the 1870s, 1890s, and 1930s. Since [1][2]
1945, business cycles have become less frequent and milder, and many Americans have never witnessed a real Depression.

What were the sources of the Great Modera- [3]
tion? Some believe that capitalism is inherently more stable now than it was in earlier times. Some of that stability comes from a larger and more predictable government sector. Equally important is a better

[1] 1870s，指南北战争后的1870年代，由于棉花价格的走低引发南方的经济衰退。

[2] 1890s，所谓的“镀金时代”，社会财富迅速增加而经济秩序极度混乱，腐败现象严重。这一时期开始出现了一批美国文学史上的大家，他们的作品通过抨击丑陋和暴露政治腐败以唤醒民众，从而促使1901年上任的罗斯福总统痛下决心改革。

[3] Great Moderation，出自哈佛大学经济学教授 James Stock（1955~）和普林斯顿大学教授 Mark Watson 联名发表在《美国国家经济研究局宏观经济年刊，2002》上的文章 *Has the Business Cycle Changed and Why?*，意为“大调整”。

understanding of macroeconomics that now permits the government to conduct its monetary and fiscal policies so as to prevent shocks from turning into recessions and to keep recessions from snowballing into depressions.

During tranquil periods, people often declare that the business cycle has been vanquished. Is this a realistic possibility? While business cycles have moderated in America over the last quarter-century, they have actually become more prevalent in other economies. So take heed of the following prophetic words of the great macroeconomist Arthur Okun, which are particularly appropriate as the world economy heads into recession in 2007–2009:

> Recessions are now generally considered to be fundamentally preventable, like airplane crashes and unlike hurricanes. But we have not banished air crashes from the land, and it is not clear that we have the wisdom or the ability to eliminate recessions. The danger has not disappeared. The forces that produce recurrent recessions are still in the wings, merely waiting for their cue. ①

乘数模型

C. THE MULTIPLIER MODEL

The basic macroeconomic theory of business cycles holds that shifts in aggregate demand produce the frequent and unpredictable fluctuations in output, prices, and employment known as business cycles. Economists try to understand the *mechanism* by which changes in spending get translated into changes in output and employment. The simplest approach to understanding business cycles is known as the *Keynesian multiplier model.* [2]

When economists attempt to understand why major increases in military spending led to rapid increases in GDP, or why the tax cuts of the 1960s or 1980s ushered in long periods of business-cycle expansions, or why the investment boom of the late 1990s produced America's longest expansion, they often turn to the Keynesian multiplier model for the simplest explanation.

What exactly is the **multiplier model?** It is a macroeconomic theory used to explain how output is determined in the short run. The name "multiplier" comes from the finding that each dollar change in exogenous expenditures (such as investment) leads to more than a dollar change (or a multiplied change) in GDP. ③ The key assumptions underlying the multiplier model are that wages and prices are fixed and that there are unemployed resources in the economy. In addition, in this introductory chapter, we are ignoring the role of monetary policy and assuming that financial markets do not react to changes in the economy. Additionally, we are for now assuming that there is no international trade and finance. These further elaborations will be introduced in later chapters.

总支出决定的产出
OUTPUT DETERMINED BY TOTAL EXPENDITURES

Our initial discussion of the multiplier model analyzes how investment and consumption spending interact with incomes to determine national output. This is called the *total expenditure approach* to determining national output.

Recall Chapter 21's picture of the national consumption function. We have drawn a reminder graph in Figure 22-6, where the consumption function is

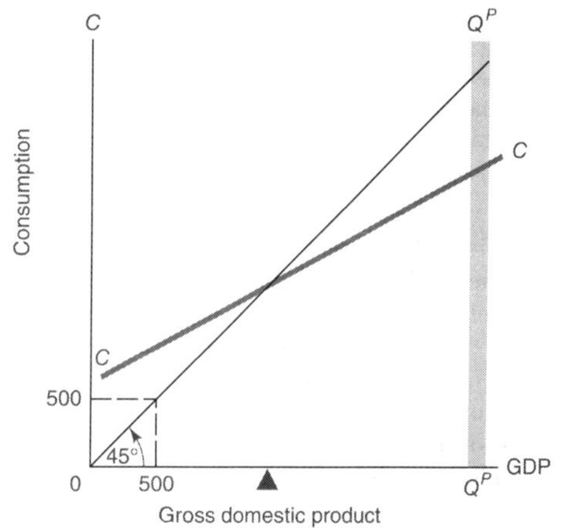

FIGURE 22-6. National Income Determines the Level of Consumption

Recall the consumption function, *CC*, that was described in Chapter 21. This shows the level of consumption expenditures corresponding to every level of income (where income equals GDP in this simple example). The two points marked "500" emphasize the important property of the 45° line. Any point on the 45° line depicts a vertical distance exactly equal to the horizontal distance. The blue band marked Q_pQ_p shows the level of potential GDP.

[2] *Keynesian multiplier model*：凯恩斯乘数模型，源自1936年在牛津大学举行的《经济学大会》上，哈罗德爵士（Roy Harrod，1900~1978），希克斯（John Hicks，1904~1989）和米德（James Meade，1907~1995，1977年和瑞典经济学家欧林分享当年的诺贝尔经济学奖）三位著名的经济学家联名宣布的 *Investment—Saving / Liquidity preference—Money supply* 数学模型，旨在诠释凯恩斯《通论》中关于利率和实际产出之间关系的宏观经济学理论。

① 现在普遍认为，衰退就好像空难一样，从本质上讲是可以阻止的，它和飓风截然不同。但是，我们却从来没有在我们的土地上根除空难事故，同样也不清楚我们消除衰退的智慧和能力。危险并未散去。引发周期性衰退的力量依然存在，只在伺机爆发。

③ 这一**乘数模型**的确切内容是什么？它是用来解释短期内如何确定产出的宏观经济学理论。"乘数"的命名来自这样一个发现，即外生支出（如投资）中每变化一美元，会带来GDP超过一美元的变化（或称乘数变化）。

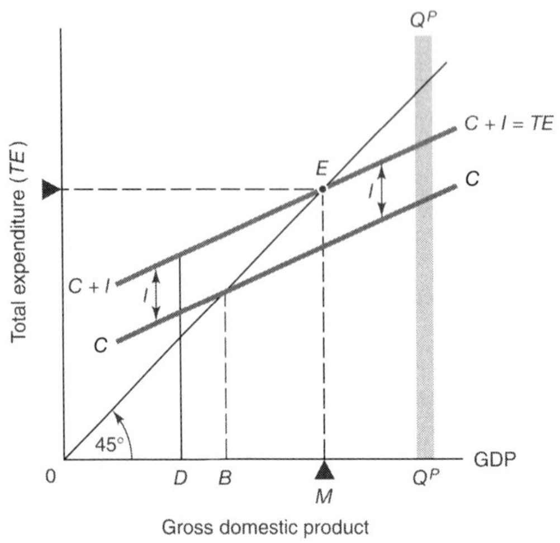

FIGURE 22-7. The Equilibrium Level of National Output Is Determined When Total Expenditure (*TE*) Equals Output

The blue *CC* line represents the consumption function (shown in Figure 22-6). The *II* arrows indicate constant investment. Adding *II* to *CC* gives the *TE* curve of total desired investment plus consumption spending. Along the 45° line, expenditures exactly equal GDP. Equilibrium GDP comes at point *E*, which is the intersection of the *TE* line and the 45° line. This is the only level of GDP at which the desired spending on $C + I$ exactly equals output.

the *CC* line. Recall that the consumption function shows the desired consumption corresponding to each level of income. We have omitted taxes, transfers, and other items, so that personal income equals national income, and national income equals GDP.

We now develop in Figure 22-7 an important new graph showing the total expenditure-output relationship. This graph is sometimes called the "Keynesian cross," [1] because it shows how output equals expenditure when the expenditure curve crosses the 45° line. (If you are not sure about the significance of the 45° line, look back at Chapter 21's explanation.)

We begin by drawing the consumption function, *CC*. We then add total investment to consumption. Normally, investment depends on interest rates, tax policy, and business confidence. To simplify things, we treat investment as an *exogenous* variable, one whose level is determined outside the model. Say that investment opportunities are such that investment would be exactly $200 billion per year regardless of the level of GDP. The investment schedule is stacked on top of the consumption schedule in Figure 22-7. Note that the $C + I$ curve is higher than the *C* curve by exactly the constant amount of *I*. This parallel feature indicates that investment is constant.

This $C + I$ curve represents total expenditures (*TE*), which equals desired investment (which is at fixed level *I*) plus consumption. This is drawn in Figure 22-7 as the green $C + I$ or *TE* curve.

Finally, we draw in a 45° line along which expenditure on the vertical axis exactly equals output on the horizontal axis. At any point on the 45° line, total desired expenditure (measured vertically) exactly equals the total level of output (measured horizontally).

We can now calculate the equilibrium level of output in Figure 22-7. Where planned expenditure, represented by the *TE* curve, equals total output, the economy is in equilibrium.

The total expenditure curve (*TE*) shows the level of expenditure desired or planned by consumers and businesses corresponding to each level of output. The economy is in equilibrium at the point where the $TE = C + I$ curve crosses the 45° line—at point *E* in Figure 22-7. Point *E* is the macroeconomic equilibrium because at that point, the level of desired expenditure on consumption and investment exactly equals the level of total output. ②

均衡含义提示
Reminder on the Meaning of Equilibrium

We often look for a macroeconomic "equilibrium" when analyzing business cycles or economic growth. What exactly does this term mean? An **equilibrium** is a situation where the different forces at work are in balance. For example, if you see a ball rolling down a hill, the ball is not in equilibrium because the forces at work are pulling the ball down. This is therefore a **disequilibrium.** When the ball comes to rest in a valley at the bottom of the hill, the forces operating on the ball are in balance. This is therefore an equilibrium. ③

Similarly, in macroeconomics, an equilibrium level of output is one where the different forces of spending and output are in balance; in equilibrium, the level of output tends to persist until there are changes in the forces affecting the economy.

---

[1] Keynesian Cross：Keynesian Cross Diagram，凯恩斯交叉图，也称 45° 线图（45-degree line diagram）。

② 总支出曲线（*TE*）系指，相对于每一项产出水平上，消费者和企业所期望或者计划的支出水平。在图 22-7 中 $TE = C + I$ 曲线和 45° 线的交点 *E*，表示经济处于均衡状态。点 *E* 是宏观经济均衡点，因为在这一点上，消费和投资期望支出水平正好等于总产出水平。

③ **均衡**是不同的作用力处于均衡时的一种状态。比如，假设你看见一个球从山上滚下来，那么，这个球就处在不平衡状态，因为所有的作用力都在将其从山上推下来。这就是**非均衡**状态。当这个球滚到山脚下的谷底停下来之后，所有作用在这个球上的力量就处于平衡状态。这就是我们所讲的均衡。

Applying the equilibrium concept to Figure 22-7, we see that point *E* is an equilibrium. At point *E*, and only at point *E*, does *desired spending on* C + I *equal actual output*. At any other level of production, desired spending would differ from production. At any level other than *E*, businesses would find themselves producing too little or too much and would want to change the level of production back toward the equilibrium level.

调节机制
The Adjustment Mechanism

It is not enough to say that point *E* is an equilibrium. We need to understand *why* a certain output is an equilibrium and what would happen if output deviated from that equilibrium. Let's consider three cases: planned spending above output, planned spending below output, and planned spending equal to output.

In the first case, suppose that spending is above output. This is represented by point *D* in Figure 22-7. At this level of output, the *C* + *I* spending line is above the 45° line, so planned *C* + *I* spending would be greater than output. This means that consumers would be buying more goods than businesses had anticipated. Auto dealers would find their lots emptying, and the backlog for computers would be getting longer and longer.

In such a disequilibrium situation, auto dealers and computer stores would respond by increasing their orders. Automakers would recall workers from layoff and gear up their production lines, while computer makers would add additional shifts. As a result ① of this increased production, output would increase. *Therefore, a discrepancy between total planned expenditure and total output leads to an adjustment of output.*

You should also work through what happens in the second case, where output is below equilibrium.

Finally, take the third case, where planned expenditure exactly equals output. At equilibrium, firms will find that their sales are equal to their forecasts. Inventories will be at their planned levels. There will not be any unexpected orders. Firms cannot improve profits by changing output because planned consumption needs have been met. So production, employment, income, and spending will remain the same. In this case GDP stays at point *E*, and we can rightly call it an *equilibrium*.

The equilibrium level of GDP occurs at point *E*, ② where planned spending equals planned production. At any other output, the total desired spending on consumption and investment differs from the planned production. Any deviation of plans from actual levels will cause businesses to change their production and employment levels, thereby returning the system to the equilibrium GDP.

数据分析
A Numerical Analysis

An example may help show why the equilibrium level of output occurs where planned spending and planned output are equal.

Table 22-2 shows a simple example of consumption, saving, and output. The break-even level of income, where consumption equals income, is \$3000 billion (\$3 trillion). Each \$300 billion change of income is assumed to lead to a \$100 billion change in saving and a \$200 billion change in consumption. In other words, the *MPC* is assumed to be constant and equal to ⅔.

We assume that investment is exogenous and always sustainable at \$200 billion, as shown in column (4) of Table 22-2.

Columns (5) and (6) are the crucial ones. Column (5) shows the total GDP. It is simply column (1) copied again into column (5). The figures in ③ column (6) represent total planned expenditures at each level of GDP; that is, it equals the planned consumption spending plus planned investment. It is the *C* + *I* schedule from Figure 22-7 in numbers.

When businesses as a whole are producing too ④ much output (higher than the sum of what consumers and businesses want to purchase), inventories of unsold goods will be piling up.

Reading from the top row of Table 22-2, we see that if firms are initially producing \$4200 billion of GDP, planned or desired spending [shown in column (6)] is only \$4000 billion. In this situation, excess inventories will be accumulating. Firms will respond by reducing their production levels, and GDP will fall. In the opposite case, represented in the bottom row of Table 22-2, total spending is \$3000 billion but output is only \$2700 billion. Inventories are being depleted and firms will expand operations, raising output.

We see, then, that when businesses as a whole are temporarily producing more than they can profitably sell, they will reduce production and GDP will fall. When they are selling more than their current production, they will increase their output, and GDP will rise.

---

① 生产增加的结果，导致产出的相应增加。由此，计划总支出与总产出之间的差异就导致了产出的调整。

② GDP 的均衡水平出现在 *E* 点，在这一点上，计划的支出与计划的产量相等。在任何其他产出水平上，在消费和投资项目上期望的总支出与计划的产量均不相同。任何偏离实际水平的计划都将导致企业改变自身的产量与就业水平，从而使得整个经济体系恢复到 GDP 的均衡状态。

③ 第六栏中的数据表示的是每一 GDP 水平上的计划总支出。这一支出，等于计划的消费支出与计划投资之和，即用数字表示的图 22-7 中的 *C* + *I* 曲线。

④ 当企业作为一个整体生产的产出过量（即高于消费者与企业应该正常购买的总量）时，未予出售的商品库存量势必出现积压。

GDP Determination Where Output Equals Planned Spending
(billions of dollars)

(1) Levels of GDP and *DI*	(2) Planned consumption	(3) Planned saving (3) = (1) − (2)	(4) Planned investment	(5) Level of GDP (5) = (1)		(6) Total planned consumption and investment, *TE* (6) = (2) + (4)	(7) Resulting tendency of output
4,200	3,800	**400**	**200**	4,200	>	4,000	Contraction
3,900	3,600	**300**	**200**	3,900	>	3,800 ↓	Contraction
3,600	**3,400**	**200**	**200**	**3,600**	=	**3,600**	**Equilibrium**
3,300	3,200	**100**	**200**	3,300	<	3,400 ↑	Expansion
3,000	3,000	**0**	**200**	3,000	<	3,200	Expansion
2,700	2,800	**−100**	**200**	2,700	<	3,000	Expansion

TABLE 22-2. Equilibrium Output Can Be Found Arithmetically at the Level Where Planned Spending Equals GDP

The darker green row depicts the equilibrium GDP level, where the $3600 that is being produced is just matched by the $3600 that households plan to consume and that firms plan to invest. In upper rows, firms will be forced into unintended inventory investment and will respond by cutting back production until equilibrium GDP is reached. Interpret the lower rows' tendency toward expansion of GDP toward equilibrium.

Only when the level of actual output in column (5) exactly equals planned expenditure (*TE*) in column (6) will the economy be in equilibrium. In equilibrium, and only in equilibrium, business sales will be exactly sufficient to justify the current level of aggregate output. In equilibrium, GDP will neither expand nor contract. ①

乘 数
THE MULTIPLIER

Where is the multiplier in all this? To answer this question, we need to examine how a change in exogenous investment spending affects GDP. It is logical that an increase in investment will raise the level of output and employment. But by how much? The multiplier model shows that an increase in investment will increase GDP by an amplified or multiplied amount—by an amount greater than itself.

The **multiplier** is the impact of a 1-dollar change in exogenous expenditures on total output. In the simple $C + I$ model, the multiplier is the ratio of the change in total output to the change in investment. ②

Note that the definition of the multiplier speaks of the change in output per unit change in *exogenous expenditures*. This indicates that we are taking certain components of spending as given outside the model. In the case in hand, the exogenous component is investment. Later, we will see that the same approach can be used to determine the effect of changes in government expenditures, exports, and other items on total output. ③

For example, suppose investment increases by $100 billion. If this causes an increase in output of $300 billion, the multiplier is 3. If, instead, the resulting increase in output is $400 billion, the multiplier is 4.

Woodsheds and Carpenters. Why is it that the multiplier is greater than 1? Let's suppose that I hire unemployed workers to build a $1000 woodshed. My carpenters and lumber producers will get an extra $1000 of income. But that is not the end of the story. If they all have a marginal propensity to consume of ⅔, they will now spend $666.67 on new consumption goods. The producers of these goods will now have extra incomes of $666.67. If their *MPC* is also ⅔, they in turn will spend $444.44, or ⅔ of $666.67 (or ⅔ of ⅔ of $1000). The process will go on, with each new round of spending being ⅔ of the previous round.

① 只有当第五栏中所示的实际产出恰好等于第六栏中的计划支出（*TE*）时，经济才处于均衡状态。在均衡状态下，也只有在达到均衡的情况下，企业的销售量才正好证明现有的总产出水平。GDP也只有在这样的均衡状态下，才能实现既不膨胀也不紧缩。

② **乘数**系指外生支出每变化一美元对总产出的影响。在简单的$C + I$模型中，乘数是总产出的变化与投资变化之间的比率。

③ 注意，乘数的定义强调的是外生支出每变化一单位，体现在产出的变化。这说明，支出的某个组成部分，是在该模型之外给定的。

Thus an endless chain of *secondary consumption spending* is set in motion by my *primary* investment of \$1000. But, although an endless chain, it is an ever-diminishing one. Eventually it adds up to a finite amount. ①

Using straightforward arithmetic, we can find the total increase in spending in the following manner:

$$\left.\begin{array}{c}\$1000.00\\+\\666.67\\+\\444.44\\+\\296.30\\+\\197.53\\+\\\vdots\\\hline\$3000.00\end{array}\right\}=\left\{\begin{array}{r}1\times\$1000\\+\\\tfrac{2}{3}\times\$1000\\+\\(\tfrac{2}{3})^2\times\$1000\\+\\(\tfrac{2}{3})^3\times\$1000\\+\\(\tfrac{2}{3})^4\times\$1000\\+\\\vdots\\\hline\dfrac{1}{1-\frac{2}{3}}\times\$1000,\text{ or }3\times\$1000\end{array}\right.$$

This shows that, with a *MPC* of ⅔, the multiplier is 3; it consists of the 1 of primary investment plus 2 extra of secondary consumption respending.

The same arithmetic would give a multiplier of 4 for a *MPC* of ¾, because $1 + \frac{3}{4} + (\frac{3}{4})^2 + (\frac{3}{4})^3 + \ldots$ eventually adds up to 4. For a *MPC* of ½, the multiplier would be 2.[1]

The size of the multiplier thus depends upon how large the *MPC* is. It can also be expressed in terms of the twin concept, the *MPS*. For a *MPS* of ¼, the *MPC* is ¾ and the multiplier is 4. For a *MPS* of ⅓, the multiplier is 3. If the *MPS* were $1/x$, the multiplier would be x.

By this time it should be clear that the simple multiplier is always the inverse, or reciprocal, of the marginal propensity to save. It is thus equal to $1/(1 - MPC)$. Our simple multiplier formula is

$$\begin{aligned}\text{Change in output} &= \frac{1}{MPS}\times\text{change in investment}\\&=\frac{1}{1-MPC}\times\text{change in investment}\end{aligned}$$

[1] The formula for an infinite geometric progression is

$$1 + r + r^2 + r^3 + \cdots + r^n + \cdots = \frac{1}{1-r}$$

as long as *MPC* (r) is less than 1 in absolute value.

乘数模型与 AS—AD 模型比较
The Multiplier Model Compared with the AS-AD Model

As you study the multiplier model, you might begin to wonder how this model fits in with the *AS-AD* model of Chapter 19. These are not, in fact, different approaches. Rather, the multiplier model is a special case of the aggregate demand-and-supply model. It explains how *AD* is affected by consumption and investment spending under certain precise assumptions.

One of the key assumptions in the multiplier analysis is that prices and wages are fixed in the short run. This is an oversimplification, for many prices adjust quickly in the real world. But this assumption captures the point that if some wages and prices are sticky—which is most definitely the case—then some of the adjustment to *AD* shifts will come through output adjustments. We will return to this important point in later chapters.

We can show the relationship between the multiplier analysis and the *AS-AD* approach in Figure 22-8. Part (*b*) displays an *AS* curve that becomes completely vertical when output equals potential output. However, when there are unemployed resources—to the left of potential output in the graph—output will be determined primarily by the strength of aggregate demand. As investment increases, this increases *AD*, and equilibrium output rises.

The same economy can be described by the multiplier diagram in the top panel of Figure 22-8. The multiplier equilibrium gives the same level of output as the *AS-AD* equilibrium—both lead to a real GDP of *Q*. They simply stress different features of output determination.

This discussion again points to a crucial feature of the multiplier model. While it is a useful model for describing recessions or even depressions, it cannot apply to periods of full employment. Once factories are operating at full capacity and all workers are employed, the economy simply cannot produce more output. ②

乘数模型中的财政政策
D. FISCAL POLICY IN THE MULTIPLIER MODEL

For centuries, economists have understood the *allocational* role of fiscal policy (government tax and spending programs). It has long been known that ③

① 这样，我最初投入的 1 000 美元，就被二次消费支出滚动起来，成为一条无休止的链条。但这是一条逐渐缩减的无休止链条。最终累加的结果是一个有限量。

② 这一节的讨论再一次指出了乘数模型的一个极其重要的特点。虽然它是一个非常有用的描述衰退甚至萧条的模型，但却无法应用于充分就业时期。一旦各家工厂以最大产能运作，所有工人都就业，很简单，该经济体就不能再增加产出了。

③ 早已众所周知的是，财政计划有助于决定国民产出如何在集体消费和个体消费之间分配，以及集体消费商品的支付负担如何在人口间分配。

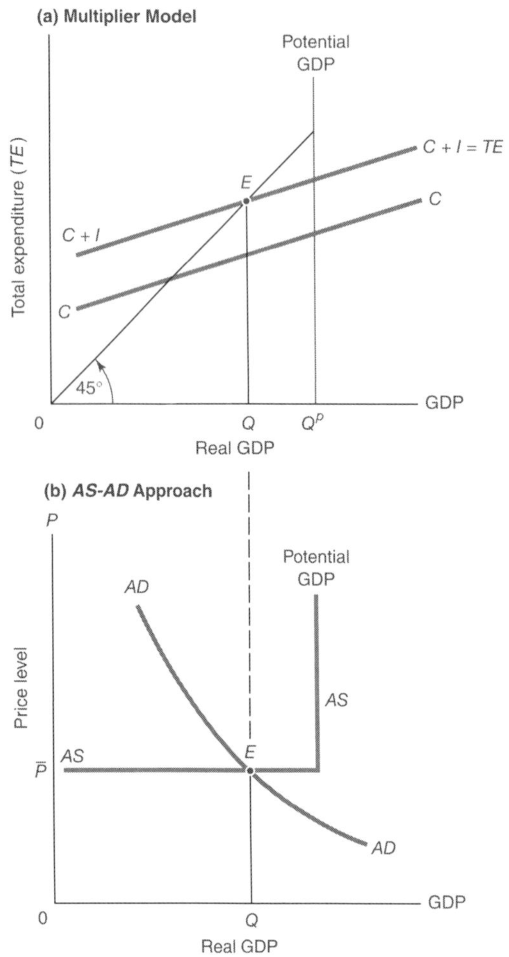

FIGURE 22-8. How the Multiplier Model Relates to the *AS-AD* Approach

The multiplier model is a way of understanding the workings of the *AS-AD* equilibrium.

(a) The top panel shows the output-expenditure equilibrium in the multiplier model. At point *E*, the spending line just cuts the 45° line, leading to equilibrium output of *Q*.

(b) The equilibrium can also be seen in the bottom panel, where the *AD* curve cuts the *AS* curve at point *E*. In this simplest business-cycle model wages and prices are assumed to be fixed, so the *AS* curve is horizontal until full employment is reached. Both approaches lead to exactly the same equilibrium output, *Q*.

fiscal programs are instrumental in deciding how the nation's output should be divided between collective and private consumption and how the burden of payment for collective goods should be divided among the population.

Only with the development of modern macroeconomic theory has a surprising fact been uncovered: Government fiscal powers also have a major *macroeconomic* impact upon the short-run movements of output, employment, and prices. The knowledge that fiscal policy has powerful effects upon economic activity led to the *Keynesian approach to macroeconomic* ① *policy,* which is the active use of government action to moderate business cycles. This approach was described by the Nobel Prize–winning macroeconomist James Tobin as follows:

> Keynesian policies are, first, the explicit dedica- ②
> tion of macroeconomic policy instruments to real economic goals, in particular full employment and real growth of national income. Second, Keynesian demand management is activist. Third, Keynesians have wished to put both fiscal and monetary policies in consistent and coordinated harness in the pursuit of macroeconomic objectives.

In this section we use the multiplier model to show how government purchases affect output.

政府财政政策对产出的影响
HOW GOVERNMENT FISCAL POLICIES AFFECT OUTPUT

To understand the role of government in economic activity, we need to look at government purchases and taxation, along with the effects of those activities on private-sector spending. We now modify our earlier analysis by adding G to $C + I$ to get a new total expenditure curve $TE = C + I + G$. This new schedule can describe the macroeconomic equilibrium when government, with its spending and taxing, is in the picture.

It will simplify our task in the beginning if we ③ analyze the effects of government purchases with total taxes collected held constant (taxes that do not change with income or other economic variables are called *lump-sum taxes*). But even with a fixed dollar value of taxes, we can no longer ignore the distinction between disposable income and gross domestic product. Under simplified conditions (including no foreign trade, transfers, or depreciation), we know

---

① *Keynesian approach to macroeconomic policy*：凯恩斯宏观经济政策理论

② 首先，凯恩斯政策体现为宏观经济政策对实际的经济目标，尤其是充分就业和国民收入的实际增长作出的显著贡献。其次，凯恩斯的需求管理是积极主动的。再次，为了实现宏观经济目标，凯恩斯主义者希望财政政策和货币政策保持一致，相互协调。

③ 在总税赋保持不变（不随收入或者其他经济变量变化的税种称为一次性总付税）的情况下，如果我们需要对政府采购的影响进行分析，第一步则必须将问题简化。

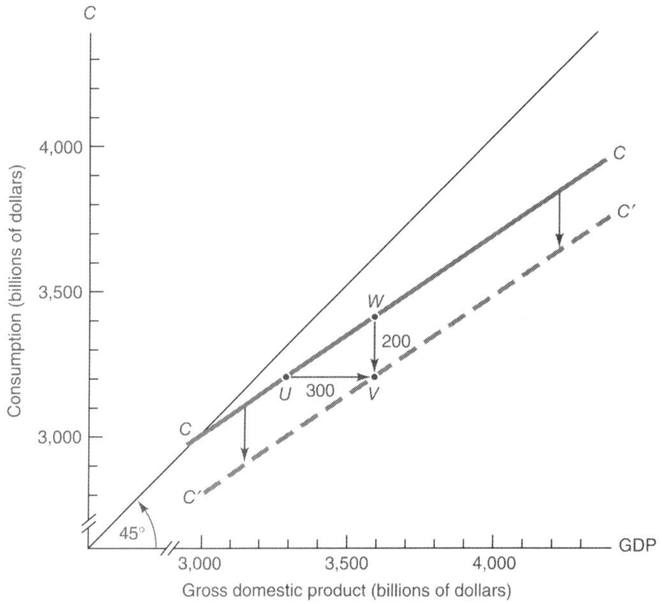

FIGURE 22-9. Taxes Reduce Disposable Income and Shift *CC* Schedule to the Right and Down ①

Each dollar of taxes paid shifts the *CC* schedule to the right by the amount of the tax. A rightward *CC* shift also means a downward *CC* shift, but the downward *CC* shift is less than the rightward shift. Why? Because the downward shift is equal to the rightward shift times the *MPC*. Thus, if the *MPC* is ⅔, the downward shift is ⅔ times \$300 billion = \$200 billion. Verify that *WV* = ⅔ *UV*.

from Chapter 20 that GDP equals disposable income plus taxes. But with tax revenues held constant, GDP and *DI* will always differ by the same amount; thus, after taking account of such taxes, we can still plot the *CC* consumption schedule against GDP rather than against *DI*.

Figure 22-9 shows how the consumption function changes when taxes are present. This figure draws the original no-tax consumption function as the blue *CC* line. In this case, GDP equals disposable income. We use the same consumption function as in Table 22-2 on page 440. Therefore, consumption is 3000 when GDP (and *DI*) is 3000, and so forth.

Now introduce taxes of 300. At a *DI* of 3000, GDP must equal 3300 = 300 + 3000. Consumption is still 3000 when GDP is 3300 because *DI* is 3000. We can therefore plot consumption as a function of GDP by shifting the consumption function rightward to the green *C′C′* curve. The amount of the rightward shift is *UV*, which is exactly equal to the amount of taxes, 300.

Alternatively, we can plot the new consumption function as a parallel *downward* shift by 200. As Figure 22-9 shows, 200 is the result of multiplying a decrease in income of 300 times the *MPC* of ⅔.

Turning next to the different components of aggregate demand, recall from Chapter 20 that GDP consists of four elements:

GDP = consumption expenditure
+ gross private domestic investment
+ government purchases of goods and services
+ net exports
$= C + I + G + X$

For now, we consider a closed economy with no foreign trade, so our GDP consists of the first three components, $C + I + G$. (We add the final component, net exports, when we consider open-economy macroeconomics.)

Figure 22-10 shows the effect of including government purchases. This diagram is very similar to the one used earlier in this chapter (see Figure 22-7). Here, we have added a new expenditure stream, *G*, to the consumption and investment amounts. Diagrammatically, we place the new variable, *G* (government

① 图 22-9：税收减少可支配收入，使 *CC* 曲线同时向右下方移动

每一美元税收会使 *CC* 曲线向右移动同样的一美元，这一移动也意味着 *CC* 曲线的下降，但其幅度小于向右移动的幅度。为什么？其原因在于，向下的移动等于向右移动与 *MPC*（边际消费倾向）的乘积。因此，如果 *MPC* 的值为 ⅔，则向下移动的幅度为 3 000 亿 × ⅔ = 2 000 亿（美元）。即 *WV* = ⅔ *UV*。

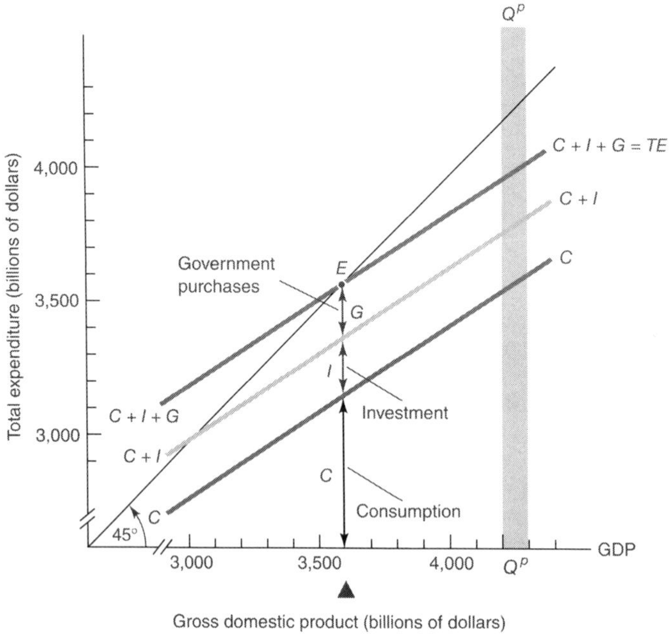

FIGURE 22-10. Government Purchases Add On Just like Investment to Determine Equilibrium GDP ①

We now add government purchases on top of consumption and investment spending. This gives us the new total planned expenditure schedule, $TE = C + I + G$. At E, where the TE schedule intersects the 45° line, we find the equilibrium level of GDP.

purchases of goods and services), on top of the consumption function and the fixed amount of investment. The vertical distance between the $C + I$ line and the new $TE = C + I + G$ line is just the quantity of G.

Why do we simply add G on the top? Because spending on government buildings (G) has the same macroeconomic impact as spending on private buildings (I); the collective expenditure involved in buying a government vehicle (G) has the same effect on jobs as private consumption expenditures on automobiles (C).

We end up with the three-layer cake of $TE = C + I + G$, calculating the amount of total spending forthcoming at each level of GDP. We now must locate the point of intersection of the TE line with the 45° line to find the equilibrium level of GDP. At this equilibrium GDP level, denoted by point E in Figure 22-10, total planned spending exactly equals total planned output. Point E thus indicates the equilibrium level of output when we add government purchases to the multiplier model. ②

征税对总需求的影响

Impact of Taxation on Aggregate Demand

How does government taxation tend to reduce aggregate demand and the level of GDP? Extra taxes lower our disposable incomes, and lower disposable incomes tend to reduce our consumption spending. Clearly, if investment and government purchases remain unchanged a reduction in consumption spending will then reduce GDP and employment. Thus, in the multiplier model, higher taxes without increases in government purchases will tend to reduce real GDP.[2]

A look back at Figure 22-9 confirms this reasoning. In this figure, the upper CC curve represents the level of the consumption function with no taxes. But the upper curve cannot be the consumption function because consumers definitely pay taxes on their incomes. Suppose that consumers pay \$300 billion in taxes at every level of income; thus, DI is exactly \$300 billion less than GDP at every level of output.

[2] Strictly speaking, by "taxes" in this chapter we mean net taxes, or taxes minus transfer payments.

① 图 22-10：如投资决定 GDP 的均衡水平一样，将政府采购加上去
我们在消费和投资支出之上，另外加上政府采购。这样就得到一个新的计划总支出曲线，$TE = C + I + G$。在 TE 与 45° 线相交的 E 点，我们就可以找到 GDP 的均衡水平。

② 我们使用三层蛋糕的方法得到三者叠加在一起的 $TE = C + I + G$，计算未来每一个 GDP 水平上的总支出量。

As shown in Figure 22-9, this level of taxes can be represented by a rightward shift in the consumption function of $300 billion. This rightward shift will also appear as a downward shift; if the *MPC* is ⅔, the rightward shift of $300 billion will be seen as a downward shift of $200 billion.

Without a doubt, taxes lower output in our multiplier model, and Figure 22-10 shows why. When taxes rise, *I* + *G* does not change, but the increase in taxes will lower disposable income, thereby shifting the *CC* consumption schedule downward. Hence, the *C* + *I* + *G* schedule shifts downward. You can pencil in a new, lower *C* + *I* + *G* schedule in Figure 22-10. Confirm that its new intersection with the 45° line must be at a lower equilibrium level of GDP.

Keep in mind that *G* is government purchases of goods and services. It excludes spending on transfers such as unemployment insurance or social security payments. These transfers are treated as negative taxes, so the taxes (*T*) considered here can best be thought of as taxes less transfers. Therefore, if direct and indirect taxes total $400 billion, while all transfer payments are $100 billion, then net taxes, *T*, are $400 − $100 = $300 billion. (Can you see why an increase in social security benefits lowers *T*, raises *DI*, shifts the *C* + *I* + *G* curve upward, and raises equilibrium GDP?) ①

数值示例

A Numerical Example

The points made up to now are illustrated in Table 22-3. This table is very similar to Table 22-2, which illustrated output determination in the simplest multiplier model. The first column shows a reference level of GDP, while the second shows a fixed level of taxes, $300 billion. Disposable income in column (3) is GDP less taxes. Planned consumption, taken as a function of *DI*, is shown in column (4). Column (5) shows the fixed level of planned investment, while column (6) exhibits the level of government purchases. To find total planned expenditures, *TE*, in column (7), we add together the *C*, *I*, and *G* in columns (4) through (6).

Finally, we compare total desired expenditures *TE* in column (7) with the initial level of GDP in column (1). If desired spending is above GDP, firms raise production to meet the level of spending, and output consequently rises; if desired spending is below GDP, output falls. This tendency, shown in the last column, assures us that output will tend toward its equilibrium level at $3600 billion.

Output Determination with Government Spending (billions of dollars)

(1) Initial level of GDP	(2) Taxes *T*	(3) Disposable income *DI*	(4) Planned consumption *C*	(5) Planned investment *I*	(6) Government expenditure *G*	(7) Total planned expenditure, *TE* (*C* + *I* + *G*)	(8) Resulting tendency of economy
4,200	300	3,900	3,600	200	200	4,000 ↓	Contraction
3,900	300	3,600	3,400	200	200	3,800 ↓	Contraction
3,600	**300**	**3,300**	**3,200**	**200**	**200**	**3,600**	**Equilibrium**
3,300	300	3,000	3,000	200	200	3,400 ↑	Expansion
3,000	300	2,700	2,800	200	200	3,200 ↑	Expansion

TABLE 22-3. Government Purchases, Taxes, and Investment Also Determine Equilibrium GDP ②

This table shows how output is determined when government purchases of goods and services are added to the multiplier model. In this example, taxes are "lump-sum" or independent of the level of income. Disposable income is thus GDP minus $300 billion. Total spending is *I* + *G* + the consumption determined by the consumption function.

At levels of output less than $3600 billion, planned spending is greater than output, so output expands. Levels of output greater than $3600 are unsustainable and lead to contraction. Only at output of $3600 is output in equilibrium—that is, planned spending equals output.

---

① 将这些转移支付按负税收处理，这里所考虑的税收（*T*）就可以确认为税收减去转移支付。

② 表 22-3：政府采购、税收及投资也决定 GDP 的均衡

本表说明，当政府对商品和服务的采购计入乘数模型时，产出是如何决定的。本例中，税收是“一次性总付税”，或者独立于收入水平。这样，可支配收入等于 GDP 减去 3 000 亿美元，总支出就等于 *I* 加 *G* 所得之和，再加上消费函数所决定的消费额。

在产出小于 36 000 亿美元的水平上，计划支出大于产出，所以扩大产出。产出水平大于 36 000 亿美元是不可持续的，同时还会导致紧缩。只有在 36 000 亿美元的水平上，产出才实现均衡，即计划支出等于产出。

财政政策乘数
FISCAL-POLICY MULTIPLIERS

The multiplier analysis shows that government fiscal policy is high-powered spending much like investment. The parallel suggests that fiscal policy should also have multiplier effects upon output. And this is exactly right.

The **government expenditure multiplier** is the ① increase in GDP resulting from an increase of $1 in government purchases of goods and services. An initial government purchase of a good or service will set in motion a chain of spending: if the government builds a road, the road-builders will spend some of their incomes on consumption goods, which in turn will generate additional incomes, some of which will be spent. In the simple model examined here, the ultimate effect on GDP of an extra dollar of *G* will be the same as the effect of an extra dollar of *I*: the multipliers are both equal to $1/(1 - MPC)$. Figure 22-11 shows how a change in *G* will result in a higher level of GDP, with the increase being a multiple of the increase in government purchases.

To show the effects of an extra $100 billion of *G*, the $C + I + G$ curve in Figure 22-11 has been shifted up by $100 billion. The ultimate increase in GDP is equal to the $100 billion of primary spending times the expenditure multiplier. In this case, because the *MPC* is ⅔, the multiplier is 3, so the equilibrium level of GDP rises by $300 billion.

This example, as well as common sense, tells ② us that the government expenditure multiplier is exactly the same number as the investment multiplier. They are both called **expenditure multipliers.**

Also, note that the multiplier horse can be ridden in both directions. If government purchases were to fall, with taxes and other influences held constant, GDP would decline by the change in *G* times the multiplier.

The effect of *G* on output can be seen as well in the numerical example of Table 22-3. You can pencil in a different level of *G*—say, $300 billion—and find the equilibrium level of GDP. It should give the same answer as Figure 22-11.

We can sum up:

Government purchases of goods and services (*G*) ③ are an important force in determining output and employment. In the multiplier model, if *G* increases, output will rise by the increase in *G* times the expenditure multiplier. Government purchases therefore have the potential to increase or decrease output over the business cycle.

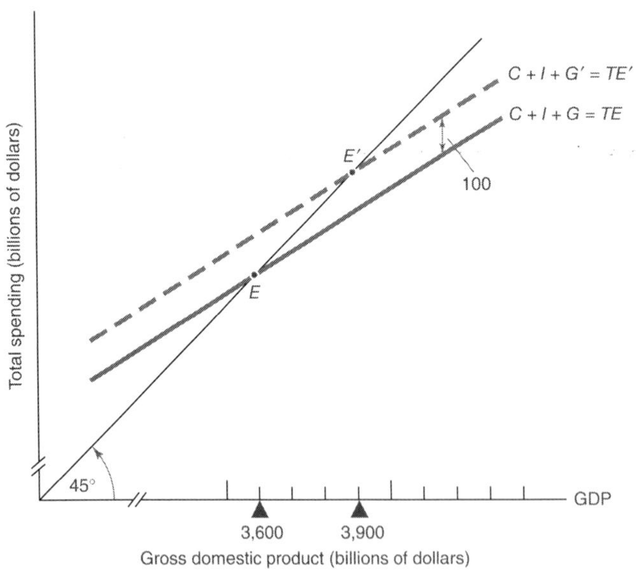

FIGURE 22-11. The Effect of Higher *G* on Output

Suppose that the government raises defense purchases by $100 billion in response to a threat to Mideast oil fields. This shifts upward the $C + I + G$ line by $100 billion to $C + I + G'$.

The new equilibrium level of GDP is thus read off the 45° line at E' rather than at E. Because the *MPC* is ⅔, the new level of output is $300 billion higher. That is, the government expenditure multiplier is

$$3 = \frac{1}{1 - \frac{2}{3}}$$

(What would the government expenditure multiplier be if the *MPC* were ¾? $\frac{9}{10}$?)

---

① **政府支出乘数**系指政府对商品和服务每增加 1 美元的采购量所带来的 GDP 的增加量。政府对某一项商品或者服务的初始采购，将会带动支出的连锁效应：如果政府新建一条公路，则道路的建设者们就会把他们收入中的一部分用于商品消费上，这些消费又会去创造另外的收入，这些收入中的一部分又会用于消费。

② 这个人所共知的常识性例子告诉我们，政府的支出乘数与投资乘数完全相等，统称为**支出乘数**。

③ 政府对商品和服务的采购（*G*）是决定产出和就业的一个重要因素。在乘数模型中，如果 *G* 增加，则产出随之增加的量就可以用 *G* 的增加量乘以支出乘数的结果来表示。这样，政府采购就具有了一种通过增加或者减少产出来影响商业周期的潜能。

Economic Stimulus from Defense Spending

War	Period of war or buildup	Increase in defense spending as percent of GDP	Real GDP growth over buildup period (%)
World War I	1916–1918	10.2	13.0
World War II			
Before Pearl Harbor	1939–1941	9.7	26.7
All years	1939–1944	41.4	69.1
Korean War	1950:3–1951:3	8.0	10.5
Vietnam War	1965:3–1967:1	1.9	9.7
Persian Gulf War	1990:3–1991:1	0.3	−1.3
Iraq War	2003:1–2003:2	0.1	0.5

TABLE 22-4. Economic Booms Accompany Large Increases in Military Spending

This table shows the period of the war or buildup, the size of the military buildup, and the resulting increase in real GDP. Major wars have produced sustained economic booms, but the last two wars, with relatively little growth in military spending, had only a small impact on the economy.

Source: Department of Commerce, National Income and Product Accounts, available at *www.bea.gov*, and estimates by authors. The dates are year and quarter. Hence, 1950:3 is the third quarter of 1950.

Are Wars Necessary for Full Employment? Historically, economic expansions were the constant companions of war. As can be seen in Table 22-4, major wars in the past were often accompanied by large increases in military spending. In World War II, for example, defense outlays rose by almost 10 percent of total GDP before Pearl Harbor was bombed in December 1941. Indeed, many scholars believe that the United States emerged from the Great Depression largely because of the buildup for World War II. Similar but smaller military buildups accompanied economic expansions in the Korean and Vietnam Wars.

By contrast, the Persian Gulf War of the early 1990s triggered a recession. The reason for this anomaly was that there was but a small increase in military spending and psychological factors triggered by the war more than offset the increase in *G*.

What were these psychological factors? After Iraq invaded Kuwait in August 1990, consumers and investors became frightened and reduced spending. Additionally, oil prices shot up, lowering real incomes. These factors then reversed after the U.S. victory in February 1991.

What was the impact of the war in Iraq in early 2003? This war resembled the Persian Gulf War more than it did major wars. There was little increase in defense spending, while cautious consumers and businesses, along with high oil prices, produced a strong headwind that slowed the economy.

The role of wartime spending in economic expansions is one of the most direct and persuasive examples of the functioning of the multiplier model. Make sure you understand the underlying mechanism as well as why the sizes of the economic expansions shown in Table 22-4 vary so much.

税收的影响
Impact of Taxes

Taxes also have an impact upon equilibrium GDP,
[1] although the size of tax multipliers is smaller than
② that of expenditure multipliers. Consider the following example: Suppose the economy is at its potential GDP and the nation raises defense spending by \$200 billion. Such sudden increases have occurred at many points in the history of the United States—in the early 1940s for World War II, in 1951 for the Korean war, in the mid-1960s for the Vietnam war, and in the early 1980s during the Reagan administration's military buildup. Furthermore, say that eco-
[3] nomic planners wish to raise taxes just enough to
④ offset the effect on GDP of the \$200 billion increase in *G*. How much would taxes have to be raised?

[3] War in Iraq：伊拉克战争，又称美伊战争或第二次海湾战争。2003年3月20日，美国和英国为主的联合部队在未经联合国授权的情况下正式宣布对伊拉克开战。到2011年12月18日，美国国防部长帕内塔正式宣布结束伊拉克战争，在近9年的战争中，有超过150万的美国人赴伊拉克服役，3万多美国士兵受伤，近4 500名美国军人牺牲。

④ 那么，2003年年初发动的伊拉克战争又产生了怎样的影响？这场战争与过去的重大战争不同，更像海湾战争。国防的支出几乎没有增加，而与此同时，消费者和企业谨小慎微，伴随着高涨的石油价格，刮起了一场强劲的逆风，减缓了经济运行。

[1] Persian Gulf War：也称海湾战争。1991年1月17日，以美国为首的多国部队在联合国安理会授权下，为恢复科威特领土完整发动了对伊拉克的战争；这是第二次世界大战之后参战国家最多、一次性投入兵力最大、投入的兵器最多最先进、空袭规模最大、战况空前激烈和发展异常迅猛、双方伤亡损失又极其悬殊的一场现代高技术条件下的局部战争；这场战争对冷战后国际新秩序的建立产生了深刻影响，所展示的现代高技术条件作战，对军事战略、战役战术和军队建设等问题带来了众多启示。历时42天，于2月28日以萨达姆政权的彻底失败结束。

② 与此形成强烈对比的是，20世纪90年代初的波斯湾战争却引发了经济衰退。对于这起非常规战争，其原因在于，当时的军费支出只有小幅的增加，但与此同时，战争所导致的心理因素却远远超越了政府采购所带来的补偿。

We are in for a surprise. To offset the \$200 billion increase in *G*, we need to increase tax collections by more than \$200 billion. In our numerical example, we can find the exact size of the tax, or *T*, increase from Figure 22-9. That figure shows that a \$300 billion increase in *T* reduces disposable income by just enough to produce a consumption decline of \$200 billion when the *MPC* is ⅔. Put differently, a tax increase of \$300 billion will shift the *CC* curve down by \$200 billion. Hence, while a \$1 billion increase in defense spending shifts up the $C + I + G$ line by \$1 billion, a \$1 billion tax increase shifts down the $C + I + G$ line by only \$⅔ billion (when the *MPC* is ⅔). Thus offsetting an increase in government purchases requires an increase in *T* larger than the increase in *G*.

Tax changes are a powerful weapon in affecting output. But the tax multiplier is smaller than the expenditure multiplier by a factor equal to the *MPC*: ①

Tax multiplier = *MPC* × expenditure multiplier

The reason the tax multiplier is smaller than the expenditure multiplier is straightforward. When government spends \$1 on *G*, that \$1 gets spent directly on GDP. On the other hand, when government cuts taxes by a dollar, only part of that dollar is spent on *C*, while a fraction of that \$1 tax cut is saved. The difference in the responses to a dollar of *G* and to a dollar of *T* is enough to lower the tax multiplier below the expenditure multiplier.[3]

乘数模型与商业周期
The Multiplier Model and the Business Cycle

The multiplier model is the simplest model of the business cycle. It can show how changes in investment due to innovation or pessimism, or fluctuations in government spending due to war, can lead to sharp changes in output. Suppose that war breaks out and the country increases military spending (as illustrated by the many cases in Table 22-4). *G* increases, and this leads to a multiplied increase in output, as seen in Figure 22-11. If you look back at Figure 22-2 on page 430, you can see how large wars were accompanied by large increases in output relative to potential output. Similarly, suppose that a burst of innovation leads to rapid growth in investment, as occurred with the new-economy boom of the 1990s. This would lead to an upward shift in the $C + I + G$ curve and to higher output. Again, you can see the results in Figure 22-2. Make sure you can graph each of these examples using the $C + I + G$ apparatus. Also, make sure you can explain why a revolution in a country that led to sharp decline in investment might lead to a recession. ②

Economists often combine the multiplier model with the accelerator principle of investment as an internal theory of the business cycle. In this approach, every expansion breeds recession and contraction, and every contraction breeds revival and expansion—in a quasi-regular, repeating chain. According to the accelerator principle, rapid output growth stimulates investment, which is amplified by the multiplier on investment. High investment, in turn, stimulates more output growth, and the process continues until the capacity of the economy is reached, at which point the economic growth rate slows. The slower growth, in turn, reduces investment spending, and this, working through the multiplier, tends to send the economy into a recession. The process then works in reverse until the trough is reached, and the economy then stabilizes and turns up again. This internal theory of the business cycle shows a mechanism, like the rise and fall of the tides in which an exogenous shock tends to propagate itself through the economy in a cyclical fashion. (See question 11 at the end of the chapter for a numerical example.)

The multiplier model, working together with the dynamics of investment, shows how alternating bouts of investment optimism and pessimism, along with changes in other exogenous expenditures, can lead to the fluctuations that we call business cycles. ③

[3] For simplicity, we take the absolute value of the tax multiplier (since the multiplier is actually negative). The different multipliers can be seen using the device of the "expenditure rounds" shown on page 441. Let the *MPC* be *r*. Then if *G* goes up by 1 unit, the total increase in spending is the sum of secondary respending rounds:

$$1 + r + r^2 + r^3 + \cdots = \frac{1}{1-r}$$

Now, if taxes are reduced by \$1, consumers save $(1 - r)$ of the increased disposable income and spend *r* dollars on the first round. With the further rounds, the total spending is thus

$$r + r^2 + r^3 + \cdots = \frac{r}{1-r}$$

Thus the tax multiplier is *r* times the expenditure multiplier, where *r* is the *MPC*.

---

① 调整税收是影响产出的强有力工具。但税收乘数小于支出乘数，其比值等于 *MPC*（边际消费倾向）。

税收乘数 = *MPC* × 支出乘数

② 乘数模型是商业周期中最为简单的模型。它说明由于创新或者悲观情绪所导致的投资变化，或者由于战争原因而引发的政府支出波动，导致产出的剧烈变化。假设战争爆发，国家的军费开支增加（如表 22-4 中的案例所示）。正如图 22-11 所示，*G* 的增加，导致产出的倍增。

③ 乘数模型与投资变化的共同作用表明，投资的乐观情绪和悲观情绪的交替，以及其他外生支出的变化，是如何导致我们所讲的商业周期波动的。

乘数模型展望
The Multiplier Model in Perspective

We have completed our introductory survey of the Keynesian multiplier model. It will be useful to put all this in perspective and see how the multiplier model fits into a broader view of the macroeconomy. Our goal is to understand what determines the level of national output in a country. In the long run, a country's production and living standards are largely determined by its potential output. But in the short run, business conditions will push the economy above or below its long-term trend. It is this deviation of output and employment from the long-term trend that we analyze with the multiplier model.

The multiplier model has been enormously ① influential in business-cycle theory over the last half-century. However, it gives an oversimplified picture of the economy. One of the most significant omissions is the impact of financial markets and monetary policy on the economy. Changes in output tend to affect interest rates, which in turn affect the economy. Additionally, the simplest multiplier model omits the interactions between the domestic economy and the rest of the world. Finally, the model omits the supply side of the economy as represented by the interaction of spending with aggregate supply and prices. All of these shortcomings will be remedied in later chapters, and it is useful to keep in mind that this first model is simply a stepping stone on the path to understanding the economy in all its complexity.

The multiplier analysis focuses primarily on ② spending changes as the factors behind short-run output movements. In this approach, fiscal policy is often used as a tool to stabilize the economy. But the government has another equally powerful weapon in monetary policy. Although monetary policy works quite differently, it has many advantages as a means of combating unemployment and inflation.

The next two chapters survey one of the most fascinating parts of all economics: money and financial markets. Once we understand how the central bank helps determine interest rates and credit conditions, we will have a fuller appreciation of how governments can tame the business cycles that have run wild through much of the history of capitalism.

SUMMARY

A. What are Business Cycles?

1. Business cycles or fluctuations are swings in total national output, income, and employment, marked by widespread expansion or contraction in many sectors of the economy. They occur in all advanced market economies. We distinguish the phases of expansion, peak, recession, and trough.
2. Most business cycles occur when shifts in aggregate demand cause changes in output, employment, and prices. Aggregate demand shifts when changes in spending by consumers, businesses, or governments change total spending relative to the economy's productive capacity. A decline in aggregate demand leads to recessions or even depressions. An upturn in economic activity can lead to inflation.
3. Business-cycle theories differ in their emphasis on exogenous and internal factors. Importance is often attached to fluctuations in such exogenous factors as technology, elections, wars, exchange-rate movements, and oil-price shocks. Most theories emphasize that these exogenous shocks interact with internal mechanisms, such as financial market bubbles and busts.

B. Aggregate Demand and Business Cycles

4. Ancient societies suffered when harvest failures produced famines. The modern market economy can suffer from poverty amidst plenty when insufficient aggregate demand leads to deteriorating business conditions and high unemployment. At other times, excessive government spending and reliance on the monetary printing press can lead to runaway inflation. Understanding the forces that affect aggregate demand, including government fiscal and monetary policies, can help economists and policymakers smooth out the cycle of boom and bust.
5. Aggregate demand represents the total quantity of output willingly bought at a given price level, other things held constant. Components of spending include (*a*) consumption, which depends primarily upon disposable income; (*b*) investment, which depends upon present and expected future output and upon interest rates and taxes; (*c*) government purchases of goods and services; and (*d*) net exports, which depend upon foreign and domestic outputs and prices and upon foreign exchange rates.

---

① 在刚刚过去的半个世纪，乘数模型对商业周期理论产生了巨大影响，但却给我们勾画了一幅过分简化的经济运行图。其中，漏掉的最重要一点是金融市场和货币政策对经济的影响。产出变化一般会影响利率，反过来又影响到经济运行。此外，这一最简单的乘数模型还忽略了国内经济与世界其他经济体之间的相互作用，最后，该模型还将支出与总供给和价格之间的互动所代表的经济中的供给方省略掉了。

② 乘数分析主要关注于短期产出背后的诸因素出现波动时，支出发生的变化。在这一模型中，财政政策常被用于作为稳定经济运行的工具。但政府还有另一件同样强大的武器——货币政策。虽然货币政策的运作机制与其他截然不同，但它却具有很多优势，可以用作遏制通货膨胀与对抗失业的手段。

6. Aggregate demand curves differ from demand curves used in microeconomic analysis. The *AD* curves relate overall spending on all components of output to the overall price level, with policy and exogenous variables held constant. The aggregate demand curve is downward-sloping because a higher price level reduces real income and real wealth.
7. Factors that change aggregate demand include (*a*) macroeconomic policies, such as fiscal and monetary policies, and (*b*) exogenous variables, such as foreign economic activity, technological advances, and shifts in asset markets. When these variables change, they shift the *AD* curve.

C. The Multiplier Model

8. The multiplier model provides a simple way to understand the impact of aggregate demand on the level of output. In the simplest approach, household consumption is a function of disposable income, while investment is fixed. People's desire to consume and the willingness of businesses to invest are brought into balance by adjustments in output. The equilibrium level of national output occurs when planned spending equals planned output. Using the expenditure-output approach, equilibrium output comes at the intersection of the total expenditure (*TE*) consumption-plus-investment schedule and the 45° line.
9. If output is temporarily above its equilibrium level, businesses find output higher than sales, with inventories piling up involuntarily and profits plummeting. Firms therefore cut production and employment back toward the equilibrium level. The only sustainable level of output comes when buyers desire to purchase exactly as much as businesses desire to produce. Thus, for the simplified Keynesian multiplier model, investment calls the tune and consumption dances to the music.
10. Investment has a *multiplied effect* on output. When investment changes, output will initially rise by an equal amount. But that output increase is also an income increase for consumers. As consumers spend a part of their additional income, this sets in motion a whole chain of additional consumption spending and employment.
11. If people always spend r of each extra dollar of income on consumption, the total of the multiplier chain will be

$$1 + r + r^2 + \cdots = \frac{1}{1-r} = \frac{1}{1-MPC} = \frac{1}{MPS}$$

The simplest multiplier is numerically equal to $1/(1 - MPC)$.

12. Key points to remember are (*a*) the basic multiplier model emphasizes the importance of shifts in aggregate demand in affecting output and income and (*b*) it is primarily applicable for situations with unemployed resources.

D. Fiscal Policy in the Multiplier Model

13. The analysis of fiscal policy elaborates the Keynesian multiplier model. It shows that an increase in government purchases—taken by itself, with taxes and investment unchanged—has an expansionary effect on national output much like that of investment. The total expenditure $TE = C + I + G$ schedule shifts upward to a higher equilibrium intersection with the 45° line.
14. A decrease in taxes—taken by itself, with investment and government purchases unchanged—raises the equilibrium level of national output. The *CC* schedule of consumption plotted against GDP is shifted upward and leftward by a tax cut. But since the extra dollars of disposable income go partly into saving, the dollar increase in consumption will not be quite as great as the increase in new disposable income. Therefore, the tax multiplier is smaller than the government-expenditure multiplier.

CONCEPTS FOR REVIEW

Business Fluctuations or Cycles

business cycle or business fluctuation
business-cycle phases: peak, trough, expansion, contraction
recession
exogenous and internal cycle theories

Aggregate Demand

aggregate demand shifts and business fluctuations
aggregate demand, *AD* curve
major components of aggregate demand: *C, I, G, X*
downward-sloping *AD* curve
factors underlying and shifting the *AD* curve

The Basic Multiplier Model

$TE = C + I + G$ schedule
output and spending: planned vs. actual levels
multiplier effect of investment

multiplier

$= 1 + MPC + (MPC)^2 + \cdots$

$= \frac{1}{1 - MPC} = \frac{1}{MPS}$

Government Purchases and Taxation

fiscal policy:
G effect on equilibrium GDP
T effect on *CC* and on GDP

multiplier effects of government purchases (*G*) and taxes (*T*)
C + *I* + *G* curve

FURTHER READING AND INTERNET WEBSITES

Further Reading

The quotation from Okun is Arthur M. Okun, *The Political Economy of Prosperity* (Norton, New York, 1970), pp. 33 ff. This is a fascinating book on the economic history of the 1960s written by one of America's great macroeconomists.

The classic study of business cycles by leading scholars at the National Bureau of Economic Research (NBER) is Arthur F. Burns and Wesley Clair Mitchell, *Measuring Business Cycles* (Columbia University Press, New York, 1946). This is available from the NBER at *www.nber.org/books/burn46-1*. The multiplier model was developed by John Maynard Keynes in *The General Theory of Employment, Interest and Money* (Harcourt, New York, first published in 1935). Advanced treatments can be found in the intermediate textbooks listed in the Further Reading section in Chapter 19. One of Keynes's most influential books, *The Economic Consequences of the Peace* (1919), predicted with uncanny accuracy that the Treaty of Versailles would lead to disastrous consequences for Europe.

Websites

A consortium of macroeconomists participates in the NBER program on economic fluctuations and growth. You can sample the writings and data at *www.nber.org/programs/efg/efg.html*. The NBER also dates business cycles for the United States. You can see the recessions and expansions along with a discussion at *www.nber.org/cycles.html*.

Business-cycle data and discussion can be found at the site of the Bureau of Economic Analysis, *www.bea.gov*. The first few pages of the *Survey of Current Business*, available at *www.bea.gov/bea/pubs.htm*, contain a discussion of recent business-cycle developments.

QUESTIONS FOR DISCUSSION

1. Define carefully the difference between movements along the *AD* curve and shifts of the *AD* curve. Explain why an increase in potential output would shift out the *AS* curve and lead to a movement along the *AD* curve. Explain why a tax cut would shift the *AD* curve outward (increase aggregate demand).
2. Construct a table parallel to Table 22-1, listing events that would lead to a *decrease* in aggregate demand. (Your table should provide different examples rather than simply changing the direction of the factors mentioned in Table 22-1.)
3. In recent years, a new theory of real business cycles (or RBCs) has been proposed (this approach is further analyzed in Chapter 31). RBC theory suggests that business fluctuations are caused by shocks to productivity, which then propagate through the economy.
   a. Show the RBC theory in the *AS-AD* framework.
   b. Discuss whether the RBC theory can explain the customary characteristics of business fluctuations described on pages 430–431.
4. In the simple multiplier model, assume that investment is always zero. Show that equilibrium output in this special case would come at the break-even point of the consumption function. Why would equilibrium output come *above* the break-even point when investment is positive?
5. Define carefully what is meant by equilibrium in the multiplier model. For each of the following, state why the situation is *not* an equilibrium. Also describe how the economy would react to each of the situations to restore equilibrium.
   a. In Table 22-2, GDP is \$3300 billion.
   b. In Figure 22-7, actual investment is zero and output is at *M*.
   c. Car dealers find that their inventories of new cars are rising unexpectedly.
6. Reconstruct Table 22-2 assuming that planned investment is equal to (*a*) \$300 billion and (*b*) \$400 billion. What is the resulting difference in GDP? Is this difference greater or smaller than the change in *I*? Why?

When I drops from \$200 billion to \$100 billion, how much must GDP drop?

7. Give (*a*) the common sense, (*b*) the arithmetic, and (*c*) the geometry of the multiplier. What are the multipliers for $MPC = 0.9$? 0.8? 0.5?
8. Explain in words and using the notion of expenditure rounds why the tax multiplier is smaller than the expenditure multiplier.
9. "Even if the government spends billions on wasteful military armaments, this action can create jobs in a recession." Discuss.
10. **Advanced problem:** The growth of nations depends crucially on saving and investment. And from youth we are taught that thrift is important and that "a penny saved is a penny earned." But will higher saving necessarily benefit the economy? In a striking argument called *the paradox of thrift,* Keynes pointed out that when people attempt to save more, this will not necessarily result in more saving for the nation as a whole.

    To see this point, assume that people decide to save more. Higher desired saving means lower desired consumption, or a downward shift in the consumption function. Illustrate how an increase in desired saving shifts down the *TE* curve in the multiplier model of Figure 22-7. Explain why this will *decrease output with no increase in saving!* Provide the intuition here that if people try to increase their saving and lower their consumption for a given level of business investment, sales will fall and businesses will cut back on production. Explain how far output will fall.

    > Here then is the paradox of thrift: When the community desires to save more, the effect may actually be a lowering of income and output with no increase of saving.

11. **Advanced problem illustrating the multiplier-accelerator mechanism:** Find two dice and use the following technique to see if you can generate something that looks like a business cycle: Record the numbers from 20 or more rolls of the dice. Take five-period moving averages of the successive numbers. Then plot these averages. They will look very much like movements in GDP, unemployment, or inflation.

    One sequence thus obtained was 7, 4, 10, 3, 7, 11, 7, 2, 9, 10, . . . The averages were (7 + 4 + 10 + 3 + 7)/5 = 6.2; (11 + 7 + 2 + 9 + 10)/5 = 7, and so forth. Why does this look like a business cycle?

    [*Hint:* The random numbers generated by the dice are like exogenous shocks of investment or wars. The moving average is like the economic system's (or a rocking chair's) internal multiplier or smoothing mechanism. Taken together, they produce what looks like a cycle.]
12. **Data problem:** Some economists prefer an objective, quantitative definition of a recession to the more subjective approach used by the NBER. These economists define a recession as any period during which real GDP declined for at least two quarters in a row. Note from the text that this is *not* the way the NBER defines a recession.
    a. Get quarterly data on real GDP for the United States for the period since 1948. This can be obtained from the website of the Bureau of Economic Analysis, *www.bea.gov.* Put the data in a column of a spreadsheet, along with the corresponding date in another column.
    b. Calculate in a spreadsheet the percent growth rate of real GDP for each quarter at an annual rate. This is calculated as follows:

    $$g_t = 400 \times \frac{x_t - x_{t-1}}{x_{t-1}}$$

    c. Under this alternative definition, which periods would you identify as recessions? For which years does this alternative objective procedure reach a conclusion different from that of the NBER?

CHAPTER

23

Money and the Financial System
货币与金融体系

[1] 约翰·肯尼斯·加尔布雷思（John Kenneth Galbraith，1908~2006），出生于加拿大的美国著名经济学家、作家、思想家和外交官，新制度学派的主要代表人物，民主党元老，被公认为公众知名度最高的经济学家。《美国的资本主义》（*American Capitalism*，1952）、《富裕社会》（*The Affluent Society*，1958）和《新工业国家》（*The New Industrial State*，1967）是其 40 部著作中最著名的三部，他的多部著作已有中文译本。本段文字出自《不确定的时代》（*The Age of Uncertainty*，1977）一书，原文如下：

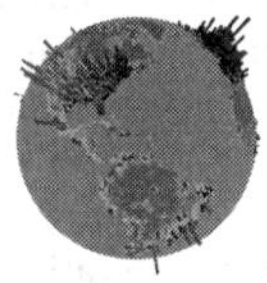

Money is a singular thing. It ranks with love as man's greatest source of joy. And with death as his greatest source of anxiety. Over all history it has oppressed nearly all people in one of two ways: either it has been abundant and very unreliable, or reliable and very scarce.

译文如下：

货币是一种独一无二的东西。你如对它爱之深切，它能使你欢乐无比。你如对它恨之入骨，它就使你焦虑不安。纵观历史，货币始终伴随在每个人的左右，困扰不已：要么腰缠万贯，却整日疑神疑鬼；要么捉襟见肘，却活得踏踏实实。

Over all history, money has oppressed people in one of two ways: either it has been abundant and very unreliable, or reliable and very scarce.

John Kenneth Galbraith [1]
The Age of Uncertainty (1977)

The financial system is one of the most important and ② innovative sectors of a modern economy. It forms the vital circulatory system that channels resources from savers to investors. Whereas finance in an earlier era consisted of banks and the country store, finance today involves a vast, worldwide banking system, securities markets, pension funds, and a wide array of financial instruments. When the financial system functions smoothly, as was the case for most of the period since World War II, it contributes greatly to healthy economic growth. However, when banks fail and people lose confidence in the financial system, as happened in the world financial crisis of 2007–2009, credit becomes scarce, investment is curbed, and economic growth slows.

货币传导机制概要
Overview of the Monetary Transmission Mechanism

One of the most important topics in macroeconomics ③ is the *monetary transmission mechanism*. This refers to the process by which monetary policy undertaken by the central bank (in the case of the U.S., the Federal Reserve), interacts with banks and the rest of the economy to determine interest rates, financial conditions, aggregate demand, output, and inflation.

We can provide an overview of the monetary transmission mechanism as a series of five logical steps:

1. The central bank announces a target short-term interest rate that depends upon its objectives and the state of the economy.
2. The central bank undertakes daily open-market operations to meet its interest-rate target.
3. The central bank's new interest-rate target and market expectations about future financial conditions help determine the entire spectrum of short- and long-term interest rates, asset prices, and exchange rates.
4. The changes in interest rates, credit conditions, asset prices, and exchange rates affect investment, consumption, and net exports.
5. Changes in investment, consumption, and net exports affect the path of output and inflation through the *AS-AD* mechanism.

We survey the different elements of this mechanism in the three chapters on money, finance, and
[4] central banking. Chapter 15 examined the major elements of interest rates and capital. The present chapter focuses on the private financial sector, including the structure of the financial system (Section A), the

② 金融系统是现代经济最为重要和最具创新性的部门之一。它构建了至关重要的循环体系，形成了一个从储蓄者到投资者的资源转移通道。早期的金融环境只由银行和农村信用社组成。然而，今天的金融体系却包括了全球性的巨大银行系统、证券市场、养老基金和一系列金融工具。

③ 货币传导机制是宏观经济学中最重要的问题之一。它指的是中央银行（在美国即联邦储备局）会同各银行以及经济体的其他部门一起，决定利率、金融状况、总需求、产出和通货膨胀水平，实施货币政策的过程。

---

[4] The Federal Reserve：美国联邦储备局，简称"美联储"，英文全称为 The Federal Reserve System，常缩写为"Fed"。该系统根据《联邦储备法》（Federal Reserve Act）于 1913 年成立，负责履行美国中央银行的职责，由核心机构联邦储备委员会（The Board of Governors of The Federal Reserve System）与另外两个主要机构联邦公开市场委员会（The Federal Open Market Committee）和遍布全美 12 个储备区的联邦储备银行（Federal Reserve Banks）组成。美联储的成立还应该追溯到美国开国元勋之一的亚历山大·汉密尔顿（Alexander Hamilton，1757~1804，美国第一任财政部长，美国宪法的起草人之一）。在美国开国之初，汉密尔顿顶着来自以杰弗逊（Thomas Jefferson，1743~1826，美国开国元勋之一，第三任总统，独立宣言的主要起草人）等人为首的众多反对者的巨大压力，于 1791 年 2 月 25 日经国会特许、华盛顿总统亲自签署，成立了履行中央银行职责的第一美国银行（First Bank of the United States），并设计和创建了全民信用体系（Credit System），使美国的国家机器从建国之初就能够较为健康有效地运行。同时，也使汉密尔顿和杰弗逊与华盛顿一道各司其责，成为美国开国和建国的真正伟人。

demand for money (Section B), banks (Section C), and the stock market (Section D). The next chapter surveys central banking as well as the way in which financial markets interact with the real economy to determine output and inflation. When you have completed these chapters, you will understand the different steps in the monetary transmission mechanism. It is one of the most important parts of all of macroeconomics.

现代金融系统

A. THE MODERN FINANCIAL SYSTEM

金融系统的作用

The Role of the Financial System

The financial sector of an economy is the circulatory system that links together goods, services, and finance in domestic and international markets. It is through money and finance that households and firms borrow from and lend to each other in order to consume and invest. People may borrow or lend because their cash incomes do not match their desired spending. For example, students generally have spending needs for tuition and living expenses that exceed their current incomes. They often finance their excess spending with student loans. Similarly, working couples will generally save some of their current incomes for retirement, perhaps by buying stocks or bonds. They are thereby financing their retirement.

The activities involved in finance take place in ① the **financial system.** This encompasses the markets, firms, and other institutions which carry out the financial decisions of households, businesses, and governments. Important parts of the financial system include the money market (discussed later in this chapter), markets for fixed-interest assets like bonds or mortgages, stock markets for the ownership of firms, and foreign exchange markets which trade the monies of different countries. Most of the financial system in the United States is composed of for-profit entities, but government institutions such as the Federal Reserve System and other regulatory bodies are particularly important for ensuring an efficient and stable financial system.

Borrowing and lending take place in finan- ② cial markets and through financial intermediaries. **Financial markets** are like other markets except that their products and services consist of financial instruments like stocks and bonds. Important financial markets are stock markets, bond markets, and foreign exchange markets.

Institutions which provide financial services and ③ products are called **financial intermediaries.** Financial institutions differ from other businesses because their assets are largely financial, rather than real assets like plant and equipment. Many retail financial transactions (such as banking or purchase of insurance) take place through financial intermediaries rather than directly in financial markets.

The most important financial intermediaries are commercial banks, which take deposits of funds from households and other groups and lend these funds to businesses and others who need funds; banks also "create" the special product known as money. Other important financial intermediaries are insurance companies and pension funds; these firms provide specialized services such as insurance policies and investments held until people retire.

Yet another group of intermediaries pools and subdivides securities. These intermediaries include mutual funds (which hold bonds and corporate stocks on behalf of small investors), government-sponsored mortgage buyers (which buy mortgages from banks and sell them to other financial institutions), and "derivative" firms (which buy assets and then subdivide them into various parts).

Table 23-1 shows the growth and composition of the assets of financial institutions in the United States. There has been substantial growth and innovation in this area, such that the ratio of all assets to GDP grew from 1.5 in 1965 to 4.5 in 2007. This growth took place because of increased *financial intermediation*, which is a process in which assets are bought, repackaged, and resold several times. The purpose of financial intermediation is to transform illiquid assets into liquid assets that small investors can buy. By the end of 2007, financial intermediaries had total assets of $61 trillion, or around $530,000 per American household. Clearly, given the investments people have in this sector, a careful study is important not only for good policy but also for wise household financial decision making.

金融系统的功能

The Functions of the Financial System

Because the financial system is such a critical part of a modern economy, let's consider its major functions:

---

① 所有涉及金融的活动都在**金融系统**内进行。金融系统包括市场、企业以及执行家庭、企业和政府金融决策的其他机构。金融系统的主要组成部分包括货币市场（本章后面讨论）、债券或者抵押贷款等固定利率资产的市场、交易公司所有者股权的股票市场，以及交易不同国家货币的外汇市场。

② 借贷行为通过金融中介在金融市场内进行。除了产品和服务由债券和股票这样的金融工具组成之外，**金融市场**与其他的市场没有区别。股票市场、债券市场和外汇市场是重要的金融市场。

③ 提供金融服务和产品的机构称作**金融中介**。金融机构同其他企业不同，其资产主要由金融资产构成，而不是像厂房和设备那样的实物财产。

	1965		2007	
	Total assets ($, billion)	Percent of total	Total assets ($, billion)	Percent of total
Federal Reserve	112	11	2,863	5
Commercial banks	342	33	11,195	18
Other credit institutions	198	19	2,575	4
Insurance and pension funds	325	31	16,557	27
Money market and mutual funds	43	4	11,509	19
Government-sponsored mortgage firms	20	2	9,322	15
Asset-backed securities	0	0	4,221	7
Security brokers, dealers, and miscellaneous	10	1	3,095	5
Total	1050	100	61,337	100
Percent of GDP	146%		450%	

TABLE 23-1. Assets of Major Financial Institutions in the United States

The financial sector has evolved rapidly over the last four decades. The table shows the total assets of all financial institutions, the grand total of which increased from 146 to 450 percent of GDP. Banks and other credit institutions declined in importance as secondary institutions like mutual funds and government-sponsored mortgage guarantors expanded sharply. Some important new areas, such as asset-backed securities, did not even exist in the 1960s.

Source: Federal Reserve Board, Flow of Funds, available at *www.federalreserve.gov/releases/z1/*, level tables.

- The financial system *transfers resources* across time, ① sectors, and regions. This function allows investments to be devoted to their most productive uses rather than being bottled up where they are least needed. We provided the examples above of student loans and retirement saving. Another example is found in international finance. Japan, which has a high saving rate, transfers resources to China, which has robust investment opportunities; this transfer occurs through both loans and direct foreign investments in China.
- The financial system *manages risks* for the economy. ② In one sense, risk management is like resource transfer: it moves risks from those people or sectors that most need to reduce their risks and transfers or spreads the risks to others who are better able to weather them. For example, fire insurance on your house takes a risk that you may lose a $200,000 investment and spreads that risk among hundreds or thousands of stockholders of the insurance company.
- The financial system *pools and subdivides funds* ③ depending upon the need of the individual saver or investor. As an investor, you might want to invest $10,000 in a diversified portfolio of common stocks. To buy efficiently a portfolio of 100 companies might require $10 million of funds. Here is where a stock mutual fund comes in: by having 1000 investors, it can buy the portfolio, subdivide it, and manage it for you. In return, a well-run mutual fund might charge $30 per year on your $10,000 portfolio. Additionally, a modern economy requires large-scale firms which have billions of dollars of invested plant and equipment. No single person is likely to be able to afford that—and if someone could, that person would not want all his or her eggs in one basket. The modern corporation can and does undertake this task because of its ability to sell shares of stock to many people and pool these funds to make large and risky investments.
- The financial system performs an important *clearinghouse function*, ④ which facilitates transactions between payers (purchasers) and payees (sellers). For example, when you write a check to buy a new computer, a clearinghouse will debit your bank and credit the bank of the company selling the computer. This function allows rapid transfers of funds around the world.

---

① 金融系统跨时间、部门和地区来转移资源。
② 金融系统对经济有管控风险的作用。
③ 金融系统根据个人储蓄者或者投资者的需要吸纳和发放资金。
④ 金融系统发挥着重要的票据交易所的功能，这一功能方便了付款人（买家）与收款人（卖家）之间的交易活动。

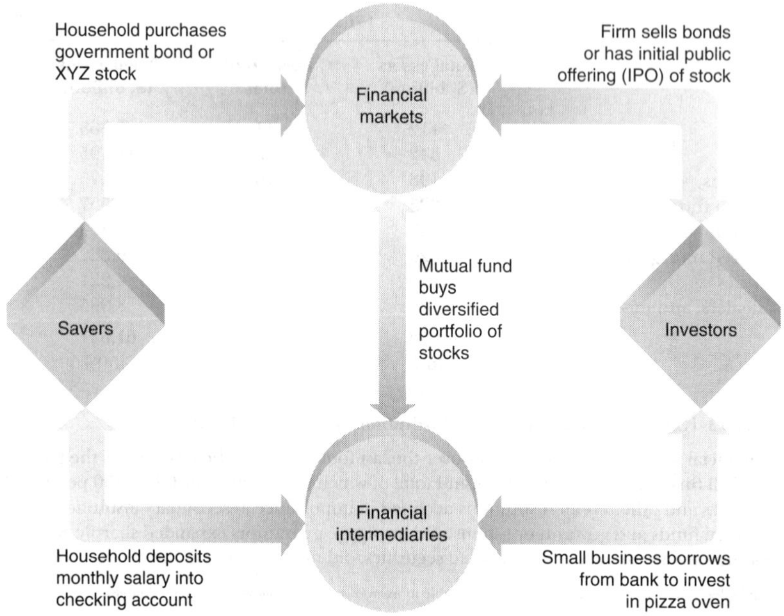

FIGURE 23-1. The Flow of Funds Tracks Financial Flows in the Economy

Savers and investors transfer funds across time, space, and sectors through financial markets and financial intermediaries. Some flows (such as buying 100 shares of XYZ) go directly through financial markets, while others (such as purchasing shares of mutual funds or depositing money in your checking account) go through financial intermediaries.

资金的流动
The Flow of Funds

We can illustrate a simplified account of financial ① markets through a picture of the **flow of funds,** shown in Figure 23-1. This shows two sets of economic agents—savers and investors—and representative examples of saving and investing through financial markets and financial intermediaries.

This picture is simplified, for there are many different kinds of financial assets or instruments, as we will see in the next section.

金融资产的类别
A MENU OF FINANCIAL ASSETS

Financial assets are claims by one party against another party. In the United States, they consist primarily of *dollar-denominated assets* (whose payments are fixed in dollar terms) and *equities* (which are claims on residual flows such as profits or on real assets). Table 23-2 shows the major financial instruments for the United States at the end of 2007. The total value of financial assets was $142 trillion, which totals an enormous $1.2 million per American household. Of course, many of these assets are offseting items, but these huge numbers show how vast the financial system has become.

Here are the major financial instruments or assets:

- *Money* and its two components are very special ② assets, and they will be defined carefully later in this chapter.
- *Savings accounts* are deposits with banks or credit ③ institutions, usually guaranteed by governments, that have a fixed-dollar principal value and interest rates determined by short-term market interest rates.

---

① 如图 23-1 所示，我们可以用**资金流动图**来说明经过简化的金融市场账户。

② 货币与它的两个组成要素都是极其特殊的资产，我们将在本章的后面认真地予以定义。

③ 储蓄账户系指银行或者信贷机构吸纳的存款，通常由政府担保，有固定的美元本金价值，利率由短期的市场利率决定。

Financial instrument	Total ($, billion)	Percent of total
Money (M_1)		
Currency	774	0.5
Checking deposits	745	0.5
Savings deposits	7,605	5.4
Money market and mutual funds	10,852	7.6
Credit market instruments		
Government and government-sponsored	12,475	8.8
Private	38,660	27.2
Corporate and noncorporate equity	29,355	20.7
Insurance and pension reserves	13,984	9.9
Miscellaneous credit and other	27,470	19.4
Total, all financial instruments	**141,921**	**100.0**

TABLE 23-2. Major Financial Instruments in the United States, 2007

This table shows the wide range of financial assets owned by households, firms, and businesses in the United States. The total value is larger than the amount issued by financial institutions alone because many assets are issued by other entities, such as governments.

Source: Federal Reserve Board, Flow of Funds, available at *www.federalreserve.gov/releases/z1/*, level tables.

- *Credit market instruments* are dollar-denominated obligations of governments or private entities. Federal securities are generally thought to be risk-free assets. Other credit market instruments, which have varying degrees of risk, are mortgages, corporate securities, and junk bonds. ①
- *Common stocks* (which are a kind of equity) are ownership rights to companies. They yield dividends, which are payments drawn from company profits. Publicly traded stocks, which are priced on stock markets, are discussed later in this chapter. Noncorporate equities are the values of partnerships, farms, and small businesses. ②
- *Money market funds* and *mutual funds* are funds that hold millions or billions of dollars in either short-term assets or stocks and can be subdivided into fractional shares to be bought by small investors. ③
- *Pension funds* represent ownership in the assets that are held by companies or pension plans. Workers and companies contribute to these funds during working years. These funds are then drawn down to support people during their retirement years. ④
- *Financial derivatives* are included in the credit market instruments. These are new forms of financial instruments whose values are based on or derived from the values of other assets. One important example is a stock option, whose value depends upon the value of the stock to which it is benchmarked. ⑤

Note that this list of financial assets excludes the single most important asset owned by most people—their houses, which are tangible as opposed to financial assets.

利率概述
Review of Interest Rates

Chapter 15 presented a full survey of rates of return, present value, and interest rates. You should review these concepts carefully. Below are the main points.

The interest rate is the price paid for borrowing money. We usually calculate interest as percent per year on the amount of borrowed funds. There are many interest rates, depending upon the maturity, risk, tax status, and other attributes of the loan. ⑥

Some examples will illustrate how interest works:

- When you graduate from college, you have only $500. You decide to keep it in the form of currency in a jar. If you don't spend any, you will still have $500 at the end of 1 year because currency has a zero interest rate.

---

① 信贷市场工具是政府或者私有实体以美元为单位发行的证券。

② 普通股（一种股本）系指对企业的所有权。

③ 货币市场基金和共同基金是持有数百万甚至数十亿美元短期资产或者股票的基金，可经过细分后供小型投资者购买。

④ 养老基金是公司或者养老金计划所持有的资产所有权。

⑤ 金融衍生产品属于信贷市场工具，它是全新形式的金融工具，其价值以其他资产价值为基础，或者衍生于其他资产价值。

⑥ 利率是借入资金应付的价格。我们通常以每年所借资金总额的百分比来计算利息。基于还款期限、风险、税负状况以及贷款的其他属性，利率分为很多种。

- A little later, you deposit $2000 in a savings account at your local bank, where the interest rate on savings accounts is 4 percent per year. At the end of 1 year, the bank will have paid $80 in interest into your account, so the account will now be worth $2080.
- You start your first job and decide to buy a small house that costs $100,000. You go to your local bank and find that a 30-year, fixed-rate mortgage has an interest rate of 5 percent per year. Each month you must make a mortgage payment of $536.83. Note that this payment is a little bit more than the pro-rated monthly interest charge of 0.417 (= $^5/_{12}$) percent per month. Why? Because the monthly payment includes not only interest but also *amortization* (the repayment of principal, the amount borrowed). By the time you have made your 360 monthly payments, you will have completely paid off the loan.

货币的特殊问题

B. THE SPECIAL CASE OF MONEY

Let's now turn to the special case of money. If you think about it for a moment, you will realize that money is a strange thing. We study for years so that we can earn a good living, yet each dollar bill is just paper, with minimal intrinsic value. Money is useless until we get rid of it.

However, money is anything but useless from a macroeconomic point of view. Monetary policy is today one of the two important tools (along with fiscal policy) the government has to stabilize the business cycle. The central bank uses its control over money, credit, and interest rates to encourage growth when the economy slows and to slow growth when inflationary pressures rise.

When the financial system is well managed, output grows smoothly and prices are stable. But an unstable financial system, as seen in many countries torn apart by war or revolution, can lead to inflation or depression. Many of the world's major macroeconomic traumas of the twentieth century can be traced to mismanaged monetary systems.

We now turn to a careful analysis of the definition of and demand for money.

货币的演变
THE EVOLUTION OF MONEY

货币的历史
The History of Money

What is money? **Money** *is anything that serves as a commonly accepted medium of exchange.* Because money has a long and fascinating history, we will begin with a description of money's evolution. ①

Barter. In an early textbook on money, when Stanley Jevons wanted to illustrate the tremendous leap forward that occurred as societies introduced money, he used the following experience: [2]

> Some years since, Mademoiselle Zélie, a singer of the Théâtre Lyrique at Paris, . . . gave a concert in the Society Islands. In exchange for an air from Norma and a few other songs, she was to receive a third part of the receipts. [3] [4] [5]
>
> When counted, her share was found to consist of three pigs, twenty-three turkeys, forty-four chickens, five thousand cocoa-nuts, besides considerable quantities of bananas, lemons, and oranges. . . . [I]n Paris . . . this amount of live stock and vegetables might have brought four thousand francs, which would have been good remuneration for five songs. In the Society Islands, however, pieces of money were scarce; and as Mademoiselle could not consume any considerable portion of the receipts herself, it became necessary in the mean time to feed the pigs and poultry with the fruit.

This example describes **barter,** which consists of the exchange of goods for other goods. Exchange through barter contrasts with exchange through money because pigs, turkeys, and lemons are not generally acceptable monies that we or Mademoiselle Zélie can use for buying things. Although barter is better than no trade at all, it operates under grave disadvantages because an elaborate division of labor would be unthinkable without the introduction of the great social invention of money.

As economies develop, people no longer barter one good for another. Instead, they sell goods for money and then use money to buy other goods they wish to have. At first glance this seems to complicate rather than simplify matters, as it replaces one transaction with two. If you have apples and want nuts, would it not be simpler to trade one for the other rather than to sell the apples for money and then use the money to buy nuts?

[5] Society Islands：俗译为“社会群岛”，应译为“学会群岛”，源于库克船长（James Cook，1728~1779）的探险发现，以英国皇家学会命名，太平洋东南部法属波利尼西亚的主要岛群，19世纪中叶为法属保护地。Norma：早期浪漫主义音乐的代表之一，19世纪意大利作曲家贝里尼（Vincenzo Bellini，1801~1835）的歌剧作品。19世纪许多著名的女中音、女高音和男高音的成名均得益于演唱其作品。

① 什么是货币？**货币**是被普遍接受的起交易媒介作用的任何东西。

[2] Stanley Jevons：全名为威廉姆·斯坦利·杰文斯（William Stanley Jevons，1835~1882），著名的英国经济学家和逻辑学家，边际效用学派的创始人之一，数理经济学派的早期代表人物。以下这段话出自其专著《货币及其交易机制》（*Money and the Mechanism of Exchange*）中第一章《以物易物》（*Barter*）的“1.1”节。

[3] Mademoiselle Zélie：19世纪中叶活跃在巴黎歌剧界的著名女中音歌唱家，以演唱贝里尼作品成名。

[4] Théâtre Lyrique：19世纪中叶巴黎的四大歌剧演出公司之一，以将外国歌剧作品译成法文并成功演出而闻名。

Actually, the reverse is true: two monetary transactions are simpler than one barter transaction. For example, some people may want to buy apples, and some may want to sell nuts. But it would be a most unusual circumstance to find a person whose desires exactly complement your own—eager to sell nuts and buy apples. To use a classic econom- ① ics phrase, instead of there being a "double coincidence of wants," there is likely to be a "want of coincidence." So, unless a hungry tailor happens to find an unclothed farmer who has both food and a desire for a pair of pants, under barter neither can make a direct trade.

Societies that want to trade extensively simply cannot overcome the overwhelming handicaps of barter. The use of a commonly accepted medium of exchange, money, permits the farmer to buy pants from the tailor, who buys shoes from the cobbler, who buys leather from the farmer.

Commodity Money. Money as a medium of exchange ② first came into human history in the form of commodities. A great variety of items have served as money at one time or another: cattle, olive oil, beer or wine, copper, iron, gold, silver, rings, diamonds, and cigarettes.

Each of the above has advantages and disadvantages. Cattle are not divisible into small change. Beer does not improve with keeping, although wine may. Olive oil provides a nice liquid currency that is as minutely divisible as one wishes, but it is rather messy to handle. And so forth.

By the eighteenth century, commodity money was almost exclusively limited to metals like silver and gold. These forms of money had *intrinsic value,* ③ meaning that they had use value in themselves. Because money had intrinsic value, there was no need for the government to guarantee its value, and the quantity of money was regulated by the market through the supply and demand for gold or silver. But metallic money has shortcomings because scarce resources are required to dig it out of the ground; moreover, it might become abundant simply because of accidental discoveries of ore deposits.

The advent of monetary control by central banks has led to a much more stable currency system. The intrinsic value of money is now its least important feature.

Modern Money. The age of commodity money gave way to the age of *paper money.* The essence of money is now laid bare. Money is wanted not for its own sake but for the things it will buy. We do not wish to consume money directly; rather, we use it by getting rid of it. Even when we choose to keep money, it is valuable only because we can spend it later on.

The use of paper currency has become widespread because it is a convenient medium of exchange. Paper currency is easily carried and stored. The value of money can be protected from counterfeiting by careful engraving. The fact that private individuals cannot legally create money keeps it scarce. Given this limitation on supply, currency has value. It can buy things. As long as people can pay their bills with currency, as long as it is accepted as a means of payment, it serves the function of money.

Paper money issued by governments was gradu- ④ ally overtaken by *bank money*—the checking accounts that we will discuss shortly.

A few years ago, many people predicted that we would soon move to a cashless society. They foresaw that cash and checking accounts would be replaced by electronic money, such as the stored-value cards found in many stores today. But, in fact, consumers have been reluctant to adopt electronic money in substantial amounts. They trust and prefer government money and checks. To some extent electronic transfers, debit cards, and e-banking have replaced paper checks, but these should be seen as different ways of *using* a checking account rather than as different *kinds* of money.

货币供给的构成

Components of the Money Supply

Let us now look more carefully at the different kinds of money, focusing on the United States. The main *monetary aggregate* studied in macroeconomics is known as M_1. This is also called *transactions money*. In earlier times, economists examined other concepts of money, such as M_2. These concepts included further assets and were often useful for looking at broad trends, but they are little used in monetary policy today. The following are the components of M_1:

- *Currency.* Currency is defined as coins and paper money held outside the banking system. Most of us know little more about a \$1 or \$5 bill than that each is inscribed with the picture of an American

---

① 借用经典的经济学术语，似乎应该是“缺乏巧合”，而不是业已成习的“需求的双重巧合”。

② 货币作为一种交易媒介，在人类历史上最初是以商品的形式出现的。

③ 这些货币形式有其固有价值，即它们本身具有使用价值。由于这些货币的固有价值，政府就没有必要对其担保，这样，货币的数量就由市场通过对黄金或者白银的供求关系来调节与管理。但是，由于稀缺资源开采于地下，金属货币有其缺点。更重要的是，矿藏的偶然发现会使稀缺资源变得丰裕。

④ 政府发行的纸币正在逐步被银行货币所取代，这就是我们将在下面讨论的支票账户问题。

statesman, bears some official signatures, and has a number showing its face value. Examine a $10 bill or some other paper bill. You will find that it says "Federal Reserve Note." But what [1] "backs" our paper currency? Many years ago, paper money was backed by gold or silver. There is no such pretense today. Today, all U.S. coins and paper currency are *fiat money*. This term signifies something declared to be money by the government even if it has no intrinsic value. Paper currency and coins are *legal tender*, which must be accepted for all debts, public and private. Currency is approximately one-half of total M_1.

- *Checking deposits*. The other component of M_1 is bank money. This consists of funds, deposited in banks and other financial institutions, on which you can write checks and withdraw your money on demand. The technical name for this component of the money supply is "demand deposits and other checkable deposits." If I have $1000 in my checking account at the Albuquerque National Bank, that deposit can be regarded as money. Why? For the simple reason that I can pay for purchases with checks drawn on it. The funds in my account are a medium of exchange, and it is therefore counted as money.

Students often wonder if credit cards are money. Actually, they are not. The reason is that a credit card is actually an easy (but not cheap!) way to *borrow* money. When paying with a credit card, you are promising to pay the credit card company—with money—at a later date.

Figure 23-2 shows the trend in the ratio of M_1 to GDP. This ratio has declined by a factor of 3 over the last half-century. At the same time, all other financial assets have grown sharply.

Money is anything that serves as a commonly accepted medium of exchange. Today, we define transactions money as M_1, which is the sum of currency held by the public and checking deposits. ②

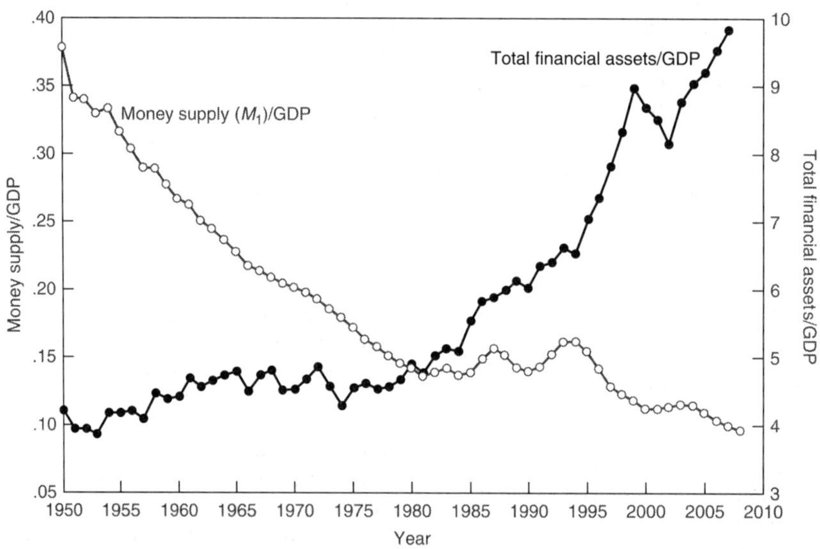

FIGURE 23-2. Money Holdings and Total Financial Assets per Unit of GDP

Total financial assets have risen sharply relative to GDP, while the ratio of the money supply to GDP has gradually declined. Note the vast difference in scale. Total financial assets are defined similarly here as in Table 23-1.

Source: Financial data from the Federal Reserve Board; GDP from the Bureau of Economic Analysis.

---

[1] Federal Reserve Note：官方名称还有 United States Banknote，简写为 U.S. Banknote，美元的正式全称。

② 货币是可以被普遍接受的起交易媒介作用的任何一种东西。现在，我们将交易货币定义为 M_1，指社会大众持有的通货与支票存款的总和。

货币需求
THE DEMAND FOR MONEY

The demand for money is different from the demand for ice cream or movies. Money is not desired for its own sake; you cannot eat nickels, and we seldom hang $100 bills on the wall for the artistic quality of their engraving. Rather, we demand money because it serves us indirectly as a lubricant to trade and exchange.

货币的功能
Money's Functions

Before we analyze the demand for money, let's note money's functions:

- The central function emphasized here is that money serves as a *medium of exchange*. Without money, we would be constantly roving around looking for someone to barter with. Money's value is often shown when the monetary system malfunctions. After Russia abandoned its central- ①
planning system in the early 1990s, for example, people spent hours waiting in line for goods and tried to get dollars or other foreign currencies because the ruble had ceased to function as an acceptable means of exchange.
- Money is also used as the *unit of account*, the unit by which we measure the value of things. Just as we measure weight in kilograms, we measure value in money. The use of a common unit of account simplifies economic life enormously.
- Money is sometimes used as a *store of value*. In comparison with risky assets like stocks or real estate or gold, money is relatively riskless. In earlier days, people held currency as a safe form of wealth. Today, when people seek a safe haven for their wealth, the vast preponderance of their wealth is held in nonmonetary assets, such as savings accounts, stocks, bonds, and real estate.

持有货币的成本
The Costs of Holding Money

What is the *cost* of holding money? Money is costly ②
because it has a lower yield than do other safe assets. Currency has a nominal interest rate of exactly zero percent per year. Checking deposits sometimes have a small interest rate, but that rate is usually well below the rate on savings accounts or money market mutual funds. For example, over the period 2000–2007, currency had a yield of 0 percent per year, checking accounts had an average yield of around 0.2 percent per year, and short-term money funds had a yield of around 4.6 percent per year. If the weighted yield on money (currency and checking accounts) was 0.1 percent per year, then the *cost of holding money* was 4.5 = 4.6 − 0.1 percent per year. Figure 23-3 on page 462 shows the interest rate on money as compared to that on safe short-term assets.

The cost of holding money is the interest forgone ③
from not holding other assets. That cost is usually very close to the short-term interest rate.

货币需求的两个起因
Two Sources of Money Demand

Transactions Demand for Money. People need money primarily because their incomes and expenditures do not come at the same time. For example, I might be paid on the last day of the month, but I buy food, newspapers, gasoline, and clothing throughout the month. The need to have money to pay for purchases, or transactions, of goods, services, and other items constitutes the *transactions demand for money.*

For example, suppose that a family earns $3000 per month, keeps it in money, and spends it evenly throughout the month. A calculation will show that the family holds $1500 on average in money balances.

This example can help us see how the demand for money responds to different economic influences. If all prices and incomes double, the nominal demand for M doubles. Thus the transactions demand for money doubles if nominal GDP doubles with no change in real GDP or other real variables.

How does the demand for money vary with interest rates? As interest rates rise, the family might say, "Let's put only half of our money in the checking account at the beginning of the month and put the other half in a savings account earning 8 percent per year. Then on day 15, we'll take that $1500 out of the savings account and put it into our checking account to pay the next 2 weeks' bills."

This means that as interest rates rose and the family decided to put half its earnings in a savings account, the average money balance of our family fell from $1500 to $750. This shows how money holdings ④
(or the demand for money) may be sensitive to interest rates: other things equal, as interest rates rise, the quantity of money demanded declines.

---

① 例如，在20世纪90年代早期，俄罗斯在放弃了中央计划体系之后，由于卢布早已失去了其作为普遍接受的交易媒介的功能，导致民众花数小时排队抢购商品，竭尽全力兑换美元或者其他外汇。

② 持有货币的成本是什么？由于持有货币的收益率低于投资其他安全资产的收益，所以成本很高。

③ 持有货币的成本是未持有其他资产所放弃的利息，通常与短期利率极为接近。

④ 这一案例说明，货币持有量（或者说货币的需要量）对于利率的敏感程度，即在其他条件保持不变的情况下，随着利率上升，货币需求量下降。

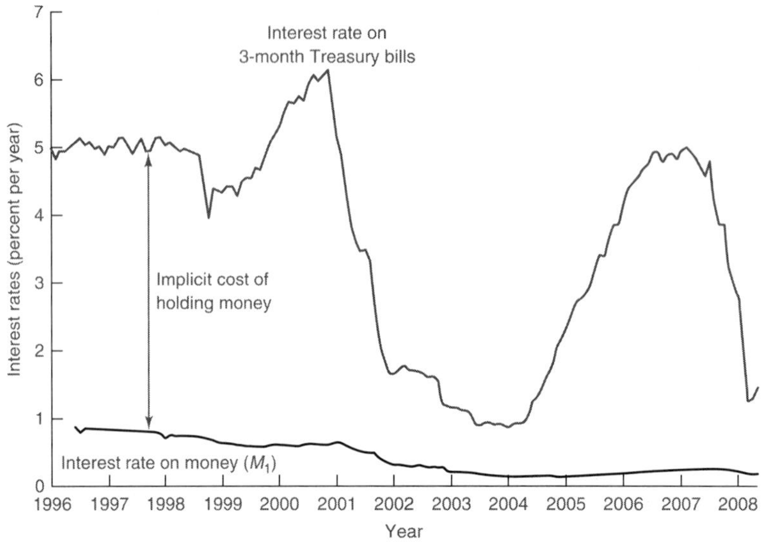

FIGURE 23-3. Interest Rates on Money and Safe Short-Term Assets

This figure shows the interest rate on money (which is the average of zero on currency and the rate on checking accounts) as compared to the interest rate on short-term Treasury securities. The difference between these two interest rates is the implicit cost of holding money.

Source: Treasury interest rate from Federal Reserve; interest rate on checking accounts from Informa Research Services, Inc.

Asset Demand. In addition to its use for transac- ① tion needs, you might wonder if money itself would ever be used as a store of value. The answer today is, not often. In a modern economy in normal times, people prefer to keep their nontransaction assets in safe, interest-bearing assets such as savings accounts or money funds. Suppose you need \$2000 a month in your checking account for your transactions, and you have another \$50,000 in savings. Surely, you would be better off putting the \$50,000 in a money market fund earning 4.6 percent per year than in a checking account earning 0.2 percent per year. After a decade, the latter would be worth only \$51,009 while the former would be worth \$78,394. (Make sure you can reproduce these numbers.)

There are some important exceptions, however, where money itself might be used as a store of value. Money might be an attractive asset in primitive financial systems where there are no other reliable assets. U.S. currency is widely held abroad as a safe asset in countries where hyperinflation occurs, or where a currency might be devalued, or where the financial system is unreliable. Additionally, in advanced countries, people might hold money as an asset when interest rates are near zero. This situation, known as a liquidity trap, terrifies central bankers because they lose the ability to affect interest rates. We will review this syndrome in the next chapter.

The main reason people hold money (M_1) is to ② meet their transactions demand. This means that money is an acceptable medium of exchange that we can use to buy our goods and pay our bills. As our incomes rise, the dollar value of the goods we buy tends to go up as well, and we therefore need more money for transactions, raising our demand for money. In a modern financial system, there is generally little or no asset demand for M_1.

① 除了满足交易需求之外，你或许想知晓货币本身是否可用作价值储藏。现实的答案是，不可经常用。在现代经济中，正常情况下，人们都优先选择将非交易性资产投放在安全的、有持续利息收益的资产中，如储蓄账户或者货币基金。

② 人们持有货币 M_1 的主要原因是满足他们的交易需求。这就意味着，货币是一种可接受的交易媒介，人们可以用它购买商品与支付账单。随着收入的增加，我们购买商品的美元价值也就会随之增加，那么，就需要更多的货币用于交易，从而提高了我们对货币的需求。在现代金融体系中，总体上几乎没有对 M_1 的资产性需求。

银行与货币供给

C. BANKS AND THE SUPPLY OF MONEY

Now that we have described the basic structure of the ① financial system, we turn to commercial banks and the supply of money. If you look back at the description of the monetary transmission mechanism at the beginning of this chapter, you will see that the activities of banks are the critical third step. While money constitutes a relatively small fraction of all financial assets, the interaction between the central bank and commercial banks turns out to play a central role in the setting of interest rates, and ultimately in influencing macroeconomic behavior.

Banks are fundamentally businesses organized to earn profits for their owners. A commercial bank provides certain services for its customers and in return receives payments from them.

Table 23-3 shows the consolidated balance sheet of all U.S. commercial banks. A *balance sheet* is a ② statement of a firm's financial position at a point in time. It lists *assets* (items that the firm owns) and *liabilities* (items that the firm owes). Each entry in a balance sheet is valued at its actual market value or its historical cost.[1] The difference between the total value of assets and total liabilities is called *net worth*.

Except for the details, a bank balance sheet looks ③ much like a balance sheet for any other business. The unique feature of a bank balance sheet is an asset called **reserves.** This is a technical term used in banking to refer to a special category of bank assets that are regulated by the central bank. Reserves equal currency held by the bank ("vault cash") plus deposits with Federal Reserve Banks. In earlier days, reserves were held to pay depositors, but today they serve primarily to meet legal reserve requirements. We will discuss reserves in detail in the next chapter.

金匠铺如何发展成银行
How Banks Developed from Goldsmith Establishments

Commercial banking began in England with the goldsmiths, who developed the practice of storing people's gold and valuables for safekeeping. At first, such establishments simply functioned as secure warehouses. Depositors left their gold for safekeeping and were given a receipt. Later they presented their receipt, paid a fee, and got back their gold.

What would the balance sheet of a typical goldsmith establishment look like? Perhaps like Table 23-4. A total of $1 million has been deposited in its vaults, and this whole sum is held as a cash asset (this is the item "Reserves" in the balance sheet). To balance this

[1] Balance sheets, assets, and liabilities are extensively discussed in Chapter 7 of the full textbook.

Balance Sheet of All Commercial Banking Institutions, 2008 (billions of dollars)

Assets		Liabilities and Net Worth	
Reserves	43	Checking deposits	629
Loans	6,250	Savings and time deposits	5,634
Investments and securities	2,265	Other liabilities	2,643
Other assets	1,404	Net worth (capital)	1,056
Total	9,961	Total	9,961

TABLE 23-3. Balance Sheet of All U.S. Commercial Banks

Commercial banks are diversified financial institutions and are the major providers of checking deposits, which is an important component of M_1. Checking accounts are payable on demand and thus can be used as a medium of exchange. Reserves are held primarily to meet legal requirements, rather than to provide against possible unexpected withdrawals. (Note that banks have a small amount of net worth or capital relative to their total assets and liabilities. The ratio of liabilities to net worth is called the "leverage ratio." Highly leveraged financial institutions produce systemic risk if the values of their assets all deteriorate at the same time, as occurred in 2007–2009.)

Source: Federal Reserve Board, available at *www.federalreserve.gov/releases/*.

① 基于我们已经把金融系统的基本结构作了详尽描述，本节开始，我们讨论商业银行和货币供给的问题。

② 资产负债表是企业在某一时间点上的财务状况表，资产（企业所拥有的项目）和负债（企业所欠的项目）均在表中列出。资产负债表中的每一项均以其实际市场价值或者历史成本计入。资产的总价值和总负债之间的差额称作净值。

③ 银行资产负债表的独特之处是称为**准备金**的资产。这是银行业使用的一个术语，表示银行资产中的一个特殊类别，由中央银行管控。准备金等于银行持有的通货（即备用现金）与联邦储备银行的存款之和。早期，准备金用来保证储户提现之需，但今天，它的主要功能是满足法定准备金要求。我们将在下一章中详细讨论准备金的问题。

Goldsmith Balance Sheet with 100% Reserves			
Assets		**Liabilities**	
Reserves	1,000,000	Demand deposits	1,000,000
Total	1,000,000	Total	1,000,000

TABLE 23-4. First Goldsmith Bank Held 100 Percent Cash Reserves against Demand Deposits

In a primitive banking system, with 100 percent backing of deposits, no creation of money out of reserves is possible.

asset, there is a demand deposit of the same amount. Reserves are therefore 100 percent of deposits.

In today's language, the goldsmiths' demand deposits would be part of the money supply; they would be "bank money." However, the bank money just offsets the amount of ordinary money (gold or currency) placed in the bank's vaults and withdrawn from active circulation. No money creation has taken place. The process is of no more interest than if the public decided to convert nickels into dimes. *A 100 percent-reserve banking system has a neutral effect on money and the macroeconomy because it has no effect on the money supply.* ①

We can go a step further and ask what would happen if there were paper money issued under a gold standard with 100 percent backing by gold. In this case, you can create a new Table 23-4 by writing "gold notes" instead of "demand deposits." The gold notes would be currency and part of M_1. Again, the money supply would be unchanged because the currency has 100 percent backing.

部分准备金银行
Fractional-Reserve Banking

Let's take another step toward today's banking system by introducing *fractional-reserve banking*. Banks soon learned that they did not need to keep 100 percent of their gold or silver as reserves against their notes and deposits. People did not all come to redeem their notes at the same time. A bank might be safe if it kept only fractional reserves to back its notes and deposits. This was a tiny first step on the road to today's vast financial system. ②

We explore the implications of fractional-reserve banking starting with a situation where a system of banks operates with a customary or legal requirement that it keep reserves equal to at least 10 percent

Goldsmith Balance Sheet with Fractional Reserves			
Assets		**Liabilities**	
Reserves	100,000	Demand deposits	
Investments	900,000	and gold notes	1,000,000
Total	1,000,000	Total	1,000,000

TABLE 23-5. Goldsmith Bank Keeps 10 Percent Reserves against Deposits and Gold Notes

Later, Goldsmith Bank learns that it does not need to keep 100 percent reserves. Here, it has decided to invest 90 percent and keep only 10 percent in reserves against deposits and notes.

of deposits. Suppose that the president of Goldsmith [3] Bank wakes up and says, "We do not need to keep all this sterile gold as reserves. In fact, we can lend out 90 percent of it and still have sufficient gold to meet the demands of depositors."

So Goldsmith Bank lends out \$900,000 and keeps the remaining \$100,000 as gold reserves. The initial result is shown in Table 23-5. The bank has invested \$900,000—perhaps lending money to Duck.com, which is building a toy factory.

But that is not the end of the process. Duck.com [4] will take the \$900,000 loan and deposit it in its own checking account to pay the bills for the factory. Suppose, for simplicity, that the firm has a checking account in Goldsmith Bank. The interesting result here, shown in Table 23-6, is that Goldsmith Bank

Goldsmith Balance Sheet after Deposit of Loan by Duck.com			
Assets		**Liabilities**	
Reserves	1,000,000	Demand deposits	
Investments	900,000	and gold notes	1,900,000
Total	1,900,000	Total	1,900,000

TABLE 23-6. After the Firm Deposits Its Loan, the Banking System Has Excess Reserves to Lend Out Again

The Duck firm deposits its \$900,000 loan into its account. This increases Goldsmith Bank's reserves of gold back to \$1,000,000. Soon the excess will be lent out again.

---

① 一个具有100%准备金率的银行系统对货币和宏观经济的影响是中性的，原因是它对货币供给不产生影响。

② 储户不可能在同一时间来银行兑现。银行只要按其票据和储蓄持有少量准备金，即可安全地运营。这就是当时向今天庞大的金融体系首先迈出的一小步。

[3] Goldsmith Bank：萨缪尔森借用传统金匠作坊虚拟，籍以隐指银行业的过渡。金匠作坊是古老的外汇交易平台，在17世纪中叶的英国内战和第二次英荷战争中，金匠作坊扮演了极其重要的角色，加速了英国的传统金匠作坊向现代银行业的转化。

[4] Duck.com：同“Goldsmith Bank”一样，用虚拟来隐喻传统的文化产业向当代过渡。Duck即家喻户晓的“唐老鸭”（Donald Fauntleroy Duck）的略称。

has recovered the \$900,000 of reserves. In essence, Duck.com took the loan of gold and then lent it back to the bank. (The process would be exactly the same if Duck.com went to another bank: that bank would have excess reserves of \$900,000.)

But now the bank needs to keep only 10 percent × \$1.9 million = \$190,000 for reserves, so it can lend out the excess \$810,000. Soon the \$810,000 will show up in a bank deposit. This process of deposit, relending, and redeposit continues in a chain of dwindling expansions.

银行系统的最终均衡
Final System Equilibrium

Now let's sum up the total of all deposits. We started with \$1,000,000 in deposits, then added \$900,000, then \$810,000 and so on. The total is given by the sum:

$$\begin{aligned}\text{Total deposits} &= 1{,}000{,}000 + 1{,}000{,}000 \times 0.9 + 1{,}000{,}000 \times 0.9^2 + \cdots \\ &= 1{,}000{,}000[1 + 0.9 + 0.9^2 + \cdots + (0.9)^n + \cdots] \\ &= 1{,}000{,}000\left(\frac{1}{1-0.9}\right) = 1{,}000{,}000\left(\frac{1}{0.1}\right) = 10{,}000{,}000\end{aligned}$$

At the end of the process, the total amount of deposits and money is \$10 million, which is 10 times the total amount of reserves. Assuming that Goldsmith is the only bank, or that we are looking at the consolidated banking system, we can show the final balance sheet in Table 23-7. The point here is that once banks require only fractional reserves, the total money supply is a multiple of the reserves.

This can be seen intuitively. The cumulative process just described must come to an end when every bank in the system has reserves equal to 10 percent of deposits. In other words, the final equilibrium of the banking system will be the point at which 10 percent of deposits (D) equals total reserves. What level of D satisfies this condition? The answer is D = \$10 million.

When banks hold fractional reserves against their deposits, they actually create money. The total bank money is generally equal to total reserves multiplied by the inverse of the reserve ratio: ①

$$\text{Bank money} = \text{total reserves} \times \left(\frac{1}{\text{reserve ratio}}\right)$$

Consolidated Balance Sheet of All Banks in Equilibrium			
Assets		**Liabilities**	
Reserves	1,000,000	Demand deposits	
Investments	9,000,000	and gold notes	10,000,000
Total	10,000,000	Total	10,000,000

TABLE 23-7. Final Equilibrium Balance Sheet When Banking System Has No Excess Reserves

We aggregate the banking system together assuming that there are \$1,000,000 of total reserves. When banks have lent out all excess reserves, so reserves are just 10 percent of deposits and notes, total money is 1/0.1 = 10 times reserves.

现代银行系统
A Modern Banking System

It is time to put our fable of goldsmiths behind us. How does all this relate to the actual banking system today? The surprising answer is that with some additional details, the process we just described fits today's banking system exactly. Here are the key elements of the modern banking system:

- Banks are required to hold at least 10 percent of their checking deposits as reserves, in the form of either currency or deposits with the Federal Reserve (more on this in the next chapter). ②
- The Federal Reserve buys and sells reserves at a target interest rate set by the Fed (again, more on this in the next chapter). ③
- The checking-deposit component of M_1 is therefore determined by the amount of reserves along with the required reserve ratio. ④

A few qualifications need to be mentioned before closing this section. First, commercial banks do much more than simply provide checking accounts, as we saw in Table 23-3. This fact may complicate the task of the regulatory authorities, but it does not change the basic operation of monetary policy.

A second complication arises if nominal interest rates approach zero. This is referred to as the liquidity trap. We will discuss this syndrome in the next chapter.

股票市场
D. THE STOCK MARKET

We close this chapter with a tour through one of the most exciting parts of a capitalist system: the stock market. A **stock market** is a place where shares

① 当银行按照其存款额来保有少量准备金时，它们实际上是在创造货币。银行的货币总量一般等于准备金总额乘以准备金率的倒数。

② 银行必须持有至少 10% 的支票存款作为准备金，形式是现金，或在联邦储备系统的存款（这个问题将在下一章进一步讨论）。

③ 美国联邦储备局以自己所确定的目标利率购入或者出售准备金（下一章中将对此再作进一步的讨论）。

④ 因此，M_1 中的支票存款由准备金的数量决定，而准备金的数量由法定准备金率决定。

in publicly owned companies—the titles to business firms—are bought and sold. In 2008, the value of corporate equities in the United States was estimated at $21 trillion. The stock market is the hub of our corporate economy.

[1] The New York Stock Exchange：纽约证券交易所。1817 年 3 月 8 日以"纽约证券交易委员会"（New York Stock & Exchange Board）正式挂牌，1863 年改为现名，它是上市公司总市值第一和交易量第二的交易所。

The New York Stock Exchange is America's main [1] stock market, listing more than a thousand securities. Another important market is the NASDAQ, [2] which had a meteoric rise and subsequent collapse in stock prices after 2000. Every large financial center has a stock exchange. Major ones are located in Tokyo, London, Frankfurt, Shanghai, and, of course, New York.

不同资产的风险与收益
Risk and Return on Different Assets

Before discussing major issues in stock market analysis, we need to introduce some basic concepts in financial economics. We noted earlier in this chapter that different assets have different characteristics. Two important characteristics are the rate of return and the risk.

The *rate of return* is the total dollar gain from a security (measured as a percent of the price at the beginning of the period). For savings accounts and short-term bonds, the return would simply be the interest rate. For most other assets, the return combines an income item (such as dividends) with a *capital gain* or *loss,* which represents the increase or decrease in the value of the asset between two periods.

We can illustrate the rate of return using data on stocks. (For this example, we ignore taxes and commissions.) Say that you bought a representative portfolio of $10,000 worth of stocks in U.S. companies at the end of 1996. Over the next 3 years, your fund would have had a total real return (including dividends plus capital gains and correcting for inflation) of 32 percent per year.

However, before you get too excited about these fantastic gains, be forewarned that the stock market also goes down. In the 3 years after 1999, real stock prices declined by 19 percent per year. An even worse experience came in 2008, when stock prices declined 38 percent during the year.

The fact that some assets have predictable rates of ③ return while others are quite risky leads to the next important characteristic of investments. **Risk** refers to the variability of the returns on an investment. If I buy a 1-year Treasury bond with a 6 percent return, the bond is a riskless investment because I am sure to get my expected dollar return. On the other hand, if I buy $10,000 worth of stocks, I am uncertain about their year-end value.

Economists often measure risk as the standard deviation of returns; this is a measure of dispersion whose range encompasses about two-thirds of the variation.[2] For example, from 1908 to 2008, common stocks had an average annual real return of 6 percent per year with an annual standard deviation of return of 16 percent. This implies that the real return was between 22(= 6 + 16) percent and −10(= 6 − 16) percent about two-thirds of the time.

Individuals generally prefer higher return, but ④ they also prefer lower risk because they are *risk-averse.* This means that they must be rewarded by higher returns to induce them to hold investments with higher risks. We would not be surprised, therefore, to learn that over the long run safe investments like bonds have lower average returns than risky investments like stocks.

Table 15-1 on page 289 showed the historical returns or interest rates on a number of important investments. We show the most important assets in the *risk-return diagram* in Figure 23-4. This diagram shows the average real (or inflation-corrected) return on the vertical axis and the historical risk (measured as a standard deviation) on the horizontal axis. Note the positive relationship between risk and return.

泡沫与崩盘
Bubbles and Crashes

The history of finance is one of the most exciting ⑤ parts of economics. Sometimes, sound judgments get put aside as markets engage in frenzies of speculation, often followed by moods of pessimism and falling prices.

Investors are sometimes divided into those who invest on firm foundations and those who try to

[2] The standard deviation is a measure of variability that can be found in any elementary statistics textbook. It is roughly equal to the average deviation of a series from its mean. The precise definition of standard deviation is the square root of the squared deviations of a variable from its mean. As an example, if a variable takes the values of 1, 3, 1, 3, the mean or expected value is 2 while the standard deviation is 1.

[2] NASDAQ：纳斯达克，National Association of Securities Dealers Automated Quotations（全美证券商协会自动报价系统）的缩写，全球最大的股票电子交易市场，始建于 1971 年，催生于信息和服务业的崛起。

③ 事实上，某些资产的收益率是可以预测的，而有些资产却具有相当大的风险。因此，风险成为投资的另一重要特征。**风险**一词系指投资收益的可变性。

④ 个人通常偏好更高的收益，但又喜欢低风险，因为他们是风险规避型的。这就意味着要引导他们持有更高风险的投资就必须给予他们更高的回报。因此，我们认识到，长远来看，像债券这样安全的投资比风险投资（如股票）的平均收益率更低就毫不奇怪了。

⑤ 金融史是经济学中最让人兴奋的部分之一。有时候，当市场陷入狂热的投机行为时，理性的判断就会搁置一边，随之而来的常常是悲观的情绪和价格下跌。

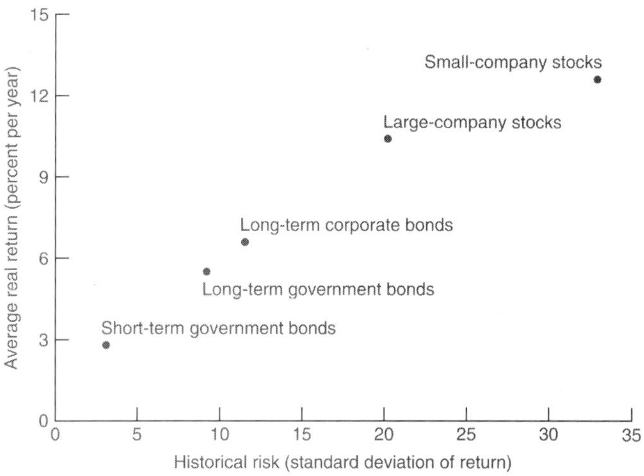

FIGURE 23-4. Risk and Return on Major Investments, 1926–2005

Investments vary in their average returns and riskiness. Bonds tend to be safe with low returns, while stocks have much higher returns but face higher risks. This diagram shows the *historical* risk and return on different financial assets. Depending upon market sentiments, the *expected* risk and return may differ markedly from the historical experience.

Source: Ibbotson Associates, 2006.

outguess the market psychology. The firm-foundation approach holds that assets should be valued on the basis of their intrinsic value. For common stocks, the intrinsic value is the expected present value of the dividends. If a stock has a constant dividend of \$2 per year and the appropriate interest rate with which to discount dividends is 5 percent per year, the intrinsic value would be \$2/.05 = \$40 per share. The firm-foundation approach is the slow but safe way of getting rich.

Impatient souls might share the view of Keynes, ①
who argued that investors are more likely to worry about market psychology and to speculate on the future value of assets rather than wait patiently for stocks to prove their intrinsic value. He argued, "It is not sensible to pay 25 for an investment which is worth 30, if you also believe that the market will value it at 20 three months hence." The market psychologist tries to guess what the average investor thinks, which requires considering what the average investor thinks about the average investor, and so on, ad infinitum.

When a psychological frenzy seizes the market, it can result in speculative bubbles and crashes. A *speculative bubble* occurs when prices rise because ②
people think they are going to rise even further in the future—it is the reverse of Keynes's just-cited dictum. A piece of land may be worth only \$1000, but if you see a land-price boom driving prices up 50 percent each year, you might buy it for \$2000 hoping you can sell it to someone else next year for \$3000.

A speculative bubble fulfills its own promises for a while. If people buy because they think stocks will rise, their act of buying sends up the price of stocks. This causes other people to buy even more and sends the dizzy dance off on another round. But, unlike people who play cards or dice, no one apparently loses what the winners gain. Of course, the prizes are all on paper and would disappear if everyone tried to cash them in. But why should anyone want to sell such lucrative securities? Prices rise because of hopes and dreams, not because the profits and dividends of companies are soaring.

History is marked by bubbles in which speculative prices were driven up far beyond the intrinsic value of the asset. In seventeenth-century Holland, a tulip mania drove tulip prices to levels higher than the price of a house. In the eighteenth century, the stock
of the South Sea Company rose to fantastic levels on [3]
empty promises that the firm would enrich its stockholders. In more recent times, similar bubbles have
been found in biotechnology, Japanese land, "emerg- [4]
ing markets," and a vacuum-cleaning company called

① 那些骚动的灵魂很可能被凯恩斯言中。凯恩斯认为，投资者更可能担心市场心理，从而去投机资产的未来价值，而不是耐心地等待股票证明其内在价值。他认为："如果有一笔价值 30 美元的投资，你也确信在今后的三个月内，其市场估价将在 20 美元的水平，但你还是付出 25 美元将它买入，这个行为就是不明智的。" 市场心理学家竭力猜测普通投资者究竟在想些什么，这就需要考虑到普通投资者之间相互对对方的思考，诸如此类的问题，没完没了。

② *a speculative bubble*：投机泡沫

[3] South Sea Company：1711 年英国政府为降低政府成本而成立的一家由民众个人持股的股份公司，以享有与南美洲贸易的垄断权而使持有股票的普通民众产生暴富的幻觉，却因西班牙战争中英国军队的惨败和南美洲易手于西班牙控制而导致该公司彻底破产。

[4] Japanese land：连续暴跌的日本地价

ZZZZ Best, whose business was laundering money for [1] the Mafia.

The most famous bubble of them all occurred in ② the American stock market in the 1920s. The "roaring twenties" saw a fabulous stock market boom, when everyone bought and sold stocks. Most purchases in this wild bull market were on margin. This means that a buyer of $10,000 worth of stocks put up only part of the price in cash and borrowed the difference, pledging the newly bought stocks as collateral for the loan. What did it matter that you had to pay the broker 6, 10, or 15 percent per year on the loan when Auburn Motors or Bethlehem Steel might jump 10 percent in value overnight?

Speculative bubbles always produce crashes and sometimes lead to economic panics. The speculation of the 1920s was soon followed by the 1929 panic and crash. This event ushered in the long and painful Great Depression of the 1930s. By the trough of the Depression in 1933, the market had declined 85 percent.

Trends in the stock market are tracked using ③ *stock-price indexes,* which are weighted averages of the prices of a basket of company stocks. Commonly followed averages include the Dow-Jones Industrial Average (DJIA) of 30 large companies; Standard and Poor's index of 500 companies (the S&P 500), which is a weighted average of the stock prices of 500 large American corporations; and the NASDAQ Composite Index, which includes more than 3000 stocks listed on that market.

Figure 23-5 shows the history of the Standard and Poor's 500 price index over the last century. The lower curve shows the nominal stock-price average, which records the actual average during a particular month. The upper line shows the real price of stocks;

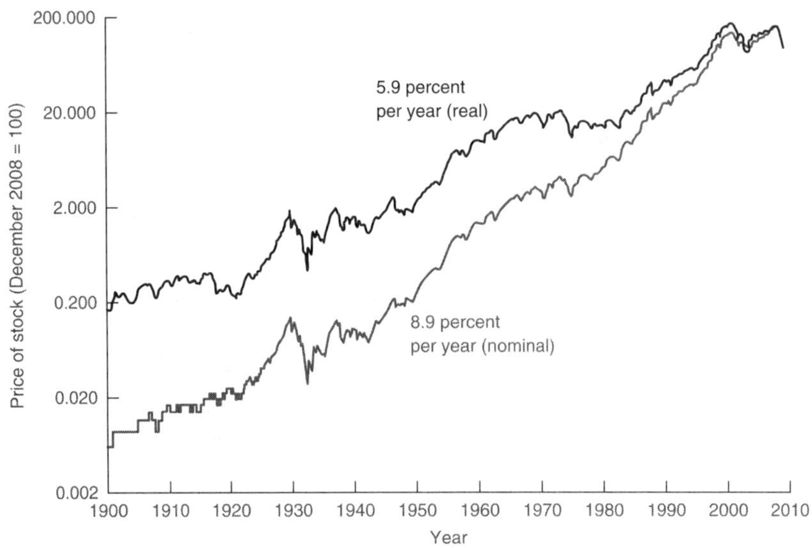

FIGURE 23-5. The Only Guarantee about Stock Prices Is That They Will Fluctuate

The Standard and Poor's index (the S&P 500) tracks the value-weighted average of the stock prices of 500 large companies traded in the U.S. It is shown here including reinvested dividends. Stock prices in nominal terms are shown by the bottom line; these averaged a growth of 8.9 percent per year from 1900 to 2008. The top line shows the "real" S&P 500, which is the S&P 500 corrected for movements in the consumer price index. It rose 5.9 percent per year on average.

Source: Standard and Poor, Bureau of Labor Statistics.

[1] ZZZZ Best：一家由地毯清洗公司起家的为黑手党洗钱的公司，1986 年出现在公众视野中，一度市值超过两亿美元，由高中二年级的学生 Barry Minkow 创办，事情败露后被判处 25 年监禁。

② 所有这些著名的泡沫均发生在 20 世纪 20 年代的美国股票市场。那个“喧闹的 20 年代”目睹了股票市场难以置信的繁荣。当时，每一个人都在买进和卖出股票。在那个疯狂的牛市中，大多数都是以保证金的形式购买的。

③ 股票市场的起伏趋势可以用股票价格指数来跟踪，它是一揽子公司股票价格的加权平均值。这个跟进的平均值通常包括 30 家大公司的道琼斯工业平均指数（DJIA）、标示美国 500 家大公司股票价格加权平均值的标准普尔指数（S&P 500），以及包括超过 3 000 家上市公司的 NASDAQ 综合指数。

this equals the nominal price divided by an index of consumer prices. Both curves are indexed to equal 100 in December 2008. The average growth rate of stocks over the period was 8.9 percent per year in dollar terms but only 5.9 percent per year after correcting for inflation.

Stocks have proven to be a good investment over the long term. But they are also extremely risky in the short run, as people learned when stock prices declined 52 percent from the peak in October 2007 to the trough in November 2008. Is there a crystal ball that can foretell the movement of stock prices? This is the subject of modern finance theory.

有效市场与随机游走
Efficient Markets and the Random Walk

Economists and finance professors have long studied prices in speculative markets such as the stock market and the foreign exchange market. One important hypothesis is that speculative markets tend to be "efficient." This finding has stirred great controversy in the economics profession and with financial analysts.

What is the essence of the **efficient-market theory?** A summary statement is the following:

> Securities markets are extremely efficient in absorbing information about individual stocks and about the stock market as a whole. When new information arrives, the news is quickly incorporated into stock prices. Systems which attempt to forecast prices on the basis of the past or of fundamentals cannot produce returns greater than those that could be obtained by holding a randomly selected portfolio of individual stocks of comparable risk.[3] ①

A colorful story illustrates the basic message. A finance professor and a student are walking across the campus when they see what looks like a $100 bill lying on the ground. The professor tells the student, "Don't bother to pick it up. If it were really a $100 bill, it wouldn't be there." In other words, you can't get rich simply by bending down on a public thoroughfare!

This paradoxical view has been generally confirmed in hundreds of studies over the last half-century. Their lesson is not that you will never become rich by following a rule or formula but that, on average, such rules do not outperform a diversified portfolio of stocks.

Rationale for the Efficient-Market View. Finance theorists have spent many years analyzing stock and bond markets in order to understand why well-functioning financial markets rule out persistent excess profits. The theory of efficient markets explains this.

An **efficient financial market** is one where all new information is quickly understood by market participants and becomes immediately incorporated into market prices. For example, say that Lazy-T Oil Company has just struck oil in the Gulf of Alaska. This event is announced at 11:30 A.M. on Tuesday. When will the price of Lazy-T's shares rise? The efficient-market theory holds that market participants will react at once, bidding the price of Lazy-T up by the correct amount. In short, at every point in time, markets have already digested and included all available information in asset prices.

> The theory of efficient markets holds that market prices contain all available information. It is not possible to make profits by acting on old information or at patterns of past price changes. Returns on stocks will be primarily determined by their riskiness relative to the market. ②

A Random Walk. The efficient-market view provides an important way of analyzing price movements in organized markets. Under this approach, the price movements of stocks should look highly erratic, like a random walk, when charted over a period of time.

A price follows a **random walk** when its movements over time are completely unpredictable. For example, toss a coin for heads or tails. Call a head "plus 1" and a tail "minus 1." Then keep track of the running score of 100 coin tosses. Draw it on graph paper. This curve is a random walk. Now, for comparison, also graph 100 days' movement of Microsoft stock and of Standard and Poor's 500 index. Note how similar all three figures appear.

Why do speculative prices resemble a random walk? Economists, on reflection, have arrived at the following truths: In an efficient market all predictable things have already been built into the prices. It

[3] This definition is adopted from Malkiel's 2003 article; see Further Readings. Note that "efficiency" is used differently in finance theory than in other parts of economics. Here, "efficiency" means that information is quickly absorbed, not that resources produce the maximal outputs.

---

① 证券市场在吸收有关个别股票信息以及股票市场的整体信息方面是非常高效的。新的信息一经披露，马上就会在股票的价格上得以具体体现。根据过去的数据或者基本理论来预测股票价格的系统，产生的收益不可能高于随机地持有风险相当的个股投资组合的投资收益。

② 有效市场理论认为，市场价格包含了所有可用信息。依赖陈旧的信息或者过去价格的变化模式来投资，是不可能获得收益的。股票的收益主要取决于股票本身相对于市场的风险。

is the arrival of *new* information that affects stock or commodity prices. Moreover, the news must be random and unpredictable (or else it would be predictable and therefore not truly news).

To summarize:

The efficient-market theory explains why movements in stock prices look so erratic. Prices respond to news, to surprises. But surprises are unpredictable events—like the flip of a coin or next month's rainstorm—that may move in any direction. Because stock prices move in response to erratic events, stock prices themselves move erratically, like a random walk. ①

Qualifications to the Efficient-Market View. Although the efficient-market view has been the canon of finance in economics and business, many believe that it is oversimplified and misleading. Here are some of the reservations:

1. Researchers have uncovered many "anomalies" in stock-price movements that lead to some predictability. For example, stocks with high dividends or earnings relative to prices appear to perform better in subsequent periods. Similarly, sharp upward or downward movements tend to be followed by "reversals" in movements. To some, these anomalies are persuasive indicators of market inefficiencies; to others, they simply reflect the tendency of analysts to mine the data looking for patterns that are in fact spurious correlations. ②
2. Economists who look at the historical record ask whether it is plausible that sharp movements in stock prices could actually reflect new information. Consider the 30 percent drop in stock prices that occurred from October 15 to October 19, 1987. Efficient-market theories imply that this drop was caused by economic events that depressed the expected present value of future corporate earnings. Critics of the efficient-market view argue that there was no news that could make a 30 percent difference in the value of stock prices over those 4 days. Efficient-market theorists fall silent before this criticism.
3. Finally, the efficient-market view applies to individual stocks but not necessarily to the market as a whole. There is persuasive evidence of long, self-reversing swings in stock market prices. These swings tend to reflect changes in the general mood of the financial community. Periods like the 1920s and 1990s saw investor optimism and rising stock prices, while the 1930s and 2007–2008 were periods of investor pessimism when stock prices declined sharply. However, say that we believed that the market reflected an "irrational exuberance" and was overvalued. What could we do? We could not individually buy or sell enough stocks to overcome the entire national mood. In addition, we might get wiped out if we bet against the market a year or two before the peak. So, from a macroeconomic perspective, speculative markets can exhibit waves of pessimism and optimism without powerful economic forces moving in to correct these mood swings.

个人金融策略 PERSONAL FINANCIAL STRATEGIES

While taking a course in economics is no guarantee of great wealth, the principles of modern finance can definitely help you invest your nest egg wisely and avoid the worst financial blunders. What lessons does economics teach about personal investment decisions? We have culled the following five rules from the wisdom of the best brains on the street:

Lesson 1: Know thy investments. The absolute bedrock of a sound investment strategy is to be realistic and prudent in your investment decisions. For important investments, study the materials and get expert advice. Be skeptical of approaches that claim to have found the quick route to success. You can't get rich by listening to your barber or consulting the stars (although, unbelievably, some financial advisers push astrology to their clients). Hunches work out to nothing in the long run. Moreover, the best brains on Wall Street do not, on average, beat the averages (Dow-Jones, Standard and Poor's, etc.). ③

Lesson 2: Diversify, diversify—that is the law of the prophets of finance. One of the major lessons of finance is the advantage of diversifying your investments. "Don't put all your eggs in one basket" is one way of expressing this rule. By putting funds in a number of different investments, you can continue to average a high yield while reducing the risk. Calculations show that by diversifying their wealth among a broad array of investments—different

---

① 有效市场理论诠释了股票价格变动为什么如此不稳定。价格会对新闻和意外事件做出反应。但意外事件是无法预测的，就像掷硬币或者下个月的暴风雨，变幻莫测。由于股票价格的变动是不规则事件的反应，因此，其变动就像随机游走，毫无规律可言。

② 对某些人来讲，这些异常现象恰是市场无效的有力佐证。对另外一些人来说，这些现象只反映出分析家们要挖掘的数据——寻找事实上本就毫无关系的模型。

③ 经验 1：了解投资。明智的投资策略的根本原则是在投资决策时要慎重和实事求是。

common stocks, conventional and inflation-indexed bonds, real estate, domestic and foreign securities—people can attain a good return while minimizing the downside risk on their investments.

Lesson 3: Consider common-stock index funds. Investors who want to invest in the stock market can achieve a good return with the least possible risk by holding a broadly diversified portfolio of common stocks. A good vehicle for diversifying is an *index fund.* This is a portfolio of the stocks of many companies, weighting each company in proportion to its market value and often tracking a major stock index like the S&P 500. One major advantage of index funds is that they have low expenses and low turnover-induced taxes.

Lesson 4: Minimize unnecessary expenses and taxes. People often find that a substantial amount of their investment earnings is nibbled away by taxes and expenses. For example, some mutual funds charge a high initial fee when you purchase the fund. Others might charge a management fee of 1 or even 2 percent of assets each year. Additionally, heavily "managed" funds have high turnover and may lead to large taxes on capital gains. Day traders may find great enjoyment in lightning movements in and out, and they may strike it rich, but they *definitely* will pay heavy brokerage and investment charges. By choosing your investments carefully, you can avoid these unnecessary drains on your investment income.

Lesson 5: Match your investments with your risk preference. You can increase your expected return by picking riskier investments (see Figure 23-4). But always consider how much risk you can afford—financially *and psychologically.* As one sage put it, investments are a tradeoff between eating well and sleeping well. If you get insomnia worrying about the ups and downs of the market, you can maximize your sleep by keeping your assets in inflation-indexed U.S. Treasury bonds. But in the long run, you might be snoozing soundly on a cot! If you want to eat well and can tolerate disappointments, you might invest more heavily in stocks, including ones in foreign countries and emerging markets, and incorporate more volatile small companies into your portfolio—rather than concentrating on short-term bonds and bank deposits.

Such are the lessons of history and economics. If, after reading all this, you still want to try your hand in the stock market, do not be daunted. But take to heart the caution of one of America's great financiers, Bernard Baruch:

> If you are ready to give up everything else—to study the whole history and background of the market and all the principal companies whose stocks are on the board as carefully as a medical student studies anatomy—if you can do all that, and, in addition, you have the cool nerves of a great gambler, the sixth sense of a kind of clairvoyant, and the courage of a lion, you have a ghost of a chance. ①

SUMMARY

A. The Modern Financial System

1. Financial systems in a modern economy transfer resources over space, time, and sectors. The flow of funds in financial systems occurs through financial markets and financial intermediaries. The major functions of a financial system are to transfer resources, to manage risk, to subdivide and pool funds, and to clear transactions.
2. Interest rates are the prices paid for borrowing funds; they are measured in dollars paid back per year per dollar borrowed. The standard way we quote interest rates is in percent per year. People willingly pay interest because borrowed funds allow them to buy goods and services to satisfy current consumption needs or make profitable investments.
3. Recall the menu of financial assets, especially money, bonds, and equities.
4. Study the *monetary transmission mechanism.* This refers to the process by which monetary policy undertaken by the central bank, our Federal Reserve, interacts with banks and the rest of the economy to determine interest rates, other financial conditions, aggregate

① 如果你已经做好准备放弃其他一切事情，像医学院的学生研究解剖学一样认真地研究市场的全部历史和背景，以及所有主要的挂牌交易的上市公司，假设你真能做到这一切，除此之外你还有一个大赌棍才具备的冷静头脑，可以洞察一切的第六感觉，以及雄狮一般的勇气，那么你才能有一丝机会。

demand, output, and inflation. Make sure you understand each of the five steps (page 453).

B. The Special Case of Money

5. Money is anything that serves as a commonly accepted medium of exchange, or a means of payment. Money also functions as a unit of account. Unlike other economic goods, money is valued because of social convention. We value money indirectly for what it buys, rather than for its direct utility. Money today is composed of currency and checking deposits and is denoted M_1.
6. People hold money primarily because they need it to pay their bills or buy goods; this is known as the transactions demand. But people keep only a small fraction of their assets in money because money has an opportunity cost: we sacrifice interest earnings when we hold money. Therefore, the asset demand for money is limited.

C. Banks and the Supply of Money

7. Banks are commercial enterprises that seek to earn profits for their owners. One major function of banks is to provide checking accounts to their customers. Banks are legally required to keep reserves on their checking deposits. These can be in the form of either vault cash or deposits at the Federal Reserve.
8. Under 100 percent reserves, banks cannot create money, as seen in the simplest goldsmith bank example. For illustrative purposes, we then examined a required reserve ratio of 10 percent. In this case, the banking system as a whole creates bank money in a ratio of 10 to 1 for each dollar of reserves. With fractional-reserve banking, the total value of checking deposits is a multiple of reserves. Remember the formula

$$\text{Bank money} = \text{total reserves} \times \left(\frac{1}{\text{reserve ratio}}\right)$$

D. The Stock Market

9. The most important factors about assets are the rate of return and the risk. The rate of return is the total dollar gain from a security over a specified period of time. Risk refers to the variability of the returns on an investment, often measured by the statistical standard deviation. Because people are risk-averse, they require higher returns to induce them to buy riskier assets.
10. Stock markets, of which the New York Stock Exchange is the most important, are places where titles of ownership to the largest companies are bought and sold. The history of stock prices is filled with violent gyrations, such as the Great Crash of 1929 or the sharp bear market of 2008. Trends are tracked using stock-price indexes, such as the Standard and Poor's 500 and the familiar Dow-Jones Industrial Average.
11. Modern economic theories of stock prices generally focus on the efficient-market theory. An "efficient" financial market is one in which all information is immediately absorbed by speculators and built into market prices. In efficient markets, there are no easy profits; looking at yesterday's news or at past patterns of prices or business cycles will not help predict future price movements. Thus, in efficient markets, prices respond to surprises. Because surprises are inherently random, stock prices and other speculative prices move erratically, as in a random walk.
12. Plant the five rules of personal finance firmly in your long-term memory: (*a*) Know thy investments. (*b*) Diversify, diversify—that is the law of the prophets of finance. (*c*) Consider common-stock index funds. (*d*) Minimize unnecessary expenses and taxes. And (*e*) Match your investments with your risk preference.

CONCEPTS FOR REVIEW

The Modern Financial System

financial system, financial markets, financial intermediaries
functions of the financial system
major financial assets or instruments
interest forgone as the cost of holding money

The Special Case of Money

Money (M_1) = currency outside the banks plus checking deposits
commodity *M*, paper *M*, bank *M*
motives for money demand:
transactions demand (today)
asset demand (in a fragile financial system)

Banking and the Money Supply

bank reserves = vault cash plus deposits with the Fed
fractional-reserve banking
bank money = reserves/required reserve ratio

The Stock Market

common stocks (corporate equities)
efficient market, random walk of stock prices
index fund
five rules for personal investing

FURTHER READING AND INTERNET WEBSITES

Further Reading

There are many fine histories of money. A good one is John Kenneth Galbraith, *Money, Whence It Came, Where It Went* (Houghton, Boston, 1975). There are many good textbooks on monetary economics. The standard reference on U.S. monetary history is Milton Friedman and Anna Jacobson Schwartz, *Monetary History of the United States 1867–1960* (Princeton University Press, Princeton, N.J., 1963).

Modern capital and finance theory are very popular subjects often covered in the macroeconomics part of an introductory course or in special courses. Good books on the subject are Burton Malkiel, *A Random Walk down Wall Street,* 9th ed. (Norton, New York, 2007). A recent book surveying financial history and theory and arguing that the stock market was extraordinarily overvalued in the bull market of 1981–2000 is Robert Shiller, *Irrational Exuberance,* 2d ed. (Princeton University Press, Princeton, N.J., 2005). A recent summary of evidence on the efficient-market theory by Burton Malkiel and Robert Shiller is found in the *Journal of Economic Perspectives,* Winter 2003.

Websites

Review our list of good blogs in Chapter 19.

Basic data on money, interest rates, and monetary policy can be found at the website of the Federal Reserve, *www.federalreserve.gov.* Interesting articles on monetary policy can be found in the *Federal Reserve Bulletin* at *www.federalreserve.gov/publications.htm.* The best comprehensive data on finance are from the Federal Reserve flow of funds at *www.federalreserve.gov/releases/z1/.*

A good source for data on financial markets is *finance.yahoo.com.* If you are interested in the latest buzz on stocks, you might visit the Motley Fool at *www.fool.com.*

QUESTIONS FOR DISCUSSION

1. Suppose that banks hold 20 percent of deposits as reserves rather than 10 percent. Assuming that reserves are unchanged, redo the balance sheet in Table 23-7. What is the new ratio of bank deposits to reserves?
2. What would be the effect of each of the following on the money demand, M_1 (with other things held equal)?
   a. An increase in real GDP
   b. An increase in the price level
   c. A rise in the interest rate on savings accounts and Treasury securities
   d. A doubling of all prices, wages, and incomes (Calculate the exact effect on the money demand.)
   e. An increase in the interest rate banks pay on checking accounts
3. The implicit cost of checking accounts is equal to the difference between the yield on safe short-term assets (such as Treasury bills) and the interest rate on checking accounts. What are the impacts of the following on the opportunity cost of holding money in checking deposits?
   a. Before 1980 (when checking deposits had a zero interest rate under law), market interest rates increased from 8 to 9 percent.
   b. In 2007 (when interest rates on money were one-quarter of market interest rates), interest rates declined from 4 to 2 percent.
   c. How would you expect the demand for checking deposits to respond to the change in market interest rates under **a** and **b** if the elasticity of demand for money with respect to the implicit cost of money is -1?
4. Explain whether you think that each of the following should be counted as part of the money supply (M_1) of the United States: savings accounts, subway tokens, postage stamps, credit cards, debit cards, Starbucks cash cards, and $20 bills used by Russians in Moscow.
5. Explain why the best portfolio should not contain any money (use information from Section D of this chapter). How does the notion of the cost of holding money fit into your answer? Would your answer change if your checking account earned a return equal to that of risk-free investments?
6. According to the efficient-market theory, what effect would the following events have on the price of GM's stock?
   a. A surprise announcement that the government is going to lower business taxes next July 1
   b. A decrease in business taxes on July 1, 6 months after Congress passed the legislation

c. An announcement, unexpected by experts, that the United States will impose quotas on imports of Chinese cars during the coming year
d. Implementation of **c** by issuing regulations on December 31

7. The Federal Reserve is scheduled to pay interest on bank reserves.
   a. Suppose that the interest rate on reserves is 1 percentage point below market rates. Would banks still desire to minimize excess reserves? Would this affect the bank money equation in Summary point 8 above?
   b. Suppose that the interest rate on reserves is equal to the market rate. How would your answer to **a** change?
   c. Using your answer to **b,** can you see why the relationship between reserves and bank money becomes very loose when market interest rates are zero (the "liquidity trap")?

8. Suppose that one giant bank, the Humongous Bank of America, held all the checking deposits of all the people, subject to a 10 percent legal reserve requirement. If reserves increased by $1 billion, could the Humongous Bank expect to lend out more than 90 percent of the reserve increase, knowing that the new deposit must come back to it? Would this change the ultimate money-supply multiplier? Explain both answers.

9. **Advanced problem:** An *option* is the right to buy or sell an asset (stocks, bonds, foreign exchange, land, etc.) for a specified price on or before a specific date. A *call option* is the right to buy the stock, while a *put option* is the right to sell the stock. Suppose you have a call option to buy 100 shares in a highly volatile stock, Fantasia.com, at any time in the next 3 months at $10 per share. Fantasia currently sells at $9 per share.
   a. Explain why the value of the option is more than $1 per share.
   b. Suppose the option were to expire tomorrow and the price of Fantasia.com had an even chance of rising $5 or falling $5 before then. What would be the value of the option today?
   c. Replace the figure "$5" with "$10" in **b**. What would happen to the value of the option? Explain why an increase in volatility *increases* the value of an option (other things unchanged).

10. This problem will illustrate the point that the prices of many speculative financial assets look like a random walk.
    a. Flip a coin 100 times. Count a head as "plus 1" and a tail as "minus 1." Keep a running score of the total. Plot your results. This is a random walk. (This is easily accomplished on a computer with a program such as Excel, which contains a random-number generator and a graphics function.)
    b. Next, keep track of the closing price of the stock of your favorite company for a few weeks, or get it online. Plot the price against time for each day. Compare the random numbers in **a** with your stock prices, or show them to a friend and ask the friend to spot the difference. If they look the same, this illustrates that stocks behave like a random walk.

CHAPTER 24

Monetary Policy and the Economy

货币政策与经济

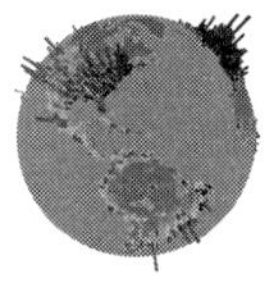

[1] 威廉·罗杰斯（Will Rogers，1879~1935），20世纪初期著名的美国牛仔、娱乐界的歌舞杂耍喜剧演员、社会评论家、哲学家……，以言简意赅并深入骨髓的朴素幽默的警语和表演而著称于世，是20世纪二三十年代享誉全球的著名人物，在美国历史上享有崇高地位。这句话是罗杰斯家喻户晓的警句之一，与其出生于印第安部落的切诺基人家族有关。考虑到印第安人的信仰属性，拟译如下：

There have been three great inventions since the beginning of time: fire, the wheel, and central banking.

Will Rogers [1]

开天辟地以来，有三大发明，火、车轮和中央银行。

[3] Federal Reserve：美国联邦储备系统（Fed），主要由联邦储备理事会（Federal Reserve Board）、联邦储备银行（Federal Reserve Banks）及联邦公开市场委员会（Federal Open Market Committee）等机构组成，履行美国中央银行的职责。

Where would you look to find the most important macroeconomic policymakers today? In the White House? In Congress? Perhaps in the United Nations or the World Bank? Surprisingly, the answer is that you would look in an obscure marble building in Washington that houses the Federal Reserve System. It is here that you will find the Federal Reserve (or "the Fed," as it is often called). The Fed determines the level of short-term interest rates and lends money to financial institutions, thereby profoundly affecting financial markets, wealth, output, employment, and prices. Indeed, the Fed's influence spreads not only throughout the 50 states but to virtually every corner of the world through financial and trade linkages.

The Federal Reserve's central goals are to ensure low inflation, steady growth in national output, low unemployment, and orderly financial markets. If output is growing rapidly and inflation is rising, the Federal Reserve Board is likely to raise interest rates, putting a brake on the economy and reducing price pressures.

The period 2007–2009 was a particularly challenging time for the Federal Reserve and other central banks. During this period, unsound investments and excessive leverage led to the deteriorating financial health of banks and other financial institutions. This in turn produced huge declines in stock and bond prices, "bank runs," and the failures of several large banks. The Federal Reserve, the European Central [6]
Bank, and U.S. and foreign governments provided
[2] *trillions* of dollars of loans, loan guarantees, nationalizations, and bailouts. All of these were designed
[3] to prevent the seizing up of financial markets and to reduce the severity of the ensuing recession.

Every country has a central bank that is responsible for managing the country's monetary affairs. This chapter begins by explaining the objectives and organization of central banks, focusing on the
④ U.S. Federal Reserve System. It explains how the Fed operates and describes the monetary transmission mechanism. The second section of the chapter then surveys some of the major issues in monetary policy.

④ 确切地讲，美联储的影响力绝不限于全美的50个州，它还通过其金融和贸易联系渗透到世界的每一个角落。

⑤ 如果产出增加过快，通货膨胀的压力增加，美联储就有可能提高利率，给经济踩一脚刹车，以减轻价格上涨的压力。

[6] European Central Bank：欧洲中央银行（ECB），也称欧元体系。根据1992年在荷兰东南部小城马斯特里赫特签署的《马斯特里赫特条约》的规定，于1998年7月1日正式成立。总部设在法兰克福，是欧洲经济一体化的重要产物。

⑤ 中央银行与联邦储备系统

A. CENTRAL BANKING AND THE FEDERAL RESERVE SYSTEM

We begin this section by providing an overview of central banking. The next section provides the details about the different tools employed by the central bank and explains how they can be used to affect short-term interest rates.

[2] World Bank：世界银行集团（The World Bank Group）的缩写和俗称。由IBRD（International Bank for Reconstruction and Development，国际开发银行）、IDA（International Development Association，国际开发协会）、IFC（International Finance Corporation，国际金融公司）、MIGA（Multilateral Investment Guarantee Agency，多边投资保障委员会）和ICSID（International Centre for Settlement of Investment Disputes，解决投资争端国际中心）五大机构组成，总部设在华盛顿，成立于1945年12月27日。最初的使命是帮助在二战中破坏严重的国家重建，现在的功能正如其宗旨"Working for a World Free of Poverty"所言，由这五大机构联合履行向发展中国家提供低息贷款、无息贷款和赠款服务。

中央银行概述

THE ESSENTIAL ELEMENTS OF CENTRAL BANKING

A central bank is a government organization that is primarily responsible for the monetary affairs of a country. In this section, we focus on the U.S. Federal Reserve System. We describe its history, objectives, and functions.

历　史

History

During the nineteenth century, the United States was plagued by banking panics. These occurred when large numbers of people attempted to convert their bank deposits into currency all at the same time. When people arrived at the banks, they found that there was insufficient currency to cover everybody's deposits because of the system of fractional reserves. Bank failures and economic downturns often ensued. After the severe panic of 1907, agitation and discussion led to the Federal Reserve Act of 1913, whose purpose was "to provide for the establishment of Federal reserve banks, to furnish an elastic currency, to afford means of rediscounting commercial paper, to establish a more effective supervision of banking in the United States, and for other purposes." That was the beginning of the Fed.

结　构

Structure

As currently constituted, the **Federal Reserve System** ① consists of the Board of Governors in Washington, D.C., and the regional Reserve Banks. The core of the Federal Reserve is the *Board of Governors,* which consists of seven members nominated by the president and confirmed by the Senate to serve overlapping terms of 14 years. Members of the board are generally economists or bankers who work full time at the job.

Additionally, there are 12 regional Federal ② Reserve Banks, located in New York, Chicago, Richmond, Dallas, San Francisco, and other major cities. The regional structure was originally designed in the populist age to ensure that different areas of the country would have an equal voice in banking matters and to avoid a great concentration of central-banking powers in Washington or in the hands of the Eastern bankers. Today, the Federal Reserve Banks supervise banks in their districts, operate the national payments system, and participate in the making of national monetary policy.

The key decision-making body in the Federal ③ Reserve System is the *Federal Open Market Committee* (FOMC). The 12 voting members of the FOMC include the seven governors plus five of the presidents of the regional Federal Reserve Banks who serve as voting members on a rotating basis. This key group controls the most important tool used in monetary policy: the setting of the short-term interest rate.

At the pinnacle of the entire system is the *chair of the Board of Governors.* The chair is nominated by the president and confirmed by the Senate for renewable four-year terms. The chair presides over the Board of Governors and the FOMC, acts as the public spokesperson for the Fed, and exercises enormous power over monetary policy. The cur- ④ [5] rent chair is Ben Bernanke, who was a distinguished academic economist, a professor of economics at Princeton University, as well as a former Fed governor before he was appointed chair in 2006. Bernanke succeeded Alan Greenspan, a conserva- [6] tive business economist who became an iconic figure in American economic affairs during his long term as Fed chair (1987–2006).

In spite of the geographically dispersed structure of the Fed, the Fed's power is actually quite centralized. The Federal Reserve Board, joined at meetings by the presidents of the 12 regional Federal Reserve Banks, operates under the Fed chair to formulate and carry out monetary policy. The structure of the Federal Reserve System is shown in Figure 24-1.

中央银行的目标

Goals of Central Banks

Before focusing primarily on the U.S. system, we discuss briefly the goals of central banks around the world. We can distinguish three different general approaches of central banks:

- *Multiple objectives.* Many central banks have general goals, such as to maintain economic stability. Among the specific objectives pursued might be low and stable inflation, low unemployment, rapid economic growth, coordination with fiscal policy, and a stable exchange rate.
- *Inflation targeting.* In recent years, many countries have adopted explicit inflation targets. Under such a mandate, the central bank is directed to undertake its policies so as to ensure that inflation stays within a range that is generally low but positive. For example, the Bank of England has

① 现在的**联邦储备系统**由设在华盛顿特区的理事会和区域性的联邦储备银行组成。理事会是美联储的核心机构，由总统提名并经国会批准通过的七名成员组成，任期为跨越总统任期的 14 年。理事会成员通常由经济学家或银行家全职出任。

② 此外，有 12 家区域性的联邦储备银行，分别设在纽约、芝加哥、里士满、达拉斯、旧金山以及其他几个主要城市。这种区域性的结构最初是在民粹主义时代设计的，宗旨是保障美国的不同区域在银行事务上享有平等的发言权，防止华盛顿或者东部银行家手中掌握的中央银行权力出现高度集中。

③ 联邦储备系统内关键的决策机构是联邦公开市场委员会（FOMC）。其 12 名享有表决权的成员包括理事会的七名成员，其余五个由各区域联邦储备银行的行长轮流出任。

---

④ 现任主席本·伯南克在 2006 年上任之前，是美联储理事会理事，杰出的经济学家，曾任普林斯顿大学经济学教授。伯南克的前任阿兰·格林斯潘是一位保守的企业经济学家，他在长达 19 年（1987~2006）之久的超长任职期间，始终是美国经济事务中的一位标杆性的人物。

[5] Ben Bernanke：本·伯南克，1953 年出生，十几岁就扛起了生活的重担，做过多种劳动强度很大的工作，被赞为“小大人”。在 2002~2005 年出任美联储理事会理事期间，率先提出了“大调整”（Great Moderation）理论，以及使用货币政策抗击通货紧缩的“伯南克主义”（Bernanke Doctrine）。

[6] Alan Greenspan：阿兰·格林斯潘，1926 年出生，2006 年卸任后重操旧业，做私人经济顾问以及在自己的公司里担任经济分析咨询师。

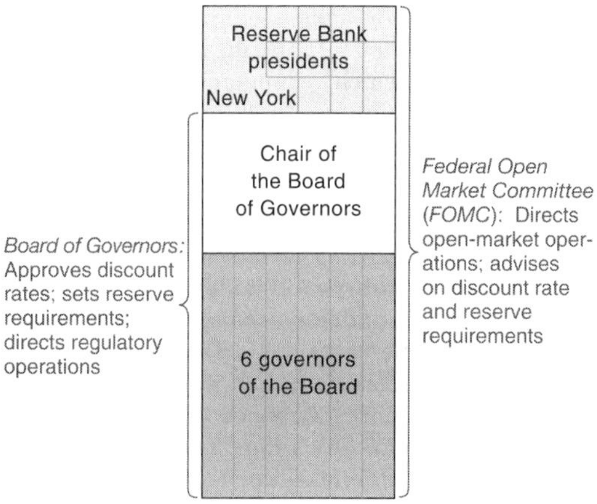

FIGURE 24-1. **The Major Players in Monetary Policy**

Two important committees are at the center of monetary policy. The seven-member Board of Governors approves changes in discount rates and sets reserve requirements. The FOMC directs the setting of bank reserves. The chair of the Board of Governors heads both committees. The size of each box indicates that person's or group's relative power; note the size of the chair's box.

been directed to set monetary policy to maintain a 2 percent annual inflation rate.

- *Exchange-rate targeting.* In a situation where a country has a fixed exchange rate and open financial markets, it can no longer conduct an independent monetary policy, as we will see in our chapters on open-economy macroeconomics. In such a case, the central bank can be described as setting its monetary policy to attain an exchange-rate target.

The Federal Reserve falls into the first category, that of "multiple objectives." Under the Federal [1] Reserve Act, the Fed is directed "to promote effectively the goals of maximum employment, stable prices, and moderate long-term interest rates." Today this is interpreted as a dual mandate to maintain low and stable inflation along with a healthy real economy. This is how the Fed sees its role today:

> [The Federal Reserve's] objectives include economic growth in line with the economy's potential to expand; a high level of employment; stable prices (that is, stability in the purchasing power of the dollar); and moderate long-term interest rates.[1]

联邦储备的功能

Functions of the Federal Reserve

The Federal Reserve has four major functions:

- Conducting monetary policy by setting short-term interest rates
- Maintaining the stability of the financial system and containing systemic risk as the lender of last resort
- Supervising and regulating banking institutions
- Providing financial services to banks and the government

We will primarily examine the first two of these functions because they have the most important impact on macroeconomic activity.

中央银行的独立性

Central-Bank Independence

On examining the structure of the Fed, you might ② naturally ask, "In which of the three branches of government does the Fed lie?" The answer is interesting. Although nominally a corporation owned by the commercial banks that are members of the Federal Reserve System, the Federal Reserve is in practice a public agency. It is directly responsible to Congress; it attends to the advice of the president; and whenever any conflict arises between making a profit and promoting the public interest, it acts unswervingly in the public interest.

② 在研究美联储的组织结构时，你会很自然地提出这样一个问题："美联储究竟归于三大政府机构中的哪一个？"答案很有趣。名义上，它是一家公司，归美联储系统内所有的成员银行所共有，但实质上它是一家公共机构。它直接对国会负责，并听取总统的意见。无论在任何时候，只要赢取利润和促进公共利益之间发生冲突，它就会坚定不移地站在公共利益一边。

Above all, the Federal Reserve is an *independent* ③ agency. While it consults with Congress and the president, in the end the Fed decides monetary policy according to its own views about the nation's economic interests. As a result, the Fed sometimes comes into conflict with the executive branch. Almost every president has words of advice for the Fed. When Fed policies clash with the administration's goals, presidents occasionally use harsh words. The Fed listens politely but generally chooses the path it deems best for the country, for its decisions do not have to be approved by anybody.

From time to time, critics argue that the Fed is too independent—that it is undemocratic for a small group of unelected people to govern the nation's

[1] See *The Federal Reserve System. Purposes and Functions*, p. 2, under "Websites" in this chapter's Further Reading section.

[1] Federal Reserve Act：联邦储备法案，于 1913 年 12 月 23 日经美国国会通过，由威尔逊总统签署生效。美国联邦储备系统即根据此法案建立。

③ 最重要的是，美联储是一个独立的机构。虽然需要咨询国会和总统的意见，但美联储最终还是从国家的整体经济利益出发，根据自身的分析制定货币政策。因此，有的时候美联储会与行政机构之间发生冲突。几乎每一任总统都曾对美联储的政策提出过建议。当美联储的政策与行政目标相冲突时，总统偶尔还会使用严厉措辞。这时，尽管美联储都会有礼貌地倾听，但通常会选择他们认为对国家最有利的做法，因为他们制定的政策不需要任何人批准。

financial markets. This is a sobering thought, for unelected bodies sometimes lose touch with social and economic realities.

Defenders of the Fed's independence respond that an independent central bank is the guardian of a nation's currency and the best protector against rampant inflation. Moreover, independence ensures that monetary policy is not subverted for partisan political objectives, as sometimes happens in countries where the executive branch controls the central bank. Historical studies show that countries with independent central banks have generally been more successful in keeping inflation down than have those whose central banks are under the control of elected officials.

To summarize:

> Every modern country has a central bank. The ①
> U.S. central bank is composed of the Federal Reserve Board in Washington, together with the 12 regional Federal Reserve Banks. The Fed's primary mission is to conduct the nation's monetary policy by influencing monetary and credit conditions in pursuit of low inflation, high employment, and stable financial markets.

中央银行如何决定短期利率

HOW THE CENTRAL BANK DETERMINES SHORT-TERM INTEREST RATES

Central banks are at the center stage of macroeconomics because they largely determine short-term interest rates. We now turn to an explanation of this function.

美联储业务概览

Overview of the Fed's Operations

The Federal Reserve conducts its policy through ②
changes in an important short-term interest rate called the **federal funds rate.** This is the interest rate that banks charge each other to trade reserve balances at the Fed. It is a short-term (overnight) risk-free interest rate in U.S. dollars. The Fed controls the federal funds rate by exercising control over the following important instruments of monetary policy:

- *Open-market operations*—buying or selling U.S. government securities in the open market to influence the level of bank reserves
- *Discount-window lending*—setting the interest rate, called the *discount rate,* and the collateral requirements with which commercial banks, other depository institutions, and, more recently, primary dealers can borrow from the Fed
- *Reserve-requirements policy*—setting and changing the legal reserve-ratio requirements on deposits with banks and other financial institutions

The basic description of monetary policy is this: When economic conditions change, the Fed determines whether the economy is departing from the desired path of inflation, output, and other goals. If so, the Fed announces a change in its target interest rate, the federal funds rate. To implement this change, the Fed undertakes open-market operations and changes the discount rate. These changes then cascade through the entire spectrum of interest rates and asset prices, and eventually change the overall direction of the economy.

联邦储备银行的资产负债表

Balance Sheet of the Federal Reserve Banks

To understand how the Fed conducts monetary policy, we first need to describe the consolidated balance sheet of the Federal Reserve System, shown in Table 24-1. U.S. government securities (e.g., bonds) have historically been the bulk of the Fed's assets. Starting in 2007, the Fed extended its operations to include term auctions, dealer credit, and loan guarantees, which by 2008 constituted a substantial fraction of its assets. The exact com- ③
position of the balance sheet is not essential for our understanding of how the Fed normally determines interest rates.

There are two unique items among the Fed's liabilities: currency and reserves. *Currency* is the Fed's principal liability. This item comprises the coins and the paper bills we use every day. The other major liability is reserve balances of banks, which are balances kept on deposit by commercial banks. These depos- ④
its, along with the banks' vault cash, are designated as **bank reserves.**

The following is our plan for the remainder of this section: First, we explain in more detail the three instruments that the Fed uses to conduct monetary policy. We will show how the supply of reserves is determined through a combination of announcements, open-market operations, and

---

① 每一个现代国家都有中央银行。美国的中央银行由设在华盛顿的美联储理事会和 12 家区域性联邦储备银行构成。美联储的主要任务就是制定货币政策，通过货币政策影响货币和信贷环境，实现低通货膨胀、高就业以及金融市场的稳定。

② 美联储通过调整短期利率来制定货币政策，短期利率被称为**联邦基金利率**。这是一种各银行间在交易联储准备金账户余额资金时所使用的利率。它是美元计价的短期（隔夜）无风险利率。

③ 资产负债表的确切构成，对于我们了解美联储如何决定利率并不是至关重要的。

④ 这些存款加上所有银行库存现金，就是我们所讲的**银行准备金**。

Combined Balance Sheet of 12 Federal Reserve Banks, September 2008 (billions of dollars)

Assets		Liabilities and Net Worth	
U.S. government securities	$479.8	Federal Reserve currency	$832.4
Loans, auction credits, and repurchase agreements	322.5	Deposits:	
Miscellaneous other assets	181.0	Reserve balances of banks	47.0
		Other deposits	14.4
		Miscellaneous liabilities	89.5
Total	$983.3	Total	$983.3

TABLE 24-1. By Changing Its Balance Sheet, the Fed Determines Short-Term Interest Rates and Credit Conditions

By buying and selling its assets (government securities and repurchase agreements), the Fed controls its liabilities (bank deposits and Federal Reserve notes). The Fed determines the federal funds interest rate by changing the volume of reserves and thereby affects GDP, unemployment, and inflation.

Source: Federal Reserve Board, at *www.federalreserve.gov/releases/h41.*

discount-window policy. Then, we show how short-term interest rates are determined, with the most important factor being the Fed's control over the supply of reserves. ①

操作程序
Operating Procedures

The FOMC meets eight times a year to decide upon monetary policy and give operating instructions to the Federal Reserve Bank of New York, which conducts open-market operations on a day-to-day basis. ②

Today, the Fed operates primarily by setting a short-term target for the *federal funds rate,* which is the interest rate that banks pay each other for the overnight use of bank reserves. Figure 24-2 shows the federal funds rate for recent years along with shaded areas for recessions. You can see how the Fed tends to lower interest rates before recessions and raise them as the economy enters expansions. If you look back to Figure 15-2 on p. 289, you can see how other interest rates tend to move along with the federal funds rate. The linkage is not a tight one, however. While the Fed sets the general level and trend in interest rates, there are many other factors at work in determining interest rates and financial conditions, as evidenced by the fact that interest rates sometime move in different directions.

美联储如何影响银行准备金
HOW THE FEDERAL RESERVE AFFECTS BANK RESERVES

The most important element of monetary policy is the determination of bank reserves through Fed policy. This is an intricate process and requires careful study. Through the combination of reserve requirements, open-market operations, and discount-window policy, the Fed can normally determine the quantity of bank reserves within very narrow limits. We start with a review of the nuts and bolts of these major policy instruments.

公开市场业务
Open-Market Operations

Open-market operations are a central bank's primary tool for implementing monetary policy. These are activities whereby the Fed affects bank reserves by buying or selling government securities on the open market.

How does the Fed decide how much to buy or sell? The Fed looks at the factors underlying reserve demand and supply and determines whether those trends are consistent with its target for the federal funds rate. On the basis of this forecast, the Fed will buy or sell a quantity of government securities that will help keep the funds rate near the target.

Suppose that, on the basis of its forecasts, the Fed desires to sell $1 billion worth of securities. The Fed

① 然后，我们来说明短期利率是如何根据由美联储掌控的准备金供给这一最重要的因素来制定的。

② 联邦公开市场委员会（FOMC）每年召开八次会议决定货币政策，并对纽约的联储银行下达操作指令，由其实施每一天的公开市场操作。

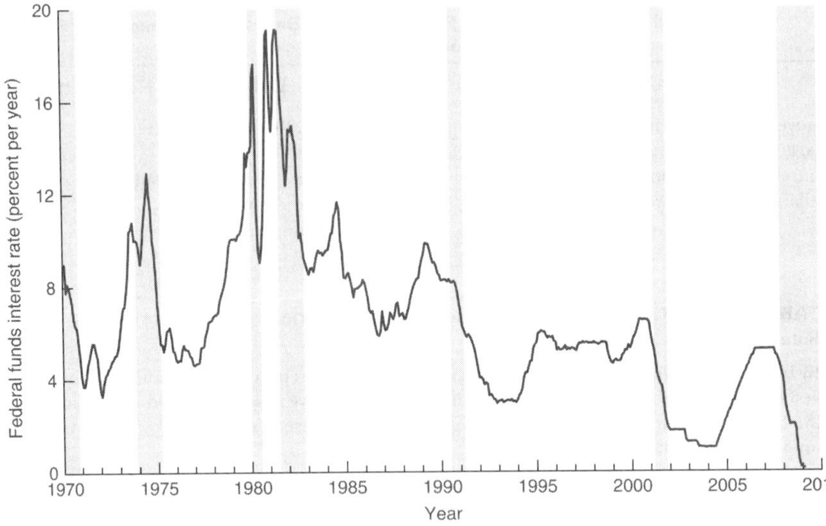

FIGURE 24-2. Federal Reserve Determines the Federal Funds Rate

The Fed sets a target for the federal funds rate, which is the interest rate charged by banks for lending reserves to each other. This rate then affects all other interest rates, although the linkage is variable and is affected by expectations of future interest rates as well as by overall financial conditions. (Look at Figure 15-2 for a graph of other major interest rates.) Note how the federal funds rate approached zero at the end of 2008 as the economy entered a liquidity trap.

Source: Federal Reserve Board.

[1] Goldman-Sachs：高盛集团（Goldman-Sachs Group, Inc.），一家向全球提供广泛投资、咨询和金融服务的国际领先的投资银行和证券公司。1869年由德裔美国商人和实业家Marcus Goldman（1821~1904）创建于纽约。1882年，其女婿Samuel Sachs（1851~1935）加盟后改名至今。现在全球的23个国家和地区设有41个办事处，其中包括上海和北京，在香港设有分部。

conducts open-market operations with primary dealers, which include about 20 large banks and securities broker-dealers such as Goldman-Sachs and J.P. [1] Morgan. [2] The dealers would buy the securities, drawing upon accounts at the Federal Reserve. After the sale, the total deposits at the Fed would decline by $1 billion. *The net effect would be that the banking system loses $1 billion in reserves.*

Table 24-2(*a*) shows the effect of a $1 billion open-market sale on a hypothetical Federal Reserve balance sheet. The blue entries show the Fed balance sheet before the open-market operation. The green entries show the effect of the open-market sale. The net effect is a $1 billion reduction in both assets and liabilities. The Fed's assets decreased with the $1 billion sale of government bonds, and its liabilities decreased by exactly the same amount, with the corresponding $1 billion decrease in bank reserves.

Now focus on the impact this has on commercial banks, whose consolidated balance sheet is shown in Table 24-2(*b*). We assume that commercial banks hold 10 percent of their deposits as reserves with the central bank. After the open-market operation, banks see that they are short of reserves because they have lost $1 billion of reserves but only lost $1 billion of deposits. The banks must then sell some of their ③ investments and call in some short-term loans to meet the legal reserve requirement. This sets off a multiple contraction of deposits. When the entire chain of impacts has unfolded, deposits are down by $10 billion, with corresponding changes on the asset

[2] J.P. Morgan：J. P. 摩根公司。19世纪早期，由著名的美国金融家和慈善家，铁路和钢铁大亨约翰·皮尔邦·摩根（John Pierpont Morgan，1837~1913）的父亲在伦敦创立，当时是一家英国商业银行。摩根公司对包括美国钢铁、通用电气以及美国电话电报等知名企业最初的创立及融资起了重大作用。该公司与大通银行（Chase Manhattan Bank）和富林明集团（Robert Fleming & Co.）合并为摩根大通公司（JPMorgan Chase & Co.），是全球历史最长、规模最大的金融服务集团之一。

③ 这样，这些商业银行就必须出售自己的部分投资，以收回一部分短期贷款，来满足法定准备金要求。其结果导致了存款的成倍收缩。当这一影响的完整链条铺开之后，存款会减少100亿美元，同时，所有银行的资产负债表中资产项也随之变化（请仔细参阅表24-2（b）中加深黑体部分）。

Federal Reserve Balance Sheet (billions of dollars)

Assets		Liabilities	
Securities	500 −1	Currency held by public	410
Loans	10	Bank reserves	100 −1
Total assets	510 −1	**Total liabilities**	510 −1

TABLE 24-2(a). **Open-Market Sale by Fed Cuts Bank Reserves**

Balance Sheet of Commercial Banks (billions of dollars)

Assets		Liabilities	
Reserves	100 −1	Demand deposits	1000 −10
Loans and investments	900 −9		
Total assets	1000 −10	**Total liabilities**	1000 −10

TABLE 24-2(b). **Decline in Reserves Leads Banks to Reduce Loans and Investments until Money Supply Is Cut by 10-to-1 Ratio**

The central bank sells securities to reduce reserves in order to raise interest rates toward its target.

In **(a)**, the Fed sells \$1 billion worth of securities on the open market. When dealers pay for the securities, this reduces reserves by \$1 billion.

Then, in **(b)**, we see the effect of the open-market operation on the balance sheet of the commercial banks. With a reserve-requirement ratio of 10 percent of deposits, banks must reduce loans and investments. The net effect will be to tighten money and raise interest rates.

side of the banks' balance sheet [look carefully at the green entries in Table 24-2(*b*)].

This contraction of loans and investments will ① tend to raise interest rates. If the Fed has forecast correctly, the interest rate will move to the Fed's new target.

But if it has forecast incorrectly, what should the ② Fed do? Simply make another adjustment by buying or selling reserves the next day!

贴现窗口政策：公开市场业务的支撑
Discount-Window Policy: A Backstop for Open-Market Operations

The Fed has a second set of instruments that it can use to meet its targets. The discount window is a facility from which banks, and more recently primary dealers, can borrow when they need additional funds. The Fed charges a "discount rate" on borrowed funds, although the discount rate will vary slightly among different uses and institutions. Generally, the primary discount rate is ¼ to ½ of a percentage point above the target federal funds rate.

The discount window serves two purposes. It ③ complements open-market operations by making reserves available when they are needed on short notice. It also serves as a backstop source of liquidity for institutions when credit conditions may suddenly become tight.

Until very recently, the discount window was ④ seldom used. In the credit crisis of 2007–2009, the Federal Reserve opened the discount window so that banks could borrow when their customers became nervous and demanded immediate withdrawals. During this period, in order to provide more liquidity to a nervous financial market, the Fed enlarged the scope of its lending capacities in several ways. The Fed broadened its definition of allowable collateral, added primary dealers to the list of institutions eligible to borrow at the discount window, put guarantees on shaky securities to help prop up failing banks, and purchased private commercial paper from nonbank entities. All these steps were intended to reduce fears that financial institutions would be unable to pay off their obligations and that the financial system would freeze up and credit would become unavailable to businesses and households.

Lender of Last Resort. Financial intermediaries like ⑤ banks are inherently unstable because, as we have seen, their liabilities are short-term and subject to

on short notice: 突然

① 贷款和投资的收缩将推高利率。如果美联储能做出准确的预测，利率就会朝着联储新的目标移动。

② 但是，如果未能有准确的预测，美联储应该做什么？很简单，用第二天买进或者卖出准备金的方法，再做一次调整。

③ 贴现窗口有两个目的。当准备金出现突发急需时，通过利用准备金来弥补公开市场业务。其次，当信贷环境突然紧张时，可以为各机构的流动性提供支撑。

④ 直到最近，贴现窗口很少使用。在 2007~2009 年间的信贷危机中，美联储曾打开过贴现窗口，以便银行客户出现紧张而需要立刻提款时，银行能够借入资金。

⑤ *Lender of last resort*：最终贷款方

[1] 前文。

② 如果我们乐意使用杠杆型的金融中介系统，则金融系统管控风险的负担绝不仅仅会落到私人机构的肩上。杠杆通常会通过连锁反应，将风险传播开来。如果其过程未被监管，违约的瀑布似的后续结果将在金融系统内部累积，引发金融危机。在这一破坏性尚未形成之前，只有中央银行有无限力量创造货币，有可能阻断这一过程的蔓延。因此，中央银行必然随时被拖入其中，成为最终的贷款方。

③ 今天，贴现窗口主要用于确保货币市场的平稳运行。它在增加了流动性的同时，也成为各商业银行在需要最终贷款方时可以求助的地方。

rapid withdrawal while their assets are often long-term and even illiquid. From time to time, banks and other financial institutions cannot meet their obligations to their customers. Perhaps there are seasonal needs for cash, or perhaps, even more ominously, depositors may lose faith in their banks and withdraw their deposits all at once. In this situation, when the bank has run out of liquid assets and lines of credit, a central bank may step in to be the *lender of last resort.* This function was well described by former Fed chair [1] Alan Greenspan:

> [If] we choose to enjoy the advantages of a system ②
> of leveraged financial intermediaries, the burden of managing risk in the financial system will not lie with the private sector alone. Leveraging always carries with it the remote possibility of a chain reaction, a cascading sequence of defaults that will culminate in financial implosion if it proceeds unchecked. Only a central bank, with its unlimited power to create money, can with a high probability thwart such a process before it becomes destructive. Hence, central banks have, of necessity, been drawn into becoming lenders of last resort.

Today the discount window is used primarily to ③
ensure that money markets are operating smoothly. It provides additional liquidity, and it is also the place to which banks can turn when they need a lender of last resort.

法定准备金的作用
The Role of Reserve Requirements

The Nature of Reserves. The previous chapter showed the relationship between bank reserves and bank money. In a free-market banking system, prudent bankers would always need to hold some reserves on hand. They would need to keep a small fraction of their deposits in cash to pay out to depositors who desired to convert their deposits to currency or who wrote checks drawn on their accounts.

Many years ago, bankers recognized that, although deposits are payable on demand, they are seldom all withdrawn together. It would be necessary to hold reserves equal to total deposits if all depositors suddenly wanted to be paid off in full at the same time, but this almost never occurred. On any given day, some people made withdrawals while others made deposits. These two kinds of transactions generally canceled each other out.

Early bankers did not need to keep 100 percent of ④
deposits as sterile reserves; reserves earned no interest when they were sitting in a vault. Banks quickly hit upon the idea of finding profitable investments for their excess deposits. By putting most of the money deposited with them into interest-bearing assets and keeping only fractional cash reserves, banks could maximize their profits.

The transformation into fractional-reserve banks—holding fractional rather than 100 percent reserves against deposits—was in fact revolutionary. It led to the leveraged financial institutions that dominate our financial system today.

Legal Reserve Requirements. In the nineteenth century, banks sometimes had insufficient reserves to meet depositors' demands, and these occasionally spiraled into bank crises. Therefore, begin- ⑤
ning at that time, and currently formalized under Federal Reserve regulations, banks were required to keep a certain fraction of their checking deposits (the Fed uses the technical term "checkable deposits") as reserves. In an earlier period, reserve requirements were an important part of controlling the quantity of money (as discussed later in this chapter). In today's environment, where the Fed primarily targets interest rates, reserve requirements are a relatively unimportant instrument of monetary policy.

Reserve requirements apply to all types of check- ⑥
ing deposits. Under Federal Reserve regulations, banks are required to hold a fixed fraction of their checking deposits as reserves. This fraction is called the **required reserve ratio.** Bank reserves take the form of vault cash (bank holdings of currency) and deposits by banks with the Federal Reserve System.

Table 24-3 shows current reserve requirements along with the Fed's discretionary power to change these requirements. The key concept is the level of required reserve ratios. They currently range from 10 percent against checking deposits down to zero for personal savings accounts. For convenience in our numerical examples, we use 10 percent reserve ratios, with the understanding that the actual ratio may differ from time to time.

In normal times, the level of required reserves is generally higher than what banks would voluntarily hold. These high requirements serve primarily to ensure that the demand for reserves is relatively

---

④ 早期的银行业者并不需要将百分之百的存款都作为没有升值功能的准备金，长期码放在金库中的准备金挣不来分毫的利息。银行很快就发现，用其超额的储蓄进行投资竟然可以找到赚钱的机会。通过把大部分存款利用起来，投入盈利性资产，同时只保持少量的现金储备，银行就能将利润最大化。

⑤ 这样，从那时候开始，就已经形成了现在的联邦储备条例，要求银行必须保留特定比例的支票存款作为准备金（美联储使用“可随时支取的支票存款”）。

⑥ 准备金要求适用于所有类型的支票账户存款。按照美联储的条例，银行必须保有支票存款的固定比例作为准备金。这一比例就叫做**法定准备金率**。银行的准备金以库存现金（银行持有的通货）和银行在联邦储备系统存款的形式保有。

Type of deposit	Reserve ratio (%)	Range in which Fed can vary (%)
Checking (transactions) accounts:		
$0–$44 million	3	No change allowed
Above $44 million	10	8–14
Time and savings deposits:		
Personal	0	
Nonpersonal:		
Up to 1½ years' maturity	0	0–9
More than 1½ years' maturity	0	0–9

TABLE 24-3. Required Reserves for Financial Institutions

Reserve requirements are governed by law and regulation. The reserve-ratio column shows the percent of deposits in each category that must be held in non-interest-bearing deposits at the Fed or as cash on hand. Checking accounts in large banks face a required reserve ratio of 10 percent, while other major deposits have no reserve requirements. The Fed has power to alter the reserve ratio within a given range but does so only on the rare occasion when economic conditions warrant a sharp change in monetary policy.

Source: *Federal Reserve Bulletin*, March 2008.

predictable so that the Fed can have more precise control over the federal funds rate.

The Fed began to pay interest on bank reserves in 2008. The idea was that the interest rate on reserves would serve as a floor under the federal funds rate, thereby allowing better control over the federal funds rate. For example, if the target federal funds rate is 3½ percent, while the interest rate on reserves is 3 percent and the discount rate is 4 percent, then the federal funds rate will effectively be constrained between 3 and 4 percent, and the Fed can more easily attain its target. The financial environment took an unusual turn during the financial crisis of 2007–2009 as the economy entered a "liquidity trap." We return to this point briefly later in this chapter.

联邦基金利率的决定

Determination of the Federal Funds Rate

Now that we have surveyed the basic instruments, we can analyze how the Fed determines short-term interest rates. The basic operation is shown in Figure 24-3. This shows the demand for and supply of bank reserves. ①

First, consider the demand for bank reserves. As we saw in the last chapter, banks are required to hold reserves as determined by the total value of their checking deposits and the required reserve ratio. Because the demand for checking deposits is an inverse function of the interest rate, this implies that the demand for bank reserves will also decline as interest rates rise. This is what lies behind the downward-sloping $D_R D_R$ curve in Figure 24-3.

Next, we need to consider the supply of reserves. This is determined by open-market operations. By purchasing and selling securities, the Fed controls the level of reserves in the system. A purchase of securities by the Fed increases the supply of bank reserves, while a sale does the opposite. ②

The equilibrium federal funds interest rate is determined where desired supply and demand are equal. The important insight here is that the Fed can achieve its target through the judicious purchase and sale of securities—that is, through open-market operations. ③

But Figure 24-3 shows only the very short run supply and demand. Because the Fed intervenes in the market daily, and because market participants know the Fed's interest-rate target, the Fed can keep the federal funds rate close to its target. Figure 24-4 shows supply and demand over the period of a month or more. The central bank in essence provides a perfectly elastic supply of reserves at the target federal funds rate. This shows how the Fed achieves its funds target on a week-to-week and month-to-month basis.

---

① 由于已经讨论了基本的货币政策工具，我们就可以来分析美联储是如何决定短期利率的。

② 联储通过对证券的买进和卖出，控制系统内准备金的规模。联储对证券的买进增加了银行准备金的供给，相反，卖出则减少了准备金的供给。

③ 联邦基金均衡利率是在期望的供给与需求相等的情况下决定的。这里重要的一点是，美联储通过审慎地买进和卖出证券，即通过公开市场业务来实现其目标。

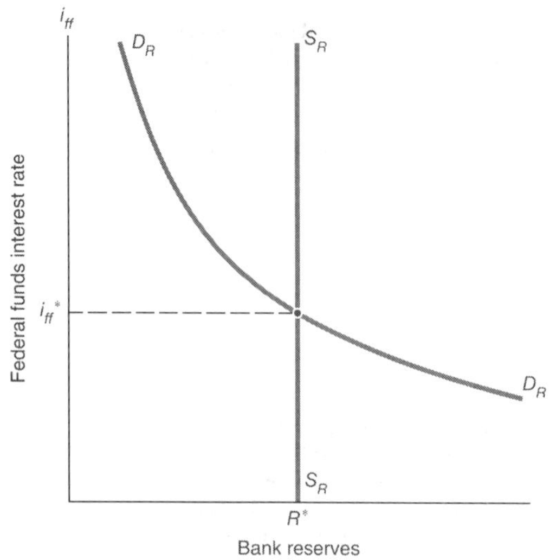

FIGURE 24-3. Supply of and Demand for Bank Reserves Determine the Federal Funds Rate

The demand for bank reserves declines as interest rates rise, reflecting that checking deposits decline as lower interest rates increase money demand. The Fed has a target interest rate at i_{ff}^*. By supplying the appropriate quantity of reserves at R^* through open-market operations, the Fed achieves its target.

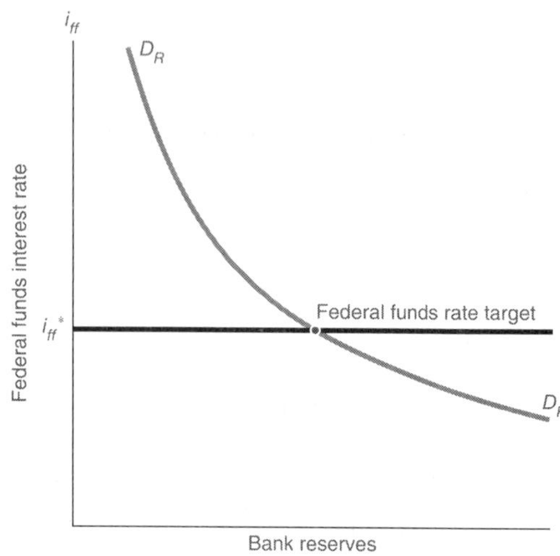

FIGURE 24-4. By Constant Intervention the Fed Can Achieve Its Interest-Rate Target

Because the Fed intervenes daily, undertaking open-market operations as illustrated in Figure 24-3, it can achieve its target with a narrow margin.

The federal funds rate, which is the most impor- ① tant short-term interest rate in the market, is determined by the supply of and demand for bank reserves. By constantly monitoring the market and providing or removing reserves as needed through open-market operations, the Federal Reserve can ensure that short-term interest rates stay very close to its target.

货币传导机制

B. THE MONETARY TRANSMISSION MECHANISM

概 述
A Summary Statement

Having examined the building blocks of monetary ② theory, we now describe the **monetary transmission mechanism,** the route by which monetary policy affects output, employment, prices, and inflation. We sketched the mechanism at the beginning of the previous chapter, and now we describe the mechanism in greater detail.

1. *The central bank raises the interest-rate target.* The central bank announces a target short-term interest rate chosen in light of its objectives and the state of the economy. The Fed may also change the discount rate and the terms of its lending facilities. These decisions are based on current economic conditions, particularly inflation, output growth, employment, and financial conditions.
2. *The central bank undertakes open-market operations.* The central bank undertakes daily open-market operations to meet its federal funds target. If the ③ Fed wished to slow the economy, it would sell securities, thereby reducing reserves and raising short-term interest rates; if a recession threatened, the Fed would buy securities, increasing the supply of reserves and lowering short-term interest rates. Through open-market operations,

① 作为市场中最为重要的短期利率，联邦基金利率是由银行准备金的供给与需求决定的。通过对市场的实时监控，以及按需要通过公开市场业务增加或减少准备金，美联储就可以确保短期利率长期保持在接近目标的水平。

② 在研究了货币理论的主要构成之后，我们现在来讨论一下**货币传导机制**，即货币政策影响产出、就业、价格和通货膨胀的途径。在上一章的开头，我们对这一机制作了概述，现在让我们进行更详细的讨论。

③ 如果美联储希望使经济放缓，它就会卖出证券，以此减少准备金并提高短期利率；如果经济面临衰退的威胁，联储就会买进证券，增加准备金供给并降低短期利率。

the Fed keeps the short-term interest rate close to its target on average.

3. *Asset markets react to the policy changes.* As the short-term interest rate changes, given expectations about future financial conditions, banks adjust their loans and investments, as well as their interest rates and credit terms. Changes in current and expected future short-term interest rates, along with other financial and macroeconomic influences, determine the entire spectrum of longer-term interest rates. Higher interest rates ① tend to reduce asset prices (such as those of stocks, bonds, and houses). Higher interest rates also tend to raise foreign-exchange rates in a flexible-exchange-rate system.
4. *Investment and other spending react to interest-rate changes.* Suppose the Fed has raised interest rates to reduce inflation. The combination of higher interest rates, tighter credit, lower wealth, and a higher exchange rate tends to reduce investment, consumption, and net exports. Businesses scale down their investment plans. Similarly, when mortgage interest rates rise, people may postpone buying a house, lowering housing investment. In addition, in an open economy, the higher foreign-exchange rate of the dollar will depress net exports. Hence, tight money will ② reduce spending on interest-sensitive components of aggregate demand.
5. *Monetary policy will ultimately affect output and price inflation.* The aggregate supply-and-demand analysis (or, equivalently, the multiplier analysis) showed how changes in investment and other autonomous spending affect output and employment. If the Fed tightens money and credit, the ③ decline in *AD* will lower output and cause prices to rise less rapidly, thereby curbing inflationary forces.

We can summarize the steps as follows:

Change in monetary policy
→ change in interest rates, asset prices, exchange rates
→ impact on *I, C, X*
→ effect on *AD*
→ effect on *Q, P*

Make sure you understand this important sequence from the central bank's change in its interest-rate target to the ultimate effect on output and prices. We have discussed the first steps of the sequence in depth, and we now follow through by exploring the effect on the overall economy.

货币政策的变化对产出的影响
The Effect of Changes in Monetary Policy on Output

We close with a graphical analysis of the monetary transmission mechanism.

Interest Rates and the Demand for Investment. We can track the first part of the mechanism in Figure 24-5. This diagram puts together two diagrams we have met before: the supply of and demand for reserves in (*a*) and the demand for investment in (*b*). We have simplified our analysis by assuming that there is no inflation, no taxes, and no risk, with the result that the federal funds interest rate in (*a*) is the same as the cost of capital paid by business and residential investors in (*b*). In this simplified situation, the real interest rate (r) equals the central bank's interest rate (i_{ff}). Monetary policy leads to interest rate r^*, which then leads to the corresponding level of investment I^*.

Next, consider what happens when economic conditions change. Suppose that economic conditions deteriorate. This could be the result of a decline in military spending after a war, or the result of a decline in investment due to the burst of a bubble, or the result of a collapse in consumer confidence after a terrorist attack. The Fed would examine economic conditions and determine that it should lower short-term interest rates through open-market purchases. This would lead to the downward shift in interest rates from r^* to r^{**} shown in Figure 24-6(*a*).

The next step in the sequence would be the reaction of investment, shown in Figure 24-6(*b*). As interest rates decline *and holding other things constant,* the demand for investment would increase from I^* to I^{**}. (We emphasize the point about holding other ④ things constant because this diagram shows the shift relative to what would otherwise occur. Taking into account that other things *are* changing, we might see a fall in *actual* investment. However, the monetary shift indicates that investment would fall less with the policy than without it.)

Changes in Investment and Output. The final link in the mechanism is the impact on aggregate demand,

---

① 利率的升高会降低资产价格（如股票、债券和房产的价格）。在浮动汇率体系，利率的升高还会抬高汇率。

② 因此，紧缩货币会降低总需求中对利率敏感的组成部分的支出。

③ 如果美联储收紧货币和信贷，则总需求 *AD* 的下降将会降低产出，从而减缓价格的快速上涨，以此抑制通货膨胀的压力。

④（我们之所以强调保持其他因素不变这一点，是因为如该图所示，其他因素发生变化会导致投资需求曲线发生移动。如果把发生变化的其他因素考虑在内，我们会看到实际投资下降。然而，相较于没有这一货币政策而言，实施货币政策后，投资减少的幅度会比较小。）

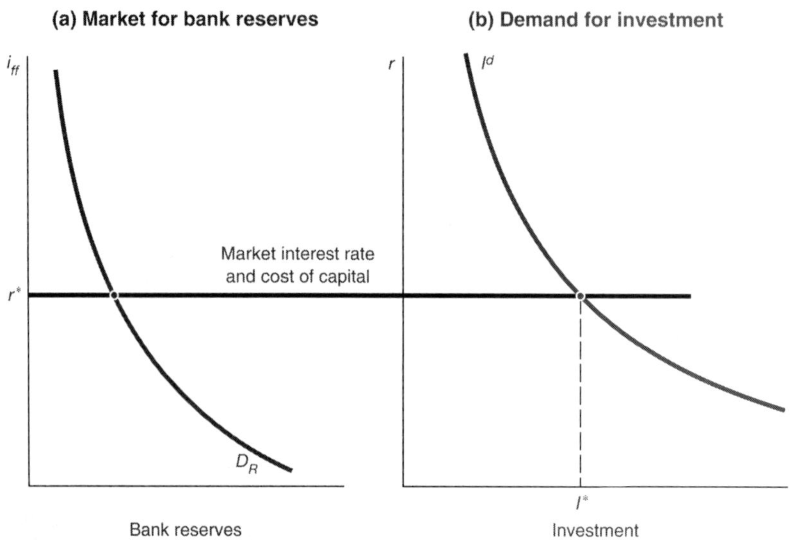

FIGURE 24-5. Interest Rate Determines Business and Residential Investment

This figure shows the linkage between monetary policy and the real economy. (**a**) The Fed uses open-market operations to determine short-term interest rates. (**b**) Assuming no inflation or risk, the interest rate determines the cost of business and residential investment; that is, $r = i_{ff}$. Total investment, which is the most interest-sensitive component of *AD*, can be found at *I**. ①

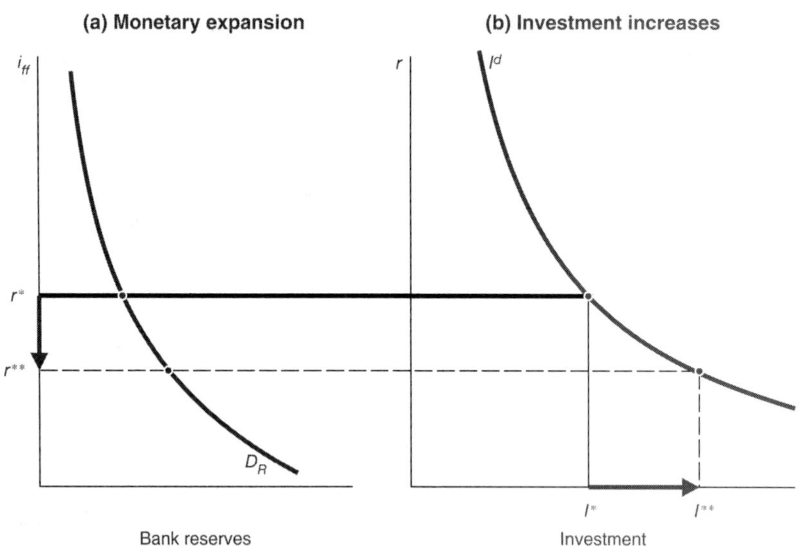

FIGURE 24-6. Monetary Expansion Leads to Lower Interest Rates and Increased Investment

Suppose that the economy weakens, as happened in 2007–2008. **(a)** The Fed buys securities and increases reserves, lowering the interest rate. **(b)** The effect (other things held constant) is that the lower interest rate raises asset prices and stimulates business and residential investment. See how investment rises from *I** to *I***. ②

① 本图表示货币政策与实体经济之间的关系。（a）联储使用公开市场业务的手段来决定短期利率；（b）假定没有通货膨胀或者风险，企业以及住宅投资的成本就由利率决定，即：$r = i_{ff}$。作为总需求中对利率最为敏感的组成部分，总投资在图中的 *I** 点。

② 假设像 2007~2008 年那样经济低迷的时期：（a）美联储买进证券，增加准备金，同时降低利率；（b）假定其他因素不变，它的作用是利率下降提高了资产价格，从而刺激企业和住宅投资。

as shown in Figure 24-7. This is the same diagram we used to illustrate the multiplier mechanism in Chapter 22. We have shown the $C + I + G$ curve of total expenditure as a function of total output on the horizontal axis. With the original interest rate r^*, output is at the depressed level Q^* before the central bank undertakes its expansionary policy.

Next, assume that the Fed takes steps to lower market interest rates, as shown in Figure 24-6. The lower interest rates increase investment from I^* to I^{**}. This is illustrated in Figure 24-7 as an upward shift in the total expenditure line to $C + I(r^{**}) + G$. The result is a higher total output at Q^{**}. This diagram shows how the sequence of monetary steps has led to higher output, just as the Fed desired in the face of deteriorating economic conditions.

This graphical device is oversimplified. It omits many other contributions to changes in aggregate demand, such as the impact of monetary policy on

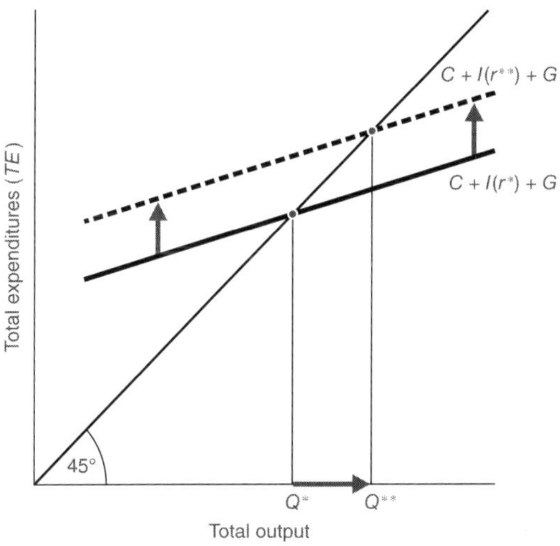

FIGURE 24-7. Monetary Expansion Lowers Interest Rate and Increases Output

As interest rates decline from r^* to r^{**}, then (other things held constant) investment increases from $I(r^*)$ to $I(r^{**})$. This increase shifts up the aggregate demand $C + I + G$ curve of total expenditure, and output increases from Q^* to Q^{**}. This completes the monetary transmission mechanism.

wealth and consequently on consumption, the effect of exchange rates on foreign trade, and the direct effect of credit conditions on spending. Additionally, we have not yet fully described how monetary policy affects inflation. Nevertheless, this simple graph illustrates the essence of the monetary transmission mechanism.

Monetary policy uses open-market operations ①
and other instruments to affect short-term interest rates. These short-term interest rates then interact with other economic influences to affect other interest rates and asset prices. By affecting interest-sensitive spending, such as business and residential investment, monetary policy helps control output, employment, and price inflation.

流动性陷阱的挑战

The Challenge of a Liquidity Trap

One of the greatest challenges for a central bank ②
arises as nominal interest rates approach zero. This is referred to as the **liquidity trap.** Such a situation
occurred in the Great Depression of the 1930s and [3]
then again in 2008–2009 in the United States.

When short-term safe interest rates are zero, short-term safe securities are equivalent to money. The demand for money becomes infinitely elastic with respect to the interest rate. In this situation, banks have no reason to economize on their reserve holdings; they get essentially the same interest rates on reserves as on riskless short-term investments. For example, in early 2009, banks could earn 0.10 percent annually on reserves and 0.12 percent on Treasury bills.

Central bank open-market operations therefore have little or no impact upon interest rates and financial markets. Instead, when the Fed purchases securities, the banks just increase their excess reserves. This syndrome appeared with a vengeance in 2008–2009 as excess reserves rose from a normal level of $1 billion to over $900 billion. In essence, banks were using the Fed as a safe deposit box for their funds! (Make sure you understand why open-market operations are ineffective in a liquidity trap.) Because the Fed cannot lower short-term interest rates, it is unable to use the normal monetary transmission mechanism to stimulate the economy in a liquidity trap.

If the central bank cannot lower short-term interest rates below zero, what other steps can it take to stimulate a depressed economy? This was

① 货币政策利用公开市场业务以及其他工具对短期利率施加影响。然后这些短期利率与其他经济影响因素相互作用于利率和资产价格。通过影响诸如企业和住宅投资这些对利率敏感的支出，货币政策强化了对产出、就业以及通货膨胀的控制力度。

② 中央银行的最大挑战之一出现在名义利率接近于零的时候。这就是所谓的**流动性陷阱**。美国在 20 世纪 30 年代经济大萧条时出现过这样的情况，并在 2008~2009 年再次出现。

[3] Great Depression：指 20 世纪 30 年代的大萧条。萨翁在 17 版的前言中将 20 世纪分为前 50 年的 *the Great Repression*，后 50 年 *the Great Peace*。这是萨缪尔森不经意间对 20 世纪 100 年做出的科学断代，正好契合了“长波论”，此后的 18 版即予删除。因此，本书的 17 版在学术上由于这个断代说和对美国网络经济泡沫破灭的反思，更有其独特的价值所在。

the dilemma that the Fed faced in early 2009. One step would be to attempt to lower *long-term interest rates*. This would require that the central bank purchase long-term bonds instead of focusing on short-term securities, which is its usual practice. A second step would be to *reduce the risk premium on risky securities*. Acting with the U.S. Treasury, the ①
Fed has been taking forceful steps in this direction since the early stages of the 2007–2009 credit crisis. The steps included buying distressed assets, opening the discount window to non-bank financial institutions, buying commercial paper, and lending against a wide range of private financial assets. The purpose of these steps was to improve liquidity and increase the availability of credit in financial markets. An excellent review of the Fed's activities during this period is contained in a 2009 speech by Fed chair Bernanke cited in the Further Readings section at the end of this chapter.

AS–AD 框架中的货币政策

Monetary Policy in the AS-AD Framework

Figures 24-5, 24-6, and 24-7 illustrate how a change in monetary policy could lead to an increase in aggregate demand. We can now show the effect of such an increase on the overall macroeconomic equilibrium by using aggregate supply and aggregate demand curves.

The increase in aggregate demand produced by a monetary expansion is shown as a rightward shift of the *AD* curve, as drawn in Figure 24-8. This shift illustrates a monetary expansion in the presence of unemployed resources, with a relatively flat *AS* curve. The monetary expansion shifts aggregate demand from *AD* to *AD*′, moving the equilibrium from *E* to *E*′. This example demonstrates how monetary expansion can increase aggregate demand and have a powerful impact on real output.

The complete sequence of impacts from expan- ②
sionary monetary policy is therefore as follows: Open-market operations lower market interest rates. Lower interest rates stimulate interest-sensitive spending on business investment, housing, net exports, and the like. Aggregate demand increases via the multiplier mechanism, raising output and prices above the levels they would otherwise attain. Therefore, the basic sequence is

$$r \text{ down} \rightarrow I, C, X \text{ up} \rightarrow AD \text{ up} \rightarrow Q \text{ and } P \text{ up}$$

Expansionary Monetary Policy

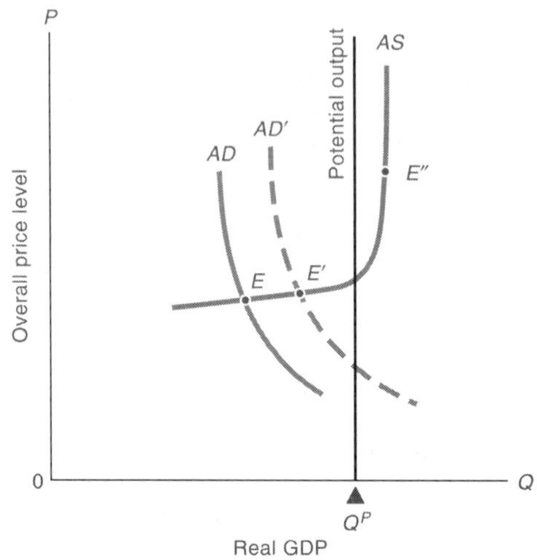

FIGURE 24-8. Expansionary Monetary Policy Shifts Out the *AD* Curve, Increasing Output and Prices

Figures 24-5 to 24-7 showed how a monetary expansion would lead to an increase in investment and thereby to a multiplied increase in output. This results in a rightward shift of the *AD* curve.

In the Keynesian region where the *AS* curve is rela- ③
tively flat, a monetary expansion has its primary effect on real output, with only a small effect on prices. In a fully employed economy, the *AS* curve is near-vertical (shown at point *E*″), and a monetary expansion will primarily raise prices and nominal GDP, with little effect on real GDP. Can you see why in the long run monetary policy would have no impact on real output if the *AS* curve is vertical?

To clinch your understanding of this vital sequence, work through the opposite case of a monetary contraction. Say that the Federal Reserve decides to raise interest rates, slow the economy, and reduce inflation. You can trace this sequence in Figures 24-5 through 24-7 by reversing the direction of the initial change in monetary policy, thereby seeing how money, interest rates, investment, and aggregate demand react when monetary policy is tightened. Then see how a corresponding leftward shift of the *AD* curve in Figure 24-8 would reduce both output and prices.

---

① 从 2007~2009 年信贷危机的早期阶段开始，美联储就在美国财政部的全力协调下，朝这个方向采取了一系列强有力的措施。

② 所以，这种扩张性的货币政策所引发的全部后续效应如下：公开市场业务降低了市场利率；较低的市场利率刺激了企业投资、住房以及净出口等对利率敏感的支出；乘数机制增加了总需求，同时也使产出和价格高出了它们通过其他手段所能达到的水平。

③ 在凯恩斯区域，即在 AS 曲线相对平缓的这一区域，货币的扩张主要对实际产出产生影响，而对价格只是小有影响而已。

长期货币政策
Monetary Policy in the Long Run

The analysis in this chapter focuses primarily on monetary policy and business cycles. That is, it considers how monetary policy and interest rates affect output in the short run.

Be aware, however, that a different set of forces will operate in the long run. Monetary policies to stimulate the economy cannot keep increasing output beyond its potential for long. If the central bank holds interest rates too low for long periods of time, the economy will overheat and inflationary forces will take hold. With low real interest rates, speculation may arise, and animal spirits may overtake rational calculations. Some analysts believe that interest rates were too low for too long in the 1990s, causing the stock market bubble; some people think that the same mechanism was behind the housing market bubble of the 2000s.

In the long run, therefore, monetary expansion mainly affects the price level with little or no impact upon real output. As shown in Figure 24-8, monetary changes will affect aggregate demand and real GDP in the short run when there are unemployed resources in the economy and the *AS* curve is relatively flat. However, in our analysis of aggregate supply in the following chapters, we will see that the *AS* curve tends to be vertical or near-vertical in the long run as wages and prices adjust. Because of such price-wage adjustments and a near-vertical *AS* curve, the effects of *AD* shifts on output will diminish in the long run, and the effects on prices will tend to dominate. *This means that, as prices and wages become more* ①
flexible in the long run, monetary-policy changes tend to have a relatively small impact on output and a relatively large impact on prices.

What is the intuition behind this difference between the short run and the long run? Suppose that monetary policy lowers interest rates. In the beginning, real output rises smartly and prices rise modestly. As time passes, however, wages and ②
prices adjust more completely to the higher price and output levels. Higher demand in both labor and product markets raises wages and prices; wages are adjusted to reflect the higher cost of living. In the end, the expansionary monetary policy would produce an economy with unchanged real output and higher prices. All dollar variables (including the money supply, reserves, government debt, wages, prices, exchange rates, etc.) would be higher, while all real variables would be unchanged. In such a case, we say that *money is neutral*, meaning that changes in monetary policy have no effect on real variables.

This discussion of monetary policy has taken place without reference to fiscal policy. In reality, whatever the philosophical predilections of the government, every advanced economy simultaneously conducts both fiscal and monetary policies. Each type of policy has both strengths and weaknesses. In the chapters that follow, we return to an integrated consideration of the roles of monetary and fiscal policies in combating the business cycle and promoting economic growth.

货币经济学的应用
C. APPLICATIONS OF MONETARY ECONOMICS

Having examined the basic elements of monetary economics and central banking, we now turn to two important applications of money to macroeconomics. We begin with a review of the influential monetarist approach, and then we examine the implications of globalization for monetary policy.

货币主义与货币和价格的数量理论
MONETARISM AND THE QUANTITY THEORY OF MONEY AND PRICES

Financial and monetary systems cannot manage ③
themselves. The government, including the central bank, must make fundamental decisions about the monetary standard, the money supply, and the ease or tightness of money and credit. Today, there are many different philosophies about the best way to manage monetary affairs. Many believe in an active policy that "leans against the wind" by raising interest rates when inflation threatens and lowering them in recessions. Others are skeptical about the ability of policymakers to use monetary policy to "fine-tune" the economy to attain the desired levels of inflation and unemployment; they would rather limit monetary policy to targeting inflation. Then there are the monetarists, who believe that discretionary monetary policy should be replaced by a fixed rule relating to the growth of the money supply.

---

① 这就意味着长期内，随着价格和工资变得更有弹性，货币政策变化的走向对产出的影响相对较小，而对价格的影响相对较大。

② 然而，随着时间的推移，工资和价格会根据更高的价格和产出水平做更充分的调整。劳动和产品两个市场的更高需求推升了工资和价格，而工资的调整又反映到更高的生活成本。最终，这种扩张性的货币政策就会导致经济中的实际产出不变，价格上升。

③ 金融和货币系统根本无法自我管理。政府，包括中央银行，必须就货币标准、货币供给量、货币和信贷的松紧制定基本决策。目前，关于货币管理问题的最优办法还存在许多不同观点。

① **货币主义**认为，货币的供给是名义 GDP 的短期波动和价格的长期波动的主要决定因素。当然，凯恩斯主义宏观经济学也承认，货币在决定总需求时具有关键作用。货币主义和凯恩斯主义之间的主要区别在于，在决定总需求时对货币作用所赋予的重要程度不同。凯恩斯理论认为，除了货币之外，还有许多其他因素也影响总需求，而货币主义坚信，货币供给量的变化是决定产出和价格波动的主要因素。

[2] Alfred Marshall：阿尔弗雷德·马歇尔（1842~1924），新古典学派的创始人，19 世纪末和 20 世纪初英国经济学界最重要的人物，在剑桥大学建立了世界上第一个经济学系，使经济学从仅仅是人文和历史学科的一门必修课发展成为一门独立学科。1881 年出版的《经济学原理》（*Principles of Economics*）是其主要代表作。

Having reviewed the basics of mainstream monetary theory, this section analyzes monetarism and traces the history of its development from the older quantity theory of money and prices. We will also see that monetarism is closely related to modern macroeconomic theory.

货币主义的根源

The Roots of Monetarism

Monetarism holds that the money supply is the pri- ①
mary determinant of both short-run movements in nominal GDP and long-run movements in prices. Of course, Keynesian macroeconomics also recognizes the key role of money in determining aggregate demand. The main difference between monetarists and Keynesians lies in the importance assigned to the role of money in the determination of aggregate demand. While Keynesian theories hold that many other forces besides money also affect aggregate demand, monetarists believe that changes in the money supply are the primary factor that determines movement in output and prices.

In order to understand monetarism, we need to understand the concept of the *velocity of money*.

交易方程与货币周转率

The Equation of Exchange and the Velocity of Money

Money sometimes turns over very slowly; it may sit under a mattress or in a bank account for long periods of time between transactions. At other times, particularly during periods of rapid inflation, money circulates quickly from hand to hand. The speed of the turnover of money is described by the concept of the velocity of money, intro-
duced by Cambridge University's Alfred Marshall [2]
and Yale University's Irving Fisher. The velocity of [3]
money measures the number of times per year that the average dollar in the money supply is spent for goods and services. When the quantity of money is large relative to the flow of expenditures, the velocity of circulation is low; when money turns over rapidly, its velocity is high.

The concept of velocity is formally introduced in the **equation of exchange.** This equation states[2]

$$MV \equiv PQ \equiv (p_1q_1 + p_2q_2 + \cdots)$$

where M is the money supply, V is the velocity of money, P is the overall price level, and Q is total real
output. This can be restated as the definition of the ④
velocity of money by dividing both sides by M:

$$V \equiv \frac{PQ}{M}$$

We generally measure PQ as total income or output (nominal GDP); the associated velocity concept is the *income velocity of money*.

Velocity is the rate at which money circulates ⑤
through the economy. The **income velocity of money** is measured as the ratio of nominal GDP to the stock of money.

As a simple example, assume that the economy produces only bread. GDP consists of 48 million loaves of bread, each selling at a price of \$1, so GDP = PQ = \$48 million per year. If the money supply is \$4 million, then by definition V = \$48/\$4 = 12 per year. This means that money turns over 12 times per year or once a month as incomes are used to buy the monthly bread.

价格的数量理论

The Quantity Theory of Prices

Having defined an interesting variable called velocity, we now describe how early monetary economists used velocity to explain movements in the overall price level. The key assumption here is that *the velocity of money is stable and predictable.* The reason for stability, according to monetarists, is that velocity mainly reflects underlying patterns in the timing of earning and spending. If people are paid once a month and tend to spend their income evenly over the course of the month, income velocity will be 12 per year. Suppose that all prices, wages, and incomes double. With unchanged spending patterns, the income velocity of money would remain unchanged and the demand for money would double. Only if people and businesses modify their spending patterns or the way in which they pay their bills would the income velocity of money change.

On the basis of this insight about the stability of ⑥
velocity, some early writers used velocity to explain changes in the price level. This approach, called the **quantity theory of money and prices,** rewrites the definition of velocity as follows:

$$P \equiv \frac{MV}{Q} \equiv \left(\frac{V}{Q}\right)M \approx kM$$

[2] The definitional equations have been written with the three-bar identity symbol rather than with the more common two-bar equality symbol. This usage emphasizes that they are "identities"—statements which hold true by definition.

[3] Irving Fisher：欧文·费希尔（1867~1947），耶鲁大学教授，美国第一位数理经济学家，经济计量学的先驱者，货币理论原则是其对经济学做出的主要贡献。

④ 两边除以 M 之后，我们可以将**货币周转率**的定义重新描述为：$V \equiv PQ/M$

⑤ 周转率是货币在该经济体中流通的速率。**货币收入周转率**是名义 GDP 与货币存量的比值。

⑥ 在深入分析周转率稳定性的基础上，一些早期的学者曾经使用周转率来解释价格水平的变化。这种称作**货币与价格数量论**的方法，对周转率重新做了定义。

This equation is obtained from the earlier definition of velocity by substituting the variable k as a shorthand for V/Q and solving for P. We write the equation in this way because many classical economists believed that if transaction patterns were stable, k would be constant or stable. In addition, they generally assumed full employment, which meant that real output would grow smoothly. Putting these two assumptions together, $k \approx (V/Q)$ would be near-constant in the short run and decline smoothly in the long run.

What are the implications of the quantity theory? As we can see from the equation, if k were constant, the price level would then move proportionally with the supply of money. A stable money supply would produce stable prices; if the money supply grew rapidly, so would prices. Similarly, if the money supply were growing a hundredfold or a millionfold each year, the economy would experience galloping inflation or hyperinflation. Indeed, the most vivid demonstrations of the quantity theory can be seen in periods of hyperinflation. Look at Figure 30-4 (on page 613). Note how prices rose a billionfold in Weimar Germany after the central [1] bank unleashed the power of the monetary printing presses. This is the quantity theory of money with a vengeance.

To understand the quantity theory of money, it is essential to recall that money differs fundamentally from ordinary goods such as bread and cars. We want bread to eat and cars to drive. But we want money only because it buys us bread and cars. If prices in Zimbabwe today are 100 million times what they were [2] a few years ago, it is natural that people will need about 100 million times as much money to buy things as they did before. Here lies the core of the quantity theory of money: the demand for money rises proportionally with the price level as long as other things are held constant.

In reality, velocity has tended to increase slowly over time, so the k ratio might also change slowly over time. Moreover, in normal times, the quantity theory is only a rough approximation to the facts. Figure 24-9 shows a scatter plot of money growth and inflation over the last half-century. While periods of faster U.S. money growth are also periods of higher inflation, other factors are clearly at work as well, as evidenced by the imperfect correlation between money supply and prices.

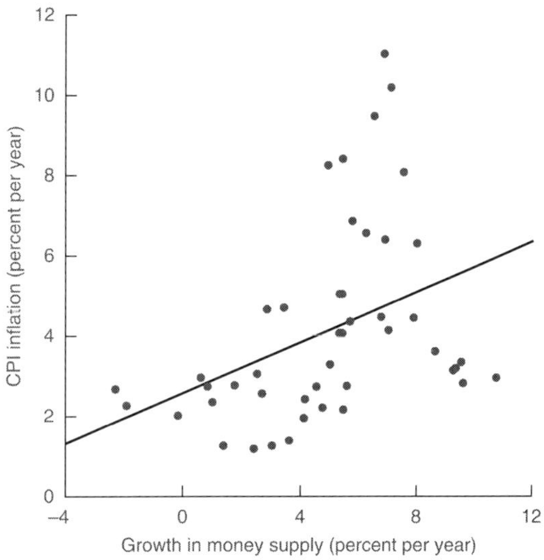

FIGURE 24-9. The Quantity Theory in the United States, 1962–2007

The quantity theory states that prices should change 1 percent for each 1 percent change in the money supply. The scatter plot and the line of best fit show how the simple quantity theory holds for data from the last half-century. Inflation is indeed correlated with money growth, but the relationship is a loose fit. As we will see in our chapters on inflation, other variables such as unemployment and commodity prices influence inflation as well. Query: Assuming velocity is constant and output grows at 3 percent per year, what scatter plot would be produced if money were neutral?

Source: Money supply from the Federal Reserve Board, and the consumer price index from the Bureau of Labor Statistics. Data are 3-year moving averages.

The quantity theory of money and prices holds ③ that prices move proportionally with the supply of money. Although the quantity theory is only a rough approximation, it does help to explain why countries with low money growth have moderate inflation while those with rapid money growth find their prices galloping along.

现代货币主义
Modern Monetarism

Modern monetary economics was developed after ④ World War II by Chicago's Milton Friedman and [5] his numerous colleagues and followers. Under

[1] Weimar Germany：魏玛德国。1919年德国国民议会在其文化中心的小城魏玛制订了第一部共和宪法，即魏玛宪法，成立了魏玛共和国，其短暂的14年历史经历了西方民主史上最严重的经济危机。

[2] Zimbabwe：按2008年7月的官方统计，津巴布韦的通货膨胀率达231 000 000%。

③ 货币与价格数量论认为，价格随货币供给按比例波动。虽然该理论得出的结果只是一个粗略的近似值，但它确实有助于解释为什么货币增长缓慢的国家通货膨胀温和，而那些货币增长过快的国家则价格一路飞涨。

④ 现代货币主义经济学是二次大战以后由芝加哥学派的米尔顿·弗里德曼与他的众多同事以及追随者们发展起来的。在弗里德曼的领导下，货币主义者向凯恩斯主义的宏观经济学发起了挑战，强化了货币政策在宏观经济稳定中的重要性。

[5] Milton Friedman：米尔顿·弗里德曼（1912~2006），美国芝加哥自由主义经济学派的杰出代表人物，著名统计学家，萨缪尔森的师兄。两人的学术观点终身相左，但生活中又是极其要好的朋友，在学术界颇受称道。

Friedman's leadership, monetarists challenged Keynesian macroeconomics and emphasized the importance of monetary policy in macroeconomic stabilization. In the 1970s, the monetarist approach branched into two separate schools of thought. One continued the monetarist tradition, which we will now describe. The younger offshoot became the influential "new classical school," which is analyzed [1] in Chapter 31.

Strict monetarists hold that "only money mat- ② ters." This means that prices and output are determined solely by the money supply and that other factors affecting aggregate demand, such as fiscal policy, have no effect on total output or prices. Moreover, while monetary changes may affect real output in the short run, in the long run output is determined by supply factors of labor, capital, and technology. This theory predicts that in the long run, *money is neutral.* This proposition means that in the long run, after expectations have been corrected and business-cycle movements have damped out, (1) nominal output moves proportionally with the money supply and (2) all real variables (output, employment, and unemployment) are independent of the money supply.

货币主义者的纲领：货币的持续增长
The Monetarist Platform: Constant Money Growth

Monetarism played a significant role in shaping macroeconomic policy in the period after World War II. Monetarists hold that money has no effect on real output in the long run, while it does affect output in the short run with long and variable lags. These views lead to the central monetarist tenet of a **fixed-money-growth rule:** The central bank should set the growth of the money supply at a fixed rate and hold firmly to that rate.

Monetarists believe that a fixed growth rate of money would eliminate the major source of instability in a modern economy—the capricious and unreliable shifts of monetary policy. They argue that we should, in effect, replace the Federal Reserve with a computer that produces a fixed-money-growth rate. Such a computerized policy would ensure that there would be no bursts in money growth. With stable velocity, nominal GDP would grow at a stable rate. With suitably low money growth, the economy would soon achieve price stability. So argue the monetarists.

货币主义者的实验
The Monetarist Experiment

When U.S. inflation moved into the double-digit range in the late 1970s, many economists and policymakers believed that monetary policy was the only hope for an effective anti-inflation policy. In October 1979, Federal Reserve chair Paul Volcker launched a [3] fierce attack against inflation in what has been called the *monetarist experiment.* In a dramatic shift from its ④ normal operating procedures, the Fed attempted to stabilize the growth of bank reserves and the money supply rather than targeting interest rates.

The Fed hoped that the quantitative approach to monetary management would lower the growth rate of nominal GDP and thereby lower inflation. In addition, some economists believed that a disciplined monetary policy would quickly reduce inflationary expectations. Once people's expectations ⑤ were reduced, the economy could experience a relatively painless reduction in the underlying rate of inflation.

The experiment succeeded in slowing the growth of nominal GDP and reducing inflation. With tight money, interest rates rose sharply. Inflation slowed from 13 percent per year in 1980 to 4 percent per year in 1982. Any lingering doubts about the efficacy of monetary policy were killed by the monetarist experiment. Money works. Money matters. Tight money can wring ⑥ inflation out of the economy. However, the decline in inflation came at the cost of a deep recession and high unemployment during the 1980–1983 period.

货币主义的衰落
The Decline of Monetarism

Paradoxically, just as the monetarist experiment succeeded in rooting inflation out of the American economy, changes in financial markets undermined the monetarist approach. During and after the monetarist experiment, velocity became extremely unstable. Careful economic studies have shown that velocity is positively affected by interest rates and cannot be considered to be a constant that is independent of monetary policy.

Figure 24-10 shows trends in velocity over the 1960–2007 period. M_1 velocity growth was relatively stable in the 1960–1979 period, leading many economists to believe that velocity was predictable. Velocity became much more unstable after 1980 as the high interest rates of the 1979–1982 period spurred financial innovations, including money market

[1] new classical school：（第二代）新古典学派。以亚当·斯密为代表的经济学称为“古典经济学”，起源于19世纪70年代的“边际革命”（Marginal Revolution）。20世纪后形成的以宏观经济学和微观经济学为基本框架的经济学称为“新古典经济学”，华人学者习惯地命名为“第一代新古典经济学”。这里的“new classical school”系华人学者所讲的“第二代新古典经济学”，指20世纪70年代形成的理性预期学派。

② 纯粹的货币主义者强调，“只有货币起决定作用”。其意思是指价格和产出只由货币供给决定，而其他影响总需求的因素，诸如财政政策，则对总产出或者价格没有任何影响。此外，尽管货币供给量的变化在短期内会影响实际产出，但长期的产出则是由劳动、资本和技术的供给要素决定的。这一理论预期，长期来讲，货币是中性的。

[3] 保罗·沃克尔（Paul Volcker，1927~）美国经济学家，卡特和里根总统时期的美联储主席，任期为1979.8~1987.8，对结束美国经济在20世纪七八十年代的通货膨胀发挥了重要作用。2009.2~2011.1出任奥巴马总统“经济复苏顾问委员会”（Economic Recovery Advisory Board）主席。

④ 在这一戏剧性的政策转向中，美联储通过调整正常的操作程序，竭力稳定银行准备金和货币供给量的增加，而不是把目标盯在利率上。

⑤ 一旦人们的预期降低，经济就可能在潜在的通货膨胀率下，经历一场相对不痛苦的下滑。

⑥ 成也货币，败也货币。紧缩货币可以使经济摆脱通货膨胀，但在1980~1983年期间，通货膨胀的降低是以经济的严重衰退和高失业率为代价的。

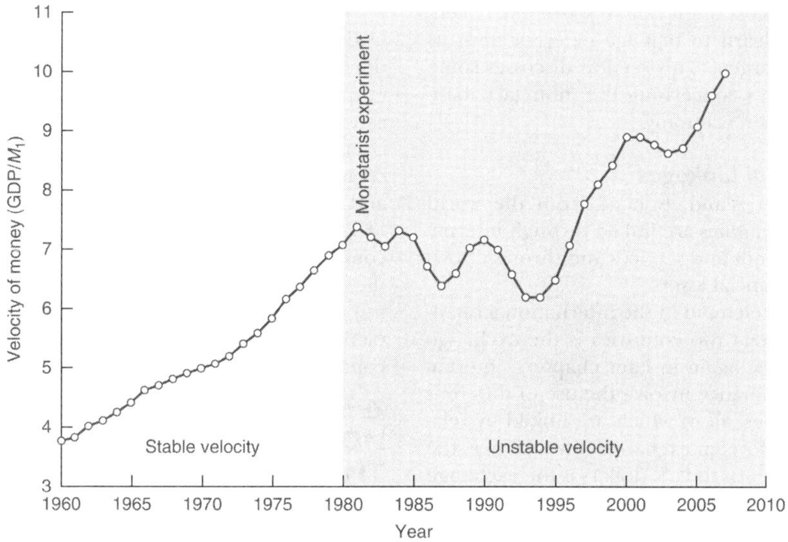

FIGURE 24-10. Income Velocity of M_1

Monetarists assume that the velocity of money is stable and thereby argue for a constant money-supply growth rate. The velocity of money grew at a steady and predictable rate until around 1979. Beginning in 1980 (the shaded area of the graph), an active monetary policy, more-volatile interest rates, and financial innovations led to the extreme instability of velocity.

Source: Velocity defined as the ratio of nominal GDP to M_1; money supply from the Federal Reserve Board, and GDP from the Commerce Department.

accounts and interest-bearing checking accounts. Some economists believe that the instability of velocity was actually *produced* by the heavy reliance on targeting monetary aggregates during this period.

As the velocity of money became increasingly unstable, the Federal Reserve gradually stopped using it as a guide for monetary policy. By the early 1990s, the Fed began to rely on macroeconomic indicators such as inflation, output, and employment to diagnose the state of the economy. Interest rates, not the money supply, became the major instrument of policy.

For most central banks today, monetarism is no ① longer a useful macroeconomic theory. Indeed, during the recession of 2007–2009, the Federal Reserve did not include monetary quantities among its objectives. But this did not diminish the importance of monetary policy, which continues to be a central partner in macroeconomic policy around the world.

Monetarism holds that "only money matters" in ② the determination of output and prices and that money is neutral in the long run. Although monetarism is no longer a dominant branch of macroeconomics, monetary policy continues to be a central tool of stabilization policy in large market economies today.

开放经济中的货币政策
MONETARY POLICY IN AN OPEN ECONOMY[3]

Central banks are particularly important in open economies, where they manage reserve flows and the exchange rate and monitor international financial developments. As economies become increasingly

[3] This section is relatively advanced and can usefully be studied after the chapters on open-economy macroeconomics (Chapters 27 and 28) have been covered.

① 对于今天的绝大多数中央银行而言，货币主义已经不再是有用的宏观经济理论。

② 货币主义认为，在产出和价格的决策中，"只有货币起决定作用"。但长期来讲，货币又是中性的。虽然货币主义已经不再是宏观经济学的一个主要分支，但在今天的大型市场经济中，货币政策依然是稳定政策的主要工具。

integrated (a process often called *globalization*), central banks must learn to manage external flows as well as internal targets. This section discusses some of the major issues concerning the monetary management of an open economy.

国际联系
International Linkages

No country is an island, isolated from the world economy. All economies are linked through international trade in goods and services and through flows of capital and financial assets. ①

An important element in the international financial linkage between two countries is the exchange rate. As we will see again in later chapters, international trade and finance involve the use of different national currencies, all of which are linked by relative prices called foreign exchange rates. Hence, the relative price of Euros to U.S. dollars is the exchange rate between those two currencies.

One important exchange-rate system is floating exchange rates, in which a country's foreign exchange rate is determined by market forces of supply and demand. Today, the United States, Europe, and Japan all operate floating-exchange-rate systems. These three regions can pursue their monetary policies independently from other countries. This chapter's analysis mainly concerns the operation of monetary policy under floating exchange rates.

Some economies—such as Hong Kong and China today, as well as virtually all countries in earlier periods—maintain fixed exchange rates. They "peg" ② their currencies to one or more external currencies. When a country has a fixed exchange rate, it must align its monetary policy with that of the country to which its currency is pegged. For example, if Hong Kong has open financial markets and an exchange rate pegged to the U.S. dollar, then it must have the same interest rates as the United States.

The Federal Reserve acts as the government's ③ operating arm in the international financial system. Under a floating-exchange-rate system, the main aim of the central bank is to prevent disorderly conditions, such as might occur during a political crisis. The Fed might buy or sell dollars or work with foreign central banks to ensure that exchange rates do not move erratically. However, unlike in the earlier era of fixed exchange rates, the Fed does not "intervene" to maintain a particular exchange rate.

In addition, the Federal Reserve often takes the lead in working with foreign countries and international agencies when international financial crises erupt. The Fed played an important role in the Mexican loan package in 1994–1995, worked with other countries to help calm markets during the East Asian crisis in 1997 and the global liquidity crisis in 1998, and helped calm markets during the Argentine crisis of 2001–2002. When financial institutions in many countries began to incur large losses in 2007–2008, the Federal Reserve joined forces with other central banks to provide liquidity and prevent investor panics in one country from spilling over into other countries.

在开放经济中的货币传导
MONETARY TRANSMISSION IN THE OPEN ECONOMY

The monetary transmission mechanism in the United States has evolved over the last three decades as the economy has become more open and changes have occurred in the exchange-rate system. The relationship between monetary policy and foreign trade has always been a major concern for smaller and more open economies like Canada and Great Britain. However, after the introduction of flexible exchange rates in 1973 and with the rapid growth of cross-border linkages, international trade and finance have come to play a new and central role in U.S. macroeconomic policy.

Let's see how monetary policy affects the economy through international trade with a flexible exchange rate. Suppose the Federal Reserve decides to tighten money. This raises interest rates on assets denominated in U.S. dollars. Attracted by higher-dollar interest rates, investors buy dollar securities, driving up the foreign exchange rate on the dollar. The higher exchange rate on the dollar encourages imports into the United States and reduces U.S. exports. As a result, net exports fall, reducing aggregate demand. This will lower real GDP and reduce the rate of inflation. We will study the international aspects of macroeconomics in more detail in Chapters 27 and 28.

Foreign trade opens up another link in the monetary transmission mechanism. Monetary policy has the same impact on international trade as it has on domestic investment: tight money lowers net exports, ④

---

① 任何一个国家都无法成为独立于世界经济之外的孤岛。所有的经济体都通过商品和服务的国际贸易以及资本和金融资产的流动联系在一起。

② "peg"：紧紧地"钉住"

③ 美联储在国际金融系统中是政府的运营工具。在浮动汇率机制下，中央银行的主要目标是防止外汇市场出现混乱局面，比如政治危机引发的乱局。

④ 对外贸易打开了货币传导机制的另外一条渠道。正如货币政策对国内投资所产生的影响一样，其对国际贸易也有同样的影响：紧缩货币使净出口减少，因而挤压了产出和价格。货币政策对国际贸易的影响加剧了对国内经济的冲击。

thereby depressing output and prices. The international-trade impact of monetary policy reinforces its domestic-economy impact.

从总需求到总供给
FROM AGGREGATE DEMAND TO AGGREGATE SUPPLY

We have completed our introductory analysis of the determinants of aggregate demand. We examined the foundations and saw that aggregate demand is determined by exogenous factors, such as investment and net exports, along with monetary and fiscal government policies. In the short run, changes in these factors lead to changes in spending and changes in both output and prices.

In today's volatile and globalized world, economies are exposed to shocks from both the inside and the outside of their borders. Wars, revolutions, stock market collapses, housing-price bubbles, financial and currency crises, oil-price shocks, and government miscalculations have led to periods of high inflation or high unemployment or both. No market mechanism provides an automatic pilot that can eliminate macroeconomic fluctuations. Governments must therefore take responsibility for moderating the swings of the business cycle. ①

While the United States experienced recessions in 1990, 2001, and 2008, it has up to now been fortunate to avoid deep and prolonged downturns. Other countries over the last quarter-century have not been so lucky. Japan, much of Europe, Latin America, Russia, and the East Asian countries have all occasionally been caught in the turbulent storms of rapid inflation, high unemployment, currency crises, or sharp declines in living standards. These events serve as a reminder that there is no universal cure for unemployment and inflation in the face of all the shocks to a modern economy.

We have now concluded our introductory chapters on short-run macroeconomics. The next part of the book turns to issues of economic growth, the open economy, and economic policy.

SUMMARY

A. Central Banking and the Federal Reserve System

1. Every modern country has a central bank. The U.S. central bank is made up of the Federal Reserve Board in Washington, together with the 12 regional Federal Reserve Banks. Its primary mission is to conduct the nation's monetary policy by influencing financial conditions in pursuit of low inflation, high employment, and stable financial markets.
2. The Federal Reserve System (or "the Fed") was created in 1913 to control the nation's money and credit and to act as the "lender of last resort." It is run by the Board of Governors and the Federal Open Market Committee (FOMC). The Fed acts as an independent government agency and has great discretion in determining monetary policy.
3. The Federal Reserve has four major functions: conducting monetary policy by setting short-term interest rates, maintaining the stability of the financial system and containing systemic risk as the lender of last resort, supervising and regulating banking institutions, and providing financial services to banks and the government.
4. The Fed has three major policy instruments: (*a*) open-market operations, (*b*) the discount window for borrowing by banks and, more recently, primary dealers, and (*c*) legal reserve requirements for depository institutions.
5. The Federal Reserve conducts its policy through changes in an important short-term interest rate called the federal funds rate. This is the short-term interest rate that banks charge each other to trade reserve balances at the Fed. The Fed controls the federal funds rate by exercising control over its instruments, primarily through open-market operations.

B. The Monetary Transmission Mechanism

6. Remember the important monetary transmission mechanism, the route by which monetary policy is translated into changes in output, employment, and inflation:

   a. The central bank announces a target short-term interest rate chosen in light of its objectives and the state of the economy.

① 在当今这个瞬息万变的全球化世界，经济会受到来自国内和国外两方面的冲击。战争、革命、股票市场崩盘、房地产价格泡沫、金融和货币危机、石油价格震荡以及政府决策上的失误，都会导致高通货膨胀、高失业，或者两者并存。没有一个市场机制具有消除宏观经济动荡的自动调节能力。因此，各国政府必须承担起减缓商业周期波动的责任。

b. The central bank undertakes daily open-market operations to meet its interest-rate target.
c. The central bank's interest-rate target and expectations about future financial conditions determine the entire spectrum of short- and long-term interest rates, asset prices, and exchange rates.
d. The level of interest rates, credit conditions, asset prices, and exchange rates affect investment, consumption, and net exports.
e. Investment, consumption, and net exports affect the path of output and inflation through the *AS-AD* mechanism.

We can write the operation of a monetary policy change as follows:

Change in monetary policy
  → change in interest rates, asset prices, exchange rates
  → impact on *I, X, C*
  → effect on *AD*
  → effect on *Q, P*

7. Although the monetary transmission mechanism is often described simply in terms of "the interest rate" and "investment," this mechanism is in fact an extremely rich and complex process whereby changes in all kinds of financial conditions influence a wide variety of spending. The affected sectors include: housing, affected by mortgage interest rates and housing prices; business investment, affected by interest rates and stock prices; spending on consumer durables, influenced by interest rates and credit availability; state and local capital spending, affected by interest rates; and net exports, determined by the effects of interest rates upon foreign exchange rates.

C. Applications of Monetary Economics

8. Monetarism holds that the money supply is the primary determinant of short-run movements in both real and nominal GDP as well as the primary determinant of long-run movements in nominal GDP. The income velocity of money (V) is defined as the ratio of the dollar-GDP flow (PQ) to the stock of money (M): $V \equiv PQ/M$. With constant velocity, prices move proportionally to the money supply. Monetarists propose that the money supply should grow at a low fixed rate. Statistical studies indicate that velocity tends to be positively correlated with interest rates, a finding that undermines the monetarist policy prescription.
9. In an open economy, the international-trade linkage reinforces the domestic impacts of monetary policy. In a regime of flexible exchange rates, changes in monetary policy affect the exchange rate and net exports, adding yet another facet to the monetary mechanism. The trade link tends to reinforce the impact of monetary policy, which operates in the same direction on net exports as it does on domestic investment.

CONCEPTS FOR REVIEW

Central Banking

bank reserves
federal funds interest rate
Federal Reserve balance sheet
open-market purchases and sales
discount rate, borrowing from the Fed
legal reserve requirements
FOMC, Board of Governors

The Monetary Transmission Mechanism and Applications

demand for and supply of reserves
monetary transmission mechanism
interest-sensitive components of spending
monetary policy in the *AS-AD* framework
"neutrality" of money
second route by which *M* affects output

FURTHER READING AND INTERNET WEBSITES

Further Reading

Alan Greenspan's memoir, *The Age of Turbulence* (Penguin, New York, 2007) is a valuable history of the last half-decade as well as of his stewardship of the Federal Reserve.

The *Federal Reserve Bulletin* contains monthly reports on Federal Reserve activities and other important financial developments. The *Bulletin* is available on the Internet at *www.federalreserve.gov/pubs/bulletin/default.htm*.

The quotation on the lender of last resort is from Alan Greenspan, "Remarks," Lancaster House, London, U.K., September 25, 2002, available at *www.federalreserve.gov/boarddocs/speeches/2002/200209253/default.htm*.

The governors of the Fed often bring informed economic expertise to monetary and other issues. See speeches at *www.federalreserve.gov/newsevents/*. A particularly influential speech by current Fed chair Ben Bernanke on the "global savings glut" is at *www.federalreserve.gov/boarddocs/speeches/2005/200503102/default.htm*.

Websites

The Federal Reserve System: Purposes and Functions, 9th ed. (Board of Governors of the Federal Reserve System, Washington, D.C., 2005), available online at *www.federalreserve.gov/pf/pf.htm*, provides a useful description of the operations of the Fed. Also, see the Further Reading and Websites sections in Chapter 25 for a more detailed list of sites on monetary policy. An excellent review of the Federal Reserve's response to the credit crisis of 2007–2009 is contained in a speech by Fed chair Ben Bernanke, "The Crisis and the Policy Response," January 2009, available at http://www.federalreserve.gov/newsevents/speech/bernanke20090113a.htm.

If you want to know which Reserve Bank region you live in, see *www.federalreserve.gov/otherfrb.htm*. Why are the eastern regions so small?

Biographies of the members of the Board of Governors can be found at *www.federalreserve.gov/bios/*. Particularly interesting are the transcripts and minutes of Fed meetings, at *www.federalreserve.gov/fomc/*.

QUESTIONS FOR DISCUSSION

1. Using Figures 24-5 through 24-7, work through each of the following:
   a. As in 2007–2008, the Federal Reserve is concerned about a decline in housing prices that is reducing investment. What steps might the Fed take to stimulate the economy? What will be the impact on bank reserves? What will be the impact on interest rates? What will be the impact on investment (other things held constant)?
   b. As in 1979, the Fed is concerned about rising inflation and wishes to reduce output. Answer the same questions as in **a**.
2. Suppose you are the chair of the Fed's Board of Governors at a time when the economy is heading into a recession and you are called to testify before a congressional committee. Write your explanation to an interrogating senator outlining what monetary steps you would take to prevent the recession.
3. Consider the balance sheet of the Fed in Table 24-1. Construct a corresponding balance sheet for banks (like the one in Table 23-3 in the previous chapter) assuming that reserve requirements are 10 percent on checking accounts and zero on everything else.
   a. Construct a new set of balance sheets, assuming that the Fed sells \$1 billion worth of government securities through open-market operations.
   b. Construct another set of balance sheets, assuming that the Fed increases reserve requirements from 10 to 20 percent.
   c. Assume that banks borrow \$1 billion worth of reserves from the Fed. How will this action change the balance sheets?
4. Assume that commercial banks have \$100 billion of checking deposits and \$4 billion of vault cash. Further assume that reserve requirements are 10 percent of checking deposits. Lastly, assume that the public holds \$200 billion of currency, which is always fixed. Central-bank assets include only government securities.
   a. Construct the balance sheets for the central bank and the banking system. Make sure you include banks' deposits with the central bank.
   b. Now assume that the central bank decides to engage in an open-market operation, selling

$1 billion worth of government securities to the public. Show the new balance sheets. What has happened to M_1?

c. Finally, using the graphical apparatus of the monetary transmission mechanism, show the qualitative impact of the policy on interest rates, investment, and output.

5. In his memoirs, Alan Greenspan wrote, "I regret to say that Federal Reserve independence is not set in stone. FOMC discretion is granted by statute and can be withdrawn by statute." (*The Age of Turbulence*, p. 478 f.) Explain why the independence of a central bank might affect the way in which monetary policy is conducted. If a central bank is not independent, how might its monetary policies change in response to electoral pressures? Would you recommend that a new country have an independent central bank? Explain.

6. One of the nightmares of central bankers is the liquidity trap. This occurs when nominal interest rates approach or even equal zero. Once the interest rate has declined to zero, monetary expansion is ineffective because interest rates on securities cannot go below zero.

   a. Explain why the nominal interest rate on government bonds cannot be negative. (*Hint:* What is the nominal interest rate on currency? Why would you hold a bond whose interest rate is below the interest rate on currency?)

   b. A liquidity trap is particularly serious when a country simultaneously experiences falling prices, also called deflation. For example, in the early 2000s, consumer prices in Japan were falling at 2 percent per year. What were Japanese real interest rates during this period if the nominal interest rate was 0? What was the *lowest* real interest rate that the Bank of Japan could have produced during this period?

   c. Explain on the basis of **b** why the liquidity trap poses such a serious problem for monetary policy during periods of deflation and depression.

7. After the reunification of Germany in 1990, payments to rebuild the East led to a major expansion of aggregate demand in Germany. The German central bank responded by slowing money growth and raising German real interest rates. Trace through why this German monetary tightening would be expected to lead to a depreciation of the dollar. Explain why such a depreciation would stimulate economic activity in the United States. Also explain why European countries that had pegged their currencies to the German mark would find themselves plunged into recessions as German interest rates rose and pulled other European rates up with them.

8. In December 2007, the Federal Open Market Committee made the following statement: "The Federal Open Market Committee seeks monetary and financial conditions that will foster price stability and promote sustainable growth in output. To further its long-run objectives, the Committee [will reduce] the federal funds rate [from 4½ percent to] 4¼ percent." Your assignment is to explain the macroeconomic rationale behind this monetary expansion. It will help to review the minutes of the FOMC meeting at *www.federalreserve.gov/monetarypolicy/files/fomcminutes20071211.pdf.*

PART SIX

Growth, Development, and the Global Economy

经济增长、经济发展与全球经济

CHAPTER

25

Economic Growth

经济增长

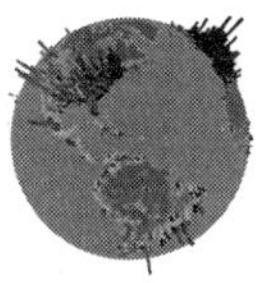

[1] 霍布斯鲍姆（E. J. Hobsbawm，2012 年 10 月 1 日病逝，享年 95 岁），出生于埃及亚历山大城的犹太中产家庭，克思主义学派历史学家，以研究 19 世纪欧洲历史的三部曲著称：《革命年代：1789~1848 的欧洲》（*The Age of Revolution: Europe: 1789~1848*）、《资本年代：1848~1875》（*The Age of Capital: 1848~1875*）和《帝国时代：1875~月 1914》（*The Age of Empire: 1875~1914*）。首部《革命年代》一书 1962 年由兰登书屋的纽约子公司 Vintage Books 出版。本段文字摘自该书第 2 章：

The Industrial Revolution was not indeed an episode with a beginning and an end. To ask when it was 'complete' is senseless, for its essence was that henceforth revolutionary change became the norm. It is still going on; at most we can ask when the economic transformations had gone far enough to establish a substantially industrialized economy, capable of producing, broadly speaking, anything it wanted within the range of the available techniques, a 'mature industrial economy' to use the technical term.

所以，本处节选的这句话应该译作：

The Industrial Revolution was not an episode with a beginning and an end. . . . It is still going on.

E. J. Hobsbawm [1]

The Age of Revolution (1962)

工业革命着实不是人类历史中一段既有开头又有结尾的插曲。……这场革命依然在继续。

If you look at photographs of an earlier era, you will quickly recognize how dramatically the living standards of the average household have changed over past decades and centuries. Today's homes are stocked with goods that could hardly be imagined a century ago. Just think of entertainment before the era of plasma televisions, high-definition DVDs, and portable media devices. Similarly, the Internet has opened up a vast array of information that could be obtained only by going to the library, and even then only a small fraction of published knowledge was available in most libraries. Or consider the health care available today as ②
compared to periods such as the U.S. Civil War, when soldiers died simply because they got an infection.

These changes in the array, quality, and quantity of goods and services available to the average household are the human face of economic growth. In macroeconomics, economic growth designates the process by which economies accumulate larger quantities of capital equipment, push out the frontiers of technological knowledge, and become steadily more productive. Over the long run of decades and gen- ③
erations, living standards, as measured by output per capita or consumption per household, are primarily determined by aggregate supply and the level of productivity of a country.

This chapter begins with a survey of the theory of economic growth and then reviews the historical trends in economic activity with particular application to wealthy countries like the United States. The ④
next chapter looks at the other end of the income spectrum by examining the plight of the developing countries, struggling to reach the level of affluence enjoyed in the West. The two chapters that follow examine the role of international trade and finance in macroeconomics.

经济增长的长期意义

The Long-Term Significance of Growth

A careful analysis of the economic history of the ⑤
United States reveals that real GDP has grown by a factor of 35 since 1900 and by a factor of over 1000 since 1800. Rapid growth of output is the distinguishing feature of modern times and contrasts sharply with human history going back to its origins millions of years ago. This is perhaps the central economic fact of the century. Continuing rapid economic growth enables advanced industrial countries to provide more of everything to their citizens—better food and bigger homes, more resources for medical care and pollution control, universal education for children, better equipment for the military, and public pensions for retirees.

---

② 再看今天享有的医疗条件。我们拿美国南北战争那个年代相比，当时的士兵仅仅因为伤口感染就会死掉。

③ 长期来看，在经过了数十年或者数代人之后，以人均产出和家庭平均消费所衡量的生活标准，则主要由一国的总供给及其生产力水平决定。

④ 下一章我们通过讨论发展中国家在努力追赶西方的富裕水平时所面临的困境，看一下收入问题的另一个侧面。

⑤ 在对美国的经济史进行仔细分析之后我们发现，美国实际 GDP 自 1900 年以来增长了 35 倍，自 1800 年以来增长了 1 000 多倍。

Because economic growth is so important for living standards, it is a central objective of policy. Countries that run swiftly in the economic-growth race, such as Britain in the nineteenth century and the United States in the twentieth century, serve as role models for other countries seeking the path to affluence. At the other extreme, countries in economic decline often experience political and social turmoil. The revolutions in Eastern Europe and the [1] Soviet Union in 1989–1991 were sparked when those nations' residents compared their economic stagnation under socialism with the rapid growth experienced by their Western, market-oriented neighbors. Economic growth is the single most important factor in the success of nations in the long run.

经济增长理论

A. THEORIES OF ECONOMIC GROWTH

Let's begin with a careful definition of exactly what we mean by economic growth: **Economic growth** represents the expansion of a country's potential GDP or national output. Put differently, economic growth occurs when a nation's production-possibility frontier (*PPF*) shifts outward.

A closely related concept is the growth rate of *output per person*. This determines the rate at which the country's living standards are rising. Countries are primarily concerned with the growth in per capita output because this leads to rising average incomes.

What are the long-term patterns of economic growth in high-income countries? Table 25-1 shows the history of economic growth since 1870 for high-income countries including the major countries of North America and Western Europe, Japan, and Australia. We see the steady growth of output over this period. Even more important for living standards is the growth in output per hour worked, which moves closely with the increase in living standards. Over the ② entire period, output per hour worked grew by an average annual rate of 2.3 percent. If we compound this rate over the 136 years, output per person at the end was 22 times higher than at the beginning (make sure you can reproduce this number).

What were the major forces behind this growth? What can nations do to speed up their economic growth rate? And what are the prospects for the twenty-first century? These are the issues that must be confronted by economic-growth analysis.

Economic growth involves the growth of potential output over the long run. The growth in output per capita is an important objective of government because it is associated with rising average real incomes and rising living standards.

经济增长的四个车轮
THE FOUR WHEELS OF GROWTH

What is the recipe for economic growth? To begin with, many roads lead to Rome. There are many successful strategies on the road to self-sustained economic growth. Britain, for example, became the

	Average Annual Growth Rate (percent per year)			
Period	GDP	GDP per hour worked	Total hours worked	Labor force
1870–1913	2.5	1.6	0.9	1.2
1913–1950	1.9	1.8	0.1	0.8
1950–1973	4.8	4.5	0.3	1.0
1973–2006	2.6	2.2	0.4	1.0
Total period	**2.8**	**2.3**	**0.5**	**1.0**

TABLE 25-1. Patterns of Growth in Advanced Countries

Over the last century-plus, major high-income countries like the United States, Germany, France, and Japan have grown rapidly. Output has grown faster than inputs of labor, reflecting increases in capital and technological advance.

Source: Angus Maddison, *Phases of Capitalist Development* (Oxford University Press, Oxford, 1982), updated by authors. The data cover 16 major countries starting in 1870, while more recent data cover 31 advanced economies.

[1] the Revolutions in Eastern Europe and the Soviet Union in 1989~1991：东欧大革命与苏联解体，系指 1989 年东欧和中欧的波兰、东德、捷克斯洛伐克、匈牙利、保加利亚、罗马尼亚和阿尔巴尼亚等前社会主义国家，除罗马尼亚的流血革命之外，先后均以自由选举的方式更迭了原有的社会主义制度，华沙条约组织解散。1991 年 12 月 25 日总统戈尔巴乔夫宣布辞职，苏联解体。

② 在这一时期的全过程，每个工时产出的年平均增长率达 2.3%。如果把这 136 年的增长率综合统计一下，最终的人均产出比一开始提高 22 倍（你也完全可以重新计算出这个结果）。

world economic leader in the 1800s by pioneering the Industrial Revolution, inventing steam engines and railroads, and emphasizing free trade. Japan, by contrast, came to the economic-growth race later. It ① made its mark by first imitating foreign technologies and protecting domestic industries from imports and then developing tremendous expertise in manufacturing and electronics.

Even though their individual paths may differ, all rapidly growing countries share certain common traits. The same fundamental process of economic growth and development that helped shape Britain and Japan is at work today in developing countries like China and India. Indeed, economists who have studied growth have found that the engine of economic progress must ride on the same four wheels, no matter how rich or poor the country. These four wheels, or factors of growth, are:

- Human resources (labor supply, education, skills, discipline, motivation)
- Natural resources (land, minerals, fuels, environmental quality)
- Capital (factories, machinery, roads, intellectual property)
- Technological change and innovation (science, engineering, management, entrepreneurship)

Often, economists write the relationship in terms of an *aggregate production function* (or *APF*), which relates total national output to inputs and technology. Algebraically, the *APF* is

$$Q = AF(K, L, R)$$

where Q = output, K = productive services of capital, L = labor inputs, R = natural-resource inputs, A represents the level of technology in the economy, and F is the production function. As the inputs of capital, labor, or resources rise, we would expect that output would increase, although output will probably show diminishing returns to additional inputs of production factors. We can think of the role of technology as augmenting the productivity of inputs. **Productivity** denotes the ratio of output to a weighted average of inputs. As technology (A) improves through new inventions or the adoption of technologies from abroad, this advance allows a country to produce more output with the same level of inputs.

Let's now see how each of the four factors contributes to growth.

人力资源
Human Resources

Labor inputs consist of quantities of workers and of the skills of the workforce. Many economists believe that the quality of labor inputs—the skills, knowledge, and discipline of the labor force—is the single most important element in economic growth. A country might buy fast computers, modern telecommunications devices, sophisticated electricity-generating equipment, and hypersonic fighter aircraft. However, these capital goods can be effectively used and maintained only by skilled and trained workers. Improvements in literacy, health, and discipline, and most recently the ability to use computers, add greatly to the productivity of labor.

自然资源
Natural Resources

The second classic factor of production is natural resources. The important resources here are arable land, oil, gas, forests, water, and mineral deposits. Some high-income countries like Canada and Norway have grown primarily on the basis of their ample resource base, with large output in oil, gas, agriculture, fisheries, and forestry. Similarly, the United States, with its fertile farmlands, is the world's largest producer and exporter of grains.

But the possession of natural resources is not necessary for economic success in the modern world. New York City prospers primarily on its high-density service industries. Many countries, such as Japan, had virtually no natural resources but thrived by concentrating on sectors that depend more on labor and capital than on indigenous resources. Indeed, tiny Hong Kong, with but a tiny fraction of the land and natural resources of Nigeria, actually has a larger GDP than does that giant country.

资　本
Capital

Capital includes tangible capital goods like roads, power plants, and equipment like trucks and computers, as well as intangible items such as patents, trademarks, and computer software. The most dramatic stories in economic history often involve the accumulation of capital. In the nineteenth century, the ② transcontinental railroads of North America brought commerce to the American heartland, which had been living in isolation. In the twentieth century, waves of investment in automobiles, roads, and power plants increased productivity and provided the infrastructure which created entire new industries. Many ③

① 日本的经济奇迹系先从效仿外国的技术开始，同时，通过限制进口来保护本国工业，然后大力发展制造业和电子工业的专门技术。

② 在 19 世纪，横跨北美大陆铁路的修建将工商业带进了美国的腹地，这里曾经是一块与世隔绝的蛮荒之地。

③ 许多人坚信，计算机与信息技术如同早期的铁路和公路一样，必将在 21 世纪发挥极其重要的作用。

believe that computers and information technology will do for the twenty-first century what railroads and highways did in earlier times.

Accumulating capital, as we have seen, requires a sacrifice of current consumption over many years. Countries that grow rapidly tend to invest heavily in new capital goods; in the most rapidly growing countries, 10 to 20 percent of output may go into net capital formation. The United States shows a stark contrast with high-saving countries. The U.S. net national saving rate, after averaging around 7 percent during the first four decades after World War II, began to decline and actually fell to near-zero in 2008. The low saving rate was the result of low personal saving and large government fiscal deficits. The low saving was seen primarily in the large external (trade) deficit. Economists worry ① that the low saving rate will retard investment and economic growth in the decades to come and that the large foreign indebtedness may require major adverse changes in exchange rates and real wages.

When we think of capital, we must not concentrate only on computers and factories. Many investments that are necessary for the efficient functioning of the private sector will be undertaken only by governments. These investments are called **social overhead capital** ② and consist of the large-scale projects that precede trade and commerce. Roads, irrigation and water projects, and public-health measures are important examples. All these involve large investments that tend to be "indivisible," or lumpy, and sometimes have increasing returns to scale. These ③ projects generally involve external economies, or spillovers that private firms cannot capture, so the government must step in to ensure that these social overhead or infrastructure investments are effectively undertaken. Some investments, such as transportation and communication systems, involve "network" externalities in which productivity depends upon the fraction of the population which uses or has access to the network.

技术变革与创新
Technological Change and Innovation

In addition to the three classic factors discussed above, technological advance has been a vital fourth ingredient in the rapid growth of living standards. Historically, growth has definitely not been a process of simple replication, adding rows of steel mills or power plants next to each other. Rather, a never-ending stream of inventions and technological advances led to a vast improvement in the production possibilities of Europe, North America, and Japan.

We are today witnessing an explosion of new technologies, particularly in computation, communication (such as the Internet), and the life sciences. But this is not the first time that American society has been shaken by fundamental inventions. Electricity, radio, the automobile, and television also diffused rapidly through the American economy in an earlier age. Figure 25-1 shows the diffusion of major inventions of the twentieth century. This S-shaped pattern is typical of the diffusion of new technologies.

Technological change denotes changes in the ④ processes of production or introduction of new products or services. Process inventions that have greatly increased productivity were the steam engine, the generation of electricity, antibiotics, the internal-combustion engine, the wide-body jet, the microprocessor, and the fax machine. Fundamental product inventions include the telephone, the radio, the airplane, the phonograph, the television, the computer, and the DVR.

The most dramatic developments of the modern era are occurring in information technology. Here, tiny notebook computers can outperform the fastest computer of the 1960s, while fiber-optic lines can carry 200,000 simultaneous conversations that required 200,000 paired copper-wire lines in an earlier period. These inventions provide the most spectacular examples of technological change. Nonetheless, techno- ⑤ logical advance is in fact a continuous process of small and large improvements, as witnessed by the fact that the United States issues over 100,000 new patents annually and that millions of other small refinements are routine activities in a modern economy.

Economists have long pondered how to encourage technological progress because of its importance in raising living standards. Technological progress is a complex and multifaceted process, and no single formula for success has been found.

Here are some historical examples: Toyota succeeded in instilling a workplace ethic of making continuous quality improvements from the bottom up; this propelled Toyota to the top of the automobile industry. Quite a different pattern arose in Sili- [6] con Valley's computer business. Here, technological ⑦ change was fostered by an entrepreneurial spirit of free inquiry, light government regulation, free international trade in intellectual property products, and the lure of lucrative stock options. Economists

① 经济学家们所担心的是，低储蓄率必将阻碍未来几十年的投资和经济增长，汇率和实际工资也必须做出大幅度的逆向调整来应对庞大的外债。

② 这些投资称作**社会分摊资本**，由促进贸易和商业的大型项目构成。

③ 通常情况下，这些大型项目涉及外部经济或者溢出效应，民营企业无法投资，所以，政府必须介入，以确保这些社会分摊投资或基础设施投资有效进行。

④ **技术变革**系指生产过程的变革，或者新产品或服务的引进。

⑤ 但是，技术进步事实上是一个持续性的小的以及大的技术改进过程，正如美国所证明的那样，它每年发布的超过 100 000 个新专利和其他数百万个小革新都是现代经济中的常规活动。

[6] Silicon Valley：硅谷，位于美国加利福尼亚州北部，旧金山湾以南，因早期以硅芯片的设计与制造而闻名于世，由加州著名的成功企业家 Ralph Vaerst 命名，而后由其朋友、著名的美国记者 Don Hoefler（1922~1986）在《电子报》（*Electronic News*）发表连载文章《美国硅谷》（*Silicon Valley in the USA*）而家喻户晓。

⑦ 硅谷的计算机产业则是截然不同的模式。在这里，技术变革孕育于自由探索的企业家精神、宽松的政府法规、知识产权的自由国际贸易，以及极具诱惑力的期权回报。

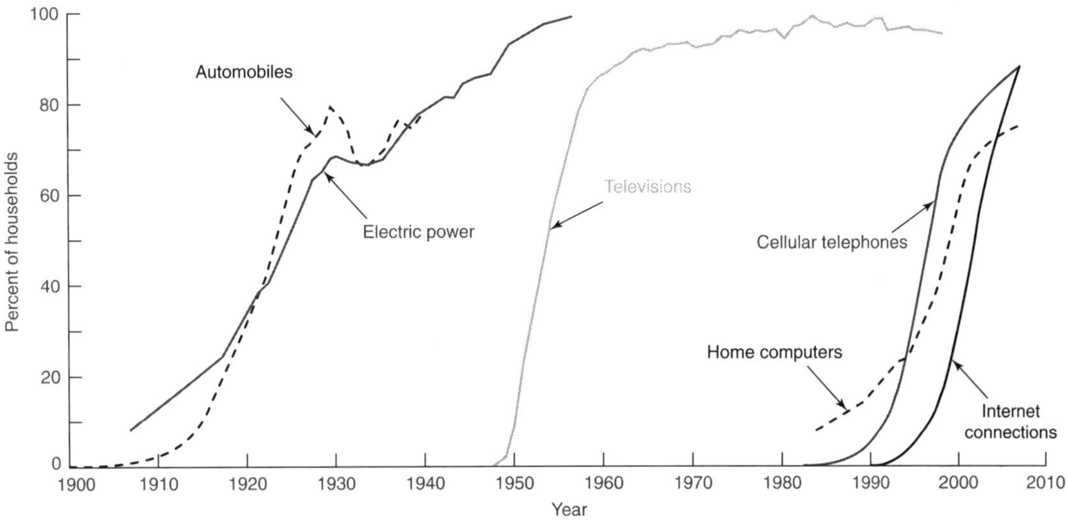

FIGURE 25-1. Diffusion of Major Technologies

Today's information technologies such as cellular telephones, computers, and the Internet are spreading rapidly through American society. Similar diffusion patterns were seen with other fundamental inventions in the past.

Source: *Economic Report of the President, 2000,* updated by authors.

Factor in economic growth	Examples
Human resources	Size of labor force Quality of workers (education, skills, discipline)
Natural resources	Oil and gas Soils and climate
Capital stock	Homes and factories Machinery Intellectual property Social overhead capital
Technology and entrepreneurship	Quality of scientific and engineering knowledge Managerial know-how Rewards for innovation

TABLE 25-2. The Four Wheels of Progress

Economic growth inevitably rides on the four wheels of labor, natural resources, capital, and technology. But the wheels may differ greatly among countries, and some countries combine them more effectively than others.

recognize that some approaches seem to kill the spirit of innovation. Many sectors of the Soviet Union ① under central planning saw technological stagnation because of the heavy hand of state regulation, lack of profit motivation, an inefficient pricing mechanism, and widespread corruption.

Table 25-2 summarizes the four wheels of economic growth.

① 由于政府管制的沉重束缚、利润驱动的缺失、效率低下的定价机制和腐败的泛滥，在中央计划体制下的前苏联的许多部门，都经历了技术的停滞不前。

Institutions, Incentives, and Innovation

In the very long run, the growth in the world's output and wealth has come primarily because of improvements in knowledge. Yet institutions to promote the creation and spread of knowledge, along with incentives to devote our human effort to that task, were developed late in human history—slowly in Western Europe over the last [1]
500 years. This point was eloquently argued by William [2]
Baumol:

> [3] The museum at Alexandria was the center of technological
> [4] innovation in the Roman Empire. By the first century B.C., that city knew of virtually every form of machine gearing that is used today, including a working steam engine. But these seemed to be used only to make what amounted to elaborate toys. The steam engine was used to open and close the doors of a temple.[1]

[5] Baumol and economic historian Joel Mokyr argue that innovation depends crucially on the development of incentives and institutions. They particularly point to the role of private ownership, the patent system, and a rule-based system of adjudicating disputes as devices for fostering innovation.

经济增长理论
THEORIES OF ECONOMIC GROWTH

Virtually everyone is in favor of economic growth. But there are strong disagreements about the best way to accomplish this goal. Some economists and policymakers stress the need to increase capital investment. Others advocate measures to stimulate research and development and technological change. Still a third group emphasizes the role of a better-educated workforce.

Economists have long studied the question of the relative importance of different factors in determining growth. In the discussion below, we look at different theories of economic growth, which offer some clues about the driving forces behind growth. Then, in the final part of this section, we see what can be learned about growth from its historical patterns over the last century.

[1] See Baumol in the Further Reading section at the end of this chapter.

斯密与马尔萨斯的古典动态模型
The Classical Dynamics of Smith and Malthus

Early economists like Adam Smith and T. R. Malthus [6]
stressed the critical role of land in economic growth. In *The Wealth of Nations* (1776), Adam Smith provided a handbook of economic development. He began with a hypothetical idyllic age: "that original state of things, which precedes both the appropriation of land and the accumulation of [capital] stock." This was a time when land was freely available to all, and before capital accumulation had begun to matter.

What would be the dynamics of economic growth in such a "golden age"? Because land is freely avail- [7]
able, people would simply spread out onto more acres as the population increases, just as the settlers did in the American West. Because there is no capi- [8]
tal, national output would exactly double as population doubles. What about real wages? The entire national income would go to wages because there is no subtraction for land rent or interest on capital. Output expands in step with population, so the real wage rate per worker would be constant over time.

But this golden age cannot continue forever. Eventually, as population growth continues, all the land will be occupied. Once the frontier disappears, balanced growth of land, labor, and output is no longer possible. New laborers begin to crowd onto already-worked soils. Land becomes scarce, and rents rise to ration it among different uses.

Population still grows, and so does the national product. But output must grow more slowly than does population. Why? With new laborers added to ⑨
fixed land, each worker now has less land to work with, and the law of diminishing returns comes into operation. The increasing labor-land ratio leads to a declining marginal product of labor and hence to declining real wage rates.[2]

How bad could things get? The dour Reverend ⑩
T. R. Malthus thought that population pressures would

[2] The theory in this chapter relies on an important finding from microeconomics. In analysis of the determination of wages under simplified conditions, including perfect competition, it is shown that the wage rate of labor will be equal to the extra or marginal product of the last worker hired. For example, if the last worker contributes goods worth $12.50 per hour to the firm's output, then under competitive conditions the firm will be willing to pay up to $12.50 per hour in wages to that worker. Similarly, the rent on land is the marginal product of the last unit of land, and the real interest rate will be determined by the marginal product of the least productive piece of capital.

[6] Adam Smith：亚当·斯密（1723~1790），古典经济学之父，苏格兰道德哲学家，老亚当·斯密的遗腹子，一生与母亲相依为命，终身未娶。1759 年出版的《道德情操论》（*The Theory of Moral Sentiments*）和 1776 年出版的《国富论》（*The Wealth of Nations*）是斯密留给全人类的跨世经典，共同建构了斯密"先有利他，才有利己"的完整的经济学思想，而多年来学术界几乎忘却了利他主义的《道德情操论》，严重地曲解了斯密的经济学理论。T. R. Malthus：托马斯·罗伯特·马尔萨斯（1766~1834），著名的英国人口学家和政治经济学家，其 1798 年出版的《人口学原理》（*An Essay on the Principle of Population*）提出，人口以几何级数上升的同时，物品供应则只能以等差级数上升。最终的人口均衡点是以饥饿淘汰不适宜生存者的局面。该书自 1798 至 1826 年间共再版五次。历史证明马尔萨斯的人口论是错误的。200 多年来，世界人口确以几何级数上升，但生活水平和平均寿命却大大提高。今天，生活在中度以上发达国家的普通中产阶级，除了居住面积与美酒佳人之外，比当时的皇帝和国王生活得还要好。

[7] golden age：黄金时代，指人类社会的最高阶段——人们生活在一个理想、幸福、和平和富裕的时代，源自希腊神话中人类社会的"五个时代说"，其余依次为白银时代、青铜时代、英雄时代以及现代的"铁器时代"。古印度文化、古代中东文明等也有与之类似和呼应的宗教信仰与哲学观。拍摄于 2006 年的英国电影 *The Golden Age*，故事情节发生在英国历史上的第一个"辉煌时代"，即伊丽莎白一世时代。2012 年 5 月 18 日，《大西洋》（*the Atlantic*）杂志发表了该刊高级编辑 Derek Thomson 对硅谷的著名实业家和"创新大师"、现伯克莱哈斯商学院、斯坦福和哥伦比亚大学商学院兼职教授史蒂夫·布兰克（Steve Blank）关于硅谷前途的专访，题目即冠予 *The Golden Age of Silicon Valley Is Over, and We're Dancing on its Grave*（硅谷的辉煌已经结束，我们只不过是在其墓冢上狂舞而已）。

[1] over the last 500 years：世界主流的西方断代观，即指文艺复兴以来的现代社会。

[2] William Baumol：威廉·鲍莫尔（1922~），美国经济学家，美国艺术与科学研究院院士，纽约大学教授，对经济思想史的研究有重大贡献，被誉为全世界最具影响力的经济学家之一。2003 年曾获诺贝尔经济学奖提名。

[3] The museum at Alexandria：著名的埃及亚历山大博物馆，拥有全世界最大和最具影响力的古代世界图书馆。

[4] Roman Empire：通常指从公元前 10 世纪初在意大利半岛中部兴起的文明，公元前一世纪前后扩张成为横跨欧洲、亚洲和非洲的庞大罗马帝国。

[5] Joel Mokyr：乔尔·莫克（1946~），美国西北大学教授，经济史学家，2006 年由于其对"现代工业经济的起因研究"而获海尼肯奖（Dr A.H. Heineken Prize）。

[8] American West：通常泛指美国西部各州，从某种美国历史意义讲，一部美国史就是一部美国的疆域向西拓展和开发的历史，所以美国西部的定义也随时代的变迁而改变。同时，它也是反映 19 世纪北美西部拓疆生活的电影、文学以及语言等艺术体裁的代名词。

⑨ 由于新增的劳动力投入到固定的土地上，所以每一位劳动者能够赖以耕作的土地就随之减少，收益递减规律即开始凸显。劳动力与土地的比率不断上升导致劳动边际产品下滑，所以实际工资率下降。

⑩ 事情的发展能糟糕到什么程度？冷峻牧师马尔萨斯认为，人口的压力会把经济推向劳工仅能维持最低的生活水平。

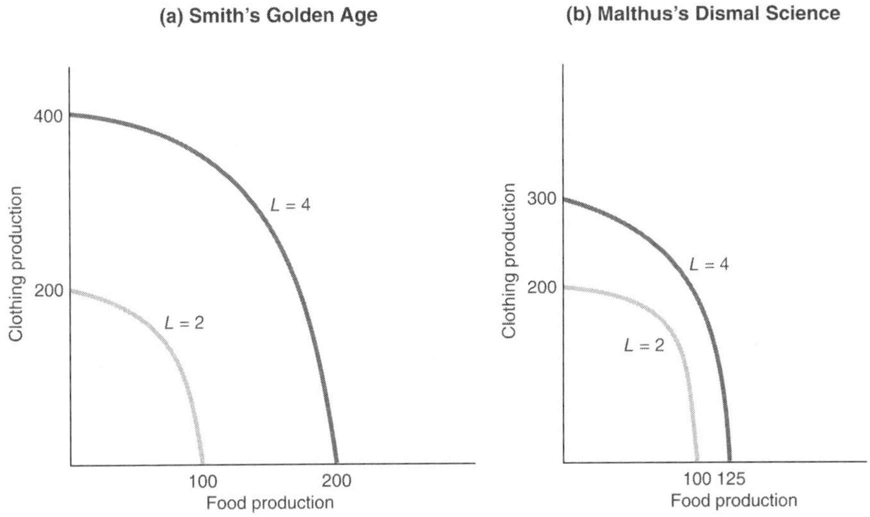

FIGURE 25-2. The Classical Dynamics of Smith and Malthus

In (**a**), unlimited land on the frontier means that when population doubles, labor can simply spread out and produce twice the quantity of any food and clothing combination. In (**b**), limited land means that increasing population from 2 million to 4 million triggers diminishing returns. Note that potential food production rises by only 25 percent with a doubling of labor inputs.

drive the economy to a point where workers were at the minimum level of subsistence. Malthus reasoned that whenever wages were above the subsistence level, population would expand; below-subsistence wages would lead to high mortality and population decline. Only at subsistence wages could there be a stable equilibrium of population. He believed the working classes were destined to a life that is brutish, nasty, and short. This gloomy picture led Thomas Carlyle to criticize economics as "the dismal science."

Figure 25-2(a) shows the process of economic growth in Smith's golden age. Here, as population doubles, the production-possibility frontier (*PPF*) shifts out by a factor of 2 in each direction, showing that there are no constraints on growth from land or resources. Figure 25-2(b) shows the pessimistic Malthusian case, where a doubling of population leads to a less-than-doubling of food and clothing, lowering per capita output, as more people crowd onto limited land and diminishing returns drive down output per person.

经济增长伴随的资本累积：新古典增长模型

Economic Growth with Capital Accumulation: The Neoclassical Growth Model

Malthus's forecast was dramatically wide of the mark because he did not recognize that technological innovation and capital investment could overcome the law of diminishing returns. Land did not become the limiting factor in production. Instead, the first ①
Industrial Revolution brought forth power-driven machinery that increased production, factories that gathered teams of workers into giant firms, railroads and steamships that linked together the far points of the world, and iron and steel that made possible stronger machines and faster locomotives. As market economies entered the twentieth century, a second Industrial Revolution grew up around the telephone, automobile, and electricity industries. Capital accumulation and new technologies became the dominant forces affecting economic development.

What will be the driving forces of economic growth in the twenty-first century? Perhaps advances

---

① 相反，第一次工业革命带来的动力机器增加了产量，工厂将工人聚集于大型企业，铁路和蒸汽轮船将遥不可及的世界连接起来，钢铁的使用使制造出更坚固的机器和更快的机车成为可能。

① 为了了解资本积累和技术变革是如何影响经济的，我们必须引入**新古典经济增长模型**。

[2] Robert Solow：罗伯特·索洛（1924~），美国经济学家，麻省理工学院教授，1961 年克拉克奖和 1987 年诺贝尔经济学奖获得者（表彰其对经济增长主要靠技术进步而不是资本和劳动力投入的研究，即对经济增长理论做出的贡献）。新古典经济增长模型是以其与澳大利亚经济学家斯万（Trevor Swan，1918~1989）的名字联合命名的：即 Solow-Swan neo-classical growth model。斯万是举世公认的澳大利亚最伟大的经济学家，他独立推导出该模型，但主要因与索洛的研究撞车而与诺贝尔奖擦肩而过。

in computation, software, and artificial intelligence will spark yet another industrial revolution. Perhaps, as some ecological pessimists warn, a present-day Malthusian specter haunts rich countries as climate change, sea-level rise, and drought-induced migrations lead to social unrest and economic decline.

To understand how capital accumulation and ①
technological change affect the economy, we must introduce the **neoclassical model of economic growth.** This approach was pioneered by Robert [2]
Solow of MIT, who was awarded the 1987 Nobel Prize for this and other contributions to economic-growth theory. The neoclassical growth model serves as the basic tool for understanding the growth process in advanced countries and has been applied in empirical studies of the sources of economic growth.

Apostle of Economic Growth

Robert M. Solow was born in Brooklyn and educated at Harvard and then moved to the MIT Economics Department in 1950. Over the next few years he developed the neoclassical growth model and applied it in the growth-accounting framework discussed later in this chapter.

One of Solow's major studies was "A Contribution to the Theory of Economic Growth" in 1956. This was a mathematical version of the neoclassical growth model surveyed in this chapter. The importance of this study was highlighted as follows in Solow's Nobel Prize citation:

> Solow's theoretical model had an enormous impact on economic analysis. From simply being a tool for the analysis of the growth process, the model has been generalized in several dif- ③
> ferent directions. It has been extended by the introduction of other types of production factors and it has been reformulated to include stochastic features. The design of dynamic links in certain "numerical" models employed in general equilibrium analysis has also been based on Solow's model. But, above all, Solow's growth model constitutes a framework within which modern macroeconomic theory can be structured.
>
> The increased interest of government to expand education and research and development was inspired by these studies. Every long-term report . . . for any country has used a Solow-type analysis.[3]

Solow has also contributed to empirical studies of economic growth, to natural-resource economics, and to the development of capital theory. In addition, Solow served as a macroeconomic adviser for the Kennedy administration.

Solow is known for his enthusiasm for economics as well as for his humor. He believed that the hunger for publicity has led some economists to exaggerate their knowledge. He criticized economists for "an apparently ④
irresistible urge to push their science further than it will go, to answer questions more delicate than our limited understanding of a complicated question will allow. Nobody likes to say 'I don't know.'"

A lively writer, Solow worries that economics is terrifically difficult to explain to the public. At his news conference after winning the Nobel Prize, Solow quipped, "The attention span of the people you write for is shorter than the length of one true sentence." Nonetheless, Solow continues to labor for his brand of economics, and the world listens carefully to the apostle of economic growth from MIT.

Basic Assumptions. The neoclassical growth model describes an economy in which a single homogeneous output is produced by two types of inputs—capital and labor. In contrast to the Malthusian analysis, labor growth is assumed to be a given. In addition, we assume that the economy is competitive and always operates at full employment, so we can analyze the growth of potential output.

The major new ingredients in the neoclassical growth model are capital and technological change. For the moment, assume that technology remains constant. Capital consists of durable produced goods that are used to make other goods. Capital goods include structures like factories and houses, equipment like computers and machine tools, and inventories of finished goods and goods in process.

For convenience, we will assume that there is a single kind of capital good (call it K). We then measure the aggregate stock of capital as the total quantity of capital goods. In our real-world calculations, we approximate the universal capital good as the total dollar value of capital goods (i.e., the constant-dollar value of equipment, structures, and inventories). If L is the number of workers, then (K/L) is equal to the quantity of capital per worker, or the *capital-labor ratio.* We can write our aggregate production function for the neoclassical growth model without technological change as $Q = F(K, L)$.

Turning now to the economic-growth process, ⑤
economists stress the need for **capital deepening,** which is the process by which the quantity of capital

[3] The citations of the committees for the Nobel Prizes in economics can be found on the Internet at *www.nobel.se/laureates.*

---

③ 这一模型已经通过引入其他类型的生产要素得以扩展，并在经过重新调整之后将随机要素包括了进来。这种在一般均衡分析中使用的某个“数理”模型的动态联系设计，同样也是建立在索洛模型的基础之上。然而最重要的问题是，索洛的增长模型构建了现代宏观经济理论赖以形成的框架。

④ 他批评经济学家说：“明显地存在着一种把科学推出超越科学本身局限的不可抑制的冲动，在超出自己有限的理解复杂问题的能力之外，想把问题回答得更精妙。根本没有人愿意站出来说一句：‘我不懂。’”

⑤ 现在来讨论一下经济增长的过程问题，即经济学家们所强调的**资本深化**的必要性。资本深化是一个人均劳动力的资本量随着时间的推移而增加的过程。

per worker increases over time. Here are some examples of capital deepening: A farmer uses a mechanical orange picker instead of unskilled manual labor; a road builder uses a backhoe instead of a worker with a pick and shovel; a bank substitutes hundreds of ATM machines for human tellers. These are all examples of how the economy increases the amount of capital per worker. As a result, the output per worker has grown enormously in agriculture, road building, and banking.

What happens to the return on capital in the process of capital deepening? For a given state of technology, a rapid rate of investment in plant and equipment tends to depress the rate of return on capital.[4] This occurs because the most worthwhile investment projects get undertaken first, after which later investments become less and less valuable. Once a full railroad network or telephone system has been constructed, new investments will branch into more sparsely populated regions or duplicate existing lines. The rates of return on these later investments will be lower than the high returns on the first lines between densely populated regions.

In addition, the wage rate paid to workers will tend to rise as capital deepening takes place. Why? Each worker has more capital to work with and his or her marginal product therefore rises. As a result, the competitive wage rate rises along with the marginal product of labor.

We can summarize the impact of capital deepening in the neoclassical growth model as follows:

> Capital deepening occurs when the stock of capital grows more rapidly than the labor force. In the absence of technological change, capital deepening will produce a growth of output per worker, of the marginal product of labor, and of real wages; it also will lead to diminishing returns on capital and therefore to a decline in the rate of return on capital. ①

新古典模型的几何分析
Geometrical Analysis of the Neoclassical Model

We can analyze the effects of capital accumulation by using Figure 25-3. This figure shows the aggregate production function graphically by depicting output

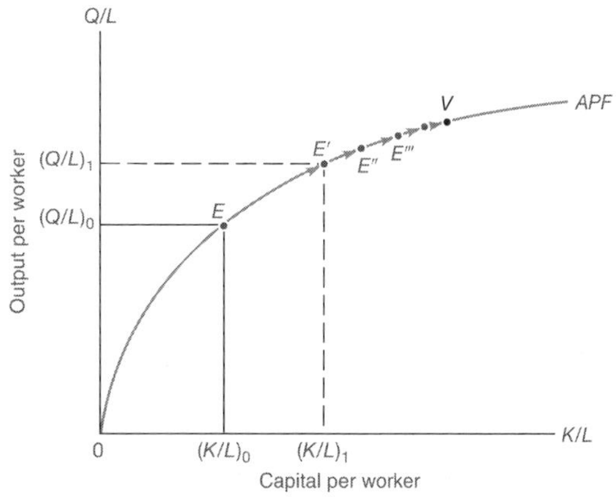

FIGURE 25-3. Economic Growth through Capital Deepening

As the amount of capital per worker increases, output per worker also increases. This graph shows the importance of "capital deepening," or increasing the amount of capital each worker has on hand. Remember, however, that other factors are held constant, such as technology, quality of the labor force, and natural resources.

per worker on the vertical axis and capital per worker on the horizontal axis. In the background, *and held constant for the moment*, are all the other variables that were discussed at the start of this section—the amount of land, the endowment of natural resources, and, most important of all, the technology used by the economy. ②

What happens as the society accumulates capital? As each worker has more and more capital to work with, the economy moves up and to the right on the aggregate production function. Say that the capital-labor ratio increases, from $(K/L)_0$ to $(K/L)_1$. Then the amount of output per worker increases, from $(Q/L)_0$ to $(Q/L)_1$.

What happens to the factor prices of labor and capital? As capital deepens, diminishing returns to capital set in, so the rate of return on capital and the real interest rate fall. (The slope of the curve in Figure 25-3 is the marginal product of capital, which is seen to fall as capital deepening occurs.) Also, because each worker can work with more capital, workers' marginal productivities rise and the real wage rate consequently also rises.

[4] Under perfect competition and without risk, taxes, or inflation, the rate of return on capital is equal to the real interest rate on bonds and other financial assets.

① 资本的深化发生在资本存量的增加远快于劳动力的时候。在忽略技术变革的条件下，资本深化必将带来人均产出、劳动边际产品以及实际工资的增加，也必将导致资本的边际收益递减，随之引起资本收益率的降低。

② 本节开头讨论的所有其他变量，诸如土地数量、自然资源的贡献，以及最重要的经济中所使用的技术，均在此保持不变。

The reverse would happen if the amount of capital per worker were to fall for some reason. For example, wars tend to reduce much of a nation's capital to rubble and lower the capital-labor ratio; after wars, therefore, we see a scarcity of capital and high returns on capital. Hence, our earlier verbal summary of the impact of capital deepening is verified by the analysis in Figure 25-3.

Long-Run Steady State. What is the long-run equilibrium in the neoclassical growth model without technological change? Eventually, the capital-labor ratio will stop rising. *In the long run, the economy will enter a steady state in which capital deepening ceases, real wages stop growing, and capital returns and real interest rates are constant.*

We can show how the economy moves toward the steady state in Figure 25-3. As capital continues to accumulate, the capital-labor ratio increases as shown by the arrows from E' to E'' to E''' until finally the capital-labor ratio stops growing at V. At that point, output per worker (Q/L) is constant, and real wages stop growing.

Without technological change, output per worker and the wage rate stagnate. This is certainly a far better outcome than the world of subsistence wages predicted by Malthus. But the long-run equilibrium of the neoclassical growth model makes it clear that if economic growth consists only of accumulating capital through replicating factories with existing methods of production, then the standard of living will eventually stop rising. ①

技术变革的主要作用

The Central Role of Technological Change

While the capital-accumulation model is a first step on the road to understanding economic growth, it leaves some major questions unanswered. To begin with, the model predicts that real wages will eventually stagnate if there is no improvement in technology. However, real wages have definitely not stagnated over the last century. Peek ahead at Figure 25-5(*c*) on page 513. This figure shows that real wages have grown by a factor of more than 8 over the last century. The simple capital-accumulation model cannot explain the tremendous growth in productivity over time, nor does it account for the tremendous differences in per capita income among countries.

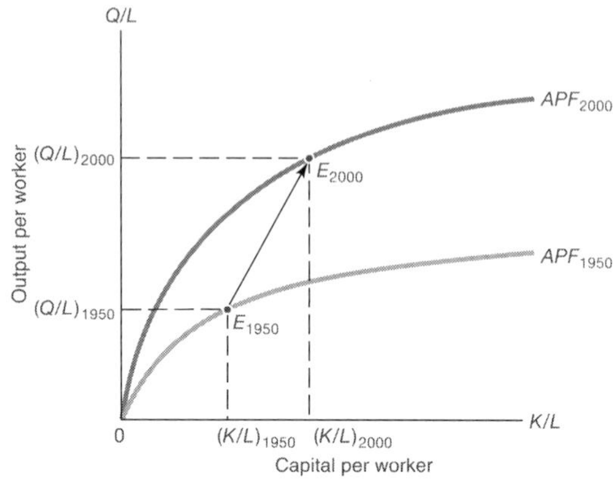

FIGURE 25-4. Technological Advance Shifts Up the Production Function

As a result of improvements in technology, the aggregate production function shifts *upward over time.* Hence improvements in technology combine with capital deepening to raise output per worker and real wages.

What is missing is technological change. We can depict technological change in our growth diagram as an upward shift in the aggregate production function, as illustrated in Figure 25-4. In this diagram, we show the aggregate production function for both 1950 and 2000. Because of technological change, the aggregate production function has shifted upward from APF_{1950} to APF_{2000}. This upward ② shift shows the advances in productivity that are generated by the vast array of new processes and products like electronics, Internet commerce, advances in metallurgy, improved medical technologies, and so forth.

Therefore, in addition to considering the capital deepening described above, we must also take into account advances in technology. The sum of capital deepening and technological change is the arrow in Figure 25-4, which indicates an increase in output per worker from $(Q/L)_{1950}$ to $(Q/L)_{2000}$. Instead of settling into a steady state, the economy enjoys rising output per worker, rising wages, and increasing living standards.

Of particular interest is the impact of changing technologies on rates of profit and real interest

---

① 没有技术变革，人均产出与工资率就会停滞不前。这当然比马尔萨斯所预言的维持生存状态工资的世界要好得多。但是，新古典经济增长模型的长期均衡清楚地表明，如果经济增长仅仅是依赖现有的生产工艺和技术来复制工厂，并通过这些工厂来积累资本的话，那么生活水准的提升最终会止步不前。

② 曲线的上移表明了生产率的提高是由新工艺和新产品的大量涌现驱动的，像电子业、电子商务、冶金技术的进步和医疗技术的改善等。

rates. As a result of technological progress, the real interest rate need not fall. Invention increases the productivity of capital and offsets the tendency for a falling rate of profit.

作为经济产出的技术变革
Technological Change as an Economic Output

Up to now we have treated technological change as something that floats mysteriously down from scientists and inventors like manna from heaven. Recent ① research on economic growth has begun to focus on the *sources of technological change*. This research, sometimes called *new growth theory* or the "theory of endogenous technological change," seeks to uncover the processes by which private market forces, public-policy decisions, and alternative institutions lead to different patterns of technological change.

One important point is that technological change is an output of the economic system. Edison's lightbulb was the result of years of research into different lightbulb designs; the transistor resulted from the efforts of scientists in Bell Labs to find a process that would improve telephone switching devices; pharmaceutical companies spend hundreds of millions of dollars developing and testing new drugs. Those who are talented and lucky may earn supernormal profits, or even become billionaires like Bill Gates of Microsoft, but many are the disappointed inventors or companies that end up with empty pockets.

The other unusual feature of technologies is that ② they are public goods, or "nonrival" goods in technical language. This means that they can be used by many people at the same time without being used up. A new computer language, a new miracle drug, a design for a new steelmaking process—I can use each of these without reducing its productivity for you and the British and the Japanese and everyone else. In addition, inventions are expensive to produce but inexpensive to reproduce. These features of technological change can produce severe market failures, which means that inventors sometimes have great difficulty profiting from their inventions because other people can copy them.

The market failures are largest for the most basic and fundamental forms of research. Public policy has an important role to play here. First, governments generally support basic science through government grants and research facilities. Without government and not-for-profit support, basic research in mathematics, the natural sciences, and the social sciences would wither away. Additionally, governments must be careful to ensure that profit-oriented inventors have adequate incentives to engage in research and development. Governments increasingly pay attention to *intellectual property rights*, such as patents and copyrights, to provide adequate market rewards for creative activities.

What is the major contribution of new growth theory? It has changed the way we think about the growth process and public policies. If technological differences are the major reason for differences in living standards among nations, and if technology is a produced factor, then economic-growth policy should focus much more sharply on how nations can improve their technological performance. This is just the lesson drawn by Stanford's Paul Romer, one of the leaders of new growth theory:

> Economists can once again make progress toward a complete understanding of the determinants of long-run economic success. Ultimately, this will put us in position to offer policymakers something more insightful than the standard neoclassical prescription—more saving and more schooling. We ③ will be able to rejoin the ongoing policy debates about tax subsidies for private research, antitrust exemptions for research joint ventures, the activities of multinational firms, the effects of government procurement, the feedback between trade policy and innovation, the scope of protection for intellectual property rights, the links between private firms and universities, the mechanisms for selecting the research areas that receive public support, and the costs and benefits of an explicit government-led technology policy.[5]

③ 我们能够重新加入正在进行的政策辩论，这些辩论是关于：为私人研究提供税收补贴、研发型合资企业反垄断豁免权、跨国公司的经营活动、政府采购的影响、贸易政策与创新之间的相互回馈、知识产权的保护范围、私人企业与大学之间的联系、获得公共资助的研究领域的筛选机制，以及明确的政府引导技术政策的成本与收益等。

To summarize:

> Technological change—which increases output ④ produced for a given bundle of inputs—is a crucial ingredient in the growth of nations. The new growth theory seeks to uncover the processes which generate technological change. This approach emphasizes that technological change is an output that is subject to severe market failures because technology is a public good that is expensive to produce but cheap to reproduce. Governments increasingly seek to provide strong intellectual property rights for those who develop new technologies.

[5] See Paul Romer in this chapter's Further Reading section.

① 近期对经济增长的研究已经开始关注技术变革的源头。这一研究，有时也被称作新增长理论，或者“内源性技术变革理论”，其目标是要揭示私有市场力量、公共政策决策以及制度创新引发不同的技术变革模式的过程。

② 技术的另外一个非同寻常的特征是其公共品的属性，换一个术语说，即“非竞争性”物品。

④ 在给定投入的条件下，技术变革能增加产出，因此是各国经济增长的关键因素。新增长理论试图揭示技术变革驱动的这一过程。该理论强调的是，技术变革是一种容易引起严重市场失灵的产出。这是因为，技术是生产成本昂贵而复制成本低廉的公共品。政府正努力为那些开发新技术的企业提供强有力的知识产权保护。

美国经济的增长模式

B. THE PATTERNS OF GROWTH IN THE UNITED STATES

经济增长实况

The Facts of Economic Growth

The first part of this chapter described the basic theories of economic growth. But economists have not been content to rest with theory. A major research area all around the world has been measuring the different components of the economic-growth process and applying them to the important theories. An understanding of the patterns of economic growth will help sort out the reasons that some nations prosper while others decline.

Figure 25-5 depicts the key trends of economic development for the United States since the start of the twentieth century. Similar patterns have been found in most of the major industrial countries.

Figure 25-5(*a*) shows the trends in real GDP, the capital stock, and population. Population and employment have more than tripled since 1900. At the same time, the stock of physical capital has risen by a factor of 14. Thus, the amount of capital per worker (the K/L ratio) has increased by a factor of more than 4. Clearly, capital deepening has been an important feature of twentieth- and early-twenty-first-century American capitalism.

What about the growth in output? In a world without technological change, output growth would be somewhere between labor growth and capital growth. In fact, the output curve in Figure 25-5(*a*) is not in between the two factor curves, but actually lies above both curves. This indicates that technological progress must have increased the productivity of capital and labor.

For most people, an economy's performance is measured by their wages, salaries, and fringe benefits. This is shown in Figure 25-5(*c*) in terms of real hourly compensation (or wages and fringe benefits corrected for inflation). Hourly earnings have grown impressively for most of the post-1900 period, as we would expect from the growth in the capital-labor ratio and from steady technological advance.

The real interest rate (which is calculated as the interest rate on long-term Treasury securities corrected for inflation) is shown in Figure 25-5(*d*). The rate of profit on capital is larger than this risk-free interest rate to reflect risk and taxes, but it shows a similar pattern. Real interest rates and profit rates fluctuated greatly in business cycles and wars but have displayed no strong upward or downward trend over the whole period. Either by coincidence or because of an economic mechanism inducing this pattern, technological change has largely offset diminishing returns to capital.

Output per worker-hour is the solid blue curve in Figure 25-5(*c*). As could be expected from the deepening of capital and from technological advance, output per worker has risen steadily.

The fact that wages rise at the same rate as output ①
per worker does not mean that labor has captured all the fruits of productivity advance. Rather, it means that labor has kept about the same *share* of total product, with capital also earning about the same relative share throughout the period. A close look at Figure 25-5(*c*) shows that real wages have grown at about the same rate as output per worker since 1900. More precisely, the average growth rate of real wages was 1.8 percent per year, while that of output per worker was 2.2 percent per year. These figures imply that labor's share of national income (and therefore also property's share) was near-constant over the last century.

Seven Basic Trends of Economic Growth

Economists studying the economic history of advanced nations have found that the following trends apply in most countries:

1. The capital stock has grown more rapidly than population and employment, resulting from capital deepening.
2. For most of the period since 1900, there has been a strong upward trend in real average hourly earnings.
3. The share of labor compensation in national income has been remarkably stable over the last century.
4. There were major oscillations in real interest rates and the rate of profit, particularly during business cycles, but there has been no strong upward or downward trend over the post-1900 period.
5. Instead of steadily rising, which would be predicted by the law of diminishing returns with unchanging technology, the capital-output ratio has actually declined since the start of the twentieth century.
6. For most of the period since 1900, the ratios of national saving and of investment to GDP were stable. Since

① 工资与人均产出两者上升速度相同这一事实并不意味着劳动要素占有了生产率提高的所有果实。但却表明，在整个时间段内，劳动要素在总产出中保持相同份额的同时，资本也获得了同样份额的利润。

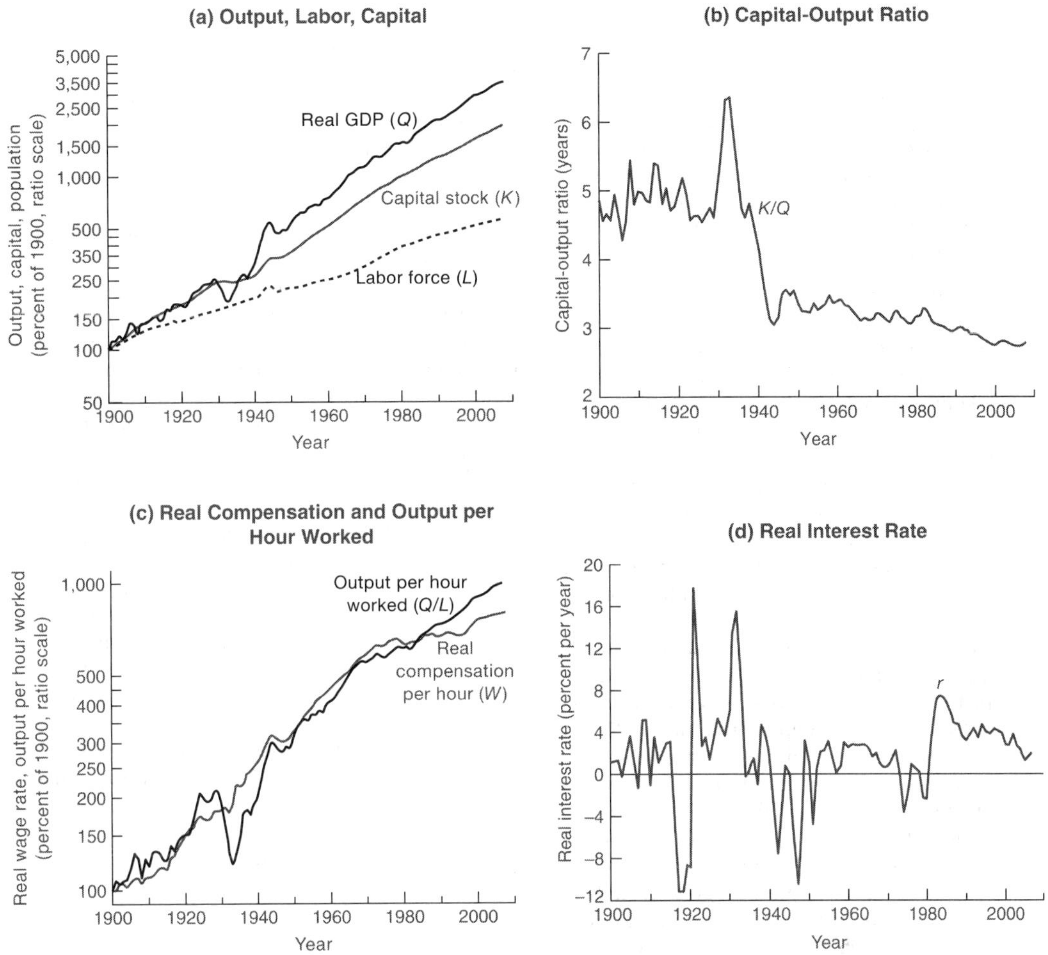

FIGURE 25-5. Economic Growth Displays Striking Regularities

(a) The capital stock has grown faster than population and labor supply. Nonetheless, total output has grown even more rapidly than capital because of improving technology. **(b)** The capital-output ratio dropped sharply during the first half of the twentieth century and has declined slowly since then. **(c)** Real earnings have grown steadily and at almost the same rate as average product per worker-hour over the entire period. **(d)** The real interest rate has been trendless since 1900, suggesting that technological change has offset diminishing returns to capital accumulation. ①

Source: U.S. Departments of Commerce and Labor, Federal Reserve Board, U.S. Bureau of the Census, and Susan Carter et al., *Historical Statistics of the United States: Millennial Edition* (Cambridge University Press, Cambridge, U.K., 2006), available online.

---

①（a）资本存量的增长始终快于人口与劳动供给的增长。然而，由于技术改进，总产出比资本增长的速度甚至更快。（b）在20世纪上半叶，资本－产出比急剧下滑，而下半叶却始终保持了缓慢下降的态势。（c）实际收益在整个时间段内增长平稳，并与每个工时的平均产出保持了几乎同样比例的增长水平。（d）1900年以来，实际利率的走势并不明朗，它说明技术变革抵消了资本积累的收益递减。

1980, the national saving rate has declined sharply in the United States.

7. After effects of the business cycle are removed, national product has grown at an average rate of 3.3 percent per year. Output growth has been much higher than a weighted average of the growth of capital, labor, and resource inputs, suggesting that technological innovation must be playing a key role in economic growth.

七大趋势与经济增长理论的关系
Relationship of the Seven Trends to Economic-Growth Theories

While the seven trends of economic history are not like the immutable laws of physics, they do portray fundamental facts about growth in the modern era. How do they fit into our economic-growth theories?

Trends 2 and 1—higher wage rates when capital deepens—fit nicely into our neoclassical growth model shown in Figure 25-3. Trend 3—that the wage share has been remarkably stable—is an interesting coincidence that is consistent with a wide variety of production functions relating Q to L and K.

Trends 4 and 5, however, show us that technological change must be playing a role here, so Figure 25-4, with its picture of advancing technology, is more realistic than the steady state depicted in Figure 25-3. A steady profit rate and a declining, or steady, capital-output ratio cannot hold if the K/L ratio rises in a world with unchanging technology; taken together, they contradict the basic law of diminishing returns under deepening of capital. We must therefore recognize the key role of technological progress in explaining the seven trends of modern economic growth. Our models confirm what our intuition suggests.

经济增长源
The Sources of Economic Growth

We have seen that advanced market economies grow through increases in labor and capital and by technological change as well. But what are the relative contributions of labor, capital, and technology? To answer this question, we turn to an analysis of the quantitative aspects of growth and of the useful approach known as growth accounting. This approach is the first step in the quantitative analysis of economic growth for any country.

The Growth-Accounting Approach. Detailed studies of economic growth rely on what is called **growth accounting.** ② This technique is not a balance sheet or national product account of the kind we met in earlier chapters. Rather, it is a way of separating out the contributions of the different ingredients driving observed growth trends. ①

Growth accounting usually begins with the aggregate production function we met earlier in this chapter, $Q = AF(K, L, R)$. Often resources are omitted because land is constant. Using elementary calculus and some simplifying assumptions, we can express the growth of output in terms of the growth of the inputs plus the contribution of technological change. Growth in output (Q) can be decomposed into three separate terms: growth in labor (L) times its weight, growth in capital (K) times its weight, and technological change itself (T.C.).

Momentarily ignoring technological change, an assumption of constant returns to scale means that a 1 percent growth in L together with a 1 percent growth in K will lead to a 1 percent growth in output. But suppose L grows at 1 percent and K at 5 percent. It is tempting, but wrong, to guess that Q will then grow at 3 percent, the simple average of 1 and 5. Why is this wrong? Because the two factors do not necessarily contribute equally to output. Rather, the fact ③ that three-fourths of national income goes to labor while only one-fourth goes to capital suggests that labor growth will contribute more to output than will capital growth.

If labor's growth rate gets 3 times the weight of capital's growth, we can calculate the answer as follows: Q will grow at 2 percent per year (= ¾ of 1 percent + ¼ of 5 percent). To growth of inputs, we add technological change and thereby obtain all the sources of growth.

Hence, output growth per year follows the *fundamental equation of growth accounting:*

$$\%\ Q\text{ growth} = \tfrac{3}{4}\,(\%\ L\text{ growth}) + \tfrac{1}{4}\,(\%\ K\text{ growth}) + \text{T.C.} \qquad (1)$$

where "T.C." represents technological change (or total factor productivity) that raises productivity and where ¾ and ¼ are the relative contributions of each input to economic growth. Under conditions of perfect competition, these fractions are equal to the shares of national income of the two factors; naturally, these fractions would be replaced by new fractions if the relative shares of the factors were to change or if other factors were added.

---

① 产出的增长始终高于资本、劳动和资源投入增长的加权平均，这一点表明，技术创新在经济增长中起着关键作用。

② ***增长核算法：***对经济增长的详细研究依赖于**增长核算**。该核算技术既不是我们前面所讲的资产负债表，也不是国民产值核算。确切地讲，它是一种将观察到的增长态势中各种不同推进因素的贡献区分开来的方法。

③ 确凿无疑的事实是，国民收入中的 3/4 是劳动创造的，只有 1/4 归功于资本。这表明，劳动的增长对产出所做的贡献大于资本增长的贡献。

To explain per capita growth, we can eliminate L as a separate growth source. Now, using the fact that capital gets one-fourth of output, we have from equation (1)

$$\% \frac{Q}{L} \text{ growth} = \% \ Q \text{ growth} - \% \ L \text{ growth} = \tfrac{1}{4}\left(\% \frac{K}{L} \text{growth}\right) + \text{T.C.} \qquad (2)$$

This relation shows clearly how capital deepening would affect per capita output if technological advance were zero. Output per worker would grow only one-fourth as fast as capital per worker, reflecting diminishing returns.

One final point remains: We can measure Q growth, K growth, and L growth, as well as the shares of K and L. But how can we measure T.C. (technological change)? We cannot. Rather, we must *infer* T.C. as the residual or leftover after the other components of output and inputs are calculated. We can therefore calculate technological change (or total factor productivity) by rearranging the terms in equation (1) as follows:

$$\text{T.C.} = \% \ Q \text{ growth} - \tfrac{3}{4} (\% \ L \text{ growth}) - \tfrac{1}{4} (\% \ K \text{ growth}) \qquad (3)$$

This equation allows us to answer critically important questions about economic growth. What part of per capita output growth is due to capital deepening, and what part is due to technological advance? Does society progress chiefly by dint of thrift and the forgoing of current consumption? Or is our rising living standard the reward for the ingenuity of inventors and the daring of innovator-entrepreneurs?

Numerical Example. To determine the contributions of labor, capital, and other factors to output growth, we substitute representative numbers for the period 1900–2008 into equation (2) for the growth of Q/L. Since 1900, hours worked have grown 1.4 percent per year, and K has grown 2.6 percent per year, while Q has grown 3.3 percent per year. Thus, by arithmetic, we find that

$$\% \frac{Q}{L} \text{growth} = \tfrac{1}{4}\left(\% \frac{K}{L} \text{growth}\right) + \text{T.C.}$$

becomes

$$1.9 = \tfrac{1}{4} (1.2) + \text{T.C.} = 0.3 + 1.6$$

Thus of the 1.9 percent-per-year increase in output per hour worked, about 0.3 percentage point is due to capital deepening, while the largest portion, 1.6 percent per year, stems from T.C. (technological change).

Detailed Studies. More thorough studies refine the simple calculation but show quite similar conclusions. Table 25-3 presents the results of studies by

Contribution of Different Elements to Growth in Real GDP, United States, 1948–2007

	In percent per year	As percent of total
Real GDP growth (private business sector)	**3.52**	**100**
Sources of growth:		
Contribution of inputs	**2.14**	**61**
Capital	1.21	34
Labor	0.94	27
Total factor productivity growth (research and development, education, advances in knowledge, and other sources)	**1.39**	**39**

TABLE 25-3. Advances in Knowledge Outweigh Capital in Contributing to Economic Growth

Using the techniques of growth accounting, studies break down the growth of GDP in the ① private business sector into contributing factors. Recent comprehensive studies find that capital growth accounted for 34 percent of output growth. Education, research and development, and other advances in knowledge made up 39 percent of total output growth and more than half of the growth of output per unit of labor.

Source: U.S. Department of Labor, "Historical Multifactor Productivity Measures (SIC 1948–87 Linked to NAICS 1987–2007)," at *www.bls.gov/mfp/home.htm.*

① 使用增长核算法这一技术，可以把私人企业部门GDP的增长分解到各贡献要素中。近期的综合研究发现，资本增长在产出增长中所占比例为34%。教育、研发以及其他知识进步占总产出的39%，单位劳动产出增长的贡献则超过了一半。

the Department of Labor for the 1948–2007 period. During this time, output (measured as gross output of the private business sector) grew at an average rate of 3.5 percent per year, while input growth (of capital, labor, and land) contributed 2.1 percentage points per year. Hence **total factor productivity**—the ① growth of output less the growth of the weighted sum of all inputs, or what we have called T.C.—averaged 1.4 percent annually.

About 60 percent of the growth in output in the United States can be accounted for by the growth in labor and capital. The remaining 40 percent is a residual factor that can be attributed to education, research and development, innovation, economies of scale, advances in knowledge, and other factors.

Other countries show different patterns of growth. For example, scholars have used growth accounting to study the Soviet Union, which grew rapidly during the period from 1930 until the mid-1960s. It appears, however, that the high growth rate came primarily from forced-draft increases in capital and labor inputs. For the last few years of the U.S.S.R.'s [2] existence, productivity actually *declined* as the central-planning apparatus became more dysfunctional, as corruption deepened, and as incentives worsened. The estimated growth of total factor productivity for the Soviet Union over the half-century before its collapse was slower than that for the United States and other major market economies. Only the ability of ③ the central government to divert output into investment (and away from consumption) offset the system's inefficiency.

目前的生产率变化趋势 RECENT TRENDS IN PRODUCTIVITY

A careful look at productivity trends indicates that there are sharp movements from year to year as well as long swings. The growth of labor productivity is shown in Figure 25-6. Productivity grew briskly from World War II until the late 1960s.

Then, beginning around 1973, there were several years of poor performance, and even decline. [4] Surveys of this period indicate that the poor productivity record stemmed from the sharp increases in ⑤

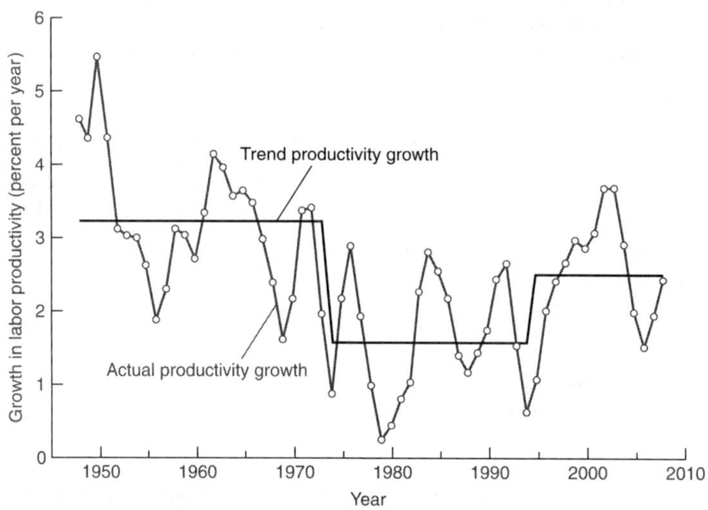

FIGURE 25-6. Labor Productivity Growth in U.S. Business, 1948–2008

Labor productivity grew rapidly until the troubled 1970s and then declined. Bolstered by impressive gains in information technology, especially computers, productivity growth has rebounded over the last decade.

Source: Bureau of Labor Statistics. Data were downloaded from the St. Louis Fed database at *research.stlouisfed.org/fred2*.

① 因此，**全要素生产率**即产出的增长减去所有投入要素加权之和的增长，也就是我们所称的技术变革——年平均值为 1.4%。

[2] U.S.S.R.：Union of Soviet Socialist Republics，苏维埃社会主义共和国联盟，即苏联。

③ 只有中央政府有能力将产出转变为投资（消费除外），它抵消了制度的低效率。

[4] beginning around 1973：1973 年 10 月第四次中东战争爆发后不久，石油输出国组织宣布石油禁运，使油价暴涨，造成石油危机，引发了 1973~1974 年的证券市场危机，是 20 世纪 30 年代经济大萧条以来对全球经济影响最持久的事件。

⑤ 对这一时期所作的研究指出，低生产率源于油价暴涨、管制变严格、物价和工资控制的影响、能源企业的全面管制，以及研发支出的削减。

Productivity and Real Wages

Period	Average Annual Percentage Growth in: Labor productivity	Real wages
1948–1973	3.1	3.3
1973–1995	1.3	1.5
1995–2008	2.6	2.6

TABLE 25-4. Real Wages Mirror Productivity Growth

Over the long run, real wages tend to move with trends in labor productivity. After the productivity slowdown in 1973, real wage growth slowed sharply.

Source: U.S. Department of Labor. Productivity is for the U.S. business sector; nominal compensation is deflated using the price index for private business.

oil prices, increasing stringency of regulations, and impacts of price and wage controls and pervasive regulation of the energy industries, as well as a slowdown in research and development spending.

Economists worry about productivity because of its close association with growth in real wages and living standards. Figure 25-5(*c*) showed how growth in real wages has tracked productivity per hour worked since 1900. This point is presented quantitatively in Table 25-4. Some elementary arithmetic shows that ① if labor's share of national income is constant, this implies that real wages will grow at the rate of growth of labor productivity.[6]

生产率的反弹
The Productivity Rebound

Economists have been waiting for an upturn in productivity growth, hoping that the revolution in information technology would spur rapid growth throughout the economy. Indeed, innovations in information technology (computer hardware, software, and communications) have produced astonishing improvements in every corner of the economy. The prices of computers have fallen more than a thousandfold in the last three decades. Electronic mail and the Internet are changing the face of retailing. Computers are the nerve system of business—running airline pricing and reservation systems, scanning price and quantity data in stores, dispatching electricity, clearing checks, dunning taxpayers, and sending students their tuition bills. Some economists think that computers are like a new fourth factor of production.

The impact of the computer revolution became apparent in the productivity statistics beginning around 1995. Having grown slowly during the 1973–1995 period, labor productivity then surged ahead at 2.6 percent per year from 1995 to 2008.

As is predicted by the model with constant income shares, real compensation moved in parallel with labor productivity (see Table 25-4). Real wages grew at an average rate of 3.3 percent from 1948 to 1973, slowed to 1.5 percent per year from 1973 to 1995, and then increased sharply to 2.6 percent from 1995 to 2008.

Enthusiasts spoke of a "new era" and a "brave new ② world of American capitalism." Fed chair Alan Greenspan, known for his Delphic pronouncements, joined the technological enthusiasts, arguing, "A perceptible quickening in the pace at which technological innovations are applied argues for the hypothesis that the recent acceleration in labor productivity is not just a cyclical phenomenon or a statistical aberration, but reflects, at least in part, a more deep-seated, still developing, shift in our economic landscape."

Economists who have looked at the numbers under a statistical microscope have uncovered some interesting facts about the productivity rebound. Among the important factors are the following:

- *Productivity explosion in computers.* The productivity explosion (and consequent price decline) in computers has been extraordinary. Economists who have studied computer technology estimate that the growth of productivity in this sector has been between 20 and 30 percent per year. This became economically important as computers penetrated ever deeper into the U.S. economy. By the late 1990s, production of information technology was contributing almost half of all productivity growth, although that slowed sharply after the [3] bursting of the technology bubble in 2000.

[6] To see this relationship, write labor's share as $W \times L = s \times P \times Q$, where s = labor's share, W = money wage rate, L = hours of work, P = price index, and Q = output. Dividing both sides by L and P yields $(W/P) = s \times (Q/L)$, which signifies that the real wage equals labor's share times labor productivity. Hence, if the share of labor of national income is constant, real wages will grow at the same rate as labor productivity.

① 使用小学的算术知识就可以计算出来，如果国民收入中劳动所占的份额保持不变，即意味着实际工资必将以劳动生产率的增长率增加。

② 热衷者们对此提出了“新纪元”和“美国资本主义的全新世界”的概念。美联储主席阿兰·格林斯潘也加入到了这些技术变革热衷者的行列。虽然他一向以谨慎著称，但也对此振振有词：“技术创新应用的步伐明显加快的事实证明了此种假设——近期劳动生产率的加速提高不只是周期现象或者统计误差，而是至少部分地反映了更加深化且仍在发展的技术，改变了我们的经济面貌。”

[3] after the bursting of the technology bubble in 2000：1994 年浏览器的出现开始引发互联网泡沫，至 2000 年 3 月 10 日 NASDAQ 指数达到顶峰，遂开始破裂。一般称为 1995~2001 年间的投机泡沫。

- *Capital deepening.* There has been a very sharp increase in investment since 1995. Companies invested heavily in computers and software to take advantage of their falling prices and the increasing power of new software.
- *Unmeasured outputs.* Many of the advances of the new economy have not been captured by the productivity statistics. The phenomenal advances of the Internet, e-mail, and cellular phones are largely missed in the productivity statistics. Some economists have found that productivity is significantly underestimated for software and communications equipment (see the discussion of price measurement in Chapter 20). Or consider, the time that consumers save by shopping on the Internet, the saving of time and postage involved in the switch from snail-mail to e-mail, and the convenience of cellular telephones—none of these shows up in measured productivity. Others think the true gains from computers lie in the future. Stanford economic historian Paul David, who has studied [1]
past inventions, believes that it takes decades for the economy to reap the full benefits of fundamental inventions.

Whether or not the more rapid productivity ②
growth is a permanent feature of our economy, it is clear that computers continue to shape our economy and our lives in surprising ways.

This concludes our introduction to the principles of economic growth. The next chapter applies these principles to the struggle of poor countries to improve their living standards. In the remaining chapters in this part, we open our inquiry to international trade and finance.

SUMMARY

A. Theories of Economic Growth

1. The analysis of economic growth examines the factors that lead to the growth of potential output over the long run. The growth in output per capita is an important objective of government because it is associated with rising average real incomes and living standards.
2. Reviewing the experience of nations over space and time, we see that the economy rides on the four wheels of economic growth: (*a*) the quantity and quality of its labor force; (*b*) the abundance of its land and other natural resources; (*c*) the stock of accumulated capital; and, perhaps most important, (*d*) the technological change and innovation that allow greater output to be produced with the same inputs. There is no unique combination of these four ingredients, however; the United States, Europe, and Asian countries have followed different paths to economic success.
3. The classical models of Smith and Malthus describe economic development in terms of land and population. In the absence of technological change, increasing population ultimately exhausts the supply of free land. The resulting increase in population density triggers the law of diminishing returns, so growth produces higher land rents with lower competitive wages. The Malthusian equilibrium is attained when the wage rate has fallen to the subsistence level, below which population cannot sustain itself. In reality, however, technological change has allowed long-term growth in real wages and productivity per worker in most countries by continually shifting the productivity curve of labor upward.
4. Capital accumulation with complementary labor forms the core of modern growth theory in the neoclassical growth model. This approach uses a tool known as the aggregate production function, which relates inputs and technology to total potential GDP. In the absence of technological change and innovation, an increase in capital per worker (capital deepening) would not be matched by a proportional increase in output per worker because of diminishing returns to capital. Hence, capital deepening would lower the rate of return on capital (equal to the real interest rate under risk-free competition) while raising real wages.
5. Technological change increases the output producible with a given bundle of inputs. This pushes upward the aggregate production function, making more output available with the same inputs of labor and capital. Recent analysis in the "new growth theory" seeks to uncover the processes which generate technological change. This approach emphasizes (*a*) that technological change is an output of the economic system, (*b*) that technology is a public or nonrival good that can be used simultaneously by many people, and (*c*) that new inventions are expensive to produce but

[1] Paul David：保罗·大卫，斯坦福大学教授，美国经济史协会前主席，美国艺术和科学院院士，其学术著作以科技变革和经济学的发展研究著称。

② 毋庸置疑，无论生产率的快速增长是否是经济中的永久特点，计算机技术都在以惊人的方式持续地重塑着我们的经济和生活。

inexpensive to reproduce. These features mean that governments must pay careful attention to ensuring that inventors have adequate incentives, through strong intellectual property rights, to engage in research and development.

B. The Patterns of Growth in the United States

6. Numerous trends of economic growth are seen in data for the twentieth and early twenty-first centuries. Among the key findings are that real wages and output per hour worked have risen steadily; that the real interest rate has shown no major trend; and that the capital-output ratio has declined. The major trends are consistent with the neoclassical growth model augmented by technological advance. Thus economic theory confirms what economic history tells us—that technological advance increases the productivity of inputs and improves wages and living standards.
7. The last trend, continual growth in potential output since 1900, raises the important question of the sources of economic growth. Applying quantitative techniques, economists have used growth accounting to determine that "residual" sources—such as technological change and education—outweigh capital deepening in their impact on GDP growth and labor productivity.
8. After 1970, productivity growth slowed under the weight of energy-price increases, increasing environmental regulation, and other structural changes. In the late 1990s, however, the explosion of productivity and the investment in computers and other information technologies have led to a sharp upturn in measured productivity growth.

CONCEPTS FOR REVIEW

four wheels of growth:
- labor
- resources
- capital
- technology

aggregate production function
Smith's golden age
capital-labor ratio
Malthus's subsistence wage
neoclassical growth model
K/L rise as capital deepens
new growth theory
technology as a produced good
seven trends of economic growth

growth accounting:
$\% Q$ growth = ¾ ($\% L$ growth) + 1/4 ($\% K$ growth) + T.C.
$\% Q/L$ growth = ¼ ($\% K/L$ growth) + T.C.

FURTHER READING AND INTERNET WEBSITES

Further Reading

One of the best surveys of economic growth is Robert Solow, *Economic Growth* (Oxford University Press, Oxford, U.K., 1970). See his pathbreaking article, "A Contribution to the Theory of Economic Growth," *Quarterly Journal of Economics,* 1956. The text reference is William Baumol, "Entrepreneurship: Productive, Unproductive, and Destructive," *Journal of Political Economy,* October 1990, pp. 893–921.

You may want to read some excellent books on economic growth. David N. Weil, *Economic Growth* (Pearson, Addison-Wesley, New York, 2006) is an advanced survey of the subject. David Warsh is an excellent economic journalist; his *Knowledge and the Wealth of Nations* (Norton, New York, 2006) explores the origins of the new growth theory. Benjamin Friedman, *The Moral Consequences of Economic Growth* (Knopf, New York, 2006) explores the moral and historical dimensions of economic growth, with some surprising conclusions.

Websites

A website devoted to economic growth is maintained by Jonathan Temple of Oxford, *www.bristol.ac.uk/Depts/Economics/Growth/*, and contains many references and links, as well as access to growth data. The articles by Solow and Baumol are available at *www.jstor.org.*

Technological change is often associated with particular inventions. The lives and patents of great inventors can be found at *www.invent.org/hall_of_fame/1_0_0_hall_of_fame.asp.*

QUESTIONS FOR DISCUSSION

1. **Reminder on compound growth:** Like financial economics, economic growth theory and measurement rely on calculations of growth rates. The one-period growth rate in percent per year is

$$g_t = 100 \times \left(\frac{x_t}{x_{t-1}} - 1\right)$$

Similarly, the n-period growth rate in percent per year is calculated as

$$g_t^{(n)} = 100 \times \left[\left(\frac{x_t}{x_{t-n}}\right)^{1/n} - 1\right]$$

   a. Now look back to the table of macroeconomic data in the Appendix to Chapter 19. Calculate the annual growth rate of real GDP for 1980–1981 and 1980–1982.
   b. Next, calculate the growth of labor productivity from 1995 to 2000, assuming the following shows indexes of real output and labor inputs.

Year	Labor inputs	Output
1995	100.00	100.00
2000	110.29	126.16

2. "If the government strengthens intellectual property rights, subsidizes basic science, and controls business cycles, we will see economic growth that would astound the classical economists." Explain what the writer meant by this statement.
3. "With zero population growth and no technological change, persistent capital accumulation would ultimately destroy the capitalist class." Explain why such a scenario might lead to a zero real interest rate and to a disappearance of profits.
4. Recall the growth-accounting equation [equation (1) on page 514]. Calculate the growth of output if labor grows at 1 percent per year, capital grows at 4 percent per year, and technological change is 1½ percent per year.

   How would your answer change if:
   a. Labor growth slowed to 0 percent per year?
   b. Capital growth increased to 5 percent per year?
   c. Labor and capital had equal shares in GDP?

   Also, calculate for each of these conditions the rate of growth of output per hour worked.
5. Use the *PPF* to illustrate the Malthusian prediction and why it is flawed. Put per capita food production on one axis and per capita manufactures on the other. Assume that there are diminishing returns to labor in food production but that manufactures have constant returns to labor.
6. **Advanced problem for those who know calculus:** Those who understand calculus can easily grasp the essentials of the growth-accounting framework of this chapter. We rely for this problem on the important Cobb-Douglas production function. This is a specific algebraic formula that is written as $Q_t = A_t K_t^{\alpha} L_t^{(1-\alpha)}$. It is widely used in empirical studies.
   a. Show that the growth rate of output is given by

$$g(Q_t) = g(A_t) + \alpha g(K_t) + (1 - \alpha)\, g(L_t)$$

   where $g(x_t)$ is the growth rate of that variable.
   b. Advanced courses will show that under perfect competition, α = the share of capital in national income and $(1 - \alpha)$ = labor's share. If the share of labor in national income is 75 percent, derive the growth-accounting equation in the text.
7. **Advanced problem:** Many fear that computers will do to humans what tractors and cars did to horses—the horse population declined precipitously early in this century after technological change made horses obsolete. If we treat computers as a particularly productive kind of K, what would their introduction do to the capital-labor ratio in Figure 25-3? Can total output go down with a fixed labor force? Under what conditions would the real wage decline? Can you see why the horse analogy might not apply?

经济发展的挑战

The Challenge of Economic Development

CHAPTER

26

I believe in materialism. I believe in all the proceeds of a healthy materialism—good cooking, dry houses, dry feet, sewers, drain pipes, hot water, baths, electric lights, automobiles, good roads, bright streets, long vacations away from the village pump, new [1] *ideas, fast horses, swift conversation, theaters, operas, orchestras, bands—I believe in them all for everybody. The man who dies without knowing these things may be as exquisite as a saint, and as rich as a poet; but it is in spite of, not because of, his deprivation.*

Francis Hackett [2]

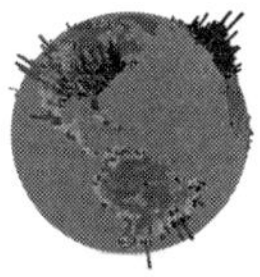

[2] 弗朗西斯·哈克特：Francis Hackett（1883~1962），著名的爱尔兰裔美国批评家和传记作家，一生著作颇多，其中最为学界称道的是《亨利八世》（*Henry VIII*）。这段文字出自哈克特《爱尔兰：民族主义研究》（*Ireland: A Study in Nationalism*）一书，1918年由纽约的B.M. Huebsch公司出版，原文如下：

I believe in materialism. I believe the one hope for Ireland is a healthy materialism. I believe in all the proceeds of a healthy materialism——good cooking, dry houses, dry feet, sewers, drain-pipes, hot water, baths, electric light, automobiles, good roads, bright streets, long vacations away from the village pump, new ideas, fast horses, swift conversation, theatres, operas, orchestras, bands—I believe, in short, in practically everything which (except the horses) is now the exclusive perquisite of the AngloIrish parasites. I believe in them all, *for everybody*. The man who dies without knowing these things may be as exquisite as a saint, and as rich as a poet; but it is in spite, not because, of his deprivation.

根据以上原文，这段文字拟译作：

我信奉物质主义。因此，我相信健康的物质主义所带来的一切——美味的菜肴、干爽的宅邸、干燥的鞋袜、缝纫机、排水管道、热水供应、洗浴设备、电灯、汽车、四通八达的路网、明亮的街区、远离喧嚣都市的长假、新思想、马会赛马、快速沟通、戏院、歌剧、交响乐、流行乐队——我相信，这一切均为我们每一个人所享有。任何一位未曾接触这一切就过世的人或许会像圣人一样高尚，像诗人一样丰富，但这是因为他们本来就高尚，而不是因为剥夺了他们应该享有的权利。

Planet Earth today contains people at vastly differ- ③ ent living standards. At one end are the affluent of North America and Western Europe, where the richest 1 percent of the people enjoy about 20 percent of world income and consumption. At the other extreme are the destitute of Africa and Asia—1 billion people living in absolute poverty, with few comforts, seldom knowing where the next meal will come from.

What causes the great differences in the wealth of ④ nations? Can the world peacefully survive with such poverty in the midst of plenty? What steps can poorer nations take to improve their living standards? What are the responsibilities of affluent countries?

These questions concerning the obstacles facing developing countries are among the greatest challenges facing modern economics. It is here that the ⑤ tools of economics can make the greatest difference in people's daily lives. It is here that economics can literally make the difference between life and death. We begin with an analysis of population and then describe the characteristics of developing countries. The second part of this chapter examines alternative approaches to economic growth in developing countries, particularly the more successful models in Asia along with the failed communist experiment in Russia.

人口增长与经济发展

A. POPULATION GROWTH AND DEVELOPMENT

马尔萨斯与沉闷的科学
MALTHUS AND THE DISMAL SCIENCE

Can technology keep pace with population growth in poor countries? Is Africa doomed to live on the ragged edge of subsistence because of its high birth rate and the burden of diseases like AIDS? These

---

[1] village pump，在当时指纽约、伦敦等特大都市生活所包罗的一切，可参阅T. S. 艾略特（Thomas Stearns Eliot，1888~1965）的著名长诗《荒原》（*Waste Land*）。现在特指由信息技术所主导的一切现代国际化大都市人生活中的所有内容和生存手段。"deprivation"语义双关。

③ 今天，地球人的生活水平有很大不同。一极是北美和西欧的富裕生活，那里最富有的人群只占人群总数的1%，却在享受着全世界20%的收入与消费。而非洲和亚洲的贫困人群则是另一极，达10亿之众，生活在绝对贫困之中，吃了上顿没下顿，更无舒适可言。

④ 为什么会造成各国如此巨大的贫富差距？世界能否在贫富悬殊状态下和平相处呢？比较穷的国家能够采取哪些措施来改善本国人民的生活水平？富国在其中应该承担哪些责任？

⑤ 也恰是这些经济学的分析工具，使人们的日常生活千差万别。这里经济学关系到人类的生死存亡。

[1] the Reverend T. R. Malthus：托马斯·罗伯特·马尔萨斯（1766~1834），著名的英国人口学家和政治经济学家。the Reverend：对牧师和神父的尊称，拟译为"尊敬的"。

questions have been a prominent part of economics for almost two centuries.

Economic analysis of population dates back to the Reverend T. R. Malthus, whom we met in the [1] context of the analysis of economic growth in the last chapter. Malthus developed his views while arguing against his father's perfectionist opinion that the human race was always improving. Finally, the son became so agitated that he wrote *An Essay on the Principle of Population* (1798), which was a best-seller and has since influenced the thinking of people all over the world about population and economic growth.

Malthus began with the observation of Benjamin [2] Franklin that in the American colonies, where resources were abundant, population tended to double every 25 years or so. He then postulated a universal tendency for population—unless checked by limited food supply—to grow exponentially, or by a geometric progression. Eventually, a population which doubles every generation—1, 2, 4, 8, 16, 32, 64, 128, 256, 512, 1024, . . . —becomes so large that there is not enough space in the world for all the people to stand.

After invoking exponential growth, Malthus had one further argument. At this point he unleashed the devil of diminishing returns. He argued that, because land is fixed, the supply of food would tend to grow only at an arithmetic progression. It could not keep pace with the exponential growth (or geometric progression) of labor. (Compare 1, 2, 3, 4, . . . , with 1, 2, 4, 8, . . .). We paraphrase Malthus's gloomy conclusions as follows:

> As population doubles and redoubles, it is as if the ③ globe were halving and halving again in size—until finally it has shrunk so much that food production is below the level necessary to support the population.

When the law of diminishing returns is applied to a fixed supply of land, food production tends not to keep up with a population's geometric-progression rate of growth.

Actually, Malthus did not say that population would *necessarily* increase at a geometric rate. This was only its tendency if unchecked. He described the checks that operate, in all times and places, to hold population down. In his first edition, he stressed the "positive" checks that increase the death rate: pestilence, famine, and war. Later, he held out hope that population growth could be slowed by "moral restraint" such as abstinence and postponed marriages.

This important application of diminishing returns illustrates the profound effects that a simple theory can have. Malthus's ideas had wide repercussions. His book was used to support a stern revision of the ④ English poor laws. Under the influence of Malthus's writings, people argued that poverty should be made as uncomfortable as possible. In this view, the government cannot improve the welfare of the poor population because any increase in the incomes of the poor would only cause workers to reproduce until all were reduced to a bare subsistence.

Compound Interest and Exponential Growth

Let us pause for a reminder on exponential growth and compound interest, which are important tools in economics. Exponential (or geometric) growth occurs when a variable increases at a constant proportional rate from period to period. Thus, if a population of 200 is growing at 3 percent per year, it would equal 200 in year 0, 200×1.03 in year 1, $200 \times 1.03 \times 1.03$ in year 2, . . . , $200 \times (1.03)^{10}$ in year 10, and so on.

When money is invested continuously, it earns compound interest, meaning that interest is earned on past interest. Money earning compound interest grows geometrically. An intriguing calculation is to determine how much the $26 received by the Indians for Manhattan Island would, if deposited at compound interest, be worth today. Say that this fund was placed in an endowment that earned 6 percent each year from 1626. It would be worth $136 billion in 2010.

A useful rule about compound interest is the **rule of 70,** which states that a magnitude growing at a rate of *g* per year will double in (70/*g*) years. For example, a human population growing at 2 percent per year will double in 35 years, whereas if you invest your funds at 7 percent per year, the funds will double in value every 10 years.

Flawed Prophecies of Malthus. Despite Malthus's careful statistical studies, demographers today think that his views were oversimplified. In his discussion of ⑤ diminishing returns, Malthus did not anticipate the technological miracle of the Industrial Revolution; nor did he understand that the birth-control movement and new technologies would provide families with the capability to reduce the birth rate. In fact, population growth in most Western nations began to

---

[2] Benjamin Franklin：本杰明·富兰克林（1706~1790），18世纪美国最伟大的科学家和发明家，著名的政治家、外交家、哲学家、文学家和航海家，由于坚持其"13种品德"而被誉为"资本主义精神最完美的代表"，其头像印在100美元的纸币上。

③ 当人口翻倍和再翻倍地增加时，就好像我们这颗星球在一半一半地收缩。直到最后，地球收缩到它所能生产的食物低于其维持人口的必要水平。

④ 他的这部著作用来支持英国贫困法的严格修订。

⑤ 在其对边际收益递减问题的讨论中，马尔萨斯没有预期到工业革命产生的科技奇迹，也无法理解人口控制活动及新技术给家庭提供了降低出生率的能力。

decline after 1870 just as living standards and real wages grew most rapidly.

In the century following Malthus, technological advance shifted out the production-possibility frontiers of countries in Europe and North America. Technological change outpaced population, resulting in a rapid rise in real wages. Nevertheless, the germs of truth in Malthus's doctrines are still important for understanding population trends in some poor countries where the race between population and food supply continues today.

Population Implosion? Before we turn to issues facing poor countries, it is important to recognize that the problem facing many rich countries is *declining population growth,* not population explosion. ① Virtually every rich country in the world today has zero or negative native population growth, meaning that the average number of adult children per woman is 2 or less. Population in most advanced countries is today growing only because of immigration. Stable or declining population with increasing life expectancy puts great stress on countries' fiscal conditions because of the need to fund health care and public pensions.

经济增长的极限与新马尔萨斯主义 Limits to Growth and Neo-Malthusianism

② Often, earlier ideas reemerge in light of new social trends or scientific findings. Again and again, neo-Malthusian ideas have surfaced as many antigrowth advocates and environmentalists argue that economic growth is limited due to the finiteness of our natural resources and because of environmental constraints.

Worries about the viability of growth emerged prominently in the early 1970s with a series of studies by an ominous-sounding group called the "Club of Rome." [3] ④ The analysis of this school appeared in a famous computer study called *The Limits to Growth* and its 1992 sequel *Beyond the Limits.* The predictions of the neo-Malthusians were even more dismal than those of Malthus himself:

> ⑤ If present growth trends in world population, industrialization, pollution, food problems, and resource depletion continue unchanged, the limits to growth on this planet will be reached within the next one hundred years. The most probable results will be a rather sudden and uncontrollable decline in both population and industrial capacity.

These growth critics found a receptive audience because of mounting alarm about rapid population growth in developing countries and, in the 1970s, an upward spiral in oil prices and the sharp decline in the growth of productivity. A second wave of growth pessimism emerged over the last decade because of concerns about environmental constraints on long-term economic growth. Among today's concerns are global warming, in which the use of fossil fuels is warming the climate; widespread evidence of acid rain; the appearance of the Antarctic "ozone hole," along with ozone depletion in temperate regions; deforestation, especially of the tropical rain forests, which may upset the global ecological balance; soil erosion, which threatens the long-term viability of agriculture; ocean acidification from increased atmospheric carbon dioxide; and species extinction, which threatens many ecosystems and precious biological resources.

The economic analysis underlying the neo-Malthusian analysis is closely related to the Malthusian theory. Whereas Malthus held that production would be limited by diminishing returns in food production, today's growth pessimists argue that growth will be limited by the absorptive capacity of our environment. We can, some say, burn only a finite amount of fossil fuel before we face the threat of dangerous climate change. The need to reduce the use of fossil fuels might well slow our long-term economic growth.

⑥ There is a key difference, however. The earlier analysis related to *market commodities* such as land, food, and oil. Many of today's concerns relate to *externalities* and *public goods,* where unregulated market prices provide distorted signals.

What is the empirical evidence on the effects of resource exhaustion and environmental limits on economic growth? The facts are that the prices of most basic commodities such as grains, energy, and timber have risen *more slowly* than the general price level. However, many economists are concerned about externalities, particularly global public goods such as global warming. Nations have not found it easy to negotiate cooperative agreements to slow global warming. We can look to the troubled history of nuclear proliferation as another example where global cooperation has been difficult to achieve. The future of the global economy may depend upon finding solutions to these new Malthusian dilemmas.

[3] Club of Rome：罗马俱乐部，1968年由意大利著名实业家佩切伊（Aurelio Peccei，1908~1984）和苏格兰科学家金（Alexander King，1909~2007）创立，由全球知名的科学家、企业家、经济学家、社会学家、教育家、国际组织、高级公务员和政治家等组成，总部设在意大利罗马，通过对人口、粮食、工业化、污染、资源、贫困、教育等全球热点问题的系统研究，从事有关全球性问题的宣传、预测和研究活动，是“未来学悲观派”的代表。

---

① 事实上，今天世界上所有富国的人口增长率是零或者负数。这就意味着，每一位女性平均只生育两个可成年子女，或者更少。现在，大多数发达国家人口依然在增长的原因，仅仅是因为移民。

② 在新的社会潮流或者科学发现的启发下，早期的一些思想往往会再度出现。

④ 这一学派的分析出现在著名的计算机研究报告《增长的极限》及其在1992年的续篇《超越极限》。

⑤ 如果现在世界人口的增长趋势、工业化、环境污染、食物短缺，以及资源枯竭问题继续持续，我们这颗星球的增长极限必将在下一个百年内出现。最可能的结果将是人口和企业的生产能力都会出现突如其来的无法控制的骤减。

⑥ 但是，其中有一个关键的区别。早期的分析主要是针对土地、食物和石油这样一些市场商品，而今天所关注的则多数是外部性和公共品。在这些领域，不受管制的市场价格释放着扭曲的信号。

穷国的经济增长

B. ECONOMIC GROWTH IN POOR COUNTRIES

发展中国家概述

ASPECTS OF A DEVELOPING COUNTRY

Exactly what is a **developing country?** The most ① important characteristic of a developing country is that it has low per capita income. In addition, people in developing countries usually have poor health, low levels of literacy, extensive malnutrition, and little capital to work with. Many poor countries have weak market and government institutions, corruption, and civil strife. These countries often have high native population growth, but they also suffer from out-migration, particularly among skilled workers.

Table 26-1 is a key source of data for understanding the major players in the world economy, as well as important indicators of underdevelopment. Low- and middle-income countries are grouped into six major regions.

A number of interesting features emerge from the table. Clearly, low-income countries are much poorer than advanced countries like the United States. People in the poorest countries earn only about one-twentieth as much as people in high-income countries. For the table's data, *purchasing-power-parity* (PPP) calculations were used to measure incomes. Market exchange rates tend to understate ② the incomes of low-wage countries. (The use of purchasing-power-parity exchange rates to evaluate living standards is discussed in Chapter 27.) Note also that the early 2000s were a period of strong

	Population			Per capita GDP		Education	Net Migration
Region	Total number, 2006 (millions)	Growth rate, 2000–2006 (% per year)	Life expectancy at birth (years)	2006 ($)	Growth, 2000–2006 (% per year)	Adult illiteracy (%, ages 15 and older)	Migration Rate (per 1,000 persons)
East Asia and Pacific (China, Indonesia, . . .)	1,900	0.9	71	6,820	7.6	9	−2.0
Eastern Europe and Central Asia (Russia, Poland, . . .)	460	0.0	69	9,660	5.7	2	−0.4
Latin America and Caribbean (Brazil, Mexico, . . .)	556	1.3	73	8,800	1.8	10	−1.2
Middle East and North Africa (Egypt, Iran, . . .)	311	1.8	70	6,450	2.3	27	−0.9
South Asia (India, Pakistan, . . .)	1,493	1.7	63	3,440	5.1	42	−0.2
Sub-Saharan Africa (Nigeria, Ethiopia, . . .)	770	2.3	47	2,030	2.3	41	−0.1

TABLE 26-1. Important Indicators for Different Country Groups

The World Bank groups developing countries into six regions. For each, a number of important indicators of economic development are shown. Note that low-income countries tend to have high illiteracy and out-migration. Some low-income countries have life expectancies close to those of rich countries.

Source: World Bank, *World Development Report*, and data at *www.worldbank.org*.

① **发展中国家**的准确定义是什么？发展中国家最重要的特征是它的人均收入很低。

② 市场汇率有低估低工资国家收入的倾向。

growth in the world economy, and that spilled over to most poor regions as well.

In addition, many social and health indicators show the effects of poverty on low-income nations. Life expectancy is lower than in high-income countries, and educational attainment and literacy are often minimal.

There is a great diversity among developing countries. Some remain at the ragged edge of starvation—these are the poorest countries like Congo, Ethiopia, and Liberia. Other countries that were in that cat- ①
egory two or three decades ago have moved to the rank of middle-income countries. The more successful ones—Slovenia, Singapore, and South Korea—have graduated from the developing group, and the most successful of these have per capita incomes that have reached the ranks of high-income countries. Yesterday's successful developing countries will be tomorrow's high-income countries.

Life in Low-Income Countries

To bring out the contrasts between advanced and developing economies, imagine that you are a typical 21-year-old in a low-income country such as Mali, India, or Bangladesh. You are poor. Even after making allowance for the goods that you produce and consume, your annual income barely averages $2000. Your counterpart in North America might have more than $30,000 in average earnings. Perhaps you can find cold comfort in the thought that only 1 person in 4 in the world averages more than $5000 in annual income.

For each of your fellow citizens who can read, there is one like you who is illiterate. Your life expectancy is four-fifths that of the average person in an advanced country; already, two of your brothers and sisters have died before reaching adulthood. Birth rates are high, particularly for families where women receive no education, but mortality rates are also much higher here than in countries with good health-care systems.

Most people in your country work on farms. Few can be spared from food production to work in factories. You work with but one-sixtieth the horsepower of a prosperous North American worker. You know little about science, but much about your village traditions.

You are often hungry, and the food you eat is mainly roughage or rice. While you were among those who got some primary schooling, like most of your friends, you did not go on to high school, and only the wealthiest go to a university. You work long hours in the fields without the benefit of machinery. At night, you sleep on a mat. You have little household furniture, perhaps a table and a radio. Your ②
only mode of transportation is an old pair of boots.

人力资源开发
Human Development

This review of life in the poorest countries of the world reminds us of the importance of adequate incomes in meeting basic needs as well as the fact that life involves
more than market incomes. Thoughtful economists ③
such as Nobel Prize recipient Amartya Sen and Yale's [4]
Gustav Ranis emphasize that other factors should be [5]
considered in appraising a country's progress: Factors such as health and life expectancy, school enrollment, adult literacy, and independence of women are important goals for developing countries along with increasing per capita market consumption.

Figure 26-1 shows a plot of life expectancy and per capita GDP. The correlation is strong, but there are exceptions to the general positive relationship. Some countries, such as Botswana, Equatorial Guinea, and South Africa, have low life expectancies relative to income because of the scourge of AIDS. No poor countries have high life expectancies, but countries like Greece and Costa Rica have life expectancies as high as or higher than those in the United States because of the poorly designed health-care system in the United States.

发展四要素
THE FOUR ELEMENTS IN DEVELOPMENT

Having seen what it means to be a developing country, we now turn to an analysis of the process by which low-income countries improve their living standards. We saw in Chapter 25 that economic growth in the United States—growth in its potential output—rides on four wheels. These are (1) human resources, (2) natural resources, (3) capital, and (4) technol-
ogy. These four wheels operate in rich and poor ⑥
countries, although the mix and strategy for combining them will differ depending on the state of development. Let's see how each of the four wheels operates in developing countries and consider how public policy can steer the growth process in favorable directions.

⑥ 无论是富国还是穷国，都是依靠这四个车轮在运行，只是根据发展状况不同，这四大要素的组合战略不同而已。

① 二三十年以前属于这类的贫困国家现在已进入中等收入国家的行列。

② 一双破旧靴子就是一个人唯一的交通工具。

③ 诸如诺奖得主昂马蒂亚·森和耶鲁的古斯塔夫·拉尼斯这样有思想的经济学家强调，在表扬一国进步的同时，还应考虑其他一些因素：

[4] Amartya Sen：昂马蒂亚·森（1933~），印度学者，先后出任过哈佛、剑桥、麻省理工、康奈尔、伦敦政治经济学院等名校教授，1998 年诺贝尔经济学奖获得者，当代最杰出的经济学家和哲学家之一，在社会选择、福利分配和贫困研究领域有突出贡献，人类发展与可行能力视角的理论奠基人，同时也是一位始终关注并肯定中国社会发展进程的重要学术领袖。

[5] Gustav Ranis：古斯塔夫·拉尼斯（1929~），德国经济学家，耶鲁大学国际经济学荣誉客座教授，在经济发展的综合性理论、发展中国家的劳动过剩和经济的发展问题领域贡献卓著。

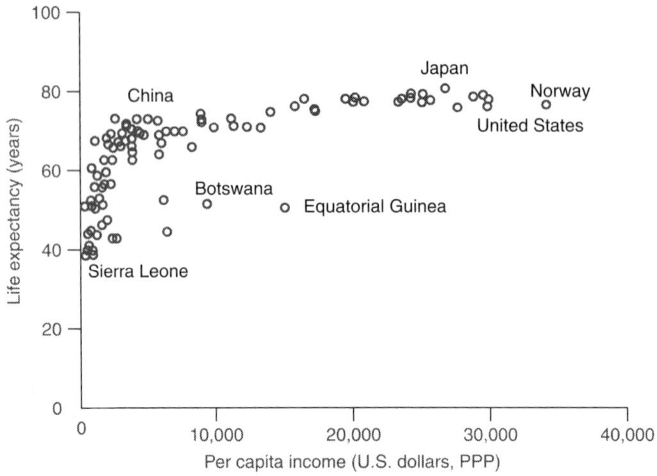

FIGURE 26-1. Life Expectancy and Incomes, 2000

Life expectancies are highly correlated with per capita incomes. Higher incomes allow greater investments in health care, but a healthier population is also more productive. Note that some middle-income African countries have been hard hit by the AIDS epidemic, threatening both health and economic development.

Source: United Nations Development Programme, *Human Development Report*, 2002.

人力资源
Human Resources

Population Explosion: The Legacy of Malthus. Many poor countries are forever running hard just to stay in place. Even as a poor nation's GDP rises, so does its population. Recall our discussion of the Malthusian population trap, where population grows so rapidly that incomes remain at subsistence levels. While the high-income countries left Malthus behind long ago, Africa is still caught in the Malthusian bind of high birth rates and stagnant incomes. And the population expansion has not stopped—demographers project that the poor countries will add about 1 billion people over the next 25 years.

It's hard for poor countries to overcome poverty with birth rates so high. But there are escape routes from overpopulation. One strategy is to take an active role in curbing population growth, even when such actions run against prevailing religious norms. Many countries have introduced educational campaigns and subsidized birth control.

And for countries which manage to boost their per capita incomes, there is the prospect of making the *demographic transition,* which occurs when a population stabilizes with low birth rates and low death rates. Once countries get rich enough, and infant mortality drops, people voluntarily reduce their birth rates. When women are educated and emerge from subservience, they usually decide to spend less of their lives in childbearing. Families substitute quality for quantity—devoting time and incomes to a better education for fewer children. Mexico, Korea, and Taiwan region have all seen their birth rates drop sharply as their incomes have risen and their populations have received more education.

Slowly, the results of economic development and birth control are being felt. The birth rate in poor countries has declined from 44 per 1000 per year in 1960 to 27 per 1000 in 2005, but that is still far higher than the birth rate of 11 per 1000 in the high-income countries. The struggle against poverty induced by excessive population growth continues.

However, the demographic transition has not been ① reached in every corner of the world. Fertility continues at a high rate in much of tropical Africa even as the AIDS epidemic rages through the population and lowers life expectancies in a way not experienced

① 但是，人口的转型并没有波及到世界的每一个角落。尽管艾滋病在人群中蔓延，以及自前几个世纪大瘟疫肆虐以来从未经历的寿命缩短，但在热带非洲的大部分地区，生育率依然居高不下。马尔萨斯的预言就像一个幽灵，始终在中部非洲游徊。

since the great plagues of earlier centuries. The specter of Malthus hangs over much of central Africa.

Human Capital. In addition to dealing with excessive population growth, developing countries must also be concerned with the quality of their human resources. Economic planners in developing countries emphasize the following strategies:

1. *Control disease and improve health and nutrition.* ① Raising the population's health standards not only makes people happier but also makes them more productive workers. Health-care clinics and provision of safe drinking water are vitally useful social capital.
2. *Improve education, reduce illiteracy, and train workers.* ② Educated people are more productive workers because they can use capital more effectively, adopt new technologies, and learn from their mistakes. For advanced learning in science, engineering, medicine, and management, countries will benefit by sending their best minds abroad to bring back the newest advances. But countries must beware of the brain drain, in which the most able people get drawn off to high-wage countries.
3. *Above all, do not underestimate the importance of human resources.* ③ Most other factors can be bought in the international marketplace. Most labor is home-grown, although labor can sometimes be augmented through immigration. The crucial role of skilled labor has been shown again and again when sophisticated mining, defense, or manufacturing machinery fell into disrepair and disuse because the labor force of developing countries had not acquired the necessary skills for its operation and maintenance.

自然资源
Natural Resources

Some poor countries of Africa and Asia have meager endowments of natural resources, and such land and minerals that they do possess must be divided among large populations. Perhaps the most valuable natural resource of developing countries is arable land. Much of the labor force in developing countries is employed in farming. Hence, the productive use of land—with appropriate conservation, fertilizers, and tillage—will go far in increasing a poor nation's output.

Moreover, land ownership patterns are a key to ④ providing farmers with strong incentives to invest in capital and technologies that will increase their land's yield. When farmers own their own land, they have better incentives to make improvements, such as in irrigation systems, and undertake appropriate conservation practices.

Some economists believe that natural wealth from oil or minerals is not an unalloyed blessing. Countries like the United States, Canada, and Norway have used their natural wealth to form the solid base of industrial expansion. In other countries, the wealth has been subject to plunder and *rent seeking* by corrupt leaders and military cliques. Countries like Nigeria and Congo (formerly Zaire), which are fabulously wealthy in terms of mineral resources, failed to convert their underground assets into productive human or tangible capital because of venal rulers who drained that wealth into their own bank accounts and conspicuous consumption.

资 本
Capital

A modern economy requires a vast array of capital. Countries must abstain from current consumption to engage in fruitful roundabout production. But there's the rub, for the poorest countries are near a subsistence standard of living. When you are poor to begin with, reducing current consumption to provide for future consumption seems impossible.

The leaders in the growth race invest at least 20 percent of output in capital formation. By contrast, the poorest agrarian countries are often able to save only 5 percent of national income. Moreover, much of the low level of saving goes to provide the growing population with housing and simple tools. Little is left over for development.

But let's say a country has succeeded in hiking up its rate of saving. Even so, it takes many decades to accumulate the highways, telecommunications systems, hospitals, electricity-generating plants, and other capital goods that underpin a productive economic structure.

Even before acquiring the most sophisticated capi- ⑤ tal, however, developing countries must first build up their *infrastructure*, or social overhead capital, which [6] consists of the large-scale projects upon which a market economy depends. For example, a regional agricultural adviser helps farmers in an area learn of new seeds or crops; a road system links up the different markets; a public-health program inoculates people against typhoid or diphtheria and protects the population beyond those inoculated. In each of these cases it would be impossible for an enterprising firm to capture the social benefits involved, because the firm cannot collect fees from the thousands or even millions of

---

① 疾病控制及健康和营养水平的改善。
② 提高教育水平、减少文盲与劳动者培训。
③ 总之，决不可低估人力资源的重要性。
④ 更为重要的是，土地所有权模式对于激励农民向土地投入资本和技术以增加其收益是关键。
⑤ 然而，在获得最重要的资本之前，发展中国家也必须首先建好自己的基础设施，即社会间接资本——它由市场经济所依托的大型项目组成。

[6] social overhead capital，缩写为 SOC，用来定义一个经济体对所有虚拟产品需要提供可靠服务的基础性资源。可译作**社会间接资本**。

beneficiaries. Because of the large indivisibilities and external effects of infrastructure, the government must step in to make or ensure the necessary investments.

In many developing countries, the single most ① pressing problem is too little saving. Particularly in the poorest regions, urgent current consumption competes with investment for scarce resources. The result is too little investment in the productive capital so indispensable for rapid economic progress.

Foreign Borrowing and Debt Crises

If there are so many obstacles to finding domestic saving for capital formation, why not borrow abroad? Economic theory tells us that a rich country, which has tapped its own high-yield investment projects, can benefit both itself and the recipient by investing in high-yield projects abroad.

However, risks are the necessary companion of reward in foreign lending. The history of lending from rich to poor ② regions shows a cycle of opportunity, lending, profits, overexpansion, speculation, crisis, and drying-up of funds, followed by a new round of lending by yet another group of starry-eyed investors. No sooner has one crisis been forgotten than another one erupts.

It is instructive to review the saga of *emerging markets,* ③ which is the name often given to rapidly growing low- and middle-income countries that are promising areas for foreign investment. In the 1990s, investors in wealthy countries sent their funds abroad in search of higher returns; poor countries, hungry for capital, welcomed this flow of foreign funds. From Thailand to South Africa, both loans and equity investments grew rapidly during the 1990s.

Figure 26-2 shows the interest-rate spread on emerging market securities. This represents the risk premium that borrowers from emerging-market countries would need to pay to attract funds. When the perceived risk is

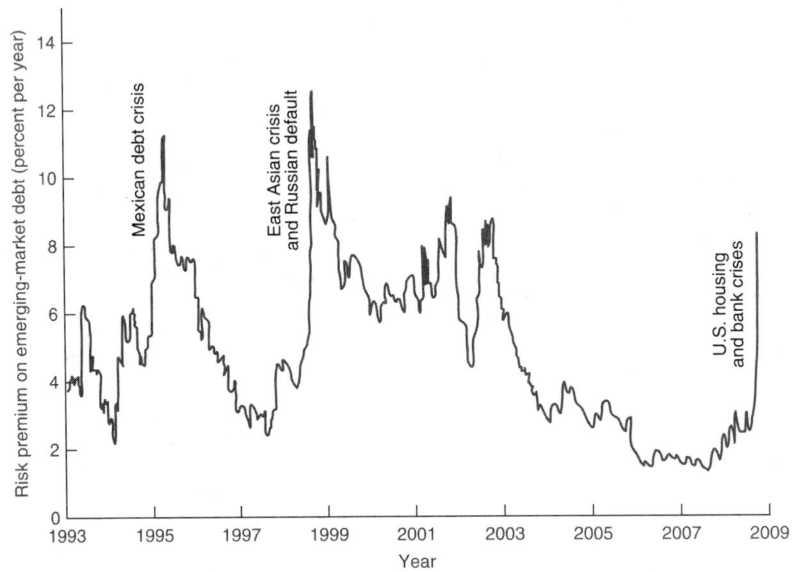

FIGURE 26-2. Spread on Emerging-Market Bonds, 1993–2008

The spread shows the risk premium that borrowers from emerging-market countries paid. It is the premium over safe U.S. dollar securities. Note how the premium shot up during the Mexican crisis in 1995 and the emerging-market crisis and Russian default in 1998. Then market participants became optimistic during the long market boom of the 2000s. All this came to an end with the credit crisis of 2007–2009 as the spread increased.

Source: International Monetary Fund.

① 在许多发展中国家，少得可怜的储蓄是一个最紧迫的难题。特别是那些最贫困的地区，当前的紧急消费始终在与长远投资争夺稀缺资源，其结果是导致经济快速发展不可或缺的生产性资本投资变得捉襟见肘。

② 富国向贫困地区贷款的历史，就是机遇、贷款、利润、过度膨胀、投机、危机和资金枯竭之间的循环，随之又是新一轮的贷款，贷款方是另外一群缺乏理性的狂热投资者。一轮的危机尚未平息，另一轮的危机已爆发在即。

③ 回顾一下新兴市场的传奇是很有启发的。新兴市场是指那些经济快速发展但收入又处于中低水平的国家，它们对外国投资来讲是一片充满希望的热土。

low, the spread is low. When investors become concerned that countries will not pay back their loans, or during periods when the price of risk rises, the spreads skyrocket.

As long as the growth in emerging markets continued, all was quiet and returns were solid. But a slowdown in growth, combined with a series of banking crises, led to massive outflows of short-term funds from Thailand, Indonesia, and South Korea. Bankers who had invested heavily called in their loans. This led to a sharp increase in the supply of the currencies of these countries. Most countries were on fixed-exchange-rate systems, and the selling overwhelmed the countries' foreign exchange reserves. One after another, the currencies of the East Asian countries depreciated sharply. Many called upon the International Monetary Fund (IMF) to provide short-term funds, but the IMF required contractionary monetary and fiscal policies. All these factors together produced sharp business recessions throughout East Asia. When Russia defaulted on its debt in 1998, the emerging-country market panicked and credit spreads shot up.

Within 3 years, most of these countries had recovered from the crisis after a period of *adjustment*—slow output growth, declining real wages, debt reschedulings, and trade surpluses. Economic growth had resumed. The world had ① survived another financial crisis. As Figure 26-2 shows, the spread or risk premium declined gradually over the next decade—until the next crisis erupted in the U.S. financial system in 2007.

技术变革与创新
Technological Change and Innovations

The final and most important wheel is technological advance. Here, developing countries have one major advantage: They can hope to benefit by relying on the technological progress of more advanced nations.

Imitating Technology. Poor countries need not find modern Newtons to discover the law of gravity; they can read about it in any physics book. They don't have to repeat the slow, meandering route to the Industrial Revolution; they can buy tractors, computers, and power looms undreamed of by the great merchants of the past.

Japan and the United States clearly illustrate this in their historical developments. The United States provides a hopeful example to the rest of the world. The key inventions involved in the automobile origi- ② nated almost exclusively abroad. Nevertheless, Ford and General Motors applied foreign inventions and rapidly became the world leaders in the automotive industry.

Japan joined the industrial race late, and only at the end of the nineteenth century did it send students abroad to study Western technology. The Japanese government took an active role in stimulating the pace of development and in building railroads and utilities. By adopting productive foreign technologies, Japan moved into its position today as the world's second-largest industrial economy. The examples of the United States and Japan show how countries can thrive by adapting foreign science and technology to local market conditions.

Entrepreneurship and Innovation. From the histories of the United States and Japan, it might appear that adaptation of foreign technology is an easy recipe for development. You might say: "Just go abroad; copy more-efficient methods; put them into effect at home; then sit back and wait for the extra output to roll in."

Alas, implementing technological change is not that simple. You can send a textbook on chemical engineering to Poorovia, but without skilled scientists, engineers, entrepreneurs, and adequate capital, Poorovia couldn't even think about building a working petrochemical plant. The advanced technology was itself developed to meet the special conditions of the advanced countries—including ample skilled engineers and workers, reliable electrical service, and quickly available spare parts and repair services. These conditions do not prevail in poor countries.

One of the key tasks of economic development is promoting an entrepreneurial spirit. A country ③ cannot thrive without a group of owners or managers willing to undertake risks, open new businesses, adopt new technologies, and import new ways of doing business. At the most fundamental level, innovation and entrepreneurship thrive when property rights are clear and complete and taxes and other drains on profits (such as corruption) are low and predictable. Government can also foster entrepreneurship through specific investments: by setting up extension services for farmers, by educating and training the workforce, and by establishing management schools.

Poor countries often suffer from pervasive corruption. The following discussion by economic

---

① 全球经济再一次从金融危机中幸存。正如图 26-2 所示，息差或风险溢价在接下来的 10 年逐步降低，直到 2007 年美国金融危机再一次爆发。

② 与汽车相关的重要发明几乎无一例外地来自于国外。但是，福特和通用两大汽车公司却将外国的发明致力于应用，从而很快成为世界汽车行业的领袖。

③ 一个国家如果没有一批乐于承担风险、开拓创新、吸纳新技术和引进企业运营新方式的企业家或管理者，就不可能繁荣兴旺起来。

[1] Robert Klitgarrd：罗伯特·科里特伽德（1947~），2005~2009 年在美国著名的克莱尔蒙特研究大学（Claremont Graduate University）出任校长，杰出的经济学家。一生论著颇丰，对全球腐败问题的研究享有盛名。

development specialist Robert Klitgaard explains how [1] corruption undermines economic development:

> At the broadest level, corruption is the misuse of ② office for unofficial ends. The catalogue of corrupt acts includes bribery, extortion, influence-peddling, nepotism, fraud, speed money, embezzlement, and more.
>
> Corruption that undercuts the rules of the ③ game—for example, the justice system or property rights or banking and credit—devastates economic and political development. Corruption that allows polluters to foul rivers or hospitals to extort patients can be environmentally and socially corrosive. When corruption becomes the norm, its effects are crippling. So, although every country has corruption, the varieties and extent differ. The killer is systematic corruption that destroys the rules of the game. It is one of the principal reasons why the most underdeveloped parts of our planet stay that way.

Battling corruption is particularly difficult because the state, which is the instrument of justice, is often itself corrupt.

从恶性循环到良性循环

Vicious Cycles to Virtuous Circles

We have emphasized that poor countries face great obstacles in combining the four elements of progress—labor, capital, resources, and innovation. In addition, countries find that the difficulties reinforce each other in a *vicious cycle of poverty.*

Figure 26-3 illustrates how one hurdle raises yet other hurdles. Low incomes lead to low saving; low saving retards the growth of capital; inadequate capital prevents introduction of new machinery and rapid growth in productivity; low productivity leads to low incomes. Other elements in poverty are also self-reinforcing. Poverty is accompanied by low levels of education, literacy, and skill; these in turn prevent the adoption of new and improved technologies and lead to rapid population growth, which eats away at improvements in output and food production.

Countries that suffer from a vicious cycle can get ④ caught in a *poverty trap.* This syndrome arises when there are multiple equilibria, and one of the equibria may be particularly pernicious. Low-level traps are found in many areas of the social and natural sciences and are illustrated in Figure 26-4. This graph shows average income in period t on the horizontal axis and average income in period $(t + 1)$ on the

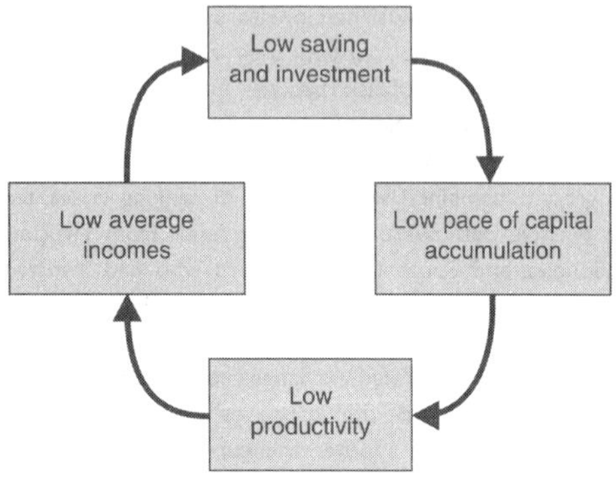

FIGURE 26-3. The Vicious Cycle of Poverty

Many obstacles to development are self-reinforcing. Low levels of income prevent saving, retard capital growth, hinder productivity growth, and keep income low. Successful development may require taking steps to break the chain at many points.

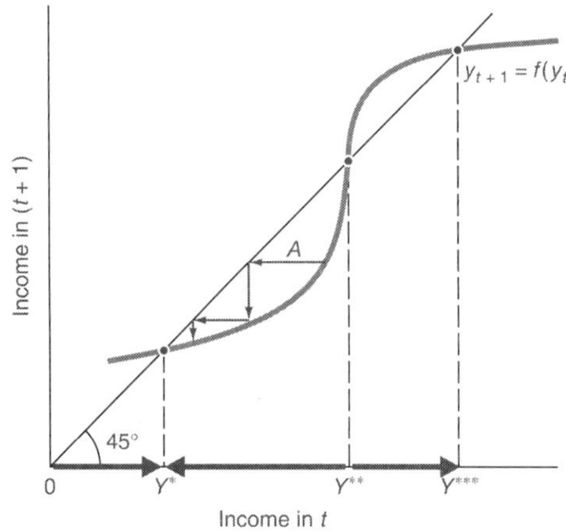

FIGURE 26-4. Countries Can Get Caught in Poverty Traps

When vicious cycles lead to downward spirals, countries can get caught in low-level traps such as Y^*. Note how a country that starts out between 0 and Y^{**} will gravitate back to the low-level trap. Follow the arrows starting at A and see how they lead to Y^*. However, if a country can make a big push to get out of the trap by pushing beyond Y^{**}, then the country enjoys a virtuous cycle of growth to the high-level of income at Y^{***}. Low-level traps can arise because of the interaction of low income, poor health, low saving, low investment, and low productivity.

---

② 从广义上讲，腐败是非官方目的的滥用职权行为。腐败行为包括受贿、以权谋利、权钱交易、任人唯亲、徇私舞弊、快速敛财、滥用公款，等等。

③ 破坏游戏规则的腐败行为，比如对司法系统、产权、银行业以及信贷的腐蚀，破坏了经济和政治发展。而允许污染者污染河流，或者听任医院敲诈病人的腐败行为会演变为环境和社会的灾难。当腐败变成常态之后，其结果是社会经济陷入瘫痪。因此，虽然每一个国家都存在腐败问题，但程度和形态各有不同。体制本身的腐败是致命性的，它可以摧毁一切游戏规则。这就是我们这颗星球上大多数欠发达地区无法摆脱贫困的主要原因之一。

④ 遭遇恶性循环的国家陷于贫困之中无法自拔。当多重均衡出现时，这一病症就会浮现，其中还可能有一种极其有害的均衡。

vertical axis. The nonlinear growth curve $y_{t+1} = f(y_t)$ shows how income moves over time. The 45° line shows the dividing line between positive growth and decline. When a point on the growth curve is above the 45° line, income in $(t + 1)$ is greater than income in t, so income is growing. When the growth curve intersects the 45° line, income is constant and we have an economic equilibrium.

The unusual feature of the *S*-shaped growth curve is that it leads to multiple equilibria. The lower crossing represents a nasty low-level equilibrium trap at Y^*, while the upper one is a benign high-level equilibrium at Y^{***}. Modern economic-development theory points to low-level traps coming from rapid population growth, low productivity, or low "connectivity."

Overcoming the poverty trap may require a concerted effort on many fronts, and some development economists recommend a "big push" forward ① to break the vicious cycle. If a country is fortunate, simultaneous steps to invest more, improve health and education, develop skills, and curb population growth can break the vicious cycle of poverty and stimulate a virtuous circle of rapid economic development. If the country can push itself to the right of Y^{**} in Figure 26-4, then it will take off into sustained economic growth.

经济发展战略
STRATEGIES OF ECONOMIC DEVELOPMENT

We see how countries must combine labor, resources, capital, and technology in order to grow rapidly. But this is no real formula; it is the equivalent of saying ② that an Olympic sprinter must run like the wind. Why do some countries succeed in running faster than others? How do poor countries ever get started down the road of economic development?

Historians and social scientists have long been fascinated by the differences in the pace of economic growth among nations. Some early theories stressed climate, noting that all advanced countries lie in the earth's temperate zone. Others have pointed to custom, culture, or religion as a key factor. Max Weber [3] emphasized the "Protestant ethic" [4] as a driving force behind capitalism. More recently, Mancur Olson [5] has argued that nations begin to decline when their decision structures become brittle and interest groups or oligarchies prevent social and economic change.

No doubt each of these theories has some validity for a particular time and place. But they do not hold up as universal explanations of economic development. Weber's theory leaves unexplained why the cradle of civilization appeared in the Near East [6] and Greece while the later-dominant Europeans [7] lived in caves, worshiped trolls, and wore bearskins. Where do we find the Protestant ethic in bustling China? How can we explain that a country like Japan, with a rigid social structure and powerful lobbies, has become one of the world's most productive economies?

Even in the modern era, people become attached to simple, holistic explanations of economic development. People once considered import substitution (the replacement of imports with domestically produced goods) to be the most secure development strategy. Then, in the 1970s, reliance on labor-intensive techniques was thought advantageous. Today, as we will see, economists tend to emphasize reliance on market forces with an outward orientation. This history should serve as a warning to be wary of oversimplified approaches to complex processes.

Nonetheless, historians and development economists have learned much from the study of the varieties of economic growth. What are some of the lessons? The following account represents a montage of important ideas developed in recent years. Each approach describes how countries might break out of the vicious cycle of poverty and begin to mobilize the four wheels of economic development.

落后假说
The Backwardness Hypothesis

One view emphasizes the international context of development. We saw above that poorer countries have important advantages that the first pioneers along the path of industrialization did not. Developing nations can now draw upon the capital, skills, and technology of more-advanced countries. A hypothesis advanced by Alexander Gerschenkron of Harvard suggests that *relative backwardness* itself may aid development. Countries can buy modern textile machinery, efficient pumps, miracle seeds, chemical fertilizers, and medical supplies. Because they can lean on the technologies of advanced countries, today's developing countries can grow more rapidly than did Britain or Western Europe in the period 1780–1850. As low-income countries draw upon the

[5] Mancur Olson：曼瑟尔·奥尔森（1932~1998），美国经济学家和社会学家，对与制度经济学相关的私有财产、税收、公共品、集体决议、合同权利等问题的研究做出了很大贡献。

[6] Near East：近东，与远东和中东一起均为欧洲中心论的产物，系欧洲人指除伊朗和阿富汗之外的亚洲西南部和非洲东北部地区，通常指地中海东部沿岸、非洲东北部和亚洲西南部地区，有时还包括巴尔干半岛。

[7] the later-dominant Europeans：通常指16世纪至18世纪晚期（一般指从文艺复兴开始至以蒸汽机为代表的工业革命这段时期），以对外掠夺和扩张性对外贸易为特征的重商主义占统治地位的欧洲国家。

---

① 克服贫困陷阱需要很多部门合力而为，有些发展经济学家建议用一种“强大的推力”来打破这种恶性循环。

② 但是，这不是一个现实可行的发展模式，其说法无异于要求一位奥运会短跑运动员以风速奔跑。

[3] Max Weber：马克斯·韦伯（1864~1920），德国社会学家、哲学家和政治经济学家，对社会学理论、社会研究和社会学科自身均具深远影响，与卡尔·马克思（Karl Marx，1818~1883）和埃米尔·杜尔凯姆（Émile Durkheim，1858~1917）一起并称为社会学的三大奠基人。

[4] Protestant ethic：马克斯·韦伯在其代表性著作《新教伦理与资本主义精神》（*The Protestant Ethic and the Spirit of Capitalism*）中主张，宗教的影响是造成东西方文化发展差距的主要原因，并且强调新教伦理在资本主义、官僚制度和法律权威的发展上所扮演的重要角色。韦伯在其另一部著作《政治学的使命》（*Politics as a Vocation*）中将国家定义为一个“拥有合法使用暴力的垄断地位”的实体，这对西方现代政治学的发展影响极大。

more productive technologies of the leaders, we would expect to see *convergence* of countries toward the technological frontier. Convergence occurs ① when those countries or regions that have initially low incomes tend to grow more rapidly than ones with high incomes.

① 当那些原本是低收入的国家和地区比这些高收入国家和地区的发展速度更快时，就会出现这种趋同现象。

工业化与农业
Industrialization vs. Agriculture

In most countries, incomes in urban areas are almost double those in rural areas. And in affluent nations, much of the economy is in industry and services. Hence, many nations jump to the conclusion that industrialization is the cause rather than the effect of affluence.

We must be wary of such inferences, which confuse the association of two characteristics with causality. Some people say, "Rich people drive BMWs, but ② driving a BMW will not make you a rich person." Similarly, there is no economic justification for a poor country to insist upon having its own national airline and large steel mill. These are not the fundamental necessities of economic growth.

The lesson of decades of attempts to accelerate ③ industrialization at the expense of agriculture has led many analysts to rethink the role of farming. Industrialization is capital-intensive, attracts workers into crowded cities, and often produces high levels of unemployment. Raising productivity on farms may require less capital, while providing productive employment for surplus labor. Indeed, if Bangladesh could increase the productivity of its farming by 20 percent, that advance would do more to release resources for the production of comforts than would trying to construct a domestic steel industry to displace imports.

国家与市场
State vs. Market

The cultures of many developing countries are hostile to the operation of markets. Often, competition ④ among firms or profit-seeking behavior is contrary to traditional practices, religious beliefs, or vested interests. Yet decades of experience suggest that extensive reliance on markets provides the most effective way of managing an economy and promoting rapid economic growth.

What are the important elements of a market-oriented policy? The important elements include the predominance of private property and ownership, an outward orientation in trade policy, low tariffs and few quantitative trade restrictions, the promotion of small business, and the fostering of competition. Moreover, markets work best in a stable macroeconomic environment—one in which taxes are predictable and inflation is low.

经济增长与外向型经济
Growth and Outward Orientation

A fundamental issue of economic development concerns a country's stance toward international trade. Should developing countries attempt to be self-sufficient, to replace most imports with domestic production? (This is known as a strategy of *import* ⑤ *substitution.*) Or should a country strive to pay for the imports it needs by improving efficiency and competitiveness, developing foreign markets, and keeping trade barriers low? (This is called a strategy of *outward orientation* or *openness.*) ⑥

Policies of import substitution were often popular in Latin America until the 1980s. [7] The policy most frequently used toward this end was to build high tariff walls around domestic manufacturing industries so that local firms could produce and sell goods that would otherwise be imported.

A policy of openness keeps trade barriers as low as practical, relying primarily on tariffs rather than quotas and other nontariff barriers. It minimizes the interference with financial flows and allows supply and demand to operate in financial markets. It avoids a state monopoly on exports and imports. It keeps government regulation to the minimum necessary for an orderly market economy. Above all, it relies primarily on a private market system of profits and losses to guide production, rather than depending on public ownership and control or the commands of a government planning system.

The success of outward-oriented policies is best illustrated by the successful East Asian countries. A generation ago, countries like South Korea and Singapore had per capita incomes one quarter to one-third of those in the wealthiest Latin American countries. Yet, by saving large fractions of their national incomes and channeling these to high-return export industries, the East Asian countries overtook every Latin American country by the late 1980s. The secret to success was not a doctrinaire laissez-faire policy, for the governments in

---

② "有钱人都开宝马，但开着宝马绝不可能把你造就为有钱人。"

③ 近几十年来的教训——为加速工业化而牺牲农业，已经唤起许多分析家重新思考农业的作用。

④ 企业间的竞争或者追逐利润的行为常常与传统习惯、宗教信仰或者既得利益背道而驰。

⑤ import substitution：进口替代

⑥ outward orientation or openness：外向型或者开放型经济

[7] often popular in Latin America until the 1980s：20 世纪 80 年代之前半个世纪，拉美国家普遍实施的进口替代政策，使拉美各国在进入 80 年代后陷入严重的债务危机、通货膨胀和经济危机之中。在西方发达国家和国际金融机构的多重压力下，他们开始了贸易自由化、放宽对外资的限制、私有化、汇率金融改革、加强市场导向等新自由主义经济发展模式的转变。

fact engaged in selective planning and intervention. Rather, the openness and outward orientation allowed the countries to reap economies of scale and the benefits of international specialization and thus to increase employment, use domestic resources effectively, enjoy rapid productivity growth, and provide enormous gains in living standards.

While openness provides many benefits, excessive openness, particularly to short-term financial flows, is an invitation to speculative attack. What investors lendeth, investors can taketh back. This syndrome can cause financial and banking crises, as we noted for the East Asian economies in our discussion earlier in this chapter.

简 评
Summary Judgment

Decades of experience in dozens of countries have led many development economists to the following summary view of the way government can best promote rapid economic development:

> The government has a vital role in establishing ①
> and maintaining a healthy economic environment. It must ensure respect for the rule of law, enforce contracts, fight corruption, and orient its policies toward competition and innovation. Government must play a leading role in investments in social overhead capital—in education, health, communications, energy, and transportation—but it should look to the private sector where it has no comparative advantage. Government should resist the temptation to produce everything at home. A firm commitment to openness to trade and foreign investment will help ensure that a country moves quickly toward the best world practices in different sectors.

经济发展的替代模式
C. ALTERNATIVE MODELS FOR DEVELOPMENT

People continually look for ways to improve their
living standards. Economic betterment is particu- ②
larly compelling for poor countries seeking a path to the riches they see around them. This textbook has surveyed in depth the mixed market economy of the United States, which combines fundamentally free markets with a sizable government sector. What other alternatives are available?

"主义"大餐
A BOUQUET OF "ISMS"

At one extreme is *free-market absolutism*, which holds that the best government is the least government. At the other extreme is complete communism, with the government operating a collectivized economic order in which the first-person singular hardly exists. Between the extremes of laissez-faire and communism lie mixed capitalism, managed markets, socialism, and many combinations of these models. In this section, we describe briefly some of the influential alternative strategies for growth and development:

1. *The Asian managed-market approach.* South Korea, ③
Singapore, and other countries of East Asia have devised their own brands of economics that combine strong government oversight with powerful market forces.
2. *Socialism.* Socialist thinking encompasses a wide variety of different approaches. In Western Europe after World War II, socialist governments operating in a democratic framework expanded the welfare state, nationalized industries, and planned their economies. In recent years, however, these countries moved back toward a free-market framework with extensive deregulation and privatization.
3. *Soviet-style communism.* For many years, the clearest alternative to the market economy existed in the Soviet Union. Under the Soviet model, the state owned all the land and most of the capital, set wages and most prices, and directed the microeconomic operation of the economy.

核心困境：市场与指令
The Central Dilemma: Market vs. Command

A survey of alternative economic systems may seem like a bewildering array of economic "isms." And indeed, there is a great variety in the way countries organize their economies.

One central issue runs through all the great ④
debates about alternative economic systems: Should economic decisions be taken primarily by the *private market* or by *government command?*

---

① 政府对于建立和维护健康经济环境有重要作用。它必须确保法规的尊严，执行契约，打击腐败，并使政策向竞争和创新倾斜。在教育、医疗保健、通信、能源和交通这些需要社会常规资本投入的领域，政府必须起到引领作用。但在那些政府并不具有比较优势的领域，就必须将目光投向私人部门。政府应该抵制本国能生产一切的诱惑。坚定地实施贸易和外资的开放政策有助于确保一个国家的不同部门快速追赶国际先进水平。

② 经济学的意义之一是驱使贫穷国家寻找到一条可行的致富之路。

③ 亚洲管理市场的模式。

④ 在所有关于经济体制选择这一重大问题的争论中，有一个核心问题始终贯穿其中：经济决策是应该主要交给私有市场，还是靠政府指令？

At one end of the spectrum is the *market economy*. In a market system, people act voluntarily and primarily for financial gain or personal satisfaction. Firms buy factors and produce outputs, selecting inputs and outputs in a way that will maximize their profits. Consumers supply factors and buy consumer goods to maximize their satisfactions. Agreements on production and consumption are made voluntarily and with the use of money, at prices determined in free markets, and on the basis of arrangements between buyers and sellers. Although individuals differ greatly in terms of economic power, the relationships between individuals and firms are horizontal in nature, essentially voluntary, and nonhierarchical.

At the other end of the spectrum is the *command economy*, where decisions are made by government bureaucracy. In this approach, people are linked by a vertical relationship, and control is exercised by a multilevel hierarchy. The planning bureaucracy determines *what* goods are produced, *how* they are produced, and *for whom* output is produced. The highest level of the pyramid makes the major decisions and develops the elements of the plan for the economy. The plan is subdivided and transmitted down the bureaucratic ladder, with the lower levels of the hierarchy executing the plan with increasing attention to detail. Individuals are motivated by coercion and legal sanctions; organizations compel individuals to accept orders from above. Transactions and commands may or may not use money; trades may or may not take place at established prices.

In between are the socialist and the managed-market economies. In both cases government plays an important role in guiding and directing the economy, though much less so than in a command economy. The tension between markets and command runs through all discussions about alternative economic systems. Let us look in more detail at some of the alternatives to the mixed market economies. ①

亚洲模式
THE ASIAN MODELS

亚洲“龙”
Asian Dragons

Development specialists sometimes look to the countries of East Asia as examples of successful development strategies. The rapid economic growth over the last half-century in South Korea and Singapore, is sometimes called the *East Asian miracle*. [2] Table 26-2 compares the performance of the "Asian dragons" with those of other major areas over recent years. Latin America and sub-Saharan Africa have been growing at a positive rate. However, look at the East Asian and Pacific region, and especially China. Countries in this region have had a phenomenal rate of growth, particularly in the last three decades.

A World Bank study analyzed the economic policies of different regions to see whether any patterns emerged.[1] The results confirmed common

[1] See this chapter's Further Reading section for the World Bank study on the East Asian miracle.

Region	Average Growth of Real per Capita GDP 1962–1973	1973–1995	1995–2006
East Asia and Pacific	3.6	4.8	6.4
China	4.0	4.7	8.2
South Asia	2.0	2.5	4.4
India	2.2	2.3	4.9
Latin America and Caribbean	4.0	1.7	1.5
Sub-Saharan Africa	2.8	0.7	1.7

TABLE 26-2. Attention to Fundamentals Spurred Growth for the Asian Dragons

Source: *World Development Indicators* (2008), available at *www.worldbank.org/*.

① 市场与指令之间的紧张关系贯穿于所有关于经济体制选择问题的讨论中。让我们更为详细地看一下混合型市场经济的某些选择模式。

[2] *East Asian miracle*：东亚奇迹。有关“亚洲四小龙”，在西方有两种表述。“Asian dragons”系含有贬义的说法，遗憾的是我们接受了这种表述。其实还有一种褒义的说法，即“Asian Tigers”，在欧洲使用较多，西方人听来很亲切，但国人知之甚少。这也从另一个侧面反映了美国和欧洲对东方文化潜意识中截然相反的不同态度。另外，18 版中这一节的题目冠以“*Dragons and Laggards*”，用“Latin Laggards”（拉美人的懒散）来强烈地映衬东亚人的勤劳。以巴西为代表的拉美新兴经济使萨缪尔森彻底修改了这一节。

views but also found a few surprises. Here are the high points:

- *Investment rates.* The Asian dragons followed the classic recipe of high investment rates to ensure that their economies benefited from the latest technology and could build up the necessary infrastructure. Investment rates among the Asian dragons were almost 20 percentage points higher than those of other regions.
- *Macroeconomic fundamentals.* Successful countries had a steady hand on macroeconomic policies, keeping inflation low and saving rates high. They invested heavily in human capital as well as in physical capital and did more to promote education than any other developing region. The financial systems were managed to ensure monetary stability and a sound currency.
- *Outward orientation.* The Asian dragons were outward-oriented, often keeping their exchange rates undervalued to promote exports, encouraging exports with fiscal incentives, and pursuing technological advance by adopting best-practice techniques of high-income countries.

中国的崛起
The Rise of China

One of the major surprises in economic development during the last three decades was the rapid growth of the Chinese economy. After the Chinese revolution of 1949, China initially adopted a Soviet-style central-planning system. The high-water mark ② of centralization came with the Cultural Revolution of 1966–1969, which led to an economic slowdown in China. After the death of the revolutionary leader Mao Tse-tung, a new generation concluded that economic reform was necessary if the Communist party was to survive. Under Deng Xiaoping's leadership from 1977 to 1997, China decentralized a great deal of economic power and promoted competition.

To spur economic growth, the Chinese leadership has taken dramatic steps such as setting up "special economic zones" which allowed capitalist and foreign enterprises to operate. The most rapidly growing parts of China have been the coastal regions, such as the southern region near Hong Kong and in greater Shanghai. These areas have become closely integrated with countries outside China and have attracted considerable foreign investment. In addition, China has allowed private and foreign firms, free from government planning or control, to operate alongside state-owned firms. These innovative forms of ownership have grown rapidly and by the 2000s were producing more than half of China's GDP.

The continued rapid growth of the Chinese economy has surprised observers almost as much as did the collapse of the Soviet economy. As shown in Table 26-2, the growth in per capita GDP accelerated from 4.0 percent per year in 1962–1973 to 8.2 percent per year in 1995–2006. Exports from China to the United States grew over 17 percent per year during the last decade. By 2008, China had annual exports of almost $2 trillion and had accumulated $1½ trillion in foreign exchange reserves.

The future of the Chinese economic model is being watched closely around the world. The undoubted success of outward orientation, particularly to foreign investment, is an especially striking feature of Chinese economic policy.

社会主义模式
SOCIALISM

[1] As a doctrine, socialism developed from the ideas of Karl Marx and other radical thinkers of the nineteenth century. Socialism is a middle ground between laissez-faire capitalism and the central-planning model, which we discuss in the next subsection. A few common elements characterize most socialist philosophies:

- *Government ownership of productive resources.* Socialists traditionally believed that the role of private property should be reduced. Key industries such as railroads and banking should be nationalized (that is, owned and operated by the state). In recent years, because of the poor performance of many state-owned enterprises, enthusiasm for nationalization has ebbed in most advanced democracies.
- *Planning.* Socialists are suspicious of the "chaos" of the marketplace and question the allocational efficiency of the invisible hand. They insist that a planning mechanism is needed to coordinate different sectors. In recent years, planners have

---

[1] *The Rise of China*：中国的崛起。18 版中本节的题目为"*The Chinese Giant: Market Leninism*"（中国巨人：市场列宁主义）。这一修改反映了萨缪尔森对中国崛起的心态变化，也是他在本版亲撰的前言冠以"*A Centrist Proclamation*"的佐证。

② 在 1966~1969 年文化大革命期间出现了高度空前的集中，导致中国经济下滑。

emphasized subsidies to promote the rapid development of high-technology industries, such as microelectronics, aircraft manufacturing, and biotechnology; these policies are sometimes called "industrial policies."

- *Redistribution of income.* Inherited wealth and the ① highest incomes are to be reduced by the militant use of government taxing powers; in some Western European countries, marginal tax rates have reached 98 percent. Government social security benefits, free medical care, and cradle-to-grave welfare services paid for with progressive taxes increase the well-being of the less privileged and guarantee minimum standards of living for all.
- *Peaceful and democratic evolution.* Socialists often advocate the peaceful and gradual extension of government ownership—evolution by ballot rather than revolution by bullet.

Socialist approaches fell out of favor with the stagnation in Europe and the success of market-oriented ② economies. Thoughtful socialists are combing through the wreckage to find a future role for this branch of economic thought.

失败的模式：中央计划经济
THE FAILED MODEL: CENTRALLY PLANNED ECONOMIES

For many years, developing countries looked to the Soviet Union and other communist countries as role models on how to industrialize. Communism offered both a theoretical critique of Western capitalism and a seemingly workable strategy for economic development. We begin by reviewing the theoretical underpinnings of Marxism and communism and then examine how the Soviet-style command economy ③ worked in practice.

Karl Marx: Economist as Revolutionary

On the surface, Karl Marx (1818–1883) lived an uneventful life, studiously poring through books in the British Museum, writing newspaper articles, and working on his scholarly studies of capitalism. Although originally attracted to German universities, his atheism, pro-constitutionalism, and radical ideas led him to journalism. He was eventually exiled to Paris and London, where he wrote his massive critique of capitalism, *Capital* (1867, 1885, 1894). [6]

The centerpiece of Marx's work is an incisive analysis of the strengths and weaknesses of capitalism. Marx argued that all commodity value is determined by labor content—both the direct labor and the indirect labor embodied in capital equipment. For example, the value of a shirt comes from the efforts of the textile workers who put it together, plus the efforts of the workers who made the looms. By imputing all the value of output to labor, Marx attempted to show that profits—the part of output that is produced by workers but received by capitalists—amount to "unearned income."

In Marx's view, the injustice of capitalists' receiving unearned income justifies transferring the ownership of factories and other means of production from capitalists to workers. He trumpeted his message in *The Communist Manifesto* [7] (1848): "Let the ruling classes tremble at a Communist revolution. The proletarians have nothing to lose but their chains." And the ruling capitalist classes did tremble at Marxism for more than a century!

Like many great economists, but with more passion than most, Marx was deeply moved by the struggle of working people and hoped to improve their lives. He penned the words that appear on his gravestone: "Up 'til now philosophers have only interpreted the world in various ways. The point, though, is to change it!" Our epitaph for Marx might echo the appraisal of the distinguished intellectual historian, Sir Isaiah Berlin: "No thinker in the nineteenth century [8] has had so direct, deliberate, and powerful an influence on mankind as Karl Marx."

马克思的预言
Marx's Prophesies

Marx saw capitalism as inevitably leading to socialism. In Marx's world, technological advances enable capitalists to replace workers with machinery as a means of earning greater profits. But this increasing accumulation of capital has two contradictory consequences. As the supply of available capital increases, the rate of profit on capital falls. At the same time, with fewer jobs, the unemployment rate rises and [4] wages fall. In Marx's terms, the "reserve army of the unemployed" would grow, and the working class [5] would become increasingly "immiserized"—by which he meant that working conditions would deteriorate and workers would grow progressively alienated from their jobs.

① 收入的再分配。严格行使政府的税收权力来减少继承的财富和高收入。在某些西欧国家，边际税率已经高达98%。累进税用于政府提供的社会保障补贴、免费的医疗保健，以及"从摇篮到坟墓"的终身福利待遇，来增加贫困人口的福利，保证所有公民的最低生活标准。

② the success of market-oriented economies：市场导向型经济的成功

③ how the Soviet-styled command economy worked in practice：苏联模式的指令经济是如何实际运行的

[4] Karl Marx：卡尔·马克思，西方学术界将其定位为在19~20世纪和达尔文、弗洛伊德一起改变世界的三位哲人之一，与马克斯·韦伯（Max Weber，1864~1920）和埃米尔·杜尔凯姆（Émile Durkheim，1858~1917）一起并称为社会学的三大奠基人。

[5] British Museum：大不列颠博物馆，俗称大英博物馆，与巴黎的卢浮宫和纽约的大都会博物馆并称西方三大博物馆。

[6] *Capital*：《资本论》。在将近整个20世纪的中国，《资本论》几乎占据着至高无上的地位，连20世纪30年代初著名的经济学家王亚南和郭大力先生为了更好地将它译为中文，竟然先拿亚当·斯密的 *The Wealth of Nations* 练手，这部"翻译习作"就是今天的中文版《国富论》。

[7] *The Communist Manifesto*：《共产党宣言》，由马克思执笔，与恩格斯一起共同起草，中文本1904年转译自日本，早期很多的中文译著均自日语译本转译，又译《共产主义宣言》。革命一生的毛泽东晚年专门在英语教师的辅导下，通过一个一个地查阅英汉词典，认真细致地圈阅了英文版的《宣言》，以自身革命领袖的亲身实践准确地求证和解读马克思理论，并质疑翻译水准。

[8] Sir Isaiah Berlin：塞亚·伯林爵士（1909~1997），拉脱维亚裔的英国哲学家、历史学家，《思想史》（*Intellectual History*）的奠基人。R.G. Collingwood（柯林伍德，1889~1943，美国哲学家、历史学家和画家）认为"人类全部的历史就是一部思想史"，其广义为基督教教义史。

As profits decline and investment opportunities at home become exhausted, the ruling capitalist classes resort to imperialism. Capital tends to seek higher rates of profit abroad. And, according to this theory (particularly as later expanded by Lenin), the [1] foreign policies of imperialist nations increasingly attempt to win colonies and then mercilessly milk surplus value from them.

Marx believed that the capitalist system could not continue this unbalanced growth forever. Marx predicted increasing inequality under capitalism, along with a gradual emergence of class consciousness among the downtrodden proletariat. Business ② cycles would become ever more violent as mass poverty resulted in macroeconomic underconsumption. Finally, a cataclysmic depression would sound the death knell of capitalism. Like feudalism before it, capitalism would contain the seeds of its own destruction.

The *economic interpretation of history* is one of Marx's lasting contributions to Western thought. Marx argued that economic interests lie behind and determine our values. Why do business executives vote for conservative candidates, while labor leaders support those who advocate raising the minimum wage or increasing unemployment benefits? The reason, Marx held, is that people's beliefs and ideologies reflect the material interests of their social and economic class. In fact, Marx's approach is hardly foreign to mainstream economics. It generalizes Adam Smith's analysis of self-interest from the dollar [3] votes of the marketplace to the ballot votes of elections and the bullet votes of the barricades.

从书本教条到应对策略：苏联式的指令经济
From Textbooks to Tactics: Soviet-Style Command Economy

Marx wrote extensively about the faults of capital- ④ ism, but he left no design for the promised socialist land. His arguments suggested that communism would arise in the most highly developed industrial countries. Instead, it was feudal Russia that adopted the Marxist vision. Let's examine this fascinating and horrifying chapter of economic history.

Historical Roots. An analysis of Soviet communism is of the utmost importance for economics because the Soviet Union served as a laboratory for theories about the functioning of a command economy. Some economists claimed that socialism simply could not work; the Soviet experience proved them wrong. Its advocates argued that communism would overtake capitalism; Soviet history also refutes this thesis.

Although czarist Russia grew rapidly from 1880 to ⑤ 1914, it was considerably less developed than industrialized countries like the United States or Britain. World War I brought great hardship to Russia and allowed the communists to seize power. From 1917 to 1933, the Soviet Union experimented with different socialist models before settling on central planning. But dissatisfaction with the pace of industrialization led Stalin to undertake a radical new venture [6] around 1928—collectivization of agriculture, forced-draft industrialization, and central planning of the economy.

⑤ 虽然沙皇俄国的经济在1880~1914年期间实现了高速的增长，但与英国和美国这样的工业化国家相比，很大程度上还是欠发达的。

[6] Stalin：斯大林（Joseph Stalin，1879~1953），原姓朱加什维利（Jughashvili，1879~1953）。前苏联联共（布）中央总书记、苏联部长会议主席。1928年放弃列宁的新经济政策，全力推行高度中央集权化的工业化，通过几个五年计划使苏联这个落后国家迅速改变了面貌。先后发动大清洗以及肃反运动大规模地清除异己，为死后遭清算埋下祸根。

The other part of the Soviet "great leap forward" came through the introduction of economic planning for rapid industrialization. The planners created the first 5-year plan to cover the period 1928–1933. The first plan established the priorities of Soviet planning: heavy industry was to be favored over light industry, and consumer goods were to be the residual sector after all the other priorities had been met. Although there were many reforms and changes in emphasis, the Stalinist model of a command economy applied in the Soviet Union and Eastern Europe countries until the fall of Soviet communism at the end of the 1980s.

How the Command Economy Functioned. In the Soviet-style command economy, the broad categories of output were determined by political decisions. Military spending in the Soviet Union was always allocated a substantial part of output and scientific resources, while the other major priority was investment. Consumption claimed the residual output after the quotas of higher-priority sectors were filled.

In large part, decisions about how goods were to be produced were made by the planning authorities. Planners first decided on the quantities of final outputs (the *what*). Then they worked backward from outputs to the required inputs and the flows among different firms. Investment decisions were specified in great detail by the planners, while firms had

[1] Lenin：弗拉基米尔·伊里奇·列宁（Vladimir Ilyich Lenin，1870~1924），"列宁"系笔名，原名乌利亚诺夫（Ulyanov），著名的马克思主义者和无产阶级革命家、布尔什维克党创建者和前苏联的缔造者，20世纪伟大的政治家、思想家和理论家。

② 大量贫困导致宏观经济消费不足，使商业周期更剧烈地波动。最终，经济大萧条敲响了资本主义的丧钟。像之前的封建主义一样，资本主义为自己播下了自身灭亡的种子。

[3] Adam Smith：亚当·斯密（1723~1790），古典经济学之父，苏格兰道德哲学家，老亚当·斯密的遗腹子，一生与母亲相依为命，终身未娶。详见5页[1]。

④ 马克思广泛地论述了资本主义的缺陷，但他没有对社会主义的美好蓝图设计任何行动方案。他预言，共产主义会在经济最为发达的工业化国家中出现。然而事实上，是封建主义的俄国接受了马克思的思想。

considerable flexibility in deciding upon their mix of labor inputs.

Clearly no planning system could specify all the activities of all the firms—this would have required trillions of commands every year. Many details were left to the managers of individual factories. It was here, in what is called the *principal-agent problem,* that the command economy ran into its deepest difficulties.

The principal-agent problem arises because the person at the top of a hierarchy (the "principal") wants to provide appropriate incentives for the people making the decisions down the hierarchy (the "agents") to behave according to the principal's wishes. In a market economy, profits and prices serve as the mechanism for coordinating consumers and producers. A command economy is plagued by an inability to find an efficient substitute for profits and prices as a way of motivating the agents.

A useful example of the failure to solve the principal-agent problem is found in Soviet book publishing. In a market economy, commercial decisions about books are made primarily on the basis of profit and loss. In the Soviet Union, because profits were taboo, planners instead used quantitative targets. A first approach was to reward firms according to the number of books produced, so publishers printed thousands of thin unread volumes. Faced with a clear incentive problem, the center (principal) changed the system so that the producers (agents) were rewarded on the basis of the number of pages printed, and the result was fat books with onion-skin paper and large type. The planners then changed the criterion to the number of words—to which the publishers responded by printing huge volumes with tiny type. None of these mechanisms was capable of signaling consumer wants effectively.

The principal-agent problem crops up in organi- ①
zations in all countries, but the Soviet model had few mechanisms (like bankruptcy in markets and elections for public goods) to provide an ultimate check on waste.

Comparative Economic Performance. From World War II until the mid-1980s, the United States and the Soviet Union engaged in a superpower competition for public opinion, military superiority, and economic dominance. How well did the command economies perform in the economic growth race? Any attempt ②
at answering this question is bedeviled by the absence of reliable statistics. Most economists believed until recently that the Soviet Union grew rapidly from 1928 until the mid-1960s, with growth rates perhaps surpassing those in North America and Western Europe. After the mid-1960s, growth in the Soviet Union stagnated and output actually began to decline.

A revealing comparison of the performance of market and command economies can be made by contrasting the experiences of East Germany and West Germany. These countries started out with roughly equal levels of productivity and similar industrial structures at the end of World War II. After four decades of capitalism in the West and Soviet-style socialism in the East, productivity in East Germany had fallen to a level estimated between one-fourth and one-third of that in West Germany. Moreover, the East German growth tended to emphasize production of intermediate goods and commodities of little value to consumers. Quantity, not quality, was the goal.

Balance Sheet. Is there a final balance sheet on Soviet central planning? The Soviet model demonstrated that a command economy can work—it is capable of mobilizing capital and labor and producing both guns and butter. But the Soviet economy, with borders closed to trade, technologies, and people, became increasingly obsolete over time. Innovation withered because of poor incentives. In competition with the open-market economies, particularly as the world turned to increasingly high-quality goods and services, Russia could export virtually nothing except raw materials and military equipment.

Growth slowed, and per capita income declined ③
in the latest period of central planning. Its leaders finally abandoned Soviet central planning as it was seen to be morally, politically, and economically bankrupt.

从马克思到市场
From Marx to Market

Beginning in 1989, the countries of Eastern Europe and the former Soviet Union rejected the communist experiment and introduced market economies.

The road back to capitalism proved a rocky one for many countries. Among the challenges were the following: (1) liberalizing prices to allow supply and demand to determine prices, (2) imposing

---

① 所有国家的组织都面临委托—代理问题。但在苏联模式中，却几乎没有制约浪费的解决机制（如市场上的破产和公共品的选择）。

② 任何回答这个问题的尝试都会受到缺少可靠统计数据的困扰。

③ 在中央计划经济的末期，人均收入下降，经济增长缓慢。

hard budget constraints on subsidized enterprises, (3) privatizing enterprises so that the decisions about buying, selling, pricing, producing, borrowing, and lending would be made by private agents, and (4) establishing the institutions of the market, such as a modern banking system, the legal framework for commerce, and the tools for monetary and fiscal policy.

Some countries, like Slovenia and the Czech Republic, made the transition relatively quickly and are now increasingly integrated into the European Union as functioning market democracies. Russia has renationalized much of its energy industry and has become an energy powerhouse. Other countries are still mired in autocracy, corruption, and rigid economic structures. The lessons here are useful for any country attempting to establish the institutions of a market economy.

最后注意：审慎乐观
A Final Note of Cautious Optimism

This chapter has described the problems and prospects of poor countries struggling to be rich and free—to provide the dry houses, education, electric lights, fast horses, automobiles, and long vacations of the excerpt that opened this chapter. What are the prospects of attaining these goals?

We close with a sober assessment by Jeffrey Sachs [1]
of Columbia University and the Earth Institute, one [2]
of the outstanding development economists of today, and his co-author Andrew Warner: [3]

> The world economy [today] looks much like the world economy at the end of the nineteenth century. A global capitalist system is taking shape, drawing almost all regions of the world into arrangements of open trade and harmonized economic institutions. As in the nineteenth century, this new round of globalization promises to lead to economic convergence for the countries that join the system. . . . ④
>
> And yet there are also profound risks for the consolidation of market reforms in Russia, China, and Africa, as well as for the maintenance of international agreements among the leading countries. . . . The spread of capitalism in the [last] twenty-five years is an historic event of great promise and significance, but whether we will be celebrating the consolidation of a democratic and market-based world system [twenty-five years hence] will depend on our own foresight and good judgments in the years to come. ⑤

[1] Jeffrey Sachs：杰弗里·萨克斯（1954~），"休克疗法"之父，29岁即成为哈佛大学经济学教授，现任美国哥伦比亚大学地球研究院院长、联合国秘书长、首席经济顾问、《联合国千年发展目标》（Millennium Development Goals）首席专家。曾于2004和2005年两度被《时代》周刊评为"全世界100位最具影响力的人物"。

[2] Earth Institute：地球学院，1995年在哥伦比亚大学成立，关注可持续发展和全球贫困问题。

SUMMARY

A. Population Growth and Development

1. Malthus's theory of population rests on the law of diminishing returns. He contended that population, if unchecked, would tend to grow at a geometric (or exponential) rate, doubling every generation or so. But each member of the growing population would have less land and natural resources to work with. Because of diminishing returns, income could grow at an arithmetic rate at best; output per person would tend to fall so low as to stabilize population at a subsistence level of near-starvation.
2. Over the last two centuries, Malthus and his followers have been criticized on several grounds. Among the major criticisms are that Malthusians ignored the possibility of technological advance and overlooked the significance of birth control as a force in lowering population growth. The neo-Malthusians see limits to growth from environmental constraints, particularly global warming, where markets provide distorted signals.

B. Economic Growth in Poor Countries

3. Most of the world's population lives in developing countries, which have relatively low per capita incomes. Such countries often exhibit rapid population growth, a low level of literacy, poor health, and a high proportion of their population living and working on farms.
4. The key to development lies in four fundamental factors: human resources, natural resources, capital, and technology. Explosive population causes problems as the Malthusian prediction of diminishing returns haunts the poorest countries. On the constructive agenda, improving the population's health, education, and technical training has high priority.
5. Investment and saving rates in poor countries are low because incomes are so depressed that little can be saved for the future. International financing of investment in poor countries has witnessed many crises over the last two centuries.

---

[3] Andrew Warner：安德鲁·华纳，美国国家经济研究院所属千年挑战社团（Millennium Challenge Corporation，National Bureau of Economic Research，NBER）首席经济学家。

④ 今天的世界经济与19世纪末期的世界经济极为相似。全球资本主义体系正在形成，几乎把全世界所有地区都带入了开放贸易和经济相调机制。正如19世纪一样，新一轮的全球化浪潮，导致了经济趋同，所有国家都卷入这一体系之中。

⑤ 然而，俄罗斯、中国和非洲国家巩固市场改革，以及所有主要国家维持国际协议，都存在着深不可测的风险。……资本主义在过去25年里的传播意义深远。但在今后的25年里，我们是否能为民主的、以市场为基础的世界体系的巩固而庆祝，取决于在未来几年我们自己的远见卓识和准确判断。

6. Technological change is often associated with investment and new machinery. It offers much hope to the developing nations because they can adopt the more productive technologies of advanced nations. This requires entrepreneurship. One task of development is to spur internal growth of the scarce entrepreneurial spirit.
7. Numerous theories of economic development help explain why the four fundamental factors are present or absent at a particular time. Development economists today emphasize the growth advantage of relative backwardness, the need to respect the role of agriculture, and the art of finding the proper boundary between state and market. The most recent consensus is on the advantages of openness.
8. Countries should be concerned about falling into the poverty trap, in which a vicious cycle of poverty leads to poor performance and locks a country into continued poverty.
9. Recall our summary judgment on the role of government policies: (*a*) Foster the rule of law. (*b*) Make the critical investments in human and social overhead capital. (*c*) Limit the public sector to clear areas of comparative advantage. (*d*) Maintain an economy open to trade and foreign investment.

C. Alternative Models for Development

10. Many "isms" have competed with the mixed market economy as models for economic development. Alternative strategies include the managed-market approach of the East Asian countries, socialism, and the Soviet-style command economy.
11. The managed-market approach of Japan and the Asian dragons, such as South Korea, Hong Kong (China), Taiwan (China), and Singapore, proved remarkably successful over the last quarter-century. Among the key ingredients were macroeconomic stability, high investment rates, a sound financial system, rapid improvements in education, and an outward orientation in trade and technology policies.
12. Socialism is a middle ground between capitalism and communism, stressing government ownership of the means of production, planning by the state, income redistribution, and peaceful transition to a more egalitarian world.
13. Historically, Marxism took its deepest economic roots in semi-feudal Russia and was then imposed on the rest of the Soviet Union and Eastern Europe. Studies of resource allocation in these countries show that resources were allocated by central planning with severe distortions of prices and outputs. The Soviet economy depended primarily on energy-intensive heavy industry and the military in its early decades. Stagnation and poor incentives for innovation left Russia and other centrally planned countries at income levels far below those of North America, Japan, and Western Europe. These countries have all rejected the centralized command economy for some variant of the mixed market economy.

CONCEPTS FOR REVIEW

Population Theory

Malthus's population theory
geometric vs. arithmetic growth

Economic Development

developing country
indicators of development
four elements in development
vicious cycles, virtuous circles, poverty trap
backwardness hypothesis

Alternative Models for Development

the central dilemma of market vs. command
socialism, communism
the principal-agent problem
command economy

FURTHER READING AND INTERNET WEBSITES

Further Reading

One of the most influential books of all times is T. R. Malthus, *Essay on Population* (1798, many publishers). An online version can be found at *www.ac.wwu.edu/~stephan/malthus/malthus.0.html*. The influential books by the new Malthusians Donella H. Meadows, Dennis L. Meadows, and Jørgen Randers are *The Limits to Growth* (Potomac, Washington, D.C., 1972) and *Beyond the Limits* (Chelsea Green, Post Mills, Vt., 1992).

The study on the East Asian miracle is contained in World Bank, *The East Asia Miracle: Economic Growth and Government Policies* (World Bank, Washington, D.C., 1993). The quotation at the end is from Jeffrey Sachs and Andrew Warner, "Economic Reform and the Process of Global Integration," *Brookings Papers on Economic Activity*, no. 1, 1995, pp. 63–64.

A highly readable account of developments in Soviet economic history is contained in Alec Nove, *An Economic History of the U.S.S.R.*, 3d ed. (Penguin, Baltimore, 1990). A careful study of the Soviet economic system is provided by Paul R. Gregory and Robert C. Stuart, *Russian and Soviet Economic Performance and Structure*, 6th ed. (Harper & Row, New York, 1997).

Websites

The World Bank has information on its programs and publications at its site, *www.worldbank.org;* the International Monetary Fund (IMF) provides similar information at *www.imf.org.* The United Nations website has links to most international institutions and their databases at *www.unsystem.org.* A good source of information about high-income countries is the Organisation for Economic Cooperation and Development (OECD) website, *www.oecd.org.* U.S. trade data are available at *www.census.gov.* You can find information on many countries through their statistical offices. A compendium of national agencies is available at *www.census.gov/main.*

Population data are available from the United Nations at *www.un.org/popin/.* One of the best sources for studies of developing countries is the World Bank, especially the annual *World Development Review* at *www.worldbank.org.* The quote from Klitgaard was published in *Finance and Development,* March 1998, and can be found at *www.gwdg.de/~uwvw/icr.htm.*

QUESTIONS FOR DISCUSSION

1. A geometric progression is a sequence of terms (g_1, g_2, . . . , g_t, g_{t+1}, . . .), in which each term is the same multiple of its predecessor:

   $$\frac{g_2}{g_1} = \frac{g_3}{g_2} = \cdots = \frac{g_{t+1}}{g_t} = \beta$$

   If $\beta = 1 + i > 1$, the terms grow exponentially like compound interest, where i is the interest rate. An arithmetic progression is a sequence (a_1, a_2, a_3, . . . , a_t, a_{t+1}, . . .), in which the difference between each term and its predecessor is the same constant:

   $$a_2 - a_1 = a_3 - a_2 = \cdots = a_{t+1} - a_t = \cdots = \lambda$$

   Give examples of each. Satisfy yourself that any geometric progression with $\beta > 1$ must eventually surpass any arithmetic progression. Relate this to Malthus's theory.
2. Recall that Malthus asserted that unchecked population would grow geometrically, while food supply—constrained by diminishing returns—would grow only arithmetically. Use a numerical example to show why per capita food production must decline if population is unchecked while diminishing returns lead food production to grow more slowly than labor inputs.
3. Do you agree with the celebration of material well-being expressed in the chapter's opening quotation? What would you add to the list of the benefits of economic development?
4. Delineate each of the four important factors driving economic development. With respect to these, how was it that the high-income oil-exporting countries became rich? What hope is there for a country like Mali, which has very low per capita resources of capital, land, and technology?
5. Some fear the "vicious cycle of underdevelopment." In a poor country, rapid population growth eats into whatever improvements in technology occur and lowers living standards. With a low per capita income, the country cannot save and invest and mainly engages in subsistence farming. With most of the population on the farm, there is little hope for education, decline in fertility, or industrialization. If you were to advise such a country, how would you break the vicious cycle?
6. Compare the situation a developing country faces today with the one it might have faced (at an equivalent level of per capita income) 200 years ago. Considering the four wheels of economic development, explain the advantages and disadvantages that today's developing country might experience.
7. Some economists today question whether it is wise to allow complete openness on both financial and current accounts. They argue that allowing free flow of short-term financial movements increases vulnerability to speculative attacks. Give the pros and cons of limiting short-term financial movements. Might you want to

use a tax on short-term flows rather than quantitative restrictions?

8. Analyze the way that *what, how,* and *for whom* are solved in a Soviet-style command economy, and compare your analysis with the solution of the three central questions in a market economy.
9. **Advanced problem** (relying upon the growth accounting of Chapter 25): We can extend our growth-accounting equation to include three factors and write the following equation:

$$g_Q = s_L g_L + s_K g_K + s_R g_R + \text{T.C.}$$

where g_Q = the growth rate of output, g_i = the growth rate of inputs (i = inputs to production: L for labor, K for capital, and R for land and other natural resources), and s_i = the contribution of each input to output growth as measured by its share of national income ($0 \le s_i \le 1$ and $s_L + s_K + s_R = 1$). T.C. measures technological change.

 a. In the poorest developing countries, the share of capital is close to zero, the main resource is agricultural land (which is constant), and there is little technological change. Can you use this to explain the Malthusian hypothesis in which per capita output is likely to be stagnant or even to decline (i.e., $g_Q < g_L$)?
 b. In advanced economies, the share of land resources drops to virtually zero. Why does this lead to the growth-accounting equation studied in the previous chapter? Can you use this to explain how countries can avoid the Malthusian trap of stagnant incomes?
 c. According to economists who are pessimistic about future prospects (including a group of *neo-Malthusians* from the Club of Rome), T.C. is close to zero, the available supply of natural resources is declining, and the share of resources is large and rising. Does this explain why the future of industrial societies might be bleak? Which assumptions of the neo-Malthusians might you question?

CHAPTER

27

Exchange Rates and the International Financial System

汇率与国际金融体系

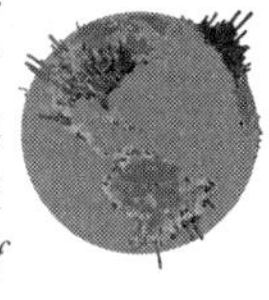

[1] 约翰·斯图尔特·米尔：John Stuart Mill（1806~1873），曾被严复译作“穆勒”，著名的英国哲学家和经济学家，19 世纪极具影响力的古典自由主义思想家。本句话改编自米尔的代表性著作《政治经济学原理》（*The Principles of Political Economy*）第三编的第 17 章，原文如下：

From this exposition we perceive in what consists the benefit of international exchange, or in other words, foreign commerce. Setting aside its enabling countries to obtain commodities which they could not themselves produce at all; its advantage consists in a more efficient employment of the productive forces of the world.

所以，这句话应译为：

The benefit of international trade—a more efficient employment of the productive forces of the world.

John Stuart Mill [1]

国际贸易的益处是将全世界的生产要素进行了更加有效的应用。

Economically, no nation is an island unto itself. When the bell tolls recession or financial crisis, the sound reverberates around the world.

We see this point illustrated dramatically in the ② twentieth century, which we can divide into two distinct periods. The period from 1914 to 1945 was characterized by destructive competition, shrinking international trade, growing financial isolation, hot and cold military and trade wars, dictatorships, and depression. By contrast, after World War II, most of the world enjoyed growing economic cooperation, widening trade linkages, increasingly integrated financial markets, an expansion of democracy, and rapid economic growth. This stark contrast empha- ③ sizes how high the stakes are in the wise management of our national and global economies.

What are the economic links among nations? The important economic concepts involve international trade and finance. International trade in goods and ser- ④ vices allows nations to raise their standards of living by specializing in areas of comparative advantage, exporting products in which they are relatively efficient while importing ones in which they are relatively inefficient. In a modern economy, trade takes place using different currencies. The international financial system is the lubricant that facilitates trade and finance by allowing people to use and exchange different currencies.

International trade is sometimes seen as a zero- ⑤ sum, Darwinian conflict. This view is misleading at best and wrong at worst. International trade and finance, like all voluntary exchange, can improve the well-being of all participants in the transactions. When the United States sells wheat to Japan and imports cars, using the medium of dollars and yen, these transactions lower prices and raise living standards in both countries.

But economic integration (sometimes called *globalization*) is not without its perils. Some periods, such as the early 2000s, were relatively tranquil, while others saw crisis after crisis. The 1930s saw the gold standard and the international trading regime collapse. The 1970s saw the failure of the fixed-exchange-rate system, oil embargoes, and a sharp increase in inflation. The 1990s saw a succession of financial crises: a crisis of confidence in the exchange-rate regime in Europe in 1991–1992, capital flight from Mexico in 1994–1995, banking and currency panics in East Asia in 1997, a default on Russian debt and a global liquidity freeze in 1998, and a series of currency problems in Latin America.

After a period of relative tranquility, the world was shocked in 2007–2009 by the bursting of a housing-price bubble, mortgage foreclosures, and financial failures in the world's most sophisticated

---

② 对于这一点，我们可以把 20 世纪分为截然不同的两个阶段来予以说明。

③ 这一鲜明的对比说明了高度智慧地管理好本国和全球经济何等重要。

④ 各国将自己相对高效的产品予以出口，而与此同时，进口自己相对低效的产品，这样，通过在自己有比较优势的领域专业化，商品和服务的国际贸易使各国提高了生活水平。在现代经济中，贸易要使用不同的货币。通过让人们使用和交换不同的货币，国际金融体系成为推动国际贸易和国际金融的润滑剂。

⑤ 国际贸易有时被视为是一种达尔文进化论式的零和游戏。这种观点往好了说是一种误导，往坏了说是错误的。

economy, the United States. The global nature of the economic system was seen in 2007–2009, when the financial crisis in the United States spread around the world. All of these crises required careful management by the fiscal and monetary authorities of the major countries involved.

This chapter and the next one survey international macroeconomics. This topic includes the principles governing the international monetary system, which is the major focus of the present chapter, as well as the impact of foreign trade on output, employment, and prices, which is covered in the next chapter.

International macroeconomics involves many of the most controversial questions of the day: Does foreign trade raise or lower our output and employment? What is the link between domestic saving, domestic investment, and the trade balance? What are the causes of the occasional financial crises that spread contagiously from country to country? What has been the effect of the European Monetary Union on Europe's macroeconomic performance? And why has the United States become ① the world's largest debtor country in the last decade? The economic stakes are high in finding wise answers to these questions.

对外贸易的发展趋势
TRENDS IN FOREIGN TRADE

An economy that engages in international trade is ② called an **open economy.** A useful measure of openness is the ratio of a country's exports or imports to its GDP. Figure 27-1 shows the trend in the shares of imports and exports for the United States over the last half-century. It shows the large export surplus in the early years after World War II as America financed the reconstruction of Europe. But the share of imports and exports was low in the 1950s and 1960s. With growth abroad and a lowering of trade barriers, the share of trade grew steadily and reached an average of 13 percent of GDP in 2008.

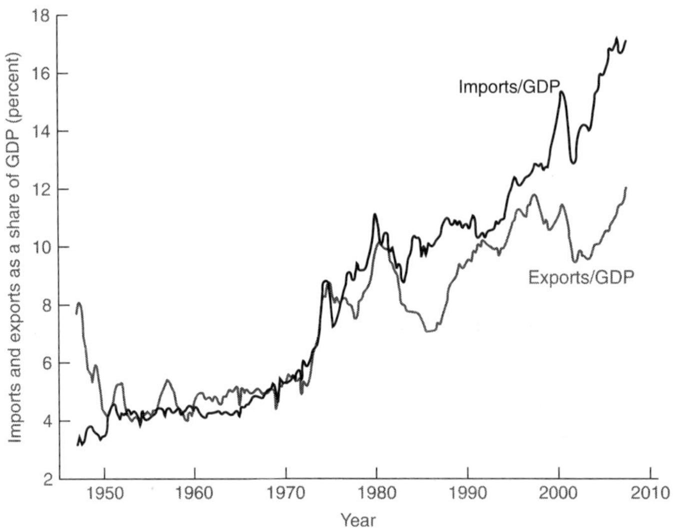

FIGURE 27-1. Growing U.S. Openness

Like all major market economies, the United States has increasingly opened its borders to foreign trade since World War II. This has led to a growing share of output and consumption involved in international trade. Since the 1980s, imports have far outdistanced exports, causing the United States to become the world's largest debtor nation.

Source: U.S. Bureau of Economic Analysis.

---

① 在过去的 10 年中，美国为什么会成为全世界最大的债务国？探寻这些问题的答案是经济学研究需要高度关切的问题。

② 所谓的**开放经济**即融入国际贸易的经济。衡量开放程度的有效指标是该国的出口和进口贸易在其 GDP 中所占的比重。

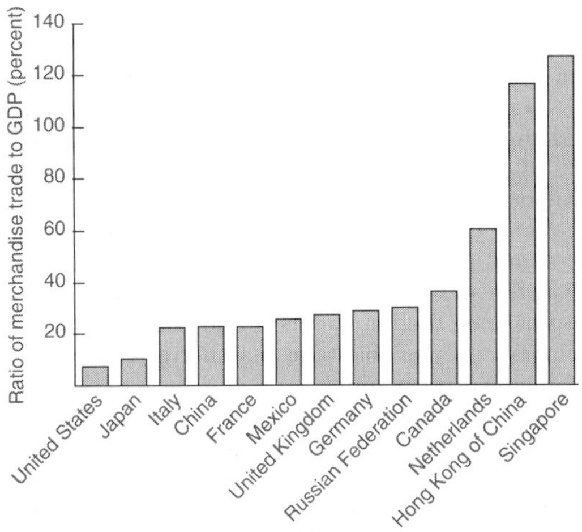

FIGURE 27-2. Openness Varies Enormously across Regions

Large countries like the United States have small trade shares, while tiny countries like Singapore trade more than they produce.

Source: World Trade Organization. Shares are the ratio of merchandise trade to GDP for the period 2002–2005.

You might be surprised to learn that the United States is a relatively self-sufficient economy. Figure 27-2 shows the trade proportions of selected countries. Small countries and those in highly integrated regions like Western Europe are more open than the United States. Moreover, the degree of openness is much higher in many U.S. industries than in the overall economy, particularly in manufacturing industries like steel, textiles, consumer electronics, and autos. Some industries, such as education and health care, are largely insulated from foreign trade.

国际收支平衡

A. THE BALANCE OF INTERNATIONAL PAYMENTS

国际收支账户

BALANCE-OF-PAYMENTS ACCOUNTS

We begin this chapter with an overview of the way nations keep their international accounts. Economists keep score by looking at income statements and balance sheets. In the area of international economics, the key accounts are a nation's **balance of international payments.** These accounts provide a systematic statement of all economic transactions between that country and the rest of the world. Its major components are the current account and the financial account. The basic structure of the balance of payments is shown in Table 27-1, and each element is discussed below.

借方与贷方

Debits and Credits

Like other accounts, the balance of payments records each transaction as either a plus or a minus. The general rule in balance-of-payments accounting is the following:

If a transaction earns foreign currency for the ①
nation, it is called a *credit* and is recorded as a plus item. If a transaction involves spending foreign currency, it is a *debit* and is recorded as a negative item. In general, exports are credits and imports are debits.

Exports earn foreign currency, so they are credits. Imports require spending foreign currency, so they are debits. How is the U.S. import of a Japanese camera recorded? Since we ultimately pay for it in Japanese yen, it is clearly a debit. How shall we

I. Current account
- Merchandise (or "trade balance")
- Services
- Investment income
- Unilateral transfers

II. Financial account
- Private
- Government
  - Official reserve changes
  - Other

TABLE 27-1. Basic Elements of the Balance of Payments

The balance of payments has two fundamental parts. The *current account* represents the spending and receipts on goods and services along with transfers. The *financial account* includes purchases and sales of financial assets and liabilities. An important principle is that the two must always sum to zero:

$$\text{Current account} + \text{financial account} = \text{I} + \text{II} = 0$$

① 如果一笔交易可以为该国赚取外汇，则被称作贷方，以正值计入账户。如果一笔交易需要支出外汇，则被称作借方，以负值计入账户。一般来讲，出口为贷方，进口则为借方。

treat interest and dividend income on investments received by Americans from abroad? Clearly, they are credit items like exports because they provide us with foreign currencies.

收支平衡明细

Details of the Balance of Payments

Balance on Current Account. The totality of items under section I in Table 27-1 is the **balance on current account.** This includes all items of income and outlay—imports and exports of goods and services, investment income, and transfer payments. The current-account balance is akin to the net ① income of a nation. It is conceptually similar to net exports in the national output accounts. In the past, many writers concentrated on the **trade balance,** which consists of merchandise imports and exports. The composition of merchandise imports and exports consists mainly of primary commodities (like food and fuels) and manufactured goods. In an earlier era, the mercantilists strove for a trade surplus (an excess of exports over imports), calling this a "favorable balance of trade." They hoped to avoid an "unfavorable trade balance," by which they meant a trade deficit (an excess of imports over exports). Even today, we find traces of mercantilism when nations seek to maintain trade surpluses.

Today, economists avoid this language because a trade deficit is not necessarily harmful. As we will see, the trade deficit is really a reflection of the imbalance between domestic investment and domestic saving. Often, a nation has a trade deficit ② because it has a low saving rate (perhaps because of a government deficit). It might also have a trade deficit because it has productive uses for domestic investment (as is the case for the United States). An opposite case of a trade surplus would arise when a country has high saving with few productive domestic investments for its saving (as, for example, Saudi Arabia, with vast oil revenues but meager investment opportunities).

In addition, *services* are increasingly important in international trade. Services consist of such items as shipping, financial services, and foreign travel. A third item in the current account is *investment income,* which includes the earnings on foreign investments (such as earnings on U.S. assets abroad). One of the major developments of the last two decades has been the growth in services and investment income. A final element is transfers, which represent payments not in return for goods and services.

Table 27-2 presents a summary of the U.S. balance of international payments for 2007. Note its two main components: current account and financial account. Each item is listed by name in column (a). Credits are listed in column (b), while column (c) shows the debits. Column (d) then lists the net credits or debits; it shows a credit if on balance the item added to our stock of foreign currencies or a debit if the total subtracted from our foreign-currency supply.

In 2007, America's merchandise exports led to credits of $1149 billion. But at the same time, merchandise imports led to debits of $1965 billion. The *net* difference was a merchandise trade deficit of $815 billion. This trade deficit is listed in column (d). (Be sure you understand why the algebraic sign is shown as − rather than as +.) From the table we see that net services and net investment income were positive. The total current-account deficit including merchandise trade, services, investment income, and unilateral transfers was $739 billion for 2007.

(We have omitted an additional item in the accounts called the capital account, which involves capital transfers. This item is extremely small and can be ignored in most circumstances.)

Financial Account. We have now completed our analysis of the current account. But how did the United States "finance" its $739 billion current-account deficit in 2007? It must have either borrowed or reduced its foreign assets, for by definition, when you buy something, you must either pay for it or borrow for it. This identity means that *the balance of international payments as a whole must by definition show a final balance of zero.*

Financial-account transactions are asset transactions between Americans and foreigners. They occur, for example, when a Japanese pension fund buys U.S. government securities or when an American buys stock in a German firm.

Credits and debits are somewhat more complicated in the financial accounts. The general rule, which is drawn from double-entry business accounting, is this: Increases in a country's assets and

---

① 经常账户余额与一个国家的净收入相类似。从概念上与国民产出账户的净出口相似。

② 一个国家经常出现贸易赤字是因为该国储蓄率低（或政府赤字）。对国内投资的高效运用（如美国就是这种情况）也是一个国家可能出现贸易赤字的原因。

U.S. Balance of Payments, 2007
(billions of dollars)

(a) Items	(b) Credits (+)	(c) Debits (−)	(d) Net credits (+) or debits (−)
I. Current account			−739
a. Merchandise trade balance	1,149	−1,965	−815
b. Services	479	−372	107
c. Investment income	782	−708	74
d. Unilateral transfers			−104
II. Financial account [lending (−) or borrowing (+)]			739
a. Private borrowing or lending	1,451	−1,183	268
b. Government			
Official U.S. reserve assets, changes			−24
Foreign official assets in the U.S., changes			413
c. Statistical discrepancy			83
III. Sum of current and financial accounts			0

TABLE 27-2. Basic Elements of the U.S. Balance of Payments, 2007

Source: U.S. Bureau of Economic Analysis. Note that the totals may not equal the sum of the components because of rounding.

decreases in its liabilities are entered as debits; conversely, decreases in a country's assets and increases in its liabilities are entered as credits. A debit entry is represented by a negative (−) sign and a credit entry by a positive (+) sign.

You can usually get the right answer more easily if you remember this simplified rule: Think of the United States as exporting and importing stocks, bonds, or other securities. Then you can treat these exports and imports of securities like other exports and imports. When we borrow abroad, we are sending IOUs (in the form of Treasury bills or corporate [1] stocks) abroad and getting foreign currencies. Is this a credit or a debit? Clearly, this is a credit because it brought foreign currencies into the United States.

Similarly, if U.S. banks lend abroad to finance a computer assembly plant in Mexico, the U.S. banks are importing IOUs from the Mexicans and the United States is losing foreign currencies; this is clearly a debit item in the U.S. balance of payments.

Line II shows that in 2007 the United States was a net *borrower:* we borrowed abroad more than we lent to foreigners. The United States was a net exporter of IOUs (a net borrower) in the amount of $739 billion.[1]

The Paradox of Wealthy Borrowers

What is the typical pattern of surpluses and deficits of nations? You might think that poor countries would have higher productivity of capital and would therefore borrow from rich countries, while rich countries would have used up their investment opportunities and should therefore lend to poor countries.

Indeed, this pattern did hold for most of U.S. history. ②
During the nineteenth century, the United States imported more than it exported. Europe lent the difference, which allowed the United States to build up its capital stock. The

[1] As with all economic statistics, the balance-of-payments accounts necessarily contain statistical errors (called the "statistical discrepancy"). These errors reflect the fact that many flows of goods and finance (from small currency transactions to the drug trade) are not recorded. We include the statistical discrepancy in line II(c) of Table 27-2.

[1] IOUs：IOU 的复数，即“I owe you”的读音缩略用大写字母表示，有“借据”、“借条”之意。

② 毫无疑问，这个模式存在于美国的大部分历史中。在整个 19 世纪，美国的进口量都大于其出口量。美国通过向欧洲借款来弥补这部分差额，这就使美国建立起了资本存量。

United States was a typical young and growing debtor nation. From about 1873 to 1914, the U.S. balance of trade moved into surplus. Then, during World War I and World War II, America lent money to its allies England and France for war equipment and postwar relief needs. The United States emerged from the wars a creditor nation, with a surplus from earnings on foreign investments matched by a deficit on merchandise trade.

The pattern around the world is quite different today because of financial globalization. In an open financial world, the pattern of trade surpluses and deficits is largely determined by the balance of saving and investment. Table 27-3 shows a summary of the major regions today. This table shows that the pattern of lending and borrowing has virtually no relationship to levels of economic development but is primarily determined by saving and investment patterns. The most interesting situation on the list is that of the United States, which is a wealthy country borrowing abroad. We will explore the reasons for this paradox of wealthy borrowers in the next chapter.

Current Account Balance (billions of dollars)

Region	2007
Rich and low saving:	
United States	−739
Rich and high saving:	
Japan	211
Other rich countries	160
Resource-rich and diversifying:	
OPEC/Middle East	257
Russia	76
Poor and high saving:	
China	372
Poor and low saving:	
Sub-Saharan Africa	−25
Other	−45

TABLE 27-3. Pattern of Current Accounts around the World, 2007

The United States is the world's largest borrower with its low saving rate and stable investment climate. Important savers are rich and high-saving countries (such as Japan), resource-rich countries looking for financial diversification (such as Russia and OPEC countries), and poor and high-saving countries (such as China, which has a saving rate even higher than its high investment rate). The poorest countries do get some small net inflows.

Source: International Monetary Fund, *World Economic Outlook*, available online at *www.imf.gov*.

汇率的决定

B. THE DETERMINATION OF FOREIGN EXCHANGE RATES

汇率
FOREIGN EXCHANGE RATES

We are all familiar with domestic trade. When I buy Florida oranges or California computers, I naturally want to pay in dollars. Luckily, the orange grower and the computer manufacturer want payment in U.S. currency, so all trade can be carried out in dollars. Economic transactions within a country are relatively simple.

But suppose I am in the business of selling Japanese bicycles. Here, the transaction becomes more complicated. The bicycle manufacturer wants to be paid in Japanese currency rather than in U.S. dollars. Therefore, in order to import the Japanese bicycles, I must first buy Japanese yen (¥) and use those yen to pay the Japanese manufacturer. Similarly, if the Japanese want to buy U.S. merchandise, they must first obtain U.S. dollars. This new complication involves foreign exchange.

Foreign trade involves the use of different ① national currencies. The **foreign exchange rate** is the price of one currency in terms of another currency. The foreign exchange rate is determined in the **foreign exchange market,** which is the market where different currencies are traded.

We begin with the fact that most major countries have their own currencies—the U.S. dollar, the Japanese yen, the Mexican peso, and so forth. (European countries are an exception in that they have a common currency, the Euro.) We follow the convention of measuring exchange rates, which we denote by the symbol e, as the amount of foreign currency that can be bought with 1 unit of the domestic currency. For example, the foreign exchange rate of the dollar might be 100 yen per U.S. dollar (¥100/$).

When we want to exchange one nation's money for that of another, we do so at the relevant foreign exchange rate. For example, if you traveled to Mexico in the summer of 2008, you would have received

① 对外贸易涉及不同国家货币的使用。**外汇汇率**是使用另外一种货币来表示一种货币的价格。外汇汇率由**外汇市场**决定，外汇交易是由不同货币进行交易的平台。

about 11 Mexican pesos for 1 U.S. dollar. There is a foreign exchange rate between U.S. dollars and the currency of every other country. In 2008, the foreign exchange rate per U.S. dollar was 0.68 Euro, 0.54 British pound, and 103 Japanese yen.

With foreign exchange, it is possible for me to buy a Japanese bicycle. Suppose its quoted price is 20,000 yen. I can look in the newspaper for the foreign exchange rate for yen. Suppose the rate is ¥100/$. I could go to the bank to convert my $200 into ¥20,000. With my Japanese money, I then can pay the exporter for my bicycle in the currency it wants.

You should be able to show what Japanese importers of American trucks have to do if they want to buy, say, a $36,000 truck from an American exporter. Here yen must be converted into dollars. You will see that, when the foreign exchange rate is 100 yen per dollar, the truck costs them ¥3,600,000.

Businesses and tourists do not have to know anything more than this for their import or export transactions. But the economics of foreign exchange rates cannot be grasped until we analyze the forces underlying the supply and demand for foreign currencies and the functioning of the foreign exchange market.

The foreign exchange rate is the price of one currency in terms of another currency. We measure the foreign exchange rate (e) as the amount of foreign currency that can be bought with 1 unit of domestic currency: ①

$$e = \frac{\text{foreign currency}}{\text{domestic currency}} = \frac{\text{yen}}{\$} = \frac{\text{Euros}}{\$} = \cdots$$

外汇市场
THE FOREIGN EXCHANGE MARKET

Like most other prices, foreign exchange rates vary from week to week and month to month according to the forces of supply and demand. The *foreign exchange market* is the market in which currencies of different countries are traded and foreign exchange rates are determined. Foreign currencies are traded at the retail level in many banks and firms specializing in that business. Organized markets in New York, Tokyo, London, and Zurich trade hundreds of billions of dollars of currencies each day.

We can use our familiar supply and demand curves to illustrate how markets determine the price of foreign currencies. Figure 27-3 shows the supply and demand for U.S. dollars that arise in dealings with Japan.[2] The *supply* of U.S. dollars comes from people in the United States who need yen to purchase Japanese goods, services, or financial assets. The *demand* for dollars comes from people in Japan who buy U.S. goods, services, or investments and who, accordingly, need dollars to pay for these items. The price of foreign exchange—the foreign exchange rate—settles at that price where supply and demand are in balance.

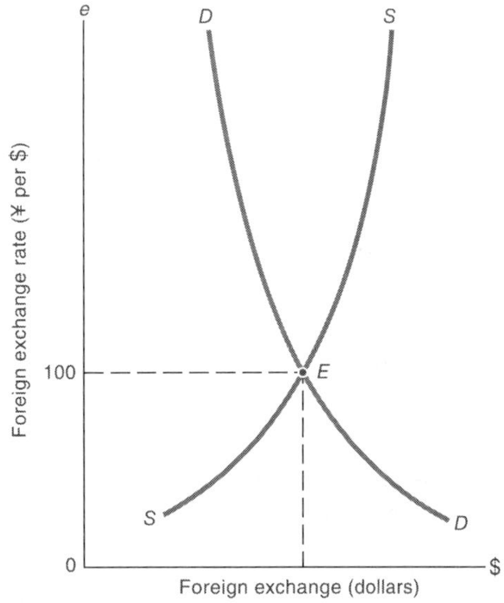

FIGURE 27-3. Exchange-Rate Determination

Behind the supplies and demands for foreign exchange lie purchases of goods, services, and financial assets. Behind the demand for dollars is the Japanese desire for American goods and investments. The supply of dollars comes from Americans desiring Japanese goods and assets. Equilibrium comes at E. If the foreign exchange rate were above E, there would be an excess supply of dollars. Unless the government bought this excess supply with official reserves, market forces would push the foreign exchange rate back down to balance supply and demand at E. ②

[2] This is a simplified example in which we consider only the bilateral trade between Japan and the United States.

① 外汇汇率是以另外一种货币来表示的一种货币的价格。我们可以使用以一个单位的本国货币所能购买的外国货币的数量来衡量汇率（e）。

② 外汇供给与需求的背后是商品、服务以及金融资产的交易。

Let us first consider the supply side. The supply of U.S. dollars to the foreign exchange market originates when Americans need yen to buy Japanese automobiles, cameras, and other commodities, to vacation in Tokyo, and so forth. In addition, foreign exchange is required if Americans want to purchase Japanese assets, such as shares in Japanese companies. In short, *Americans supply dollars when they purchase foreign goods, services, and assets.*

In Figure 27-3, the vertical axis is the foreign exchange rate (e), measured in units of foreign currency per unit of domestic currency—that is, in yen per dollar, in Mexican pesos per dollar, and so forth. Make sure you understand the units here. The horizontal axis shows the quantity of dollars bought and sold in the foreign exchange market.

The supply of U.S. dollars is represented by the upward-sloping *SS* curve. The upward slope indicates that as the foreign exchange rate rises, the number of yen that can be bought per dollar increases. This means, with other things held constant, that the prices of Japanese goods fall relative to those of American goods. Hence, Americans will tend to buy more Japanese goods, and the supply of U.S. dollars therefore increases.

To see why the supply curve slopes upward, take the example of bicycles. If the foreign exchange rate were to rise from ¥100/$ to ¥200/$, the bicycle which costs ¥20,000 would fall in price from $200 to $100. If other things are constant, Japanese bicycles would be more attractive, and Americans would sell more dollars in the foreign exchange market to buy more bicycles. Hence, the quantity supplied of dollars would be higher at a higher exchange rate.

What lies behind the demand for dollars (represented in Figure 27-3 by the *DD* demand curve? Foreigners demand U.S. dollars when they buy American goods, services, and assets. For example, suppose a Japanese student buys an American economics textbook or takes a trip to the United States. She will require U.S. dollars to pay for these items. Or when Japan Airlines buys a Boeing 787 for its fleet, this transaction increases the demand for U.S. dollars. If Japanese pension funds invest in U.S. stocks, this would require a purchase of dollars. *Foreigners demand U.S. dollars to pay for their purchases of American goods, services, and assets.*

The demand curve in Figure 27-3 slopes downward to indicate that as the dollar's value falls (and the yen therefore becomes more expensive), Japanese residents will want to buy more foreign goods, services, and investments. They will therefore demand more U.S. dollars in the foreign exchange market. Consider what happens when the foreign exchange rate on the dollar falls from ¥100/$ to ¥50/$. American computers, which had sold at $2000 × (¥100/$) = ¥200,000 now sell for only $2000 × (¥50/$) = ¥100,000. Japanese purchasers will therefore tend to buy more American computers, and the quantity demanded of U.S. foreign exchange will increase.

Market forces move the foreign exchange rate ①
up or down to balance the supply and demand. The price will settle at the *equilibrium foreign exchange rate,* which is the rate at which the dollars willingly bought just equal the dollars willingly sold.

The balance of supply and demand for foreign ②
exchange determines the foreign exchange rate of a currency. At the market exchange rate of 100 yen per dollar shown at point E in Figure 27-3, the exchange rate is in equilibrium and has no tendency to rise or fall.

We have discussed the foreign exchange market in terms of the supply and demand for dollars. But in this market, there are two currencies involved, so we could just as easily analyze the supply and demand for Japanese yen. To see this, you should sketch a supply-and-demand diagram with yen foreign exchange on the horizontal axis and the yen rate ($ per ¥) on the vertical axis. If ¥100/$ is the equilibrium looking from the point of view of the dollar, then $0.01/¥ is the *reciprocal exchange rate.* As an exercise, go through the analysis in this section for the reciprocal market. You will see that in this simple bilateral world, for every point made about dollars there is an exact yen counterpart: supply of dollars is demand for yen; demand for dollars is supply of yen.

There is just one further extension necessary to get to actual foreign exchange markets. In reality, there are many different currencies. We therefore need to find the supplies and demands for each and every currency. And in a world of many nations, it is the many-sided exchange and trade relationships, with demands and supplies coming from all parts of the globe, that determine the entire array of foreign exchange rates.

---

① 市场力量驱使汇率的升降，以实现供给与需求的平衡。其价格将在均衡的汇率水平稳定下来。在这一汇率水平上，美元的自愿买进量正好等于自愿卖出量。

② 外汇的供给与需求的平衡决定了一种货币的汇率。图 27-3 中 E 点所表示的在每一美元兑换 100 日元的市场汇率水平上，汇率即处于既没有上升也没有下跌趋势的均衡状态。

Terminology for Exchange-Rate Changes

Foreign exchange markets have a special
vocabulary. By definition, a fall in the price ①
of one currency in terms of one or all others is called a *depreciation*. A rise in the price of a currency in terms of another currency is called an *appreciation*. In our example above, when the price of the dollar rose from ¥100/$ to ¥200/$, the dollar appreciated. We also know that the yen depreciated.

In the supply-and-demand diagram for U.S. dollars, a fall in the foreign exchange rate (e) is a depreciation of the U.S. dollar, and a rise in e represents an appreciation.

A different set of terms is used when a currency has a fixed exchange rate. When a country lowers the official price of its currency in the market, this is called a *devaluation*. A *revaluation* occurs when the official foreign exchange rate is raised.

For example, in December 1994 Mexico devalued its currency when it lowered the official price or parity of the peso from 3.5 pesos per dollar to 3.8 pesos per dollar. Mexico soon found it could not defend the new parity and "floated" its exchange rate. At that point, the peso fell, or depreciated, even further.

When a country's currency falls in value relative to ②
that of another country, we say that the domestic currency has undergone a **depreciation** while the foreign currency has undergone an **appreciation.**

When a country's official foreign exchange rate is ③
lowered, we say that the currency has undergone a **devaluation.** An increase in the official foreign exchange rate is called a **revaluation.**

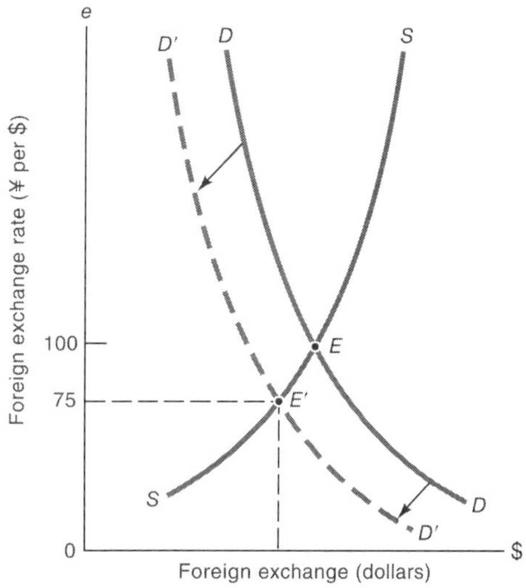

FIGURE 27-4. A Decrease in Demand for Dollars Leads to Dollar Depreciation

Suppose that a recession or deflation in Japan reduces the Japanese demand for dollars. This would shift the demand for dollars to the left from *DD* to *D'D'*. The exchange rate of the dollar depreciates, while the yen appreciates. Why would the new exchange rate discourage American purchases of Japanese goods?

贸易波动的影响

Effects of Changes in Trade

What would happen if there were changes in foreign exchange demand? For example, if Japan has a recession, its demand for imports declines. As a result, the demand for American dollars would decrease. The result is shown in Figure 27-4. The decline in purchases of American goods, services, and investments decreases the demand for dollars in the market. This change is represented by a leftward shift in the demand curve. The result will be a lower foreign exchange rate—that is, the dollar will depreciate and the yen will appreciate. At the lower exchange rate, the quantity of dollars supplied by Americans to the market will decrease because Japanese goods are now more expensive. Moreover, the quantity of dollars demanded by the Japanese will decline because of the recession. How much will
exchange rates change? Just enough so that the sup- ④
ply and demand are again in balance. In the example shown in Figure 27-4, the dollar has depreciated from ¥100/$ to ¥75/$.

In today's world, exchange rates often react to
changes involving the financial account. Suppose ⑤
that the Federal Reserve raises U.S. interest rates. This would make U.S. dollar assets more attractive than foreign assets as dollar interest rates rise relative to interest rates on foreign securities. As a result, the demand for dollars increases and the dollar appreciates. This sequence is shown in Figure 27-5.

汇率与国际收支平衡

Exchange Rates and the Balance of Payments

What is the connection between exchange rates and adjustments in the balance of payments? In the simplest case, assume that exchange rates are

① 根据定义，当一种货币对于另外一种或者其他所有币种的价格下跌时，就称为贬值。反之，一种货币以另外一种货币表示的价格上升则称为升值。

② 当一个国家的货币价值相对于另外一个国家的货币价值下降时，我们说，本国货币遭受了一次**贬值**，外国货币经历了一次**升值**。

③ 当一个国家的官方汇率调低时，我们说该国货币遭受了一次**降值**。当官方的汇率调高时，则被称为**增值**。

④ 其满足条件仅仅是供给与需求再一次达到平衡。

⑤ 假如美联储调高了美元利率，就会使美元资产比外汇资产更具吸引力。这是因为相对于外国证券的利率来讲美元利率升高了。

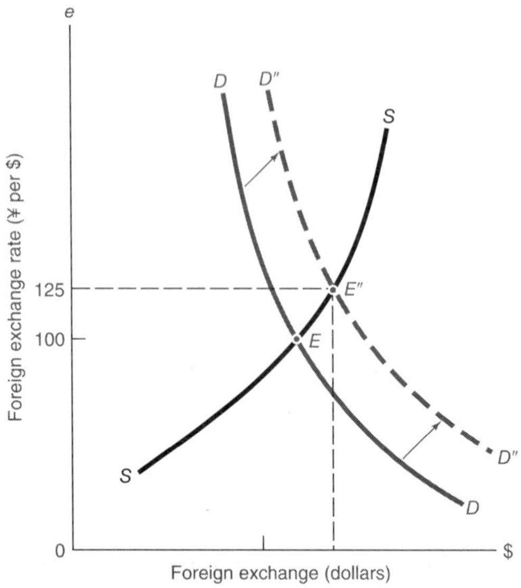

FIGURE 27-5. Monetary Tightening Increases Demand for Dollars and Produces Dollar Appreciation

Monetary policy can affect the exchange rate through the financial account. If the Federal Reserve raises dollar interest rates, this induces investors into dollar securities and raises the demand for dollar foreign exchange. The result is an appreciation of the dollar. (Explain why this leads to depreciation of the Euro.)

determined by private supply and demand with no government intervention. Consider what happened in 1990 after German unification when the German central bank decided to raise interest rates to curb inflation. After the monetary tightening, foreigners moved some of their assets into German marks to benefit from high German interest rates. This produced an excess demand for the German mark at the old exchange rate. In other words, at the old foreign exchange rate, people were, on balance, buying German marks and selling other currencies. (You can redraw Figure 27-5 to show this situation.)

Here is where the exchange rate plays its role as equilibrator. As the demand for German marks increased, it led to an appreciation of the German mark and a depreciation of other currencies, such as the U.S. dollar. The movement in the exchange rate continued until the financial and current accounts were back in balance.

Such a change in the foreign exchange rate has an important effect on trade flows. As the German mark appreciated, German goods became more expensive in foreign markets and foreign goods became less expensive in Germany. This led to a decrease in German exports and an increase in German imports. As a result, the trade balance moved toward deficit. The current-account deficit was the counterpart of the financial-account surplus induced by the higher interest rates.

Exchange-rate movements serve as a balance ① wheel to remove disequilibria in the balance of payments.

汇率与购买力平价
Purchasing-Power Parity and Exchange Rates

In the short run, market-determined exchange rates are highly volatile in response to monetary policy, political events, and changes in expectations. But over the longer run, exchange rates are determined primarily by the relative prices of goods in different countries. An important implication is the *purchasing-power-parity (PPP) theory of exchange rates.* Under this ② theory, a nation's exchange rate will tend to equalize the cost of buying traded goods at home with the cost of buying those goods abroad.

The PPP theory can be illustrated with a simple example. Suppose the price of a market basket of goods (automobiles, jewelry, oil, food, and so forth) costs \$1000 in the United States and 10,000 pesos in Mexico. At an exchange rate of 100 pesos to a dollar, this bundle would cost \$100 in Mexico. Given these relative prices and the free trade between the two countries, we would expect to see American firms and consumers streaming across the border to take advantage of the lower Mexican prices. The result would be higher imports from Mexico and an increased demand for Mexican pesos. That would cause the Mexican peso to appreciate relative to the U.S. dollar, so you would need more dollars to buy the same number of pesos. As a result, the prices ③ of the Mexican goods *in dollar terms* would rise even though the prices in pesos have not changed.

Where would this process end? Assuming that domestic prices are unchanged, it would end when the peso's exchange rate falls to 10 pesos to the dollar. Only at this exchange rate would the price of the

① 汇率变动可以作为一个平衡器，消除国际收支账户中的不平衡现象。

② 按照这一理论，一国的汇率可以使在国内购买交易商品的成本与到国外购买这些商品的成本相同。

③ 其结果是，即便比索的价格没有发生变化，以美元计价的墨西哥商品的价格也会上升。

market basket of goods be equal in the two countries. At 10 pesos to the dollar, we say that the currencies have equal purchasing power in terms of the traded goods. (You can firm up your understanding of this discussion by calculating the price of the market basket in both Mexican pesos and U.S. dollars before and after the appreciation of the peso.)

The PPP doctrine also holds that countries with high inflation rates will tend to have depreciating currencies. For example, if Country A's inflation rate is 10 percent while inflation in Country B is 2 percent, the currency of Country A will tend to depreciate relative to that of Country B by the difference in the inflation rates, that is, 8 percent annually. Alternatively, let's say that runaway inflation leads to a hundredfold rise of prices in Russia over the course of a year, while prices in the United States are unchanged. According to the PPP theory, the Russian ruble should depreciate by 99 percent in order to bring the prices of American and Russian goods back into equilibrium.

We should caution that the PPP theory only approximates and cannot predict the precise movements in the exchange rate. One reason it does not hold exactly is that many of the goods and services covered in price indexes are not traded. For example, if the PPP uses the consumer price index, then we must take into account that housing is a nontraded service and that the prices for housing of comparable quality can vary greatly over space. Additionally, even for traded goods, there is no "law of one price" that applies uniformly to all goods. If you look at the price of the same item on amazon.com and amazon.co.uk, you will find that (even after applying the current exchange rate) the price is usually different. Price differences for the same good can arise because of tariffs, taxes, and transportation costs. In addition, financial flows can overwhelm the effects of prices in the short run. Therefore, while the PPP theory is a useful guide to exchange rates in the long run, exchange rates can diverge from their PPP levels for many years.

PPP and the Size of Nations

By any measure, the United States still has the largest economy in the world. But which country has the second largest? Is it Japan, Germany, Russia, or some other country? You would think this would be an easy question to answer, like measuring height or weight. The problem, however, is that Japan totes up its national output in yen, while Russia's national output is given in rubles, and America's is in dollars. To be compared, they all need to be converted into the same currency.

The customary approach is to use the market exchange rate to convert each currency into dollars, and by that yardstick Japan has the second-largest economy. However, there are two difficulties with using the market rate. First, because market rates can rise and fall sharply, the "size" of countries might change by 10 or 20 percent overnight. Moreover, the use of market exchange rates tends to underestimate the national output of low-income countries.

Today, economists generally prefer to use PPP exchange rates to compare living standards in different countries. The difference between market exchange rates and PPP exchange rates can be dramatic, as Figure 27-6 shows. When market exchange rates are used, the ① incomes and outputs of low-income countries like China and India tend to be understated. This understatement occurs because a substantial part of the output of such countries comes from labor-intensive services, which are usually extremely inexpensive in low-wage countries. Hence, when we calculate PPP exchange rates including the prices of nontraded goods, the GDPs of low-income countries rise relative to those of high-income countries.

国际货币体系

C. THE INTERNATIONAL MONETARY SYSTEM

While the simple supply-and-demand diagrams for the foreign exchange market explain the major determinants, they do not capture the drama and central importance of the international monetary system. We saw crisis after crisis in international finance—in Europe in 1991–1992, in Mexico and Latin America in 1994–1995, in East Asia and Russia in 1997–1998, and then back to Latin America in 1998–2002.

What is the **international monetary system?** This term denotes the institutions under which payments

---

① 在使用市场汇率之后，像印度这样低收入国家的收入和产出就会被低估。这种现象的出现是因为这些国家产出中的大部分来自于劳动密集型服务，这些服务在低工资国家通常比较便宜。因此，我们在计算包括非贸易商品价格在内的购买力平价汇率时，相对于高收入国家，低收入国家的国内生产总值就会上升。

FIGURE 27-6. PPP Calculations Change the Relative Sizes of Nations' Economies, 2006

Using PPP exchange rates instead of market exchange rates changes the economic ranking of nations. After correcting for the purchasing power of incomes, China moves from being the fourth largest to being the second largest. Note that points along the 45° line are ones for which GDPs calculated using the two exchange rates are equal. Points above the line, such as China, are ones for which the PPP estimates of GDP are above those estimated using market exchange rates. Japan is below the line because relative prices in Japan are high due to high rents and trade barriers.

Source: World Bank. Note that outputs are shown on a ratio scale.

are made for transactions that cross national boundaries. In particular, the international monetary system determines how foreign exchange rates are set and how governments can affect exchange rates.

The importance of the international monetary system was well described by economist Robert Solomon:

> Like the traffic lights in a city, the international monetary system is taken for granted until it begins to malfunction and to disrupt people's lives. . . . A well-functioning monetary system will facilitate international trade and investment and smooth adaptation to change. A monetary system that functions poorly may not only discourage the development of trade and investment among nations but subject their economies to disruptive shocks when necessary adjustments to change are prevented or delayed. ①

The central element of the international monetary system involves the arrangements by which exchange rates are set. In recent years, nations have used one of three major exchange-rate systems:

- A system of fixed exchange rates
- A system of flexible or floating exchange rates, where exchange rates are determined by market forces
- Managed exchange rates, in which nations intervene to smooth exchange-rate fluctuations or to move their currency toward a target zone ②

固定汇率制：古典的金本位制
FIXED EXCHANGE RATES: THE CLASSICAL GOLD STANDARD

At one extreme is a system of **fixed exchange rates,** where governments specify the exact rate at which dollars will be converted into pesos, yen, and other currencies. Historically, the most important fixed-exchange-rate system was the **gold standard,** which

① 国际货币体系就像一个城市中的红绿灯一样，它的存在往往被认为是理所当然的，直到其开始发生故障，扰乱人们的生活。一个高效运行的货币制度会促进国际贸易与投资，并使其平稳地适应变化。而一个运行不畅的货币制度不仅会抑制各国之间的贸易和投资发展，而且在对变化不能做出调整时，经常会使其经济受到破坏性打击。

② 有管理的汇率，即各国借助于对汇率的干预平抑汇率波动，或者使其货币运行在目标汇率区间。

was used off and on from 1717 until 1936. In this system, each country defined the value of its currency in terms of a fixed amount of gold, thereby establishing fixed exchange rates among the countries on the gold standard.[3]

The functioning of the gold standard can be seen easily in a simplified example. Suppose people ① everywhere insisted on being paid in bits of pure gold metal. Then buying a bicycle in Britain would merely require payment in gold at a price expressed in ounces of gold. By definition there would be no foreign-exchange-rate problem. Gold would be the common world currency.

This example captures the essence of the gold standard. Once gold became the medium of exchange or money, foreign trade was no different from domestic trade; everything could be paid for in gold. The only difference between countries was that they could choose different *units* for their gold coins. Thus, Queen Victoria chose to make British coins about ¼ ounce of gold (the pound) and President McKinley chose to make the U.S. unit ¹⁄₂₀ ounce of gold (the dollar). In that case, the British pound, being 5 times as heavy as the dollar, had an exchange rate of \$5/£1.

This was the essence of the gold standard. In practice, countries tended to use their own coins. But anyone was free to melt down coins and sell them at the going price of gold. So exchange rates were fixed for all countries on the gold standard. The exchange rates (also called "par values" or "parities") for different currencies were determined by the gold content of their monetary units.

休谟的调整机制
Hume's Adjustment Mechanism

The purpose of an exchange-rate system is to promote international trade and finance while facilitating adjustment to shocks. How exactly does the *international adjustment mechanism* function? What happens if a country's wages and prices rise so sharply that its goods are no longer competitive in the world market? Under flexible exchange rates, the country's exchange rate could depreciate to offset the domestic inflation. But under fixed exchange rates, equilibrium must be restored by deflation at home or inflation abroad.

Let's examine the international adjustment mechanism under a fixed-exchange-rate system with two countries, America and Britain. Suppose that American inflation has made American goods uncompetitive. Consequently, America's imports rise and its exports fall. It therefore runs a trade deficit with Britain. To pay for its deficit, America would have to ship gold to Britain. Eventually—if there were no adjustments in either America or Britain—America would run out of gold.

In fact, an automatic adjustment mechanism does exist, as was demonstrated by the British philosopher David Hume in 1752. He showed that the outflow of gold was part of a mechanism that tended to keep international payments in balance. His argument, though nearly 250 years old, offers important insights for understanding how trade flows get balanced in today's economy.

Hume's explanation rested in part upon the ③ quantity theory of prices, which is a theory of the overall price level that is analyzed in macroeconomics. This doctrine holds that the overall price level in an economy is proportional to the supply of money. Under the gold standard, gold was an important part of the money supply—either directly, in the form of gold coins, or indirectly, when governments used gold as backing for paper money.

③ 某种程度上，休谟的解释是基于价格的数量论，在宏观经济学领域，它是一种分析整体价格水平的理论。这一理论强调，经济的总体价格水平与货币的供给是成比例的。在金本位制度下，无论是以金币作为交易媒介的直接形式，还是政府以黄金为基础发行纸币的间接形式，黄金都是货币供给的重要部分。

What would be the impact of a country's losing gold? First, the country's money supply would ④ decline either because gold coins would be exported
[2] or because some of the gold backing for the currency would leave the country. Putting both these consequences together, a loss of gold leads to a reduction in the money supply. According to the quantity theory, the next step is that prices and costs would change proportionally to the change in the money supply. If the United States loses 10 percent of its gold to pay for a trade deficit, the quantity theory predicts that U.S. prices, costs, and incomes would fall 10 percent. In other words, the economy would experience a deflation.

The Four-Pronged Mechanism. Now consider Hume's theory of international payments equilibrium. Suppose that America runs a large trade deficit and

[3] Why was gold used as the standard of exchange and means of payment, rather than some other commodity? Certainly other materials could have been used, but gold had the advantages of being in limited supply, being relatively indestructible, and having few industrial uses. Can you see why wine, wheat, or cattle would not be a useful means of payment among countries?

---

① 假设每个地方都坚持使用纯黄金支付，那么，在英国买一辆自行车就只有拿以盎司为标价单位的黄金来埋单。根据定义，这样的交易不存在汇率问题，因为黄金是全世界的通用货币。

[2] *Hume*：大卫·休谟（David Hume，1711~1776），苏格兰哲学家、经济学家和历史学家，苏格兰启蒙运动和西方哲学史上最主要的人物之一，在爱丁堡的国家名人堂与亚当·斯密并排而立。其为期八年出齐的六卷本《英格兰史》（*History of England, or, History of Great Britain*）风靡一个甲子以上。

④ 首先，该国的货币供给量会下降。这既是因为金币出口，也是因为作为纸币发行基础的黄金从该国流失。

begins to lose gold. According to the quantity theory of prices, this loss of gold reduces America's money supply, driving down America's prices and costs. As a result, (1) America decreases its imports of British and other foreign goods, which have become relatively expensive; and (2) because America's domestically produced goods have become relatively inexpensive on world markets, America's exports increase.

The opposite effect occurs in Britain and other foreign countries. Because Britain's exports are growing rapidly, it receives gold in return. Britain's money supply therefore increases, driving up British prices and costs according to the quantity theory. At this point, ① two more prongs of the Hume mechanism come into play: (3) British and other foreign exports have become more expensive, so the volume of goods exported to America and elsewhere declines; and (4) British citizens, faced with a higher domestic price level, now import more of America's low-priced goods.

Figure 27-7 illustrates the logic in Hume's mechanism. Make sure you can follow the logical chain from

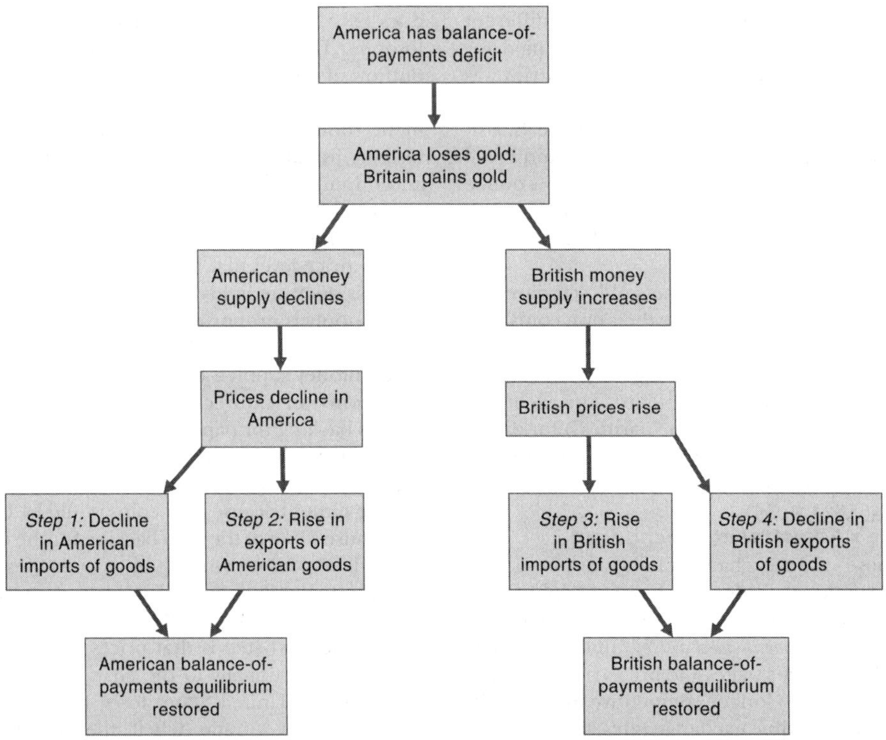

FIGURE 27-7. Hume's Four-Pronged International Adjustment Mechanism

Hume explained how a balance-of-payments disequilibrium would automatically produce equilibrating adjustments under a gold standard. Trace the lines from the original disequilibrium at the top through the changes in prices to the restored equilibrium at the bottom. This mechanism works in modified form under any fixed-exchange-rate system. Modern economics augments the mechanism by replacing the fourth row with "Prices, output, and employment decline in America" and "Prices, output, and employment rise in Britain."

---

① 就这个问题来讲，休谟机制中的另外两个分支开始出现：（3）英国以及其他国家的出口已经变得更加昂贵，使出口到美国或者其他国家商品的数量减少；（4）由于面临国内价格水平的提高，所以英国民众进口更多的美国低价商品。

the original deficit at the top through the adjustment to the new equilibrium at the bottom.

The result of Hume's four-pronged gold-flow ① mechanism is an improvement in the balance of payments of the country losing gold and a worsening in that of the country gaining gold. In the end, an equilibrium of international trade and finance is reestablished at new relative prices, which keep trade and international lending in balance with no net gold flow. This equilibrium is a stable one and requires no tariffs or other government intervention.

当代宏观经济学对休谟理论的更新

Updating Hume to Modern Macroeconomics

Hume's theories are no longer completely relevant today. We do not have a gold standard, and the quantity theory of prices is no longer used to explain price movements. However, the basis of Hume's theory can be reinterpreted in the light of modern macroeconomics. The essence of Hume's argument is to explain the adjustment mechanism for imbalances between countries under a fixed exchange rate. The fixed exchange rate might be a gold standard (as existed before 1936), a dollar standard (as under the Bretton Woods system from 1945 to 1971), or a Euro standard (among European Union countries today).

If exchange rates are not free to move when the ② prices or incomes of different countries get out of line, *then domestic output and prices must adjust to restore equilibrium.* If, under a fixed exchange rate, domestic prices become too high relative to import prices, full adjustment can come only when domestic prices fall. This will occur when domestic output falls sufficiently so that the country's price level will decline relative to world prices. At that point, the country's balance of payments will return to equilibrium. Suppose that Greece's prices rise too far above those in the rest of the European Union and it becomes uncompetitive in the market. Greece will find its exports declining and its imports rising, lowering net exports. Eventually, as wages and prices in Greece decline relative to those in the rest of Europe, Greece will once again be competitive and will be able to restore full employment.

When a country adopts a fixed exchange rate, it ③ faces an inescapable fact: Domestic real output and employment must adjust to ensure that the country's relative prices are aligned with those of its trading partners.

战后国际货币体系

INTERNATIONAL MONETARY INSTITUTIONS AFTER WORLD WAR II

In the early part of the twentieth century, even nations which were ostensibly at peace engaged in debilitating trade wars and competitive devaluations. After World War II, international institutions were developed to foster economic cooperation among nations. These institutions continue to be the means by which nations coordinate their economic policies and seek solutions to common problems.

The United States emerged from World War II with its economy intact—able and willing to help rebuild the countries of friends and foes alike. The postwar international political system responded to the needs of war-torn nations by establishing durable institutions that facilitated the quick recovery of the international economy. The major international economic institutions of the postwar period were the General Agreement on Tariffs and Trade (rechar- [4] tered as the World Trade Organization in 1995), the [5] Bretton Woods exchange-rate system, the Interna- [6] tional Monetary Fund, and the World Bank. These [7] four institutions helped the industrial democracies rebuild themselves and grow rapidly after the devastation of World War II, and they continue to be the major international institutions today.

国际货币基金组织

The International Monetary Fund

An integral part of the Bretton Woods system was the establishment of the International Monetary Fund (or IMF), which still administers the international monetary system and operates as a central bank for central banks. Member nations subscribe by lending their currencies to the IMF; the IMF then relends these funds to help countries in balance-of-payments difficulties. The main function of the IMF is to make temporary loans to countries which have balance-of-payments problems or are under speculative attack in financial markets.

世界银行

The World Bank

Another international financial institution created [8] after World War II was the World Bank. The Bank is ⑨ capitalized by high-income nations that subscribe in proportion to their economic importance in terms of GDP and other factors. The Bank makes long-term low-interest loans to countries for projects which are

[6] Bretton Woods：布雷顿森林货币体系，由1944年7月在美国新罕布什尔州布雷顿森林举行的联合国国际货币金融会议得名。此次会议确立了以美元和黄金为基础的金融汇兑本位制，其实质是建立了以美元为中心的国际货币体系，即美元与黄金挂钩，其他国家的货币与美元挂钩，以及实行固定汇率制度。布雷顿森林货币体系的运转与美元的信誉和地位密切相关。1971年8月15日，尼克松政府宣布休克性的新经济政策（Nixon Shock），停止履行外国政府或中央银行可用美元向美国兑换黄金的义务，美元随之成为名义货币，形成许多国家把美元作为储存货币的格局。

[7] International Monetary Fund：国际货币基金组织，缩写为IMF，根据1944年7月布雷顿森林会议所签协议于次年年底在华盛顿与世界银行同时成立，以监察汇率和各国贸易情况，提供技术和资金协助，确保全球金融制度运作正常。1969年创设特别提款权（Special Drawing Right，SDR，也称“纸黄金”），以保证会员国在发生国际收支逆差时，向其他会员国换取外汇的权利，实质是一种记账单位。

[8] World Bank：世界银行与1945~1988年间先后建立的国际复兴开发银行（International Bank for Reconstruction and Development，IBRD，1945）、国际金融公司（International Finance Corporation，IFC，1956）、国际开发协会（International Development Association，IDA，1960）、国际投资争端解决中心（International Centre for Settlement of Investment Disputes，ICSID，1966）和多边投资担保机构（Multilateral Investment Guarantee Agency，MIGA，1988）五家机构一起组成世界银行集团（World Bank Group），联合向发展中国家提供低息贷款、无息贷款和赠款，通常简单地俗称为“世界银行”。

① 休谟黄金流通的四重机制，导致黄金流出国家的收支平衡问题得以改善，而黄金流入国家的收支平衡问题却日益恶化。最终，国际贸易和国际金融在新的相对价格水平上重新建立均衡。这一相对价格使贸易和国际信贷处于均衡状态，不存在黄金的净流动。这样一种稳定的均衡状态不需要关税或者政府的其他干预。

② 如果不同国家的价格和收入波动过大，而汇率又无法自由浮动，那么国内的产出和价格就必须做出调整以恢复平衡。

③ 一个国家在实行了固定汇率之后，就必须面对一个无法回避的事实：国内的实际产出和就业必须予以调整，以确保本国的相对价格水平与其贸易伙伴的价格水平相一致。

[4] General Agreement on Tariffs and Trade:《关税及贸易总协定》，简称《关贸总协定》，缩写为GATT，1947年10月30日在日内瓦签署，直到1995年由世界贸易组织（World Trade Organization，WTO）取代。

[5] World Trade Organization：世界贸易组织，简称WTO，以促进贸易自由化和经济增长为宗旨，但也由于穷国和富国之间的鸿沟日益扩大早已远离了其初衷而备受诟病。

⑨ 该银行由高收入国家提供资金，资金比例以GDP以及其他因素衡量的经济重要性确定。

economically sound but which cannot get private-sector financing. As a result of such long-term loans, goods and services flow from advanced nations to developing countries.

布雷顿森林体系
The Bretton Woods System

After World War II, governments were determined to replace the gold standard with a more flexible system. They set up the **Bretton Woods system,** which ① was a system with fixed exchange rates. The innovation here was that exchange rates were *fixed but adjustable*. When one currency got too far out of line with its appropriate or "fundamental" value, the parity could be adjusted.

The Bretton Woods system functioned effectively for the quarter-century after World War II. The system eventually broke down when the dollar became overvalued. The United States abandoned the Bretton Woods system in 1973, and the world moved into the modern era.

How to Ensure a Credibly Fixed Exchange Rate through the "Hard Fix"

Although the collapse of the Bretton Woods system marked the end of a predominantly fixed exchange-rate system, many countries continue to opt for fixed exchange rates. A recurrent problem with fixed-exchange-rate systems is that they are prey to speculative attacks when the country runs low on foreign exchange reserves. (We will return to this problem in the next chapter.) How can countries improve the credibility of their fixed-exchange-rate systems? Are there "hard" fixed-exchange-rate systems that will better withstand speculative attacks?

Specialists in this area emphasize the importance of establishing credibility. In this instance, credibility may be enhanced by creating a system that would actually make it *hard* for the country to change its exchange rate. This approach is similar to a military strategy of burning the bridges behind the army so that there is no retreat and the soldiers will have to fight to the death. Indeed, Argentina's president tried to instill credibility in Argentina's system by proclaiming that he would choose "death before devaluation."

② One solution is to create **currency boards.** A currency board is a monetary institution that issues only currency that is fully backed by foreign assets in a key foreign currency, usually the U.S. dollar or the Euro. A currency board defends an exchange rate that is fixed by law rather than just by policy, and the currency board is usually independent, and sometimes even private. Under currency boards, a payments deficit will generally trigger Hume's automatic adjustment mechanism. That is, a balance-of-payments deficit will reduce the money supply, leading to an economic contraction, eventually reducing domestic prices and restoring equilibrium. A currency board system has worked effectively in Hong Kong, but the system in Argentina was unable to withstand economic and political turmoil and collapsed in 2002.

A fixed exchange rate is even more credible when countries adopt a **common currency** through monetary union. The United States has had a common currency since 1789. The most important recent example is the Euro, which has been adopted by 15 countries of the European Union. This is a most unusual arrangement because the currency joins together many powerful sovereign countries. From a macroeconomic point of view, a common currency is the hardest fix of all because the currencies of the different countries are all defined to be the same. A variant of ③ this approach is called "dollarization," which occurs when a country (usually a small one) adopts a key currency for its own money. About a dozen small countries, such as El Salvador, have gone this route.

浮动汇率制
FLEXIBLE EXCHANGE RATES

The international monetary system for major countries today relies primarily on **flexible exchange rates.** (Another term often used is **floating exchange rates,** which means the same thing.) Under this system, exchange rates are determined by supply and demand. Here, the government neither announces ④ an official exchange rate nor takes steps to enforce one, and the changes in exchange rates are determined primarily by private supply of and demand for goods, services, and investments.

As noted above, virtually all large and medium-sized countries rely upon flexible exchange rates. We can use the example of Mexico to illustrate how such a system works. In 1994, the peso was under attack in foreign exchange mar-

---

① 他们建立了固定汇率制的**布雷顿森林体系**，其创新之处是，汇率既是固定的，又是可以调整的。当一国货币与其应有的或者“基础”价值相去甚远时，即使用平价机制予以调整。

② 一种解决办法是创建**货币委员会**。货币委员会是一个货币管理机构，发行唯一的完全由某一关键外币标定的外汇资产作为支撑货币，这种外币通常为美元或者欧元。

③ 这种模式的一种变异被称为“美元化”，出现在一个国家（通常为小国）将一种关键货币作为本国货币的情况。大约有 12 个小国走这样的道路，比如萨尔瓦多。

④ 在这种汇率机制下，政府既不发布官方汇率，也不采取任何措施强制汇率改变，汇率的任何变化主要由私人对商品、服务与投资的供给和需求来决定。

kets, and the Mexicans allowed the peso to float. At the original exchange rate of approximately 4 pesos per U.S. dollar, there was an excess supply of pesos. This meant that at that exchange rate, the supply of pesos by Mexicans who wanted to buy American and other foreign goods and assets outweighed the demand for pesos by Americans and others who wanted to purchase Mexican goods and assets.

What was the outcome? As a result of the excess supply, the peso depreciated relative to the dollar. How far did the exchange rates move? Just far enough so that—at the depreciated exchange rate of about 6 pesos to the dollar—the quantities supplied and demanded were balanced.

What is behind the equilibration of supply and demand? Two main forces are involved: (1) With the dollar more expensive, it costs more for Mexicans to buy American goods, services, and investments, causing the supply of pesos to fall off in the usual fashion. (2) With the depreciation of the peso, Mexican goods and assets become less expensive for foreigners. This increases the demand for pesos in the marketplace. (Note that this simplified discussion assumes that all transactions occur only between the two countries; a more complete discussion would involve the demands and supplies of currencies from all countries.)

当今的混合体系
TODAY'S HYBRID SYSTEM

Unlike the earlier uniform system under either the gold standard or Bretton Woods, today's exchange-rate system fits into no tidy mold. Without anyone's having planned it, the world has moved to a hybrid exchange-rate system. The major features are as follows:

- A few countries allow their currencies to *float freely*. In this approach, a country allows markets to determine its currency's value and it rarely intervenes. The United States has fit this pattern for most of the last three decades. While the Euro is just an infant as a common currency, Europe is clearly in the freely floating group.
- Some major countries have *managed but flexible* exchange rates. Today, this group includes Canada, Japan, and many developing countries. Under this system, a country will buy or sell its currency to reduce the day-to-day volatility of currency fluctuations. In addition, a country will ①
sometimes engage in systematic intervention to move its currency toward what it believes to be a more appropriate level.
- A few small countries and some large country peg their currencies to a major currency or to a "basket" of currencies in a *fixed exchange rate*. Sometimes, the peg is allowed to glide smoothly upward or downward in a system known as a gliding or crawling peg. A few countries have the hard fix of a currency board, and others set their currencies equal to the dollar in a process called dollarization.
- In addition, almost all countries tend to intervene either when markets become "disorderly" or when exchange rates seem far out of line with the "fundamentals"—that is, when they are highly inappropriate for existing price levels and trade flows.

结 语
Concluding Thoughts

The world has made a major transition in its international financial system over the last three decades. In earlier periods, most currencies were linked together in a system of fixed exchange rates, with parities linked either to gold or to the dollar. Today, all major countries have almost flexible exchange rates. This new system has the disadvantage that exchange rates are volatile and can deviate greatly from underlying economic fundamentals. But this system also has the advantage of reducing the perils of speculation that undermined earlier fixed-rate systems. Even ②
more important in a world of increasingly open financial markets is that flexible exchange rates allow countries to pursue monetary policies designed to stabilize domestic business cycles. It is this macroeconomic advantage that most economists find most important about the new regime.

---

① 此外，一国有时也会进行系统干预，以使本国货币向着它所认为更趋合适的汇率水平浮动。

② 在金融市场越来越开放的国际大环境下，更为重要的是浮动汇率允许各国实行各自设计的货币政策，来稳定本国商业周期。这就是宏观经济学的优势所在，大多数经济学家都认为，这一新机制是最为重要的。

SUMMARY

A. The Balance of International Payments

1. The balance of international payments is the set of accounts that measures all the economic transactions between a nation and the rest of the world. It includes exports and imports of goods, services, and financial instruments. Exports are credit items, while imports are debits. More generally, credit items are transactions that increase a country's holdings of foreign currencies; debit items are ones that reduce its holdings of foreign currencies.

2. The major components of the balance of payments are:
   I. Current account (merchandise trade, services, investment income, transfers)
   II. Financial account (private, government, and official-reserve changes)

   The fundamental rule of balance-of-payments accounting is that the sum of all items must equal zero: I + II = 0

B. The Determination of Foreign Exchange Rates

3. International trade and finance involve the new element of different national currencies, which are linked by relative prices called foreign exchange rates. When Americans import Japanese goods, they ultimately need to pay in Japanese yen. In the foreign exchange market, Japanese yen might trade at ¥100/$ (or, reciprocally, ¥1 would trade for $0.01). This price is called the foreign exchange rate.
4. In a foreign exchange market involving only two countries, the supply of U.S. dollars comes from Americans who want to purchase goods, services, and investments from Japan; the demand for U.S. dollars comes from Japanese who want to import commodities or financial assets from America. The interaction of these supplies and demands determines the foreign exchange rate. More generally, foreign exchange rates are determined by the complex interplay of many countries buying and selling among themselves. When trade or financial flows change, supply and demand shift and the equilibrium exchange rate changes.
5. A fall in the market price of a currency is a depreciation; a rise in a currency's value is called an appreciation. In a system where governments announce official foreign exchange rates, a decrease in the official exchange rate is called a devaluation, while an increase is a revaluation.
6. According to the purchasing-power-parity (PPP) theory of exchange rates, exchange rates tend to move with changes in relative price levels of different countries. The PPP theory applies better to the long run than the short run. When this theory is applied to measure the purchasing power of incomes in different countries, it raises the per capita outputs of low-income countries.

C. The International Monetary System

7. A well-functioning international economy requires a smoothly operating exchange-rate system, which denotes the institutions that govern financial transactions among nations. Two important exchange-rate systems are (*a*) flexible exchange rates, in which a country's foreign exchange rate is determined by market forces of supply and demand; and (*b*) fixed exchange rates, such as the gold standard or the Bretton Woods system, in which countries set and defend a given structure of exchange rates.
8. Classical economists like David Hume explained international adjustments to trade imbalances by the gold-flow mechanism. Under this process, gold movements would change the money supply and the price level. For example, a trade deficit would lead to a gold outflow and a decline in domestic prices that would (*a*) raise exports and (*b*) curb imports of the gold-losing country while (*c*) reducing exports and (*d*) raising imports of the gold-gaining country. This mechanism shows that under fixed exchange rates, countries which have balance-of-payments problems must adjust through changes in domestic price and output levels.
9. After World War II, countries created a group of international economic institutions to organize international trade and finance. Under the Bretton Woods system, countries "pegged" their currencies to the dollar and to gold, providing fixed but adjustable exchange rates. After the Bretton Woods system collapsed in 1973, it was replaced by today's hybrid system. Today, virtually all large and medium-sized countries have flexible exchange rates.

CONCEPTS FOR REVIEW

Balance of Payments

balance of payments
- I. current account
- II. financial account

balance-of-payments identity:
- I + II = 0

debits and credits

Foreign Exchange Rates

foreign exchange rate, foreign exchange market
supply of and demand for foreign exchange
exchange-rate terminology:
- appreciation and depreciation
- revaluation and devaluation

International Monetary System

exchange-rate systems:
- flexible
- fixed rates (gold standard, Bretton Woods, currency board)
- common currency

international adjustment mechanism
Hume's four-pronged gold-flow mechanism

FURTHER READING AND INTERNET WEBSITES

Further Reading

A fascinating collection of essays on international macroeconomics is Paul Krugman, *Pop International* (MIT Press, Cambridge, Mass., 1997). The quotation on the international monetary system is from Robert Solomon, *The International Monetary System, 1945–1981: An Insider's View* (Harper & Row, New York, 1982), pp. 1, 7.

Websites

Data on trade and finance for different countries can be found in the websites listed for Chapter 12.

Some of the best popular writing on international economics is found in *The Economist*, which is available on the Web at *www.economist.com*. One of the best sources for policy writing on international economics is *www.iie.com/homepage.htm*, the website of the Peterson Institute for International Economics. One of the leading scholar-journalists of today is Paul Krugman of Princeton. His blog at *krugman.blogs.nytimes.com* contains many interesting readings on international economics.

QUESTIONS FOR DISCUSSION

1. Table 27-4 shows some foreign exchange rates (in units of foreign currency per dollar) as of late 2008. Fill in the last column of the table with the reciprocal price of the dollar in terms of each foreign currency, being

	Price	
Currency	**Units of foreign currency per U.S. dollar**	**U.S. dollars per unit of foreign currency**
Dollar (Canada)	0.9861	1.014 (US$/Canadian dollar)
Real (Brazil)	1.656	_____ (_____)
Yuan (China)	6.942	_____ (_____)
Peso (Mexico)	10.38	_____ (_____)
Pound (Britain)	0.5054	_____ (_____)
Euro	0.6368	_____ (_____)
Dollar (Zimbabwe)	255,771,415	_____ (_____)

TABLE 27-4.

especially careful to write down the relevant units in the parentheses.

2. Figure 13-3 shows the demand and supply for U.S. dollars in an example in which Japan and the United States trade only with each other.
   a. Describe and draw the reciprocal supply and demand schedules for Japanese yen. Explain why the supply of yen is equivalent to the demand for dollars. Also explain and draw the schedule that corresponds to the supply of dollars. Find the equilibrium price of yen in this new diagram and relate it to the equilibrium in Figure 13-3.
   b. Assume that Americans develop a taste for Japanese goods. Show what would happen to the supply and demand for yen. Would the yen appreciate or depreciate relative to the dollar? Explain.
3. Draw up a list of items that belong on the credit side of the balance of international payments and another list of items that belong on the debit side. What is meant by a trade surplus? By the balance on current account?
4. Consider the situation for Germany described on page 268. Using a figure like Figure 13-3, show the supply and demand for German marks before and after the shock. Identify on your figure the excess demand for marks *before* the appreciation of the mark. Then show how an appreciation of the mark would wipe out the excess demand.
5. A Middle East nation suddenly discovers huge oil resources. Show how its balance of trade and current account suddenly turn to surplus. Show how it can acquire assets in New York as a financial-account offset. Later, when it uses the assets for domestic capital investment, show how its current and financial items reverse their roles.
6. Consider the following quotation from the 1984 *Economic Report of the President:*

   > In the long run, the exchange rate tends to follow the differential trend in the domestic and foreign price level. If one country's price level gets too far out of line with prices in other countries, there will eventually be a fall in demand for its goods, which will lead to a real depreciation of its currency.

   Explain how the first sentence relates to the PPP theory of exchange rates. Explain the reasoning behind the PPP theory. In addition, using a supply-and-demand diagram like that of Figure 13-3, explain the sequence of events, described in the second sentence of the quotation, whereby a country whose price level is relatively high will find that its exchange rate depreciates.
7. A nation records the following data for 2008: exports of automobiles ($100) and corn ($150); imports of oil ($150) and steel ($75); tourist expenditures abroad ($25); private lending to foreign countries ($50); private borrowing from foreign countries ($40); official-reserve changes ($30 of foreign exchange bought by domestic central bank). Calculate the statistical discrepancy and include it in private lending to foreign countries. Create a balance-of-payments table like Table 13-2.
8. Consider the following three exchange-rate systems: the classical gold standard, freely flexible exchange rates, and the Bretton Woods system. Compare and contrast the three systems with respect to the following characteristics:
   a. Role of government vs. market in determining exchange rates
   b. Degree of exchange-rate volatility
   c. Method of adjustment of relative prices across countries
   d. Need for international cooperation and consultation in determining exchange rates
   e. Potential for establishment and maintenance of severe exchange-rate misalignment
9. Consider the European monetary union. List the pros and cons. How do you come down on the question of the advisability of monetary union? Would your answer change if the question concerned the United States?

CHAPTER

28

Open-Economy Macroeconomics
开放经济的宏观经济学

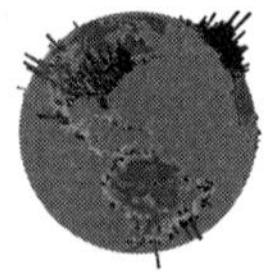

Before I built a wall I'd ask to know
What I was walling in or walling out . . .

Robert Frost [1]

The international business cycle exerts a powerful effect on every nation of the globe. Shocks in one area can have ripple effects around the world. Political disturbances in the Middle East can set off a spiral in oil prices that triggers inflation and unemployment. Defaults can rock stock markets and shake business confidence in distant lands. The interconnectedness of countries was illustrated dramatically in the financial crisis of 2007–2009. When U.S. financial institutions suffered huge losses, stock and bond markets around the world also declined, and a banking crisis in Europe erupted almost simultaneously with that in the United States.

The previous chapter surveyed the major concepts of international macroeconomics—the balance of payments, the determination of exchange rates, and the international monetary system. The present ② chapter continues the story by showing how macroeconomic shocks in one country have ripple effects on the output and inflation of other countries. We explore the paradoxical finding that trade balances are largely determined by the balances between domestic saving and investment. The chapter concludes with a review of some of the key international issues of today.

对外贸易与经济活动

A. FOREIGN TRADE AND ECONOMIC ACTIVITY

开放经济的净出口与产出
Net Exports and Output in the Open Economy

Open-economy macroeconomics is the study of how economies behave when the trade and financial linkages among nations are considered. The previous chapter described the basic concepts of the balance of payments. We can restate those concepts here in terms of the national income and product accounts.

Foreign trade involves imports and exports. Although the United States produces most of what it consumes, it nonetheless has a large quantity of **imports,** which are goods and services produced abroad and consumed domestically. **Exports** are goods and services produced domestically and purchased by foreigners.

Net exports are defined as exports of goods and services minus imports of goods and services. In 2007, net exports for the United States were minus $708 billion, as calculated from $1662 billion worth

[1] 罗伯特·弗罗斯特：Robert Frost（1874~1963），一位兼跨古典和现代的美国大诗人，曾四次获得普利策诗歌奖。其诗歌从乡村生活中汲取营养，既崇尚生活的现实又富有神秘色彩。这两行诗出自1914年伦敦David Nutt出版的弗罗斯特诗集《波士顿的北方》（*North of Boston*）中的一首45行抒情诗 *Mending Wall*（《修墙》)，系一首五音步诗行的无韵诗（即每行五音步，十音节。)，诗中"wall"象征阻碍社会进步与和谐的障碍，"whom"为诗人的父亲。原文为：
Before I built a wall I'd ask to know
What I was walling in or walling out,
And to whom I was like to give offense.
根据上下文，这两句拟译为：
（父亲大人恕我言，）
未曾修墙问在先，
隔断内外为哪般……

② 本章我们通过描述一国宏观经济震荡是如何波及影响其他国家的产出和通货膨胀，来继续讨论这些问题。我们还要探讨一个矛盾的发现：国内储蓄和投资之间的差额很大程度上决定了贸易余额。

of exports minus $2370 billion worth of imports. When a country has positive net exports, it is accumulating foreign assets. The counterpart of net exports is **net foreign investment,** which denotes net U.S. savings abroad and is approximately equal to the value of net exports. Because the U.S. had negative net exports, its net foreign investment was negative, implying that the U.S. foreign indebtedness was growing.

In other words, *foreigners were making a significant contribution to U.S. investment.* Why is it that rich America borrowed so much from abroad? As we will see later in this chapter, this paradoxical phenomenon is explained by a relatively low U.S. saving rate, a high foreign saving rate, and an attractive investment climate in the United States. ①

In an open economy, a nation's expenditures may differ from its production. Total *domestic expenditures* (sometimes called *domestic demand*) are equal to consumption plus domestic investment plus government purchases. This measure differs from total *domestic product* (or GDP) for two reasons. First, some part of domestic expenditures will be on goods produced abroad, these items being imports (denoted by *Im*) like Mexican oil and Japanese automobiles. In addition, some part of America's domestic production will be sold abroad as exports (denoted by *Ex*)—items like Iowa wheat and Boeing aircraft. The difference between national output and domestic expenditures is exports minus imports, which equals net exports, or $Ex - Im = X$.

To calculate the *total production* of American goods and services, we need to add trade to domestic demand. That is, we need to know the total production for American residents as well as the net production for foreigners. This total includes domestic expenditures $(C + I + G)$ plus sales to foreigners (Ex) minus domestic purchases from foreigners (Im). Total output, or GDP, equals consumption plus domestic investment plus government purchases plus net exports:

$$\text{Total domestic output} = \text{GDP} = C + I + G + X$$

贸易与净出口的决定因素
Determinants of Trade and Net Exports

What determines the levels of exports and imports and therefore of net exports? It is best to think of the import and export components of net exports separately.

Imports into the United States are positively related to U.S. income and output. When U.S. GDP rises, imports into the U.S. increase (1) because some of the increased $C + I + G$ purchases (such as cars and shoes) come from foreign production and also (2) because America uses foreign-made inputs (like oil or lumber) in producing its own goods. The demand for imports depends upon the relative price of foreign and domestic goods. If the price of domestic cars rises relative to the price of Japanese cars, say, because the dollar's exchange rate appreciates, Americans will buy more Japanese cars and fewer American ones. Hence *the volume and value of imports will be affected by domestic output and the relative prices of domestic and foreign goods.*

Exports are the mirror image of imports: U.S. exports are other countries' imports. American exports therefore depend primarily upon foreign output as well as upon the prices of U.S. exports relative to the prices of foreign goods. As foreign output rises, or as the exchange rate of the dollar depreciates, the volume and value of American exports tend to grow.

Figure 28-1 shows the ratio of U.S. net exports to GDP. For most of the period after World War II, the U.S. external accounts were in surplus or balance. Starting in the early 1980s, a decline in national saving, fueled by large federal budget deficits, led to a sharp appreciation of the dollar. Foreign economies grew less rapidly than the U.S. economy, depressing exports. The net effect was a large trade deficit and growing foreign indebtedness. Was it a good thing or a bad thing? The following discussion by the president's Council of Economic Advisers puts the U.S. trade deficit in an economic context:

> By themselves, external trade and current account deficits are neither inherently good nor inherently bad. What matters are the reasons for the deficits. The main reason for the deficits today appears to be the strength of the U.S. economic expansion relative to the slow or negative growth in many other countries. . . . These deficits are essentially a macroeconomic phenomenon, reflecting a higher rate of domestic investment than of national saving. The deficit's growth . . . reflects rising investment rather than falling saving. ②

① 换句话讲，是外国人一直在对美国的投资做着重要贡献。问题是为什么富裕的美国向外国借如此多的债？本章后面的部分将会讨论：这种自相矛盾的现象，可以用美国相对低的储蓄率、国外的高储蓄率，以及美国诱人的投资环境来予以解释。

② 就其自身来讲，对外贸易和经常账户赤字都没有一定的好与坏的问题。造成赤字的原因是问题的关键。今天看赤字产生的主要原因似乎是美国经济的强劲扩张，而许多其他国家的经济增长却相对缓慢或者为负，……从根本上讲，这些赤字都是宏观经济现象，它反映了国内的投资率高于国民储蓄率。赤字的增加……反映出投资在增加，而非储蓄在下降。

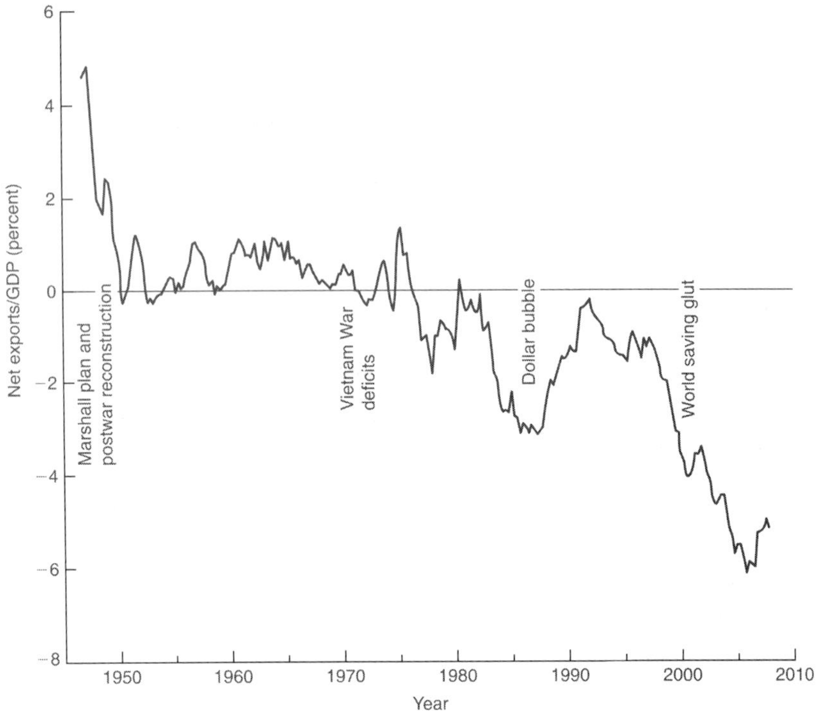

FIGURE 28-1. U.S. Net Exports Have Been in Deficit for Many Years

The United States had a large trade surplus after World War II as it helped rebuild Europe. Note how net exports turned sharply negative in the early 1980s as America's saving declined. Net exports grew even more negative in the last decade with the global savings glut.

Source: U.S. Bureau of Economic Analysis.

贸易对 GDP 的短期影响

SHORT-RUN IMPACT OF TRADE ON GDP

How do changes in a nation's trade flows affect its GDP and employment? We first analyze this question in the context of our short-run model of output determination, the multiplier model of Chapter 22. The multiplier model shows how, in the short run ① when there are unemployed resources, changes in trade will affect aggregate demand, output, and employment.

There are two major new macroeconomic elements in the presence of international trade: First, we have a fourth component of spending, net exports, which adds to aggregate demand. Second, ② an open economy has different multipliers for private investment and government domestic spending because some spending leaks out to the rest of the world.

Table 28-1 on the next page shows how introducing net exports affects output determination. This table begins with the same components as those for a closed economy. (Look back to Table 22-2 on page 440 to refresh your memory about the major components and the way they sum to total spending.) Total domestic demand in

① 乘数模型说明，在短期内存在闲置资源时，贸易的变化将如何影响总需求、总产出及就业。

② 其次，由于一些支出会流漏到世界的其他地方，因此在开放经济中，对于私人投资和政府的国内支出就会有不同的乘数。

Output Determination with Foreign Trade (billions of dollars)						
(1) Initial level of GDP	(2) Domestic demand $(C+I+G)$	(3) Exports *Ex*	(4) Imports *Im*	(5) Net exports $(X = Ex - Im)$	(6) Total spending $(C+I+G+X)$	(7) Resulting tendency of economy
4,100	4,000	250	410	−160	3,840 ↓	Contraction
3,800	3,800	250	380	−130	3,670 ↓	Contraction
3,500	**3,600**	**250**	**350**	**−100**	**3,500**	**Equilibrium**
3,200	3,400	250	320	−70	3,330 ↑	Expansion
2,900	3,200	250	290	−40	3,160 ↑	Expansion

TABLE 28-1. Net Exports Add to Aggregate Demand of Economy

To the domestic demand of $C + I + G$, we must add net exports of $X = Ex - Im$ to get total aggregate demand for a country's output. Higher net exports affect aggregate demand just as do investment and government purchases.

column (2) is composed of the consumption, investment, and government purchases we analyzed earlier. Column (3) then adds the exports of goods and services. As described above, exports depend upon foreign incomes and outputs and upon prices and exchange rates, all of which are also taken as given for this analysis. Exports are assumed to be a constant level of $250 billion of foreign spending on domestic goods and services.

The interesting new element arises from imports, shown in column (4). Like exports, imports depend upon exogenous variables such as prices and exchange rates. But, in addition, imports depend upon domestic incomes and output, which clearly change in the different rows of Table 28-1. For simplicity, we assume that the country always imports 10 percent of its total output, so imports in column (4) are 10 percent of column (1).

Subtracting column (4) from column (3) gives net exports in column (5). Net exports are a negative number when imports exceed exports and a positive ① number when exports are greater than imports. Net exports in column (5) are the net addition to the spending stream contributed by foreign trade. Total spending on domestic output in column (6) equals domestic demand in column (2) plus net exports in column (5). Equilibrium output in an open economy occurs where total net domestic and foreign spending in column (6) exactly equals total domestic output in column (1). In this case, equilibrium comes with net exports of −100, indicating that the country is importing more than it is exporting. At this equilibrium, note as well that domestic demand is greater than output.

Figure 28-2 shows the open-economy equilibrium graphically. The upward-sloping blue line marked $C + I + G$ is the same curve used in Figure 22-10. To this line we must add the level of net exports that is forthcoming at each level of GDP. Net exports from column (5) of Table 28-1 are added to get the green line of total aggregate demand or total spending. When the green line lies below the blue curve, imports exceed exports and net exports are negative. When the green line is above the blue line, the country has a net-export surplus and output is greater than domestic demand.

Equilibrium GDP occurs where the green line of total spending intersects the 45° line. This intersection comes at exactly the same point, at $3500 billion, that is shown as equilibrium GDP in Table 28-1. Only at $3500 billion does GDP exactly equal what ② consumers, businesses, governments, and foreigners want to spend on goods and services produced in the domestic economy.

---

① 当进口额超过出口额时，净出口为负值；当出口额大于进口额时，净出口为正值。

② 只有在 35 000 亿美元这一水平上，GDP 才正好等于消费者、企业、政府以及外国人想要在国内经济所生产的商品和服务上的支出。

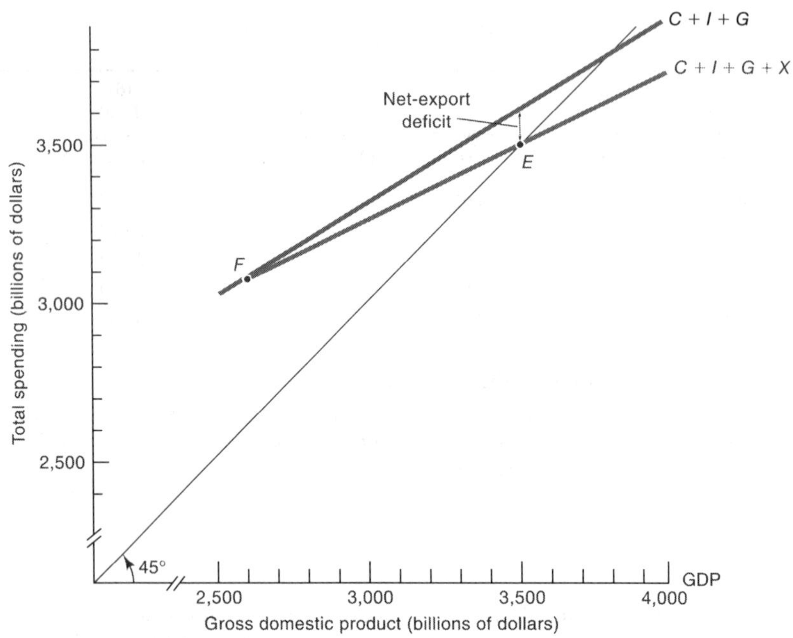

FIGURE 28-2. Adding Net Exports to Domestic Demand Gives Equilibrium GDP in the Open Economy

The blue line represents domestic demand ($C + I + G$), which are purchases by domestic consumers, businesses, and governments. To this must be added net foreign spending. Net exports plus domestic demand give the green line of total spending. Equilibrium comes at point *E*, where total GDP equals total spending on goods and services produced in the United States. Note that the slope of the green total demand curve is less than that of domestic demand to reflect the leakage from spending into imports.

边际进口倾向与支出线

The Marginal Propensity to Import and the Spending Line

Note that the aggregate demand curve, the green $C + I + G + X$ curve in Figure 28-2, has a slightly smaller slope than the blue curve of domestic demand. The explanation of this is that *there is an additional leakage from spending into imports.* ① This new leakage arises from our assumption that 10 cents of every dollar of income is spent on imports. To handle this requires introducing a new term, the **marginal propensity to import.** The marginal propensity to import, which we will denote *MPm*, is the increase in the dollar value of imports for each $1 increase in GDP.

The marginal propensity to import is closely related to the marginal propensity to save (*MPS*). Recall that the *MPS* tells us what fraction of an additional dollar of income is not spent but leaks into saving. The marginal propensity to import tells how much of additional output and income leaks into imports. In our example, the *MPm* is 0.10 because every $300 billion of increased income leads to $30 billion of increased imports. (What is the marginal propensity to import in an economy with no foreign trade? Zero.)

① 对这个问题的解释是，有一个支出中的额外漏出量进入到进口。这一新的漏出量来源于我们的假设，即每一美元收入中有 10 美分用于支付进口。为便于理解，我们需要引入一个新术语，即**边际进口倾向**。

Now examine the slope of the total spending line in Figure 28-2—that line shows total spending on $C + I + G + X$. Note that the slope of the total spending line is less than the slope of the domestic demand line of $C + I + G$. As GDP and total incomes rise by \$300, spending on consumption rises by the income change times the *MPC* (assumed to be two-thirds), or by \$200. At the same time, spending on imports, or foreign goods, also rises by \$30. Hence spending on domestic goods rises by only \$170(= \$200 − \$30), and the slope of the total spending line falls from 0.667 in our closed economy to \$170/\$300 = 0.567 in our open economy.

开放经济的乘数
The Open-Economy Multiplier

Surprisingly, opening up an economy lowers the expenditure multiplier.

One way of understanding the expenditure mul- ①
tiplier in an open economy is to calculate the rounds of spending and respending generated by an additional dollar of government spending, investment, or exports. Suppose that Germany needs to buy American computers to modernize antiquated facilities in what used to be East Germany. Each extra dollar of U.S. computers will generate \$1 of income in the United States, of which \$2/3 = \$0.667 will be spent by Americans on consumption. However, because the marginal propensity to import is 0.10, one-tenth of the extra dollar of income, or \$0.10, will be spent on foreign goods and services, leaving only \$0.567 of spending on domestically produced goods. That \$0.567 of domestic spending will generate \$0.567 of U.S. income, from which 0.567 × \$0.567 = \$0.321 will be spent on consumption of domestic goods and services in the next round. Hence the total increase in output, or the open-economy multiplier, will be

$$\begin{aligned}\text{Open-economy multiplier} &= 1 + 0.567 + (0.567)^2 + \cdots \\ &= 1 + (\tfrac{2}{3} - \tfrac{1}{10}) + (\tfrac{2}{3} - \tfrac{1}{10})^2 + \cdots \\ &= \frac{1}{1 - \frac{2}{3} + \frac{1}{10}} = \frac{1}{\frac{13}{30}} = 2.3\end{aligned}$$

This compares with a closed-economy multiplier of $1/(1 - \tfrac{2}{3}) = 3$.

Another way of calculating the multiplier is as follows: Recall that the multiplier in our simplest model was $1/MPS$, where *MPS* is the "leakage" into saving. As we noted above, imports are another leakage. The total leakage is the dollars leaking into saving ②
(the *MPS*) plus the dollars leaking into imports (the *MPm*). Hence, the open-economy multiplier should be $1/(MPS + MPm) = 1/(0.333 + 0.1) = 1/0.433 = 2.3$. Note that both the leakage analysis and the rounds analysis provide exactly the same answer.

To summarize:

> Because a fraction of any income increase leaks ③
> into imports in an open economy, the **open-economy multiplier** is smaller than the multiplier for a closed economy. The exact relationship is
>
> $$\text{Open-economy multiplier} = \frac{1}{MPS + MPm}$$
>
> where *MPS* = marginal propensity to save and *MPm* = marginal propensity to import.

浮动汇率制下美国的贸易与金融
TRADE AND FINANCE FOR THE UNITED STATES UNDER FLEXIBLE EXCHANGE RATES

We begin with a review of major trends in trade and finance for the United States over the period of flexible exchange rates, which began after the abandonment of the Bretton Woods system in 1973 (recall the discussion in the previous chapter).

First, examine the movements in the dollar exchange rate, shown in Figure 28-3. This is an index of the *real exchange rate* of the U.S. dollar against other major currencies. The real exchange rate corrects for movements in the price levels in different countries. Note how the exchange rate was relatively stable under fixed rates. Then, as with all market-determined asset prices, exchange rates became volatile in the flexible-rate era.

Figure 28-4 shows the *real* component of net exports. This is the ratio of real net exports to real GDP. We saw above that an increase in real net exports tends to be expansionary, while a decrease in real net exports tends to reduce output. We describe two periods in the history of the United States to help understand the role of international trade in domestic production.

Trade Movements Reinforce Tight Money in the 1980s. The decade of the 1980s witnessed a dramatic cycle of dollar appreciation and depreciation. The rise in the value of the dollar began in 1980 after tight

---

① 有一种理解开放经济支出乘数的方法，即计算政府支出、投资和出口中每增加一美元所驱动的一轮又一轮的支出和再支出。

② 总漏出量是流漏入储蓄的美元（*MPS*）与流漏入进口（*MPm*）的美元之和。

③ 在开放经济中，由于收入的任一增加中都有一小部分流入进口，因此，**开放经济乘数**小于封闭经济的乘数。其精确的关系式为：

开放经济乘数 =1/（*MPS* + *MPm*）

式中：*MPS* = 边际储蓄倾向，*MPm* = 边际进口倾向。

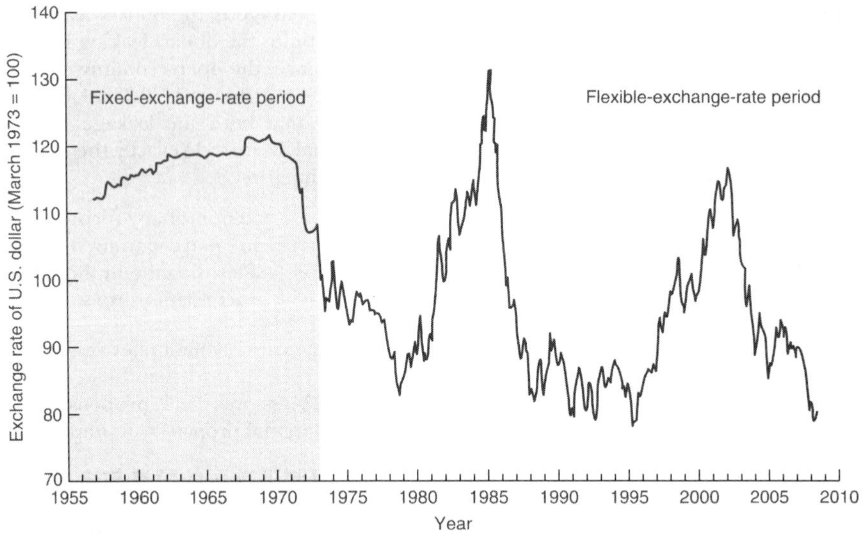

FIGURE 28-3. The Foreign Exchange Rate of the Dollar

During the fixed-exchange-rate (Bretton Woods) period, the dollar's value was stable in exchange markets. After the United States moved to flexible exchange rates in 1973, the dollar's value became more volatile. When the United States pursued its tight-money policies in the early 1980s, the high interest rates pulled up the dollar. With large current-account deficits and the foreign accumulation of dollar-denominated assets, the dollar began to depreciate after 2000.

Source: Federal Reserve System, at *www.federalreserve.gov/releases/h10/summary*.

U.S. monetary policy and loose U.S. fiscal policy drove interest rates up sharply. High interest rates ① at home and economic turmoil abroad attracted funds into financial investments in U.S. dollars. Figure 28-3 shows that during the period from 1979 to early 1985, the real exchange rate on the dollar rose by 80 percent. Many economists believe the dollar was overvalued in 1985—an *overvalued currency* is one whose value is high relative to its long-run or sustainable level.

As the dollar rose, American export prices ② increased and the prices of goods imported into the United States fell. Figure 28-5 shows the important relationship between real exchange rates and the trade deficit. It illustrates the dramatic effect of the appreciating dollar on trade flows. From the trough in 1980 to the peak in 1986, the trade deficit increased by 3 percent of GDP as the dollar appreciated.

By itself, this sharp increase in the trade deficit would be contractionary. The decline in net exports reinforced a decline in domestic demand induced by tight monetary policy. The result was the deepest recession in 50 years.

Countercyclical Net Exports in the 1995–2000 Period. The late 1990s were the opposite story. After 1995, [3] the combination of low real interest rates and a booming stock market led to the rapid growth of domestic demand in the United States, particularly in private investment. Unemployment fell sharply. A rapid increase in foreign demand for U.S. assets led to the sharp appreciation of the dollar.

In contrast with the early 1980s, the macroeconomic impact of the dollar appreciation in this period was appropriate. As the American economy approached full employment, import prices rose, net exports declined, and the foreign sector exercised

---

① 国内的高利率和国外经济的混乱吸引各种资金进入美元的金融投资。

② 由于美元的升值，美国的出口价格随之上涨，进入美国的进口商品价格下跌。

[3] 这句话在 17 版和 18 版中的原文均为：

The late 1990s were the opposite—and a happier—story. 19 版中 “*and a happier*” 的删除隐含了对 20 世纪 90 年代后期互联网泡沫开始破灭的冷静思考。

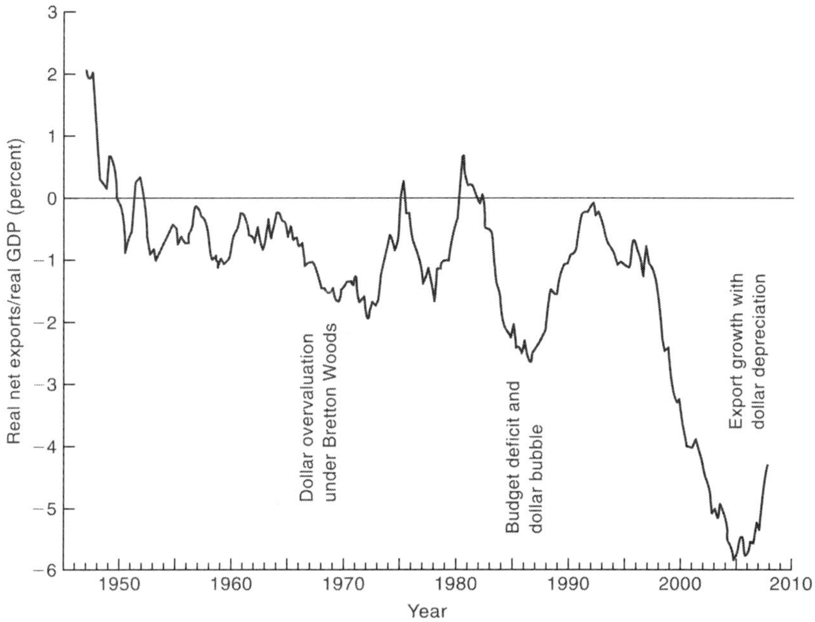

FIGURE 28-4. Real Net Exports Have Been an Important Component of Demand

With a strong rise in the dollar exchange rate and weak economic growth abroad, U.S. real net exports turned sharply negative in the early 1980s. This shift produced a massive drag on aggregate spending in the $C + I + G + X$ equation and helped produce the deep recession of 1982. The growing deficit from the period after 1990 moderated the growth of output. Note how net exports increased after the dollar's depreciation in the late 2000s.

Source: U.S. Bureau of Economic Analysis.

a drag on the economy. Had the dollar depreciated ① rather than appreciated, the foreign sector would have been expansionary, the American economy would have experienced rising inflation, and the Fed would have found it necessary to tighten money to choke off the boom. In the late 1990s, therefore, an appreciation of the dollar and a decline in net exports were just what the macroeconomic doctor ordered.

开放经济的货币传导机制
THE MONETARY TRANSMISSION MECHANISM IN AN OPEN ECONOMY

Our earlier multiplier analysis of business cycles and economic growth focused on policies in a closed economy. We analyzed the way that monetary and fiscal policies can help stabilize the business cycle. How do the impacts of macroeconomic policies change in an open economy? How is the monetary transmission mechanism different in this situation? Surprisingly, the answer to these questions depends crucially on whether the country has a fixed or a flexible exchange rate.

Our survey here will concentrate on high-income countries whose financial markets are closely linked together—the United States, Japan, and the countries of the European Union. When financial investments ② can flow easily among countries and the regulatory barriers to financial investments are low, we say that these countries have *high mobility of financial capital.*

Fixed Exchange Rates. The key feature of countries with fixed exchange rates and high capital mobility is

① 如果当时美元贬值而不是升值的话，外贸部门一定会扩张，美国经济会经历高涨的通货膨胀，美联储就会发现有必要紧缩银根以抑制通货膨胀的迅猛势头。因此在20世纪90年代后期，美元的升值和净出口额的下降，恰恰是宏观经济当局所希望的。

② 当金融投资在各国之间很容易流动，且金融投资的监管门槛又低时，我们就可以说，这些国家具备金融资本的高流动性。

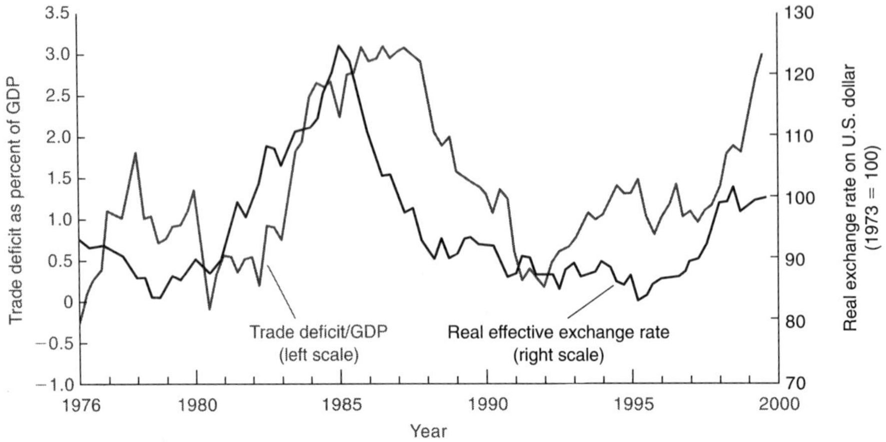

FIGURE 28-5. Trade and Exchange Rates

Trade flows respond to exchange-rate changes, but with a time lag. The real appreciation of the dollar during the early 1980s increased U.S. export prices and reduced prices of goods imported into the United States. As a result, the trade deficit rose sharply. When the dollar depreciated after 1985, the trade deficit began to shrink. The increase in the current-account deficit resulted from dollar appreciation and slow growth outside the United States.

Source: Council of Economic Advisers, *Economic Report of the President, 2000.*

that their interest rates must be very closely aligned. Any divergence in the interest rates between two such countries will attract speculators who will sell one currency and buy the other until the interest rates are equalized.

Consider a small country which pegs its exchange ① rate to the currency of a larger country. *Because the small country's interest rates are determined by the monetary policy of the large country, the small country can no longer conduct independent monetary policy.* The small country's monetary policy must be devoted to ensuring that its interest rates are aligned with those of its partner.

Macroeconomic policy in such a situation is therefore exactly the case described in our multiplier model discussed earlier. From the small country's point of view, investment is exogenous, because it is determined by world interest rates. Fiscal policy is highly effective because there is no monetary reaction to changes in government spending or taxes.

Flexible Exchange Rates. One important insight in this area is that macroeconomic policy with flexible exchange rates operates in quite a different way from the case of fixed exchange rates. A flexible exchange rate has a reinforcing effect on monetary policy.

Let's consider the case of the United States. The ② monetary transmission mechanism in the United States has changed significantly in recent decades as a result of increased openness and the change to a flexible exchange rate. In the modern era, international trade and finance have come to play an increasingly important role in U.S. macroeconomic policy.

Figure 28-6 shows the monetary transmission mechanism under flexible exchange rates. Panel (*a*) shows the relationship between net exports and the exchange rate, the actual history of which we saw in Figure 28-5. This is an inverse relationship because a depreciation stimulates exports and discourages imports. Suppose that the Fed decides to reduce interest rates to stimulate the economy. The decline in interest rates would lead to a depreciation in the dollar as financial investors moved from

① 假设一个小国将其汇率钉住比较大的国家的货币。由于小国的利率是由大国的货币政策决定的，所以小国就不能制定独立的货币政策。小国的货币政策必须致力于确保其利率与其伙伴国的利率相一致。

② 让我们以美国为例来做一分析。近几十年来，由于经济日趋开放和浮动汇率变化所带来的结果，美国的货币传导机制已经发生了重大变化。在当今这个时代，国际贸易与国际金融已经在美国的宏观经济政策中起到越来越重要的作用。

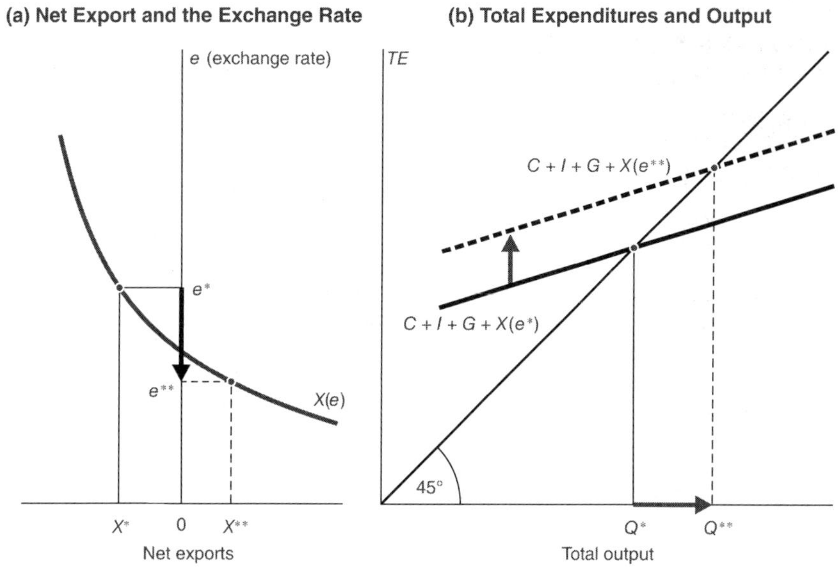

FIGURE 28-6. With Flexible Exchange Rates, the Monetary Transmission Mechanism Is Reinforced

Suppose that the central bank lowers interest rates. This will tend to lower the exchange rate from e^* to e^{**} in a flexible-exchange-rate system. Such a depreciation will stimulate net exports by moving down *along* the net-export curve. This increase in net exports from $X(e^*)$ to $X(e^{**})$ shifts up the total expenditure curve, increasing total output from Q^* to Q^{**}.

dollar to nondollar stocks and bonds. The depreciation is shown in Figure 28-6 as a movement from e^* to e^{**}. This depreciation changes a net export deficit of X^* to a net export surplus of X^{**}. The decline in interest rates would also tend to increase domestic investment, but we omit that effect from our discussion.

We show the result of this net export expansion in Figure 28-6(*b*). (This assumes, as with all our multiplier analyses, a situation where there are unemployed resources.) The increase in net exports shifts the total expenditure curve up from $C + I + G + X(e^*)$ to $C + I + G + X(e^{**})$. The result is an increase in total expenditure and an increase in output from Q^* to Q^{**}. All the changes shown in Figure 28-6 illustrate the policies and reactions during the 1995–2000 period discussed in the previous section.

① Alternatively, take the opposite case. Suppose that the Fed decides to slow the economy, as it did after 1979. The monetary tightening raised U.S. interest rates, which attracted funds into dollar securities. This increase in the demand for dollars led to an appreciation of the dollar. The high dollar exchange rate reduced net exports and contributed to the recession of 1981–1983, as we described earlier. The impact on net exports in such a situation would be the opposite of that shown in Figure 28-6.

Foreign trade produces a new and powerful link ② in the monetary transmission mechanism when a country has a flexible exchange rate. When monetary policy changes interest rates, this affects exchange rates and net exports as well as domestic investment. Monetary tightening leads to an appreciation in the exchange rate and a corresponding decline in net exports; monetary easing does the opposite. The impact of changes in interest rates on net exports reinforces the impact on domestic investment.

① 换一个角度，我们来分析一个截然相反的案例。假设美联储决定减缓经济发展的速度，这一举措美联储早在 1979 年之后就曾使用过。货币紧缩提高了美国利率，这就吸引了资金涌入以美元标价的证券市场。这种对美元的需求增加导致了美元的升值。居于高位的美元汇率降低了美国的净出口，引发了前面我们所讨论过的 1981~1983 年期间的经济衰退。

② 一个国家在实施了浮动利率制之后，其对外贸易就为货币传导机制建构了一条崭新而强有力的链接。当货币政策改变了利率时，又将影响到汇率、净出口以及国内投资。货币的紧缩引发汇率升值，从而导致净出口的下滑。货币的宽松则与此正好相反。利率变化对净出口所产生的这些影响，使其对国内投资的影响得以加强。

全球经济中的相互依存

B. INTERDEPENDENCE IN THE GLOBAL ECONOMY

开放经济的经济增长
ECONOMIC GROWTH IN THE OPEN ECONOMY

The first section described the short-run impact of international trade and policy changes in the open economy. These issues are crucial for open economies combating unemployment and inflation. But countries must also keep their eye on the implications of their policies for long-run economic growth. Particularly for small open economies, effective use of international trade and international finance is central for promoting economic growth.

Economic growth involves a wide variety of issues, as we saw in Chapter 25. Perhaps the single most important approach for promoting rapid economic growth is to ensure high levels of saving and investment.

But economic growth involves more than just ① capital. It requires moving toward the technological frontier by adopting the best technological practices. It requires developing institutions that nurture investment and the spirit of enterprise. Other issues—trade policies, intellectual property rights, policies toward direct investment, and the overall macroeconomic climate—are essential ingredients in the growth of open economies.

开放经济的储蓄与投资
SAVING AND INVESTMENT IN THE OPEN ECONOMY

In a closed economy, total investment equals domes- ②
tic saving. Open economies, however, can draw upon world financial markets for investment funds, and other countries can be an outlet for domestic saving. (Recall Table 27-3, which shows the net saving of important regions.) We first review the investment-saving relationship, and then we examine the mechanisms for allocating saving among different countries.

The Saving-Investment Relation in an Open Economy

Let's pause to recall our saving-investment identities from Chapter 20:

$$I_T = I + X = S + (T - G)$$

This states that total national investment (I_T) consists of investment in domestic capital (I) plus net foreign

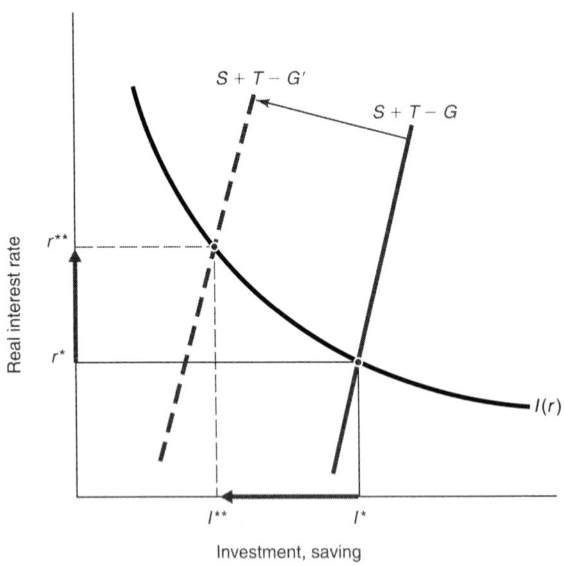

FIGURE 28-7. Saving and Investment in the Closed Economy

Investment is inversely related to the real interest rate, while private saving and public saving are relatively unresponsive to the interest rate. Equilibrium saving and investment comes at r^*. Suppose that government military spending increases. This increases the government deficit and therefore reduces public saving. The result is a shift in the national saving curve to the left to $S + T - G'$, raising the market interest rate to r^{**} and reducing national saving and investment to I^{**}.

① 但是，经济增长不仅仅是资本的问题。它需要通过采用最佳技术实践，尽可能地向科学技术的最前沿靠拢。它还需要制定制度，以培育投资和企业家精神。贸易政策、知识产权保护、鼓励直接投资的政策，以及总体的宏观经济环境等其他因素，都是开放经济必要的组成部分。

② 在封闭经济中，总投资等于国内储蓄。但是，开放经济却能从国际金融市场吸收投资所需的资金，同时，其他国家也可以成为其国内储蓄的出口。

investment or net exports (X). This must equal total private saving (S) by households and businesses plus total public saving, which is given by the government surplus ($T - G$).

We can rewrite the identity as follows to emphasize the components of net exports:

$$X = S + (T - G) - I$$

or

Net exports = (private saving + government saving) − domestic investment

This important equation shows that net exports are the difference between domestic saving and domestic investment. The components of total U.S. national investment for recent decades are shown in Table 28-2.

充分就业条件下储蓄与投资的决定
Determination of Saving and Investment at Full Employment

We need to go beyond the identities to understand the ① *mechanism* by which saving and investment are equalized in the open economy. This analysis concerns primarily the long run in which there is full employment and output equals its potential. That is, we consider how saving and investment are allocated in the long run in a "classical" economy.

Closed Economy. We begin with a closed economy where there is no inflation and no uncertainty. In this situation, investment must equal private saving plus the government surplus. The equilibrating price is the real interest rate, which adjusts to balance the levels of saving and investment.

Figure 28-7 shows how national saving and investment are equilibrated in a full-employment closed economy. The $S + T - G$ curve shows national saving, which is assumed to increase slightly with the real interest rate. Additionally, as we learned in Chapter 21, there is an inverse relationship between investment and the interest rate. Higher interest rates reduce spending on housing and on business plant and equipment. We therefore write our investment schedule as $I(r)$ to indicate that investment depends upon the real interest rate, r.

The saving and investment schedules intersect in Figure 28-7 to determine an interest rate at r^* with high levels of saving and investment.

Now suppose that the government increases its purchases without increasing taxes, say, because of an increase in military spending to fight foreign wars. This will shift the saving schedule to the left to $S + T - G'$. As a result, the real interest rate increases to equilibrate saving and investment, and the level of investment falls. A similar outcome would occur if ② the government lowered taxes or if the private sector lowered its desired savings.

In a full-employment closed economy (always ③ holding other things constant), higher government

Saving and Investment as Percentage of NNP			
Sector	**1959–1981**	**1982–2001**	**2002–2007**
Net domestic saving	**11.5**	**6.4**	**1.7**
Net private saving	11.6	8.8	4.6
Net government saving	−0.1	−2.5	−2.8
Net domestic investment (in capital)	**11.1**	**8.5**	**7.7**
Net foreign investment	**0.4**	**−2.1**	**−6.0**

TABLE 28-2. The Declining U.S. Saving Rate

This table shows the changing structure of U.S. saving over the last half-century. For most of the 1959–1981 period, saving and investment were about equal and at a high level. Then, after 1981, government saving declined as the federal budget moved into deficit. This decline was reinforced in the 2000s as personal and other private saving dropped sharply. By the 2002–2007 period, most U.S. capital investment was financed by foreign saving, which is the counterpart to the large current-account deficit.

Source: Bureau of Economic Analysis.

① 我们需要透过这些等式，深入地了解一下开放经济中导致储蓄与投资相等的机制是如何运作的。这一分析主要关注长期——实现充分就业，产出等于潜在产出。也就是说，我们是在思考在“古典”经济中，储蓄与投资在长期是如何进行分配的。

② 如果政府降低税收，或者私人部门预期的储蓄额降低，则会出现类似的结果。

③ 在充分就业的封闭经济中（保持其他因素不变），较高的政府支出、较低的税收，以及预期的私人低储蓄率将会提高实际利率，降低储蓄与投资的均衡水平。

spending, lower taxes, or lower desired private saving will raise the real interest rate and lower equilibrium saving and investment.

Open-Economy Equilibrium. Now consider the situation of an open economy in which financial markets are integrated with world markets. An open economy has alternative sources of investment and alternative outlets for saving. We simplify by assuming that the economy is small and cannot affect world interest rates. We show this situation in Figure 28-8 for a small open economy with a high degree of mobility of financial capital. A small open economy must equate its domestic real interest rate with the world real interest rate, r^W. Because financial markets are open, financial capital will move to equilibrate interest rates at home and abroad. ①

Figure 28-8 helps explain the determination of saving, investment, and net exports in the open economy. At the prevailing world interest rate, domestic investment is shown at point *A*, which is the intersection of the investment schedule and the interest rate. Total national saving is given at point *B* on the total saving schedule, $S + T - G$. The difference between them—given by the line segment *AB*—is net exports. (This equality is shown by the saving-investment identity in the box on page 574.)

Hence net exports are determined by the difference between national saving and national ②

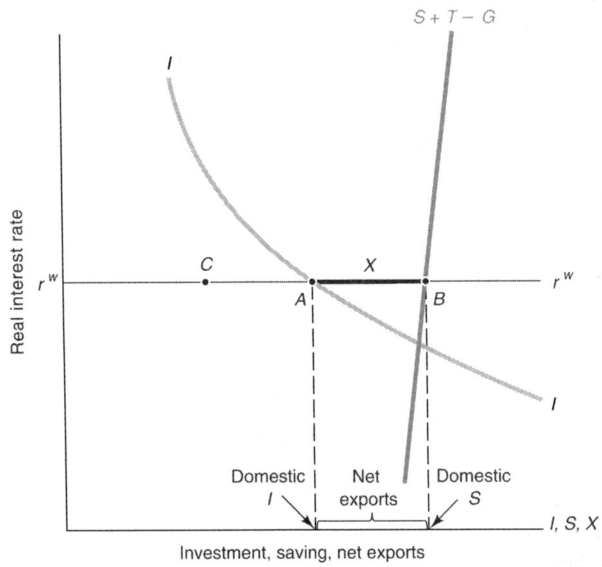

FIGURE 28-8. Saving and Investment in a Small Open Economy

Domestic investment and domestic saving are determined by income, interest rates, and government fiscal policy, as in Fig. 28-7. But the small open economy with mobile financial capital has its real interest rates determined in world financial markets. At the relatively high real interest rate at r^W, domestic saving exceeds domestic investment and the excess saving flows to more lucrative investment opportunities abroad. The difference between national saving and domestic investment is net exports (also equal to net foreign investment), shown as *X* in the figure. A trade surplus such as has been seen in Japan and China is caused by the interaction of high domestic saving and low domestic investment.

① 现在我们来分析一下开放经济中金融市场与国际市场整合的状况。一个开放的经济体拥有各种可供选择的投资来源及多种储蓄出口。

② 因此，净出口额是由国民储蓄和国民投资之间的差额决定的，同时又受国内因素和国际利率的共同影响。

investment, which is determined by domestic factors plus the world interest rate.

This discussion pushes into the background the ① mechanism by which a country adjusts its trade, saving, and investment. It is here that the exchange rate plays the crucial equilibrating role. *Changes in exchange rates are the mechanism by which saving and investment adjust.* That is, exchange rates move to ensure that the level of net exports balances the difference between domestic saving and investment.

This analysis can help explain the trends in saving, investment, and trade patterns in major countries in recent years. Figure 28-8 describes well the role of Japan in the world economy. Japan has traditionally had a high domestic saving rate. Yet in recent ② years—because of high production costs at home and competitive conditions in neighboring newly industrialized countries—the return on Japanese capital has been depressed. Japanese saving therefore seeks outlets abroad, with the consequence that Japan has had a large trade surplus and high net exports.

The United States has seen an interesting twist in its saving and investment position, as was shown in Table 28-2. Until 1980, the United States had a modestly positive net-export position. But in the early 1980s the U.S. government's fiscal position shifted sharply toward deficit. You can depict this by drawing a new $S + T' - G'$ line in Figure 28-8 that intersects the real-interest-rate line at point *C*. You can see that total national saving would decline with a larger government deficit. Domestic investment would be unchanged. Net exports would turn negative and be given by the line segment *CA*.

We can also use this analysis to explain the mechanism by which net exports adjust to provide the necessary investment when the government runs a budget deficit. Consider a country with a net-export surplus as shown in Figure 28-8. Suppose that the government suddenly begins to run a large budget deficit. This change will lead to an imbalance in the ③ saving-investment market, which would tend to push up domestic interest rates relative to world interest rates. The rise in domestic interest rates will attract funds from abroad and will lead to an appreciation in the foreign exchange rate of the country running the budget deficit. The appreciation will lead to falling exports and rising imports, or a decrease in net exports. This trend will continue until net exports have fallen sufficiently to close the saving-investment gap.

Other important examples of the open-economy saving-investment theory in the small open economy are the following:

- An increase in private saving or lower government spending will increase national saving as represented by a rightward shift in the national saving schedule in Figure 28-8. This will lead to a depreciation of the exchange rate until net exports have increased enough to balance the increase in domestic saving.
- An increase in domestic investment, say, because of an improved business climate or a burst of innovations, will lead to a shift in the investment schedule. This will lead to an appreciation of the exchange rate until net exports decline enough to balance saving and investment. In this case, domestic investment crowds out foreign investment.
- An increase in world interest rates will reduce the level of investment. This will lead to an increase in the difference between saving and investment, to a depreciation in the foreign exchange rate, and to an increase in net exports and foreign investment. (This would be a shift along the investment schedule.)

Table 28-3 summarizes the major results for the small open economy. Make sure you can also work through the cases of decreases in the government's fiscal deficit, in private saving, in investment, and in world interest rates. This handy table and its explanation deserve careful study.[1]

Integration of a country into the world economy ④
adds an important new dimension to macroeconomic performance and policy. Key findings are:

- The foreign sector provides an important source of domestic investment and a potential outlet for domestic saving.
- Higher saving at home—whether in the form of higher private saving or higher public saving—will lead to higher net exports.

[1] This discussion covers "small" open economies that cannot affect the world interest rate. For "large" open economies like the United States, the impact would be somewhere between the small-economy and the closed-economy cases. This more complex case is covered in intermediate textbooks (see the Further Reading section in Chapter 19).

① 这一讨论将深入到一国对其贸易、储蓄和投资进行调节的运作机制。这里，汇率起着关键的平衡作用。汇率的变化是储蓄和投资赖以调整的机制。

② 然而近几年，国内的高生产成本，以及邻近的新工业化国家形成的竞争格局，致使日元资本的收益率受到挤压。因此，日元的储蓄也在寻找国外的出口，其结果是日本有庞大的贸易顺差和高的净出口额。

③ 这一变化导致了储蓄－投资市场的失衡，从而推高相对于国际利率的国内利率。

④ 一国融入世界经济对宏观经济运行和政策的制定都增添了极其重要的新的扩展空间。主要有以下几点：

- 国外部门给国内投资提供了重要来源，也给国内储蓄提供了一个潜在的出路。
- 无论是国内较高的私人储蓄率，还是较高的公共储蓄率，两种形式的高储蓄率都可导致净出口的升高。

Change in policy or exogenous variable	Change in exchange rate	Change in investment	Change in net exports
Increase in G or decrease in T	$e\uparrow$	0	$X\downarrow$
Increase in private S	$e\downarrow$	0	$X\uparrow$
Increase in investment demand	$e\uparrow$	$I\uparrow$	$X\downarrow$
Increase in world interest rates	$e\downarrow$	$I\downarrow$	$X\uparrow$

TABLE 28-3. Major Conclusions of Saving-Investment Model in Small Open Economy

Make sure you understand the mechanism by which each of these occurs.

- A country's trade balance is primarily a reflection ① of its national saving and investment balance rather than of its absolute productivity or wealth.
- Adjustments in a country's trade accounts require a change in domestic saving or investment.
- In the long run, adjustments in trade accounts will be brought about by movements in the country's relative prices, often through exchange-rate changes.

开放经济中促进经济增长的问题 PROMOTING GROWTH IN THE OPEN ECONOMY

Increasing the growth of output in open economies involves more than just waving a magic wand that will attract investors or savers. A favorable saving and investing climate involves a wide array of policies, including a stable macroeconomic environment, secure property rights, and, above all, a predictable and attractive returns on investment. We review in this section some of the ways that open economies can improve their growth rates by using the global marketplace to their best advantage.

Over the long run, the single most important way of increasing per capita output and living standards is to ensure that the country *adopts best-practice techniques* in its production processes. It does little good to have a high investment rate if the investments are in the wrong technology. This point was abundantly ② shown in the last years of Soviet central planning (discussed in Chapter 26), when the investment rate was extremely high but much investment was poorly designed, left unfinished, or put in unproductive sectors. Moreover, individual poor countries do not need to start from scratch in designing their own turbines, machinery, computers, and management systems. Often, reaching the technological frontier will involve engaging in joint ventures with foreign firms, which in turn requires that the institutional framework be hospitable to foreign capital.

Another important set of policies is *trade policies*. Evidence shows that an open trading system promotes competitiveness and adoption of best-practice technologies. By keeping tariffs and other barriers to trade low, countries can ensure that domestic firms feel the spur of competition and that foreign firms are permitted to enter domestic markets when domestic producers sell at inefficiently high prices or monopolize particular sectors.

When countries consider their saving and investment, they must not concentrate entirely on physical capital. *Intangible capital* is just as important. Studies show that countries that invest in human capital through education tend to perform well and be resilient in the face of shocks. Many countries have valuable stocks of natural resources—forests, minerals, oil and gas, fisheries, and arable land—that must be managed carefully to ensure that they provide the highest yield for the country.

One of the most complex factors in a country's growth involves *immigration* and *emigration*. Historically, the United States has attracted large flows of immigrants that not only have increased the size of its labor force but also have enhanced the quality of its culture and scientific research. More recently, however, the immigrants have possessed less education and lower skills than the domestic labor force. As a result, according to some studies, immigration has depressed the relative wages of low-wage workers in the United States. Countries that "export" workers, such as Mexico, often

---

① • 一国的贸易余额主要是反映国民储蓄和投资的平衡，而不完全是其生产率或财富。
- 一国贸易账户的调节，需要国内储蓄或者投资做相应的变动。
- 长期来讲，贸易账户的调节必须由该国相对价格的变动来完成，通常是通过汇率的变化来实现的。

② 这一点在苏联计划经济的最后几年里（请参阅第26章）表现得非常充分。虽然投资率极高，但其中很大部分都是盲目投资，或沦为烂尾工程，或者投给了生产效率很低的部门。

have a steady stream of earnings that are sent home by citizens to their relatives, and this can provide a nice supplement to export earnings.

① One of the most important yet subtle influences concerns the *institutions of the market.* The most successful open economies—like the Netherlands and Luxembourg in Europe or Taiwan and Hong Kong of China in Asia—have provided a secure environment for investment and entrepreneurship. This involved establishing a secure set of property rights, guided by the rule of law. Increasingly important is the development of intellectual property rights so that inventors and creative artists are assured that they will be able to profit from their activities. Countries must fight corruption, which is a kind of private taxation system that preys on the most profitable enterprises, creates uncertainty about property rights, raises costs, and has a chilling effect on investment.

A *stable macroeconomic climate* means that taxes are ② reasonable and predictable and that inflation is low, so lenders need not worry about inflation confiscating their investments. It is crucial that exchange rates be relatively stable, with a convertibility that allows easy and inexpensive entry into and exit out of the domestic currency. Countries that provide a favorable institu- ③ tional structure attract large flows of foreign financial capital, while countries that have unstable institutions attract relatively little foreign funds and suffer "capital flight," in which local residents move their funds abroad to avoid taxes, expropriation, or loss of value.

Figure 28-9 illustrates the impact of the investment climate on national investment. The left-hand panel

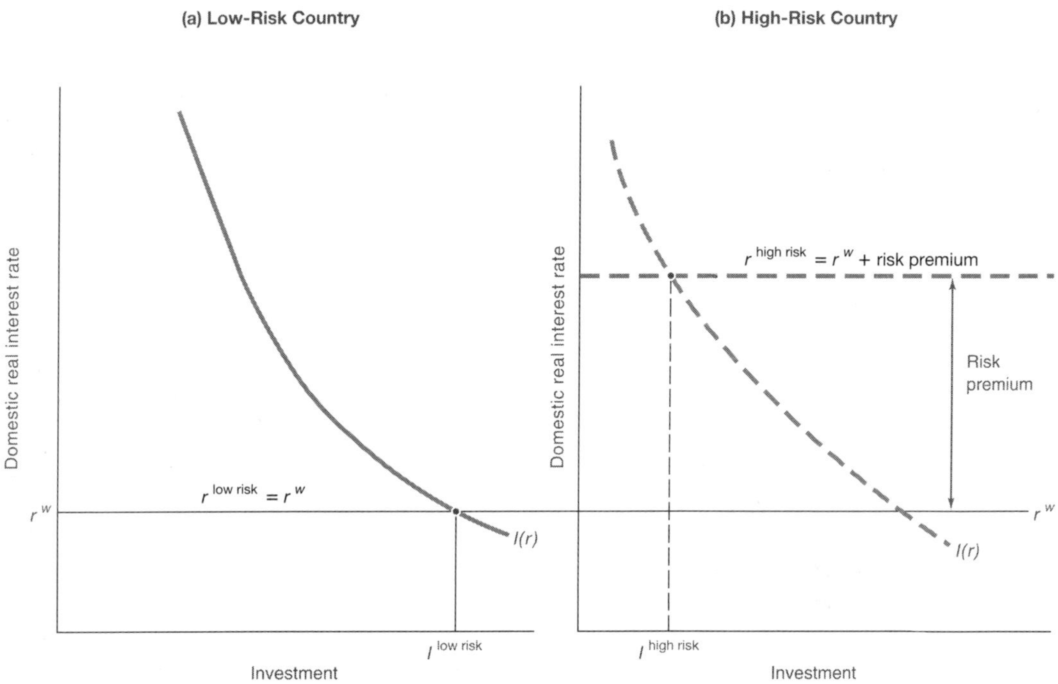

FIGURE 28-9. Business Climate Affects Interest Rate and Investment Level

In the low-risk country in (**a**), a stable economic climate leads to a low domestic interest rate at r^W and a high level of investment at $I^{\text{low risk}}$. In the high-risk country, racked by political turmoil, corruption, and economic uncertainty, investors require a large risk premium on their investments, so the domestic interest rate is far above the world interest rate. The result is a depressed level of investment as foreign investors seek safer terrain.

① 市场机制是其中最为重大而又微妙的影响之一。
② 一个稳定的宏观经济环境意味着税收是合理的、可预测的，且通货膨胀率较低，所以，贷方不需要担忧由于通货膨胀的原因其投资被"没收"的风险。
③ 那些提供了有利的制度结构的国家吸引了大量流动性的外国金融资本，而那些没有稳定制度的国家几乎无法吸引外国资金，并且还得忍受"资本外逃"之苦——在这些国家，当地居民将其资金转移至国外，以规避税收、被征用或者贬值的风险。

depicts a country that has a favorable investment climate, so the domestic interest rate is equal to the world interest rate. The overall level of investment there is high, and the country can attract foreign funds to finance domestic investment.

Panel (*b*) shows a high-risk country. Look back at Figure 26-2 on page 528, which shows the premium on emerging-market bonds. In periods of crisis, these countries might pay interest rates 8 or 10 or 12 percentage points above the rate paid by investors in advanced countries. The high risk premium might ①
arise because of high inflation, unpredictable taxes, nationalizations, default, corruption, an unstable foreign exchange rate, or sometimes just panic and contagion. The real cost of capital would therefore be extremely high. The risky country will have trouble attracting both domestic *and* foreign investment, and the resulting level of investment will be low. Compare the equilibrium level of investment in low-risk panel (*a*) to that of high-risk panel (*b*).

② 在开放经济中，促进经济的增长必须确保企业对国内外投资者的吸引力——这些投资者在世界经济中有大量的投资机会。制定政策的最终目标是在高生产率的部门实现高储蓄率和高投资率，并能确保企业采用最成熟的技术。实现这些目标需要营造稳定的宏观经济环境，对有形投资和知识产权都能提供可靠的产权保障；实现货币兑换以允许投资者将其利润带回家；保持对该国政治和经济稳定的信心。

Promoting economic growth in an open economy involves ensuring that business is attractive for foreign and domestic investors who have a wide array of investment opportunities in the world economy. The ultimate goals of policy are to have high rates of saving and investment in productive channels and to ensure that businesses use best-practice techniques. Achieving these goals involves setting a stable macroeconomic climate, guaranteeing dependable property rights for both tangible investments and intellectual property, providing exchange-rate convertibility that allows investors to take home their profits, and maintaining confidence in the political and economic stability of the country. ②

国际经济问题

C. INTERNATIONAL ECONOMIC ISSUES

In this final section, we apply the tools of international economics to examine two of the central issues that have concerned nations in recent years. In the first part, we examine the issue of the difference between competitiveness and productivity. In the second part, we examine the birth of the European Monetary Union.

竞争力与生产率
COMPETITIVENESS AND PRODUCTIVITY

“美国的去工业化”
“The Deindustrialization of America”

Often, when the trade deficit becomes large, people become concerned and worry about the nation's productivity and competitiveness. Just such a situation occurred in the United States in the 1980s, and later resurfaced in the 2000s. A review of this history is a helpful reminder about the determinants of trade flows.

The appreciation of the dollar in the 1980s pro- ③
duced severe economic hardships in many U.S. sectors exposed to international trade. Industries like automobiles, steel, and textiles found the demand for their products shrinking as an appreciation of the exchange rate led to a rise in their prices relative to those of their foreign competitors. Unemployment in America's manufacturing heartland increased sharply, factories were closed, and the Midwest became known as the "rust belt."

Many noneconomists interpreted U.S. trade problems as indicative of "America in decline." They fretted that America's technological leadership was eroding because of what they saw as unfair trade practices, excessive regulation, declining innovation, and managerial sloth. Some called for a reversal of ④
trade agreements such as the North American Free Trade Agreement (NAFTA). America was pictured as [5]
a land condemned to serving potato chips while others were manufacturing our computer chips.

Economists saw a different syndrome at work—this situation is a classic disease of an overvalued exchange rate. To understand the fundamentals, we must distinguish a nation's competitiveness from its productivity. *Competitiveness* refers to the extent to which a nation's goods can compete in the marketplace; this depends primarily upon the relative prices of domestic and foreign products. Competitiveness should not be confused with *productivity*, which is measured by the output per unit of input. Productivity is fundamental to the growth of living standards in a nation; to a first approximation, a nation's real income grows in step with its productivity growth.

It is true that U.S. competitiveness fell sharply during the 1980s and again in the early 2000s. However, these changes were not caused by a deterioration in productivity growth. Actually, productivity

① 高通货膨胀、不可预测的税收、国有化、违约、腐败、不稳定的汇率，以及不时发生的社会恐慌和疫病等都是引发高风险溢价的原因。

③ 20 世纪 80 年代美元的升值给美国经济中受国际贸易影响的许多部门带来了严重的经济困难。像汽车、钢铁和纺织等行业，均遭遇了需求萎缩。这都是由于汇率上升，导致其产品价格相较于那些国外竞争对手的价格升高造成的。

④ 还有一些人大声呼吁废除像《北美自由贸易协定》（NAFTA）这样的贸易协议。

[5] North American Free Trade Agreement：美国和加拿大于 1989 年签署了《美加自由贸易协定》，1992 年墨西哥加入成为三边自由贸易的《北美自由贸易协定》，1994 年 1 月 1 日正式生效。

growth increased just as the trade deficit increased. Macroeconomists believe that deteriorating competitiveness arose because the decline in national saving in the United States led to an appreciation of the dollar and raised American prices relative to those of its trading partners.

生产率的发展趋势
Trends in Productivity

The real story about U.S. real incomes is not about competitiveness but about productivity. Recall that productivity measures the output per unit of input (such as labor-hours). Our chapter on economic growth showed that increases in real wages depend primarily on the growth of domestic labor productivity.

Competitiveness is important for trade but has no intrinsic relationship to the level or growth of real incomes. China enjoyed a massive trade surplus in the 2000s at the same time as the United States ran a large trade deficit. But would Americans therefore trade their living standards for those in China with jobs paying $1 an hour? Loss of competitiveness in international markets results from a nation's *prices* being out of line with those of its trading partners; it has no necessary connection with how a nation's *productivity* compares with that of other countries.

Studies of productivity differences among countries emphasize the importance of *competition* and *outward orientation*. An essential aspect of policy designed to increase productivity is to force domestic industries to compete with foreign firms, who often have superior, frontier technologies. Foreign direct investment by the most productive countries (such as the Japanese automobile plants operating in the United States) has contributed to dramatic productivity improvements through both the introduction of cutting-edge technologies and the stimulation of competition.

Conclusion on productivity and competitiveness: As ①
the theory of comparative advantage demonstrates, nations are not inherently uncompetitive. Rather, they become uncompetitive when their prices move out of line with those of their trading partners. The surest route to high productivity and high living standards is to expose domestic industries to world markets and to encourage vigorous domestic competition with foreign companies that have adopted the most advanced technologies.

欧洲货币联盟
THE EUROPEAN MONETARY UNION

An ideal exchange-rate system is one that allows high levels of predictability of relative prices while stabilizing the economy in the face of economic shocks. In a well-functioning system, people can trade and invest in other countries without worrying that exchange rates will suddenly change and make their ventures unprofitable.

From the early 1990s, however, fixed-exchange-rate systems were often *destabilizing* rather than stabilizing. Time and again, fixed-exchange-rate systems were the subject of intense speculative attacks that spread to other countries through contagion. They were seen in Europe in 1991–1992, Mexico in 1994–1995, Russia and East Asia in 1997–1998, and Latin America from 1998 to 2002.

Nowhere were problems with the exchange- ②
rate system more persistent and profound than in Western Europe. As a result, the countries of the European Union took the giant step of linking their economic fortunes through the European Monetary Union, which forged a common currency, the Euro.

The Fundamental Trilemma of Fixed Exchange Rates

"You can't have it all" is one of the central tenets of economics. This was driven home in macroeconomic affairs on several occasions during the 1990s. As countries on fixed exchange rates liberalized their financial markets, they encountered a *fundamental trilemma of fixed exchange rates: A country can have only two of the following (a) a fixed but adjustable exchange rate, (b) free capital and financial movements, and (c) an independent domestic monetary policy.*

This inconsistency among the three objectives was explained by Paul Krugman as follows: [3]

> ④ The point is that you can't have it all: A country must pick two out of three. [5] It can fix its exchange rate without emasculating its central bank, but only by maintaining controls on capital flows (like China today); it can leave capital movement free and retain monetary autonomy, but only by letting the exchange rate fluctuate (like Britain—or Canada); or it can choose to leave capital free and stabilize the currency, but only by abandoning any ability to adjust interest rates to fight inflation or recession (like Argentina today, or for that matter most of Europe).[2]

---

[2] See this chapter's Further Reading section.

④ 问题的关键是一个人不可能将一切据为己有：一国必须在三个目标中选择两个。通过维持对资本流动的控制这个唯一手段，一个国家（比如今天的中国）可以在不削弱中央银行的前提下固定其汇率。但是，通过让汇率浮动起来（如英国和加拿大），一国能让资本自由流动，并可以保持货币的自主权。一个国家还可以选择让资本自由流动，稳定货币，但只能通过放弃调整利率来抑制通货膨胀和经济衰退的能力（比如今天的阿根廷以及类似的大多数欧洲国家）。

[5] pick two out of three：相当于中国传统经商逻辑——赊三不如现二。

---

① 关于劳动生产率和竞争力的结论：正如比较优势理论所揭示的那样，没有一个国家是生来就不具备竞争力的。一些国家的价格超出了其贸易伙伴的的价格，他们就失去了竞争力。通向高生产率和高生活水平的最可靠途径是将本国的产业向国际市场开放，鼓励本国企业与采用最先进技术的外国企业竞争。

② 世界上没有一个地方的汇率体系问题比西欧的更持久、更根深蒂固。但结果是，欧盟国家迈出了巨大的一步，通过欧洲货币联盟将各国的经济命运连在一起，打造了统一货币——欧元。

[3] Paul Krugman：保罗·克鲁格曼（1953~），普林斯顿大学教授，美国经济学家，《纽约时报》专栏作家。由于其对“新贸易理论”和“新经济地理”的突出贡献获 2008 年诺贝尔经济学奖。他是诺贝尔经济学奖得主中少有的几位具备人文史哲修养和文笔俱佳的人物之一。

迈向统一货币：欧元

Toward a Common Currency: The Euro

Since World War II, the democratic countries of Western Europe have pursued ever-closer economic integration, primarily to promote political stability after two devastating wars. Peace and trade go hand in hand, according to many political scientists. Beginning in 1957 with a free-trade agreement, Western Europeans gradually removed all barriers to trade in goods, services, and finance. The final step in economic integration was to adopt a common currency. This would not only foster closer economic ties but also resolve the problem of unstable currencies that plagued the earlier fixed-exchange-rate systems.

Eleven European countries joined the European ① Monetary Union (EMU) in 1999. These countries, sometimes called Euroland, adopted the Euro as their unit of account and medium of exchange. The first step was to begin transactions in Euros. The trickiest step came on January 1, 2002, when the countries of Euroland replaced their national currencies with Euro coins and notes, saying, in effect, "*Au revoir,* French franc; *bonjour,* Euro." The Euro was launched smoothly and has now taken its place among the world's major currencies.

The monetary structure under the European Monetary Union resembles that of the United States. Control over European monetary policy is exercised by the *European Central Bank (ECB),* which conducts monetary policy for countries in the accord. The ECB undertakes open-market operations and thereby determines interest rates for the Euro.

One of the major questions for monetary policy involves the objectives of the central bank. The ECB ② is directed under its charter to pursue "price stability" as its primary objective, although it can pursue other communitywide goals as long as these do not compromise price stability. The ECB defines price stability as an increase in Euroland consumer prices of below 2 percent per year over the medium term.

货币联盟的成本与收益

Costs and Benefits of Monetary Union

What are the costs and benefits of European monetary union? Advocates of monetary union see important *benefits.* Under a common currency, exchange-rate volatility within Europe will be reduced to zero, so trade and finance will no longer have to contend with the uncertainties about prices induced by changing exchange rates. The primary result will be a reduction in transactions costs among countries. To the extent that national financial markets are segmented, moving to a common currency may allow a more efficient allocation of capital across countries. Some believe that firm macroeconomic discipline will be preserved by having an independent European central bank committed to strict inflation targets. Perhaps the most important benefit may be political integration and stability of Western Europe—a region that has been at peace for half a century after being at war with itself for most of its recorded history.

Some economists are skeptical about the wisdom of monetary union in Europe and point to significant *costs* of such a union. The dominant concern is that the individual countries will lose the use of both monetary policy and exchange rates as tools for macroeconomic adjustment. This question concerns the optimal currency area, a concept first proposed by Columbia's Robert Mundell, who won the 1999 Nobel Prize for his contributions in this field. An **optimal currency area** is one whose regions have high labor mobility or have common and synchronous aggregate supply or demand shocks. In an optimal currency area, significant changes in exchange rates are not necessary to ensure rapid macroeconomic adjustment.

Most economists believe that the United States is an optimal currency area. When the United States is faced with a shock that affects the different regions asymmetrically, labor migration tends to restore balance. For example, workers left the hard-hit northern states and migrated to the oil-rich southwestern states after the oil shocks of the 1970s.

Is Europe an optimal currency area? Some economists think it is not because of the rigidity of its wage structures and the low degree of labor mobility among the different countries. When a shock has occurred—for example, after the 1990 reunification of Germany—inflexible wages and prices led to rising inflation in the regions with a demand increase and rising unemployment in depressed regions. Monetary union might therefore condemn unfortunate regions to persistent low growth and high unemployment.

What is the initial verdict on the European Monetary Union? The creation of the Euro has removed one of the major sources of instability in the European economy—intra-European exchange-rate movements. In addition, it has led to a convergence of interest rates and inflation rates among European countries. On the other hand, Europe has

① 1999年，11个欧洲国家加入了欧洲货币联盟（EMU）。这些国家有时被称为欧元区，他们将欧元作为他们的记账单位和交易媒介。

② 根据欧洲中央银行的章程，稳定价格是欧洲央行追求的主要目标。只要不危及价格稳定，欧洲央行当然可以去追求欧盟范围内的其他目标。

continued to experience high unemployment rates since the Euro's introduction. The financial crisis of 2007–2009 was the first major test of the European Monetary System, and economists will study how well this new multinational institution weathers the storm.

The European Monetary Union is one of history's great economic experiments. Never before has such a large and powerful group of countries turned its economic fortunes over to a multinational body like the European Central Bank. Never before has a central bank been charged with the macroeconomic fortunes of a large group of nations with 325 million people producing \$16 trillion of goods and services. While optimists point to the microeconomic benefits of a larger market and lower transactions costs, pessimists worry that monetary union threatens stagnation and unemployment because of the lack of price and wage flexibility and insufficient labor mobility among countries. The financial crisis of 2007–2009 is the first major test of this new monetary system. ①

最后的评价 FINAL ASSESSMENT

This survey of international economics must acknowledge a mixed picture, with both successes and failures. It is true that market economies occasionally suffer from inflation and recession. Moreover, in the most recent downturn in 2007–2009, unemployment rose sharply and many financial giants teetered on the edge of bankruptcy. Nonetheless, if we step back, an impartial jury of historians would surely rate the last half-century as one of unparalleled success for the countries of North America and Western Europe:

- *Robust economic performance.* The period has seen the most rapid and sustained economic growth in recorded history. It is the only period since the Industrial Revolution in which these countries have avoided deep depression and the cancer of hyperinflation.
- *The emerging monetary system.* The international monetary system continues to be a source of turmoil, with frequent crises as countries encounter balance-of-payments or currency difficulties. Nonetheless, we can see an emerging system in ② which the major economic regions—the United States, Europe, and Japan—conduct independent monetary policies with flexible exchange rates, while smaller countries either float or have "hard" fixed exchange rates tied to one of the major blocks. A major challenge for the future will be to integrate the Asian giants China and India into the international trade and financial systems.
- *The reemergence of free markets.* You often hear that imitation is the sincerest form of flattery. In economics, imitation occurs when a nation adopts the economic structure of another in the hope that it will produce growth and stability. In the last two decades, country after country threw off the shackles of communism and stifling central planning. This occurred not only because economics textbooks explained the miracle of the free market but primarily because people could see with their own eyes how the market-oriented countries of the West prospered while the centrally planned command economies collapsed. *For the first time, an empire collapsed because it could not produce sufficient butter along with its guns.*

② 尽管如此，我们还是看到，在美国、欧洲和日本这样的主要经济区，新形成的货币体系在浮动汇率制下独立地制定货币政策。与此同时，一些较小的国家，既有浮动汇率，也有捆绑于一个主要区块的严格的固定汇率。

SUMMARY

A. Foreign Trade and Economic Activity

1. An open economy is one that engages in international exchange of goods, services, and investments. Exports are goods and services sold to buyers outside the country, while imports are those purchased from foreigners. The difference between exports and imports of goods and services is called net exports.

2. When foreign trade is introduced, domestic demand can differ from national output. Domestic demand comprises consumption, investment, and government purchases ($C + I + G$). To obtain GDP, exports (Ex) must be added and imports (Im) subtracted, so

$$\text{GDP} = C + I + G + X$$

① 欧洲货币联盟是历史上伟大的经济学实验之一。之前，从来没有如此多庞大而又强大的国家将本国的经济命运交给像欧洲中央银行这样的多国实体。从来没有一家中央银行管理这么多国家（拥有 3.25 亿人口，创造 16 万亿美元的商品和服务）的宏观经济命运。尽管乐观主义者认为更大的市场和更低的交易成本会带来宏观经济收益，但悲观主义者担忧，由于缺乏价格和工资弹性，以及国家间劳动力流动性不足，货币联盟可能会带来经济停滞和失业。2007~2009 年的金融危机就是对这个新货币体系的第一次重大考验。

where X = net exports = $Ex - Im$. Imports are determined by domestic income and output along with the prices of domestic goods relative to those of foreign goods; exports are the mirror image, determined by foreign income and output along with relative prices. The dollar increase of imports for each dollar increase in GDP is called the marginal propensity to import (MPm).

3. Foreign trade has an effect on GDP similar to that of investment or government purchases. As net exports rise, there is an increase in aggregate demand for domestic output. Net exports hence have a multiplier effect on output. But the expenditure multiplier in an open economy will be smaller than that in a closed economy because of leakages from spending into imports. The multiplier is

$$\text{Open-economy multiplier} = \frac{1}{MPS + MPm}$$

Clearly, other things equal, the open-economy multiplier is smaller than the closed-economy multiplier, where $MPm = 0$.

4. The operation of monetary policy has new implications in an open economy. An important example involves the operation of monetary policy in a small open economy that has a high degree of capital mobility. Such a country must align its interest rates with those in the countries to whom it pegs its exchange rate. This means that countries operating on a fixed exchange rate essentially lose monetary policy as an independent instrument of macroeconomic policy. Fiscal policy, by contrast, becomes a powerful instrument because fiscal stimulus is not offset by changes in interest rates.

5. An open economy operating with flexible exchange rates can use monetary policy for macroeconomic stabilization which operates independently of other countries. In this case, the international link adds another powerful channel to the domestic monetary transmission mechanism. A monetary tightening leads to higher interest rates, attracting foreign financial capital and leading to a rise (or appreciation) of the exchange rate. The exchange-rate appreciation tends to depress net exports, so this impact reinforces the contractionary impact of higher interest rates on domestic investment.

B. Interdependence in the Global Economy

6. In the longer run, operating in the global marketplace provides new constraints and opportunities for countries to improve their economic growth. Perhaps the most important element concerns saving and investment, which are highly mobile and respond to incentives and the investment climate in different countries.

7. The foreign sector provides another source of funds for investment and another outlet for saving. Higher domestic saving—whether through private saving or government fiscal surpluses—will increase the sum of domestic investment and net exports. Recall the identity

$$X = S + (T - G) - I$$

or

$$\begin{aligned}\text{Net exports} = {} & \text{private saving} \\ & + \text{government saving} \\ & - \text{domestic investment}\end{aligned}$$

In the long run, a country's trade position primarily reflects its national saving and investment rates. Reducing a trade deficit requires changing domestic saving and investment. One important mechanism for bringing trade flows in line with domestic saving and investment is the exchange rate.

8. Besides promoting high saving and investment, countries increase their growth through a wide array of policies and institutions. Important considerations are a stable macroeconomic climate, strong property rights for both tangible investments and intellectual property, a convertible currency with few restrictions on financial flows, and political and economic stability.

C. International Economic Issues

9. Popular analysis looks at large trade deficits and sees "deindustrialization." But this analysis overlooks the important distinction between productivity and competitiveness. Competitiveness refers to how well a nation's goods can compete in the global marketplace and is determined primarily by relative prices. Productivity denotes the level of output per unit of input. Real incomes and living standards depend primarily upon productivity, whereas the trade and current-account positions depend upon competitiveness. There is no close linkage between competitiveness and productivity.

10. Fixed exchange rates are a source of instability in a world of highly mobile financial capital. Recall the fundamental trilemma of fixed exchange rates: A country cannot simultaneously have a fixed but adjustable exchange rate, free capital and financial movements, and an independent domestic monetary policy.

11. In 1999, European countries chose to move to a common currency and a unitary central bank. A common currency is appropriate when a region forms an optimal currency area. Advocates of European monetary union point to the improved predictability, lower transactions costs, and potential for better capital allocation. Skeptics worry that a common currency—like any irrevocably fixed exchange-rate system—will require flexible wages and prices to promote adjustment to macroeconomic shocks.

CONCEPTS FOR REVIEW

$C + I + G + X$ curve for open economy
net exports $= X = Ex - Im$
domestic demand vs. spending on GDP
marginal propensity to import (MPm)
expenditure multiplier:
in closed economy $= 1/MPS$
in open economy $= 1/(MPS + MPm)$
impact of trade flows and exchange rates on GDP
saving-investment identity in open economies: $X = S + (T - G) - I$
equilibration in saving-investment market in closed and open economies
growth policies in the open economy
competitiveness vs. productivity

FURTHER READING AND INTERNET WEBSITES

Further Reading

The quotation from the *Economic Report of the President, 2000* (Government Printing Office, Washington, D.C., 2000), can also be found at *fraser.stlouisfed.org/publications/ERP,* pp. 231–235.

Websites

Data on trade and finance for different countries can be found in the section on websites for Chapter 26.

Robert Mundell won the Nobel Prize in 1999 for his contribution to international macroeconomics. Visit *www.nobel.se/laureates* to read about his contribution.

The website of the European Central Bank, at *www.ecb.int/ecb/html/index.en.html,* explains some of the issues involved in the management of the Euro. Also see the sites listed for Chapter 26.

QUESTIONS FOR DISCUSSION

1. Assume that an expansionary monetary policy leads to a decline or depreciation of the U.S. dollar relative to the currencies of America's trading partners in the short run with unemployed resources. Explain the mechanism by which this will produce an economic expansion in the United States. Explain how the trade impact reinforces the impact on domestic investment.
2. Explain the short-run impact upon net exports and GDP of the following in the multiplier model, using Table 28-1 where possible:
   a. An increase in investment (I) of $100 billion
   b. A decrease in government purchases (G) of $50 billion
   c. An increase in foreign output which increased exports by $10 billion
   d. A depreciation of the exchange rate that raised exports by $30 billion and lowered imports by $20 billion at every level of GDP
3. What would the expenditure multiplier be in an economy without government spending or taxes where the MPC is 0.8 and the MPm is 0? Where the MPm is 0.1? Where the MPm is 0.9? Explain why the multiplier might even be less than 1.
4. Consider Table 28-3.
   a. Explain each of the entries in the table.
   b. Add another column with the heading "Change in interest rates" to Table 28-3. Then, on the basis of the graph in Figure 28-7, fill in the table for a closed economy.
5. An eminent macroeconomist recently wrote: "Moving toward a monetary union by adopting a common currency is not really about the currency. The most important factor is that countries in the union must agree on a single monetary policy for the entire region." Explain this statement. Why might adopting a single monetary policy cause troubles?
6. Consider the city of New Heaven, which is a very open economy. The city exports reliquaries and has no investment or taxes. The city's residents consume 50 percent of their disposable incomes, and 90 percent

of all purchases are imports from the rest of the country. The mayor proposes levying a tax of $100 million to spend on a public-works program. Mayor Cains argues that output and incomes in the city will rise nicely because of something called "the multiplier." Estimate the impact of the public-works program on the incomes and output of New Heaven. Do you agree with the mayor's assessment?

7. Review the bulleted list of the three interactions of saving, investment, and trade on page 577. Make a graph like that of Figure 28-8 to illustrate each of the impacts. Make sure that you can explain the reverse cases mentioned in the paragraph that follows the bulleted list.
8. Politicians often decry the large trade deficit of the United States. Economists reply that to reduce the trade deficit would require a tax increase or a cut in government expenditures. Explain the economists' view using the analysis of the saving-investment balance in Figure 28-8. Also, explain the quotation from the *Economic Report 2000* on page 565.
9. Look back at Figure 26-2 and make sure you understand it. Now, consider an emerging-market country like Brazil or Argentina.
   a. Draw a diagram like Figure 28-9(*b*) for the country in good times, when the risk premium on its borrowing is low. Call this Figure A.
   b. Next, consider a shock that raises the risk premium by a large amount. Draw a new figure with the high premium and the new equilibrium. Call this Figure B.
   c. Now compare the equilibria in Figures A and B. Specifically, explain the difference in (i) the equilibrium domestic real interest rate, (ii) domestic investment, (iii) the exchange rate, and (iv) net exports.
10. Consider the example of small open economies like Belgium and the Netherlands that have highly mobile financial capital and fixed exchange rates but also have high government budget deficits. Suppose that these countries find themselves in a depressed economic condition, with low output and high unemployment. Explain why they cannot use monetary policy to stimulate their economies. Why would fiscal expansion be effective if they could tolerate higher budget deficits?
11. **Advanced problem.** After the reunification of Germany, payments to rebuild the former East Germany led to a major expansion of aggregate demand in Germany. The German central bank responded by raising German real interest rates. These actions took place in the context of the European Monetary System, in which most countries had fixed exchange rates and where the German central bank was dominant in monetary policy.
   a. Explain why European countries having fixed exchange rates and following the lead of the German central bank would find their interest rates rising along with German interest rates. Explain why other European countries would thereby be plunged into deep recessions.
   b. Explain why countries would prefer the European Monetary Union to the earlier system.
   c. Trace through why this German monetary tightening would be expected to lead to a depreciation of the dollar. Explain why the depreciation would stimulate economic activity in the United States.
12. **Advanced problem.** Reread the definition of the fundamental trilemma as well as the discussion by Paul Krugman on page 297. Explain why the three elements cannot go together. Why is there not a fundamental trilemma for the fixed-exchange-rate system between "California dollars" and "Texas dollars"? Explain the arguments for and against each of the three possible choices in the trilemma described by Krugman.

PART SEVEN

Unemployment, Inflation, and Economic Policy

失业、通货膨胀与经济政策

CHAPTER 29

Unemployment and the Foundations of Aggregate Supply
失业与总供给的基础

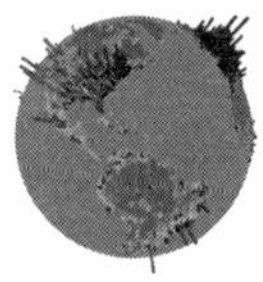

Be nice to people on your way up because you'll meet them on your way down.

Wilson Mizner [1]

春风得意之时要善待旁人，失意之时才不致被人冷落。

Among the persistent features of a market economy ② are business recessions, in which employment and output fall and unemployment rises. For most of the period since World War II, the United States avoided prolonged and deep recessions. However, even during the mild business contractions, joblessness increased and incomes fell sharply.

Occasionally, and often without much warning, countries suffer severe recessions or even decade-long depressions, and high unemployment persists for several years or even a decade. Such a situation was seen in the U.S. during the 1930s, when the unemployment rate was above 10 percent of the labor force for ten years.

The world's richest economies entered a recession in 2007, and it turned sharply worse in 2008–2009. Faced with a housing bubble, failing banks, a loss of confidence in the economy, weak investment, and a liquidity trap, the unemployment rate rose sharply in the 2007–2009 period. Although a better ③ understanding of macroeconomics has allowed most countries to take countercyclical measures, prospects for a strong recovery of output and employment were slim.

This chapter presents an analysis of the macroeconomics of unemployment. It begins by analyzing the foundations of aggregate supply. This analysis shows how rising unemployment is the result of slow growth of aggregate demand relative to potential output. We then examine the major policy issues surrounding unemployment.

总供给的基础

A. THE FOUNDATIONS OF AGGREGATE SUPPLY

Earlier chapters focused on aggregate demand and economic growth. This section describes the factors determining aggregate supply. In the short run, the nature of the inflationary process and the effectiveness of government countercyclical policies depend on aggregate demand. In the long run of a decade or more, economic growth and rising living standards are closely linked with increases in aggregate supply.

This distinction between short-run and long-run aggregate supply is crucial to modern macroeconomics. In the short run, it is the interaction of aggregate supply and demand that determines business-cycle fluctuations, inflation, unemployment, recessions, and booms. But in the long run, it is the growth of potential output working through aggregate supply which explains the trend in output and living standards.

[1] 威尔森·米兹纳：Wilson Mizner（1876~1933），著名的美国剧作家、实业家，以擅长谈论哲理性的人文轶事和警句著称，晚年签约华纳兄弟娱乐公司出任首席剧作家。本句话即是米兹纳家喻户晓的诲人为善的名言之一。

② 经济衰退是市场经济的常态性特征之一，即就业和产出下滑，失业上升。

③ 虽然更好地理解宏观经济学能使大多数国家采取反周期措施，但产出和就业强劲复苏的前景依然渺茫。

It will be useful to summarize the key points at the outset:

- **Aggregate supply** describes the behavior of the production side of the economy. The **aggregate supply curve,** or *AS* curve, is the schedule showing the level of total national output that will be produced at each possible price level, other things held constant.
- In analyzing aggregate supply, we will make the central distinction between the long run and the short run. The short run, corresponding to the behavior over periods of a few months to a few years, involves the **short-run aggregate supply schedule.** In the short run, prices and wages have elements of inflexibility. As a result, higher prices are associated with higher production of goods and services. This is shown as an *upward-sloping AS* curve.
- The long run refers to periods associated with economic growth, after most of the elements of business cycles have damped out; it refers to a period of several years or decades. In the long run, prices and wages are perfectly flexible. Output is determined by potential output and is independent of the price level. We depict the **long-run aggregate supply schedule** as *vertical.*

This section is devoted to explaining these central points.

总供给的决定因素
DETERMINANTS OF AGGREGATE SUPPLY

Aggregate supply depends fundamentally upon two distinct sets of forces: potential output and input costs. Let us examine each of these influences.

潜在产出
Potential Output

The key concept for understanding aggregate supply is *potential output* or *potential GDP.* **Potential output** is the maximum sustainable output that can be produced without triggering rising inflationary pressures.

Over the long run, aggregate supply depends primarily upon potential output. Hence, long-run *AS* ①
is determined by the same factors which influence long-run economic growth: the quantity and quality of labor, the supply of capital and natural resources, and the level of technology.

Macroeconomists generally use the following definition of potential output:

> Potential GDP is the highest sustainable level of ②
> national output. It is the level of output that would be produced if we remove business-cycle influences. As an operational measure, we measure potential GDP as the output that would be produced at a benchmark level of the unemployment rate called the *nonaccelerating inflation rate of unemployment* (or the *NAIRU*).

Potential output is a growing target. As the economy grows, potential output increases as well, and the aggregate supply curve shifts to the right. Table 29-1 shows the key determinants of aggregate supply, broken down into factors affecting potential output and production costs. From our analysis of economic growth, we know that the prime factors determining the growth in potential output are the growth in inputs and technological progress.

Potential Output Is Not Maximum Output

We must emphasize a subtle point about ③
potential output: Potential output is the maximum sustainable output but not the absolute maximum output that an economy can produce. The economy can operate with output levels above potential output for a short time. Factories and workers can work overtime for a while, but production above potential is not indefinitely sustainable. If the economy produces more than its potential output for long, price inflation tends to rise as unemployment falls, factories are worked intensively, and workers and businesses try to extract higher wages and profits.

A useful analogy is someone running a marathon. Think of potential output as the maximum speed that a marathoner can run without becoming "overheated" and dropping out from exhaustion. Clearly, the runner can run faster than the sustainable pace for a while, just as the U.S. economy grew faster than its potential growth rate during the 1990s. But over the entire course, the economy, like the marathoner, can produce only at a maximum sustainable "speed," and this sustainable output speed is what we call potential output.

投入成本
Input Costs

It is not surprising that increased potential output would lead to increased aggregate supply. The role

---

① 因此，长期总供给曲线是由影响经济长期增长的下述因素决定的：劳动力的数量与质量、资本与自然资源的供给，以及技术水平。

② 潜在 GDP 是国民产出最高的可持续水平。如果我们排除商业周期的影响，则所能获得的产出水平即潜在的 GDP。从可操作性角度出发，我们用失业率处于非加速通货膨胀的失业率时的产出来测量潜在 GDP。

③ 我们在这里必须强调关于潜在产出的微妙之处：潜在产出是可持续产出的最大值，但却不是一个经济体可以生产的最大绝对产出。

Variable	Impact on aggregate supply
Potential output	
Inputs	Supplies of capital, labor, and natural resources are the important inputs. Potential output comes when employment of labor and other inputs is at the maximum sustainable level. Growth of inputs increases potential output and aggregate supply.
Technology and efficiency	Innovation, technological improvement, and increased efficiency increase the level of potential output and raise aggregate supply.
Production costs	
Wages	Lower wages lead to lower production costs; lower costs mean that quantity supplied will be higher at every price level for a given potential output.
Import prices	A decline in foreign prices or an appreciation in the exchange rate reduces import prices. This leads to lower production costs and raises aggregate supply.
Other input costs	Lower oil prices lower production costs and thereby raise aggregate supply.

TABLE 29-1. Aggregate Supply Depends upon Potential Output and Production Costs

Aggregate supply relates total output supplied to the price level. The *AS* curve depends upon fundamental factors such as potential output and production costs. The factors listed in the table would increase aggregate supply, shifting the *AS* curve down or to the right.

of costs in *AS* is less obvious. We will see, however, ① that aggregate supply *in the short run* is affected by the costs of production.

The intuition behind this point is the following: Businesses have certain costs that are inflexible in the short run. For example, consider an airline that has a long-term lease and a multiyear labor contract. If the demand for air travel increases, the airline will find it profitable to add flights and to raise its ticket prices. In other words, both prices and output increase with an increase in demand in the short run.

We can also see that changes in production costs will affect aggregate supply in the short run. For example, consider what happened in the early 2000s when oil prices rose sharply, increasing the price of jet fuel. Airlines were unable to adjust their operations and ticket prices sufficiently to offset the higher costs. They were making record losses. They therefore cut some of their operations, abandoned routes, cut back on food service, and mothballed a substantial number of airplanes. This example shows how input costs can affect supply behavior.

Table 29-1 shows some of the cost factors affecting aggregate supply. These examples are ones in ② which lower costs will increase *AS*, meaning that the *AS* curve shifts down.

AS *Shifts*. We can illustrate the effects of changes in costs and potential output graphically in Figure 29-1. The left-hand panel shows that an increase in potential output with no change in production costs would shift the aggregate supply curve outward from *AS* to *AS*′. If production costs were to increase with no change in potential output, the curve would shift straight up from *AS* to *AS*″, as shown in Figure 29-1(*b*).

The real-world shifting of *AS* is displayed in Figure 29-2. The curves are realistic empirical estimates for two different years, the recession year of 1982 and the peak year of 2000. The vertical lines indicate the levels of potential output in the two years. According to studies, real potential output grew about 72 percent over this period.

The figure shows how the *AS* curve shifted outward and upward over the period. The *outward* shift ③ was caused by the increase in potential output that came from growth in the labor force and the capital stock as well as from improvements in technology. The *upward* shift was caused by increases in the cost of production, as wages, oil prices, and other production costs rose. Putting together the cost increases and the potential-output growth gives the aggregate supply shift shown in Figure 29-2.

---

① 但是，我们会看到，短期内总供给受生产成本的影响。

② 这些例子说明一点，降低成本会增加总供给，即意味着 *AS* 曲线下移。

③ 向外移动源于潜在产出的增加，而潜在产出的增加来源于劳动力与资本存量的增加以及技术进步。

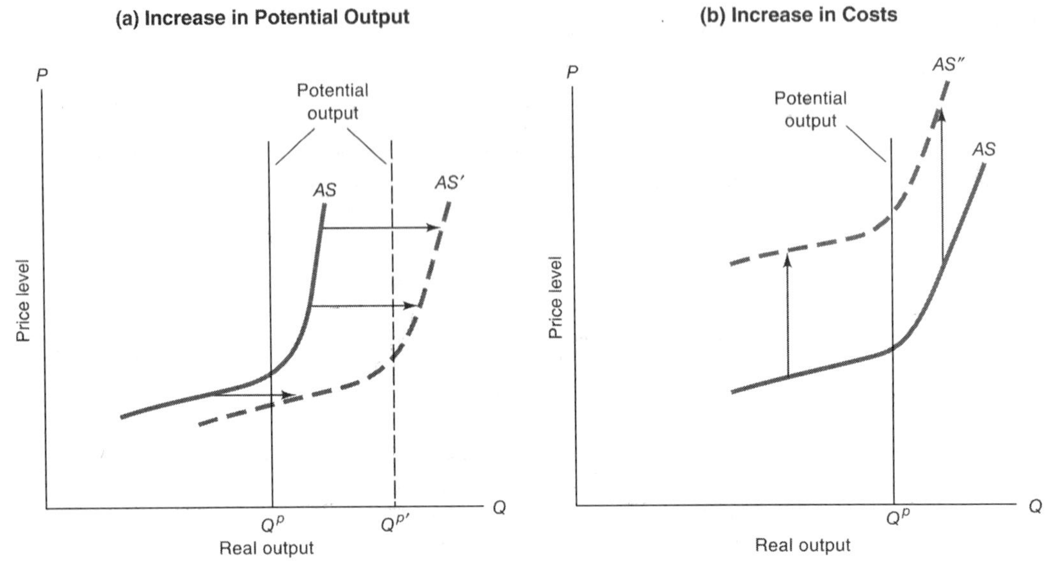

FIGURE 29-1. How Do Growth in Potential Output and Cost Increases Affect Aggregate Supply?

In (**a**), growth in potential output with unchanged production costs shifts the *AS* curve rightward from *AS* to *AS′*. When production costs increase, say, because of higher wages or oil costs, but with unchanged potential output, the *AS* curve shifts vertically upward, as from *AS* to *AS″* in (**b**).

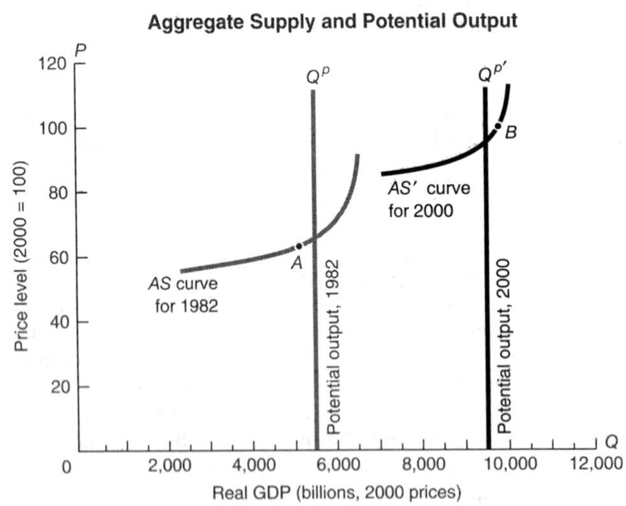

FIGURE 29-2. In Reality, Aggregate Supply Shifts Combine Cost Increases and Increased Potential Output

Between 1982 and 2000, potential output grew ① due to increases in capital and labor inputs along with technological improvements, shifting out the *AS* curve. At the same time, increases in production costs shifted up the *AS* curve. The net effect was to shift the *AS* curve upward and to the right.

① 在 1982~2000 年，潜在产出增长，*AS* 曲线外移，这是由于资本和劳动投入的增加，以及技术进步的驱动。

短期与长期总供给
AGGREGATE SUPPLY IN THE SHORT RUN AND LONG RUN

How do shifts in aggregate demand affect output and employment? The answer to this question differs between the short run (which applies to business cycles) and the long run (which applies to comparisons of countries over long periods of time or to comparisons among countries). The two approaches are illustrated in Figure 29-3.

The upward-sloping, short-run aggregate supply curve is associated with the analysis called **Keynesian macroeconomics.** In this situation, changes in aggregate demand have a significant effect on output. In ① other words, if aggregate demand falls because of a monetary tightening or a falloff in consumer spending, this will lead to falling output and prices. In terms of our curves, this means that the *AS* curve is upward-sloping, so a decline in *AD* will lead to a decline in both prices and output.

The long-run approach, sometimes called **classical** ② **macroeconomics,** holds that changes in *AD* affect prices but have no effect on real output. In the long run, prices and wages adjust fully to changes in aggregate demand. The classical or long-run *AS* curve is vertical; changes in aggregate demand therefore have no effect on output.

We can summarize the reasons for the difference as follows: The short-run *AS* curve in Figure 29-3(*a*) indicates that firms are willing to increase their output levels in response to changes in aggregate demand. Clearly, there must be unemployed resources in the economy. But the expansion of output cannot go on forever. As output rises, labor shortages appear and factories operate close to capacity. Wages and prices begin to rise more rapidly. A larger fraction of the response to aggregate demand increase comes in the form of price increases and a smaller fraction comes in output increases.

Figure 29-3(*b*) shows what happens in the long run—after wages and prices have had time to react fully. When all adjustments have taken place, the long-run *AS* curve becomes vertical or classical. In the long run, the level of output supplied is independent of aggregate demand.

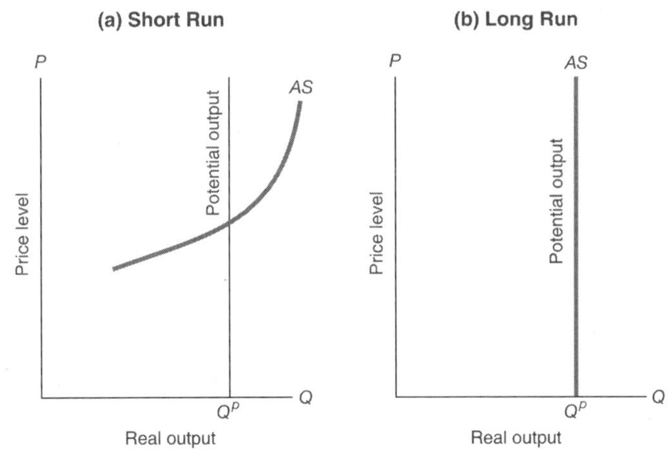

FIGURE 29-3. ***AS* Is Upward-Sloping in the Short Run but Turns Vertical in the Long Run**

The short-run *AS* curve in (**a**) slopes upward because many costs are inflexible in the short run. But sticky prices and wages become unstuck as time passes, so the long-run *AS* curve in (**b**) is vertical and output is determined by potential output. Can you see why a Keynesian economist in (**a**) might desire to stabilize the economy through policies that change aggregate demand while a classical economist in (**b**) would concentrate primarily on increasing potential output?

---

① 换言之，如果由于货币紧缩或消费者支出下降而导致总需求下滑的话，则必然引起产出和价格的下跌。如果用曲线来描述，即表现为 *AS* 曲线向上倾斜，这样，总需求的下降势必导致价格和产出的双重下滑。

② 这种有时也称作**古典宏观经济学**的长期分析法认为，总需求的变动会对价格产生影响，但对实际产出没有任何作用。长期来讲，价格和工资会根据总需求的变化进行调节。古典或长期 *AS* 曲线是垂直的，因此，总需求的变化对产出没有影响。

粘性工资、价格和向上倾斜的 AS 曲线

Sticky Wages and Prices and the Upward-Sloping AS Curve

Economists generally agree that the *AS* curve slopes up in the short run—which is to say that both output and prices respond to demand shifts. It has proved very difficult to develop a complete theory to explain this relationship, and controversies about aggregate supply are among the most heated in all of economics. We will describe one of the important and durable theories here—one involving sticky wages and prices—but don't be surprised if you hear other ones as well.

The puzzle is why firms raise both prices and output in the short run as aggregate demand increases, whereas increases in demand lead primarily to price changes in the long run. The key to this puzzle lies in the behavior of wages and prices in a modern market economy. Some elements of business costs are *inflexible* or *sticky* in the short run. As a result of this inflexibility, businesses can profit from higher levels of aggregate demand by producing more output.

For example, suppose that a wartime emergency leads to an increase in military spending. Firms know that in the short run many of their production costs are fixed in dollar terms—workers are paid $15 per hour, rentals are $1500 per month, and so forth. In response to the higher demand, firms will generally raise their output prices and increase production. This positive association between prices and output is seen in the upward-sloping *AS* curve in Figure 29-3(*a*).

We have spoken repeatedly of "sticky" or "inflexible" costs. What are some examples? The most ① significant is wages. Take unionized workers as an example. They are usually paid according to a long-term union contract which specifies a dollar wage rate. For the life of the labor agreement, the wage rate faced by the firm will be largely fixed in dollar terms. It is quite rare for wages to be raised more than once a year even for nonunion workers. It is even more uncommon for money wages or salaries actually to be cut, except when a company is visibly facing the threat of bankruptcy.

Other prices and costs are similarly sticky in the short run. When a firm rents a building, the lease will often last for a year or more and the rental is generally set in dollar terms. In addition, firms often sign contracts with their suppliers specifying the prices to be paid for materials or components.

Putting all these cases together, you can see how a certain short-run stickiness of wages and prices exists in a modern market economy.

What happens in the long run? Eventually, the inflexible or sticky elements of cost—wage contracts, rental agreements, regulated prices, and so forth—become unstuck and negotiable. Firms cannot take advantage of fixed-money wage rates in their labor agreements forever; labor will soon recognize that prices have risen and insist on compensating increases in wages. Ultimately, all costs will adjust to the higher output prices. If the general price level rises by *x* percent because of the higher demand, then money wages, rents, regulated prices, and other costs will in the end respond by moving up around *x* percent as well.

Once costs have adjusted upward as much as prices, firms will be unable to profit from the higher level of aggregate demand. In the long run, after all elements of cost have fully adjusted, firms will face the same ratio of price to costs as they did before the change in demand. There will be no incentive for firms to increase their output. The long-run *AS* curve therefore tends to be vertical, which means that output supplied is independent of the level of prices and costs.

Aggregate supply differs depending upon the ② period. In the short run, inflexible elements in wages and prices lead firms to respond to higher demand by raising both production and prices. In the longer run, as costs respond fully, all of the response to increased demand takes the form of higher prices. Whereas the short-run *AS* curve is upward-sloping, the long-run *AS* curve is vertical because, given sufficient time, all prices and costs adjust fully.

失 业

B. UNEMPLOYMENT

During the recession that began in 2007, the number of unemployed people in the United States rose by more than 4 million. Of the 11 million unemployed people at the end of 2008, half were "job losers," people who lost their jobs involuntarily. In earlier periods, such as the Great Depression or the early 1980s, the unemployment rate rose much more, reaching an all-time high of 25 percent in 1933.

---

① 最突出的例子是工资。以工会工人为例，这些工人的工资通常根据与工会签订的长期合同发放，该合同具体说明了美元工资率。

② 总供给会基于时段的长短而不同。短期来讲，工资和价格不变会导致厂家提高产量和价格，以应对需求的增加。长期来讲，由于成本的充分调整，对需求增加的全部反应形式就是更高的价格。无论短期 *AS* 曲线是否向上倾斜，长期 *AS* 曲线都是垂直的，因为在充足的时间内，所有的价格和成本都可做充分调整。

The presence of involuntary unemployment in a market economy raises important questions: How can millions of people be unemployed when there is so much useful work to be done? Is there some flaw in the market mechanism that forces so many who want to work to remain idle? Alternatively, is high unemployment primarily due to flawed government programs (such as unemployment insurance) that reduce the incentive to work, or is it due to inherent properties of a market economy? The balance of this chapter provides a survey of the meaning of unemployment and some answers to these important questions.

失业统计
MEASURING UNEMPLOYMENT

Changes in the unemployment rate make monthly headlines. Look back to Figure 19-3 on page 373 to refresh your memory about the long-term trend. What lies behind the numbers? Statistics on unemployment and the labor force are among the most carefully designed and comprehensive economic data the nation collects. The data are gathered monthly in a procedure known as *random sampling* of the population. Each month about 60,000 households are interviewed about their recent work history.

The survey divides the population of those 16 years and older into four groups:

- **Employed.** These are people who perform any paid work, as well as those who have jobs but are absent from work because of illness, strikes, or vacations. ①
- **Unemployed.** Persons are classified as unemployed if they do not have a job, have actively looked for work in the prior 4 weeks, and are currently available for work. An important point to note is that unemployment requires more than being without a job—it requires taking steps to find a job.
- **Not in the labor force.** This includes the 34 percent of the adult population that is keeping house, retired, too ill to work, or simply not looking for work.
- **Labor force.** This includes all those who are either employed or unemployed.

Figure 29-4 shows how the population in the United States is divided among the categories of employed, unemployed, and not in the labor force. (The status of students is examined in question 6 at the end of this chapter.)

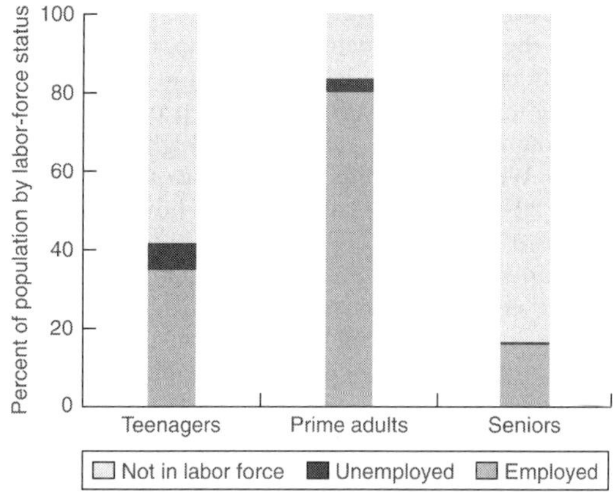

FIGURE 29-4. Labor-Force Status of the Population, 2007

How do Americans spend their time? This figure shows how teenagers (ages 16–19), prime-age adults (ages 25–54), and seniors (65 and older) divided their time among employment, unemployment, and not in the labor force. Many young workers are out of the labor force and in school, while most older workers are retired.

Source: Bureau of Labor Statistics.

The definition of labor-force status used by the government is the following:

> People with jobs are employed; people without jobs but looking for work are unemployed; people without jobs who are not looking for work are outside the labor force. The **unemployment rate** is the number of unemployed divided by the total labor force. ②

失业的影响
IMPACT OF UNEMPLOYMENT

High unemployment is both an economic and a social problem. Unemployment is an economic problem because it represents waste of a valuable resource. Unemployment is a major social problem because it causes enormous suffering as unemployed workers struggle with reduced incomes. During periods of high unemployment, economic distress spills over to affect people's emotions and family lives.

---

① **就业者**：指任何从事领取报酬工作的人，同时包括那些因病、罢工或者休假而缺勤的有工作的人。

② 有工作的人即为就业者；没有工作但正在找工作的人为失业者；没有工作但又不找工作的人排除在劳动力之外。**失业率**是失业总人口与劳动力总人口之比。

经济影响
Economic Impact

When the unemployment rate goes up, the economy ① is in effect throwing away the goods and services that the unemployed workers could have produced.

How much waste results from high unemployment? What is the opportunity cost of recessions? Table 29-2 provides a calculation of how far output ② fell short of potential GDP during three periods of high unemployment over the last half-century. The largest economic loss occurred during the Great Depression, but the oil and inflation crises of the 1970s and 1980s also generated more than a trillion dollars of lost output.

The economic losses during periods of high unemployment are the greatest documented wastes in a modern economy. They are many times larger than the estimated inefficiencies from microeconomic waste due to monopoly or from the waste induced by tariffs and quotas.

社会影响
Social Impact

The economic cost of unemployment is certainly large, but no dollar figure can adequately convey the human and psychological toll of long periods of persistent involuntary unemployment. The personal tragedy of unemployment has been proved again and again. We can read of the futility of a job search in San Francisco during the Great Depression: [3]

> I'd get up at five in the morning and head for the waterfront. Outside the Spreckles Sugar Refinery, outside the gates, there would be a thousand men. You know dang well there's only three or four jobs. The guy would come out with two little Pinkerton cops: "I need two guys for the bull gang. Two guys to go into the hole." A thousand men would fight like a pack of Alaskan dogs to get through. Only four of us would get through.

Or we can listen to the recollection of an unemployed construction worker:

> I called the roofing outfits and they didn't need me because they already had men that had been working for them five or six years. There wasn't that many openings. You had to have a college education for most of them. And I was looking for anything, from car wash to anything else.
>
> So what do you do all day? You go home and you sit. And you begin to get frustrated sitting home. Everybody in the household starts getting on edge. They start arguing with each other over stupid things 'cause they're all cramped in that space all the time. The whole family kind of got crushed by it.

		Lost Output	
	Average unemployment rate (%)	GDP loss ($, billion, 2008 prices)	As percentage of GDP during the period
Great Depression (1930–1939)	18.2	2,796	30.0
Oil and inflation crises (1975–1984)	7.7	1,694	2.7
Slump after dot.com bust (2001–2003)	5.5	509	1.4

TABLE 29-2. Economic Costs from Periods of High Unemployment

The two major periods of high unemployment since 1929 occurred during the Great Depression and during the oil shocks and high inflation from 1975 to 1984. The lost output is calculated as the cumulative difference between potential GDP and actual GDP. Note that during the Great Depression losses relative to GDP were 10 times greater than losses in the oil-inflation slump. The slowdown in the early 2000s was mild by comparison to earlier downturns.

Source: Authors' estimates on the basis of official GDP and unemployment data.

---

① 当失业率攀升时，经济实质上是在抛弃那些失业工人本应该生产出来的商品与服务。

② 表 29-2 计算了最近半个世纪的三个高失业率时期，实际产出相对潜在 GDP 的减少程度。虽然大萧条时期承受的经济损失最为沉重，但 20 世纪 70 年代和 80 年代的石油危机和通货膨胀也将损失的产出推高到了 1 万亿美元以上。

[3] Great Depression：指 20 世纪 30 年代的大萧条时期。萨翁在 17 版的前言中将 20 世纪的前 50 年用它来定义（笔者译为“危机四伏时期”），后 50 年则相应地定义为“伟大的和平时期”（the Great Peace），这是迄今为止国际学术界对 20 世纪 100 年符合“长波论”断代思想的唯一论述，但在此后的 18 版即予删除（见本书前言部分笔者对此的注疏内容）。因此，本书的 17 版在学术上由于这个断代说和对美国网络经济泡沫破灭的反思，更有其独特的价值。

Unemployment is not limited to the unskilled, as ① many well-paid managers, professionals, and white-collar workers learned in the corporate downsizings of the last two decades. Listen to the story of one middle-aged corporate manager who lost his job in 1988 and was still without permanent work in 1992:

> I have lost the fight to stay ahead in today's economy.... I was determined to find work, but as the months and years wore on, depression set in. You can only be rejected so many times; then you start questioning your self-worth.

奥肯法则 OKUN'S LAW [2]

The most traumatic consequence of a recession is the accompanying rise in unemployment. As output falls, firms need fewer labor inputs, so new workers are not hired and current workers are laid off. We see that the unemployment rate usually moves inversely with output over the business cycle. This co-movement is known as Okun's Law.

Okun's Law states that for every 2 percent that ③ GDP falls relative to potential GDP, the unemployment rate rises about 1 percentage point.

This means that if GDP begins at 100 percent of its potential and falls to 98 percent of potential, the unemployment rate rises by 1 percentage point, say, from 6 to 7 percent. Figure 29-5 shows how output and unemployment have moved together over time.

We can illustrate Okun's Law by examining output and unemployment trends in the 1990s. At the trough of the recession of 1991, the unemployment rate rose to 7 percent. At that point, actual GDP was estimated to be 3 percent below potential output. Then, over the next 8 years, output grew 5 percent faster than potential output, so in 1999 actual GDP was estimated to be 2 percent above potential output. According to Okun's Law, the unemployment rate should have fallen by 2½ percentage points (5/2) to 4½ percent (7 − 2½). In fact, the unemployment rate for 1999 was 4¼ percent—a remarkably accurate prediction. This shows how Okun's Law can be used to relate changes in the unemployment rate to the growth in output.

One important consequence of Okun's Law is that actual GDP must grow as rapidly as potential GDP just to keep the unemployment rate from rising. In a sense, GDP has to keep running just to keep unemployment in the same place. Moreover, if you want to bring the unemployment rate down, actual GDP must be growing faster than potential GDP.

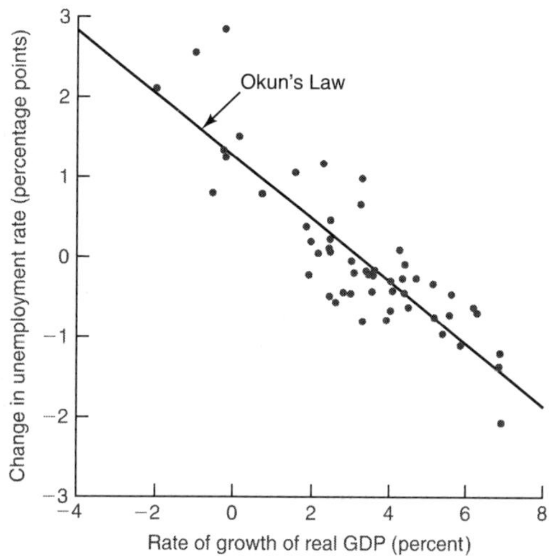

FIGURE 29-5. Okun's Law Illustrated, 1955–2007

According to Okun's Law, whenever output grows 2 percent faster than potential GDP, the unemployment rate declines 1 percentage point. This graph shows that unemployment changes are well predicted by the rate of GDP growth. What output growth would lead to no change in unemployment according to the line?

Source: U.S. Departments of Commerce and Labor.

③ 奥肯法则指出，相对于潜在GDP来讲，GDP每下降2%，失业率大约就会上升1%。

Okun's Law provides the vital link between the ④ output market and the labor market. It describes the association between short-run movements in real GDP and changes in unemployment.

④ 奥肯法则在产出市场和劳动市场之间提供了重要联系。它描述了实际GDP的短期变动与失业率变化之间的联系。

失业的经济学解释 ECONOMIC INTERPRETATION OF UNEMPLOYMENT

On the face of it, the cause of unemployment seems clear: too many workers chasing too few jobs. Yet this simple phenomenon has presented a tremendous puzzle for economists for many years. Experience shows that prices rise or fall to clear competitive markets. At the market-clearing price, buyers willingly buy what sellers willingly sell. But something is

---

① 在刚刚过去的20年里，失业问题绝不仅仅限于非技术工人，许多原本收入颇丰的经理人、专业人士和白领工作人员也都在公司裁员中经历了失业的痛苦。

[2] OKUN：Arthur Okun，阿瑟·奥肯（1928~1980），美国经济学家，1961年之后长期担任肯尼迪和约翰逊两任总统的经济顾问委员会委员，1968年被任命为该委员会主席。奥肯对于经济学的突出贡献是分析了失业率与GNP之间的线性变化关系，总结出了著名的奥肯法则（Okun's Law），即失业率每下降1%，实际GNP将上升3%。奥肯的研究是基于从第二次世界大战开始至1960年间美国政府公布的详细的官方统计数据分析出来的，尤其在失业率居于3%~7.5%时更为准确。

gumming up the workings of the labor market when many hospitals are searching for nurses but cannot find them while thousands of coal miners want to work at the going wage but cannot find a job. Similar symptoms of labor market failures are found in all market economies.

Let's turn now to the economic analysis of unemployment. As with other economic phenomena, we would like to understand the reasons for unemployment. Can we understand why unemployment varies sharply over the business cycle, as well as why some groups have higher unemployment rates than other groups? We will see that a combination of imperfections in the labor market, as well as personal search dynamics, lies behind the observed behavior.

均衡失业
Equilibrium Unemployment

We begin by analyzing unemployment in a supply-and-demand framework. To begin with, we will consider equilibrium unemployment. **Equilibrium unemployment** ① arises when people become unemployed voluntarily as they move from job to job or into and out of the labor force. This is also sometimes called *frictional unemployment* because people cannot move instantaneously between jobs. Here are some examples: Someone working at the local hamburger stand might decide that the pay is too low, or the hours are too inconvenient, and quit to look for a better job. Others might decide to take time off between school and their first job. A new mother might take 3 months of unpaid maternity leave. These workers have chosen unemployment rather than work in balancing their relative preferences of income, job characteristics, leisure, and family responsibilities.

This kind of unemployment is equilibrium because firms and workers are on their supply and demand schedules. The market is clearing properly in the sense that all workers who desire jobs at the going wages and working conditions have them and all firms that wish to hire workers at the going compensation can find them. Some economists label this *voluntary unemployment* to denote that people are unemployed because they prefer that state over other labor market states.

Equilibrium unemployment is shown in Figure 29-6(a). The workers have a labor supply schedule shown as SS. The left-hand panel shows the usual picture of competitive supply and demand, with a market equilibrium at point E and a wage of W^*. At the competitive, market-clearing equilibrium, firms willingly hire all qualified workers who desire to work at the market wage. The number of employed is represented by the line from A to E.

However, even though the market is in equilibrium, some people would like to work but only at a higher wage rate. These unemployed workers, represented by the segment EF, are unemployed in the sense that they choose not to work at the market wage rate. But this is equilibrium unemployment in the sense that they are not working because of their choice between work and nonwork given the market wages.

The existence of equilibrium unemployment ② leads to an often misunderstood point: *Unemployment may be an efficient outcome in a situation where heterogeneous workers are searching for work or testing different kinds of jobs.* The voluntarily unemployed workers might prefer leisure or other activities to jobs at the going wage rate. Or they may be frictionally unemployed, perhaps searching for their first job. Or they might be low-productivity workers who prefer retirement or unemployment insurance to low-paid work. There are countless reasons why people might voluntarily choose not to work at the going wage rate, and yet these people might be counted as unemployed in the official statistics.

非均衡失业
Disequilibrium Unemployment

Go back to reread the paragraphs above on the experiences of the three workers. The situation outside the Spreckles Sugar Refinery hardly sounds like equilibrium conditions. The unemployed workers surely do not seem like people carefully balancing the value of work against the value of leisure. Nor do they resemble people choosing unemployment as they search for a better job. Rather, these workers are in a situation of disequilibrium unemployment. This occurs when the labor market or the macroeconomy is not functioning properly and some qualified people who are willing to work at the going wage cannot find jobs. Two examples of disequilibrium are structural and cyclical unemployment.

Structural unemployment signifies a mismatch ③ between the supply of and the demand for workers. Mismatches can occur because the demand for one kind of labor is rising while the demand for another kind is falling and markets do not quickly adjust. We often see structural imbalances across occupations or

---

① 当一个人不断地跳槽或者出入于劳动力队伍，也就是处于自愿失业时，就会出现**均衡失业**。有时我也称之为摩擦性失业，这是因为，一个人不可能在失掉一份工作的瞬间找到另一份工作。

② 均衡失业的存在会引起一种误解：各种不同工种和类型的工人正在寻找工作，或者尝试不同种类的工作，在这种条件下，失业或许是个有效结果。

③ **结构性失业**说明劳动者的需求和供给之间不匹配。不匹配现象的出现是由于对某一种劳动需求上升的同时，对另一种劳动的需求却在下降，而市场又不能很快地予以调整。

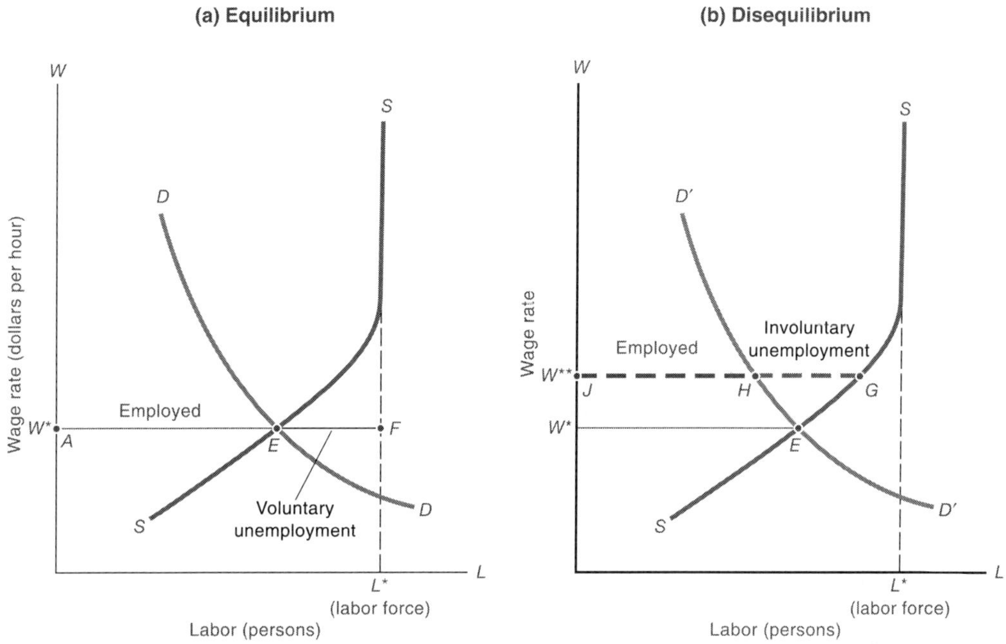

FIGURE 29-6. Equilibrium vs. Disequilibrium Unemployment

We can depict different kinds of unemployment by using the microeconomic supply-and-demand framework.

Panel **(a)** shows a standard market-clearing equilibrium with flexible wages. Here, wages decline to W^* to clear the labor market and balance supply and demand. All unemployment is voluntary.

Panel **(b)** shows disequilibrium unemployment, with sticky wages that do not adjust to clear the labor market. At the too high wage at W^{**}, *JH* workers are employed, but *HG* workers are involuntarily unemployed.

regions as certain sectors grow while others decline. For example, an acute shortage of nurses arose recently as the number of skilled nurses grew slowly while the demand for nursing care grew rapidly because of an aging population. Not until nurses' salaries rose rapidly and the supply adjusted did the structural shortage of nurses decline. By contrast, the demand for coal miners has been depressed for decades because of the lack of geographic mobility of labor and capital; unemployment rates in coal-mining communities remain high today.

Cyclical unemployment exists when the overall ① demand for labor declines in business-cycle downturns, as described in the Keynesian business-cycle theory. For example, in the major recession of 2007–2009, the demand for labor declined and unemployment rose in virtually every industry and region. Similarly, in the long expansion of the 2000s, the unemployment rate fell in virtually every state in the United States. The labor market consequences ② of business cycles differ from case to case, from mild declines in employment growth to job losses totaling a sizable fraction of the population.

The key to understanding disequilibrium unem- ③ ployment is to see that labor markets are not at their supply-and-demand equilibrium, as is shown in Figure 29-6(*b*). For this example, we assume that wages are sticky in the short run at the initial level of W^{**}.

① 正如凯恩斯在商业周期理论中所描述的那样，**周期性失业**存在的原因是在商业周期的低迷期，对劳动的总需求下降。

② 商业周期对劳动力市场的后续影响因不同的个案而异，从就业增长出现温和下滑，到总人口中出现规模庞大的失业大军，不一而足。

③ 理解非均衡失业的关键一点是要看到劳动力市场未处于供给与需求平衡的状态，如图 29-6（b）所示。

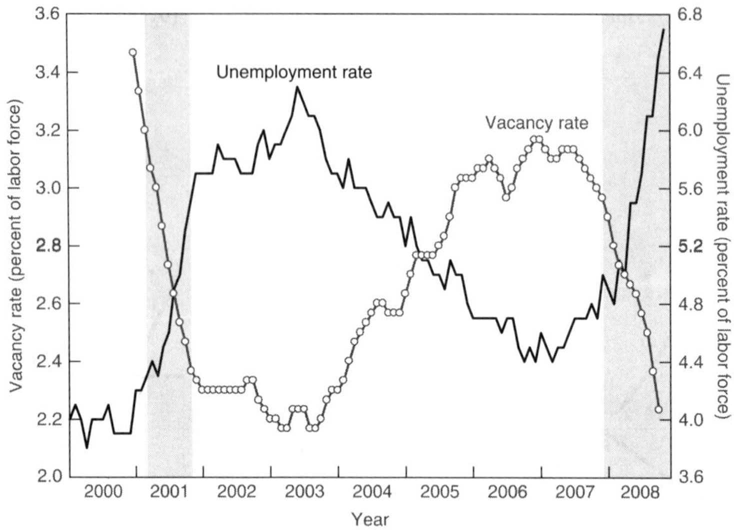

Shaded areas are NBER recessions.

FIGURE 29-7. Vacancy and Unemployment Rates

The vacancy and unemployment rates move inversely over the business cycle. This is an important prediction of the Keynesian sticky-wage theory of unemployment.

Source: Bureau of Labor Statistics.

Hence, when there is a decline in the demand for labor, and labor demand declines to the $D'D'$ curve in (b), the market wage at W^{**} is above the market-clearing wage at W^*.

At the too high wage rate, there are more qualified workers looking for work than there are vacancies looking for workers. The number of workers desiring to work at wage W^{**} is at point G on the supply curve, but firms want to hire only H workers, as shown by the demand curve. Because the wage exceeds the market-clearing level, there is a surplus of workers. The unemployed workers represented by the dashed line segment HG constitute *disequilibrium unemployment.* Alternatively, we may call them "involuntarily unemployed," signifying that they are qualified workers who want to work at the prevailing wage but cannot find jobs.

The opposite case occurs when the wage is below ① the market-clearing rate. Here, in a labor-shortage economy, employers cannot find enough workers to fill the existing vacancies. Firms put help-wanted signs in their windows, advertise in newspapers or on Monster. [2] com, and even recruit people from other towns.

Figure 29-7 shows the vacancy rate along with the unemployment rate for the last decade. The two curves move inversely, as predicted by the sticky-wage theory shown in Figure 29-6.

The Analogy of College Admissions. The example of college admissions illustrates the kind of adjustment that takes place when shortages or gluts occur because prices do not adjust. Many colleges have enjoyed soaring applications in recent years. How did they react? Did they raise their tuition enough to choke off the excess demand? No. Instead, they raised their ③ admission standards, requiring better grades in high school and higher average SAT scores. Upgrading the requirements rather than changing wages and prices is exactly what happens in the short run when firms experience an excess supply of labor.

① 相反的情况出现在工资低于市场出清率时。此时，在劳动力短缺的经济环境下，雇主无法找到足够的工人来填补现存的岗位空缺。企业在他们的窗口张贴招工告示，在报纸和求职网站刊登招工广告，甚至跑到其他城镇招人。

[2] Monster.com：全世界最大的招聘搜索引擎，由Monster Worldwide公司创办并经营，据称，它动态地拥有1.5亿以上的人用它投递简历。

③ 不是的。相反，他们提高了录取标准，要求更高的高中学业的级点分以及更高的SAT平均分。提高标准和要求而不是靠改变工资和价格也恰恰是短期内企业经历劳动力供给过剩时发生的事情。

刚性工资的微观经济基础
Microeconomic Foundations of Inflexible Wages

Economists have developed many approaches to understanding the microeconomic foundations of unemployment. This issue remains one of the deepest unresolved mysteries of modern macroeconomics. Our survey emphasizes the importance of inflexibility of wages and prices. But this raises the further question: Why are wages and prices inflexible? Why do wages not move up or down to clear markets?

These are controversial questions. Few economists today would argue that wages move quickly to erase labor shortages and surpluses. Yet no one completely understands the reasons for the sluggish behavior of wages and salaries. We can therefore provide no more than a tentative assessment of the sources of wage inflexibility.

Auction vs. Administered Markets. A helpful distinc- ① tion is that between auction markets and administered markets. An *auction market* is a highly organized and competitive market at which the price floats up or down to balance supply and demand. At the Chicago Board of Trade, for example, the price of "number 2 hard red wheat delivered in Kansas City" or "dressed 'A' broiler chickens delivered in New York" changes every minute to reflect market conditions.

Auction markets are the exception. Most goods and all labor are sold in administered markets. Nobody grades labor into "grade B Web page developer" or "class AAA assistant professor of economics." No market specialist ensures that every job and worker is quickly matched at a market-clearing wage.

Rather, most firms *administer* their wages and salaries, setting pay scales and hiring people at an entry-level wage or salary. These wage scales are generally fixed for a year or so, and when they are adjusted, the pay goes up for all categories. For example, every pay grade in a hospital might get a 4 percent pay increase for this year. Sometimes, the firm might decide to move one category up or down more than the average. Under standard procedures, firms will make only partial adjustments when there are shortages or gluts in a particular area.

For unionized labor markets, the wage patterns ② are even more rigid. Wage scales are typically set for a 3-year contract period; during that period, there are no adjustments in wages if shortages or gluts appear in particular jobs.

Menu Costs of Adjusting Wages and Prices. What is ③ the economic reason for inflexible wages and salaries? Many economists believe that the inflexibility arises because of the costs of administering compensation (these are called "menu costs"). To take the example of union wages, negotiating a contract is a long process that requires much worker and management time and produces no output. Because collective bargaining is so costly, such agreements are generally negotiated only once every 3 years.

Setting compensation for nonunion workers is less costly, but it nevertheless requires scarce management time and has important effects on worker morale. Every time wages or salaries are set, every time fringe benefits are changed, earlier compensation agreements are changed as well. Some workers will feel the changes are unfair, others will complain about unjust procedures, and grievances may be triggered.

Personnel managers therefore prefer a system in which wages are adjusted infrequently and most workers in a firm get the same pay increase, regardless of the market conditions for different skills or categories. This system may appear inefficient because it does not allow for a perfect adjustment of wages to reflect market supply and demand. But it does economize on scarce managerial time and helps promote a sense of fair play and equity in the firm. In the end, it may be cheaper to recruit workers more vigorously or to change the required qualifications than to upset the entire wage structure of a firm simply to hire a few new workers.

We can summarize the microeconomic foundations as follows:

> Most wages in market economies are administered ④ by firms or contracts. Wages and salaries are adjusted infrequently because of the costs of negotiation and wage setting. When labor supply or demand changes, because of sticky wages, the reaction is primarily in quantities of labor employed rather than wages.

劳动市场问题
LABOR MARKET ISSUES

Having analyzed the causes of unemployment, we turn next to major labor market issues for today. Which groups are most likely to be unemployed? How long are they unemployed? What explains differences in unemployment across countries?

---

① 拍卖型市场与管理型市场
② 在工会化的劳动市场，工资模式更加僵化。典型的工资等级合同以 3 年为期。在合同期内，即便某些特殊岗位出现短缺或过剩，也不能调整工资。
③ 工资和价格调整的菜单成本
④ 市场经济中的大多数工资都受到企业或合同的制约。由于谈判和工资设定存在成本，因此工资和薪金不能经常调整。当劳动的供给和需求发生变化时，由于刚性工资的原因，反应主要表现在已雇佣劳动力的数量，而不是工资。

	Unemployment Rate of Different Groups (% of labor force)		Distribution of Total Unemployment across Different Groups (% of total unemployed)	
Labor market group	Trough (1982)	Peak (March 2000)	Trough (1982)	Peak (March 2000)
By age:				
16–19	23.2	13.3	18.5	20.2
20 years and older	8.6	3.3	81.5	80.0
By race:				
White	8.6	3.6	77.2	77.6
Black and other	17.3	7.3	22.8	22.4
By sex (adults only):				
Male	8.8	3.8	58.5	50.5
Female	8.3	4.3	41.5	49.5
All workers	**9.7**	**4.1**	**100.0**	**100.0**

TABLE 29-3. Unemployment by Demographic Group

This table shows how unemployment varies across different demographic groups in peak and trough years. The first set of figures shows the unemployment rate for each group in 1982 and during the peak period of 2000. The last two columns show the percent of the total pool of unemployed that is in each group.

Source: U.S. Department of Labor, *Employment and Earnings*.

哪些人失业

Who Are the Unemployed?

We can diagnose labor market conditions by comparing years in which output is above its potential (of which 1999–2000 was a recent period) with those of deep recessions (such as was seen in 1982). Differences between these years show how business cycles affect the amount, sources, duration, and distribution of unemployment.

Table 29-3 shows unemployment statistics for peak and trough years. The first two columns of numbers are the unemployment rates by age, race, and sex. These data show that the unemployment rate of every group tends to rise during recession. The last two columns show how the total pool of unemployment is distributed among different groups; observe that the distribution of unemployment across groups changes relatively little throughout the business cycle.

Note also that nonwhite workers tend to experience unemployment rates more than twice those of whites in both trough and peak periods. Until the 1980s, women tended to have higher unemployment rates than men, but in the last two decades unemployment rates differed little by gender. Teenagers, with high frictional unemployment, have generally had unemployment rates much higher than adults. ①

失业的持续时间

Duration of Unemployment

Another key question concerns duration. How much of the unemployment experience is long-term and of major social concern, and how much is short-term as people move quickly between jobs?

Figure 29-8 shows the duration of unemployment in 2000–2007. A surprising feature of American labor markets is that a very large fraction of unemployment is of short duration. In 2003, one-third of unemployed workers were jobless for less than 5 weeks, and long-term unemployment was relatively rare.

In Europe, with lower mobility and greater legal obstacles to economic change, long-term unemployment in the mid-1990s reached 50 percent of the ②

① 同时需要提醒注意的是，无论经济处于低谷期还是高峰期，有色人种的失业率是白人失业率的两倍以上。

② 在欧洲，由于流动性较低和经济变化的法律障碍更大，在20世纪90年代中期，长期失业人口达到失业总人口的50%。

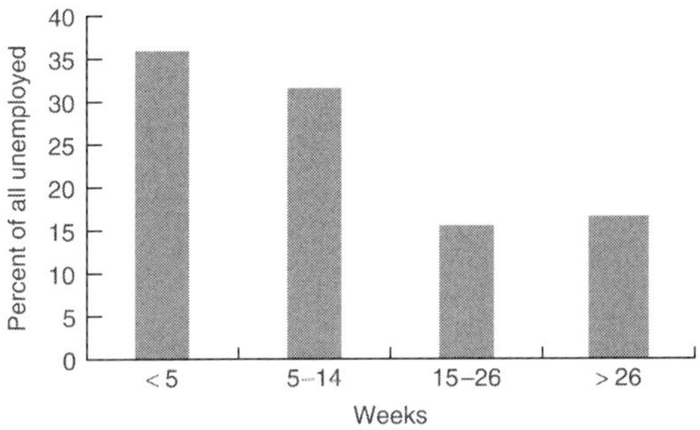

FIGURE 29-8. Duration of Unemployment in the United States, 2000–2007

Most unemployment is short-term in the United States. This suggests a frictional interpretation, where people move quickly between jobs.

Source: Bureau of Labor Statistics.

unemployed. Long-term unemployment poses a serious social problem because the resources that families have available—their savings, unemployment insurance, and goodwill toward one another—begin to run out after a few months.

无业可就的根源
Sources of Joblessness

Why are people unemployed? Figure 29-9 shows how people responded when asked the source of their unemployment, looking at the recession year of 1982 and the full-employment year of 2000.

There is always some frictional unemployment that results from changes in people's residence or from the life cycle—moving, entering the labor force for the first time, and so forth. The major changes in ①
the unemployment rate over the business cycle arise from the increase in job losers. This source swells enormously in a recession for two reasons: First, the number of people who lose their jobs increases, and then it takes longer to find a new job.

由年龄问题导致的失业
Unemployment by Age

How does unemployment vary over the life cycle? Teenagers generally have the highest unemployment rate of any demographic group, and nonwhite teenagers in recent years have experienced unemployment rates between 30 and 50 percent. Is this unemployment frictional, structural, or cyclical?

Recent evidence indicates that, particularly for whites, teenage unemployment has a large frictional component. Teenagers move in and out of the labor force very frequently. They get jobs quickly and change jobs often. The average duration of teenage unemployment is only half that of adult unemployment; by contrast, the average length of a typical job is 12 times greater for adults than teenagers. In most years, half the unemployed teenagers are "new entrants" who have never had a paying job before. All these factors suggest that teenage unemployment is largely frictional; that is, it represents the job search and turnover necessary for young people to discover their personal skills and to learn what working is all about.

But teenagers do eventually learn the skills and work habits of experienced workers. The acquisition ②
of experience and training, along with a greater desire and need for full-time work, is the reason middle-aged workers have much lower unemployment rates than teenagers.

Teenage Unemployment of Minority Groups. While most evidence suggests that unemployment is largely frictional for white teenagers, the labor market for young African-American workers has behaved quite differently. For the first decade after World War II, the labor-force participation rates and unemployment rates of black and white teenagers were virtually identical. After that time, however, unemployment rates for black teenagers rose sharply relative to those of other groups while their labor-force participation rates have fallen. By 2008, only 20 percent of black teenagers (16 to 19 years of age) were employed, compared to 35 percent of white teenagers.

What accounts for this extraordinary divergence in the experience of minority teenagers from that of other groups? One explanation might be that labor market forces (such as the composition or location of jobs) have worked against black workers in general. This explanation does not tell the whole story. While ③
adult black workers have always suffered higher unemployment rates than adult white workers—because of lower education attainment, fewer contacts with people who can provide jobs, less on-the-job training, and racial discrimination—the ratio of black to white adult unemployment rates has not increased since World War II.

---

① 在整个商业周期期间，失业率的变化主要源自失业人口数的增加。这一根源在经济衰退期间被极度地强化，其原因有二：一为失业人口数量增加；二为找到一份新工作花的时间更长。

② 中年劳动力的失业率大幅低于青少年劳动力的原因是其获得的工作经验和培训，以及对全职工作更强烈的渴望和需要。

③ 由于成年的黑人劳动力受教育程度较低，很少有同提供工作岗位的雇方接触的机会，缺乏在岗培训以及种族歧视问题，因此，成年的黑人劳动力一直比成年白人劳动力的失业率高。但是，自从二次大战以来，成年黑人劳动力的失业率与成年白人劳动力的失业率之比却始终没有增加。

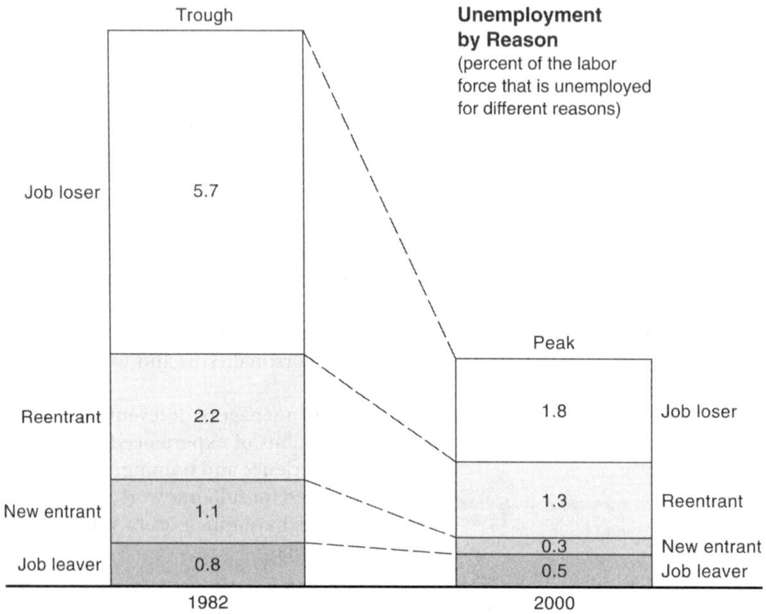

FIGURE 29-9. Distribution of Unemployment by Reason, 1982 and 2000

Why do people become unemployed? Very few were unemployed in the full-employment year of 2000 because they left their jobs, and almost 2 percent were new entrants into the labor force (say, because they just graduated from college) or reentrants (people who earlier left the labor force and are back looking for a job). The major change in unemployment from peak to trough, however, is found in the number of job losers. From 1982 to 2000 the fraction of workers who became unemployed because they lost their jobs fell from 5.7 to 1.8 percent.

Source: Bureau of Labor Statistics, at *www.bls.gov/data.*

Numerous studies of the sources of the rising black teenage unemployment rate have turned up no clear explanations for the trend. One possible source ① is discrimination, but a rise in the black-white unemployment differential would require an increase in racial discrimination—even in the face of increased legal protection for minority workers. Another theory holds that a high minimum wage along with rising costs of fringe benefits tends to drive low-productivity black teenagers into unemployment.

Does high teenage unemployment lead to long-lasting labor market damage, with permanently lower levels of skills and wage rates? This question is a topic ② of intensive ongoing research, and the tentative answer is yes, particularly for minority teenagers. It appears that when youths are unable to develop on-the-job skills and work attitudes, they earn lower wages and experience higher unemployment when they are older. This finding suggests that public policy has an important stake in devising programs to reduce teenage unemployment among minority groups.

Unemployment Trends in America and Europe

Unemployment rates in the United States and Europe show different trends in recent years. European unemployment was low until the supply shocks of the 1970s and has been relatively high since that time. American unemployment rates were generally lower than those in

① 一个可能的原因即种族歧视问题。尽管对少数族裔提供了更多的法律保护，但黑人与白人之间的失业率差异的升高要求我们更加重视种族歧视问题。

② 这是需要进一步研究的课题，初步的回答是肯定的，尤其对于少数族群青少年更是如此。

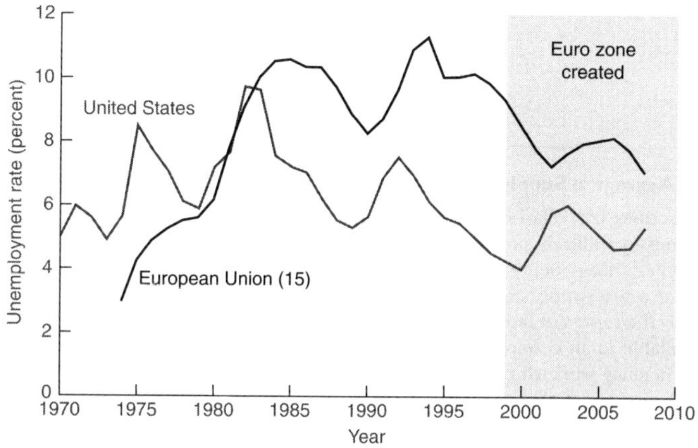

FIGURE 29-10. Unemployment in the United States and Europe

While unemployment has remained low in the United States, European unemployment has risen sharply over the last two decades. Many believe that the rising unemployment was due to labor market rigidities, while others think a fragmented monetary policy was to blame. With the introduction of the Euro and the integrated European Central Bank in 1999, European unemployment has declined gradually.

Source: U.S. Department of Labor, the OECD, and Eurostat. Data are for the EU 15 countries.

Europe over the last quarter-century. Figure 29-10 shows the unemployment-rate history for the two regions.

How can we explain the divergent labor markets of these two regions? Part of the reason probably lies in differences in macroeconomic policies. The United States has for almost a century had a single central bank, the Federal Reserve, which keeps careful watch over the American economy. When unemployment begins to rise, the Fed lowers interest rates to stimulate aggregate demand, increase output, and stem the unemployment increase.

Central banking in Europe was fragmented until very recently. ① Until 1999, Europe was a confederation of countries whose monetary policies were dominated by the German central bank, the Bundesbank. The Bundesbank was fiercely independent and aimed primarily at maintaining price stability *in Germany*. When unemployment rose in the rest of Europe and inflation rose in Germany—as happened after the reunification of Germany in 1990—the Bundesbank increased interest rates. This tended to depress output and raise unemployment in countries whose monetary policies were tied to Germany's. You can see this syndrome in the rise in unemployment in Europe after 1990.

A second feature of European unemployment relates to rising structural unemployment. Europe was the birthplace of the welfare state; countries like Germany, France, and Sweden legislated generous welfare benefits, unemployment insurance, minimum wages, and job protection for workers. These policies tend to increase real wages because workers possess greater bargaining power and have more attractive alternative uses for their time. ② Persons who are collecting welfare or unemployment benefits might be voluntarily unemployed, but they are generally counted as unemployed in the actual statistics. The United States has been less generous in its unemployment and welfare benefits.

What is the remedy for the high level of unemployment in Europe? Some economists emphasize reducing labor market barriers and welfare benefits. Other economists believe that the new European Central Bank may maintain a better balance of aggregate supply and demand in that region. (Recall our discussion of the European Monetary Union in Chapter 28.) It does appear that European unemployment has declined since the introduction of the Euro in 1999, although it is still above that in the United States.

① 直到最近，欧洲的中央银行依然脆弱。在 1999 年之前，欧洲还是个国家联盟，其货币政策由德国的中央银行，即德意志联邦银行主导。

② 那些敛收各种福利和失业救济金的人很有可能成为自愿失业者，但在实际的统计中，他们通常都被作为失业人数计算在内。在美国没有这样慷慨的失业救济金和福利津贴。

SUMMARY

A. The Foundations of Aggregate Supply

1. Aggregate supply describes the relationship between the output that businesses willingly produce and the overall price level, other things being constant. The factors underlying aggregate supply are (*a*) potential output, determined by the inputs of labor, capital, and natural resources available to an economy, along with the technology or efficiency with which these inputs are used, and (*b*) input costs, such as wages and oil prices. Changes in these underlying factors will shift the *AS* curve.
2. A central distinction in *AS* analysis is between the long run and the short run. The short run, corresponding to the behavior in business cycles of a few months to a few years, involves the short-run aggregate supply schedule. In the short run, prices and wages have elements of inflexibility. As a result, higher prices are associated with increases in the production of goods and services. This is shown as an upward-sloping *AS* curve. The short-run *AS* and *AD* analyses are used in Keynesian analysis of the business cycle.
3. The long run refers to periods associated with economic growth, after most of the elements of business cycles have damped out. In the long run, prices and wages are perfectly flexible; output is determined by potential output and is independent of the price level. The long-run aggregate supply schedule is *vertical*. The long-run *AS* and *AD* analyses are used in the classical analysis of economic growth.

B. Unemployment

4. The government gathers monthly statistics on unemployment, employment, and the labor force in a sample survey of the population. People with jobs are categorized as employed; people without jobs who are looking for work are said to be unemployed; people without jobs who are not looking for work are considered outside the labor force.
5. There is a clear connection between movements in output and the unemployment rate over the business cycle. According to Okun's Law, for every 2 percent that actual GDP declines relative to potential GDP, the unemployment rate rises 1 percentage point. This rule is useful in translating cyclical movements of GDP into their effects on unemployment.
6. Economists distinguish between equilibrium and disequilibrium unemployment. Equilibrium unemployment arises when people become unemployed voluntarily as they move from job to job or into and out of the labor force. This is also called frictional unemployment.
7. Disequilibrium unemployment occurs when the labor market or the macroeconomy is not functioning properly and some qualified people who are willing to work at the going wage cannot find jobs. Two examples of disequilibrium are structural and cyclical unemployment. Structural unemployment arises for workers who are in regions or industries that are in a persistent slump because of labor market imbalances or high real wages. Cyclical unemployment is a situation where workers are laid off when the overall economy suffers a downturn.
8. Understanding the causes of unemployment has proved to be one of the major challenges of modern macroeconomics. The discussion here emphasizes that involuntary unemployment arises because the slow adjustment of wages produces surpluses (unemployment) and shortages (vacancies) in individual labor markets. If inflexible wages are above market-clearing levels, some workers are employed but other equally qualified workers cannot find jobs.
9. Wages are inflexible because of the costs involved in administering the compensation system. Frequent changes of compensation for market conditions would command too large a share of management time, would upset workers' perceptions of fairness, and would undermine worker morale and productivity.
10. A careful look at the unemployment statistics reveals several regularities:
    a. Recessions hit all segments of the labor force, from the unskilled to the most skilled and educated.
    b. A very substantial part of U.S. unemployment is short-term. The average duration of unemployment rises sharply in deep and prolonged recessions.
    c. In most years, a substantial amount of unemployment is due to simple turnover, or frictional causes, as people enter the labor force for the first time or reenter it. Only during recessions is the pool of unemployed composed primarily of job losers.
    d. The difference in unemployment rates in Europe and the United States reflects both structural policies and the effectiveness of monetary management.

CONCEPTS FOR REVIEW

Foundations of Aggregate Supply

aggregate supply, *AS* curve
factors underlying and shifting aggregate supply
aggregate supply: role of potential output and production costs
short-run vs. long-run *AS*

Unemployment

population status:
- unemployed
- employed
- labor force
- not in labor force

unemployment rate

Okun's Law
equilibrium vs. disequilibrium unemployment
inflexible wages, unemployment, vacancies

FURTHER READING AND INTERNET WEBSITES

Further Reading

The quotations in the text are from Studs Terkel, *Hard Times: An Oral History of the Great Depression in America* (Pantheon, New York, 1970) for the Great Depression; Harry Maurer, *Not Working: An Oral History of the Unemployed* (Holt, New York, 1979) for the construction worker; and *Business Week*, March 23, 1992, for the corporate manager.

Websites

Analysis of employment and unemployment for the United States comes from the Bureau of Labor Statistics, at *www.bls.gov*. Statistics on unemployment in Europe and other OECD countries can be found at *www.oecd.org*. The BLS site also has an online version of *The Monthly Labor Review* at *www.bls.gov/opub/mlr/mlrhome.htm*, which is an excellent source for studies about employment, labor issues, and compensation. It contains articles on everything from "The Sandwich Generation" (*www.bls.gov/opub/mlr/2006/09/contents.htm*) to an analysis of the effect of going to war on labor market performance (*www.bls.gov/opub/mlr/2007/12/contents.htm*).

QUESTIONS FOR DISCUSSION

1. Explain carefully what is meant by the aggregate supply curve. Distinguish between movements along the curve and shifts of the curve. What might increase output by moving along the *AS* curve? What could increase output by shifting the *AS* curve?
2. Construct a table parallel to Table 29-1, illustrating events that would lead to a decrease in aggregate supply. (Be imaginative rather than simply using the same examples.)
3. What, if anything, would be the effect of each of the following on the *AS* curve in both the short run and the long run, other things being constant?
   a. Potential output increases by 25 percent.
   b. Oil prices double because of rising demand from China and India with a fixed supply of oil.
   c. Consumers become pessimistic and increase their saving rate.
4. Assume that the unemployment rate is 7 percent and GDP is $4000 billion. What is a rough estimate of potential GDP if the NAIRU is 5 percent? Assume that potential GDP is growing at 3 percent annually. What will potential GDP be in 2 years? How fast will GDP have to grow to reach potential GDP in 2 years?
5. What is the labor-force status of each of the following?
   a. A teenager who sends out résumés in searching for a first job
   b. An autoworker who has been laid off and would like to work but has given up hope of finding work or being recalled
   c. A retired person who moved to Florida and answers advertisements for part-time positions
   d. A parent who works part-time, wants a full-time job, but doesn't have time to look
   e. A teacher who has a job but is too ill to work

6. In explaining its procedures, the Department of Labor gives the following examples:
   a. "Joan Howard told the interviewer that she has filed applications with three companies for summer jobs. However, it is only April and she doesn't wish to start work until at least June 15, because she is attending school. Although she has taken specific steps to find a job, Joan is classified as not in the labor force because she is not currently available for work."
   b. "James Kelly and Elyse Martin attend Jefferson High School. James works after school at the North Star Café, and Elyse is seeking a part-time job at the same establishment (also after school). James' job takes precedence over his non-labor force activity of going to school, as does Elyse's search for work; therefore, James is counted as employed and Elyse is counted as unemployed."

   Explain each of these examples. Take a survey of your classmates. Using the examples above, have people classify themselves in terms of their labor-force status as employed, unemployed, or not in the labor force.
7. Assume that Congress is considering a law that would set the minimum wage above the market-clearing wage for teenagers but below that for adult workers. Using supply-and-demand diagrams, show the impact of the minimum wage on the employment, unemployment, and incomes of both sets of workers. Is any unemployment voluntary or involuntary? What would you recommend to Congress if you were called to testify about the wisdom of this measure?
8. Do you think that the economic costs and personal stress of a teenager unemployed for 1 month of the summer might be less or more than those of a head-of-household unemployed for 1 year? Do you think that this suggests that public policy should have a different stance with respect to these two groups?

CHAPTER

Inflation
通货膨胀

30

[1] 约翰·梅纳德·凯恩斯：J. M. Keynes（John Maynard Keynes，1883~1946），英国人，现代西方经济学最有影响的经济学家之一，开创了经济学的"凯恩斯革命"，被誉为"20世纪30年代经济大萧条的终结者"，其创立的宏观经济学被称为20世纪人类知识界的三大革命之一。《就业、利息和货币通论》（*General Theory of Employment, Interest and Money*，简称《通论》）是其革命性的代表作。本段文字出自凯恩斯另一本奠定其左翼经济学家领袖地位的著作《凡尔赛和约的经济效应》（*The Economic Consequences of the Peace*）第六章中第13自然段的开头。作为英国财政部的代表，凯恩斯在1919年的凡尔赛和会上对《凡尔赛和约》的签订起了至关重要的作用，本书即是其出席和会期间陈述和平理念和和约精神的专著，是一本遍布全球的畅销著作，出版于1919年。这段话是萨缪尔森《经济学》中难得的一段一字未改的原文。拟译如下：

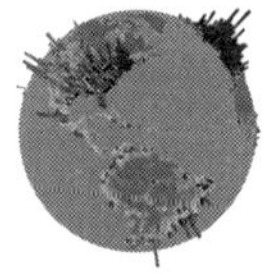

Lenin is said to have declared that the best way to destroy the capitalist system was to debauch the currency. By a continuing process of inflation, governments can confiscate, secretly and unobserved, an important part of the wealth of their citizens.

J. M. Keynes [1]

据说列宁曾经断言，推翻资本主义制度的最佳途径就是挖其货币的墙角。通过持续不停的通货膨胀侵蚀，政府就能神不知鬼不觉地将自己公民的主要财富收归公有。——J.M. 凯恩斯

For most of the last quarter-century, the United States succeeded in maintaining low and stable inflation. This experience was primarily due to the success of ②
monetary and fiscal policies in keeping output in a narrow corridor between inflationary excesses and sharp downturns, but favorable experience with commodity prices as well as moderation of wage increases helped reinforce the policies.

One new factor in the inflation equation was the growing "globalization" of production. As the United States became more integrated in world markets, domestic firms found that their prices were constrained by the prices of their international competitors.

Even when sales of clothing and electronic goods were booming, domestic companies could not raise their prices too much for fear of losing market share to foreign producers.

The 2000s were a turbulent period for prices. In the first part of the decade, inflation awoke from its long slumber. Particularly under the impetus of rising oil and food prices, prices rose rapidly. Then a steep recession starting in 2007 caused commodity prices to drop sharply, and countries were faced with the peril of deflation.

What are the macroeconomic dynamics of inflation? Why does deflation pose such a challenge for policy makers? The present chapter will examine the meaning and determinants of inflation and describe the important public-policy issues that arise in this area.

通货膨胀的定义及影响
A. DEFINITION AND IMPACT OF INFLATION

什么是通货膨胀
WHAT IS INFLATION?

We described the major price indexes and defined inflation in Chapter 20, but it will be useful to reiterate the basic definitions here:

Inflation occurs when the general level of prices ③
is rising. Today, we calculate inflation by using price indexes—weighted averages of the prices of thousands of individual products. The consumer price index (CPI) measures the cost of a market basket of consumer goods and services relative to the cost of that bundle during a particular base year. The GDP deflator is the price of all of the different components of GDP.

② 其经验主要归于成功的货币政策和财政政策，在过度的通货膨胀与经济剧烈下滑的狭窄夹缝之间保证了产出。但是，控制商品价格的成功经验以及工资的温和上涨也有助于加强政策的执行效果。

③ 通货膨胀由价格水平的普遍上涨引发。今天我们使用价格指数将数千种单个产品的价格加权平均来计算通货膨胀水平。消费者价格指数（CPI）是以某个基年的价格水平为基础，衡量市场上的一揽子消费品和服务的相对成本。GDP紧缩指数系指GDP中所有不同组成部分的价格水平。

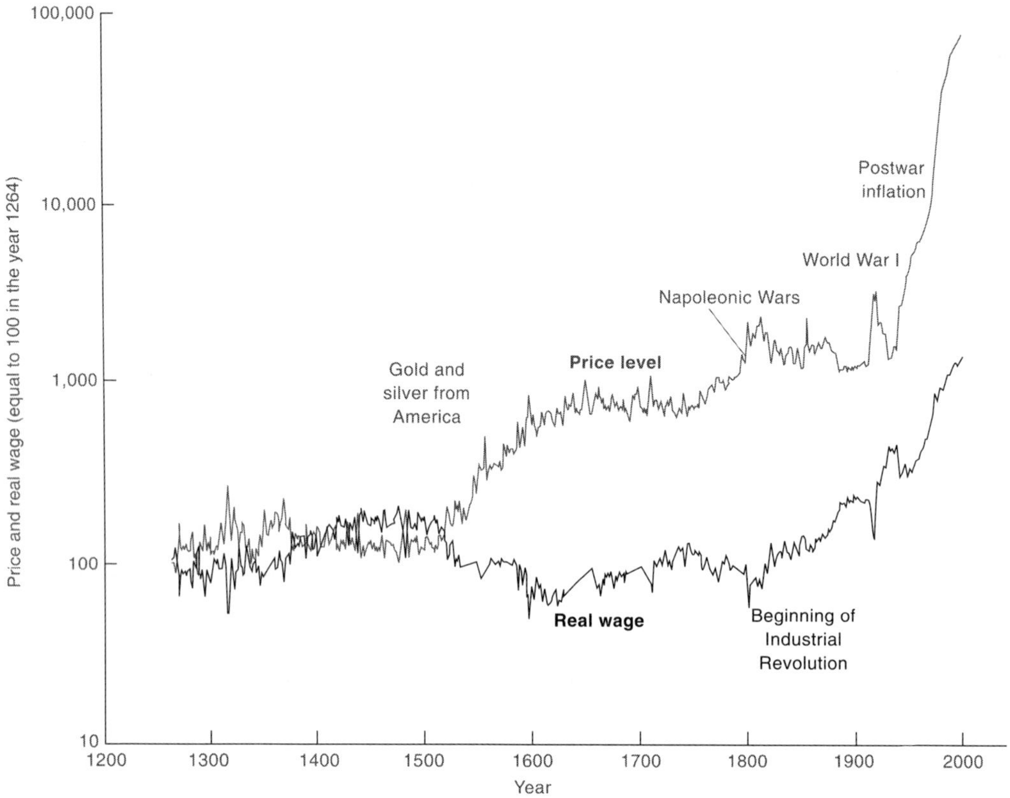

FIGURE 30-1. English Price Level and Real Wage, 1264–2007 (1270 = 100)

The graph shows England's history of prices and real wages since the Middle Ages. In early years, price increases were associated with increases in the money supply, such as from discoveries of New World treasure and the printing of money during the Napoleonic Wars. Note the meandering of the real wage prior to the Industrial Revolution. Since then, real wages have risen sharply and steadily.

Source: E. H. Phelps Brown and S. V. Hopkins, *Economica,* 1956, updated by the authors.

The rate of inflation is the percentage change in the price level:

$$\text{Rate of inflation in year } t = 100 \times \frac{P_t - P_{t-1}}{P_{t-1}}$$

If you are unclear on the definitions, refresh your memory by reviewing Chapter 20.

通货膨胀的历史

The History of Inflation

Inflation is as old as market economies. Figure 30-1 ① depicts the history of prices in England since the thirteenth century. Over the long haul, prices have generally risen, as the green line reveals. But examine also the blue line, which plots the path of *real wages* (the wage rate divided by consumer prices).

① 通货膨胀与市场经济一样古老。图 30-1 描绘出 13 世纪以来英格兰的价格变化史。正如图中上面的曲线所示，长期内价格水平总体呈上升态势。

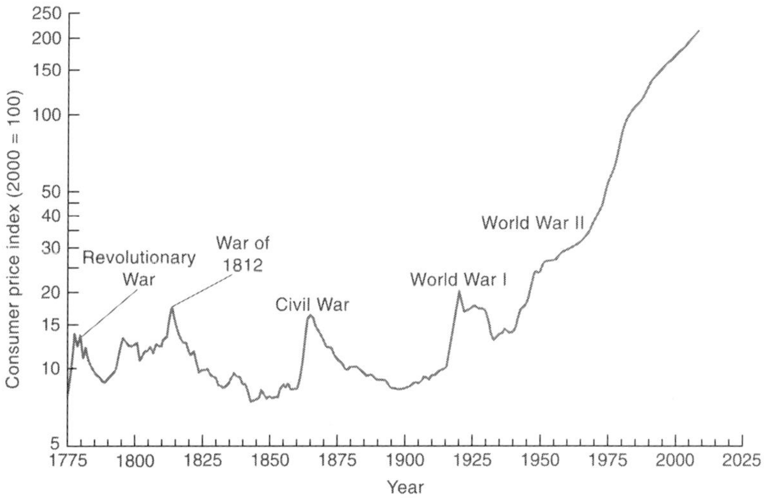

FIGURE 30-2. Consumer Prices in the United States, 1776–2008

Until World War II, prices fluctuated trendlessly—rising rapidly with each war and then drifting down afterward. But since then, the trend has been upward, both here and abroad.

Source: U.S. Department of Labor, Bureau of Labor Statistics for data since 1919.

Real wages meandered along until the Industrial Revolution. Comparing the two lines shows that inflation is not necessarily accompanied by a decline in real income. You can see, too, that real wages have climbed steadily since around 1800, rising more than tenfold.

Figure 30-2 focuses on the behavior of consumer prices in the United States since the Revolutionary War. [1] Until World War II, the United States was generally on a combination of gold and ② silver standards, and the pattern of price changes was regular: Prices would soar during wartime and then fall back during the postwar slump. But the pattern changed dramatically after World War II. Prices and wages now travel on a one-way street that goes only upward. They rise rapidly in periods of economic expansion and slow down in periods of slack.

Figure 30-3 shows CPI inflation over the last half-century. You can see that inflation in recent years has moved in a narrow range, fluctuating primarily because of volatile food and energy prices.

通货膨胀的三种形态

Three Strains of Inflation

Like diseases, inflations exhibit different levels of severity. It is useful to classify them into three categories: low inflation, galloping inflation, and hyperinflation.

Low Inflation. Low inflation is characterized by prices that rise slowly and predictably. We might define this as single-digit annual inflation rates. When prices are relatively stable, *people trust money* because it retains its value from month to month and year to year. People are willing to write long-term contracts in money terms because they are confident that the relative prices of goods they buy and sell will not get too far out of line. Most countries have experienced low inflation over the last decade.

Galloping Inflation. Inflation in the double-digit or ③ triple-digit range of 20, 100, or 200 percent per year is called **galloping inflation** or "very high inflation." Galloping inflation is relatively common, particularly in countries suffering from weak governments, war, or revolution. Many Latin American countries, such

[1] Revolutionary War：即 1775~1783 的美国独立战争，主要始于对抗英国的经济政策，开始阶段是英国与其北美 13 个州殖民地革命者之间的战争，之后有法国、荷兰和西班牙等几个欧洲强国加入对抗英国，使战争的范围远远超过了英属北美洲之外，成为世界历史上规模最大的一次反殖民战争。1776 年 7 月 4 日在费城举行的大陆会议通过了《独立宣言》，宣告了美国的诞生。1783 年的《巴黎条约》承认了美国的独立。战争之后，许多殖民地居民逃离到北方安顿下来，为日后加拿大的建立奠定了基础。

② 直到第二次世界大战，美国在总体上使用金银复本位制，价格变化的模式是有规律的：价格在战争期间都会飞涨，而在战后的整个萧条期回落。但在二次大战之后，该模式却发生了戏剧性变化。

③ **急剧通货膨胀**。通货膨胀以每年 20%、100% 或者 200% 的两位数或者三位数的速度飞涨称为**急剧通货膨胀**，或者“高通货膨胀”。急剧通货膨胀是一种比较常见的通胀，在那些政府弱势、爆发战争或者革命的国家，尤其如此。

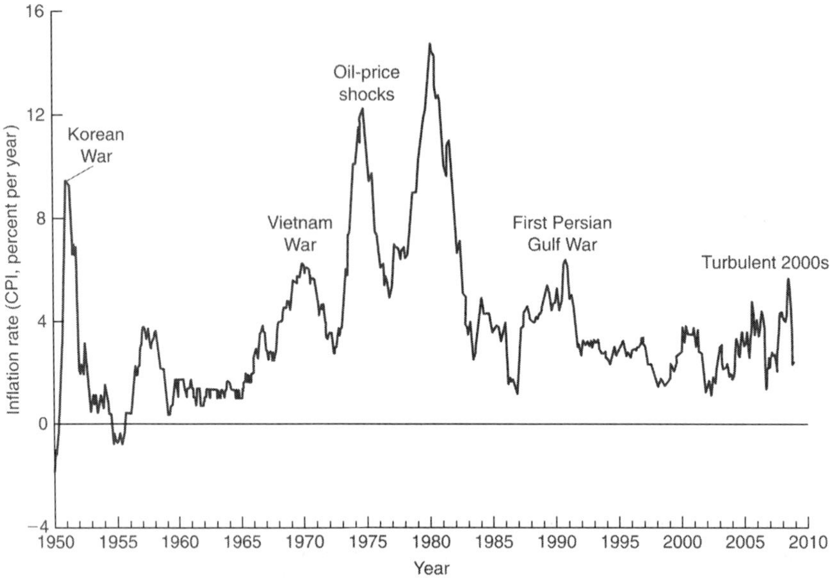

FIGURE 30-3. Inflation Has Remained Low and Stable in Recent Years

Historically, inflation in the United States was variable, and it reached unacceptably high rates in the early 1980s. In the last decade, skillful monetary management by the Federal Reserve along with favorable supply shocks has kept inflation low and in a narrow range.

Source: Bureau of Labor Statistics, *www.bls.gov.* This graph shows inflation of the consumer price index. The graph shows the rate of inflation over the prior 12 months.

[4] the Weimar Republic of Germany in the 1920s：20 世纪 20 年代的魏玛共和国，德国有史以来第一次走向共和的尝试，1919~1933 年期间统治德国的共和政体之历史名词。其宪法在魏玛召开的国民议会上通过，故称魏玛共和国，该宪法也称《魏玛宪法》。

as Argentina, Chile, and Brazil, had inflation rates of 50 to 700 percent per year in the 1970s and 1980s.

Once galloping inflation becomes entrenched, serious economic distortions arise. Generally, most ① contracts get indexed to a price index or to a foreign currency like the dollar. In these conditions, money loses its value very quickly, so people hold only the bare-minimum amount of money needed for daily transactions. Financial markets wither away, as capital flees abroad. People hoard goods, buy houses, and never, ever lend money at low nominal interest rates.

Hyperinflation. While economies seem to survive ② under galloping inflation, a third and deadly strain takes hold when the cancer of **hyperinflation** strikes. Nothing good can be said about an economy in which prices are rising a million or even a trillion percent per year.

Hyperinflations are particularly interesting to students of inflation because they highlight its disastrous impacts. Consider this description of hyperinflation in the Confederacy during the Civil War: [3]

> We used to go to the stores with money in our pockets and come back with food in our baskets. Now we go with money in baskets and return with food in our pockets. Everything is scarce except money! Prices are chaotic and production disorganized. A meal that used to cost the same amount as an opera ticket now costs twenty times as much. Everybody tends to hoard "things" and to try to get rid of the "bad" paper money, which drives the "good" metal money out of circulation. A partial return to barter inconvenience is the result.

The most thoroughly documented case of hyperinflation took place in the Weimar Republic of [4] Germany in the 1920s. Figure 30-4 shows how the government unleashed the monetary printing presses,

① 一般情况下，大多数合同都会以某种价格指数或者像美元一样的某种外币为基准，将其指数化。

② **恶性通货膨胀**：虽然在急剧通货膨胀下经济体似乎可以幸存，但当癌症般的**恶性通货膨胀**爆发时，这第三种通货膨胀足以使经济彻底崩溃。

[3] the Confederacy：即 the Confederate States of America，（美国南北战争时期的）南部邦联。the Civil War：全称为 the American Civil War，是美国历史上一场大规模的内战，参战双方为北方的美利坚合众国（简称联邦）和南方的美利坚联盟国（简称邦联）。这场战争改变了当时美国的政经情势，导致奴隶制度在美国南方最终被废除，对美国社会产生了巨大的影响。

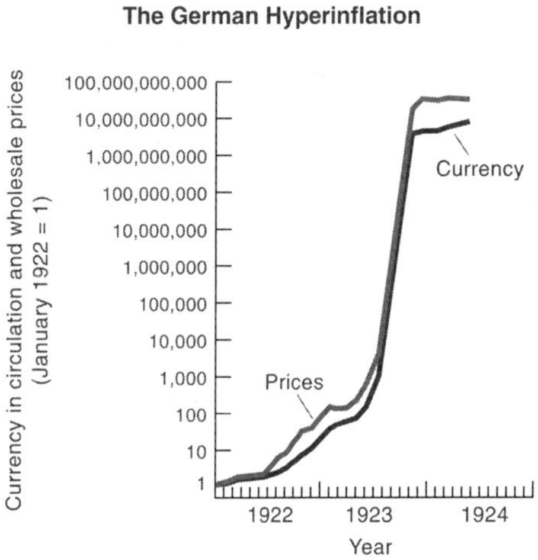

FIGURE 30-4. Money and Hyperinflation in Germany, 1922–1924

In the early 1920s, Germany could not raise enough taxes, so it used the monetary printing press to pay the government's bills. The stock of currency rose astronomically from January 1922 to December 1923, and prices spiraled upward as people frantically tried to spend their money before it lost all value.

driving both money and prices to astronomical levels. From January 1922 to November 1923, the price index rose from 1 to 10,000,000,000. If a person had owned 300 million marks worth of German bonds in early 1922, this amount would not have bought a piece of candy 2 years later.

Studies have found several common features in hyperinflations. First, the real money stock (measured by the money stock divided by the price level) falls drastically. By the end of the German hyperinflation, real money demand was only one-thirtieth of its level 2 years earlier. People were seen running from ① store to store, dumping their money like hot potatoes before they get burned by money's loss of value. Second, relative prices become highly unstable. Under normal conditions, a person's real wages move only a percent or less from month to month. During 1923, German real wages changed on average one-third (up or down) each month. This huge variation in relative prices and real wages—and the inequities and distortions caused by these fluctuations—took an enormous toll on workers and businesses, highlighting one of the major costs of inflation.

The impact of inflation was eloquently expressed by J. M. Keynes:

> As inflation proceeds and the real value of the currency fluctuates wildly from month to month, all ② permanent relations between debtors and creditors, which form the ultimate foundation of capitalism, become so utterly disordered as to be almost meaningless; and the process of wealth-getting degenerates into a game and a lottery.

可预期通货膨胀与不可预期通货膨胀
Anticipated vs. Unanticipated Inflation

An important distinction in the analysis of inflation ③ is whether the price increases are anticipated or unanticipated. Suppose that all prices are rising at 3 percent each year and everyone expects this trend to continue. Would there be any reason to get excited about inflation? Would it make any difference if both the actual and the expected inflation rates were 1 or 3 or 5 percent each year? Economists generally believe that anticipated inflation at low rates has little effect on economic efficiency or on the distribution of income and wealth. People would simply be adapting their behavior to a changing monetary yardstick.

But the reality is that inflation is usually unanticipated. For example, the Russian people had become accustomed to stable prices for many decades. When prices were freed from controls of central planning in 1992, no one, not even the professional economists, guessed that prices would rise by 400,000 percent over the next 5 years. People who naïvely put their money into ruble savings accounts saw their net worth evaporate. Those who were more sophisticated manipulated the system, and some even became fabulously wealthy "oligarchs."

In more stable countries like the United States, the impact of unanticipated inflation is less dramatic, but the same general point applies. An unexpected jump in prices will impoverish some and enrich others. How costly is this redistribution? Perhaps "cost" does not describe the problem. The effects may be more social than economic. An epidemic of burglaries may not lower GDP, but it causes great distress. Similarly, randomly redistributing wealth by inflation is like forcing people to play a lottery they would prefer to avoid.

---

① 人们都在匆匆忙忙地一家商店一家商店地出出进进，手里的钱就好像烫手的山芋，急着在货币贬值前将其甩出去。

② 通货膨胀发生时，货币的实际价值逐月地在剧烈波动，构建资本主义根基的债权人与债务人之间所有的永久性关系成为完全被扭曲的状态，并因此完全失去了意义，同时，挣取财富的方法也退化到了靠赌博和购买彩票的境地。

③ 价格增长可否预测是分析通货膨胀的显著特征。

The Quagmire of Deflation

If inflation is so bad, should societies instead strive for *deflation*—a situation where prices are actually falling rather than rising? Historical experience and macroeconomic analysis suggest that deflation combined with low interest rates can produce serious macroeconomic difficulties.

A gentle deflation by itself is not particularly harmful. Rather, deflations generally trigger economic problems because they may lead to a situation where monetary policy becomes impotent.

Normally, if prices begin to fall because of a recession, the central bank can stimulate the economy by increasing bank reserves and lowering interest rates. But if prices are falling rapidly, then real interest rates may be relatively high. For example, if the nominal interest rate is ¼ percent and prices are falling at 3¾ percent per year, then the real interest rate is 4 percent per year. At such a high real interest rate, investment may be choked off, with recessionary consequences.

The central bank may decide to lower interest rates. ① *But the lower limit on nominal interest rates is zero.* Why so? Because when interest rates are zero, then bonds are essentially money, and people will hardly want to hold a bond paying negative interest when money has a zero interest rate. Now, when the central bank has lowered interest rates to zero, in our example, real interest rates would still be 3¾ percent per year, which might still be too high to stimulate the economy. The central bank is trapped in a quagmire—a quagmire called the *liquidity trap*—in which it can lower short-term interest rates no further. The central bank has run out of ammunition.

Deflation was frequently observed in the nineteenth and early twentieth centuries but largely disappeared by the late twentieth century. However, at the end of the 1990s, Japan entered a period of sustained deflation. This was in part caused by a tremendous fall in asset prices, particularly land and stocks, but also by a long recession. Short-term interest rates were essentially zero after 2000. For example, the yield on 1-year bank deposits was 0.032 percent per year in mid-2003. The Bank of Japan was helpless in the face of deflation and zero interest rates.

The United States entered liquidity-trap territory in late 2008. Short-term, risk-free dollar securities (such as 90-day Treasury bills) fell to under 1/10th of 1 percent in late 2008 and early 2009. At that point, many economists believed, the Fed had "run out of ammunition"—that is, there was no further room to lower short-run interest rates.

Are there any remedies for deflation and the liquidity trap? One solution is to use fiscal policy, as was emphasized by the new Obama administration in emphasizing a large fiscal stimulus plan in early 2009. A fiscal stimulus will increase aggregate demand, and it will do so without any crowding out from higher interest rates.

Monetary policy could also expand its range of instruments, as discussed in Chapter 24. For example, the Fed could attempt to lower long-run interest rates or to lower the risk premium on risky assets, but these steps have proven difficult to achieve. Many economists believe that ② the best defense against a liquidity trap is a good offense. Policy makers should ensure that the economy stays safely away from deflation and the liquidity trap by maintaining full employment, ensuring a gradually rising price level, and avoiding the asset-price booms and busts that have been experienced over the last decade.

通货膨胀的经济影响
THE ECONOMIC IMPACTS OF INFLATION

Central bankers are united in their determination to contain inflation. During periods of high inflation, opinion polls often find that inflation is economic enemy number one. What is so dangerous and costly about inflation? We noted above that during periods of inflation all prices and wages do not move at the same rate; that is, changes in *relative prices* occur. As a result of the diverging relative prices, two definite effects of inflation are:

- A *redistribution* of income and wealth among different groups
- *Distortions* in the relative prices and outputs of different goods, or sometimes in output and employment for the economy as a whole

对收入与财富分配的影响
Impacts on Income and Wealth Distribution

Inflation affects the distribution of income and wealth primarily because of differences in the assets and liabilities that people hold. When people owe money, a sharp rise in prices is a windfall gain for them. Suppose you borrow $100,000 to buy a house and your annual fixed-interest-rate mortgage payments are $10,000. Suddenly, a great inflation doubles all wages and incomes. Your *nominal* mortgage payment is still $10,000 per year, but its real cost is halved. You will need to work only half as long as before to make your mortgage payment. The great inflation has increased

① 中央银行可以决定降低利率，但零利率是名义利率的极限。为什么？这是因为利率为零时，债券实质上就变成了货币。而零利率的货币，就意味着人们几乎不愿意持有负利率的债券。

② 许多经济学家坚信，防止流动性陷阱最好的方法是有效地主动进攻。政策制定者应该通过维持充分就业、确保价格水平的逐步上涨，以及避免过去十年来经历过的资产价格泡沫的形成和破裂，来确保经济运行远离通货紧缩和流动性陷阱。

your wealth by cutting in half the real value of your mortgage debt.

If you are a lender and have assets in fixed-interest-rate mortgages or long-term bonds, the shoe is on the other foot. An unexpected rise in prices will leave you the poorer because the dollars repaid to you are worth much less than the dollars you lent.

If an inflation persists for a long time, people ① come to anticipate it and markets begin to adapt. An allowance for inflation will gradually be built into the market interest rate. Say the economy starts out with interest rates of 3 percent and stable prices. Once people expect prices to rise at 9 percent per year, bonds and mortgages will tend to pay 12 percent rather than 3 percent. The 12 percent nominal interest rate reflects a 3 percent real interest rate plus a 9 percent inflation premium. There are no further major redistributions of income and wealth once interest rates have adapted to the new inflation rate. The adjustment of interest rates to chronic inflation has been observed in all countries with a long history of rising prices.

Because of institutional changes, some old myths no longer apply. It used to be thought that common stocks were a good inflation hedge, but stocks generally move inversely with inflation today. A common saying was that inflation hurts widows and orphans; today, they are insulated from inflation because social security benefits are indexed to consumer prices. Also, unanticipated inflation benefits debtors and hurts lenders less than before because many kinds of debt (like "floating-rate" mortgages) have interest rates that move up and down with market interest rates.

The major redistributive impact of inflation ② comes through its effect on the real value of people's wealth. In general, unanticipated inflation redistributes wealth from creditors to debtors, helping borrowers and hurting lenders. An unanticipated deflation has the opposite effect. But inflation mostly churns incomes and assets, randomly redistributing wealth among the population with little significant impact on any single group.

对经济效率的影响
Impacts on Economic Efficiency

In addition to redistributing incomes, inflation affects the real economy in two specific areas: It can harm economic efficiency, and it can affect total output. We begin with the efficiency impacts.

Inflation impairs economic efficiency because ③ it *distorts prices and price signals.* In a low-inflation economy, if the market price of a good rises, both buyers and sellers know that there has been an actual change in the supply and/or demand conditions for that good, and they can react appropriately. For example, if the neighborhood supermarkets all boost their beef prices by 50 percent, perceptive consumers know that it's time to start eating more chicken. Similarly, if the prices of new computers fall by 90 percent, you may decide it's time to turn in your old model.

By contrast, in a high-inflation economy it's much harder to distinguish between changes in relative prices and changes in the overall price level. If inflation is running at 20 or 30 percent per month, price changes are so frequent that changes in relative prices get missed in the confusion.

Inflation also *distorts the use of money.* Currency is money that bears a zero nominal interest rate. If the inflation rate rises from 0 to 10 percent per year, the real interest rate on currency falls from 0 to −10 percent per year. There is no way to correct this distortion.

As a result of the negative real interest rate on money, people devote real resources to reducing their money holdings during inflationary times. They go to the bank more often—using up "shoe leather" and valuable time. Corporations set up elaborate cash-management schemes. Real resources are thereby consumed simply to adapt to a changing monetary yardstick rather than to make productive investments.

Economists point to the *distortionary effect of inflation on taxes.* ④ Part of the tax code is written in dollar terms. When prices rise, the real value of the taxes paid rises even though real incomes have not changed. For example, suppose you were taxed at a rate of 30 percent on your income. Further suppose that the nominal interest rate was 6 percent and the inflation rate was 3 percent. You would, in reality, be paying a 60 percent tax rate on the real interest earnings of 3 percent. Many similar distortions are present in the tax code today.

But these are not the only costs; some economists point to *menu costs* of inflation. The idea is that when prices are changed, firms must spend real resources adjusting their prices. For instance, restaurants reprint their menus, mail-order firms reprint their catalogs, taxi companies remeter their cabs, cities adjust parking meters, and stores change the price tags of goods. Sometimes, the costs are intangible, such as those involved in gathering people to make new pricing decisions.

---

① 如果通货膨胀持续很长时间，人们就可以逐渐预测其走势，市场也开始与之相适应。市场利率也将逐渐地构建起包容通货膨胀的调整空间。

② 通货膨胀对再分配的影响主要是通过影响人们所拥有财富的实际价值实现的。总体来讲，无法预测的通货膨胀是将债权人手中的财富再分配给债务人，债权人受害，而债务人受益。一场无法预测的通货紧缩的作用正好相反。但是，通货膨胀多半是将收入和资产搅在一起，随机地将财富在全体民众中进行重新分配，很少对任何单个群体有重大影响。

③ 通货膨胀对价格和价格信号的扭曲作用损害了经济运行的效率。

④ 经济学家们指出了通货膨胀对税收产生的扭曲性影响。税法中有些规定以美元计价。价格上涨时，即便实际收入没有发生任何变化，但纳税总额的实际价值也会随之上升。

宏观经济影响
Macroeconomic Impacts

What are the macroeconomic effects of inflation? This question is addressed in the next section, so we merely highlight the major points here. Until the 1970s, high inflation in the United States usually went hand in hand with economic expansions; inflation tended to increase when investment was brisk and jobs were plentiful. Periods of deflation or declining inflation—the 1890s, the 1930s, some of the 1950s—were times of high unemployment of labor and capital.

But a more careful examination of the historical record reveals an interesting fact: The positive association between output and inflation appears to be only a temporary relationship. Over the longer run, there seems to be an inverse-U-shaped relationship between inflation and output growth. Table 30-1 shows the results of a multicountry study of the association between inflation and growth. It indicates that economic growth is strongest in countries with low inflation, while countries with high inflation or deflation tend to grow more slowly. (But beware the *ex post* fallacy here, as explored in question 7 at the end of this chapter.)

理想的通货膨胀率是多少
What Is the Optimal Rate of Inflation?

Most nations seek rapid economic growth, full employment, and price stability. But just what is meant by "price stability"? Exactly zero inflation? Over what period? Or is it perhaps low inflation?

One school of thought holds that policy should aim for absolutely stable prices or zero inflation. If we are confident that the price level in 20 years will be very close to the price level today, we can make better long-term investment and saving decisions.

Many macroeconomists believe that, while a zero-inflation target might be sensible in an ideal economy, we do not live in a frictionless system. One friction arises from the resistance of workers to declines in money wages. When inflation is literally zero, efficient labor markets would require that the money wages in some sectors are reduced while wages in other sectors are increased. Yet workers and firms are extremely reluctant to cut money wages. Some economists believe that, in the context of downward rigidity of nominal wages, a zero rate of inflation would lead to higher unemployment on average. ①

An additional and more serious concern about zero inflation is that economies might find themselves in the liquidity trap discussed above. If a country in a zero-inflation situation were to encounter a major contractionary shock, it might need negative real interest rates to climb out of the recession with monetary policy. While fiscal policy would still be effective, most macroeconomists believe that a better solution is to aim for a positive inflation rate so that the threat of liquidity traps is minimized. ②

We can summarize our discussion in the following way:

> Most economists agree that a predictable and gently rising price level provides the best climate for healthy economic growth. A careful analysis of the evidence suggests that low inflation has little impact on productivity or real output. By contrast, galloping inflation or hyperinflation can harm productivity and redistribute income and wealth in an arbitrary fashion. A gradual rise in prices will help avoid the deadly liquidity trap. ③

Inflation rate (% per year)	Growth of per capita GDP (% per year)
−20–0	0.7
0–10	2.4
10–20	1.8
20–40	0.4
100–200	−1.7
1,000+	−6.5

TABLE 30-1. Inflation and Economic Growth

The pooled experience of 127 countries shows that the most rapid growth is associated with low inflation rates. Deflation and moderate inflation accompany slow growth, while hyperinflations are associated with sharp downturns.

Source: Michael Bruno and William Easterly, "Inflation Crises and Long-Run Growth," *Journal of Monetary Economics*, 1998.

现代通货膨胀理论
B. MODERN INFLATION THEORY

What are the economic forces that cause inflation? What is the relationship between unemployment and inflation in the short run and in the long run? How

① 许多宏观经济学家坚持认为，虽然零通货膨胀目标在一个理想的经济体中是合理的，但我们不可能生活在无摩擦的社会体制里。

② 零通货膨胀的另外一个更为严重的问题是经济自身有可能陷入前面所讨论过的流动性陷阱中。

③ 大多数经济学家有一个共识，即可预测的温和上升的价格水平为经济的健康发展提供了最佳环境。对经济表现所作的详细分析表明，低通货膨胀对生产率和实际产出影响甚微。与此形成鲜明对比的是，急剧通货膨胀或者恶性通货膨胀会对生产率造成损害，并以任意方式对收入和财富进行再分配。逐渐上涨的价格有助于避开致命的流动性陷阱。

can nations reduce an unacceptably high inflation rate? What is the role of inflation targeting in central-bank policies?

Questions, questions, questions. Yet answers to these are critical to the economic health of modern mixed economies. In the balance of this chapter we explore modern inflation theory and analyze the costs of lowering inflation.

AS–AD 框架中的价格
PRICES IN THE *AS-AD* FRAMEWORK

There is no single source of inflation. Like illnesses, inflations occur for many reasons. Some inflations come from the demand side; others, from the supply side. But one key fact about modern inflations is that they develop an internal momentum and are costly to stop once underway.

预期通货膨胀
Expected Inflation

In modern economies like that of the United States, inflation has great momentum and tends to persist at the same rate. Expected inflation is like a lazy old dog. If the dog is not "shocked" by the push of a foot or the pull of a cat, it will stay put. Once disturbed, the dog may chase the cat, but then it eventually lies down in a new spot where it stays until the next shock.

Over the last three decades, prices in the United States rose on average around 3 percent annually, and most people came to expect this rate of inflation. This expected rate was built into the economy's institutions: wage agreements between labor and management were designed around a 3 percent inflation rate; government monetary and fiscal plans assumed a 3 percent rate as well. During this period, the *expected rate of inflation* was 3 percent per year.

Another closely related concept is the *core rate of* ①
inflation, which is a term often used in monetary policy. This is the inflation rate without volatile elements such as food and energy prices.

While inflation can persist at the same rate for a while, history shows that shocks to the economy tend to push inflation up or down. The economy is constantly subject to changes in aggregate demand, sharp oil- and commodity-price changes, poor harvests, movements in the foreign exchange rate, productivity changes, and countless other economic events that push inflation away from its expected rate.

Inflation has a high degree of inertia in a mod- ②
ern economy. People form an **expected rate of inflation,** and that rate is built into labor contracts and other agreements. The expected rate of inflation tends to persist until a shock causes it to move up or down.

需求拉动型通货膨胀
Demand-Pull Inflation

One of the major shocks to inflation is a change in aggregate demand. In earlier chapters we saw that changes in investment, government spending, or net exports can change aggregate demand and propel output beyond its potential. We also saw how a nation's central bank can affect economic activity.
Whatever the reason, **demand-pull inflation** occurs ③
when aggregate demand rises more rapidly than the economy's productive potential, pulling prices up to equilibrate aggregate supply and demand. In effect, demand dollars are competing for the limited supply of commodities and bid up their prices. As unemployment falls and workers become scarce, wages are bid up and the inflationary process accelerates.

A particularly damaging form of demand-pull inflation occurs when governments engage in deficit spending and rely on the monetary printing press to finance their deficits. The large deficits and the rapid money growth increase aggregate demand, which in turn increases the price level. Thus, when the German government financed its spending in 1922–1923 by printing billions and billions of paper marks, which came into the marketplace in search of bread and fuel, it was no wonder that the German price level rose a billionfold. This was demand-pull inflation with a vengeance. This scene was replayed in the early 1990s when the Russian government financed its budget deficit by printing monetary rubles. The result was an inflation rate that averaged 25 percent *per month,* or 1355 percent per year. (Make sure you understand how 25 percent per month becomes 1355 percent per year.)

Figure 30-5 illustrates the process of demand-pull inflation in terms of aggregate supply and demand. Starting from an initial equilibrium at point *E,* suppose there is an expansion of spending that pushes the *AD* curve up and to the right. The economy's equilibrium moves from *E* to E'. At this higher level of demand, prices have risen from *P* to P'. Demand-pull inflation has taken place.

---

① 另外一个与此密切相关的概念是核心通货膨胀率，这是一个常在货币政策中使用的术语，系指排除食品和能源价格等易变因素之后的通货膨胀率。

② 在现代经济中，通货膨胀具有很高的惯性。人们形成**预期通货膨胀率**，并把它置入劳动合同与其他协议。预期通货膨胀率一般不变，直至出现某种冲击使其上升或者下降。

③ 无论出于什么原因，**需求拉动型通货膨胀**总会在总需求上升的速度高于经济的潜在生产能力时出现，从而推高价格以平衡总需求与总供给。

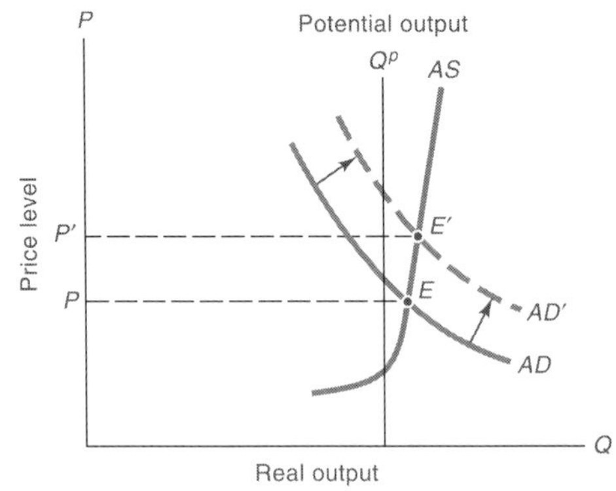

FIGURE 30-5. Demand-Pull Inflation Occurs When Too Much Spending Chases Too Few Goods

When aggregate demand increases, the rising spending is competing for limited goods. Prices rise from P to P' in demand-pull inflation.

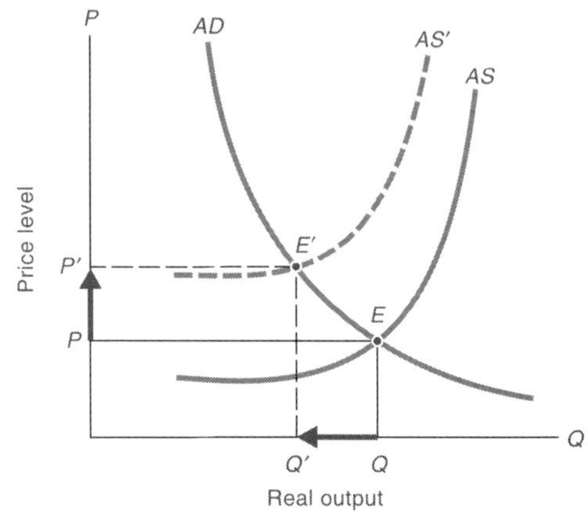

FIGURE 30-6. Increases in Production Costs Can Cause Stagflation, with Falling Output and Rising Prices

In periods marked by rapid increases in production costs, such as with the oil-price shocks, countries can experience the dilemma of rising inflation along with falling output, the combination of which is called stagflation. Policies to affect aggregate demand can cure one problem or the other but not both simultaneously.

成本推动型通货膨胀和“滞胀”
Cost-Push Inflation and "Stagflation"

The classical economists understood the rudiments of demand-pull inflation and used that theory to explain historical price movements. But a new phe- ①
nomenon has emerged over the last half-century. We see today that inflation sometimes increases because of increases in costs rather than because of increases in demand. This phenomenon is known as *cost-push* or *supply-shock* inflation. Often, it leads to an economic slowdown and to a syndrome called "stagflation," or *stag*nation with in*flation.*

Figure 30-6 shows the workings of supply-shock inflation. In 1973, 1978, 1999, and again in the late 2000s, countries were minding their macroeconomic business when severe shortages occurred in oil markets. Oil prices rose sharply, business costs of production increased, and a sharp burst of cost-push inflation followed. These situations can be seen as an upward shift in the *AS* curve. Equilibrium output falls while prices and inflation rise.

Stagflation poses a major dilemma for policymakers. They can use monetary and fiscal policies to change aggregate demand. However, *AD* shifts cannot simultaneously increase output *and* lower prices and inflation. An outward shift of the *AD* curve in Figure 30-6 through monetary expansion would offset the decline in output but raise prices further. Or an attempt to curb inflation by tightening monetary policy would only lower output even further. Economists explain this situation by saying that policymakers have two targets or goals (low inflation and low unemployment) but only one instrument (aggregate demand).

Such a dilemma is often faced by monetary policy makers. When inflation and unemployment are rising at the same time, what stance should the Federal Reserve or the European Central Bank take? Should it tighten money to reduce inflation? Or focus primarily on reducing unemployment? Or make some compromise between the two? Economics can provide no definitive answer to this dilemma. The response will depend upon society's values as well as the mandates imposed by the national legislatures (such as inflation targeting for the ECB versus a dual mandate for the Fed).

Inflation resulting from rising costs during peri- ②
ods of high unemployment and slack resource utilization is called **supply-shock inflation.** It can lead to the policy dilemma of stagflation when output declines at the same time as inflation is rising.

---

① 但是，在刚刚过去的半个世纪里，出现了一种全新的现象。今天我们明白，有的时候通货膨胀的上升是由于成本的上涨引起的，而不是需求的增长在作祟。这种现象就是众所周知的成本推动型或者供给冲击型通货膨胀。这种膨胀通常都能导致经济放缓以及称作“滞涨”的症状，即通货膨胀与经济停滞并存。

② 在高失业率和资源利用不足期间，由成本上升引发的通货膨胀称作**供给冲击型通货膨胀**。当产出的下降和通货膨胀的上升在同一时间发生时，供给冲击型通货膨胀就会导致滞胀的政策困境。

预期与通货膨胀

Expectations and Inflation

Why, you might ask, does inflation have such strong momentum? The answer is that most prices and wages are set with an eye to future economic conditions. When prices and wages are rising rapidly and are expected to continue doing so, businesses and workers tend to build the rapid rate of inflation into their price and wage decisions. High or ① low inflation expectations tend to be self-fulfilling prophecies.

We can use a hypothetical example to illustrate the role of expectations in the inflation process. Say that in 2009, Brass Mills Inc., a nonunionized light-manufacturing firm, was contemplating its annual wage and salary decisions for 2010. Its sales were growing as well. Brass Mills' chief economist reported that no major inflationary or deflationary shocks were foreseen, and the major forecasting services were expecting national wage growth of 4 percent in 2010. Brass Mills had conducted a survey of local companies and found that most employers were planning on increases in compensation of 3 to 5 percent during the next year. All the signals, then, pointed to wage increases of around 4 percent from 2009 to 2010.

In examining its own internal labor market, Brass Mills determined that its wages were in line with the local labor market. Because the managers did not want to fall behind local wages, Brass Mills decided that it would try to match local wage increases. It therefore set wage increases at the expected market increase, an average 4 percent wage increase for 2010.

The process of setting wages and salaries with an eye to expected future economic conditions can be extended to virtually all employers. This kind of reasoning also applies to many product prices—such as college tuitions, automobile prices, and long-distance telephone rates—that cannot be easily changed after they have been set. Because of the length of time involved in modifying inflation expectations and in adjusting most wages and many prices, expected inflation will change only if there are major shocks or changes in economic policy.

Figure 30-7 illustrates the process of expected inflation. Suppose that potential output is constant and that there are no supply or demand shocks. If everyone expects average costs and prices to rise at 3 percent each year, the *AS* curve will shift upward at 3 percent per year. If there are no demand shocks, the *AD* curve will also shift up at that rate. The intersection of the *AD* and *AS* curves will come at a price that is 3 percent higher each year. Hence, the macroeconomic equilibrium moves from E to E' to E''. Prices are rising 3 percent from one year to the next; expected inflation has set in at 3 percent.

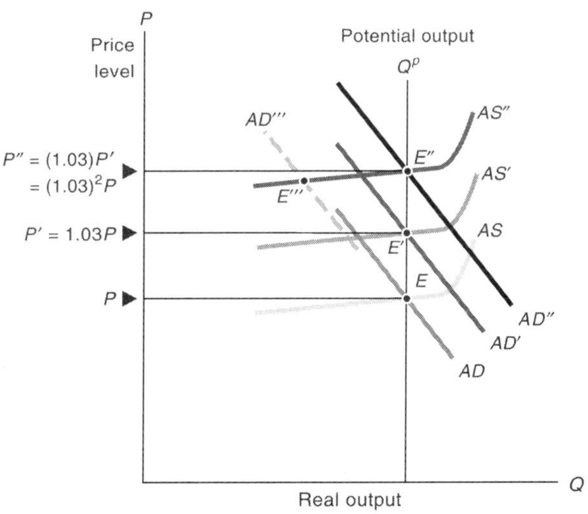

FIGURE 30-7. An Upward Spiral of Prices and Wages Occurs When Aggregate Supply and Demand Shift Up Together

Suppose that production costs and *AD* rise by 3 percent each year. *AS* and *AD* curves would shift up 3 percent each year. As the equilibrium moves from E to E' to E'', prices march up steadily because of expected inflation.

① 高通货膨胀或者低通货膨胀预期均为自我实现的预言。

Steady inflation occurs when the *AS* and *AD* curves are moving steadily upward at the same rate.

价格水平与通货膨胀
Price Levels vs. Inflation

Using Figure 30-7, we can make the useful distinction between movements in the price level and movements in inflation. In general, an increase in aggregate demand will raise prices, other things being equal. Similarly, an upward shift in the *AS* curve resulting from an increase in wages and other costs will raise prices, other things being equal.

But of course other things always change; in particular, *AD* and *AS* curves never sit still. Figure 30-7 shows, for example, the *AS* and *AD* curves marching up together.

What if there were an unexpected shift in the *AS* or *AD* curve during the third period? How would prices and inflation be affected? Suppose, for example, that the third period's *AD*″ curve shifted to the left to *AD*‴ because of a monetary contraction. This might cause a recession, with a new equilibrium at *E*‴ on the *AS*″ curve. At this point, output would have fallen below potential; prices and the inflation rate would be lower than at *E*″, but the economy would still be experiencing inflation because the price level at *E*‴ is still above the previous period's equilibrium *E*′ with price *P*′.

This example is a reminder that supply or ① demand shocks may reduce the price level below the level it would otherwise have attained. Nonetheless, because of inflation's momentum, the economy may continue to experience inflation.

菲利普斯曲线
THE PHILLIPS CURVE

The major macroeconomic tool used to understand inflation is the **Phillips curve.** This curve shows the [2] relationship between the unemployment rate and inflation. The basic idea is that when output is high and unemployment is low, wages and prices tend to rise more rapidly. This occurs because workers and unions can press more strongly for wage increases when jobs are plentiful and firms can more easily raise prices when sales are brisk. The converse also holds—high unemployment tends to slow inflation.

短期菲利普斯曲线
Short-Run Phillips Curve

Macroeconomists distinguish between the short-run Phillips curve and the long-run Phillips curve. A typical short-run Phillips curve is shown in Figure 30-8. On the diagram's horizontal axis is the unemployment rate. On the blue left-hand vertical scale is the annual rate of price inflation. The green right-hand vertical scale shows the rate of money-wage inflation. As you move leftward on the Phillips curve by reducing unemployment, the rate of price and wage increase indicated by the curve becomes higher.

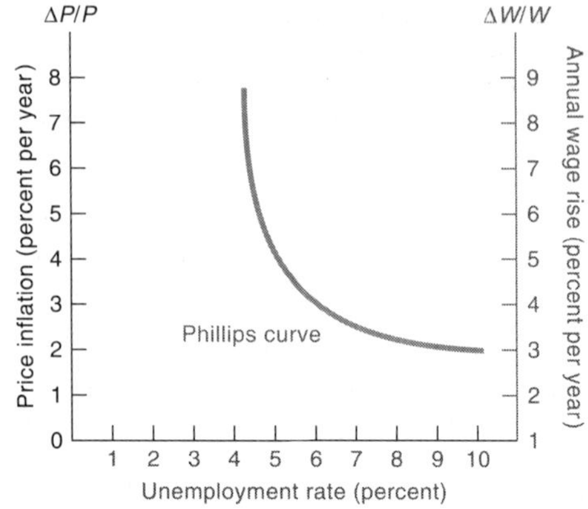

FIGURE 30-8. The Short-Run Phillips Curve Depicts the Tradeoff between Inflation and Unemployment

A short-run Phillips curve shows the inverse relationship between inflation and unemployment. The green wage-change scale on the right-hand vertical axis is higher than the blue left-hand inflation scale by the assumed 1 percent rate of growth of average labor productivity.

An important piece of inflation arithmetic underlies this curve. Say that labor productivity (output per worker) rises at a steady rate of 1 percent each year. Further, assume that firms set prices on the basis of average labor costs, so prices always change just as much as average labor costs per unit of output. If wages are rising at 4 percent, and productivity is rising at 1 percent, then average labor costs will rise at 3 percent. Consequently, prices will also rise at 3 percent.

Using this inflation arithmetic, we can see the relation between wage and price increases in Figure 30-8. The two scales in the figure differ only by the assumed rate of productivity growth (so the price change of 4 percent per year would correspond to a wage change of 5 percent per year

---

① 该例分析提醒我们，供给或者需求冲击可以使价格水平降低至其他途径所能达到的价格水平之下。但是，由于通货膨胀的内在能量，该经济体还会继续经历通货膨胀。

[2] Phillips Curve：菲利普斯曲线，新西兰统计学家威廉·菲利普斯（A.W. Phillips，1914~1975）于 1958 年根据英国 19 世纪中叶至 20 世纪中叶的百年宏观经济数据，画出的一条表现通货膨胀与失业率关系的曲线。

if productivity grew by 1 percent per year and if prices always rose as fast as average labor costs).

The Logic of Wage-Price Arithmetic

This relationship between prices, wages, and productivity can be formalized as follows: The fact that prices are based on average labor costs per unit of output implies that P is always proportional to WL/Q, where P is the price level, W is the wage rate, L is labor-hours, and Q is output. Assume that average labor productivity (Q/L) is growing smoothly at 1 percent per year. Hence, if wages are growing at 4 percent annually, prices will grow at 3 percent annually (= 4 percent growth in wages − 1 percent growth in productivity). More generally,

$$\text{Rate of inflation} = \text{rate of wage growth} - \text{rate of productivity growth}$$

This shows the relationship between price inflation and wage inflation.

We can illustrate how closely this relationship holds with actual numbers for a high-inflation period and for a low-inflation period. The following table shows the major long-run determinants of inflation to be wage growth and productivity change. From the first to the second period, inflation rose because wage growth increased slightly while productivity fell sharply. In the third period, inflation was low because wage growth was restrained while productivity growth rebounded.

	Rate of CPI inflation (%)	Rate of wage growth (%)	Rate of productivity growth (%)
1958–1973	2.9	5.4	3.1
1973–1995	5.6	5.9	1.5
1995–2007	2.6	4.3	2.6

Source: Bureau of Labor Statistics data on the business sector, at *www.bls.gov*.

非加速通货膨胀的失业率
The Nonaccelerating Inflation Rate of Unemployment

Economists who looked carefully at inflationary periods noticed that the simple two-variable Phillips curve drawn in Figure 30-8 was unstable. On the basis of theoretical work of Edmund Phelps and Milton Friedman, along with statistical tests of the actual history, macroeconomists developed the modern theory of inflation, which distinguishes between the long run and the short run. The downward-sloping Phillips curve of Figure 30-8 holds only in the short run. In the long run, the Phillips curve is *vertical,* not downward-sloping. This approach implies that in the long-run there is a minimum unemployment rate that is consistent with steady inflation. This is the *nonaccelerating inflation rate of unemployment* or *NAIRU* (pronounced "nay-rew").[1]

The **nonaccelerating inflation rate of unemployment** (or **NAIRU**) is that unemployment rate consistent with a constant inflation rate. At the NAIRU, upward and downward forces on price and wage inflation are in balance, so there is no tendency for inflation to change. The NAIRU is the lowest unemployment rate that can be sustained without upward pressure on inflation. ①

The idea behind the NAIRU is that the state of the economy can be divided into three situations:

- *Excess demand.* When markets are extremely tight, with low unemployment and high utilization of capacity, then prices and wages will be subject to demand-pull inflation.
- *Excess supply.* In recessionary situations, with high unemployment and idled factories, firms tend to sell at discounts and workers push less aggressively for wage increases. Wage and price inflation tend to moderate.
- *Neutral pressures.* Sometimes the economy is operating "in neutral." The upward wage pressures from job vacancies just match the downward wage pressures from unemployment. There are no supply shocks from oil or other exogenous sources. Here, the economy is at the NAIRU, and inflation neither rises nor falls. ②

从短期到长期
From Short Run to Long Run

How does the economy move from the short run to the long run? The basic idea is that when price changes are unanticipated, the short-run Phillips curve tends to shift up or down. This point is

[1] Other terms will sometimes be encountered. The original name for the NAIRU was the "natural rate of unemployment." This term is unsatisfactory because there is nothing natural about the NAIRU.

---

① **非加速通货膨胀的失业率（NAIRU）**系指与稳定的通货膨胀率相一致的失业率。在这一失业率水平上，价格和工资的通胀上升和下降的压力获得平衡，使通货膨胀不存在变化的倾向。非加速通货膨胀的失业率是最低的失业率，它在没有通货膨胀上升压力的条件下得以维持。

② 中性压力：有的时候经济会在一种“中性”的状态下运行。源自岗位空缺的工资上升压力正好与源自失业的工资下降压力相抵，没有任何来自于石油和其他外部资源供给的冲击。因此，经济在此时处于非加速通货膨胀的失业率水平，通货膨胀既没有上升也没有下降。

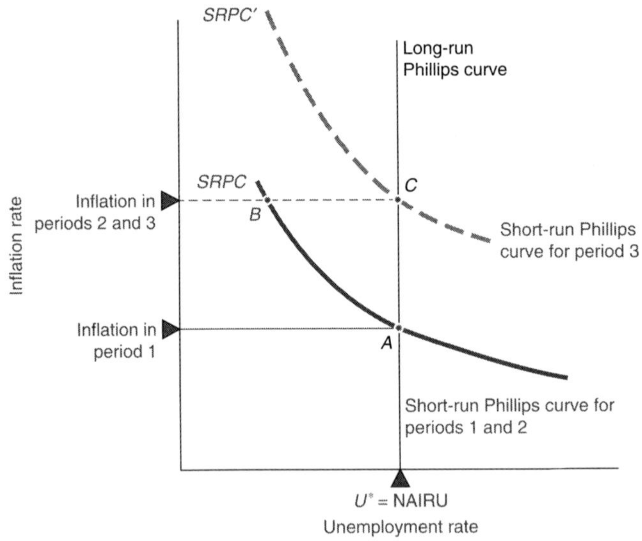

FIGURE 30-9. The Shifting Phillips Curve

This figure shows how economic expansion leads to an inflationary surprise and an upward shift in the short-run Phillips curve. The steps in the shift are explained by the bullets in the text. Note that if you connect points *A, B,* and *C,* the shifting curve produces a clockwise loop.

illustrated by a series of steps in a "boom cycle" here [1] and in Figure 30-9:

- *Period 1.* In the first period, unemployment is at the NAIRU. There are no demand or supply surprises, and the economy is at point *A* on the lower short-run Phillips curve (*SRPC*) in Figure 30-9.
- *Period 2.* Next, suppose there is an economic expansion which lowers the unemployment rate. As unemployment declines, firms recruit workers more vigorously, giving larger wage increases than formerly. As output approaches capacity, price markups rise. Wages and prices begin to accelerate. In terms of our Phillips curve, the economy moves up and to the left to point *B* on its short-run Phillips curve (along *SRPC* in Figure 30-9). As shown in the figure, inflation expectations have not yet changed, so the economy stays on the original Phillips curve, on *SRPC*. The lower unemployment rate raises inflation during the second period.
- *Period 3.* Because inflation has risen, firms and workers are surprised, and they revise upward their inflationary expectations. They begin to incorporate the higher expected inflation into their wage and price decisions. The result is a *shift in the short-run Phillips curve.* We can see the new curve as *SRPC′* in Figure 30-9. The new short-run Phillips curve lies above the original Phillips curve, reflecting the higher expected rate of inflation. We have drawn the curve so that the new expected inflation rate for period 3 equals the actual inflation rate in period 2. If a slowdown in economic activity brings the unemployment rate back to the NAIRU in period 3, the economy moves to point *C.* Even though the unemployment rate is the same as it was in period 1, actual inflation will be higher, reflecting the upward shift in the short-run Phillips curve.

Note the surprising outcome. Because the expected inflation rate has increased, the rate of

[1] boom cycle：繁荣周期，该周期内金融业高速增长，GDP 增速强劲，消费者需求旺盛，企业销售兴旺，利润丰硕。

inflation is higher in period 3 than during period 1 even though the unemployment rate is the same. The economy in period 3 will have the same *real* GDP and unemployment rate as it did in period 1, even though the *nominal* magnitudes (prices and nominal GDP) are now growing more rapidly than they did before the expansion raised the expected rate of inflation.

We can also track a "recession cycle" that occurs ① when unemployment rises and the actual inflation rate falls below its expected rate. The expected rate of inflation declines in recessions, and the economy enjoys a lower inflation rate when it returns to the NAIRU. This painful cycle of austerity occurred during the Carter-Volcker-Reagan wars against inflation during 1979–1984.

垂直的长期菲利普斯曲线
The Vertical Long-Run Phillips Curve

When the unemployment rate departs from the NAIRU, the inflation rate will tend to change. What happens if the gap between the actual unemployment rate and the NAIRU persists? For example, say that the NAIRU is 5 percent while the actual unemployment rate is 3 percent. Because of the gap, inflation will tend to rise from year to year. Inflation might be 3 percent in the first year, 4 percent in the second year, 5 percent in the third year—and might continue to move upward thereafter. When would ② this upward spiral stop? It stops only when unemployment moves back to the NAIRU. Put differently, as long as unemployment is below the NAIRU, wage inflation will tend to increase.

The opposite behavior will be seen at high unemployment. In that case, inflation will tend to fall as long as unemployment is above the NAIRU.

Only when unemployment is *at* the NAIRU will inflation stabilize; only then will the shifts of supply and demand in different labor markets be in balance; only then will inflation—at whatever is its inertial rate—tend neither to increase nor to decrease.

The modern theory of inflation has important implications for economic policy. It implies that there is a minimum level of unemployment that an economy can enjoy in the long run. If the economy is pushed to very high levels of output and employment, this will ignite an upward spiral of wage and price inflation. This theory also provides a formula for curbing inflation. When the inflation rate is too high, a country can tighten money, trigger a recession, raise the unemployment rate above the NAIRU, and thereby reduce inflation.

The NAIRU defines the neutral zone between ③ excessive tightness/rising inflation and high unemployment/falling inflation. In the short run, inflation can be reduced by raising unemployment above the NAIRU, but in the long run, the NAIRU is the lowest sustainable rate of unemployment.

数量估计
Quantitative Estimates

Although the NAIRU is a crucial macroeconomic concept, precise numerical estimates of the NAIRU have proved elusive. Many macroeconomists have used advanced techniques to estimate the NAIRU. For this text, we have adopted the estimates prepared by the Congressional Budget Office (CBO). According to the CBO, the NAIRU rose gradually from the 1950s, peaked at 6.3 percent of the labor force around 1980, and declined to 4.8 percent by 2008. CBO estimates, along with the actual unemployment rate through the end of 2008, are shown in Figure 30-10.

对非加速通货膨胀失业率的质疑
Doubts about the NAIRU

The concept of the nonaccelerating inflation rate of unemployment, along with its output twin of potential GDP, is crucial for understanding inflation and the connection between the short run and the long run in macroeconomics. But the mainstream view remains controversial.

Critics wonder whether the NAIRU is a stable and reliable concept. The inflation experience of the United States has led economists to question whether there is in fact a stable NAIRU for the country. Another question is whether an extended period of high unemployment will lead to a deterioration of job skills, to loss of on-the-job training and experience, and thereby to a higher NAIRU. Might not slow growth of real GDP reduce investment and leave the country with a diminished capital stock? Might not that capacity shortage produce rising inflation even with unemployment rates above the NAIRU?

Experience in Europe over the last two decades confirms some of these worries (recall our discussion of the European unemployment puzzle at the end of the previous chapter). In the early 1960s, labor markets in Germany, France, and Britain appeared to be in equilibrium with unemployment rates between 1 and 2 percent. By the late 1990s, after a decade of stagnation and slow job growth, labor market

---

① 当失业率上升，实际通货膨胀率低至预期通货膨胀率之下时，我们就会观察到一种"衰退周期"现象的发生。

② 这种螺旋式上升什么时候才能停止？只有当失业率回到非加速通货膨胀的失业率水平时，才会停止。换一种不同的说法，只要失业率低于非加速通货膨胀的失业率水平，工资的通胀就势必趋向上涨。

③ 非加速通货膨胀的失业率水平定义了过渡紧缩 / 通货膨胀上升与高失业率 / 通货膨胀下降两者之间的中性区域。在短期，通过将失业率提高到非加速通货膨胀失业率水平之上可以降低通货膨胀率，但在长期，非加速通货膨胀的失业率是可维持的最低失业率。

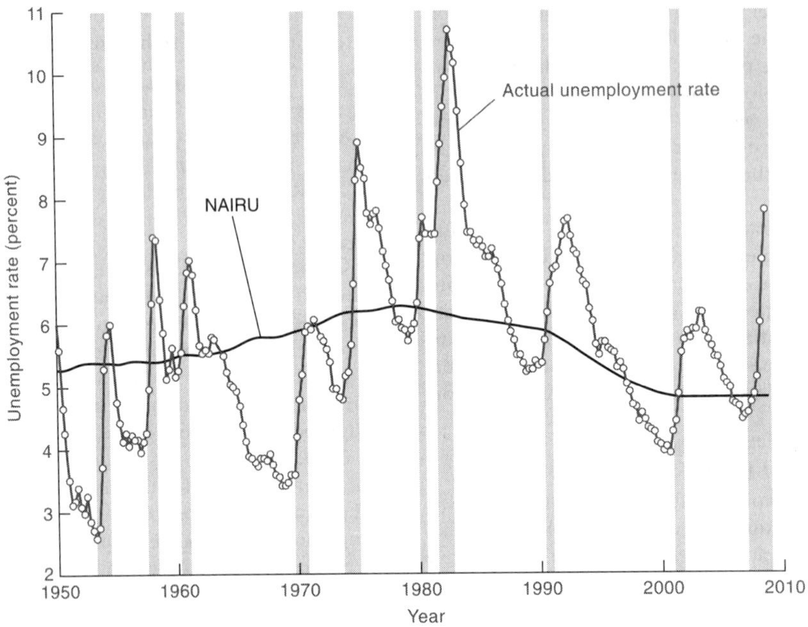

Shaded areas are NBER recessions.

FIGURE 30-10. Actual Unemployment Rate and NAIRU for the United States

The NAIRU is the unemployment rate at which upward and downward forces acting on inflation are in balance.

Source: Actual unemployment rate from Bureau of Labor Statistics; NAIRU from estimates of the Congressional Budget Office.

equilibrium seemed to be in balance with unemployment rates in the 6 to 12 percent range. On the basis of recent European experience, many macroeconomists are looking for ways to explain the instability of the NAIRU and its dependence upon actual unemployment as well as labor market institutions.

复习 Review

The major points to understand are the following:

- In the short run, an increase in aggregate demand which lowers the unemployment rate below the NAIRU will tend to increase the inflation rate. Recessions and high unemployment tend to lower inflation. In the short run, there is a tradeoff between inflation and unemployment.
- When inflation is higher or lower than what ① people expect, inflation expectations adjust. The changed inflation expectations will generally shift the short-run Phillips curve up or down.
- The long-run Phillips curve is vertical at the non- ② accelerating inflation rate of unemployment (NAIRU). Unemployment above (below) the NAIRU will tend to lower (increase) the rate of inflation.

抗通货膨胀的政策困境

C. DILEMMAS OF ANTI-INFLATION POLICY

The economy evolves in response to political forces and technological change. Our economic theories, designed to explain issues like inflation and unemployment, must also adapt. In this final section on

① 当通货膨胀高于或者低于人们的预期时，该预期即会做出调整。调整之后的预期一般会推动短期菲利普斯曲线上升或者下降。

② 长期菲利普斯曲线在非加速通货膨胀的失业率水平上是垂直的，失业率高于（低于）非加速通货膨胀的失业率水平往往会降低（提高）通货膨胀率。

inflation theory, we discuss the pressing issues that arise in combating inflation.

长期究竟有多长

How Long Is the Long Run?

The NAIRU theory holds that the Phillips curve is vertical in the long run. Just how long is the long run for this purpose? The length of time that it takes the economy to adjust fully to a shock is not known with precision. Recent studies suggest that full adjustment takes at least 5 years or perhaps even a decade. The reason for the long delay is that it takes years for expectations to adjust, for labor and other long-term contracts to be renegotiated, and for all these effects to percolate through the economy.

降低通货膨胀率的代价有多大

How Much Does It Cost to Reduce Inflation?

Our analysis suggests that a nation can reduce the expected rate of inflation by temporarily reducing output and raising unemployment. But policymakers may want to know just how much it costs to squeeze inflation out of the economy. How costly is *disinflation,* which denotes the policy of lowering the rate of inflation?

Studies of this subject find that the cost of reducing inflation varies depending upon the country, the initial inflation rate, and the policy used. Analyses for the United States give a reasonably consistent answer: Lowering the expected inflation rate by 1 percentage point costs the nation about 4 percent of 1 year's GDP. In terms of the current level of GDP, this amounts to an output loss of about \$600 billion (in 2008 prices) to reduce the inflation rate by 1 percentage point.

To understand the cost of disinflation, consider the Phillips curve. If the Phillips curve is relatively ① flat, reducing inflation will require much unemployment and loss in output; if the Phillips curve is steep, a small rise in unemployment will bring down inflation quickly and relatively painlessly. Statistical analyses indicate that when the unemployment rate rises 1 percentage point above the NAIRU for 1 year and then returns to the NAIRU, the inflation rate will decline about ½ percentage point. Therefore, to reduce inflation by 1 full percentage point, unemployment must be held 2 percentage points above the NAIRU for 1 year.

The loss associated with disinflationary policies is ② called the **sacrifice ratio.** More precisely, the sacrifice ratio is the cumulative loss in output, measured as a percent of 1 year's GDP, associated with a 1-percentage-point permanent reduction in inflation.

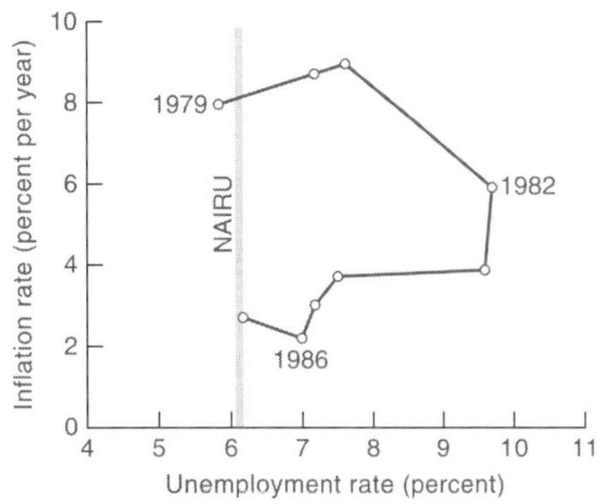

FIGURE 30-11. The Costs of Disinflation, 1979–1987

This graph shows a disinflation cycle. High interest rates led to slow economic growth and high unemployment in the early 1980s. The result was unemployment above the NAIRU and output below potential. Core inflation declined by about 5 percentage points, while cumulative output loss was about 20 percent of GDP, which leads to a sacrifice ratio of 4 percent.

We can illustrate the sacrifice ratio using the period of disinflation after 1979. The scatter plot of inflation and unemployment during this period is shown in Figure 30-11. This is an *austerity cycle* or *disinflation cycle,* which is the opposite of the boom cycle illustrated in Figure 30-9. During these years, the Federal Reserve took strong steps to reduce inflation. Tight money drove the unemployment rate up above 10 percent for 2 years, and output was below its potential for 7 years. We have shown the average NAIRU as the vertical line, which would also be the long-run Phillips curve for this period.

Tight money did reduce core inflation from around 8 to 3 percent per year during this period. The cumulative loss of output associated with this disinflation is estimated to be about 20 percent of GDP. This provides an estimate of the sacrifice ratio for this period of 4 percent [= (20 percent of GDP)/(5 percentage points of disinflation)]. In the American economy today, this implies that lowering the core inflation rate by 1 percentage point would cost about \$600 billion, or around \$6000 per American household.

① 如果菲利普斯曲线相对平缓，降低通货膨胀率就会以牺牲失业率和减少产出为代价。如果菲利普斯曲线是陡峭的，失业率的小幅上升将很快地压低通货膨胀率，其代价相对较小。

② 与反通货膨胀政策有关的损失称作**牺牲率**。更确切一点讲，牺牲率系产出的累积损失，可用年损失占年度GDP的百分比衡量，与通货膨胀持续下降一个百分点相联系。

① 这些持不同意见的人坚持认为，信用以及公开颁布的政策，如采用固定的货币条例和名义 GDP 目标等，可以比较低的产出和失业率为代价来执行抗通货膨胀政策，降低通货膨胀。

② 一项信用货币政策，如强行确定一个低通货膨胀率目标，就会让人们预期通货膨胀未来会更低，而且在某种程度上，这种信念可能就是可以自我实现的预言。

③ 当失业率快速升高以及农民和建筑工人的罢工潮席卷国会大厦并且包围白宫时，国会和总统往往都会在与通货膨胀的博弈中乱了阵脚。

The Phillips-curve theory illustrates how policy can reduce inflation by raising unemployment above the NAIRU for a period of time. Estimates of the cost of disinflation are typically around 4 percent of 1 year's GDP for 1 point of disinflation. This calculation shows why containing inflation is a costly policy and one not undertaken lightly.

信用与通货膨胀 Credibility and Inflation

One of the most important questions in anti-inflation policy concerns the role of credibility of policy. Many economists argue that the Phillips-curve approach is too pessimistic. The dissenters hold that credible and ① publicly announced policies—for example, adopting fixed monetary rules or targeting nominal GDP—would allow anti-inflation policies to reduce inflation with lower output and unemployment costs.

The idea relies on the fact that inflation is a process that depends on people's expectations of future inflation. A credible monetary policy—such as one ② that relentlessly targets a fixed, low inflation rate—might lead people to expect that inflation would be lower in the future and that this belief might in some measure be a self-fulfilling prophecy. Those emphasizing credibility backed their theories by citing fundamental policy changes, such as occurred with monetary and fiscal reforms that ended Austrian and Bolivian hyperinflations at relatively low cost in terms of unemployment or lost GDP.

Many economists were skeptical about claims that credibility would significantly lower the output costs of disinflation. While such policies might work in countries torn by hyperinflation, war, or revolution, Draconian anti-inflation policies would be less credible in the United States. Congress and the ③ president often lose heart in the fight against inflation when unemployment rises sharply and farmers or construction workers storm the Capitol and circle the White House.

The U.S. experience during the 1980s, shown in Figure 30-11, provides a good laboratory to test the credibility critique. During this period, monetary policy was tightened in a clear and forceful manner. Yet the price tag was still high, as the sacrifice calculations indicate. Using tough, preannounced policies to enhance credibility does not appear to have lowered the cost of disinflation in the United States.

Because the United States has such a high degree of stability of its political and economic institutions, its experience may be unusual. Economists have examined anti-inflation policies in other countries and have determined that anti-inflation policies can sometimes be *expansionary*. A recent study by Stanley [4] Fischer, Ratna Sahay, and Carlos A. Végh concluded [5] as follows:

> Periods of high inflation are associated with bad ⑥ macroeconomic performance. In particular, high inflation is bad for growth. The evidence is based on a sample of 18 countries which have experienced very high inflation episodes. During such periods, real GDP per capita fell on average by 1.6 percent per annum (compared to positive growth of 1.4 percent in low inflation years). . . . Exchange rate-based stabilizations appear to lead to an initial expansion in real GDP and real private consumption. [7]

降低失业的政策 Policies to Lower Unemployment

Given the costs of high unemployment, we might ask: Is the NAIRU the optimal level of unemployment? If not, what can we do to lower it toward a more desirable level? Some economists believe that the NAIRU (sometimes also called the "natural rate of unemployment") represents the economy's efficient unemployment level. They hold that it is the outcome of an efficient pattern of employment, job vacancies, and job search. In their view, holding the unemployment rate below the NAIRU would be like driving your car without a spare tire.

Other economists strongly disagree, reasoning that the NAIRU is likely to be above the optimal unemployment rate. In their view, economic welfare would be increased if the NAIRU could be lowered. This group argues that there are many spillovers or externalities in the labor market. For example, workers who have been laid off suffer from a variety of social and economic hardships. Yet employers do not pay the costs of unemployment; most of the costs (unemployment insurance, medical costs, family distress, etc.) spill over as external costs and are absorbed by the worker or by the government. Moreover, there may be congestion externalities when an additional unemployed worker makes it harder for other workers to find jobs. To the extent that unemployment has external costs, the NAIRU is likely to be higher than the optimal unemployment

[4] Stanley Fischer：斯坦利·费希尔（1943~），出生于美国的以色列经济学家，以色列中央银行行长，曾出任世界银行首席经济学家。

[5] Ratna Sahay：拉特纳·撒哈，国际货币基金组织驻埃及、中东和中亚发展执行主任，女经济学家。
Carlos A. Végh：柯劳斯·维赫（1958~），乌拉圭经济学家，马里兰大学教授。

⑥ 高通货膨胀时期与宏观经济的表现不佳是联系在一起的。尤其对经济增长，高通货膨胀的作用是负面的。这个结论是从对 18 个经历过高通货膨胀国家的样本数据得出的。在这样的高通胀期间，人均实际 GDP 年均降低 1.6%（相比较而言，低通货膨胀期间的这个数据却上升 1.4%）。……基础汇率的稳定似乎引发了实际 GDP 与个人实际消费的初始扩张。

[7] 本段文字出自斯坦利·费希尔、拉特纳·撒哈、柯劳斯·维赫为国际货币基金组织完成的项目结题报告《东欧到布鲁塞尔还有多远》（*How Far is Eastern Europe from Brussels?*）。

rate; consequently, lowering the unemployment rate would raise the nation's net economic welfare.

A large social dividend would reward the society that discovers how to lower the NAIRU. What measures might lower the NAIRU?

- *Improve labor market services.* Some unemployment occurs because job vacancies are not matched up with unemployed workers. Through better information, the amount of frictional and structural unemployment can be reduced. A recent innovation is Internet matching, run by states or private companies, which can help people find jobs and firms find qualified workers more quickly.
- *Bolster training programs.* If you look at the Internet or at help-wanted ads in the newspaper, you will see that most of the job vacancies call for skilled workers. Conversely, most of the unemployed are unskilled or semiskilled workers, or workers who are in a depressed industry. Many economists believe that government or private training programs can help unemployed workers retool for better jobs in growing sectors. If suc- ① cessful, such programs provide the double bonus of allowing people to lead productive lives and of reducing the burden on government transfer programs.
- *Reduce disincentives to work.* In protecting people from the hardships of unemployment and poverty, the government has at the same time removed the sting of unemployment and reduced incentives to seek work. Some economists call for ② reforming the unemployment-insurance system and reforming health care, disability, and social security programs to improve work incentives. Others note that the lack of a national health insurance system may increase "job lock" and reduce the mobility of workers.

* * *

Having surveyed the history and theory of unemployment and inflation, we conclude with the following cautious summary:

Critics believe that the high unemployment that often prevails in North America and Europe is a central flaw in modern capitalism. Indeed, unemployment must sometimes be kept above its socially optimal level to ensure price stability, and the tension between price stability and low unemployment is one of the cruelest dilemmas of modern society.

SUMMARY

A. Definition and Impact of Inflation

1. Recall that inflation occurs when the general level of prices is rising. The rate of inflation is the percentage change in a price index from one period to the next. The major price indexes are the consumer price index (CPI) and the GDP deflator.
2. Like diseases, inflations come in different strains. We generally see low inflation in the United States (a few percentage points annually). Sometimes, galloping inflation produces price rises of 50 or 100 or 200 percent each year. Hyperinflation takes over when the printing presses spew out currency and prices start rising many times each month. Historically, hyperinflations have almost always been associated with war and revolution.
3. Inflation affects the economy by redistributing income and wealth and by impairing efficiency. Unanticipated inflation usually favors debtors, profit seekers, and risk-taking speculators. It hurts creditors, fixed-income classes, and timid investors. Inflation leads to distortions in relative prices, tax rates, and real interest rates. People take more trips to the bank, taxes may creep up, and measured income may become distorted.

B. Modern Inflation Theory

4. At any time, an economy has a given expected inflation rate. This is the rate that people have come to anticipate and that is built into labor contracts and other agreements. The expected rate of inflation is a short-run equilibrium and persists until the economy is shocked.
5. In reality, the economy receives incessant price shocks. The major kinds of shocks that propel inflation away from its expected rate are demand-pull and supply-shock. Demand-pull inflation results from too much spending chasing too few goods, causing

① 如果这些计划获得成功，就可以实现双重收益——既可以让人们过上富足的生活，又可以减轻政府转移支付计划的负担。

② 有些经济学家呼吁改革失业保险制度，改革医疗保健、残疾人及社会保障制度，以改善工作激励。

the aggregate demand curve to shift up and to the right. Wages and prices are then bid up in markets. Supply-shock inflation is a new phenomenon of modern industrial economies and occurs when the costs of production rise even in periods of high unemployment and idle capacity.

6. The Phillips curve shows the relationship between inflation and unemployment. In the short run, lowering one rate means raising the other. But the short-run Phillips curve tends to shift over time as expected inflation and other factors change. If policymakers attempt to hold unemployment below the NAIRU for long periods, inflation will tend to spiral upward.
7. Modern inflation theory relies on the concept of the nonaccelerating inflation rate of unemployment, or NAIRU, which is the lowest sustainable unemployment rate that the nation can enjoy without risking an upward spiral of inflation. It represents the level of unemployment of resources at which labor and product markets are in inflationary balance. Under the NAIRU theory, there is no permanent tradeoff between unemployment and inflation, and the long-run Phillips curve is vertical.

C. Dilemmas of Anti-inflation Policy

8. A central concern for policymakers is the cost of reducing inflation. Current estimates indicate that a substantial recession is necessary to slow expected inflation.
9. Economists have put forth many proposals for lowering the NAIRU; notable proposals include improving labor market information, improving education and training programs, and refashioning government programs so that workers have greater incentives to work.

CONCEPTS FOR REVIEW

History and Theories of Inflation

Rate of inflation in year t

$$= 100 \times \frac{P_t - P_{t-1}}{P_{t-1}}$$

strains of inflation:
- low
- galloping
- hyperinflation

impacts of inflation (redistributive, on output and employment)
anticipated and unanticipated inflation
costs of inflation:
- "shoe leather"
- menu costs
- income and tax distortions
- loss of information

short-run and long-run Phillips curves
nonaccelerating inflation rate of unemployment (NAIRU) and the long-run Phillips curve

Anti-inflation Policy

costs of disinflation
measures to lower the NAIRU
sacrifice ratio

FURTHER READING AND INTERNET WEBSITES

Further Reading

The quotation from Stanley Fischer, Ratna Sahay, and Carlos A. Végh is from their article, "Modern Hyper- and High Inflations," *Journal of Economic Literature,* September 2002, pp. 837–880.

A discussion of factors influencing the NAIRU can be found in Congressional Budget Office, *The Effect of Changes in Labor Markets on the Natural Rate of Unemployment,* April 2002, available at *www.cbo.gov.*

Websites

Analysis of the consumer price data for the United States comes from the Bureau of Labor Statistics, at *www.bls.gov.* This site also contains useful discussions of inflation trends in the *Monthly Labor Review,* online at *www.bls.gov/opub/mlr/mlrhome.htm.*

QUESTIONS FOR DISCUSSION

1. Consider the following impacts of inflation: tax distortions, income and wealth redistribution, shoe-leather costs, and menu costs. For each, define the cost and provide an example.
2. "During periods of inflation, people use real resources to reduce their holdings of fiat money. Such activities produce a private benefit with no corresponding social gain, which illustrates the social cost of inflation." Explain this quotation and give an example.
3. Unanticipated deflation also produces serious social costs. For each of the following, describe the deflation and analyze the associated costs:
   a. During the Great Depression, prices of major crops fell along with the prices of other commodities. What would happen to farmers who had large mortgages?
   b. Japan experienced a mild deflation in the 1990s. Assume that Japanese students each borrowed 2,000,000 yen (about $20,000) to pay for their education, hoping that inflation would allow them to pay off their loans in inflated yen. What would happen to these students if wages and prices began to *fall* at 5 percent per year?
4. The data in Table 30-2 describe inflation and unemployment in the United States from 1979 to 1987. Note that the economy started out near the NAIRU in 1979 and ended near the NAIRU in 1987. Can you explain the decline of inflation over the intervening years? Do so by drawing the short-run and long-run Phillips curves for each of the years from 1979 to 1987.
5. Many economists argue as follows: "Because there is no long-run tradeoff between unemployment and inflation, there is no point in trying to shave the peaks and troughs from the business cycle." This view suggests that we should not care whether the economy is stable or fluctuating widely as long as the average level of unemployment is the same. Discuss critically.
6. A leading economist has written: "If you think of the social costs of inflation, at least of moderate inflation, it is hard to avoid coming away with the impression that they are minor compared with the costs of unemployment and depressed production." Write a short essay describing your views on this issue.
7. Consider the data on annual inflation rates and growth of per capita GDP shown in Table 30-1. Can you see that low inflation is associated with the highest growth rates? What are the economic reasons that growth might be lower for deflation and for hyperinflation. Explain why the *ex post* fallacy might apply here (see the discussion in Chapter 1).
8. The following policies and phenomena affected labor markets over the last three decades. Explain the likely effect of each on the NAIRU:
   a. Unemployment insurance became subject to taxation.
   b. Funds for training programs for unemployed workers were cut sharply by the federal government.
   c. The fraction of the workforce in labor unions fell sharply.
   d. The welfare-reform act of 1996 sharply reduced payments to low-income families and required them to work if they were to receive government payments.

Year	Unemployment rate (%)	Inflation rate, CPI (% per year)
1979	5.8	11.3
1980	7.1	13.5
1981	7.6	10.3
1982	9.7	6.2
1983	9.6	3.2
1984	7.5	4.4
1985	7.2	3.6
1986	7.0	1.9
1987	6.2	3.6

TABLE 30-2. Unemployment and Inflation Data for the United States, 1979–1987

CHAPTER

31

Frontiers of Macroeconomics
宏观经济学的前沿问题

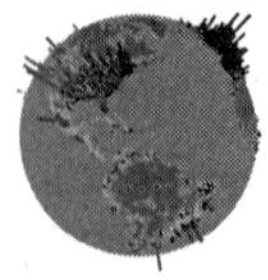

The task of economic stabilization requires keeping the economy from straying too far above or below the path of steady high employment. One way lies inflation, and the other lies recession. Flexible and vigilant fiscal and monetary policy will allow us to hold the narrow middle course.

President John F. Kennedy [1]
(1962)

The U.S. economy has changed enormously over the last 50 years. The shares of farming and manufacturing have declined. People work with computers instead of with tractors. Trade is a growing share of production and consumption. Technology has revolutionized daily life. Advanced telecommunications systems enable businesses to control their operations across the country and around the world, and ever more powerful computers have eliminated many of the tedious tasks that used to employ so many people.

Yet, even with these tectonic shifts in our eco- ②
nomic structure, the central goals of macroeconomic policy remain the same: stable employment, good pay, low unemployment, rising productivity and real incomes, and low and stable inflation. The challenge remains to find policies that can achieve these objectives.

This chapter uses the tools of macroeconomics to examine some of today's major policy issues. We begin with an assessment of the consequences of government deficits and debt on economic activity. We then present some of the new approaches to macroeconomics. Some of these theories are on the frontiers of our science today but will be the staples of classroom economics in a generation. We analyze controversies involving short-run economic stabilization, including current questions on the roles of monetary and fiscal policy. Should the government stop trying to smooth out business cycles? Should policy makers rely on fixed rules rather than discretion? We then conclude with an epilogue on the importance of economic growth.

政府债务的经济后果

A. THE ECONOMIC CONSEQUENCES OF THE GOVERNMENT DEBT

As the United States entered the twenty-first century, its fiscal policies were stable and the federal government was running a budget surplus. Then, like a monster rising from the deep, the budget deficit rose up to swallow the nation's fiscal resources and terrify its populace.

---

[1] 约翰·肯尼迪总统：President John F. Kennedy（1917~1963），美国第35任总统，著名的肯尼迪家族成员。47岁（1961年）入主白宫，1963年11月22日，在得克萨斯州达拉斯市遇刺身亡。肯尼迪总统治理宏观经济的思想基本上源自萨缪尔森的苦谏（请参阅笔者的前言）。这段话的译文如下：

经济稳定的任务，要求经济不能偏离持续的高就业太远。就业率过高意味着通货膨胀；就业率过低，则衰退不可避免。只有灵活而谨慎的财政政策和货币政策才能让我们守住这条狭窄的中间通道。

——约翰·肯尼迪总统（1962）

② 然而，即便我们的经济结构发生了巨变，宏观经济政策的中心目标依然没有改变：稳定的就业、良好的薪酬、低失业率、生产率和实际收入的持续增长，以及稳定的低通货膨胀率。找到能够实现这些目标的良策始终是我们面临的挑战。

The budget deficit increased even during the prosperous years of the mid-2000s as taxes were cut and spending increased on new entitlement programs and seemingly endless wars in Iraq and Afghanistan. Then, the nation's banking system ran mammoth losses and the economy went into a deep recession. Tax revenues fell sharply, and hundreds of billions of dollars were spent to prop up the financial system and stimulate the economy. For 2009, the federal government was running an annual deficit of close to $2 trillion, which was the largest percent of GDP since World War II.

How did the budget deficit get so high? What are the economic impacts of fiscal deficits? These important questions will be addressed in this section. We will see that the popular concern with deficits has a firm economic foundation. Deficit spending may be necessary to reduce the length and depth of recessions, particularly when the economy is in a liquidity trap. But high deficits during periods of full employment carry serious consequences, including reduced national saving and investment and slower long-run economic growth.

Government Budgets. Governments use budgets to plan and control their fiscal affairs. A **budget** shows, for a given year, the planned expenditures of government programs and the expected revenues from tax systems. The budget typically contains a list of specific programs (education, welfare, defense, etc.), as well as tax sources (individual income tax, social-insurance taxes, etc.).

A **budget surplus** occurs when all taxes and other revenues exceed government expenditures for a year. A **budget deficit** is incurred when expenditures exceed taxes. When revenues and expenditures are equal during a given period—a rare event on the federal level—the government has a **balanced budget.**

When the government incurs a budget deficit, it must borrow from the public to pay its bills. To borrow, the government issues bonds, which are IOUs that promise to pay money in the future. The **government debt** (sometimes called the *public debt*) consists of the total or accumulated borrowings by the government; it is the total dollar value of government bonds.

It is useful to distinguish between the total debt and the net debt. The *net debt,* also called the *debt held by the public,* excludes debt held by the government itself. Net debt is owned by households, banks, businesses, foreigners, and other nonfederal entities. The *gross debt* equals the net debt plus bonds owned by the government, primarily by the social security trust fund. The social security trust fund is running a large surplus, so the difference between these two concepts is growing rapidly today.

Debt versus Deficit

People often confuse the debt with the deficit. You can remember the difference as follows: Debt is water in the tub, while a deficit is water flowing into the tub. The government debt is the *stock* of liabilities of the government. The deficit is a *flow* of new debt incurred when the government spends more than it raises in taxes. For example, when the government ran a deficit of $640 billion in 2008, it added that amount to the stock of government debt. By contrast, when the government enjoyed a surplus of $200 billion in 2000, this reduced the government debt by that amount.

财政史
FISCAL HISTORY

Like Sisyphus, federal policymakers toil endlessly to ① [2]
push the stone of fiscal balance up the hill only to have it roll down to crush them again. The government passed law after law in the 1980s and 1990s to stop the rising deficit. No sooner was the deficit vanquished than it reappeared and grew rapidly after 2001. Was this typical, or was it a new feature of the American economy?

Deficits were not new to the American economy, but large deficits during peacetime are a unique feature of recent economic history. For the first two centuries after the American Revolution, the federal government of the United States generally balanced its budget. Heavy military spending during wartime was financed by borrowing, so the government debt soared in wartime. In peacetime, the government would pay off some of its debt, and the debt burden would shrink.

Then, starting in 1940, the fiscal affairs of state began to change rapidly. Table 31-1 illuminates the major trends. This table lists the major federal budget categories and their shares in GDP for the period from 1940 to 2008. The key features were the following:

- The share of federal spending and taxes grew sharply from 1940 to 1960 primarily because of the expansion of military and civilian spending. This growth was financed by a significant increase in individual and corporate taxation.

① 像古希腊神话中的西西弗斯一样，联邦的政策制定者们不屈不挠地将财政收支平衡的这块巨石苦苦推到了山顶，而最终的结局又让这块巨石滚下山来再一次碾压了自己。在 20 世纪 80 和 90 年代，政府出台了一部又一部的法律来阻止不断高涨的财政赤字。然而，赤字刚刚得到压制，2001 年之后却又出现了更快的上涨。这究竟是美国经济的典型特征，还是一个未知的新特点？

[2] Sisyphus：西西弗斯，一位超越了自身命运的古希腊神话人物。在不屈不挠地往山顶推巨石的壮举中西西弗斯发现了庞然曼妙背后的力量之美，并沉浸在看似苦难的幸福之中，最终感动了诸神，不再让巨石从山顶滚下来。

	Percent of GDP				
Federal budget component	**1940**	**1960**	**1980**	**2000**	**2008**
Revenues	**6.4**	**17.6**	**18.5**	**20.6**	**17.7**
Individual income taxes	0.9	7.7	8.8	10.2	8.1
Corporation income taxes	1.2	4.1	2.3	2.1	2.1
Social insurance and retirement receipts	1.8	2.8	5.7	6.7	6.3
Other	2.7	3.0	1.8	1.6	1.2
Expenditures	**9.4**	**17.5**	**21.2**	**18.2**	**20.9**
National defense and international affairs	1.8	9.7	5.3	3.2	4.4
Health	0.1	0.2	2.0	3.6	4.7
Income security	1.5	1.4	3.1	2.6	3.0
Social security	0.0	2.2	4.2	4.2	4.3
Net interest	0.9	1.3	1.9	2.3	1.7
Other	5.2	2.7	4.7	2.4	2.5
Surplus or deficit	**−2.9**	**0.1**	**−2.6**	**2.4**	**−3.2**

TABLE 31-1. Federal Budget Trends, 1940–2008

The federal share of the economy grew sharply from 1940 to 1960 as the United States took an active military role in world affairs during the hot and cold wars. After 1960, the federal-spending share stabilized, but the composition of spending moved from military to health care and other social spending. The federal government deficit grew sharply in the 2000s as revenues declined sharply due to individual income-tax cuts.

Source: Data are for fiscal years and come from the Department of the Treasury, Office of Management and Budget, and Department of Commerce. They are summarized in *Economic Indicators*, available at *origin.www.gpoaccess.gov/indicators/*.

- The period from 1960 to 1980 marked the "New Society" programs for health, income security, and expanded social security. As a result, the expenditure share grew sharply. The share of federal revenues in GDP stabilized over this period.
- Beginning in 1981, both political parties declared that the era of big government was over. Presidents Ronald Reagan and George W. Bush introduced large tax cuts, which in each case led to large government budget deficits. From 1980 to 2008, as shown in Table 31-1, the ratio of total federal spending to GDP was essentially constant. Spending on health care rose sharply as other civilian programs were squeezed.

政府预算政策
GOVERNMENT BUDGET POLICY

The government budget serves two major economic functions. First, it is a device by which the government can set national priorities, allocating national output among private and public consumption and investment and providing incentives to increase or reduce output in particular sectors. From a macroeconomic point of view, it is through fiscal policy that the budget affects the key macroeconomic goals. More pre- ①
cisely, by **fiscal policy** we mean the setting of taxes and public expenditures to help dampen the swings of the business cycle and contribute to the maintenance of a growing, high-employment economy, free from high or volatile inflation.

Some early enthusiasts of the Keynesian approach ② believed that fiscal policy was like a knob they could turn to control or "fine-tune" the pace of the economy. A bigger budget deficit meant more stimulus for aggregate demand, which could lower unemployment and pull the economy out of recession. A budget surplus could slow down an overheated economy and dampen the threat of inflation.

Few today hold such an idealized view of fiscal policy. With many decades of practice, economies

① 更确切地讲，**财政政策**的含义系指税收和公共支出的规划和决策，以期抑制商业周期的波动，尽可能地确保经济的增长与高就业，以免过高或急剧的通货膨胀。

② 早期一些凯恩斯学派的热衷者们坚信，财政政策就像一柄门闩，可以通过它来控制或者“精准地调控”经济运行的节奏。更高的预算赤字意味着对总需求的更大刺激，降低失业率和推动经济摆脱衰退。预算的盈余可以为过热的经济降温，并能减少通货膨胀的威胁。

still experience recessions and inflations. Fiscal policy works better in theory than in practice. Moreover, monetary policy has become the preferred tool for moderating business-cycle swings. Still, when unemployment rises, there is usually strong public pressure for the government to boost spending. In this section, we will review the major ways in which the government can employ fiscal policy, and we will examine the practical shortcomings that have become apparent.

实际预算、结构性预算与周期性预算
Actual, Structural, and Cyclical Budgets

Modern public finance distinguishes between structural and cyclical deficits. The idea is simple. The ① *structural* part of the budget is active—determined by discretionary policies such as those covering tax rates, public-works or education spending, or the size of defense purchases. In contrast, the *cyclical* part of the budget is determined passively by the state of the business cycle, that is, by the extent to which national income and output are high or low. The precise definitions follow:

> The **actual budget** records the actual dollar expenditures, revenues, and deficits in a given period. ②
>
> The **structural budget** calculates what government revenues, expenditures, and deficits would be if the economy were operating at potential output. ③
>
> The **cyclical budget** is the difference between the actual budget and the structural budget. It measures the impact of the business cycle on the budget, taking into account the effect of the cycle on revenues, expenditures, and the deficit. ④

The distinction between the actual and the structural budgets is important for policymakers who want to distinguish between long-term or trend budget changes and short-term changes that are primarily driven by the business cycle. Structural spending and revenues consist of the discretionary programs enacted by the legislature; cyclical spending and deficits consist of the taxes and spending that react automatically to the state of the economy.

The nation's saving and investment balance is primarily affected by the structural budget. Efforts to change government saving should focus on the structural budget because no durable change comes simply from higher revenues due to an economic boom.

债务与赤字经济学
THE ECONOMICS OF THE DEBT AND DEFICITS

No macroeconomic issue is more controversial today than the impact of large government deficits upon the economy. Some argue that large deficits are placing a heavy burden on future generations. Others rejoin that there is little evidence of an impact of deficits on interest rates or investment. Yet a third group argues that deficits are favorable for the economy in recessionary times.

How can we sort through the conflicting points of view? At one extreme, we must avoid the customary practice of assuming that a public debt is bad because private debtors are punished. On the other hand, we must recognize the genuine problems associated with large government deficits and the advantages that come from a lower government debt.

政府赤字的短期影响
THE SHORT-RUN IMPACT OF GOVERNMENT DEFICITS

短期与长期
Short Run vs. Long Run

It is useful to separate the impact of fiscal policy into the short run and the long run. The *short run* in macroeconomics considers situations where less than full employment may prevail—that is, where actual output may differ from potential output. This is the world of the Keynesian multiplier model. The *long run* refers to a full-employment situation, where actual output equals potential output. This is the world of our economic-growth analysis.

We have already discussed the role of fiscal policy in the short run, so that needs only a brief review in this section. The impact in the long run is more novel and will be presented in the next section.

财政政策与乘数模型
Fiscal Policy and the Multiplier Model

We discussed in earlier chapters the way that fiscal policy affects the economy in the short run—that is, in an economy with less than full employment.

Suppose that the government purchases computers for its schools or missiles for its army. Our multiplier model says that in the short run, with no change in interest or exchange rates, GDP will rise by a multiple (perhaps 1½ or 2) times the increase in *G*. The same argument applies (with a smaller multiplier) to reductions in taxes, *T*. At the same time, the

---

① 预算的结构性部分是主动的——取决于相机抉择的政策，诸如确定税率、公共工程或者教育的支出，以及国防开支的规模等。相比较而言，预算的周期性部分则是被动地取决于商业周期的状况，即国民收入和产出高或者低的程度。

② **实际预算**系指既定时期内，以美元标定的实际支出、收入和赤字。

③ **结构性预算**系指如果经济在潜在产出水平上运行，所计算的政府收入、支出和赤字。

④ **周期性预算**系指实际预算与结构性预算之间的差额。它所衡量的是商业周期对预算的影响，同时考虑了商业周期对收入、支出及赤字的影响。

government deficit will rise because the deficit equals $T - G$ and thus rises with T cuts or G increases.

① 在未充分就业的情况下，由于消减税收 T 和增加政府支出 G 而引发的结构性赤字上升一般会导致更高的产出与更低的失业率，还可能导致更高的通货膨胀率。

This then is the basic result for the short run: With less than full employment, increases in the ① structural deficit arising from discretionary T cuts or G increases will tend to produce higher output and lower unemployment, and perhaps higher inflation.

We must, however, expand on the simplest multiplier analysis to incorporate the reactions of financial markets and monetary policy. As output rises and inflation threatens, central banks may raise interest rates, discouraging domestic investment. Higher interest rates may also cause a country's foreign exchange rate to appreciate if the country has a flexible exchange rate; the appreciation leads to a decline in net exports. These financial reactions ② would tend to choke off or "crowd out" investment, with a resulting decrease in the expenditure multiplier of our simplest model.

Fiscal policy tends to expand the economy in ③ the short run—that is, when there are unemployed resources. Higher spending and lower tax rates increase aggregate demand, output, employment, and inflation. However, this expansionary impact is reduced by the subsequent financial reactions of interest rates and foreign exchange rates.

政府债务与经济增长
GOVERNMENT DEBT AND ECONOMIC GROWTH

We turn now from the short run to the long run—to the impact of fiscal policy, and particularly a large government debt, on investment and economic growth. The analysis here deals with the costs of servicing a large external debt, the inefficiencies of levying taxes to pay interest on the debt, and the impact of the debt on capital accumulation.

历史趋势
Historical Trends

Before we begin our analysis of government debt, it is useful to review historical trends. Long-run data for the United States appear in the figure on page 716 of this text, which shows the ratio of net federal debt to GDP since 1789. Notice how wars drove up the ratio of debt to GDP, while rapid output growth with generally balanced budgets in peacetime reduced the ratio of debt to GDP.

Figure 31-1 shows the debt-GDP ratio for the United States over the last seven decades. You can see the dramatic effect of government deficits during World War II, as well as during the 1980s and the 2000s.

Most industrialized countries are today saddled with large public debts. Table 31-2 compares the United States with seven other large countries. Japan's debt-GDP ratio has climbed sharply over the ④ last two decades because of the nation's aggressive fiscal policy and a prolonged recession. Many economists worry that Japan is caught in a vicious cycle of high debt leading to high interest payments, which in turn increase the growth of the debt.

外债与内债
External vs. Internal Debt

The first distinction to be made is between an internal debt and an external debt. *Internal government debt* is owed by a nation to its own residents. Many argue that an internal debt poses no burden because "we owe it all to ourselves." While this statement is oversimplified, it does represent a genuine insight. If each citizen owned $10,000 of government bonds and were liable for the taxes to service just that debt, it would make no sense to think of debt as a heavy load of rocks that each citizen must carry. People simply owe the debt to themselves.

An external debt is quite a different situation. An *external debt* occurs when foreigners own a fraction of the assets of a country. For example, because of

	Ratio of Gross Government Debt to GDP (%)			
	1980	**1990**	**2000**	**2007**
Japan	37	47	106	161
Italy	53	93	104	96
France	30	40	47	52
United Kingdom	51	35	43	43
Germany	13	20	34	39
United States	26	41	34	36
South Korea	4	13	17	32
Mexico	18	46	23	24

TABLE 31-2. Central-Government Debt in Eight Major Countries

Slow economic growth and rising spending on entitlement programs led to growing public debts in most major countries in the last three decades. Japan's debt-GDP ratio led to a downgrading of the nation's debt rating even though Japan is one of the world's richest countries.

Source: OECD at *webnet.oecd.org/wbos/index.aspx.*

② 这些金融反应导致阻止或"挤出"投资，其结果便是基本模型中支出乘数降低。

③ 短期内，或者说在资源尚未充分利用的情况下，财政政策都有扩张经济的倾向。更大的支出和更低的税率增加了总需求、产出、就业和通货膨胀。但是，由于利率和汇率这些金融工具的后续金融反应，其扩张性的影响被降低。

④ 日本债务在其 GDP 中所占的比例在过去的 20 年里剧烈地攀升，这是因为国家实行积极的财政政策并且经济长期处于衰退。许多经济学家担忧，日本已经深陷高债务引发高利息的恶性循环中，反过来，高利息又将推高债务的增长。

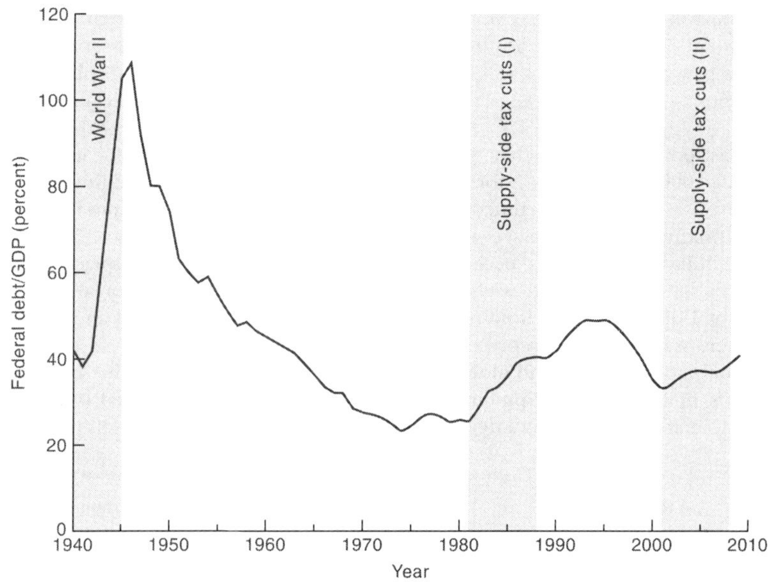

FIGURE 31-1. Debt-GDP Ratio for the U.S. Federal Government

This figure shows the ratio of net debt, or debt in the hands of the public, to GDP. See the effect of World War II and the two periods of supply-side tax cuts on the ratio.

Source: U.S. Office of Management and Budget, available at *www.gpoaccess.gov/eop/tables08.html*, Table B-78.

its large current-account deficits, the United States owed the rest of the world \$3 trillion at the end of 2008. What this means is that U.S. residents will eventually have to export that much in goods and services or sell that much of the nation's assets to foreigners. Suppose that the real interest rate on that debt is 5 percent per year. Then, each year, U.S. residents would need to ship abroad \$150 billion (about \$500 per capita) to "service" the external debt.

So an external debt definitely does involve a net ① subtraction from the resources available for consumption in the debtor nation. This lesson has been learned time and again by developing countries—particularly when their creditors wanted their debts paid back quickly.

税收导致的效率损失

Efficiency Losses from Taxation

An internal debt requires payments of interest to bondholders, and taxes must be levied for this purpose. But ② even if the same people were taxed to pay the same amounts they receive in interest, there would still be the *distorting effects on incentives* that are inescapably present in the case of any taxes. Taxing Paula's interest income or wages to pay Paula interest would intro- [3] duce microeconomic distortions. Paula might work less and save less; either of these outcomes must be reckoned as a distortion of efficiency and well-being.

资本的替代

Displacement of Capital

Perhaps the most serious consequence of a large public debt is that it displaces capital from the nation's stock of private wealth. As a result, the pace of economic growth slows and future living standards will decline.

What is the mechanism by which debt affects capital? Recall from our earlier discussion that people accumulate wealth for a variety of purposes, such as retirement, education, and housing. We can separate the assets people hold into two groups: (1) government debt and (2) capital like houses and financial assets like corporate stocks that represent ownership of private capital.

---

① 所以，外债确实导致了债务国可消费资源的净减少。这样的教训已经一而再再而三地被发展中国家所汲取，特别是当债权国快速地催索借款时。

② 但即使是向相同的人征收相同数量的利息税时，仍然会存在激励效应的扭曲，这是任何税收案例中不可避免的现实。

[3] Paula interest：即公共利息（public interest），源自本领域领军人物澳大利亚墨尔本大学法学院高级讲师 Paula O'Brien 女士发表在 *Alternative Law Journal* 的论文 *Changing Public Interest Law: Overcoming the law's barriers to social change lawyering*。

The effect of government debt is that people will ① accumulate government debt instead of private capital, and the nation's private capital stock will be displaced by public debt.

To illustrate this point, suppose that people desire to hold exactly 1000 units of wealth for retirement and other purposes. As the government debt increases, people's holdings of other assets will be reduced dollar for dollar. This occurs because as the government sells its bonds, other assets must be reduced, since total desired wealth holdings are fixed. But these other assets ultimately represent the stock of private capital; stocks, bonds, and mortgages are the counterparts of factories, equipment, and houses. In this example, if the government debt goes up 100 units, we would see that people's holdings of capital and other private assets fall by 100 units. This is the case of 100 percent displacement (which is the long-run analog of 100 percent crowding out).

Full displacement is unlikely to hold in practice. ② The higher debt may increase interest rates and stimulate domestic saving. In addition, the country may borrow abroad rather than reduce its domestic investment (as has been the case for the U.S. in recent years). The exact amount of capital displacement will depend on the conditions of production and on the saving behavior of domestic households and foreigners.

A Geometric Analysis. The process by which the stock of capital is displaced in the long run is illustrated in Figure 31-2. The left panel shows the supply

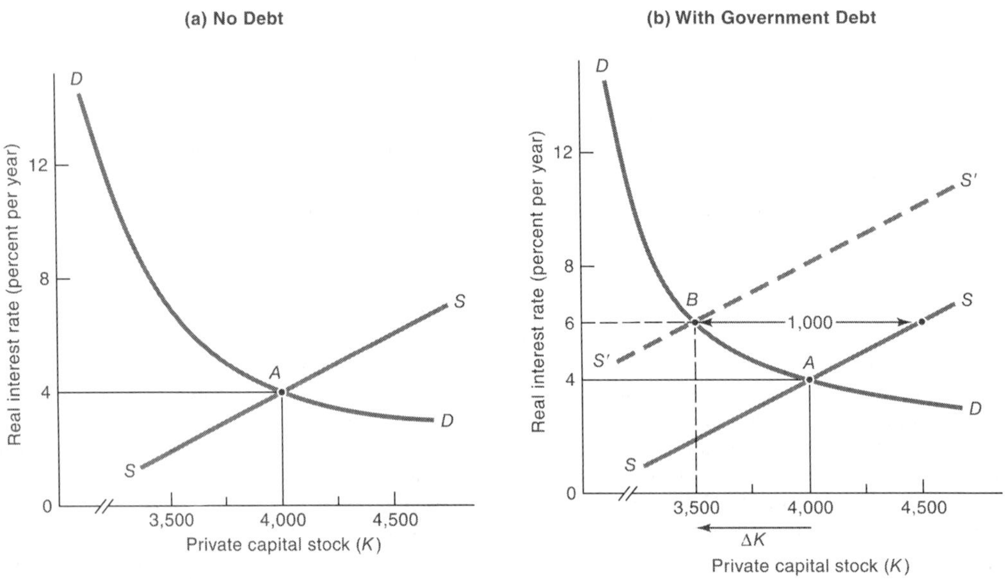

FIGURE 31-2. Government Debt Displaces Private Capital

Firms demand capital, while households supply capital by saving in private and public assets. The demand curve is the downward-sloping business demand for *K*, while the supply curve is the upward-sloping household supply of wealth.

Before-debt case in **(a)** shows the equilibrium without government debt: *K* is 4000 and the real interest rate is 4 percent.

After-debt case in **(b)** shows the impact of 1000 units of government debt. Debt shifts the net supply of *K* to the left by the 1000 units of the government debt. The new equilibrium arises northwest along the demand-for-*K* curve, moving from point *A* to point *B*. The interest rate is higher, firms are discouraged from holding *K*, and the capital stock falls.

① 政府债的作用是人们将积累政府债务，而非私人资本，国家私人资本的存量将由公共债务所替代。

② 完全的替代在实际中是不可能的。较高的债务可能会推高利率并刺激国内储蓄。此外，国家会向国外举债，而不是减少国内投资（如美国政府近几年的做法）。

and demand for capital as a function of the real interest rate or return on capital. As interest rates rise, firms demand less capital while individuals may want to supply more. The equilibrium shown is for a capital stock of 4000 units with a real interest rate of 4 percent.

Now say that the government debt rises from 0 to 1000—because of war, recession, supply-side fiscal policies, or some other reason. The impact of the increase in debt can be seen in the right-hand diagram of Figure 31-2. This figure shows the 1000-unit increase in debt as a shift in the supply-of-capital (or *SS*) curve. As depicted, the households' supply-of-capital schedule shifts 1000 units to the left, to $S'S'$.

We represent an increase in government debt as a leftward shift in the households' supply-of-capital schedule. Note that, because the *SS* curve represents the amount of private capital that people willingly hold at each interest rate, the capital holdings are equal to the total wealth holdings minus the holdings of government debt. Since the amount of government debt (or assets other than capital) rises by 1000, the amount of private capital that people can buy after they own the 1000 units of government debt is 1000 less than total wealth at each interest rate. Therefore, if *SS* represents the total wealth held by people, $S'S'$ (equal to *SS* less 1000) represents the total amount of capital held by people. In short, after 1000 units of government debt are sold, the new supply-of-capital schedule is $S'S'$.

As the supply of capital dries up—with national ① saving going into government bonds rather than into housing or into companies' stocks and bonds—the market equilibrium moves northwest along the demand-for-*K* curve. Interest rates rise. Firms slow their purchases of new factories, trucks, and computers.

In the illustrative new long-run equilibrium, the capital stock falls from 4000 to 3500. Thus, in this example, 1000 units of government debt have displaced 500 units of private capital. Such a reduction has significant economic effects, of course. With less capital, potential output, wages, and the nation's income are lower than they would otherwise be.

The diagrams in Figure 31-2 are illustrative. Economists do not have a firm estimate of the magnitude of the displacement effect. In a look at historical trends, the best evidence suggests that domestic capital is partially displaced by government debt but that some of the impact comes in higher foreign debt.

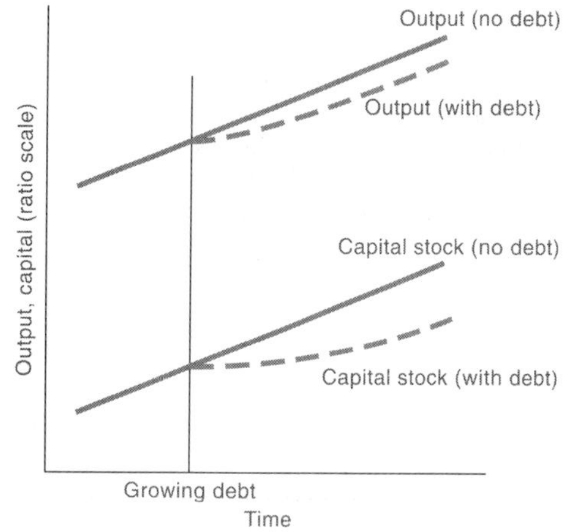

FIGURE 31-3. Impact of Government Debt on Economic Growth

The solid lines show the paths of capital and output if the government balances its books and has no debt. When the government incurs a debt, private capital is reduced. The dashed lines illustrate the impact on capital and output of the higher government debt.

债务与经济增长
Debt and Growth

If we consider all the effects of government debt on the economy, a large public debt is likely to reduce long-run economic growth. Figure 31-3 illustrates this connection. Say that an economy were to operate over time with no debt. According to the principles of economic growth outlined in Chapter 25, the capital stock and potential output would follow the hypothetical paths indicated by the solid blue lines in Figure 31-3.

Next consider a situation with a growing national debt. As the debt accumulates over time, more and more capital is displaced, as shown by the dashed green line for the capital stock in the bottom of Figure 31-3. As taxes are raised to pay interest on the debt, inefficiencies further lower output. Also, an increase in external debt lowers national income and raises the fraction of national output that has to be set aside for servicing the external debt. All the effects taken together, output and consumption will grow more slowly than they would have had there been no large government debt and deficit, as can be seen by comparing the top lines in Figure 31-3.

---

① 由于资本供给枯竭——国民储蓄流入政府债券，而不是住房或者公司的股票和债券——所以市场均衡就会沿着资本需求曲线向西北方向运动，利率升高。结果导致企业减少对新工厂、卡车和计算机的购置。

What is the impact of a budget surplus and a *declining* government debt? Here, the argument works in the other direction. A lower national debt means that more of national wealth is put into capital rather than government bonds. A higher capital stock increases the growth of output and increases wages and consumption per person.

This is the major point about the long-run impact of ① a large government debt on economic growth: A large government debt tends to reduce the growth in potential output because it displaces private capital, increases the inefficiency from taxation, and forces a nation to reduce consumption to service its foreign borrowing.

Deficit Confusions Unraveled

Having completed our analysis of the economic impacts of deficits and debt, we can summarize the key points by unraveling some of the major confusions in this area.

The impact of fiscal policy on the economy is one of the most misunderstood facets of macroeconomics. The confusion arises because fiscal policy operates differently depending upon the time period:

- *In the short run, higher spending and lower tax rates tend to increase aggregate demand and thereby to raise output and lower unemployment*. This is the Keynesian impact of fiscal policy, which operates by raising actual output relative to potential output. We would expect that the ② expansionary impact of fiscal policy—the increase in capacity utilization—would last at most for a few years. It might be offset by a monetary tightening, especially if the central bank thought the economy was operating near the inflation danger zone.
- *In the long run, higher spending and lower tax rates tend to depress the growth rate of the economy*. This is the growth impact of fiscal policy. The growth impact concerns the impact of government deficits on the national saving and investment balance in a full-employment economy. If taxes are lower, this will decrease public saving and, because private saving is unlikely to rise as much as public saving falls, total national saving and investment will decline. The investment decline will lead to slower growth in the capital stock and therefore in potential output.

These two impacts of fiscal policy can easily confuse people and are the source of many debates about fiscal policy. Consider the following debate between Senators Hawk and Dove:

Senator Dove: The economy is tipping into recession. [3] We cannot afford to sit around while millions of people lose their jobs. Now is the time for a big stimulus package with tax cuts and new spending on infrastructure and pressing public needs. Recessions are not the time for old-fashioned dogmas about deficits.

Senator Hawk: A huge stimulus package today would [4] be the height of fiscal irresponsibility. With higher government spending, the deficit will grow even larger, interest rates will rise, and businesses will reduce their spending on new plant, equipment, and information technology. With all the critical needs facing the nation, we can ill-afford slower economic growth over the next decade. [5]

Make sure that you understand the implicit theories underlying the positions of the two distinguished senators. They are both right . . . and both wrong.

现代宏观经济学的新进展

B. ADVANCES IN MODERN MACROECONOMICS

Our philosophy in this textbook is to consider all the important schools of thought. We emphasize the modern mainstream Keynesian approach as the best way to explain the business cycle in market economies. At the same time, the forces behind long-run economic growth are best understood by using the neoclassical growth model.

While our key task has been to present mainstream thinking, experience shows how important it is to keep our minds open to alternative points of view. Time and again in science, the orthodoxies of one era are overturned by new discoveries in the next. Schools, like people, are subject to hardening of the arteries. Students learn the embalmed truth from their teachers and sacred textbooks, and the imperfections in the orthodox doctrines are glossed over as unimportant. For example, John Stuart Mill, one of the greatest economists and philosophers of all time, wrote in his 1848 classic, *Principles of Political Economy:* "Happily, there is nothing in the laws of Value which remains for the present and any future writer to clear up." Yet the next century and a half

---

① 由于政府的庞大债务取代了私人资本，增加了税收的低效性，以及迫使一国降低消费以应对外债，因此它会降低潜在产出的增长。这就是政府的庞大债务对经济增长长期影响的关键点所在。

② 我们预期，财政政策的扩张性影响，即产能利用率的上升，最多仅能持续几年。尤其是如果中央银行认为经济运行接近通货膨胀的危险区，其扩张性影响就会被货币的紧缩政策所抵消。

[3] Senator Dove：参议员德夫，喜剧电影《2000 恋爱法则》(*Chain of Fools*) 中的人物。

[4] Senator Hawk：参议员霍克，畅销的连环漫画《铁人》(*Iron Man*) 中的主人公。

[5] 此处引入两个轻松的喜剧电影和连环漫画中的人物，旨在强调本节话题的戏剧性，彰显了萨翁的幽默。

saw two major revolutions in economics—the marginal revolution in microeconomics and the discovery of macroeconomics.

Historians of science observe that the progress ① of science is discontinuous. New schools of thought rise, spread their influence, and convince skeptics. In this section, we sketch some of the leading new lines of thinking in modern macroeconomics.

古典宏观经济学与萨伊定律
CLASSICAL MACROECONOMICS AND SAY'S LAW

Since the dawn of economics two centuries ago, economists have wondered if a market economy has a tendency to move spontaneously toward a long-run, full-employment equilibrium without the need for government intervention. Using modern language, we label as **classical** those approaches that emphasize the self-correcting forces in an economy. The classical approach holds that prices and wages are flexible and that the economy is stable, so the economy moves automatically and quickly to its full-employment equilibrium.

萨伊的市场定律
Say's Law of Markets

Before Keynes developed his macroeconomic theories, the major economic thinkers generally adhered to the classical view of the economy, at least in good times. Early economists knew about business cycles, but they viewed them as temporary and self-correcting aberrations.

Classical analysis revolved around **Say's Law of Markets.** This theory, advocated in 1803 by the French economist J. B. Say, states that overproduc- [2] tion is impossible by its very nature. This is sometimes expressed as "supply creates its own demand." This law rests on a view that there is no essential difference between a monetary economy and a barter economy—in other words, people can afford to buy whatever factories can produce. Say's Law is illustrated in Figure 31-4. In the classical world, output is determined by aggregate supply, and aggregate demand affects only the price level.

A long line of the most distinguished economists, including David Ricardo (1817), John Stuart Mill [3] (1848), and Alfred Marshall (1890), subscribed to [4] the classical macroeconomic view that overproduction is impossible.

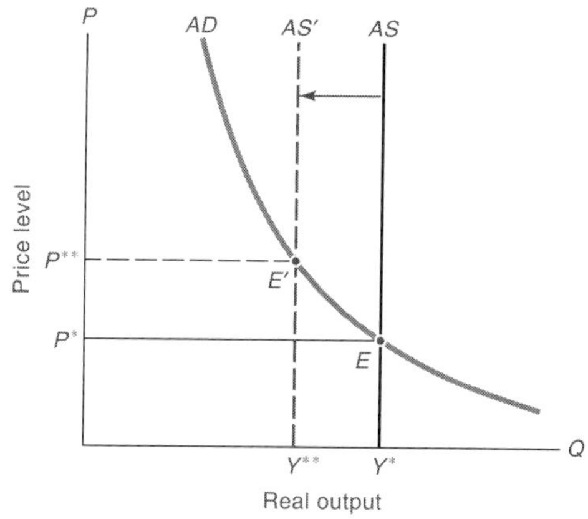

FIGURE 31-4. In the Real Business Cycle, Output Changes Come from Technological Shocks

In the classical as well as the real-business-cycle (RBC) approach, *AS* reflects classical flexible wages and prices and is therefore vertical. Output fluctuations come as technological shocks percolate through the economy. This figure shows how a decline in productivity can be the cause of a RBC recession. Can you see why policies to increase *AD* will affect prices but not output?

The classical view is that the economy moves ⑤ automatically toward its full-employment equilibrium. Changes in the money supply, fiscal policy, investment, or other spending factors have no lasting impact upon output or employment. Prices and wages adjust quickly and flexibly to maintain full employment.

现代古典宏观经济学
MODERN CLASSICAL MACROECONOMICS

While classical economists were preaching the impossibility of persistent unemployment, eclectic economists of the 1930s could hardly ignore the vast army of unemployed workers begging for work and selling pencils on street corners. Keynes's *The General Theory of Employment, Interest and Money* [6] (1936) offered an alternative macroeconomic theory—a new set of theoretical spectacles for looking at the impacts of shocks and economic policies. The analysis of business cycles and short-run aggregate demand presented in this text reflects the modern synthesis of the Keynesian approach.

---

① 科学史学家们发现，科学的发展过程是不连续的。新思想学派兴起并传播其影响，使那些持怀疑态度的人折服。在这一节，我们分析一下现代宏观经济学前沿的一些新主流思想。

[4] Alfred Marshall：阿尔弗雷德·马歇尔（1842~1924），新古典学派的创始人，19 世纪末 20 世纪初英国经济学界最重要的人物，在剑桥大学建立了世界上第一个经济学系，使经济学从仅仅是人文和历史学科的一门必修课发展成为一门独立的学科。"1890"即指该年出版的《经济学原理》(*Principles of Economics*)。

⑤ 古典经济学派认为，经济本身会自动向充分就业的均衡状态运行。货币供给、财政政策、投资或其他支出因素的变化对产出或者就业没有持久影响。价格和工资迅速而灵活的调整能够维持充分就业。

[6] 凯恩斯 1936 年出版的《就业、利息和货币通论》

[2] J. B. Say：萨伊（1767~1832），法国经济学家，实业家，古典自由主义经济学派的重要人物，以其命名的萨氏定律（*Say's Law*）强调每个生产者之所以愿意从事生产活动，是为了满足自己对该产品的消费欲望，并用自己所生产的物品换取他人的物品或服务。其核心思想即本段所讲的"供给能够创造自身的需求"。

[3] David Ricardo：大卫·李嘉图（1772~1823），英国资产阶级古典政治经济学的主要代表之一，是最有影响力的古典经济学家。李嘉图早期的职业是证券经纪人，亚当·斯密的《国富论》激发了他对经济学研究的兴趣。"1817"即指其主要的经济学代表作《政治经济学及税赋原理》(*Principles of Political Economy and Taxation*)。书中论述了货币流通量的规律、对外贸易中的比较优势学说等。李嘉图只关注经济范畴中的数量关系，很难在价值规律基础上说明资本和劳动的交换、等量资本获等量利润等，是资本主义制度忠实的卫道士。李嘉图自负有加，坚持认为在英国，能看懂自己著作的人不会超过 25 人。

John Stuart Mill：约翰·斯图尔特·米尔（1806~1873），曾被严复译作"穆勒"，著名的英国哲学家和经济学家，19 世纪极具影响力的古典自由主义思想家。"1848"即指其 1848 年出版的代表性著作《政治经济学原理》(*The Principles of Political Economy*，全名为 *Principles of Political Economy with some of their Applications to Social Philosophy*)。

⑤ **rational-expectations hypothesis：理性预期假说。**

[6] Finn Kydland and Edward C. Prescott：冯恩·凯德兰德（1943~，挪威经济学家）和爱德华·普里克特（1940~，美国经济学家）分获2004年度诺贝尔经济学奖，以表彰两人对商业周期驱动力和经济政策时间一致性的研究成果。

While mainstream business-cycle analysis relies primarily on the Keynesian *AS* and *AD* model, a new branch of the classical school challenges the standard approach. This theory, called **new classical macroeconomics,** was developed by Robert Lucas (University of Chicago), Thomas Sargent (Stanford University and New York University), and Robert Barro (Harvard University). This approach is much in the spirit of the classical approach in emphasizing the role of flexible wages and prices, but it also adds a new feature called rational expectations to explain observations such as the Phillips curve. ① [2] [3] [4]

理性预期

Rational Expectations

The major innovation of new classical economics has been to introduce the principle of rational expectations into macroeconomics. Some background on expectations will help to explain this new approach. In many areas of economics, particularly those involving investment and financial decisions, expectations are a central factor in decision making. They influence how much businesses will spend on investment goods and whether consumers spend now or save for the future. For example, assume that you are considering how much to spend on your first house. Your decision will be affected by your *expectations* about your future income, family size, and future housing prices.

How do people form their expectations? According to the **rational-expectations hypothesis,** expectations are unbiased and based on all available information. ⑤

We pause for a statistical aside: A forecast is unbiased if it contains no systematic forecasting errors. Clearly, a forecast cannot always be perfectly accurate—you cannot foresee how a coin flip will come up on a single toss. However, you should not commit the statistical sin of *bias* by predicting that a fair coin will come up tails 25 percent of the time. You would be making an unbiased forecast if you predicted that the coin would come up tails 50 percent of the time or that each of the numbers on a die would, on average, come up one-sixth of the time.

People have **rational expectations** when, in addition to lacking bias, they use all available information in making their decisions. This implies that people understand how the economy works and what the government is doing. Thus, suppose that the government always boosts spending in election years to promote its election prospects. Under rational expectations, people will anticipate this kind of behavior and act accordingly. (Recall that this principle is also an important assumption behind the efficient-market hypothesis of financial markets, as described in Chapter 23.)

实际商业周期

Real Business Cycles

The major application of modern classical macroeconomics is an exciting field known as **real-business-cycle (RBC) theory.** This theory was developed principally by Finn Kydland and Edward C. Prescott, [6] who won the Nobel Prize for their work in this area. This approach holds that business cycles are primarily due to technological shocks and do not invoke any monetary or demand-side forces.

In the RBC approach, shocks to technology, investment, or the labor supply change the potential output of the economy. In other words, the shocks shift a *vertical AS* curve. These supply shocks are transmitted into actual output by the fluctuations of aggregate supply and are completely independent of *AD*. Similarly, movements in the unemployment rate are the result of movements in the natural rate of unemployment (the NAIRU) due either to microeconomic forces, such as the intensity of sectoral shocks, or to tax and regulatory policies. Standard Keynesian monetary and fiscal policies have no effect on output or employment in RBC models; they affect only *AD* and the price level. Figure 31-4 shows an example of a RBC recession caused by a decline in productivity.

财政政策的李嘉图法则

The Ricardian View of Fiscal Policy

One of the most influential criticisms of Keynesian macroeconomics was a new view of the role of fiscal policy. This view, known as the **Ricardian view of fiscal policy** and developed by Harvard University's Robert Barro, argues that changes in tax rates have no impact upon consumption spending.

This idea is a logical extension of the life-cycle model of consumption, introduced in Chapter 21. Under the Ricardian view, individuals are farsighted and form part of a succession of family members, like a dynasty. Parents care not only about their own consumption but also about the well-being of their children; the children, in turn, care about the well-being of their own children; and so on. This structure, called "dynastic preferences," implies that the current generation's horizon stretches into the

① **new classical macroeconomics：新古典宏观经济学**

[2] Robert Lucas：罗伯特·卢卡斯（1937~），美国经济学家，芝加哥大学教授，斯坦福大学胡佛研究院高级研究员。1995年获得诺贝尔经济学奖，以表彰其改造了宏观经济分析和深化了经济政策理解的理性预期假说。

[3] Thomas Sargent：汤姆斯·萨金特（1943~），美国经济学家，纽约大学教授，斯坦福大学胡佛研究院高级研究员，2011年与克里斯托弗·西姆斯（Christopher A. Sims，普林斯顿大学教授）分获当年的诺贝尔经济学奖，以表彰他们对宏观经济因果关系的实证性研究。

[4] Robert Barro：罗伯特·巴洛（1944~），哈佛大学教授，斯坦福大学胡佛研究院高级研究员，美国古典宏观经济学家。

indefinite future through the overlapping concerns of each generation about its offspring.

Here is where the surprising result comes: If the government cuts taxes but leaves expenditures unchanged, this necessarily requires increased government borrowing. But, with unchanged expenditures, the government will have to raise taxes at some point in the future to pay the interest on its new borrowing. In the Ricardian view, consumers have rational expectations about future policies, so when a tax cut occurs, they know they must plan for a future tax increase. They will therefore increase their saving by the amount of the tax cut, and their consumption will remain unchanged. Moreover, people take into account the well-being of their children. So, even if the future tax increase comes after their lifetime, they will save enough to increase their bequests to their children so that their children can pay the extra taxes.

The net result in the Ricardian view is that tax changes have no impact upon consumption. Moreover, government debt is not net debt from the point of view of households because they offset these assets in their mental calculations with the present value of taxes that must be paid to service the government debt.

The Ricardian view of debt and deficits has stirred much controversy among macroeconomists. Critics point out that it requires that households be extremely farsighted, planning to give bequests to their children and constantly weighing their own interests against those of their descendants. The chain would be broken if there were no children, no bequests, no concern for children, or poor foresight. The empirical evidence to date provides little support for the Ricardian view, but it is a useful reminder of the logical limitations on fiscal policy.

效率工资

Efficiency Wages

Another important recent development, fusing elements of both classical and Keynesian economics, is called **efficiency-wage theory.** This approach was developed by Edmund Phelps (Columbia University), Joseph Stiglitz (Columbia University), and Janet Yellen (president of the Federal Reserve Bank of San Francisco). It explains the rigidity of real wages and the existence of involuntary unemployment in terms of firms' attempts to increase productivity by keeping wages above the market-clearing level. According to this theory, higher wages lead to higher productivity because workers are healthier, because workers will have higher morale and be less likely to surf the Internet at work for fear of losing their jobs, because good workers are less likely to quit and look for new jobs, and because higher wages may attract better workers.

As firms raise their wages to increase worker productivity, job seekers may be willing to stand in line for these high-paying jobs, thereby producing involuntary unemployment. The innovation in this theory is that involuntary unemployment is an equilibrium feature and will not disappear over time.

供给学派经济学

Supply-Side Economics

In the early 1980s, a group of economists and journalists developed a popular school known as **supply-side economics,** which emphasized incentives and tax cuts as a means of increasing economic growth. Supply-side economics was espoused forcefully by President Reagan in the United States (1981–1989) [4] and by Prime Minister Thatcher in Great Britain [5] (1979–1990).

Supply siders argued that Keynesians, in their excessive concern with the business cycle, had ignored the impact of tax rates and incentives on economic growth. According to supply siders, high taxes lead people to reduce their labor and capital supply. Indeed, supply-side economists like Arthur Laffer [6] suggested that high tax rates might actually lower tax revenues. This *Laffer-curve* proposition holds that high tax rates shrink the tax base because they reduce economic activity. To fix what they view as an inefficient tax system, supply-side economists proposed a radical restructuring of the tax system, through an approach sometimes called "supply-side tax cuts."

After occupying center stage during the 1980s, the supply-side theories largely waned after Ronald Reagan left office. In studying this period, economists have generally found that many of the supply-side assertions were not supported by economic experience. Supply-side tax cuts produced lower, not higher, revenues.

Many of the supply-side policies were revived in 2001, when President George W. Bush [7] successfully negotiated another round of income-tax cuts. These cuts were rationalized not by the argument that they would raise revenues but, instead, by the theory that they would improve the efficiency of the tax system

[5] Prime Minister Thatcher：撒切尔（Margaret Thatcher，1925~），20世纪英国任期最长的首相（1979~1990），以"铁娘子"著称，奉行所谓撒切尔主义的保守政策。

[6] Arthur Laffer：阿瑟·拉弗（1940~），美国经济学家，长期（1981~1989）担任里根政府经济政策顾问委员会委员。

[7] George W. Bush：小布什，第43任（2001~2009）美国总统，其父"老布什"（George H. Bush）是第41任（1989~1993）美国总统。

[1] Edmund Phelps：埃德蒙·菲尔普斯（1933~），2006年诺贝尔经济学奖得主，其在加深人们对通货膨胀和失业预期关系的理解方面做出了巨大贡献。

[2] Joseph Stiglitz：2001年约瑟夫·斯蒂格利茨（1943~，美国经济学家）和乔治·阿卡洛夫（George A. Akerlof, 1940~, 美国经济学家）及迈克尔·斯彭斯（A. Michael Spence，1943~，美国经济学家）分享了当年的诺贝尔经济学奖，以表彰他们用信息不对称理论对市场分析所做出的贡献。

[3] Janet Yellen：珍妮特·耶伦（1946~），美国经济学家，现为美联储副主席。

[4] President Reagan：里根（Ronald Reagan，1911~2004），美国第40任（1981~1989）总统，曾是电影演员以及电台和电视节目主持人。

and raise the long-run rate of economic growth. Like their precursor in 1981, these tax cuts led to lower, rather than higher, tax revenues (see Table 31-1).

政策含义
POLICY IMPLICATIONS

政策的无效性
Policy Ineffectiveness

The new classical approaches have several important implications for macroeconomic policy. One of the ① most important contentions is the *ineffectiveness of systematic fiscal and monetary policies in reducing unemployment.* The basic idea here is that a predictable attempt to stimulate the economy would be known in advance and would therefore have no effect on the economy.

For example, suppose that the government has always stimulated the economy whenever elections were approaching. After a couple of episodes of politically motivated fiscal policy, people would rationally come to expect that behavior. They might say to themselves:

> Elections are coming. From experience I know that ② the government always pumps up the economy before elections. I will probably get an election-year tax cut, but that will be followed by a stealth tax increase next year. They can't fool me into consuming more, working harder, and voting for incumbents.

② 大选就要来了。从过去的经验我得出一点，政府总会在选前给经济打气。或许我还能享受一次选举年的减税，但紧跟着在来年必定会偷偷地增税。我们不能傻到中他们的圈套，什么多消费，什么更努力地工作，什么为他连任投票，统统见鬼去吧！

This is the **policy-ineffectiveness theorem** of classical macroeconomics. With rational expectations and flexible prices and wages, anticipated government policy cannot affect real output or unemployment.

固定规则的可取性
The Desirability of Fixed Rules

We described the monetarist case for fixed rules in Chapter 24. New classical macroeconomics puts this argument on firmer footing. This approach holds that an economic policy can be divided into two parts, a predictable part (the "rule") and an unpredictable part ("discretion").

New classical macroeconomists argue that discretion is a snare and a delusion. Policymakers, they contend, cannot forecast the economy any better than can the private sector. Therefore, by the time policymakers act on the news, flexibly moving prices in markets populated by well-informed buyers and sellers have already adapted to the news and reached their efficient supply-and-demand equilibrium. There are ③ no further *discretionary* steps the government can take to improve the outcome or prevent the unemployment that is caused by temporary misperceptions or real-business-cycle shocks.

Although they cannot make things better, government policies can definitely make things worse. The government can generate unpredictable discretionary policies that give misleading economic signals, confuse people, distort their economic behavior, and cause waste. According to new classical macroeconomists, governments should avoid any discretionary macroeconomic policies rather than risk producing such confusing "noise."

新的融合
A New Synthesis?

After three decades of digesting the new classical approach to macroeconomics, elements of a synthesis of old and new theories are beginning to appear. Economists today emphasize the importance of expectations. A useful distinction is between the adaptive (or "backward-looking") approach and the rational (or "forward-looking") approach. The adaptive assumption holds that people form their expectations on the basis of past information; the forward-looking or rational approach was described above. The importance of forward-looking expectations is crucial to understanding behavior, particularly in competitive auction markets like those in the financial sector.

Some macroeconomists have begun to fuse the ④ new classical view of expectations with the Keynesian view of product and labor markets. This synthesis is embodied in macroeconomic models that assume (1) labor and goods markets display inflexible wages and prices, (2) the prices in financial auction markets adjust rapidly to economic shocks and expectations, and (3) the expectations in auction markets are formed in a forward-looking way.

One important forecast of such new approaches is that forward-looking models tend to have large "jumps" or discontinuous changes in interest rates, stock prices, foreign exchange rates, and oil prices in reaction to major news. Sharp reactions are often seen after elections or when wars break out. For example, when the United States invaded Iraq in March 2003, oil prices declined by 35 percent and stock prices rose by 10 percent *in a single week.* The ⑤ new classical prediction of "jumpy" prices replicates one realistic feature of auction markets and thus suggests one area where forward-looking expectations might be important in the real world.

---

① 其中最重要的论点之一是系统的财政政策和货币政策在降低失业率时的无效性。

③ 政府已经没有可进一步采取的措施来扭转困局，或者阻止由一时的误判或者实际商业周期冲击引发的失业。

④ 某些宏观经济学家已经开始将新古典经济学的预期理论与凯恩斯主义关于产品市场与劳动市场的理论融合在一起。

⑤ "跳跃式"价格的新古典预期完全是拍卖市场中真实场景的一种翻版，因此，它说明在现实世界中前瞻性预期或许是很重要的。

The new classical approach to macroeconomics ① has brought many fruitful insights. Most important, it reminds us that the economy is populated by intelligent consumers and investors who react to and often anticipate policy. This reaction and counterreaction can actually change the way the economy behaves.

稳定经济
C. STABILIZING THE ECONOMY

The period since World War II has been one of remarkable economic progress for the high-income market democracies. Average incomes and employment grew rapidly, international trade broadened and deepened, and many poor countries, notably India and China, began to close the gap with rich countries.

The economies performed so well that some ② proclaimed a "Great Moderation," in which business cycles were disappearing. Some "new" economics textbooks virtually ignored the macroeconomics of business cycles.

This fantasy was dispelled with the financial crisis and deep recession that began in 2007. Words like "recession" and "depression"—which had been banished to the history books—again took on meaning in people's daily lives.

It is critical to find policies which can help avoid the excesses of the business cycle. We have seen that the path of output and prices is determined by the interaction of aggregate supply and aggregate demand. *However, policies designed to stabilize the business cycle must* ③ *operate primarily through their impact on aggregate demand.* The government can affect the growth of aggregate demand primarily through the use of its monetary and fiscal levers and thereby counter recessions.

These observations leave open two crucial questions: What is the best mix of monetary and fiscal policies for stabilizing the economy? Should there be tight rules on policy-making, or should policymakers be allowed great discretion in their actions?

货币政策与财政政策的相互作用
THE INTERACTION OF MONETARY AND FISCAL POLICIES

For large economies like the United States or Euroland, the best combination of monetary and fiscal policies will depend upon two factors: the need for demand management and the desired fiscal-monetary mix.

需求管理
Demand Management

The top consideration in business-cycle management is the overall state of the economy and the need to adjust aggregate demand. When the economy is stagnating, fiscal and monetary policies can be used to stimulate the economy and promote economic recovery. When inflation threatens, monetary and fiscal policies can help slow the economy and dampen inflationary fires. These are examples of *demand management*, which refers to the active use of monetary and fiscal policies to affect the level of aggregate demand. ④ 这些关于需求管理的例子，涉及到积极应用货币政策与财政政策来影响总需求水平。

Suppose, for example, that the economy is entering a severe recession. Output is low relative to its potential. What can the government do to revive the lagging economy? It can increase aggregate demand by raising money growth or by boosting government spending or both. After the economy has responded to the monetary and fiscal stimulus, output growth and employment will increase and unemployment will fall. (What steps could the government take during inflationary periods?)

Let's review the relative strengths and weaknesses of monetary policy and fiscal policy.

The Role of Fiscal Policy. In the early stages of the Keynesian revolution, macroeconomists emphasized fiscal policy as the most powerful and balanced remedy for demand management. Critics of fiscal policy pointed to shortcomings stemming from timing, politics, and macroeconomic theory.

One concern is the time span between cyclical shock and policy response. It takes time to recognize that a cyclical turning point has been reached—the policy lag. For example, it took one year for the NBER to declare the latest business-cycle peak. [5] NBER：National Bureau of Economic Research，（美国）联邦经济研究局。 (The December 2007 peak was not announced until December 2008.) After a turning point is identified, it takes time for the President to decide what policies are necessary and then still more time for the Congress to act. Finally, even when taxation or spending is changed, there is an effectiveness lag before the economy responds.

Critics also point out that it is easier to cut taxes than to raise them, and easier to raise spending than to cut it. During the 1960s, Congress was enthusiastic about passing the Kennedy-Johnson tax cuts. [6] Two years later, when the Vietnam War expansion ignited inflationary pressures, contractionary policies were called for.

---

① 宏观经济学的新古典学派已经取得了许多丰硕的成果。最重要的一点是，它提醒我们，在经济中，能够预测政策以及对政策做出应对的聪明消费者和投资者大有人在。这样的作用和反作用实际上能改变经济行为的方式。

② 经济运行得如此良好，以至于有人将它冠以“太平稳顺时期”。在这一时期，商业周期始终没有出现。一些“新”的经济学教科书实际上已经略去了宏观经济学中的商业周期内容。。

③ 但是，用来稳定商业周期的既定政策必须通过它对总需求的影响来运作。

[6] Kennedy-Johnson tax cuts，系萨缪尔森为肯尼迪设计的一套减税方案，使美国避免了一次潜在的经济危机。请参阅前言。

There are two situations when countercyclical fiscal policies appear to be particularly useful. One case is temporary tax cuts in recessions. Temporary tax cuts may be aimed primarily at low- and middle-income households. The reason is that these households have high marginal propensities to consume because they have little excess saving to fall back on in hard times. Statistical studies indicate that these measures have indeed been effective in increasing aggregate demand in the short run without leading to long-run fiscal deficits.

An even more important situation is when the economy is in a liquidity trap and the central bank has no further room to lower short-term interest rates. (Recall our discussion of the liquidity trap in Chapter 24.) This was the case during the 2007–2009 recession. In its effort to revive the economy, the Obama administration worked with Congress in early 2009 to pass the largest fiscal stimulus package in U.S. history. While some people worried about the long-term impact of the fiscal stimulus on the government debt, most macroeconomists believed that fiscal policy was the only feasible way to reduce the depth and the severity of the downturn in this circumstance.

Effectiveness of Monetary Policy. Compared to fiscal policy, monetary policy operates much more indirectly on the economy. Whereas an expansive fiscal policy actually buys goods and services or puts income into the hands of consumers and businesses, monetary policy affects spending by altering interest rates, credit conditions, exchange rates, and asset prices. In the early years of the Keynesian revolution, some macroeconomists were skeptical about the effectiveness of monetary policy—some said, "Monetary policy was like pushing on a string." Over the last two decades, however, these concerns have been put to rest as the Federal Reserve has shown itself quite capable of slowing down, or speeding up, the economy.

The Federal Reserve is much better placed to conduct stabilization policy than are the fiscal-policy makers. Its staff of professional economists can recognize cyclical movements as well as anyone. And it can move quickly when the need arises. For example, a cascade of failures of financial institutions caused a major financial crisis when the investment-banking firm Bear, Stearns had severe liquidity problems on [1] Friday, March 14, 2008. The Fed needed to come up with a solution before markets opened on Monday morning. By Sunday, working with the U.S. Treasury Department, the Fed had engineered a takeover of Bear by J.P. Morgan and had opened an entire new credit facility for its primary dealers. It is difficult to conceive of any legislature taking such complex measures in such a short time.

A key ingredient in Fed policy is its independence, and the Fed has proved that it can stand the heat of making politically unpopular decisions when they are necessary to slow inflation. Most important is that—with some qualifications—from the point of view of demand management, monetary policy can do, or undo, anything that fiscal policy can accomplish. The major reservation is that if the economy gets stuck in a liquidity trap, with nominal interest rates at or near zero, then monetary policy loses its ability to stimulate the economy. When the economy is in or near a liquidity trap, fiscal policy must therefore take over the major expansionary role.

We can summarize the current state of fiscal and monetary policy as follows:

> Because of their political independence and rapid decision making, central banks are well placed to be on the front line of defense in stabilizing the economy against business-cycle shocks. Discretionary fiscal policy is useful in recessions as a one-time stimulus. When the economy approaches a liquidity trap, fiscal policy must be the primary source of economic stimulus. ②

财政政策与货币政策的组合
The Fiscal-Monetary Mix

The second factor affecting fiscal and monetary policy is the desired **fiscal-monetary mix,** which refers to the relative strength of fiscal and monetary policies and their effect on different sectors of the economy. A *change in the fiscal-monetary mix* is an approach which tightens one policy while easing the other in such a way that aggregate demand and therefore total output remain constant. The basic idea is that fiscal policy and monetary policy are substitutes in demand management. But while alternative combinations of monetary and fiscal policies can be used to stabilize the economy, they have different impacts upon the *composition* of output. By varying the mix of taxes, government spending, and monetary policy, the government can change the fraction of GDP devoted to business investment, consumption, net exports, and government purchases of goods and services.

---

[1] Bear, Stearns：即 Bear Stearns Companies, Inc.，贝尔斯登公司，在 2008 年的金融危机中被摩根大通收购，它曾经是全球领先的金融服务公司。1923 年由 Joseph Bear 和 Robert Stearns 联合 Harold Mayer 共同投资组建。

② 由于政治独立性与快速的决策，中央银行在稳定经济抵御商业周期的冲击上被置于防线的最前沿。作为一次性的经济刺激政策，相机抉择的财政政策是遏制衰退的有用手段。而当经济的运行接近流动性陷阱时，财政政策就必然成为刺激经济的首选。

Sector			Change in output ($, billion, 2008 prices)
Investment sectors			**132**
Gross private domestic investment		48	
Housing	18		
Business fixed investment	30		
Net exports		83	
Consumption sectors			**−106**
Government purchases of goods and services		−68	
Personal consumption expenditures		−38	
Memoranda:			
Change in real GDP			26
Change in federal deficit			−100

TABLE 31-3. Changing the Fiscal-Monetary Mix

What would be the impact of a change in the fiscal-monetary mix for the United States? This simulation assumes that the federal deficit is cut by $100 billion through higher personal taxes and lower federal nondefense expenditures while the Federal Reserve uses monetary policy to keep unemployment on an unchanged trajectory. The simulation takes the average of the changes from the baseline path over the period 2000–2009.

Source: Simulation using the DRI model of the U.S. economy.

Effect of Changing the Mix of Monetary and Fiscal Policies. To understand the impact of changing the fiscal-monetary mix, let's examine a specific set of policies. Suppose that the federal government reduces the federal budget deficit by $100 billion and that the Fed lowers interest rates to offset the contractionary impact of such a fiscal policy.

We can estimate the impact using a quantitative economic model. Table 31-3 shows the results of this experiment. Two interesting features emerge: First, the simulation indicates that a change in the fiscal-monetary mix would indeed change the composition of real GDP. While the deficit declines by $100 billion, business investment goes up by $30 billion. Investment in housing also increases as interest rates fall. At the same time, personal consumption declines, freeing up resources for investment. This simulation shows how a change in the fiscal-monetary mix might change the composition of output.

The simulation contains one particularly interesting result: Net exports rise far more than either housing or business fixed investment. This occurs because of the strong depreciation of the dollar which results from the lower interest rates. While this ①
result is clearly sensitive to the reaction of financial markets and exchange rates to the deficit-reduction package, it suggests that some of the popular analyses of the impact of such a package may be misleading. Many analysts have argued that a deficit-reduction package would have a significant impact upon domestic business investment and upon productivity. However, to the extent that lower deficits mainly ②
increase net exports and housing, the nation is likely to experience relatively little increase in productivity growth. According to the estimates, cutting the budget deficit by $100 billion will raise the growth rate of potential output from 2.3 percent per year to 2.5 percent per year over a 10-year period. Perhaps the small size of the payoff explains why it is so hard to muster the political will to cut the deficit.

Alternative Mixes in Practice

The fiscal-monetary mix has been sharply debated in American economic policy. Here are two major alternatives:

- *Loose fiscal—tight monetary policy.* Assume that the economy begins in an initial situation with low inflation

① 结果很清楚，金融市场和汇率对一揽子削减赤字计划的反应是敏感的，但这表明，某些对这一计划影响的普遍性分析是一种误导。

② 然而，某种程度上，较低的赤字主要是增加了净出口和住房，但该国生产率的提高可能是微不足道的。

and output at its potential. A new president decides that it is necessary to increase defense spending sharply without raising taxes. By itself, this would increase the government deficit and increase aggregate demand. In this situation, the Federal Reserve would need to tighten monetary policy to prevent the economy from overheating. The result would be higher real interest rates and an appreciation of the dollar exchange rate. The higher interest rates would squeeze investment, while the appreciated dollar would reduce net exports. The net effect therefore would be that the higher defense spending would crowd out domestic investment and net exports. This policy was the one followed by the United States in the 1980s and again in the 2000s.

- *Tight fiscal—loose monetary policy.* Suppose that a country becomes concerned about a low national saving rate and desires to raise investment so as to increase the capital stock and boost the growth rate of potential output. To implement this approach, the country could raise consumption taxes and squeeze transfer payments so as to reduce disposable income and thereby lower consumption (tight fiscal policy). This would be accompanied by an expansionary monetary policy to lower interest rates and raise investment, lower the exchange rate, and expand net exports. This course would encourage private investment by increasing public saving. This was the economic philosophy of President Clinton which was embodied in the 1993 Budget Act and led to the budget surplus at decade's end.

规则与相机抉择
RULES VS. DISCRETION

We have seen that fiscal and monetary policy can *in principle* stabilize the economy. Many economists believe that countries should *in practice* take steps to shave the peaks and troughs off the business cycle. Other economists are skeptical of our ability to forecast cycles and take the right steps at the right time for the right reasons; this second group concludes that government cannot be trusted to make good economic policy, so its freedom to act should be strictly limited.

For example, fiscal conservatives worry that it's easier for Congress to increase spending and cut taxes than to do the reverse. That means it's easy ① to increase the budget deficit during recessions but much harder to turn around and shrink the deficit again during booms, as a countercyclical fiscal policy would require. For that reason, conservatives have made several attempts to limit the ability of Congress to appropriate new funds or increase the deficit.

At the same time, monetary conservatives would like to tie the hands of central banks and force them to target inflation. Such a policy would eliminate the uncertainty about policy and enhance the credibility of the central bank as an inflation fighter.

At the most general level, the debate about ② "rules versus discretion" boils down to whether the advantages of flexibility in decision making are outweighed by the uncertainties and potential abuse in unconstrained decisions. Those who believe that the economy is inherently unstable and complex and that governments generally make wise decisions are comfortable with giving policymakers wide discretion to react aggressively to stabilize the economy. Those who believe that the government is the major destabilizing force in the economy and that policymakers are prone to selfishness and misjudgments favor tying the hands of the fiscal and monetary authorities.

立法机构的预算约束
Budget Constraints on Legislatures?

As deficits began to grow during the 1980s, many people argued that Congress lacks the self-control to curb excessive spending and a burgeoning government debt. One proposal put forth by conservatives was a *constitutional amendment requiring a balanced budget.* Such an amendment was criticized by economists because it would make it difficult to use fiscal policy to fight recessions. To date, none of the proposed constitutional amendments has passed Congress.

Instead, Congress legislated a series of *budgetary rules to limit spending and tax reductions.* The first attempt was the Gramm-Rudman Act in 1985, which required that the deficit be reduced by a specified dollar amount each year and that the budget be balanced by 1991. This approach failed to limit spending and was abandoned.

A second approach was a *pay-as-you-go budget rule,* which was adopted in 1990. This required that Congress find the revenues to pay for any new spending program. In a sense, pay-as-you-go imposes a budget constraint on Congress, requiring that the costs of new programs be explicitly recognized either through higher taxes or through a reduction in other spending.

What was the impact of the budget constraints on Congress? Economic studies indicate that the

① 在经济衰退期间，这样的政策意味着增加预算赤字是一件轻而易举的事情。但在经济繁荣时期进行回调和缩小赤字，就变成了一件更难的事情。

② 全方位来讲，关于“规则与相机抉择”的争论可以归结为一点，即决策灵活性的优势是否会被不确定性以及决策不受约束的潜在的滥用职权所抵消。

budget rules produced significant fiscal discipline, helped reduce the deficit over the 1990s, and eventually produced the surplus after 1998. However, when the deficit changed to surplus and the urgency of deficit-reduction declined, policymakers evaded the earlier budget caps with gimmicks like "emergency spending" for predictable items like the decennial census. Finally, in 2002, the budget caps were allowed to expire. Many economists believe that a pay-as-you-go rule is a useful mechanism to impose budget constraints on legislatures, and there were proposals to reinstate these in 2009.

联储的货币规则

Monetary Rules for the Fed?

In our discussion of monetarism in Chapter 24, we laid out the case for fixed policy rules. The traditional argument for fixed rules is that the private economy is relatively stable and active policy-making is likely to destabilize rather than stabilize the economy. Moreover, to the extent that a central bank under the thumb of the government may be tempted to expand the economy before elections and to create a political business cycle, fixed rules will tie its hands. In addition, modern macroeconomists point to the value of being able to commit to action in advance. If the central bank can commit to follow a noninflationary rule, people's expectations will adapt to this rule and inflationary expectations may be dampened.

One of the most important new developments in the last decade has been the trend toward inflation targeting in many countries. **Inflation targeting** is the ① announcement of official target ranges for the inflation rate along with an explicit statement that low and stable inflation is the overriding goal of monetary policy. Inflation targeting in hard or soft varieties has been adopted in recent years by many industrialized countries, including Canada, Britain, Australia, and New Zealand. Moreover, the treaty authorizing the new European Central Bank mandates that price stability be the ECB's primary objective, although it is not formally required to target inflation. A number of economists and legislators are advocating this approach for the United States as well.

Inflation targeting involves the following:

- The government or central bank announces that monetary policy will strive to keep inflation near a numerically specified target.
- The target usually involves a range, such as 1 to 3 percent per year, rather than literal price stability. Generally, the government targets a core inflation rate, such as the CPI excluding volatile food and energy prices.
- Inflation is the primary or overriding target of policy in the medium run and long run. However, countries always make room for short-run stabilization objectives, particularly with respect to output, unemployment, financial stability, and the foreign exchange rate. These short-run objectives recognize that supply shocks can affect output and unemployment and that it may be desirable to have temporary departures from the inflation target to avoid excessive unemployment or output losses.

Proponents of inflation targeting point to many advantages. If there is no long-run tradeoff between ② unemployment and inflation, a sensible inflation target is that rate which maximizes the efficiency of the price system. Our analysis of inflation in Chapter 30 suggested that a low and stable rate of inflation would promote efficiency and minimize unnecessary redistribution of income and wealth. In addition, some economists believe that a strong and credible commitment to low and stable inflation will improve the short-run inflation-unemployment tradeoff. Finally, an explicit inflation target would increase the transparency of monetary policy.

Inflation targeting is a compromise between rule-based approaches and purely discretionary policies. The main disadvantage would come if the central bank began to rely too rigidly on the inflation rule and thereby allowed excessive unemployment in periods of severe supply shocks. Skeptics worry that the economy is too complex to be governed by fixed rules. Arguing by analogy, they ask whether one would advocate a fixed speed limit for cars or an automatic pilot for aircraft in all kinds of weather and emergencies.

Critics point to the financial crisis of 2007–2009 as an example of the peril of relying on rigid targets. The Fed lowered interest rates and expanded credit throughout this period, even though supply shocks were raising inflation above the Fed's "comfort zone." If the Fed had focused entirely on inflation under an inflation-targeting approach, it would have raised interest rates, tightened credit, and reinforced the recessionary tendencies and economic distress in

---

① **设定通货膨胀目标**系指官方公布的通货膨胀率目标区间，它明确说明了稳定的低通货膨胀率是货币政策的首要目标。

② 如果失业率和通货膨胀率之间不存在长期的此消彼长的权衡关系，则合理的通货膨胀率目标就是使价格体系效率实现最大化。

this period. Instead, the Fed concentrated on trying to cushion the economy from a deep recession and to prevent wholesale bankruptcies of financial institutions (see the discussion of Bear, Stearns above).

Monetary policy cannot banish all recessions or remove every temporary spike of inflation. However, working with fiscal policy, it can reduce the chance of spiraling contractions or hyperinflation.

The debate over rules versus discretion is one ① of the oldest debates of political economy. This dilemma reflects the difficult tradeoffs that democratic societies face in making decisions between short-run policies intended to attract political support and long-run policies designed to improve the general welfare. There is no single best approach for all times and places. For monetary policy, the United States has resolved the dilemma by creating an independent central bank, accountable to the legislature but given discretion to act forcefully when economic or financial crises arise.

Country	Per capita GDP, 2006
United States	44,070
United Kingdom	33,650
Japan	32,840
Germany	32,680
Slovenia	23,970
South Korea	22,990
Poland	14,250
Mexico	11,990
Botswana	11,730
Argentina	11,670
China	4,660
Nigeria	1,410
Congo	270

TABLE 31-4. Current Incomes Represent Effects of Past Growth

Those countries that have grown most rapidly in the past have reached the highest levels of per capita GDP today.

Source: World Bank.

经济增长与居民福利

D. ECONOMIC GROWTH AND HUMAN WELFARE

We have come to the end of our survey of modern macroeconomics. Let us step back and reflect on the central long-run message as stated by economist-journalist Paul Krugman:

> Productivity isn't everything, but in the long run it is ② almost everything. A country's ability to improve its living standards over time depends almost entirely on its ability to raise its output per worker.

Promoting a high and growing standard of living for the nation's residents is one of the fundamental goals of macroeconomic policy. Because the current *level* of real income reflects the history of the *growth* of productivity, we can measure the relative success of past growth by examining the per capita GDPs of different countries. A short list is presented in Table 31-4. This table compares incomes by using *purchasing-power-parity* exchange rates that measure the purchasing power of (or quantity of goods and services that can be bought by) different national currencies. Evidently, the United States has been successful in its past growth performance. Perhaps the most worrisome issue in recent years is that the growth in living standards has not been universally shared around the world.

In discussions of growth rates, the numbers often seem tiny. A successful policy might increase a country's growth rate by only 1 percentage point per year (recall the estimated impact of the deficit-reduction package in the last section). But over long periods, this makes a big difference. Table 31-5 shows how tiny acorns grow into mighty oaks as small growth-rate differences cumulate and compound over time. A 4 percent-per-year growth difference leads to a 50-fold difference in income levels over a century.

How can public policy boost economic growth? As we emphasized in our chapters on economic growth, the growth of output per worker and of living standards depends upon a country's saving rate and upon its technological advance. Issues involving saving were discussed earlier in this chapter. Technological change includes not only new products and processes but also improvements in management as well as entrepreneurship and the spirit of enterprise—and we close our discussion with this topic.

---

① 有关规则与相机抉择的争论是政治经济学中最古老的争论焦点之一。这一两难问题反映出民主社会所面临的权衡难题：如何在旨在获得政治支持的短期政策和提高国民福利的长期政策之间进行决策。没有适用于任何时间和任何地点的最佳方案。就货币政策而言，美国政府已经通过创设独立的中央银行解决了这一两难问题。中央银行虽然对立法机构负责，但在经济危机或者金融危机爆发时，也被授予强有力的相机抉择权。

② 生产率并不代表一切，但长期来讲，它几乎又意味着一切。随着时间的推移，一个国家提高国民生活水平的能力几乎完全取决于其提高人均产出的能力。

Growth rate (% per year)	Real Income per Capita (constant prices) 2000	2050	2100
0	$ 24,000	$ 24,000	$ 24,000
1	24,000	39,471	64,916
2	24,000	64,598	173,872
4	24,000	170,560	1,212,118

TABLE 31-5. Small Differences in Growth Rates Compound into Large Income Differentials over the Decades

企业精神
THE SPIRIT OF ENTERPRISE

Although investment is a central factor in economic growth, technological advance is perhaps even more important. If we took the workers in 1900 and doubled or tripled their capital in mules, saddles, picks, and cow paths, their productivity still could not come close to that of today's workers using huge tractors, superhighways, and supercomputers. ①

鼓励科技进步
Fostering Technological Advance

While it is easy to see how technological advance promotes growth in productivity and living standards, governments cannot simply command people to think harder or be smarter. Centrally planned socialist countries used "sticks" to promote science, technology, and innovation, but their efforts failed because neither the institutions nor the "carrots" were present to encourage both innovation and introduction of new technologies. ② Governments often promote rapid technological change best when they set a sound economic and legal framework with strong intellectual property rights and then allow great economic freedom within that framework. *Free markets in labor, capital, products, and ideas have proved to be the most fertile soil for innovation and technological change.*

Within the framework of free markets, governments can foster rapid technological change both by encouraging new ideas and by ensuring that technologies are effectively used. Policies can focus on both the supply side and the demand side.

Promoting Demand for Better Technologies. The world is full of superior technologies that have not been adopted; otherwise, how could we explain the vast differences in productivity shown in Table 31-4? In considering technology policies, therefore, governments must ensure that firms and industries move toward the *technological frontier,* adopting the best-practice technology available in the global marketplace.

The major lesson here is that "necessity is the mother of invention." In other words, vigorous competition among firms and industries is the ultimate discipline that ensures innovation. Just as athletes perform better when they are trying to outrun their competitors, so are firms spurred to improve their products and processes when the victors are given fame and fortune while the laggards may go bankrupt.

Vigorous competition involves both domestic and foreign competitors. For large countries on the technological frontier, domestic competition is necessary to promote innovation. The movement to deregulation over the last three decades has brought competition to airlines, energy, telecommunications, and finance, and the positive impact on innovation has been dramatic. For small or technologically backward countries, import competition is crucial to adopting advanced technologies and ensuring product market competition.

Promoting Supply of New Technologies. Rapid economic growth requires pushing out the technological frontier by increasing the supply of inventions as well as ensuring that there is adequate demand for existing advanced technologies. There are three ways by which governments can encourage the supply of new technologies. ③

First, governments can ensure that the basic science, engineering, and technology are appropriately supported. In this respect, the world leader in the

---

① 以1900年的农工为例，即便将骡子、鞍具、镐和牛车道等资本扩大至原有的两倍或者三倍，其生产率仍然无法接近今天的工人使用大型拖拉机、高速公路和超级计算机所创造的生产率。

② 实行中央计划经济的社会主义国家使用“大棒”政策来促进科学发展、技术进步和创新，但这些努力均告失败。这是因为这些国家既没有有效的机制，也没有“胡萝卜”来鼓励创新和引进新技术。

③ 经济的快速增长要求通过不断的发明创造以及确保现有的先进技术有足够的需求来推动新技术领域。

last half-century has been the United States, which combines company support for applied research with top-notch university basic research generously supported by government funding. Particularly outstanding have been the impressive improvements in biomedical technology in the form of new drugs and equipment that benefit consumers directly in daily life. The government's role in supporting for-profit research is accomplished by a strong patent system, predictable and cost-effective regulations, and fiscal incentives such as the current R&D tax credit. ①

Second, governments can advance technologies at home through encouraging investment by foreign firms. As foreign countries reach and pass the American technological frontier, they can also contribute to American know-how by establishing operations in the United States. The last two decades have brought ②
a number of Japanese automakers to the United States, and Japanese-owned plants have introduced new technologies and managerial practices to the benefit of both the profits of Japanese shareholders and the productivity of American workers.

Third, governments can promote new technologies by pursuing sound macroeconomic policies. These include low and stable taxes on capital income and a low cost of capital to firms. Indeed, the importance of the cost of capital brings us back full circle to the issue of the low saving rate and high real interest rate. American firms are sometimes accused of being myopic and being unwilling to invest for the long run. At least part of this myopia comes from being faced with high real interest rates—high real interest rates *force* rational American firms to look for quick payoffs in their investments. A change in economic policy that lowered real interest rates would change the "economic spectacles" through which firms look when considering their technological policies. If real interest rates were lower, firms would view long-term, high-risk projects such as investments in technology more favorably, and the increased investment in knowledge would lead to more rapid improvements in technology and productivity.

Valediction on Economic Growth

Following the Keynesian revolution, the leaders of the market democracies believed that they could flourish and grow rapidly. By using the tools of modern economics, countries could moderate the extremes of unemployment and inflation, poverty and wealth, privilege and deprivation. Indeed, many of these goals were achieved as the market economies experienced a period of output expansion and employment growth never seen before.

At the same time, Marxists carped that capitalism was doomed to crash in a cataclysmic depression; ecologists fretted that market economies would choke on their own fumes; and libertarians worried that government planning was leading us down the road to serfdom. But the pessimists overlooked the spirit of enterprise, which was nurtured by an open society and free markets and which led to a continuous stream of technological improvements.

A valediction from John Maynard Keynes, as timely today as it was in an earlier age, provides a fitting summary of our survey of modern economics:

> It is Enterprise which builds and improves the world's possessions. If Enterprise is afoot, wealth accumulates whatever happens to Thrift; and if Enterprise is asleep, wealth decays whatever Thrift may be doing. ③

SUMMARY

A. The Economic Consequences of the Government Debt

1. Budgets are systems used by governments and organizations to plan and control expenditures and revenues. Budgets are in surplus (or deficit) when the government has revenues greater (or less) than its expenditures. Macroeconomic policy depends upon fiscal policy, which comprises the overall stance of spending and taxes.
2. Economists separate the actual budget into its structural and cyclical components. The structural budget calculates how much the government would collect

---

① R&D tax credit：研发税收抵免。

② 在过去的 20 年中，许多日本的汽车制造商进入了美国市场，他们的生产工厂引入了新技术和管理实践，使日本股东的收益和美国工人的生产率双双受益。

③ 恰恰是企业在为全世界创造并增加财富。如果企业在正常运营，无论人们是否节俭，财富都在增加。但是，如果企业停止运营，则无论人们如何节俭，财富都在衰竭。

and spend if the economy were operating at potential output. The cyclical budget accounts for the impact of the business cycle on tax revenues, expenditures, and the deficit. To assess fiscal policy, we should pay close attention to the structural deficit; changes in the cyclical deficit are a *result* of changes in the economy, while structural deficits are a *cause* of changes in the economy.

3. The government debt represents the accumulated borrowings from the public. It is the sum of past deficits. A useful measure of the size of the debt is the debt-GDP ratio, which for the United States has tended to rise during wartime and fall during peacetime.
4. In understanding the impact of government deficits and debt, it is crucial to distinguish between the short run and the long run. Review the box on page 638 and make sure you understand why a larger deficit can increase output in the short run while decreasing output in the long run.
5. To the degree that we borrow from abroad for consumption and pledge posterity to pay back the interest and principal on such external debt, our descendants will indeed find themselves sacrificing consumption to service this debt. If we leave future generations an internal debt but no change in capital stock, there are various internal effects. The process of taxing Peter to pay Paula, or taxing Paula to pay Paula, can involve various microeconomic distortions of productivity and efficiency but should not be confused with owing money to another country.
6. Economic growth may slow if the public debt displaces capital. This syndrome occurs when people substitute public debt for capital or private assets, thereby reducing the economy's private capital stock. In the long run, a larger government debt may slow the growth of potential output and consumption because of the costs of servicing an external debt, the inefficiencies that arise from taxing to pay the interest on the debt, and the diminished capital accumulation that comes from capital displacement.

B. Advances in Modern Macroeconomics

7. Classical economists relied upon Say's Law of Markets, which holds that "supply creates its own demand." In modern language, the classical approach means that flexible wages and prices quickly remove any excess supply or demand and thereby reestablish full employment. In a classical system, macroeconomic policy has no role to play in stabilizing the real economy, although it will still affect the path of prices.
8. New classical macroeconomics holds that expectations are rational, prices and wages are flexible, and unemployment is largely voluntary. The policy-ineffectiveness theorem holds that predictable government policies cannot affect real output and unemployment. The theory of the real business cycle points to supply-side technological disturbances and to labor market shifts as the clues to business-cycle fluctuations.
9. What is our appraisal of the contribution of the new classical approach to short-run macroeconomics? The new classical approach properly insists that the economy is populated by forward-looking consumers and investors. These economic actors react to and often anticipate policy and can thereby change economic behavior. This lesson is particularly important in financial markets, where reactions and anticipations often have dramatic effects.

C. Stabilizing the Economy

10. Nations face two considerations in setting monetary and fiscal policies: the appropriate level of aggregate demand and the best monetary-fiscal mix. The mix of fiscal and monetary policies helps determine the composition of GDP. A high-investment strategy would call for a budget surplus along with low real interest rates.
11. Should governments follow fixed rules or discretion? The answer involves both positive economics and normative values. Conservatives often espouse rules, while liberals often advocate active fine-tuning to attain economic goals. More basic is the question of whether active and discretionary policies stabilize or destabilize the economy. Economists often stress the need for *credible* policies, whether credibility is generated by rigid rules or by wise leadership. A recent trend among countries is inflation targeting for monetary policy, which is a flexible rule-based system that sets a medium-term inflation target while allowing short-run flexibility when economic shocks make attaining a rigid inflation target too costly.

D. Economic Growth and Human Welfare

12. Remember the dictum: "Productivity isn't everything, but in the long run it is almost everything." A country's ability to improve its living standards over time depends almost entirely on its ability to improve the technologies and capital used by the workforce.
13. Promoting economic growth entails advancing technology. The major role of government is to ensure free markets, protect strong intellectual property rights, promote vigorous competition, and support basic science and technology.

CONCEPTS FOR REVIEW

The Economics of Debt and Deficits

government budget
budget deficit, surplus, and balance
budget:
- actual
- structural
- cyclical

short-run impact of G and T on output
long-run impacts on economic growth:
- internal vs. external debt
- distortions from taxation
- displacement of capital

Advances in Modern Macroeconomics

Say's Law of Markets
rational (forward-looking) expectations, adaptive (backward-looking) expectations
policy-ineffectiveness theorem
real business cycle, efficiency wages
Ricardian view of fiscal policy

Stabilization

demand management
fiscal-monetary mix
fixed rules vs. discretion
inflation targeting

Long-Run Growth

reaching the technological frontier vs. moving it outward
Keynes's spirit of enterprise

FURTHER READING AND INTERNET WEBSITES

Further Reading

The Krugman quotation is from Paul Krugman, *The Age of Diminished Expectations* (MIT Press, Cambridge, Mass., 1990), p. 9. Many of the foundations of new classical economics were developed by Robert Lucas and republished in *Studies in Business-Cycle Theory* (MIT Press, Cambridge, Mass., 1990). Modern efficiency-wage theory is presented in Edmund Phelps, *Structural Slumps: The Modern Equilibrium Theory of Unemployment, Interest, and Assets* (Harvard University Press, Cambridge, Mass., 1994).

A nontechnical review of the different schools of macroeconomics is provided by Paul Krugman, *Peddling Prosperity: Economic Sense and Nonsense in the Age of Diminished Expectations* (Norton, New York, 1994).

Websites

Economic issues and data on fiscal policy, budgets, and the debt are regularly provided by the nonpartisan Congressional Budget Office, which is staffed by professional economists. Recent documents are available at *www.cbo.gov.*

A survey of issues involved in inflation targeting can be found in a 2003 speech by Fed chair Ben Bernanke, "A Perspective on Inflation Targeting," at *www.federalreserve.gov/Boarddocs/Speeches/2003/20030325/default.htm.* Real-business-cycle theory has its own website at *dge.repec.org/index.html.*

QUESTIONS FOR DISCUSSION

1. A common confusion is that between the debt and the deficit. Explain each of the following:
   a. A budget deficit leads to a growing government debt.
   b. Reducing the deficit does not reduce the government debt.
   c. Reducing the government debt requires running a budget surplus.
   d. Even though the government deficit was reduced in the 1993–1998 period, the government debt still rose in these years.
2. Is it possible that government *promises* might have a displacement effect along with government debt? Thus, if the government were to promise large future social security benefits to workers, would workers feel richer? Might they reduce saving as a result? Could

the capital stock end up smaller? Illustrate using Figure 31-2.

3. Trace the impact upon the government debt, the nation's capital stock, and real output of a government program that borrows abroad and spends the money on the following:
   a. Capital to drill for oil, which is exported (as did Mexico in the 1970s)
   b. Grain to feed its population (as did Nigeria in the 2000s)
4. Construct a graph like that in Figure 31-3 showing:
   a. The paths of consumption and net exports with and without a large government debt
   b. The paths of consumption with a balanced budget and with a government fiscal surplus
5. Review the debate between the senators on page 638. Explain which senator would be correct in the following situations:
   a. The government increased military spending during the Great Depression.
   b. The government reduced tax rates during a period of full employment in the early 1960s.
   c. The government refused to raise taxes during the full-employment period of the Vietnam War.
6. Suppose someone advocates that monetary policy should target a specific inflation rate every year—say, 2 percent per year for the CPI. What are the various arguments for and against this proposal? Specifically, consider the difficulties of attaining a strict inflation target after a sharp supply shock shifts the Phillips curve up. Compare a rigid inflation target with a flexible inflation target in which the target would be attained at the end of a 5-year period.
7. Political candidates have proposed the policies listed below to speed economic growth in recent years. For each, explain qualitatively the impact upon the growth of potential output and upon the growth of per capita potential output. If possible, give a quantitative estimate of the increase in the growth of potential output and per capita potential output over the next decade.
   a. Cut the federal budget deficit (or raise the surplus) by 2 percent of GDP, increasing the ratio of investment to GDP by the same amount.
   b. Increase the federal subsidy to R&D by ½ percent of GDP, assuming that this subsidy will increase private R&D by the same amount and that R&D has a social rate of return that is 4 times that of private investment.
   c. Decrease defense spending by 1 percent of GDP at full employment.
   d. Decrease the number of immigrants so that the labor force declines by 5 percent.
   e. Increase investments in human capital (or education and on-the-job training) by 1 percent of GDP.
8. J. M. Keynes wrote, "If the Treasury were to fill old bottles with banknotes, bury them in disused coal mines, and leave it to private enterprise to dig the notes up again, there need be no more unemployment and the real income of the community would probably become a good deal greater than it actually is" (*The General Theory*, p. 129). Explain why Keynes's analysis of the utility of a discretionary public-works program might be correct during a depression. How could well-designed monetary policies have the same impact on employment while producing a larger quantity of useful goods and services?
9. What would Keynesians and new classical macroeconomists predict to be the impacts of each of the following on the course of prices, output, and employment? In each case, hold tax rates and interest rates constant unless specifically mentioned:
   a. A large tax cut
   b. A large cut in interest rates
   c. A wave of innovations that increases potential output by 10 percent
   d. A burst of exports
10. **Advanced problem** (on rational expectations): Consider the effect of rational expectations on consumption behavior.
   a. Say that the government proposes a temporary tax cut of $20 billion, lasting for a year. Consumers with adaptive expectations consequently assume that their disposable incomes would be $20 billion higher every year. What would be the resulting impact on consumption spending and GDP in the simple multiplier model of Chapter 22?
   b. Next suppose that consumers have rational expectations. They rationally forecast that the tax cut is only for 1 year. Being "life-cycle" consumers, they recognize that their average lifetime incomes will increase by only $2 billion per year, not by $20 billion per year. What would be the reaction of such consumers? Analyze, then, the impact of rational expectations on the effectiveness of temporary tax cuts.
   c. Finally, assume that consumers behave according to the Ricardian view. What would be the impact of the tax cut on saving and consumption? Explain the differences between the models discussed in **a, b,** and **c.**

专业术语表 [1]

A

支付能力原则

Ability-to-pay principle (of taxation). The principle that one's tax burden should depend upon the ability to pay as measured by income or wealth. This principle does not specify *how much* more those who are better off should pay.

（国际贸易中的）绝对优势

Absolute advantage (in international trade). The ability of Country A to produce a commodity more efficiently (i.e., with greater output per unit of input) than Country B. Possession of such an absolute advantage does not necessarily mean that A can export this commodity to B successfully. Country B may still have the comparative advantage.

实际预算、周期性预算和结构性预算

Actual, cyclical, and structural budget. The *actual budget* deficit or surplus is the amount recorded in a given year. This is composed of the *structural budget,* which calculates what government revenues, expenditures, and deficits would be if the economy were operating at potential output, and the *cyclical budget,* which measures the effect of the business cycle on the budget.

适应性预期

Adaptive expectations. See **expectations.**

逆向选择

Adverse selection. A type of market failure in which those people with the highest risk are the most likely to buy insurance. More broadly, adverse selection encompasses situations in which sellers and buyers have different information about a product, such as in the market for used cars.

总需求

Aggregate demand. Total planned or desired spending in the economy during a given period. It is determined by the aggregate price level and influenced by domestic investment, net exports, government spending, the consumption function, and the money supply.

总需求曲线（*AD*）

Aggregate demand (*AD*) curve. The curve showing the relationship between the quantity of goods and services that people are willing to buy and the aggregate price level, other things equal. As with any demand curve, important variables lie behind the aggregate demand curve, e.g., government spending, exports, and the money supply.

总供给

Aggregate supply. The total value of goods and services that firms would willingly produce in a given time period. Aggregate supply is a function of available inputs, technology, and the price level.

总供给曲线（*AS*）

Aggregate supply (*AS*) curve. The curve showing the relationship between the output firms would willingly supply and the aggregate price level, other things equal. The *AS* curve tends to be vertical at potential output in the very long run but may be upward-sloping in the short run.

配置效率

Allocative efficiency. See **Pareto efficiency.**

（通货）升值

Appreciation (of a currency). See **depreciation** (of a currency).

可分拨的

Appropriable. Term applied to resources for which the owner can capture the full economic value. In a well-functioning competitive market, appropriable resources are priced and allocated efficiently. Also refer to **inappropriable.**

套　利

Arbitrage. The purchase of a good or asset in one market for immediate resale in another market in order to profit from a price discrepancy. Arbitrage is an important force in eliminating price discrepancies, thereby making markets function more efficiently.

---

[1] Words in bold type within definitions appear as separate entries in the glossary. For a more detailed discussion of particular terms, the text will provide a useful starting point. More complete discussions are contained in Douglas Greenwald, ed., *The McGraw-Hill Encyclopedia of Economics* (McGraw-Hill, New York, 1994), and David W. Pearce, *The MIT Dictionary of Modern Economics*, 4th ed. (Macmillan, London, 1992). For a comprehensive encyclopedia, see Steven N. Durlauf and Lawrence E. Blume, *The New Palgrave Dictionary of Economics,* 8 vols. (Macmillan, London, 2008). A reasonably accurate online dictionary by *The Economist* is at *www.economist.com/research/economics/.*

资　产
Asset. A physical property or intangible right that has economic value. Important examples are plant, equipment, land, patents, copyrights, and financial instruments such as money or bonds.

信息不对称
Asymmetric information. A situation where one party to a transaction has better information than the other party. This often leads to a market failure or even to no market at all.

自动（或内在）稳定器
Automatic (or built-in) stabilizers. The property of a government tax and spending system that cushions income changes in the private sector. Examples include unemployment compensation and progressive income taxes.

平均成本
Average cost. Refer to **cost, average.**

长期平均成本曲线（*LRAC*或*LAC*）
Average cost curve, long-run (*LRAC*, or *LAC*). The graph of the minimum average cost of producing a commodity for each level of output, assuming that technology and input prices are given but that the producer is free to choose the optimal size of plants.

短期平均成本曲线（*SRAC*或*SAC*）
Average cost curve, short-run (*SRAC*, or *SAC*). The graph of the minimum average cost of producing a commodity for each level of output, using the given state of technology, input prices, and existing plant.

平均固定成本
Average fixed cost. Refer to **cost, average fixed.**

平均产量
Average product. Total product or output divided by the quantity of one of the inputs. Hence, the average product of labor is defined as total product divided by the amount of labor input, and similarly for other inputs.

平均收入
Average revenue. Total revenue divided by total number of units sold—i.e., revenue per unit. Average revenue is generally equal to price.

平均税率
Average tax rate. Total taxes divided by total income; also known as *effective tax rate.*

平均可变成本
Average variable cost. Refer to **cost, average variable.**

B

国际收支平衡表
Balance of international payments. A statement showing all of a nation's transactions with the rest of the world for a given period. It includes purchases and sales of goods and services, gifts, government transactions, and capital movements.

贸易余额
Balance of trade. The part of a nation's balance of payments that deals with imports or exports of *goods,* including such items as oil, capital goods, and automobiles. When services and other current items are included, this measures the *balance on current account.* In balance-of-payments accounting, the current account is financed by the *financial account.*

经常账户余额
Balance on current account. See **balance of trade.**

资产负债表
Balance sheet. A statement of the financial position of an entity (person, firm, government) as of a given date, listing **assets** in one column and **liabilities** plus **net worth** in the other. Each item is listed at its actual or estimated money value. Totals of the two columns must balance because net worth is defined as assets minus liabilities.

平衡预算
Balanced budget. Refer to **budget, balanced.**

商业银行
Bank, commercial. A financial intermediary whose prime distinguishing feature is that it accepts checkable deposits. All financial institutions that hold savings and checkable deposits are called depository institutions.

银行货币
Bank money. Money created by banks, particularly the checking accounts (part of M_1) that are generated by a multiple expansion of bank reserves.

银行准备金
Bank reserves. Refer to **reserves, bank.**

进入壁垒
Barriers to entry. Factors that impede entry into a market and thereby reduce the amount of competition or the number of producers in an industry. Important examples are legal barriers, regulation, and product differentiation.

以物易物
Barter. The direct exchange of one good for another without using anything as money or as a medium of exchange.

（税收的）收益原则
Benefit principle (of taxation). The principle that people should be taxed in proportion to the benefits they receive from government programs.

债　券
Bond. An interest-bearing certificate issued by a government or corporation, promising to repay a sum of money (the principal) plus interest at a specified date in the future.

（宏观经济学中的）盈亏平衡点
Break-even point (in macroeconomics). For an individual, family, or community, that level of income at which 100 percent is spent on consumption (i.e., the point where there is neither saving nor dissaving). Positive saving begins at higher income levels.

广义货币 (M_2)
Broad money (M_2). A measure of the **money supply** that includes transactions money (or M_1) as well as savings accounts in banks and similar assets that are very close substitutes for transactions money.

预　算
Budget. An account, usually for a year, of planned expenditures and expected receipts. For a government, the receipts are tax revenues. See also **actual, cyclical,** and **structural budget.**

预算平衡
Budget, balanced. A budget in which total expenditures just equal total receipts (excluding any receipts from borrowing).

预算约束
Budget constraint. See **budget line.**

预算赤字
Budget deficit. For a government, the excess of total expenditures over total receipts, with borrowing not included among receipts. This difference (the deficit) is ordinarily financed by borrowing.

预算线
Budget line. A line indicating the combination of commodities that a consumer can buy with a given income at a given set of prices. Also sometimes called the *budget constraint.*

预算盈余
Budget surplus. Excess of government revenues over government spending; the opposite of *budget deficit.*

商业周期
Business cycles. Fluctuations in total national output, income, and employment, usually lasting for a period of 2 to 10 years, marked by widespread and simultaneous expansion or contraction in many sectors of the economy.

C

消费+投资+政府支出+净出口
$C + I + G + NX$ schedule. A schedule showing the planned or desired levels of aggregate demand for each level of GDP, or the graph on which this schedule is depicted. The schedule includes consumption (C), investment (I), government spending on goods and services (G), and net exports (NX).

资本（资本品，资本设备）
Capital (capital goods, capital equipment). (1) In economic theory, one of the triad of productive inputs (land, labor, and capital). Capital consists of durable produced items that are in turn used in production. (2) In accounting and finance, "capital" means the total amount of money subscribed by the shareholder-owners of a corporation, in return for which they receive shares of the company's stock.

资本消耗补偿
Capital consumption allowance. See **depreciation** (of an asset).

资本深化
Capital deepening. In economic-growth theory, an increase in the capital-labor ratio. (Contrast with **capital widening.**)

资本利得
Capital gains. The rise in value of a capital asset, such as land or common stocks, the gain being the difference between the sales price and the purchase price of the asset.

资本市场（也称金融市场）
Capital markets (also **financial markets**). Markets in which financial resources (money, bonds, stocks) are traded. These, along with **financial intermediaries,** are institutions through which saving in the economy is transferred to investors.

资本－产出比率
Capital-output ratio. In economic-growth theory, the ratio of the total capital stock to annual GDP.

资本广化
Capital widening. A rate of growth in real capital stock just equal to the growth of the labor force (or of the population), so the ratio between total capital and total labor remains unchanged. (Contrast with **capital deepening.**)

资本主义
Capitalism. An economic system in which most property (land and capital) is privately owned. In such an economy, private markets are the primary vehicles used to allocate resources and generate incomes.

基数效用
Cardinal utility. See **ordinal utility.**

卡特尔
Cartel. An organization of independent firms producing similar products that work together to raise prices and restrict output. Cartels are illegal under U.S. antitrust laws.

中央银行
Central bank. A government-established agency (in the United States, the Federal Reserve System) responsible for controlling the nation's money supply and credit conditions and for supervising the financial system, especially commercial banks and other depository institutions.

需求变化与需求量的变化
Change in demand vs. change in quantity demanded. A change in the quantity buyers want to purchase, prompted by any reason other than a change in price (e.g., increase in income, change in tastes), is a *change in demand.* In graphical terms, it is a shift of the demand curve. If, in contrast, the decision to buy more or less is prompted by a change in the good's price, then it is a *change in quantity demanded.* In graphical terms, a change in quantity demanded is a movement along an unchanging demand curve.

供给变化与供给量的变化
Change in supply vs. change in quantity supplied. This distinction for supply is the same as that for demand, so see **change in demand vs. change in quantity demanded.**

支票账户（或支票存款，银行货币）
Checking accounts (also **checkable deposits** and **bank money**). A deposit in a commercial bank or other financial intermediary upon which checks can be written and which is therefore transactions money (or $\boldsymbol{M}_1$). Checkable deposits are about half of M_1.

芝加哥经济学派
Chicago School of Economics. A group of economists (among whom Henry Simons, F. A. von Hayek, and Milton Friedman have been the most prominent) who believe that competitive markets free of government intervention will lead to the most efficient operation of the economy.

古典理论
Classical approach. See **classical economics.**

古典经济学
Classical economics. The predominant school of economic thought prior to the appearance of Keynes's work; founded by Adam Smith in 1776. Other major figures who followed Smith include David Ricardo, Thomas Malthus, and John Stuart Mill. By and large, this school believed that economic laws (particularly individual self-interest and competition) determine prices and factor rewards and that the price system is the best possible device for resource allocation.

古典宏观经济学
Classical macroeconomics. See **classical theories**.

（宏观经济学中的）古典理论
Classical theories (in **macroeconomics**). Theories emphasizing the self-correcting forces in the economy. In the classical approach, there is generally full employment, and policies to stimulate aggregate demand have no impact upon output.

市场出清
Clearing market. A market in which prices are sufficiently flexible to equilibrate supply and demand very quickly. In markets that clear, there is no rationing, unemployed resources, or excess demand or supply. In practice, this is thought to apply to many commodity and financial markets but not to labor or many product markets.

封闭经济
Closed economy. See **open economy.**

集体协议
Collective bargaining. The process of negotiations between a group of workers (usually a union) and their employer. Such bargaining leads to an agreement about wages, fringe benefits, and working conditions.

共 谋
Collusion. An agreement between different firms to cooperate by raising prices, dividing markets, or otherwise restraining competition.

勾结寡头
Collusive oligopoly. A market structure in which a small number of firms (i.e., a few oligopolists) collude and jointly make their decisions. When they succeed in maximizing their joint profits, the price and quantity in the market closely approach those prevailing under monopoly.

指令经济
Command economy. A mode of economic organization in which the key economic functions—*what, how,* and *for whom* — are principally determined by government directive. Sometimes called a *centrally planned economy.*

商品货币
Commodity money. Money with **intrinsic value;** also, the use of some commodity (cattle, beads, etc.) as money.

共同货币
Common currency. A situation where several countries form a monetary union with a single currency and a unified central bank; e.g., the European Monetary Union (EMU), which introduced the Euro in 1999.

普通股票
Common stock. The financial instrument representing ownership and, generally, voting rights in a corporation. A certain share of a company's stock gives the owner title to that fraction of the votes, net earnings, and assets of the corporation.

共产主义
Communism. A communist economic system (also called *Soviet-style central planning*) is one in which the state owns and controls the means of production, particularly industrial capital. Such economies are also characterized by extensive central planning, with the state setting many prices, output levels, and other important economic variables.

（国际贸易中的）比较优势
Comparative advantage (in international trade). The law of comparative advantage says that a nation should specialize in producing and exporting those commodities which it can produce at *relatively* lower cost and that it should import those goods for which it is a *relatively* high-cost producer. Thus it is a comparative advantage, not an absolute advantage, that should dictate trade patterns.

补偿性差异
Compensating differentials. Differences in wage rates among jobs that serve to offset or compensate for the nonmonetary differences of the jobs. For example, unpleasant jobs that require isolation for many months in Alaska pay wages much higher than those for similar jobs nearer to civilization.

不完全竞争
Competition, imperfect. Term applied to markets in which perfect competition does not hold because at least one seller (or buyer) is large enough to affect the market price and therefore faces a downward-sloping demand (or supply) curve. Imperfect competition refers to any kind of market imperfection—pure **monopoly, oligopoly,** or **monopolistic competition.**

完全竞争
Competition, perfect. Term applied to markets in which no firm or consumer is large enough to affect the market price. This situation arises where (1) the number of sellers and buyers is very large and (2) the products offered by sellers are homogeneous (or indistinguishable). Under such conditions, each firm faces a horizontal (or perfectly elastic) demand curve.

竞争均衡
Competitive equilibrium. The balancing of supply and demand in a market or economy characterized by **perfect competition.** Because perfectly competitive sellers and buyers individually have no power to influence the market, price will move to the point at which it equals both marginal cost and marginal utility.

竞争性市场
Competitive market. See **competition, perfect.**

互补品
Complements. Two goods which "go together" in the eyes of consumers (e.g., left shoes and right shoes). Goods are *substitutes* when they compete with each other (as do gloves and mittens).

复　利
Compound interest. Interest computed on the accrued total of interest and principal. For example, suppose $100 (the principal) is deposited in an account earning 10 percent interest compounded annually. At the end of year 1, interest of $10 is earned. At the end of year 2, the interest payment is $11, $10 on the original principal and $1 on the interest—and so on in future years.

集中率，集中度
Concentration ratio. The percentage of an industry's total output accounted for by the largest firms. A typical measure is the *four-firm concentration ratio,* which is the fraction of output accounted for by the four largest firms.

规模报酬不变
Constant returns to scale. See **returns to scale.**

消费者价格指数（CPI）
Consumer price index (CPI). A price index that measures the cost of a fixed basket of consumer goods in which the weight assigned to each commodity is the share of expenditures on that commodity in a base year.

消费者剩余
Consumer surplus. The difference between the amount that a consumer would be willing to pay for a commodity and the amount actually paid. This difference arises because the marginal utilities (in dollar terms) of all but the last unit exceed the price. Under certain conditions, the money value of consumer surplus can be measured (using a demand curve diagram) as the area under the demand curve but above the price line.

消　费
Consumption. In macroeconomics, the total spending, by individuals or a nation, on consumer goods during a given period. Strictly speaking, consumption should apply only to those goods totally used, enjoyed, or "eaten up" within that period. In practice, consumption expenditures include all consumer goods bought, many of which last well beyond the period in question—e.g., furniture, clothing, and automobiles.

消费函数
Consumption function. A schedule relating total consumption to personal **disposable income** (*DI*). Total wealth and other variables are also frequently assumed to influence consumption.

消费可能线
Consumption-possibility line. See **budget line.**

合作性均衡
Cooperative equilibrium. In game theory, an outcome in which the parties act in unison to find strategies that will optimize their joint payoffs.

核心通货膨胀率
Core rate of inflation. Inflation after removing the influence of volatile elements like food and energy prices. This concept is often used by central banks in inflation targeting.

公司所得税
Corporate income tax. A tax levied on the annual net income of a corporation.

公　司
Corporation. The dominant form of business organization in modern capitalist economies. A corporation is a firm owned by individuals or other corporations. It has the same rights to buy, sell, and make contracts as a person would have. It is legally separate from those who own it and has **limited liability.**

相　关
Correlation. The degree to which two variables are systematically associated with each other.

平均成本
Cost, average. Total cost (refer to **cost, total**) divided by the number of units produced.

平均固定成本
Cost, average fixed. Fixed cost (refer to **cost, fixed**) divided by the number of units produced.

平均可变成本
Cost, average variable. Variable cost (refer to **cost, variable**) divided by the number of units produced.

固定成本
Cost, fixed. The cost a firm would incur even if its output for the period in question were zero. Total fixed cost is made up of such individual contractual costs as interest payments, mortgage payments, and directors' fees.

边际成本
Cost, marginal. The extra cost (or the increase in total cost) required to produce 1 extra unit of output (or the reduction in total cost from producing 1 unit less).

最低成本
Cost, minimum. The lowest attainable cost per unit (whether average, variable, or marginal). Every point on an average cost curve is a minimum in the sense that it is the best the firm can do with respect to cost for the output which that point represents. Minimum average cost is the lowest point, or points, on that curve.

总成本
Cost, total. The minimum attainable total cost, given a particular level of technology and set of input prices. *Short-run total cost* takes existing plant and other fixed costs as given. *Long-run total cost* is the cost that would be incurred if the firm had complete flexibility with respect to all inputs and decisions.

可变成本
Cost, variable. A cost that varies with the level of output, such as raw-material, labor, and fuel costs. Variable costs equal total cost minus fixed cost.

成本推动型通货膨胀
Cost-push inflation. See **supply-shock inflation.**

信　贷
Credit. (1) In monetary theory, the use of someone else's funds in exchange for a promise to pay (usually with interest) at a later date. The major examples are short-term loans from a bank, credit extended by suppliers, and commercial paper. (2) In balance-of-payments accounting, an item such as exports that earns a country foreign currency.

需求的交叉弹性
Cross elasticity of demand. A measure of the influence of a change in one good's price on the demand for another good. More precisely, the cross elasticity of demand equals the percentage change in demand for good A when the price of good B changes by 1 percent, assuming other variables are held constant.

通　货
Currency. Coins and paper money.

通货升值（或贬值）
Currency appreciation (or **depreciation).** See **depreciation** (of a currency).

货币委员会
Currency board. A monetary institution operating like a central bank for a country that issues only currency that is fully backed by assets denominated in a key foreign currency, often the U.S. dollar.

经常账户
Current account. See **balance of trade.**

周期性预算
Cyclical budget. See **actual, cyclical, and structural budget.**

周期性失业
Cyclical unemployment. See **frictional unemployment.**

D

净损失
Deadweight loss. The loss in real income or consumer and producer surplus that arises because of monopoly, tariffs and quotas, taxes, or other distortions. For example, when a monopolist raises its price, the loss in consumer satisfaction is more than the gain in the monopolist's revenue—the difference being the deadweight loss to society due to monopoly.

借　方
Debit. (1) An accounting term signifying an increase in assets or decrease in liabilities. (2) In balance-of-payments accounting, a debit is an item such as imports that reduces a country's stock of foreign currencies.

规模报酬递减
Decreasing returns to scale. See **returns to scale.**

赤字性支出
Deficit spending. Government's expenditures on goods and services and transfer payments in excess of its receipts from taxation and other revenue sources. The difference must be financed by borrowing from the public.

（经济数据）紧缩
Deflating (of economic data). The process of converting "nominal" or current-dollar variables into "real" terms. This is accomplished by dividing current-dollar variables by a **price index.**

通货紧缩
Deflation. A fall in the general level of prices.

需求曲线（或需求表）
Demand curve (or **demand schedule).** A schedule or curve showing the quantity of a good that buyers would purchase at each price, other things equal. Normally a demand curve has price on the vertical or *Y* axis and quantity demanded on the horizontal or *X* axis. Also see **change in demand vs. change in quantity demanded.**

货币需求
Demand for money. A summary term used by economists to explain why individuals and businesses hold money balances. The major motivations for holding money are (1) *transactions demand,* signifying that people need money to purchase things, and (2) *asset demand,* relating to the desire to hold a very liquid, risk-free asset.

需求拉动型通货膨胀
Demand-pull inflation. Price inflation caused by an excess demand for goods in general, caused, e.g., by a major increase in aggregate demand. Often contrasted with **supply-shock inflation.**

人口统计学
Demography. The study of the behavior of a population.

（资产）折旧
Depreciation (of an asset). A decline in the value of an asset. In both business and national accounts, depreciation is the dollar estimate of the extent to which capital has been "used up" or worn out over the period in question. Also termed *capital consumption allowance* in national-income accounting.

（通货）贬值
Depreciation (of a currency). A nation's currency is said to depreciate when it declines relative to other currencies. For example, if the foreign exchange rate of the dollar falls from 200 to 100 Japanese Yen per U.S. dollar, the dollar's value has fallen, and the dollar has undergone a depreciation. The opposite of a depreciation is an *appreciation,* which occurs when the foreign exchange rate of a currency rises.

萧　条
Depression. A prolonged period characterized by high unemployment, low output and investment, depressed business confidence, falling prices, and widespread business failures. A milder form of business downturn is a **recession,** which has many of the features of a depression to a lesser extent.

派生需求
Derived demand. The demand for a factor of production that results (is "derived") from the demand for the final good to which it contributes. Thus the demand for tires is derived from the demand for automobile transportation.

货币降值
Devaluation. A decrease in the official price of a nation's currency, usually expressed in the currency of another nations (such as the U.S. dollar) or in terms of gold (in a gold standard). The opposite of devaluation is *revaluation,* which occurs when a nation raises its official foreign exchange rate relative to another currency.

发展中国家
Developing country. A country with a per capita income far below that of "developed" nations (the latter usually includes most nations of North America and Western Europe). Same as *less developed country.*

差异化产品
Differentiated products. Products which compete with each other and are close substitutes but are not identical. Differences may be manifest in the product's function, appearance, location, quality, or other attributes.

边际效用递减规律
Diminishing marginal utility, law of. The law which says that as more and more of any one commodity is consumed, its marginal utility declines.

收益递减规律
Diminishing returns, law of. A law stating that the additional output from successive increases of one input will eventually diminish when other inputs are held constant. Technically, the law is equivalent to saying that the marginal product of the varying input declines after a point.

直接税
Direct taxes. Taxes levied directly on individuals or firms, including taxes on income, labor earnings, and profits. Direct taxes contrast with *indirect taxes,* which are levied on goods and services and thus only indirectly on people, such as sales taxes and taxes on property, alcohol, imports, and gasoline.

贴现率
Discount rate. (1) The interest rate charged by a Federal Reserve Bank (the central bank) on a loan that it makes to a commercial bank. (2) The rate used to calculate the present value of some asset.

（未来收入）折现
Discounting (of future income). The process of converting future income into an equivalent present value. This process takes a future dollar amount and reduces it by a discount factor that reflects the appropriate interest rate. For example, if someone promises you \$121 in 2 years, and the appropriate interest rate or discount rate is 10 percent per year, then we can calculate the present value by discounting the \$121 by a discount factor of $(1.10)^2$. The rate at which future incomes are discounted is called the **discount rate.**

歧　视
Discrimination. Differences in earnings that arise because of personal characteristics that are unrelated to job performance, especially those related to gender, race, ethnicity, sexual orientation, or religion.

非均衡
Disequilibrium. The state in which an economy is not in **equilibrium.** This may arise when shocks (to income or prices) have shifted demand or supply schedules but the market price (or quantity) has not yet adjusted fully. In macroeconomics, unemployment is often thought to stem from market disequilibria.

反通货膨胀
Disinflation. The process of reducing a high inflation rate. For example, the deep recession of 1980–1983 led to a sharp disinflation over that period.

可支配收入（*DI*）
Disposable income (*DI*). Roughly, take-home pay, or that part of the total national income that is available to households for consumption or saving. More precisely, it is equal to GDP less all taxes, business saving, and depreciation plus government and other transfer payments and government interest payments.

个人可支配收入
Disposable personal income. Same as **disposable income.**

负储蓄
Dissaving. Negative saving; spending more on consumption goods during a period than the disposable income available for that period (the difference being financed by borrowing or drawing on past savings).

分　配
Distribution. In economics, the manner in which total output and income is distributed among individuals or factors (e.g., the distribution of income between labor and capital).

分配理论
Distribution theory. See **theory of income distribution.**

劳动分工
Division of labor. A method of organizing production whereby each worker specializes in part of the productive process. Specialization of labor yields higher total output because labor can become more skilled at a particular task and because specialized machinery can be introduced to perform more carefully defined subtasks.

占优均衡
Dominant equilibrium. See **dominant strategy.**

占优策略
Dominant strategy. In game theory, a situation where one player has a best strategy no matter what strategy the other player follows. When all players have a dominant strategy, we say that the outcome is a *dominant equilibrium.*

需求向下倾斜规律
Downward-sloping demand, law of. The rule which says that when the price of some commodity falls, consumers will purchase more of that good, other things held equal.

双寡头垄断的市场
Duopoly. A market structure in which there are only two sellers. (Compare with **oligopoly.**)

E

经济计量学
Econometrics. The branch of economics that uses the methods of statistics to measure and estimate quantitative economic relationships.

经济效率
Economic efficiency. See **efficiency.**

经济品
Economic good. A good that is scarce relative to the total amount of it that is desired. It must therefore be rationed, usually by charging a positive price.

经济增长
Economic growth. An increase in the total output of a nation over time. Economic growth is usually measured as the annual rate of increase in a nation's real GDP (or real potential GDP).

经济管制
Economic regulation. See **regulation.**

经济租金
Economic rent. Refer to **rent, economic.**

经济剩余
Economic surplus. A term denoting the excess in total satisfaction or utility over the costs of production; equals the sum of consumer surplus (the excess of consumer satisfaction over total value of purchases) and producer surplus (the excess of producer revenues over costs).

经济学
Economics. The study of how societies use scarce resources to produce valuable commodities and distribute them among different people.

信息经济学
Economics of information. Analysis of economic situations that involve information as a commodity. Because information is costly to produce but cheap to reproduce, market failures are common in markets for informational goods and services such as invention, publishing, and software.

规模经济
Economies of scale. Increases in productivity, or decreases in average cost of production, that arise from increasing all the factors of production in the same proportion.

有效税率
Effective tax rate. Total taxes paid as a percentage of the total income or other tax base; also known as *average tax rate.*

效　率
Efficiency. Absence of waste, or the use of economic resources that produces the maximum level of satisfaction possible with the given inputs and technology. A shorthand expression for **Pareto efficiency.**

有效工资理论
Efficiency-wage theory. According to this theory, higher wages lead to higher productivity. This occurs because with higher wages workers are healthier, have higher morale, and have lower turnover.

有效的金融市场
Efficient financial market. A financial market displaying the characteristics of an **efficient market.**

有效市场（或有效市场理论）
Efficient market (also **efficient-market theory**). A market or theory in which all new information is quickly absorbed by market participants and becomes immediately incorporated into market prices. In economics, efficient-market theory holds that all currently available information is already incorporated into the price of common stocks (or other assets).

弹 性
Elasticity. A term widely used in economics to denote the responsiveness of one variable to changes in another. Thus the elasticity of X with respect to Y means the percentage change in X for every 1 percent change in Y. For especially important examples, see **price elasticity of demand** and **price elasticity of supply.**

就 业
Employed. According to official U.S. definitions, persons are employed if they perform any paid work or if they hold jobs but are absent because of illness, strike, or vacations.

等成本线
Equal-cost line. A line in a graph showing the various possible combinations of factor inputs that can be purchased with a given quantity of money.

等产量曲线
Equal-product curve (or **isoquant**). A line in a graph showing the various possible combinations of factor inputs which will yield a given quantity of output.

交易方程式
Equation of exchange. A definitional equation which states that $MVP \equiv PQ$, or the money stock times velocity of money equals the price level times output. This equation forms the core of **monetarism.**

均 衡
Equilibrium. The state in which an economic entity is at rest or in which the forces operating on the entity are in balance so that there is no tendency for change.

（厂商）均衡
Equilibrium (for a business firm). That position or level of output in which the firm is maximizing its profit, subject to any constraints it may face, and therefore has no incentive to change its output or price level. In the standard theory of the firm, this means that the firm has chosen an output at which marginal revenue is just equal to marginal cost.

（单个消费者的）均衡
Equilibrium (for the individual consumer). That position in which the consumer is maximizing utility, i.e., has chosen the bundle of goods which, given income and prices, best satisfies the consumer's wants.

竞争均衡
Equilibrium, competitive. Refer to **competitive equilibrium.**

一般均衡
Equilibrium, general. Refer to **general-equilibrium analysis.**

宏观经济均衡
Equilibrium, macroeconomic. A GDP level at which intended aggregate demand equals intended aggregate supply. At the equilibrium, desired consumption (C), government expenditures (G), investment (I), and net exports (X) just equal the quantity that businesses wish to sell at the going price level.

均衡失业
Equilibrium unemployment. Equilibrium unemployment arises when people are voluntarily unemployed rather than unemployed because of a failure of labor markets to clear. An example is the frictional unemployed that occurs when people move voluntarily from job to job or in and out of the labor force.

等边际法则
Equimarginal principle. A principle for deciding the allocation of income among different consumption goods. Under this principle, a consumer's utility is maximized by choosing the consumption bundle such that the marginal utility per dollar spent is equal for all goods.

汇 率
Exchange rate. See **foreign exchange rate.**

汇率制度
Exchange-rate system. The set of rules, arrangements, and institutions under which payments are made among nations. Historically, the most important exchange-rate systems have been the gold exchange standard, the Bretton Woods system, and today's flexible-exchange-rate system.

消费税和销售税
Excise tax vs. sales tax. An excise tax is one levied on the purchase of a specific commodity or group of commodities (e.g., alcohol or tobacco). A *sales tax* is one levied on all commodities with only a few specific exclusions (e.g., all purchases except food).

排他原则
Exclusion principle. A criterion by which public goods are distinguished from private goods. When a producer sells a commodity to person A and can easily exclude B, C, D, etc., from enjoying the benefits of the commodity, the exclusion principle holds and the good is a private good. If, as in public health or national defense, people cannot easily be excluded from enjoying the benefits of the good's production, then the good has public-good characteristics.

外生变量和引致变量
Exogenous vs. induced variables. Exogenous variables are those determined by conditions outside the economy. They are contrasted with *induced variables,* which are determined by the internal workings of the economic system. Changes in the weather are exogenous; changes in consumption are often induced by changes in income.

预　期
Expectations. Views or beliefs about uncertain variables (such as future interest rates, prices, or tax rates). Expectations are said to be *rational* if they are not systematically wrong (or "biased") and use all available information. Expectations are said to be *adaptive* if people form their expectations on the basis of past behavior.

预期的通货膨胀率
Expected rate of inflation. A process of steady inflation that occurs when inflation is expected to persist and the ongoing rate of inflation is built into contracts and people's expectations.

支出乘数
Expenditure multiplier. See **multiplier.**

出　口
Exports. Goods or services that are produced in the home country and sold to another country. These include merchandise trade (like cars), services (like transportation), and interest on loans and investments. *Imports* are simply flows in the opposite direction—into the home country from another country.

外部不经济
External diseconomies. Situations in which production or consumption imposes uncompensated costs on other parties. Steel factories that emit smoke and sulfurous fumes harm local property and public health, yet the injured parties are not paid for the damage. The pollution is an external diseconomy.

外部经济
External economies. Situations in which production or consumption yields positive benefits to others without those others paying. A firm that hires a security guard scares thieves from the neighborhood, thus providing external security services. Together with external diseconomies, these are often referred to as **externalities.**

外部变量
External variables. Same as **exogenous variables.**

外部性
Externalities. Activities that affect others for better or worse, without those others paying or being compensated for the activity. Externalities exist when private costs or benefits do not equal social costs or benefits. The two major species are **external economies** and **external diseconomies.**

F

生产要素
Factors of production. Productive inputs, such as labor, land, and capital; the resources needed to produce goods and services. Also called *inputs.*

合成谬误
Fallacy of composition. The fallacy of assuming that what holds for individuals also holds for the group or the entire system.

联邦基金利率
Federal funds rate. The interest rate that banks pay each other for the overnight use of bank reserves.

联邦储备系统
Federal Reserve System. The **central bank** of the United States; consists of the Board of Governors and 12 regional Federal Reserve Banks.

法定货币
Fiat money. Money, like today's paper currency, without **intrinsic value** but decreed (by fiat) to be legal tender by the government. Fiat money is accepted only as long as people have confidence that it will be accepted.

最终产品
Final good. A good that is produced for final use and not for resale or further manufacture. (Compare with **intermediate goods.**)

融　资
Finance. The process by which economic agents borrow from and lend to other agents in order to save and spend.

金融账户，资本账户
Financial account. See **balance of trade.**

金融资产
Financial assets. Monetary claims or obligations by one party against another party. Examples are bonds, mortgages, bank loans, and equities.

金融经济学
Financial economics. That branch of economics which analyzes how rational investors should invest their funds to attain their objectives in the best possible manner.

金融中介
Financial intermediaries. Institutions which provide financial services and products. These include depository institutions (such as commercial or savings banks) and nondepository institutions (such as money market mutual funds, brokerage houses, insurance companies, or pension funds).

金融市场
Financial markets. Markets whose products and services consist of financial instruments like stocks and bonds.

金融体系
Financial system. The markets, firms, and other institutions which carry out the financial decisions of households, businesses, governments, and the rest of the world. Important parts of the financial system include the money market, markets for fixed-interest assets like bonds or mortgages, stock markets for the ownership of firms, and foreign exchange markets which trade the monies of different countries.

厂商（企业）
Firm (business firm). The basic, private producing unit in an economy. It hires labor, rents or owns capital and land,

and buys other inputs in order to make and sell goods and services.

财政—货币政策组合
Fiscal-monetary mix. The combination of fiscal and monetary policies used to influence macroeconomic activity. A tight monetary–loose fiscal policy will tend to encourage consumption and retard investment, while an easy monetary–tight fiscal policy will have the opposite effect.

财政政策
Fiscal policy. A government's program with respect to (1) the purchase of goods and services and spending on transfer payments and (2) the amount and type of taxes.

固定成本
Fixed cost. Refer to **cost, fixed.**

固定汇率
Fixed exchange rate. See **foreign exchange rate.**

弹性汇率制
Flexible exchange rates. A system of foreign exchange rates among countries wherein the exchange rates are predominantly determined by private market forces (i.e., by supply and demand) without governments' setting and maintaining a particular pattern of exchange rates; also sometimes called *floating exchange rates.* When the government refrains from any intervention in exchange markets, the system is called a pure flexible-exchange-rate system.

浮动汇率制
Floating exchange rates. See **flexible exchange rates.**

资金流量
Flow of funds. The account which traces how money and other financial instruments flow through the economy.

流量与存量
Flow vs. stock. A *flow* variable is one that has a time dimension or flows over time (like the flow through a stream). A *stock* variable is one that measures a quantity at a point of time (like the water in a lake). Income represents dollars per year and is thus a flow. Wealth as of December 2005 is a stock.

外　汇
Foreign exchange. Currency (or other financial instruments) of different countries that allow one country to settle amounts owed to other countries.

外汇市场
Foreign exchange market. The market in which currencies of different countries are traded.

外汇汇率
Foreign exchange rate. The rate, or price, at which one country's currency is exchanged for the currency of another country. For example, if you can buy 10 Mexican pesos for 1 U.S. dollar, then the exchange rate for the peso is 10. A country has a *fixed exchange rate* if it pegs its currency at a given exchange rate and stands ready to defend that rate. Exchange rates which are determined by market supply and demand are called **flexible exchange rates.**

四企业集中率，四企业集中度
Four-firm concentration ratio. See **concentration ratio.**

部分准备金银行制度
Fractional-reserve banking. A regulation in modern banking systems whereby financial institutions are legally required to keep a specified fraction of their deposits in the form of deposits with the central bank (or in vault cash).

免费品
Free goods. Those goods that are not **economic goods.** Like air or seawater, they exist in such large quantities that they need not be rationed out among those wishing to use them. Thus, their market price is zero.

自由贸易
Free trade. A policy whereby the government does not intervene in trading between nations by tariffs, quotas, or other means.

摩擦性失业
Frictional unemployment. Temporary unemployment caused by changes in individual markets. It takes time, for example, for new workers to search among different job possibilities; even experienced workers often spend a minimum period of unemployed time moving from one job to another. Frictional is thus distinct from *cyclical unemployment,* which results from a low level of aggregate demand in the context of sticky wages and prices.

充分就业
Full employment. A term that is used in many senses. Historically, it was taken to be that level of employment at which no (or minimal) involuntary unemployment exists. Today, economists rely upon the concept of the **nonaccelerating inflation rate of unemployment** (**NAIRU**) to indicate the highest sustainable level of employment over the long run.

G

贸易利得
Gains from trade. The aggregate increase in welfare accruing from voluntary exchange; equal to the sum of consumer surplus and gains in producer profits.

急剧的通货膨胀
Galloping inflation. See **inflation.**

博弈论
Game theory. An analysis of situations involving two or more decision makers with at least partially conflicting interests. It can be applied to the interaction of oligopolistic markets as well as to bargaining situations such as strikes or to conflicts such as games and war.

GDP紧缩指数
GDP deflator. The "price" of GDP, i.e., the price index that measures the average price of the components in GDP relative to a base year.

一般均衡分析
General-equilibrium analysis. Analysis of the equilibrium state for the economy as a whole in which the markets for all goods and services are simultaneously in equilibrium. By contrast, **partial-equilibrium analysis** concerns the equilibrium in a single market.

国民生产总值
GNP. See **gross national product.**

金本位制
Gold standard. A system under which a nation (1) declares its currency unit to be equivalent to some fixed weight of gold, (2) holds gold reserves against its money, and (3) will buy or sell gold freely at the price so proclaimed, with no restrictions on the export or import of gold.

政府债务
Government debt. The total of government obligations in the form of bonds and shorter-term borrowings. Government debt held by the public excludes bonds held by quasi-governmental agencies such as the central bank.

政府支出乘数
Government expenditure multiplier. The increase in GDP resulting from an increase of $1 in government purchases.

名义国内生产总值（或名义GDP）
Gross domestic product, nominal (or **nominal GDP**). The value, at current market prices, of the total final output produced inside a country during a given year.

实际国内生产总值（或实际GDP）
Gross domestic product, real (or **real GDP**). The quantity of goods and services produced in a nation during a year. Real GDP takes nominal GDP and corrects for price increases.

实际国民生产总值（或实际GNP）
Gross national product, real (or **real GNP**). Nominal GNP corrected for inflation; i.e., real GNP equals nominal GNP divided by the GNP deflator. This was the central accounting concept in earlier times but has been replaced by **gross domestic product.**

增长核算
Growth accounting. A technique for estimating the contribution of different factors to economic growth. Using marginal productivity theory, growth accounting decomposes the growth of output into the growth in labor, land, capital, education, technical knowledge, and other miscellaneous sources.

H

套期保值
Hedging. A technique for avoiding a risk by making a counteracting transaction. For example, if a farmer produces wheat that will be harvested in the fall, the risk of price fluctuations can be offset, or hedged, by selling in the spring or summer the quantity of wheat that will be produced.

赫芬达尔—赫希曼指数
Herfindahl-Hirschman Index (HHI). A measure of market power often used in analysis of market structure. It is calculated by summing the squares of the percentage market shares of all participants in a market. Perfect competition would have an HHI of near zero, while complete monopoly has an HHI of 10,000.

高能货币
High-powered money. Same as **monetary base.**

横向公平与纵向公平
Horizontal equity vs. vertical equity. *Horizontal equity* refers to the fairness or equity in treatment of persons in similar situations; the principle of horizontal equity states that those who are essentially equal should receive equal treatment. *Vertical equity* refers to the equitable treatment of those who are in different circumstances.

横向整合
Horizontal integration. See **integration, vertical vs. horizontal.**

横向兼并
Horizontal merger. See **merger.**

人力资本
Human capital. The stock of technical knowledge and skill embodied in a nation's workforce, resulting from investments in formal education and on-the-job training.

恶性通货膨胀
Hyperinflation. See **inflation.**

I

不完全竞争
Imperfect competition. Refer to **competition, imperfect.**

不完全竞争者
Imperfect competitor. Any firm that buys or sells a good in large enough quantities to be able to affect the price of that good.

隐性成本要素
Implicit-cost elements. Costs that do not show up as explicit money costs but nevertheless should be counted as such (such as the labor cost of the owner of a small store). Sometimes called **opportunity cost,** although "opportunity cost" has a broader meaning.

进　口
Imports. See **exports.**

不可分拨性
Inappropriability. See **inappropriable.**

不可分拨的
Inappropriable. Term applied to resources for which the individual cost of use is free or less than the full social costs. These resources are characterized by the presence of externalities, and thus markets will allocate their use inefficiently from a social point of view.

归宿（或税收归宿）
Incidence (or **tax incidence).** The ultimate economic effect of a tax on the real incomes of producers or consumers (as opposed to the legal requirement for payment). Thus a sales tax may be paid by a retailer, but it is likely that the incidence falls upon the consumer. The exact incidence of a tax depends on the price elasticities of supply and demand.

收入，收益
Income. The flow of wages, interest payments, dividends, and other receipts accruing to an individual or nation during a period of time (usually a year).

（价格变动的）收入效应
Income effect (of a price change). Change in the quantity demanded of a commodity because the change in its price has the effect of changing a consumer's real income. Thus it supplements the **substitution effect** of a price change.

需求的收入弹性
Income elasticity of demand. The demand for any given good is influenced not only by the good's price but by buyers' incomes. Income elasticity measures this responsiveness. Its precise definition is percentage change in quantity demanded divided by percentage change in income. (Compare with **price elasticity of demand.**)

收益表，利润表，损益表
Income statement. A company's statement, covering a specified time period (usually a year), showing sales or revenue earned during that period, all costs properly charged against the goods sold, and the profit (net income) remaining after deduction of such costs. Also called a *profit-and-loss statement.*

个人所得税
Income tax, personal. Tax levied on the income received by individuals in the form of either wages and salaries or income from property, such as rents, dividends, or interest. In the United States, personal income tax is **progressive,** meaning that people with higher incomes pay taxes at a higher average rate than people with lower incomes.

货币的收入周转率
Income velocity of money. See **velocity of money.**

规模报酬递增
Increasing returns to scale. See **returns to scale.**

独立品
Independent goods. Goods whose demands are relatively separate from each other. More precisely, goods A and B are independent when a change in the price of good A has no effect on the quantity demanded of good B, other things equal.

指数化
Indexing (or **indexation).** A mechanism by which wages, prices, and contracts are partially or wholly adjusted to compensate for changes in the general price level.

无差异曲线
Indifference curve. A curve drawn on a graph whose two axes measure amounts of different goods consumed. Each point on one curve (indicating different combinations of the two goods) yields exactly the same level of satisfaction for a given consumer.

无差异曲线图
Indifference map. A graph showing a family of indifference curves for a consumer. In general, curves that lie farther northeast from the graph's origin represent higher levels of satisfaction.

间接税
Indirect taxes. See **direct taxes.**

引致变量
Induced variables. See **exogenous vs. induced variables.**

产　业
Industry. A group of firms producing similar or identical products.

幼稚产业
Infant industry. In foreign-trade theory, an industry that has not had sufficient time to develop the experience or expertise to exploit the economies of scale needed to compete successfully with more mature industries producing the same commodity in other countries. Infant industries are often thought to need tariffs or quotas to protect them while they develop.

低档品或劣等品
Inferior good. A good whose consumption goes down as income rises.

通货膨胀（或通货膨胀率）
Inflation (or **inflation rate).** The inflation rate is the percentage of annual increase in a general price level. *Hyperinflation* is inflation at extremely high rates (say, 1000, 1 million, or even 1 billion percent a year). *Galloping inflation* is a rate of 50 or 100 or 200 percent annually. *Moderate inflation* is a price-level rise that does not distort relative prices or incomes severely.

设定通货膨胀目标
Inflation targeting. The announcement of official target ranges for the inflation rate along with an explicit statement that low and stable inflation is the overriding goal of monetary policy. Inflation targeting in hard or soft varieties has been adopted in recent years by many industrial countries.

创　新
Innovation. A term particularly associated with Joseph Schumpeter, who meant by it (1) the bringing to market of a new and significantly different product, (2) the introduction of a new production technique, or (3) the opening up of a new market. (Contrast with **invention.**)

投　入
Inputs. Commodities or services used by firms in their production processes; also called *factors of production.*

保　险

Insurance. A system by which individuals can reduce their exposure to risk of large losses by spreading the risks among a large number of persons.

纵向一体化和横向一体化

Integration, vertical vs. horizontal. The production process is one of stages—e.g., iron ore into steel ingots, steel ingots into rolled steel sheets, rolled steel sheets into an automobile body. *Vertical integration* is the combination in a single firm of two or more different stages of this process (e.g., iron ore with steel ingots). *Horizontal integration* is the combination in a single firm of different units that operate at the same stage of production.

知识产权

Intellectual property rights. Laws governing patents, copyrights, trade secrets, electronic media, and other commodities comprised primarily of information. These laws generally provide the original creator the right to control and be compensated for reproduction of the work.

利　息

Interest. The return paid to those who lend money.

利　率

Interest rate. The price paid for borrowing money for a period of time, usually expressed as a percentage of the principal per year. Thus, if the interest rate is 10 percent per year, then $100 would be paid for a loan of $1000 for 1 year.

中间产品

Intermediate goods. Goods that have undergone some manufacturing or processing but have not yet reached the stage of becoming final products. For example, steel and cotton yarn are intermediate goods.

国际货币制度（国际金融体系）

International monetary system (also international financial system). The institutions under which payments are made for transactions that reach across national boundaries. A central policy issue concerns the arrangement for determining how foreign exchange rates are set and how governments can affect exchange rates.

干　预

Intervention. An activity in which a government buys or sells its currency in the foreign exchange market in order to affect its currency's exchange rate.

（货币的）内在价值

Intrinsic value (of money). The commodity value of a piece of money (e.g., the market value of the weight of copper in a copper coin).

发　明

Invention. The creation of a new product or discovery of a new production technique. (Distinguish from **innovation.**)

投　资

Investment. (1) Economic activity that forgoes consumption today with an eye to increasing output in the future. It includes tangible capital such as houses and intangible investments such as education. *Net investment* is the value of total investment after an allowance has been made for depreciation. *Gross investment* is investment without allowance for depreciation. (2) In finance terms, "investment" has an altogether different meaning and denotes the purchase of a security, such as a stock or a bond.

投资需求（或投资需求曲线）

Investment demand (or investment demand curve). The schedule showing the relationship between the level of investment and the cost of capital (or, more specifically, the real interest rate); also, the graph of that relationship.

看不见的手

Invisible hand. A concept introduced by Adam Smith in 1776 to describe the paradox of a laissez-faire market economy. The invisible-hand doctrine holds that, with each participant pursuing his or her own private interest, a market system nevertheless works to the benefit of all as though a benevolent invisible hand were directing the whole process.

非自愿失业

Involuntarily unemployed. See **unemployment.**

等产量

Isoquant. See **equal-product curve.**

K

凯恩斯经济学

Keynesian economics. The body of macroeconomic analysis developed by John Maynard Keynes holding that a market economy does not automatically tend toward a full-employment equilibrium. According to Keynes, the resulting underemployment equilibrium could be cured by fiscal or monetary policies to raise aggregate demand.

凯恩斯宏观经济学

Keynesian macroeconomics. A theory of macroeconomic activity used to explain business cycles. It relies on an upward-sloping aggregate supply curve, so that changes in aggregate demand can affect output and employment.

凯恩斯学派

Keynesian school. See **Keynesian economics.**

L

劳动力

Labor force. In official U.S. statistics, that group of people 16 years of age and older who are either employed or unemployed.

劳动力参与率

Labor-force participation rate. The ratio of those in the labor force to the entire population 16 years of age or older.

劳动生产率
Labor productivity. See **productivity.**

劳动供给
Labor supply. The number of workers (or, more generally, the number of labor-hours) available to an economy. The principal determinants of labor supply are population, real wages, and social traditions.

劳动价值论
Labor theory of value. The view, often associated with Karl Marx, that every commodity should be valued solely according to the quantity of labor required for its production.

自由放任（“别来管我”）
Laissez-faire (“Leave us alone”). The view that government should interfere as little as possible in economic activity and leave decisions to the marketplace. As expressed by classical economists like Adam Smith, this view held that the role of government should be limited to maintenance of law and order, national defense, and provision of certain public goods that private business would not undertake (e.g., public health and sanitation).

土 地
Land. In classical and neoclassical economics, one of the three basic factors of production (along with labor and capital). More generally, land is taken to include land used for agricultural or industrial purposes as well as natural resources taken from above or below the soil.

边际效用递减规律
Law of diminishing marginal utility. See **diminishing marginal utility, law of.**

边际收益递减规律
Law of diminishing returns. See **diminishing returns, law of.**

需求向下倾斜规律
Law of downward-sloping demand. The nearly universal observation that when the price of a commodity is raised (and other things are held constant), buyers buy less of the commodity. Similarly, when the price is lowered, other things being constant, quantity demanded increases.

（生产的）最低成本法则
Least-cost rule (of production). The rule that the cost of producing a specific level of output is minimized when the ratio of the marginal revenue product of each input to the price of that input is the same for all inputs.

法定清偿物
Legal tender. Money that by law must be accepted as payment for debts. All U.S. coins and currency are legal tender, but checks are not.

负 债
Liabilities. In accounting, debts or financial obligations owed to other firms or persons.

自由放任主义
Libertarianism. An economic philosophy that emphasizes the importance of personal freedom in economic and political affairs; also sometimes called “liberalism.”

有限责任
Limited liability. The restriction of an owner's loss in a business to the amount of capital that the owner has contributed to the company. Limited liability was an important factor in the rise of large corporations. By contrast, owners in partnerships and individual proprietorships generally have *unlimited liability* for the debts of those firms.

长 期
Long run. A term used to denote a period over which full adjustment to changes can take place. In microeconomics, it denotes the time over which firms can enter or leave an industry and the capital stock can be replaced. In macroeconomics, it is often used to mean the period over which all prices, wage contracts, tax rates, and expectations can fully adjust.

长期总供给表
Long-run aggregate supply schedule. A schedule showing the relationship between output and the price level after all price and wage adjustments have taken place, and the *AS* curve is therefore vertical.

洛伦茨曲线
Lorenz curve. A graph used to show the extent of inequality of income or wealth.

M

M_1. See **money supply.**

宏观经济均衡
Macroeconomic equilibrium. Refer to **equilibrium, macroeconomic.**

宏观经济学
Macroeconomics. Analysis dealing with the behavior of the economy as a whole with respect to output, income, the price level, foreign trade, unemployment, and other aggregate economic variables. (Contrast with **microeconomics.**)

马尔萨斯人口增长理论
Malthusian theory of population growth. The hypothesis, first expressed by Thomas Malthus, that the “natural” tendency of population is to grow more rapidly than the food supply. Per capita food production would thus decline over time, thereby putting a check on population. In general, a view that population tends to grow more rapidly as incomes or living standards of the population rise.

有管理的汇率
Managed exchange rate. The most prevalent exchange-rate system today. In this system, a country occasionally intervenes to stabilize its currency but there is no fixed or announced parity.

边际成本
Marginal cost. Refer to **cost, marginal.**

边际原则
Marginal principle. The fundamental notion that people will maximize their income or profits when the marginal

costs and marginal benefits of their actions are equal.

边际产品（*MP*）
Marginal product (*MP*). The extra output resulting from 1 extra unit of a specified input when all other inputs are held constant. Sometimes called *marginal physical product.*

分配的边际产品理论
Marginal product theory of distribution. A theory of the distribution of income proposed by John B. Clark, according to which each productive input is paid according to its **marginal product.**

边际消费倾向（*MPC*）
Marginal propensity to consume (*MPC*). The extra amount that people consume when they receive an extra dollar of disposable income. To be distinguished from the *average propensity to consume,* which is the ratio of total consumption to total disposable income.

边际进口倾向（*MPm*）
Marginal propensity to import (*MPm*). In macroeconomics, the increase in the dollar value of imports resulting from each dollar increase in the value of GDP.

边际储蓄倾向（*MPS*）
Marginal propensity to save (*MPS*). That fraction of an additional dollar of disposable income that is saved. Note that, by definition, *MRC* + *MPS* = *1.*

边际收益（*MR*）
Marginal revenue (*MR*). The additional revenue a firm would earn if it sold 1 extra unit of output. In perfect competition, *MR* equals price. Under imperfect competition, *MR* is less than price because, in order to sell the extra unit, the price must be reduced on all prior units sold.

（一种投入的）边际收益产品（*MRP*）
Marginal revenue product (*MRP*) (of an input). Marginal revenue multiplied by marginal product. It is the extra revenue that would be brought in if a firm were to buy 1 extra unit of an input, put it to work, and sell the extra product it produced.

边际税率
Marginal tax rate. For an income tax, the percentage of the last dollar of income paid in taxes. If a tax system is progressive, the marginal tax rate is higher than the average tax rate.

边际效用（*MU*）
Marginal utility (*MU*). The additional or extra satisfaction yielded from consuming 1 additional unit of a commodity, with amounts of all other goods consumed held constant.

市　场
Market. An arrangement whereby buyers and sellers interact to determine the prices and quantities of a commodity. Some markets (such as the stock market or a flea market) take place in physical locations; other markets are conducted over the telephone or are organized by computers, and some markets now are organized on the Internet.

市场出清价格
Market-clearing price. The price in a supply-and-demand equilibrium. This denotes that all supply and demand orders are filled at that price, so that the books are "cleared" of orders.

市场经济
Market economy. An economy in which the ***what, how,* and *for whom*** questions concerning resource allocation are primarily determined by supply and demand in markets. In this form of economic organization, firms, motivated by the desire to maximize profits, buy inputs and produce and sell outputs. Households, armed with their factor incomes, go to markets and determine the demand for commodities. The interaction of firms' supply and households' demand then determines the prices and quantities of goods.

市场均衡
Market equilibrium. Same as **competitive equilibrium.**

市场不灵
Market failure. An imperfection in a price system that prevents an efficient allocation of resources. Important examples are **externalities** and **imperfect competition.**

市场力量
Market power. The degree of control that a firm or group of firms has over the price and production decisions in an industry. In a monopoly, the firm has a high degree of market power; firms in perfectly competitive industries have no market power. **Concentration ratios** are the most widely used measures of market power.

市场份额
Market share. That fraction of an industry's output accounted for by an individual firm or group of firms.

马克思主义
Marxism. The set of social, political, and economic doctrines developed by Karl Marx in the nineteenth century. As an economic theory, Marxism predicted that capitalism would collapse as a result of its own internal contradictions, especially its tendency to exploit the working classes.

均　值
Mean. In statistics, the same thing as "average." Thus for the numbers 1, 3, 6, 10, 20, the mean is 8.

中位数
Median. In statistics, the figure exactly in the middle of a series of numbers ordered or ranked from lowest to highest (e.g., incomes or examination grades). Thus for the numbers 1, 3, 6, 10, 20, the median is 6.

重商主义
Mercantilism. A political doctrine emphasizing the importance of balance-of-payments surpluses as a device to accumulate gold. Proponents therefore advocated tight government control of economic policies, believing that laissez-faire policies might lead to a loss of gold.

商品贸易余额
Merchandise trade balance. See **balance of trade.**

兼　并
Merger. The acquisition of one corporation by another, which usually occurs when one firm buys the stock of another. Important examples are (1) *vertical mergers,* which occur when the two firms are at different stages of a production process (e.g., iron ore and steel), (2) *horizontal mergers,* which occur when the two firms produce in the same market (e.g., two automobile manufacturers), and (3) *conglomerate mergers,* which occur when the two firms operate in unrelated markets (e.g., shoelaces and oil refining).

微观经济学
Microeconomics. Analysis dealing with the behavior of individual elements in an economy—such as the determination of the price of a single product or the behavior of a single consumer or business firm. (Contrast with **macroeconomics.**)

最低成本
Minimum cost. Refer to **cost, minimum.**

混合经济
Mixed economy. The dominant form of economic organization in noncommunist countries. Mixed economies rely primarily on the price system for their economic organization but use a variety of government interventions (such as taxes, spending, and regulation) to handle macroeconomic instability and market failures.

模　型
Model. A formal framework for representing the basic features of a complex system by a few central relationships. Models take the form of graphs, mathematical equations, and computer programs.

瞬　期
Momentary run. A period of time that is so short that production is fixed.

货币主义
Monetarism. A school of thought holding that changes in the money supply are the major cause of macroeconomic fluctuations.

货币基础
Monetary base. The net monetary liabilities of the government that are held by the public. In the United States, the monetary base is equal to currency and bank reserves. Sometimes called *high-powered money.*

货币经济
Monetary economy. An economy in which the trade takes place through a commonly accepted medium of exchange.

货币政策
Monetary policy. The objectives of the central bank in exercising its control over money, interest rates, and credit conditions. The instruments of monetary policy are primarily open-market operations, reserve requirements, and the discount rate.

货币规则
Monetary rule. The cardinal tenet of monetarist economic philosophy is the monetary rule which asserts that optimal monetary policy sets the growth of the money supply at a fixed rate and holds to that rate through thick and thin.

货币传导机制
Monetary transmission mechanism. In macroeconomics, the route by which changes in the supply of money are translated into changes in output, employment, prices, and inflation.

货币联盟
Monetary union. An arrangement by which several nations adopt a common currency as a unit of account and medium of exchange. The European Monetary Union adopted the Euro as the common currency in 1999.

货　币
Money. The means of payment or medium of exchange. For the items constituting money, see **money supply.**

货币周转率
Money, velocity of. Refer to **velocity of money.**

货币需求表
Money demand schedule. The relationship between holdings of money and interest rates. As interest rates rise, bonds and other securities become more attractive, lowering the quantity of money demanded. See also **demand for money.**

货币资金
Money funds. Shorthand expression for very liquid short-term financial instruments whose interest rates are not regulated. The major examples are money market mutual funds and commercial-bank money market deposit accounts.

货币市场
Money market. A term denoting the set of institutions that handle the purchase or sale of short-term credit instruments like Treasury bills and commercial paper.

货币供给
Money supply. The narrowly defined money supply (narrow money, or M_1) consists of coins, paper currency, and all demand or checking deposits; this is transactions money. The broadly defined supply (broad money) includes all items in M_1 plus certain liquid assets or near-monies—savings deposits, money market funds, and the like.

货币供给效应
Money-supply effect. The relationship whereby a price rise operating on a fixed nominal money supply produces tight money and lowers aggregate spending.

货币供给乘数
Money-supply multiplier. The ratio of the increase in the money supply (or in deposits) to the increase in bank reserves. Generally, the money-supply multiplier is equal to the inverse of the required reserve ratio. For example, if the required reserve ratio is 0.125, then the money-supply multiplier is 8.

垄断竞争
Monopolistic competition. A market structure in which there are many sellers supplying goods that are close, but not perfect, substitutes. In such a market, each firm can exercise some effect on its product's price.

垄　断
Monopoly. A market structure in which a commodity is supplied by a single firm. Also see **natural monopoly.**

买方垄断
Monopsony. The mirror image of monopoly: a market in which there is a single buyer; a "buyer's monopoly."

道德风险
Moral hazard. A type of market failure in which the presence of insurance against an insured risk increases the likelihood that the risky event will occur. For example, a car owner insured 100 percent against auto theft may be careless about locking the car because the presence of insurance reduces the incentive to prevent the theft.

MPC. See **marginal propensity to consume.**

MPS. See **marginal propensity to save.**

乘　数
Multiplier. A term in macroeconomics denoting the change in an induced variable (such as GDP or money supply) per unit of change in an external variable (such as government spending or bank reserves). The *expenditure multiplier* denotes the increase in GDP that would result from a $1 increase in expenditure (say, on investment).

乘数模型
Multiplier model. In macroeconomics, a theory developed by J. M. Keynes that emphasizes the importance of changes in autonomous expenditures (especially investment, government spending, and net exports) in determining changes in output and employment. Also see **multiplier.**

N

非加速通货膨胀的失业率
NAIRU. See **nonaccelerating inflation rate of unemployment.**

纳什均衡
Nash equilibrium. In game theory, a set of strategies for the players where no player can improve his or her payoff given the other player's strategy. That is, given player A's strategy, player B can do no better, and given B's strategy, A can do no better. The Nash equilibrium is also sometimes called the *noncooperative equilibrium*.

国家债务
National debt. Same as **government debt.**

国民收入和生产账户（NIPA）
National income and product accounts (NIPA). A set of accounts that measures the spending, income, and output of the entire nation for a quarter or a year.

国民储蓄率
National saving rate. Total saving, private and public, divided by net domestic product.

自然垄断
Natural monopoly. A firm or industry whose average cost per unit of production falls sharply over the entire range of its output, as, e.g., in local electricity distribution. Thus a single firm, a monopoly, can supply the industry output more efficiently than can multiple firms.

自然失业率
Natural rate of unemployment. The same concept as the **nonaccelerating inflation rate of unemployment (NAIRU).**

新古典增长模型
Neoclassical model of growth. A theory or model used to explain long-term trends in the economic growth of industrial economies. This model emphasizes the importance of capital deepening (i.e., a growing capital-labor ratio) and technological change in explaining the growth of potential real GDP.

国内生产净值（NDP）
Net domestic product (NDP). GDP less an allowance for depreciation of capital goods.

净出口
Net exports. In the national product accounts, the value of exports of goods and services minus the value of imports of goods and services.

净国外投资
Net foreign investment. Net saving by a country abroad; approximately equal to net exports.

净投资
Net investment. Gross investment minus depreciation of capital goods.

净值，净资产
Net worth. In accounting, total assets minus total liabilities.

新古典宏观经济学
New classical macroeconomics. A theory which holds that (1) prices and wages are flexible and (2) people make forecasts in accordance with the **rational-expectations hypothesis.**

名义GDP
Nominal GDP. See **gross domestic product, nominal.**

名义（或货币）利率
Nominal (or money) interest rate. The **interest rate** paid on different assets. This represents a dollar return per year per dollar invested. Compare with the **real interest rate,** which

represents the return per year in goods per unit of goods invested.

非加速通货膨胀的失业率（NAIRU）

Nonaccelerating inflation rate of unemployment (NAIRU). An unemployment rate that is consistent with a constant inflation rate. At the NAIRU, upward and downward forces on price and wage inflation are in balance, so there is no tendency for inflation to change. The NAIRU is the unemployment rate at which the long-run Phillips curve is vertical.

非合作性均衡

Noncooperative equilibrium. See **Nash equilibrium.**

不可再生资源

Nonrenewable resources. Those natural resources, like oil and gas, that are essentially fixed in supply and whose regeneration is not quick enough to be economically relevant.

规范经济学与实证经济学

Normative vs. positive economics. *Normative economics* considers "what ought to be"—value judgments, or goals, of public policy. *Positive economics,* by contrast, is the analysis of facts and behavior in an economy, or "the way things are."

非劳动力

Not in the labor force. That part of the adult population that is neither working nor looking for work.

O

奥肯法则

Okun's Law. The empirical relationship, discovered by Arthur Okun, between cyclical movements in GDP and unemployment. The law states that when actual GDP declines 2 percent relative to potential GDP, the unemployment rate increases by about 1 percentage point. (Earlier estimates placed the ratio at 3 to 1.)

寡　头

Oligopoly. A situation of imperfect competition in which an industry is dominated by a small number of suppliers.

开放经济

Open economy. An economy that engages in international trade (i.e., imports and exports) of goods and capital with other countries. A *closed economy* is one that has no imports or exports.

开放经济乘数

Open-economy multiplier. Multiplier analysis as applied to economies that have foreign trade. The open-economy multiplier is smaller than the closed-economy multiplier because there is a leakage of spending into imports as well as into saving.

公开市场业务

Open-market operations. The activity of a central bank in buying or selling government bonds to influence bank reserves, the money supply, and interest rates. If securities are bought, the money paid out by the central bank increases commercial-bank reserves, and the money supply increases. If securities are sold, the money supply contracts.

机会成本

Opportunity cost. The value of the best alternative use of an economic good. Thus, say that the best alternative use of the inputs employed to mine a ton of coal was to grow 10 bushels of wheat. The opportunity cost of a ton of coal is thus the 10 bushels of wheat that *could* have been produced but were not. Opportunity cost is particularly useful for valuing nonmarketed goods such as environmental health or safety.

理想货币区

Optimal currency area. A grouping of regions or countries which have high labor mobility or have common and synchronous aggregate supply or demand shocks. Under such conditions, significant changes in exchange rates are not necessary to ensure rapid macroeconomic adjustment, and the countries can have fixed exchange rates or a common currency.

序数效用

Ordinal utility. A dimensionless utility measure used in demand theory. Ordinal utility enables one to state that A is preferred to B, but we cannot say by how much. That is, any two bundles of goods can be ranked relative to each other, but the absolute difference between bundles cannot be measured. This contrasts with *cardinal utility,* or dimensional utility, which is sometimes used in the analysis of behavior toward risk. An example of a cardinal measure comes when we say that a substance at 100 K (kelvin) is twice as hot as one at 50 K.

其他条件保持不变

Other things constant. A phrase (sometimes stated "*ceteris paribus*") which signifies that a factor under consideration is changed while all other factors are held constant or unchanged. For example, a downward-sloping demand curve shows that the quantity demanded will decline as the price rises, as long as other things (such as incomes) are held constant.

产　出

Outputs. The various useful goods or services that are either consumed or used in further production.

P

节约悖论

Paradox of thrift. The principle, first proposed by John Maynard Keynes, that an attempt by a society to increase its saving may result in a reduction in the amount which it actually saves.

价值悖论

Paradox of value. The paradox that many necessities of life (e.g., water) have a low "market" value while many luxuries (e.g., diamonds) with little "use" value have a high market price. It is explained by the fact that a price reflects not the total utility of a commodity but its marginal utility.

帕累托效率（或帕累托最优）
Pareto efficiency (or **Pareto optimality**). A situation in which no reorganization or trade could raise the utility or satisfaction of one individual without lowering the utility or satisfaction of another individual. Under certain limited conditions, perfect competition leads to allocative efficiency. Also called *allocative efficiency*.

局部均衡分析
Partial-equilibrium analysis. Analysis concentrating on the effect of changes in an individual market, holding other things equal (e.g., disregarding changes in income).

合伙制
Partnership. An association of two or more persons to conduct a business which is not in corporate form and does not enjoy limited liability.

专 利
Patent. An exclusive right granted to an inventor to control the use of an invention for, in the United States, a period of 20 years. Patents create temporary monopolies as a way of rewarding inventive activity and, like other intellectual property rights, are a tool for promoting invention among individuals or small firms.

回报矩阵（也称支付矩阵）
Payoff table. In game theory, a table used to describe the strategies and payoffs of a game with two or more players. The profits or utilities of the different players are the *payoffs*.

回 报
Payoffs. See **payoff table.**

完全竞争
Perfect competition. Refer to **competition, perfect.**

个人可支配收入
Personal disposable income. Personal income minus taxes plus transfers. The amount households have for consumption and saving.

个人收入
Personal income. A measure of income before taxes have been deducted. More precisely, it equals disposable personal income plus net taxes.

个人储蓄
Personal saving. That part of income which is not consumed; in other words, the difference between disposable income and consumption.

个人储蓄率
Personal saving rate. The ratio of personal saving to personal disposable income, in percent.

菲利普斯曲线
Phillips curve. A graph, first devised by A. W. Phillips, showing the tradeoff between unemployment and inflation. In modern mainstream macroeconomics, the downward-sloping "tradeoff" Phillips curve is generally held to be valid only in the short run; in the long run, the Phillips curve is usually thought to be vertical at the nonaccelerating inflation rate of unemployment (NAIRU).

政策无效性定理
Policy-ineffectiveness theorem. A theorem which asserts that, with rational expectations and flexible prices and wages, anticipated government monetary or fiscal policy cannot affect real output or unemployment.

投资组合理论
Portfolio theory. An economic theory that describes how rational investors allocate their wealth among different financial assets—that is, how they put their wealth into a "portfolio."

实证经济学
Positive economics. See **normative vs. positive economics.**

前因后果谬误
Post hoc fallacy. From the Latin, *post hoc, ergo propter hoc,* which translates as "after this, therefore because of this." This fallacy arises when it is assumed that because event A precedes event B, it follows that A *causes* B.

潜在GDP
Potential GDP. High-employment GDP; more precisely, the maximum level of GDP that can be sustained with a given state of technology and population size without accelerating inflation. Today, it is generally taken to be equivalent to the level of output corresponding to the **nonaccelerating inflation rate of unemployment (NAIRU).** Potential output is not necessarily maximum output.

潜在产出
Potential output. Same as **potential GDP.**

贫 困
Poverty. Today, the U.S. government defines the "poverty line" to be the minimum adequate standard of living.

PPF. See **production-possibility frontier.**

（资产的）现值
Present value (of an asset). Today's value for an asset that yields a stream of income over time. Valuation of such time streams of returns requires calculating the present worth of each component of the income, which is done by applying a discount rate (or interest rate) to future incomes.

价 格
Price. The money cost of a good, service, or asset. Price is measured in monetary units per unit of the good (as in 3 dollars per 1 hamburger).

价格歧视
Price discrimination. A situation where the same product is sold to different consumers for different prices.

富有价格弹性的需求（或有弹性的需求）
Price-elastic demand (or **elastic demand**). The situation in which price elasticity of demand exceeds 1 in absolute value. This signifies that the percentage change in quantity demanded is greater than the percentage change in price. In addition, elastic demand implies that total revenue

(price times quantity) rises when price falls because the increase in quantity demanded is so large. (Contrast with **price-inelastic demand.**)

需求的价格弹性
Price elasticity of demand. A measure of the extent to which quantity demanded responds to a price change. The elasticity coefficient (price elasticity of demand E_p) is the percentage change in quantity demanded divided by percentage change in price. In figuring percentages, use the averages of old and new quantities in the numerator and of old and new prices in the denominator; disregard the minus sign. Refer also to **price-elastic demand, price-inelastic demand,** and **unit-elastic demand.**

供给的价格弹性
Price elasticity of supply. Conceptually similar to **price elasticity of demand,** except that it measures the supply responsiveness to a price change. More precisely, the price elasticity of supply measures the percentage change in quantity supplied divided by the percentage change in price. Supply elasticities are most useful in perfect competition.

价格灵活性
Price flexibility. Price behavior in "auction" markets (e.g., for many raw commodities or the stock market), in which prices immediately respond to changes in demand or in supply.

价格指数
Price index. An index number that shows how the average price of a bundle of goods changes over time. In computation of the average, the prices of the different goods are generally weighted by their economic importance (e.g., by each commodity's share of total consumer expenditures in the **consumer price index**).

缺乏价格弹性的需求（或缺乏弹性的需求）
Price-inelastic demand (or **inelastic demand**). The situation in which price elasticity of demand is below 1 in absolute value. In this case, when price declines, total revenue declines, and when price is increased, total revenue goes up. Perfectly inelastic demand means that there is no change at all in quantity demanded when price goes up or down. (Contrast with **price-elastic demand** and **unit-elastic demand.**)

GDP的价格
Price of GDP. See **GDP deflator.**

私人品
Private good. See **public good.**

生产者价格指数
Producer price index. The price index of goods sold at the wholesale level (such as steel, wheat, oil).

生产者剩余
Producer surplus. The difference between the producer sales revenue and the producer cost. The producer surplus is generally measured as the area above the supply curve but under the price line up to the amount sold.

平均产量
Product, average. Refer to **average product.**

边际产品
Product, marginal. Refer to **marginal product.**

产品差异化
Product differentiation. The existence of characteristics that make similar goods less-than-perfect substitutes. Thus locational differences make similar types of gasoline sold at separate points imperfect substitutes. Firms enjoying product differentiation face a downward-sloping demand curve instead of the horizontal demand curve of the perfect competitor.

生产函数
Production function. A relation (or mathematical function) specifying the maximum output that can be produced with given inputs for a given level of technology; applies to a firm or, as an aggregate production function, to the economy as a whole.

生产可能性边界
Production-possibility frontier (*PPF*). A graph showing the menu of goods that can be produced by an economy. In a frequently cited case, the choice is reduced to two goods, guns and butter. Points outside the *PPF* (to the northeast of it) are unattainable. Points inside it are inefficient since resources are not being fully employed, resources are not being used properly, or outdated production techniques are being utilized.

有效率的生产
Productive efficiency. A situation in which an economy cannot produce more of one good without producing less of another good; this implies that the economy is on its production-possibility frontier.

生产率
Productivity. A term referring to the ratio of output to inputs (total output divided by labor inputs is *labor productivity*). Productivity increases if the same quantity of inputs produces more output. Labor productivity increases because of improved technology, improvements in labor skills, or capital deepening.

生产率增长
Productivity growth. The rate of increase in **productivity** from one period to another. For example, if an index of labor productivity is 100 in 2004 and 101.7 in 2005, the rate of productivity growth is 1.7 percent per year for 2005 over 2004.

净资本生产率
Productivity of capital, net. See **rate of return on capital.**

利 润
Profit. (1) In accounting terms, total revenue minus costs properly chargeable against the goods sold (see **income statement**). (2) In economic theory, the difference between sales revenue and the full opportunity cost of resources involved in producing the goods.

损益表
Profit-and-loss statement. See **income statement.**

累进税、比例税和累退税
Progressive, proportional, and regressive taxes. A progressive tax weighs more heavily upon the rich; a regressive tax does the opposite. More precisely, a tax is *progressive* if the average tax rate (i.e., taxes divided by income) is higher for those with higher incomes; it is a *regressive* tax if the average tax rate declines with higher incomes; it is a *proportional* tax if the average tax rate is equal at all income levels.

产 权
Property rights. Rights that define the ability of individuals or firms to own, buy, sell, and use the capital goods and other property in a market economy.

比例税
Proportional tax. See **progressive, proportional, and regressive taxes.**

独资经营
Proprietorship, individual. A business firm owned and operated by one person.

保护主义
Protectionism. Any policy adopted by a country to protect domestic industries against competition from imports (most commonly, a tariff or quota imposed on such imports).

公共选择（也称公共选择理论）
Public choice (also **public-choice theory**). Branch of economics and political science dealing with the way that governments make choices and direct the economy. This theory differs from the theory of markets in emphasizing the influence of vote maximizing for politicians, which contrasts to profit maximizing by firms.

公共债务
Public debt. See **government debt.**

公共品
Public good. A commodity whose benefits are indivisibly spread among the entire community, whether or not particular individuals desire to consume the public good. For example, a public-health measure that eradicates polio protects all, not just those paying for the vaccinations. To be contrasted with *private goods,* such as bread, which, if consumed by one person, cannot be consumed by another person.

纯经济租金
Pure economic rent. See **rent, economic.**

Q

需求量
Quantity demanded. See **change in demand vs. change in quantity demanded.**

交易数量方程
Quantity equation of exchange. A tautology, $MV \equiv PQ$, where M is the money supply, V is the income velocity of money, and PQ (price times quantity) is the money value of total output (nominal GDP). The equation must always hold exactly since V is defined as PQ/M.

供给量
Quantity supplied. See **change in supply vs. change in quantity supplied.**

货币价格数量理论
Quantity theory of money and prices. A theory of the determination of output and the overall price level holding that prices move proportionately with the money supply. A more cautious approach put forth by monetarists holds that the money supply is the most important determinant of changes in nominal GDP (see **monetarism**).

配 额
Quota. A form of import protectionism in which the total quantity of imports of a particular commodity (e.g., sugar or cars) during a given period is limited.

R

（股市价格的）随机游走理论
Random-walk theory (of stock market prices). See **efficient market.**

通货膨胀率
Rate of inflation. See **inflation.**

资本收益率（或资本收益）
Rate of return (or **return**) **on capital.** The yield on an investment or on a capital good. Thus, an investment costing \$100 and yielding \$12 annually has a rate of return of 12 percent per year.

投资收益率
Rate of return on investment. The net dollar return per year for every dollar of invested capital. For example, if \$100 of investment yields \$12 per year of return, the rate of return on investment is 12 percent per year.

理性预期
Rational expectations. See **expectations.**

理性预期假说
Rational-expectations hypothesis. A hypothesis which holds that people make unbiased forecasts and, further, that people use all available information and economic theory to make these forecasts.

理性预期宏观经济学
Rational-expectations macroeconomics. A school holding that markets clear quickly and that expectations are rational. Under these and other conditions it can be shown that predictable macroeconomic policies have no effect on real output or unemployment. Sometimes called **new classical macroeconomics.**

实际商业周期理论
Real-business-cycle (RBC) theory. A theory that explains business cycles purely as shifts in aggregate supply, primarily due to technological disturbances, without any reference

to monetary or other demand-side forces.

实际GDP
Real GDP. See **gross domestic product, real.**

实际利率
Real interest rate. The interest rate measured in terms of goods rather than money. It is thus equal to the money (or nominal) interest rate less the rate of inflation.

实际工资
Real wages. The purchasing power of a worker's wages in terms of goods and services. It is measured by the ratio of the money wage rate to the consumer price index.

衰 退
Recession. A period of significant decline in total output, income, and employment, usually lasting from 6 months to a year and marked by widespread contractions in many sectors of the economy. See also **depression.**

累退税
Regressive tax. See **progressive, proportional, and regressive taxes.**

管 制
Regulation. Government laws or rules designed to control the behavior of firms. The major kinds are *economic regulation* (which affects the prices, entry, or service of a single industry, such as telephone service) and *social regulation* (which attempts to correct externalities that prevail across a number of industries, such as air or water pollution).

可再生资源
Renewable resources. Natural resources (like agricultural land) whose services replenish regularly and which, if properly managed, can yield useful services indefinitely.

经济租（或纯经济租金）
Rent, economic (or **pure economic rent**). Term applied to income earned from land. The total supply of land available is (with minor qualifications) fixed, and the return paid to the landowner is rent. The term is often extended to the return paid to any factor in fixed supply—i.e., to any input having a perfectly inelastic or vertical supply curve.

法定准备金率
Required reserve ratio. See **reserves, bank.**

银行准备金
Reserves, bank. That portion of deposits that a bank sets aside in the form of vault cash or non-interest-earning deposits with Federal Reserve Banks. In the United States, banks are required to hold 10 percent of checking deposits (or transactions accounts) in the form of reserves.

国际储备
Reserves, international. International money held by a nation to stabilize or "peg" its foreign exchange rate or provide financing when the nation faces balance-of-payments difficulties. Today, the bulk of reserves are U.S. dollars, with Euros and Japanese yen the other major reserve currencies.

资源配置
Resource allocation. The manner in which an economy distributes its resources (its factors of production) among the potential uses so as to produce a particular set of final goods.

规模报酬
Returns to scale. The rate at which output increases when all inputs are increased proportionately. For example, if all the inputs double and output is exactly doubled, that process is said to exhibit *constant returns to scale.* If, however, output grows by less than 100 percent when all inputs are doubled, the process shows *decreasing returns to scale;* if output more than doubles, the process demonstrates *increasing returns to scale.*

货币增值
Revaluation. An increase in the official foreign exchange rate of a currency. See also **devaluation.**

财政政策的李嘉图法则
Ricardian view of fiscal policy. A theory developed by Harvard's Robert Barro which holds that changes in tax rates have no impact upon consumption spending because households foresee, say, that tax cuts today will require tax increases tomorrow to finance the government's financing requirements.

风 险
Risk. In financial economics, refers to the variability of the returns on an investment.

风险厌恶
Risk averse. A person is risk-averse when, faced with an uncertain situation, the displeasure from losing a given amount of income is greater than the pleasure from gaining the same amount of income.

风险分摊
Risk spreading. The process of taking large risks and spreading them around so that they are but small risks for a large number of people. The major form of risk spreading is **insurance,** which is a kind of gambling in reverse.

70法则
Rule of 70. A useful shortcut for approximating compound interest. A quantity that grows at r percent per year will double in about $70/r$ years.

S

牺牲率
Sacrifice ratio. The sacrifice ratio is the cumulative loss in output, measured as a percent of one year's GDP, associated with a one-percentage-point permanent reduction in inflation.

销售税
Sales tax. See **excise tax vs. sales tax.**

储蓄函数
Saving function. The schedule showing the amount of saving that households or a nation will undertake at each level of income.

萨伊的市场定律
Say's Law of Markets. The theory that "supply creates its own demand." J. B. Say argued in 1803 that, because total purchasing power is exactly equal to total incomes and outputs, excess demand or supply is impossible. Keynes attacked Say's Law, pointing out that an extra dollar of income need not be spent entirely (i.e., the marginal propensity to spend is not necessarily unity).

稀　缺
Scarcity. The distinguishing characteristic of an economic good. That an economic good is scarce means not that it is rare but only that it is not freely available for the taking. To obtain such a good, one must either produce it or offer other economic goods in exchange.

稀缺规律
Scarcity, law of. The principle that most things that people want are available only in limited supply (the exception being **free goods**). Thus goods are generally scarce and must somehow be rationed, whether by price or some other means.

（总）需求表，（总）供给表
Schedule (demand, supply, aggregate demand, aggregate supply). Term used interchangeably with "curve," as in demand curve, supply curve, etc.

证　券
Securities. A term used to designate a wide variety of financial assets, such as stocks, bonds, options, and notes; more precisely, the documents used to establish ownership of these assets.

短　期
Short run. A period in which not all factors can adjust fully. In microeconomics, the capital stock and other "fixed" inputs cannot be adjusted and entry is not free in the short run. In macroeconomics, prices, wage contracts, tax rates, and expectations may not fully adjust in the short run.

短期总供给表
Short-run aggregate supply schedule. The schedule showing the relationship between output and prices in the short run wherein changes in aggregate demand can affect output; represented by an upward-sloping or horizontal *AS* curve.

停业价格（或停业点、停业原则）
Shutdown price (or **point** or **rule**). In the theory of the firm, the shutdown point comes at that point where the market price is just sufficient to cover average variable cost and no more. Hence, the firm's losses per period just equal its fixed costs; it might as well shut down.

单一税运动
Single-tax movement. A nineteenth-century movement, originated by Henry George, holding that continued poverty in the midst of steady economic progress was attributable to the scarcity of land and the large rents flowing to landowners. The "single tax" was to be a tax on economic rent earned from landownership.

斜　率
Slope. In a graph, the change in the variable on the vertical axis per unit of change in the variable on the horizontal axis. Upward-sloping lines have positive slopes, downward-sloping curves (like demand curves) have negative slopes, and horizontal lines have slopes of zero.

社会保险
Social insurance. Mandatory insurance provided by government to improve social welfare by preventing the losses created by market failures such as moral hazard or adverse selection.

社会基础资本
Social overhead capital. The essential investments on which economic development depends, particularly for sanitation and drinking water, transportation, and communications; sometimes called *infrastructure*.

社会管制
Social regulation. See **regulation.**

社会主义
Socialism. A political theory which holds that all (or almost all) the means of production, other than labor, should be owned by the community. This allows the return on capital to be shared more equally than under capitalism.

投机者
Speculator. Someone engaged in speculation, i.e., someone who buys (or sells) a commodity or financial asset with the aim of profiting from later selling (or buying) the item at a higher (or lower) price.

外　溢
Spillovers. Same as **externalities.**

滞　胀
Stagflation. A term, coined in the early 1970s, describing the coexistence of high unemployment, or *stag*nation, with persistent in*flation*. Its explanation lies primarily in the inertial nature of the inflationary process.

统计性歧视
Statistical discrimination. Treatment of individuals on the basis of the average behavior or characteristics of members of the group to which they belong. Statistical discrimination can be self-fulfilling by reducing incentives for individuals to overcome the stereotype.

普通股股票
Stock, common. Refer to **common stock.**

股票市场
Stock market. An organized marketplace in which common stocks are traded. In the United States, the largest stock market is the New York Stock Exchange, on which are traded the stocks of the largest U.S. companies.

存量与流量
Stock vs. flow. See **flow vs. stock.**

策略互动
Strategic interaction. A situation in oligopolistic markets in which each firm's business strategies depend upon its rival's plans. A formal analysis of strategic interaction is given in **game theory.**

结构性预算
Structural budget. See **actual, cyclical, and structural budget.**

结构性失业
Structural unemployment. Unemployment resulting because the regional or occupational pattern of job vacancies does not match the pattern of worker availability. There may be jobs available, but unemployed workers may not have the required skill or the jobs may be in different regions from where the unemployed workers live.

补 贴
Subsidy. A payment by a government to a firm or household that provides or consumes a commodity. For example, governments often subsidize food by paying for part of the food expenditures of low-income households.

替代品
Substitutes. Goods that compete with each other (as do gloves and mittens). By contrast, goods that go together in the eyes of consumers (such as left shoes and right shoes) are *complements.*

（价格变动的）替代效应
Substitution effect (of a price change). The tendency of consumers to consume more of a good when its relative price falls (to "substitute" in favor of that good) and to consume less of the good when its relative price increases (to "substitute" away from that good). This substitution effect of a price change leads to a downward-sloping demand curve. (Compare with **income effect.**)

替代法则
Substitution rule. A rule which asserts that if the price of one factor falls while all other factor prices remain the same, firms will profit by substituting the now-cheaper factor for all the other factors. The rule is a corollary of the **least-cost rule.**

供给曲线（或供给表）
Supply curve (or supply schedule). A schedule showing the quantity of a good that suppliers in a given market desire to sell at each price, holding other things equal.

供给冲击
Supply shock. In macroeconomics, a sudden change in production costs or productivity that has a large and unexpected impact upon aggregate supply. As a result of a supply shock, real GDP and the price level change unexpectedly.

供给冲击通货膨胀
Supply-shock inflation. Inflation originating on the supply side of markets from a sharp increase in costs. In the aggregate supply-and-demand framework, cost-push is illustrated as an upward shift of the *AS* curve. Also called *cost-push inflation.*

供给学派经济学
Supply-side economics. A view emphasizing policy measures to affect aggregate supply or potential output. This approach holds that high marginal tax rates on labor and capital incomes reduce work effort and saving.

T

有形资产
Tangible assets. Those assets, such as land or capital goods like computers, buildings, and automobiles, that are used to produce further goods and services.

关 税
Tariff. A levy or tax imposed upon each unit of a commodity imported into a country.

税收归宿
Tax incidence. See **incidence.**

技术变革
Technological change. A change in the process of production or an introduction of a new product such that more or improved output can be obtained from the same bundle of inputs. It results in an outward shift in the production-possibility curve. Often called *technological progress.*

技术进步
Technological progress. See **technological change.**

（国际贸易中的）贸易条件
Terms of trade (in international trade). The "real" terms at which a nation sells its export products and buys its import products. This measure equals the ratio of an index of export prices to an index of import prices.

收入分配理论
Theory of income distribution. A theory explaining the manner in which personal income and wealth are distributed in a society.

定期存款
Time deposit. Funds, held in a bank, that have a minimum "time of withdrawal"; included in broad money but not in M_1 because they are not accepted as a means of payment. Similar to *savings deposits.*

总成本
Total cost. Refer to **cost, total.**

全要素生产率
Total factor productivity. An index of productivity that measures total output per unit of total input. The numerator of the index is total output (say, GDP), while the denominator is a weighted average of inputs of capital, labor, and resources. The growth of total factor productivity is often taken as an index of the rate of technological progress. Also sometimes called *multifactor productivity.*

总产品（或总产量）

Total product (or output). The total amount of a commodity produced, measured in physical units such as bushels of wheat, tons of steel, or number of haircuts.

总收益，总收入

Total revenue (*TR*). Price times quantity, or total sales.

贸易余额或商品贸易余额

Trade balance or **merchandise trade balance.** See **balance of trade.**

贸易壁垒

Trade barrier. Any of a number of protectionist devices by which nations discourage imports. Tariffs and quotas are the most visible barriers, but in recent years nontariff barriers (or NTBs), such as burdensome regulatory proceedings, have replaced more traditional measures.

货币的交易需求

Transactions demand for money. See **demand for money.**

交易货币

Transactions money (M_1). A measure of the **money supply** which consists of items that are actually for transactions, namely, currency and checking accounts.

政府转移支付

Transfer payments, government. Payments made by a government to individuals, for which the individual performs no current service in return. Examples are social security payments and unemployment insurance.

短期国库券

Treasury bills (T-bills). Short-term bonds or securities issued by the federal government.

U

失业者

Unemployed. People who are not employed but are actively looking for work or waiting to return to work.

失 业

Unemployment. (1) In economic terms, *involuntary unemployment* occurs when there are qualified workers who are willing to work at prevailing wages but cannot find jobs. (2) In the official (U.S. Bureau of Labor Statistics) definition, a worker is unemployed if he or she (*a*) is not working and (*b*) either is waiting for recall from layoff or has actively looked for work in the last 4 weeks. See also **frictional unemployment** and **structural unemployment.**

失业率

Unemployment rate. The percentage of the labor force that is unemployed.

单位价格弹性需求

Unit-elastic demand. The situation, between **price-elastic demand** and **price-inelastic demand,** in which price elasticity is just equal to 1 in absolute value. See also **price elasticity of demand.**

无限责任

Unlimited liability. See **limited liability.**

高利贷

Usury. The charging of an interest rate above a legal maximum on borrowed money.

效用（或总效用）

Utility (also **total utility**). The total satisfaction derived from the consumption of goods or services. To be contrasted with *marginal utility,* which is the additional utility arising from consumption of an additional unit of the commodity.

V

价值悖论

Value, paradox of. Refer to **paradox of value.**

附加价值

Value added. The difference between the value of goods produced and the cost of materials and supplies used in producing them. In a \$1 loaf of bread embodying \$0.60 worth of wheat and other materials, the value added is \$0.40. Value added consists of the wages, interest, and profit components added to the output by a firm or industry.

增值税（VAT）

Value-added tax (VAT). A tax levied upon a firm as a percentage of its value added.

变 量

Variable. A magnitude of interest that can be defined and measured. Important variables in economics include prices, quantities, interest rates, exchange rates, dollars of wealth, and so forth.

可变成本

Variable cost. Refer to **cost, variable.**

货币周转率

Velocity of money. In serving its function as a medium of exchange, money moves from buyer to seller to new buyer and so on. Its "velocity" refers to the speed of this movement.

纵向公平

Vertical equity. See **horizontal equity vs. vertical equity.**

纵向一体化

Vertical integration. See **integration, vertical vs. horizontal.**

纵向兼并

Vertical merger. See **merger.**

W

财 富

Wealth. The net value of tangible and financial items owned by a nation or person at a point in time. It equals all assets less all liabilities.

福利经济学

Welfare economics. The normative analysis of economic systems, i.e., the study of what is "wrong" or "right" about the economy's functioning.

福利国家
Welfare state. A concept of the mixed economy arising in Europe in the late nineteenth century and introduced in the United States in the 1930s. In the modern conception of the welfare state, markets direct the detailed activities of day-to-day economic life while governments regulate social conditions and provide pensions, health care, and other aspects of the social safety net.

生产什么、如何生产以及为谁生产
What, how,* and *for whom. The three fundamental problems of economic organization. *What* is the problem of how much of each possible good and service will be produced with the society's limited stock of resources or inputs. *How* is the choice of the particular technique by which each good shall be produced. *For whom* refers to the distribution of consumption goods among the members of that society.

Y

收 益
Yield. Same as the **interest rate** or **rate of return** on an asset.

Z

零经济利润
Zero economic profit. In a perfectly competitive industry in long-run equilibrium, there will be zero economic profit. This definition pertains to all revenues less all costs, including the implicit costs of factors owned by the firms.

零利润点
Zero-profit point. For a business firm, that level of price at which the firm breaks even, covering all costs but earning zero profit.

Index

Note: Page references in **boldface** indicate Glossary terms; page numbers followed by n indicate footnotes.

E

L

N

O

后　记

——从几个小故事讲起

2012年4月28日下午，萨缪尔森《微观经济学》第19版双语注疏本样书由印厂送达新曲线。时值五一长假，员工回家心切，数催无果。30日晨八时许，陆瑜君短信至，参加环城马拉松之前专程回办公室取出，久盼之中的样书终于如面。

自1994年秋季始授第12版原著至今，经14、16、17、18至本19版，历时十八年，磨此一剑，开国人注疏西典之先河，终成正果。出版社为一书排版长达两年之久的精雕细琢，亦创当今国内出版界之纪录。本书，萨缪尔森《经济学》第19版双语注疏本的出版，与其《微观经济学》和《宏观经济学》的第19版双语注疏本一起，完成了萨缪尔森绝笔之作的双语注疏工程，历时四年，可喜可贺。其余五部经典，当十年左右逐一完成。此系列承中西先贤千年之文脉与哲思，及余毕生对国家和民族拳拳之心所致。倚窗远眺，情思泉涌，端详书而吟，慰告天国之萨翁：

一剑磨砺已廿载，
移山愚公今开怀；
待到八部出齐日，
告慰先贤再奏恺。

合璧东西精注疏，
纵贯历史古今无；
连横十九蓦回首，
凝眉乐眸七秩途。

从1948年萨缪尔森《经济学》第一版问世至今，时已七秩。战后60余年的人类社会波澜壮阔，是萨缪尔森在第17版的前言中，不经意间定义的“伟大和平时期”（Great Peace）。这一时期，以“中国人民从此站起来了”为开端，至中国的经济总量一跃而居世界第二，写就了人类文明史上最辉煌的一页。

第16版虽然是50周年的纪念版，但1998这个年份，美国互联网的泡沫也使得萨缪尔森不得不很快地重新修订，2000年底即推出第17版样书。从此，学术界对刚刚结束的20世纪有了一个明晰的断代。第18版是中国经济快速地融入世界的印记，而中国加入世贸组织十年所成就的世界经济格局，成为第19版修订中最为丰厚的滋养，是奠定第19版历史地位的重要基础，是人类历史赏赐给萨缪尔森绝笔的机遇窗口。

西方经济学是一门纯粹的舶来学科。作为改革开放重要指标之一的萨缪尔森《经济学》教材的中文译本，从第10版开始，经第12、14、16、17、18到此版，萨翁绝笔的第19版，各中译本均与萨氏原著的意蕴相去甚远，体现萨缪尔森经济哲学思想的精髓部分，尤为如此。

1948年第一版的畅销使萨缪尔森一夜之间成为拜伦式的英雄。在最近的四五十年中，曾有几本经济学的教科书对萨氏奇迹形成挑战，有的甚至一度超过该书的销量，日文版译者所得的版税也曾经创下超过萨缪尔森原版的记录。但是，迄今为止，仍然没有任何一本经济学教材，像萨翁的经济学教科书这样历经61年，18次再版，版版精品，版版畅销。

与学术界和社会大众对其定位不同，萨缪尔森认为，自己首先是一位哲学家。萨翁极其深厚的人文修养从第12版开始，在版式设计中表现得淋漓尽致，令克隆其模式的所有经济学教材只能望其项背，相形见绌。著名的美国宏观经济学家曼昆（Greg Mankiw，1958~）坦言，现在流行的经济学教材比起萨翁的所有版本来，只是小巫见大巫而已。美国经济学界把萨缪尔森的经济学教材尊为“天书”，书中深厚的人文史哲底蕴让经济学家们崇拜有加的同时，常常望而却步。欧美的学术界则将其视为集人文史哲各学科大成的“圣经”。教授萨缪尔森原版经济学教材的各国学者，也如沐春光，在欧美的学术界备受尊重。

2002年赴美讲学期间，适逢德高望重的Maureen Lally-Green教授甫任宾州高等法院大法官，邀我们造访其位于匹茨堡市中心的大法官官邸，一件小小的事情让我始终记忆犹新。老人与老布什、小布什总统会见时单独合影的大幅照片悬挂在私人办公室的显要位置，这是美国上层精英们的潜习惯，通常是迎待客人的首选。但此次例外。老太太迎我进入她私有办公空间的第一件事，是郑重地向我推荐了她刚刚买到的一本百科辞典，兰登书屋（Random House）新修订的*Webster's Encyclopedic Unabridged Dictionary of the English Language*。随着老人展开该书的瞬间，一股大部头新工具书特有的墨香扑鼻而来，让人爱不释手。这样的全节本辞典收词均在40万左右，比案头工具书多约一倍。这样的英文辞典，今天国内的读书人见过的很少，用过的就更可想而知了。事也凑巧，我赴美前在中国图书进出口公司的总部，将刚刚通关的几十本该书全部买下，给属下的同仁每人发了一本，喜出望外者有，但不屑一顾者居多。Maureen在听到来美之前我刚刚为Faculty的老师们每人赠送一册时，西方上流社会老人特有的天真顷刻喷涌而出，给我一个惊喜，也使我们的关系顿时升级。此访期间，美方罕见地主动安排了一系列意想不到的高层活动，字典的故事恐是其中的原因之一。在本书写作的过程中，这本辞典也做出了她应有的贡献，犹如她为我的访美所做的贡献一般。

20世纪80年代初在北京大学读书期间，富尔布莱特项目的普林斯顿大学著名教授、思想极右的德裔学者E. Stein对莎士比亚、美国当代文学悲剧的讲习令我记忆深刻，其中一件小事更让我恍如昨日。先生授课时所携的硕大皮箱里永远随身装一本 *Webster's New World Dictionary of American English*。现在回想起来，那是先生在刻意地给我们这些如饥似渴的中国学子传递一种信息。之后多年，在自己能有机会在欧美的各著名大学游访及讲学期间意外地发现，此案头工具书是各大学校长办公室走廊、会议室等客人候见的茶几上必备的几本权威工具书之一。

2009 年 10 月 25 日，“股神”巴菲特在接受英国 BBC 著名主持人、经济学家伊万·大卫（Evan Davis，1962~）专访时，除去其特有的以灌装可乐为标志的待客之道之外，下意识的动作也引起了大卫及摄像师的注意。一组特写镜头在巴菲特手扶《韦氏大词典》的瞬间定格，让巴菲特自誉为哲学家背后的严谨思维和主持人的职业敏感用镜头的无声语言表露无遗。

在国际学术界，分别由梅里厄姆－韦伯斯特公司（Merriam-Webster，Incorporated）和牛津大学出版社出版的 *Webster's Third New International Dictionary* 和 *Oxford English Dictionary* 是公认的最权威的英文工具书，收词均在 60 万左右。两者在欧美各大学的图书馆、各院系资料室等场所，都有专用的托台供人们随时查阅。上世纪 80 年代初期在北京大学各相关系里的资料室和学校的图书馆里还保留了这样的传统。从抗战前的各国立、私立以及教会大学到西南联大，再到抗战胜利后各归原址，这些一次又一次盖上那些特定时期印章的珍贵辞书，早已成了之后一代又一代学人心中的图腾。每每站在她们的面前，就好像自己也经历过那难忘的岁月，仿佛那些大师们多年前也站在她们的面前，从中汲取过无尽的营养。但是，令人遗憾的是，这些前人在国难当头的危亡时刻，不顾个人安危，用生命护行着她们一起规避战火的宝贵辞书们，在 1952 年被“院系调整”出北大、清华、燕京……之后，始终在某些国内顶尖大学的图书馆里被封存在“令人遗忘的角落”里，五花大绑地在睡大觉，时刻面临被送入废品收购站永远蒸发的危险。这些极其珍贵的辞书，在当年的各国立大学和南开、燕京这样的私立和教会大学都属于重点保护对象。当年的这些大学，有资格与当时世界上的一流大学对话甚至比肩，有她们的一份功劳。

权威的达沃斯《世界经济论坛》早在 2007 年的年度报告中就将中国的教育排在负面现象之首，伦敦的《金融时报》更将中国的高等教育斥之以“Collapsed”的程度。2010 年的 5 月 2 日到 5 日，在南京举办的中外大学校长论坛上，美国斯坦福大学的 John L. Hennessy 校长和牛津大学 Andrew Hamilton 副校长几乎是异口同声地在演讲中客气地对主人预测，中国的一流大学需 20 年以后才有可能出现。

2002 年 6 月 27 日，光明日报以《一流大学应超越基础阶段的外语教育》为题发表了对笔者的专访，据笔者对一流大学的探索和理解，对国内一流大学的定义给出了一个具体诠释。这一具体的诠释很简单，就是引进像萨缪尔森的《经济学》这样的大师亲自编撰的经典教材，硬着头皮上，去赏析，去找感觉，去找差距。在此基础上，有计划地让所谓的“大学英语”在国内某些励志向前的重点院校中退出历史舞台之日，就是国内出现一流大学曙光之时。然而，八年多过去了，随着教育的快速产业化，变相地飞速商业化，我国的高等教育在某些方面，似乎离国际一流大学越来越远。

但是，令笔者唯一聊以自慰的是，在20多年关注萨缪尔森，关注萨缪尔森《经济学》的今天，在萨翁辞世三年半之际，继第19版的前半部——《微观经济学》双语注疏本出版之后，其后半部——《宏观经济学》双语注疏本及精装典藏版的《经济学》双语注疏本也终于可以和读者见面了。与当前教育的产业化和商业化以及学术界的歪风邪气相悖逆的是，这本书是用构筑在现代技术手段基础上的传统方式、使用最原始的方法，以蚂蚁啃骨头的精神，一点一滴地独立自主完成的。本着文责自负的基本文德，精心地将每一笔作为自己的心血所致，不聘任何助手，不申请招一个研究生，全书注疏部分的每一个字都由笔者负全责。这就是，虽然能力有限，但为读者负责、对自己负责、对国家和民族负责的心力未敢有丝毫的懈怠。总之，近20年来，以对学术的本质负责和对学术的良心负责为己任，在一键一键敲击键盘的过程中，无时无刻不在仰望着那些天国的大师，是他们在鞭策着我脚踏实地地一步一步为我国能够出现一流大学贡献一点绵薄之力。本书之后，第一版的中译本以及各个时期不同大师经典著作的注疏本也将逐一精雕细琢地完成。

国人所作注疏体应始于先秦时期对典籍的注释。汉武帝的“罢黜百家，独尊儒术”催生了经注，两汉之后出现了义疏，范围逐渐扩大到了经、史、子、集各类。义疏又称讲疏，原本为佛门讲经和清谈玄学的一种方式，以疏通文字、讲解义理为主，方式自由，内容详尽。宋、元、明时期“求变求新”，摒弃门户之见，出现了一批理学注疏大家。清代的典籍注疏更是盛极一时，倡导了以训诂考据为主的务实学风，考据学兴盛，注疏也迅速发展，出现了补注、集注、评注、校注等一系列的注疏方法。

如果说佛经的翻译在唐代达到顶峰，以及与之相伴随的讲经是国人对外来经典的最早的注疏的话，国人对西方经典的注疏则是一项两千多年以来几近空白的领域。萨缪尔森的《经济学》是被国外经济学界和学术界公认为“天书”与“圣经”的有史以来为数不多的经典。从这个意义上讲，萨缪尔森《微观经济学》、《宏观经济学》和《经济学》注疏本的出现是国内学术界一项开创性的探索。由于本人水平所限，衷心地希望本书的读者和使用者对书中的疏漏之处不吝赐教，共同呵护这棵刚刚破土的幼苗。

注疏与考证是极其严肃的学术研究，其中的一点一滴均需大量的查证与比对研究，更考验注疏者的全方位素养。东施效颦，后患无穷。对于萨缪尔森《经济学》这样的“天书”与“圣经”而言，尤为如此。

西方经济学作为一门舶来的新兴学科，国人对其的真正引进是从译介萨缪尔森的《经济学》第10版开始的，是伴随着中国的改革开放发展起来的。笔者衷心地感谢已故的高鸿业先生率其弟子们（共8人）翻译和介绍第12版及其之前的版本；胡代光先生率其弟子们（共7人）对第14版的翻译；萧琛先生亲率众弟子对第16~19版的翻译以及第18版的译注（参译人数也随着版本的递增而增多，第16版7人、第17版11人、第18版最多，达20人之众；第19版的中译本以及将其拆分为数分册"加注本"，分别由商务印书馆和人民邮电出版社出版，也是这20人团队的集体成果。)；特别是前辈范家骧先生的力作《一部世界性的经济学教科书》对第1版至第16版跨越整整半个世纪的萨翁《经济学》的梳理。为方便读者阅读起见，笔者尽可能地沿用了包括上述版本在内的国内经济学界已经基本通用的术语。比如，虽然market equilibrium译为"市场均势"更贴近市场的定义和经济学的核心哲学内核，market failure译作"市场机制缺失"，比"市场失灵"或者"市场不灵"更加到位，但本书还是将其译作"市场均衡"、"市场失灵"等等，望读者谅知。

翻译界也是当前国内学术界被世人诟病的重灾区之一。笔者在本书的每一页中精选了若干典型和较难解读以及容易出现"关公战秦琼"（侯宝林先生经典相声中的著名包袱）式错误的内容精心地为读者提供了译文。翻译是一门再创作的艺术。百年前的严复，朱生豪先生的31部莎士比亚剧本，傅雷先生在每天译作不超过500字的严谨基础上为我们留下的美妙译文，都是笔者在翻译这些文字中追寻的目标。萨缪尔森的英语语言文字功底，是专事语言文字研究的大师们也难以企及的。其语言逻辑与语法结构所要表达的外延与内涵是翻译本书最大的拦路虎之一。更为悲剧的是看似理解但其实相去甚远的译作组建了中文译本中典型的"善意误导"大军。这也是本书提供部分典型段落译文的初衷之一。本书精选段落的译文，系笔者精雕细琢之作，均可与此比肩。"入戏"舞键，伏案而作，每日之功课，必逊傅雷先师，实难突破500字也。与当今经济学界每天万字之"神笔"，或"众僧拾材"之译著与"注释"相比，余愧难趋之。在充分忠实于原文的基础上，力争使译文可读、可点、可评，让所译文字对得起萨缪尔森深邃的哲思，对得起读者，对得起后代，对得起我们这个古老的民族。关于翻译内容的选择，考虑到版次的延续性，笔者参考了先前版本所选的内容，并根据编辑的建议，做了适量的补充。借此向萧琛先生及其弟子致以深深的谢意。每一章前面的名言引语，从第12版起就成为了本书的画龙点睛之笔，笔者对此均作了精心的注疏与翻译，请读者在赏析的同时，不吝指正。

同时，也借此机会衷心地表达对新曲线公司的刘力、陆瑜诸君策划此书出版的远见卓识和年轻的责任编辑徐向娟一丝不苟的敬业精神，以及麦格劳－希尔出版集团的纽约和芝加哥总部、中国代表处、香港代表处、新加坡代表处以及台北代表处，中国图书进出口公司、中国教育图书进出口公司等机构内相关朋友多年来支持的感佩与谢意。在本书出版之际，特别要表达对麦格劳－希尔前任驻中国总代表姜峰先生在任期间以及卸任之后的鼎力支持与倾力合作致以真挚的感谢。本书的出版与诸君的共同努力是分不开的，愿我们以此书，向崛起的当代中国贡献出一份别样的礼物，为古老的中华民族的真正复兴尽一份独特的心力。这也是你们所有人的心血所致。

之所以敢于开倡这样一种探索，还有一个重要的原因源于本人几十年来的积累，以及拥有的较为丰富的藏书的缘故。这些藏书对此贡献菲薄，主要有：

1. *Webster's Third New International Dictionary of English Language*，Merriam-Webster, Incorporated，2002，收词 60 万。
2. *Oxford English Dictionary*，Oxford University Press，2005，收词 60 万。
3. 萨缪尔森《经济学》从第一版至本版的各时期主要版本，特别是第 12 版之后的各版（原版）。
4. N. G. Mankiw、P. R. Krugman、M. Obstfeld、J. Stiglitz、G. Hubbard、A. P. O'Brien、M. Parkin、C. R. McConnell、S. Brue、A. R. Thompson、W. J. Baumol、A. S. Blinder、W. W. Scarth、R. A. Arnold 等著名经济学大家各个版本的原作。
5. *Webster's New World Dictionary of American English*、*Merriam-Webster's Collegiate Dictionary* 和 *The American Heritage Dictionary of the English Language* 这三本举世公认的作为受过或者正在接受良好教育的公民随时查阅和定夺的日常使用的权威案头工具书。
6. *Webster's New Twentieth Century Dictionary*，Unabridged, Simon and Schlister，2nd Edition-Deluxe Color，William Collins Publishers Inc.，收词 45 万。
7. *The Random House Encyclopedia*，Random House，1977。
8. *The Oxford Dictionary of English Etymology*，Oxford Press，1982。
9. *Webster's New Biographical Dictionary*，Merriam-Webster Inc.，1983。
10. *Webster's New Geographical Dictionary*，Merriam-Webster Inc.，1983。
11. *The New Columbia Encyclopedia*，Columbia University Press，1982。
12. 《远东英汉大辞典》，梁实秋，远东图书公司，1977，台北。

等等。

这些经典带我回到了那些浩瀚的历史典籍之中，帮我破解了其中的许多密码，寻找到了多年来始终未解的答案，它们的精髓已经深深地融进了本书的注疏之中。这一切也是笔者完成这部注疏的初衷之一。

2009 年年中，在本人的文集《中国英语教育改革探思录》一书出版后不久，笔者步五代时期布袋和尚《插秧诗》，作了一首随感，录以为记：

传道授业解惑田，
大胆改革谱新篇；
六根清净遂成道，
后退方可大步前。

2010年毕业生离校前夕，应有关的学生社团之邀，为即将走向社会和继续读书的我校同学赋诗两首，中英各一，格式古典，内容等效。中文一首师承儒家八木、汉书与尽心之篇，心继天国的周总理，哲思源自苏格拉底。英文一首上溯莎士比亚14行诗，下接罗伯特·弗罗斯特（Robert Frost，1874~1963）。莎翁和弗罗斯特均是萨缪尔森的一生钟爱。莎士比亚自不必说，19版全书中至少有三处论及弗罗斯特，其中两处引自其经典 *Road Not Taken*，本诗亦然。无论中英，均为笔者改良后的古典格式。今转帖于此，望读者和使用者指正。

寄语即将走出校门的同学

正心修身身欲宁，
悬梁刺股善其行；
四载军都图破壁，
齐家治国天下平。

To My Students, 2010

All four winters have besieged your brows,
And dug deeper trenches into your growth;
Try to take the road less taken by, hence,
And, that shall have made all the difference.

以注疏的体式引进原版经典教材，是本人在国内率先的实践。20年来，始终以坚持不懈并耕耘不怠的“牧羊”模式，学生受益，我更得惠，既是“技术”的提高，也是“艺术”的升华。笔者才疏学浅，更非经济学科班出身，只是印证了在实践中学、在实践中用、在实践中思考、在实践中研究、在实践中升华的前人楷范，钱穆为师、启功为范、傅斯年为榜，华罗庚为样。

1997年9、10月间，应欧盟10司、13司和意大利米兰理工大学（Politecnico Di Milano）的邀请，本人作为欧中教育网（Euro Sino Educational Network）项目的中方首席主持人，遍访了欧洲各主要大国。在德国当时的首都波恩，一次小小的经历让我终身难忘。随身携带的日立牌电动刮胡刀那时在国内还是很难享有的“奢侈品”，在德国期间电已耗尽，亟待充电。由于欧洲各国220伏低压民用电气的安全标准远高于国内，以及欧洲各大国标准各异的电源插座无法转接，在国内使用的双单片插头在欧洲根本没有可匹配的插座可供充电。77届上大学之前，我曾是全山西省电工技术考试的第一名，这点困难岂在话下！项目的硬件系统集成方德国电信全球教育事业部（Department of Global Learning, Deutsch Telecom）的老板Leopold Reif和总工程师通过之前在北京的交往，已经是很好的朋友了。遂利用在波恩德国电信总部开会的机会，让二位帮忙找一小截普通的电线。二人的诧异让我深感意外。他们说，在德国的任何地方你都找不到这样一截电线，也没有任何电气商店会卖给顾客这样一截电线，太危险了！我在工厂时，在当地是出了名的电气“大拿”，又以技术上的一丝不苟著称，干出的活很漂亮，几乎无人可及。但在以严谨著称的德国人目前，我的那点雕虫小技让我汗颜。作为中方首席主持人的我，可能的话，真想在那一刻找个地缝钻下去！

当时，我使用萨缪尔森第 12 版的原版教材已经三个学年有余，这次小小的经历对我以后伴随着萨翁的第 14、16、17、18 和 19 版，走到即将面世的第 19 版的注疏本，好像总有一个无形的影子在鞭策着我，督促着我。这可能就是我思维逻辑当中建构“技术”和“艺术”最高境界的一砖或一瓦。我们的教育需要这样的一块砖、一片瓦；我们的民族复兴需要这样的一块砖、一片瓦。但愿笔者奉献的这本萨缪尔森《经济学》双语注疏本是一块合格的长城砖，一片风吹不蚀、雨下不透、既能透气又能呼吸的汉瓦，秦汉未央宫上的一片普普通通的瓦当。

经济学是一门与时俱进的动态科学。萨缪尔森《微观经济学》第 19 版双语注疏本问世一年多来，我们这颗越来越小的星球已经在越来越纷杂多变的轨道上逐渐加速与变轨。与此同时，国际政治与经济发展中大国的演弈，小国的摇旗鸣锣或者魑魅魍魉，以及自然规律中新陈代谢与优胜劣汰的最新现状与可见未来的轨迹，均在这本典藏版的萨翁《经济学》第 19 版的注疏中尽可能地予以更新、调适与修订。只有这样，才可后记本书的出版。

2012 年 7 月，应山东大学威海校区商学院之邀，作了一场《圣经与天书——The Samuelson's *ECONOMICSes*》的演讲，初步将这些优秀的 90 后学子带入到了萨缪尔森的哲学王国之中，带入到了全书的哲学思想精髓之中。

萨缪尔森的这些哲思精髓，基本上隐匿于全书的字里行间。笔者将其初步厘至九条：

1. *Small is beautiful;*
2. *Visible vs. Invisible;*
3. *Americanization;*
4. *Chimericanism;*
5. *Chinese-Styled Globalization;*
6. *The Business of America;*
7. *Long Wave Theory;*
8. *Great Depression & Great Peace;*
9. *Anglo-Saxon Club.*

这九条均系笔者受萨缪尔森的优美文辞与深邃思想启发，提炼和引深而就，是笔者与弟子们穷极一生思考的问题。对这些问题的思考，已使我的学生们受益匪浅，获得了各种大考、大赛的最高成绩和奖誉，也使我进入了萨缪尔森“天书”和“圣经”的“自由王国”。

演讲瑕余，有感于下榻“山东大学国际学术中心”海浪、海风之不胜美景，吟五言小诗附后，是为后记：

保罗珠玑字，
天书千年新；
独辟新天地，
绝顶天籁音。

高楼望天涯，
憔悴终无悔；
海尽沁晚霞，
回首蓦为水。

倚窗天尽头，
梦回南山中；
日落羞山后，
宏观扬晚钟。

浪花轻拂岸，
旖旎入梦乡；
文登酒醉仙，
翩跹羽自昂。

极目海天外，
千里目欲穷；
一色弥天海，
寥廓入朦胧。

听涛沐星空，
万里枕月光；
千古论英雄，
百年议沧桑。

于 健

2013年7月1日晨于北京医院C0203，时吾孙廿二月。

FAMILY TREE OF ECONOMICS

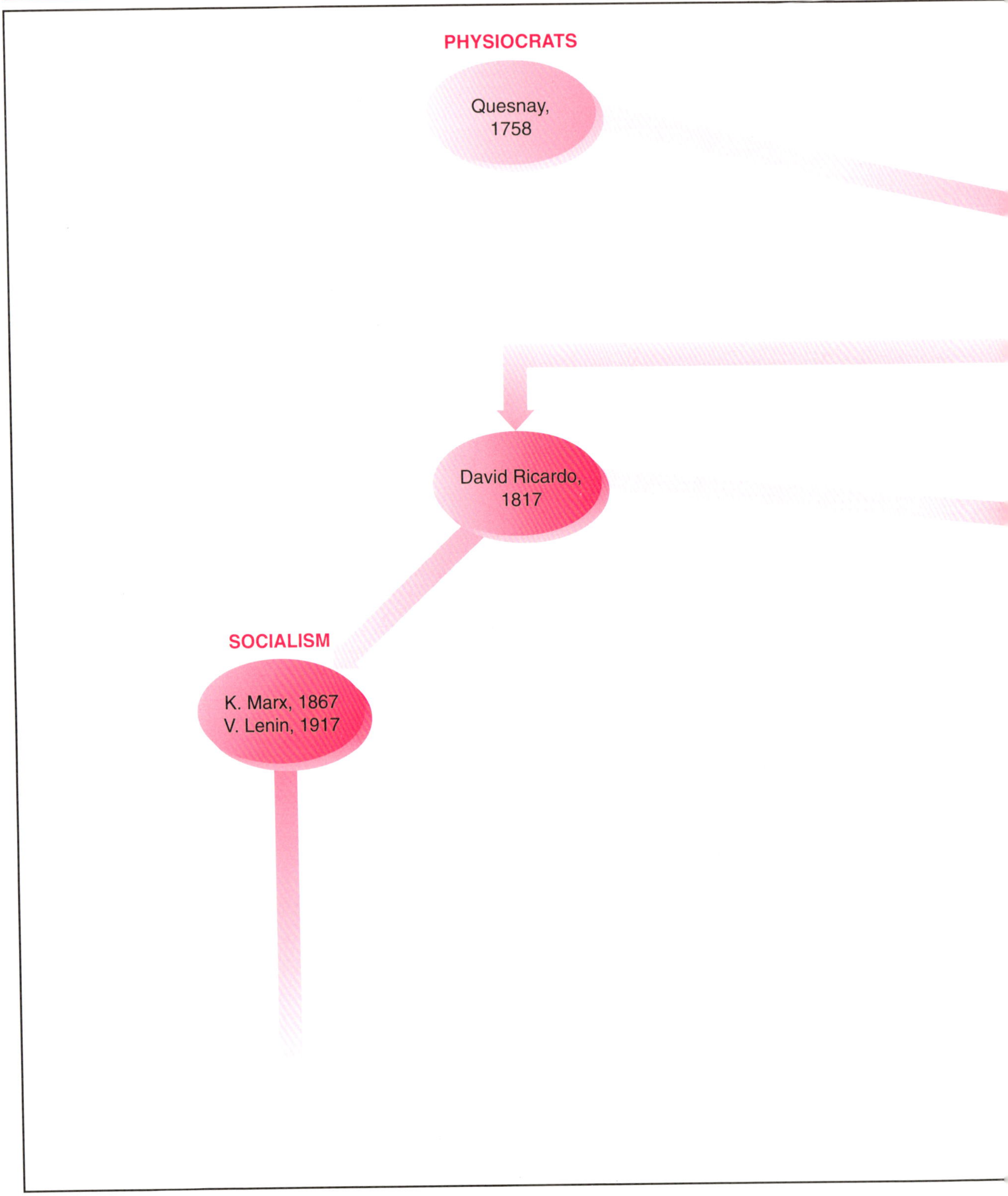